The Diaries of
Evelyn Waugh

The Diaries of Evelyn Waugh

Edited by Michael Davie

Weidenfeld and Nicolson   London

Designed by Simon Bell for
George Weidenfeld and Nicolson Limited
11 St John's Hill
London SW11

ISBN 0 297 77126 4
Filmset by Keyspools Limited, Golborne, Lancs.
Printed by Cox & Wyman Limited
London, Fakenham and Reading

Contents

Preface

Evelyn Waugh kept a diary, intermittently, for most of his life. The earliest surviving entry dates from September 1911, when he was seven; the last entry was made on Easter Day 1965, a year before he died. The complete diary runs to some 340,000 words.

After Waugh's death, the manuscript was transferred from his home at Combe Florey House, near Taunton, to the University of Texas in Austin, where it is now kept in dark blue boxes on the air-conditioned shelves of the Humanities Research Center. The juvenile diary is in two parts: the diary for 1911 and 1912, decorated with lively drawings in coloured crayons, is on loose sheets; the diaries for 1914 and 1916 are in small notebooks. The extensive diaries that Waugh kept at his boarding school, Lancing, between 1919 and 1921, and after he left Oxford, between 1924 and 1926, were written in folio notebooks subsequently bound by Maltby, the Oxford bookbinder. The diary from 2 October 1926 to 4 August 1927 is in a red exercise book. The bulk of the subsequent diary is on loose pages, predominantly folio; the entries for 1930, after Waugh had achieved literary celebrity with the publication of his first two novels, *Decline and Fall* (1928) and *Vile Bodies* (1930), are on double sheets of good paper embossed at the head of the first page with the entwined initials 'E.W.' Throughout, the MS is handwritten in pen and ink.

The diary, as it survives, is incomplete. At Lancing, on 10 October 1919, Waugh recorded that he had torn out entries about the holidays. Unpublished correspondence in the archives of the University of Texas contains a letter written by Waugh from Oxford to a schoolfriend, Dudley Carew. 'For the last fortnight I have been nearly insane. I am a little saner now. My diary for the period is destroyed.' In a second letter to the same correspondent, evidently written at about the same time, Waugh says that he has been 'quite incredibly depraved morally'. Taken together, these letters suggest that he destroyed the diary 'for the period' because it reflected the undergraduate homosexual experiences referred to by his authorized biographer, Christopher Sykes.[1] It is noticeable that no diary exists for two other periods of emotional crisis: the

[1] Christopher Sykes, *Evelyn Waugh, A Biography* (London 1975), p. 48.

collapse of his first marriage in 1929, and his 'lunacy' of 1954 – the hallucinations described in *The Ordeal of Gilbert Pinfold*.

Few members of Waugh's circle knew that he kept a diary. Alastair Graham, a close friend during the middle 1920s, was unaware of it; so was Waugh's first wife; so was Lord Birkenhead, who lived cheek by jowl with Waugh in a small farmhouse in occupied Jugoslavia during the Second World War. Yet it would have been out of character for Waugh to have behaved furtively, concealing his diary. Why did he keep it at all? His motive for doing so during his travels, especially the travels of the 1930s, is plain enough: he needed an *aide-mémoire* for the articles and travel books he had it in mind, or had been commissioned, to write. In keeping (in defiance of military regulations) a diary during the Second World War, while he was in the armed forces, he was no doubt aware that he was laying down a store of experience on which he might later wish to draw, as indeed he did; the *Sword of Honour* trilogy, written between 1951 and 1961, in many places closely parallels the diary. The Lancing diary and the 1920s diary became a source, discreetly used and quoted, for the 'first volume' of his unfinished autobiography, published in 1964. When in December 1960 he resumed his diary after an interval, he wrote: 'Fading memory and a senile itch to write to *The Times* on all topics have determined me to keep irregular notes of what passes through my mind.' The diary was not written for publication. The decision to publish was taken, before her death in 1973, by Mrs Laura Waugh, his second wife, in conjunction with her eldest son Mr Auberon Waugh, and with the approval of Waugh's elder brother, Mr Alec Waugh.

Publication of the verbatim text will not be possible for some years, because of the English laws of libel. In this edition, twenty-three libellous references have been altogether excised. Another twenty phrases have been omitted, not because they are libellous, but because I have concluded that their publication would be intolerably offensive or distressing to living persons or to the surviving relations of persons recently dead. To the delicate problems raised by these offensive, though not libellous, references, no general solution can be applied; each instance has required a separate decision; and each decision has been, necessarily, subjective. I have, however, attempted to distinguish between passages capable in my opinion of causing lasting distress, and those – again in my opinion – likely to cause only temporary embarrassment, irritation, or anger. I carefully considered, and at length rejected, the notion of showing to all those mentioned in the diary the references to themselves; but some of those mentioned could not be traced, and those who could be traced could not be given a right of veto, so that in any event the decision to publish or to suppress would have remained with the editor. Removal of all disparaging references to all living persons would have distorted the text unduly. In deciding what should be published and what should not, I have borne in mind

Waugh's own response to a newspaper editor who asked him if he would care to read, before publication, the text of an unflattering article: Waugh declined the offer, saying that if he took offence he would seek a remedy either with a horsewhip or in the courts.

My most difficult task has been to balance my duty to the text against the sensibilities of those mentioned and – given Waugh's taste for exaggeration and fantasy – possibly misrepresented. In some places, instead of cutting out libellous or offensive passages altogether, I have replaced a name with a dash. This device may at first sight appear to sensationalize the text, but that is not my intention; the purpose of the device is to protect the reputation or privacy of the person named while retaining as much as possible of the text. Where there can be no possibility of identification, I have employed a more conventional device: the initial of the person named, followed by a dash.

Since in any event the full text cannot yet be published, the question arose whether further cuts should be made – not to protect the publishers from libel actions or named persons from offence but the reader from boredom. Nothing, I decided, would be lost, and liveliness would be gained, by cautious abbreviation of the boyhood and Lancing diary and of some parts of the travel diaries. From the Lancing diary I have removed about 10,000 words, for the sole reason that they are tedious: repetitious accounts of games, lessons and debates. Ample, perhaps excessive, accounts of these activities have even so been kept. From the travel diaries I have removed occasional sentences, and I have omitted altogether the staccato notes he kept on his return journey to British Guiana in 1961–2. In both school and travel diaries I have always retained a phrase or passage if I was in doubt about its possible interest. The entire original text, it should be pointed out, is open to inspection (by permission of Waugh's executors) at the University of Texas.

In the rest of the diary, nothing has been omitted except for reasons of libel, or personal offence, or, in a few places, unintelligibility. It was suggested that the rest of the diary should be shortened also, especially when Waugh kept little more than a record of his social engagements, since repetition of trivialities may weary the reader and perhaps give him a false impression of Waugh's life. I decided against this course of action for two reasons: first, I concluded that although the general reader would accept as reasonable the excision of accounts of football matches played by fifteen-year-olds in 1919, or the names of Brazilians encountered on the banks of the Ireng river in 1933, he would feel unsettled, and justifiably aggrieved, if he knew that the entire diary had been tampered with. Besides, in working on the diaries, I have become increasingly aware of the interest of certain entries that may, at first sight, appear boring.

Waugh's spelling was invariably poor, though it improved in later life; as a convenience to the reader, I have silently corrected his errors while recording some of his eccentricities in footnotes. Capitalization and datelines have been standardized; where the dateline is not in the style 'Hampstead, 24 January 1925', the form is Waugh's. Punctuation, to which Waugh paid little attention in his diary, has been added where its absence might have confused the reader; in quotations, though, Waugh's own punctuation, or lack of it, has always been followed. Question marks in brackets – (?) – are Waugh's; a question mark in square brackets – [?] – indicates editorial doubt about the word immediately preceding the symbol. Footnotes have been added when they appeared to contribute to an understanding of Waugh and his relations to his contemporaries and predecessors, or where further explanation seemed necessary; in general I have tried to avoid an over-pedantic use of footnotes. I have added a footnote about characters, not necessarily on their first but on their first significant appearance; an Appendix of Names supplies further information about those who most notably reflected Waugh's life or writings.

The accurate transcription of proper names has presented special difficulty, for Waugh's handwriting is often hard to decipher; in addition, he took little trouble about getting names right, sometimes spelling them phonetically, sometimes using different spellings for the same person. Where I have been unable to identify a person, I have usually followed what I take to be Waugh's spelling. In places where he inadvertently omitted a word but the identity of the missing word is plain from the context, I have supplied it without a footnote: e.g. Waugh wrote, 'Diana and Conrad arrived two and a half late', but the context makes it clear that the missing word is 'hours', not 'days'; I have accordingly inserted 'hours'. Apart from these trivial amendments, I have conscientiously tried to reproduce Waugh's own words as accurately as possible.

Over the edited text, the Waugh Estate has retained a veto; and has exercised it in seven instances, making brief cuts in entries that might otherwise have caused unnecessary distress.

The editor of a modern diary depends on the help of many people. I must record my particular thanks to Sir Harold Acton, Father M. C. D'Arcy SJ, Mrs Basil Bennett, the late Earl of Birkenhead, Lord Campbell of Eskan, Mr Dudley Carew, Miss Anne Chisholm, Colonel John Clarke, Mr Stephen Clissold, Lady Diana Cooper, the late Sir Noel Coward, Lord Bradwell, Lady Mary Dunn, Mrs Ann Fleming, Mr Roger Fulford, Mr and Mrs Donat Gallagher, Mr Val Gielgud, Mr Alastair Graham, Major-General F. C. C. Graham, Mr Graham Greene, Mr Richard Plunket Greene, Mr Hamish Hamilton, Mr B. W. T. Handford, Comte and Comtesse Anne-Pierre d'Harcourt, Sir Roy Harrod, Sir John Heygate, the Hon. Edmund Howard, Mr John St John, Lady Jones, Lord Kinross, Lady Pansy Lamb, Miss Nili Limon, Lord Lovat, Lady Dorothy Lygon, Lady Mary Lygon, Mr Felix Markham, Sir Fitzroy Maclean, Mr Ian McDonald, Miss Jessica Mitford, Mrs

Alan Moorehead, the Hon. Mrs Nightingale, Mr C. H. Rolph, the Earl of Rosse, Sir John Rothenstein, Mr John Sparrow, Mr James Stern, Mr John Sutro, the late Mr Derek Verschoyle, Mr Alec Waugh, Mr Auberon Waugh, the late Mrs Evelyn Waugh, the late Sir Pelham Wodehouse and the Hon. Mrs Yorke. They are not, of course, responsible for any errors of fact, still less of judgement, that this edition of Waugh's diaries may contain.

At the University of Texas, Dr Warren Roberts, Dr David Farmer, Mrs Sally Leach and Mrs Carolyn Harris, of the Humanities Research Centre Staff, were consistently obliging. In London, my task was greatly eased by the professional skills of Miss M. R. Silverman and her cheerful staff of transcribers at the Palantype Organization, particularly Mrs Joan Melman.

Michael Davie
London
March 1976

Chronological Table

1903 Born at 11 Hillfield Road, Hampstead (28 October).

1907 Family moves to North End Road, Hampstead.

1910–17 At Heath Mount preparatory school.

1917–21 At Lancing College, Sussex.

1921–4 At Hertford College, Oxford. Homosexual phase. Leaves Oxford without prospects.

1924 Art school (Sept.–Dec.). Falls 'in love with an entire family', the Plunket Greenes.

1925 Schoolmaster in Wales; attempts suicide.

1926 Schoolmaster in Berkshire. First short story published. *P.R.B.*, *An Essay on the Pre-Raphaelite Brotherhood 1847–1854*, privately printed by Alastair Graham.

1927 Sacked from Berkshire school (Feb.). Temporary schoolmaster in Notting Hill, London (March). *Daily Express* (April–May). Begins to write *Decline and Fall*.

1928 First book, *Rossetti*, published. Marries Evelyn Gardner (June). *Decline and Fall* published (Sept.).

1929 Wife leaves him (July). From 1929 to 1937, 'no fixed home' and continuous travel.

1930 *Vile Bodies*; literary and social success; columnist in *Daily Mail*; first travel book, *Labels*. Becomes Roman Catholic. Travels to Abyssinia and central Africa.

1931 *Remote People*. In love with 'Baby' Jungman. Meets Lady Diana Cooper. Christmas at Madresfield with the Lygons.

1932 *Black Mischief*. Travels to British Guiana and Brazil (Nov.–Feb. 1933).

1933 Mediterranean cruise. Marriage nullity hearings (Oct.–Nov.).

1934 Winter of 1933–4 in Morocco. Spitzbergen 'expedition'. *Ninety-Two Days*. *A Handful of Dust* (Oct.).

1935 Covers Italian–Abyssinian war for *Daily Mail*; interviews Mussolini. *Edmund Campion*.

1936 Rome confirms the annulment of his marriage, enabling him to re-marry. Third visit to Abyssinia. *Waugh in Abyssinia*.

1937 Marries Laura Herbert (April); settles at Piers Court, Stinchcombe, Gloucestershire.

1938 *Scoop*. Visits Hungary in spring and Mexico in autumn.

1939 *Robbery Under Law: The Mexican Object-lesson*. Joins Royal Marines (Dec.).

1940 Goes on Dakar expedition. Transfers to Commandos.

1941 At Battle of Crete; disillusion with brother-officers and, following entry of Russia into the war, with the war itself.

1942 *Put Out More Flags. Work Suspended*. 'A good year,' spent in the UK.

1943 Enforced resignation from Commandos. His father, Arthur Waugh, dies.

1944 Obtains special leave to write *Brideshead Revisited* (Jan.–June). Goes to German-occupied Jugoslavia with the British Military Mission to the Partisans (Sept.). In December, becomes liaison officer in Dubrovnik, Jugoslavia.

1945 *Brideshead Revisited* published (May). Demobilized (Sept.): returns to Piers Court.

1946 Visits Spain, which stimulates *Scott-King's Modern Europe*, published 1947.

1947 Visits Hollywood, which stimulates *The Loved One*, published 1948.

1948–9 US lecture tour.

1950 *Helena*.

1951 Near East tour for *Life* magazine, which produces *The Holy Places*, 1952.

1952 *Men At Arms*. Christmas in Goa.

1953 *Love Among the Ruins*.

1954 Sets out on voyage that produces 'Pinfold' experiences. His mother, Catherine Waugh, dies.

1955 *Officers and Gentlemen*.

1956 Moves to Combe Florey House, near Taunton, Somerset.

1957 *The Ordeal of Gilbert Pinfold*.

1958 Travels to Rhodesia, collecting material for a life of Ronald Knox.

1959 *The Life of the Right Reverend Ronald Knox*.

1960 *A Tourist in Africa*. European tour for *Daily Mail*.

1961 *Unconditional Surrender*. Winter in British Guiana.

1964 *A Little Learning, The First Volume of an Autobiography*.

1966 On Easter Sunday, 10 April, dies at Combe Florey House.

Laura and Evelyn Waugh had six children (another died at birth):

> Teresa, born March 1938; she married in 1961 John D'Arms, professor of Latin and Greek at the University of Michigan.
>
> Auberon, born November 1939; he married in 1961 Lady Teresa Onslow.
>
> Margaret, born June 1942; she married in 1962 Giles FitzHerbert, of the Foreign and Commonwealth Office.
>
> Harriet, born May 1944.
>
> James, born June 1946.
>
> Septimus, born July 1950.

1 The Boyhood Diary 1911-16

Introduction

Arthur Evelyn St John Waugh was born on 28 October 1903 at 11 Hillfield Road, Hampstead. In his unfinished autobiography, published in 1964, Waugh describes Hillfield Road as 'a cul-de-sac . . . near the Hampstead cricket ground, off the Finchley Road'.[1] The description is mildly misleading. Hillfield Road is less sequestered than Waugh's phrasing implies, and nearer to Hampstead Cemetery than to the cricket ground. This part of west Hampstead, bordering Kilburn, was developed in the 1880s by a firm of speculative builders for the *petite bourgeoisie* who could not afford to live higher up the Hampstead slopes; Hillfield Road was, and is, a bleak terraced street of small and uniform Victorian dwellings.

Waugh's forebears on his father's side were Scots farmers in Berwickshire: his great-great-grandfather was a Nonconformist minister who was sent south to a chapel, now demolished, off Oxford Street; his great-grandfather became a Church of England clergyman and rector of Corsley, near Frome; his grandfather was a doctor of sadistic temperament who settled at Midsomer Norton, near Bath.

His father, Arthur Waugh, was educated at Sherborne and New College, Oxford, where he won the Newdigate Prize for poetry. After he came down, he established himself in London as a man of letters, 'a category, like maiden aunts, that is now almost extinct'. He wrote biographies, reviewed for the *Daily Telegraph*, read manuscripts for publishers, edited the Nonesuch Dickens, and – surprisingly, in view of his preference for robust literature – contributed to the first number of *The Yellow Book*. In religion, he was a practising Anglican; in politics, a conservative. He married Catherine Raban in 1893, and the first of their two children, Alec, who became a prolific and popular writer, mainly of novels, was born in 1898. Both sons have recorded their recollections of their father, and he himself wrote an autobiography, *One Man's Road*. From all these accounts Arthur Waugh emerges as a pleasant, sociable and generous man, respected in the London literary world, keen on cricket, devoted to his

---

[1] Evelyn Waugh, *A Little Learning, The First Volume of an Autobiography* (London 1964), p. 27.

family, and a lover of Shakespeare, the Bible and the established authors of the nineteenth century. In 1902 he became managing director of Chapman & Hall, the publishers of Dickens; and five years later he moved with his family to a new house he had built in what was then the relatively rural district – certainly by comparison with Hillfield Road – between Hampstead and Golders Green. In his autobiography, Arthur Waugh confesses to his own sentimentality, and his sons have described his theatrical manner; he named his new house 'Underhill' and spoke proudly of its 'stout timbers'. Since 1907, the 'grim cyclorama of despoilation', in Evelyn Waugh's phrase, has overtaken what used to be the village of North End, but Arthur Waugh's house – 145 North End Road – survives, a modest Edwardian villa, now divided into small flats and bordered by a row of decrepit garages, yet still able to convey not only why Arthur Waugh took pride in it, but also why his younger son came to 'detest' it.

Catherine Raban, Waugh's mother, was born in India, with which the Raban family had long been connected. Her father was a magistrate in the Bengal Civil Service; he died during her infancy, and she was brought up in Shirehampton, now a suburb of Bristol. In *A Little Learning*, Waugh describes his mother as 'small, neat, reticent, and until her last decade, very active'. She was an enthusiastic gardener and would have preferred the country to London. Friends of the family have testified that she possessed a stronger character than her husband.

The earliest relic of Evelyn Waugh is a short story written when he was, in all probability, six: *The Curse of the Horse Race*. The evidence of the earliest fragment of diary, written at the age of seven, is of a high-spirited, friendly, happy child who was given much parental affection and encouragement – an impression confirmed by his autobiography. He was, he says, never bored; he adored his nurse, Lucy Hodges; he was taken on regular outings into London proper by his mother and father. When, with the children of a neighbouring family, he formed the Pistol Troop, to defend the country from German invasion, the *Pistol Troop Magazine* was typed by his father's secretary.

He went to his first school, Heath Mount preparatory school in Heath Street, Hampstead, in September 1910, when he was seven. As the diary shows, the Great War, when it came, keenly excited him; he and his friends collected and sold empty jam jars for the Red Cross; he joined the Boy Scouts; and in 1915 he briefly acted as a War Office messenger. At about the same time he was captivated by Anglo-Catholicism, partly through his attendance, with his parents, at the flamboyant services of a fashionable clergyman, the Reverend Basil Bourchier, at St Jude's, Hampstead Garden Suburb, and partly through a friendship he formed with an Anglo-Catholic curate when, during the holidays, he stayed with his father's sisters at Midsomer Norton.

In the diary before August 1916, Waugh's own spelling has been retained.

My History

My name is Evelyn Waugh I go to Heath Mount school I am in the Vth Form, Our Form Master is Mr Stebbing.

We all hate Mr Cooper, our arith master. It is the 7th day of the Winter Term which is my 4th. Today is Sunday so I am not at school. We allways have sausages for breakfast on Sundays I have been waching Lucy fry them they do look funny befor their kooked. Daddy is a Publisher he goes to Chapman and Hall office it looks a offely dull plase. I am just going to Church. Alec, my big brother has just gorn to Sherborne. The wind is blowing dreadfuly I am afraid that when I go up to Church I shall be blown away. I was not blown away after all.

June, 1912 ; aged 8

Vol. I.

My history by Evelyn Waugh.
& Diary. Big Print.
Begining at June 10th 1912 at school & at home.
My HISTORY
  BY E. WAUGH
   AT SCHOOL & HOME
    ILASTRATED BY THE AUTHER
     WRITEN AT THE AGE OF EIGHT
  AT SCHOOL & AT HOME & at the seaside CHEEFLY AT HOME.

My name is Evelyn. I live in a house called Underhill. I have been in bed with something wrong with my stomach & have got to stay in bed for the hole of this *week* it is awful. This morning Maxwell, my great chum, came round to see me It was his birthday & he showed me all his presents. He had a riping pair of pads & a pair of wickekeeping gloves & bat. In the evening Dady came back from office & brought me a lot of paper to draw on. The next morning I read 'How Heat Travels' in the Childs 'Encyclopaedia' then I had breakfast and read the Boy's Friend.

In the afternoon Miss Hoar[1] came to see me & brought me a dear little hand bag with some soldiers of the regiment of the 'Black Watch'.

Mother read me a article the following morning called 'How To Join the Navy' & I have made up my mind that I am going to be a 'Merry Jack tar', if my eyes will pass Mother dous not think they will. If they do not I shall go board a 'Merchantman' for I must go to sea.

I am just go to make my little elaphant a coat.

> If I should be a sailor bold
> I'd stand up on the deck
>
> I'd lock my prisoners in the hold
> And make thier ship a wreck

Chap IV

Next morning Mrs Simmons came to to see me & showed me some carvings she had done and Max came to tea with me. On the following morning I found I had the appendicitis & had an operation. Mother had a nurse in. This happened VI days ago for I have not been able to write this till now. I have had IX presants since the opeation cheafly soldiers.

This is a list of them

1. Pen 2 Gordon Hilanders 3. Camel corps 4. Mule battery 5. Caesar 6. Puzel 7. French soldier 8. Stories from Iliad 9. Stories of Roland.

> A lot of presants have I had
> That makes me very, very glad
>
> The soldiers I like best of all
> They look so very strong and tall.

The end of Vol. I

June, 1913; aged 9

MY HISTORY
AN DIARY BY E. WAUGH
VOLLUME II
A POEM WITH EACH CHAPTER

CHAPTER I

I do not think that in Voll I I told you I go to Heath Mount school and that I am in Class VB. But even if I did I have told you now so I can go on. One year

---

[1] Miss Hoare of North End House, one of the two large houses in the neighbourhood, was a member of the Hoare family of bankers: the sister of the first baronet, who was MP for Norwich 1886–1906, and an aunt of Samuel Hoare, Lord Templewood, who was Foreign Secretary in 1935.

has past since Voll I and the date is June 21st 1913. I would have been the day of the sports only our cricket field is having a road cut through it.

Haward is on daily reports and got caned because 'Latin Very Poor!!!' was writen on his report.

> Poor old Hayward had the cane
> Which gave him tremendous pain

Chapter II

The lessons for today were Scripture $\frac{7}{7}$ History $\frac{19}{20}$ Spelling $\frac{8}{20}$ French $\frac{15}{18}$ Latin $\frac{2}{2}$. In French we had a ripping row. About Fletcher who we always tell 'My nose is bleeding. It's rude to look up peoples noses' which come from an old joke.

Chapter III

The first lesson this morning was history in which Mr Stebbing 'heard us' our 'notes' on the Peninsular War. Then Latin in which Mr Cooper was in a rotten bate about what Stebbing had set us. Then we had break. After break we had French in which I translated 'Here is the church' into 'Ici est lêglise.' Then Spelling in which I got 13 marks out of 20 (not bad). Then we had Arith. I got the arith 'prep' right and got full marks ($\frac{8}{8}$) 3 for the Prep and 5 for the other sum. Then break and dinner. After dinner I fought Geogan. Then Rep in which we had to say 'Tall are the oacks whos ackorns drop in dark Auserrill, Fat are the stags that champ the boughs of the Ciminian Hill & ect' (it comes in Horatios) for which I got $\frac{19}{20}$. Then Extra Geog for which I got $\frac{18}{20}$. Then Cricket. I was on Roscoe's side and made 0 (Mr Stebbing's bowling).

August 18th 1914; aged 10

Journey

On the journey down all the bridges and signal boxes were gaurded by sentries untill we got to Reading and there was not one more to be seen.

Bath

We would have had a nice journey down if it was not for the presence of a drunk man in our carriage who kept on making wierd signs to his son who answered them with equally wierd gesticalations. When we got out we went to the Roman Baths and had a grand time there was an ass of a guide who showed the others round but Daddy and I did not, prefering our guide book to the repulsive look of that awful guide.

Christmas Term, 1914; aged 11

The miseries of scool

I have come to the conclusion that Heath Mount is the worst managed school in England.

We had 3 classics today which was something awful Mr Hynchcliffe is getting more obnoxious every day and his nose is getting pereceptably longer every day. He spent the greatest part of the first Latin in slobbering over the unfortunate Spenser who has the bad luck to be the favorite of a man like Hynchcliffe.

At Duty's call

Today was Mr Vernon's last day at school. At prayers Edwards gave him the watch we had subscribed to get. When the clapping had died away Mr Grenfell leaned forward 'Boys' he said in a husky sort of voice I had never heard him use before 'Mr Vernon has answered to his country's call. I know you all wish him a happy time and a safe return. Three cheers for him!' By now most of the chaps were blubbing and as the cheers rang out there were many chaps who hid behind each other so as not to be caught blubbing. Brown and I were playing cards in the afternoon in the dining room when the door opened and in came Mr Vernon. 'Goodby V.' cried Brown and then he was gone. That was the last of Mr Vernon that any of the chaps saw. I feel rather sorry now I used to rag him so.

1915 ; aged 11

Brighton

The halfe term has come at last and we (I and Mother) started off for Brighton.

In the evening we went to church. We struck a horrible low one. I was the only person who crossed myself and bowed to the alter.

Zeplin Raid

Alec woke me up in the night at about 11 o'clock saying the Zeps had come. We came downstairs and the special constable was rushing about yelling 'Lights Out' and telling us the Zeppelin was right overhead. We heard two bombs and then the Parliament Hill guns were going and the Zep went away in their smoke cloud to do some baby-killing elswear.

Lost, stolen or strayed?

Strayed to be correct. But where is the point. Praps in the next desk. Why Yes! Here's my Richie and my Primer by George! But who's have I got then. I could swear I put my own in my locker – No I haven't got your Primer Oh! Yes I have though that's funny I'm sure . . . *My* idea – Great what? Changed every jolly book in Dumpy's class room. Bravo *me*!

Easter Term, 1916 ; aged 12

My fight with Rostail

It being a wet day and it being above all Heath Mount we had to change our boots like a kindergarten. While engrossed in this exilerating occupation (in the company of a few others) Rostail entered and squatting temptingly on the edge of a basin proceeded to call me 'Wuffles'. I informed him that unless he refrain from using my name in a corupted form I would have to chastise him. He knowing that he was larger than me continued in the name whereupon I fulfiled my promise one hundredfold.

Heath Mount v Street cads

Hooper and I were going home when a kid about 10 yelled out 'Silly old green caps'! We chased him about 300 yards when out came a biger brother who came at us with the usual 'Ere d'you want a fight?' I answered yes and we set to with a mixture of wrestling and boxing ending in my victory.

War Work

On the first day of the holls we went to the Golders Green depot and asked for war work. They received us with open arms and the next day we set to work in cutting out soles for soldiers shoes. All the same I think I shall chuck it soon as it cuts into the holls so frightfully. Dove and Max are of the same opinion. Some of our soles were dreadfully cut out specially Maxwell's.

My shrine

I had started a shrine and mentioned this to the aunts who instantly promised to make me a frontal. Aunt Elsie is going to give me a crucifix when I'm confirmed and Aunt Trissie has given me two sweet brass bowls to fill with flowers.

Summer Term, 1916

Water Rat

We have had the most gorgeous rags with Cameron lately we have ever had with any master. We call him Water Rat to his face and make the desks skweak. One time after they creaked with extra vim he asked the reason. 'Well' said Brown 'You can come and and sit here yourself and see if they don't creak.' Then Nobel found a washer and sugested it had come off the desk. It's almost as funny as Mr Vernon.

Finis Vol 2

Westcliffe-on-Sea, Saturday 12 August 1916

Started down with the carriage fairly empty but we soon filled up with vile Southend trippers. The tide was in so as soon as we arrived we left the hotel and went down to the front where I was suddenly struck by an overwhelming desire to bathe. We hurried back and greatly anoyed the domestics who were hard at work getting our room ready by opening our bags and driving them away but I had to change in the bathroom. I had a delicious bathe – the water was positively hot – but as the time was but a few minutes to dinner I had to get out dreadfully soon. Had dinner and then we went and had an ice each, bought some cheap lite attire and encamped on deckchairs on the esplanade. In the evening we went to the *Olympians*. It was a good show but frightfully crowded. We are going to book seats for the last night.

Sunday 13 August 1916

We went for a church hunt and found quite a high one, St Albans. It was rather like an Orientle temple inside, as it was adorned with painted patterns on wood. We went to High Mass there and came back in time for lunch. Immediately after lunch I had a bathe it was choppy and the waves were just perfect. Then we walked up to Leigh and back again. Dinner was lovely and soon after we went up to Southend. They have built some huge baths there and I shall bathe there sometime, but it is cheaper and quite as nice to bathe in the sea.

Monday 14 August 1916

In the morning Mother and I went shopping and she bought a hat and I after great difficulty obtained a sketchbook and drew bad pictures in it until just before lunch when we bathed. It was rougher than ever and not quite so warm. The waves were simply lovely and I could make quite a bit of headway against them. After lunch I bathed again and came back frightfully hungry to a tea which was to say the least scanty. In fact it consisted of one tiny piece of thin bread and butter and a little finger of cake, verging upon the microscopic. But the dinner well made up for this trifling deficiency. After dinner we went to the *Happy Valley* not a bad show but not a patch on the *Olympians*. The funny men were as good but the ladies – I mean females – were so aged and so cockney and so dreadfuly painted that they simply spoilt the whole show. They had quite a decent song called *Follow the Sergeant* but their choruses were ragged and out of tune. Still they gave us a happy and amusing evening.

Tuesday 15 August 1916

In the morning we went out, wrote letters on the cliffs, and went back and only just arrived in time to avoid a tremendous storm of rain; then as it cleared up a bit I went and had a bathe off the jetty. It was the first time Mother had allowed me out of my depth in the sea. I tried diving but with small result. It poured all the afternoon but at about three o'clock I and four or five other people from the hotel went and bathed again. Then we went back and devoured our would-be tea without much relish. Then we went out and bought a *Pearsons* which we afterwards found was for MAY! and returned home and read practicly all the evening.

Wednesday 16 August 1916

I didn't feel very well so we had a terribly quiet day. In the morning I went and saw the lucky people bathing and went back to lunch then I went out sketching on the esplanade. Before tea we walked into Southend and found there a most enthralling slot [machine] at which I practised with little result.

Thursday 17 August 1916

We went up to Southend in the morning and spent a small fortune at the slots. Then we took a train to Prittlewell. It is a sweet little village with old houses with wobly roofs. And a mad lovely old church. There is still the little staircase in the wall leading up to where the Rood-Screne ought to be. There is a lovely black oak carved fourteenth century door. After tea I and Girlie then had a single at Babmington and were soon joined by Nora and Jessie and Mrs Paine. Then Mrs Freeman turned up with an atrocity of about seven and spoilt our game. Whenever he 'no-served' she used to say, 'Never mind darling try again'.

Friday 18 August 1916

In the morning we went to Leigh and saw the church. It is a beautiful old one and is very spikey. It has got some very Roman candles on sort of rings standing on the ground but without the image in the centre. The Blessed Sacrament is reserved in the Lady Chapel. The East windows are very faintly coloured and we think they must be very old. After lunch I had three or four ripping sets of Babmington and a lovely bathe; after tea Girlie and I went and got an ice and had some more Babmington. In the evening we went to the *Olympians*. It was a frightfully good show but they weren't half so nice in evening dress as in the pierot's clothes. Winnie Melville was simply sweet and the funny men were good but oh the sentimental singers! There were two of them and they got encored nearly every time. They had *Shall us – Let's* and two or three others I knew, but their *Drum-major* was easily the best thing I've seen for ages and was very well sung.

Saturday 19 August 1916

Girlie and I went to the Southend baths as the tide was out and I wanted to get in a bathe before I left but it was not too nice as the towels were filthy and the baths crowded. We had a tremendous rush to get the train and only just bundled into a carriage where there were *three* babies and two females who drank evil-smelling stout to revive themselves the whole time. We had some dificulty with the baggage at Golders Green as there was not a single taxi or cab but we got a tubeman to take them.

2 The Lancing Diary 1919-21

Introduction

No diary exists between the summer of 1916 and the autumn of 1919. Waugh left his prep school in 1917, at the end of the Easter Term, and in May went to Lancing College. Like his father and brother, he had been intended for Sherborne, but in 1915 Alec, then a senior boy, had been involved in a scandal. In those days, Alec Waugh has written, 'A conspiracy of silence shrouded the main moral of school life. Today the danger is recognized with frankness; and I wonder how many ex-public schoolboys would deny that at some point in their schooldays they indulged in homosexual practices; practices that had no lasting effect, that they instantly abandoned on finding themselves in an adult heterosexual world. I was not the immaculate exception, and had the bad luck to be found out.' Head of the batting averages though he was, Alec Waugh was asked to leave.

That winter, aged seventeen, he wrote *The Loom of Youth*. It was undisguisedly autobiographical and caused a considerable stir: in many schools the book was banned and boys were thrashed for reading it; a former headmaster of Eton, Canon Edward Lyttleton, announced that it was 'almost wholly untrue'. Not only Alec but also his father were struck off the roll of Sherborne Old Boys (they were readmitted in 1933); Evelyn's entry to Sherborne was barred. Compelled to find an alternative at short notice, his father lighted on Lancing – a school with which he had no connection and which he had never seen – mainly because he had noted Evelyn's piety and knew that Lancing had been founded to inculcate High Church principles.

At the time, Lancing was a monastic, solitary, and – three years after the outbreak of the Great War – run-down institution. In his autobiography, Waugh describes his early days there as 'black misery'. Roger Fulford, also a new boy at Head's House in the summer of 1917, has written: 'Regimentation was the thing. Scholarship, skill in athletics and good looks made regimentation possible to bear and opened the door to popularity. Now Evelyn, in those days, was clever but not a scholarship-boy, courageous but no games-player, pleasant-featured but not good-looking. On arrival, he therefore sank to a low place in the esteem of the House and school. In the narrow setting of Head's House and in the wider setting of Lancing College, he was too independent, too prone to notice oddities and comment on them, to be popular. How often in those early days did I hear those ominous words "that awful little tick Waugh".[1]

In chapel, his devotion was pronounced. He walked with a strange and ungainly trudge – the result of having his feet 'strapped down for a week or ten days'[2] when he was operated on for appendicitis in the summer of 1912 – and was mocked for having 'trench feet', an affliction his contemporaries had read about in the newspapers. He wore spectacles; he was small for his age. He joined in all games with enthusiasm, but he was no athlete.

The diary that Waugh kept at Lancing may well be a unique document. During this century, public-school novels and retrospective accounts of public-school life have proliferated, but Waugh seems to be the only writer of the front rank – or indeed of any rank – to have preserved a day-by-day record of school life while it happened. To follow the diary, it is necessary to grasp the structure of the school. It was divided into six houses: Headmaster's (known as Head's), Second's, Olds, Field's, Gibbs', and Sanderson's. The houses other than Head's were collectively known as out-houses. Head's, during Waugh's time there, accommodated some fifty boys and charged extra fees for which, according to Fulford, 'there was no obvious return'. The Headmaster of the school was also *de facto* House-master of Head's: the Reverend Henry Bowlby, 'a tall lean man, distinctly handsome except when the keen winds of the place caught and encrimsoned his narrow nose'.[3] The Headmaster read House-prayers on Sunday evenings, and sometimes limped round the dormitories. Other matters in the House were left to the House-tutor, a post always given to the master next in line for a House, so that during Waugh's time in Head's there were four different House-tutors.

The school buildings comprised, essentially, two large quadrangles, Upper Quad and Lower Quad, dominated by the vast and spectacular neo-Gothic chapel. The Houses occupied the opposing sides of the quadrangles; and the principal characteristic of each was its House Room, which accommodated some forty boys. The elongated House Room of Head's House contained an oak settle; to be promoted to 'the settle' with the top eight boys was the first step up the hierarchy towards the position of House-captain. Dining hall (where the food, according to Waugh, 'would have provoked mutiny in a mid-Victorian poor-house') and lavatories, known as 'Groves', were separate. Academically, the boys were divided into the Upper and Lower School.

Besides Roger Fulford, subsequently the author and editor of a number of

[1] *Evelyn Waugh and his World* (London 1973), p. 17.

[2] *A Little Learning*, p. 56.

[3] *A Little Learning*, p. 98. The Revd. Henry Bowlby (1864–1940): educated Charterhouse and Balliol College, Oxford; Assistant master Eton, 1887–1909; Headmaster of Lancing, 1909–25; Canon Residentiary at Chichester, 1925–30.

historical works, several of Waugh's contemporaries later became well-known: from his own House, Max Mallowan, as an archaeologist; from other Houses, Dudley Carew, as a journalist on *The Times*; Tom Driberg, as the first William Hickey of the *Daily Express* and a left-wing Labour MP; and Hugh (later Lord) Molson, as a Conservative MP.

Of the adults, Waugh was particularly concerned with two men whom he called his 'mentors': J. F. Roxburgh – known as 'J.F.' – and Francis Crease. They crop up regularly in his diary. Roxburgh, then in his early thirties and teaching the Sixth Form, was a Scotsman who subsequently became celebrated as the creator and first Headmaster of Stowe School: an elegant, cultivated classicist of sceptical beliefs who impressed Waugh with his worldliness and panache and stimulated his pupils' interest in prose style, inculculating, before the publication of Fowler's *Modern English Usage*, 'in almost the same terms precision of grammar and contempt of cliché'.[1] The other 'mentor', Francis Crease, Waugh recognized as J.F.'s opposite: a mysterious aesthete who had no formal connection with the school but lived in rented rooms at a farm near by. Waugh was given permission to visit Crease one afternoon a week, 'golden hours', to be instructed in the technique of writing illuminated scripts.

Besides Waugh's transfer to Lancing, another important change in the circumstances of his life since 1916 had been caused by the end of the war and the return home of his elder brother. Alec had been a prisoner-of-war; he already enjoyed, because of *The Loom of Youth*, a reputation as a writer. Evelyn had grown up in his father's Hampstead world of men of letters – Edmund Gosse, E. V. Lucas, Ernest Rhys, St John Ervine, W. W. Jacobs – but after his brother's return from Germany, he soon came into contact with a younger, more Bohemian set of authors and literary men who are now obscure but were then prominent: Clifford Bax, Douglas Goldring, E. S. P. Haynes. Alec's first marriage was to Barbara Jacobs, daughter of W. W. Jacobs the short-story writer, and Evelyn's first flirtation was with her younger sister, Luned.

His early intellectual tastes were romantic: in architecture, he was drawn to the medieval; in drawing, to Beardsley; in books, to *Morte d'Arthur* and *Sinister Street*. When he was seventeen, he made an approving mark, in an *Oxford Book of Victorian Verse* belonging to Dudley Carew, against the poems of Richard Middleton, Hilaire Belloc, Ernest Dowson, Arthur Symons, Richard Le Gallienne, 'Q', and Oscar Wilde.[2] He had no ear, either then or later, for music, but he had a lively interest inherited from his father in the theatre and cinema.

In later life, Waugh reread his Lancing diary with shame, appalled by what he described as its 'consistent caddishness'. Other readers will note characteristics that persist throughout his life: the interest in prose style, intel-

[1] *Ibid.*, p. 159.
[2] Dudley Carew, *A Fragment of Friendship* (London 1974), p. 19.

lectual self-confidence, a sceptical attitude towards those in authority, detachment, a certain puritanism. Thirty-four years after he left Lancing, writing the self-portrait that opens *The Ordeal of Gilbert Pinfold*, Waugh observed of himself: 'As a little boy he had been acutely sensitive to ridicule. His adult shell seemed impervious.' The Lancing diary, which begins a month before Waugh's sixteenth birthday, offers evidence that bears on this transition.

Lancing College, Tuesday 23 September 1919

Alec once said that he kept his life in 'watertight' compartments. It is very true; here I am flung suddenly into an entirely different world, different friends, and different mode of life. All the comforts of home are gone but one doesn't really miss them much.

Great changes have happened. Gordon[1], whose new name is Pussy-foot, has played hell with the House. Easton has greased into a pit[2] and O'Connor has gone on the Settle. He is a terrible man.

Wednesday 24 September 1919

First day is generally damnable. The Head has begun some ridiculous scheme of having Upper Fifths A and B instead of the old Classical and Modern Side. It is an absurd arrangement, the only change being that the poor Moderns do Latin.

Thursday 25 September 1919

Writing in evening school. Today we have started the usual routine beginning with early school. Our form-master is one Woodard, a new parson who, people say, is related to the misguided old gentleman who founded us.[3] He seems quite decent but undoubtedly means to make us work – a fad I abhor in masters. PT is starting again, I am in IA at last. In the afternoon we had a senior House game. We were all fearfully out of training and puffing and sweating but it is a splendid reaction after the long, lazy insipidity of last term. 'Pussy-foot' is taking evening school and wanders (or rather prowls) about looking at our books. We have got to write an explanation of a cartoon in the *Bystander* for tonight. A truly fatuous subject. Money is fast decreasing but I have still got 30s banked with Super[4] and my allowances and a promissary tip

---

[1] E. B. Gordon, House-tutor of Headmaster's (Head's) House.
[2] Oiled his way into obtaining a study.
[3] He was a grandson.
[4] 'Super' or 'Super-spy' – another name for Pussy-foot Gordon.

from my good sister-in-law (I hope she remembers it) and a birthday, so things might be worse.

Friday 26 September 1919

Roxburgh's French is really a joy. It is almost worth doing the wretched subject. He announced the work we were going to do in the 'four delicious hours at our disposal'. The Head made some far-fetched joke about UVA and a bunch of grapes;[1] Roxburgh's comment was, 'Really, the Headmaster's profound classical witticisms are getting on my nerves'. Woodard is going to be awfully dull. English was rather a bright spot, when Savory completed the line 'A damsel with a dulcimer' by 'sackbut, psaltery, and divers kinds of music'. In the afternoon there was an organisation parade. Fremlin, Trenam and I have got into A company. I am rather glad although it means more sweat; one has to start moving sometime, even in the Corps. Fox has put up a notice, 'New boys will be caned upon their sixth late'. As Fremlin remarked, this seems a humane mitigation of the usual crude place for corporal punishment.

Last night we caught Pussy-foot out beautifully. My bed is next to the door and there is a hideous match-boarding partition to keep the draught out. Fremlin, a few beds further down, was enlarging on an interview with him, about ragging Puttass, when I heard a rustling and gentle squeaking of India-rubber boots, the other side of the partition. I peeped round and there was Gordon caught in the act of listening to our conversation. As soon as he saw me, he came striding into the room like a Second's House corps-maniac, as if he had only just come. He went out to light a gas so, at once, O'Connor advised us to say our dibs.[2] He came back to find us all in elaborate devotions. Taking the snub in the spirit in which it was given, he slunk out again, and has been very subdued and pensive all today. Why can't he go to his ruddy Field's House where he is appreciated, instead of interfering with gentlemen in the House.

Saturday 27 September 1919

I don't think we shall be able to rag Woodard long, but meanwhile we are making hay. He is trying to make us use the new pronunciation in Latin, and it is an endless source for supposed misunderstanding.[3] We have also some splendid attempts such as SOOBYOONGTEEWAY for the pronunciation of Subjunctive. He got quite bored when, on his using the new pronunciation in Greek, his pronunciation was greeted with a longdrawn wail of oooh! He threatened to send us all to our House-masters, and I believe he will carry out

[1] UVA: both the initials of a form, Upper Fifth A, and the Latin word meaning 'grape'.

[2] Prayers.

[3] A reformed pronunciation of Latin was formulated around 1870 by various Oxford and Cambridge scholars; but opposition was so powerful that it only began to be taught in schools in the early part of the twentieth century.

the threat. At present he sets very little work which enables me to keep this chronicle in evening school. The library opened today, and incidentally the baths did too (several misguided men went and came out blue and wretched, loudly declaring that it was quite priceless). I have found another of Andrew Lang's book-collecting books. My opinion of the value of my much-valued Elzevir has been rudely shocked.[1] Lun[2] has not written yet so I trust she realizes the ridiculous affair is at an end. Anyhow, if she does open the subject again I think I shall have to snub her. She is really not worth it. Tonight we had the service of Installation of Prefects and House-captains. It seems rather a farce now, but I suppose it is really a good thing to keep it up. We shall soon lose all touch with the old Lancing, and it served as a connecting link. Last night, waiting for a bath, I had to endure seven solid minutes of the Head's conversation. He is a bore, though rather an old dear, I'm beginning to think.

Sunday 28 September 1919

I went to the second service in common with most of the house. The only light relief was caused by faints by small boys. We then adjourned to the unappetizing Sunday breakfast. Being first Sunday there was no Sunday lesson and as this railway strike[3] is making the destination of letters very uncertain it hardly seemed worthwhile expending much energy on my Sunday letter. Some men took the opportunity of not writing at all. We then went to the library, where the library privileges list was up. I missed them by one place, Apthorpe got them and Southwell and I, who were equal next to him, missed ours. It is very hard as I would have almost given anything to get them. I seem to miss everything by just a hair's breadth, first my House colours and now this. I expect when I die, I shall miss getting into heaven by one place and the golden gates will clang to in my face.

In the afternoon, that Spartan system, which the authorities, being unaffected, keep up, of shutting the House Room, drove us out into the cold for a dismal walk along the Coombes road. The blackberries are ripening however, a fact which somewhat alleviated our distress. In the evening the Head preached a not too bad for him sermon on 'Seek first the kingdom of God and then all these shall be added unto you' on the rise of Lancing. It is rather a point of interest with me.

St Michael's Day, Monday 29 September 1919

This strike is causing the rather pleasant sensation of being besieged. We feel so remote from the outer world in our flint-girt fortress without letters, and

---

[1] Andrew Lang (1844–1912), scholar, historian, bibliographer; Elzevir, a long-established Netherlands publishing house celebrated for its fine editions.

[2] Luned Jacobs.

[3] The railwaymen were on strike against a threatened reduction in wages.

the *Sussex Daily* the only paper that has succeeded in penetrating our seclusion. Being a Saint's Day it has been pleasantly slack. The Clubs[1] were voluntary but I had put down for them, fearing boredom more than anything. We had a terrible game however. It does not encourage one to be enthusiastic when you see the company you have to enthuse with. Woodard has had the inordinate bad taste to remember to set us a Greek prose. But for that we have a perfectly immaculate evening. Last week this time we were just having dinner before going to Wyndham's for *The Choice*. Watertight compartments – well, they might be worse but mine leak a bit sometimes.

Tuesday 30 September 1919

Last night Pussy-foot committed another awful breach of good manners. On leaving the dormitory, where he had been but coldly received, he stopped at my bed and said, 'Waugh, I've come to the conclusion that your father must be a very broadminded and enlightened man'. It really is most fearful impertinence for him to try and patronize a man who, even if he doesn't realize that he's very distinguished, is double his own age. The more I see of the man the less I like him. If only we had Dick.[2] This system of moving House-masters about is stinking.

This afternoon our Third League played against the Olds and lost 1–2. It was a fearfully hot game; I was playing centre half, and we all staggered up feeling battered and racked. This is perhaps sufficient excuse for drinking four drinks at the Grubber,[3] a feat I accomplished today.

To the library again after callover.[4] It is amazing how common-room offences mount up. They have now made it one to have a library book out without having it entered or having out more than your ration. I wonder what you *will* be allowed to do in fifty years' time, but perhaps the difficulty will be solved by a revolutionary government's abolition of public schools.

The strike has allowed a few papers and quite a large post to get through. I got letters from Mother and Father.

Wednesday 1 October 1919

At 12.30 there was a parade but by a merciful dispensation it was only an organization one, without arms or side-arms. The morning had been pleasantly slack as the benevolent followers of Mr Thomas[5] are holding up all our books in London, and even the exacting Woodard cannot expect us to work without

---

[1] Games.

[2] Dick Harris, an 'extremely agreeable young man' (*A Little Learning*, p. 100) who had been House-tutor of Head's House when Waugh arrived.

[3] Tuck-shop.

[4] Roll-call.

[5] J. H. Thomas (1874–1949): general secretary National Union of Railwaymen, 1917–31.

them. That is the good part of this strike, that small things like letters (incidentally I got one from Lun today, but a poor three halfpence worth) get through while great consignments of books are kept back. As long as food continues to arrive I see no reason for wishing it to stop. To resume – the parade was organization, chiefly of military-school, and to my horror I was put down as a PT comer-on[1] and have to spend military-school with Staff. Still it is better than musketry which the other poor devils are doing.

Thursday 2 October 1919

Our enterprising timetable today is Greek, double Maths, double Greek. Of this little can be said.

In the evening we went to the library, where the amazing Molson[2] engaged me in conversation, and, having edged me into one of the bays, confessed to having written a book on education which he means to publish and for which he wishes Alec to write a preface. I can hardly think that either will come off but I have not yet had time to read it. He is undoubtedly clever and he has the true aristocrat's capacity of being perfectly at home in anyone's company. He was guilty however of the terrible effusion in the last *Literary Supplement*, so there does not seem much hope for him unless his literary style has greatly improved since then. Still he has great guts. I hope it is some good. By the way, I heard a rather good addition to the large collection of biblical jests. 'The best high jump ever recorded in history – when Our Lord cleared the temple.' Quite good after the usual sort of biblical pun.

Friday 3 October 1919

Friday has always been a particularly unpleasant day, since they fixed on it for their uniform parade. The disgusting part is the preparatory cleaning, when the filthy stuff gets up one's nostrils.

I have spent a lot ot today pondering on the very important question of bindings. I think that if I live like a hermit this term I ought to be able to get one book bound, and with any luck I might get the wherewithal for another at Christmas. I have just thought what an excellent binding could be made of half black morocco, and half cloth of gold, but I have only enough of it to do a very small book and it would only be suitable for certain sorts, such as Oscar Wilde. It would be rather a good idea to go through my little store next holidays and mark each with what I think would suit them best, and get them done, as best I can. I think there are great possibilities in the half-bindings. If only I could do it myself. We have to write an essay on 'Fairytales' this week. Rather a good

[1] A candidate for advancement in the Physical Training hierarchy. PT was organized in groups under boy instructors.

[2] Hugh (now Lord) Molson. See Appendix of Names, p. 794.

subject for Woodard, who, by the way, has quite good taste to judge from his books.

Saturday 4 October 1919

Days are growing very uneventful. It is just about now that one begins thoroughly to settle down to the humdrum course of term. One bright spot was the arrival this morning of a letter from Chapman & Hall's[1] enclosing a note from Stewart Caven, the author of *A Pair of Idols*, saying that he liked my cover drawing very much. They also said that they hoped to be able to give me some more work to do later. This is really most encouraging and is the sort of thing that cheers one up more than all the rags and jokes Lancing has to offer.

I must look up some material for my fairy essay tomorrow. I have a few ideas but not many facts. The strike seems as unmoving as ever so it looks as if we may expect to do without our books for some days yet. As a matter of fact, however, this slackness begins to pall. After all, we do want to get our Certificates most awfully. One advantage of this diary that I had not thought of is that it provides a great deal of material for letters. I must write to Lun tomorrow, I suppose.

Sunday 5 October 1919

Sunday, here, is an amazingly dismal day. In the morning there was a congregational singing practice. After that I went to the library, where, chancing to stray into the poetry bay, I found a copy of Andrew Lang's *Leaves of Parnassus* that I suddenly coveted more than anything in the library. It is printed very well on the most beautiful handmade paper and the feel of its crisp edges made me feel that I could buy no book on anything else again. I wrote off at once to the publishers to know if *Books and Bookmen* was published in the same edition. I also wrote to Dent's for Everyman, Wayfarer, and Temple Classics catalogues. In the evening Fulford[2] and I went to a debate in the provost's room, 'This House prefers Lenin to Pussy-foot'.[3] The result was a draw, thirty-four votes each way. I longed to speak but couldn't summon up enough courage. I will some time this term.

As bibliographical curiosities, I will get one or two of the most ultramodern products of the Bomb Shop, Beaumont's, and the Poetry Bookshop,[4] and have

---

[1] The publishing firm of which Evelyn Waugh's father, Arthur Waugh, had become managing director in 1902.

[2] Roger Fulford. See Appendix of Names, p. 794.

[3] Not Waugh's House-master, but Pussy-foot Johnson, the American temperance advocate, then prominent.

[4] The Bomb Shop was run by an anarchist in the Charing Cross Road; the Beaumont Press in 1919 published, among other writers, Herbert Read and D. H. Lawrence; the Poetry Bookshop, run by Harold Munro, was a publishing firm as well as a bookshop.

them bound. They should prove interesting to future generations. It will cost some money, however, but if I get work from Chapman & Hall's I can manage it.

Monday 6 October 1919

As we have been persuaded to go in for this fives competition, I thought it would be well to take some steps to learn how to play. At any rate I got an order for a pair of gloves, which of course the Grubber had not got, and got Fulford to bag me a court. It was no good however as I was down to play goal for a very senior senior House game. It was a fearful shock, I only found it by a mere chance. I had no idea how big a goal is until I started keeping it. After half-time I began to lose count of the goals I let through, but I rather think they reached double figures. I will never make disparaging comments on Gilbey's performances again. The only explanation I can think of, to account for Crowe's extraordinary conduct in putting me there, is that he has realized that we have no goal for the Under Sixteen House matches and intends training me. I only hope that this afternoon has discouraged the experiment.

Tuesday 7 October 1919

This morning at 12.30 I played my first game of fives and returned very sore. It is a most painful game unless you hit the thing square every time. I can't think how some people manage to play without gloves.

I was eleventh for the week, equal with Mallowan.[1] Much better than I expected; if I can keep up that level with the same amount of work, this form looks as if it might be quite a cushy show.

In the afternoon our Third League played Field's, and much to our discredit were badly beaten 3–1. We all got quite dispirited towards the end and my boots hurt like the devil.

Afterwards I heroically avoided the Grubber and rushed off fifty lines for Streatfeild. I don't think I shall see my way to doing the seventy-two that Puttock had the bad taste to set me this morning. He is going very much on the 'Oderint, dum metuant'[2] principle and ticks people off right and left. He swept down and ticked Fremlin off today for ragging before grace. I really don't wonder that all the out-House men loathe him so.

I have taken a Thomas Hardy out of the library today as I feel I ought to read something of him.

Last night we had a rather good rag with O'Connor in the dormitory by saying our dibs before he came up and then refusing to when he told us. He is

---

[1] Max Mallowan (1904–): Professor of Western Asiatic Archaeology at London University 1947–62; Fellow of All Souls College, Oxford, 1962–71. Knighted 1968. Husband of Dame Agatha Christie.

[2] 'Let them hate so long as they fear.' Quoted in Cicero's *Philippic*, 1.14.

really awfully officious considering how lately he was one of the leaders of our set. We are rapidly dwindling now with Newman, Boyd and he on the Settle and Pratt leaving. Even I am going to do comers-on. I suppose we must be growing up but it is a pity; we had some wonderful rags.

Wednesday 8 October 1919

Today at breakfast among other letters (one from Longman, Green & Co. saying that the handmade paper edition of *Books and Bookmen* was out of print, and another from Lun with an incoherent enclosure from Mrs Jacobs) came one from Father in which he suggested my doing a cover for *Invisible Tides* by one Beatrice Seymour. It is awfully nice of him not only for the money, which will buy several books or pay for another theatre, but it is so priceless getting one's things printed. I have sketched out two or three ideas already. I am very glad I took my paints and inks back with me this time.

We have found that Woodard has the amiable weakness of letting one get books, so now hardly anyone ever brings any in and the stampede to House Rooms and pits[1] always wastes some ten minutes. By arranging it by relays we waste quite a lot of time.

Tonight we have only one subject so I can plan my drawing. I wonder if Pussy-foot would let me draw in third evenings[2] instead of reading. He might and anyhow it's worth trying.

Thursday 9 October 1919

I went to Gordon this morning and he, albeit grudgingly, gave me permission to draw in third evening tonight. It does not however look as if I shall have time if I am to finish this work, as Woodard has set us a fearful anagram in Latin to work out. It quite beats me. I have made some efforts during the day but the atmosphere here is so uncongenial that they came to little. The Dent catalogues arrived today and I have found many things I want badly. They do do things well.

Friday 10 October 1919

This morning I tore out and destroyed all the first part of this diary about the holidays. There was little worth preserving and a very great deal that could not possibly be read and was really too dangerous without being funny, so all this book, now reduced to a very meagre pamphlet, must be this term and I shall have to be wiser next holidays in what I record.

[1] Studies.
[2] 'First Evening': prep. before supper. 'Second Evening': prep. after supper, from about 8.15 pm to 8.45 pm; the smaller boys then went to bed. 'Third Evening': a more casual prep. period when boys were allowed to read books of their own choice, but had to keep to their places in the House Room.

Today was frightfully cold and there was a wretched uniform parade, quite unrelieved by any touch of humour. No one even dropped their rifle and got defaulters.[1] It however had the good result of making me so sick of the machinations of the Corps that I crossed my name off the comers-on list just in time for tomorrow. It hardly looks as if I shall ever be able to get a game of fives before the tournament as the accommodation in the way of courts is so ludicrously bad. I should think that some benevolent old boy could present at least another four. The present number is too fatuous.

Father returned Molson's essay today with a very excellent letter of criticism. He is always emphasizing how much more advanced our generation is than his was. I wonder if we are really going to produce any great men or if we will fizzle into mediocrity. We certainly seem more precocious if that is at all a good sign.

Saturday 11 October 1919

At 12.30 I played fives again with Newman. I am beginning to pick it up much more and it grows less painful as one gets on. Today the post brought a letter from Father in which he suggests my putting a crescent moon into my cover design. I think that it would be a mistake artistically however appropriate it may be symbolically. Anyhow I shall do everything else first and then see how it looks. A book on *Ancient Art and Ritual* came from Mrs Jacobs in that lamentable piece of production the Home University Library service. I suppose I ought to try and read it. This afternoon our First XI beat the Old Westminster 1–0. They played awfully well. Our amiable form-master has forgotten to set us any work which gives me time for my drawing to which I added the framework last night and which now shows up, I think, rather well. Altogether I am fairly content with it. I hope I don't make a mess of the lettering. If only I can do that all right I think my guinea is secure.

Sunday 12 October 1919

Sunday is always a monochrome day here. In the morning there was the 'new men's concert',[2] a curious relic of barbarism. I don't think anyone really enjoys it. The performers certainly do not and it is seldom really funny. This time it was particularly vapid. I tried to do the last part of the lettering for *Invisible Tides* but it is quite impossible to work in the House Room and as I did not get my library privileges I was forced to get leave from Gordon to use his classroom and eventually got it finished but not very satisfactorily. I do hope

[1] Punishment parade.

[2] After three weeks the new boys in turn stood on a table in the House Room and sang a song. They were occasionally applauded, but usually bombarded with missiles. In 1917 Waugh as a new boy sang, 'My wife's gone to the country – Hurray Hurrah'; the words were provided by his father.

they take it. In the afternoon, as it was raining, Fremlin and I returned early
from our walk and helped Gordon to mend his printing press. It would be
priceless to have one but they are rather costly. He invited us to tea and we sat
round his fire talking scandal and eating toast till chapel. Perhaps he isn't really
so bad after all.

Monday 13 October 1919

Very little doing in the morning. The ordinary round of work, PT, and work
again. In the afternoon there was a root-about and I had to stand in goal while
all the Hamertons and Leas and Rowes shot at me. It is really an awful place. I
am sure I shall make a fool of myself in the Under Sixteens.

I am very anxious about the result of my cover design. I hope I hear by the
first post tomorrow and don't have to wait all day for an answer. The posts out
are so bad here that it may only reach them last post tonight.

Tuesday 14 October 1919

I am afraid that my design cannot have reached Father until last night. I
have not heard from him yet, though the reply from Arthur Humphreys to my
inquiry about the Rossetti arrived first post. It is still in print and at the modest
price of 6s 6d. If Father accepts my design, as I really at heart expect him to, I
think I will get it. But there are so many books I want badly. I could easily
spend three times the price. Still, I may score something for my birthday on the
28th, though birthdays decrease greatly in value as they get more. This
afternoon our Third League lost against Sanderson's 2–3. Up till the last five
minutes they were losing and then I did my leg in and let through two goals in
succession. I hope, however, my leg will stand me leave off the parade
tomorrow. It certainly hurts like the devil now, but there is always the danger
of its getting well in the night. Other letters were one from Lun and a *World*
from Alec with an article and portrait by and of him. Life is awfully dull just
now and Father's silence makes it anxious too, a terrible mixture. If he accepts
Invisible Tides I think I shall ask him to let me try for the *Chanson de Roland*.
That is a subject I should really love doing.

Wednesday 15 October 1919

In the morning, by the merciful orders of the doctor, I stayed in bed for early
school and came down to find a letter from Father accepting my cover and a
guinea from Chapman & Hall's. Sitting out all the morning I busied myself
with catalogues and at last decided to get Marlowe's *Hero and Leander* in
Dent's Renaissance Series at 16s with my money.

Thursday 16 October 1919

A letter arrived from Alec saying that he and Barbara were stopping in Brighton for the weekend for a football match and that they will stagger up here to see me on Sunday. Quite a good arrangement. If I get off parade tomorrow life looks as if it were going to be reasonably comfortable for the next day or so. I have asked for the *Chanson de Roland* but can hardly hope to get it. It may not be having a wrapper at all. After callover to the library as usual and there the boy Molson said that Father had written him a long letter and sent him a copy of *Tradition and Change*.[1] Jolly nice of him. I really think Molson is going to do something in life after he gets over his affection and delittantism. What a ridiculous generation we are. In the last generation people never began to think until they were about nineteen, to say nothing of thinking about publishing books and pictures. Time can only show if we are going to be any better for it.

Friday 17 October 1919

'Life is as tedious as a twice-told tale, vexing the dull ear of a drowsy man'.

There has been absolutely nothing doing today. No letters have arrived and nothing funny has happened here. I got leave off parade and spent all day reading Marlowe and Conan Doyle, except some of the time when I looked through Gordon's books. He has a beautiful edition of the *Odyssey*, but I suppose some people would call the type precious. I got a postal order for 16s 6d and sent off to Dent's for *Hero and Leander*. I have read it in the library's shaving-paper edition and it seems very Elizabethan in expression.

My fairy-story essay came off quite well with 27 out of 30, but my spelling is still awfully bad. I had spelt imagination with two 'm's' three or four times. Tomorrow is a Saint's Day and most men are going on Veniams,[2] so it promises to be as dull as today has been.

Saturday 18 October 1919

Saints' Days, when one has not got a Veniam, are perfectly godless. After morning school, two hours of which were spent doing a précis of almost inconceivable dullness and incoherence, there was absolutely nothing to do until chapel. In the afternoon we got the news that Carter ma. has died suddenly at Cambridge. It is rather disconcerting to hear it of a man whom last term you used to rag. I pity his brother. In the evening I went to the library but more as a social function than to read. I there had another long conversation with Molson. He tells me Alec has refused to do a preface as, really, he could hardly help doing. He seems rather bored by it, however.

---

[1] Arthur Waugh's second book of collected essays.
[2] On 'Veniam' Days, 'Red-letter' Saints' Days, boys could obtain leave to go out with parents or friends.

Sunday 19 October 1919

It was as if a Brangwyn painting suddenly found its way into an exhibition of etchings. Alec and Barbara came over after Sunday lesson, which was more dull than one could have thought possible, and we went over Alma Mater. Both Barbara and the school were looking their best and I was proud of them both. We had lunch at the Pad, and quite a good lunch too, and then went up to see the library. Unfortunately they had to rush off again at three but it was a very jolly time. Apparently Father is at present engaged on his autobiography, which perhaps accounts for his not having written for so long. I gave Barbara my Sunday letter to take back; I hope she doesn't lose it, as there are far too many luxuries to be got at school for one to be able to afford necessities like stamps. In the evening there was a debate on 'This House thinks suicide the most reasonable form of death'. I again looked to speak but had not the courage or conceit. Molson did, however, but not to much purpose, I thought.

Monday 20 October 1919

Back among the etchings again. The morning was unrelieved by any humour or incident. In the afternoon there was another root-about and I had to stand in goal and be shot at. I dread the Under Sixteens. My *Hero and Leander* hasn't turned up yet. I hope the letter hasn't got mislaid or anything. A rule has been made forbidding one to have one's own food at lunch. It really looks as if we shall have to live by bread alone. It is certainly the only palatable food that is provided in any quantity at all.

Tuesday 21 October 1919

Little happened in the morning except that the proofs of the block for *Invisible Tides* came by the morning post. It has reproduced rather well and with the exception of the lettering, which looks worse than ever, is I think quite good. In the afternoon we played the Gibbs' with our Third League. The Dyke Field grounds are quite ludicrous and we had the worst of all. On the goal which I was called upon to defend first half there was no crossbar but only a piece of rope which sagged enough to make a difference of about a foot and a half in the middle. The first shot went over this but, I think, under the place where the crossbar would have been. Baker came bustling up, saying that the rope made no difference and that it was to count a goal. We disagreed and expressed our opinions perhaps rather honestly. Anyway he threatened to turn O'Connor off the field, quite an unconstitutional proceeding, and when he shouted out, 'Well anyhow, lay 'em out' said he would have him common-roomed.[1] I don't know if he will or not. Eventually the score was 3–3, as they made it, or 3–1 as we did (there was another discussion about the next goal!) It

[1] Disciplined.

really is a bad system to let prefects play in Third Leagues as it is a great advantage having a captain who cannot be contradicted. All our prefects and House-captains are much too good and play First League or First Club. Most people seem rather to hope he does get common-roomed, but I think it would be damnably unfair. Still, there's no knowing what these out-House prefects will do.

Wednesday 22 October 1919

Today, when coming back to the House Room after early school we found the notice 'D. M. O'Connor has been suspended playing in leagues for a month' up on the House Room board. Besides weakening our League this is rather bad for the House reputation, but I'm jolly glad he didn't get common-roomed as I don't really think he deserved it. In break, my *Hero and Leander* arrived. It is really a beautiful edition, bound far better than I expected in quarter leather (I think it looks like pigskin), and three-quarters parchment. The paper and type are splendid. It is a numbered edition too.

Thursday 23 October 1919

In the afternoon we played Field's with our Third League and considering that we had been deprived of O'Connor did better than might have been expected, eventually losing 3–2. One I let through was most awfully easy and I let it go right through my feet, but the others were almost impossible. On the whole for me it was a failure. In the library Molson told me that he had had another article accepted in some periodical on education. I must try and write one next holidays.

Friday 24 October 1919

This afternoon we had one of the funniest parades I have ever been on. The only bad point about it was that the Corps with its military thoroughness rather overdid things.

It was the Certificate A candidates examination and Roxburgh's address beforehand gave us to expect the most fearful blood of the Guards-major type we get for the inspection. When we got down there we found the most blatantly risen-from-the-ranks I've ever seen. He was not even a Temporary Gentleman but a Permanent Oik. He addressed Fox with a 'come here – boy!'. As Roxburgh said, he was 'quite monstrous'. He, however, fairly tied the miserable candidates up with his amazing orders. There was a wonderful period of stupefied hysteria after each of the orders, which were certainly somewhat involved. The first hour and a half was sheer delight but as it grew later even the sight of dropped rifles began to pall. Candidate after candidate tried to drill us but the cry was still 'They come'. It got quite desperate when at the end no mention was made of the expected half-holiday. On going into chapel a notice was found on the Corps board saying that everyone had passed. How Bond and Roxburgh wangled the little grocer, God knows.

Saturday 25 October 1919

A pleasant reaction after yesterday's exertions. In the morning we had a very fine hour with Woodard. When two forms are taken together things generally begin to move. After the usual preliminary stampede for books he settled down to give us church history questions and rashly asked for any legend we knew connected with the Early Church. It was a golden opportunity and we did not fail to take advantage of it. We filled paper with obscure legends and there was a storm of questions as to what constituted a legend and what was the exact line between the Early Church and stories about the Disciples and minor saints generally. Some amazing anecdotes of St Dunstan were cited and the hour went merrily by, everyone cribbing like sin.

It looks as if the government are not going to resign after all. Lloyd George seems glued to office, the little beast. Still, if he is in the minority in the House he can't keep on long and then perhaps he'll get turned out. But a terrible amount of people seem to trust him still.

Sunday 26 October 1919

A more than usually uneventful day. One Temple,[1] who appears to be rather a leading light, came to preach and talked socialism to some purpose but greatly to the disgust of the great washed.

Monday 27 October 1919

Some birthday presents have rolled up. Some books from the Jacobs crowd, an Everyman *Divine Comedy* and *Child's* (!) *Book of Saints* and a book of drawings of Rome. Most thoughtful and kind and useless. I have written an essay on 'Romance', quite off the subject but it gives me some pleasure working out an idea I had had some time.

Tuesday 28 October 1919

It is extraordinary how unimportant birthdays become after a few years. Today has been a pleasant enough day but little out of the ordinary. At breakfast a letter came from Muriel[2] and from Alec, on Chelsea football paper, 'with the manager's compliments', 'NO PRESENT: THANKS FOR INSULTING MY FRIENDS'. I suppose he means my disparaging remarks about his Lunn friends.[3] I hope he isn't really bored. I learned that I was bottom for the week, a feat I have seldom accomplished before; other than that,

---

[1] William Temple, later Archbishop of Canterbury.

[2] Muriel Silk, Arthur Waugh's secretary.

[3] Hugh Lunn, better known as Hugh Kingsmill, biographer and man of letters.

little marked it off as any different from any other Tuesday. A splendid parcel of confectionery arrived from home after lunch on which we sublimely overate ourselves. Nothing has yet arrived from the Flemings, but they are generally a day or so late, or from my aunts. I think 10s may reasonably be expected from Aunt Elsie. Father sent Walter Crane's *Bases of Design* for which I asked. Meanwhile there is no work except a little Greek testament.

Wednesday 29 October 1919

This morning at breakfast a quid arrived from the Norton aunts, which was jolly decent of them. It is no good my thinking of buying another of those Dent's Renaissance books as I have only thirty bob to last out the term with. I must wait until Christmas. Nothing has turned up from the Flemings so I must conclude that they have forgotten. In the afternoon we had PT comers-on again, which is getting rather awful. I rather hope however I do get in the Under Sixteen PT squad as it would be rather a disgrace not to be. Still, I hate taking these things seriously.

Thursday 30 October 1919

Last night we ragged O'Connor somewhat. This morning Lea comes up to Fremlin in the Groves quad and tells him that he got a late last night (he had been having a bath). Apparently O'Connor to revenge his ragging had lied to Lea about it. Fremlin soon got off the late and it will give us a splendid handle against O'Connor. I can see we are working up for a big row. We can't go on as we are and either O'Connor will be degraded or we'll find ourselves all up in the common room. From O'Connor's previous escapades I should think the first not unlikely.

A letter came from Father today from which I gather that he does not like my 'Romance' essay. Apparently the satirical parts have put his back up. However I shall try it on Woodward, and if he snubs me over it I shall not try again. I think I shall either write journalese or *Spectator* essays. But I don't think he will. I am convinced there is some merit in it.

We had a senior House game today and I think I kept goal a bit better, though I still always hit it out instead of catching it.

Friday 31 October 1919

Parade was quite pleasant; the inspecting general was quite a gentleman, or at any rate knew how to behave as such. Bevan dropped a rifle. At the band practice afterwards the bandmaster appears to have called Cordner-James a 'bugger' and he at once retaliated by calling him 'a bloody fool'. The bandmaster rushed off to Bond and had him degraded to the ranks and put in defaulters next Monday. It seems rather unfair, but it is rather bad form to swear at one's social inferiors.

Saturday 1 November 1919

This morning we had a full choral before breakfast. I can't conceive why we should be subjected to such an amazing time. Being a Saint's Day there was little work, and being Lancing it was far too cold to watch the match, so I went for a short run and lay longer than was good for me in a splendidly hot, hot bath. Apparently Dick is starting a scheme for a Fifth Form debating club and general literary gathering. It sounds feasible but smacks rather of the awful Mais.[1]

Boyd returned from his Veniam full of having spent the day with his Dorothy. He has rashly promised to take her to Sheerness next holidays and now realizes that the evening will run him up to two or three quid. It is rather funny that I have also been proposing taking Phil[2] and Lun to the Finchley Road dancing hall. I feel now that if I had money I should spend it all on dress and amusements.

Tuesday 4 November 1919

In the afternoon we played Second's Third League and of course won. The score was I think 9–0. It was desperately dull for me in goal. I only had one save to do and no behinds or corners. Goal is a terrible place, much too much in the fore when their forwards are strong and no look-in when they are bad.

Our ideas about Dick's Society are that it should be divided into groups – literary, artistic, political, musical etc. – who should read papers, exchange criticism on work, and hold informal discussions. Now and then formal debates should be held. I should also like to hold a sort of dramatic club in connection with it. The only thing is that very possibly not enough people could be interested and certainly very few would know enough to read a paper on anything. I could read several, and E. J. Carter ought to be able to, and Carew[3] will, but I am afraid that the discussions will have to be very elementary at first.

Wednesday 5 November 1919

Last night Fulford, Molson, Carew and I went to Dick and sat in his room in front of his fire discussing the Society till well after the end of third evening. We arranged that the groups should be political, literary and artistic; music was decided impracticable owing to Brenter's[4] jealousy. For the present Molson has taken over the political, with the help of Carew, Fulford the literary, and I the art, to canvass suitable members. We decided after a great many suggestions on the Dilettantes as our name. With any luck I think that it might be a success. I know several subjects I would like to read papers on: 'The

---

[1] Presumably the writer, S. P. B. Mais.
[2] Phil Fleming.
[3] Dudley Carew. See Appendix of Names, p. 794.
[4] Brent-Smith, the school organist and choirmaster.

Tendencies of Modern Painting'; 'The Failure of the Pre-Raphaelites'; 'The Limerick as the Most Perfect Form of Poetical Expression'. I think if I am elected president or secretary that I shall try and arrange that the first artistic debate shall be 'This House is of the opinion that the nineteenth century Gothicist revival may be justified by the school buildings', proposed by E. J. Carter and opposed by myself. I have managed to assemble a small circle today which will, I think, be enough for the present. I expect that the first two or three discussions will have to be entirely done by Barnsley, Carter, and myself but I hope others may take heart soon.

Thursday 6 November 1919

The Dilettanti – apparently that is the plural of dilettante – are going merrily. Recruits pour in, though certainly hardly the ones we might want. The chief difficulty is dissuading self-confident undesirables. Quite strange boys I had never heard of accost me and ask to become members. I have enrolled one Chalker who has few qualifications, but we want it to be perfectly democratic. Above all, we must behave entirely as equal to each other. It is a great pleasure being able to work under Dick again. We spent a long time with him tonight talking and have booked spending first evening Saturday with him. We are having the elections on Saturday after callover. I do hope I get either president or secretaryship. I do honestly think I am the most suitable man for the job. The difficulty is that Barnsley, Carter and I all wish to hold office, but I think that I shall be able to buy off Carter by getting him O.C.[1] debates. Today our Third League were beaten 4–2 by Sanderson's. Two of their goals, however, were shot by our side. At 12.30 I was subjected to a goal-keeping practice. Athletics, however, seem very unimportant when we are having so much activity with the Dilettanti.

Friday 7 November 1919

A few more converts trickled in. I have great difficulty in warding off boys who obviously know nothing. One youth wished to join whose favourite painter was Landseer.

The slothful Woodard has not yet corrected our essays. I wished he would brace himself up. I am anxious to hear the philistine's verdict upon mine.

Saturday 8 November 1919

At 12.30 I had to do another awful goal-keeping practice. It is rumoured that the Under Sixteens are on Monday. I shall be awfully nervous but it is not quite as bad as the awful House swimming match. At five we had our election. I got made chairman and Carew made secretary. I really think I shall be able to

[1] Officer Commanding.

make it a success. We made lists of the subjects on which we were willing to read papers and everyone seemed full of ideas. We are much more compact than any of the other groups. The boy Woodward seems to be very nice, but Carter tells me he was much sought after his first term; he thinks, however, he kept out of it all.

Sunday 9 November 1919

After Sunday lesson we had our first Dilettanti general meeting and went on after lunch. Most things were referred to the groups to decide. We then adjourned but I assembled my little family and we drew up a programme for the term. I am reading on Tuesday on 'Book Illustration and Decoration'. It will not be at all carefully prepared as I have no time, but it will set the show going and I like to have my show working before everyone else gets going. I think my group is easily the best, nicest men and most ideas. The boy Chalker is the only blot. In the evening there was the school debate and it was a flagrant instance of how those in authority can wangle themselves to win. If I was one of 'the unkillable children of the very poor' I am sure I should be a raving revolutionary. I feel very much the way power can crush any rising. It came to this, that either we voted for the old constitution or ceased to be members. Roxburgh said that if we passed our proposed vote of no-confidence he and the whole committee would dissolve the house and no one could call another meeting. If the 'labour' party formed a house on their own it would be a private society. The old School Debating Society would reform but without us as members. We would thus be expelled from the house. Of course the motion was lost, most of us not voting at all. Of course it was quite 'in order' but a glaring injustice all the same.

Monday 10 November 1919

This afternoon the much-dreaded Under Sixteens came off and quite came up to expectations. It could scarcely have been worse. They won 10–2. I played badly, as the score shows; the backs had better not have been playing at all. It was altogether an absolutely vile show. After hot baths however – we got leave to use the Upper Head's lav.[1] as our water was cold as usual – things looked brighter. Games don't really matter awfully and there are the Dilettanti and such things to pass the term. Last night too we had a splendid rag with O'Connor (Sunday night is obviously our time) and it looks as if there will be a lot doing in that way before the end of term. We have decided to cut off his fly-buttons last night of term.

Tuesday 11 November 1919

This morning Hill asked me in the armoury whether I was willing to speak in

---

[1] Changing room and wash room.

a debate. It really is a great compliment. I am to propose the motion that 'This House believes that reincarnation of souls is the most reasonable solution to the problem of human immortality'; of course, it isn't, but I have a few ideas to defend it with. It is obviously Roxburgh's idea to see if the Fifth Forms really are willing to take the responsibilities we have been claiming.

At 11 am today we had the King's amazing proposition of two minutes silence to commemorate last year. It was really a disgusting idea of artificial nonsense and sentimentality. If people have lost sons and fathers they should think of them whenever the grass is green or Shaftesbury Avenue brightly lighted, not for two minutes on the anniversary of a disgraceful day of national hysteria. No one thought of the dead last year, why should they now?

Wednesday 12 November 1919

Today we had an extra half for no very apparent reason, and we took advantage of it to have our first Dilettanti meeting. More than that, we had all the first half of morning school open, as our benign form-master was away for the day. In the afternoon there was a First Eleven match against Westminster. We were infinitely the better team but they kept the score down wonderfully. After the match we had our Art Group meeting. I had been too occupied with the school debate – I am afraid that I must admit that I have been bought over from the democratic party by the distinction – to prepare much of a paper. I managed to talk however more or less coherently, though I found myself repeating once or twice (no doubt the effect of trying to remember the rest of the quotation 'Yet would you tread again all the path over'), on 'Book Illustration and Decoration'. I hope I speak better at the school debate. I think my performance today was good enough for the Group but no better. I could have done it better. I forgot to post my Sunday letter until last night and am rather afraid that it may have caused some anxiety at home.

Thursday 13 November 1919

I have written a little of my debate speech but it is not going very well. Hill has rather put the wind up me by giving me a long preparation, very kindly meant but rather frightening.

Friday 14 November 1919

The Corps took over today almost, in its bellumnial manner. We had a horrible parade with dud blanks. Newman and I managed to disengage ourselves from our platoon on an errand of 'first-ditching', whatever that may be. We did not rejoin it until the final standfast and had quite a good time joining in with different sections in turn – we kept fairly warm too. Woodard has at last corrected our essays. As I expected, I was first. I wish there were form prizes for English.

Saturday 15 November 1919

Whittall got beaten for asking O'Connor if he might do a soprano cough.

Sunday 16 November 1919

We had a good Dilettanti show of Fulford's Literature Group this afternoon. We had quite a good rag in the private business but the actual show, poem reading, was poor. Mallowan read part of *The Everlasting Mercy* quite well; I read Belloc's *Song of the South Downs*. The debate in the evening was rather good fun. We lost hopelessly (29–59 votes) but I think that I might have got a few more people round if I had had more time for the summing up. As it was, everyone, with the exception of Molson who will take any view if it is unconventional, spoke against us and I had no time for a defence. My speech however seems to have been quite a success and many people since, I think sincerely, have congratulated me on it.

Monday 17 November 1919

Another dull day but infinitely better than the alarms and discursions of last Monday. In the afternoon, although the Menu on the Clubs Board said 'All change and do anything', our bloods decreed a run to Nearer Steep Down. No small affliction but once one has established a reputation of being able to do better one need not sweat, so I took things easy. The boy Woodward has lettered out our Dilettanti notice for tomorrow, extremely well, in red and black.

Tuesday 18 November 1919

We had a Dilettanti Art Group meeting this evening. The boy Woodward read us an excellent paper on 'Lettering and Illuminating', but it provided little food for discussion. I managed to raise one point about colour which made them talk a bit, but it is still always just one or two of us who do the talking and the rest remain inarticulate.

Wednesday 19 November 1919

We again had PT comers-on with Staff bounding about like a pantomime fairy.

It looks rather as if Alec is overwriting himself. He has used exactly the same phrase in two articles, in a thing on Compton Mackenzie in *John O'London's Weekly* and in a review in the ill-famed *Herald*. I should hardly have thought he could afford to do that sort of thing yet.

Thursday 20 November 1919

Last night Mallowan was told by O'Connor that he was going to report him, but I don't think he intends to. It would be an admission of incompetence to say that his juniors whistled after lights out. We have almost given up ragging him and have turned our attention to the bumptious Boothby. There is nothing of interest in the term. 'Life is one long process of getting tired.' From all I hear from home, the Jacobs household are having a fair share of excitement. They have at last determined to separate; she's going to take the children, however. Their final row apparently was about the children being boarders. I must say I think the woman's right over that. It is about the only thing that could brace them up.

Friday 21 November 1919

Parade today was splendidly slack after the last two weeks. It only took an hour. The War Office have sent down a lorryful of new rifles. They are rather a score as they are lighter than the old ones but arrived in a terrible state of grease. After parade there was a committee meeting to discuss the behaviour of the men who have formed the Head's House group. It is rotten that house jealousy must enter into everything. Dick has got rather a blood down to talk to the Political Group tomorrow week. We are all going to be allowed to be there. He is one Davidson[1], Bonar Law's secretary, and ought to be good.

Saturday 22 November 1919

Writing in science most 'unoriginally prolix'. Little happened.

Sunday 23 November 1919

The Art Group meeting in the afternoon was quite a good show. Barnsley read a not too bad paper on 'The Tendencies of Modern Art'.

Monday 24 November 1919

We had a half today for some quite unexplained reason. Anyway we didn't question the gift of the Lord and took it with thanks. It was however a desperately dull day. I wasn't playing in the House game so all I could do was to sit over the fire all the afternoon. Gordon has done a most damnable thing today. Even Fulford can find nothing to say to defend him for it. The boy Trenam had to be common-roomed for lates. His last late was got by him being unable to get on a boot as he had hurt his foot. This same bad foot sent him up to the San. this morning before he could be beaten. Gordon fetched him down, made him dress, be beaten, and go up again!

Tuesday 25 November 1919

A thoroughly unsatisfactory day. The only bright spot was my place in form which was sixth. I have had to scrap my paper on 'Limericks'. I saw that they

[1] J. C. Davidson, a leading Conservative; a close friend of Baldwin.

hadn't got the right sense of humour to enjoy it and might even think that they were being ragged and resent it. I don't know what I'm going to talk about. I wanted to read some of the lesser-known poets of the last twenty years, Dowson, Middleton, A. E. Housman, etc but I cannot find a copy of the Oxford *Victorian Verse* anywhere. We played Second's and won 6–1 in the Third League. But none of these things cheer. I am weary of an old passion and thoroughly depressed. Anyhow there are only a little over three weeks more of term. I almost think I am homesick. A long letter came yesterday from Lun which I had perforce to answer. She seems quite unaware of her people's proposed separation.

Wednesday 26 November 1919

Today is always bad with PT and parade and PT comers-on. Today it was rather slacker than usual as the haircutters came. Tonight too there is a lecture which may prove quite entertaining by Hamilton-Fyfe[1] on the 'Reconstruction of Modern Europe'.

Friday 28 November 1919

The weather is really most curious, snow in the morning, rain in the afternoon and thunderstorm in the evening. Apparently some American professor puts it down to the approaching end of the world by collision with some fragment of the sun. Our form could hardly conceivably be slacker. We have only two pages of principal parts for tonight and a sort of anagram acrostic for tomorrow. I heard from O'Connor another excellent story of Gordon. When O'Connor was suspended from playing in Leagues for a month he took up fives and the only man he could find to play with was the little boy Lushington. That evening Gordon had O'Connor into his room and accused him of having a keenness on the child. He really has the manners of an Olds House underschool.[2]

Saturday 29 November 1919

This afternoon we had a rather enjoyable House paper-chase. This evening Davidson gave his lecture. It was amazingly interesting and he seemed to be well up in all the political byways and hedges. He took George's[3] announcement of the signing of peace to the King. His views were most enlightening and rather cynical. The chief memory of the Peace Treaty was that they all came away in their wrong hats. Apparently the railway strike was entirely due to the

[1] H. Hamilton Fyfe (1869–1951), author and journalist; editor *Daily Herald* 1922–6.
[2] Junior.
[3] Lloyd George.

personal jealousy of Thomas and Cramp.[1] D'Annunzio appears to be entirely a put-up job by Italy.[2] The more I see of politics the more dishonest and fascinating they appear.

Sunday 30 November 1919

In the morning our big Parliamentary Debate came off but I didn't think that it went awfully well. The imbecile Molson produced much too long a Bill altogether. We Independents were tucked away at the far end, and these treble orators will not speak up.

Some sensational American scientist has produced some theory that by conjunction of planets or something the world will end or at any rate become extinct on the 17th December. We can hardly hope that this is true but the weather seems rather hysterical if that is any sign.

Monday 1 December 1919

An utterly dull day. A steady downpour of rain all day made Clubs impossible so we had ridiculous PT games in the Great School. Slackness is ever so much more tiring than energy and I feel quite washed out.

Tuesday 2 December 1919

This morning started with a terrific hurricane. A big pane of glass was blown out of one of the top windows in chapel and crashed into the side pew next to the boy Hutton. Unfortunately the storm abated so that we had to do a school run, after which I spent much more than I can afford at the Grubber. I have suddenly realized that it will be very hard to make ends meet in the next ten days. I have got very poor suddenly but really one cannot live under a bob a day under present conditions. Today I have spent five. In the evening we had an Art Group meeting, which was not too bad, upon the destruction of the Victorian age. I spoke rottenly. I am sick of body and soul and can't connect sentences or think.

If ever I paint anything really fine I shall make a huge collection of all my other work and have a jolly old bonfire. If I ever do anything better than that I shall destroy the first. The idea sounds familiar. I believe it's O. Henry. (Why does one always think of O. Henry as if it was O'Henry?) My God, I can't think tonight. There's more work than usual too. I believe I am getting most fearfully moody and melancholy. What's the quotation about 'moody, melancholy, mad, pipe a tune to dance to bed' or is it 'moping'? *Shropshire*

---

[1] J. H. Thomas was general secretary, and C. T. Cramp was president of the National Union of Railwaymen.

[2] In September 1919 the romantic Italian poet d'Annunzio seized Fiume and turned it into an independent state.

Lad. This is quite incoherent like a page from Wells. Oh hell what rot I'm writing.

Wednesday 3 December 1919

We went for a House run to Nearer Steep Down today. No one could find the way. We stopped a hundred yards too soon; a great white sea mist hung all over the downs and was wet on our bare chests; it seemed to heave and creep up the edges of the slopes. And Mr Einstein has discovered a new theory of the universe!

Thursday 4 December 1919

This morning Pratt gave a farewell tea to all his friends at the Grubber. It was awfully good fun. Dick was there and the life and soul of the whole thing. We had an excellent tea and he gave us leave off callover; we sat on until just in time for chapel and capped funny stories, chiefly about ragging masters. He is a splendid man and to think that we've got the reptile in his place. Tonight Beckett and Carpentier are giving their show.[1] If Carpentier doesn't win I stand to lose my last bob. It seems very unpatriotic betting against Beckett but he has got such a bull-neck.

Friday 5 December 1919

Last night Carpentier laid Beckett out in the first round. This has somewhat alleviated my financial distress.

Apparently Mr and Mrs Jacobs have decided not to separate this time.

Saturday 6 December 1919

The concert today was a most god-forsaken bore. Sir John Sankey[2] the coal report man came to give away the prizes in a huge frock-coat and spoke such a speech as I have never heard before. Either he is a most brilliant and profound cynic and did it out of rag or he must be semi-imbecile. He was just like a rather exaggerated parody. He called a minute's silence for the old boys who had been killed and quoted statistics and percentages about the numbers who had served.

Sunday 7 December 1919

A pretty dismal day. In Sunday lesson Dick talked to us about the mission. It was most interesting. I think that I must go down there next holidays.

---

[1] A heavyweight boxing match: Georges Carpentier was French; Joe Beckett English.
[2] Lancing old boy and High Court judge; as chairman of the Coal Commission, he had just recommended nationalization of the mines. Lord Chancellor, 1929–35.

Monday 8 December 1919

This morning we had nothing but interminable revision for exams. It was terrible. Thank God early school's stopped though.

Tuesday 9 December 1919

Today I was third at reading over,[1] rather an achievement which made me feel I had earned the 7s 6d that came from Father this morning. Parade this afternoon was awful. Very long and very cold. The attack was really rather a wonderful sight though. All over the face of the downs little knots of men strolling aimlessly about, benignly lost, firing blanks into the air at intervals.

Wednesday 10 December 1919

Last day of ordinary work, otherwise uneventful. Great plots are being discussed for sacking O'Connor on the last night. It seems rather a brutal beginning for a Christmas holiday but he is so self-confident.

Thursday 11 December 1919

Today the Art Exhibition was held and judged. I got first prize again but could not take it as the year was not up. It was but a poor show and rather quaintly judged, I thought.

Friday 12 December 1919

Exams this morning were fairly bad. Latin Prose and Science. In Science I have come out 5th with 50, better than I expected. In the afternoon we had Under Sixteen PT again. I can hardly think what the squad would be like that we could beat. The afternoon exam was English, a paper simply on the *Macbeth* with the usual characters and contexts.

Saturday 13 December 1919

This morning we had Maths II and Latin Books. I did, I think, about moderately in both. I am not, however, doing as well in exams as I generally do. I am afraid that with Woodard I have lost the knack of working. Fulford, Fremlin and I still continue to propound schemes for the discomfiture of O'Connor on the last night but I cannot think they will come to very much. Everyone is far too bored at the end of the term to be vindictive enough to make the show a success.

Monday 15 December 1919

Exams continue to be most unsatisfactory. I have done poorly so far.

---

[1] A ceremony at which the Headmaster stood in Great School and read out the class placings; as he did so, the boys formed themselves into line in order of achievement.

Divinity was bad this morning. How I do wish these last days would hurry up and go. We have almost given up the idea of ragging O'Connor.

Tuesday 16 December 1919

The last evening school this year! I think I look forward to these holidays more than I have ever before. Christmas holidays are always the best. Only two more days anyhow thank the Lord.

I had to go and be shown off to an illuminator friend of Gordon's.[1] He was most contemptuous over my script but praised the illumination. Apparently if one is ever going to do good work one has to give one's whole life to it. I suppose this is really true of everything. There is no place for the dilettanti.

Wednesday 17 December 1919

Exams over at last. All the afternoon spent packing. How splendid the end of the term is. Much better than most of the holidays ever are. In the evening we packed Alken's jerry in his box again. It really is most subtly funny.

Thursday 18 December 1919

Last day is always an anticlimax. Today is lamentably dull. Fulford and Fremlin are off to Worthing for a visit to a mythical dentist. The consolation is picturing tomorrow this time and the ragging last night. We have quite given up the idea of laying O'Connor out. I didn't think it would ever come to much.

Hampstead, Friday 19 December 1919

Up this morning at six and off to Brighton in a taxi. We cheered our way through Hove. We had a good time to spare at the station, got good seats in a Pullman and arrived at Victoria at 9.30. There I got breakfast and ate a most inconceivable amount. The ineffable sweetness of London was all round again. We went home and after lunch set about hunting out clothes. We found an old blue double-breasted coat which we decided to convert into a smoking jacket, which we were doing when, with that genius of the Jacobs family for arriving just when they aren't wanted, Lun and Barbara turned up. This was so depressing that I went off to see Phil. After dinner Father read me the first two chapters of his autobiography. It is an awful pity he has scrapped it. It is very sentimental but I thought awfully good. I hope these holidays are going to be a decent show. I shall always, I think, look on last Christmas holidays as the best I have ever had. The war was just over and Alec back and money being spent quicker than ever before since 1913. We have got a few invitations to dinners but not much.

[1] Francis Crease. See Appendix of Names, p. 794. Waugh had maintained an interest in illuminated manuscripts since childhood; in 1919 he won the school art competition with an illuminated prayer.

Saturday 20 December 1919

This morning I went to Matisse's show at the Leicester Galleries. It was rather disappointing. I cannot find it in me to admire his crude ill-drawn things. There was an exceptionally good show of Sheringham's though, which was well worth going for. He has a wonderful knowledge of colour and design. They had a wonderful daylight apparatus there made of reflection of silver light from check [?] of green, mauve, and purple. In the afternoon Dad and I went to Pond Street where we had an excellent film and met the Ensors with whom we had tea.

Sunday 21 December 1919

In the morning we went over to St Jude's for High Mass. Bourchier[1] celebrated and made a characteristic address about the attack on French.[2] In the evening Father read some more of his autobiography. It seems awfully good. I am trying to persuade him to go on with it.

Monday 22 December 1919

Today Barbara and I went for a long shopping expedition. Town was more crowded than I have ever seen it; all the suburbs seemed to converge there. The people in the west were not so bad but at Gamages, where we rashly ventured, there was a terrible mob. It seemed to have been chosen for an elementary school treat. We had lunch at a meal-mongers' [?] morgue in Holborn and then got inextricably lost in the City. We eventually arrived at civilization, fought down Regent Street and into Oxford Street and Selfridge's. There we had a terrible fight but wisely they had an icecream soda bar on and we returned refreshed. After tea Alec, Barbara, and I went to the cinema but had a poor show. On the way back I dropped in at the Rhys'[3] and accepted for the New Year dance.

Tuesday 23 December 1919

In the morning I tried to shop but with little result. I managed however to book some dancing lessons at Valhalla. In the afternoon Father came home to lunch and stayed at home for the afternoon, so we went off to Pond Street where we got an excellent show. We had tea at the little Continental Restaurant there and walked back over the Heath.

[1] The Revd. Basil Bourchier: a flamboyant and unorthodox clergyman then in charge of St Jude's, Hampstead Garden Suburb. 'His sermons were dramatic, topical, irrational and quite without theological content.' *A Little Learning*, p. 92.

[2] The 1st Viscount French, (1852–1925), then Lord Lieutenant of Ireland.

[3] Ernest Rhys (1859–1946) was the first editor of Everyman's Library.

Wednesday 24 December 1919

I had a dancing lesson this morning and made, I think, a little progress. All the dances have altered since last year. The hesitation is absolutely different. I then went into town and lunched with Father, Alec and Jock at Roche's. After that we had an awful literary bunfight at the Rhys'.[1] Mrs Rhys was trotting out everyone and showing them off. One was a wonderful young poet, or another a rising musical genius, or at least a distant cousin of a peer. She really drove me wild and I was proud that Alec refused to read anything. She even suggested that I should take lessons in dancing from that half-caste son of a profligate, Chauncy Charan! It doesn't feel the least Christmassy with our having our Christmas dinner on Friday so that Alec may entertain his friends.

Thursday 25 December 1919

A poor Christmas day. In the morning we had a magnificent High Mass at S. Jude's with Messe Solennelle. Other than that no festivities. Dear Imbecile Mission Dick wrote yesterday asking me to come down for Christmas! I have arranged to go down on Sunday however. Stella Rhys came to tea and we played games. It was a poor Christmas, however. Like birthdays, Christmas gets duller and duller. Soon it will merely be a day when the shops are most inconveniently shut.

Friday 26 December 1919

The dinner party in the evening was quite good fun. Marjorie, Christopher, and Toby Dawson-Scott came. The latter struck me as rather the Palmer type, likely to be too popular with the bloods. Hugh Swan arrived halfway through dinner but made up amply in drink what he lost in oysters. Besides a lot of burgundy he had seven liqueur brandies. We played charades until eleven which was quite funny but none of us knew each other quite well enough to go into it with the complete abandonment necessary.

Saturday 27 December 1919

In the afternoon Phil and I went to a Thé Dansant at Valhalla. It was quite good fun, an excellent jazz band and floor; the 'thé' was not so good but quite all right. We didn't get on very well at first, but when we got used to each

---

[1] Arthur Waugh, in his autobiography, gives a different picture of the Rhys's literary evenings: 'How many delightful evenings we spent with Ernest Rhys and his wife in their weatherboarded cottage in the Vale of Health! Richard Le Gallienne would read aloud one of his new "Prose Fancies", his amazing hair glittering like flame in the lamplight. James Welch, the actor, who was married to Le Gallienne's sister, was renowned for his sketch of a man trying to make a speech and perpetually interrupted by a sneezing fit. We were none of us self-conscious, or suspected one another of showing off. Most of the company contributed something to the impromptu programme.'

other's steps we began moving. The tango's a most beautiful dance to watch. I hope I can learn it. The hesitation is still beyond me.

Sunday 28 December 1919

I went down to the mission for the day. It is a dreary neighbourhood but a little better than I had expected. I went to High Mass. There was a small congregation as the men were still sleeping off their Bank Holiday drink. There is a huge gathering of parsons there, mostly risen from the ranks. A dear old, very old, bishop was there too and he fastened on to me and talked all the time about Lancing in his day. He was a dear old dodderer but rather a strain to talk to. I saw their club rooms and fixed up some times for going down, and then went back to civilization.

Monday 29 December 1919

In the morning I finished my dancing lessons and to some purpose. I at last mastered the hesitation and learned more foxtrot steps. Dear old Hooper[1] turned up in the afternoon and I went off to tea with him. He seems to be getting quite a blood at Sherborne and expects to be a House-prefect next term. In the morning Olive, Muriel, Guy Silk and I went to a Cinderella dance at Caxton Hall. It was very jolly but for the rest like any other dance before or at least for the last three years. There were nothing but maxixes, and quadrilles and cotillions and things like that. Still, it was good fun and I was pleasantly conscious of being the best-dressed man in the room.

Tuesday 30 December 1919

Little doing. In the morning Hooper and I went for a book hunt in Charing Cross Road. In the evening I went down to the nativity and mystery plays by the girls at Camberwell. A poor show but amusing.

Wednesday 31 December 1919

After a long walk in the morning I danced in the New Year at East Heath Lodge. It was a delightful dance and I enjoyed it thoroughly. The bobbed-haired MacLeary [?] girl was there and made up in attractiveness what she lost in dancing.

Thursday 1 January 1920

The Manor House dance in the evening was a splendid show. I stayed on till past two and loved every dance. Two partners asked whether I was at Oxford or Cambridge and several said they liked my hesitation. Generally it was splendid.

[1] A contemporary of Waugh's at Heath Mount prep school.

Friday 2 January 1920

Didn't get up till one and then went for a walk and off to the mission to talk to the boys' club. They were a very friendly lot. One charming fellow asked, 'Lancing College's run by this institute too, ain't it?'

Saturday 3 January 1920

Lun arrived. In the evening we went to a funny dance at St Jude's hut with a floor like a ploughed field and a band like a street organ, but it was quite good fun.

Sunday 4 January 1920

Excessively dull. Lun of course read all the time except for a few minutes when she hoisted herself out of a chair to make me call on her damn grandparents and that diabolical aunt.

Monday 5 January 1920

Mother was not well this morning and stayed in bed. Lun and I went to the War Paintings at the Royal Academy. It was a more broadminded show than the gloomy portals of Burlington House have ever let pass, and very interesting. Charles Pears had some fine things but o the Nash brothers! In the afternoon we had a few friends in to tea. Gwynneth [?] MacLeary and Max and Phil and Hooper and played some quite jolly games.

Tuesday 6 January 1920

After the usual indefinite arrangement of that woman[1] Hugh and Olive came up to town and nearly drove me mad. Lun, Hugh and I did a pit for *Tilly of Bloomsbury* at the Apollo. A very jolly show on the whole. Hugh was most irritating all day with his eternal questions. We had tea at one of Lyons pretentious houses and then back.

Wednesday 7 January to Saturday 10 January 1920

Spent in the unpleasant atmosphere of Beechcroft[2]. After scurrying to Euston we found our train was a 'Saturdays only' one, looked up by their imbecile grandfather. So we had two and a half hours to waste at Euston. We went to the Refreshment Room where the children overate themselves revoltingly. Eventually we got a train of sorts and arrived in time for a rather depressing high tea, after which we dressed and went off in a car hired from a local pub for the occasion – the Jacobs spend money on their guests if they

---

[1] Mrs W. W. Jacobs, mother of Hugh and Olive.
[2] A large, modern house on the outskirts of Berkhamsted; the home of W. W. Jacobs and his family.

don't entertain them. The studio dance at the Dixons was fancy dress but we went in mufti and it was quite delightful. The floor was just right – quite smooth but with the essential grip. Our host was a wizened, pleasant little oik who makes the delightful brooches the Jacobs deal so extensively in and perpetrates the most nerve-shattering pseudo-Pre-Raphaelite pictures. The band was only a piano but it was quite enough for so small a floor. There were fifteen couples which just fitted nicely. The supper was sufficient. One Dulcie Buchanan, the belle of Berkhamsted, was there. I could only get one dance with her as she was eternally compassed about by a great cloud of admirers. It is said that at the club the best tennis player plays croquet with her because she doesn't like tennis. She was a beautiful dancer. At the end they had a cotillion with 'Favour' 'Flirtation' and 'Fanfare'. All very jolly.

The next morning, after waiting half an hour or so for breakfast, the entertainment offered me was to sit before the fire of their dining-room with not a window open all day. The only variation being a shopping expedition for the tyrannical Annie. Our heads having been turned by this debauch we embarked upon further reckless dissipation by sitting before the fire until eight, when we went to the local cinema. Luned and I again held hands. I think she would like to carry on the flirtation again and would have let me kiss her had I wanted to. Next morning, after further fireside orgies, we went down to meet their friend Pat Owen, the daughter of Will Owen the black and white man[1]. A pleasant enough child, rather prim but a not unpleasing opposite to the Jacobs! The dance in the evening was excellent. They should, however, have had more music for such a large hall. I had excellent partners. Barbara and I did one wonderful one-step when we spun in and out only holding by one hand.

Next morning in a frantic whirlwind of halfpacked dress clothes we were swept away in the fiery chariots of God (first-class carriage with third-class tickets) with, like Elijah, more than one mantle left behind. We went after many changes to Putney where Alec gave us an excellent lunch, soup, omelette, fruit salad, coffee and cider, at a restaurant opposite the river. From there we went to the ground to see the first Cup Tie round, Swindon v. Fulham. I gather that Swindon won. The crowds were astounding. It is extraordinary the people who can pay 10s 6d for a seat. We returned tired and weary to find the Meynells to dinner (he smoked American gaspers) and Mrs Meynell stopped the night for a religious debauch at St Jude's.

Sunday 11 January 1920

Having been ill in the night I spent the day in bed. Unpleasantly like the Jacobs family.

[1] Black and White Minstrel.

Monday 12 January 1920

This morning arrived: 'Dear Waugh, I met Gordon the other day and write this hoping to be the first to congratulate you on being head of the dormitory. Yrs etc D. M. O'Connor'. It is utterly godless unless, of course, it means I am going on the Settle. Anyway it is more a liability than an asset. With it came a communication from Miss Hadon, the woman I wrote to about dancing. She has offered me membership of her dancing club. I think I shall join if it looks all right. In the afternoon we went to the cinema which was none too bad.

Tuesday 13 January 1920

In the morning Barbara being suddenly possessed of energy we went over to Mill Hill to see Maxwell's school. We had a long walk from Finchley but it was worth it. It is really quite a decent place, infinitely better than I had expected. In the afternoon we staggered over to Pond Street to a fairly decent show.

Wednesday 14 January 1920

We went to the Zoo of all places. It was really most amusing. I hadn't been for ages and thoroughly enjoyed it. The bears and monkeys were divine. In the evening Phil and I went to an awfully good dance at the town hall. It was one of the Private Subscription ones that Mrs MacFadden [?] and Mrs Kendall are running. The people were all right and the supper most excellent with ices and claret cup and éclairs. The band was large but none too good. On the whole however it was one of the best I've been to this holidays.

Thursday 15 January 1920

Nothing much doing. We went to the cinema with the infernal Chris.[1] He has come up to town to launch himself to Claymore as they didn't think they could get him in there any other way.

Friday 16 January 1920

Mother and I rushed off far too early for my liking to Harley Street to see an oculist. After this reckless debauch we waited hours at Curry & Paxton's then had a meal at a mealmongers and hunted bargains in dress materials at Liberty's. We got back in time for a swell party of Barbara's. It was jolly good fun; we had charades and all the usual games. Some awful friends of Alec's called Goldrings came to dinner. I understand that he is a novelist of sorts.[2] They were awful and we gladly escaped to the amazing impropriety of *A Weekend* at the local Hippodrome. The main theme was the arrival of two men

---

[1] Christopher Jacobs, later an architect.

[2] Douglas Goldring: as a literary agent he was responsible for the publication of James Elroy Flecker's *Golden Journey to Samarkand*; as a novelist he wrote a 'Years of Chaos' trilogy: *Nobody Knows, Cuckoo, The Facade.*

in the same house to spend the weekend with little bits of fluff. The wives and the owner of this house arrived.

Saturday 17 January 1920

Hooper and I went to buy some stolen property but it hardly looked worth stealing. In the afternoon Pond Street. Awful Chris staying with us.

Sunday 18 January 1920

Father, Mother, and I went to early service and spent the rest of the morning doing nothing. In the afternoon, as they had no other guests, Alec and Barbara invited me up to tea with them. We thought we wanted to do something to amuse ourselves and distract the melancholy Chris. So we rushed off to fetch him from his aunts. He was not there so we pursued him to his grandparents. We rushed to break the Sabbath at Maida Vale Cinema.

Monday 19 January 1920

More Jacobean trouble. Mrs Jacobs came up to see him [Chris] and without any warning took him away back to Berkhamsted. He cut going to Maskelyne and Devants with us and behaved rather badly all round. That woman is maddening. He is a beastly child but she is steadily making him worse.

Tuesday 20 January 1920

A pretty full day. In the morning Barbara and I rushed off to the Dawson-Scotts for particulars about the evening show. We then went up to Finchley Road where, having refreshed ourselves with coffee and éclairs at a Stewart's we bought some clothes (socks, ties, and collars) at Meakers. At Golders Green we bought a quid's worth of food for me to take back. I then had my hair cut and changed into a better suit before lunch. I went back with Father to the office to take Alec his dress things and then after cashing a cheque went and got a bowler. It was so astoundingly cheap 12s 6d that I spent fifteen bob on a pair of gloves at Swan and Edgar's. I then rushed back and went up to call on Miss Hoare. We then dressed, had dinner, and went off to the Hyde Park Hotel for the Tomorrow Club 'At Home'. The speeches were awful, and Father and I escaped after half an hour's boredom and went to the American bar. When we came back we found lots of people had followed our example. We had some excellent refreshments and then left at about half-past eleven. Alec stayed on a little.

Wednesday 21 January 1920

Little doing in the morning. After an early lunch we went off to pit a Joy-Bells matinée. There was no pit but we went into some seats called the amphitheatre which were a mixture between gallery and upper circle. It was a good show; George Robey was wonderful but the rest was a shade too spectacular.

Thursday 22 January 1920

After lunch Mother and I went to rather a depressing show at the cinema. We then dressed for an early dinner and went off to Ainley's *Julius Caesar* at the St James's. It was a magnificent show. The last two scenes were badly hurried but all the rest was splendid. The tent scene was as good as anyone could wish. Casca came out much more than I thought in reading it. They cut all the part that reflected upon Antony's character, like the scene with Octavius about Lepidus, which seemed a liberty.

Lancing, Friday 23 January 1920

Going back today. I don't know what this term's going to be like at all. It's certain to be an awful sweat with House Trials and the House Platoon competition. Anyhow the holidays have been very good fun.

I travelled down with Fremlin and E. J. Carter. After a good deal of fighting we secured a taxi and arrived here at about six-thirty. O'Connor's card, greatly to my relief, proved to be a lie. Our anteroom has got the most terrible new arrivals, Lushington, Haworth-Booth and Lowther. He isn't so bad but the other two are hateful little ticks. This term promises to be quite good fun.

Saturday 24 January 1920

Spent as usual in loafing about doing nothing. Several journeys to the Grubber and a little hauling about of boxes was all we did. We collected the books for the Art Group library. Rather a good show. That infernal Woodard has just sent round some work for us. It is really an awful bore. I thought that this evening at any rate we might be free.

Sunday 25 January 1920

Today was as dismal as only a first Sunday can be. I have joined Molson's Political Group and become secretary of Literature. In the evening the Head preached a wonderful sermon. He shouted out, 'Some people think God a sort of Super-spy'. The whole Head's House collapsed.

Tuesday 27 January 1920

A dull morning. Work is gradually beginning to become oppressive. A letter arrived from Lun but it was elaborately hurried. After lunch we had the first run of the term. It was pouring with rain and very cold. I ran with O'Connor and he set a terrible pace after the dissipations of the holidays. I am afraid that there is little chance of my getting a place in the five-mile team, none of House colours. I slacked all the way back, more from necessity than from inclination.

The water supply could only run to one bath, shallow, tepid, and dirty. It was a discouraging afternoon. After callover I went to the library and talked to Molson. I am getting more reconciled to him. He runs his Political Group quite amazingly well.

Wednesday 28 January 1920

Last night Gordon told me that he was arranging with Crease about my illumination lessons. This afternoon, after a morning which was somewhat brightened by a double Treble,[1] I ran over to see him about it. I had some considerable difficulty in finding his place, as he has rooms at Lychpole Farm, and went a long way out of my way in the mist. I found him eventually, however, and although I was wet through he took me in and showed me some of his work. When I arrived he was doing a large piece of embroidery in delicate-coloured silks. He is very effeminate and decadent and cultured and affected and nice. His room was beautifully furnished in old oak and old china, with a very few good prints on he walls. The carpet was dull brown. He has arranged to give me lessons every Thursday, starting tomorrow afternoon. It makes one feel rather romantic, like the old things that used to ride miles before breakfast to hear Mass, having a six-mile run to get art lessons. I am afraid however that it will make me awfully shaky for work. Perhaps I may have to walk.

Thursday 29 January 1920

This afternoon I went over for my first lesson from Crease. I walked over, as I thought it would be more seemly than to go in running change, and got caught on the top of Steep Down in the most tremendous hailstorm. Luckily I had borrowed Fulford's trenchcoat but even so it was pretty awful. It was too violent to last long however and I arrived at Lychpole early. Crease met me at the door and led me to his bedroom where he lent me dry socks, trousers, and shoes. He then took me into another upstairs sitting-room where he had a fire and all his things arranged for me. He showed me some of Johnston's work[2] and some of his own. I don't admire his script awfully, it seems to me rather too far spaced and affected, but he can undoubtedly teach me a lot of technique. He started writing Alec's *Sherborne Abbey* as, he said, it was most worthy of beautiful work. He then made me do some and was most flattering, saying that

[1] Two consecutive lessons with the science master Treble.
[2] Edward Johnston, a pioneer in the rediscovery of calligraphy; author of *Writing and Illuminating and Lettering* (1906); designer of the long-lasting sanserif type used by the London Underground (1916); member of the Ditchling Colony, a group of craftsmen, founded by Eric Gill, eight miles from Brighton. Waugh, aged fourteen, met Johnston through a printer friend of Arthur Waugh's and had been shown, by Johnston, how to cut a turkey-quill into a chisel-pointed pen. See *A Little Learning*, p. 146.

I had real instinct for it and had the makings of a better scribe than he. Time passed very quickly and at half-past four we had tea. It was then that I saw most of his character. He strikes me as being a man who may have a big influence over my Lancing life. He is not nearly as affected as he struck me at first. Very well-bred and very individualist. He is most my ideal of the true dilettante of anyone I have yet met. He is a great student of character and claims to be able to sum anyone up by intuition at first sight. He has taken a great interest in Roberts and hates O'Connor. He was most kind to me and I think rather likes me. I could gather practically nothing of his life; he learns all he can without giving anything out. His secretiveness is his only bad quality as far as I can see. All I can gather of him is that his career has been spoiled by ill-health and that he was in some rather distinguished post at Corpus, Oxford. He has asked me to bring Fulford over sometime. On the whole he has impressed me a lot, and will, I hope, be a really decent friend.

Friday 30 January 1920

Today is Lun's birthday, but I have forgotten to write to her. I must get her a packet of chocolate or something at the Grubber. Today was quite beautiful after yesterday's storms, but of course it was quite wasted on a parade day. I should like to have gone for a training run but I mustn't train too palpably as it is only too probable that I shan't get a place at all. At quarter to one today we had a general Dilettanti show but very few people turned up.

The Paisley election is awfully exciting. I can't help admiring the way Asquith is sticking to his guns, even though I loathe his policy.

Saturday 31 January 1920

A dull, damp day. In morning school Woodard put me into detention, but as there was none today we got off. There was a run in the afternoon. Alken, realising that this is his last term and wishing to finish in style, has decided to get his House colours for running and will probably succeed. He could have before if he hadn't been too slack. I have practically given up hope of a place and mean to concentrate on doing something in the sports. We have thought of a Co-education Bill as the subject of our next Parliamentary Debate.

Sunday 1 February 1920

A day of many meetings. In the morning Molson's Political Group had a show at which Roxburgh read a most brilliant paper on the 'Economics of Peace'. The whole world seems to have ceased to live upon a paying basis at all. Only America sits there slowly piling up money. In the afternoon our Lit. Group had a really rather poor show. The debate was 'Beauty should come after Utility' – a rather crude re-wording of my motion 'In the Applied Arts, Beauty should be subordinate to Utility'. People talked a good deal of rot, and finally Beauty won. In the evening there was a school debate. I was speaking third in the motion 'The War having ended the Corps should do likewise'. It resulted in an astounding victory for militarism 9–37. Charnock was proposing and spoke very well. Molson also spoke for us, but man after man got up and talked the imperialist trash about discipline and the capacity for leading.

Monday 2 February 1920

A Saint's Day. Purification of the BVM. There was a very dismal choral in the morning. Brenter went thundering on with the full organ while the school remained sullen and silent.

In the afternoon I went for a long walk with Molson, against all conventions. We discussed religion most of the time. I suppose it is ridiculous for two boys of sixteen seriously to discuss these questions, but it was an awfully interesting discussion and it clears up one's ideas tremendously having to put them into words. I had no idea that I was such an individualist until I had to defend my standpoint. It is extraordinary how one builds up one's convictions quite unconsciously. The great charm in argument is really finding one's own opinions, not other people's.

Tuesday 3 February 1920

Carew and Fulford found that they could not draw up a Bill or get a party together so after reading over (at which I figured rather ingloriously) we had a committee meeting. We there decided to add two clauses to the Co-education show; one making all privileges and official positions purchasable by auction; and another abolishing the Grubber and running Hall as an *à la carte* restaurant. I have joined the coalition and left Barnsley to run the independents. We all had to be weighed and have our chest expansions taken after lunch, apparently with a view to seeing just how bad an effect school food and training do have on us. After that there was a cheerless senior house and a Literary Group show. Our Group is really rather dud; when they rag they go too far and when they are serious they are merely very dull.

Thursday 5 February 1920

Owing to my visits to Crease, Thursday has become the best day of the week, by far. I believe he is beginning to take a real interest in my work. This afternoon he cut a pen but not at all a good one so that I didn't get on nearly so well; but he seems fairly satisfied with me still. The best part is when work is put away and we have tea in his beautiful blue and white china. It is such a relief to get into refined surroundings, if only for an afternoon. We had a great discussion on Gordon and temperament. I went some of the way there on the back of Gordon's motor bike at a splendid pace and I must own he was extremely pleasant.

Friday 6 February 1920

The first parade of the long series of horrors for the House Platoon Shield. Other than the discomfort of uniform and the revolting touch of cleaning materials, it was not very bad, but it is most depressing getting into uniform again and remembering how I slung it into my locker in the armoury after the last parade of last term with a 'Thank God that's over for this year'.

Saturday 7 February 1920

A dull cheerless day. Uneventful morning school, lines till lunch, dull House game, extravagance at Grubber, detention, chapel, and the infernal evening school.

Sunday 8 February 1920

A rather wretched day. In the morning there was the new men's concert. It was as dull as ever. No one enjoys it at all but people still keep it up because they think it is an old tradition. It is ridiculous in so modern a school. Then there was a Political Group meeting on Ireland – very good. After lunch everything went wrong with our literary. We all disbanded and then reorganized and dragged Dick into it. It is beginning to look as though the whole Dilettanti were going to collapse. Personally I should not be sorry as then we could start our inner group as we want to.

Monday 9 February 1920

People say that library privileges are going to be posted soon and I can reasonably hope for mine at last. It will make all the difference if I can get them. I see the only way to get any pleasure out of life here is to cut oneself off as much as possible from the tide of events. I have tried plunging in and trying to enjoy the cold water but it was no good. Crease's life is about the best after all.

Tuesday 10 February 1920

Still no library privileges up but Dick has taken down the old list so it looks hopeful. I was eighth in form this week. Rather good.

Wednesday 11 February 1920

No library privileges up yet. One very cheering incident in the day however was the arrival of a letter from Alec accepting Dick's offer to put him up for the weekend to lecture to the Dilettanti, and enclosing a cheque for ten bob. Accordingly, after a short run to the crossroads, I went to the Grubber where I overate myself disgustingly. The religious tracts have arrived from Edinburgh for which Nattrass and I sent. *Not One Drop* is most entertaining, but *Growing Boys* is perfectly filthy and is now I believe enjoying immense acclamation in the Olds House. I have written out my speech for Sunday's Parliamentary

Debate on 'Girls'. It is not too bad, I think, though quite short. The great sensation will be in the food clause when Fremlin is going to produce a sausage in the house and hurl it at the feet of the opposition, like Cato's figs.

I have been to the much-dreaded Debate Committee and the bloods have sunk much in my opinion. Fox forgot to turn up but we met in the barbaric splendour of his pit. His furniture was poor and his pictures execrable. Ford's ideas for motions were 'something about national guilds' and 'This House favours a Labour Government'. Churchill's were poor. Harris had one good one about 'unwarrantable optimism of religion'. I suggested, 'This House, far from accepting the opinions of parsons and politicians, considers that the war has been an unwarrantable waste and has produced no good results whatever'; and 'This House considers money the most important and desirable thing in the world'. We drew lots for motions and decided on one of Churchill's: 'This House thinks the bachelor to be better off than the paterfamilias'. It is sure to be a frost. We also decided to take Minutes in alphabetical order. Some advantages in Ws after all.

Thursday 12 February 1920

Today the House beat the Olds 2–0. It was a good game and under ordinary conditions I should have been delirious with enjoyment, but, to be quite honest with myself, I am afraid my chief emotion, as I cheered the back of my throat raw, was of extreme vexation. We have no conceivable chance of winning in the Finals and it means that next Thursday I shall have to watch an ignominious defeat instead of going over to Crease. We had an Art Group meeting this evening and heard Barnsley's minutes. He broached a scheme for having them printed, but they were really quite awful. Perhaps I shouldn't have been so disgusted with them had I not spent the morning reading Quiller-Couch on Jargon. Every fault he held up to execration was there! The Grubber had éclairs today – Alec's ten bob is rapidly decreasing.

Friday 13 February 1920

Last night the imbecile astronomer's book arrived. It is really well worth a place in any collection of curiosities. He has had it produced quite well with diagrams in red and black. The elaborate way in which he has worked out his absurdities and his confidence in the conclusiveness of his proofs are rather pathetic. It only cost two bob, too, so I think I have made a good investment. Tomorrow the best event of the week, my visit to Crease. I have done as much practice as possible and hope he will be pleased with me.

Saturday 14 February 1920

I went over to Crease again this afternoon, bearing, rather proudly, the fruits of assiduous practice during the week. He would, however, have none of it and was most critical of all my work. It appears to be part of his system to give great encouragement at first, but as soon as I make any progress, and show signs of confidence, to find innumerable faults. It is a little disappointing and discouraging, but I know that I did better work today than I ever have before and am really learning a great deal. We talked a lot and he criticized my taste in socks most justly and scathingly. He was as nice as ever apart from the script and we discussed art. I am going to try and do a sketch of the view from his window, but it is about the hardest he could find.

Sunday 15 February 1920

The Parliamentary Debate this morning was quite good fun. Molson was very depressed by it but I thought it was better than the one before. The great crowds of underschools are a little trying. They shout all the time and vote *en bloc* for the nearest lobby. My speech proposing the co-education clause was quite a success, I think, but we lost the clause by an overwhelming majority. After lunch I catalogued the art library. Wade told me I had my library privileges. That is some comfort but I do wish they'd hurry up and bring them into force. I went to tea with Gordon and Crease was coming. The tea was quite nice, but I never think Crease is so nice in Gordon's company. He does get so awfully affected and hysterical. Roxburgh came in and talked for a bit.

I think *Old Moore's Almanac* is a good thing to take in and bind. They are most entertaining. I always have a passion for bound volumes of anything. Even *Punch*. I am very pleased with the lunatic philosopher's book. It is so charmingly sincere that I keep looking at it. If I go to Norton next holidays I think that I shall call on him and get him to write on the flyleaf some personal note.

Monday 16 February 1920

Gordon said this morning that he thought Crease loathed Roxburgh. I must say that I thought he showed up rather badly. His 'The Sage of Lychpole, I believe' seemed too patronizing.

Tuesday 17 February 1920

Shrove Tuesday. After lunch there was a run to the Ring and back by Cowbottom. The day was as hot as Southend in August and hardly conducive of energy. As we were allowed plenty of time I walked nearly all the way and even so got quite tired. While we were changing Boothby and O'Connor had a fight. It was screamingly funny, quite in the school story vein, and as we disliked both combatants equally and did not mind who won, we thoroughly enjoyed it. They didn't fight long but they hit each other energetically for quite long enough to leave us limp with laughter. In the library after callover, I read Johnston's book again. It is amazingly fascinating but I despair of ever being able to approach his work. If Crease will let me I should much prefer to do a small manuscript book to the huge sheet of script he wants me to do for the next Art Show. But I'm afraid he won't.

Wednesday 18 February 1920

The Commination Service this morning was what the Head described as 'unrelieved, unexplained, gloom'. Nattrass next to me was rather a wit. He marched into chapel, sat down and said quite audibly, 'Damned if I'm going to dib' and lolled back. Southwell wishes to start a Club here modelled on Barry Pain's Problem Club. It ought to be good fun but I see it developing into a meeting place for lawless desperadoes. Soon the problem will be 'to remove as many fly-buttons as possible from the Headmaster's dress trousers' or 'blocking up all the high notes on the big organ'. It would have to be carefully managed. I think that I shall be forced into Lenten self-denial as my funds are rapidly decreasing and there is little prospect of more for a long time yet.

Thursday 19 February 1920

We've won the footer jerry. It seems almost incredible, the out-Houses are blank with amazement. It is really too wonderful. As a matter of fact when the decisive goal was scored I was looking the other way and talking of something else. It didn't make any difference however to sharing in the general delirium. This ecstatic joy is worth a life of serene happiness. All lines and fines have been cancelled, a thing I've only known happen once before – on Armistice Day. It is simply wonderful to see it there now and to know we've got it for a whole year. All the team have been given their House colours. God, it's too good to be true.

Friday 20 February 1920

A most infernal parade, bitterly cold and dull – arms drill with frozen fingers and rifles gnawingly cold. Most depressing; still, Crease tomorrow, and a letter arrived from home this morning to say they are quite ready to put him up if I can persuade him to come. Dick has put up rather an incoherent notice about library privileges. Today I had to vote on the school debate motions. I voted for 'Manners un-make man' and 'All religion is an instance of the wishing being father to the thought'. I expect that they will decide on 'In the next war the rifle will be obsolete' or something equally absurd.

Saturday 21 February 1920

The library privileges are up this morning and I head the list. It is a great thing to have as I shall be able to do drawing and script there. My lesson this afternoon was in rather aristocratic and most comfortable surroundings. The Tristrams of Sompting Abbots are great friends of Crease's and he is staying there, although they are away, as he felt he wanted civilization again after his landlady's cookery. They claim to be the Tristrams of Lyonesse but I can hardly believe the story. Anyway they have a comfortable house and good servants and have fairly plastered the church at Sompting with their three boars' heads. Poor Crease was not at all well, but he cheered up a bit after a time. He was much more tolerant of my lettering, however, and has invited me over to lunch on Tuesday. The surroundings at Sompting Abbots are not so conducive of Art perhaps as Lychpole – the heavy mouldings and family portraits are quite ugly – but they cook well and make one comfortabler than his hermit's cell. He has practically agreed to coming up next holidays.

Sunday 22 February 1920

The usual dull Sunday only cheered by the universal apprehension before the House Trials. A Political Group meeting in the morning discussed the Enabling Bill and Asquith's chances at Paisley. In the afternoon an Art Group meeting discussed the Pre-Raphaelites. I have been paid rather a compliment by the invitation of the Upper Sixth to be a speaker on the paper at their visitors' debate a week next Thursday, the other visitors being Whitworth and Brenters. They are a very exclusive if not a distinguished society.

A rather touching letter arrived in the evening from Crease to say he could not afford to pay for any of the shows we should do if he comes up. He cannot be nearly as well off as Gordon told me. I must make it quite clear that we shall pay all expenses.

Monday 23 February 1920

A jolly little row with that tick Treble in the morning. We had an explosion with our legitimate experiment at the inauspicious moment that Nattrass was doing one of his own. Treble came raving up thinking that at last he had got a good excuse for a row and gave me an hour's detention for impertinence and said he would report me to Gordon. Later Nattrass explained that I had had no share in his experiment. Treble then had to wash out the beating, which he did not transfer to Nattrass and remained firm of the detention and would listen to no comments. I foresee that we are going to disagree quite a lot in the near future. The much-dreaded House Trials were not nearly as bad as last year. I took things quite easily and came in fourteenth.

Tuesday 24 February 1920

S. Matthias. Immediately after reading over I went over to Sompting Abbots. Crease met me at the garden gate and we went down to see over Sompting Church before lunch. We then came back and ate an excellent and well-served lunch of soup, a meat pie, rhubarb, and cheese and coffee, quite simple but the very best stuff and well cooked. I then played with one of the wild stable kittens, which to the horror of the servants Crease insists on having in with him, while he had a cigarette. We then went over to Lychpole and the rest of the day was not quite so jolly. I had some shots at the sketch he wants me to do, but it is awfully hard and I was singularly unsuccessful. He gave me an excellent tea but would talk all the time of schemes to get Roberts over to see him. Apparently he wants to see him eat as he thinks he is like a kitten! After tea he walked back some of the way with me but was very gloomy and I am afraid my company made him feel worse. I am going over to my next lesson on Thursday.

Wednesday 25 February 1920

Little doing. In the morning we had science with Treble. I did my level best to be rude to him but he is quite impervious to any insult more subtle than physical assault.

Thursday 26 February 1920

Asquith got in by a majority of three thousand. It is really awfully good news. Now there is someone to organize the Opposition properly. This afternoon I went over to Crease at Sompting Abbots; he was much nicer today and seemed better. My script is going pretty well, but it still goes against the grain having to do large work. As soon as I have learned how to do it properly I shall go back to minute work. He walked all the way back with me and tried to make me see the beauty of those irridescent flaky clouds that always strike me as quite ugly. I saw the envelope of his invitation on the mantelpiece.

Saturday 28 February 1920

Very little happened. In the afternoon there was a long fives match v. Olds. It was successful for the House but most tiresome for the spectators. The most exciting event was the simultaneous outbreak of pinkeye, flu, german measles and scarlet fever, and tantalizing rumours of being sent home.

Sunday 29 February 1920

One of the very few good Sundays that I have known here. The library opened at last, and we could first use our privileges. The Political Group had a show in the morning. I, quite insincerely, opposed the motion 'That this House approves of the education of the masses'. It was only a mediocre debate however. The Art Group after Hall was a bit better. They had my scheme for a series of five-minute papers. I spoke upon the humour of Art. By far the best paper was a satire by Woodward on the Ditchling Colony.[1] It was most entertaining to anyone who knows their affections and conceits, but was I think

[1] See note 2, p. 53.

a trifle lost on the rest. We then avoided the House Room, which has become perfectly uninhabitable now on Sunday afternoons with underschool orgies, and went to the library. The school debate in the evening was on one of Harris's motions that 'This House thinks curiosity the best trait in human character'. The 'trays' and 'trates' were as closely divided as the division on the motion.

Monday 1 March 1920

Another double Treble this morning. I have shown up my science in blank verse to see if he is too illiterate to spot it. I think he will be, but hell knows what he'll do if he isn't. This afternoon was most sweaty. I first had to go for a long run – crossroads and back by water-works – then go off to the gym for boxing. I had to fight Wallis and got rather knocked about. It was not too unequal however to be quite void of interest. However I have survived though stiff and sore, and must now do some Plato to appease Woodard.

Tuesday 2 March 1920

Ten bob arrived from Father. In the evening there was a lecture on Art for the Sixths and Art Group. I am to write an account of it for the school magazine. Rather a compliment but it is a difficult thing to write up.

Wednesday 3 March 1920

Wednesday are very full days now. There was a parade at 12.30 but luckily the hair-cutters were up in the afternoon so we had 'Run anywhere' for Clubs. Afterwards Trenam and I did some sparring. Father's ten bob rapidly decreasing.

Sunday 7 March 1920

We had a Dilettanti political meeting after Sunday. Booth read a paper attacking the Coalition. It was very funny. 'As a profound admirer of Mr George and a staunch supporter of the Coalition' I felt compelled to defend my idol. Not too bad a speech, I think. At lunch a card arrived from Crease saying that if Fremlin wished to see the Iris Stylosa he was to come over that afternoon.

Wednesday 10 March 1920

Little enough doing. Parade at 12.30 was quite a wit as we had to get our belts right with the new leather equipment. The fairy godmother department of the War Office sent us another immense gun yesterday. It came today and will probably sink into the earth if it doesn't have a concrete base.

Thursday 11 March 1920

I ran over to Crease today still nursing the unconquerable hope of reducing my weight. He was very scornful of my work and so disheartened that he did not give me any script. At tea a charming but plain young man turned up, indulging in the name of Osbert Burdett. I know his name quite well but can't place it.[1] He seemed very brilliant and began holding forth so fluently that I invited him to come and chat to our Literary Group. He says he will talk about 'Exceptions'. I think I shall bring him a small general audience, no special group. He was most entertaining on the philosophy of the evasion of duty, and the interest script gives to tomb stones.

Friday 12 March 1920

A dull day consecrated to Mars. I have broken training badly today, eating much too much and taking no exercise other than the parade afforded. The conversation of the lav. is really getting too bad although I join in readily enough. We ought to write round the walls, 'Filth is Silver, Silence is Golden'.

Saturday 13 March 1920

The career of Flynn this week has been rather amazing. I have noticed that when people get their House colours it nearly always has a terrible effect on their morals. Flynn started the week with a report card and got three NSs and a VS before a day was up.[2] He burnt the card and went and told the Head he had lost it and got another. He got three NS on this report and in two days lost it genuinely and was reported by Howitt and Bond in one day. Accordingly yesterday he got six from Gordon. Today he had to go and tell the Head that he had lost his report card again. The Head was furious and told him to start his new card with two NS. Howitt had told him to bring his new card as soon as he got it, to sign it NS! The persecution is rather sad though most amusing. There was a running match against some hare and hounds club today. Their team had never seen dykes before and were ludicrously beaten. I should think that it must have been rather a dismal outing for them.

Sunday 14 March 1920

Burdett's visit was fairly successful. It is something of an ordeal for a boy of my age to entertain two grown men in someone else's house, but it went off all right. There was one bad moment when the applause after his speech was over and no one started a discussion or proposed a vote of thanks. But it passed and a lively argument took place between Roxburgh and him. His speech on individual freedom and the tyranny of the community was splendid. 'The

---

[1] Osbert Burdett (1885–1936): educated Marlborough and King's College, Cambridge; author of *The Silent Heavens, A Modern Mystery Play*, 1914; *The Beardsley Period*, 1925; *Blake* (English Men of Letters series), 1926; *A Little Book of Cheese*, 1935.

[2] Boys doing badly were given a report card, which they had to take to their form-master after each lesson. He marked it either 'S', for 'Satis.'; 'VS' for 'Vix Satis.' (scarcely satisfactory); or 'NS' for 'Non Satis.'. If a boy got three NS marks in a week he was liable to be thrashed.

public has given, the public has taken away. Blessed be the name of the public' was one of his epigrams.

Monday 15 March 1920

On Sunday evening I finished a coloured caricature of Puttock which I sold to Southwell for four cream slices and four halfpenny stamps. It earned an immediate success quite out of proportion to its deserts and has been praised ecstatically by half the school, including Roxburgh. If my work is to be popular I see I must forswear script and take to caricature. Anyhow I may make a little food out of it.

Tuesday 16 March 1920

We had boxing at 12.30 again today. I had to fight Alken and rather laid him out. He can't box at all, for all his strength. I feel rather guilty though, as he has felt quite done in since.

Thursday 18 March 1920

Today after the heats for the open hundred (in which I got a third place) the boxing House Trials came off. I fought Alken first and knocked him about fairly considerably but with little enjoyment. There is no satisfaction in so tame a victory. After that Streatfeild asked if I was willing to fight Wallis. I was very tired and refused but while the bantams were fighting I thought it would be best to get it over, as if I did not I should not be able to go to Crease on Saturday. It was a pretty good fight, both of us were pretty done in. I didn't know what I was hitting at all in the last round. Of course he won. A very hot bath restored comfort and satisfaction.

Saturday 20 March 1920

I went over to Crease at Lychpole for a lesson. We did some handbills for a parish entertainment at Sompting. He was awfully nice as usual, and has invited Carew and me over to tea on Thursday.

Sunday 21 March 1920

The Dilettanti is really rather clamorous with its meetings. Today there were three. A quite dud political one in the morning, a fairly good art one after lunch, and an excellent literary one after chapel. At the art one, Barnsley read a thing called the Apolloniad purporting to be a discovery of his in the Fellows' Library. It was in pseudo 'translationese', and I spotted it at once as a rather clever satire on the group, but it took in everyone else. It is extraordinary how dense they are. Barnsley never thought it would deceive for a minute. At the literary one, Carew read an excellent paper on 'The Character of Hamlet'. As he and I were the only two with any workable knowledge of the play it was rather a two-man discussion, but I enjoyed it awfully.

Tuesday 23 March 1920

At five we had a House platoons' parade. The tyranny of the corps is awful, trying to justify its pseudo-militarism under House patriotism.

Wednesday 24 March 1920

Nothing doing.

Thursday 25 March 1920

I am rather disillusioned in Dick. Lately Gordon has been very jealous of Crease's influence at Lancing and has been subtly trying to put me off him. I have often noticed that, but I never thought Dick would descend to that sort of petty intrigue. This morning he refused to allow Carew to come over to tea with me at Lychpole. He gave as a reason that his people did not know, but he also said he did not wish him to. It may not be jealousy, of course. Perhaps Burdett's speech put him off, but I am awfully disappointed in him whatever his reason. It's no good putting people on pedestals. They come down with an almighty big crash. It has made me rather unhappy and is certainly awkward when Alec is coming to stay with him.

Friday 26 March 1920

Today the House Platoon show came off. We were magnificently bad.

Saturday 27 March 1920

Alec came down today for his weekend and to speak to the Dilettanti. In the afternoon he, Dick, and I watched the heats. I ran in the mile but only just got a place. In first evening his speech was awfully good, I think, a great success. He spoke on the growth and functions of the novel. I asked Carew about Dick's objection to Crease. Apparently he does not know anything against him but has heard scandal of him.

Sunday 28 March 1920

In the morning Alec and I went for a walk. He and Dick got on pretty well together. In the afternoon Dick, he, and I went for a short walk. A most amusing question was raised by talking about the reversion of cinema films. What would our life be like lived backwards? We worked out some most amusing situations. Having a bath you get into a dirty bath, slowly the water clears and deposits the dirt on you. You then gradually get cleaner until your next bath dirties you again. Reading a book you start with complete knowledge and slowly forget it as you progress. It was a most entertaining discussion.

Tuesday 30 March 1920

By an amazing piece of luck – I have not yet made up my mind if it was bad or good – I got a place in the half-mile finals today.

Wednesday 31 March 1920

Work has practically ceased for us now. There are no order and marks. Crease is very upset at the slander by Dick and wants to send the Tristrams to the Head to witness to his purity.

Thursday 1 April 1920

Much to my relief I lost my place in the half mile today. The House is doing excellently in sports and well in boxing. We stand a good chance of both jerries. Other than that little happened. Work has ceased.

Friday 2 April to Tuesday 6 April 1920

Writing in the beautiful calm of the end of term. Sports are over and we have got the jerry. I ran in the 220 relay race. Everything is over for the term. The end of this term is so much better than the others. Tomorrow I go off by the early train. Life seems very pleasant now. The end of the term is the best part of the holidays.

Hampstead, Wednesday 7 April 1920

Came home. In the afternoon I went into tea at the Criterion with Barbara, in the evening to our local music-hall for a very bad show.

Thursday 8 April 1920

Went to an At Home at the Rhys' in the afternoon. One Solomon, an appalling little Jew and great musician, played but did not convey anything to me. It is rather awful to be such a barbarian at music. I miss an awful lot by it. There was I sitting bored to distraction with Stella trembling and swaying in ecstasies. In the evening Barbara and Alec took me to the Tomorrow Club for their weekly meeting. An engaging little Jewish oik read a paper on 'Sitwellism & petrefaction in poetry', rather deep and very journalistic.

Friday 9 April 1920

Went to Chancery Lane to get pens and paper which I left in the West End Cinema.

Saturday 10 April 1920

Crease arrived. Mother and Father are being very charming to him.

Monday 12 April 1920

Went with Crease to Phoenix Society show at the Lyric Hammersmith. *A Fair Maid of the West*. Very good.

Tuesday 13 April 1920

National Gallery in morning. Lunch at St Stephen's Club, Westminster, with a friend of Crease. Bad report from school.

Wednesday 14 April 1920

Poor Crease did not sleep at all well last night. We had purposed to go to the Stoll with Father, but in the morning Barbara and I took him to the Zoo and it was too tiring for him so we had to give it up.

Thursday 15 April 1920

A more successful day. In the morning Crease and I went to the British Museum's illuminated manuscripts. There was one French manuscript (a translation of the *De Bello Gallico*) which had almost perfect script. We could find no reproduction of it for sale, so we had the official photographer over to do it for us. The place is most extraordinarily well run; every man seems to know his business.

In the afternoon we set out to find a Mr West who had been at New College with Father and with whom Crease had some business. He is Vicar of St Dunstan-in-the-East, Idol Lane. We emerged from the station and as we approached the church it began to drizzle. It was raining hard when we reached it. It was ugly and dark but with a few lights still burning. We could see no one and were going to leave but the rain drove us in again. Then we saw a light under the vestry door, knocked and went in. Mr West was sitting there in a high-backed chair fast asleep. He was a short stout person with a yellow sunken face. Crease roused him but he was still quite in a stupor – talked incoherently for a few seconds and then dropped off to sleep again. I realized that he was drugged. It was really rather awful finding a thing like that. The man must be an absolute slave to it, if he can't keep away from it even in his own church. We tried to shake off the impression and hurried to Father's office for tea and then we went with Mother and him to the Stoll where we got an excellent show. We are beginning to convert Crease to the cinema. He had never seen a good show before. We shall soon find him going to Worthing with the cinema habit.

Friday 16 April 1920

We took a quiet morning and I did some script of Marcus Aurelius's *About Fame*. In the afternoon we tried to do the Wallace Collection but found it shut. So we pottered about and had tea at the Thistle.

Saturday 17 April 1920

In the morning Crease and I set off for St Albans. It was an inauspicious day to choose but we got there all right. We reviewed the atrocities of Grimthorpe[1] at the Abbey but found much still remaining to admire, particularly the painted roof. We had lunch at a quaint little restaurant and came back very crowded in time for tea. After tea we went out to the cinema. Crease is quite contented.

Sunday 18 April 1920

To St Mary's, Primrose Hill, for High Mass. This mediaevalism suited Crease better than the more Renaissance service at St Jude's. It was certainly very beautiful.

Monday 19 April 1920

South Kensington Museum.

Tuesday 20 April 1920

Today Crease left for a Lady Florence Proctor in Baron's Court. In the morning we got some paper at Roberson's. We also found a charming little shop headed OLD MASTERS. On one was an inscription

NOTICE
Unless I can get the sum of £100 for this picture
before the end of the week, it will have to leave
this country for America. It is a shame that this
country should lose such a splendid old Portrait but
GAUDEAMUS DUM IUVENES SUMUS
I am now 20 years of age.

Rather a gem.
I saw Crease off and returned a little sad.[2]

Wednesday 21 April 1920

In the morning shopping with Mother. My next pair of shoes are going to cost four guineas to make.

---

[1] The 1st Baron (1816–1905), who designed Big Ben and restored St Albans.

[2] Waugh wrote later of this visit: 'My father's most obvious characteristic was theatricality, but I did not become conscious of this until it was pointed out to me at the age of sixteen by the first adult visitor I introduced into the house. . . . This friend said to me: "Charming, entirely charming, and acting all the time." When I consulted her, my mother confirmed this judgement.' *A Little Learning*, p. 69. Others made a similar judgement about Waugh: 'Evelyn referred to his father as a born actor who performed in private life instead of on the stage; Evelyn inherited that particular characteristic.' Dudley Carew, *A Fragment of Friendship* (London 1974), p. 15.

Midsomer Norton, Thursday 22 April 1920

Came down to Norton.[1] The journey down was quite jolly after we passed Bath where an appalling man got out who would discourse to the whole carriage about the scenery. Aunt Connie, with an invitation from the Bulleids for nursery tea, met me at the station. We went up to a very cranky meal – mutton broth, liver, cheese, junket and ordinary tea and cakes. I think, in her way, Mrs Bulleid would be as awful a mother in-law as Mrs Jacobs. Betty was looking sweetly pretty. Much better than Luned. After this picnic we played games.

Friday 23 April 1920

Went for a walk in the morning. In the afternoon Betty, Nancy and Hilary came to tea and played games. Betty again beautiful. They have invited us to a motor picnic to Stratford tomorrow. I want to do a piece of script for Betty's birthday but can think of nothing.

Saturday 24 April 1920

A very jolly picnic with the Bulleids at Stratford. We took sketching materials but did not use them but explored a haunted house instead. In the evening Aunt Trissie and I went up to dinner at the Bulleids. The dinner was excellent but after dinner I made one of the worst faux pas in my tactless life. Mademoiselle was sitting by herself listening intently to the conversation attempting to learn French idioms. Oblivious to her presence I began voicing my opinions on the French menace to Europe! I feel quite cold and clammy to think of it now.

Sunday 25 April 1920

Church twice in the morning. My Holmes cousins were there, Agnes very flirtatious. I went to tea with them in the afternoon to see my old nurse Lucy. She has now four stalwart boys of her own. The Holmes girls came back here to dinner and games. They are a most vivacious pair after the almost insipid coyness of the Bulleids. Mrs Bulleid brought me down a book of Betty's favourite quotations she kept, for me to select one to do. I decided on either Browning's 'The Year's at the Spring' from *Pippa Passes* or an anonymous thing about 'the kiss of the sun for pardon', though I should like to give a more material token than the kiss of the sun.

---

[1] To visit three unmarried aunts, sisters of Arthur Waugh's. Their house had originally been acquired by Evelyn's grandparents, Dr and Mrs Alexander Waugh, who lived in it for forty-two years, until their death. 'When I first knew it, little had been changed since the 1870s . . . the place captured my imagination as my true home never did.' *A Little Learning*, p. 44.

Monday 26 April 1920

Norton fair-day. It was great fun. The country crowd is so infinitely preferable to the East End importation we get at Hampstead. There were very much the same amusements as Hampstead – swingboats, roundabouts (not much like Gertler's[1]), hoopla, freaks and so on. There was one most engaging sportsman who ate fire. He simply crammed himself with burning cotton wool and then put some not burning in, which caught fire in his mouth and he breathed out clouds of smoke and sparks. He also ate a burning torch. The rifle ranges proved an alluring and costly joy. I spent all my spare money on them. After tea we went down to a football match but the incorrigible Humphrey[2] made that part of the day hideous for me by sitting on my knees and inquisiting me about the game all the time. After dinner we went to the room over the tailor's shop and watched the fair from there for some time. It gets jolliest at night when it's all lit up.

Tuesday 27 April 1920

I took a slack morning and in the afternoon we had a small party. Fortunately the Miall boys could not come or Grace. The Bulleids came in force; my two cousins; Nancy Williams (she is an astoundingly pretty child – I should fall in love with her were she older); and a rather nice Downside boy, Costobadie.[3] He wanted me to go out riding with him but as I can't ride I thought it wisest to be engaged; as a matter of fact I had got an indefinite invitation from the Bulleids.

Wednesday 28 April 1920

Spent entirely at Dimboro. A walk in the morning marred by Humphrey. He would be quite impossible as a brother-in-law. I went úp to tea (junket, hard-boiled eggs and lettuce) with them and played exhausting games in their stable yard. Poor Betty is very piano with the prospects of approaching school.

Thursday 29 April 1920

In the morning I went for a long walk with the Bulleids. Humphrey was as usual simply awful. We went a perilous walk by the bank of a stream and I tore my least shabby suit. In the afternoon Aunt Connie and I went over to Chilcompton to tea with the Holmes. Eva was there and very mad; also a Miss Harty. We went back early as Aunt Connie had a political jaunt. Aunt Trissie leads the Tory faction and they have teas and At Homes at intervals to bribe their votes. One old cottage woman, asked if she was Conservative, said: 'Yes,

---

[1] Mark Gertler (1891–1939), the painter.

[2] Humphrey Bulleid, Betty's brother.

[3] Later Commander A. N. P. Costobadie, DSC, RN; he was the son of a Midsomer Norton doctor who was also medical officer for Downside School.

miss, I should just about think I am. Why the woman next door's Labour and her hens do eat all my greens.' I suppose that really is what makes and ruins ministries. That is really democracy.

Friday 30 April 1920

Betty's birthday. Aunt Trissie and I went up to Dimboro bearing our small gifts. She had kept it a week before because she knew that she would be unhappy at going back to school and would not enjoy it. The aunts sent her a china hen to add to her collection of model animals. I brought my bit of script. I think that she was really very pleased with it. In the afternoon I went over to tea at my cousins and they came back to us to dinner.

Hampstead, Saturday 1 May 1920

Aunt Connie and I returned to Hampstead. It was Labour Day and everything was very crowded. At Bath we got into a slow train instead of a fast one, but luckily no one came to meet us. In the evening I had to go down to Mrs Rhys to read *Twelfth Night*. Aunt Connie kindly came too. It was a melancholy show. The Fordham boy for whom the party was organized was unspeakably bad as Viola. Old Professor Gardner read Orsino and Malvolio, quite intelligently but with no histrionic powers. I had to sit next to the genius Delphis Gardner. We had biscuits and claret cup between the acts.

Sunday 2 May 1920

Went to High Mass at S. Jude's in the morning. Hugh Mackintosh came back with us looking immaculate. Guy Kendall[1] and his small son called in the afternoon.

Monday 3 May 1920

The morning was spent in the many duties before going back to school – visits to watchmaker and provision vendor and tailor's, and helping in packing. The afternoon Molson and I did our afternoon we had arranged. We met under the Cupid in Piccadilly Circus. Quite irresponsibly we rushed off to Chelsea to see John's[2] show. After some difficulty we found it and it well repaid our trouble. His portraits were splendid, but I did not much like his other things. From the proprietor I learned the truth about the scandal of his being turned down at the Academy. Apparently he only consented to put his name down very grudgingly at the clamorous entreaties of all the young men of the Academy. The old men had promised, or declared that they had, their votes before, and the young men were in the minority. The man at the show was

[1]Headmaster of University College School, Hampstead, and a regular visitor to the Waugh home; the father of Ursula Kendall. See Appendix of Names, p. 794.

[2] Augustus John.

awfully pleased and said John had no right to try to start hobnobbing with them.

We then rushed back to civilization and had tea at the Cri. After tea we went to the National Gallery. I am afraid Preters[1] has no eye for beauty at all. He is just clever and cannot see the charm of things like the early Flemish Madonnas. He calls the serenity, vacancy. Then we set out to find the little shop in the Long Acre neighbourhood that I found with Crease (the old masters' one). We did not find it but we had quite good fun and found a printing works into which we rushed and got estimates for the Dilettanti magazine. I returned by tube where I found Hugh who showed me a set of jade dress-waistcoat buttons he had bought.

Tuesday 4 May 1920

In the morning Aunt Connie, Mother and I set out for the Academy. I was greatly surprised at the show. I had always been led to think that nothing good ever got there at all. Several very good pictures indeed slipped in. Notably *Oratio Obliqua*, a picture of the inside of a cinema, and two clean oils by Harold Hankey. Greiffenhagen had a good thing in too. The worst part, I thought, was the miniatures, none of which were a patch on the commonplace of a hundred years ago or could touch the family ones at Norton or Mother's Raban and Cockburn ones. We saw Mrs Bulleid's watercolour which seemed one with the surrounding mediocrity – no worse than its fellows. After this intellectual debauch we pandered to the physical at Roche's where we were joined by Alec and Father. Aunt Connie stood us an excellent lunch. Then for want of other idleness I went to a cinema where I saw a most amorous French film, *Sappho*. I then went off to the backwoods of Bloomsbury to pay the bill for the photo Crease and I had taken at the British Museum. I had considerable difficulty getting back as everything was crowded. Eventually however I got back in time for dinner. The last of all my evenings did not crown the last of all my days particularly memorably. Aunt Connie and I went down to our local theatre to see a touring edition of *Peg o' My Heart*. It was not at all badly played and the play itself was excellent. We returned to find Father back from his rehearsal and after a little refreshment went up, rather slowly, to bed.

Wednesday 5 May 1920

And so with the holidays my book[2] comes to an end. I must not drag out the measured stanzas of most last pages, as like *Jean Christophe* it is a book that

---

[1] A nickname for Molson. Waugh, in *A Little Learning*, derives the name from Molson saying that he was preternaturally interested in politics.

[2] The book in which he was keeping his diary.

doesn't end. But next term is going to be rather a turning point with the Certificate that makes so much difference.

Explicit liber tertius

Lancing, Thursday 6 May 1920

This morning the locker list was posted and I am junior man on the demi-Settle. I did not expect it at all, but am not as elated as I should have expected. I suppose it is the natural gloom of the beginning of term. Today has been most melancholy. After lunch I played a foursome at squash rackets, which was quite jolly, and came down to find an impromptu Settle tea nearing its completion. However they made me welcome. I was rather the new one but I suppose that I shall get used to my position soon. The lav. is somewhat of a wilderness, full of the children and very few of our old sort of a year ago. O'Connor and Fulford, Brennan and Easton are downstairs, Pratt and Boyd left. Still I know I should have been very hurt if I had been passed over.

Friday 7 May 1920

I am not enjoying this term very much so far. I have not yet become familiar with the other men on the Settle and my old friends are a little cold already. The lav. is appallingly dull. There was a parade today and we got the charming news that camp is going to be made virtually compulsory. After parade there was nothing doing. I talked to Preters in the library for some time. Everything seems fairly cheerless except school which might be worse. I seem to have gained a very shallow sort of officialdom and lost my friends. Small boys seem to have become quite shy of me and get out of my way quite deferentially, but it isn't much consolation for the way being lonely. I shall be very glad indeed to get over to Crease tomorrow. It does seem ridiculous to get so depressed at gaining a position which I should have been more depressed to miss. One advantage anyway is evening school, where on a cushioned seat at a demi-Settle I can do what I like without fear of interruption. I need no longer keep this diary surreptitiously.

Saturday 8 May 1920

I went to Crease in the rain and returned in sunlight. The morning was sad and cheerless. It was raining hard so we could not play rackets as we had intended. I went to the library and felt rather lonely. Promotion is by no means a panacea for unhappiness. I have however gained more position so that it does not matter so much being lonely. School was dull and uneventful. I was really feeling very much depressed. I persuaded Carew to walk with me over the downs and we discussed things generally. As soon as I got in the Lychpole atmosphere I became happy. Crease was as charming as he has ever been. I loved every minute of my visit. He perfectly understood 'Roses', admired and hated it. He suggests a twin picture of paganism, a beautiful ethereal man, a golden-haired Apollo magnificently unprepared for the long littleness of life. It would be rather a clever contrast to the hideous face of lust and debauch if only I could achieve it. We had tea in his handleless Crown Derby cups. Then we swung back over the downs, I with a very great content at heart. After all there is no physical comfort to compare with aesthetic pleasure. I owe anything at Lancing worth remembering to him.

Sunday 9 May 1920

The morning was wretched. No fire in the House Room drove me to the library where I met with the usual habitués, Carew and Molson. Those two between them have been muddling furiously about Molson going over to Crease. Molson appears to have been trying to avoid a row between Dick and Crease. Carew seems to have been entirely aimless and, carried away by the exuberance of his own mendacity, has been talking quite purposeless little lies to all parties concerned. The whole thing has become as ludicrously complicated as a Renaissance intrigue or a Criterion farce. Finally, however, Dick has decided that however evil an influence Crease may be, Molson can look after himself. It's all very unsatisfactory, but I can see no other way than to let the matter rest.

In the afternoon I went to the library and tried the picture that Crease suggested, but I have only created a rather plain prig. There was a gloomy debauch of a Settle tea in the afternoon. There is no conscionable satisfaction in overeating unless in good fellowship. It is like secret drinking. Hall for me has become a draughty reading interval. I hardly spoke a word the whole time.

There was something of a fiasco in the dormitory. We are always allowed to talk on Sunday nights after the House-captain has been up. Last night as no one came for about quarter of an house I despaired and let them talk. Ford immediately came up. He did not make a row but he must have thought that I was being ragged and am quite incompetent.

Monday 10 May 1920

Morning and afternoon rackets. They are one of the few amusements that the summer term affords. They were really quite enjoyable and passed the time quickly. I heard the water running into the baths which means that the tyranny of House swimming will begin soon. I am hating this term almost as much as my first term three years ago. It is going to be much worse and culminates in camp at the end. A letter from Father arrived saying that *His Excellency* had been a great success. I wish I could have seen it, but it would have been on the one happy afternoon I've had this term.

Tuesday 11 May 1920

Nothing of interest or amusement in school. Puttock talked through a double period on the calculus and Woodard started a brush-up for the Certificate. I have started working quite assiduously. At 12.30 I had a very good game of rackets with Whittall, Boothby and Booth. I had got a court for after lunch but I had to play in a House game. At first it was awful. I got caught for two in the first innings but things got a little brighter later as I took four wickets, three of them in four balls, and in the second innings I made fifty-one not out which was quite good fun although I can claim no credit for it as the bowling was bad and I was dropped four times by one man. I am arranging to go to Cowfold[1] with Molson on Ascension Day. I hope it will be a success as one can't afford to waste whole holidays on failures. What filthy ink this is.

Ascension Day, Thursday 13 May 1920

Without exception the best Ascension Day I have spent. Molson and I set out soon after breakfast. Our train was not until 12.14 but he has joined a local country club – the Sussex Aero Club – and we thought it would be jollier to wait there than up here. He showed me all over it and I was quite delighted at how well run it was. It is very well furnished, obviously by a man with some taste. Very plain. Black floors with rush mats and rugs round oak tables and every comfort in the way of washing and cooking. We began a game of ping-pong and were soon engrossed. After a time I said, 'I say, Preters, I suppose there's still plenty of time?' He went out to look and returned with the reassuring news that it was only about 10.55. We played for about twenty minutes more and then he went out to look at the time. He came back grinning: 'Evelyn, it's 12.15'. After a little bad language we looked up a Bradshaw and found that there was not another train until 2.15. So we decided to have lunch there. This was the next mistake. It was an excellent lunch but costly. When we got to Shoreham with about ten minutes to spare we found that we hadn't enough money to go there with. Luckily, school credit is good. We rushed to Sayers & Hedgecock but found them shut. Finally we borrowed ten bob off Glasspool. Eventually we arrived at Partridge Green and after a beautiful walk reached the monastery. We had to wait for an hour until a service was over so we ate our picnic lunch as tea. We then went to the monastery. The monks all wore the most attractive habits. We could not see much but what we did impressed us immensely. We walked all round the outside, and saw the cells, each with its own garden so arranged that no windows overlooked the outside world or even each other's gardens. It made one feel an awful tripper and vulgarian. Of course it reminded us of Dowson

---

[1] St Hugh's Charterhouse, Cowfold, established (1877–83) by monks from the Grande Chartreuse, the mother-house of the Carthusian Order in the Dauphiné Alps.

'Nuns of the perpetual adoration'. Well, we shook off the monastic gloom and walking back Molson told me the history of his less reputable past at Dartmouth. We thought, and the Bradshaw supported our heresy, that there was a train at 6.30. We waited half an hour for that train and then found that there wasn't. We got a train that landed us at Shoreham at 7.50. We had to charter a taxi to scramble up in time, at perfectly appalling cost. I shall have simply not to spend a penny for the rest of the term if I'm to pay for my Settle tea, and I do not feel justified in getting more money from Father when I shall have to ask for some more as it is for the Brighton match.

Saturday 15 May 1920

Made sixteen and thirty-nine in a Third League. I had a brilliant thought yesterday in chapel that some play on 'te deum' and 'tedium' should be made. I started with the idea of an epigram but the following resulted, the original 'motif' being somewhat lost.

Lancing Chapel

O God, who blessed the chapel's height and founded it on chalk and
    flint,
Canst not thou hear the coin debased that's loudly jingled in thy
    mint
Or hear the long, mute, listless prayers, our prayerless lips are
    forced to raise?
Accept, for 'tis our widow's mite, this plainsong tedium of praise.

The coin they gave us rings untrue; it swells the purse but leaves us
    poor.
It will not pay the incessant tolls that wait beyond the chapel door.
When we are hungry, tired, oppressed, it will not stay our failing
    health.
Then help us, God, lest in that hour we lose all hope of future
    wealth!

So if on judgment day I stand, I broken abject, hungry, cold,
Remember in thy timeless love who turned to copper thy fine gold.
Remember all and say of me: 'They paid their score in lead and tin.
They gave thee nothing; thou hast brought thyself. Poor servant
    enter in!'

I have started a scheme for scoring off Treble by washing out our whole set. I have impressed on Woodard that it is an appalling waste of time to do science before the Certificate. I think it would be rather a score even if it did let him off some work.

Sunday 16 May 1920

Averagely unprofitable. In the morning there was a dud Art Group meeting, which decided nothing, and Mrs B. invited me to tea.[1] Later in the day I was reprieved but I am afraid it is only an averted evil. I tried to do the names on the House team photo for the House Room but with little success and I have induced Gordon to have it remounted. The Settle tea was a subscription one but fortunately very cheap; it was very interrupted by the House bathe. Rest of the day in the library.

Monday 17 May 1920

Today I sent 'Roses' off to *Colour*. I do not expect that they will accept it but it is worth trying. My poverty and future monetary obligations prey on me a lot. I have never been so poor so early in the term. In the morning I carried on my guerilla warfare with Treble, the honours being still equally divided. House nets wasted the afternoon.

Wednesday 19 May 1920

Today *Colour* returned 'Roses'. As soon as I heard that there was a registered envelope for me in Miss Owen's room, I was in tea, I guessed what it was. I had only the customary euphemism about 'lack of space'. I must own that, though I hardly expected it to be taken, I felt rather crushed. Father was very kind to my verses on Lancing Chapel in his letter this morning.

Thursday 20 May 1920

A letter at breakfast from Ensor asking me to do him some script. At lunch a letter from Mother. I was promoted into the Second League this afternoon where I made ten, being caught out largely owing to the fault of the bat. After our League, when, of course, we were beaten, I broke my fast and spent a bob at the Grubber. It doesn't sound much after my usual extravagances, but when I have the weight of a Settle tea on my purse it is a great self-indulgence. I had determined not to spend anything at all. At 12.30 I had rather a good single with Boothby at rackets. It is an excellent form of exercise. After Leagues the wretched doctor had to take all weights and measures. I do wish I could get a little taller. The prospect of parade tomorrow is sickening. Thank God I shall be able to get away over to Lychpole on Saturday. I must set about Crease's *Bells of Heaven*. I have had my knife sharpened but it does not seem much improved, and it is not sharp enough near the point, where I need it most.

Friday 21 May 1920

Life goes rather unsatisfactorily here. Today was chiefly commandeered by the Corps. After the ceremonial parade there was a bathe where my swimming

---

[1] Mrs Bowlby, wife of the Headmaster.

went much faster and better. Still, I am feeling very depressed and unhappy. Crease will be away a month and he is the only real friend I have here. I do believe that I am getting homesick again after three years. Evening school is an unpleasant opening for retrospection and introspection. Sorely and sadly afternoon chills into evening. A great gloom lies over the whole House Room. The prefect taking it looks out on the life he knows with fierce contempt; at the new men's table the small boys are still in a strange inconsequent incoherent world. The placid bourgeoisie of the House sit depressed and aimless. I can see how little it all means and how tremendously it all matters. We are all drifting without rudders; whatever aims we started with have long since been lost. We all really live for the holidays and are all at most times happy enough, but there are times like this when we are so physically and morally exhausted that we cannot help thinking. And it is 'only thinking lays boys underground'.

Saturday 22 May 1920

I spent the afternoon at Lychpole. Only one episode blotted the contentment of the afternoon. I broke a blade of one of Crease's quill-cutting knives. This was a peculiarly elaborate weapon in a leather case and I was doing the final cut with a very thin, exquisitely sharp blade. I put too much pressure and it snapped in two. Apart from this the afternoon was charming. I always find that the Lychpole atmosphere sends me back contented, even without Crease there. I did pretty good work there too, I think. I have done the script of the *Bells of Heaven* and now have only to work out a design. Mrs Fuller was very nice to me and gave me a decent tea. A rapidly rising cloud on my horizon is the first round of the House swimming matches that has been fixed for next Wednesday. However, I have less reason, I suppose, for nerves than I had last year. A letter arrived from Father today. He has been unwell at Norton and is in bed with a temperature. It is rather bad luck on his holiday.

Whit Monday, 24 May 1920

After school there was a splendid bathe for House teams only. I did pretty well. I am acquiring the racing flat dive and getting a better crawl.

Tuesday 25 May 1920

Heat. Afternoon, I had to shoot on the big range, appalling noise, things still echo. After Leagues, bathe, swam badly, got to start in the House match tomorrow, awful bore. Too hot to think, let alone write. Just read Ecclesiastes, magnificent. Like to do it in script. Too long. Hot as hell.

Wednesday 26 May 1920

Today the House swimming matches came off. We were all prostrate with nerves beforehand. I had to start and our match was first. I do not dislike starting as much as I had expected; one gets it over quicker anyway. We lost but did more creditably than I had expected.

Thursday 27 May 1920

I am getting less sanguine of my chances for the Certificate. Yesterday I was looking through some old papers and found I could do scarcely a word.

Friday 28 May 1920

At lunch a very nice letter from Father offering to send a quid whenever I needed it. On the strength of it I made another raid on the Grubber. I have written a satire of the Modern Pharisee showing the Arnold Lunn[1] type who talk about the man from the east with burning eyes and all that as the real pharisees. I am reading *The New Machiavelli* which I do not like as much as I had hoped. H.G.W's eternal sex obsession gets trying when it ceases to be shocking. The cold-blooded introspection is rather revolting too. Thank God Lychpole tomorrow.

Saturday 29 May 1920

The enchantment of Lychpole still holds me with its spell. I had some difficulty in getting there as Gordon's motor bike broke down. I did not do very much script except the names on a House team group. I looked at his books and did a little drawing, so very quickly and contentedly the afternoon passed and I had to plunge back in the shouting and fighting of Lancing.

Sunday 30 May 1920

Today the tea with Mrs B. could be no longer averted. It was particularly annoying as it was Bevan's Settle tea; however, I ate a good deal before I went. Booth, Boothby, Trenam and Parker were my appalling fellow-sufferers in the persecution. We went about four and were kept waiting a long time. Finally the good woman turned up and insisted upon seeing my drawings. I took 'Roses' and the script I had done for Crease. Of course she did not understand them at all, and was very silly over them. She showed me a fifteenth century Book of Hours of the Head's which was really very beautiful. Tea was a farce, with everyone trying to behave very well and behaving very badly. Boothby talked motor shop to Margy[2] all the time and Mrs B. would try to talk art to me. She seems to think it is a sort of obsession of mine that should be humoured. When we were just finishing tea the Head rolled up and made me leave my pictures for him to see. Then with profound relief we escaped to chapel.

[1] Arnold Lunn, author of *Loose Ends*, an anti-religious book cast in the form of an argument between two schoolboys; Waugh's House-tutor read it aloud to the boys. Lunn later became a Roman Catholic.
[2] One of the Headmaster's daughters.

Monday 31 May 1920

The day which might have been rather a pleasant one was spoiled by a letter from Crease at breakfast. He is very bored about my breaking his knife and says that I had no right to be using it at all. All he intended to lend me was his ink and he had put the box of other things away purposely. The knife is very old, quite irreplaceable, and he was passionately fond of it. If I have any hope of its being mended I must send it at once by registered post to the best place in London. I am very hurt that he should take that line about it. If anywhere in this bloody place, I did look for kindness and sympathy at Lychpole. Oh well another broken pencil point. . . .

The rest of the day was fairly all wrong. I have had difficulty about getting my script back as Parker was going to frame it today. At about one, taking my courage in both clammy hands, I waylaid the Head in the cloister by his door and asked for it. He was most ungracious and merely limped straight on without a word. I followed and waited half-in and half-out of his door while he went down his big staircase and glanced nonchalantly about the hall. He came up again and merely growled, 'My wife must have put it away. I'll bring it into the dining hall'. He did not, and I have not dared ask him for it again, so it has to go for another week unframed; though I don't mind quite so much as I should have if Crease had not been unkind to me. After lunch I again escaped nets and played a rackets single with Fremlin and a borrowed ball which we, of course, lost. It now only remains for me to get a nasty letter from home and into some bad row here to complete the canvas. I am laying a few shillings on the Derby and with Barnsley organizing a sweepstake; perhaps I shall lose all my cash too, as well as the one friend I have made here. Work is going none too well and my script and drawing worse. I shall have nothing for the Art Show, with Mrs B. destroying what little I have accomplished.

Tuesday 1 June 1920

Gordon was most characteristic last night about the sweepstake. I went to him as we are always supposed to get leave. He said he would think about it, and later in the evening had me in. 'Waugh', he said, 'I think you've put me in a damned awkward position about this sweepstake. If I give you leave, and of course personally I don't mind a bit, some little fool will write and tell his parsonic parents he has won something in a sweepstake and they'll write to the Head, and I'll have to blurt out that I gave you leave. So I am afraid that I have no choice but to refuse you leave, but you may get one up unofficially.'

In the Second League I made one, out second ball. A card arrived from Crease: 'I hope you do not think my letter unkind. Please do not read that into it.'

Other than this nothing happened, except that I was fifth in form, and ten bob, most of which is already blued, arrived from home.

Wednesday 2 June 1920

Hell's own Field Day. Tonbridge, owing to the difficulty of travelling on Derby Day, neglected to arrive. We left Shoreham at 10 for Preston Park, where we had a long walk through an avenue of the most hideous houses of the very pretentious Beechcroft type I have seen. We had a short but large lunch and immense quantities of fizzy drinks at a ludicrously early hour and then began the show. The government sent us a battery of RFA who made an appalling noise. Their sleek, well-groomed horses were a great contrast to us, sweating and dishevelled. I have seldom been so hot. The actual battle seemed pretty futile and indecisive, but I think the officers enjoyed themselves prancing about on horses, and I think that all things considered I would have as soon been on as off. There is always something vaguely romantic about a train journey. Spion Kop is said to have won the Derby, and Archaic second, but rumours do not agree. Anyhow I've lost money all right.

Thursday 3 June 1920

Weary and stiff after yesterday's excesses. In morning school we had quite a rag with Puttass. A bumble bee came in and we jumped about and yelled for sometime.

Friday 4 June 1920

Better than most Fridays. All the afternoon I spent in the library over old *Punches*.

Saturday 5 June 1920

To Lychpole in the afternoon. I had rather expected that after Crease's letter I should find the illusion shattered, but I had a very good afternoon and did a little quite good script. In the morning Woodard asked us to write about any religious difficulties we had, for him to explain. I covered two pages with it. In second evening I wrote the following for Whittall about his love for Lea mi.

> *Ars Amoris* for C.F.W.
> They love, the gold head and the black,
> With the heat of a 'tortoise' stove,
> They love with a love platonic
> As pure as a Gibbs' House Grove,[1]
> Passing the love of women;
> Passing the lust for gold;
> Beside their white hot passion
> Launcelot's love was cold
> Endymion's hair was golden,

[1] Latrine.

> It shone for many miles
> But Diana the great, pure huntress
> Ne'er basked in such amorous smiles.
> What though the brutal brother
> With toast his leisure tasks,
> and makes him fetch his clothing?
> One thing in vain he asks;
> His love can never be given
> to any at Dunley Hall, [1]
> it is given in reckless rapture
> to the classical swell Whittall.

I don't think that it is bad considering I wrote it in twenty minutes at the fag end of the day. Whittall greatly resents the liberty with the scanning of his name.

Sunday 6 June 1920

One Kirk, leader of some Church Bolshevik association, took Sunday lesson and droned on his political clichés for three quarters of an hour. I don't think people should talk politics where they cannot be heckled. I am making negotiations about mending Crease's knife.

Tuesday 8 June 1920

The only cheering thing was the arrival of a card from the makers of Crease's knife to say that they can replace the blade. It is no good trying script. I cannot write at all decently if I try to go at any pace and my thoughts will not wait for my pen. I have sent the knife off by registered post.

Thursday 10 June 1920

Tomorrow the First Eleven are going to play cricket against Tonbridge. The ridiculous homage of a minor school to a better is perfectly disgusting. It was given out that among other injunctions we were to sing lustily in chapel on Saturday morning as the Tonbridge team would be there. Snobbery is fairly healthy but that sort of thing is most morbid.

Friday 11 June 1920

To Lychpole today because I must watch us being beaten by Tonbridge tomorrow. I did a lot of script. In my thick notebook I carried out the scheme I had pondered for some time of the decorative treatment of a theorem in geometry. It was quite a success. I also began a heraldic blazoning of Mother's

---

[1] Dunley Hall, near Stourport, Worcestershire; home of the Lea brothers.

and Father's arms marshalled together, which, if satisfactory, I will give Father for his birthday. Returning from Lychpole I thought of a rather good Dowsonian first line:

'I loved you, dear, as madly as a hatter.'

Saturday 12 June 1920

We are all painting or drawing our lives. Some draw with pencil, weakly and timidly, continually breaking the point and taking up another, continually trying to rub things out and always leaving an ugly smear. Some use ink and draw firmly and irrevocably with strong, broad lines. Their work is often ugly, often grotesque, but always purposeful and deliberate. Some use colour, rich and lurid, laid on in full glowing brushfuls, with big sweeps of the wrist. Some draw a straggling haphazard design, the motive being eternally confused with unnecessary and meaningless parts. The threads pass out of the picture and are lost. The whole is an intricate incoherent maze. But some, and these are the elect, draw their design clearly and fully. No part is unnecessary. Each twist and curl of the fanciful foliage adds to and carries on the original motive. Each part works into the whole and there is no climax or end to it.

Sunday 13 June 1920

O'Connor and I are getting a trifle worried about the little boy ——, in whom both of us have a friendly interest. He has been getting in with a very unpleasant set lately, as his case[1] Wilson has left and we have rather suspicions that they may be making him foul. He has seen far too much of ——, who is a corrupt little brute in every way, and now he has started going out with out-House men like —— whose life in the Olds is quite notorious. It will be more than a pity if he does go to the devil as he was a charming little man as well as the possessor of a profile that excites my artistic senses. Heaven knows O'Connor's and my interest in him is pure enough.

In the evening I had to break my resolution of running the dormitory without punishments. I had to give Flynn a late. I am rather sorry as it had always been a theory of mine that if you treat people decently they won't abuse it. However, I was mistaken. Flynn is an absolute fool, and deliberately challenged my authority before the whole dormitory so I had no other choice. I am bored all the same. People will always interpret laxity as weakness and I'll be damned if I am going to have them thinking that of me.

Monday 14 June 1920

This afternoon I had to go into Shoreham to get my spectacles mended. I had an ice and saw the church and bought some new halfpenny buns.

[1] Friend.

Tuesday 15 June to Saturday 19 June 1920

In self-love, Man created God in his own image. He thought what a fine creature he was and so formed an ideal of the genius that could create him; he found what a weak creature he was and so found an ideal of the genius on whose almighty arms he could cast his cares and say, 'God's in his heaven, all's right with the world.'

This was a thought which occurred to me the other day; the expression of it has become rather mangled as Ford has been standing over me for the last five minutes and I have been afraid that he will ask me if I am doing work. He suspected it wasn't but couldn't read it as it was upside down and was afraid of a rebuff and of seeming officious if he asked me and was wrong. Anyway he has spoiled the fall of what was once a good sentence.

I have sent in an entry for Woodard's competition for a translation of Horace's *Sapphic Odes*, hoping to earn some money.

The great disadvantage of silver pen-holders is that if once ink gets on them it spreads everywhere.

I should like to write an Ode on the Intimations of Immorality. It might be quite funnily done but I will resist the temptation.

Sunday 20 June 1920

Pouring with rain and so spent largely in the library. There was no Settle tea and none of us were too eager for the expense of a subscription tea and Grimes and Snow were going out and the others had invitations to the pits.

I had to take the House bathe in the afternoon. I was a little nervous particularly as Shine and Newman arrived but it went all right. I had a windy moment however before shouting the 'all out'.

Monday 21 June 1920

Rackets and a dud bathe and work.

This morning Barnsley referred to O'Connor as 'your case'. I had not realized before that everyone must now think us bosom friends. It is rather funny as I used at one time cordially to detest him and have now no very great affection or respect for him. We seem just to have drifted together through being of equal position in the House, and have been going about together as it would be *infra dig* for us or them if we did with anyone else. A poor sentence.

Tuesday 22 June 1920

In the morning a letter from Father, with an unsolicited gratuity of ten bob, and a pleasant letter from Crease. He returns to the 'Downland cloister' in the first week of next month and wishes to see Molson and me over there this term. I had my hair cut and was bowled first ball in the Third League; I however caught a boy out and blew half-a-crown and lent a bob more which I expect will prove a gift.

Wednesday 23 June 1920

In the evening Gordon made me very bad-tempered – rather childishly perhaps, I begin to see in the cool forgetfulness of retrospection – but I have decided to put up a barrier or two between us. I refuse to become friendly with a man who has been as rude to me as he was. Lately, the senior people of the House have been going to dig on the Head's memorial cloister after third evening. When I write 'senior people', I mean the House-captains and lower lav., including people like Fremlin who are my juniors. I had had no exercise at all that day and felt that digging for half an hour in the cool evening was just what I would like. Accordingly I went to Gordon to get leave and he simply snapped out, 'No, Waugh, I'm sorry. You're in the wrong dormitory for that sort of thing.' If he had not intended to be rude he was at any rate inexcusably tactless. He might have said that he would sooner I went to look after my dormitory, but the way he put it could only mean that I was too junior for 'that sort of thing' and was presumptuous to ask. 'That sort of thing' was only for the upper classes like Fremlin. It is bad enough the insufferable little bounder keeping me up with the children when all my friends have been moved down. Last term he asked if I would very much mind staying up to oblige him and now it's 'you're in the wrong dormitory to take the place you ought in House society'. One good result of this, however, was that I went up to the dormitory fuming with rage and sulky and soon put a stop to any freedom after lights out. People were beginning to believe, I think, that I was lenient through weakness and not from strength, and I was beginning to distrust myself, too. My bad temper has at any rate restored my self-confidence in that direction, even if Gordon has succeeded in wounding my pride pretty severely.

Thursday 24 June 1920

A Saint's Day. In the early hours of the morning there was a House river bathe. Gordon apologized in an awkward, inadequate way first thing for his rudeness last night and made overtures of friendship, which I managed to keep at arm's length. The bathe was cheerless and windy but the day grew very hot. I played rackets with O'Connor, Mallowan, and Thubron at 12 and with Whittall for most of the afternoon. I also did a little cleaning for Major Bond's inspection tomorrow. One, Lord Horne[1], is coming to pry into our affairs. I am reading *Sinister Street* Vol II again to get the Oxford atmosphere, since Father and I have started discussing what college I am to go to. It is incomparably

[1] Lord Horne (1861–1929): educated Harrow; commissioned Royal Artillery, 1880; South African War, 1899–1902; commanded 1st Army in France, 1916; ADC General to the King, 1920–4.

good and I am quite enchanted. I have written to Father to suggest a few days at the Mitre next hols to see the place. The time I stopped there I saw far too little.

Friday 25 June 1920

It is very 'contenting' to have the inspection over. It was hot and long and all the morning was hideous with the scrubbing of brushes and smell of Brasso. At the end of it all Lord Horne made a speech which seems to me the epitome of all that is most fine and most false in the old school. He was a fine old man and so obviously sincere that it is hard not to be cheaply cynical about it. It was astoundingly like a parody by Alec. He spoke of the glory of discipline and militarism, of the power of leading men which could only be acquired by being born a gentleman and having spent one's youth at a public school and 'varsity. He told us that it was for officers that we were being trained, of our obligations to the state owing to the gap in British manhood (caused by his principles), of the danger of the present situation and how any minute we might be called up to fight Turks or Indians or Sinn Feiners or Bolsheviks or Welsh miners. It was really an excellent speech and was so true up to a point, even if all his ideals died with Palmerston and Disraeli. I could not help admiring him when he said how much more was required of us than of his generation. They nearly always say that when they were young they had to do so much more than us.

Saturday 26 June 1930

To Lychpole on the back of Gordon's motor bike. There I wrote out the thing of Cannan's Alec quotes in *The Loom*[1] about 'To him who desireth much, much is given' for his birthday. I am going to exhibit it at the Art Show first. In the evening Gordon read some more of *Loose Ends*. Other than this nothing at all happened. Molson has been suspended the use of his club again for cutting chapel. Dick is a very long-suffering House-master.

Sunday 27 June 1920

When I had interviewed the chef about my Settle tea and written an appeal home for more funds I went for a walk with O'Connor and Fremlin. The House bathe was very dud – the water was quite tepid and rather dirty. After the bathe we had Grimes's Settle tea, which was rather inadequate except for an excellent iced pudding he had sent over from the kitchens. We have taken to wearing crimson poppies as rather a pleasant affectation for our set. Dear Carew has written a poem to me.

[1] *The Loom of Youth:* Alec Waugh's autobiographical novel about Sherborne.

To E.A.W.
You have broken all my idols,
Given me fresh creeds to keep.
You have waked me from my dreaming,
Shattered my sweet, careless sleep.
Some are born to high endeavours.
For them much easier lies the way.
To me 'tis dark, unknown forbidding.
Guide me lest I go astray.
Change is not always for the better.
Perhaps the road I trod before
Contained less evil than the future
And progress only damns me more.
For you despise those who advance but little
Whose spirits and whose purposes are frail
Who stop at every inn upon the road-way
Who falter, quicken, falter and then fail.
For you I've given up all that I cherish,
Curses I find now where once friendships grew.
Give me then freely of your knowledge.
Be fair, my friend, 'tis all I ask of you.

It is rather embarrassing to have so large an influence which works out in such a bad poem. Lines in it are good; I don't dislike the last couplet; but most of it doesn't scan at all and some of it is not even true, such as the line 3 from the end. I'm sure my friendship has never gone to make anyone unpopular or earn him curses.

Monday 28 June 1920

At 12.30 there was an excellent team bathe. The water was a bit dirty but otherwise it was splendid and very empty. After lunch I escaped the House game and played rackets. The Bowlby family were having a smart wedding, Cuthbert marrying money and J.F. and the Head radiant in morning dress and white spats.

Tuesday 29 June 1920

S. Peter's day and my confirmation day. How things have changed in four years. When I was confirmed everything seemed to matter most awfully. I think I must have been rather a prig. Today was very pleasant except for the gloom of the imminent concert. Two quid came from Father by the breakfast post. I went for a walk with Preters until callover. At least we walked a little way and lay down in the grass and talked. He always shocks me rather pleasurably. I wonder if he will entirely go to the devil when he gets older or sober down and become a hardened old conventionalist. I think that he must do one or the other.

Wednesday 30 June 1920

It was not nearly so grey a Concert Day as I had anticipated. The day was bright and warm, and soon after lunch the gravel began crunching under cars and the quads and cloisters bright with summer dresses. Up in the gallery I had borrowed some cushions from Gordon, and, sprawling in comparative comfort with Ian Hay and G. K. Chesterton, the concert passed pleasantly enough. Music makes a pleasant background for indolence and, particularly in a recital by Brenter and some distinguished woman friend of his on a violin, it was not unlike an orchestra at a dinner or a dull turn at a music-hall, the sound gently flitting in and out of one's preoccupation. After the concert there was a bathe to which I did not go but instead had a shave and, feeling clean and scented with the soap and cream, came to the library till tea. This was as usual a stand-up one, with better food and flowers on the tables. Altogether it was very pleasant compared with the usual fierce loneliness of a stunt day without people.

Thursday 1 July 1920

was wet so there were no Leagues. I went to the library with the pious intention of doing some work, but old *Punches* soon scattered that illusion.

Saturday 3 July 1920

In the short morning school Woodard announced the result of the Horace prize. Rather to my surprise I won. At 10.45 we had Hall and tried to make a good meal to keep money for tea, but it is a strange time to eat much. The school cavalcade, straggling out for about half a mile, started for the station immediately after lunch. On the way down we bought some new buns from Gigins! The train was rather late; when we arrived at Hove we put our coats into the cloakroom at the station as the sun had come out. A perfect stranger accosted us and told us that we had got Brighton all out for sixty. This was the first of many encounters with enthusiastic natives. It was rather amusing that while Brighton were only taking a casual interest and we were frankly apathetic, all the onlookers and inhabitants outside seem frantically worked up about it, and numberless men and street urchins asked us the score with tense anxiety (and of course we didn't know it). We lunched modestly at one of the little tables by the ground off buns, bananas, chocolate, and ginger beer. We however made up for it at tea. Of the actual cricket I recall but vague memories. It lacked the green and white pageantry of Lords and the audience were for the most part blatantly semitic. We won, I gather, pretty easily. Hilder knocked up forty-nine in seventeen minutes, mostly in boundaries. At about 3.30 we went off for tea. We went by bus to the Pavilion Creamery where we had a royal orgy. We made the rule that the one that ate the smallest tea should pay the tip and, having thus established a healthy spirit of competition, I ate three plates of strawberries and Devonshire cream, a cream ice and three meringues, and later about half a pound of cherries, and felt none the worse for it. The cost, however, has severely crippled me.

Monday 5 July 1920

The House swimming matches are over and I have not got my House colours. I am hardly at all disappointed, although I had expected to get them.

In the morning there was a good rag with Tarbat[1] in Treble's absence. Barnsley was persecuting him, so he threw a brace of inkpots at him with more force than precision which made splendid smashes on the floor. Barnsley accordingly pursued Tarbat and began punching him; he gave one soul-rending scream and fled down the passage. Barnsley told so many lies about it that he got off with the price of the inkpots. Molson has won the Scarlyn Wilson Literature prize.

Tuesday 6 July 1920

Another filthily wet day. At breakfast a letter came from Father in which he concludes that I intend to pay for the things I ordered for my tea. This is something of a blow; unless I win the Art Show, and that very quickly, I don't see how I am going to make both ends meet for the next few weeks. I took no form of exercise at all today (except PT) and feel thoroughly discontented. I spent all the day – except a short time watching us beat Harrow at swimming – reading a Balzac, *The Wild Ass's Skin*, a most morbid and fantastic and engrossing story.

Wednesday 7 July to Sunday 11 July 1920

The weather has been perfectly vile. For exercise I was constrained on Friday to dig on the Head's cloister which got us off watching a match and gave me a comforting fatigue and made the old man so pleased. He met Fremlin and me going into chapel that evening and was most effusive and thanked us for our work. Saturday was Old Boys' day. All sorts of quaint creatures in OL ties turned up to feed on salmon mayonnaise at the school's expense.

Molson and I went over to tea at Lychpole and got thoroughly wet, but had a fairly good afternoon of it. I was very much afraid that my Settle tea today was going to be an utter failure as my raspberries never turned up. It was most annoying but I got the chef to whip the cream and doubled the amount of toast and, to judge by the Settle table's appetite in Hall this evening, I think it was quite a success. We put the surplus cream into the vase on Grimes's desk to

---

[1] A senior boy.

stink him out in a few days. I have made the pious resolve not to read any novel
or book for pleasure until after the Certificate and have taken out four large
volumes, two on History and two on the English. Eighteenth-century history is
most attractive. I can't abide the battles and colonies but I love all the corrupt
politics and diplomacy, particularly Alberoni. It is so healthily cynical. The
Certificate is only three days off now but I am fairly confident of all but the
Maths; under Puttock's mild and magnificent eye I have forgotten all that
successions of mathematicians have taught me. I hope to get credits in English
and History and possibly in Latin too. If I fail, I think I shall adopt the
precedent of Ahitophel.

Monday 12 July to Friday 16 July 1920

As I work all evening school now – and a long time out of school – my diary is
becoming more desultory. This sweat is really telling on me. Every night I go
to bed with a splitting headache. The days before the exam were quite
uneventful. One could have a lyrical time if one didn't care a damn about the
Certificate. Thursday was a very full day. Besides the Certificate there was a
Provost's garden party and the introduction of a thing called an Archimandrite
which, I gather, is a sort of Greek pope. He looked more like a fantasy of Jean
de Bochiere's than anything, with a huge black draped hat and an immense
many-pleated cope of purple and silver and a tinkle of hundreds of little bells
all about him. A rather charming contrast to the mediaevalism of the
procession was his interpreter, who paced behind the choir with their
Gregorians, the corporations in their S. Nicholas copes, and the ex-Provost in
his mitre, looking like a well-bred shop-walker in tight-fitting morning dress.
The garden party was, I think, on the whole a complete failure. The Head
showed off all our little tricks: the bands of Lancing and Ardingly played
military dirges; the choir sang with 'profuse strains of unpremeditated art';
and the PT maniacs ruined their white trousers. But all to no purpose: the
guests were, not unnaturally, bored stiff, and all through the afternoon their
cars were surreptitiously slipping away.

The exams were very trying. To start with we had a paper for two hours on
Algebra and Trigonometry which we were not meant to pass but were only
given, it appears, to keep us out of mischief. This was rather discouraging for a
start. In the afternoon we had the English Books at which I had put in so much
work. I think I must have got credit but there was not nearly enough time. The
most depressing thought is the amazing amount of quite unnecessary work I
have done. I had fairly sweated up Wordsworth's poetic diction and connection
with the French Revolution and had written out a great analysis of the happy
warrior's character, all to no purpose. However, I think I must have done fairly
well. One appalling result of nerves, I found, was that all my knowledge of
spelling – slender at the best of times – left me and I had to avoid perfectly

ordinary words through being unable to spell them: 'succeed' and 'subtle' and several others. Mallowan found the same. The culmination of a hard day was the amazing conduct of Gordon. He seems to get sudden manias at intervals for making himself unpleasant. He made us go into early school today. No one in our set in the out-Houses was going and very few other sets. It was a ludicrous act as of course Puttock never turned up at all.

Saturday 17 July to Wednesday 21 July 1920

But for the anxiety over the exam, these Certificate days would be very pleasant. We live all day in change, go into school at queer hours and sit out the usual ones. We do few chapels and callovers. In early school we play rackets; after breakfast we have long exams with a pleasant atmosphere of importance and long breaks spent in feverish comparisons of results. So far I have done none too badly. The best paper was the History Special Period. I hardly think I can have failed to get about 70% on it. I think that I have passed in everything important so far, but the worst are yet to come, herded together into the last two days. There has been nothing else of interest. A House match to watch in which we were easily beaten, the official announcement of Gordon's leaving, and the fortunate appointment of Woodard.[1]

One thing only of real interest happened. The Dilettanti supper party was an immense success: We had it on Sunday evening after chapel and were all very boisterous. It was hard to believe that it was the festival of an aesthetic society. Roxburgh was splendid. The supper was good – tongue, eggs, cucumber, radishes, meringues, and cakes, with lime juice to drink – and excellently managed by Dick. We were very uproarious. Bolshie Ferguson fell in a cow pat and girt only with a rug continued to fight with Fife all over the hill. Afterwards we soaked each other with water and played a hysterical game of rounders, to return sweaty, wet, and dishevelled, but wonderfully happy.

Thursday 22 July to Sunday 25 July 1920

At last the Certificate is over. I think that I must have passed. Last night we sung, 'For all thy Saints who from their labours rest'. From now onward the term is consecrated to straps and buckles and all the jingling trappings of the Corps.

OTC Camp, Tidworth Park, Salisbury Plain
27 July to 5 August 1920

I want rather carefully to record, while I can still remember it vividly, what camp was really like. Already the opiate of comfortable retrospection is beginning to blur the unpleasant part and I am afraid that by the time I have

---

[1] As House-tutor of Head's House.

again to decide about going, all that I shall remember will be a series of comfortable evenings and military bands. These indeed were the only things which made life at Tidworth at all tolerable; the rest of the day was wretched.

It was always very cold indeed in the early mornings, and, if reveillé had been the last trump it so much resembles, I think that many of us would have welcomed it as the opening of a warmer, if not a more pleasant, life. The valances had to be rolled up. They were generally wet and always allowed a piercing gust of wind to remove any feeling of comfort or warmth which the thick army blankets, rough and redolent of fumigation, had permitted. One had then to dress and put one's discarded clothes into one's kit-bag. There was seldom time to wash but the cold water in the windy shed was most uninviting. Bed piles had then to be made and the tent swept clean of the straw which was strewn thickly from our palliasses and bolsters. A peculiarly unenjoyable meal followed. The food was moderately good and plentiful, but served most revoltingly. Queer-tasting, orange, stewed tea had to be drunk from enamelled mugs. The metal was laid bare round the rims and made everything taste nasty. After this meal uniforms and equipments had to be cleaned. We soon had to fall in, be inspected, and marched to the battalion parade ground for most uninspiring prayers. Our battalion commander was an unpleasant little OL with the unmelodious name of Stubbs. His horsemanship was one of the few brightening features of the parades. These were not excessively sweaty but intolerable, dull, and full of trivial inconveniences. We were marched back to a fairly adequate lunch. The afternoon parade was generally an exhibition of sorts, but it rained so often that we did not have many. Those we did have were dull and uninstructive, even if we had wanted to learn anything. The most instructive thing I saw was that when the drum-major of the Gloucesters knocked his hat off with his wand not a single man smiled.

After parade came the social part of the camp. This I thoroughly enjoyed. We changed from uniform to fatigue dress and after a rather good high tea meal were free for the evening. I spent most of the time playing bridge in the canteen and listening to the sing-songs. The canteen was excellent. A large marquee, with flags and lights and flowers, it was the nearest approach to comfort which the camp provided, except the barber's tent. Here we spent a great deal of unnecessary money for the very pleasure of having someone attendant on our comfort; here anyway, among the oils and scents and soap, we could escape from the pervading reek of army grease. The sing-songs were quite amusing, all songs with choruses to be sung and times to be rapped out with swagger poles. Except for one little lad, who soon got hissed down, the entertaining was done almost entirely by the better schools – Charterhouse, Tonbridge, Christ's Hospital, Wellington, Sherborne and ourselves. (Sherborne were far more friendly and a much better set of fellows than I had expected. Hooper introduced me to several of his friends and I like most of them very much. *The Loom* does not seem to have embittered them as much as I had been led to suppose. Ross[1] came and looked me up which I thought not ungracious of him. 'John'[2] came down for the PT and went off again in a sulk having argued for two hours on a wet day with Dick.) Then came a dark unpalatable supper and bed. After the first night I slept fairly well but it was an immense joy last night to get back to sheets and pillows. The latrines were horrible and we had all to smoke in protection against the smell. Tent orderly was one of the torments of the damned. I shudder now to remember washing up army stew in cold water kneeling in mud.

The advantages were small. A certain democracy was not unpleasant and I got to know Longe, whom I have always liked very much, but the chief result of the increased insight into people's characters led, I found, mainly to increased dislike. The Ox[3] and I were extremely rude to each other and O'Connor sulked most of the time; Easton was officious. The only people who showed up well were Longe and Fulford. Altogether it was not at all worth the cost of the first week of the holidays. It is quite probable that even this faithful account will not deter me from going next year, but if it does not, I am sure that I shall regret it again. Eventually the last morning came. As we were the fire picket, we slept in our clothes and were up at five packing blankets and waterproof sheets and emptying palliasses. I left camp at 7 am and arrived at Waterloo at about 11.

Hampstead, Thursday 5 August 1920

Mother met me at Waterloo and after a short breakfast started for home. I had adventures with motor-buses but eventually reached home to luxuriate in hot water and clean clothes. After lunch Mother, Barbara, and I rushed into town and bought an excellent overcoat at Moss Bros. for nine guineas. I then rushed back for tea and dressed for the show with the Molsons. I got to Ashley Gardens at about 6.30 and was introduced to Mrs Molson, a short, ugly, pleasant little woman, fashionably dressed and much encompassed about by the many duties of an MP's wife. At the House of Commons we met Mr Molson, a very nice handsome man. We had dinner in one of the small private dining-rooms. The dinner was not nearly as good as I would have expected; it was most palpably the work of a Briton. We had coffee out on the terrace. There was some difficulty about getting seats for so important a debate, but we managed to get in. It was the Restoration of Order in Ireland Bill and was being fiercely attacked. When we arrived it was dinner hour, and a prolix Irishman was engaged on the thankless job of keeping the floor. He managed, however, to do it with some semblance of vehemence. Soon the debate warmed up.

[1] A. H. Trelawney Ross, a Sherborne housemaster.
[2] G. M. Carey, who appears in *The Loom of Youth* as 'the Bull', the games master.
[3] F. M. Hamerton of Head's House.

Almost everyone attacked the Government, but I am afraid that the dumb majority will carry the bill. Clynes made a very good speech; Lord Hugh Cecil was brilliant; and then Devlin lost his temper and in a broad Irish brogue delivered a tremendous attack. 'It's easy enough', said he, 'to laugh at the Labour Party' – here there were shouts of 'hear hear' and 'yes' – 'but you don't laugh at the by-elections'. Here someone called out, 'Sir, I defeated a Labour candidate.' 'Yes sir, but surely you are the epitome of all that is most noble in the Unionist Party?' Eventually I staggered home at about 12 having had rather a full day.

Friday 6 August 1920

Slept until 11.30. After lunch I went with my sister-in-law to a tailor in the Strand where we saw a ludicrously cheap suit yesterday, under seven pounds, in very attractive greenish blue cloth. Having ordered this we ate ices at Selfridge's and came home to tea.

Saturday 7 August 1920

In the afternoon Barbara and I went out and careered about on buses for some time, had tea at the Thistle and came home. On the way back we bought tickets for our local music-hall. We struck a peculiarly disreputable show. All the usual jokes about immorality and prostitution and one peculiarly repulsive comedian whose entertainment was a fable about venereal disease. There were however quite amusing parts; one rather good jest – 'King Solomon had a thousand wives and the damn fool slept with his fathers.' Father is getting very frightened about this ludicrous capitalist war in Poland.[1] It really looks as if we were going to fight, in which case Alec would be called up.

Sunday 8 August 1920

Mass at St Jude's in the morning. In the afternoon the awful Herbert came to tea so I rushed off to the Flemings but was coldly received.

Monday 9 August 1920

Little doing. Barbara and I went down to explore Cheyne Walk in the morning and in the afternoon to a cinema. In the evening Hugh came to see us, immaculately dressed, and told long and rather indecent stories for some time. We then began the spiritualist game with the swinging ring but with little success. Then we did the wine glass show but could get nothing intelligible. If it was sane it spoke a different language from us.

[1] Early in 1920 Poland set out to conquer the Ukraine from Soviet Russia. She was repulsed, and in July the Red Army advanced on Warsaw. The British government seemed inclined to intervene on the side of Poland, but dropped the idea when a united Labour movement, led by Ernest Bevin, threatened a general strike.

Tuesday 10 August 1920

Barbara and I went down to Ditchling for the day to see her little house.[1] It is getting on very well; the skeleton of the roof is up now, and looks charming. We intended having tea with the Meynells, but were so coldly received that we pretended we had forgotten an important injunction to the builder about gas taps, went and had tea in a shop, and bought a puppy. This was the triumph. He is a charming little spaniel we have christened Boke.[2] I have seldom seen such an engaging dog. We bought him for the modest sum of two guineas from an old farmer. We brought him back in a taxi from Victoria. Mother is, of course, delighted with him.

I have written this parody of Landor's epigram, to a decadent modernist.

> I strove with none, lest he should strive too well;
> Nature I feared, but safely toyed with art;
> I warmed both feet before the fires of Hell,
> They rise a little; comfort bids depart.

Wednesday 11 August 1920

We took the puppy down to the vet's in the morning and learned that he had mange.

Thursday 12 August 1920

Today the Jacobs children, Luned and Hugh, came up to town for the day. I find little attraction in Luned now. She has coarsened out a lot. I went to my tailor's but found that the suit was not ready yet. We then went to the National Gallery. I escaped under the pretext of being too proud to lunch at a Lyons and came home.

Friday 13 August 1920

To my tailor's in the morning. The suit is divine. It could hardly be better if it had cost eighteen guineas at Savile Row. After an early lunch Mother and I went to stand in the pit for Galsworthy's *Skin Game* at the St Martin's. We got very good seats. It is the most terrible tragedy I have seen and most magnificently played. Father made a remark worth recording. The new puppy was howling dismally, during dinner, in the bathroom. Father said, 'He's unhappy and wants to tell us about it, which, after all, is all that most literature is!'.

---

[1] Barbara Jacobs and Alec Waugh married on 29 July 1919, but lived at the Waugh house in Hampstead until the summer of 1920, when they moved to Ditchling, near Lancing.

[2] The name embodied a family joke: Alec Waugh, as a child, used to hold up objects he had broken and say, 'boke'.

Saturday 14 August 1920

Little doing. In the afternoon I went to the baths but found the water dirty and full of the most dreadful greasy-haired cads.

Sunday 15 August 1920

To church in the morning. I did not wear my new suit as I didn't want to spoil the cut of the trousers. Basil,[1] to enliven the time when all his swell friends are out of town, has invented a new festival 'The Coronation of the blessed Mother of God' which he observed with all pomp of copes and processions. No one called in the afternoon so Father and I went to see the Flemings and Mrs Carew. Poor Boggy[2] has had an accident with a garden rake and nearly blinded herself. Mrs Carew was a little saner than usual.

Monday 16 August 1920

I went down to the baths in the morning but for no very apparent reason they had no towels. Defrauded of this I went to the show at the Hampstead Art Gallery to which Mrs Fleming has been urging me to go. There was little really interesting: one or two Gertlers I had seen in his studio, some ludicrous still lifes, and several would-be moderns. Alec came back from his cricket week profoundly depressed. He appears to have had rather a good time and has cheered us all up with threats of suicide. We, however, opened a bottle of pink fizz which although it was not very good restored general good humour. I managed to put down three glasses without getting at all screwed, rather to my satisfaction.

Tuesday 17 August 1920

Barbara and I went on the lake at Regent's Park in the morning. After lunch, having put on purple and fine linen, we fared sumptuously at the Thistle and went on to Chapman & Hall's to pick up Father and Jock Ledward. We went to an excellent show at the Cinema de Paris and home to a good dinner. Alec fairly sepulchral. After dinner we played paper games which became less decent as the whiskies were drunk. However it was a good evening. Some of the drawings were really awfully funny and all appeared so. Jock is most excellent company. Alec stirred a little from his lethargy to deliver a few obscenities.

Wednesday 18 August 1920

After lunch Mother and I set out by bus to find great-great-grandfather's church in Wells Street, but found that it had been pulled down.[3] We then went

[1] The Revd. Basil Bourchier.

[2] 'Boggy' Fleming.

[3] The Revd. Alexander Waugh, DD (1754–1827), a Calvinist, was educated for the Ministry at Edinburgh and Aberdeen. In 1782, at the age of twenty-eight, he was sent to London to a chapel in Wells Street, off Oxford Street, which he served until his death.

to the shop in Bloomsbury which Jock had told me about and got a very nice plain stick for 6s 6d. If I get my five quid I will have a gold or silver band put on it. We then went to the Stoll because Mother wished to see *Wagon Tracks* and I was quite ready to see it again.

Friday 20 August 1920

In the afternoon to a cinema. Morning to vet. In the evening I met Father at his office and we plunged into the wilds of Hammersmith for *Iolanthe* at King's. We had an excellent dinner first at the Clarendon. *Iolanthe* was perfectly enchanting and utterly different from anything I had seen before. I loved every minute of it.

Saturday 21 August 1920

Father and Alec spent the whole day perched on the Pavilion at the Oval. Barbara, Mother and I to cinema after lunch. Alec far more cheerful after dinner.

Sunday 22 August 1920

To Saint Jude's in the morning. After lunch Barbara and I set out to see the Labour demonstration in Trafalgar Square.[1] It was a queer sight. There were thousands of people there, very few of whom could have heard anything of the speakers. It was rather like a fair with barrels of fruit and queer-looking confectionery and women selling Labour and Sinn Fein colours crying, 'Wear your colours, sir, wear your colours'.

Monday 23 August 1920

Marjorie Scott came to stay for a couple of days. Barbara very hysterical in the morning because she had a few housewifely duties to do. God knows what life at Halfacre will be like. In the afternoon, as neither of the girls seemed bent on doing anything exciting, I journeyed off alone to look at the bookshops. In the evening we played games. One rather good limerick said:

> 'There once was a man called Wymark,
> Whose daughter set out for a lark;
> When she met Gilbert Cannan,
> She turned round and ran on
> But the sequel matured after dark.'

Tuesday 24 August 1920

After lunch Mother, Marjorie, Barbara and I went to the private view of the film version of *Little Dorritt*. Very bad. Dickens always seems so fantastic and

[1] To oppose British aid to Poland in her war with Russia.

grotesque on the cinema with all his doddering old men and semi-imbeciles. The plot too seemed peculiarly inconsequent and insipid.

Midsomer Norton, Wednesday 25 August 1920

The journey down couldn't have been better if I had travelled first class. Two bob to the guard got me a lunching car with only one other person. I had a reasonably good lunch. At Salisbury the guard hunted me out and put me in the Temple Combe part of the train, locking me in an all-but-empty carriage. I had a short wait at Temple Combe and arrived at Norton at 3.17. I had then to go down to a party at the Costobadies. The aunts had accepted for me as they thought that Betty was going to be there. It turned out to be a children's athletic sports without her – not a success. I returned and after dinner played bridge. Dear Aunt Connie is not very good, being preoccupied with beatific visions, and her partners are always badly down.

Thursday 26 August 1920

Basked in the sun on the veranda all the morning. The aunts have got a charming new cat. Immeasurably wild. In the afternoon I went up to play tennis at Dimboro with Nancy. Betty eluded me again.

Saturday 28 August 1920

In the morning Aunt Elsie and I went out sketching. I did a fairly satisfactory one of one of the big hills with the trees getting more and more blurred in the distance. After lunch, Aunt Trissie and I went over to tea and tennis at the Mialls. We came back in time for me to change for dinner at Dimboro. They call it 'supper' – rather a charming affectation, I think; so many people have a sort of high tea and call it 'dinner'.

Sunday 29 August 1920

Not much doing. I went to early service and not again during the day. A queer woman came to lunch who talked church shop all the time. It is queer that it could have interested me once. She wanted badly to go to Oxford to see St Barnabas! I did a sketch, not wholly unsuccessfully, of part of the stable yard while the others were at evensong.

Monday 30 August 1920

We went out for a lunch picnic to sketch but I could find no inspiration so I read all the time. We were invited to a hay picnic by one Mr Beauchamp, a prosperous farmer, cousin of the baronet, the only one who could keep his place of that family. He fetched us and took us back in a car and had two smart maids waiting on us. He was a dear old thing, very proud of entertaining the 'gentry'. The vicar's wife and child and a Miss Thatcher were there too. He gave us a very good tea and afterwards showed us how all his agricultural machines worked. It was really extraordinarily interesting. After dinner the Thatchers came in for bridge. Léonie Thatcher was one who Alec said was the most attractive girl he had seen, next to Barbara. She was hideous and nearly mad.

Tuesday 31 August 1920

There was a small tennis party at the Bulleids in the afternoon. Betty was looking divine. My two cousins were there. Grace Miall also, looking pretty but so shy and a terrible Bulleid cousin, son of Lawrence the painter. The tennis was very good fun but not too well organized.

Wednesday 1 September 1920

At Dimboro most of the day. After dinner the aunts and I went up to bridge and were given no refreshments! Not so much as a cup of coffee, so we had to make tea and forage for buns when we got back.

Thursday 2 September 1920

Nothing doing in the morning. In the afternoon we had the Holmeses and Bulleids to tea. Humphrey came uninvited and was quite appalling. I think that the aunts had rashly said, when Betty couldn't come, 'Never mind we shall be glad to see any of you who care to turn up', and the beggars left the byways and hedges. Anyway, Nancy and Hilary seemed thoroughly to be ashamed of him. We played cards after tea.

Hampstead, Friday 3 September 1920

Came home comfortably in a lunch train by Bristol. After dinner we all, except Father, who was going out to some acting committee meeting, went down to *Milestones* at the local theatre, excellently played.

Saturday 4 September 1920

Our expedition to Oxford had to be scratched as the weather was bad and I was unwell. I spent the day uneventfully in bed feeding on rusks and tea.

Sunday 5 September 1920

Clothed and to a certain extent in my right mind, but still feeling a little depressed. Practically nothing happened.

Monday 6 September 1920

With the morning post, as I was drearily awaiting breakfast in bed, the exam list came with the notice that I had got through the Certificate with credit in all seven subjects. I am astoundingly elated. It does mean a lot to be sure of being in the Sixth. Next term ought really to be splendid. Father gave me five guineas most of which I have already blued on theatre tickets. I am taking Alec and Barbara to *French Leave* at the Globe, and Mother, Father, and Hooper to the St James's for Hawtrey's show about *His Lady Friends*. Hooper came round after lunch to take me out on his motor bike, a fearsome exploding thing. As we began to gather speed he leant back and said cheerily, 'I hope you don't mind, old thing, I haven't got a brake on it yet'. Luckily we had no cause to use it. After that I went to meet Father for a cinema.

What a futile thing this diary really is. I hardly record anything worth the trouble. Everything important I think had better be stored in my memory and it consists chiefly of 'shops in morning. cinema in afternoon'. I ought to try and make it more ——[1] but it becomes so dangerous.

Thursday 9 September 1920

In the morning Barbara and I went into the city see about gas fittings. In the evening we went to *French Leave*, a thoroughly merry play. I induced Alec to dress. He did not go to the office as he had sprained his ankle at the nets. He has offered to write a novel if I will find him the plot. I have worked out an analysis for one which ought to be thoroughly amusing if well written. He has not yet decided whether he will do it. He talks of doing it under another name with Herbert Jenkins. If that fails he will own up to it and place it with Grant Richards; in that case it will be dedicated to me. My plot is the disappearance of a literary eccentric who disappears deliberately to avoid his former mistress, and to observe, as a psychological study, the effect of the murder on the guests, arrives in the guise of the detective's assistant. I shall try Ensor with it as a play if it falls through.

Friday 10 September 1920

To tea with the Hoopers. First of all Hooper took me out on his motor bike for a long and peculiarly dangerous drive which I enjoyed a lot, but one needs nerves and bottom of iron ever really to be free from discomfort. Mrs Hooper was charming. They have invited me to dinner and theatre on Wednesday.

Saturday 11 September 1920

Our expedition to Oxford. I have never seen anything so beautiful. In places like Wells there are beautiful buildings and closes, but I have never seen anything like New College Cloisters or Tom Quad or the Founder's Tower. Father has put my name down for New College and I am going to try for a scholarship at the House. We saw the Sheldonian and the rostrum from which

---

[1] Word heavily crossed out in MS.

Father recited the Newdigate; we saw the gate of Trinity which James Waugh my great-uncle scaled at two o'clock in the morning; and the Union where I hope to speak. We saw all over the good colleges and the front quad of them all. We went down to the river through Christ Church Meadows, had lunch at the Mitre and tea at Boffins. It was a splendid day; Father told me disreputable stories of his time. We returned at last very tired by the dining train.

Sunday 12 September 1920

In the morning to St Jude's. After tea Alec and I went down to call on Mrs Rhys. She was very excited about the swell house where she has been staying. Ernest read a poem beginning with: 'I have known purple and gold in my time'.

Wednesday 15th September 1920

Barbara and I went with Mother to call on the Flemings to greet Jean and Philla who had arrived late the night before. Jean was looking very beautiful but Philla had, I thought, become rather too vivacious. However she was very jolly. I then dressed and went out to dinner at the Hoopers. We had an excellent meal and as it was wet they had hired a car for the evening. We drove off to *Cherry* at the Apollo. It was singularly bad but we enjoyed it. Mr and Mrs Hooper were charming. Hooper and I had adventures between the acts trying to get a smoke. When I got back Alec's guests had not gone. He called me up and introduced me. Lowe and Bax.[1] Bax was charming, very kind and quiet and gentle. I liked the other man too. It is pleasant to find Alec with such decent friends as well as his usual sort.

Thursday 16 September 1920

It poured with rain all the morning so I stayed in and tried to finish *Madame Bovary*. After lunch Barbara and I went to a matinée at the Coliseum. It was an excellent show. Arthur Prince was splendid; there was a short sketch with Violet Vanburgh in it, and a good Norwegian dancer. We came back and dressed for *His Lady Friends*. Hooper came, very cheery. The show was splendid. I had never seen Hawtrey before. We met Reed there, very cheery too.

Lancing, Friday 17 September 1920

Barbara and I, after fetching Boke from the vet's, went to call on Jean de Bochiere. He was perfectly sweet with a sort of mediaeval courtesy of manners. He showed me his *Macbeth* pictures and several others. After lunch I changed into my customary suits of solemn black and went off to Victoria. The station

[1] Clifford Bax (1886–1962); studied art at the Slade and Heatherley's; prolific playwright and novelist.

was appallingly crowded. The whole line is run for the Jewish first-class season-ticket holders who have no luggage.

I am, as I expected, in the Lower Dormitory and have the left-hand desk in the House Room.

Saturday 18 September 1920

I have been put in the Upper Sixth. Roxburgh has given me a time table which suits me very well. I am doing no French, Greek, or Maths, a little English, a lot of History, some Latin and Divinity. I upholstered my desk and it looks very distinguished in blue with Father's brass candlesticks. Woodard has given us leave to have a bridge club. The term opens with great prospects. I am happier than I have ever been before at school. Being in the Sixth has greatly raised my social position in the House.

Monday 20 September 1920

Work starts in the Sixth. I am thoroughly enjoying it. There are only seven in our history squad. We are doing much more interesting work, Political Economy, Social and European History.

Wednesday 22 September 1920

Nothing doing. Dull House game, no work.

Friday 24 September 1920

A farcical parade, and bridge at which Fulford and I lost five pence. It is a cheap amusement.

Saturday 25 September to Thursday 30th September 1920

Very little has happened. I am enjoying the work in the Sixth awfully. Our bridge has been stopped. Ford went to the Head behind Woodard's back. We went and argued with the old man, who was courteous but adamantine. Yesterday we took tea out and I attempted a sketch.

In the debate on Sunday evening I opposed the motion that 'This House deplores the disrespect for age by modern youth'.

'Anyone, sir, who has toiled through the two volumes of dreaming spires and squalid gutters of *Sinister Street*, will have found on the last page a word of consolation for the time which it has taken him to reach it. Michael is told that there is no tragedy of age. Now this is in part true; I am the first person to agree with the honourable proposer in this statement of the immense gulf between youth and age. Age is of itself a tragedy, the most hideous and ubiquitous tragedy in the world.

'Age, like most virulent poisons, is an excellent stimulant in small doses. Its results are quite satisfactory until a man reaches his prime. Then it begins gradually to undo what it has done, torments, degrades and finally kills him.

'Most people, I suppose, would, like the honourable proposer, fix the prime of a man's life somewhere about thirty or thirty-five. Personally – I am open to conversion and do not hold this out as an essential article in my creed – I should place it at between fifteen and sixteen. It is then, it always seems to me, that his vitality is at its highest; he has greatest sense of the ludicrous and least sense of dignity. After that time, decay begins to set in. Possibly he attains to the "ungainly wisdom" of the Sixth Form and in that languorous atmosphere drinks deep of the opiate of specialization; possibly he attains to some abnormal form of muscular development and in his gyrations upon the football field loses his sense of the ludicrous; possibly he attains to an official position in the school and loses that still greater gift, his sense of humour. After these first steps on the downward path his decadence grows rapidly. Experience leads only to intellectual domesticity. Every day he wakes with his body a little more feeble, his brain a little more haphazard, his soul a little more damned. He becomes narrow and querulous and finally, after the puerility of old age, his jaw drops in the complete imbecility of death.

'And so we come to the one argument that can be urged for this motion. It is the nature of a fool to revere deformity, but it is the nature of a cad to sneer at it. It might be said that the least we can do is to pity these poor phantoms of ourselves. Well, magnanimity is a fine thing towards a beaten people but, as Gladstone found, it is a peculiarly dangerous one to a people who refuse to acknowledge defeat. Too few people follow the precedent of the men of Grantchester and "up and shoot themselves when they get to feeling old". They seem positively to glory in their affliction.

'It is easy enough to laugh at the great uncle's "My-boy-when-I-was-your-age" manner. It is altogether too easy to laugh at terrible things. This pride in their deformity is one of the most hideous symptoms of their horrible disease. These grotesque, decaying old men, with the supreme arrogance of the impotent, take upon themselves to dictate to their youngers and betters how they should paint their pictures and write their sonnets and lay down their lives.

'The old men have just been having a war which the young men have had to fight. The result, to quote a distinguished preacher of a year or so ago, is that his generation is now one of broken and tired men. There are now practically only two generations – the very young and the very old.

'The result is the extraordinary boom of youth, which everyone must have noticed during the last few years. Every boy is writing about his school, every child about her doll's house, every baby about its bottle. The very young have gained an almost complete monopoly of bookshop, press, and picture gallery. Youth is coming into its own.

'Though, I suppose, most members of this house have now passed what I have fixed as the prime of their lives, I think that all can claim a place in the younger generation; and it is to this generation and to themselves that they will be doing a grave wrong if they allow this iniquitous motion to be carried. Respect, if it is to be of any value at all, must include an acknowledgement of superiority. If they pass this motion they will condemn themselves to their own consciences as the inferiors of a generation of narrow, decadent malformities. No generation has ever wreaked such disasters as the last. After numerous small indiscretions it has had its fling of a war which has left the civilized world pauperized, ravaged, shaken to its foundations. By passing this motion they will have registered their complete lack of confidence in themselves to do better, and their profound admiration for the perpetrators of this calamity, and I firmly contend that no man could exist if this was his true estimate of himself.

'I therefore appeal to this house not to let any scruples of maudlin sentimentality outweigh their pride in their own souls. Let them sympathize with the honourable proposer in the quite unjustifiable pessimism with which he appears to regard his own abilities; but let it end there. To vote for this motion would be to betray themselves and their whole generation.'

On Thursday Bevan and I had the lugubrious distinction of going to tea with the Gods.[1]

Friday 1 October 1920

Parade in the afternoon was a farce. Boothby and I got brought up before the OC for laughing while we were being inspected. Only the timely arrival of his young wife saved us from defaulters. It caused considerable merriment. Ford was very priggish about it.

Saturday 2 October 1920

In early school we were doing Horace and I suddenly got the bright idea of putting up

'dis te minorem quod geris, imperas'[2]

over my desk in script. Molson and I went over to tea at Lychpole in the afternoon. Crease leaves on Monday and is going to spend a few days at Underhill before he goes to Oxford.

Sunday 3 October 1920

I did the script notice for the top of my desk; it looks very well. We had a Political Group meeting at twelve and discussed the miners' strike. A gloomy Settle tea.

---

[1] House-captains and prefects. A Waugh word, not general Lancing slang.
[2] Only as servants of the gods in heaven can you rule earth. *The Odes of Horace*, Book 3, Ode 6.

Tuesday 5 October 1920

By the first post the woodcuts I ordered from the 'serendipity' shop arrived. They are a most attractive little pamphlet on handmade paper in red and black. When I am rich I will get it bound. In the afternoon I was raised to the First League and played, I think, none too badly. Fremlin and I went up to tea with Fulford. The hospitality of the pits this term has been splendid.

Wednesday 6 October 1920

The parade at 12.30 was a splendid farce. We had a thoroughly jolly four and ragged the whole time. Hill tells me that Molson is agitating to resign the Corps; personally I think that it is far jollier to stay in and rag it. After a strenuous afternoon's boxing there was another military show. This proved our undoing. We had to go to the BSM.[1] for musketry. We ragged the whole time and at the end Fulford, Fremlin and I were hauled up before the O.C.

Thursday 7 October 1920

We were marched up to the orderly room this morning and given defaulters. We have devised a great number of rags, such as coming on in running things or great-coats, but I doubt if we shall carry any of them out.

Friday 8 October 1920

Today the Corps show reached its climax. The whole of the uniform parade our sect behaved most uproariously, the junior people took it up too and the parade, as far as our half of the platoon went, was quite ludicrous. After supper Fulford, Whittall, Parker (God knows why!), and I were summoned to the House-captains' room to discuss things with Ford. He ingeniously appealed to our vanity; he said that hitherto he had not ticked us off openly as it was bad for the House if senior people seemed up against the head of it. He said that he quite saw our point of view (people always say that when they mean to be particularly overbearing) but things could not go on as they had been. I told him that I should like to use any influence I might have to make the Corps look ridiculous. We argued a bit, not because I had a thought of winning, but just to show that we had something to say, and then gracefully capitulated. He thanked us and we went out with the prospect of solid gloom for the rest of our military existences.

Saturday 9 October 1920

At 12.30 I went to Woodard to ask him what could be done about resigning the Corps. He was very sensible about it, but said that it would stop any chance of my ever being made a House-captain.

[1] Battalion Sergeant Major.

Sunday 10 October 1920

In the evening there was a debate on 'This House considers that man's one and only aim in life is his own pleasure'. It was not very good. I spoke twice, not badly. With the exception of Hill, I think that Lister and I are really the best speakers. I endeavoured to show that the ideals of pleasure and pain were not diametrically opposed. The only criterion by which we could judge right and wrong was our conscience, and this was only an educated instinct that showed us what courses would end in unpleasant consequences.

Monday 11 October 1920

We had our defaulters in the morning. Fremlin was got at by the militarist set and boasted his quiescence in mufti. Fulford wore running shorts, tweed coat with huge sprigs of holly, and socks (with suspenders), and corps boots. I wore running things and a great coat and woollen muffler. It was dull but not the least sweaty. In the afternoon, boxing. I am beginning to like Hale very much. He is much more than a brilliant athlete. He showed me some verses which he writes, not very good but naive. I can quite understand the way in which he was pursued in his youth. He is extraordinarily charming.

Thursday 14 October 1920

In the morning O'Connor sent Riley up to me to ask if he might join the Literary Group. I punted[1] him all round the Chapel Quad before PT. He has now lost his only friend in the House.

Friday 15 October 1920

Parade. O'Connor bagged the last cleaning stuff and took it up to his pit. General indignation against him. The library privilege list is up. Hale is rather hurt at not getting his. I sent the list in to Woodard and feel rather conscience-stricken because I gave them to Lowther just because he is pretty and forgot a man like Hale who really deserves them. I told Dick about it after chapel. He said he would think about it which means he will forget all about it. In second and third evenings the UVB had a peculiarly revolting debate. I thought that it took a pretty honest conversation to shock me, but they were simply disgusting. I can't conceive how Dick countenanced it at all. The motion was, 'This House approves of mixed bathing', but they digressed about brothels and syphilis and eunuchs and abortion *ad nauseam*. C. F. D. Long[2] proved a most morbid little tick with an immense knowledge of the technicalities of sex.

[1] Kicked.

[2] Later a pioneer explorer of underground caves, particularly White Scar Cave. He committed suicide in 1924.

Sunday 17 October 1920

I was in the House Room contemplating a dull day of a couple of Dilettanti meetings and a badly-attended Settle tea when a telephone message arrived that Alec and Barbara were in Brighton and asking me out to lunch. The world was recoloured. I rushed back, finished off my letters, made hasty apologies to my Dilettanti presidents, got leave from Woodard, fumed through a lecture by Howitt on the synoptic problem and then rushed off for one of the best days I have spent. They were staying at the Albion, by far the best hotel, and we had an excellent lunch there, among other things a peculiarly good dressed crab and a glass of port. We discovered a new drink of ginger beer and burgundy which was very good. We played with the slot machines on the pier − an everlasting joy − and saw an octopus fed at the aquarium. A meringue, some chocolates, and an unexpected and quite unsolicited ten bob and then back to bondage.

Monday 18 October 1920

Alec's ten bob blued. Hale and I spent our Saint's Day walking over to Washington. We had a fairly good lunch at a pub there, Hale a little screwed, walked back to Steyning where we had tea, and got a bus to Old Shoreham and so back.

Tuesday 19 October to Monday 25 October 1920

Nothing much doing. On Tuesday evening we had the modern play-reading society. We did Shaw's *Candida*, a thoroughly jolly evening. I have decided to do my first novel next holidays. I have got a scheme − the study of a man with two characters, by his brother − but I never realized what an immense amount of labour it entails. I have been making elaborate calculations and find that each chapter will have to be about two sections of College bumph.

Tuesday 26 October to Monday 1 November 1920

I have not time adequately to keep a diary. All my energies are being devoted to my novel which goes fairly well.

Tuesday 2 November to Monday 8 November 1920

Another week.

Tuesday 9 November to Monday 15 November 1920

Another and very full week. A debate conspiracy, ragging some Rabelaisians, and the novel have taken up all my time.

Tuesday 16 November to Thursday 2 December 1920

Art Comp.

Friday 3 December to Tuesday 21 December 1920

On Monday 6 December I heard from Father that Mother had gone into a nursing home and had had an operation.

I arrived home last Friday. At last the family are beginning to take a little interest in my novel: Alec apprehensive of a rival, Mother of my ruin through becoming a public figure too soon. Father likes it. Meanwhile I plod on and on at it, trying to make it take some form or shape. At present it seems a mere succession of indifferently interesting conversations. However, I believe it is fairly good and I am pretty sure to be able to get it published. It's a bloody sweat however.

On Sunday to a show in Clifford Bax's studio. Brilliant plays.

Hampstead, Monday 10 January 1921

I have a lot to make up – almost the whole of the holidays – and now that my family's disapproval and my own innate sloth have led me to abandon my novel, I must set about doing it.

At present Carew is nursing the abortion – frantically admiring, dear fellow! My only literary achievements have been a short story, on which I am still waiting *Pan*'s verdict, and some things for the *Bookman* competitions.

On Christmas Day Hooper and the Rhys family came to dinner and, mellowed by champagne, we acted some charades which were to us most uproariously funny.

In the evening of Sunday we went down to one of the Rhys' 'genii' parties. A niece of Katherine Tynan and I acted a charade. I think it must have been on the Wednesday following that Stella took me to the dance. There I renewed my acquaintance with Di Brewer whom I had only met before as Maria in that awful *Twelfth Night* reading. She improves on acquaintance and I found her rather attractive. Next day I got an invitation to her dance. That, I see from the card, was on January 3, Monday. It was a very jolly show, excellent supper and partners. I only got one dance with Di, however. On Tuesday or the Tuesday before, I cannot quite remember which, Alec took me to *The Beggar's Opera* – it was simply perfect – and introduced me to Lovat Fraser[1] who was in one of the boxes.

On New Year's Eve – this is getting as bad as Warner and Martin's *History* – Barbara and I went to the *Knight of the Burning Pestle* and went round to see Noel Coward and the leading lady behind the scenes.

Monday 24 January 1921

Keeping a diary is a habit that it is very easy to drop. Ever since I allowed myself to get slack about it last term when I was at work on my novel it has

---

[1] Claud Lovat Fraser (1890–1921), artist and designer; designed settings and costumes for *The Beggar's Opera*, 1920; book designer.

languished and even when, at the beginning of last holidays, I determined to give that up, I did not begin it again. The unfinished volume is now in the bureau at home and is a most haphazard and half-hearted thing. But now that I am back in the languorous atmosphere of Lancing, with a pit and privileges, I feel that it is a salutary activity to begin again.

This, then, as preface. Last holidays passed quickly with dances and shopping. The only thing that happened not entirely trivial was my meeting with Ursula Kendall. She is beautiful and gracious and womanly, but I am afraid that others, better than I, have seen this too. However I have shut down, I think finally, the Luned affair. She wrote me a rather touching, but hysterical and, I fear, rather a self-conscious letter, asking me in almost as many words to go on kissing her. I wrote her a long letter back in which I explained my share in the whole thing and told her it was over. The last week passed in a whirl of shopping for the pit, none of which, except perhaps the crockery, was very successful. On Friday I came back here.

Saturday was hideous. All the morning I was at work trying to make the pit look decent and finding it inconceivably hard. The walls below about shoulder level defy all attempts with hammer and nails, and above that the least tap brings down half the wall in a cloud of plaster. After lunch I was going down to Shoreham with Hale, who is being very kind to me this term, and that imponderable ass Boothby tacked himself on to us. The rest of the day was spent in finishing nailing up the ragged wall stuff until to bed tired out, impoverished, and very disappointed with everything.

Sunday was more cheerful. I was initiated into the innumerable duties of junior sacristan. These are far worse than I had expected. In the afternoon I had my first tea party – Fremlin and Hale. It was not an unrelieved success but, as they are my best friends, I thought I ought to have them first, although they are 'temperamentally incompatible'. Still it wasn't altogether a failure. After Hall we had a 'social' in my pit. Just the same party we used to have last term – Bevan, Hale, Barnsley and Fulford, and Longe came up from the God-box. He is behaving splendidly as a god, making no difference with his old friends.

Today was fairly pleasant. School and a House game. Hale had been awfully nice to me the last three days. He is the only man whose friendship I really want – and Longe. Hill and Lister came up for a few minutes to discuss the debating society. Fulford has been more friendly too. A pit is a great social asset in the House, however much it costs in other ways.

Tuesday 25 January 1921

A Saint's Day of sorts. In the morning Hale went up to the San. We had three periods of Lucas on end with nothing amusing at all. The House game in the afternoon was short and very good. Fulford and I had Carew up to tea –

quite jolly. A letter arrived from Luned – very pathetic: 'what a fool is a fond wench'.

Wednesday 26 January 1921

I have begun my scheme of sponging the wall and it has been splendidly successful, except in one place where the pink has come through from the wall below.

Thursday 27 January 1921

Nothing doing again. It is extraordinary, considering how little I see of him, what a difference there is when Hale is not here. I have to train with the football team, but there is little chance of a place for me. I am pretty certain to get into the boxing however.

Friday 28 January 1921

History, parade, training run, tea, history.

Sunday 30 January 1921

Fulford very worked up as it was St Charles's day. He wanted Howitt to pray for him in chapel but was told that it would be liturgically incorrect. I have been made a member of the Shakespeare Society! Also Dick has asked me to begin studying librarianship so as to be it when Ox leaves. Another distinction.

Monday 31 January 1921

The training goes on unabated. After the run I went to spar in the gym. O'Connor is training down to lightweight so I doubt whether I shall get into the House team after all. No news yet from the *Bookman*. I am afraid I haven't won anything after all. Carew showed me the draft of another novel. None too bad, I thought.

Tuesday 1 February 1921

In the evening we had the meeting of the Shakespearean Society. It was a most aristocratic affair; there were only two other commoners besides myself there. We were reading *Lear*, none too badly. Mrs B. was in her best form. 'Isn't it dreadful how all the tragedies work up to the end' after 'Oh let me not be mad'! Afterwards we had tea and cakes.

Thursday 3 February 1921

Another day of feverish training. In the evening, during evening school, I suddenly thought of the 'mute magnificence of death' and so wrote some verses which I dispatched this morning to the *Public School Verse*. The original phrase was lost, as is usual in verbal inspirations, and the whole was very self-conscious – 'mean adventurings', etc. – but I hope that they take it so that I can collect the signed copy 1 had thought of months ago.

Friday 4 February 1921

A sad day. Parade and training run. All my money spent. Match tomorrow.

Saturday 5 February 1921

The House match was on the whole 'very pleasant'. We were all very nervous beforehand and hung about in shivering groups frantically talking filth to keep our spirits. When the game started it was extraordinarily fast. A sort of languidness, not unlike the feeling one has in dreams when one tries to catch trains, quite spoiled my pace. I think it must have come from overtraining. I played a poor game and dropped some very bad bricks. We lost eventually 2–1. Hale, Streatfeild and Boothby played well. Afterwards Mallowan and I had a huge toast tea and for the rest of the evening I lay full length on cushions doing no work.

Sunday 6 February 1921

Stiff and sore. We had a social in Barnsley's pit in second evening but I at least found it a complete failure. We had no decent conversation the whole time. Fulford and I tried to talk, but Hale and Longe had strange jokes of their own which kept them catching each other's eyes and giggling.

Monday 7 February 1921

Indolent. Borrowed a quid from Bevan, invited John Woodward to tea, told Carew how to write his novel, and wrote my own 'Sunday letter'.

Thursday 10 February 1921

This morning at 12.30, while I was impatiently waiting with a tinful of dirty china, Ford had Fulford into his pit and ticked him off about his keenness on young Woodard.[1] He said that he was quite prepared to believe that their relations were at present perfectly moral, but that they had to cease. It was unfair on Woodard to accustom him to the company of his seniors; when Fulford left he would be friendless and quite probably with a bad reputation, in which state he might well become a prey to his many admirers whose affections were less Platonic. He was sorry that Fulford could not see things in the same light, but was afraid that it would have to stop. All this Fulford told me when at last he came to help with the crockery.

[1] Not to be confused with the boy Woodward. Woodard was a nephew of the Head's House-tutor, a grandson of the founder of Lancing, and a neighbour of Fulford's in Suffolk. When Fulford said to Ford, 'But I know him in the holidays!' Ford replied: 'Everyone says that'.

I am convinced Ford is wrong and that Hill, who presumably instigated the scene, has been making a complete fool of himself. He, at least, ought to be able to differentiate between men like Tubbs and Wisden and Fulford and Hale. I do not approve of keennesses, myself, and have always tried, I think with some success, to suppress any such emotions; but I do think that to Woodard, with a pretty face in a house like Olds, Fulford's friendship has been one of the most fortunate things that could happen. Hale, to my disappointment, has caved in once. I do not understand him. Fulford at my advice has had the whole thing out with Woodard, and they have agreed to keep on their friendship less ostentatiously and to discuss it all with Dick. I think they are both very sensible in rather an awkward situation.

Friday 11 February 1921

The more I see of Lancing the more convinced I become of the fact that our generation, and in this I include all who came in the terms on either side of Fulford's and mine, was a very exceptional one. One day I must try and work out the many influences which contributed to this. I think that if I do I shall find that the war is directly responsible for most of us, but lately I have been fearing that we shall have left no mark upon the House. I was afraid that the 'system', as Crease would call it, is stronger than we. The dilettantism which marked us out above everything is, I am convinced, going to collapse now we have all left it, but we had a tremendous ragging spirit and I think that we are handing this at least on to our successors. The House was most energetic and Spartan under Donovan and most damnably languid under Smallwood. Both these were opposed to us, but in the first we were too utterly insignificant and, in the second, turbulent underschools who were ingloriously beaten. Now we are at the top we are a real force, and a force against exclusiveness and snobbery. This I am afraid will not last; but I do think that the hatred of the Corps, into which I have always tried to focus our high spirits, will outlive us. Fashions change with each generation here, but if we have done this I think we have done more than any before us. I rather pride myself, too, that much of it has been my doing.

Saturday 12 February to Tuesday 15 February

Another blank not worth making up. Pit teas and a debate made a dull weekend. This evening I am very disconsolate. All the term I had been determining not to sweat in the House Trials, feeling I could justify myself better if I had no intention of doing well. Yesterday, I don't know why, partly because of Hale, I think, I determined to get a place. I came in about fifteenth this afternoon. I really wanted to do well. Whether or not it is worth while laying yourself out is beside the point. What matters is that I decided to and couldn't and when passing people showed my exhaustion more than I need have. I hate myself accordingly and have lost confidence in my personality and guts. It is no excuse for me to plead bad training. I am a contemptible, clever, little coward[1] and, worst of all, I know it.

Sunday 20 February 1921

Rather interesting on the whole. There is a good deal of worry about the evening's social. The others, apparently, disliked the last as much as I. The trouble is that even if we were good talkers, six is far too many for a decent conversation. The only things our particular six had in common were our positions in the House. This has been amicably settled by my dropping out and letting them have a sing-song. I am glad of this, among other things, because I have to eat little for the weighing-in tomorrow and have already had an ample tea with Carew, but chiefly because I dislike seeing Hale 'show off' as he does on these occasions.

There have been fresh developments in the Fulford and Woodard show. On Wednesday Fulford went to Dick and he, rather to my surprise, was quite on our side and thought it would be wrong for Fulford to give in. The Gods saw Fulford give him a letter and went to Dick to find out what advice he had given. Dick most gallantly refused to say and told Fulford all about it. Today we went out for a walk and discussed it. I can't conceive what Hill is driving at and mean to ask him. I can't see that he has any right at all to order people to stop being friends unless he thinks they are immoral. He knows Fulford isn't. If he thinks it bad for Woodard he can ask him to stop, but cannot possibly demand it officially. Another thing has been that Ford has just asked me to train for the school relay team for the half and the two-twenty.

Monday 21 February 1921

The weighing-in for the boxing. I got down to well under my weight. In the gym I met Hill and told him I wanted to talk about Fulford and Woodard.

Tuesday 22 February 1921

This afternoon Hill and I talked over the Fulford show. He came to my pit and for about twenty minutes argued in the way he had all along; we of course got no further towards a settlement. Then Fulford called me to the telephone. Hill met me outside the porter's lodge and we walked out behind the chapel down the prefects' garden and round by the farm. There he told me a good deal which quite alters the case. Where I was wrong was in supposing that Woodard

---

[1] 'The race was the House Trial for the Five Mile and it was regarded as something of a triumph to finish. A group of Head's House undesirables had gone, well wrapped-up, to watch the race. We were amazed by Evelyn's spirit as he jumped into one of those filthy dykes, and he was loudly cheered. His independence and courage were the secret of his standing in the Head's.' Roger Fulford, in a letter to the editor.

was like Fulford thinks he is. He appears to be greatly flattered at the notice taken of him, only fond of Fulford's position in the school. He doesn't understand Fulford at all. All this forced me to see that the Gods are in the right. I am sorry.

Afterwards I had to go down with Fulford to Shoreham. He wanted to know all about our interview. I couldn't tell him all that Hill told me and he was naturally enough hurt at my deserting him on such obviously half-hearted grounds as I could suggest.

I am in rather an awkward position. Fulford will still rely on Dick's support. Dick will still think him in the right until he knows what Hill told me about Woodard. I can't tell Dick because I was told in strict confidence. I can't ask Hill to tell him as I should be betraying Dick's part in the show. I have got in a devilish difficulty over someone else's affairs. I don't know what I ought to do.

Sunday 27 February 1921

A walk with —— in the morning. He is very much all over himself as he has just stolen more cocaine from the doctor. I see myself having a fairly hectic time with him in France. After lunch Hale and I went with Fulford to meet Woodard on the downs – a damn compromising thing of his to do. The latest complexity is that Hill may well have been lying to me. Much of what he said – what I could tell Fulford – has proved to be exaggerated and some either untrue or Woodard is lying – bad sentence, misspelt.[1]

Alec and Barbara came to tea and were in quite good form. I have thought of an idea for the Prize Poem. Spenserean stanzas on any incident in Malory. Bedivere when Arthur is dead and Lancelot sums things up cynically but not very bitterly. It's all over, things like that don't last. Men aren't like that really. Unfortunately this is not 'narrative'. The Essays do not tempt me but I will think more about them.

Tuesday 1 March 1921

We had to watch a gloomy fives match. *Public School Verse* sent back my verses.[2]

Friday 4 March 1921

In break today it occurred to me that it would not be without humour if some of us went on parade with one boot scrupulously polished and the other filthy.

---

[1] Spelling in MS is in fact correct.

[2] Two of Waugh's Lancing contemporaries, Dudley Carew and J. L. Hill, appeared in *Public School Verse 1921-22*; other contributors included Graham Greene, Christopher Isherwood, Peter Quennell and A. L. Rowse.

We suggested it to the pits and the more senior of the House Room, but owing to five-mile stress very few were coming on parade. Eventually about six of us decided to do it but we thought it wouldn't be much of a jest. When we came to fall in we found the news had got all round the House and about three-quarters of the platoon had followed our lead. Although it is doubtful policy to appear to be setting the lower half of the House against Ford, I must say that it shows an excellent spirit if they were willing to do it without any coaching, and is also something of a testimony to our influence for good. The parade started well, with Bond falling us in three times, but I must confess I found the rest of it rather dull. I think that the proletariate enjoyed it though.

Saturday 5 March 1921

Sat out practically the whole day and read a book of detective stories (the school library is closed for stock-taking). Tea with Bevan and Fulford. In the afternoon, rugger; as usual it was a duel between a few enthusiasts and was very dull for the rest of us. Bevan at tea made one or two witty remarks about crests and butlers. I thought it would be rather an idea to start illustrating but to judge by this it would not.[1]

Sunday 6 March 1921

Fulford and I went up to see Hale at San. for a few moments after lunch; then he went on for a walk with Woodard and I back to an essay on Mirabeau. The social in the evening was a great success; at least, it was incomparably better than the Hale, Bevan and Longe ones.

Monday 7 March 1921

Poor old Hale has come down from the San. with a strained heart. He will never be allowed to run further than the half again. I am very sorry.

The Head has started a scheme by which a committee will be elected to run the mission, one member of each House; I see possibilities for a rag. One thing I am beginning to realize, though, is that one must limit one's Bolshevism. It is no use leading a *Loom of Youth* existence, ragging everything. One's attentions must be confined to certain deserving cases such as the Corps. It is a great mistake to start trying to rag everything.

These illustrations are not an unrelieved success. I shall have to drop them soon if I can't make a better thing of them.

Tuesday 8 March 1921

Lucas thought an essay of mine, dashed off in a moment, 'thoughtful'.

---

[1] Henceforward the Lancing diary is spasmodically illustrated by pen and ink drawings.

Wednesday 9 March 1921

I got checked off today by Ford for ragging on PT. 'Limited Bolshevism' must be our motto.

Thursday 10 March 1921

Today started rather ingloriously by my being turned out of Lucas's form; he must have decided while dressing that I needed snubbing and worked up his courage all the way from Steyning. He walked straight into the room and before he had put down his cap or books said, 'Leave the room please Waugh. I've had enough of your talking. Leave the room'. I had a pleasant sit-out and after breakfast went up to him prepared to be magnanimous and make concessions and apologize. Breakfast and a pipe, however, had softened him and we parted, if not on the best of terms, at least civilly.

Friday 11 March 1921

Last night Woodard made a speech to the House about the Corps. He did not express any particularly new or profound views but he told us that he would do all in his power to stop any Bolshevist being made a House-captain. This worried me a lot. It gave us the worst possible reason for being good, but one which is rather important with me. I do want to be a House-captain, chiefly because I know Father wants it very much and because I want other distinctions like editor of the magazine and president of the literary society for which one has to be one. I thought about it most of evening school but could come to no decision. Woodard had made me ashamed to stop. In the evening we discussed it all in the dormitory. Someone, I rather think it was I, suggested how witty it would be if we won the ridiculous shield.[1] Immediately several people said we could if we really tried and so we decided to have a shot and, if successful, rag the 'jerry-run'.[2] At night I suddenly got the idea of having a meeting of the House and explaining it all to them. This morning I suggested it to Barnsley and Fulford and, rather to my surprise, they took it up. It was an wholly unprecedented thing to do. We wrote out three notices and signed them.

> 'The Members of the Lower Dormitory would be grateful if all
> who can would be in the House Room at 12.30 for a few minutes,
> as they have an announcement to make.'

[1] In his autobiography, Waugh says that he made this proposal 'disingenuously'. 'I was not, as I pretended, free from ambition. This covert self-seeking, more than the cruelty to individual boys – odious as that was – constitutes the "caddishness" which I found revealed in my diary.' *A Little Learning*, p. 133.

[2] When, at Lancing, a cup ('jerry') passed from one House to another, it was the custom for the captain of the winning team to collect the trophy from the defeated House; his supporters, cheering wildly, then lifted him shoulder high and carried him back in triumph to his own House.

During morning school I became quite nervous, expecting the House to be hostile or interruptions from the Gods. However it went off splendidly. Barnsley, Fulford and I came down soon after half past and found the whole House waiting for us. The pits and Settle were standing round the fire, the rest of the House sitting round looking most good-natured and interested. Bevan shut the door and Barnsley as senior man made a short speech apologizing for the inconvenience of the time and calling on me to explain the situation.

I said: 'Gentlemen, we were not converted by Mr Woodard's speech last night, but in a discussion arising out of it, we decided that the Corps ragging couldn't go on. It's been perfectly splendid but it doesn't really do. Among other things it is making a quite intolerable position for one of the best heads the House has ever had. But we also decided that it must not be allowed merely to splutter out. We must end it in a way worthy of the Head's House. Samson must quit himself like Samson. So we began to look for some really magnificent final rag. Well, we have thought of one which, I think, is one of the best that have ever been organized; it scores off most people but it is one which needs the hard work of every member of the House. We have decided to get the House Platoons' Shield. If we can do this we shall have scored off the Corps-maniacs in the out-Houses. I expect you have heard that Eve told the Gibbs' the other night that his greatest ambition since his first term had been to be platoon sergeant of the winning platoon. The out-Houses are full of people like that. We should also score off the people who say that we started deliberately ragging and are now simply incompetent and losing our grip on everything. We should also score off the whole idea of House platoons by showing that in a week's work a platoon who utterly despise the whole thing can win it. Then, when we've got it, we'll do the best 'jerry-run' there has ever been. We'll march in a slow funereal procession in dead silence with heads down. It ought to be splendid, but it will be very difficult. It will be quite impossible if we haven't got the complete support of the whole House. We shall have to sweat like hell this week. We are asking a big sacrifice, but I hope you will agree that it is worth the sacrifice.'

Barnsley then asked all who would help us to put up their hands. There was a breathless moment when I was afraid that the whole thing was going to collapse, and then every man voted for us. It was a splendid show.[1] After that I went down to the armoury and found half the House cleaning and polishing. The parade was fairly good, all things considered. It was a hot day and I am rather afraid that a lot of the smaller people lost their enthusiasm by the end of the day, but it was incomparable with our usual show. I think we may win. It all

[1] 'This particular episode deserves emphasis because it illustrates the authority which Evelyn's personality stamped on his fellows. Virtually the entire House followed his leadership.' Roger Fulford, *Evelyn Waugh and his World*, p. 20.

depends on whether we can keep the House worked up. Dear Woodard is so braced because he thinks it is all due to his influence. Indirectly, of course, it is.

Saturday 12 March 1921

Longe came up to tea today. The Gods know all about our Friday show – how, heaven knows! Either they must have heard through the window, or overheard some conversation in the dormitories or have some tweetle; but apparently they don't know what I said.

Sunday 13 March 1921

We offered a prize of 2s. 0d. to the smartest man on the Monday Parade.

Monday 14 March 1921

This morning there was quite a demand for Corps books, but I fear mostly out of wit. In the afternoon we had the semi-finals of the 100 yards. Everything seemed to conspire against me. I came in last – bloody bad.

Tuesday 15 March 1921

A grotesque confirmation service. I have never noticed how menacing it is before. Some small frightened children taking a lot of oaths they will never keep, with a dressed-up coloured thing like a Dulac figure and gloomy threatening masters and provosts all round.[1] I was spared some of the horrors Lancing can offer anyway.[2] I won my heat in the quarter.

Wednesday 16 March 1921

Today I went on a Veniam with Carew. I am afraid that we came at rather an inconvenient time, as they were just moving. We had lunch out. Carew is a most affectionate brother and I should think a most satisfying son. We had a jolly day away from everyone playing with the slots on the pier – when I find that joy empty I shall feel I am really grown up at last. In that, at least, I am still unsophisticated. It was thoroughly happy. Then I came back to the web of House politics again. They seem less satisfying than ever. It is all vanity and vexation of spirit. Everything this term seems to be conspiring to drive me into making a fool of myself. I started this term popular with almost everyone. The Gods looked on me with favour – I was to have been a House-captain by now. The first two or three weeks were very full of successes. Then everything seemed to turn against and drive me on. From mildly ragging the Corps, I have

---

[1] 'This was stark nonsense. The confirmation candidates were not frightened and I knew it. All I meant was that I was losing my taste for everything ecclesiastical. But in my last two years at Lancing I was eager to dispute the intellectual foundations of Christianity.' *A Little Learning*, p. 142.

[2] Waugh had been confirmed at St Jude's, Hampstead Garden Suburb.

been driven into an organized rebellion against the Gods. I don't see how I can get out of it. I am pledged to the House and my friends. If only something could happen: the Head make me a House-captain on spec., or if I could break an arm or get ill. I seem absolutely in a net. I am bitterly unhappy. This evening, coming back to it all, I seriously began considering running away. I might have filled my diary all this term with, 'This day I was a fool – tomorrow?'

Longe depresses me too. I like him. All this term I have been watching him gradually being broken by the God system. The extreme Bolshevism into which I am being driven is, I think, largely responsible for it. He could have kept in with us while we were working, more or less, with Ford, but now that we are directly opposed to him he has really no choice. I am doing no good but how can I get out of it? I wish Crease were here to help me. I might confide in Dick.

Thursday 17 March 1921

Verldsmets[1] almost passed. Today in free ballot, without any influence and without pits or Settle voting, the House declared in favour of a rag 'jerry-run'. We accordingly had the Ox up to Barnsley's pit and delivered our ultimatum. He was perfectly fair and courteous about it and promised to let us know the authorities' decision. He was, I thought, a trifle on our side. This evening he let us know the result. Quite reasonably he showed that it was an untenable position for officials to allow a vote of the House to rule them. He is quite right; both of us are in quite impossible positions. We are up against the God spirit again: conscientious and serious-minded, always looking on the official side of things. I am now resigned to a row and looking forward with interest to what will happen.

I was running in the school sports team today against Oxford. Of course they did not try much or give us a chance.

Friday 18th March 1921

The Gods have won. This afternoon we were third in the competition. If we had been first there would have been a splendid fight and I think we should have won. As it was, all that we can say is that we gave them an anxious twenty-four hours. After we declared war on the Ox last night the Gods had been going about in chattering groups discussing nothing else. This morning I went to Hill[2] for an official ruling about whether a 'jerry-run' was compulsory. He hedged – the Gods had been there before us – but what he said was in our favour. I think that the authorities were really frightened. We fell in wonderfully clean. I had sent a message round in the morning:

'It is more than ever vitally necessary for the honour and

[1] 'World-weariness' (Weltschmerz).
[2] Head of the school.

compulsory. He hedged & the Gods had been there before us but what he said was in our favour. I think that the

authorities were really frightened. but fell in wonderfully clean. I had sent a message round in the morning :—

'It is more than ever vitally necessary for the honour and self-respect of the House, that we should win the Platoon Shield; we have the House's promise and are confident. Trust in God and stand steady in the ranks.'

self-respect of the Houses, that we should win the Platoon
Shield; we have the House's promise and are confident.
Trust in God and stand steady in the ranks.'

The House were really very good. I suppose it is ungrateful of me to be
disappointed in them. We really did the first part very well. The arms-drill and
steadiness during the inspection were quite splendid. There were one or two
bricks in the platoon-drill but not very awful ones. Where we failed was in the
open order. Two and Three Sections were chosen – the worst men with the
worst NCOs and they were quite pathetic. If One Section had been called
out, I think we might have won the show. As it was, we had to lie down and see
our chances of success slowly melting away. The Gods were quite gleeful with
relief. We knew we had lost almost at once. I was surprised that we were as high
as third. It would have been the greatest thing the House had ever done if we
had won.

Saturday 19 March 1921

In the House heats I was third in the 220. Hale complained that I ran across
him. I am beginning to believe that there must be some malignant fate which
makes me foul. I never think of the man behind at all. I spend all my attention
on trying to get in front of the man in front.

Thursday 24 March 1921

Today was more nearly happy than any this term. Mother and Father came
over from Ditchling for lunch and tea. We had lunch at the Pad – all they could
offer were eggs and bacon – and then went over the manor. It is really a
delightful house and garden, now full of workmen despoiling it. We then went
up to the downs and met J.F., who made himself very pleasant. Then back to
tea in my pit. Carew came up and the chef had done his work well. I think it was
a success. Anyway it has made me feel more cheered than I have felt for several
weeks.

Friday 25 March 1921

I can remember nothing of the day so presumably it was not very eventful. It
was Good Friday I believe.

Saturday 26 March 1921

The Steeplechase. I came in about three from the end.

Easter Day, Sunday 27 March 1921

After lunch I went for a walk with ——. He became confidential and
revealed depths of lust and depravity for which I never gave him credit.
Apparently he has had a lust on —— for some time and Dick has found out and

quarrelled with him rather severely. He is amazingly candid. I begin to see that his diaries will need some editing. Fulford, Mallowan and I had a toast tea. After Hall, Woodard gave us leave to go for a walk in the dark – very jolly. Hale has been awfully nice to me all this term – it has been about the only good thing about it. Tomorrow Father and Mother are coming over to lunch and I am having him down. I expect that it will be a filthy meal however.

Monday 28 March 1921

Father, Mother, and Barbara came down. The weather was filthy and I don't think that they can have enjoyed it much. We had Hale down to lunch at the Pad. After lunch the relays in which we were signally successful. It was not wholly pleasant running however.

Thursday 31 March 1921

I had to go and see Woodard. He had asked me after breakfast and I guessed at once that it was about Bolshevism and being made a House-captain. He began at once.

'Ah Waugh. I wanted to see you – sit down. You see we have got to make another House-captain next term and of course you are the obvious person. You have immense influence in the House and it really amounts to this, that if you will not accept the attitude of a Head's House official I shall have to ask your people to take you away. I know that you often say and write a lot which you don't really believe; now what do you really think about it?'

I got going on the God tradition and the war gap and our generation. He was very reasonable. I said that I was prepared, and already determined, to lead a steadier life and do all I could to see rules kept, but that I refused to drop any of my friends or in any way put on the airs of a brat. I also told him I was not going to play cricket. All this he took like a lamb and we parted on the best terms. I only confided in Mallowan. I expected the Head to say something to me that night but he passed by without a word, so presumably it is not yet officially settled. One of the most subtly funny things was watching Bevan waiting about before undressing expecting to be summoned. Poor fellow, he would love all the petty pomp of it! I am in a way pleased. Although it will in all probability make next term even less enjoyable, it is rather gratifying that I have won through my own way. They made the first advances and I did not work for it like Bevan and perhaps Boothby.

By far the most delightful part of the day I have forgotten. J.F. asked me to tea with him. He was simply charming the whole time. We had it by ourselves up in his pit. It was the first time I had been there; he has done it very well with plain furniture and Medici prints, Botticelli and Murillo mostly. We talked poetry and most abstruse philosophy most of the time. I am afraid I must have been rather disappointing to him conversationally, but I enjoyed it thoroughly.

Hampstead, Friday 1 April 1921

Today home by the 7.36. The house is full of stray guests, Bobby Shaw and Eustace Heriz-Smith.[1] Alec was here in the morning. He has found it impossible to write near Barbara so hired a typist and dictated eight thousand words of his new novel straight off this morning and for another hour after lunch. I went to call on the Flemings. Boggy drivelling – Philla frowsy but pleasant. Maxwell apparently did something in his sports.

Saturday 2 April 1921

I am writing at 10.55 in my room before settling down to work on my poem. I am going to try and cultivate the habit of working at night. Besides the fact that it appeals strongly to my imagination, it is the only time when the house is at all quiet, and I think that with a little training I shall find I work best at night. This is my second night. Last night I did about an hour and a half's work. I hope to do the same tonight and more on Tuesday. Tomorrow I am doing *The Beggar's Opera* binge. Today and yesterday were not very exciting. Bobby and I went to an excellent show at the Stoll yesterday afternoon. I like him awfully, though he is quite brainless and slow. This afternoon I went with Father to hear him lecture on Dickens' women to the St Augustine's Guild. A good lecture but incorrigibly theatrical, as usual.

As sometimes walking in the middle of London one has a sudden impulse to run, I feel that I must write prose or burst. I have been tinkering away for two hours and shall not sleep unless I can clear my brain. To express oneself in the Spenserian stanza is as though one had to paint a picture on little bits of paper and fit them together like a jigsaw puzzle.

I am doing badly. I have only done about half a dozen verses and most of them are complete balls. I find myself forced into the most hideous rhymes.

Monday 4 April 1921

We did our *Beggar's Opera* binge last night. It was a splendid show. We had dinner at the Clarendon first. Preters was about quarter of an hour late, but soon softened in voice and became more amiable as he became more tight. Bevan didn't enjoy it much I'm afraid. I think we were too far from Piccadilly for him to be quite at his ease. I loved the show more second time than the first. Preters loved it. Carew stopped with us for the night.

Tuesday 5 April 1921

Carew and I had a hectic morning, meeting relations of his among them a pretty cousin, Joan Laking, whose younger brother is a baronet and complete

---

[1] The Revd. E. E. A. Heriz-Smith, a master at Sherborne.

little roué. In the evening Heriz-Smith took me to *Bulldog Drummond* at Wyndham's.

Saturday 9 April 1921

A war fever has taken hold upon us just as it did in August 1914. All the week has been fiercely exciting with strike news.[1] On Wednesday Mother and I went to the wedding of one of our cousins, and the bridegroom, a regular officer, was called up that night. Yesterday the Triple Alliance came out. I am anxious to get some work, but the only people at present being called up are those over eighteen who can join for ninety days and to my disgust Mother and Father refuse to let me do this. I have written to the local Labour Bureau but I doubt if they will give me anything to do. It is quite exasperating. It looks as if we were going to have a civil war and I shall be out of it. I mean to try and get in somehow. It seems to me that it has now ceased to be a matter of right or wrong and is merely war. One does not blame the miners particularly. If I was a miner I know that I should be only too anxious to strike; since I am not, I try to break them.

Sunday 10 April 1921

It looks as though some strike settlement may be reached. The men seem to be frightened now that they find how strongly the rest of the nation is against them.

I have hammered out another couple of verses in my prize poem. I get no sort of pleasure from it.

Sunday 17 April 1921

It looks as if trades unionism was broken, at any rate for the time. The *Daily Herald* admitted that it was the 'biggest defeat of the labour cause in memory of man'. The miners are still holding out, but there is no fear of the Triple Alliance strike. I suppose that all along they expected the country to give way and then got frightened of the volunteer movement. I signed on for fatigue work.

On Friday our colonial relatives came. I do not dislike my aunt but Eric is terrible. How Uncle Alick,[2] who appears to have been one of the stoutest Waughs for some time, can have produced him defies eugenics. I am quite

[1] On 1 April 1921, after the miners had demanded higher wages, the mineowners began a lockout. The miners called on their fellow-members of the 'Triple Alliance' – the railway and transport workers – to strike in sympathy. On Friday 15 April – 'Black Friday' in the Labour movement – the railway and transport workers called off their strike a few hours before it was due to begin. The miners held out until 1 July.

[2] Arthur Waugh's naval officer brother, who married a Tasmanian and died in 1900.

miserable in his company. He is fat, uncouth, self-complacent, good-hearted, and vulgar.

Monday 18 April 1921

Writing at night again. I have put in a hard two hours' work on the essay. I have chosen 'Money' as the subject and have a good deal to say, but I feel it is all rather like damp fireworks. This morning Ursula Kendall invited me to a little dance for Saturday. My relations still torment me. They talk at bridge incessantly. Eric leeches onto me everywhere and I have to try and be friendly. Well, I must get to bed now; it's filthily cold.

Saturday 23 April 1921

This has been a wretched week. Thank God I can get away from my relatives and dance tonight. Father has been ineffably silly the whole holidays. The extraordinary thing is that the more I see through my Father the more I appreciate Mother. I always think I am discovering some new trait in his character and find that she knew it long ago. She is a very wonderful woman.

Last night we went to *Bulldog Drummond*. It was my second visit but I liked it as much as the first time.

Lancing, Tuesday 3 May 1921

This diary appears entirely to be kept in big chunks. The last week of the holidays was rather fun. Barbara came up and we rushed about together. On the last night she took me to dinner at the d'Italie and to the *Bill of Divorcement*. I also saw Preters twice. We had one thoroughly good evening at *The Beggar's Opera*. I got there without enough money so we saw the manager and he gave us tickets on our appearance. Now I am back at school and pretty wretched. The first thing I heard on arriving was that I had been made a House-captain. Since then I have been in a miserable position. I sit next to Newman who can't speak a word. Longe is reasonably kind to me but it is rather lonely.

Friday 6 May 1921

I have always tried to keep clear of the vulgarer forms of conceit, but I feel that in my present position I am in great danger of becoming self-important and even officious. Rowe is the worst I might become. Still, as long as I have the friendship of people like Hale and Longe, I ought to keep sane. This evening I have been taking evening school and putting the Upper Head's to bed.[1] I hope I was not patronizing. The whole position of House-captain is wholly illogical. Tonight Newman, who never thinks of doing any work and hinders us doing any, had a small boy beaten with positive glee for writing a letter in evening

[1] The dormitory of the youngest boys.

school. (Incidentally he read the whole letter which I consider unforgivable.) But as Longe pointed out it would have been still worse if he let people slack like himself. My position is really impossible – a House-captain as a bribe to make me sober.

Yesterday, Ascension Day, was great. Molson and I went out driving. He drank: a neat whisky, a whisky and water, a gin and bitters, two whisky and sodas, two liqueurs, a double whisky almost neat, two bottles of cider, two glasses of port, one neat whisky. He was rampaging[?] drunk[1] and sober and melancholy in gusts. In the car he was a trifle risky and used the most filthy language. The dinner at Goring was excellent and beautifully served. He lives comfortably.

Monday 23 May 1921

The last fortnight has been most extraordinarily indolent. I have played a little tennis rather badly and done a good deal of sketching rather well. I am getting on much better with the other brats. The Ox is awfully nice, Longe is splendid, Ford still rather aloof. The others I dislike and despise.

The only outlet for my Bolshevism has been in going out at night. Longe and I went out for a walk on the downs on Saturday night. Last night Woodard took us for a walk after hot air[2] and as we came back we were confronted by a man who demanded, 'I must ask the names of you gentlemen, please'. Apparently the school keeps a night-watchman now. It was wonderfully lucky that Longe and I didn't meet him. Hill and I and he intend to go down to the sea tomorrow. It ought to be rather exciting.

I am arranging to do a fortnight's reading alone next holidays. It ought to be rather fun besides jolly good for me. I haven't yet decided on the village. I hope near the sea somewhere.

Wednesday 25 May 1921

Last night Hill and Longe and I went out for another walk. It was the happiest time of the term. We walked down to the sea and paddled and talked intellectual nonsense. We got back about two and had a meal before going to bed.

Tuesday 31 May 1921

1.15 am. I am getting into very good training for work. In the last week I have put in any amount of work without feeling perceptibly the worse for it. I have been at work on the Scarlyn Literature Prize. Longe has become infected with my same craving for work, so I am not alone. If I can keep it up I ought to get a scholarship next term.

---

[1] 'Ramping' in MS.
[2] A social occasion on Sunday evenings when House-captains were entertained by their House-masters.

Friday 3 June 1921

2.30 am. Hill and I had determined to go out for a walk on Saturday night and have some supper. We were just going down to Shoreham to get some wine when I got a frenzied letter from Father who has heard, from Bobby presumably, about my going out. He was quite unconvincingly rhetorical about it and threatened to take me away if I didn't promise never to do it again. I think he is absurd, but I am rather glad he has taken a strong line about something at last.[1]

Monday 13 June 1921

As I expected I have won the Scarlyn. I am sorry for Sangar who has not even got second. However £3 in books isn't bad. I should really like to pull off the Essay and Poem too.

The play is going fairly well but not nearly as well as it should considering how near it is to the performance. On Saturday night Gordon and I printed the invitations and I addressed them all before going to bed.[2] The answers are coming in. All have accepted so far except Woodward. I think he must dislike me.

Meynell wrote and offered to print it. I have told him that I can't possibly sell them but it is very good of him to offer. He has also shown it to Squire who might stick it in the *Mercury*. This is of course inconceivable. Still it is, I suppose, just possible he might do it out of friendship, but such a master of parody would see through it awfully I am afraid.

In the last few weeks I have ceased to be a Christian (sensation off!) I have realized that for the last two terms at least I have been an atheist in all except the courage to admit it to myself. I am sure it is only a phase and am not much worried except if it cut me off from Longe at all. I don't think that it will for a moment. If I thought it would, I would believe anything. He has been one of the few things that make school worth while. I have written a poem to him and Hale.

> I suppose that when I leave
> I shall think as others do,
> Storing in my memory

---

[1] Arthur Waugh wrote to Evelyn: 'It is years since we heard anything that has so disturbed us.' He feared a repetition of the trouble that had led to the expulsion of Alec from Sherborne. See *A Little Learning*, p. 136.

[2] The invitations read: 'The Headmaster's House requests the honour of your company on Sunday, June 19th. at 7.45 p.m. in the Great School at a performance of *Conversion*, the tragedy of Youth in three burlesques, by Evelyn Waugh. Act I. School, as maiden Aunts think it is. Act II. School, as modern authors say it is. Act III. School, as we all know it is. R.S.V.P. F. E. Ford.' Ford was head-boy of Head's House.

Things refreshing and untrue.
I shall think that I have known
Comfort in the flint and stone
In the light the evening shews
When I leave, I suppose.
Light on china, white and blue,
Memories of study teas
I shall think that I loved these
Just as all the others do.
Fellowship, I shall believe
Cheered my way when I was young;
I shall hunger for old friends,
I suppose when I leave.
Yet I know that just you two
Mattered out of all I knew –
But I may lose the thought of you
Just as all the others do.

The only really bad thing about my life this term is the way I find myself imbibing the official atmosphere. I am convinced that it is wrong. Longe, who is incomparably kind to me in all else, tries to give me still more gravitas. I obey him in most things, perhaps tamely. It is rather fun subordinating one's personality to another after so much turmoil as last term.

Sunday 19 June 1921

The play on Friday was, I think, quite a success. All my company acted very well. The audience was fairly appreciative and eminently amiable. The House were happy in getting off evening school and in seeing the bloods making fools of themselves. There were one or two distinguished visitors who could not come on Monday.

I think Fulford has been playing a dirty game the last week or so. It has been rather a beastly slew. He heard from Hale, who apparently had been told by one of his tweetles, that the Upper Dormitory are very immoral. I expect it is quite true. Overcome by reforming fervour, he reported this to Ford, who commissioned him to find out more. He accordingly set up a sort of competition with Hale to find out the more. Hale, by a despicable breach of trust, told Fulford all he could find out from his junior friends, and Fulford, without his knowing, has passed it all on to Ford. I think both of them have behaved contemptibly. Longe attempted Jesuitically to justify them. We had a long talk about it in the bathroom last night. I rather foresee that we may quarrel next term when we are the most important people in the House. I think, though, that my views on House-governance are not worth sacrificing his friendship for. But if he takes Hale up more I expect we shall not be on speaking terms by the end of next term. It is a pity that the people I like best are always those with whom I differ profoundly in everything. He and Hale are the only people I like. Hale's gone already. I suppose he will have to. 'He travels the fastest who travels alone' anyway. Longe was very charming the other night. He had been down at the Pad late with his people on the night of the play and he came in to see me to ask how it had gone. It doesn't sound much but it cheered me awfully. God, I am getting sentimental.

Sunday 26 June 1921

At present, whenever I do anything, I say, 'In three years I shall despise this', but eventually a time will come when I shall find myself able to do a little less and see a little less clearly. A time will come when muscles will get weaker, sight dimmer, the brain slacker. I shall consciously lose grip on things, I shall find it harder to concentrate on anything; things will become clouded in sentiment and recollection. And yet they say, triumphing, that through all this the soul – the vital personality – will remain immutable. Dear God! I don't ask much of life, I ask it from myself, but this I demand in justice. When you take from me that body and brain which I have built up, take from me all. Never let this soul live when all that has made it worthwhile is gone. Grant it to weaken with my body and give it in my death utter extinction.

The play was a tremendous success on Monday. The bloods were a far more appreciative audience than the House and were awfully nice about it. Dick sent me a letter congratulating me, after the show. J.F. said that the epilogue was a touch of genius. Even Parnell and Smith became tolerably polite. It was really awfully cheering. Yesterday we had the laying of the foundation stone for the Cloister and Old Boys day. I hate old boys. They remind me of too much I would forget.

Saturday 9 July 1921

Alec's birthday yesterday.

> Ode on the Intimations of Immmaturity
> Evelyn to Alec Waugh, July 8th 1921
>
> Come, Muse, bring out your usual togs
> Dress you in myrtle boughs and bay
> For Alec Waugh the novelist
> Is twenty-three years old today.
>
> Youth hot upon his flaming quest
> At length sinks sobbing into age,
> And Gordon – brave Byronic soul –
> Grows to a shrewd, sardonic sage.

Let others, less profound than he,
Indulge in vain, athletic fads
Screening their minds paucacity[1]
In square legs, popping crease and pads,

Let others dote on averages
And yearn for centuries or ducks,
The Sage, composed and cynical,
Observes that all things are in flux.

Shall he be ticketed and laid
Deep in the dust of God's great shelf?
No, let the angels say of him
'Poor chap, he grew into himself'.

So let the rhythm of the words
Bring more familiar attitudes;
Let him find hope for human kind
In pantheistic platitudes.

Envoi
Let Bergson prate of memory,
Potential relativity
Whatever that may be
Alec's twenty three.

Tuesday 19 July 1921

It is very hard to keep a record of this part of the term; things are slipping by in the indolence of hard work. Everything is rather pleasant; no early school, living all day in change, bathing at night and in the river. Newman is getting friendly with me; Longe is kind. I might almost at times think I was happy. I am not doing badly at the exams; I think that if I work I am pretty certain for a scholarship next term, and then Paris and Oxford. I know I'm not really a bit happy though.

Hale is leaving this term to learn farming. Longe is awfully cut up about it. Except for that, I think I should be rather glad. He is rather a disturbing influence to one's self-complacency.

The other night I went down onto the field with Hill. He is leaving this term. He says he has lived wonderfully happily and loved everyone and regrets nothing; he has gone just as far and lived just as dangerously as he wanted. If he doesn't get the scholarship to Oxford he is working for he means to commit suicide. He has a horror of getting into a rut. After all, if he can feel like that

---

[1] *sic.*

about things it seems a sufficient defence for his life here, whatever the official view may be of it. One can't live for the House and for discipline. I suppose most people would put him down as a failure; he has not lived up to the promise he gave, but I think he has been something better than scholar or athlete.

I think a lot about suicide. I really think that if I were without parents I should kill myself; as it is I owe them a certain obligation. 'He has lived well who died when he wished.' The other night I sat up in my window seat until one, composing last letters.

To Carew: 'My dear Carey, I'm afraid that the biography will be rather short but you may print this in full to swell it, if you like. Whatever happens I hope that the jury will not bring in "while temporarily insane". The supreme conceit of the living is imagining that a man must be lunatic if a deliberate train of thought leads him to the conclusion that not to be born is best. If I have ever been normal, I am now. I am perhaps a little excited as one about to meet new friends, but I can see everything as clearly as I ever have. At least one takes back one's brain unfogged, dying young.

'I have no really definite cause for killing myself. It certainly is not sorrow at my people's death. That has just removed all obstacles. I suppose it is really fear of failure. I know I have something in me but I am desperately afraid it may never come to anything. Suicide is cowardice really, you see. I am sure that if I have genius, it will survive; if not it isn't worth living anyway. Nox est perpetua una dormienda. Cheerily, Evelyn.'

And to Longe. 'I can see you being very intolerant of this my last act of leniency, John. I am sure it is unliturgical. Well you're the only man here who mattered a damn to me – I'll remember you to God if I see him but I somehow think that if he's your sort of God he'll know all about you already and if he's mine he won't much care, I'm afraid. I hope to see you in Abraham's bosom. I'm sure you'd be the first to get across the palpable obscure with a drop of water for my tongue. With love, Evelyn Waugh.'

Rather a morbid taste, I dare say.

Omnipotence is absurd. One cannot have it without omniscience and that limits it. I mean, if one knows what is going to happen, one can't do anything at all except the things you know. Knowledge controls action and limits possibility. But, as Dobson said, if one is going to allow an omnipotent being one must allow him to be illogical.

On Sunday Dick and I went over to Ditchling in his two-seater. A jolly run.

I had not meant to work at all for the Certificate. I am more or less taking it as it comes, but doing a certain amount of work. The only thing one can do this weather is to bathe. I ought to be doing divinity now.

What wonderful stuff mud is. Yesterday Longe, Newman and I went down to the river. The mud banks were firm and hot and very slippery on top. I never knew anything more luxurious except perhaps very hot water in winter. To think that God, with a world of mud, went and shaped a man!

Crease is back at Lychpole. The spell is broken. His influence is quite gone. I just see a rather silly perhaps casually interesting little man. Carew is coming under his shadow now.

Sunday 24 July 1921

Today I went for a walk with Hill. Last week I was thinking that his life here had been most perfect and he had got most from Lancing. Today he was awfully depressed. It had come out practically by accident that all his House-captains, even, hate and distrust him. It makes him rather bitter and very glad to leave.

I am very unhappy tonight. I have been for the last few days. It is the time, too, when I should be most happy – work over, end of term.

The atmosphere all round is very unpleasant. Most of the people leaving are very sentimental. The whole talk is of promotions, everyone preparing for the next person to take his place. I have been made editor of the magazine and president of the debating society. Of neither of these am I very proud. Woodard apparently was very much opposed to my having the magazine and it was only after it had been offered to all the conventionalists that they offered it to me. This piqued me and only filial piety constrained me to take it. It makes me want to justify their opinions of me though. With unusual brilliancy, Longe has suggested an athletic supplement. This appeals to me immensely. Of the presidency too I am ashamed. Molson in his customary parliamentary way offered to pack the house and have me elected. I said that of course I could not sanction it but would be pleased if he succeeded. Yesterday evening I was discussing the project with Lister and felt awfully ashamed of the intrigue. I told Molson this morning but he said it was too late. So neither of these things cheer me.

Newman has also transferred his company to me. He sees that since Rowe is leaving he is no more use to him, so he has taken me up to ensure a friend for next term. I can't like him much.

I am burdened with failure this term, when I have been most successful really. Everything I have had has come to me shop-soiled and second-hand. Longe and Hale, the only two people I have met whom I love more than myself, have both offered me a third-rate friendship with many inadequacies and misunderstandings. I have been a failure as a House-captain from all points of view. I have not justified Ford's faith in me and become sound and able; I have not kept gloriously on my own way. I have worked fairly hard and done fairly badly in the Higher Certificate. I have led an unhealthy life. I have done a great deal of which I am ashamed. Petty and silly and spiteful things. Last term I was dissatisfied enough and Bolshevik, but it was dramatic – a perfect pattern. Last term I ruled the House. I ran it into indiscipline. I stopped it when it had gone too far; it ended in a dramatic capitulation by the authorities. I started this term with everything on my side and I have only been ineffectual and silly – liked, but not respected. I have got under the shadow of Ford and the Gods. It has been so much wasted time.

Well, Ford and the Gods are leaving this term. Everything's going to be pretty different in September. I shall have to settle myself into the rut for the time. I think Oxford and Paris ought to keep me safe. I shall work like blazes and get a scholarship and run a nice orderly debating society and a nice magazine which the clerical old boys will like. But the prospect seems as damnable as hell ever has been.

Hampstead, Sunday 7 August 1921

The term ended unmemorably. Hill and I spent the whole of the last day together. I shall miss him, I think, next term. We went to Steyning and ate eggs and bacon and then into the church where a communion service was going on. He told me afterwards that while I was sitting looking at the architecture he had wanted to pray but been too shy. We came back on an oil cart and in a private car and after lunch we went on the river and then lay on the bank smoking. We were very nearly late for chapel. Afterwards I went up to the pits and drank cider with Fremlin and Nattrass. I suppose it ought to have been a sentimental day, but I can say quite honestly that it wasn't. Next morning we went off to camp. It was a pleasant tent: Ford, Bevan, self, Fulford, Shaw, Lowther, de Bruyne, Kenrick. After a time I did not like Shaw but the others were dears. I suppose I was, on the whole, reasonably happy in camp – certainly I was happier than last year. There was one day that was quite unbearable but every other one had compensations. I had extraordinarily good luck at bridge every night.

I saw very little of Longe or Hale. He went off without saying goodbye – my last remark to him was something bitter about his motor glasses. I hope he has left for good. Longe came on to stay with me for two nights.

As we left, the whole camp melted away. It is like some strange growth that has no life of its own. A school has continuity; a camp assembles for ten days, develops a character, and then entirely disappears.

Longe and I got back at about twelve, glad to wash and change. I was very happy in having his company uninterruptedly for three days. We went to *The Beggar's Opera* again on the Thursday. I could not help feeling how vulgarized it is becoming. There is a new Mrs Peachem whom I loathed. I was afraid at first I was not going to enjoy it, but the moment Macheath came on everything was perfect again. I loved it more than ever.

Next morning to the National Gallery. I think Longe liked it. Barbara and I made a new discovery. A lady and gentleman in a sort of chariot. English eighteenth-century at its most charming. We lunched lightly on Graves, salmon mayonnaise, meringues, and iced coffee and then went to see the Greek sculpture in Bloomsbury. Then to Liverpool Street to see Longe off. Barbara and I went to a cinema and after dinner went to the Shaw show at Queen's. This was splendid. There was a delightful little indecent sketch by Schnitzler first, then *The Dark Lady of the Sonnets*, then *The Shewing up of Blanco Posnet*. All excellent. Shaw is really supreme in his own way. (Trite remark. Will future editor kindly omit from published version. E.A.W.)

This morning to church where I thought of a blasphemous vision of judgement I will write eventually. After lunch to Barnet with Barbara. I must settle down to history again now. I mean to get this scholarship or be damned. Probably both.

Sunday 14 August 1921

I have done a lot of work this week – about four hours a day on the European history. Other than this I have done nothing much. Mother and I rowed on Regent's Park lake twice and I have been to the Stoll. Barbara rejoined her family in Deal. Alec is still at his cricket week. The boy Higgins has made overtures of friendship to me. I went off to the National Gallery with him, lunch, Tate, and tea at his home. He bored me stiff. I thought him a prig.

Monday 15 August 1921

Carew came up to stay with us.

Tuesday 16 August 1921

Wandered about with Carew, met Sylvia Gosse.[1]

Monday 22 August 1921

Carew has been up all this week. He has picked up a girl at the Oval with whom he spends a lot of his time. While he was at Lord's with her on Wednesday Father, Mother, I and Mrs Marston went to the Stoll to see *The Kid*, the new Charlie Chaplin film. I confess I was disappointed with it. It was too self-conscious and sentimental. The part I liked best was that in which he was most like his older knockabout films. He did one splendid fight with a brick which cheered me a lot.

Thursday I spent reading. I found it most unconscionably dull. The *Cambridge Modern History* can wring all the human interest out of even the French Revolution. It shows how one's brain gets dulled and one's judgement

[1] Daughter of Edmund Gosse.

debauched, that when I read *Rich Relatives*, Compton Mackenzie's new novel – the first novel I had read for some months – I thought it the funniest thing I'd seen for years. A mad Prince Adelbert afforded me infinite pleasure after Joseph II and Leopold. Everyone else says it is quite amusing and thoroughly exaggerated.

On Friday night we went to *Abraham Lincoln*[1] at the Lyceum. I don't know that I did like it awfully. The chorus were incorrigibly prolix and a lot of it was sentimental and obvious. The two cabinet meeting scenes were by far the best. It is typical of my father that he thought the only bit of true drama in it was the scene with the sentry condemned to death!

Yesterday Bobby turned up, having just come back from the Kendalls at Dieppe. He is in a mess about Ursula. Apparently she and he are pretty desperately in love and it has got to such a stage that Kendall has had to warn him off. She seems 'most infernally bit'. Came to his room the morning he went after a sleepless night and threw herself weeping into his arms, told him she couldn't live without him and God knows what all.[2] Kendall was very sensible. It is interesting that the example he held up of a tragedy of people marrying young was Barbara and Alec. However –

Today Carew, Mother and I took our lunch out to Edgware. In the evening Carew and I were going to *The Beggar's Opera* with his cousin Joan Laking and a friend of hers. Carew was quite positive that they meant to pay for us. Luckily we took some money however. When they arrived five minutes late we found that they expected us to pay for our two stalls. The show was of course perfect. The old Mrs Peachem was back and the old Lucy. The awful disappointment was Macheath, who was not played by Ranalow. His understudy had nearly as good a voice but couldn't act a bit. He was just a decadent amorist and looked quite incapable of leading a band. We had decided to walk home and were strengthened in our resolution by the fact that neither of us had any money left. Carew volunteered to guide us and got hopelessly lost by Notting Hill Gate and Royal Oak. However we got home eventually at about two and ate sandwiches and drank coffee. I rather liked Joan Laking but she didn't talk much.

Wednesday 24 August 1921

Molson and I went down for our reading fortnight at Birchington. The appearance of the house was forbidding. We had both expected a sort of Lychpole. When the taxi stopped at a little red brick semi-detached villa and Molson said, 'You know, I have an awful suspicion that this is it', I thought it impossible. But it wasn't. The rooms were tiny and execrably furnished and very few of the windows would open, but the food was tolerable and Kemp and his wife very pleasant people. We got through a lot of work. Eight hours a day

[1] By John Drinkwater.
[2] Ursula Kendall later became Mrs Corris Evans; her husband was solicitor to the RAC.

always, generally more. I read a volume of the *Cambridge Modern History*, a volume of Lecky's *Eighteenth Century*, Bryce's *Holy Roman Empire*, the best part of O'Connor, Morris's *Napoleon*; and skipped through *Leviathan*, and Mill on *Representative Government*. Not a bad fortnight's work really.

We did very little else but work. One Sunday we went over to Canterbury for the afternoon. I liked the town but was disappointed by the cathedral. The episcopal authority left much to be desired. When we went there we were told that we must not see over it because a service was in progress. We returned in half an hour and learnt that it was shut because the service was over. We bathed twice and walked over to the surrounding villages several times. On the second Sunday we went to a delightful religious service at St Nicholas. When we had been over to see the old church there we had seen a funny little room out of one of the cottages with a notice up.

> 'Lords Day blessing of Bread at 11.
> The Gospel will be preached here every Sabbath
> evening at Six. Visitors cordially welcome.'

Molson immediately decided that we must go there. We arrived a little late and came into a low, rather pleasant little room, hung in places with faded red stuff and texts. There were about a dozen people in it counting the acting minister. This sketch[1] gives no idea of the room or of the men. They read through an execrable hymn and then sang it. I never heard such singing anywhere and so loud. Their God had endued them with a most phenomenal capacity of self-unconsciousness. Then one of them prayed: 'Our Father, when we think of all youve a bin a doing for us and how wonderful youve kep' us. We thank you for bringing us together and we pray for them as is gathered together like us. And when we think of ow you sent you're son Jesus to save us –' and so on for about ten minutes. Then they sang again, always reading through the whole hymn first. Molson all this time was prostrate with laughter; I, by repeating the diplomatic situation of 1789, managed to keep fairly quiet. Then they read a chapter of the Bible and discussed it verse by verse. The protagonists, a Mr Cole and the minister, were I suppose the most intellectual there. They seemed incapable of consequent thought. Molson felt drawn to enter the discussion and made a peculiarly fatuous remark which they thought out at great length. Luckily his laughter would not allow another question. Then they sang again. The minister came and shook hands with us afterwards and spoke to us. It was obviously very unusual for them to have a visitor.

Molson had been determining to spend the night after our reading weeks whoring. Apparently it had been an experience he had long desired. I expressed my disapproval but he seemed immovable so I let it be. I don't know

[1] A Waugh sketch in his diary (opposite).

Sabbath evening at Six. Visitors cordially welcome.
Inodson immediately decided that we must go there.
We arrived a little late and came into a low, rather
pleasant little room, hung in places with faded
red stuff and texts. There were about a dozen
people in it counting to acting minister.

if it was some telepathic wave by the minister praying for us, or the studious atmosphere, but next morning he came down saying he wondered if it was worth while. All that day I wrestled with him in spirit and at last he decided it wasn't worth it. We decided that he should come to dinner with us and go on to *The Beggar's Opera*. The dinner was good and the show, of course, perfect. I think it was probably more profitable than an attack of syphilis. He said he didn't really regret it. Ranalow wasn't back yet but it is an unfailing delight.

Thursday 8 September 1921

A most satisfactory day's shopping. I got shoes – at last I am reduced to ready made ones – shirts at very low prices, and ordered what I think should be a delightful new suit from Alderton's. Best of all though, I got the stick I had been wanting for so long. It is English oak, about as formidable and heavy as a rifle, with a large knob and a leather thong. I am awfully pleased with it. It only cost 6s at Smith's in New Oxford Street.

Lancing, Saturday 17 September 1921

On Friday[1] I was going down to Fulford's but a desperate interchange of wires put it off so I went to the Stoll with Father instead. We struck two extraordinarily good films, albeit British. Next day I went down to Bury.

The Fulford family are: the Canon, a genial gentlemanly fool; Mrs Fulford, an honest, kindly old-fashioned woman whose bridge drove me wild – you should no more trust a woman's declarations in bridge than in love; a brother whom I thought rather a prig; and a pretty, fragile, shy sort of sister called Monica. I went down rather expecting to fall in love with her but returned safely. Their house is a most delightful old rectory some way out of Bury – part of it Edward I, part of it Henry V, and the rest Georgian. Inside it was all staircases. There was a severe water shortage the first day – three of their four wells were dry and the other would only work for a few minutes a day. They kept an excellent table. In the evenings, except Sunday, we played bridge. Sunday was observed most archaically. The whole place was a survival of the Fairchild family; the villagers played quoits on the green from Good Friday to Harvest Mass. Every evening with the coffee, at about 9.30, the servants' alarm clock was brought into the drawing room and given to the Canon, who solemnly wound it up, set it, and returned it to the maid. The maids themselves were called Bessy and Rachel and strange names like that. The only thing which took the edge off its charm was that it was quite impossible not to feel an intruder. All the conversation at meals was entirely local, county families and village shop; this I found dismally dull. On Monday Fullers and I went over to Ely to interview a prep school master about a job for him. I had to pay my fare

[1] Friday 9 September.

and lunch, which came to over ten bob. The cathedral is beautiful, easily the finest I have seen. That evening Fullers was ill. Next day he was still ill, so Monica and I went for a bus ride to a distant village. We got on better but not uproariously. After lunch we went golfing, I with little success; after tea we went over to Hengrave, a beautiful old Tudor house near them. The owners, a fairly nouveau riche baronet, were away but we got shown over by a maid. It was extremely interesting. On Wednesday I returned home. Thursday was spent in riotous living at dentists, tailors, and cinemas, and on Friday I returned here. It was a sad journey with two Olds House men. I found Newman alone and rather ill at ease and wandered round in the usual way. My dormitory are a sad lot after my anteroom last term. They have all got pits or have left. Preters has gone up to San. with gout – a sad result of his happy evenings alone at Goring. I went up to see him; he was quite cheery.

Wednesday 21 September 1921

I have managed to get in a good deal of work the last few days, but Lucas is proving rather 'tarsame' over timetable arrangements. He seems to resent any attempt to make him do some work as a personal insult.

Friday 30 September 1921

I am beginning to find more interest in some of my official jobs. We have at last closed the debating society. We had a committee meeting on Tuesday night and, after a little tentative opposition from Carew, carried it unanimously. I am going to try and innovate some affectations, a tie, and Latin incantations. The magazine has not begun to worry me at all yet. Now and then the announcement of some prolific old boy arrives, now and then an In Memoriam; a huge correspondence arrived the other day which I cannot wholly dissociate from my jovial brother. I am beginning rather to enjoy taking my PT squad. I don't think they dislike it awfully. We take it quite as a rag and they really do the official part quite efficiently. They are pretty certain to rag if they are going to enjoy it at all, so it is best to rag with them, I think.

Another job I have enjoyed has been clearing out the librarian's room. There is an extraordinary satisfaction in getting things straightened out, even if it is only sweeping up. The literary refuse of the last fifty years has been allowed to accumulate there – old periodicals, novels so popular as to be incapable of being mended and unworthy of being replaced, obsolete books of science and biography, bound volumes of parish magazines, a portentous mass of biblical and devotional rubbish, tomes of topography and travel. At last I have got all these sorted out. I previously found myself two perquisites from the heap: rather a charming book of rural reminiscences by a Sussex parson, and a work on popular science with a poem in it which is either the most ludicrous in the language or is meant to be funny and has been taken seriously by the pious author. In any case it is amusing.

I have heard from Luned again. Her misconstruction of my 'Hall' for 'Hell' has led to a letter of passion and sympathy – an amusing contingency which I have not explained. As a matter of fact I am reasonably happy. I do much as I like; I am interested in much of my work; I have Longe's almost undivided friendship; I am young enough rather to enjoy authority and dignity and being busy over public affairs. I suppose I am stupified by the official atmosphere. As a matter of fact, though, this seems much clearer this term; there is none of the self-importance and restraint about this term's God-box that sickened me last term.

Yesterday was a Saint's Day and as Newman, Longe and Bevan were out we decided to have Bobby Lea to tea. It was a trifle risky but it went off very well; he was quite at home, talking and bitching away. The colleagues turned up early but were not very disgusted – only a little jealous. Driberg[1] has suggested reviewing J.F.'s brochure in the magazine – a sound idea I think. I want to make my magazines different from the usual school records. Life has compensations, whatever I tell Luned.

Friday 7 October 1921

The sale of books last Saturday was quite a success. I cleared over seventeen bob on them. It was quite inconceivable what some people thought were worth buying – old magazines, books of theology, and God knows what all.

I have been getting through a steady amount of work. The effect of Lecky[2] on the set has been electric. Everyone can now stump Lux[3] on every point. I can't think he enjoys this new enthusiasm much. I managed to finish Maine's *Ancient Law* – a most phenomenal task.

On Wednesday we had a Field Day. My section was at first sent to bear the forefront of the battle. We were what was, I thought tactlessly, called 'the point' of the whole advance and I spent the first hour or so explaining myself to fierce riding officers and shouting men. Soon however God gave his beloved sleep. An umpire galloped up and said 'Do you realise, man, that you are marching your section across the enfilade fire of two companies and a dozen Lewis guns?' I dissociated myself with any share in this daring conception and modestly remarked that those was my orders. Accordingly he told me that I must hang up my advance for a time. He would tell me when we might move. There are few men for whom I have a more fixed sense of gratitude; I never saw that officer again. Perhaps he was thrown from his horse and is now in hospital deliriously babbling 'enfilade fire – two companies – exterminated –

---

[1] Tom Driberg. See Appendix of Names, p. 794.
[2] W. E. H. Lecky's *History of England in the Eighteenth Century*.
[3] Nickname for Lucas, Waugh's form-master.

hang up advance'; perhaps he was moved by a sudden unmilitary feeling of compassion for my weary section; or perhaps he will have to be handed down to posterity as one of the men who have been able to forget Evelyn Waugh. I should think that this is the most likely.

Today there was a 12.30 parade but Molson achieved a diplomatic triumph over the adjutant and got us exemption for extra work. J.F. gave me a copy of *The Poetic Procession*.[1] I have written a review of it, not too badly I think.

Tuesday 11 October 1921

Driberg has got a scandal about J.F. He went to his room the other night and found it in darkness but J.F. and someone else in a chair very embarrassed. The boy turned out to be ——. ——'s reputation would of course stand anything but I should have thought J.F. had better taste.

I have sent *The Poetic Procession* off to be bound. I don't know how much it will cost me. I am having rather a busy time getting things ready for the magazine. One of the preposterous governors has sent in a huge and infantile contribution.

Sunday 16 October 1921

I have had a desperately busy week. The magazine has had to go off to press and the corps and football authorities have held it up. It is off now and I feel a great weight off my mind.

I have sent the poem I found in the Buckland work to be bound.

Today I have sent off some state papers to Father discussing the present situation at some length. I have told him that I find the idea of staying on here another term is very repugnant, and that if I don't get a scholarship I am prepared to go up to Oxford on a minimum wage. I have also asked to be allowed to take up a job in London between Christmas and then.

I am really hating this term; I am certainly making myself hateful. I wonder John[2] stands me at all. I think that too much work is making me nervously-strung. Anyway I am quite conscious of behaving like a cad all the time. I have become quite different in the House, too, now. Strict and dignified, as far as a man of my height can be, and extremely full of the official spirit. If all this has been for nothing and I don't get a scholarship I shall be pretty fed up.

I don't really know what I want, but I know I can't stay on here as things are. I should far sooner go as a prep school master like Fulford or Nattrass.

Carew and I are starting the Corpse Club for people who are bored stiff. I am to be president.

---

[1] Two lectures given by Roxburgh to the Workers' Educational Association in Brighton and published by Basil Blackwell.
[2] John Longe.

Wednesday 19 October 1921

I have got my reprieve. Last night I got my reply from Father – very sympathetic and consenting to my leaving this term and either going straight up to Oxford or out to France. It is very cheering. Meanwhile I must work like hell for a scholarship. I cannot think at all what my chances are. At present I feel that I shall be deliriously happy if I win and abysmally depressed if I lose. It is not perhaps a wholly logical view to take.

The Corpse Club prospers. We have decided on a black silk tassel as the badge of membership to be worn in the buttonhole. The members are Newman, Lister, Longe, Carew, P. F. Machin, and Molson. Longe and Carew are not really corpse-like. How bloody bad my handwriting is getting. The last few days have been pretty purposeless. The Shakespeare Society last night was wretched. I do honestly feel that it is an excellent thing to leave. I should have only stagnated and fallen in love with some underschool, if I had stayed on.

Sunday 23 October 1921

New College will make a vacancy for me next term if I do particularly well in the scholarship exam – they expect a good deal higher standard than the ordinary matric. I think I ought to be able to manage that. The other colleges in the group are Univ., Queen's, Exeter, Worcester, Hertford – all well worth going to, I think. I manage to get through a book a day now.

The Corpse Club is causing some amusement in the school. Yesterday we all wore our tassels for the first time; today I have put up a notice on our mourning stationery.

The proofs of the magazine have come. The compositor seems to have had some difficulty with my writing. An idea for a book to write next term: 'Reconsiderations: an Oxford book of Wild Oats', consisting of essays disparaging established reputations. Dr Johnson no conversationalist, etc. I don't think I find scholarship dulls one's brain as I expected it would.

This morning I cut chapel. It is a serious breach of trust and all that but I think I shall make it a habit on Sunday mornings. If one can combine rest and work, I think God and honour may be safely left in abeyance for a time.

Lucas tells me that it is better to go up to Oxford as a scholar in a smaller college than New, from the educational point of view. Apparently the dons make more of you. As a commoner, however, New College is far the best, as you are in a really intellectual atmosphere.

Oxford is the only thing which makes life tolerable here. The God-box is awful. Filthy stories, cocoa, and out-House guests at all hours. I think poor Longe loathes it far more than I. I at least can enjoy filth, but he finds it more trying than their ordinary conversation. I think that it is better for them to talk of a subject which is generally interesting and sometimes witty than to be as desperately dull as they are on any other. Searching[1] was the only thing which made Walker's tea sufferable last Sunday.

Sunday 23 October 1921[2]

As an experiment in the departure from the usual subjects for debate, the show on Sunday evening cannot be said to have been an unrelieved success. The motion was 'This House considers that the day of institutional religion is over'. The debate was wretched. De Bruyne was very scientific but could not arrange his ideas at all. Preters was blasphemous; he did not offend me but I think I was alone in this; J.F. was crushing and prolix; everyone else irrelevant.

'We have heard with our ears and our fathers have declared unto us the noble works which they did in their days and in the old time before us.' This struck me in chapel the other day. I don't think it's bad.

Tuesday 25 October 1921

The Corpse tea was quite a success I thought. There was quite a lot of wit; the actual tea was bad.

Thursday 27 October 1921

The scandalous Head seems to have been stirring up a conspiracy with my Father to make me stay on and try again for a scholarship, if I fail. This makes it all the more necessary for me to get one; I am less hopeful. I talked to Lux about it the other day and he seemed to think our chances pretty thin. One might try working at home next term. Anyway, I don't mean to take any risks. I am going to spend the next fortnight simply on textbooks. I have won the English Verse but it causes me no interest.

Friday 28 October 1921

My birthday. Spent, as most days, in history. Father sent me the Waterman pen I wanted, Mother a delightful tie, my aunts ten bob; other than this a few letters and nothing.

In the evening I had an interview with the Head. He was very courteous and sympathetic. I was surprised how charming and cultivated he is really. We didn't come to any decision however except that, if I fail, I had better try again in April or March or whenever it is. I would sooner work at home. On analysing it I find one of my chief motives for wanting to be sure of leaving is so that I shall be able to use that farewell editorial. Also I don't feel that Lux can teach me much. If I was a classic under J.F. things would be different, but that little ass spends all his time digressing and generalizing and hedging over

[1] A game in which Waugh's circle looked for double meanings in conversation with masters or boys.

[2] Date as in MS.

questions and recommending little books in the Home University series. I get sick to death of him.

Saturday 29 October 1921

The magazine came out today. I had thought it awfully ordinary but several people have much to my surprise congratulated me on it. J.F. has written me a perfectly charming letter. 'If you use what the Gods have given you, you will do as much as anyone I know to shape the course of your generation.' It has elated me a lot.

I am gradually getting in a state when I am open to fall in love with someone. All my friends, of course, have before. Now I find that people like Onslow and Kimmerling interest me too much. I shall have to take care if I want to leave with credit and self-respect.

Sunday 30 October 1921

A gloomy day as usual. Rather a pleasant special preacher with queer contorting legs. We had as the anthem : 'How beautiful are the feet of them that preach the gospel of peace'.

I have come to the conclusion that it was all rot what the Head said to me. I shouldn't do any good by coming back here.

Monday 31 October 1921

I simply can't write today – not even diary or letters. I don't know if it is the effect of history. I had two excellent ideas for editorials and I can't write either.

Friday 4 November 1921

This morning my application form for the scholarships arrived. It is a formidable document. There are more scholarships and exhibitions than I had expected.

I have another idea now of going as a prep school master for the next two terms, but I doubt if my father will countenance it.

Monday 7 November 1921

On Saturday the man Lucas excelled himself in slackness. He gave us a note on the Regeneration of Prussia which was absolutely useless. He didn't know a thing about it – I really felt rather wild.

This afternoon I have been looking through some old history essays and have come to the conclusion that the more I know the more dully I write. There was much more brilliancy in the things I was doing three terms ago. I am afraid that what I feared has happened and my brain is getting dulled with learning.

Yesterday Pim came down.[1] He is a district commissioner in Ireland – most immoral and amusing. We went down to the Pad to dinner with him – an excellent dinner for once and plenty to drink. I had two sherries, some claret and port.

The debate afterwards was great fun but quite frivolous. It was a pity that the private business set the house in a frivolous mood. My speech had been a prepared essay on the elimination of sound from the drama, but fortunately the wine stood me in good stead and I was able to carry through.

I am thoroughly depressed over those essays. I simply can't write now.

Friday 11 November 1921

Most depressed as usual. Yesterday some academical underling returned my application form saying it was improperly filled up and that two modern languages were required from History candidates. I can only imagine this is some satanic secretarial witticism; if it is true, it simply isn't worth my while going in for the scholarship at all; as it is the French will be a pretty good farce. I am pretty despairing of my chances of even a £25 exhibition at Worcester. My father refuses to become further entangled in discussions of what I shall do for the next six months. Meanwhile life is dull and unpleasant.

This morning we had two minutes silence for the glorious dead. This afternoon a parade. I am sure I am wasting time here. I can't get really interested in history. I don't want an academic career. I don't even know that I want Oxford awfully. Well, I must get on with the diplomatic situation, I suppose.

Saturday 12 November 1921

This morning a letter arrived from the Warden himself apologizing for the mistake of his clerk and saying that Latin and French are enough. Today has been much as usual. This afternoon I did some magazine work and for a time watched a match against some Corinthians but it was too cold. It is really monstrous making the school stand still watching the match on an afternoon like today. After a sad tea in the infernal God-box I went for a short walk with Carew and showed off. I always talk best to him.

Monday 14 November 1921

Yesterday I took a day off work and felt better for it. Today the cloud has settled down. We had a constitutional history paper this morning which bored me stiff. My books have not come from Higham, much to my disgust. Yesterday was rather pleasant. I cut chapel, spent the morning eating

[1] A Head's House old boy; later Sir Richard Pim, Inspector-General of the Royal Ulster Constabulary. During the Second World War he was in charge of Churchill's Map Room at Downing Street.

meringues and drinking tea and talking filth. Lux came to tea. We walked all the evening and made up filthy limericks. Rather good some of them. Perhaps the best was:

> There once was a tweetle called ——
> Whom —— invited to tea,
> He was promptly debagged
> And buggered and shagged,
> Till his tool simply grew like a tree.

In hot air Sir Sydney Lea[1] – the good soul I shocked with *Conversion* – came in and talked small talk steadily and complacently for two hours. Travelling and lighting systems in country houses. My God.

Wednesday 16 November 1921

I see that I have forgotten to record that on Monday evening Woodard sent to me and ticked me off for bad manners on Sunday night. I can't claim to have been very impressed – it will give me an excellent excuse for cutting his hot airs in future anyway. It will make borrowing money rather awkward though.

This morning a letter from Father bitterly opposing any thought of working in town. If I don't get anything from Oxford I have got to stay on here. He suspects that I have been caught in a brothel and am being blackmailed into finding an honourable excuse for leaving. I almost wish I was. It would at least ensure my release. The more I think of it, the more despondent I become of getting anything except a Worcester £25 exhibition.

Monday 21 November 1921

Yesterday a longish walk with Carew. He waxed introspective as usual. I had just worked him up into a state of mind to renounce the devil and all his works, when he fell in a dyke. It probably did his immortal soul more good than any renunciations.

This morning we had a general paper for Lux which simply bored me stiff. I find it almost impossible to make a decent essay out of an abstract political question. I abominate constitutions.

A rather amusing incident the other day showed me what sort of reputation I've got. The Head took me out of Hall to speak to me about my prizes and the 'In Memoriam' for Percy Bates.[2] Longe asked me what happened and I told him I had been sacked for immorality. He of course didn't believe it, but he reported it to Davis who did. Not only did he tell half the Upper Class in the school, but he also told everyone, 'Of course I'm not a bit surprised, really. I

---

[1] Sir Sydney Lea (1867–1946): JP for Worcestershire and a member of the Church Assembly; father of two boys in Head's House.
[2] The school bursar.

expected something like that would happen.' The result is that for the last few days I have been repeatedly accosted with people saying, 'My dear fellow, bad luck! Who was the other man?' Any amount of people believed it, including Carew. I don't care a lot, of course, but it is really rather witty considering that I lead as pure a life as any Christian in the place, always excepting conversation of course; but I generally think that the people who don't talk filth are as bad in their lives.

Tuesday 22 November 1921

Today in the interval between tea and my bath, while the underschools were making toast, I came to the library and recoiling from Tudor politics I began Rupert Brooke's poems and the memoir at the beginning. I was extraordinarily impressed, particularly by the letters – they, I think, bring out more than anything the situation I have tried to show in my editorial, that the beauty of living has gone out of the youngest generation. His letters are awfully like Hill's, whether because they are both poets – Hill at least in life if not in ink – I do not know. The same pleasure in their own work. Brooke's description of his romance with the dropsical leper in it is exactly like Hill's *Solomon*, but even Hill is more bitter and sophisticated. I felt very envious reading, particularly the parts about Rugby and friendship. I do honestly think that that is something that went out of the world in 1914, at least for one generation.

Wednesday 23 November 1921

Three weeks this time, before if I have failed hopelessly, I shall know the result of the scholarship exam.

I think that one of the chief things that has gone out of life is friendship. No one here seems to have made any real friends – there are several lusts but I don't count that. I wonder how much they ever did and how much friendship is simply created by memory – a good deal, I should imagine.

This evening Carew came up to me and poured out his soul on the hearthrug as usual. I think the mistake I've made all along with my friends is attempting to make them see things as I do.

Saturday 26 November 1921

The Head, graciously and to my surprise, has proved amicable about the weekend at home and offers me one before or after the exam. He favours the former, as a rest; I the latter, as a bust. However I don't much care – it will be delightful either way.

This week has been wholly without interest. I am more and more confused and confounded at my own ignorance and above all my complete incompetence at essay-writing. It is really rather formidable to tackle the most important paper without having done an essay for nearly two years. Time is too short;

there is a lot I want to do in the next six days that I shall not have time for – English prose, parts of Lecky, maps, Macaulay, biographies, etc. I am not doing as many hours a day as I ought, either. I shall have to try and get into decent training physically too, next week too I suppose, if I am going to do anything. I am very frightened for the result of it all.

Sunday 27 November 1921

Last night the man Woodard made himself trying over the magazine. He has cut out a quite unexceptionable letter on education and the specialist, which I think was of some merit and perhaps value. If he must be conscientious he would do far better to cut out some of the lust poetry which appears regularly enough.

This morning, Christmas carols. I defy anyone not to like them. Whatever one's views on Christianity and promiscuous private charity, one cannot resist them – or so I find. I only wish that the men next to me would not sing them. They are best from a distance, unless one sings oneself.

I am very much pleased with the DNB. Before, I had always read up lives in the *Encyclopaedia Britannica*. I have been doing Canning, Castlereagh, and Palmerston – excellent.

Tuesday 29 November 1921

There has been a rapid interchange of diplomatic notes this weekend about the three days the Head is allowing me at home. We have eventually decided on next weekend. This morning a delightful note from Mallowan asking us out to dinner. I am getting tired of work but I've got the hell of a lot to get through before the end of the week. I've done a good day's work yesterday and the day before.

Friday 2 December 1921

This is the last day of work. Tomorrow I go home for two days and then on to Oxford. I have been finishing off notes, learning to draw maps, and reading up things I had forgotten. I shall not be the least surprised if I fail. I am continually appalled by how little I know. It is simply on the knees of the Gods. If I get the questions I want, I should do well. I am looking forward to this weekend as much as to any holidays my first term. I must try and make myself less unpleasant at home.

Friday evening. The last day over – I haven't felt so relieved for years. I am looking forward to the next two days immeasurably. I had meant to work today but have found myself physically incapable; I think I have been working up to the bone the last week or so. I couldn't have stood any more. As it is I am not too well. It's quite like the end of term. I daren't think what the Oxford adventure will bring forth – I quite expect failure.

We had the last parade of the term – perhaps of my life – today. A route march more than usually dull and not very strenuous, but it made me thoroughly tired. I haven't taken enough exercise lately. Rufus made a farewell speech to our half of the platoon. I am accustomed to his making himself offensive but not ridiculous. This afternoon he did both. I think he was feeling very sentimental at this last uniform parade and the House certainly did nothing to encourage him. I was a little sorry for him, but he is one of the excellent men I have no use for.

Hampstead, Saturday 3 December 1921

At home. Mother met me at the station and after lunch Father, Mother and I went off to the Everyman theatre. It was the first time I had been there and I thought it perfectly delightful. It is a tiny room, one floor and most uncomfortable seats – I am told they are worse in the cheaper seats – but the scenery was delightful, designed by MacDermott.[1] It was not very full; Ensor who is working there tells us it will shut up in a fortnight if it can't do better – a great pity. They were fashionable and economical in having no footlights or music.

The show was four plays by Lord Dunsany.[2] Excellently played and staged, and good plays. The first – a profiteer pushing patent foods, and a conventional curate – was charming to a certain extent but a little Shavian. The second was a poetic Arab romance – a terrible boy has just interrupted me singing outside the window 'when the sneow ly reound abeout'. I swore at him and he went away – which we did not like awfully. It was charmingly set but tedious and sloppy. The third, a Grand Guignol sort of *Moonstone*, was brilliantly played. The appearance of an idol which had travelled from Timbuctoo was ludicrous and spoiled the air of mystery, but the first half was splendid. The last, *The Lost Silk Hat*, was perfectly delightful, particularly a navvy.

Sunday 4 December 1921

A very delightful day. It was excellently wise of the Head to suggest this weekend. I feel immensely better, albeit with a premonition of failure. Yesterday I did not go to church but just sat in an armchair pretending to read all the morning. Herbert Gatliff[3] came in and gave advice about the exam – write at huge length on two questions. After lunch I went over to Hendon to see Fulford. Fortunately he was at home and most unacademical – full of a project

---

[1] Norman MacDermott founded the Everyman theatre in 1919, in a drill hall erected in 1888–9 to celebrate Queen Victoria's jubilee. The theatre became famous in the 1920s for the range and quality of its productions; Noel Coward's play *The Vortex* was first staged there. It was supplanted by the Everyman cinema in 1933.

[2] See footnote p. 328.

[3] An Assistant Principal in the Treasury.

for taking a correspondence course on 'sales letter' writing. A minor poet called
Moult and his wife, charming Lancashire people, came to tea. Fulford stayed
to supper but had to go early. As a preparation for my pilgrimage Father read
us the introduction to *Essays in Criticism* – very fine I thought. And so early to
bed, very contented.

Oxford, Monday 5 December 1921

I am meeting Preters this morning to go down by the lunch train to what will
for me, I am afraid, be a 'city of lost causes'. I am fairly hopeless of success. The
arrangement we have come to is that if I fail so badly as not to do the *viva voce* I
shall leave and go up as a commoner next term; if I fail but do the *viva* I shall go
back to school and sweat for another hideous term; if I get anything I shall
leave and earn a living somehow until October.

We arrived at about 10 to 3 and met Hill coming down to meet us. We
stopped the cab, took him in, and brought him here to the Mitre with us. This
is really a very charming old hotel – cooking excellent and comfortable rooms
to reach which we have to walk some three-quarters of a mile of passages and go
up and down about a dozen staircases. We found a small pile of letters of
invitation and cards to greet us; during the evening nearly every Lancing man
in Oxford came in to see us. Having made investigations about our exams – the
college notices were wrong in almost every particular – we dropped in and had
tea with Southwell at Boffins and then looked Mallowan up. After a good
dinner we went to Balliol and had cocoa. And so to bed.

Tuesday 6 December 1921

This morning at 9.30 we had the general paper. I simply loved it, but so I
imagine must have everybody else. There were fifty or sixty other competitors
all looking absolute oiks but monstrously intellectual. I did four questions. One
on my favourite biography. I chose Arthur Symons's *Beardsley* and did fairly
well – well enough I think to interest them. Then I did my flutter on 'Did the
nineteenth century produce any original contribution to painting or architecture?' and did five pages, pretty good stuff. Then a cynical thing about Tacitus
being the most 'modern' classical author, and a rather feeble answer to 'Are any
subjects particularly unsuited to poetic treatment?' – this lapsed into an
extravagant eulogy of Rupert Brooke. However, I think I did well enough on
the paper to create a favourable impression.

In the Unseen, a piece of Livy, I did adequately but no more. I made good
sense of it in most parts, but of course it is only a pass paper. At 8.30 tonight we
are having to do a French Unseen which will be an absolute farce. Tomorrow
the serious business of life begins with English History and Essay.

Lancing, Saturday 10 December 1921

I think that this last week has been one of the happiest I have ever known. I simply don't know how I have done in the exam. I should not be surprised if I got something, or disappointed if I fail. I did a better French Unseen than I had expected and a fairly good English History Paper. My flutter was on the English Reformation and the younger Pitt. The essay was, I think, my worst piece of work; it was heavy and logical and pretentious. The European History was just all right: Cavour, Kaunitz and the French Revolution. The *viva* was delightful. They cross-examined me about eighteenth-century agriculture but were very charming and I was, I think, intelligent.

Apart from the papers we had a delightful time. On Wednesday we went to tea at Lincoln with Dobson and in the evening to a debate at the Union. We were disappointed in this. Considering how much older they were and how much cleverer they are supposed to be, I don't think they were much better than Lancing. The motion was on Egypt and was proposed by an awful man[1] from the House who spoke with incredible dullness for over half an hour. An Indian[2] followed who was really good, then a sarcastic aristocrat,[3] and then the guest of the evening, one Barnes or Banks, a wee Free.[4] Considering that he was a man among boys he was not much use. The Labour Party seemed a rowdy lot.

On Thursday we went to tea with Mathews at New College and then binged with Mallowan – dinner at the Clarendon and a show at the New Theatre. Neither were very good but most enjoyable! After the show we drank coffee with Whittall at Balliol. Turned out at 12, Molson and I went for a long walk by the river and then to bed.

We ought of course to have returned next morning, but neither of us felt much like it. We had Hill and Mallowan to breakfast and then I went up to town and Molson stayed on at the Mitre.

I went to lunch with Alec at the Spanish restaurant in Dean Street. There was an excellent meal and with him a Miss Richards whom he addressed as 'Goldy'. I don't know quite what their relationship is. I don't think she is his mistress, but they seemed to be on very familiar terms. Anyway she was most enchanting. 'Mothers always seem to be afraid of me. You don't think me dangerous, do you Mr Waugh?', she said to me. I must confess I did. Apparently she is living with Clifford Bax at present and is going out to Sweden soon to marry!

[1] R. A. M. Harris.

[2] S. W. R. D. Bandaranaike, later prime minister of Ceylon.

[3] H. J. Scrymgeour-Wedderburn, later the 11th Earl of Dundee, and Minister of State for Foreign Affairs, 1961–4.

[4] Major H. Barnes, MP, a member of the minority of the Free Church of Scotland that refused in 1900 to join the United Presbyterian Church to form the United Free Church.

We came to Lancing by the slow train to avoid changing. I spent second evening smoking out on Coombes road with my colleagues. Then to bed.

Lancing, Sunday 11 December 1921

Cut chapel as usual and drank tea and ate meringues. We took a lazy morning and then Newman and I went over to lunch with Ox. We went on his motor bicycle; it was very slippery; after we had been about a couple of miles the thing skidded and flung us into the road. We arose shaken, dirty, but whole and continued more cautiously. Lunch was quite good; Mrs Hamerton a fool. After chapel we went out and smoked. To my disgust the absurd Davis and Moule have insisted on asking the Head whether we should do the divinity exam. Of course he has made us. In hot air we had a more lively time than usual. Woodard made us a rum punch – most cheering. The Gibbs' House came to visit us and we ragged them and they us. We hunted the night-watchman. At last to bed. It is very cheering having no further work to do.

Monday 12 December 1921

The divinity exam was quite a joke. I had not looked anything up or taken a single note. However I found three questions to do. I went for a long walk with Preters and had a smoke – the Gibbs' House sounds intolerable. This afternoon I played in a House game and quite enjoyed it. I have got my prizes – the Samuel Butler books and the Riccardi sonnets and am well content with them.

Tuesday 13 December 1921

All the morning in sitting about and chatting and drinking – very pleasant. The afternoon the same. These days make up for a lot. Evening school we went out smoking with Reid, Newman and Plowright. The evening we sat up late talking. Newman told me an anecdote of —— which interested me a lot. That night when we went up to his pit last term to coffee he tried to get off with him.

Wednesday 14 December 1921

The day of election at Oxford. Apparently we should have arranged with the college porters if we wanted telegrams. In the evening, I had round games with my dormitory. I think they really enjoyed themselves. We played musical chairs, general post, blind man's buff, etc. They are rather dears. Bevan and Booth came up too. It cheered me – I was pretty anxious about the scholarship. Also harassed with luggage, etc.

Thursday 15 December 1921

This morning I came into breakfast rather late to find on the table two letters from Oxford. A formal announcement that I had won the £100 Hertford

Scholarship and a private letter of congratulations from the Vice-Principal.[1] I was not a little cheered at this. The good man of the house says, as I supposed, that I got it on my English style, and that my General Paper and English History were the best and my European History the worst.

It has made a very jolly day out of what would otherwise have been a very dull one. Everyone has been full of congratulations. Brent-Smith wrote me a letter. What is best is that now I can leave with a clear conscience. A hundred pounds is financially as good as anything I could get.

I have spent most of the day arranging for my successors: P. F. Machin to take on the library; Molson, if he stays on, the magazine – if not, Carew.

This morning I went for a walk with Dick and talked of school, but we did not get on awfully well together; there is a reserve between us; the time when we were in sympathy is over. I have not been able to do my duty by the servants. I have hardly enough money to get back with.

Bevan and I went up to the San. to say goodbye to people but found only O'Neil. He was looking very sweet sitting up in bed but he cannot talk. As I said to Molson I think the only reason why I have never had any keennesses is because they can never talk intelligently.

Most of the people who are leaving are getting most sentimental. Bevan and I are sane. I am only too pleased to be getting away.

It was rather a wonderful last evening. There was of course much rejoicing everywhere – more I think than I have heard at the end of any term – and I felt very much part of it. I played musical chairs with my dormitory till late and then went to say goodbye to the Head. He talked lengthily and seriously but with considerable reasonableness. We got on to philosophy and religion and he pressed two pious books on me.

One of the most charming compliments I received was from Mrs Neville-Smith, a woman I had never spoken to before. She met me on the steps in the evening. 'Do let me congratulate you on your scholarship, Waugh; I do hope you are allowing yourself to be a little pleased. Everyone else is, you know.' Most gracious I thought.

Bevan and I went to have a final drink with Mr Lowe at the Pad. He was a little tight and very sentimental.

'Well gentlemen, whenever you've been down here you've always behaved yourselves. I'm sure I wish you the best luck in life. I hope you'll sometimes think of the old Pad when you're away – a tidy little place, couldn't be much better in its way.'

[1] This was Waugh's first contact with C. R. M. F. Cruttwell (1887–1941), Principal of Hertford, 1930–9. When Waugh went up to Oxford, Cruttwell was his history tutor, but their 'mutual dislike became incurable' (*A Little Learning*, p. 175). Waugh attached Cruttwell's name to a series of shady or absurd characters in his early novels; and Cruttwell, until his death, awaited each new Waugh novel with apprehension.

We assured him we would stay there when we came back as old boys and left with great good humour.

I did not go to the entertainer for long but went to the House Room. A lot of people came in and talked – I was in rather good form, I think: Harrison, Driberg, Longe, Molson, Carew, P. F. Machin, and later my colleagues who had been smoking on the field.

Friday 16 December 1921

I left without regret and went by a late train to Ditchling. I said goodbye to many people, most cursorily to Woodard as became our relationship.

I have left the magazine in the hands of Carew, the debating society with Lister, and the library with P. F. Machin.

I am sure I have left at the right time – as early as possible and with success.

3　The Twenties Diary 1924-28

Introduction

Waugh went up to Hertford College, Oxford, in January 1922. No Oxford diary survives; as noted in the Preface, he certainly kept a diary during at least part of his time there, but destroyed it. The original plan had been that, if he won a scholarship, he would spend nine months in France learning the language. But Arthur Waugh, with what Evelyn later described as 'his habitual impatience to get a task finished; in this case my education',[1] decided he should go up at once.

Hertford was not one of the most prominent colleges, and Waugh at first lived unobtrusively. In a letter to Dudley Carew, who was still at Lancing, he reported that he spent most of his time 'with Mallowan and his New College friends'. Then, through an eccentric new acquaintance in Hertford, Terence Greenidge, the orphan son of a don and the ward of the Hertford bursar, he was introduced to the Hypocrites' Club. It was a decisive introduction. The Hypocrites had been started by pipe-smoking Rugbeians and Wykehamists, but it was, 'by the time I joined, in process of invasion and occupation by a group of wanton Etonians who brought it to speedy dissolution. It then became notorious not only for drunkenness but for flamboyance of dress and manner which was in some cases patently homosexual. . . . The Hypocrites, like Gatsby's swimming pool, saw the passage, as members or guests, of the best and the worst of that year [1923]. It was the stamping ground of half my Oxford life and the source of friendships still warm today.'[2] Waugh's range of activities soon widened. He made speeches at the Union and reported debates for the undergraduate journals, *Isis* and *Cherwell*. He belonged to the Liberal New Reform Club and to the Conservative Carlton Club. He published a short story in the *Oxford Broom*, a magazine started by Harold Acton. He made decorative drawings for magazines, bookplates, and the programmes of the Oxford University Dramatic Society. He attended the Ruskin School of Art. He became a member of the Oxford Railway Club, whose first dinner was held on 28 November 1923 in a private dining-car attached to the Penzance–Aberdeen train.

[1] *A Little Learning*, p. 163.
[2] Ibid, p. 181.

His circle of acquaintances grew wide. He met rich, aristocratic friends, among them Lord Elmley and his brother Hugh Lygon; intellectual friends, including Peter Quennell, Richard Pares, Robert Byron, David Talbot-Rice, Christopher Hollis, Claud Cockburn, Anthony Powell and Cyril Connolly; and undesirable friends, the 'satanic' Basil Murray and the 'incorrigibly homosexual' Brian Howard. Above all he met Harold Acton, who had been brought up in splendour at La Pietra, a villa overlooking Florence, and who seemed to his Oxford contemporaries, by reason of his international interests and connections, to be years ahead of any other undergraduate in the university. A friend of the Sitwells and Norman Douglas, and an inconoclastic aesthete who collected Victoriana, Acton thought little of the Georgian writers admired by Arthur Waugh and Evelyn's Lancing friends, proclaiming instead the merits of T. S. Eliot and Gertrude Stein.

When Waugh came down in the summer of 1924, owing £200, his prospects were not good. He had no money of his own; his father was not well off; Chapman & Hall was not prospering, and Alec had already been accommodated, part-time, on its staff. In any event, Waugh's talents at that stage appeared to lie in the direction of arts and crafts rather than literature; Acton thought he might become a minor William Morris, drawing and carpentering and designing stained glass.

The years between his formal departure from Oxford and his secret engagement in the winter of 1927 were probably the unhappiest stretch of his life, though they were enlivened by his friendship with Alastair Graham and they supplied the material for two of his best-known 'comic' novels, *Decline and Fall* and *Vile Bodies*. He had no settled job or ambition. During those years Waugh attended Heatherley's Art School; investigated the possibility of becoming an apprentice printer; spent two terms on the staff of a prep school in north Wales; taught, until he was sacked, allegedly for assaulting the matron, at a school for backward boys at Aston Clinton; took another teaching job in Notting Hill Gate; investigated the idea of becoming a parson; became a reporter for five weeks on the *Daily Express*; started a novel that he did not finish; wrote a serio-comic dissertation called *Noah; or the Future of Intoxication* that was turned down; and enrolled for a course at the Institute of Carpentry in Southampton Row. Until the publishing firm of Duckworth commissioned him in 1927 to write a life of Rossetti, for which he was paid an advance of £50, his only success was the publication of a short story in a collection edited by his brother.

His personal relationships were scarcely more satisfactory. Oxford had induced a certain contempt for the bourgeois, literary Hampstead world to which his father and brother were proud to belong. From 1923 onwards, according to Alec Waugh, his family found him increasingly aggressive and cantankerous, hiding what they believed to be a warm and generous nature behind a protective front. Alec concluded that part of the reason for the mask was that Evelyn had come to despise what he regarded as his father's weakness and sentimentality, and was determined to be different.

His insecure, often humiliating, series of jobs was accompanied by an unsatisfactory emotional life. At Oxford, his principal attachments had been to other male undergraduates. He was twenty-one, on the evidence of the diaries, before he fell seriously in love with a girl, Olivia Plunket Greene, a strange, disconcerting, secretive girl, younger than himself, who was never exclusively attached to Evelyn; she did little for his self-confidence either as a would-be writer or as a would-be lover.

At times, escaping from jobs he loathed, he led an intense social life, at first among those of his old circle who were still at Oxford, and later among the Bright Young People – whom the newspapers invented in 1924 and thereafter occasionally revived. They were not a coherent group and were often led by girls – Elizabeth Ponsonby, the Jungman sisters, Diana Guinness, Olivia herself – who belonged to a generation that had found a new emancipation after the war and, with their shingled hair and motor cars and wayward independence, often confused the young men who pursued them.

In the public mind, the Bright Young People became notorious through their parties. 'Oh Nina, what a lot of parties,' says Adam Fenwick Symes in *Vile Bodies*: 'Masked parties, Savage parties, Victorian parties, Greek parties, Wild West parties, Russian parties, Circus parties, parties where one had to dress as somebody else, almost naked parties in St John's Wood, parties in flats and studios and houses and ships and hotels and night clubs, in windmills and swimming-baths, tea parties at school where one ate muffins and meringues and tinned crab, parties at Oxford where one drank brown sherry and smoked Turkish cigarettes, dull dances in London and comic dances in Scotland and disgusting dances in Paris – all that succession and repetition of massed humanity. . . . Those vile bodies. . . .' Waugh was on the fringe rather than at the centre of this world. Survivors of the parties of those days recall him egging on others to join in, but hesitating to do so himself, unless drunk. These recollections seem to be confirmed by the diaries, which reflect a certain detachment, with an undercurrent of despair. In *Vile Bodies*, published in 1930 but begun during and dealing with the 1920s, the Prime Minister of the day discusses the 'Younger Generation' with a Jesuit, Father Rothschild, and complains that 'there's something wanton about these young people today'. Rothschild demurs. 'I don't think people ever want to lose their faith either in religion or in anything else. I know very few young people, but it seems to me that they possess an almost fatal hunger for permanence.' On 1 February 1925, hearing of the engagement of two friends, Waugh wrote in his diary: 'It makes me sad for them because any sort of happiness or permanence seems so infinitely remote from any one of us.'

The style of the post-Oxford diaries is described by Waugh in *A Little Learning* as 'mock-whimsical'. He finds its origin in the manner that he and Alastair Graham had adopted in their correspondence.

Hampstead, Saturday 21 June 1924

At 12 o'clock, so far as I at all clearly remember, I was in the room of poor Michael Leroy-Beaulieu in Balliol. Much of the evening he had spent in tears because Peter had frightened him by breaking a plate. There was a prodigious crowd and everything quite insufferably hot. After 12 there were only left the Balliol people and a few incapable drunks. Piers Synnott was put to bed. Benoit and Patrick Balfour[1] let me out of Richard's window by a string at a little before 1 o'clock. I returned over the New Quad water-closets, to the great detriment of my clothes, for a few hours' sleep.

After a harassing morning of labels and taxis Philip Machin and I found ourselves in the 1.45 luncheon car at the next table to poor Brian Howard.[2] We found nothing to eat that seemed tolerable except bread and cheese but we drank some brown sherries, some champagne, many liqueurs and, smoking great cigars, got out at Paddington with the conviction that we had lunched well.

At home I found my parents surprisingly agreeable; my father very healthy and full of conversation about the places he had visited in France. He had found an obscenity in the Bayeux tapestry which pleased him.

Sunday 22 June 1924

I did not leave the house all day but read and pondered *The Temple at Thatch*.[3]

Monday 23 June 1924

As soon as I was up I went to an exhibition of Lovat Fraser's printed work at the First Edition Club. I was again strengthened in my conviction of his bewildering charm and my contempt for those who abuse him as a 1920 fashion. I went abroad to Kensington where I stole Alec's large paper copy of

[1] Later the 3rd Baron Kinross. See Appendix of Names, p. 794.

[2] 'The characters in my novels often wrongly identified with Harold Acton were to a great extent drawn from him.' *A Little Learning*, p. 204. See Appendix of Names, p. 794.

[3] A novel that Waugh started but never finished.

Max's *Works*. I gave luncheon to Tony[1] at the Previtali and returned home. By far the most important event of the morning was my ordering of a new stick. I tried to get one as like as possible to the old one but found nothing so beautiful – and indeed I think it would have seemed to me rather indecent had I done so. The one I have chosen is of English oak but lighter and a little longer than my other one. I am having a small golden plate about the size of a shilling let into the top, engraved with my name and crest. I think it will be a success. I arrived home to find a wire from Alastair[2] asking me to meet him for dinner at the Previtali. We had a quiet and pleasant dinner and wandered down by way of many pubs to the Embankment and back in the same manner to the Café Royal. There we found a sweet drunk man called Wilkinson who had been at Radley. Soon we were joined by the foul Tasha Gielgud[3] and in her company a pert young woman dressed almost wholly as a man. They had many drinks with us and attracted a great deal of attention. We managed in the end to get rid of them only by leaving the restaurant ourselves and putting them to lesbianize in a taxi. And so home.

Tuesday 24 June 1924

I had engaged to spend the day with Tony but Rudolph[4] called him away. Alastair and I went to Kew on a bus and walked several miles in great heat round the gardens. They were very very beautiful. I had forgotten them almost entirely. From there we went to Hampton Court; there also my liveliest admiration was excited more by the buildings than the pictures, particularly the William and Mary and Anne additions. The maze we found ugly and ill kept and, except for the flustered and wild-eyed children who cannoned into our stomachs at each corner, quite unexciting. We will build a maze of brick with a really exquisite grotto inside. At Hampton Court after a long walk one only reaches a dusty, tiny yard with two comical carved seats and about twenty paper bags.

From Hampton Court we found a comical boat which took us in a leisurely fashion past a preposterous house-boat called *La Bohème* to the Star and Garter for dinner – at least it called itself the Star and Garter but it was a horrible place all unlike the *Doctor's Dilemma* or *Sinister Street*. That is not overwhelmed with a maternity home or Venereal Disease Hospital or other monument to governmental charity. To London by an omnibus.

---

[1] Tony Bushell, actor. See Appendix of Names, p. 794.
[2] Alastair Graham, the 'friend of my heart' to whom Waugh gave the name of 'Hamish Lennox' in *A Little Learning*. See Appendix of Names, p. 794.
[3] The step-daughter of the Grand-Duke Michael of Russia. See Appendix of Names, p. 794.
[4] Rudolph Messel, cousin of Oliver Messel, the stage designer.

Wednesday 25 June 1924

I called for Alastair at about 11 and went with him through the heart-breaking business of ordering his passage to Africa.[1] Rather sadly I went for my stick and took him home to luncheon. The afternoon we spent at Golders Green – he in reading *The Golden Bough* and I in drawing my baroque Passing of Arthur. The stick, despite the contempt of Alastair, pleases me greatly. It is of course very raw at present. I intend to bury it in a peat bog for a little to colour it. I think it is a good piece of wood. We dined with the Queen Mother[2] at Previtali and I left them to go to a cinema while I went on with the Passing of Arthur.

Thursday 26 June 1924

I did, I think, nothing.

Friday 27 June 1924

Alastair's birthday. He came out to Golders Green for luncheon and dinner and slept here for the night. Joyce[3] came to dinner too and we had rather an agreeable evening.

Saturday 28 June 1924

Alastair and I spent most of the day at Paddington Station drinking and eating buns and watching trains. We went to the Stoll Cinema and came home to dinner. At about 11 we went for a walk and lost ourselves. A very remarkable thing occurred. God took away Parliament Hill entirely for some time; it was very puzzling. When we came home Alastair cooked an omelette which tasted remarkably and looked like a buttered egg.

Sunday 29 June 1924

Alastair and I went to the church of the emigrés in Buckingham Palace Road. I liked the Russian service enormously. The priests hid themselves in a little room and only appeared at rare moments through windows and doors like a cuckoo clock. A large plate of buns was brought up for them and lots of tiny children. All the while the choir, also hidden, kept up a long chant. The service seemed infinitely long. It was in full progress when we arrived at 11 and

---

[1] He was going to stay with a sister in Kenya as a holiday from his mother.

[2] Alastair Graham's mother, also referred to in the diary as 'Mrs G.'; she was the model for 'Lady Circumference' in Waugh's first novel, *Decline and Fall*. See Appendix of Names, p. 794.

[3] Joyce Fagan; earlier in 1924 Waugh introduced her, dressed as a man, to an all-male Oxford party. The party was raided by the University authorities, the Proctor and his bulldogs, but they failed to penetrate her disguise. 'I have never seen in a whole half-century since anything that looked so degenerate. . . . It implied some criticism of the contemporary *mores* that so repellent an object could pass as a man.' Alec Waugh, *The Fatal Gift* (London 1974), pp. 9–11.

showed no sign of stopping at 12.30 when we left. The congregation were acutely pathetic and mostly exiled archdukes and strange shabby women who were pointed out as mistresses of the Emperor. There was one poor old man in a very dissipated officer's overcoat. Chris[1] came to luncheon and we drank together on the verandah until tea. That was a dreary meal from which we escaped to burgle Baldhead's[2] flat and steal his whisky. We came home at about 10 with bowels seething with hunger and ate cold meat and hardboiled eggs and things like that.

Monday 30 June 1924

Alastair and I wasted a lot of time in shops and things and went to his architecture place[3] where they were very friendly. We lunched at Previtali, borrowed £1 from Chapman & Hall,[4] and found ourselves at about tea-time at the Empire Exhibition at Wembley. We went to the Palace of Arts and walked through a blazing nightmare of colonial paintings to some peculiarly charming period rooms. The 1840 one had been made by one of Alastair's professors. The William Morris one was the best, I thought. I saw sculpture and desired with all my heart to become a sculptor and then I saw jewels and wanted to be a jeweller and then I saw all manner of preposterous things being made in the Palace of Industry and wanted to devote my life to that too.

A remarkable thing happened to us. At about 6.30 we got a drink and then went to an Indian theatre. We saw some singularly incompetent Thibetan dancers and a man with a beard who did a few of the simplest tricks which every children's party conjurer with a dress suit and a cockney accent can do. We left the tent thinking it had been a very poor entertainment. It was not until we found that it was 8 o'clock and that we had both cut our respective hosts' dinners that we realized the magical powers of the black man with the beard. Luckily when I arrived at Baldhead's dinner they were all quite drunk. I soon drank all I could find and was well contented. A ghastly hulloing outside the windows announced the arrival of Tony Bushell, indescribably drunken, waving a bowler hat in one hand and an umbrella in the other and carolling his desire to rape Lady Calthrop. He was unsuccessful in this but stripped himself naked in preparation for the act. Alastair put him to bed on some chairs. We came back very drunk and slept. Chris slept here too.

Tuesday 1 July 1924

I went in the evening to *The Merry Widow* at the Lyceum expecting to be

[1] Christopher Hollis, later an MP. See Appendix of Names, p. 794.
[2] The Evelyn Waugh circle's nickname for Alec Waugh.
[3] Bartlett school of architecture, London University.
[4] Nickname for Evelyn's father, Arthur Waugh.

greatly bored. Betty Holmes[1] had drawn a box in some competition at the theatrical garden party and into it she crowded herself, an uncle, a cousin, Grace Miall, and Mrs Hipsley. Desite all this however I enjoyed my evening very greatly. The uncle proved to be an excellent man who gave me many drinks and the play was quite delightful. There was a very attractive young foreigner called Carl Brisson who played the leading part. There were some excellent romantical scenes. Altogether I liked it.

Wednesday 2 July 1924

In the evening a great crowd of people mostly OUDS[2] came to rehearse in our garden and the rain. Joan Buckmaster was beautiful but the rest were a shabby lot. Alastair and I spent most of the time dispensing drinks. The morning we had spent in shops and the afternoon in a cinema. We bought each other at Bumpus & Blackwell the most delightful book which the Nonesuch Press have just produced called *The Week End Book*.

Thursday 3 July 1924

This morning I awoke to find a letter from my bank refusing me a further overdraft. It is sad. I spent some hours in writing begging letters to my friends and some more in drawing pictures and sending them up. After lunch I went off, my mother deserting me at the last moment, to Dudley Carew's 21st birthday party. It proved, as I had expected, a sorry evening. It rained, of course, unceasingly; the folk were mostly foul, the lavatory accommodation most inadequate. The supper however and particularly the cocktails were pleasant enough. Jack Squire[3] made a speech proposing his health which in a more graceful speaker might have been amusing; it was not very lively, however, when delivered by Squire all unshaven and dirty with a Gold Flake in the corner of his mouth. I took a strong dislike to the man Squire. There was a very beautiful girl there called Rachel Mayne[4] who had been engaged to George MacDonald at one time. I think I was rather rude to her. Joan Laking,[5]

---

[1] A Waugh cousin.

[2] Oxford University Dramatic Society.

[3] J. C. Squire, a considerable literary force in the 1920s as editor of the *London Mercury* and chief reviewer of *The Observer*; a leader of the cricket-playing, beer-drinking literary establishment opposed to and by the Sitwells, T. S. Eliot, etc. Knighted 1933. The embodiment of the world from which Waugh wished to escape. Carew worked on the *London Mercury* under Squire.

[4] Head girl of Bedales co-educational school, near Petersfield, in the same term that Malcolm MacDonald, the then Prime Minister's son, was head boy.

[5] Lesbian sister of Sir Francis Laking, Bart.; she went to South Africa in the Second World War saying that she wished to be certain of the supply of gin; taken up by Smuts; died in South Africa. Waugh first met her while he was at Lancing.

of course, looking more than ever like a big game shooter. She and I discussed the *affaires* of Tasha and Tony and the repulsive Sheridan girl to the amazement of all who overheard us.

I had a bath and changed at Alec's and went on to Faith's [1] at a little after midnight. All the usual people were there including Tallulah Bankhead and the foul Gwen Farrar.[2] Francis Laking[3] was very nearly sober and to my poor brother's great gratification made serious attempts upon his virtue. Everyone mourned the passing of Alastair.

Friday 4 July 1924

Chris arrived to stay with us. He had arranged to stay with the Sutros[4] but they put him off at the last moment with rather inadequate excuses. We suspect that after the drunkenness of John he has been forbidden to invite Chris to the home again. We went in the evening to the Everyman where there was an amusing play called *Her Daughter*. Chris and I sat up beer drinking until about 1.

Saturday 5 July 1924

I went to a matinée of *Saint Joan*. Reduced by poverty I was forced to go to the gallery where after waiting for a long time in a queue I received a seat of incredible discomfort. The play however is very fine and the dresses far superior to anything which I thought could come out of Ricketts. In the evening Chris and I went to see a performance of the Hypocrites'[5] film at Great Ormond Street. It was a typically Terentian[6] evening. He had told us that Hugh Lygon[7] and the Bastard [8] and other friends would be there. When we arrived we found in their stead a sorry congregation of shits including Charles Gray and Arthur Reade and an awful journalistic major.

---

[1] Faith Wigglesworth, a hostess.

[2] Actress; popularized the song, 'It ain't gonna rain no mo', no mo'.'

[3] 3rd and last baronet. Suffered from lisp; after his father died, he answered the telephone by saying, 'Thir Guy Laking ith dead. Thith ith thir Franthith thpeaking.' Became secretary to Tallulah Bankhead, the actress; and drank himself to death on yellow chartreuse, aged twenty-eight.

[4] Wealthy St John's Wood family whose son John (see Appendix of Names, p. 794) was a lifelong friend of Waugh's.

[5] Oxford club in St Aldate's frequented by Waugh's Oxford circle. No lavatory; infested by rats; eventually closed down by the university authorities because of the drunkenness of its members.

[6] Of Terence Greenidge, an eccentric Oxford contemporary. See Appendix of Names, p. 794.

[7] Younger son of the 7th Earl Beauchamp. See Appendix of Names, p. 794.

[8] Terence Greenidge's illegitimate brother John.

Sunday 6 July 1924

We rose late and went to hear Ronnie Knox[1] preach at Westminster. The cathedral was crowded and we had to stand in one of the side aisles. He was very amusing. I lunched *tête-à-tête* with Gwen Otter[2] who brought out a collection of Wilde pamphlets which I had not seen – his preface to Rennell Rodd's poems and his correspondence with Whistler – the 'vulgarity, my dear James, begins at home and should remain there' correspondence.

I had to fetch some seats for the 300 Club from Harrington Road so I took the opportunity of calling on Jessie and Francis.[3] They were abed when I arrived and I was left with Mrs Mason for half an hour's frantic small talk. At length they arrived and were very charming. Poor Francis is already falling very much in the role of uxorious and rather jealous husband.

I dashed home to change and met Alec at the Court. The play by Richard Hughes despite excellent acting was despicable. We went on afterwards to a party at Mrs Geoffrey Whitworth's[4] where we had to say how good it was. From there we went in the Playfairs'[5] car to Elsa's[6] dance club where Ernest Milton was acting Pirandello's *Man with the flower on his lip*. It was a brilliant performance and in some measure compensated for the sorry mumming at the Court. H. G. Wells was there and nearly lost his life by a mock tree falling on his head.

Monday 7 July 1924

I awoke to find myself at Earl's Terrace[7] and 6.30. I had to get into evening clothes and travel home in the grey morning to Golders Green to wash and change and go to my dentist who entreated me despitefully.

Tuesday 8 July 1924

Alec's birthday. I went to his luncheon party and rather enjoyed it. Marston, Mrs de Lembke, Faith and a Miss Carmina or Carsima. Lots to drink. I made a cocktail first which I thought was the best part of the lunch. We went on to

[1] Ronald A. Knox (1888–1957), Roman Catholic churchman, scholar and writer. See Appendix of Names, p. 794.

[2] An 'inexhaustibly hospitable unmarried woman of middle age and slightly reduced means with the appearance of a Red Indian.' *A Little Learning*, p. 212.

[3] A moneyed couple named Palmer who ran a hairdressing establishment in Duke Street.

[4] A celebrated hostess.

[5] Nigel Playfair (1874–1934); actor–manager; at the Lyric Theatre, Hammersmith, 1920–34; famous revival of *The Beggar's Opera*, 1924. Knighted 1928.

[6] Elsa Lanchester, redheaded film actress who married Charles Laughton. In the 1920s she ran, with Harold Scott, a cabaret-nightclub named the Cave of Harmony in Charlotte Street. Her later films included *The Constant Nymph*, *The Private Life of Henry VIII* and *Mary Poppins*. The Cave of Harmony appears in Aldous Huxley's *Antic Hay* (1924).

[7] Alec Waugh lived at 22 Earl's Terrace, Kensington.

Lord's where the cricket was slow and the crowd almost entirely made up of shits.

I went back to supper at Faith's. I liked her guests and she made some exquisite pancakes. She has lost all her money poor thing.

Wednesday 9 July 1924

I made a pilgrimage to the Coliseum to see a new sort of film called 'Plastigram'. They claim for it that by means of stereoscopic photography they can obtain an impression of a third dimension. There was an elaborate apparatus of coloured celluloid to fit over one's nose and so far as we were concerned a most ineffective impression of depth. There was gasps of amazement and admiration behind us, however, so perhaps it seemed better in the more distant seats. The rest of the show was pretty good.

Thursday 10 July 1924

All Thursday I spent cricketing with Alec at a school called Clayesmore in Hampshire. We were badly beaten and I cannot claim that my contribution did much to support the honour of the side. I was caught out by the second ball and I dropped a catch. But the good cricketers behaved as ignominiously. It was quite a good day all the same. Jack Squire drove me down. He has bought a nice shabby Buick which has an amusing speedometer. When we were puffing along at a comfortable thirty-five it registered about fifty, much to poor Squire's gratification. He could not make out why the journey took so long. He has the good habit of stopping at pubs. Some of us went back afterwards to the Poetry Bookshop and drank with Harold Munro.[1]

Friday 11 July 1924

Adrian[2] came to dinner and told travellers' tales to interest my parents.

Chris turned up in the morning and told me a good story. Mr Justice Phillimore was trying a sodomy case and brooded greatly whether his judgement had been right. He went to consult Birkenhead. 'Excuse me, my lord, but could you tell me – What do you think one ought to give a man who allows himself to be buggered?' 'Oh, 30s or £2 – anything you happen to have on you.'

Saturday 12 July 1924

I went in the morning to the Mestrovic exhibition and was overwhelmed by its excellence. I must go on a pilgrimage to the chapel he has designed near Ragusa. After that in great heat I went down Bond Street and St James's – the

---

[1] Proprietor of the Poetry Bookshop in Great Russell Street, whose purpose was to promote modern poetry.

[2] Adrian Stokes, philosopher of art. See Appendix of Names, p. 794.

pavements quite red hot – to the London Museum at Stafford House and was lost in admiration of the delightful disarrangements of Battersea enamels and Chelsea figures and murder broadsheets.

In the evening Keith Chesterton[1] was giving a party at her garret at 3 Fleet Street. There were a comic collection of all the early Cave of Harmony set – pansies, prostitutes and journalists and struggling actors all quite quite drunk and in patches lusty. —— with whom —— sodomizes was there, and Elsa, but they were practically the only people I knew so I contented myself with climbing the roofs. Alec turned up late and a little drunk and, after his fashion, fixed upon the ugliest woman in the room, bore her off and lechered with her. Elsa sang some few cockney songs including the *Yiddisher Boy* which I love. The man who wrote that delightful parody of *Our Betters* in the Little Revue was there; he acted a rather ineffective melodrama and then went off to bed with Evadne Price. I got home in broad daylight at 5 and this morning feel more than a little weary.

Monday 21 July 1924

More than a week has passed but I cannot quite remember how. I went out with Adrian one evening and overdrank mysef with Terence another and I have been to many cinemas. The dentist has taken up several mornings. I have drawn a book cover for Gustave.[2] Alastair is at Barford and yesterday I answered a despairing letter from Mrs G. asking me to persuade Alastair to remain in England for the winter. John the Bastard has introduced me to a lovely new game by which one makes a short circuit on the telephone and causes it to sing, but only a few instruments are capable of making the sound.

I began *The Temple at Thatch* last night and have written a dozen pages of the first chapter.[3] I think it is quite good.

Terence and I purpose to produce a cinema film[4] about the Pope and the Prince of Wales.

[1] Mrs Cecil Chesterton, always referred to as 'Keith'. She wrote under the name J. K. Prothero.

[2] The publisher Cecil Palmer.

[3] The plot concerned an undergraduate who inherited an eighteenth-century folly.

[4] Waugh and Greenidge bought a small camera and produced a film that ran for twenty minutes, using as background Oxford, the Waughs' garden and Hampstead Heath. The story was a fantasy of the attempts of 'Sligger' Urquhart, the Dean of Balliol, to convert the King to Roman Catholicism. Waugh played the Dean, Elsa Lanchester played Beatrice de Carolle, a cabaret singer of 'Evangelical principles', John Sutro played Cardinal Montefiasco, Lord Elmley played the Lord Chamberlain, Guy Hemingway played the Pope, Alec Waugh played the Cardinal's old mother, and Greenidge played the Prince of Wales, who approaches the Pope with homosexual intent. The titles read: 'Evelyn Waugh by arrangement with Terence Greenidge presents THE SCARLET WOMAN, An Ecclesiastical Melodrama; story by Evelyn Waugh.' Later, the words 'Nihil obstat – Projiciatur C. C. Martindale, sj' were added to the titles. Four copies of the film exist.

Written on 1 September 1924

There is an enormous gap to be made up in which I have done a thousand things. On Sunday 27 July I left London quite suddenly for Beckley.[1] The week before was hectic with cinema work and extremely expensive. Looking back on it I think the money was ill spent. The film cost us each £6, the hire of the dresses and taxi fares added heavily, and on Saturday night I gave a dinner to Elsa Lanchester which cost £4. This last item, however, I do not regret because it was a most jolly evening. Alec and Terence and Elsa and I had dinner at Previtali's and then drank at a Bodega and then at the Café Royal. In the end we went back to Great Ormond Street where we found Major Whitaker entertaining his woman and her mother and sister. We were all a little drunk. Terence put on the cinema and I was quite disgusted with the badness of the film. Elsa and I discovered that we were born on the same day and fought all over the floor for a pound note which eventually became destroyed. Alec and I took back one of the banisters in our taxi so I think we must have been consoled for the badness of the film.

The film is not finished yet owing to the desertion of Elmley and I feel no enthusiasm to finish it.

Just before I left Graham Pollard[2] nearly stopped my whole expedition by behaving atrociously about my money.

I arrived at Beckley in the late evening having walked all the way from the station bearing a bag and found Alastair in the caravan. We spent a quiet evening in the pub.

The next day was I think one of the most wretched that ever I spent. It began at about 2 with pouring rain coming through the roof of the caravan. Alastair was ill in the morning. I cooked myself a breakfast and ate it alone and in silence and went out to read Gibbon in the church. On my return at about 11 I found Alastair restored to health and nearly dressed. We walked, in the rain, into Oxford where he had promised a luncheon to Richard Plunket Greene.[3] We ate it expensively at the George where the cooking was as always foul. We found all sorts of most unattractive acquaintances. We drank about four vodkas each. We went down to Richard's rooms in the old Hypocrites' Club and drank whisky until dinner. After dinner Alastair had to take a woman of the town to a cinema. I ordered some bottles of champagne at the George and gave a post-

---

[1] Village near Oxford. Waugh and Alastair Graham stayed regularly at the pub during this period, sometimes in a caravan in the garden.

[2] Author and bibliographer, b. 1903. Partner in Birrell & Garnett, antiquarian booksellers, 1924–38.

[3] 'In the course of the autumn [of 1924] I had fallen in love. I had in fact fallen in love with an entire family.' *A Little Learning*, p. 216. The family, the Plunket Greenes, consisted of Mrs Plunket Greene (Gwen), Richard, David and Olivia. Richard Plunket Greene and Waugh first met at an Oxford party, where they had a fight. See Appendix of Names, p. 794.

dated cheque for them and became utterly drunk. All sorts of queer persons turned up, Bullock and David Rice in his car; we went into some pubs and I broke a glass and quarrelled with a man. We went back to Richard's rooms and drank more. Everyone went out on some quest and left Alastair and me to quarrel alone. Eventually I went to bed and slept.

Things were more cheerful next morning. I ate melons and walked before breakfast and then went about hiring a bicycle and doing some shopping. At lunch-time I got back to the caravan to find Alastair already arrived and strangely enough Joyce Fagan who had slept the night there. We ate part of the ham we had bought and drank beer. It still rained. Joyce had to go off in the evening and we went to dinner with Squire Cooke[1] who had a nephew − Tommy Beechcroft's elder brother − staying with him. He gave us some admirable ducks grown by Mr Higgs[2] and plenty to drink. When he had lapsed into muttering we went home to our caravan.

Wednesday 28 July 1924

In the morning I wrestled with a cover design for Dudley Carew's novel, which by the way I thought much better of than I had expected. After luncheon Alastair and I went on bicycles to his old home at Bucknell[3] and thence to Bicester where we drank in a pub until about 8. There was a big feast on at Beckley to which we had been invited. First there were sports and a cricket match and then at 4 an enormous meal in the big barn next to the pub. From then until about 3 in the morning the whole village sat and ate and drank and danced and sang. It was a most delightful evening. Harold Claire[4] was very, very drunk, but an excellent host to Alastair and myself, continually filling our glasses and introducing us to people. We danced with Mrs Mattingley[5] several times and drank pints of beer. Mr Higgs was well drunk. Cooke came in for a little and embraced a small boy. We went to bed long before it was over. Later we heard that it ended with Harold hitting the policeman on the head and then falling down in the road and cutting himself open.

Thursday 29 July–Saturday 30 August 1924

In the morning I had my viva. I went to the Schools at 9.30 am dressed in a dark coat, a scholar's gown and a white tie. I was told to come back again in an hour. I went out and was given a large whisky by my kindly wine merchant. I then went to a jeweller called Payne and bought for Alastair a little 1800

---

[1] Elderly local squire living in the village manor house.
[2] Local farmer.
[3] Bucknell Manor, where Alastair Graham was born.
[4] Local farmer's boy.
[5] Landlady of the Beckley pub.

mourning ring and for myself a very beautiful cameo which cost £7 10s, a sum I can ill afford. I do not in any way regret having bought it however. I do not yet know what the heads signify. There are two bearded ones, one clean-shaven of either a woman or youth, and a ram; in the centre a ram's horn. It is cut in four layers of onyx and three colours. The setting is plain and pleasant. My viva was purely formal. I telegraphed to my parents to inform them of my certain third and returned much dispirited to Beckley.

Next morning on the way to the station to meet Philip Machin I looked in at the Schools and learned that my forebodings had been fully justified. We met Philip, lunched heavily at the George, drank with Richard Greene, drank at the Union, and rode back to Beckley where we drank champagne. Philip was not feeling at all well but the rest of us were happy. It was a very drunken night at the Abingdon Arms. Next day we dined with Cooke and Harold,[1] and he and Mrs Mattingley came back to the caravan when the pub shut and drank champagne with us and Alastair and I gave a brooch to Mrs Mattingley which we had bought at Payne's.

Next morning Sunday we asked for our bill and found it very heavy. We went into Oxford in the car and took a train to Leamington leaving Philip to go by another train to Pershore. The mechanical Mr Shaw met us and drove us very late for luncheon to Barford.[2] The house was full of folk – the Hicksons[3] and child and nurse, Daisy Lowe, and some nice people called Anderson, Lord Derby's agent. On Sunday night we played bridge and on Monday roulette; I won a little at both games. We discovered to our consternation that Monday was bank holiday and that our train on Tuesday left before the hour for the opening of banks. We managed however by clearing the entire household of cash to get £10. With this we set off for Ireland. The Queen Mother was angry at our going because she wanted us to accompany her on a motor tour. I have omitted to record a singularly grim day when she had come over to Beckley to see us with an enormous luncheon and the amorous Mrs Fenton.[4] She was in sorrow and anger about Alastair's African expedition and made everything hideously uncomfortable. Alastair did little to brighten things.

We went by train from Stratford to Holyhead and from there by boat to Kingstown and by train to Dublin. On the boat, to the first-class part of which

[1] Harold Claire.

[2] Barford House, near Warwick, Alastair Graham's home. Between January 1924 and August 1932 Waugh stayed at Barford at least twenty-one times, sometimes staying as long as three weeks. He would often retreat there when he was broke, or wanting to escape. There was a room under roof that had been a lady's maid 'cutting out' room, furnished only with a table and chair and an armless and legless dummy, of stuffed scarlet rep, representing the Victorian lady's ideal figure. This room was called the Cock-loft, and Waugh would retire there to be undisturbed. He wrote part of *Decline and Fall* in this room.

[3] Alastair Graham's sister and her husband from Kenya.

[4] Mrs Graham's companion.

we had drifted unawares, we found L. A. G. Strong[1] returning to Ireland after ten years' absence. The crossing was extremely smooth, the boat rather laden with people going to the Horse Show. We arrived in Dublin at dusk and took a cab to Jammet's, the hotel which Billy[2] had recommended. We found that it was only a restaurant – during the next few weeks we gradually learned that all Billy had told us about his country was wholly false. We accordingly ordered a table there for dinner and drove to a large, pretentious, incompetent, and exceedingly expensive hostelry called Jury's where we were given a minute double-bedroom in the attics which a simple calculation showed us we could not possibly afford for more than one night. We looked at Dublin and, hungry and dispirited, found it a most unattractive place full of barbed wire and ruins and soldiers and unemployed. We found a Bodega however and drank some sherry and we ate a most admirable dinner and drank some port at the Bodega and felt happier. I think that I have never been so much attracted by any restaurant as by Jammet's. The decorations are bad, but it is in a decent house, eighteenth-century with balcony. The tables are steady and a long way apart; the waiters elderly, the cooking distinctly good. All the people who used it looked decent people too, which could not be said for Jury's. We were surprised in the Bodega by a switching on and off of the lights at 9 o'clock. We asked what this meant and were told that public houses closed at 9 in Dublin (Billy had told us that they stayed open until 12). I suppose it is because all big political movements in Ireland start in the pubs. We wandered out and with more tolerant eyes saw a little more of Dublin, but even now I did not like it much. We retired to bed and slept badly. Outside the cobbled street sent up a continual clatter; inside the servants shouted and crashed and even on one occasion invaded our bedroom.

In the morning, being poor, we had to choose between a bad breakfast and a bad luncheon, a good breakfast and no luncheon, or no breakfast and good luncheon. We wisely chose the last and, fasting, rose up and went to the Irish National Gallery. It really is not at all a bad collection, rich in the cheaper things such as seventeenth-century Dutch game and still life. There was an exquisitely bonny Madonna and Child by one Lorenzo d'Angelo which made us laugh loudly and shock some Dublin souls. There was also some pleasant British painting of the last two centuries. We also visited Trinity Library to see the Book of Kells. I was much amused at the binding on a copy of Parnell's poems.

We lunched at Jammet's. In the lavatory, drying my hands, I dropped the ring and chipped off a piece of stone – a curl on one of the foreheads. We went to Rathdrum by an afternoon train full of uninteresting people. Rathdrum, like, as I found later, most towns in Ireland, reminded me strongly of

[1] Irish-born writer (1896–1958) of novels, verse, criticism and plays.
[2] Lord Clonmore, later the 8th Earl of Wicklow. See Appendix of Names, p. 794.

Shoreham. In about ten minutes of our arrival a jaunting car arrived from Glenmalure driven by a cheery old man who told us long and unintelligible stories all the way to the hotel – about seven miles.

At Glenmalure we spent nine days which were for me the least amusing part of our wanderings. The hotel was uncomfortable; Terence had decamped to Lundy with Alastair's money, and all the time we were suffering from acute financial embarrassments; the hills which delighted Alastair's heart did not excite me overmuch. We had an awful fear on the first night that we had come to a Temperance Hotel. All the ash-trays and things advertised mineral-waters, and a pot of tea was brought to us at dinner. We found, however, that at great expense we could obtain a ghastly sort of ale, very fizzy and tasting strongly of baking powder, or a spirituous liquor – a mixture of bad rum, bad gin, and bad vodka called whisky – or, of course, the ubiquitous Bass. There were, besides ourselves, two parties staying at the pub. A terrible woman with bald husband and friend called Mrs Gwatkin who came from Cambridge and whipped everyone, and a party of little boys and girls all very vicious and *tiers d'état*. Later a melancholy soldier came to shoot grouse but without any success. He was poor and engaged to be married but was friendlily disposed and not a bad man really.

We walked a lot at Glenmalure and telegraphed for money a good deal which eventually arrived. The day I enjoyed most was when we walked to Glendaloch and saw the seven churches and lay in St Kevin's bed. It rained a lot and the flies were most trying. On the whole I did not enjoy Glenmalure. One thing of profit happened. We buried my stick in a peat bog to see if it would colour it and it turned quite black.

On the day after our money arrived we left Glenmalure. It was the day of the Assumption and everyone was going to Mass as we went to the station. We travelled to Dublin with a rather amusing mad woman who discussed very seriously the relative merits, as a drink, of whisky or methylated spirit.

In Dublin we lunched at Jammet's and drank at our Bodega until our train at 5. This took us through a much desolated land to Cahir. Our telegram had not been delivered but we were given a room at the only hotel in the town – a very good place called Burke's. From there in the morning we took, after some successful bargaining, an unspeakably dissolute motor in which we went as far as Newcastle. We gave our man a drink and parted company with him and walked to Mount Mellorey Abbey about seven miles over the hills.

The approach to the abbey was rather ghastly. The whole road up to it was filled with shabby and crowded cars – apparently it is a great place for holidaymakers for miles round. There was a little shop where they could buy horrible pious emblems and books. I bought an amusing temperance reader there and Alastair a prayer book in a celluloid cover. We were led to the guest house which is shut away from the trippers and kept waiting for some time in a hall. We discovered here that the monastery did not keep new time[1] which was rather a relief because it was, by our clock, 3, and we had had no luncheon. We were given a large meal of bread and cold meat and milk in a large refectory decorated with bad religious pictures and led to our bedroom which tho' cold was quite comfortable. All the time we were at Mellorey I was cold – it was altogether very much like Lancing. We stayed at the abbey for two nights. It rained all the time and we felt the need of some sitting-room sorely. There were hosts of other visitors, mostly I think on retreat. We went over the seminary and the farm and some of the monastery and we went to several services which were very well done – at Glenmalure the priest had belched into the chalice.

On Monday we took a jaunting car as far as Cappoquin and from there walked to Cappagh arriving in the middle of the Usshers' luncheon. The household consisted of Beverley[2] – very mad – a nymphomaniacal housekeeper and Percy,[3] whose appearance was extraordinary but his heart of gold. We stayed at Cappagh until Friday night. Terence's money was waiting there for us so we were able to drink much with Percy who proved an excellent pub man. At Beverley's table there was only bad claret.

On our last morning we got very drunk. The House of Ussher was very ugly, built by his father in 1860. The old house just below was now used for stables, bailiff's house, and the headquarters of some incredible ruffians called the Civic Guard whose chief activity was mocking the village idiot. His servants were a dozen or so rebellious farm-labourers and, in the house, two raw girls whose excitement at the presence of two strange young men was sufficient to drive them into hysteria whenever we met them. The journey home at Mrs G.'s urgent summons was most uncomfortable particularly for one just recovering from drunkenness. I did not feel well until I had had a long and very hot bath at Barford, changed, and eaten a large dinner. The taste of draught beer was very welcome again.

When we arrived Mrs G. said she would not now go for the motor tour. All through the week I spent at Barford she was extremely quarrelsome. On Monday morning she was furious because we wanted the car to take to Oxford. We got it in the end however and spent a pleasant enough day. We went to Beckley for half an hour to call for a stick Alastair had left there. Mrs Mattingley gave us a drink and told us the village gossip. It seems that Cooke is really selling his house. Mr Higgs, who had never left Oxfordshire, went to the Empire Exhibition at Wembley and returned very drunk but much impressed by its beauty and grandeur. We called on Cooke and drank with him.

I should have said that on our way home we had some time to waste in

[1] The standard time, in advance of ordinary time, adopted in the summer of 1916.

[2] Father of the Ussher family.

[3] Percy Ussher (b. 1897): Irish poet whose portrait by Augustus John hangs in the Swedish National Gallery in Stockholm.

Bristol. We saw the Church of St Mary Redcliffe and bought some books, I a book on Salisbury Cathedral of which the binding fascinated me for the modest sum of 6s. Jane[1] and the Hicksons arrived soon after us. Jane was extremely friendly to me and led me about the gardens burbling quite incoherent narrations. I liked her.

On Friday Alastair and I drove to a village called Chesterton where there is a lovely little church and a magnificent 1880 coloured alabaster tomb of one of the Peytos.

On Saturday I returned by a luncheon train. There is in the house a horrible wireless apparatus but no dog. My father brought out for my use a silver mug which I like greatly.

Hampstead, Monday 1 September 1924

Most of the day writing this diary. In the afternoon to a cinema. *Resolved* to go to no more cinemas promiscuously.

Wednesday 3 September 1924

In spite of my earnest resolution never again to waste time at a cinema I have spent both yesterday and this afternoon in that unprofitable way. I am ashamed and more than ever strengthened in my resolution. I have written some more of *The Temple*. I have also fixed to go to Heatherley's[2] on the 18th of this month – the day of Alastair's embarkation. My mother has invited her half-sister Emma to stay next week with us, to the profound dismay of her husband and son. Eugene Goossens[3] is in the bankruptcy court. I have just been listening to my father's new electrical machine. I think it a tiresome toy.

Thursday 4 September 1924

Last night I slept ill; I think through excess of cinemas. I went to two yesterday. One, alone, to fill in the time until dinner, and one after dinner with Adrian. Adrian gave me dinner at a beastly place in Charlotte Street full of niggers. The food too was not good. Afterwards we drank yellow chartreuse at the Café Royal which restored me to a good opinion of the universe.

Saturday 6 September 1924

At work industriously on *The Temple*. I find it in serious danger of becoming dull. Rather an amusing incident has happened about the Queen's Dolls' House. One, John Pennell, is a manager at Rivieres, the binders who have done all the work for the royal library. As a small perquisite it was allowed him to

[1] Alastair Graham's infant niece.

[2] Art school; then in Newman Street, London.

[3] Musician and conductor (1893–1962); conductor of the Cincinnati Symphony Orchestra, 1931–47.

have the honour of inserting some small contribution by himself. He accordingly compiled a little book of unspeakable futility and called it *Thoughts*. This innocent work would have gone quite unnoticed had not Her Majesty decided that it would be a seemly act of grace personally to thank all who had contributed to her toy. When it came to Mr Pennell's turn it was not unnaturally assumed that J. Pennell must be Joseph Pennell[1] and a letter was accordingly sent to him in America. He has published a letter asserting with considerable asperity that not only was he never invited to contribute but that he was prepared to see the entire Royal Family damned before he would have considered such an offer. The result is that poor Mr Pennell's little book of platitudes has attained a most humiliating prominence. E. V. Lucas[2] the librarian has made the statement that the book seemed to him so silly that he assumed its author must have been Joseph Pennell.

Sunday 7 September 1924

Still at work on *The Temple*. A suspicion settles on me that it will never be finished.

Tuesday 9 September 1924

There has arrived in the house one Emma Raban, an half-sister to my mother, who makes life very heavy to me. I cannot write or think or eat, I hate her so.

Yesterday the importunance of my mother induced me to suffer the degrading ordeal of being photographed. A place in New Bond Street called Swaine had offered to do it free. I think it must be the worst shop in London. I waited half an hour in a drawing-room furnished with enormous photographs of the Royal Family. Then I was taken up to the 'studio' where a repulsive little man attempted to be genial while two other men worked a camera. I am confident that it will be an abominable photograph.

I dined with Dudley Carew at his expense at the Previtali and went with him to the gallery at Covent Garden to see the first night of Pavlova's season. The seats were most discomfortable, and to see at all well we were forced to stand up. The theatre was inexpressibly hot. Mme Pavlova herself was of course enchanting but the big ballet *Don Quixote* did not seem to me very remarkable. I gained most pleasure from a tiny Chinese dance by two people whose names I have forgotten.

The audience was most curious. I think I have never seen so many repulsive people in so short a space of time as I saw in the gallery bar. There was one young Jew in sandals who caused comment.

[1] American graphic artist (1857–1926); lived in London, 1884–1918; vast output of etchings and lithographs; his lithograph is the only pictorial record of the 1911 Coronation.

[2] Essayist and man of letters (1868–1938).

Wednesday 10 September 1924

All day yesterday I read with great interest Harold Speed's book on Oil Painting. The horrid visit of Emma Raban continues and my nerves are stretched to a tension which makes all writing impossible.

Friday 12 September 1924

Emma Raban left us. I went to London in the hope of selling a book but ended in buying a set of Chesterton's letters to his son from Mr Hatchard at the price of 35s. I hope that the cheque will be honoured.

Saturday 13 September 1924

Alastair joined the Italian Church. I met him at Paddington and he came out to Golders Green.

Sunday 14 September 1924

I went with Alastair to Mass at a church in Hampstead – very ugly – and drank with him at the Bull and Bush at fairly frequent intervals during the day.

Oxford, Monday 15 September 1924

Alastair and I went marketing during the morning. We bought him a very shoddy little suit of thin tropical stuff and some snuff. He bought me a Bible which I like very much indeed. It contains Common Prayer (1663), Old Testament (1608), New Testament (1663), and Metrical Psalms (1663), bound together in dark olive-green morocco with tooling and silver corners and boss in the middle. The New Testament is largely illustrated with engravings. Alastair bought a breviary. Dudley Carew gave us luncheon at the Previtali and we set off to go to Oxford where Alastair had engaged to take communion and to breakfast with Father Martindale. We went on the dinner train having waited for it in a cinema and journeyed down comfortably. I was wholly without money and Alastair was paying all my expenses. We spent the evening saying goodbye to everyone at the Nag's Head and went back to sleep discomfortably enough at 31 St Aldate's[1] in clothes and on benches.

Tuesday 16 September 1924

Next morning we did a round of pubs and were tired by the companionship of Freddy Maxse whom I was rash enough to invite to drink with us. I should have liked to go home that evening but in respect for Alastair's reluctance and the shortness of the time left to him in England I agreed to stay. I am sure now that it will be the last night I shall spend in Oxford for a long time. Everything was inexpressibly sordid; I hated 31 St Aldate's for its discomfort and its

[1] Richard Plunket Greene's digs; formerly the premises of the Hyprocrites' Club.

associations; I found Richard Plunket Greene very exasperating. We dined with him at the George where the food was as usual disgusting and to make things less agreeable he insisted on arranging with the waitress to lie with her after the meal. Even the pubs were not comforting because, since we had made so many farewells, we could hardly return to the Nag's Head and were forced to go to a place called the Paviour's Arms where there was nothing except pimps and procuresses, except one mad man. Another uncomfortable night and we returned home very early. We bathed and ate and then Alastair went away to see his mother and I went to tea at Jane Marston's. She was looking more beautiful than I had seen her since her first pregnancy; the babies are like all others except that the girl is bald. The midwife who took tea with us was beastly. I told her Alastair's theory that cancer is caused by wireless but it did not amuse her.

After dinner, heralded by a telephone call, Mrs G. and Alastair arrived. I felt that the house was too small for the electrical energy of the Queen Mother. We drank a little after her departure and then glad of sleep went to bed.

Hampstead, Thursday 18 September 1924

Alastair left London at 11.40. We were not allowed to come to the boat with him. Before he went we had to spend a great time hectically finding luggage and relatives. Hamish Guthrie[1] and his wife came to see him off. Sybil Graham[2] carried a thousand parcels. After he went, feeling more than a little disconsolate, I wandered about London all day. I lunched with the Queen Mother and dined with Adrian. Between those times I went to a cinema which I could not bear and to the British Museum and to a Bodega where I spent all the little money that was left of my month's wages. With Adrian I walked miles and went to a cinema and drank beer.

The most important thing I have forgotten. I went almost immediately after luncheon to examine Heatherley's. There are things about it that I find most forbidding; for instance a palette of various colours is hung out of the window for a sign, the students whom I passed on the stairs and saw during a glance into the studio seemed to me very much 'students'. However I expect that it will serve.

Friday 19 September 1924

Today my life of poverty, chastity and obedience commences. My mother is purchasing a dog.

Sunday 21 September 1924

My mother's dog[3] is really rather charming; all the interest of the household

---

[1] Friend of Alastair Graham's; married four times; all four wives attended his funeral.
[2] Alastair Graham's sister.
[3] A poodle named Gaspard.

centres upon him. This morning I received communion with my parents at St Alban's Church; there was much flustering and retching by my father before the ceremony.

The last two days I have spent in working at my book. I do not think it is very good.

Monday 22 September 1924

Today I went for the first time to Heatherley's. I have not yet mastered the geography of the place but I have discovered two studios, an office, and a passage for the hanging of coats and hats. It is all agreeable, unlike the government-office atmosphere of the Slade. The studios are hung with skeletons and paintings and armour. I was put into the downstairs studio with a sketch-book of tissue paper and (to my surprise) a BBB pencil and set to draw a thin man with no clothes but a bag about his genitalia sitting cross-legged. I made an amateurish little sketch for which the kindly Mr Massey praised me. He, the headmaster, must I think be a good bottle man; he has a purple nose above a little white beard and a hand which trembles so much that when he attempts a demonstration the chalk breaks into a hundred pieces. Then all the girls giggle at him.

The whole place is full of girls – underbred houris most of them in gaudy overalls; they draw very badly and get much in the way of the youths who seem to be all of them bent upon making commercial careers for themselves by illustrating *Punch* or advertising things. It does not seem to me likely that I shall find any pals among them.

I lunched on minestrone and cheese to the open contempt of the new waiter at the Previtali and returned to find a 'quick sketch' class in progress which I found exceedingly diverting. The model was a young girl with a very graceful body and a face rather like Hugh Lygon's when he is very drunk. She would have been more pleasure to draw had she been able to keep still in the longer poses.

The day's work ended at 4 o'clock.

Saturday 27 September 1924

Ill-accustomed as I am to work I find my drawing school most exhausting. Every evening I return wishing to do nothing except eat a prodigious dinner and go early to bed after an evening of desultory conversation or, less profitably still, in 'listening in' to Chapman & Hall's horrible wireless. The result is that I have read nothing or written nothing for a week. On Wednesday I had a bad luncheon with Mrs Neville-Smith whom I liked greatly. I think I will go to spend a weekend with her some time in the term. I should like to see Dick again.

I think that my drawing is getting a little better.

On Friday I took tea en famille with Charles James and found him restless and his sisters noisy and his father's butler in pince-nez.

Sunday 28 September 1924

There came to tea, among other and less exciting people, D. S. McColl, who was curator of the Tate and is now at the Wallace Collection. Father after his usual custom talked about the accomplishments of his sons and sheepishly enough I was made to show some of my drawings. McColl was extremely kind about them. I think he may be useful.

Monday 29 September 1924

Again to Heatherley's, which I find somewhat unsatisfactory. Massey today insisted upon everyone giving a title to his or her drawing which seemed to me a silly sort of imposition. I lunched with Adrian and gave tea to my cousin Betty Holmes at Ridgeways.

Tuesday 30 September 1924

In the morning I drew so entirely to my own satisfaction that I decided not to return in the afternoon. Instead I went to the Soane's Museum in Lincoln's Inn Fields where I saw much to amuse me. The pride of the curator would appear to be a sarcophagus of great antiquity in the basement, but this caused me far less pleasure than the arrangements of the lighting in the rooms and such preposterous things as the Shakespeare Shrine halfway upstairs and the Bank of England Shrine in the study. They have several original Turners and Hogarths – *The Rake's Progress* and the *Election* set exquisitely composed but very ill painted. A sad couple from the Dominions went round with me. Their only interest was in the signatures on the paintings. They were fresh from the glories of Wembley but as they left the man said, 'Extraordinary thing, but there seem to be a lot of things we aren't any better at doing.' So perhaps he had learned something.

With my father later to *The Hunchback of Notre Dame*. Very gorgeous and sadistical and so home.

Wednesday 1 October 1924

This morning I received from my father the sum of £80 to pay some bills with and support the expenses of life.

Thursday 2 October 1924

This morning I drew very badly and became exceedingly weary of the model and of charcoal. I lunched at Previtali alone and returned to do much better. On my way home across the top of the Heath there was a smell of couch fire and

I became curiously cheered. This evening however a woman called White-house has come to stay and the pleasure is departed.

Monday 6 October 1924

Again I have many days to account for of such unvarying monotony as hardly to allow my mention. On Friday I lunched with Alec at Previtali, which, I observe, is gradually becoming more expensive, and returned to Newman Street to draw very well indeed. On Friday evening I read again and with vast delight Drummond of Hawthornden's *Cypress Grove*. On Saturday I wrote more of *The Temple of Thatch* which I consider calling *The Fabulous Paladins* after a passage from a *Cypress Grove*.

On Sunday for the first time for many days I broke from my seclusion and went to tea with Alec to the house of a woman called Hansard[1] with whom I fell immoderately in love. She is all pearls and lace and ivory and a most intelligent collector of furniture and china and fans and pictures.

Today I have developed a cold which saddens me. I have also drawn badly.

Friday 10 October 1924

I stayed at home on Tuesday and Wednesday being troubled with a cold and employed myself in drawing bookplates. One for Dudley Carew a pastoral of pot-boiling and one for my father – armorial. Yesterday and today I have been at Heatherley's, where I progressed a little but not as much as I should like.

The Government fell yesterday and everyone is again beginning election campaigns; I have offered to help Squire at Chiswick.[2] I lunched yesterday at Hatchett's with Driberg on his way to Oxford – anyone going that way has my sympathy. Dudley's book is being held back over the election.

Saturday 11 October 1924

I went in the morning to the private view of the London Group's exhibition at Heal's. It was indeed a show to make one sad. Two still lives by Gertler, some pretty, clean painting by Ethelbert White and one or two caricatures were the only remotely interesting pictures. Everything else was so much mud: tedious, slovenly, and self-assertive. We met Oliver Simon there also who edits the *Fleuron* and plays cricket.

Wednesday 29 October 1924

Yesterday I became a man and put away childish things. I did little to celebrate the occasion except to go to luncheon with Tony at Previtali and

[1] Mrs Hansard, owner of a large house in Cadogan Gardens containing a collection of Limoges; married to a descendant of Luke Hansard (1752–1828), the printer of the House of Commons journals from 1774.

[2] Squire was standing as a Liberal.

afterward to the Stoll Cinema alone instead of returning to Heatherley's. Joyce came to dinner. I have received more presents than I expected – my father, besides the silver mug, remitted the 4 guineas which I have owed him since the Glenmalure telegram and gave me £5 besides – 'most like a gentleman' I think. Jean Fleming and her sister sent me an exquisite snuff-box which hourly affords me greater delight. At first I did not like it overmuch. It has on a casual inspection much the appearance of those tiresome toys which black men make out of brass and steel. But it was made a long time ago by white men out of silver and gold and is work in the most subtle and delicate manner. I think that it must originally have been a tinder-box, because there are two little screws inexplicable except as the remains of one of those hinged nutmeg graters one sees in tinder-boxes.

I was signally neglected by Oxford except by Fulford and Fremlin who sent me the Beaumont Press edition of Symons's *Café Royal and Other Essays* – a book which I have sometimes wanted to buy. On the whole I enjoyed yesterday infinitely more than I enjoyed the same day last year. I remember I gave a tiny dinner party with prodigious quantities of champagne at the Carlton Club and that Alastair could not come because he had drunk too much the night before and that we went back to John Sutro's room in Oriel Street and cheered a man called Walsh and lots of people came in with presents of alcohol which they drank. It was rather a dreary evening as far as I remember it.

In the week following the last entry in this diary I learned that it is not possible to lead a gay life and to draw well. On the Sunday I went with Alec to luncheon with E. S. P. Haynes.[1] He is a highly intelligent man so corpulent that he has to bear the weight of his belly upon his shoulders by means of a patent truss built for him by Arbuthnot Lane. He gave us to drink a bottle each of vintage burgundy, two different kinds of port, and an infinite amount of 1870 brandy drunk out of tumblers as is fitting and right. By the time that I left his house I was, I regret to record, far from sober.[2] My next clear memory is being found at dinner-time in the Long Bar of the Trocadero by Tony and a friend of his called Bill Silk. I had in the intervening time taken tea with Gwen Otter, but I cannot remember what occurred there except that she invited me to luncheon to meet Ernest Thesiger.[3] With Tony and the man Silk, who appeared to be a good fellow, deeply devoted to Tony, I dined at Previtali and drank chartreuse at the Café Royal until it closed. Then much the worse for drink we went to Elsa's cabaret where I bought a bottle of whisky. I met Joyce there and insisted on presenting her with my ring which she was generous

[1] Lawyer. See Appendix of Names, p. 794.
[2] Mrs Waugh subsequently reproved Alec for taking Evelyn to this lunch with Haynes; she thought it disrupted the orderly life to which Evelyn was beginning to settle down and started his subsequent decline.
[3] Prominent actor.

enough to give back to me later. I am afraid I was over rude to poor Goldring[1] and to the exquisite Angela Baddeley.[2] Baldhead hated me. My cousins Holmes were there and cannot have formed a high opinion of my reformed London life.

It was a lot to drink after so quiet a month and next day I felt far from happy. I could not draw anything at all, all day, and returned disconsolate and in debt to Elsa to the extent of 30s. On Tuesday I spent a drinking night with Franky Filleul; also expensive on Wednesday with Joyce, and on Thursday with Tony and Bill Silk at his mother's flat who, curiously, is called Mrs Bonham-Carter.[3] By the end of the week I felt fit for very little. On Sunday I went to luncheon with Gwen to meet Ernest Thesiger but the meal was not a success. Thesiger was incredibly rude to me and for some time I could not discover why. I learned next day that Tony had been very drunk at a homosexual party the night before and had told Thesiger that he was to have come to lunch at Ralston Street next day but that I had refused to arrange the meeting on account of Thesiger's well-known tastes. Tony seems also to have mocked pretty heavily. I took tea with poor lecherous Mrs Jepson and after dinner went to a literary party at Mrs Geoffrey Whitworth's. I liked it more than I had expected. Nigel Playfair drove me on to Elsa's at about 11.30 where we found a highly indecent but very incoherent seventeenth-century Italian comedy being enacted. I thought it as well to put in a sober appearance there. I am afraid Joyce went off to copulate with the toad Goldring but this may not be so.

The next week due chiefly to poverty was much more quiet. On Friday Denise Peel whom Alec wants to marry came to dinner. I liked her but discerned at once that she was flagellant – a suspicion which Alec has confirmed. On Saturday Rupert Fremlin came to London and we lunched together and went to Kennington's[4] exhibition at the Leicester Galleries – some very distinguished draughtsmanship and some mighty tedious landscape painting. There was also some insufferable stuff by Lucien Pissarro (Junior).

Mad Beverley spent the weekend with us and bought a car. He announced the sorrowful news, which Alastair and I had suspected at Cappagh, that Percy Ussher will marry the housekeeper.

I have come to the conclusion that accurate drawing only matters in this way, that one must have complete complete control of one's tool and that a very excellent test of this control is one's ability to draw a human figure accurately,

---

[1] Douglas Goldring, literary agent and novelist. Responsible for the publication of J. E. Flecker's *The Golden Journey to Samarkand*. His novel *The Fortune* was hailed by T. S. Eliot as 'unquestionably a brilliant novel'.

[2] Actress (1904–76). She married in 1929 the producer and director Glen Byam Shaw.

[3] Silk's mother, an Irish widow, Mrs Eileen Silk, married Norman Bonham-Carter of the East Bengal Police. Silk died of drink in the early 1930s.

[4] Eric Kennington (1888–1960), artist; friend of T. E. Lawrence; illustrated the 1926 edition of *The Seven Pillars of Wisdom*.

because in doing so one is setting oneself a standard to which it is possible to apply pertinent criticism. I do not think that form or the vision of form matter at all. If one has control one may draw what one pleases and it cannot matter what one is pleased to see.

Friday 7 November 1924

In a short time I start for Barford. During the last week I have lived a life of sombre decency quite unbroken. My aunt Constance, in the absence of my mother with her relatives, came to keep house for us. I was surprised on seeing her again after a considerable time to find she is every bit as crazy as my Raban relatives. I think that perhaps it is virginity which makes elderly women mad when they suddenly realize that it is too late to hope for beastly pleasures.

On last Friday I went to eat a good dinner in Alec's flat with Mr and Mrs Mitchison[1] (Naomi Haldane) and the woman who played Lucy in *The Beggar's Opera* and a lesbian sister of the infamous A. S. M. Hutchinson.[2] There was plenty to eat and to drink. I am making two drawings which I think are going to be good, one of a battle between Amazons and satyrs, and one of the Duchess of Malfi among the zanies, both in black and brown ink only. Last night we had rather a dismal drunk party at Alec's – Alec, Tony, Bill Silk, Luke Hansard and I. Tony got very drunk and unhappy. We went on later to Mary Butts[3] who is sweet. Tony locked himself in the lavatory all the evening. There is a quarrel on between Alec and the Jessie gang.[4] I went to her barber's shop yesterday and had my hairs cut. I have discovered such a nice new game. When I come home in the evenings from Hampstead Tube I hide pennies – and last night because I was drunk, sixpences – all the way along and next day see how many are left. It is so cheap and charitable and amusing.

The Radicals[5] are well rooted in the election. Richard[6] has been made a Fellow of All Souls.

Barford, Sunday 9 November 1924

I arrived in time for dinner on Friday after a rather unprofitable day spent in writing letters, packing, and a cinema with Bill Silk. The house is just the same and a place of many ghosts. Mrs Graham stands like some baffled archangel beating in the void her voluminous wings in vain while anger fills the room up of her absent son. Nora, Mrs Fenton, is now installed as companion for a short

---

[1] Naomi Mitchison (b. 1897), daughter of J. B. S. Haldane, CH, FRS; a prolific writer. She married in 1916 G. R. Mitchison (d. 1970), Labour MP who was made a life peer in 1964.

[2] A. S. M. Hutchinson (1879–1971), author of the bestseller *If Winter Comes*. His sister, Vere, was also a novelist.

[3] 'A genial, voluptuous lady of the *avant garde*' (*A Little Learning*, p. 211); short story writer; great grand-daughter of Thomas Butts, the friend and patron of William Blake.

[4] The circle round Jessie (also known as Sylvia) and Francis Palmer.

[5] The Labour government of 1924.

[6] Richard Pares. See Appendix of Names, p. 794.

time until her man can get a dispensation to marry her from His Holiness the Bishop of Rome. She drove me into Leamington for marketing on Saturday morning and I found it a little sad to pass all the public houses where Alastair and I have drunk. At 7 o'clock yesterday morning the wife of the head-gardener was called by God and without warning died. It has caused some trouble because her sudden death involves a post-mortem and an inquest and all manner of such horrors. The body might not be moved, and since there was only one bed in the cottage I am much afraid that the poor husband must have been driven to the horrid vice of necrophily. Alastair's setter bitch has grown vastly long and far too fat but is a lovely creature.

On Saturday afternoon we went into Leamington for a matinée of a new play which Henry Edwards and Chrissie White are 'trying on the dog'. I think it will not be any success in London tho' it was quite amusing. In the evening Nora's soldier – a good chap – and some people called Howard came to dinner.

Today John Sutro came over from Oxford to luncheon. I had hoped he would bring with him Hugh Lygon but apparently he was at Eton yesterday and too drunk to get up this morning. He has asked me to lunch tomorrow (John), an invitation which I am more than half-inclined to accept. Besides John hundreds of people came to lunch including Violet Barker who appeared to have become extremely pretty. We played Cooncan[1] after lunch and I enjoyed the afternoon considerably. John was very sweet in that regretful and reminiscent melancholy which he always assumes with me. The defection of Richard to All Souls has saddened him.

Last week, he told me, Rudolph[2] rang up a number of elderly ladies in North Oxford and Boars Hill and told them that a jumble sale was being organized in All Souls – would they send their old clothes to the Warden? They did.

Wednesday 12 November 1924

I went to Oxford on Monday and contrary to my intentions stayed the night.[3] John's luncheon party consisted of Harold Acton, Mark Ogilvie-Grant, Hugh Lygon, Robert Byron,[4] Arden Hilliard and Richard Pares. My arrival had been kept a close secret and everyone was very sweet to me. After luncheon, which was hot lobster, partridges and plum pudding, sherry, mulled claret and a strange rum-like liqueur, I left Hugh and John drinking and went to call on a number of people all of whom were out. I went to a tea party at M. O.-G.'s all tepid tea and Etonian ties and then to the New Reform Club where I

[1] Card game; a type of Rummy.

[2] Rudolph Messel.

[3] Waugh dated his 'decline' as a conscientious art student from this visit to Oxford. 'It was the lure of Oxford, still full of friends, which finally made me despair of myself at Heatherley's.' *A Little Learning*, p. 212.

[4] Harold Acton, Mark Ogilvie-Grant, Robert Byron: see Appendix of Names, p. 794.

found Terence and Elmley drinking beer. I drank with them and went to dinner with Robert Byron in Merton Hall. I found Billy there looking very healthy and clean and after dinner we went up to the rooms of a charming hunting man called Reynolds and drank beer. I then got a message from the OUDS from Hugh and John to come immediately to Banbury. I went to the station but could not persuade them to abandon the expedition. I went on to the Nag's Head where I had arranged to meet Elmley. Claud Cockburn[1] turned up there with mad Yorke-Lodge and a beastly man in an eye glass all very drunk. When we were turned out we went to see Mrs Heritage and then to the old Hypocrites' rooms for a drinking of whisky and the performance of the Elsa film. After about this stage of the evening my recollections become somewhat blurred. I got a sword from somewhere and got into Balliol somehow and was let out of a window at some time having mocked Arden and Tony Powell[2] and talked very seriously to Peter Quennell.[3] When I got back to Beaumont Street I found that there had been a fire in John's rooms. Next morning I drank beer with Hugh and port with Hot Lunch Molson,[4] lunched with Hugh, drank gin with Gyles Isham, met Desmond Harmsworth[5] and Billy and was seen off at the station by Harold and Billy feeling woefully tired. In the train I gradually realized that I had engaged myself to dine with Gwen Otter. I dashed to Golders Green carrying my bag in crowded trains, being too poor for a cab, changed and dashed to Gwen's where I had a lovely dinner with only one other person there, a musical woman with a Scotch name.

Aubrey Hammond, Barbara Mole, Henry Savage and others of the old Cave of Harmony type dropped in and we went on to Charlotte Street at about 11. I was too tired to move but did not dislike the evening. A beautiful woman called Marjory Dixon or Dickson was there with Louis Golding. I talked to her most of the evening. Jessie and Francis and Co. were there but distinctly hostile, I do not know why. The play was amusing, consisting mostly of Margaret Yard slapping the buttocks of Angela Baddeley. Still too poor for a cab I was forced to walk home in pouring rain at about 3. I have promised to go out with Keith Chesterton tonight but shall do no such thing.

Tuesday 18 November 1924

Last weekend I spent again in Oxford. On Friday morning in the tube I met Cecil Maitland, rather drunk, and for something to fill up the difficult conversational pauses tube travelling always makes I said, 'Will you come down to Oxford with me tonight?' To my horror he assented readily and the

---

[1] Described by Waugh as 'my Communist cousin'. See Appendix of Names, p. 794.

[2] Anthony Powell, the novelist. See Appendix of Names, p. 794.

[3] See Appendix of Names, p. 794.

[4] Molson, Waugh's Lancing contemporary, had acquired his nickname at Oxford through his insistence on eating, daily, a hot lunch.

[5] Nephew of the 1st Viscount Northcliffe. See Appendix of Names, p. 794.

rest of the day I was consumed with distress at the prospect of a ruined weekend. I contrived however to wire to Billy not to wait dinner for me and to go by a later train without meeting Cecil Maitland. Philip Machin met me and took me off to dinner at the Carlton Club. At about 9 we went on to Merton where we found Billy's party in full swing. There was a vast crowd ranging from Godfrey Adams and Hudson to my Lords of Rosse and Stavordale and other débutants. There was a vast amount of drink but not overmuch drunkenness. One man was sick and two or three in rut. Everyone was wearing a new sort of jumper with a high collar rather becoming and most convenient for lechery because it dispenses with all unromantic gadgets like studs and ties. It also hides the boils with which most of the young men seem to have encrusted their necks. The man who owned the rooms, James Reynolds, was very drunk and most offensive to Harold and Hugh and me. He apologized later in the weekend and was forgiven. Gavin Henderson[1] was up for the weekend and most trying. I drank a good deal but went to bed eventually alone and fairly sober.

On Saturday I breakfasted with John Sutro and was called on by Peter Quennell. Roy Harrod[2] the Chinese don also came and offered me a bed in Christ Church for that night. I lunched at Harold's – Elmley, Robert Byron, Teddy Steel and a freshman called Yorke.[3] Not a very good luncheon. Later Gavin and Brian Howard and Eric Whitley came in. I left and went to tea in Balliol with Henri Lubomirski who was very sweet. Peter had asked me to dinner but put me off, much to my disgust, as I had already refused an invitation to dinner. Feeling very depressed and foresaken I went to dine alone at the New Reform Club where I found Guy Dixon entertaining a large party before the Univ. Smoker. He asked me to join him. It was a grisly evening. Never have I seen so many men being sick together or being so infernally dangerous. They threw about chairs and soda water syphons and lavatory seats. Only one man was seriously injured. We escaped with our lives and after hopping in to Keith Douglas for a drink went to sleep in the House.[4] —— had the male prostitute —— with him so I passed a quiet night unmolested. Next day to breakfast at the OUDS with Hugh Lygon, to Mass with Billy at Pusey House, to sherry in Beaumont Street with Kolkhorst[5] and to lunch in

---

[1] Later the 2nd Baron Faringdon.

[2] Economics don at Christ Church, Oxford, 1922–67.

[3] Henry Yorke; who later wrote novels under the name of Henry Green. See Appendix of Names, p. 794.

[4] Christ Church.

[5] Known as Colonel Kolkhorst; University Reader in Spanish and Portuguese; reputed owner of the Lisbon tramway system; a 'highly ridiculous but dearly loved' figure who was 'discovered' by Billy Clonmore and cultivated by John Betjeman. He was 'dedicated to the maintenance of the values and traditions of the nineties'. Osbert Lancaster, *With an Eye to the Future* (London 1967), p. 72.

Worcester with Fulford. Chris's brother[1] was there – a good bottle man – also Patrick Gamble, Arden Hilliard and Driberg. A good luncheon. Then home by the 4.37 train on which I caught a cold which has saddened me ever since.

Sunday 30 November 1924

. I have spent a very quiet week going to Heatherley's every day and spending all the evenings at home. Most days, even at the cost of 6d, I have been to the National Gallery where I find I gradually like more and more pictures. I am beginning to 'discover' Velasquez, Rubens and Poussin. Poussin the least, however.

There is a new film called *Warning Shadows* which I saw yesterday with Terence who suddenly appeared from Oxford in the Rising Sun. It is quite superb.

There is a most amusing case on now about a Mrs Robinson who lay with the Shah of Persia. Everyone in the case is a complete blackguard. Even the witness at Robinson's wedding was a convicted card-sharper.

Monday 8 December 1924

My last entry is untrue. The 'potentate' in the Robinson case was Sir Hari Singh of Kashmir. A friend of Alec's came to dinner who had committed sodomy with the black secretary and knew all the people intimately. It was an exquisitely amusing case; there was a superb man called Newton who was cross-examined by Lord Halsbury and mocked him on every point.

I am at the moment just recovering from a very heavy bout of drinking. On the evening of the last day about which I have written I had a good drinking evening with Alec, Terence, and Richard Greene. Exactly a week later I suddenly went to Oxford by the most impossible train which stopped at every station. I arrived at 10.30 and drove to 31 St Aldate's where I found an enormous orgy in progress. Billy and I unearthed a strap and whipped Tony. Everyone was hideously drunk except strangely enough myself. Next day I moved to 40 Beaumont Street and began a vastly expensive career of alcohol. After a quiet day in cinemas, I had a dinner party of Claud, Elmley, Terence, Roger Hollis and a poor drunk called Macgregor. I arrived quite blind after a great number of cocktails at the George with Claud. Eventually the dinner broke up and Claud, Roger Hollis and I went off for a pub-crawl which after sundry indecorous adventures ended up at the Hypocrites where another blind was going on. Poor Mr Macgregor turned up after having lain with a woman but almost immediately fell backwards downstairs. I think he was killed. Next day I drank all the morning from pub to pub and invited to lunch with me at the

[1] Roger Hollis, later head of the British Intelligence organization, MI5.

New Reform John Sutro, Roger Hollis, Claud, and Alfred Duggan.[1] I am not sure if there was anyone else. I ate no lunch but drank solidly and was soon in the middle of a bitter quarrel with the president – a preposterous person called Cotts – who expelled me from the club. Alfred and I then drank double brandies until I could not walk. He carried me to Worcester where I fell out of a window and then relapsed into unconsciousness punctuated with severe but well-directed vomitings. I dined four times at various places and went to a drunk party at Worcester in someone's rooms I did not know.

On Wednesday I was sober. I lunched with Robert Byron at the New Reform and the man Cotts tried to throw me out again. Robert said I was his guest and would do nothing about it until the committee expelled me. The committee met that evening and decided unanimously against Cotts. I gave dinner to Billy Clonmore and ex-service Steel and went to the Merton Smoker where everyone was congregated in James Reynolds's room. Next day I lunched with Hugh[2] and drank with him all the afternoon and sallied out with him fighting drunk at tea-time when we drank at the New Reform till dinner. I dined with Terence and went to Hertford to see the film but as I was too drunk to stand went away and drank with poor Hamerton at some clubs and pubs until he was sick. I went to the Hypocrites and then with Harding to a dance in the town hall.

Next day feeling deathly ill I returned to London having spent two months' wages. I had to dine with Richard Greene in company with Alec, Julia Strachey,[3] Olivia Greene and Elizabeth Russell. We went to the Empire and then back to Richard's home to drink. Home at 2. Since then I have decided that a gay life is not to be borne and have asked James Guthrie[4] to take me as a pupil in the country. I hope that he will do this but I see no reason why he should.

Monday 15 December 1924

Guthrie did answer my letter or rather his wife did which shows an incredible degree of conjugal intimacy. She told me that her husband was in London at the moment and seemed rather to welcome the idea of a pupil. Guthrie himself got on to me on the telephone before I was dressed and agreed to lunch with me at Previtali's. This, it should be mentioned, occurred on Wednesday. On Tuesday I had given luncheon to Professor Hind and my father. I had also been to the woodcutters' exhibition at the St George's

---

[1] Stepson of the then Lord President in Baldwin's cabinet and Chancellor of Oxford University, Lord Curzon. See Appendix of Names, p.794.

[2] The Hon. Hugh Lygon.

[3] Later a novelist; daughter of Oliver and niece of Lytton Strachey.

[4] Owner of a one-man private press, the Pear Tree Press, from 1899 until the 1930s; a member of William Morris's Arts and Crafts movement, but much influenced by William Blake.

Gallery, dominated of course by Craig and Gill (who is becoming so secular),[1] and to the Laurencin Exhibition in Leicester Square. Laurencin I did not like – steeped in that vapid obscenity that the newspaper reports called feminine charm, but there were some quite uncanny flower paintings by a man called Wood. One literally had to be within a few inches of them before one could persuade oneself that they were painted and not modelled in wax – it was quite stereoscopic. How Leonardo would have admired them! I also went to Truman & Knightley's and said that I wanted to be a schoolmaster, ever since which time I have been filling in forms to say that I was in my House-team for swimming. I also went to tea with Mrs Fremlin at a wicked women's club and ordered the drink for Audrey's[2] party – four whisky, one gin, one brandy, one curaçao, four Chianti, ten Livadia, it should have been enough but wasn't, and two bottles of ready-made cocktail.

Guthrie was a very sweet and modest man and seemed quite ready to take me as a pupil. He showed me some books printed from plates. I cannot but think that he makes a great mistake in printing only such trivial books of nursery rhymes, etc.

On Thursday in the most unspeakable fog Audrey had her party. As far as I was concerned it was not a good evening. I dined with Gwen first with several other folks including Mr Pratt who knows everything and then fetched the Stallybrass and Richard Hughes.[3] When we arrived everyone was very crowded and noisy and I had an amazingly busy hour introducing people and mixing cocktails. Tasha Gielgud came and also her husband! Another amusing meeting was Julia Strachey and her father. At the end when just everything was drunk and almost everyone had gone there arrived uninvited David Greene, Brian Howard, Earl of Rosse, Bryan Guinness and Waters-Welch. I was furious with them. Rosse said to me, 'What is this hall I am in?' I told him it was hired for the occasion. 'What an extraordinary arrangement and who are all these people actresses I suppose or what?' I told him that they were my friends. 'Indeed and are any of them anyone one has ever heard of?' I think his manners are not good.

Yesterday I went to a 300 Club performance of *Bartons Folly*. Most 'Ibscure'. Today I await with growing impatience the replies of the private schoolmasters, attempting meanwhile to push on with *The Temple*.

Wednesday 17 December 1924

Still writing out letters in praise of myself to obscure private schools and still attempting to rewrite *The Temple*. A man from Arnold House, Denbighshire, and another from Plymouth seem to show a little interest in me, but none of the

[1] Gordon Craig, the stage designer, and Eric Gill, the sculptor, letterist and wood-engraver.
[2] Audrey Lucas.
[3] Nancy Stallybrass; engaged to Richard Hughes, the novelist.

others answer at all. I am going down to see the Pear Tree Press on Friday and hope to work in luncheon at Goring too. Yesterday Gwen, in tears, rang me up to ask me to dinner. Some man has been bloody to her. She gave me the best soup ever I drank, made of chestnuts.

Thursday 18 December 1924

Jean[1] was married to the man Crowden. It was a sordid business but the champagne was surprisingly good. All the Fleming uncles got a little drunk and began 'yodelling'. I had engaged to go to a tea-dance at Mrs James but decided I could not bear it. In the evening I dined with Joyce Fagan at Previtali's. She has been making me a horoscope which threatens me with all manner of disaster. I have Uranus in my fifth house which is also in square with Venus and the Moon. We went on to the Café Royal and drank quantities of chartreuse. Frank Dobson was there also one or two rather disagreeable Oxford people. A man called Burghe who used to be at Balliol came and sat down opposite us. I introduced Joyce to him as my wife and was believed. We went back romantically in a cab to Bayswater.

Friday 19 December 1924

I caught the 10 o'clock train from Victoria in very easy time and arrived at Bognor at about 12.45. John Guthrie met me in a very light-blue rain-coat and we walked out to Flansham – about three miles. He is a pleasant enough youth though not particularly intelligent. He showed me, later, a number of linoleum-cut stage designs which I thought rather good. He is very industrious as indeed are all his family. Flansham is a very pretty village just clear of the bungalows. The Pear Tree Press is in a very ugly little house which has had a porch and windows built on by a local builder. We ate a large hot luncheon of pork, apple pie and, to drink, water. Mrs Guthrie is a fine figure of a woman. White hair, rosy cheeks, and most maternal. The daughter of a Scotch farmer. The whole family admire each other to excess. Robin seems the general idol. He has been practically adopted by a wealthy Dutchman named de Graaf who sent him to the Slade where he won all the prizes. They showed me several of his drawings which were certainly very efficient.

The best things about the household were Mrs Guthrie and the obvious creative exuberance of them all. The discomforts were very considerable. I slept in a terrible bed. The methods of the Press saddened me a little because they are directly dependent on trade photography, though of course all the quality of the printing comes from the Press work. Guthrie has zinc intaglio plates made from his drawings. It seems a pity. His drawing is most interesting. He builds it up by going over and over it again with ink on Chinese white until

[1] Jean Fleming.

it loses all quality of any ordinary technical method. After high tea Mrs Guthrie talked politics of the robust radical sort of 1880.

Next day I walked miles and miles with John Guthrie, looking for rooms. I had decided that I did not want to live with the Guthries and returned to a most sad family.

Sunday 21 December 1924

I lunched with Gwen Otter. The luncheon was not very good and I was a little sad because all the conversation was in French. Yvonne George was there and sang songs and mimicked people deliciously. Terence had suddenly appeared in London and my father most reluctantly asked him to tea. We decided that we would go to see Elsa so ate an early dinner before the rest of the family and went to the 1917 Club and drank with Richard and Olivia Greene and Elizabeth Russell – at least we all drank except Elizabeth, who sipped like a hen at a glass of water. I did not particularly want Olivia to come on to Elsa's but she decided to be 'feminine' and came. Elizabeth went home. Terence got very drunk and lapsed into muttered confessions to Olivia of his unnatural offences. It was not a particularly good evening. Elsa sang a song and bored Richard. I took Terence back and put him to sleep on a sofa.

Monday 22 December 1924

Terence and I walked with Mrs Waugh's dog and went to a cinema. Alec took us to drink at the Savile where we drank excellent wines and became a little drunk. Tony joined us and we went and drank more at the 1917 Club. Tony came back and slept at Golders Green and slept there.

Tuesday 23 December 1924

Terence and I had a lovely evening. We met Olivia at the 1917 Club and went to dinner at the Gourmet. Then we drank until the club closed and it suddenly occurred to me that it was too pleasant an evening to be broken up so we induced Olivia to come back with us. We found a huge dish of fruit which someone had sent and a decanterful of white port. Olivia was quite delightful. After a time Alec came in and we went up to my bedroom in search of a gas fire. We lit candles and talked and drank while Olivia curled herself up with my hot water bottle. At about 3 we got her a cab and gave her all our money to go home with. Terence did not want to sleep with her.

Wednesday 24 December 1924

I sent off Alec's copy of *Irais*[1] to Olivia. I wonder whether I am falling in

---

[1] Anonymous lesbian book, privately printed and rare, which Alec Waugh had obtained from Vyvyan Holland, Oscar Wilde's son.

love with this woman. I went to the Niebelungs with Terence and at length saw him off to Oxford. Tomorrow is Christmas Day.

Christmas Day 1924

I have decided to try and grow a moustache because I cannot afford any new clothes for several years and I want to see some change in myself. Also if I am to be a schoolmaster it will help to impress the urchins with my age. I look so intolerably young now that I have had to give up regular excessive drinking. Christmas Day always makes me feel a little sad; for one reason because strangely enough my few romances have always culminated in Christmas week – Luned, Richard, Alastair.[1] Now with Alastair a thousand miles away and my heart leaden and the future drearily uncertain things are not as they were. My only letter this morning was a notice of a vacancy from Truman & Knightley. There are coming to dinner tonight Stella Rhys and Audrey Lucas and Philippa Fleming. I should scarcely think that it will be a jovial evening.

Wednesday 31 December 1924

It was not as a matter of fact at all a bad evening. Since then I have been waiting with growing impatience letters from schoolmasters and Olivia. On Sunday I went to dinner at Audrey's flat to meet the Geoffrey Morrises. Mrs Morris was just like Brian Howard.

On Monday I ordered a new overcoat at a new tailor called Gotlop whom Teddy Steel told me about. In the evening Mother and I went to see Tony's first performance in *Diplomacy*. He looked very charming and acted adequately. It is rather a good play. Gladys Cooper exquisitely lovely. Yesterday morning Olivia rang up so I asked her to luncheon with me at the Rising Sun Saloon Bar. I waited for her for about twenty-five minutes drinking gin and bitters and at last she arrived absurdly well dressed and incongruous. All the poor men in the bar were most sheepish and stopped swearing, finished their drinks and slunk away. We ate veal-and-ham pies and drank gin and Benedictine. We then went to Maskelyne and Devants[2] where we saw at least one wholly miraculous performance. We drank some tea at Ridgeways and then went away. She is coming here to luncheon today. Still no news from the private schools. I have shaved away the beginnings of my moustache.

Olivia came to luncheon and afterwards we sat by the fire and talked until tea when we suddenly realized that there was no time for her to keep an appointment to go with David[3] to tea with Tom Douglas.[4] We did some very skilful work with a telephone and a district messenger and went to a cinema.

[1] Luned Jacobs, Richard Pares, Alastair Graham.
[2] Conjuring show.
[3] David Plunket Greene.
[4] American matinée idol.

Thursday 1 January 1925

I lunched with Faith and Black Torry[1] who tried to poison me. They had some snuff which had made Faith sick and sent Francis Laking to sleep for thirty six hours. They made me take it and imagining myself very ill I went off to tea with the Greenes. I met Mrs Greene for the first time and loved her. Then she and David went off and Olivia and Richard[2] began to teach me to dance. I took Richard back to dinner and he spent the night with us.

Friday 2 January 1925

A telegram has arrived from Mr Banks of Denbighshire telling me to meet him on Monday. I pray to God that this means a job and some money. In the evening Lady Pares's dance which Alec enjoyed. I was utterly bored. Ursula Pares is a pretty child.

Saturday 3 January 1925

With Jane Marston and a Mrs Crabbe-Watt to a matinée at the Everyman Theatre of *The Philanderer*. In the evening I went out and drank beer with Olivia and Richard and learned more dancing.

Sunday 4 January 1925

To luncheon with Audrey Lucas. Her mother was there and John Armstrong. The luncheon cooked by Mrs Lucas was frightfully good and the drinks bought by Audrey bad. In the evening I dined with Adrian Stokes at the Commercio and then went on to the Café Royal where Olivia joined us and Richard and a woman and a good painter called Seabrooke. We went on to Elsa's and I made love to Olivia in a corner.

Monday 5 January 1925

I wrote to Olivia to tell her I was sober (untrue) and sincere (nearly true) the evening before. At 4.30 Alastair suddenly walked in having travelled for weeks without eating anything or washing and looking very ugly in an impossible French ready-made overcoat. When he was washed and shaved he began to be more beautiful. I had to go to tea with Mr Banks of Arnold House, Denbighshire. He was a tall old man with stupid eyes. He was staying at the Berners Hotel. He is going to pay me £160 to teach little boys for him for a year. I think this will be bloody but most useful to a man as poor as I. Apparently the school is so far away from any sort of place of entertainment that it is just quite

[1] Mrs Torry, a rich hostess of Indian origins.
[2] Richard Plunket Greene.

impossible to spend any money at all there. Richard came in the evening and drank with us. Chapman & Hall has a 'quinsy'.

Tuesday 6 January 1925

After a rather dreary day of seeing to luggage and shopping, Alastair and I had a most amusing evening. John Sutro came to dinner, and afterwards, Alastair in my evening clothes, we went off to meet everyone at Oddenino's. We ate mushrooms and drank burgundy first at the Café Royal. At about 10.45 we went to Oddenino's where we found Audrey waiting for us under the suspicious eyes of the waiters who will not serve 'unaccompanied ladies'. We drank chartreuse and gradually everyone arrived. Olivia, Richard, Elizabeth Russell, Black Torry and Faith, Basil Maine, Tony Bushell and many hundreds more. A sweet man called Mr Best sat next to Olivia and smoked cigars and drank beer. At closing time we went on to dance at the 50–50. It is a bad club full of everyone one has ever heard of. I did not like it because we could not drink there, so after greeting Hugh Lygon and a few other friends Tony and I went off to 43 Gerrard Street where Miss Meyrick[1] is carrying on in her mother's place exactly the same as ever. We drank some whisky there and wandered about and resisted the assaults of the harlots and then returned to the 50–50 where David Greene had joined the party. It was proposed to go back to Audrey's flat so Richard and I went off in search of liquor. Miss Meyrick would not sell us a bottle but she introduced us to the most astonishing man who kept a brothel in Paris who led us to a tea shop in Frith Street called the Bohemian where a syphilitic old man sold us a bottle of gin at just over double the proper price. We gave this to Audrey and then set out to Park Crescent to look for Black Torry who had disappeared. We beat all the bells but could get no answer so we went on to Audrey where she had already arrived with two bottles of champagne. The party lasted until about 5 when we secured a taxi with infinite difficulty and saw everyone home; Alastair fell asleep. He also at some stage in the evening lost my waistcoat. Audrey made declarations of love to me, and Richard to Elizabeth and I to Olivia. I do not think Black Torry seduced anyone.

Wednesday 7 January 1925

Getting up at 8.30 next morning was hell. I saw Alastair off and lived for the rest of the day on caffeine. I went to tea with the Greenes and stayed to supper – eaten in the kitchen – such fun. The whole family were in a state of collapse and most of the time slept. Richard and I went to a cinema and had some supper at a restaurant in Swallow Street. So home.

[1] Daughter of the indomitable nightclub owner Mrs Meyrick who, as fast as the police closed one club, opened another. Constantly fined and imprisoned. Two of her daughters married peers.

Thursday 8 January 1925

Slept until luncheon and then took Jane Marston to a cinema. Ghastly evening at home. Muriel[1] to dinner.

Friday 9 January 1925

Nothing. Chapman & Hall still in bed.

Saturday 10 January 1925

All day at work on the wrapper for *Kept*. I think it is going to be rather good. I have arranged to go down to Barford next week.

Sunday 11 January 1925

I have bought one of those ugly high-necked jumpers and look exactly ten years old in it.

In the jumper and the most hideous fog I ever saw I went to luncheon at Gwen Otter's. I found the house only after terrible hardships and difficulties – at the corner of Kings Road and Royal Avenue I ran straight into a wall and found chalked on it ARE YOU WASHED IN THE BLOOD OF THE LAMB most disturbing.

No one else succeeded in reaching Gwen's so we ate together a huge dish of *gnocchi* which had been prepared for 5,000 and then could eat no more. We sat in front of the fire and drank until about 4.15 when Audrey arrived. Gwen sang bawdy songs. I had promised to go to tea with Olivia and after wandering for miles in fogs arrived at Hanover Terrace at about 5. We had a desolate tea alone in front of a gas fire quarrelling in a half-hearted sort of way. Most of the time she insisted monotonously, 'I don't think you love me any more' and then became aloof when I attempted to prove that I did. At about 8, deeply depressed, we set out to drink, and after some champagne cocktails at the Criterion we ate oysters and drank Chablis at the Café Royal. Lady Plunket[2] and Richard joined us. We went to Elsa's, not Lady P., where they acted a play by Laurence Housman about Queen Victoria which was not very good. Olivia very drunk. Great difficulty in getting taxi-cab in fog.

Monday 12 January 1925

In the evening Mrs G. took me to dinner and to Noel Coward's *Vortex*. Not really a very good play but fun.

Barford, Tuesday 13 January 1925

To Barford with Mrs G. Alastair and I had to go to a dinner party with some

[1] Muriel Silk, Arthur Waugh's secretary.
[2] Nickname for Mrs Plunket Greene.

people called Paton who have a very new house. Rather a dreary evening. Up-Jenkins[1] and such sports.

Wednesday 14 January 1925

Walked to nearest pub – Hampton Lucy – with dogs. Lunch tea dinner. Did some drawings for Olivia's bookplate.

Thursday 15 January 1925

A post full of bills. Wired to Alec for money which he did. Walked to pub. Luncheon. Wired to Fulford to give us luncheon in Oxford on Saturday.

Friday 16 January 1925

In the evening we went to a dance at the Barkers. There was a parrot there but otherwise it was just like all dances. Alastair and I drank all the whisky.

Saturday 17 January 1925

Alastair and I went to Oxford for the day. There had been a scene about the car so we were compelled to go in an expensive railway train. It was on the whole a very expensive day indeed. We lunched with Fulford, not in his rooms because his hearties object to me for some reason, and Roger Hollis and Claud Cockburn. Claud paid me £8 with comforted me a lot. We drank all the afternoon, tried on some clothes at Hall and returned sleepily. After dinner I succeeded in beating Alastair at chess.

Hampstead, Tuesday 20 January 1925

Just recovering from rather severe drunkenness last night and feeling most weary. I went with Alastair to half of his Mass in Leamington on Sunday and came up by the luncheon train. Unfortunately I was too poor to eat any luncheon. Alec's dinner party was almost wholly spoiled by the abominable manners of the Greene family who arrived fifty minutes late. Julia came soon afterwards. On the whole I did not enjoy the evening overmuch. We had three stalls and a box and I think the show should have been amusing but all my time was spent in running about getting drinks and cabs and collecting stray members of the party. I was also very vexed with Olivia who kissed Tony[2] in the box and drank too much cherry brandy. We went on to Elsa's with Mary Butts who joined our box on finding her mother two seats away from her. It was bitterly cold and we all stood about for hours over the fire sipping gin. Eventually more people arrived and we started dancing. I could not get drunk try as I might and was very rude to Olivia who was too drunk to mind. Richard[3]

[1] Parlour game played with a coin.
[2] Tony Bushell.
[3] Richard Plunket Greene.

and Tony and I drank white wine in the lavatory of an hotel after hours. Home at about 2.30 which was earlier than I had feared.

Next day I woke with a glowing resentment against the Greene family and sent a lot of flowers to Lady Plunket *pour prendre congé* and told her I would not dine with her as I was going to the country. This high attitude was a little shaken later in the evening because I got quite, quite drunk with Tony and Bill Silk and called at Hanover Terrace at about 12.30. At least Tony and I called. Bill lost his way between the taxi and the door and was never seen again. Tony tells me he is angry about it. I think I must have been exceedingly tiresome last night. I refused to go until Olivia knelt down and apologized to me; she quite rightly did not do this. I also broke a gramophone record.

I woke up this morning with the dreary knowledge that I had spent all the money I wanted to go to Denbighshire with. However I pawned my ring and snuff-box and Audrey's watch at one of kind Mr Attenborough's shops and raised £4. The pawnbroker was sweet. I had imagined a wicked and grubby Jew who would insult me and disparage my goods. Instead a charming and handsome gentleman rather like a distinguished civil servant who admired the cameo and bowed us out, Audrey and me, as if we had bought a pearl necklace. Lunch with Dudley at Previtali's. Home to bathe and write this and some letters.

I went to the Alhambra between tea and dinner and saw Layton and Johnstone[1] again, also Alec's friend Milton Hayes.[2] Then to dinner at Previtali's with Richard. We drank little and talked and then ate some supper at the Florence where Tony joined us.

Wednesday 21 January 1925

On my last day in London Olivia and I became friends. She rang me up and said she wanted to see me; her family were coming to tea so I asked her to luncheon. She arrived five minutes early and was very sweet. We sat in the bookroom and she told me that I was a great artist and must not be a schoolmaster. We took Gaspard for a walk and then Lady Plunket came and later Richard and Elizabeth. I think the tea party was a success. I went to bed feeling more desolate than I had felt since the embarkation of Alastair.

Friday 23 January 1925

Arnold House, Llanddulas, Denbighshire. I packed my drawing things, my clothes, the abortive notes for *The Temple*, and Horace Walpole, *Alice in Wonderland*, *The Golden Bough* and a few other books, and took them to Euston. There and at Chester I picked up bleak little groups of boys in red caps

---

[1] Black American 'duettists' and 'syncopated singers'.

[2] Celebrated music-hall artist; author of the monologue, 'The Green Eye of the Little Yellow God'.

and tears. In the carriage they ate prodigious quantities of sweetmeats and when at luncheon they drank quarts of ginger-ales and lemonades I became convinced that someone or other of them would soon be sick. To my intense relief we reached Llanddulas in safety and in spite of Mr Banks's telegrams the train stopped there. A tiny taxi took me and two hundred handbags to the house. It is built on a hill so steep that one has the perplexing experience of going in to the front door, going up two stories, and on looking out of a window finding oneself still on the ground floot. There are three pitch-pine staircases, one carpeted, but the other two indistinguishable, and several miles of passage covered with highly polished linoleum. There is a common-room where I have to live. There the linoleum is still more highly (or as Alec would say 'highlier') polished, the walls are red and covered with repulsive pictures; there are two easy chairs and some others, an acetylene gas jet, very weak, a fire and a gramophone. There are also four young men. One called Chaplin was at Saint Edmund's Hall and shared rooms with Jim Hill; he adores Flecker and is a nephew of Mr Banks. He is the best. There is a dull thing called Gordon in rimless pince-nez who is strict with the little boys. Chaplin, Gordon and I live in a little house called Sanatorium which is reached by a precipitous path between dung heaps, gooseberry bushes and stone walls. There are two new men, one very tall and grand and elderly called Watson who has been a master at Stowe and Egypt and places like that. He has an aquiline nose and a Scots accent and intends to buy a school soon. There is also a new man called Dean, very squalid, with a blue chin, discoloured cheeks, cockney accent and severe cold. He is the worst. Mr Banks has a wife who is not nearly as nice as Lady Plunket or Mrs Heritage. He has also a married son whom I have not seen but whose voice I have heard among the passages and do not like. That is my school except for an army of housemaids who scurry about the passages laden with urine, and some boys. I have only met a very few of these so far but some seem quite nice.

The school is run most curiously. There are no timetables or syllabi or such offal. All that happens is that the Headmaster Banks wanders into the common-room in a blank kind of way and says, 'Oh I say, there are some boys in that end classroom. I don't know who they are. They may be Set B in History or perhaps the Fourth Form or are they the Dancing Class. Anyway they've got their Latin books and they shouldn't have those so I think it would be best if someone took them in English.'

Then the least lazy gets up and does that and I stay on and cut wood for Olivia. Poor Mr Watson groans for a timetable but I find the arrangement quite agreeable. I sat out all the morning today.

This afternoon I took a form for the first time. They were called Set B History and I found I was supposed to teach them about William and Mary. They were a rowdy lot and I cannot pretend that I made much success with them. After three-quarters of an hour I went next door where Set A had been subdued by the excellent Watson. There were some quite intelligent children – one particularly who came from Galway I liked. I told them what little I knew about Henry VII and Henry VIII.

Sunday 25 January 1925

Yesterday morning the bell rang for school and everyone went up in a great shouting crowd, the masters in the midst. Soon Banks arrived with a list and started directing them into various rooms under various masters until I was left with nothing to do and no boys so I went down to the common-room and cut wood for Olivia until break. After break I went up again and as Dean had been at work all the morning Banks put me on to his job. I bored myself and the Fourth Form with some Latin verbs for fifty minutes. Then I went next door and tried to make the Fifth understand what 'metre' meant with some little success.

In the afternoon I went for a walk and discovered that besides the sea, the railway and the quarry there are some mountains. It is a highly geological country. Everyone in Wales has black spittle and whenever he meets you he says '*borra-da*' and spits. I was frightened at first but after a time I became accustomed to it. Also I discovered that everyone's manners are so good that when you say, 'Am I going the right way to Llanddulas?' they always say 'yes'. This courtesy led me many miles astray. I conducted a table at tea who behaved abominably and saddened me.

After dinner I went to the billiard table and thought of Richard's party that evening while Dean performed prodigies of cannoning and Chaplin mumbled sweetmeats.

This morning I was late getting up, missed chapel and came in halfway through breakfast. I finished Olivia's bookplate and went with the boys to a depressing service at the local conventicle. After luncheon I led some noisy children for a walk and played games with them until they all cut their knees.

I think that things may become amusing here after all because poor Mr Watson feels very strongly about discipline and is stirring up a mutiny against the amiable Banks; in the common-room he has just delivered an oration – very Scotsmanlike – stirring us up to a campaign of sticks and impositions and shoutings, little Dean's cockney echo supporting him. I hope there will be trouble.

A short time ago I poured the milk into the teapot instead of the hot water and said 'damn'. The two little boys next to me looked inexpressibly shocked and then gave a ghastly snigger.

Thursday 29 January 1925

Things get steadily more busy and as they become more busy more tedious.

I find I have practically no spare time until after 8 o'clock, and then if I have no papers to correct or things to learn myself I am too tired to do much. Today I went for a walk in the rain which was pleasant. First proofs have come of the Olivia bookplate – pretty good but disappointing. Glasses broken.

Sunday 1 February 1925

After lecturing all day upon the Irish problem I get this sort of answer. 'Parnell was an Irishman in Victoria's reign who was murdered in Felix Park because of a divorce.' I have to tell myself all day long that I sincerely hope that they will all fail to get into any public school or I might lose heart.

On Friday morning I received a letter from Richard Greene telling me that he is become definitely engaged with Elizabeth. It makes me sad for them because any sort of happiness or permanence seems so infinitely remote from any one of us.

Sunday 8 February 1925

The most dreary service conceivable. Matins, ante-communion, hymns and sermon all in the most abominable accent. Even the pennies in the red bags chinked in Welsh.

Watson has given the old man notice and rather shaken him. Letters during the week from Olivia and Lady Plunket.

Monday 9 February 1925

Today I beat two boys with a slipper but did not hurt either much. They were a nuisance. I have ordered a pair of shoes to cheer myself up.

Wednesday 18 February 1925

Last night I was drunk – very drunk – and feel a little the better for it. The sherry and whisky I had ordered in Oxford came. Before dinner Gordon and I drank the sherry – which brought back a thousand sentimental associations. After dinner we took the whisky to Watson's room and I drank about half of it while Watson and Dean drank a quarter each. The result was that I was sick. I have not yet met Amy and am rather unwilling to do so. I think she will not report it to proprietor Banks. The debauch has caused something of a feud in the common-room – I must confess to finding Chaplin somewhat tiresome.

Today I have had a delightful afternoon and evening. I went to Rhyl for the afternoon and got permission to stay out to dinner. I bought a lot of things which I do not particularly want and spent most of the time in the hands of a most interesting barber who talked of phallic symbolism and the Gnostics. A lovely dinner and good wines and brandy. On Saturday I went to the Naples of the North with one of the ushers called Gordon and had dinner at the Grand Hotel. It was not very grand but there was some of the burgundy which I last drank on the regrettable evening when I went to the home of Lady Plunket – Clos de Vougeot 1911. A kind man took us home in an automatic carriage. No letter from Olivia, no shoes from Oxford, no money from anywhere.

On Sunday I started on an awful thing called week's duty. It means that I have no time at all from dawn to dusk so much to read a postcard or visit a water-closet. Already – today is Tuesday, Shrove Tuesday – my nerves are distraught. Yesterday I beat a charming boy called Clegg and kicked a hideous boy called Cooper and sent Cooke to the proprietor. Yesterday afternoon I had my first riding lesson and enjoyed it greatly. It is not an easy sport or a cheap one but most agreeable. No letter from Olivia.

Yesterday in a history paper the boy Howarth wrote: 'In this year James II gave birth to a son but many people refused to believe it and said it had been brought to him in a hot water bottle.'

Monday 2 March 1925

The week's duty passed but I am still very busy with half-term reports. Last night I went to the Queen's Hotel, Colwyn, and Gordon got drunk. I am going to give up whisky I think. Mr Ducker has sent me my shoes – they are very lovely indeed and comfort me more than a chatty and impersonal letter which came yesterday from Olivia. I wrote her a very short answer full of sorrow and devotion. I wonder what she will make of it. Tomorrow I ride again.

Sunday 15 March 1925

There are rather less than three weeks left of this term and when that is said it seems that no other record can be of any interest. The riding still goes on. On Wednesday Gordon and I and the attendant rode miles over the hills. There was a brilliant sun and the fields were full of preposterous white things on legs which the farmers call 'lambs' and keep in the fields to amuse the sheep. That evening for the first time I enjoyed smoking my pipe.

There is some chance of my getting a tutoring job after all next holidays. I should dearly like to spend it at the feet of Olivia but can hardly afford it; even my bill at the village shop where I buy oranges and tobacco is more than I can meet with comfort.

During the last few days I have been quarrelling with Cramsie and Perceval, the only two boys I really like.

Mr Banks frequently expresses himself dissatisfied with the work I am doing – perhaps not without cause.

Watson is ill most of the time and the atmosphere in the common-room not very friendly. My moustache shows some signs of visible existence.

I have an idea for a book about Silenus which may or may not even be written. Richard and Elizabeth are soon to be married. And this is the last page of this dismal book.

St Patrick's Day 1925

I got up late for chapel and arrived in breakfast to find it looking very much like my idea of a Masonic banquet; all the boys had been up for hours decorating themselves like maypoles with red, white, blue, green, and orange rosettes and streamers. Mr Dean had draped a red curtain round his shoulders and looked so strange. Some of the older and more opulent boys wore green shirts and stockings. It was a horrid carnival. After luncheon they had a football match which the Irish won without difficulty. Halfway through it, I went up to Colwyn Bay where a man charged me 4s for cutting and washing my hair. In the evening we went to Mrs Roberts's public house where an eunuch taught me a new Welsh toast which I wrote down on an envelope and later lost; it meant 'Here's success to the temperance workers'.

Wednesday 18 March 1925

Feeling very weary and doing nothing. The boxing competition after tea. I have been choosing some patterns for a suit. Finished the Impieta woodcut.

Sunday 29 March 1925

There are only two more days – a thing I find it very hard to believe. Today there was a dreadful concert at which all the boys played the pieces they had learned during the term and Mrs Banks said polite things about the women who had taught them. During the last ten days we have spent most evenings at the village pub where an aged eunuch has tried to teach us Welsh. I have learned very little, however, except *Iechyd da i bob un* and *llywddiant ir archos*, which are toasts, because he gets too drunk to say anything else. On Saturday I felt so sad that I very nearly gave notice – proprietor Banks was rude to me unjustly and before a number of boys but the prospect of the holidays has buoyed me up a little. I think that I am going to enjoy them enormously. Olivia is going to be one of the Lundy party – all the term I have been allowing her to become a focus for all the decencies of life, which is foolish of me and not very fair to her. I think I shall go to Barford for a week. Martin wants me to go to an island of monks near Ireland. On Wednesday Gordon and Dean and I gave dinner to Watson at the Queen's Hotel and we drank a lot and sang all the way home. Watson goes away tomorrow, the Irish boys on Wednesday, and I on Thursday. I find that no cuts however slight ever heal in this climate. The Impieta wood engraving is rather good. A man called Gregg whose father is an archbishop came the other evening and talked bawdy until I wanted to cry. We all do nothing but talk bawdy and lay absurd wagers – 6d in the pool for the man who can keep the ash on his cigar longest, etc. Audrey gave a party a week ago which I think was unfriendly of her. Baldhead writes despondently that no one is giving any parties now.

Hampstead, Monday 6 April 1925

This morning, having retired to bed early after a pleasant and porty evening at the Savile with Alec, I woke up at 3 and could not sleep. I wandered about the house in search of *Those Barren Leaves* and when I had found it I just lay awake and considered gravely how very little I have really enjoyed the last three days. I came up from Llanddulas on Thursday and, basely deserting poor Emma Rothwell, travelled alone and in comfort. I went to Mr Gotlop and ordered lots of clothes and to a shirtmaker and a hatter and a glove merchant and bought two walking sticks and then with no money left drove to Golders Green. That evening we went to *Fata Morgana, en famille*. I was tired but I was interested to see this Tom Douglas of whom everyone writes to me.

Next day in a pair of voluminous pantaloons which kind Mr Gotlop made for me in the few hours, I went to the Norman Lindsay Exhibition and was confirmed in my contempt of him. Then to Hatchett's where Audrey had engaged to meet me. We missed each other and I ate a large and bibulous luncheon by myself. I went to the Savile in search of Alec and found Johnny Rothenstein.[1] We drank together and then bought some bottles of champagne which, after going to the Alhambra for a few minutes to see Layton and Johnstone, we took to tea at Olivia's. John Sutro was there and after a time some Talbots came to dinner. I went off by now very drunk to dinner with Tony at Previtali's – also very poor. We quarrelled with the proprietor who disapproved of my drunkenness and poverty and then drank with a bearded man called Reid or perhaps Reade at the 1917 Club, later at the 50–50, and then at Olivia's where Audrey had arrived; we danced and drank and at about 3 I found myself in Hammersmith having walked miles in totally the wrong direction – so home asleep in a taxi.

On Saturday I went with my mother and Olivia to a matinée of *Boodle* at the Empire, a musical comedy with June in it and Jack Buchanan. Fairly good. To bed early.

Yesterday Olivia came to luncheon and tea. She is agitating for a party tonight and who am I to deny her anything, so for many hours I have been at work on the telephone, getting trunk calls through to Oxford wine merchants and waking harlots from their beds to persuade them to come tonight. There is some hope, Alec tells me, of a secretaryship in Florence with a homosexual translator.[2]

Wednesday 8 April 1925

The party on Monday night so far as I was concerned was a failure. The first panic was at tea with Olivia when it was discovered that the case of drink from

---

[1] Director of the Tate Gallery, 1938–64.
[2] C. K. Scott Moncrieff, the translator of Proust.

Oxford had not arrived – after frantic work on the telephone we traced it to the Addison Road parcels office and Matthew Ponsonby[1] and I set off to find it in the Ponsonby family Ford. Olivia insisted on my changing, so it occurred to us to pub-crawl to Golders Green. We did that and pub-crawled back and at about 10 were arrested by two stalwart policemen in Oxford Street. Every effort of mine to prove my sobriety was unavailing and I had to sit for about four hours in an awful little cell just like an urinal while the police confused about six telephone messages with the result that Olivia thought that it would be no good to try and bail us out. Arthur Ponsonby[2] rescued Matthew but, rather ill-naturedly I thought, refused to do anything for me. At last I was let out and hurried to Hanover Terrace where the party was just breaking up and so home.[3] At the court next morning I was fined 15s 6d but poor Matthew is almost certainly going to prison. He had a very grand barrister who 'took a serious view of the case'. We lunched at Olivia's and then went with Tony to the Alhambra. Tea with Olivia and then home to a sorrowful family.

Lundy Island, Maundy Thursday 9 April 1925

Luncheon with Dudley Carew at such an old nightclub then on to Hanover Terrace where Elizabeth and Richard had arrived. Packing, supper at Florence, and then to Waterloo at midnight. It was quite a tolerable journey. Richard, Olivia and Elizabeth sprawled in various ungraceful attitudes of Slade composition while I drank whisky and smoked cigars and sat upright between an elderly woman and her husband and daughter. For some of the time Anne and I tossed for shillings and bet upon curious issues. She did not know what was meant by a phallic symbol. A very silly person called Martin Wilson who giggles without ceasing joined the party but spent the night in the next carriage. He is a friend of David's. We had breakfast at Barnstaple and some went on to Instow by car while Richard, Anne and I walked. We slept in the morning and lay about in the sun drinking gin. Martin did not appear all day. We walked over to Bideford and Olivia and Anne went back while Richard and Elizabeth and I stayed there for dinner. We went to the public house of a man called Butler who has written a poem about Lundy.

Breakfast was supposed to be at 7.30 for the 8 o'clock boat but it was very very late. Captain Dark did not start without us. No one was sick (and this lost

---

[1] Son of Arthur Ponsonby (see below). Later the 2nd Baron Ponsonby of Shulbrede.

[2] The son of Queen Victoria's private secretary; Eton and Balliol; page of honour to Queen Victoria; Labour MP for Sheffield, Brightside, 1922–30; Under Secretary of State for Foreign Affairs, January to November 1924; created Baron Ponsonby of Shulbrede 1930. Married the daughter of Sir Hubert Parry; Mrs Plunket Greene was his sister-in-law.

[3] The police document read: 'Metropolitan Police. E Division. Bow St Station. Take notice that you Evelyn Waugh are bound in the sum of £2.0.0 (Two) Pounds to appear at the Bow St Police Court, situated at Covent Garden at 10 o'clock A.M., on the 7th day of April 1925, to answer the charge of Drunk & Incapable.'

me some shillings to Richard). At about 11.30 we landed. The island is larger and higher than I had expected. I have not seen very much of it so far. There are two lighthouses, a coastguard station presided over by a charming person called 'Admiral', and a number of curiously bred dogs – one particularly tiresome one called Nanky lives in the hotel and is loved by everyone. Lady Plunket and David and Terence met us, Julia being in bed still. We rested all day and in the evening Lady Plunket read to us such a dull shocker while David drew unrecognizable caricatures. So far as I can see my friends in the party will be Richard, Terence and Elizabeth and, if she will allow it, Olivia.

Wednesday 15 April 1925

On the whole, except for the insistent sorrows of unrequited love which are ever with me in their most conventional form, I am enjoying this party very well. We do practically nothing all day. Sometimes Lady Plunket reads to us, sometimes we play obscene paper games. Richard and Elizabeth and I walk sometimes and climb rocks. On Monday there was a dance or rather, in Miss Sage's phrase, 'a swingabout' in the canteen. Richard and I made a great jug full of mulled claret and everyone became rather drunk. Admiral Steep[?] shed more garments and more sweat as the evening went on. Terence as always started superbly and ended in incoherent repetitions and belchings. Martin was most daring and drank two glasses of wine and squeaked uncontrollably. When everyone had gone to bed Olivia and I sat in the dark until nearly 4 and I became very sentimental and no doubt tedious, but she bore it with much kindness.

As I supposed it would, the party divides itself up into two camps. Richard and Elizabeth live infinitely remote and a rather exquisite world of their own making. I go about with them most of the time and find them very delightful. Elizabeth I like more every day. Often I have seen her looking really lovely which is odd because at first I could see no attraction in her at all. Terence is definitely of the first camp but is usually immersed in Anglo-Saxon syntax or playing bagatelle in the canteen. He drinks beer continually and has become quite pot-bellied; he also makes love to the impossible bitch Nanky and feeds it from his plate and kisses its mouth. David is so much more charming here than in Oxford or London. Poor thing he does draw so badly. Julia sleeps all day – in bed in the morning, on the grass in the afternoon, and on the sofa in the evening. When she speaks it is generally very wittily. Martin causes a lot of noise. Richard detests him and growls like a great bear whenever he comes into the room. He certainly is rather trying and once succeeded in infuriating me – last night when he sat on Olivia's chair and offered to 'burnish her bust'. This was in front of Lady Plunket too.

Yesterday evening there was a most depraved scene. After a quiet evening in the canteen I went down to the villa and talked in Elizabeth's bedroom until about 11. I came back to find an amazing orgy in progress. Everyone drunk or pretending drunkenness, except —— who was sitting in the middle of it all unusually sedate. —— almost naked was being slapped on the buttocks and enjoying herself ecstatically. Every two minutes she ran to the lavatory and as soon as she was out of the room everyone said, 'My dear, the things we are finding out about ——.' It was all rather cruel. She looked so awful, with enormous shining legs cut and bleeding in places and slapped rosy in others and her eyes shining with desire. She kept making the most terrible remarks, too, whether consciously or unconsciously I do not know, about blood and grease and to my surprise Olivia saw them all. These girls must talk a terrible lot of bawdy amongst themselves. David became quite incredibly obscene before the evening broke up and I went to bed, as always, with rather a heavy heart.

Saturday 18 April 1925

This morning Martin, David, Anne and Julia left the island and we waved them away rather gladly. I think that the party will be delightful now. After an orgy the other night I had to get up at 6 to row Captain Benson off, which was exhausting. Anne told two stories the other morning about self-abuse which she must have made up though she claimed and, I think, believed them to be personal experiences. She was much mocked about them but did not seem to mind very much. Yesterday morning Elizabeth, Richard and I went out in a boat and I tried to climb a cliff and fell down.

This morning's mail has been a little disturbing. Gaspard is ill and Audrey Lucas is engaged immediately to marry Harold Scott. It seems to be a most improper arrangement and one for which I am largely responsible. On the Monday morning of the party at Hanover Terrace I received a letter from Audrey begging me not to be drunk again – she had been shocked on Friday evening. I forgot to answer it and spent the evening in prison. I am so afraid that she was hurt about this and is marrying this vulgar man out of mockery. But perhaps she likes him. Alastair sent me £5 and the news that he is putting off his blind so that I can come to it.

The sad thing – the only sad thing about this party – is that I cannot cure myself of being in love with Olivia. It is so trying for us both. While I was in Denbighshire I had hoped that I only loved her as a personification of all the jolly things I had left behind, but here I am with Terence mouthing Kant into a pint glass and David making endless jokes about Lesbos and lavatories, and Richard rowing unseaworthy boats in fearnought trousers, and Lady Plunket serene over it all, but I am still sad and uneasy and awkward whenever I am with Olivia, and she of course is more than half in love with Tony which makes things less possible and now here is Audrey linking herself up for life with a person whom I am sure she does not much like. Amen. So be it.

Friday 24 April 1925

In a short time we are going, and by the look of the sea and of the passengers who came across this morning it will be a nauseous journey. During the last two days I have been immersed in gloom which has suddenly and quite unaccountably broken this morning. Last night we were quite drunk. At least Terence and I were, and Olivia was tipsy – I think that there is no one to whom the word 'tipsy' applies better than to her. All manner of sad things were said and I retired to bed rather savagely. I have stolen a postcard of a drunken sailor embracing a postbox from the canteen.

The Matthew Ponsonby blind has endless repercussions. A piteous letter this morning from Lady Maud Parry[1] about it – from Mrs Ponsonby no answer at all.

Tonight we spend at Exeter and after that I go to Barford for a few days to drink with Alastair.

I am stranded naked and ashamed because my mother will not send me clothes from London and my washing has been lost here. It is sad. Terence has developed a new and disagreeable mannerism. He is continuously licking the backs of his hands. I suppose it must have some Freudian implication.

Barford House, Monday 27 April 1925

As I had feared I was sick on the boat but quite discreetly behind the cabin so that no one saw except a tactful mariner in a blue jumper who was, I suppose, accustomed to such sights.

From Instow, where we ate eggs, we took an empty and leisurely train to Exeter. We arrived at about 10 at an hotel called Rougemont where were assembled a staff of the most delightful servants I ever met. We drank Liebfraumilch and ate supper and went to bed very early, Richard and Elizabeth having to go early to The Ridgeway.[2]

Next day to everyone's surprise Olivia came down dressed and having finished her Elizabeth Arden in time for breakfast. We went out to see the cathedral and the Guildhall and Woolworth's sixpenny bazaar. Soon after 12 I got into a train full of people and waited in the corridor until I ate a very bad luncheon and arrived at Bristol feeling more than a little depressed. There I changed into an empty carriage and finished the journey to Stratford in peace. Alastair met me and we had a heavy drinking evening in the little room he has fitted up for himself over the stables.

Next morning, Sunday, heard Mass at Warwick with special intention for Mrs Ponsonby. After breakfast we took Mrs G.'s very grand new car to Oxford

[1] Matthew Ponsonby's grandmother.
[2] Home at Shere, Surrey, of Harold and Lady Victoria (née Leveson-Gower) Russell, the parents of Elizabeth Russell.

where at first we found no one. Then quite suddenly in Beaumont Street we met Gyles Isham and Jim Wedderburn and Robert Byron and David Greene and John Sutro and most curiously of all Tony Bushell. We had luncheon with John at the New Reform and then drove out to Beckley and called on Mr Cooke who is a sad and scorbutic figure. We drove back to Barford where there was a lovely drunk tea party – Tony, Claud Cockburn, David, Robert, Rudolph, John Sutro, Harold Acton and a most distressing rich vulgar woman whose breath smelled horribly.

A peaceful evening, Alastair soaking port over the fire in the library. It seems unkind but I much prefer Barford when it is being run by Mrs G. Things are very vague now and there are not enough fires. Alastair is coming to London for Wednesday evening.

This morning a very sad letter from Lady P. who is overmuch worried by these Ponsonbys. I have written what I consider to be an astute letter to Matthew. I hope his parents see it.

This morning Alastair has gone away to print[1] and I am left alone awaiting the replies to several telegrams to Oxford hoping that they will bring me money.

Arnold House, Denbighshire, Friday 1 May 1925

I arrived here yesterday in immeasurable gloom – only relieved by a deathly sleepiness which with the morning has passed to leave me to the naked prospect of fourteen weeks' exile.

On Tuesday Alastair and I went into Oxford by train and lunched at 10 Oriel Street with Harold[2] – Elizabeth, Richard and David were there. David and Harold very nearly quarrelled about Martin Wilson. We all had tea with David and then went to call on various people. Everyone in Oxford looked very spotted and shabby, I thought. I had meant to get home to dinner but we were prevailed upon to stay in Oxford and Alastair had an enormous and costly dinner party at the George. Rather drunk we started home at about 9 or half-past, I in the back of Elizabeth's car. Before we reached Henley I was frozen sober and almost insensible. By the time we reached Hanover Terrace I felt disinclined to move anywhere so I slept there on the sofa after having kept poor Olivia up for hours talking to her. I got up next morning at 5.30 and slipped away to breakfast at Golders Green. Chapman & Hall becomes more melancholy daily which is sad for my mother.

I met Alastair just before luncheon at the Max Beerbohm exhibition – which was quite marvellous – and took him to luncheon at Lady Plunket's. We went to Paddington for a case of drink and to Harrods for some gramophone records

[1] Alastair Graham had become apprenticed to the Shakespeare Head Press in Stratford-on-Avon.
[2] Harold Acton.

and hairdressing and then back to tea at Hanover Terrace where Elizabeth and Richard had arrived. More talk of the *affaire* Ponsonby. Home in time to dress. To the Globe Theatre to see Noel Coward's new play *Fallen Angels* which had I been less tired I should probably have enjoyed more. In the bar we met Peter Rodd and Gavin Henderson. My party was the family Greene, Alastair, and Peter Quennell. The evening as a whole was rather dismal. We had supper at the Florence and then I went to a party at Audrey's for a few minutes and then on with Johnny Rothenstein to join them at Harry Plunket Greene's[1] studio. We stayed there drinking very little until about 2.30, Olivia at first complaining of cold and then of sleepiness.

Yesterday I came here. There is a new usher called Young[2] in Watson's place. I think that my finances have never been so desperate or my spirits so depressed.

Tuesday morning 5 May 1925

During the last three days I have been sunk in Julian apathy. The sports are being held this week so that there is very little work for me to do. In school I find a certain perverse pleasure in making all I teach as dreary to the boys as it is to myself. A crowd of urchins have come up into the Fifth from the Sixth who know nothing and cannot hear what I say to them. I set them in sullen rows all day long to learn grammatical definitions – 'a syllable is a single sound made by one simple effort of the voice,' etc. – *ad nauseam*. Anne sent me some photographs of the Lundy party. I have bought a tin of Royal Yacht which reminds me of it poignantly. I am reading a book of essays by Bertrand Russell which come in by every post and the unbroken silence of Olivia. Young, the new paradoxes of suicide and achievement, work out the scheme for a new book, and negotiate with the man Young to buy a revolver from him.

Thursday 14 May 1925

Rather more than a seventh of the term is gone and now that I have recovered from caffeine poisoning, from which I think I must have been suffering, I can face the future with equanimity in spite of the piles of bills which come in by every post and the unbroken silence of Olivia. Young, the new usher, is monotonously pederastic and talks only of the beauty of sleeping boys. Most evenings I go out with Gordon and guns and shoot at jackdaws but with more noise than bloodshed. The other evening I bought a bottle of Dow's 1908 port. Dean mixed his with lime juice and soda and when I offered him sugar too said that he preferred it 'dry'. This story is not really quite true but I have recounted it in so many letters that I have begun to believe it. 'Summer Hours'

---

[1] The separated husband of Gwen Plunket Greene; a singer and professor of music.
[2] The model for 'Captain Grimes' in *Decline and Fall*.

have started, which means less work for me in various ways. I have bought a sketch-book and want to do some serious drawing now that it is warm enough and light enough to sit in my bedroom at the San.

Yesterday there were sports. I made a book on it and was doing fairly well until an outsider won the 220 yards Under Thirteen at 6–1, and 'Jammy' won the egg-and-spoon race at 10–1. I won the masters' egg-and-spoon race to my intense gratification and the surprise of all. Lady P. wrote to me this morning, but a sorrowful letter rather. There is no news of the secretaryship at Pisa. Audrey's engagement is reported darkly to be all over.

Monday 18 May 1925

This morning a letter from Richard telling me that the Greene family are quarrelling with me. I just don't mind. This sort of thing has happened before so often that it has ceased to shock me. I shall have to regard all my friendships as things of three to six months. It makes everything easier. Also a letter from Mrs G. saying that she will come down in a motor to see me.

Also a letter from Billy telling me only amusing thing I have heard about the *affaire* Ponsonby yet. The old Duchess of Abercorn will have it that it was Arthur Ponsonby who was imprisoned for drunkenness and has been everywhere telling people how sad it is for the poor children to have a drunkard for their father.

Thursday 28 May 1925

The Greene quarrel has been healed. Richard and Lady P. and Olivia have all written to me. Alastair and Mrs G. came down to see me on Saturday and Sunday. They were both very sweet. Mrs Banks has been markedly more polite since she saw them.

I have quite suddenly received inspiration about my book. I am making the first chapter a cinema film and have been writing furiously ever since. I honestly think that it is going to be rather good.

Wednesday 1 July 1925

The last few weeks have been very pleasant. I do not know exactly how long ago, but I should think it must be nearly a month now, the news arrived from Alec that C. K. Scott Moncrieff was ready to take me as his secretary at Pisa. I promptly gave in my notice to the Banks family and made Gordon and Young and myself agreeably drunk at the Queen's Hotel. From then until yesterday I lived in the benign contemplation of a year abroad drinking Chianti under olive trees and listening to discussions of all the most iniquitous outcasts of Europe. I even became quite interested in my work – refreshed by the prospect of almost immediate release – and quite touchingly fond of a few of the boys. I stopped work on my novel and spent English afternoons pottering around in the sunshine with a pipe and a bag of sweetmeats, bathing after dinner, and sleeping soundly with dreams of the Renaissance. I even approached kindly feeling towards my father and contracted with him to surrender my allowance in exchange for my debts. Alas, yesterday came the news that Scott Moncrieff does not want me. It looks rather like being the end of the tether. At the moment I can see no sort of comfort anywhere. I had already decided on a dolorous charabanc expedition that, no doubt justly, the boys – or at least such of them as I liked – had no kind of affection for me. I think that the proprietor would be quite unwilling to take me back even if I wanted to return. I can scarcely expect my poor father to give me any more money. The phrase 'the end of the tether' besets me with unshakable persistence all the time.[1]

Friday 3 July 1925

Two things have happened to comfort me a little. Professor Dawkins[2] has come back from Oxford. He arrived on the field the day before yesterday and we spent the afternoon talking in complete neglect of the game which I should have been taking. He told me a pleasing Curzonism. 'I myself should deprecate anything in the nature of a beano' (pronounced 'bayāno'). The other thing was that Young and I went out and made ourselves drunk and he confessed all his previous career. He was expelled from Wellington, sent down from Oxford, and forced to resign his commission in the army. He has left four schools precipitately, three in the middle of the term through his being taken in sodomy and one through his being drunk six nights in succession. And yet he goes on getting better and better jobs without difficulty. It was all very like Bruce and the spider.

Saturday 4 July 1925

Last night Gordon and I dined at Professor Dawkins. We did not get drunk, which was what Gordon wanted, but I enjoyed the evening none the less.

This morning a letter from Grenfell[3] encouraging me in the idea of going to his school as an usher. It would have advantages. I should be near Gaspard and Olivia but I fear it would not be cheap living in London.

Friday 10 July 1925

Heath Mount has fallen through as I am no cricketer. Everyone is intensely doleful here. Dean has vexed the proprietor's wife and is to leave and can find

---

[1] 'One night, soon after I got the news from Pisa, I went down alone to the beach with my thoughts full of death. I took off my clothes and began swimming out to sea. Did I really intend to drown myself? That certainly was in my mind. . . .' *A Little Learning*, p. 229. Waugh encountered a shoal of jelly-fish and turned back.

[2] Sometime President of the Hypocrites' Club. See Appendix of Names, p. 794.

[3] Granville Grenfell, Headmaster of Waugh's prep school, Heath Mount, in Hampstead.

no work. Gordon's father is dying and will leave his mother and sister with no means of support. Young thinks he is getting old and Chaplin does not like the rain. For myself I have a heart of lead and nerves of fire and can see no hope of anything ever happening. Lady Plunket is to go to a hospital to be operated on. An aunt of Elizabeth's will give Richard £200 a year. The last two evenings I have spent at the village pub. Rowley Conway[?] fell down and broke his arm and had to be carried up the hill on such a hot afternoon. Alastair is with Claud Cockburn in Germany.

Sunday 26 July 1925

Tomorrow – a day before the others – I have got leave to go to London to have dinner with Alec. The proprietor was not gracious about it, but he gave way. The last week or two we have spent either at Mrs Roberts's public house and Professor Dawkins's raspberry canes. Dean and I had dinner at the Queen's one night and were drunk. I shall go home without money or any hope of earning any.

I was surprised and a little pleased to find in the history examination that I had taught some of the boys something.

Hampstead, Tuesday 28 July 1925

After some few valedictory discourtesies Mr Banks let me go early yesterday morning. Mr Hughes, the sot, drove me to Abergele and after a weary journey I arrived in London in the early afternoon. Gaspard is grown enormous but is still vastly charming. At 7.45 I met Alec at the Ritz and ate and drank well with him; we went on to the Savile for port and from there to Tony's dressing-room at the Adelphi. He is superbly important nowadays with Cabinet ministers waiting on him with their cars and amorous Jewesses offering him their beds. He also seems rather rich.

Saturday 1 August 1925

I have enjoyed the last few days. On Tuesday I spent the morning writing letters to the directors of all the art galleries or editors of all the art magazines in London. After luncheon my mother compelled me to take her to a wedding in Cheyne Walk. I dined at home and went to bed early.

Next day I went to luncheon at the Sutros. There were hundreds of people and extremely good things to eat. After tea I drank with Ronald Matthews, who is rather a sad figure now plunged in penury and unrequited love, at the 1917 Club. Elsa was there and told me that there had been committee meetings about Tony's drunkenness and mine last holidays. I went on to dinner at the Greenes' new house in Sumner Place which I don't like nearly as much as Hanover Terrace. There was just the family and Elizabeth there – David was staying in a grand party at Goodwood. I enjoyed the evening a lot. After it I went off to the Adelphi again to drink with Tony. The poor eunuch Addinsell[1] was there who is now a success too, writing ballets for the young man Dolin.[2] We drank at Oddenino's and then at Alec's flat where I slept.

Next day another vast luncheon party at the Sutros, from which I withdrew Billy Clonmore and took him off to drink beer with Gaspard. We had such an odd photograph made of us. Olivia, Elizabeth and Richard came to dinner. Richard stayed the night. I bought a new suit next day, lunched at home with Jane Marston, and went to a cinema with her. In the evening Mother and I went to see Tony act. He was so bad that I felt hot and cold all over. Henry Ainley was marvellous but the play was most old-fashioned and clumsy. There was one dreadful moment when Tony had to say, 'But this man, can he be a wrong 'un?'

Saturday. I went to see the Pirandello *Henry IV* at the Everyman Theatre. It is an intriguing mixture of Bergson and melodrama. In the evening[3] I drank with Richard and Elizabeth at the Café Royal.

Sunday 2 August 1925

Spent the day with Richard and Elizabeth.

Monday 3 August 1925

Richard and Elizabeth came in Richard's new car – very shabby and noisy but quite fast. We went on to Hampstead Heath Fair and threw darts and balls. They went off to The Ridgeway. I went to dinner at the Queen's Restaurant, Sloane Square, with Gwen Otter. Alec is giving a party on Friday night.

Tuesday 4 August 1925

Such a tiring day ordering clothes and interviewing agents. I bought a paint-box for Percival's birthday present, had tea with Tom Driberg who is becoming odder than ever, and gave Ronald Matthews dinner. He drank such a lot of whisky and bored me rather.

Wednesday 5 August 1925

All the morning I have been applying for jobs. Richard's schoolmaster[4] is looking for another usher. It would be fun if I got it.

Friday 7 August 1925

Yesterday evening, after a dreary day interviewing the directors of various

---

[1] Richard Addinsell (b. 1904), composer of songs and music for many stage productions and films.

[2] Anton Dolin.

[3] i.e., 31 July.

[4] Richard Plunket Greene was teaching at a school at Aston Clinton.

art galleries who were very polite and useless, I went to *The Cherry Orchard* – a perfectly marvellous play. I also went to a very odd kind of entertainment in Charing Cross which has just opened. It is a continuous musical hall which lasts from 4 until 11 on three stages. The audience have to stand. There was a man who claimed to remember every event in the world's history but really knew only the winners of the chief horse-races and the dimensions of the *Titanic*. I dined on Wednesday with Dudley Carew who is still committing adulteries too much.

Baldhead's party was quite a success. Young of Denbighshire arrived first and drank himself quietly insensible throughout the evening. My friends all arrived rather late but there was plenty of champagne for all who came.

I am writing in the middle of the night because I am tired of trying to sleep. I never can nowadays for hours and hours after I go to bed.

Thursday 13 August 1925

On Saturday Liza,[1] Richard and I drove down to Friendly Green to luncheon with Olivia and Joan Talbot whom I liked rather. Olivia was peculiarly sweet to me. We left Elizabeth there and came back terribly tired. We found a letter from Crawford of Clinton encouraging me in the hope of getting to his school as an usher but I have no doubt that it will fall through like everything else.

On Sunday we went down to Aston Clinton. It is an inconceivably ugly house but a lovely park. We fetched Claud Cockburn from Tring on the way and ate sandwiches and drank beer in one of the class-rooms. We had tea with Chinese Harry[2] and brought Claud home for the night. This morning Richard went down to Friendly Green. I spent the morning in trying to buy Chapman & Hall a present for Gosse's[3] golden wedding. In the afternoon I slept. Dinner at the Spanish Restaurant, Swallow Street, with Gwen Otter and John Rothenstein. I brought John back to sleep here – I can't conceive why. It is time I tried to go to sleep again I suppose.

Sunday 16 August 1925

I have got the Aston Clinton job. The news arrived – so oddly expressed – on Friday evening, just before Richard and Elizabeth and Olivia and Alastair came for dinner. It should have made the party a jolly one but somehow it did not – as far as I was concerned anyway. I was tired and ill at ease, as I usually am with Olivia, and my father's jollity seemed more than usually distressing.

[1] Elizabeth Russell.

[2] Claud Cockburn's father, for many years 'Chinese Secretary' at the British Legation in Peking.

[3] Sir Edmund Gosse (1849–1928), critic, essayist, and author of *Father and Son*; kinsman of Arthur Waugh.

The dinner at any rate was good. After the others had left Alastair and I sat up until 4 talking and drinking beer and smoking.

Next day I went to order the morning coat which I must have to be a master at Aston Clinton. Alastair and I lunched at Kettners – needless to say at his expense. In the evening he took me to a revue I had long wanted to see, called *On with the Dance*. Ernest Thesiger was quite marvellous. It was an acutely class-conscious show, I thought. When we got home we made omelettes in the kitchen.

This morning Alastair went away. I shall join him at Barford on Wednesday. I lunched at Gwen Otter's; her cook has at last recovered from her parturition and made us some excellent food. John Rothenstein was there; he has promised to find me a wife and suggests Daphne Graham or a Cecilia Balfour who is a cousin of all those Talbots.

Dinner at home with family and dog.

Monday 17 August 1925

To a cinema with my mother. I am buying some check trousers which I think will be amusing. Overdrawn at the bank again.

Barford, Thursday 20 August 1925

I have left my spectacles somewhere, probably I think in John Rothenstein's office. I lunched with him yesterday and one of my prospective wives – a Miss Balfour whom I liked.

Friday 21 August 1925

This morning I am restored to sight. The house is extremely noisy because Daisy, Mrs Lowe, is staying here. She and Mrs G. quarrel incessantly and tumultuously. Yesterday I tried to drive a motor car.

Saturday 22 August 1925

Alastair and I drove over to luncheon at Oddington where David Talbot Rice[1] lives. He has such a charming house with polo sticks and skis in the lavatory and a spiral staircase and we waited on ourselves at luncheon which was nice. Franky Filleul was staying there. He has become more tedious than ever. After luncheon we walked miles round David's park with a disobedient dog called Tim. At Barford we were met with the excellent news that Mrs Lowe had at last left the house, so that everything since has been comparatively quiet.

[1] b. 1903; educated Eton and Oxford; Oxford expedition to Kish, Mesopotamia, 1925; with Robert Byron, author of *The Birth of Western Painting*, the result of a journey to the Near East, including Mount Athos, in 1927; Professor of the History of Art at Edinburgh University, 1931; *Byzantine Art*, 1935.

Sunday 23 August 1925

I heard Mass in a hideous church in Leamington. There was a monstrous boy sitting immediately in front of me who somewhat distracted my thoughts from the contemplation of the divine attributes. We drove to Broadway after luncheon to call on Faith who was in Scotland.

Wednesday 26 August 1925

It is horrible to use red ink but Alastair's black ink is all congealed. On Monday Mrs G. found out that Alastair was guaranteeing my overdraft and was in a rage about it. Yesterday she left for East Haddon.[1] Alastair and I took her over laden with luggage and dogs and maids and had tea there and returned to a peaceful house. East Haddon was quite full of very gaga old people. All the servants are over sixty. Superannuated governesses or nurses are in all the rooms. Mrs Guthrie mistook me for Alastair. It must be rather a dreary house for Hamish and his wife. She had the best shingle that ever I saw. I finished my story which I have called *The Balance* and took it to be typed. It is odd but, I think, quite good.

I spent a most peaceful morning writing a few letters and reading a little Bergson and at 12 took a bus to Stratford to lunch with Alastair. I went to his wine merchant to buy some hock for us to drink but in the end bought some claret because it was called Mouton de Baron de Rothschild. It was quite nice. We drank a cocktail at the Shakespeare Hotel and lunched at a restaurant called Arden. Then Alastair went to print books and I to a performance of *Two Gentlemen of Verona* – such a silly play. The theatre is not quite as monstrous inside as out, but it is badly made and uncomfortable. The audience most bardolatrous, laughing religiously at the most pathetic puns. Alastair and I had tea together and went back to Barford where we dined in high-necked jumpers and did much that could not have been done if Mrs Graham had been here.

Thursday 27 August 1925

Slept most of the morning and lunched alone.

Friday 28 August 1925

Mrs G. returned with much noise.

Saturday 29 August 1925

I left Barford in Alastair's car, meaning to go to London from Oxford. We lunched in Banbury on bread and cheese and then went to Beckley where everyone was so sweet that I decided to spend the night there. Cooke has been

---

[1] Home of a family named Guthrie.

away and looks a little better than when I last saw him. Harold Claire has nearly killed himself in his car again.

Beckley, Sunday 30 August 1925

It was pleasant waking up in Beckley. I sat in the inn porch reading a newspaper until 12 when Mr Cooke and Mr Higgs came down for their morning drink. At lunch-time Alastair arrived from Barford and we ate roast beef and celery with Mr Cooke. Cooke, without saying anything to me, paid for my board and lodging. I thought it was extraordinarily sweet of him. We drove to Tring, took Claud away to tea at Aston Clinton, and from there to dinner at Aylesbury. During dinner they read my story which I have had typed at great expense – in Leamington. I decided it was too late to return to London and slept at Chinese Harry's house.

Monday 31 August 1925

I have forgotten to say that throughout these journeyings I have been carrying a kitten with me for Olivia. We arrived a little before lunch-time to find the house in the possession of a poor mad woman who thinks she has murdered her brother. I am glad I have been away for these two days.

Happisburgh, Tuesday 1 September 1925

A dreary journey to Happisburgh with children and things in the train. I spent two hours at Norwich feeding Olivia's cat and looking at a cathedral – very cylindrical and solid. Then I came to a station called North Walsham where Richard and his car were waiting and so to St Anne's. I am sleeping at the house of a blacksmith – a large room but a horrible woman who hates giving me water to wash in. St Anne's is rather charming but has no bath.

Wednesday 2 September 1925

We bathed in the morning. Olivia thinks she is very fat but is not really. Richard, Elizabeth and I went to some public houses in the car. Crossword puzzles and detective stories.

Thursday 3 September 1925

My landlady gave me some hot water and cleaned my shoes which was kind of her.

Barford, Wednesday 9 September 1925

I feel so sleepy. I have just eaten a large luncheon and drunk some burgundy and last night I slept very little. I think soon I shall go to sleep.

The Happisburgh week passed so quickly. After the second day Olivia decided to menstruate and could not bathe so no one did, tho' I wanted to often. Most of the time David read detective stories to us. Richard and I made a book on one of them and lost a lot of money.

On Monday Richard and Elizabeth and I went to a horrible place called Yarmouth. Half of it was just like Wembley but Richard was very happy discerning sloops and brigantines and trawlers and such things. Yesterday I got up very early and went to North Walsham and drank whisky in a commercial hotel and then took a train to London. I ate breakfast on it. I went to Oxford from Paddington where Alastair and Claud met me. We hardly spent any time at the fair – they had been there the night before very drunk. We went to Beckley and drank with Mrs Mattingley and from there to Barford. Mrs G. is at Harrogate but threatens to return tomorrow. There are practically no servants either. I must go to sleep.

Thursday 10 September 1925

I slept yesterday afternoon and then went in by bus to meet Alastair in Stratford. We drank a pint of beer at the Shakespeare Hotel and then came back in the rain and stuck stamps on a bottle as I had seen done in a public house at Happisburgh. Today Mrs Graham is returning – telegrams have been sent to every servant and everywhere fires are being lit and plants carried about. Chris Hollis is coming back to England. It is possible that Alastair and I will go to Paris to meet him.

Hampstead, Friday 11 September 1925

I went to Birmingham yesterday to meet Mrs G. It is a disgusting town with villas and slums and ready-made clothes shops and Chambers of Commerce. I bought a book of Dr Johnson's prayers for 2d in John Bright Street. Alastair and I purpose to spend Sunday in Shropshire.

On Saturday morning we left Stratford at 12 o'clock and, lunching at Droitwich, drove to tea at Ludlow in a very much timbered inn. I find that I am beginning to detest Elizabethan architecture owing to the vulgarities of Stratford-on-Avon. Ludlow Castle is much ruined but interesting and in certain aspects not unlovely. We had to pay 1s each for admission. In the twilight we drove to Bridgnorth and put up at an inn called – I think – the Swan where everyone was most hospitable. We walked about the town and went to a public house full of evil spirits and risked our lives on a funicular railway and then to bed.

Very sleepy next morning. We drove through Clungunford and Clunbury and over Wenlock Edge to luncheon at Church Stretton which both decided was too hideous to eat in.

Back to Barford at 6 and at 7 in a crowded and exceedingly dilatory train to Paddington. Eventually to Golders Green where I found my bald brother and Luned Jacobs. To bed very sleepy.

Monday 14 September 1925

I paid a bill at Dunhill's and redeemed my ring from Mr Attenborough and then lunched with Alec at the Savile and afterwards drank some excellent sherry. Then to a distressing film by Charles Chaplin which was being presented for the first time to an enormous crowd at the Tivoli. I hated it. I talked to Dudley Carew in a public house and then home to dinner. Reading Clifford Bax's *Inland Far*. There is to be a party at Mary Butts to which I must go.

Tuesday 15 September 1925

The party at Mary's was quite fun. I dined first at Joyce's flat[1] in an odd place called Percy Circus near King's Cross Station. Dudley Carew was there. After dinner I cut Joyce's hair and we waited rather impatiently for the arrival of a friend of Dudley's called Cecil Roberts[2] – not the one who writes books but an agreeable boy fresh from Wellington who is working with Squire on the *Mercury*. At last he arrived and after we had drunk some beer in a slum bar we went on to Mary's[3] where we found some very odd painters quite drunk and rather naked. They were for the most part what Mary called 'Paris Queers'. I liked a tall man who, from a drawing on the chimney-piece, I think is a good artist. Later when everyone was gone Mary told us his story. Cecil Roberts, whom everyone seems to address as 'Bobbie', was rather shocked at it all I think, but comforted himself in the reflection that Mary comes of a 'good county family'. Dudley behaved a little foolishly. Chid with his sobriety he filled one of Mary's vast glasses with neat brandy and drank it straight down. For some minutes he talked with only a slight quickening of his animation and then disappeared to be discovered some time later insensible in the lavatory. Joyce of her charity took him home.

After a time, complaints came in from the man above – who is called Boffin – and the party broke up. Bobbie and Joyce and I stayed on for a little while talking until Mary disappeared and we heard unmistakable sounds of something from the lavatory. We thought it was time to go and were fortunate enough to secure taxis without difficulty. The party was given in honour of a negro[4] who is acting a play called *Emperor Jones* but he had a fit in his dressing-room and would not come.

Wednesday 16 September 1925

In the morning I began Plato's *Republic*. After luncheon to a cinema. How I

[1] Joyce Fagan's.

[2] Cecil A. (Bobbie) Roberts, a nephew of the 1st Baron Clwyd, a Welsh MP from 1892 to 1918 and a passionate 'Total Abstainer' (President of the Anglo-Indian Temperance Association). He did not share his uncle's temperance views.

[3] Mary Butts' house in Belsize Park.

[4] Paul Robeson.

hate cinemas. In the evening Joyce and Dudley came to dinner. I have some check trousers.

Thursday 17 September 1925

Read more Plato. In the evening with my mother to Barry Jackson's *Hamlet* at the Kingsway Theatre. I did not find the modern clothes at all disturbing except that they were such singularly shabby modern clothes – particularly the women. Hamlet was poor and Horatio pathetic but the King and Polonius excellent. They cut the 'recorders' scene with Rosencrantz and Guildenstern which I thought a pity. The duel was exceptionally well managed.

It is all very vague about Chris.[1] We cannot discover by what boat he is arriving or when. He may turn up at any moment expecting hundreds of friends drawn up drunk to meet him.

Friday 18 September 1925

I sent *The Balance* to Leonard Woolf.[2] Dined with Mrs Fremlin at her club and afterwards to *Hay Fever* which made me laugh. Chris returns tomorrow. Desmond O'Connor[3] has shot himself in India.

Saturday 19 September 1925

Chris returned. Claud, Alastair and I spent several hours at Victoria meeting various boat trains before at last he arrived – quite unchanged except for the accretion of rather more dirt. He was wearing a Mexican ready-made suit and brought with him some books wrapped in a dirty towel and two halves of a suitcase. We went to Golders Green and drank a little beer and then went to meet my bald brother at the long bar at the Trocadero. We went to the Florence for dinner where we drank a lot and Chris discovered that he had no money so Baldhead and Alastair had to pay for practically everything all the evening. We went to the Savile and drank good port and then to the Café Royal and then to Oddenino's. At the Café Royal we found two men, one of whom Chris appeared to have met in America. We took them to drink with us at Oddenino's. Baldhead threw plates on the floor. We went to Baldhead's flat and drank more. One of the Americans turned out to be the man who played the monster in a film called *Merry-Go-Round*. We left Baldhead and drank at a place called Engineers' Club and then to the Savoy where the mummer was staying. I got into his bed and Claud sat on the lavatory and worked the plug with his foot for hours. The monster carried round packets of tooth-powder

[1] Christopher Hollis, with Douglas Woodruff, later editor of *The Tablet*, was returning from a round-the-world debating tour.

[2] At the Hogarth Press.

[3] Lancing contemporary of Waugh's.

which he said was heroin and everyone took. We returned home at about 4 and cooked sausages – all very drunk.

Sunday 20 September 1925

Alastair and Chris went to Mass in the morning and Claud and I walked with Gaspard. Harold Acton came to luncheon – very late because he had gone to Highgate. After Harold and Claud had gone, Chris and Alastair began a conversation of incredible inanity which lasted with brief breaks from 6 to 12 and nearly drove me mad. We went on a bus and idled in gutters and drank in a pub and dined here and sat in the bookroom afterwards and still they talked of drink and zanies *ad nauseam*. I did not know Chris had it in him to be such a bore. Catholicism and the Colonies seem rather stultifying.

Monday 21 September 1925

Chris left and tho' it breaks my heart to say so I was glad of it. I went to a very sexual play with Mrs G. She keeps a bottle of ancient brandy in her bedroom. We drank it out of tooth mugs before going to *Cobra*.

Tuesday 22 September 1925

Alastair and I went to a cinema at King's Cross and after dinner to call on Joyce at Percy Circus. I am afraid that Dudley Carew lay with her that night.[1]

Wednesday 23 September 1925

Alastair left in the morning. I am afraid that I was exceedingly disagreeable all the weekend and am sorry for it. I lunched with Harold Acton at Claridge's and spent the afternoon with him there hearing him read some amusing 'Lives of the Saints' which he has been writing. His mother and William[2] arrived at about 4 and we went to call on my bald brother. After dinner I went to a party given by one of the homosexual painters I had met at Mary Butts. He wanted to dance with me and Bobbie but it seemed too repulsive and I am afraid we were rude. A lovely woman called Varda who is a mannequin came just as I was leaving.

Thursday 24 September 1925

I am tired with packing. In a short time Elizabeth and Richard are coming to fetch me away to Aston Clinton.

Aston Clinton, Thursday 24 September 1925

It was a dreary beginning of term. Richard's car was affected with a 'wheel

---

[1] Dudley Carew (in a letter to the editor), says that Waugh's fear was misplaced.
[2] William Acton.

wobble' or 'woggle' and he arrived very late; we drove down in cold twilight and reached Aston Clinton just early enough for us to go in to dinner very late. Elizabeth came with us. She and I went in first and there was a dead silence while we sat down at a bleak table in front of a prodigious ewer of water. Richard came in and then the usher they call the cavalry officer.[1] After a wretched dinner we took Richard's car to have the wheels mended and sat for a little huddled over the fire at the Bell, all three of us deeply depressed. Soon Elizabeth drove back to London and left us to a house of echoing and ill-lit passages and a frightful common-room.

Friday 25 September 1925

The timetable is not finished and I have had a fairly easy time. The Headmaster made a speech to the boys telling them how different he was from other headmasters who, when boys broke things, would beat them for it, while he appealed to them as gentlemen not to do such a thing again. All this in a most unattractive and affected manner. I took languid, lengthy,[2] and incredibly ignorant boys in English. After luncheon Richard and I walked about rather dismally until tea. After tea I supervised an examination and taught boys English. Dinner. I discovered that the boy next to me had been superannuated from my House at Lancing. Richard took preparation. I bought him some beer at the Bell which we drank in his bedroom.

Saturday 26 September 1925

I taught boys in the morning and after a rather glum awakening began to be a little more at home in this frightful school. There is a boy I like the look of called Westby who is not mad but diseased. After luncheon I played football and after that had a bath in a marvellously luxurious bath – the only physical comfort I have been able to discern in this prodigious house. I was dozing from the effects of this when Claud Cockburn came in, brought over by Richard from Tring. I went off with him to dinner at Chinese Harry's where they were kind to me. Richard came later and we drank beer until late. Home by way of the speech-room windows.

Sunday 27 September 1925

We went to church dressed in tall hats and tail coats. Richard was covered in dung by a dog just before service and I had to take snuff. Elizabeth was waiting for us outside. Claud came over for tea. We drank beer. I dined in hall.

---

[1] Captain Hyde-Upward; it was his custom to polish and clean out his pipe while standing naked at his bedroom window.
[2] *Sic.*

Monday 28 September 1925

I dined and drank beer at China Harry's again. Claud lent me a novel by Virginia Woolf which I refuse to believe is good.

Tuesday 29 September 1925

By one post both my MSS of *The Balance* were returned to me, one from Whitworth and one from Woolf. Richard may be getting a job at Lancing through the good offices of Lady Vita.[1] He went off to London. I played football. A swaggering boy called Kelly, who is a subject to epilepsy, made friendly overtures to me as a result of my reading him some of *Trivia* – also borrowed from Claud.

Wednesday 30 September 1925

In the afternoon I played rugby football – very exhausting – and in the evening drank at the Bell with Claud.

Thursday 1 October 1925

I had to teach shooting in the morning which was rather a farce because I let them shoot with the guard over the foresight and the wind gauge registering a hurricane. However even when this was put right they failed to hit the targets, so it did not matter very much. After luncheon, while Richard was waiting to take me to London, Crawford[2] drew me aside 'to compare our ideals'. I got some money out of him for the library and drawing class. We went to London in a little over an hour and went straight to Summer Place. Olivia was at Eton for the day and we found Liza and Lady Plunket alone. After tea I bought plaster casts for the mad boys who draw, and dined with my father who gave me partridges to eat shot by Samuel Hoare. Richard came and drank beer and we arrived home at about 2.

Friday 2 October 1925

Taught lunatics. Played rugby football. Drank at Bell. As usual with Chris's arrangements everything is very vague about the weekend party. We are expecting him to give us dinner at Aylesbury, but do not know if he will come.

Saturday 3 October 1925

Alastair came and Beckley Harold[3] and Liza, but not Chris. In his own devastating phraseology he had to 'jaw to chaps'. As usual, poor Alastair had to pay for dinner. We went to the Bull's Head, Aylesbury, all a little embarrassed

---

[1] As music master. Lady Victoria Russell was his prospective mother-in-law.
[2] The Headmaster.
[3] Harold Claire, the farmer's boy from Beckley.

by Harold Claire who would force double whiskies upon us when we didn't want them and could talk only of his own drunkenness and his own daring as a driver. As the evening progressed and he drank more he became more and more boastful and made Richard lay bets with him about their motor cars. We went to drink at Chinese Harry's house.

Sunday 4 October 1925

Much embarrassed by the presence of Harold Claire. After the drink of the evening before none of us felt strong enough to meet him, so the poor youth was left alone at Aylesbury until nearly luncheon-time when we sent Claud off to entertain him. It was rather a relief when at about 5 all our guests went away and left Liza and Richard and me to eat nuts together in the Bell by ourselves.

The usher Tetley flew into a rage, because Crawford is keeping on summer-time a little longer, and is leaving at once. It means very little more work and I am glad he is gone.

Monday, Tuesday and Wednesday 5, 6, and 7 October 1925

Taught the poor mad boys and played football with them. On Tuesday we suddenly found Terence's voice at the Bell and later Terence himself and his illegitimate brother. We drank with him until very late. Today – Wednesday – one of the few purely disinterested acts of kindness I have met with was done to me by P. F. Machin who has sent me £2 for a birthday present. I will remember him in my prayers.

Thursday 8 October 1925

Richard and I went up to London, in spite of an attempt by Crawford and the cavalry officer to keep us at Clinton. We arrived, owing to the time which the school keeps, at the same time as we started and lunched at my home with Elizabeth. Then Richard and Eliza went to Summer Place and I went to a hairdresser. In Bond Street I suddenly ran into John Sutro, and he and I went to Betty Holmes's club and later to his hotel and drank absinthe. He sent us home in his car. I gave dinner to my mother and Olivia at the Spanish Restaurant in Swallow Street. While we were there a telephone message arrived from Richard that he had just been left £100 and proposed celebrating it at the Café Royal. It was not altogether a cheerful party. Julia[1] came and Elizabeth Ponsonby[2], whom I met for the first time. Two years ago, or less even, I suppose I should have been rather thrilled by her. We drank red wine which made us feel rather unwell. When the Café Royal closed we went to Manson Place and found Hester Pellett. David turned up later very drunk. Home at about 3.

[1] Julia Strachey.

[2] Matthew Ponsonby's sister and a leader of the Bright Young People.

Friday 9 October 1925

Both of us felt utterly weary and by a strange good chance Crawford ordained a half-holiday.

Saturday 10 October 1925

Eliza came early in the morning. There was a fog which persuaded her to stay the night at the Bell. We spent a very quiet weekend which I much preferred to the preceding one. On Saturday evening we went to a cinema in Aylesbury to see Harold Lloyd.

Monday 12 October 1925

After a very busy day teaching the mad boys and watching them play games we went to Oxford. We were afraid that we should not know anyone but we found Hugh Lygon and Mark Ogilvie-Grant and John Sutro dining at the New Reform Club. They gave us champagne and we gave them brandy and then Claud arrived with a host of friends of whom I knew Archie Harding and James Reynolds. We drank at the OUDS and in someone's rooms and we found Arden in the street and we drank at Buols[?] and Matthew Ponsonby came to see us there and seemed friendlily disposed. We drank to Bow Street. Many of them have promised to come here on Thursday but I doubt if they will.

Tuesday 13 October 1925

I woke up with a violent cold which has greatly embittered my day.

Wednesday 14 October 1925

Whole day hideous through my cold. Except for one excursion to order tomorrow's dinner at the Bell I stayed indoors all day.

Thursday 15 October 1925

Reading *The Brothers Karamazov*. The dinner was a complete failure. David Greene and Anthony Russell[1] came down from London and Richard brought Elizabeth. But no one came from Oxford. David had hiccoughs and Richard was morose. At last they went away. David announces his engagement to a girl called Babe whose surname I cannot spell – McGusty or Magustie – her mother is called Bendir[2] and is hugely rich. No one takes them at all seriously, David complains.

Friday 16 October 1925

A full school day with drawing and a game to take and boxing. By tea-time

---

[1] Elizabeth Russell's brother.
[2] Arthur Bendir was chairman of Ladbroke's, the bookmaker's.

Richard and I had fallen asleep from sheer depression on opposite ends of the sofa. Suddenly 'some ladies' were announced and we went down to find an enormous Rolls-Royce with in it Olivia, David, Robert Byron and Babe McGusty or Magustie. They had tea at the Bell while we took afternoon school and then drove up to dinner at the George in Oxford. We had to go early for fear of Mrs Bendir, but before we went stole a bottle of vodka from David Rice – he is living in the old Hypocrites' rooms. Peter Quennell has been sent down for consorting with a woman called Cara who threatens to bring an action against the Proctors. No one seemed to have any very good excuse for failing us on Thursday.

Saturday 17 October 1925

Liza came down. There was a match in which the school played ignominiously. A quiet evening.

Sunday 18 October 1925

Liza came again. Vodka gives one marvellous dreams I have discovered, but prevents one from sleeping. Every night lately I have dreamed luxuriously but slept ill. Richard fetched me meat and bread to eat from China Harry's because I was so hungry.

Monday 19 October 1925

A full day of dreary work. I hope that my mother may be coming tomorrow and possibly Gaspard too. I hope to get some money from the Carlton Club soon. A little while ago I gave a cheque which, if it is honoured, will only be honoured by the kindness of my bank. However it was to a club of which Roger Fulford is the president.

On looking through what I have written tonight I am surprised to see that I have not recorded any impression of Babe. I suppose it is because she did not impress me in any definite way. She is quiet and good-natured and pretty and well dressed with round eyes and rather a shiny nose. She seems ten years younger than Olivia and indeed when Olivia is there I found she attracts my attention very little. I should have supposed her the last person to excite David, particularly as, apparently, none of the Bendir money will come to her. I gather too that her mother's position in the society to which David aspires is very uncertain.

Tuesday 20 October 1925

A day of pouring rain. My mother did not come after all and by lunch-time I felt that I could not live another day without getting away from the school, so I borrowed 10s from Richard and took a bus to Oxford. The journey took nearly two hours but I had *The Brothers Karamazov* with me. I went to Hall's to talk about check trousers and then on to Harold Acton. He was going to a party given by William Acton and Bryan Guinness where apparently everyone was to be, so I agreed to join him there later in the evening. I made Tom Driberg give me dinner – he could ill afford it I am afraid – at the George. —— was there with —— – they had just had another motor-accident killing or at any rate seriously injuring a small boy when they were drunk. Michael Tandy, looking rather clean, asked me to a party at 69 the High Street and gave me 10s to find Claud. I could not do this, but I spent the money dashing about Oxford in a taxi in pursuit of him. At about 9.30 I went to the Christ Church party. All the tales which had been told me about the temperance of the youngest generation are utterly false. I never saw so much champagne drunk so quickly. I found Richard and brought him in and we drank large quantities of a dangerous mixture by William which consisted chiefly of champagne, gin and absinthe. We went for a short time to 69 the High where all the people who felt they should have been asked to Christ Church were drowning their chagrin. We were by now raging drunk and I can remember very little about the party except that I fought someone. It was a pathetic party I should think. About two miles out of Thame, Richard began to be sick and lay immovable in the side of the road alternately dozing and vomiting for two hours, while I sheltered as best I could under the broken hood of the car and pacified a suspicious night-watchman. Eventually we got back soaking wet at about 4 and so to bed.

Wednesday 21 October 1925

Very tired but not as ill as we had expected. I played soccer in the afternoon. Tomorrow to London where I must pawn my ring again.

Thursday 22 October 1925

Rather a disappointing day in London. I pawned my ring and redeemed my snuff-box for Elizabeth, bought some hair grease and powder with my mother, and had tea with her in a shop at a table opposite an imbecile woman in charge of a nurse. Then I went to Sumner Place where I was rather ill and rather bored tho' everyone was nice to me and we ate herrings and marmalade. Richard's car broke a chain so we ate supper while it was being mended and then home. I have sciatica and feel ill always now. I don't know why unless it is my bedroom.

Friday 23 October 1925

Very tired and sad. Kelly had a futile football practice in the rain. My drawing class will not draw well and have neither taste nor skill nor humility.

Saturday 24 October 1925

There was a match in the rain which, oddly enough, we won. Liza and Alastair came and as Crawford had given me some money we had champagne to drink and much else besides, but it was rather an ill-spent 3 guineas because no one felt moved to drink except me. Liza was particularly charming. Richard's car broke again so she had to spend the night at the Bell.

Sunday 25 October 1925

Richard did all the work for me today so that I could spend the day with Alastair. We went in the Humber to fetch Mrs G. from St Albans where she had been staying the night with Lady Verulam. Richard is gone back to London with Liza, and Alastair is gone to Barford again, and I am attacked by depression and have burned my tongue with overmuch smoking. In a few days' time I shall be twenty-two years old.

I have forgotten to say that on Saturday evening Captain Hyde-Upward made a joke about a skull and Dunhill's tobacco.

Monday 26 October 1925

Richard went to London to try on a suit and broke his motor car so we had a good dinner and a lot to drink at the Bell. The food at the school is getting quite monstrously bad.

Tuesday 27 October 1925

Richard and I again dined at the Bell. The boys went on a deputation to the Headmaster carrying a piece of stinking meat in an envelope but were repulsed. I have started a drawing for Hugh Lygon's 21st birthday.

Wednesday 28 October 1925

Chapman & Hall sent me £2 and my bald brother £1, because it is my birthday. My aunts sent me a disgusting tobacco pouch. Some shops sent me bills. It has been rather a dreary day. I tried to play football but had to stop because I felt so tired. Richard has gone off to buy hardboiled eggs for us to eat when this preparation is over.

I think that I should have been incredulous last year or the year before if I had been told how this birthday was to be spent.

Richard has a new suit.

Monday 2 November 1925

During the last few days Richard has become laden with good things like some patriarch of the Old Testament. On Thursday night he and Liza and Anthony came back with a bottle of white rum and the news that he has got his job at Lancing.[1] Today the news has arrived that the Russell parents have at last abandoned all idea of opposition to his marriage. Liza is staying a week at

---

[1] As music master.

the Bell under the supposed chaperonage of Julia and we are all very jubilant. While they sit on the sofa and make jokes about each other's faces, I sit and drink white rum and draw a picture called 'Grand Vin 1925 1ᵉʳ Août' which is going to be rather good. Yesterday evening Liza kissed me – in the most sisterly manner conceivable. Richard and I had carried her down the drive in the dark and when we put her down she kissed him and then, quite suddenly, me. We were on the way to the Bell. Claud was there unexpectedly with three friends called Archie Harding, Benvenuto Sheard, and another who never spoke all the evening except quite at the end to assure Liza, quite untruthfully, that he was drunk. He was there because he had a motor and was a most Aristotelian mechanic. We made a rum punch.

Tomorrow Anne is coming down rather to the distress of all of us. On Wednesday Claud's friends have promised to come over to play football against the boys.

I have again spent all my money.

> Say I'm weary, say I'm sad
> Say that health and wealth have missed me,
> Say I'm getting old – but add,
> Liza kissed me.

Anne arrived and I dined with her and Liza at the Bell.

Wednesday 4 November 1925

In spite of my expectations an enormous body arrived from Oxford in three cars: Arden Hilliard, Claud, Matthew Ponsonby, two Hardings, Michael Tandy, Patrick Gamble and others. They were a little drunk when they arrived and drank masses of beer at the Bell. The match was a great success. Our side won but not as easily as I had feared. I made some tries. There was a little school after tea – one period during which they broke their motor cars and overran Dr Crawford's flower beds and drank more beer. Dinner was amusing too. We drank a good deal and some got drunk and pranced. Anne was assaulted by the mechanic Clark. —— made love to me. Everything that I said about him cut him to the very soul; throughout the giddy whirligig of his life – and he had been up against things, in his time, face to face with the scalding realities of existence – the one constant thing that had remained inviolate in spite of all else had been his love of me. All of which took some time in saying and bored me inexpressibly.

Afterwards, when they had all gone away, and Anne was quivering with emotion recollected in tranquillity and Mr Gladding was lamenting the cheap red wine which Arden had poured over his Dutch table, we found that no one had paid any money at all and Richard and I were left to face a bill of some £8 or £9.

Thursday 5 November 1925

Pink men chased a fox about the park and excited the mad boys. Anne said she was always a little afraid that Richard and Liza thought she was a fool.

Hampstead, Friday 6 November 1925

Anne went away, after missing her bus, in the Ford car of a strange and common man whom she found drinking in the Bell. The Russell parents insist on a marriage in church.

In the evening Matthew Ponsonby, Michael Tandy, Patrick Gamble and an awful person whose name no one knew came in a motor car and took us to dinner at Thame where the soup was good and the awful man found pictures to discuss. Richard, Liza and I got a little drunk. Matthew is trying to exclude me from the independent party at dinner tomorrow and to put me on to Chris. We do not like each other, I am afraid. We stole a bottle of vodka from the car.

The Long Leave was, for my part, a dismal failure. On Saturday morning Richard, Liza and I spent some hours drinking cocktails and looking up the road for Anthony. At last, at about 12 o'clock – we had been up since 7 – he arrived and took us in great discomfort to Oxford. I lunched head to head[1] with Tom Driberg who gave me among other things an oyster omelette and mushrooms, and had then to go to Woodstock Road to act in Terence's film. He had managed to assemble all the people I most detest – Archie Gordon, Malcolm, Hemingway, his brother. After an hour I could bear it no more and when we came to a scene in which a taxi was to be used I got into it and drove away, rather to everyone's annoyance. Liza and Richard and I bought things and soon got very tired. We went to a tea party at Matthew's rooms – very dark and angular – and wished ourselves asleep. Then we went to the George Bar. Robert Byron has introduced into Oxford a syndicate of homosexual business men – one of them owns 107 newspapers and has platinum suspenders – who gave me a number of champagne cocktails. To everyone's surprise Chris arrived. For some odd reason I cannot now remember I refused to dine with either party and, finding two of Claud's Keble friends on the stairs, took them off to dinner at the Carlton Club. Went back to the George. Met Liza and her party looking for me in the Cornmarket. To avoid them – I was behaving very oddly, I think – I took refuge in the Clarendon bar. They followed and I climbed out of the window and fell on my ankle.

I hobbled down to Christ Church in growing discomfort and found Tom's party beginning. There were masses of men I did not know. After about an hour I succeeded in persuading people that my ankle really was hurt and they took me to Dr Counsel who pummelled and tweaked it and told me it was

---

[1] i.e., *tête-à-tête*.

broken. I returned to the party and drank a lot. Alastair and I slept at Pat Gamble's house.

The next day was dreary. Richard went round to call on old friends, Alastair went to Mass. Liza and I drove about in taxis. I was X-rayed. I lunched with Professor Dawkins – a typical don's luncheon: excellent food, masses of various wines, and abominable people, among others that common, conceited man Gill.[1] At 3 I had promised to act for Terence again. It was worse than the day before because it was colder. At tea-time Anthony, Liza, Richard and I drove back to London and arrived at Sumner Place frozen to find no fire and no food and all the family scattering to various engagements. I went home where my parents were full of sympathy for my foot and I far from gracious I am afraid.

For the next three days I remained on a sofa in my father's delightful house. Gwen,[2] Liza and Richard came in for quarter of an hour on Monday, but remote from me behind an impenetrable wall of happiness. They brought me a silver flask. Their income has now reached £1,100. On Tuesday the same sofa with Leighton's *Solitude* and an enlarged photograph of the Grand Canal. As I was going to sleep, Richard came in on his way to Aston Clinton, quite drunk with wealth, and only able to wave his arms and pour out an inarticulate description of his new acquisitions – suits, shirts, rings, watches, motor cars and so on. Wednesday was uninterrupted by any attention from my friends but by now I was deep in the study of the Pre-Raphaelites. I want to write a book about them. On Thursday Liza came to luncheon and drove me down to Aston Clinton. They went off to Oxford to arrange about the music for their wedding, which is now fixed for the 21st, and I pored over the Pre-Raphaelites in preparation.

Friday 13 November 1925

The sofa at Golders Green has been replaced by the sofa at Aston Clinton. The Pre-Raphaelites go on.

Saturday 14 November 1925

Elizabeth and Richard went off for the day to London.

The Pre-Raphaelites still absorb me. I think I can say without affectation that during this last week I have lived with them night and day. Early in the morning with Holman Hunt – the only Pre-Raphaelite – untiring, fearless, conscientious. Later in the day with Millais – never with *him* but with my biography of him – a modish Lytton Strachey biography. How he shines through Holman Hunt's loyal pictures of him. Later, when firelight and rum and loneliness have done their worst, with Rossetti, soaked in chloral and

[1] Exeter College undergraduate.
[2] Mrs Plunket Greene.

Philip Marston's 'Why is he not some great exiled king, that we might give our lives in trying to restore him to his kingdom?'

Sunday 15 November 1925

I had been warned that Olivia and David and Babe intended visiting us and had hoped to avoid them. They insisted, however, on coming up to the school after luncheon and not only they but Anne and Matthew Ponsonby and Arden Hilliard too. They made me promise to dine with them in Oxford. —— stayed behind after they had gone and drunk masses of vodka at a surprising rate and told he that he has decided to marry a pregnant whore and that he is suffering from gonorrhea and is in love with young Byam Shaw, a lot of which I think is swagger but plenty true. Richard grew moody but drove him back to Oxford, and I followed at dinner-time alone in an enormous Daimler hired for the day by Babe. They had finished dinner when I arrived and seemed rather gloomy. I ate a sole and paid £1 which I could ill afford. Anne to the wrath of Richard paid nothing. We went on to a party at Matthew Ponsonby's which I had expected to be awful but enjoyed enormously. Olivia as usual behaved like a whore and was embraced on a bed by various people, chiefly Arden and David Rice. Richard and I drank masses of brandy to Liza's health. Babe kissed me. We went for less than a moment to Robert Byron's and for a moment to David Rice's and then home. Anne was sick from and over the car.

Monday 16 November 1925

Nothing.

Tuesday 17 November 1925

Liza came down. We dined at the Bell. More talk of marriage.

Wednesday 18 November 1925

Nothing.

Thursday 19 November 1925

Liza came down. We went to see the Cockburns who were giving tea to two very odd relatives. Then we went the Hudsons. Richard thrust us through the door and disappeared. Old Mr Hudson seemed mad. He did not know us and called Liza 'Mrs Waugh'. We sat in a corner while he taught the classics to a lunatic boy. Eventually Richard came back, and Mrs Hudson and an ugly Miss Hudson. Back to the Bell. Took prep. Ate sausages with the prefects. Sent *The Balance* off to Gustave[1] – it had come back from Arrowsmith with a curt note some days before.

---

[1] The publisher Cecil Palmer.

Friday 20 November 1925

Nothing.

Saturday 21 November 1925

Elizabeth spent the weekend at the house of some people called Blezard who live near Tring. Richard went over to spend the evening with her, and when I was feeling rather disconsolate a telephone message came from the Bell that Alastair and Claud were there. I dined with them and afterwards drank masses of rum. They left and I sat up drinking until Richard returned from Stocks in no very sympathetic mood.

Sunday 22 November 1925

I did some work at the picture for Hugh Lygon's birthday which has now been past some weeks. After luncheon I was in doubt whether Alastair and Claud were going to come or not, and so after waiting half an hour I went off with Richard to Stocks. I learned later that they did arrive and were angry at not finding me. The Blezards' house is large and peopled by footmen but not particularly attractive and all far too bright and clean and highly coloured and healthy. Rather like the Queen's Dolls' House (only larger). There was no one except Liza staying there. We sat in front of the fire in a billiard room and talked about waistcoats. Richard went to sleep. Ruth Blezard is a fat woman with ugly hair and a puzzled expression in her eyes. Her father is paralysed through evil living; her mother a fool – rather like what I imagine Mary Guthrie[1] to have been in her saner days.

Monday 23 November 1925

Elizabeth spent the day at the Bell and we had meals with her. In the evening the mad boys were allowed to listen to a concert on the wireless because Richard's father[2] was singing. It confirmed me in my detestation of the invention.

Tuesday 24 November 1925

Richard went to London to talk to Frazer Nash[3] about his 'dark horse' as he described his motor car.

Wednesday 25 November 1925

I think nothing happened.

[1] Wife of the owner of the Pear Tree Press.
[2] Harry Plunket Greene.
[3] Motor car manufacturer.

Thursday 26 November 1925

Babe McGustie came down in a motor car called a Phantom Rolls-Royce with Liza and David and took us back to London for tea. She lives in an opulent house in Grosvenor Square with a common stepfather called Bendir and an animal called a lemur which is half a cat and half a squirrel and half a monkey. Bendir was learning to dance the Charleston from Barbara Back and a girl called Thirza. I found Alfred Duggan in a barber's shop and brought him on to tea with Babe. We went to an excellent tie shop called Sulka and to Hawes & Curtis for a waistcoat and then to Sumner Place for Olivia and then to Kettners for dinner. The fish was very good but the rest of the dinner rather dull and Richard morose and Liza overcome with mumps and David sad because Babe couldn't come and Olivia sad because she could afford so few cocktails. Home by a late train and very weary.

Friday 27 November 1925

Nothing.

Saturday 28 November 1925

Richard had a concert. The mad boys and Captain Hyde-Upward sang songs. I had all my meals at the Bell because I was so depressed. Alastair did not come so I rang him up. This alarmed Mrs G. out of measure because she thought he had been killed by his motor car. As a matter of fact he was alive all the time at Oxford. She was rude to a Miss Crawford.[1]

Sunday 29 November 1925

Liza came down. Snow. Dinner at Bell – celery soup. Rum and vodka. I went to tea to see China Harry but he was out.

Monday 30 November 1925

Ice and snow.

Tuesday 1 December 1925

Ice.

Wednesday 2 December 1925

Ice. No news from Alastair or Cecil Palmer.

Thursday 3 December 1925

The Crawford girls asked me and Richard and Liza to tea. It was such an amusing meal in an enormous drawing-room with nakedness on the roof and a

---

[1] One of the Headmaster's daughters.

prodigious fire. I talked about Lady Battersea's memories and Job's scabs and waistcoats. Richard muttered to Liza inaudibly about Lady Victoria's[1] taste in hymns and said, 'Oh you beautiful' very loudly and suddenly. After tea we felt rather cheerful and drank masses of very bad cocktails at the Bell and ate quite a good dinner and drank rum. A wheel came off Liza's car. We thought of a marvellous idea to mock the Ponsonbys. I am having Arthur Ponsonby's *No More War* enlarged and bound to be displayed among the presents.[2]

Monday 14 December 1925

I find now to my extreme regret that there is no such book as *No More War*. It is sad that so good a joke should go wrong.

There are only two more days left in this term and I am glad of it. I have had rather a hectic time in the last few days. Richard's new motor car has come and it employs most of his time. Claud is back at Tring and I have seen him a lot. Yesterday and today Alastair came to see me. On Thursday I went to London to play with the lemur in Grosvenor Square.

I have bought some trousers in Aylesbury and Richard has bought me rather a lovely waistcoat. I am tired of this term and of most of the boys. Some are charming. I go and talk to them in the evenings usually, and that is the nicest part of the day. I am rehearsing a scene from *The Tempest* with them. They act contemptibly. My plans for next holidays are extremely vague. I am afraid I shall have to give up the idea of going to Paris.

Tuesday 22 December 1925

I have had such a tiring week. I came up to London with Richard on Wednesday and his car broke and I had to go back by train just as the concert was finishing. It must have been a dreary concert. Next day, half-packed, I came up to London with Claud. I had asked the boy Westby to luncheon but he couldn't come, so Claud and I lunched at the Ritz and drank rather a lot. Olivia joined us. We went to tea with Hester Pellett and argued a lot and then drank some of Alec's whisky and took Olivia to Sumner Place and then home.

On Friday we had luncheon with Chris in the Café Royal and went to bed early. I liked Chris rather more than before. He paid for nearly all the luncheon, too. On Saturday Claud went to arrange about my passport and I went to a futile play with my mother. Rowland Leigh sat behind me and it was hard to decide which was the more imbecile and obscene – his conversation or the conversation in front on the stage. Claud and I took Audrey to supper and sat up until 7 in the morning arguing about the Roman Church. We lunched next day at Gwen Otter's and went to bed early.

[1] Elizabeth's mother.
[2] At the Richard Plunket Greene–Elizabeth Russell wedding. Arthur Ponsonby was an uncle by marriage of Richard Plunket Greene. See p. 206, note 2.

Yesterday Richard and Liza were married. Richard and I lunched together first at the Berkeley and arrived at the church rather late. The service went off without disaster though Matthew wore check trousers and Joan Talbot was 'taken queer' in the vestry and the priest called Richard 'Robert'. Liza said she would kiss me and did not. I spent a lot of time and Richard's money in tipping the servants of the church and nearly gave one of Liza's dowager aunts 5s for cleaning it.

There was a huge crowd at Halkin Street and Lady Mary[1] would not let anyone smoke. The champagne was warm and sweet but it made Giana[2] quite drunk. They drove away in the Frazer Nash – whose maker was at the wedding – at about 5 o'clock. I only just had time to change for Lady Victoria's dinner party which was quite awful. Plunket Greene, Olivia, David, Giana, Joan and a girl called Peggy Morrison who was about fifteen and hideously dressed. We ate masses of tasteless food and went to the Chauve Souris which was delightful. I was struck by the devastating suspicion that all the heroines of Russian novels are really like the red-cheeked woman who screamed. After the theatre we went on to the Berkeley – at least all except Lady Victoria and Harold Russell and Peggy Morrison – and drank beer and ate eggs until 2 and Olivia did that disgusting dance of hers and they discussed the chances of Liza being a virgin.

This morning I have been helping Lady Victoria with presents and am tired. There is a party tonight but I don't think I shall go to it. Tomorrow I am going to Paris by a third-class excursion which I am afraid will be most uncomfortable. How tired I am. Whenever I begin to worry about money I know I am in a low state of health.

Christmas Day 1925

I did go to the party with the result that I was too tired next day to go to Paris. Not that it was at all a debauched party – quite the reverse. Olivia and I arrived in day clothes to find everyone else decorously dressed sipping champagne. They were mostly Russian emigrés. Olivia, who is becoming literally 'Charleston crazy', was miserable until in an interval after supper she found a fairly empty room to dance it in. After that they all began singing Russian songs and she relapsed into rather drunken melancholy.

Next day a toping actor-manager I used to know called Bill Silk rang me up and I lunched with him and in a moment of weakness which I have been regretting bitterly ever since I consented to wait until tomorrow and then go to Paris with him. I dined with him and went to a play called *White Cargo* about white man and black woman and neat spirits. We went afterwards to the 50–50

---

[1] Lady Mary Herbert, a relation of Richard Plunket Greene.

[2] Georgiana Blakiston, Elizabeth's sister, married to Noel Blakiston, a close friend of Cyril Connolly and an official at the Public Record Office.

where they make the tables light up from inside rather abominably. Bill was so stupid about scenery.

Yesterday except for a brief excursion to Cook's office I rested and feel a little the better for it.

Today we are going to Earl's Terrace for two nights.

Hôtel des Empereurs, Paris, Sunday 27 December 1925

Christmas at Earl's Terrace was rather dreary. John Rothenstein and his sister and Audrey Lucas had been invited to dinner. Audrey arrived at the right time but the Rothensteins went by mistake to Golders Green and were an hour and a half late. All Alec's servants were quite drunk and Gaspard[1] was very ill at ease. On Saturday I walked with my mother and Gaspard in Kensington Gardens and after luncheon, with Gwen and Olivia and Gaspard, Olivia incited him to behave atrociously. We had tea at Earl's Terrace and went back to Sumner Place where we found Richard and Liza. At 8.20 I took a train with Bill Silk to Newhaven and from there a ship called *Brighton* which would not keep still. Neither of us were sick and fortunately the ship was very empty. Bill had drinks with a very good-looking sailor but I lay and fought nausea with sexual imaginings. At Dieppe we ate an omelette which made Bill sick and took a train, also mercifully empty, to Paris. It was raining hard and a taxi-driver in a fur coat drove us to an hotel called Regina in a street off the Boulevard Bonne Nouvelle where we had to pay 65 francs for an overheated room. We slept until about 11 when I went for a walk as far as the Rue de la Paix. We lunched well at a restaurant called Marguery where I ate caviare, consommé, sole Marguery, and a truffle omelette and drank half a bottle of champagne for 60 francs. We then looked for another hotel and found this one which is much cheaper and better than the other and nearer to the Louvre and the river. It is raining so hard that I do not think we shall go out tonight. Men wear awful clothes in Paris except for one man with a bright green jumper with an enormous collar.

Tuesday 29 December 1925

Yesterday to my dismay I found that the Louvre and all the galleries were shut. I went to Notre-Dame in the morning and was quite happy until Bill got up. Then it began to rain heavily and there was nothing to do. We walked down the Champs-Élysées and drank some liqueurs near the river and then went to sleep. At about 6 we went to the Chatham Bar and had some cocktails and Bill questioned the waiters about the addresses of brothels and then to the Café de la Rotonde for more cocktails. Dinner at Prunier's where I ate Clam Chowder, Homarde Americaine,[2] and artichokes and drank some white wine. Then for

---

[1] Mrs Waugh's poodle.
[2] *Sic.*

brandy to the Café de la Paix. From there to a brothel. The porter of the Chatham had given us the wrong number but the right street, Rue des Ourses, I think, but we were directed a few doors down to a dreary-looking café called Roland. Inside we asked how we could amuse ourselves. '*Montez, messieurs, des petits enfants.*' Upstairs was a hot little room with some tables and a waiter with a face exactly like My Lord Swinfen, but I do not think it can have been him. We drank some expensive champagne – 120 francs – and presently the *petits enfants* came down with many cries all in dowdy fancy-dresses. A gawky peasant boy arrested Bill's attention and for the rest of the evening they sat and chatted while the rest of the troupe howled and squealed and danced and pointed to their buttocks and genitalia. A boy dressed as an Egyptian woman sat himself beside me and pretended to understand my French. He admired my check trousers and made that an opportunity to squeeze my legs and then without more ado he put his arms round me and started to kiss me. He was nineteen he said and had been at the house for four years. I thought him attractive but had better uses for the 300 francs which the patron – a most agreeable young man in evening dress – demanded for his enjoyment. Bill, rather drunk, began an enormous argument in execrable French about the price of his peasant boy. I arranged a tableau by which my boy should be enjoyed by a large negro who was there but at the last minute, after we had ascended to a squalid divan at the top of the house and he was lying waiting for the negro's advances, the price proved prohibitive and, losing patience with Bill's protracted argument with the patron, I took a taxi home and to bed in chastity. I think I do not regret it.

This morning, Bill still sleeping off his excesses, I went to the Louvre. The Nike of Samothrace is superb and the Aphrodite of Melos very competent. I have not yet investigated the Egyptian rooms. In the paintings, I soon got very tired of the Le Brun and Le Sueur et Cie and even a little glutted with Poussin, but among the French painters discovered Philippe de Champaigne. The Mantegnas are excellent. I love the tree of knowledge in the 'Sagesse Victorieuse'. Bill shows signs of getting up. I must return there.

145 North End Road, Friday 1 January 1926

I hear that they are talking of starting a new year. I hope that it will be more of a success than the last.

We arrived home at about 6.30 yesterday morning and since then I have been asleep.

On the evening after the Rue des Ourses episode we went down to the river to dinner at La Tour d'Argent where there was a marvellous view of Notre-Dame and the most marvellous duck called caneton à la presse for which we were given number cards. Afterwards we drank a bottle of champagne each at a café called Prado and Bill talked about Tony[1] for several hours and was drunk.

Next day I walked to St Sulpice and liked the streets I went through and then to the Louvre again where I tried to see the Ingres drawings but found it too dark. In the evening we dined at Voisin where, after the caneton at La Tour d'Argent, the pommes de terre Anna seemed an insipid dish. The wine was excellent but I spilt most of mine. We drank chartreuse at the Prado and then returned.

Next morning I went to the Luxembourg and the Musée Rodin, where the drawings interested me greatly, up the Eiffel Tower and back to luncheon. Bill as usual still asleep. In the afternoon I went to tea with Tamara Abelson who has cut her hair and washed her face and put on pretty clothes and generally improved out of all knowledge. There was an Englishman called Burns, I think, who knew me, and a countess who gobbled cherry-jam and talked scandal in four languages. We dined at the Crillon where the food was excellent and the servants worse than anywhere in Paris and then to the Gare St Lazare. The journey was disgusting and I think that I am so unlikely to forget it that I will not write about it at all.

Saturday 2 January 1926

I went to tea at Sumner Place and we went on to dinner at a new restaurant called Favas which Richard has discovered which is very cheap indeed. I gave Richard the ties I had bought in Paris. I enjoyed the evening very much.

On Sunday I was bored.

On Monday I went to luncheon at Sumner Place and to a cinema in Shaftesbury Avenue to see the new Harold Lloyd film. Richard found an harlot who took us to drink at a club called John's in Gerard Street where there was a slot machine which gave me a lot of money and Alfred Duggan who gave me a lot of brandy. We went to dinner again at Favas with Anthony Russell. He brought me back and I made him drunk.

Tuesday 5 January 1926

I lunched with Dudley Carew and Cecil Roberts at Favas and went to Heatherley's where I drew execrably. It was odd to see the same people still drawing away there after all that has happened since I was last there. Tonight I have to go out with Anne. Her brother is being married too.

Barford House, Warwick, Monday 11 January 1926

I came here on Friday very much tired of London. On Wednesday I dined with Anne and talked to her seriously at the Café Royal. On Thursday she

---

[1] Tony Bushell.

dined with me. Chapman & Hall was entertaining quite a lot of his friends, including a woman called Ruth with whom he is in love who smoked a cigarette on the end of an hair-pin; he entertained them by making jokes which hardly amused me at all. Indeed they made me most uncomfortable. Anne thought the port was good which was odd of her.

I lunched with Bobbie on Friday after going to the private view of the London Group, and he saw me off at Paddington. I met —— in the Strand looking quite unlike a prostitute.

Since I came here I have been resting. On Saturday I saw some beautiful horses and pink-coated men meeting to hunt a fox. In the afternoon I drove with Alastair to his home at East Hendred[1] which is better than I had expected. We stopped on the way at Oxford and bought a waistcoat and some books – including T. S. Eliot's poems which seem to me marvellously good but very hard to understand. There is a most impressive flavour of the major prophets about them. The home of Sheard is typical of a second-rate painter's house – dark oak and brass and flowers and not much room. Benvenuto[2] read me some of the guide book he wants me to illustrate – it is impossibly dull and undistinguished.

On Sunday I went to mass with Alastair at a church with a humorous priest who did not think it important to baptize black men. All the congregation was called Dormer. We went over to lunch at East Haddon. I sat next to Mad Mary and had a grim time. There were a great number of children and some young women who had voices like Edna Best.[3] They had borne the children or most of them. Stella walked us round the farm and was the complete 'young lady up at the Hall'. Poor thing it is sad to see her among so many dark rooms and decaying old people, panting for gramophones and sunny verandahs and rather vulgar young men in riding britches drinking gins and lime.

Tonight Alastair and I are being made to go to a dance – only it is called a 'ball' because it is in the country. I know that I shall hate it very much indeed.

Wednesday 13 January 1926

Mrs Graham is gone up to London with a merry noise and except for a good deal of hammering and furniture-removing and chattering of housemaids there is peace in the house.

The ball was worse than I could have expected and lasted until 4.30. Alastair drank champagne and drove the car up the bank on the way home.

Yesterday we rested. T. S. Eliot's poems are incredibly good.

[1] House rented by Alastair Graham from people named Sheard in order to get away from his mother.
[2] Benvenuto Sheard.
[3] The actress.

Wednesday 20 January 1926

Exactly a year ago today – not on this date but on the Wednesday of this week – Olivia and Gwen and Richard and Elizabeth came to tea to say goodbye to me before I went to Denbighshire for the first time and on their way home Richard and Elizabeth decided that they would marry each other. How odd that seems.

I left Barford with Alastair on Saturday. We lunched with Claud in Oxford on the way and took some bedding to his house. Richard and Elizabeth met us at Paddington. We dined at Kettners where we saw a woman called Lady Ankaret Howard and the man who was head of the 'syndicate'. We drank at John's and played with the slots and drank rum – Gwen being absent – at Sumner Place. Murdocke and two friends came for a little. We slept at Sumner Place. Next day we borrowed the Russells' car and drove out to Golders Green for luncheon and back to Sumner Place for tea. Ankaret Howard came too, and spent the evening with us. I think I like her, but not as much as everyone has told me to. She 'shows off' incorrigibly – even in rather unimpressive ways such as the drinking of spirits and jumping over chairs. She is so proud of knowing bookies and common men which I suppose is creditable considering her social position,[1] but she does not seem to realize that the only reason why they like her is this same social position she is so triumphantly being independent of – or so it seems to me.

On Monday Alastair went away and Richard bought me a motor bicycle from a shop in Sussex Place. It is called Douglas and cost £25. Eliza and Richard came to dinner at my father's house. It was a dreary evening.

On Tuesday I learned to ride it at Kingston. Frazer Nash said there was only one way to learn and that was to 'find my way about it myself', so he launched me down a long road in Richmond Park on second gear. After an hour I could manage it a little. We went back to London in 'the dark horse' which has now a new engine and dined with Julia Strachey who has cut off all her hair and looks like Hugh Lygon.

Today in some nervous disquiet I drove Queensbury to London. It shook off 12s 6d worth of its lamp on the way up, and broke its front brake and stand and number-plate. Otherwise it went creditably. Lunched at a shop in the Strand called Gow's where the oysters are cheap and very excellent. Tea with Gwen who has lent me Von Hugel's letters to her to read.[2] Dinner at home – rather tired.

We saw Richard and Liza off to Shoreham. I am to join them there on Saturday for a night.

[1] As a daughter of the 10th Earl of Carlisle and a descendant of the Dukes of Norfolk and Devonshire.

[2] The Roman Catholic 'modernist' theologian von Hügel, who married Gwen Plunket Greene's aunt, had died in 1925. The letters were published in 1928, edited by Gwen Plunket Greene, with the title, *Letters from Baron Friedrich von Hügel to a Niece*.

Aston Clinton again, Tuesday 26 January 1926

I went to Gow's again to give dinner to Cecil Roberts who is Welsh. He went off later to sleep with Varda. I went, I do not know why, to call on Bill Silk. He had a horrible cousin there and it was a dreary call except that I heard that Alec was giving a dinner party on the next day to which I invited myself.

The dinner party was surprising. Julia, as I had expected, did not see fit to turn up. Audrey went early. Rather to my surprise but considerably to my gratification Elizabeth Ponsonby made vigorous love to me which I am sorry now I did not accept. She has furry arms.

Next day I went down to Lancing. I could not face the prospect of going there on the bicycle so I went by train instead. I enjoyed my visit to them very much. I did not see much of the school. We called on Kelly in a hand-made house. Back to London by train and to dinner most luxuriously at the Berkeley where I drank a bottle of champagne and smoked a vastly expensive cigar. We fetched Elizabeth Ponsonby who seems entirely to have overcome her attraction to me. Got very drunk later at a party at Bill Silk's among rather repulsive actors.

Yesterday to this school on my bicycle which did not go well and finally outside Tring made me wheel it a long way and buy it a new tyre.

There are two new masters – one quite nice in a Brasenose way called Gleed and one quite definitely dotty called Chambers.

Friday 29 January 1926

I have a cold, first from coming here in the rain on Monday, then from coming here late last night in the rain from Oxford, and now from having played football all the afternoon in a hailstorm.

The journey to Oxford was quite a success and the bicycle went along as well as could be expected. I met Alastair and Claud at the New Reform Club and went with them to East Hendred to Alastair's studio which flames with the unsold pictures of the late Mr Sheard. It was cold and draughty and I was not surprised that Alastair soon felt too ill to give me any dinner. Crumpled up and very malarial he drove us to Oxford. I went to the George and ate fried oysters with Harold[1] and Brian Howard. The journey back was beastly wet and windy and no light on my bicycle. Once I fell right over and all the time was sliding all over the road. I feel the worse for it.

Saturday 30 January 1926

I went to Barford to meet Alastair and Claud. It was a dolorous journey. It rained almost from the moment I started – after nightfall very heavily. At Aylesbury a nut came off my clutch and had to be renewed at some expense and

[1] Harold Acton.

after great delay. I reached Banbury in the dark at about 6 and set off up the Warwick road expecting to reach Barford before 7. About three miles out the bicycle stopped − the engine still going quite well but refusing to grapple with the wheel. After some time a taxi picked me up and dropped me at a garage. I rang up Barford to learn that Alastair and Claud had left soon after luncheon. They sent a car out for the bicycle which had 'sheared off a key', whatever that may be. We went back again to Banbury still in heavy rain. I could not pay for repairs and had to leave my silver flask as surety. I left Banbury a little before 9 after again ringing up Mrs G. and telling her that I should have to sleep the night. About five miles from Barford I was misdirected and sent on a detour round Kineton where my lights failed. I rode in the dark to Wellesbourne where I found a garage open and put more carbide in the lamp. At about 10 I got to Barford very, very wet having eaten nothing since luncheon. Mrs G. was kind to me and gave me a dried-up but hot dinner and masses of beer and port, while Miss Goodchild hunted me out pyjamas and handkerchiefs and dry socks from Alastair's room. At last to bed rather well contented. Next day the bicycle flew back and I was able to shave and put on a black coat in time for luncheon.

On Tuesday night Richard and Liza suddenly arrived and I got drunk with them. I have had to start another account at the Bell.

Nothing more happened until Saturday. I played games and talked to the children and ate a few meals at the Bell. On Saturday Richard and Elizabeth came again and we went to Oxford where I tried on a suit − grey tweed − at Hall's and then joined them at tea at Harold Acton's.

How absurd of me. I have forgotten that on Thursday Harold came over in a car from Oxford for the day and was quite charming. We lunched and had tea at the Bell and dined at Thame.

We all dined at the George and became enormously drunk. It was quite like the old Hypocrite days: trying on the hats of strange men, riding strange bicycles and reciting Edith Sitwell to the chimneys of Oriel Street. Eventually, I found my way to a party at the House given by William Acton where I think we were not well received, but I was too drunk by then to mind. I slept at the Bell.

On Sunday Richard and Liza went back. They have persuaded me to buy a new bicycle called Francis-Barnett. I had tea with the Crawford girls. Today I feel exceedingly tired and none too well and am vexed that it is my prep.

Ash Wednesday 1926

Last Thursday I went to London and left the Douglas at a garage in Camden Town to be collected by a man from Taylor's. The Francis-Barnett is minute but simple. At first I was most unfavourably impressed by it but now I like it more. I had tea with Julia who is ill in Sloane Avenue and dined at home where my father gave me an enormous cigar. Home by train.

On Saturday I went to dinner at Tring with the Cockburns after I had made myself rather unpopular at the school by having a number of them beaten for riding bicycles. I found Claud there who has the use of Alastair's car in his absence.

Next day I was woken early with the news that five gentlemen wished me to breakfast with them and when I reached the Bell I found Claud and the Hardings and Matthew Ponsonby and a nameless man in evening clothes having been to some celebration at Oxford. We breakfasted as they went off early. During the day I drew rather a charming cover design for the school magazine. A debate in the evening and after that dinner at the Bell. My account there must be getting very large.

Yesterday – because of the officer's absence[1] not for any religious reason – we had a whole holiday. The Francis-Barnett had arrived in Aylesbury so I rode it – very slowly because it has to be 'run in' – to Oxford. I lunched with Claud on bread and cheese and brown sherry and liked talking to him. Then we went to Hall's and to dinner at the George where we were joined by the Hardings whose mutual admiration, I find, rather depresses me. We ate an expensive but rather disagreeable dinner and picked up a lot of odd men who took us to a party in Merton which did not seem very gay to me. I went to see John Sutro for a very short time and then drove back. It did not rain until I had only a few miles left to go. Just opposite the Bell, the engine stopped. I could not make out why and was afraid it had broken, but I was glad this morning to discover that it had used up all its petrol. This seems to me gross over-consumption when I consider the promises of the catalogue. I did not get back until 2 and am tired today and I am afraid rather ill-tempered. I am at work on the magazine. My head aches and the children, even the nicest of them, get on my nerves more than a little. Tomorrow, God willing, to London.

Sunday 21 February 1926

Today Charles and Edmund took me to see a pond which they have been making in great secret in a corner of the park. They have dug it out of the mud and diverted a stream to flow through it and bordered it with moss and stones. We went to a pond near the stables and caught some fish to put in it.

After dinner, still unable to write or read, I persuaded poor Mr Chambers to come down to the Bell to drink sherry, said goodnight to the children and went to bed.

Monday 22 February 1926

By this morning's post my glasses were sent to me and also the proofs of the

---

[1] Perhaps the absence of Captain Hyde-Upward.

photographs taken by the man from Tring. They are rather amusing, particularly the one in ordinary clothes in which I have the expression of a popular preacher.

Friday 26 February 1926

I am very vexed tonight because after a fairly late night yesterday and with a formidable pile of uncorrected essays and exercises I have allowed myself to be induced to go to a dance in Tring with Claud and a girl he is in love with called Ruth Stevenson. On Tuesday I went first to Oxford to have tea with Claud and to try on a good suit Hall has made me, and after that on a wet and strange road to Shenley where Alec was staying in the village public house. I dined with him on chops and beer, spent the night there rather restlessly, and got back in time for breakfast. On Wednesday, still lame from my accident, I played no games but went to dinner with the Cockburns and returned in time to talk to the children.

Yesterday I went up to London in lovely weather and returned late through belts of impenetrable fog alternating with lengths of clear moonlit road. I took Mother to tea at Sumner Place where we found Giana Russell and left her to drink cocktails at the Ritz with Bobbie. I had hoped that Liz Ponsonby would come too – I had sent her a card – but she did not. Dinner at home.

The Doctor has let me have one of the rooms in the stable to turn into a sitting-room. Edmund and I went down this afternoon to explore them. I liked two, one of them with a delightful window but, I am afraid, too large for my money.

Monday 1 March 1926

As a matter of fact the dance was not so dreary as I had expected. I arrived very much chilled with essay-correcting and motor-cycling and was greeted by Claud with a prodigious glass of brandy and soda. Besides Ruth Stevenson there was a woman called Lecky or some name like that who was rather a woman of the world and drove me out of my pose of polite schoolmaster to talk of caviare and saxophones and such things. I only danced once with Ruth and was exhausted by her animal vigour. She seems to me an odd match for Claud at his age.

I spent the next days as usual: teaching and playing with the children, dined at the Bell on Saturday and on Sunday. Claud came over on Sunday quite early, before I had returned from sitting on the golf course with Edmund, and to my disgust brought Yorke-Lodge with him. His lecture to the Literary Society was incoherent and inarticulate and an icy failure. It needed a lot of drink to bring me back to the content in which he had found me.

This afternoon I have been for a run while Edmund and Charles dusted the room in the stables which Crawford has given me. Tonight I have some rum to drink with the Captain.

Monday 8 March 1926

The Captain and I drank all the rum with the result that I woke up with my cold almost cured while he spent the next day in bed. I went to London on Tuesday and bought some furniture from Mr Drage who was more like his advertisements than I should have thought possible. Some chairs, a rug and two tables – very common-looking.

On Thursday I went to London again, feeling rather tired in unpleasant weather, and found my mother depressed and depressing. I dined at Earl's Terrace but did not get enough to eat. John Rothenstein, whom I taxed with his false witness in the *affaire* Ponsonby,[1] Joyce Fagan, and a girl who plays the piano. Tony came in later, theatrical but prosperous. I drove back on Friday morning on frozen roads which gradually thawed as I got nearer to Aston Clinton. All day I was very tired and only Edmund to call me next day reconciled me with the prospect of the match against Oxford.

It was rather a jolly game which they won entirely through Archie Harding. Our side played well – particularly Charles. Afterwards we dined at the Bell and drank a good deal and I smoked the prodigious cigar my father had given me. Richard came for a few minutes to try to get me to a dance. We danced instead with the boys and carried off the situation without disgrace until Matthew Ponsonby, having been sick at the gates, attempted to force an entry. Luckily we got him away. At the Bell he broke an electric light bulb and went away abusing his family without attempting to pay his share of the bill.

Next day Alec and I rested. I went down to the pond and watched the children digging in it – Charles covered in mud from head to foot. Edmund with his Eton trousers turned up to the knee leaving an absurd pink hiatus between them and his socks. Alec's address in the evening was audible and intelligible and adequate. They seem to have liked it. We dined with Claud at the Bell.

Alastair is returning soon – I have missed him more than I would have thought. Tomorrow I have to go to London to drink cocktails at Earl's Terrace and introduce Alec and Murdocke at Sherry's but I am determined that it shall be my last expedition there this term. I find I am always tired out.

Saturday 13 March 1926

The cocktail party at Alec's was quite fun although Elizabeth Ponsonby never came. I got drunk. Tony was there. Alec has fallen in love with a hideous and stupid woman who is married. We went to Sherry's and ate a good dinner. Hors d'oeuvres, chicken broth, grilled salmon, caneton à la presse (but all unlike the duck of the silver tower) and omelette surprise. Murdocke mistook

[1] John Rothenstein comments: 'I was a close friend of the Ponsonbys, yet knew nothing of the arrest, and told him so; evidently he didn't believe me.'

the place of meeting. I drove home that night instead of waiting until morning and found it bitterly cold.

I have had three tea parties this week, the first on Tuesday consisting of Gleed, the two Miss Crawfords and Bill Holmes à Court who is not as frightful as everyone has led me to suppose; on Thursday Charles and Edmund; and today the prefects and Baxendale who ate prodigiously and I think enjoyed it. Tomorrow I purpose to go to communion if I can wake up early enough. I think it is just to record that Matthew sent me a letter of apology for his drunkenness – but no money for his dinner.

The children have begun to be a little naughty so I have started being strict with them, which is a bore.

Claud has broken Alastair's motor car against a lorry. Alastair has not returned yet – Mrs G. wired for me to come and see her on Thursday but I could not.

Monday 15 March 1926

I lay late in bed yesterday and did not go to church. I called on Claud in the morning and after luncheon Liza and Richard arrived unexpectedly in their red car. They came to tea with Stuart, Campbell, and Blackburn in the stables, and I decided, as I now much regret, to go to London to see Olivia. We found her packing bottles in a bedroom littered with stockings and newspaper. Fatter and larger generally, unable to talk of much except herself and that in an impersonal and incoherent way. I sat on her bed for some time trying to talk to her with my heart sinking and sinking until Richard and I went out to drink cocktails. The dinner at Favas was worse. I sat opposite David showing a lot of rather grubby striped silk cuff and next to Babe who did not speak one word all the time. We had a table which was too small for us so that all the plates were in the way. I returned by train more depressed than I have been for some weeks. On the way back I thought of a novel to write – but doubtless I shall do nothing of the sort.

Friday 26 March 1926

Today I have been entertaining Young – the lecher from Denbighshire. He came on a marvellous bicycle – a Sunbeam. We lunched at the Bell and went to see the children at football. He fell in love with R ——. I fell down rather painfully trying to take the corner up to the speed-hill. I am very much tired tonight.

Yesterday I went to a point-to-point meeting at Kimble and lost £4 which I can very ill afford.

We had a party at the Bell. We got drunk. When we were all in bed David and Babe and Eliza arrived with a car full of Charleston records from London.

Chris Hollis sent me £5 which shames me of the many things I have thought and said about him.

All Fools Day 1926

Chris's £5 did not last long. I went to a local point-to-point meeting and lost them there. Alastair disappeared for nine or ten days leaving no address and Claud and I suffered considerably from Mrs G. He was eventually discovered drunk in the Lotti at Paris. Young of Denbighshire came down and was rather a bore – drunk all the time. He seduced a garage boy in the hedge.

Midsomer Norton, Monday 12 April 1926

The term came to an end drearily. I went to Barford for the last weekend and came to London on Wednesday in the rain, ate oysters and saw Alastair off to Constantinople in my only respectable suit. Dined at home. On Thursday I hunted for luggage which Charles had lost for me, had tea at Sumner Place, drank cocktails at the Ritz with Bobbie, dined with Gwen Otter where the soup was excellent, and home. On Friday I could bear London no more and got on a bicycle and went to Hungerford for the night in a nice pub called the Bear. From there I came on to Midsomer Norton on Saturday morning through rather lovely country. Since than I have read out-of-date novels in shabby easy chairs and listened to my aunts' condemnations of everything they know nothing about. There is a Welsh woman staying in the house. There is also a ferocious maid.

Tuesday 13 April 1926

Rather an amusing afternoon at Wells. Roger Hollis and I lunched at the Swan and drank champagne and brandy mixed. After a time we were turned out. There was a market at Farrington Gurney. It was odd that we were not killed going there. After a time the man in that pub refused us drinks. I said I was Hobhouse of Castle Cary and that I would have him out of the pub in a month. He believed me and gave us heaps more to drink. We lay in a field for some time. Roger lit a pipe. I think the aunts thought I had been drinking.

Next day we went to a place called Clevedon on the sea.

Sunday 18 April 1926

I have just read such a good book called *The Orissers*.[1]

Ever since Lancing Debating Society days 'Revolution in May' or 'Revolution in October' has seemed a commonplace of polite conversation, but during the last few days I have been allowing people to arouse me to the fact that there is probably to be a general coal strike at the end of the month and the hope that its consequences are incalculable. And I have begun to think whether perhaps April 1926 may not in time take rank with July 1914 for the staging of house parties in sociological novels. I suppose that the desire to merge one's

[1] The first novel, published 1921, of L. H. Myers (1881–1944).

individual destiny in forces outside oneself, which seems to me deeply rooted in most people and shows itself in social service and mysticism and in some manner in debauchery, is really only a consciousness that this is already the real mechanism of life which requires so much concentration to perceive that one wishes to objectify it in more immediate (and themselves subordinate) forces. How badly I write when there is no audience to arrange my thoughts for.

Monday 19 April 1926

The *Herald* and the *Daily Mail* this morning are both marked by a studied moderation which is very far from being reassuring. It seems as though both sides were afraid to speak for fear of what may happen.

Thursday 22 April 1926

Nothing more has happened about the strike. Every one seems anxious to make peace. On Tuesday I went to Sherborne and saw the school under the guidance of a porter who knew C. & H.[1] well and thought Alec was dotty. It is a very charming place. Today to Taunton, tomorrow to Fowey.

Saturday 1 May 1926

I spent a night at Bishop's Hull and then went on to Fowey arriving there very wet at about 5.30. A kindly butler called Smith gave me a bath and a drink, and it was not until I was clean and in evening clothes that I was presented to the family. Lady Poole[2] is hideous but hospitable – rather like Gwen Otter to look at. The General also hideous and hospitable – a bull neck, close-cropped hair, small eyes – exactly like every caricature of a Prussian officer. There was also a brother at Eton whom I liked. I enjoyed my visit there very much. We spent most of the day on the water or else driving about the country. I met an ugly girl called Fay Quiller-Couch who was described in a paper as 'Titled author's Grace Darling daughter'.

I came back from Fowey in one day which means to me quite an achievement.

The coal strike has begun but no one except me and Mr Baldwin seems to realize how serious it is.

Hampstead, Monday 3 May 1926

On Saturday, on coming out of a cinema where we saw the world's worst film, the evening papers were full of headlines confirming all my prophecies of the last few weeks. The transport and all other big unions are coming out at 12

---

[1] 'Chapman & Hall', i.e. Arthur Waugh.
[2] Daughter of a Lord Mayor of London, and wife of Major-General Sir Cuthbert Poole, KBE, CB, CMG, DSO.

tonight. Yesterday I went to a meeting in Hyde Park where very revolutionary stuff went down frightfully well. Much talk of shooting.

This morning Carmelite House[1] struck and refused to print the *Daily Mail* leader 'For King and Country'.

Tuesday 4 May 1926

A very drunken and expensive day yesterday. I set out in the morning to the Academy where there were two or three good pictures – two by the Procters, one by Sims and some quite agreeable landscapes, the rest very painful. I went to find Bobbie and found instead Dudley Carew and a good-looking Cambridge boy called Bill. We drank a good deal and smoked cigars and then I took Bobbie off to luncheon with Audrey, drank more and smoked more cigars and went to a pub and were turned out, went to Mrs Lucas's shop, went to John's club and threw some eggs out of a window, went to a pawnbroker's and pawned my ring. Found a public house open and another and another, met Adrian Stokes, turned out of one restaurant, quieter at the next, went to a cinema where I saw double, went to see Tony who is being locked out of his theatre. Home feeling pretty ill, having spent about £3 in drink and 30s in cigars.

Today Crawford has wired curtly that term starts as arranged. I went out on my bicycle to see the stricken areas and found the traffic quite fantastic. *The Times*, much reduced, came out this morning. No other papers then or this evening.

Aston Clinton, Tuesday 11 May 1926

On Thursday I went back to Aston Clinton. In the morning I went with Alec to Limehouse where, with the same rigid orthodoxy which sends him to Jermyn Street for his shirts and Paris for his fornication, he enrolled himself as a special constable. We lunched at the Berkeley and drank port in the Savile until Winifred Macintosh picked us up and drove us home.

On Wednesday reports of rioting had come in from all big towns and they have gone on ever since. Richard and I had gone down to Hammersmith to see what was going on, but arrived too late, after the police had made a baton charge and recaptured six motor buses which the strikers had broken.

At Aston Clinton I found five boys and those the ugliest and dullest. Crawford went away early on Friday morning. It was a bloody day. Towards evening Captain Hyde-Upward and some boys came in; on Saturday, most of which I spent in London, a few more.

By Sunday, cold and beastly, there were fifteen in all. The appeals for special constables had become more and more insistent, so rather suddenly I decided

---

[1] The *Daily Mail* building.

to escape the boredom under a colour of duty – which I am afraid Crawford will see through – and came to London.

On Monday evening I was sent from the RAC to Scotland Yard where I was given an armlet, sworn in as a police despatch rider, and sent off to Scotland House where after some considerable delay I was sent off with three foul youths to East Ham Police Station. The ride there on wet tram lines was beastly. One of our party disappeared. At East Ham, Inspector James said he didn't want us at all. Back to Scotland House, where everything seemed inextricably confused, where we were dismissed for the day.

This morning only one of the East Ham contingent arrived. We waited an hour in a passage while harassed civil servants trotted to and fro and occasionally read out lists of names none of which were answered. Then told to go away and report again in an hour and a half. A pint of bitter. Told to report again in two hours and a half. Half a pint of bitter. Dudley Carew, a Mrs Gill in a charming flat, the High History of Sangreal, an hour in the passage, dismissed for the day. Alec off duty, has bought champagne and theatre seats.

Next day I thought it would be as well to find some more useful way of serving 'Jix'[1] and the constitution so I went to a territorial barracks in Camden Town and joined a force called the Civil Constabulary Reserve. It was comprised partly of the same sort of frightful youth I had met at Scotland Yard but chiefly of what I take to be the dregs of civilization – battered little men of middle age, debased and down at heel who grumbled all the time, refused to get up in the mornings, talked on parade, and fought for their food. In the evenings they got drunk in a canteen upstairs. The officers were solicitors' clerks in military clothes. We spent the morning drawing blankets, tin hats, field dressings, and such military necessaries. At luncheon the strike was called off unconditionally by the TUC. We stood fast until about 10 when I got home to bed. Next morning at lunch-time I got my discharge and returned to Aston Clinton where I found Upward still in command, no news having been heard of Crawford.

Friday 28 May 1926

I have spent quite an agreeable week. I dined in London with Richard and Liza and Anthony and a man called Cheak one night. At the Bell once or twice. On Wednesday I had a superb day in Oxford and arrived home in safety only by the Grace of God.

Sunday 30 May 1926

I have spent a peaceable week without leaving Aston Clinton at all. I dined with the Cockburns one night. I have taken the children to bathe and have

[1] Sir William Joynson-Hicks, Home Secretary, 1924–9.

played tennis with them. Last Monday, Whit Monday, I went to play with Alec and his team against Shenley but made only 0 and 3. I do not think his elderly friends like me much. I had to play in plus-fours and all the women cried 'There goes 'Arry Lauder' when I went in to bat. The nice tobacconist Somerset Johnson was there. We got drunk afterwards on Colne Spring – an excellent drink and I had to drive back in the dark among beetles[?] which hurt excessively. Alec is coming to stay next week at the Bell.

Today Richard has been here and has made me a little drunk on Colne Spring – an excellent drink. How delightful Liza is. We have arranged to go to Tours together next holidays. Olivia's cat has had kittens which is odd considering that it was a Thom or Tom.

Monday 7 June 1926

I have just returned from a delightful weekend at Barford. A barber has made savage inroads on the rather scant beauty of the school and I was glad to be away from it. I seem to have been rather drunk when I wrote the last entry in this diary.[1]

Alec spent last week at the Bell and after a brotherly reunion on the first night I have been forced to revise my opinion of Colne Spring. I have not felt really well since. There was a cricket match on Thursday when I was out first ball – caught ingloriously in the deep. On Saturday I set out for Barford, lunching on the way at Bicester. The gardens were looking very lovely and it was hot all the time. I lay in the sun and drew a green china cat. In the evening we went into Warwick to a cinema, a most amusing Harold Lloyd film. Next day Mrs G. had numberless people to luncheon and we went on to a tennis party given by some people called Grazebrooke where I was made to play in socks with a borrowed racquet. Dinner *tête-à-tête* with Mrs G. She produced champagne. A restless night, awake at 5.30.

Thursday 10 June 1926

Too little sleep last night. Richard and Liza came to see me last Friday. Crawford has told me that he proposed to get rid of Gleed. I half-hoped Richard might come back, but he will not. It has rained steadily all the week. On Sunday I went to Oxford and found everyone deeply depressed except Claud, who gave me dinner at the OUDS.

On Monday afternoon I found Edmund out of bounds and beat him with mixed feelings and an ash plant. He was very sweet and brave about it all. I have given him a Sulka tie as recompense.

Yesterday afternoon I went to London, visited Sulka's and Bobbie, went to a cinema, ate an early dinner at a chop-house in Fleet Street, and started for

---

[1] In the MS, the writing straggles down the page.

Aston Clinton. From then on everything went wrong. I had a puncture in the Strand and got it mended only after pushing it a long way. In Kilburn I ran out of petrol and spent half an hour getting some. Then the tyre went flat again. I pushed it to Cricklewood, being refused help at every garage on the way, and finally left it there. A kindly man at a coffee-stall told me that a milk-lorry left his stall at 5 for Aylesbury. The early trains are all off and this seemed the only way to get back. I walked to Golders Green and got to Mrs Waugh's house soon after 11. The aunts were there and fussed hospitably about me. I had a bath, drank some beer, and soon after 12 was asleep in the bookroom in an armchair. At 3 Alec came home from some night club in evening dress and a paper hat. I talked to him until 4 and then walked to Cricklewood. The milk-lorry never turned up. At 5.30 a man in a newspaper van offered me a lift as far as Elstree. From there I walked to Bushey, got a bus to Watford, a train to Rickmansworth, another train to Wendover, and a taxi to the school at about 9. Since then I have been rather tired.

Wednesday 23 June 1926

Some other late nights. On Thursday the Doctor ordained a whole holiday. I started for London to fetch back my motor bicycle and met Pat Grinling on the platform so we travelled up together. Feeling rich I took him to luncheon at the Ritz where we found Alec entertaining numberless elderly women. Bobbie joined us. He promised to drive my bicycle down to me next day so I went to Cobham to Pat's home. This was unwise as I was due at the school at 5 o'clock. His family were at Ascot – such a vulgar house by the way – and there was no car to take us back so we dined there – I was due to take prep – and came back by a very late train. Poor Captain Hyde-Upward was engaged for dinner that night and had to stay at the school. I feel rather ashamed of that. Bobbie came down next day. We had an agreeable dinner at the Bell and he missed his train back and woke me up to borrow pyjamas.

On Saturday Edmund went away for the weekend. Richard was in Oxford so I went over to see him. We dined at the George and had a party in Matthew's rooms. I sat up till 3.30 talking to him and liked him more than usual. His landlord cooked us eggs. As soon as it began to be light I rode back.

I was very tired next day and talked to Charles most of the afternoon who was inconsolable at Edmund's going away.

A quiet day. I went to see Claud who is back in Tring. On Tuesday there was trouble with Gladding over a cheque returned 'Payment stopped' which I had to go to Oxford to solve, missing luncheon. There was a tennis match in the afternoon. Gleed's stock went up considerably; he played very well.

Today Edmund and Charles had tea with me and ate masses of strawberries and spilt milk.

Thursday 1 July 1926

Last Thursday Richard and Liza turned up suddenly with a Lancing boy. We got drunk at the Bell and I came back and behaved myself unseemly.

As half the team were away I was made to play cricket last Saturday. I made ten runs and caught a catch and was very much bored.

On Sunday I went to London to greet my parents who are returned from France – my father very Gallic and full of stories about his experiences.

On Tuesday Claud came to dinner here. A pleasant evening. Apart from this I have been earning my wages rather conscientiously – teaching, playing tennis, bathing, etc. It is very hot usually and Mr Gleed complains of the toothache.

Sunday 11 July 1926

Last weekend Charles went away and left Edmund to play with me. On Sunday my mother and father came to see the school but it rained all the time. I have read Edmund *The Wind in the Willows*. Today it is too hot. I went to London on Thursday and found that Alastair was back. He spent the night at Golders Green. I went back to Clinton before breakfast and returned in an hour or two – the Headmaster having ordained a whole holiday. We lunched with Bobbie and that Cambridge boy at the Connaught Rooms. Bobbie had my hair cut for me at Francis Palmer's shop and gave me a bottle of face cream. Dinner at home and back to Clinton early morning.

Dined with the Cockburns yesterday – back in time to say goodnight to the children.

Saturday 24 July 1926

The last weeks have gone very quickly. Alastair came to stay at the Bell on Friday. That evening we drove up to London and went to see Cochran's revue. Afterwards we went to see Tony Bushell at his theatre. Any hard thoughts I harbour against him in his absence invariably disappear when I meet him. We went to his rooms in Percy Street, exquisitely furnished, and drank whisky and smoked good cigars. Then we drove to my home and ate fried eggs and bacon and Bath Olivers and drank prodigious quantities of beer. Just before dawn we started back for Clinton and arrived at about 5. Tony slept in my room in the stables, Alastair in his car. Next day, oddly enough, was a success too. Richard and Liza came and we had dinner at the Bell with Claud and Benvenuto. There were a lot of the boys dining with an old boy. We took them away to the pub by the canal and got very drunk and Alastair swam the canal with a glass of beer in each hand and drank them.

On Sunday I was tired. Alastair and I went to Windsor for dinner. He suggested my writing something for him to print. All this week accordingly I have been writing the essay which I made notes for when my ankle was sprained last year, on the PRB.[1] I think it is quite good. I got it done in four and a half days, in between correcting exam papers. On Tuesday I went to London and took Mrs Waugh to see Tony's play. Faith Wigglesworth and a husband were in the next seats to us.

Last night I finished the essay. Nick Kelly has been very kindly typing it for me.

The term came to an end on July 28th without any particular interest. I came up to London by motor bicycle. At his own invitation, upon some slight encouragement from my father, Kelly came for a week. On my own invitation, upon some slight encouragement from Alastair, I am going to Scotland next week with Mrs Graham. She does not take kindly to the arrangement, I am afraid. I think I shall enjoy it. I leave for Barford this afternoon, Saturday. On Thursday I ordered some clothes and dined with Gwen Otter. Yesterday I lunched with Chris Hollis and Richard and went to see a good painter called Elliott Seabrooke.

My father likes the PRB essay very much. John Rothenstein proposes to interest himself in its sale. Chris is somewhat improved.

Kelly pissed in his bed.

Saturday 31 July 1926

I came down to Barford by train because I felt that it was too difficult to drive a bicycle with so much luggage. Chris was to have come that evening but did not. Alastair and I went to a public house in Stratford. Chris arrived on August 1st by an evening train. We got drunk in the evening and argued about foreigners and absolution.

Bank holiday, Monday 2 August 1926

Mrs G. in a fury about gum-boots. She and Alastair most rude to each other. After luncheon we went to a horse show at Henley-in-Arden and drank bottled Bass – very gaseous.

Higham, Bassenthwaite Lake, Cockermouth, Cumberland
Wednesday 4 August 1926

I arrived here last night after what was on the whole quite a pleasant journey. Mrs G. raged a good deal at first and at every crossroads was tormented by the conviction that Alastair had taken the wrong turning. But as I say, on the whole things went smoothly. We lunched on bread and chicken at the side of the road and got to Carlisle at about 5. Sir Richard Graham's house is small and ugly and full of enormous oil portraits and a stuffed badger. It has a very regal

---

[1] Pre-Raphaelite Brotherhood.

lavatory. Soon after we arrived the Fishers sent a big red motor car to bring me here. This is a very Gothic house with turrets and castellations and a perfectly lovely view across the lake to a mountain called Skiddaw. There was plenty to drink at dinner and no nonsense about 'joining the ladies'. There are quite a number of odd-looking women, mostly called 'Aunt Effie'. After dinner they never appeared again. We just went straight to the library and smoked cigars and drank whisky. There is a young brother rather like Allan who was reported to have mumps but appears to have recovered surprisingly quickly.

Next day we had breakfast – a prodigious meal – at 7 o'clock and went out to hunt for an otter. Mr Fisher wore a suit of flannel plus-fours with brass buttons and a pink collar. He and I and all the men were armed with long spiked sticks, the women with cameras. We met some hairy dogs on a bridge and the hunt started. It was a most ill-disciplined affair, rather like poor Mr Gleed's drill at Aston Clinton. Two men seemed of importance – a very fat old man who, besides Mr Fisher's clothes, wore a pink waistcoat, and a young man called Jack who had a trumpet and a whip. Jack would not do what the fat man said, and the dogs would not do what Jack said. We walked along the river (called Derwent) for some time, when suddenly the dogs started making noises like sea-lions and all the men ran into the river except the master who danced on the bank saying 'put terriers in'. Jack tried to dig a hole and while he dug the dogs stood round and kicked the earth in again as fast as he threw it out. Then there was a long pause and we started walking again. Then there was another sudden noise and Jack danced about in water so deep that only the tip of his trumpet appeared. We caught an otter to the great delight of the ladies with the cameras who took 'snapshots' of all the more barbarous details and were rewarded with bits of bloody otter's meat like the dogs. Then we went on walking until the Master was tired and Jack fell down in the water and hurt his knee and then we got into a Ford van and drove back very wet with a deaf terrier we found on the road.

After luncheon we went for a drive – me and Mr Fisher and an Aunt Effie and the brother who had mumps and a chauffeur called Thomas. We saw a lot of lakes and a seat where Wordsworth wrote and a very Welsh lake with piers and jetties and promenades and ice-cream carts called Windermere. When we came back we played tennis – Allan and his father were both worse than me. Dinner, cigars, bed.

Next day we went to stay with some people called Callander at a house called Preston Hall near Edinburgh. Mrs G. had insisted on an early start for no very convincing reason, so at some inconvenience to the Fisher household they drove me into Carlisle at 9 in the morning. I met Sir Richard Graham for a few minutes – a dear old man. The drive was fairly tumultuous – Mrs G., like the opera enthusiasts who follow the score a page behind, spread a map upside down on her knee and stormed at Alastair for driving in the wrong direction.

We stopped at Netherby to call on a lady called Lady Cynthia Graham in her new grave and met a one-legged sexton whom Alastair's father used to bang on the head. I also saw some eels from a bridge and a charming tower where Alastair means to live. Owing to our early start, and in spite of Alastair's wanderings, we arrived at Preston Hall far too early. It is a perfectly charming house built and decorated by the Adams. Mrs Callander dressed rather like Lady Quiller-Couch and talked in an abrupt, jolly way; she has a daughter called Ruth who is a Girl Guide and looks like Princess Mary. The daughter took us to an octagonal tower which was furnished like a curiosity shop and talked about Greece to us there. After tea we walked round the park which is large and in parts rather lovely. There was not very much to drink at dinner. The Callanders are teetotallers and live on fruit mostly. After dinner we all talked about Greece until 10, read papers until half-past, and then took candles to bed with us.

Next morning we talked about Greece for an hour after breakfast and then Alastair and I took Mrs G.'s car to Edinburgh. It is a perfectly charming town built on two sides of a valley with a railway down the middle. There is a castle and some steep and ancient slums on one side and on the other a lovely row of shops called Princes Street which are a mixture between Bond Street and the High at Oxford. I bought some Edinburgh rock for Edmund and a long shepherd's crooked stick and a new band for my hat – for which I had taken a sudden dislike – and quite a number of glasses of drink at various public houses and some luncheon. Alastair bought me a whin stick covered in bunions with a top rather like a skull, which I like very much. We went for a short drive and saw the National Gallery – mostly Raeburns – presided over by a man in a cape and a three-cornered hat. We met a tiny girl who talked to us in Esperanto.

We had dinner, talked about Greece and Mr Cook the collier, until 10, read papers until half-past and then took candles to bed.

I have forgotten to say that on this day Alastair and I thought of some good manners. It was raining very heavily when we got back from Edinburgh and we were told that the ladies were in the garden so we ran out into the rain laden with umbrellas to the octagonal tower to rescue them. Unfortunately the butler had thought of doing that too and arrived before us.

We went across a ferry near the Forth Bridge and drove to Muchalls where Alastair's old nurse lives. On the way we went to a house called Tannadice to see a lady called N——. She had a thick beard, a bald dog, a drunken husband and a paederastic son. Muchalls was distinctly Welsh. We stayed in a teetotal public house which had once been a castle. It was full of nasty little boys and girls. The food was horrid. There was only one public house in the village and that was spoiled by a rude bartender.

On Sunday we lunched on cheese and chocolate in the car and took Alastair's nurse for a drive and ate tea with her in her cottage.

Monday 9 August 1926

We waited after loading the car for a long time for the postman, but when he came there were no letters for us. At Stonehaven we took the wrong turning and had a long drive out of the way up a hill which made the car overboil. Mrs Graham furious. At about 4 we reached Strathdon.

We went first to call on the Forbeses. They are living in what used to be their laundry. It makes rather a delightful little house – absurdly baronial, carpeted and curtained in tartan, and hung with arms. We left Mrs G. to stay with a negro doctor called Howie[1] and came to this public house – the Newe Arms – which is much nicer than everyone told us it would be.

On Tuesday we had to wash the car under Mrs G.'s orders which was a disagreeable undertaking involving some brushes and sponges and a hose and a good deal of rather violent language from Mrs G. We had luncheon at the Forbes. Such a good meal but made very restless with everyone taking everyone's plate about. Sir Charles is a futile little man[2] who feels ill a lot and seems just the sort of person one would expect to lose his inheritance. He invents three-cornered loudspeakers and an apparatus for striking matches. Lady Forbes is dull and has a sister who is stone deaf. The Forbes girls are nicer than I thought them in London. After luncheon we carried enormous stones about and they took us down to see the castle, the garden entirely run to seed in two years, the house vastly dismal. We went to the top of the tower and walked down some echoing passages and came out rather chilled.

We went up to tea at a house called Candacraig which belongs to a man called Faulkner Wallace who is extremely rich. He has the oddest wife – very tall and misshapen with jet-black shingled hair and wrinkles. She danced Charleston while she played tennis – both so badly. Their home is furnished with the remains of lots of other houses – beautiful panelling and some good furniture and a lot of arty trash which Mrs Wallace thinks modern. She doesn't like Scots people or poor people, she said.

We dined at the Forbes – Sir Charles by now in bed. Again good, and restless. After dinner Kitty Forbes had to sing a song at a mothers' meeting so

---

[1] As a baby, Dr Howie had been found abandoned in a desert beyond the Jordan after a bedouin tribal battle; he was saved and adopted by Scottish missionaries who named him Howie after his native tribe, the Howeitat; his first and only language was broad Scots.

[2] Alastair Graham (in a letter to the editor, November 1975) comments: 'The Forbeses of Newe were my cousins by marriage. I was devoted to both my uncle Charles and his wife. When Evelyn describes him as "a futile little man", he was on his deathbed and died a month or two later. In fact, he was a brilliantly clever little man, bright and gay, and one of the most charming and generous persons I have ever known. There were always large house parties at Newe, and it was his generosity and the First War that finally ruined him; the Castle had to be abandoned and finally demolished. It was not far from Balmoral and every year the King and Queen would come to a function or a meal.'

we took her there in the car. After the meeting was over we danced Highland reels – so difficult to learn.

Wednesday 11 August 1926

This morning we did not feel we could face Mrs G. so we went out for a longish walk on the hills with sandwiches. It rained most of the time. No one lives in any of the cottages and their windows are broken and their roofs fallen in.

Thursday 12 August 1926

Grouse shooting started much to everyone's excitement. We cleaned the car in the morning and I did some work at a detestable poster that I had committed myself to. It was a huge sheet of board to be covered with poster paint. I tried to draw a monk; it was hideously bad. In the afternoon we went to call on some people called Farquarson who lived at a house called Allargue which they claim is the highest home in the United Kingdom.

Le Mortier, St Symphorien, Tours
Wednesday 25 August 1926

I have rather forgotten the order in which things have happened in the last fortnight. On the day after my last entry the Lonach games were held. Everyone had spent some time assuring us that they were not what they had been now that the Forbeses had left Newe. They began with the march of the Highlanders. Originally, apparently, the laird had marched right down the Strath collecting his men, stopping for drinks at every house, and leading them back to Newe for luncheon. Sir Charles did not see his way to turning out this year, but contented himself by remaining at home fingering an enormous Cairngorm and saying, 'I daresay Mr Faulkner Wallace would like to be wearing this today.' About a dozen Highlanders did march from the Lonach Village Hall to the Bellabeg paddock, all of them I should say over fifty and most of them over eighty years of age. They trailed spears behind them and shuffled along in a sad sort of way. All the young men who have not emigrated to America or to the towns think it smarter to wear ill-fitting serge suits than the kilt. The games lasted a long time. There was a lot of piping and some dancing, notably by a lot of detestable children covered in medals. The competitors in the open events were professionals from Aberdeen. I saw them tossing the caber but I did not see anyone get it over. The Wallace boy and Alastair and I had entered for the obstacle race, but when the time came we did not compete. We dined with the Forbes and went afterwards to the Lonach Ball where I danced some of the dances I had learned. It was terribly hot. Mrs F.W. lay swathed in tartan on a chaise longue with an enormous man called Lumsden of Balmedie to carry her about. She had sprained her ankle in doing

Charleston on the tennis court. On Saturday we called on a woman called Lady Annabel Dodds.[1] On Sunday Alastair and I had luncheon at Braemar. We were in search of James Alexander Watson, the Welsh usher, but we found that his house did not exist.

We started early on Monday. It rained all the time. It was a hateful drive, Alastair and Mrs G. being unusually unpleasant. At these moments I wish only to jump out of the car and go back by train. We reached the hotel where we were staying at a place called Killin. It still rained. We walked in the rain to see some tweed mills which were shut, dinner, bed. A melancholy day.

The next two nights we spent with a woman called Cicely MacLellan at a house near Glasgow. She had been called Hicks-Beach and was as morbidly snobbish as only a woman who has married beneath her can be. Her house was very full of plaster decorations of her own making in the Italian style. Breakfast eaten from salad plate, coloured-glass finger bowls, etc. We went for a long drive in the rain next day as a birthday treat for one of her children.

From there we went to York lunching on the way with Sir Richard Graham and Vitie, Duchess of Montrose. York is lovely. I saw the minster by evening light first. By daylight it lost something. We stayed, after bustling through two other hotels, first at an enormous place called the Station Hotel or the Railway Hotel – Mrs G. in a furious rage all the time and, I think, drinking heavily. There are more harlots in York than ever I saw elsewhere. I went to communion at the Minster. Mrs G. was in a furious rage all the time from York to Barford and was intolerably rude not only to Alastair who provoked her but to me who did not. Arrived at Barford she proceeded to attack me violently for having been consistently rude to her all through the expedition. It ended with my resolving heartily never to visit her again.

Next day, Saturday, we went to London. I had tea with Olivia. She seems sad. Ronald Matthews came to see us after dinner. He has a job on the *Daily Express* and is doing rather interesting work and earning quite a lot of money.

On Sunday we went to Paris. It was a pleasant journey with a very smooth passage. We spent an hour or two at Boulogne, which Alastair loved, and arrived in Paris at about 9. We found an hotel called Suez miles on the other side of the river, left our luggage there, and then had a lot of drinks and went to an intolerable cabaret in Montmartre where women made indelicate suggestions to me. We had supper and drank disgusting champagne, then we went to a better pub called Jockey where a nigger was dancing, then to bed in an overheated and noisy room where I could sleep little.

I had meant to go to Tours on Monday but things prevented me. Hugh Lygon and Elmley were in Paris so I spent the evening with them. We dined at a restaurant called La Rue or Roue and then went to Luna Park. Most of the

[1] Alastair Graham's cousin and the mother of the 3rd Baron O'Neill, the first husband of Mrs Ian Fleming, who became a friend of Waugh's nearly thirty years later.

day we spent drinking champagne cocktails. I did not see much of Alastair, nor did I want to. He is so ignorant about Paris and French. This surprised me. I think I have seen too much of Alastair lately.

I came here yesterday, Tuesday, arriving in the middle of luncheon. It is a charming old house. M. Bricoin I think delightful. There are some rather awful English students staying here but we see nothing of them. Yesterday afternoon we went to see a château at Villandry full of forged pictures. On the way back I drove the car and ran over a dog. I don't think it was seriously hurt but its paw was cut. It was a beastly beginning. After dinner we drank some eau de vie which tasted like vodka, made by our host. We played Cooncan. I slept so well.

Monday 30 August 1926

It continues to be hot, but not intolerable. We are leading a lazy and agreeable life; getting up late, lunching heavily, perhaps going to visit a château, perhaps doing some shopping in Tours and having tea at Massie and going to the cinema at the Café de Commerce, dining heavily and then sleeping heavily. I am reading Richards' *Principles of Literary Criticism* again. My French is making no progress. On Saturday we went to Chenonceaux for luncheon where the *pâté de maison* was excellent. I do not much like seeing over châteaux. We then went to Chaumont and arrived at Amboise just too late to go over the château. Instead we drank some wine at a restaurant to which an importunate little boy directed us. There is little temptation to dine out as the cooking here is so excellent.

A charming and quite incredibly learned man called Hayward[1] has been here. He suffers from curvature of the spine but otherwise looks rather like Brian Howard.

Thursday 2 September 1926

It has rained a good deal in the last few days, bringing all manner of rank smells out of the country. On Monday we did a big round of châteaux, Azay-le-Rideau, Langres, Chinon, Langeais, Ussé. They were less crowded than on Saturday. The chapel at Ussé is very fine. I do not much like seeing châteaux. Yesterday the day was spent at garages inspecting the organs of the little car Richard has bought from a grocer. Julia and Howit are expected.

Tuesday 7 September 1926

Julia and Howit came on Friday. We dined at the Unwins and drank Chinon 1919. Julia went to bed early. Howit was accompanied by a raw youth from Lancing called Burra. On Saturday we set out for Blois in the two motor cars,

---

[1] John Hayward: bibliophile, writer, and editor of Donne, Swift, *The Oxford Book of Nineteenth Century Verse*, etc. Friend of T. S. Eliot. Died 1965.

but the Frazer Nash broke its springs. We arranged to spend the night at Blois at an hotel called Angleterre. We saw the château and rested and ate a dreadful dinner and then Julia and I went off in search of a music hall and we found a fair all along the Loire where we were photographed. We also saw a patriotic drama and Julia fell in love with a redheaded American girl chewing nuts. When we got back to the hotel we were told that Richard and Elizabeth had gone back to Tours. I may be old-fashioned, but it seemed to me an improper proceeding, particularly as the manageress could only very hardly [?] be persuaded that Julia and I did not want to sleep together. I went for a walk round the town. Next day I went to see a very beautiful church called, as far as I could make out, St Nichole and St Laurent. We lunched at the Angleterre, paid an immense bill, and drove to Chambord – a monstrous building. With what the book on Touraine calls 'a dream city' on its roof.

Yesterday we pottered about Tours drinking tasteless French beer.

Today we leave for Chartres. Julia has spots and may have to go back early.

145 North End Road, Monday 13 September 1926

We spent two nights at Chartres at an hotel called the Grand Monarque. There was some sort of festival at the cathedral: the whole building crowded – people selling gingerbread pigs, little children pissing on the pillars, women asleep or gossiping and eating, and innumerable little processions with veils and candles and a good deal of money-taking. There was also a fair in the town where Julia bought picture-frames of pink celluloid and I won a live pigeon which caused us some embarrassment and made me climb the railings into the cathedral garden.

From Chartres we went to Rouen over very bad roads. Elizabeth and I had a puncture, Richard broke all his springs. We stayed in a grand hotel called the Poste where there were thousands of servants. Lady Isham and Gyles were there. From Rouen to Le Havre, which is a detestable town. By getting drunk Richard managed to enlist all the porters and dockers on our side and was able to secure a passage. I travelled second class sitting sleepless in one of the cars. At Southampton Elizabeth was ill and there were continual complications about customs and number-plates. Elizabeth and I got off first and reached London at about 3. I slept a lot after that. Stella Rhys is staying here. This morning I received the welcome news that Alastair is getting on with the book.

Wednesday 22 September 1926

I have spent some quiet days but not many. Cecil Roberts came here to dinner one evening and we went to a revue called Blackbirds[1] where all the 'artists' were negroes and negresses. Next day I was rung up and asked to

[1] American musical show that helped to make blacks fashionable in London during the 1920s.

dinner by someone calling himself 'Billy'. Thinking it was Billy Clonmore I accepted readily and then found it was Bill Silk. I dined with him at his flat. We went out to a public house to get some whisky and met Joan Laking and a rather nice girl called Heather Chapman who is a descendant of the original Chapman & Hall. She took us to her flat in Gloucester Road where there were a whole lot of perverse young women with eyeglasses and whisky. 'Dicky' who used to play at the Hambone was there. I went from there to Tony who was about to sleep with a nice American woman called Bunny. Dick Addinsell was there and Cecil Roberts. Back to the lesbian party. I had no money for a taxi and had to wait hours in the Mall before the first bus.

Next day Audrey had a party. I went with Bobbie. All the people I used to know two years ago were there – Keith Chesterton and Francis Palmer and Jessie (now Sylvia) Ferguson. She has grown very much uglier in the last two years, Francis cleaner and smarter. Ronald Matthews took me back in a taxi and slept here for the night. My mother did not like him at all. On Sunday the wife of the mad Ussher came to tea, also a lot of Holmeses.

On Monday Alastair arrived. We spent the afternoon shopping – mostly in choosing ties at Sulka. We ate some oysters in King Street. In the evening we went to the Alhambra and then on to a party given by the lesbian girls I met the other day. It was a party. Sir Francis Laking, dressed first as a girl and then stark naked, attempted a Charleston. A Russian played a saw like a violin. Lulu Waters-Welch came. He is living in sin with Effingham.[1] Brian O'Brien came; also the leader of the syndicate. Alastair and I both got very drunk indeed. I think I was rude to Bobbie. There was a fight between two men. Also a policewoman who scared everyone and made Joan very pugnacious.

Next day Alastair and I lunched with Tony Bushell at a public house called Stone's and went to see the new Harold Lloyd film *For Heaven's Sake*. I found it excellent, contrary to most reports. In the evening I drank brandy at the Kit Kat Club.

Recorded badly like this it seems rather a vigorous ten days, but they are to be my last days of this sort of life – or so I am determined. My mother has given me £150 to pay my debts, and with next term I am resolved to attempt again a life of sobriety, chastity and obedience. On a surer foundation this time I think.

Monday 27 September 1926

This so far as I can remember is the day I have to go back to Aston Clinton. I am afraid that it will be bitterly cold driving down, but I shall not be sorry to get there.

On Wednesday night I went to a detestable pantomime called *The Mikado*.

---

[1] The 5th Earl of Effingham.

On Thursday to Sybil Thorndike's *Henry VIII*. On Friday Mother and I spent the day shopping. I paid my bill at Dunhill's and took my ring and flask out of Mr Attenborough's keeping – surely for the last time. I persuaded Mother to let Mr Truefitt cut off her hair. I think it is a success. Tea at Gunter's. Home to dinner.

On Saturday some friends of Father's called Jock and Ruth Ledward came to stay with him. I had been asked by Francis Palmer and Sylvia (née Jessie) Ferguson to go down to Bourne End for the weekend. I did not want to and wired that my bicycle was injured. However, they would take no refusal and I was forced to go by train.

It is an odious neighbourhood well suited to Sylvia. Bobbie was staying the weekend there and Geoffrey Biddulph and a youth by the name of Pippin. It was all gramophones and cocktails and restlessness. I slept out in a pub. During the night Pippin, who claims to have slept with Jessie and Francis, attempted Bobbie's virginity but without success.

Next day we sat about over the fire and there were little quarrels about things and we played tennis and a Jew called Sir Henry Slesser came to tea and a Mrs Graham whom I misinformed about were-wolves. She was not the same as that Mrs Graham at Barford.

It is pouring with rain. I think I will go to Aston Clinton by train.

Aston Clinton, Saturday 2 October 1926

Last Tuesday I took my diaries for the year to be bound at Maltby's. Since then very little has happened. I paid off all my debts in Oxford, marching from shop to shop in dragging[1] overalls with pocket book full of £5-notes. Most of the shops seem glad to get me off their books except Hall's who I do believe have some real personal feeling for Alastair and me. I have paid the Aylesbury tailor too, and sent cheques to Chris and Richard.

Alastair sent me some 'paste up' proofs of *P.R.B.*[2] I think he is doing it very well; better in fact than it deserves. Between writing and proof-reading I have greatly lost interest in it.

I am not finding Aston Clinton very gay at present. After nine weeks of comparatively civilized society I find it very hard to adapt myself to the children's prattle.

'Please, sir, Cobham must find motoring awfully slow mustn't he, sir?'

I am afraid I was hurting their feelings a little by neglect so I have asked a whole lot of them to tea. I expect little pleasure from the entertainment.

[1] *Sic.*

[2] Waugh's twenty-five-page essay on the Pre-Raphaelite Brotherhood was dedicated 'To Elizabeth Plunket Greene', Richard's wife, and privately printed by Alastair Graham at the Shakespeare Head Press.

Thursday 7 October 1926

I was right in expecting that the tea party on Sunday would be dull.

On Tuesday I went to London from which I have returned with a slight but disagreeable cold. I lunched with my father and mother and then went to Anderson & Sheppard where I ordered a suit that is to cost 15 guineas. I then went to see Bobbie and went with him to Wigmore Street where I joined the Times Book Club and took away with me Adrian Stokes's book, and Eddie Sackville West's *The Ruin* and Keyserling's *Travel Diary*. We ate oysters at the Horseshoe in Tottenham Court Road and back to dinner at my father's house where Alastair had arrived with the sheets of *P.R.B.* Home by train.

Yesterday I spent huddled in a chair trying to read. Today I suppose that I shall do the same.

Bobbie came down to the Bell last weekend. I gave tea to some of the new boys. We talked together rather creditably. On Sunday we took a taxi out to Thame and dined at the Spreadeagle as I have just been paid £2 5s 6d for *The Balance*.[1] The dinner was good and Mr Fothergill made me some mulled claret.

David Greene is to be married on November 10th. I think I shall give him writing-paper for a present.

On Tuesday I dined at the Cockburns to meet a Canadian young man. My cold is nearly well. I have to go to London today to try on my new suit at Anderson & Sheppard.

On Thursday I went to London again, looked at paper for David's wedding present, had my hair cut, went to an exhibition of Douanier Rousseau's painting, and tried on the suit Anderson & Sheppard are making. It is well made, of course, but I am a little disappointed with it. It makes me look distressingly 'dapper'. I also met a binder called Bain and made arrangements with him for binding *P.R.B.* I dined at home on partridges, smoked one of my father's cigars, and returned by train.

Saturday 23 October 1926

We have fires at last, but they are made of elm wood and are noisy. I went up to London on Tuesday, Crawford having ordained a holiday, and fetched my bicycle. I found my mother alone and lunched with her. On Thursday I went again to try on my suit at Anderson & Sheppard whom, I notice, I have been spelling wrongly[2] up till now. It is going to be good. It was a depressing day. I left my bicycle at Wendover and went up by train missing luncheon. I walked miles from shop to shop and returned home to find my father ill, my mother

---

[1] Waugh's first published short story.

[2] Waugh spelled many, if not most, proper names wrongly. For 'Sheppard', he had written 'Shepherd'.

away at Bishop's Hull tending her mother's death-bed, and a woman called Crabbe-Watt, who used to be mad but has regained her reason, staying in the house. After a bad dinner – my mother had left without ordering any food – I went back by train, fell asleep, and woke up at Aylesbury. There were no taxis to be got and I had to walk all the way out.

Yesterday, in consequence, I slept most of the day.

Bain sent me a proof copy of *P.R.B.* It was agreeable to see it looking like a book at last, but it is full of misprints.

This morning a note from Olivia. The family are changing house again, this time to a three-roomed flat over a stable in a mews in Mayfair so the march from Hanover Terrace is complete.

Harold has been writing and wiring to me a lot about his poems, for which he cannot find a publisher.

Saturday 30 October 1926

On Thursday I attained the age of twenty-three years. My father gave me, besides some very expensive underclothes, £1 to buy some dinner with. Edmund and Charles gave me a penknife with a highly coloured, variegated handle, an aunt a tobacco pouch, the cook at the Bell a cake, and John Sutro a telegram. It rained all the time. I ate luncheon at the Bell, and dinner, drank a good deal and smoked cigars and had tea with Edmund and Charles in the stables. Nick Kelly gave me a story by Hueffer and Conrad.

Some days ago I wrote to the publishers of the *Today and Tomorrow* series suggesting that I should write them a book on *Noah; or the Future of Intoxication*. To my surprise and pleasure they welcome the idea enthusiastically.

A very silly review in the *Manchester Guardian* this morning commends my contribution[1] to *Georgian Stories* highly, but for the most futile reasons.

Bain is being so quick and kind about binding *P.R.B.*

Coal is very short and the days wet and cold. The food gets worse and worse here. I have so much work to do and am neglecting it shamefully. Gleed, now that he is leaving, is very voluble and satiric about the school. The boys mock him more and more and more. Also he plays football worse and worse.

How dull this diary is becoming. I think it is important to record every day, every evening. I will try this.

All Hallows' Eve 1926

Yesterday I played football and scored a lot of tries. I find that I can always do that whenever I want to now. The games are so dull with only about ten children on each side. I went down to dinner at the Bell and drank a lot of beer.

---

[1] Waugh's story, *The Balance, A Yarn of the Good Old Days of Broad Trousers and High Necked Jumpers*.

Tuesday 2 November 1926

The Headmaster spent most of the day showing a man over the school. Not only over the speech-room and class-rooms but the kitchens and stables and bathrooms and playing fields. I suppose that he is trying to sell it.

I have done no more on *Noah*.

Today has been deeply depressing.

Wednesday 3 November 1926

A peculiarly dreary day. At the end of it I went down after prep and dined at the Bell.

Thursday 4 November 1926

I went to London, had my hair cut, tried on my suit at Anderson & Sheppard, took Harold's poems to Jonathan Cape and went home to tea where I found Jane Marston. Dined at home and returned by train as far as Wendover.

Guy Fawkes Day 1926

Gabbitas & Thring have sent me a notice from a woman in Golders Green who wants a companion-tutor for an infant son for next holidays. It will mean giving up the idea of going to Athens, but I think if I can I will take it. Four guineas a week is not to be despised.

Sunday 7 November 1926

The prospect of working next holidays instead of spending money has filled me with a self-righteousness which quiets my conscience when I spend money. Yesterday and the day before I dined out and drank rum. Last night with Charles Poole who came over from Cambridge for the night. He got rather drunk and spoke enthusiastically of fornication.

I have written up to the moment about 2,000 words of *Noah*, some of them fairly satisfactory.

Wednesday 10 November 1926

Today David is being married to 'Babe' at St George's, Hanover Square. I am not going.

I finished the first chapter of *Noah* yesterday.

Through the badness of the food and their own uncleanly habits, the children are all struck down with putrefying flesh. This has stopped all games and made them dismal.

This morning the matron marched out of the house in a rage carrying her tin trunk on her head.

Yesterday morning I dined with Gleed and walking home took the wrong turning at the canal bank. It was 12 before I reached home.

It rains ceaselessly.

Two more reviews of *Georgian Stories* omit any mention of me. Bain shows no sign of sending *P.R.B.* The woman at Golders Green has not answered my letter suggesting that I shall accompany her son next holidays.

On Thursday I went to London. The woman at Golders Green will not take me as tutor for her son. My father seemed more cheerful than usual. I rode a push-bicycle back from Wendover.

Friday, Saturday and Sunday were unspeakably dismal, and I have not the smallest doubt that today will be as bad. The boys are still covered with suppurating sores on all parts of their bodies and are increasingly given to sordid malefactions.

I had a letter from Elizabeth to say she was coming to see me next weekend. I have written a good deal more of *Noah*. It is mannered and 'literary'.

Gleed, very nervous, caned a boy on Saturday, but apparently did it quite well. A boy called Blackburn has been put into the dormitory with Charles and Edmund so I don't go to see them now. I find myself shouting at the children and neglecting to make my corrections and losing my mark book and reading Edgar Wallace and being quite unable to understand the essays of Herbert Read – and there are five more weeks of this term nearly.

Wednesday 17 November 1926

P.R.B. has arrived with an uncorrected mistake I had noticed before and forgotten to put into the errata.

All day I have been rude to the boys and am ashamed of it.

Thursday 18 November 1926

I went to London and spent more than I could afford at a chemist's shop buying hair oils and cosmetics. My father gave me a very good dinner. Met a bad man called Bloomfield.

Friday 19 November 1926

Bored.

Oxford, Saturday 20 November 1926

Richard and Elizabeth came in their new car and somewhat against my will bore me off to Oxford for the night. We dined at the George where the food was as bad as always and extremely expensive. After dinner we went to Marcus Clarke's rooms who bores me. Anthony[1] was there and some nameless youths. After that we went down to St Aldate's and saw David Rice and Elliott

---

[1] Anthony Russell.

Seabrooke. Then Richard and Elizabeth went to bed and I went to the Mitre where I found not only Harold but Hugh Lygon, Tom Douglas, Roland Leigh, Robert Byron and some others, all pretty drunk. Harold came back to the Randolph with me and we talked until about 3.

Sunday 21 November 1926

To breakfast first with David Rice and later with Marcus Clarke. I called on Roger Fulford, whom I found in bed, and Henry Yorke. Luncheon at the House with Roy Harrod. An enormous luncheon party of all the 'smart set'. Admirable food and drink and poor conversation. The one thing about that set to my mind is that, awful as their standards are, they at least do not take people like Fulford and Molson seriously. After luncheon there was some delay in finding Richard and the car, but at last we went off – I still more confirmed, as after every exodus into social life, of the futility of talking to people.

I wore my new suit from Anderson & Sheppard and for the first time did not feel the worst-dressed person in every room.

Aston Clinton, Monday 22 November 1926

The headmaster told me that he thinks after all he may take Cecil Roberts to be an usher here. I am not sure now how much I shall approve of this arrangement.

No one has received *P.R.B.* because Edmund forgot to post them.

Tuesday 23 November 1926

Tired and bored.

Wednesday 24 November 1926

I did some work chopping wood with the children.

Thursday 25 November 1926

By this morning's post Hatchard's refuse to buy any copies of *P.R.B.* I don't blame them, it is so full of misprints. Also a note from Cecil Roberts saying that on his father's advice he has decided not to apply for a mastership here. I rejoice at his decision. Ever since Monday I have been filled with dismay at the prospect of too close association with him.

To my real delight Claud has come back to Tring for some little time. The headmaster ordained a holiday today so I walked over to see him. I met a stoat, ferret, or weasel on the way. I talked to him for several hours, lunching and having tea at his house, and returned much stimulated to get on with *Noah*. I had meant to spend an evening peacefully at work on it, but the boy I am hopelessly coaching for Cambridge demands my attention. Damn him.

The handle of the common-room door is broken and I am forced to choose between sitting in a draught and getting up to open it at every knock.

Saturday 27 November–Tuesday 30 November 1926

Cold and beastly. Played games, taught, chopped wood. On Tuesday I dined with Claud and his family and rode home on a foot-bicycle. Mad Mary Guthrie wants some copies of *P.R.B.*

Monday 6 December 1926

There is nothing to relate about the last few days. I have had an idea or two for the finishing of *Noah* but lack the energy to put them into form. Yesterday I caned a boy for blasphemy.

The last Sunday of term and all the children very excited at the prospect of holidays and Switzerland and Christmas. I have had a lot of work lately besides. *Noah*, which drags along somehow and am very tired. The captain has been off duty for the weekend and I am confined to the house and burdened with all manner of odd duties – even to the rubbing of embrocation into the boys' backs. I am tired of words and want a holiday badly when I shall read and write nothing but just see things and try to draw a little.

145 North End Road, NW11

Term ended on Friday. The Headmaster, after his promise to raise my wages, gave me a cheque for the usual £40. I tackled him on the subject and he grudgingly gave me another £10 a year. I think next term will be my last.

The Marstons are moving into a new house and have most of their meals here. Claud lunched here on Friday.

On Saturday morning I went into London to have my hair cut, buy socks and gloves and get my tickets from Cook's.

In the afternoon with my father to a matinée of an indecent play called *The Country Wife*.[1] It was all about impotence and adultery and very restless to watch.

In the evening I dined with Jessie (Sylvia) Ferguson and Francis Palmer (Beaufort-Palmer). A badly organized dinner. Caviare and good hock but atrocious servants. We went on to the Berkeley where Bobbie was reprimanded by the headmaster M. Feraro, for lechery. Then to a party in a theatre. I do not know who the host was. He had not provided enough drink. The guests ranged from Lady Elizabeth Howard through the Stracheys and Guevaras and Elliott Seabrooke to cockney models and painters in short sleeves frankly enjoying themselves. Peter Rodd was there and Tom Douglas.

[1] By William Wycherley (1675).

Francis drove me back – a real kindness – at about 5. After I left, Cecil Roberts fought a man and was given a black eye.

On Sunday, very tired, to luncheon with Gwen Otter. A homosexual Scot called Ernest Thesiger has decorated a lot of her house so badly. Hugh Macintosh[1] and wife (pregnant) to tea here.

Christmas Day 1926, Saturday
Patris II, Mediterranean

Before I left London I finished off *Noah*, though badly, and sent it to Kegan Paul. Crease arrived on Thursday evening. I was glad to see him before I went.

Yesterday I started off soon after breakfast with very little luggage. The crossing to Calais was extremely rough, but I was delighted to find that I did not feel ill at all. I expect that my previous bitter experiences were mostly due to drink. The journey from Calais to Marseilles was most disagreeable. The carriage was crowded. A woman sat next to me with a little girl which she fed with chocolate and cake and fruits and aperient water every twenty minutes throughout the night. I was very thirsty and slept little.

Everyone in Marseilles seemed most dishonest. They all tried to swindle me mostly with complete success. I had an admirable luncheon at a restaurant called Basso.

This ship is much smarter and cleaner than I expected. None of the other passengers attract me much. I sit at table with a young Greek – very black – and a middle-aged and incredibly provincial American. I have not yet seen my cabin companion. It is getting quite rough and the captain is so drunk below shouting at the top of his voice. I am so afraid that if I lie down I shall be ill.

Sunday 26 December 1926

I am not enjoying this voyage any more than I expected. I have not been sick yet but it is very rough and the boat greatly overheated and badly ventilated. There is a good deal of fuss about the food, long French names, many courses, stewards in white gloves, finger bowls etcetera but it is completely tasteless. There is also a disagreeable Greek wine tasting like varnish and brown sugar; quite good Turkish coffee.

I sit all day either in the spray on deck or the heat below and doze and read *The Varieties of Religious Experience*[2] and attempt drawings for a book I intend doing to be called the Annals of Constitutional Monarchy.

I have just dined with two Americans, the Greek youth having taken to his bed. One of them is vulgar and boastful and blasphemous, but he knows Greece well and most of Europe and is a heavy drinker. The other one, whom I

---

[1] H. S. M. Macintosh, a writer of ballades.
[2] A classic analysis, published 1902, of the psychology of conversion, by William James.

sat with the first evening, is unbelievably ignorant and mean-minded. I did not think anyone outside Wales could be so awful.

The Greek who lives in my cabin seems rather charming. He has been in bed all day. Almost everyone has been. We shall not arrive before Wednesday they tell me.

Monday 27 December 1926

A brilliant sun and a calm sea. All manner of odd and scented women have emerged from their cabins this morning. Also some very dapper little men. Also a whole horde of savages who crouch on a little bit of deck and eat dry bread.

After luncheon on Wednesday, 29 December 1926

We should have arrived yesterday afternoon but we are still some hours away. The ship goes so slowly. The last two days have been calm enough and wonderfully sunny and warm. I am getting bored with these people, particularly of the two Americans. The young Greek who played his gramophone to me on the first evening has emerged again. I have a feeling that all Greeks are going to be rather like him: very friendly and gentle with hair too low on the forehead.

Yesterday the man who sleeps (with odd whistling noises) in my cabin woke me at 7 in the morning beckoning me excitedly to the porthole with cries of 'Italia! Italia!'

Athens, Saturday 1 January 1927

It was 8 o'clock on Wednesday before I got off the ship. We were kept waiting for nearly two hours before we were allowed to land while the policemen tried to read our passports. Alastair and a servant called Nikolas came to meet me on a little boat. We drank cocktails at an hotel called Grande Bretagne which is just like the Crillon. The whole of Athens is very much more modern and smart than I expected – trams, cocktail bars and enormous blocks of flats. The flat that Alastair shares with Leonard Bower[1] is very modern indeed with baths and lavatories and electric lights. There is no furniture except a few *objets d'art* and it smells strongly of plaster. We have to have our meals out at various restaurants. Generally we lunch at one called Costi and dine at *Ταβερνα*. On the first night I got very drunk at a cabaret kept by a one-legged Maltese. He gave me some poisonous cocktails which made me quite insane and next day very ill.

Nikolas calls us with soup at about 9.30 but it takes a long time for us all to have baths – Leonard has to get off first to the Legation so we are never dressed

---

[1] An attaché at the British Embassy; Alastair Graham took over his job in February 1928.

until 11. Everything in Greece takes just twice as long as it would anywhere else. In the country they just do not use time at all. In Athens the waiters take ten minutes or quarter of an hour to bring each dish and all conversations are quite interminable. No one dines before 9 or, apparently, goes to bed before about 3 or 4. For a bustling European the system has disadvantages. It is usually bank holiday too.

There is another Englishman here with a red beard called R——. I used to meet him in my Great Ormond Street, 1917 Club days. He wants to seduce Alastair and his talk – and indeed everyone's in Athens – is only of male prostitutes. The flat is usually full of dreadful Dago youths called by heroic names such as Miltiades and Agamemnon with blue chins and greasy clothes who sleep with the English colony for 25 drachmas a night.

There is an English club where there are comfortable chairs. We go from café to café – all the drinks taste either of camphor or medicine and everything smells of drains.

I have been to see a very beautiful church at Daphni full of mosaics. Also a deserted monastery. We tried to go to the Parthenon but found it shut.

Last night we dined at the Grande Bretagne and then went to drink in a library with two skittish English spinsters. We stayed there until 4. I brought a policeman in who had his fortune told again and again and got rather drunk.

This afternoon we went for a drive to some villages just outside the town. The car flies a Union Jack and has a diplomatic number which means that the police cannot interfere if we run over people or drive without lights – as frequently happens.

I have just left Alastair and R—— at a café which looks like a suburban parish hall. They all look either like that or like potting-sheds.

Sunday 2 January 1927

We went to a race meeting at Phaleron in the afternoon. They have a totalizator there run by the state on the principle that if you back a winner your stake is returned, if for a place you get half and everyone else loses. It must be a substantial source of revenue. In the morning we went to the Parthenon.

Monday 3 January 1927

I went early to Cook's to see about tickets back. As always I am very much poorer than I expected and have to wire for funds to my bank. I want to go to Olympia, Delphi and Rome on the way back. We drove into the country to a place called Vari in the afternoon. Alastair has given me an ikon I like very much. It is terribly worm-eaten and I am so afraid that it will crumble entirely to pieces on the journey home.

Tuesday 4 January 1927

We went to the National Museum in the morning and for a walk after luncheon. Wherever we went Greek soldiers appeared and shot at us. There is a nice café called the Pine Tree, underground. They dance Pyrrhic dances there. I get tired of the restaurants where we have our meals. I am afraid I have inherited overmuch of my father's homely sentiments. The truth is that I do not really like being abroad much. I want to see as much as I can this holiday and from February shut myself up for the rest of my life in the British Isles. I think I shall like the country. From what I saw of them at Vari the peasants are very childlike and charming.

I have learned some Greek words. The drink that tastes like camphorated oil is called ρετεινα, the one that looks like quinine and tastes like aniseed is ούςο, the pieces of bad meat on matches that they provide 'to take the taste away' are μεςεδε. The language which no one speaks is Καθαρευονεα.

Athens–Itea, Wednesday 5 January 1927

We had meant to go to Phile but weather prevented us. The money I had wired for arrived, so suddenly overwhelmed by claustrophobia I set out alone for Delphi. Alastair and Nikolas took me to Piraeus in a storm and left me there at 4. The boat, tiny and execrably uncomfortable, left at 9. I walked about in the mud of Piraeus for a little, sorry that the Athenian adventure had been such a failure. It is possible Alastair may get the 'bag'[1] to carry and meet me again in Rome. He was very sweet at the last filling my flask with brandy and my bag with razor blades and lavatory paper for the journey.

Itea–Olympia, Thursday 6 January 1927

I spent a more comfortable night than I might have expected. We arrived at Itea at 6.30 to learn that there is no boat to Patras tomorrow – or so they said – so I have to go straight to Patras without seeing Delphi. Dawn over Itea was very beautiful. The boat is more empty this way. It was noisy last night.

They put me off the boat at a place called Aiyion because I should miss my train at Patras if I stayed there while the boat called at all the little ports. I met a German and his wife and a Russian woman with whom I had luncheon. They knew even less French than I and conversation was difficult but I was glad of their company.

At 1.30 my train arrived. The journey to Pirgos was intolerably long but uneventful. A Greek gave me his card and said he would write to me because he loved the English. A little boy tore up a 5-drachma note in rage because it was not enough. At Pirgos, at about 7.30 I changed into a carriage which was more like the cabin of a very small sailing ship than anything, lit by a tiny oil lamp. A

[1] Diplomatic 'bag'.

young man opposite me in a bow tie talked excellent French and advised me to
go to the Hôtel de Chemin de Fer. After a very long time I realized that he was
a waiter – or else the son of the house; I have not yet discovered – and that he had
been marketing at Pirgos and that the fowl, alive, under his arm was for my
dinner.

We arrived at Olympia at about 8.30 and walked up rocky precipices for
about ten minutes guided by a peasant girl with a lantern. I began to be
apprehensive about what the hotel would be, and feared some public house
with bugs and draughts and goats in the bedrooms. We arrived at an enormous
building at the top of a hill, with high doors and most ill-lit uncarpeted
passages leading in all directions. A very courteous old man received me and
led me to a bedroom, also huge. I was the sole guest but at a moment's notice
they provided an excellent dinner – including part of the fowl I had travelled
with. And so to bed.

Olympia, Friday 7 January 1927

I awoke to find much of the impression of grandeur had disappeared but the
pleasure remained. The hotel is large but exceedingly dilapidated. They gave
me French coffee and bitter bread and I went out to see the museum. That too
was almost in ruins. One man looks after it and the real ruins which extend for
acres and acres of waste land at the bottom of the hill; I should imagine he has
an easy job. He seemed rather to resent my arrival. There is a good deal of fairly
interesting sculpture in the museum and it kept me employed until luncheon.
That again was excellent. After luncheon I went to see the Hermes of Praxiteles
(or as R—— calls him Praxilites) which is kept in a separate shed in charge of
the village idiot, embedded in concrete before a grey plush curtain. It is quite
marvellous and well worth all the trouble I have taken to see it. I went for a
short walk among goats and olive trees, two or three unsuccessful excursions to
the post office to find whether Alastair had wired his plans, and then returned.

They are expecting an American woman tonight. The young man with the
bow tie has been shopping all day in Pirgos. It is conceivable that Alastair may
arrive tonight but not likely I should think.

Tomorrow I have another heavy bout of travelling. I have to catch the boat
to Brindisi at 5 on Sunday morning.

Olympia–Brindisi, Saturday 8 January 1927

Alastair did not arrive. The American woman was a lonely spinster doing a
three weeks' tour of the whole of Greece. She declaimed loudly against
American trippers. I left after luncheon. A deaf-and-dumb boy carried my bag
to the station and for some reason would not take any money, so I gave him my
pocket knife which I happened to find in my pocket. The journey to Patras was

tedious enlivened by entirely unintelligible 'Americanos'. At every station everyone got out of the train and talked, then a bell was rung and the guard blew a trumpet, and then the engine whistled, and then they all shouted and said goodbye to each other again and off the train went at walking pace. I had a bad but cheap *table d'hôte* dinner at Patras and found a very helpful hotel porter who arranged for a man to fetch my bag and tell me as soon as the boat was in sight. I was beset by an insane interpreter who spoke no language known to man. I had to make him drunk before I could get rid of him. He left promising in execrable French and English that he would arrange for the boat to come into the cinema to fetch me. This did not actually happen but everything went very smoothly. I was just three-quarters of the way through an admirable German film called *Fire* when a man arrived and led me to the boat. After a little trouble with passports I got on board and found an empty cabin in the second class. The boat is small and of course dirty but it is at any rate better than the one to Itea.

Sunday 9 January 1927

It was very rough all the morning and I felt very ill. The deck is entirely usurped by third-class passengers who have nowhere else to go.

After luncheon we reached Corfu and spent two hours there. I landed. A very clean and rather attractive town. It reminded me of Brighton. I had my photograph taken. It is cold now because the sun has set. We are stopped at some obscure island. Tomorrow morning we are due at Brindisi.

.

Brindisi–Rome, Monday 10 January 1927

In the train an hour from Rome. I am so tired. We reached Brindisi at 4 this morning and after military and medical examinations were at last allowed to land. My train left at 9. I found an amiable Smyrnese interpreter. He got me breakfast and changed my money and walked about Brindisi with me until it was time for the train. Since 9 I have been in this carriage – sometimes alone sometimes in a crowd. At one stage of the journey a whole family with whooping cough who shared one handkerchief and retched unashamedly. At another a woman with the smile of the Gioconda and the voice of a parrot. We seem to have stopped at every station in Italy, all decorated with grubby stencilled pictures of Il Duce looking as if they were advertising Hassals[?] Press Art School.

All common Italian women have voices like parrots.

Rome, Tuesday 11 January 1927

I went straight to the Hôtel de Russie last night and found that neither Alastair nor Leonard was here. However I took a comparatively cheap room and had a bath and went to sleep in great content.

Today I got up at about 10, wired to my father for £5, and drove to St Peter's. On the way every corner showed something beautiful. I gaped like any peasant at the size of St Peter's – how bad the frescoes were compared with those at Daphni. I climbed to the highest point of the dome. I lunched for 11 lira at a small restaurant opposite St Peter's. From there I took a cab to the Forum and enjoyed myself shamelessly marching about with a guide book identifying the various ruins. Then back to the hotel where a tea-dance is going on. I drank two gin fizzes which each cost as much as my luncheon and watched the same sort of people dancing as I should have seen at the Berkeley or the Crillon. I think I shall dine here tonight and go away tomorrow evening.

Friday 14 January 1927

In the train again, between Rome and Paris. On Tuesday I dined at the Russie, not a remarkably good dinner considering the price. Afterwards I went out to try and find a little of the night life but learned that it had been stopped by Il Duce. I went to a sort of music hall where ladies did voluptuous dances in wrinkled tights and a cadaverous man in a tail coat balanced shining things on his head.

On Wednesday I went for a personally conducted Cook's tour and I must say that it is not a bad way of seeing things. The other tourists were mostly women – governesses I should imagine – who asked inane questions and made whistling noises at the things they admired. The guide seemed well informed. We went to the Vatican Museum in the morning. The Sistine Chapel is disappointing. The roof is magnificent but the Last Judgement has lost all its colouring and has been repainted with a very weak blue. It does not seem to me as perfectly composed as I had expected. The great islands of figures seemed rather unsatisfactory. In the afternoon to the Colosseum and catacomb of St Calixtus and the church of St Sebastian without the Walls where I saw the footprints of Our Lord and the arrows of St Sebastian. That night I moved to a garret in an awful public house called Nuova Roma. It only cost 11 lira so cannot complain. I should have left that night but could not cash my father's money cable. Next day to matins at St Peter's and to S. Maria Maggiore and S. Giovanni in Laterano. I had so little money that everything was rather difficult. At 10 I took this train and spent a very long night alone in the carriage except for one quite agreeable Italian. This morning three very noisy men have got in. I have just 10 francs left to get back with, and one bottle of Vichy water to drink.

Hampstead, Monday 24 January 1927

I arrived home on Saturday evening very dirty and very hungry. I found some people called Warren staying in the house and my father in bed with influenza. After Paris the journey was quite agreeable. I met an Italian ice-cream seller and lost him in the Metro but he turned up again on the boat and gave me a drink. There were a lot of very healthy-looking people coming back from Switzerland among them E. B. Gordon[1] and Christine[?] Riley.

For the last week I have been resting. The Warrens left on Wednesday. I have not told anyone that I am home and have spent most of the time here doing very little. I have spent two mornings at the Flemish exhibition at the Academy – the drawings particularly interesting.

On Saturday I went to dinner with the Sutros – and a good dinner. Today I go back to Aston Clinton.

Kegan Paul have turned *Noah* down. It is rather a blow as I was counting on the money for it but perhaps it is a good thing. I was not pleased with it.

Aston Clinton, Tuesday 8 February 1927

There have been three weeks of this term. There are four new boys more or less sane and a new usher called Attwell for whom at first I conceived an intense dislike which has begun to soften a little. He is dull-looking with a small moustache, cheap and tidy clothes, and – usually – boots. He was educated at King's School, Worcester, and retains a slight accent, and at Christ Church, Oxford, where he seems to have led the dullest life imaginable. He is very keen on education and I have only just begun to cure him of talking to me seriously about it. He was almost a teetotaller when he came but I have so far corrupted him that last night he was sick. I am gradually persuading him to pay for some of his own drinks. He took a second in English Literature and is not wholly uneducated, but he has a mean and ill-digested mind with a sort of part rationalism and part idealism. I should imagine rather a Sanderson of Oundle[2] type.

Edmund did not come back for some days.

I have used the stables more than usual and had one or two tea parties.

There is an admirable new matron who was at one time dame at Goodharts[?] and knew some of my friends there. She gave me a ham the other day. Claud came over to dinner one night, and Richard and Elizabeth another.

On Thursday I went to London, ate a good luncheon at the Ritz and bought some collars and ties at Hawes & Curtis and cigars at Dunhill's, dined at home, and came back by a very good train and taxi. I have had to take £25 of my wages already and a fiver from Alec and have about £2 to last the term on.

Sunday 20 February 1927

Most of the last days have been profitless. A man wrote to me from Oxford offering to pay me 10 guineas for a story to put in a book he edits called the *New Decameron*.

[1] Waugh's schoolmaster colleague at Arnold House.

[2] F. W. Sanderson (1857–1922), headmaster who revitalized Oundle School.

I went to London on Thursday by a very quick and comfortable train and did some shopping. Next Thursday I am to visit a Father Underhill about being a parson. Last night I was very drunk. How odd those two sentences seem together.

About five minutes after I wrote the last sentence, while Attwell and I were sitting over the fire laughing about our drunkenness of the night before, Crawford suddenly arrived and sacked us both, on the spot, Attwell to leave at the end of the term. Apparently that matron had been making trouble.[1] From then onwards it was rather a harassing day. Upward very grave and helpful, the boys shy of being seen speaking to me. I walked in the rain to Stoke Mandeville to meet Bobbie. Richard arrived for luncheon with about thirty awful men from Oxford whom he was trying to sell cars to. I packed hurriedly leaving my books to come on by goods and slipped away feeling rather like a housemaid who has been caught stealing gloves. I rang up my parents first to apprise them of my coming, and dined in a very sorrowful household.

Hampstead, Monday 21 February 1927

Today the 21st I have been trying to do something about getting a job and am tired and discouraged. It is all an infernal nuisance. I wrote to Edmund and Charles to say goodbye to them. It seems to me the time has arrived to set about being a man of letters.

Monday 28 February 1927

On Tuesday I received a very charming letter from Edmund. I spent two days writing a story about a duke. Cecil Roberts came to dinner unfortunately quite drunk. On Thursday I lunched with Gwen Greene and Olivia in their little flat in Bourdon Street. Olivia could talk of nothing except black men. I went to tea with a parson called Father Underhill who spoke respectfully of the Duke of Westminster and disrespectfully of my vocation to the Church. I called on Anne Talbot and then to dinner at Ladbroke Grove with Dudley Carew. He is engaged to a girl named Garvin, daughter of the journalist. She was there, also Sylvia Ferguson and Francis Palmer. The dinner was disgusting and everyone was late. We went later to the Blackbirds and called on Florence Mills and other niggers and negresses in their dressing-rooms. Then to a night club called Victor's to see another nigger – Leslie Hutchinson.[2] Claud came to stay on Friday. On Saturday we went to tea with Harold Acton. He has taken rather a charming flat in John Street, Adelphi, with a Chinese servant and many paintings of himself. I dined at Victor's in a large and I should think

---

[1] 'Though he told his mother that he was dismissed for drunkenness, the fact, as he confessed to me, was that he was dismissed for trying to seduce the matron.' Christopher Hollis, *Oxford in the Twenties* (London, 1976), p. 80.

[2] Pianist and singer.

enormously expensive party given by a man called Langton Douglas.[1] His illegitimate daughter Zena Naylor lives with Hutchinson. His legitimate daughter is fourteen and looks eighty. His son was also up from Eton on long leave. Besides them Francis and Sylvia with whom I was spending the night. Olivia joined us later. We went on to a party given by a Mrs Goossens which was entirely taken up by black people playing poker, and white people getting drunk and cutting each other. Next day with Claud to luncheon at Otter's. A comic luncheon party. To tea at Hill Street with the Douglases. The situation of a distinguished old man's illegitimate daughter receiving in his house her black lover and her black lover's black wife and baby might seem improbable in a book. However there it was.

This morning, Monday, I was told by the Future Career Association that a man in Notting Hill wanted an usher for a few weeks. I went to see him and got the job at £5 a week. This relieves me of immediate anxiety but it looks like being a dreary job.

Monday 7 March 1927

The school in Notting Hill is quite awful. All the masters drop their aitches · and spit in the fire and scratch their genitals. The boys have close-cropped heads and steel-rimmed spectacles wound about with worsted. They pick their noses and scream at each other in a cockney accent. For the first three days I had nothing to do but 'invigilate' while one of the urchins did an exam. Since then I have been turned onto some coaching.

On Wednesday I went with Anne to a play called *Dracula* and to call on Harold Acton. On Friday I went by appointment to the editor of the *Daily Express*. He will take me for three weeks' trial at the end of the term at £4 a week. I don't know how much I shall like that but it will be worth trying.

The *Decameron* accepted my story so I took Harold to dinner at Kettners. We went later to the Tour d'Eiffel and drank hock. When I arrived home I found, to my delight, that Alec had arrived suddenly on the *Aquitania*.

On Saturday there was a party at Oliver Messel's. Alec and Harold and I dined first at the Ritz. Then to call on E. S. P. Haynes and then to Oliver's. It was a crowded party with all the Blackbirds and all the Oxford Brian Howard set and stray and squalid stragglers uninvited from Otter's and Francis. Cecil Roberts became insensible with drink and, curled in overcoat, vomited and pissed intermittently. Robert Byron made an ostentatious entry as Queen Victoria. The Earl of Rosse and I cut each other throughout the evening. Olivia and I both felt more than a little lonely.

Next day I took Olivia to luncheon at an admirable new restaurant called Chez Taglioni in Gerrard Street where the café diabolo made us feel so well.

[1] Art dealer and art historian of ambiguous reputation. See Appendix of Names, p. 794.

This morning back again to work. I have sold my motor bicycle for £10 to little Hollins.

Thursday 10 March 1927

On Wednesday I lunched at Taglioni again and dined with Harold and Sacheverell Sitwell.[1] Chinese food. H. with severe cold. After dinner we looked at books for a long time. Sachie was extraordinarily nice to me. He drove me to a party in his car and offered to write to Baxter about me on the *Express*. The party was given by Layton the black man at Stuart Hill's studio. All very refined – hot lobster, champagne cup, and music. Florence Mills, Delysia, John Huggins, Layton and Johnston and others sang songs. Sylvia too affectionate.

On Friday Olivia, Francis and Sylvia lunched with me at Taglioni's. We called on black Hutchinson who is having a row with Zena. To dinner at Hill Street with Zena. To a box at the Blackbirds with Olivia, Tony Butts and Mrs Hutchinson. Afterwards, after infinite delay and driving about, to a noisy and cheap nightclub. May and Bessie, two Blackbirds, came back to Golders Green and thrilled Sylvia with intimate gossip.

Slept all Sunday.

Today I ordered some studs and buttons in black onyx. An absurd man called Grubb wrote asking for my autograph.

Sunday 27 March 1927

I spent several nights at Ladbroke Grove in Dudley Carew's flat. On Wednesday I went to a party at Francis Meynell's, on Thursday at Faith Wigglesworth's. On Friday I took Mrs W.[2] to a theatre. On Saturday I lunched with Joyce Fagan and her American and drove to Richmond. Dined with an ill-looking but intelligent Jew called Haskell in a very highly designed home in Hornton Street. He is starting a magazine called *Europe* and was willing to offer me work. After dinner to a party at Zena's. On Sunday I went down to Henley for luncheon with Berta Ruck[3] – an all-Welsh luncheon party. Dined Zena, Alec, Richard and Elizabeth at Taglioni's. On Monday I ordered a suit, dined Richard and Eliza at Taglioni's – *blinis* – and went to the first night of *Metropolis*. Mrs Garland asked me to a party. China Harry died. On Wednesday Claud came to London and I spent the evening with him. China H. seems to have made a characteristic death – reading Ludwig's *William II* and making sarcastic remarks about himself. Mrs Harry is going to be rather poor

[1] Younger brother (b. 1897) of Sir Osbert Sitwell; chiefly known for his art criticism and travel writings; succeeded as 6th Bart., 1969.

[2] His mother.

[3] Novelist; in March 1927 she published *The Mind of a Minx*.

but Claud has his fellowship all right. Thursday dined with Audrey Lucas – very squalid little flat. Met Peter Ruffer in a pub. Today I am going to Erringham[?] for the night and looking forward to it, so much. Taking caviare, cigars and Bristol Milk.

Thursday 7 April 1927

The job in Holland Park is over but it does not seem at all difficult to earn a living. I am in doubt at the moment whether to go on the *Express* or write a biography[1] that Duckworth show some interest in. I have been to several parties and spent such a lot of money. I have met such a nice girl called Evelyn Gardner[2] and renewed friendship with Peter Quennell and Robert Byron. I went to Erringham[?] for one weekend.

Monday 9 May 1927

I am just starting on my fifth week on the *Express*.

Duckworth's commissioned the Rossetti biography and gave me £20 on the spot which I spent in a week. Since then I have made no money except the £5 a week they pay me in Shoe Lane. I find the work most exhilarating tho' much of it is just sitting about in the office – noisy and at the present time very hot.

A charming girl called Inez Holden works on the paper. I have been to a few parties and joined a club called the Gargoyle.

I went for a weekend to Plymouth and for a day to Paris. Everything looks so lovely in the sun.

Monday 23 May 1927

I have got the sack from the *Express* and am looking forward to a holiday. There have been some parties, rather a pleasing little one by Evelyn Gardner and Pansy Pakenham[3] in Ebury Street. Papers are full of lies. C. & H. gave a party to his office staff. He and my mother go abroad at the end of the week.

Friday 1 July 1927

After a month's holiday I have settled down to work on the Rossetti book.

My father and mother went off to France luxuriously on the Blue Train leaving me quite a lot of money to live with until their return. On the day they left I spent the morning at the Gargoyle, took Evelyn Gardner to luncheon at the new Green Park Hotel – very much better than the Mayfair – and went to the *Express* office. Attended a fire in Soho where an Italian girl was supposed to

[1] Of Dante Gabriel Rossetti. Waugh had been introduced to Duckworth's by Anthony Powell.

[2] The Hon. Evelyn Gardner, who became Waugh's first wife. See Appendix of Names, p. 794.

[3] Lady Pansy Pakenham, daughter of the 5th Earl of Longford and sister of Frank Pakenham. She and Evelyn Gardner had rooms in a bed and breakfast house in Ebury Street at 35s a week.

have been brave but had actually done nothing at all and then went off with Inez Holden. We sat in the Savoy for a long time then went to a cinema, then to the Gargoyle, then to the Night Light where she spent all my money on a shilling in the slot machine then back to the Gargoyle. Eddie Gathorne-Hardy, Madge Garland, Bobbie, Wilma Bernhard and hundreds of such people were there. Next day I went to the *Express* for the last time to collect my wages, lunched with Elizabeth Greene and Julia Strachey, drove down to Kingston to see Richard, dined Lady Victoria Russell, then Gargoyle, home.

Next day I went down to Erringham[?] and spent a pleasant week undisturbed except by ghosts, reading old *Punches*, sleeping, eating very little and never shaving. From there, shaven, to Salisbury. Bus to Amesbury, spent night at Avon Hotel there. Bus next morning, train to Savernake, train to Pewsey, found Bobbie in train, drove to Mary Hope-Morley's[1] home at Oare for Whitsun weekend. A young man called Alan Hillgarth[2] very sure of himself, writes shockers, ex-sailor, and Evelyn were other people in house. Played vingt-et-un. Bobbie won. Told fortunes. Pansy Pakenham and Henry Lamb[3] were to have come down but didn't. On Monday Robert Byron arrived on a horse. We went to some pony races at Hungerford. Bobbie got tremendously drunk. Rather a strained evening. Bobbie went early. I stayed on till Wednesday when I went up to London for Alec's farewell cocktail party and decided to accompany him to Nîmes. Beastly party. Gave E.G. a pipe. Night journey via Dieppe. Arrived late next evening at Nîmes. Rather pleasant dinner at Tarascon; drank Royal Provençe.

Spent two weeks abroad with parents first at Nîmes and then at Les Baux. Visited Arles, Avignon, Aigues-Mortes, etc. Drank Tavel, Châteauneuf-du-Pape and Hermitage. Saw Alec off from Marseilles after amusing evening beginning decorously at Basso's with caviare and Meursault and ending less creditably in the slums. A street called Rue Ventomargy[4] is said to be the toughest in Europe.

Alec's boat looked repulsive.

Excellent wine called Royal Provençe at Baux. Worst crossing in the world. Quiet week since at Golders Green.

Hampstead, Friday 22 July 1927

I have finished about 12,000 words of the book on Rossetti without much

[1] The Hon. Evelyn Gardner's sister.
[2] He became Mary Hope-Morley's second husband.
[3] Landscape and portrait painter (1883–1960).
[4] In *Decline and Fall*, Paul Pennyfeather dines at Basso's, drinks Meursault, and visits the Rue Ventomargy in search of two protégées of Margot Best-Chetwynde.

real difficulty. I think it will be fairly amusing. There are to be several other books about him next year[1] unfortunately.

Richard and Liza gave a party in Eddie Gathorne-Hardy's rooms. I also went to another party the other night in Brook Street. I don't know who the host was. Everyone was dressed up and for the most part looking rather ridiculous. Olivia had had her hair dyed and curled and was dressed to look like Brenda Dean-Paul.[2] She seemed so unhappy.

I have been to the ballet – crowded with people like Mark Ogilvie-Grant, and Eddie, with Sachie Sitwell and a party of claqueurs to make a noise about rather a trivial little ballet called *Mercury*. I am going again tonight with John Sutro.

Monday 25 July 1927

On Friday I went to tea with Zena – Bobbie was there. Then to fetch Olivia and Eddie Gathorne-Hardy for a cocktail party by Wilma. Then changed and went to the ballet with John Sutro; ate ham rolls at Garrick. To David and Brian's party which was quite amusing. Talked to Olivia until 6 o'clock.

On Saturday I rested. On Sunday, yesterday a despairing telephone call from Olivia. Rudolph Dunbar – a black man – was on his way from Manchester for the day. David and Babe and everyone were away for the weekend.

Luncheon at the Sutros. Very luxurious. Roy Harrod and Mrs Dawbarn[?] wife of an architect there. After luncheon to Knightsbridge to help Olivia out with Rudolph. Secured Peter and Gwen Otter. Noisy gramophone all the time made my head ache. Home to dinner with my father. My mother being at Bishop's Hull. Gaspard lame.

I liked Eddie G.H. more on Friday.

Thursday 4 August 1927

I have been feeling rather ill all the last ten days and have done no work.

I lunched with the Sutros again and played croquet. I have been to no parties but spent a good deal of time with Olivia who is much afflicted with melancholy which I have shared to some extent lately. An absurd letter from Francis Palmer asking for money. Alastair back in England. Zena ill. Everyone I know has left London.

The Abingdon Arms, Beckley, Oxon.
Tuesday 23 August 1927

I came here rather suddenly ten days ago. Alastair came to London and we had a tedious and debauched night that sickened me of London for the time. We dined at Kettners with Richard and Elizabeth and drank a great deal and

---

[1] The 100th anniversary of Rossetti's birth.
[2] Celebrated 'beauty' who became a drug addict.

then went to the Gargoyle and drank a great deal more and then to Victor's and drank a great deal more. Gavin[1] was there with his wife, whom, tho' it sounds absurd, I rather liked. Lady Kinloss, Patrick Balfour and an absurd French nobleman and masses of other people. I talked endlessly to Hutchinson who was wearing a terribly smart French waistcoat.

Next day I felt deathly ill. Alastair went up to Scotland to stay with that Forbes family at Newe and I came down here. Since then I have been happier and felt better than I have for months. I go into Oxford most days to work in the Union Library. It is all very quiet and nice without all those gawky young men. I have written 40,000 words of my book and sent them off to be typed and feel easier in my mind about it. I think it is quite amusing in parts.

Beckley is very much altered. Old Cooke is dead. I have been surprised to realize how little I want to go and sit in the parlour in the evenings now he isn't there. Harold Claire has left the village and is reported badly of by everyone. Only Mr Higgs survives. He got very drunk the other evening and giggled and tried to dance with Mrs Mattingley. Her little boy is very spoilt and looks ill. The central figure nowadays seems to be a scorbutic baronet called Wilfred Moon.[2] He keeps arriving in rather a smart car with hosts of disreputable men and stands drinks all round and makes jokes. He is just the sort of man whom Chris[3] and I would have adored four years ago. I must say I find him rather a bore when I want to work. Besides I have lost the capacity for swilling down pint after pint of watery beer. How priggish that all looks.

I met Billy Clonmore who is studying to be a parson. He took me to luncheon at his theological college – a young man opposite me suddenly said 'I must go to box.' He meant confession, Billy told me.

I often call in on Crease[4] who I find particularly charming and witty in a way I had forgotten.

I have decided to make up my quarrel with Mrs Graham and to go to Barford for next weekend. when Wilfred Moon announces his intention of coming here.

Such an amusing letter from Olivia.

Wednesday 24 August 1927

I am going to Barford on Friday instead of Saturday. Today and for the last two days I have done no work. I feel somehow that with those first three chapters my work at Beckley is over and I must go somewhere else.

I went to Oxford this morning, just missing a heavy storm by lunching on

---

[1] The Hon. Gavin Henderson.
[2] The 4th baronet; later ADC to the Governor of Fiji.
[3] Christopher Hollis.
[4] Francis Crease had moved to Marston, a village near Oxford.

the way back at Marston. Lent Crease Roger Fry's *Flemish Art*. I am getting a little short of money again.

I have noticed some rather interesting things about Rossetti's composition so the day has not been entirely wasted.

A young man called Hudson has just arrived with a large gauche boy of sixteen. He tells me he will stand for Parliament and be ordained. It is extraordinary how Mrs Mattingley collects that sort of person. I have also found that he is the author of an entry in the visitors' book that has excited my contempt for some time.

Thursday 25 August 1927

I went into Oxford with Hudson and his boy and went to a cinema show and a revue and came back with a headache.

Barford House, Warwick, Friday 26 August 1927

Arrived at Barford at lunch-time. Mrs H., governess, Jane and Miss Goodchild all there besides Alastair and Mrs G. High tension at luncheon. Mrs H. eating nothing, mixing salad dressing in wine glass. 'No oil.' Mrs G.: 'There never is anything in this house that *you* want.' Exit butler and Mrs G. Butler brings oil. Ten minutes later Mrs G. enters with oil. Mrs H.: 'I don't want it now.' Mrs G.: 'Of course you don't want it now *I've* got it.' Exit Mrs H. saying, 'She only does this to put us off our food and save money.'

Saturday 27 August 1927

Mrs H. left. Things easier. Went to a quarry with four dogs where Mrs G. bought mountains of mustard-coloured stone from a deaf man with second sight who rode a tricycle. His son made archaic statues.

Sunday 28 August 1927

Jane very voluble about the 'Vermin Mary'. Alastair went to pray to Lord Dormer. Went to meet. Drove Stratford for cocktails. Fetched old, old women to tea.

Monday 29 August 1927

A Scotsman covered in blood came to dig a pond in the garden.

Hampstead, Tuesday 30 August 1927

Alastair and I came up to London. Dined at home and went to a revue called *One Damn Thing after Another*. Nothing in it particularly good but the whole quite brisk and jolly and well organized. Then to the Gargoyle where we found Bobbie and with him, he drunk, to the 43. Talked to a whore about Bulgaria where she had obviously never been. Then to another club called Manhattan which turned out to be a brothel.

Wednesday 31 August 1927

Saw a bloke about a job, went to a cinema. The *Bookman* have had the kindness to send me three books to review.

Saturday 3 September 1927

How I detest this house and how ill I feel in it. The whole place volleys and thunders with traffic. I can't sleep or work. I reviewed the books and have begun on a comic novel.[1] Mother is away at Midsomer Norton where Aunt Trissie is dying. The telephone bell is continually ringing, my father scampering up and down stairs, Gaspard barking, the gardener rolling the gravel under the window and all the time the traffic. Another week of this will drive me mad.

Sunday 4 September 1927

I sat up last night unable to sleep, reading my Lancing diaries. Wrote to Balston[2] about my comic novel which I think is amusing.

Wednesday 7 September 1927

The *Bookman* sent me some more books to review.

I find it hard to sleep and impossible to work. I saw a woman at Golders Green about a singularly repulsive job which I think I shall have to take.

Thursday 8 September 1927

Lunched at the Gargoyle with Tony Powell and Inez Holden having sold some review copies. Afterwards to a cinema with Inez and to her club. Tony dined here.

Friday 9 September 1927

A most amusing morning with Hall Caine.[3] He received me in bed at the top of many flights of stairs. He wore a white woollen dressing-gown and looked like a Carthusian abbot. Enormously vain and theatrical but more genial and humorous than I had expected. He told me a lot of really profitable things about Rossetti and Fanny Cornforth and Lizzie's suicide and C. A. Howell.

The Bell, Aston Clinton, September 1927

I came here on Monday after a disturbed weekend. I dined with Inez on Saturday and sat a long time with her in William Street so that, for poverty, I was obliged to walk home. On Sunday I dined with Tony Powell. I got some

---

[1] *Decline and Fall.*
[2] Tom Balston, publisher with the firm of Duckworth.
[3] Novelist (1853–1931); friend of Rossetti.

money out of my father and came here on Monday, my Aunt Trissie having died in the meantime.

They seem genuinely pleased to see me here and it is very comfortable and quiet. Before leaving I applied for a fantastic job about toothbrushes which I don't suppose will come to anything.

On Saturday I had finished 20,000 words and felt deeply depressed so I went back to London where I found the house empty. I dined alone and went to see Inez who was in bed eating *cachets de faivre*.[1] Stayed fairly late with her.

Next day she came to luncheon and my parents to dinner. I stayed at home doing very little for the next few days. On Wednesday I went to call on Evelyn Gardner and then to 15 Beaufort Gardens where Richard[2] was alone and ill. Anthony came back and we bought a bottle of gin and drank. Liza did not return till 10, we having had no dinner. She was not pleased to see me and I went off crossly. I was to have gone to Barford next day but there was a chance of a job so I stayed on, but it fell through after a prolonged and rather painful interview with the headmaster. That night I dined at the Gargoyle with Dudley who was very drunk and Ursula Garvin and Evelyn Gardner and a kind old American lady called Porterfield and an American youth. We played vingt-et-un at the American lady's flat and I lost heavily.

Next day I came here.

Barford House, Warwick, September 1927

Sunday. Drew a diagram for Rossetti, went to lunch, drove to a field where the dogs ran about.

As usual Barford is in a ferment of reorganization – a lodge being torn down, and pond dug, paving being laid, all the bath water being pumped into the pond, two gardeners threatening to cut each other's throats and being placated by the construction of an earth-closet, Miss Goodchild going, the cook ruptured, a housemaid in bed with an ulcer, Mrs G. full of port roaring about directing everything.

Today that unquiet lady went off to London for two nights much to Miss G.'s relief. I hope to be able to get some work done. I went for a very long walk this morning.

Sunday 2 October 2927

I have done terribly little work in the last week. Yesterday I wrote two-thirds of a preface for Francis Crease's designs.

Mrs G. came back on Friday. We play most astonishing cut-throat bridge in which Mrs G. makes what she calls 'plunges', which means a fantastic declaration, usually with complete success. This morning there was great

---

[1] A medicament.
[2] Richard Plunket Greene.

trouble with a large truculent under-gardener who is under notice to go and will not allow his successor to use his cottage. Mrs G. : 'Here am I left without a *man* in the house' – looking hard at me – 'if Hugh were alive he'd have *kicked* him out.'

This afternoon we went to Bromson Hall to call on the Holdens. Lots of people there but not Inez. A brother looking like death. He showed indecent pictures and talked of night haunts. I said to Mrs H. that Inez was so ill last time I saw her and living on *cachets de faivre*. Mrs H. : 'I don't think I know the de Faivres.'

Great trouble getting Colley out of his cottage. Mrs G. and I went to the lawyers and found that he could not be moved for a month. I was sent to talk to him and found him stupid but perfectly civil.

Tuesday 4 October 1927

An enormous lead statue of Mercury arrived which all the gardeners and I set up in the middle of the pond with infinite labour.

Lady Verulam[1] died yesterday.

A letter from Crease about the preface which he appears to like.

Thursday 6 October 1927

We went over to tea at Kelmscott.[2] The house much smaller than I expected, no drive, only a little locked gate opening on to the road. A small paved path with large yews – one a dragon designed by William Morris. The rooms very low and dark and the whole effect rather cramped and constricted. We could not conceive how so many people lived there. Miss Morris[3] a singularly forbidding woman – very awkward and disagreeable dressed in a slipshod ramshackle way in hand-woven stuffs. A hermaphrodite lives with her. Two exquisite Rossetti crayons of her and her sister as children – innumerable sketches of Jane Morris and a large painting and the studies for the predella of Dante's Dream. The furniture and decoration untouched since Morris's death. The tapestry that worried R. is not by Morris but some old work found there when they took the house. The garden very cramped too, the paths so narrow. I had imagined it all so spacious – perhaps it is just because it lacks Morris and has that extraordinary woman and her hermaphrodite.

Friday 7 October 1927

Mrs G. away at Lady Verulam's funeral. Dined with the Peytons. Very dull evening.

---

[1] Wife of the 3rd Earl of Verulam; she was related to Alastair Graham.

[2] Kelmscott Manor House, near Lechlade, Oxfordshire; acquired by William Morris in 1871.

[3] May Morris (1862–1938), daughter of Jane Morris, William Morris's wife.

Hampstead, Saturday 22 October 1927

I returned from Barford last week. Nothing much happened there except the continual fuss and trafficking over the eviction of Mr Colley. Mother came down for a day. We went to Stratford Mop and had our fortunes told.

On Saturday evening Evelyn Gardner had a party at the Gargoyle of Una and Pansy and Dudley and Jim Byam Shaw and a person called Commander Drage. We went back to his very large and glooming house in Cadogan Square where we drank whisky and he read pages from his diary – then to Sloane Square where we played cards until about 3.

On Monday I went to the Academy of Carpentry[1] at Southampton Row and saw a very rude secretary and an amiable principal and arranged to go to a great many classes. Tea with Evelyn and Pansy.

Tuesday 25 October 1927

Started work drawing sections and projections. In the evening, carving. Supper afterwards with Tony Powell.

Wednesday 26 October 1927

Drew plaster ornaments. Terence to dinner.

Thursday 27 October 1927

Drew sections and projections. Tea and cinema. Inez.

Friday 28 October 1927

Planed boards. Tea Dudley. Pansy. Lunch Fulford.

Saturday 29 October 1927

Not feeling terribly well, so have not gone on personally conducted tour of the Victoria and Albert Museum.

Pansy came to tea with me bringing chrysanthemums.

Sunday 30 October 1927

Feeling a little less ill I went to church in Margaret Street where I was discomposed to observe Tom Driberg's satanic face in the congregation. He told me he was starving but would not come to luncheon. It is so like *Sinister Street* meeting school friends at Mass. I gave him a penny.

---

[1] The Department of Furniture and Cabinet-making at the Central School of Arts and Crafts. The School, founded in 1896, derived from the Art Workers' Guild and drew its inspiration from Ruskin, Philip Webb and William Morris.

Saturday 5 November 1927

I quite enjoy my carpentry lessons, all except the carving in the evenings. Last Sunday I had luncheon and tea with Olivia who can talk of nothing except David's approaching divorce. It has been so good for her. She is quite a different girl from the one that depressed me so last time I met her in the spring. She has got a real fighting look, just as she had when she beat Lady Samuel at croquet.

Dined Sutros. Large party all Jews. Monday dined Elizabeth in their new house after rather a gay little cocktail party with Mary Hope-Morley and her children. Tuesday; sent flowers to H.M. children. Drew Christmas card.[1]

Friday: tea Pansy Pakenham, Lamb, Mary P.,[2] Lord and Lady Dunsany, some Irishmen, Evelyn and Dudley. Difficulties later with keys. Joined dinner party at Simpsons.

Sunday 20 November 1927

Bobbie had a party on Friday. Not very amusing. He terribly drunk. An American woman called Arota[?] turned us out of her flat. Alec is back. We dined at the Ritz with John Sutro and Peter Quennell and Evelyn and to my disgust Otter. He then went away to the country in depression. Dined with a ghastly club to hear Rebecca West yesterday. I think Bobbie is bound to die of drink soon.

Tuesday 29 November 1927

I am getting infinitely tired of London and its incessant fogs. Very little has happened lately. I see Evelyn a lot and a certain amount of Olivia. On Sunday I went to the first night of the Sitwell[3] but was bitterly disappointed and bored. There had been a Sitwell party at Balston's on the preceding Tuesday. I am getting on with the carpentry – Henry Lamb knows of a place in the country where I might work.

Friday 9 December 1927

I spent last weekend at the Fremlins. Francis Crease was there. Mrs Fremlin talks more than I should have thought possible. Rupert very irritable. The Nigerian climate can't be good for him.

Zena returned and I sent her flowers I could ill afford. She is in love with David and declares Hutchinson slept with Babe. Honor Henderson[4] also in love with David.

[1] A line drawing of holly, two turtledoves, a saw and a fret-saw.
[2] Lady Mary Pakenham; Lady Pansy Pakenham's sister.
[3] A play called *All At Sea*.
[4] Daughter of the 1st Baron Kylsant; married the Hon. Gavin Henderson, 1927 (marriage annulled, 1931).

I have nearly finished making a mahogany bed table. Not very well. Lamb very kindly offers to take me down to Bournemouth to see Romney Green,[1] a carpenter. We are going next Wednesday. Evelyn talks of going to Canada.

Very good cocktail party on Tuesday at Richard and Elizabeth. Very dreary at the Gargoyle. Olivia particularly sweet to me and drunk.

Charles Sutro asked me to spend Christmas with him. Shall do so unless engaged to be married before then.

Cecil Roberts is returning to London.

Monday 12 December 1927

Dined with Evelyn at the Ritz. Proposed marriage. Inconclusive. Went on to Ursula's party. Rang up Pansy who advised in favour of marriage. Went to Sloane Square and discussed it. Went to Bourdon Street and told Olivia. Home late and unable to sleep.

Tuesday 13 December 1927

Evelyn rang up to say she had made up her mind to accept. Went to Southampton Row but was unable to work. Went to pub with Dudley and told him of engagement. Tea Evelyn. Pansy interviewed Alathea Fry[2] and supported me. Play Phil Coddington. Home very tired.

There is a gap of six months in the diary at this point. Early in 1928 Evelyn Gardner and Pansy Pakenham left their furnished maisonette off Sloane Square – where they spent the winter of 1927–8 – and took rooms in a boarding house in Wimborne, Dorset, until May, when they returned to London. Pansy Pakenham was secretly engaged to the painter Henry Lamb, who was endeavouring to divorce his first wife, Euphemia, from whom he had long been separated. Lamb had a house in Poole and used to visit the two girls in Wimborne. Waugh took a room in a pub called the Barley Mow, about two miles from Wimborne on the Cranborne Road, where he could live very cheaply, and there wrote much of *Decline and Fall*.

Friday 22 June 1928

Evelyn and I began to go to Dulwich to see the pictures there but got bored waiting for the right bus so went instead to the vicar-general's office and bought a marriage licence. Lunched at Taglioni. Went to Warwick Square to

---

[1] A cabinet-maker, with a workshop at Christchurch, near Bournemouth.
[2] An elder sister of Evelyn Gardner; married to Sir Geoffrey Fry, private secretary to Bonar Law when Prime Minister 1922–3, and to Stanley Baldwin 1923–37.

see Harold and show him our licence. With him to Alec where we drank champagne.

Wednesday 27 June 1928

Evelyn and I were married at St Paul's, Portman Square, at 12 o'clock. A woman was typewriting on the altar. Harold best man. Robert Byron gave away the bride, Alec and Pansy the witnesses. Evelyn wore a new black and yellow jumper suit with scarf. Went to the 500 Club and drank champagne cocktails under the suspicious eyes of Winifred Mackintosh and Prince George of Russia. From there to luncheon at Boulestin. Very good luncheon. Then to Paddington and by train to Oxford and taxi to Beckley.

July 6th. Our honeymoon came to an end. Everyone at Beckley was very sweet to us. The women of the village brought bouquets of flowers for our room. Evelyn a great success with Mr Higgs.

Went over to Barford for luncheon. Lord and Lady Verulam[1] and two small boys. Mrs G. supposes Alastair to be dying of consumption.

Spent the following week at Hampstead. On Friday Alathea gave a party at which an ex-policeman sang. From there to a bad party in Chelsea. Saturday Pansy returned from country and I wrote to Lady Burghclere[2] announcing my marriage. Returned to 25 Adam Street.

Lady B. 'quite inexpressibly pained'.

Marriage announced in *Times* Wednesday.

In the evening dinner at Osbert Sitwell's. Drank too much.

Thursday dined Balston.

Friday. Saw Lady B. in the morning. Lunched Cavalry Club with Australian admirer of Mary's. Charles Drage's wedding. St Margaret's and Claridge's; preferred St Paul's and Boulestin. Tea party at Pansy's.

Saturday drew wrapper for novel for Chapman & Hall. Also hard at work on proofs of *Decline and Fall*.[3] Chapman's *not* an easy firm to deal with.

Sunday luncheon Sutro's. Dinner Taglioni.

Monday left 25 Adam Street and came to live at 145 North End Road.

Heatwave most oppressive. Went to drink cocktails with Elizabeth Pelham.[4] Nancy Mitford[5] and Mrs Drage sent wedding presents.

[1] The 4th Earl of Verulam and his wife.
[2] His new mother-in-law.
[3] Duckworth, who commissioned and published Waugh's first book, *Rossetti*, rejected *Decline and Fall* on the grounds of its indelicacy. Waugh took the manuscript eight doors down Henrietta Street to the firm of which his father was managing director; his father was abroad, and the decision to accept the novel was taken in his absence by Mr Ralph Straus. Thereafter, Waugh's travel books were usually published by Duckworth, and his novels by Chapman & Hall.
[4] Lady Elizabeth Pelham, daughter of the 6th Earl of Chichester.
[5] The Hon. Nancy Mitford, a friend of Waugh's wife. See Appendix of Names, p. 794.

Tuesday still too hot. Finished wrapper for C. & H. Joyce Fagan and husband came to dinner.

Wednesday. Worked at Wesley.[1] Cocktail party Audrey Lucas. Alec Waugh there and other dim hot people. Photograph of me and my wife in *Sketch*.

Islington,[2] Thursday 4 October 1928

Immediately after breakfast Chapman & Hall rang up to say that Doubleday and Doran wanted to take *Decline and Fall* for America and would give me a $500 advance. The prospect seemed less brilliant later in the day when I discovered that by the time Brandt,[3] Chapman & Hall and the American State had taken their share I should get a little over half of the sum and that I should not get it until the spring of next year. Even so it is most agreeable news. In the afternoon some furniture arrived from the carpenter's. Tony Powell came to see us after dinner full of scandal about the Sitwells.

Friday 5 October 1928

Evelyn's dinner party: Tom Balston, Alec Waugh and Charles Drage with his wife. She is albino with a mind like a damp biscuit and too much of my evening was occupied with her. The dinner was admirable, eggs and sweet corn, poussin, passion fruit and savoury. The wine not so good from my wine merchant. I spent the morning pasting newspapers on to the black chest and sizing them.

Saturday 6 October 1928

The size was not a success and the coat of varnish has discoloured the papers on the chest. Harold came to luncheon bringing an advance copy of his novel *Humdrum*. He stayed until about 5, talking with his usual opulence and luminousness but with every sign of a slightly deranged mind, continually losing himself in his sentences, calling things by their wrong names and muddling his words in the way Dr Spooner is supposed to do. His book shows none of these defects. Most competent and controlled. Nicholas Durham came to tea and stayed to dinner. We went to the Islington Empire where in a 12s 6d box we watched a review called *The League of Neighbours* with a little amusement.

Sunday 7 October 1928

I went to Margaret Street to church but was unable to get in. We lunched and dined at Hampstead where I read the new Aldous Huxley.[4] Infinitely long

---

[1] Waugh planned a biography of Charles Wesley; he lost confidence in the idea after he discovered that his new mother-in-law, Lady Burghclere, knew more about Wesley than he did.

[2] The Waughs had taken a flat in Canonbury Square.

[3] Waugh's American agent.

[4] *Point Counter Point*.

with all the same characters as *Antic Hay*, all the same social uncertainties, bored lovemaking, another Mrs Viveash, another Coleman, odd pages of conversation and biology. It might have been written by an educated Alec Waugh.

Monday 8 October 1928

Lunched at the Savile with Harold, Reggie Turner[1] and Raymond Mortimer,[2] A good luncheon with good wine. Reggie Turner was a very ugly, amusing little man, rather anxious to keep up to date. 'Tell me, what do you and Margot Oxford think of Aldous Huxley these days?' Full of stories about Wilde and 'Bosie'[3] and of how visiting Wilde in prison he asked whether he had enough to eat. 'They throw me sausages as the British public give buns[?][4] to the bears.' Raymond Mortimer, after his kind review of me, was a disappointment. Charvet hosiery, an unfinished face described by Reggie Turner as 'faunlike', and nasty hair. A good deal of the sort of conversation 'My dear, if I caught a cold from *you*, I should cherish it', and 'I've rather taken to Berlin, lately.' I detected him talking about *Point Counter Point* before he had read it. Several attempts to get introductions. 'D'you know it sounds absurd but I've never yet met Bosie Douglas. Will you take me round to him one day, Reggie?' 'Oh, do you know Ricketts,[5] Harold? I wish you'd take me to see him. I do so love *period* things like that, don't you?' A number of French phrases and names from de Gotha. A second-rate young man. I had tea with Olivia and returned to find Evelyn rather ill with a temperature. I imagine a touch of influenza. I see *Decline and Fall* quoted as a bestseller in one list. A letter from Robert[6] *very* cross about Gavin Henderson and Kevin Saunderson.

Tuesday 9 October 1928

Evelyn's influenza became rather bad and her temperature rose to 104 degrees. My mother came and we spent the night sitting up with her.

Wednesday 10 October 1928

Evelyn's ''flu' better. Myself with heavy cold. Spent afternoon and evening at Hampstead. There is a chance apparently of there being a review of me in tomorrow's *Evening Standard* by Bennett.[7] I read *Humdrum* which is rather a

---

[1] Prolific novelist and friend of Oscar Wilde.
[2] The critic; then aged 33.
[3] Lord Alfred Douglas.
[4] MS appears to read 'bibles', which makes no sense.
[5] Charles Ricketts (1866–1931); painter, designer. He designed the scenery and costumes for Oscar Wilde's *Salome* (1906).
[6] Probably Robert Byron.
[7] Arnold Bennett.

Barry Jackson production of *Coriolanus*. Harold Acton for the masses. Still it is very amusing in places. It will irritate Babe Greene and Brian Howard I should think.

Thursday 11 October 1928

A man named Minton wrote to me on Muriel Silk's introduction to suggest that I might write rhymes for advertisements. I went to see him and he took me to see Stanley Morison[1] of the Monotype Company who wanted me to design printing types. Leaving his office I found that Bennett had given me a very nice little notice in the *Evening Standard*. Lunched with Chapman & Hall at the Florence. Went to exhibition of Chiricos – some vulgar and like posters but rather impressive faceless seated figures in classical surroundings with laps full of skyscrapers and musical instruments. Tea at Hampstead and home to find Evelyn a bit better. Peter Quennell rang up to congratulate me on Bennett's notice.

Friday 12 October 1928

The Canonbury doctor, who is a cross between a butcher and vet in appearance, pronounced Evelyn's illness to be German measles – on the undeniable evidence of a crimson and white mottled face. Lady Burghclere called while I was out with grapes and chicken and more or less kindly comments on the flat. Attempted to draw types. Poor Chapman[2] has a book on gorillas to review. Sales for the week of *Decline and Fall* 157, total 1,093. When we touch 2,000 I shall begin to feel more at ease about it.

Saturday 13 October 1928

Evelyn goes on in bed. Her nurse is here most of the day to look after her.

Sunday 14 October 1928

Evelyn still in bed. Nurse still in flat. Lady B. sends plenty of food.

Monday 15 October 1928

Evelyn still in bed. Nurse still in flat. Reading *Orlando*. £20 from Lady Margaret Duckworth.[3]

Tuesday 16 October 1928

Evelyn still in bed. Nurse still in flat. I went to tea with Olivia who had just been to consult a slightly unorthodox gland specialist. He says she has some

---

[1] The typographer; later of *The Times*.

[2] Arthur Waugh, Evelyn's father.

[3] A daughter of the 4th Earl of Carnarvon and an aunt of Waugh's wife. She was also the aunt, through the earl's second wife, of Waugh's second wife, Laura Herbert.

nervous defect and would have been completely prostrate by Christmas. She will have to give up cocktails and be under treatment for about two years, when, in the doctor's sinister and Barrie-esque phrase, she will be 'what she should always have been'. I await her metamorphosis into some skittish golf-girl galvanized with the secretions of goats and monkeys with some alarm.

Wednesday 17 October 1928

Alathea and Geoffrey rang up and offered us Oare for Evelyn's convalescence thus relieving us of what had become a considerable anxiety about an hotel. I went to see the Chirico exhibition. They are simply *Vogue* covers writ large.

Thursday 18 October 1928

I wrote a short article on Censors for the *Daily Express*. A parcel of turtle jelly, ham mousse, and other invalid delicacies from Fortnum and Mason attested to Alathea's continued interest in our welfare.

Friday 19 October 1928

Sale of *Decline and Fall* 827 for the week. Second edition has 'gone to bed'.

Saturday 20 October 1928

The *Evening Standard* wrote asking for an article on 'England has youth: make use of it'.

Sunday 21 October 1928

Church at Margaret Street. Evelyn went out for a short walk round the square.

Monday 22 October 1928

I had my hair cut and met Martin Wilson. He seems to bear no malice for *Decline and Fall*. From there to the exhibition of Maillols. The sculpture magnificent but the wood engravings not particularly meritorious. Alathea lunched with me at Taglioni's, very lovely and vague, with an air of just waking up after an uneasy night. Extraordinarily ingenuous with a fluttery eagerness to skate and go to the theatre and see the latest pictures. After luncheon to my tailor's to try on a check suit.

Tuesday 23 October 1928

Viola Garvin[1] gave me some more books to review.

---

[1] Literary editor of *The Observer* and daughter of J. L. Garvin, editor of *The Observer*.

Oare House, near Marlborough, Wednesday 24 October 1928

A long journey down with a wait of nearly half an hour at Newbury which I had not counted on. We arrived in the dark and cold and Evelyn went up to bed. I was left to find my way about and finally settled in a small study full of illustrated books on architecture with, I was amused to find, Marie Stopes's *Married Love* fallen down behind them. Most of the servants seem to be in London and we are left the cooking of the kitchenmaid and the waiting of a slightly disagreeable housemaid. A very comfortable bed.

Thursday 25 October 1928

I went to bed feeling the atmosphere of the house to be Jamesian and awoke to find it Logan Pearsall Smith. There is an epicene preciosity or nicety about everything that goes better with cigarettes and London clothes than my tweeds and pipe. The decorations are in combed-painted[?] panels, innumerable lampshades on carefully planned lamps, the gardens too formal, but there is some lovely furniture, a fine library and a very beautiful vista from my windows, across the bathing pool to the downs. I went for a walk on the downs in the morning and felt myself back at Lancing hurrying across Steep Down from tea at Lychpole.

Friday 26 October 1928

Rain – review books and an article on 'Too Old at Forty' for the *Standard* who are giving me £10 for it. In the evening Geoffrey arrived. First Holder[1] was observed on the stairs; later the car appeared from London laden with a cock, provisions and a pile of French novels; finally by the evening train Geoffrey with a young man called John Weyman.[2] A enormous dinner, claret, port, cigars, conversation about architecture, whisky.

Saturday 27 October 1928

More servants arrived and finally Alathea. Young Mr Weyman appeared first in riding clothes and rode, then in white flannels and played tennis, then in tweeds and went out shooting – 'having a smack at the longtails' as someone described it to Geoffrey – then in evening clothes and talked about architecture. Alathea dined in the drawing-room and after dinner made a carpet.

Sunday 28 October 1928

Alathea and some servants disappeared before dinner. Talk of architecture.

[1] The butler; later employed at 10 Downing Street.
[2] Retired early from the City to Portugal, where he died in 1974.

Monday 29 October 1928

The young man disappeared before breakfast to do accounting. Finally Geoffrey and Holder and the car disappeared. Evelyn and I went over to dinner at Savernake with Robert.[1] Curiously barbaric after the refinement of Oare. Rutting stags in the forest outside. Inside, long uncarpeted, unlit passages. Furniture unrelieved 1840. Robert, having just finished his history of Byzantine art, rather at a loose end; roads deep in leaves. It was my birthday yesterday.

Tuesday 30 October 1928

A letter from Charles Scott Moncrieff praising *Decline and Fall* and suggesting that I should illustrate a ballad of his. We drove to Marlborough this afternoon. A beautiful sunny day. Evelyn engrossed in a novel and articles for the *Evening News*.

Sunday 11 November 1928

We stayed at Oare until Monday the 5th. Alathea and Geoffrey did not appear again. Towards the end of our visit I managed to do quite a lot of work. On the 5th we went to Chiseldon to spend two nights with Laurence. He is a good if rather self-conscious host – too much pressing to eat, but plenty to drink. A very cold house with most grudging fires. The church extremely well kept. Laurence obviously popular in his village – full of kind words and physical sustenance to everyone – port for the poor and sweets for the schoolchildren. We went up to call on his brother-in-law at Burdrop (?) a gouty old soldier with an engaging simplicity of mind and a house[?] of superb and ruthless Victorian ugliness. Mrs Laurence was a curiously cretinous savage woman – a voice like Gwen Otter and a mind like Mrs Graham. We came back to London to find that none of the furniture we expected had arrived and that the electrician had done nothing about the chandelier or bell.

On Thursday Bobbie brought a man called Henry Williamson round to see us. He won a prize with a book called *Tarka the Otter* and has now had a great success with a novel. He is quite elderly[2] – though I find him coupled with me in reviews as promising young writers – and wholly without culture. Very gauche and suddenly earnest-minded, but capable of fun. He stayed some time and took away a copy of *Decline and Fall*.

Friday 23 November 1928

Sales for fortnight 398. We are now in the second edition. Evelyn and I went to a cocktail party at Cyril Connolly and Patrick Balfour's. Dined at Taglioni's. Returned to find that our cook had given notice. Met Inez.

Saturday. Engaged new servant, lunched Previtali. Saw bad film, dined Hampstead. Met Inez and Veronica Poindestre, oddly enough at Hampstead.

[1] Robert Byron.
[2] Born in 1895.

4 The Thirties Diary 1930-39

Introduction

The period between the winter of 1928 and the spring of 1930 was a watershed in Waugh's life. No diary exists, however, between 23 November 1928 and 19 May 1930, and his autobiography does not go beyond 1925. He wrote seven manuscript pages of the second volume and stopped – perhaps, as his brother has conjectured, because he found himself unwilling to write about his first marriage.

The formal circumstances of its breakdown are commonplace. Neither party had had much experience of the opposite sex; and both behaved in a way that showed their immaturity. When Waugh proposed to Evelyn Gardner over dinner in the Ritz Grill, he suggested that they should get married 'and see how it goes'. It was a fatal phrase, for it gave Evelyn Gardner the sense that Waugh was not wholly committed to the alliance. Nor perhaps was she: one of her reasons for accepting Waugh's proposal was that the girl with whom she shared rooms, Pansy Pakenham, was herself on the verge of marriage, to the painter Henry Lamb, and Evelyn was not anxious to return home. She had always been intimidated by her mother and had long wanted to lead a settled life.

As Waugh's diary records, She-Evelyn (as a few of her friends called her) fell ill soon after the wedding. During the year that the marriage lasted, She-Evelyn was ill twice and operated on once. In February 1929 a shipping company gave the Waughs free tickets for a Mediterranean cruise, starting from Monte Carlo, on the understanding that Waugh would publicize the ship. In Paris, She-Evelyn was already unwell; on the train to Monte Carlo, Waugh persuaded her to drink *crème de menthe* to aid her recovery. By the time they reached Haifa, She-Evelyn needed a nurse; by Port Said, she was seriously ill with pneumonia and had to be lowered ashore on a stretcher and taken to the English Hospital. Waugh sent an enigmatic postcard to a mutual friend saying that when the card arrived, She-Evelyn would probably be dead. While she was still in hospital, though out of danger, Waugh travelled to Cyprus in response to an invitation to himself and his wife from Alastair Graham.

Back in England, in the early summer, Waugh left his wife in London and went to the country to work on his second novel, *Vile Bodies*. While he was away, She-Evelyn fell in love with a young Etonian working as news editor at the BBC, John Heygate, the son of an Eton housemaster. In July 1929 She-

Evelyn told her husband what had happened; an attempt at reconciliation was made, but without success; and in September Waugh decided on a divorce, consulting, as solicitor, his brother Alec's friend E. S. P. Haynes. On 18 January 1930 a notice of the divorce appeared in *The Times* under the heading, 'Decree Nisi against Peer's Daughter':

> There was no defence to the petition of Mr Evelyn Arthur St John Waugh of Canonbury Square, Islington, for the dissolution of his marriage with the Hon. Evelyn Florence Margaret Winifred Waugh, née Gardner, on the ground of her adultery with Mr John Heygate at an address in Cornwall-Gardens, Kensington.
>
> The marriage took place on 27 June, 1928 at St Paul's Church, Portman Square. Mr Raglan Somerset appeared for the petitioner. His lordship granted a decree *nisi* with costs against the co-respondent.
>
> Solicitor – Mr E. S. P. Haynes.

The two Evelyns met only once after the divorce. At Waugh's initiative, they lunched together, after he had joined the Roman Catholic church, to discuss She-Evelyn's appearance as a witness before the ecclesiastical court that was to hear evidence about the annulment of the marriage. Over lunch, Waugh told his former wife that his father would never again receive her; but he added that his mother took a less censorious view and indeed held him partly responsible for the marriage's failure; she had told him that he had left his wife too much alone.

Brief though the marriage was, its breakdown had important consequences for Waugh's life and career. First, it deprived him of a settled base, with the result that from 1930 until his second marriage in 1937 he travelled constantly, both in Britain and – much more adventurously than hitherto – abroad. Next, the marriage breakdown propelled him into the Roman Catholic church, though he had spoken of the attractions of Rome before 1929. Third, his old friends noted a new harshness in his character; both Harold Acton and Alastair Graham found it impossible to comfort him or to help him repair what he evidently felt as a deep humiliation; the theme of the betrayed husband recurs continually in his subsequent novels. Finally, the combination of his marriage, its breakdown and his simultaneous literary success with *Vile Bodies* (which was published early in 1930 and at once became highly successful, much more talked about than *Decline and Fall*), launched him into new and fashionable social circles. Evelyn Gardner had been a close friend of Nancy Mitford. After the breakdown, She-Evelyn's relations with her old circle were permanently ruptured, but Evelyn's prospered. The house of Nancy Mitford's sister Diana, then married to Bryan Guinness, became his principal refuge. He was taken up, too – as a successful, unattached, and amusing young man – by London hostesses; it was at Lady Cunard's dinner table that he met Lady Diana

Cooper, who became a lifelong friend. The change in Waugh's circumstances is reflected in his diary; when it resumes, in the spring of 1930, the tone is brisk, impersonal, and Tatler-ish.

Dixon of the *Daily Mail* rang up and asked me to come and see him. When I got there he said would I do a monthly article for 15 guineas a time. I said yes. When I got back to Hampstead he rang up and said would I come back at once and see the chief editor. I changed into evening clothes and went back. The chief editor said would I do him a weekly article. I said yes. He said would I sign an agreement to write for no other paper for three months. I said yes. He said how much did I want. I said I must ask Peters.[1] He said what sort of sum did I regard as a minimum. I would have been overjoyed with £15. I said £20. He was overjoyed with that. I went to the Savoy and rang up Peters and said say £25. Then I had a drink and went to dinner at Radnor Place with Henry and Dig.[2] We went to a play called *Down Our Street*. Then to Quaglino's and drank champagne, and then to a supper party at Buckingham Street. Everyone had begun supper. I sat next to Nancy[3] and Anna May Wong.[4] Very tired. Lord Redesdale[5] said A.M.W. like a brontosaurus. Gavin too talkative. Good *foie gras mousse*.

Tuesday 20 May 1930

Peters made Dixon pay £30. That brings my regular income temporarily up to about £2,500 a year. I feel rather elated about it. The *Weekend Review* very insistent about an article I promised to write for them and forgot. Luncheon at the Ivy with Jonathan Cape and my American publisher. Called on Olivia. Had tea at the Ritz with Inez and Peter Rodd. Cocktail party at Cyril Connolly's. Logan Pearsall Smith, Christopher Sykes, Ankaret Jackson, etc.[6] Wrote *Weekend Review*'s article. Very bad.

[1] A. D. Peters, Waugh's literary agent.
[2] Henry and Dig (Adelaide) Yorke.
[3] The Hon. Nancy Mitford.
[4] Film actress.
[5] The 2nd baron, and head of the Mitford family.
[6] Inez Holden, whom Waugh had met on the *Daily Express*; the Hon. Peter Rodd, who later married the Hon. Nancy Mitford; Cyril Connolly, the author and critic (see Appendix of Names, p. 794); Logan Pearsall Smith, man of letters (1865–1946) of American Quaker origin; Christopher Sykes, later Waugh's biographer (see Appendix of Names, p. 794); Lady Ankaret Howard married William Jackson in 1927.

Wednesday 21 May 1930

Cocktail party at Cecil Beaton's. Took Eleanor Smith[1] off to dinner at Quaglino's then to cinema and then to Eiffel Tower. Came back and wrote *Daily Mail* article. I talked of lesbians and constipation.

Thursday 22 May 1930

Lunched with Rudolf. Sat next to a nice Labour MP who told me that Government Whips were giving it out that if MacDonald had thirty votes against him on Mosley motion he would resign. Labour MP said Mosley had fifty certain supporters.[2] Audrey[3] cocktail party. Dined Gargoyle A. P. Herbert, John Armstrong and Mrs Gerald Barry.[4] A. affectionate. Wondered why and found later she wanted me to give her some money. Gave her what she wanted. Had photograph taken.

Friday 23 May 1930

Worked in the morning on review books. Went to London and ordered cigars. Tea at Buckingham Street, cocktail party at Francis Meynell's. He has taken Duncan Grant's house which was covered in frescoes by him and Vanessa Bell and has painted them all out except one. So sensible. Talked with Harriet Cohen[5] and Eddie Marsh.[6]

Saturday 24 May 1930

Worked in the morning. Went to tea with Edith Sitwell. Stale buns and no chairs. Numerous works by Tchelitchew in wire and wax. Harold[7] there. Diana[8] in a hat of the grossest eccentricity. Edith talked only of poetry. Home to change, then to 500 Club to meet Anthony Bradley who took me to dinner with a beastly woman called Lady Jean Mackintosh.[9] From there to a dance by Mrs Gurling [?]. No one I knew. Eventually I talked to a young man who turned out to be Jim Laurence. He stole a car and drove me home.

[1] Lady Eleanor Smith, daughter of F. E. Smith, the 1st Earl of Birkenhead. See Appendix of Names, p. 794.

[2] Sir Oswald Mosley resigned from the Labour government, in which he was a junior minister, in May 1930 after the Cabinet rejected his economic proposals. The parliamentary party followed suit, by 202 votes to 29.

[3] Audrey Lucas, daughter of E. V. Lucas, the man of letters.

[4] The MP; the painter; and journalist's wife.

[5] The pianist.

[6] Sir Edward Marsh, civil servant, sometime private secretary to Winston Churchill. In May 1930 he was private secretary to the Dominions Secretary, Lord Passfield (Sidney Webb).

[7] Harold Acton.

[8] The Hon. Diana Guinness, née Mitford, subsequently (1936) Sir Oswald Mosley's second wife.

[9] Daughter of the 13th Duke of Hamilton.

Sunday 25 May 1930

Went to church at Margaret Street and worked all day.

Monday 26 May 1930

My parents went away to Midsomer Norton. I gave Anne Talbot luncheon at Quaglino's. Poor lunch. Back to work. Then to dinner at Waldorf with my American publisher. After dinner I went to the Savoy Theatre and said 'I am Evelyn Waugh. Please give me a seat.' So they did. I saw the last two acts of Robeson's *Othello*. Hopeless production but I like his great black booby face. It seemed to make all that silly stuff with the handkerchief quite convincing. After the theatre Frank Pakenham[1] had a supper party at the Savoy. Eleanor, Baby, Maureen, Basil,[2] John Betjeman,[3] a man called Fleming and a man called Warner. Maureen deadly stupid. Baby anxious to be friendly and very sweet. Basil Murray[4] quite drunk would join us.

Tuesday 27 May 1930

I finished my *Graphic* article and went to luncheon at Buckingham Street. Nancy and John Armstrong. After luncheon to the *Mail* office to see another editor named Pulvermacher who had summoned me all the way there to tell me how glad he was that I had joined his staff. Then to tea at Olivia Greene's. The house very much disorganized by her bitch's parturition. Then to a cocktail party of Jim Laurence's at the Berkeley. Wanda Baillie-Hamilton,[5] Maureen, Eileen Plunket, Donegall[6] – full of Rosa's[7] possible [?] action against him in which I shall make an incongruous appearance as witness for the prosecution. Nancy Beaton,[8] etc.

Wednesday 28 May 1930

I spent a great part of the day reading the first part of Harold's[9] *History of the Later Medici*. It is most unsatisfactory and I am afraid will do him no more good than his novel – full of pompous little clichés and involved, illiterate passages. Now and then a characteristic gay flash but deadly dull for the most part. There are long citations from Reresby, Evelyn and contemporary

[1] See Appendix of Names, p. 794.

[2] Eleanor Smith; Baby Jungman (see Appendix of Names, p. 794); Maureen Guinness, who in July 1930 married the Earl of Ava, later the 4th Marquess of Dufferin and Ava; Earl of Ava.

[3] See Appendix of Names, p. 794.

[4] Son of Lady Mary and Professor Gilbert Murray, the Greek scholar.

[5] See Appendix of Names, p. 794.

[6] The 6th Marquess of Donegall, journalist.

[7] Rosa Lewis of the Cavendish Hotel; the model for 'Lottie Crump' in Waugh's second novel *Vile Bodies* (1930).

[8] Sister of Cecil Beaton, the photographer.

[9] Harold Acton's.

travellers. Also endless descriptions of fêtes and processions. My parents write that they will return tomorrow. I corrected the proofs of an article for the *Weekend Review*. They have cut out my impatience with the Ye olde libertie grumblers [?].

Thursday 29 May 1930

Proofs arrived of *Labels*.[1] I have let myself in for giving a luncheon party at the end of next week and have sent out many invitations. I hope I can get Maurice[2] up from Oxford or I shall be bored. Lunched alone at North End Road.

William and Harold[3] gave a delightful cocktail party at Lancaster Gate. I stayed on to dinner. Billy Clonmore appeared just back from Bonn. He drank a lot and was very genial until late in the evening when he became a little overcome by his wine, dropped his cigar and made a sudden exit with glazed eyes. As he came in, in his clergyman's clothes, Robert[4] overheard someone say, 'Damned bad taste coming in like that.' Eleanor Smith was there with a little horse in her hat made of platinum and rubies in the shape of a wagon given her by her father in honour of the book.[5] Diana but not Bryan.[6] Audrey says she thinks she is going to have a baby. I don't much care either way really so long as it is a boy. There was a great deal of adoration of Tom Mitford[7] – he sitting like a sly archdeacon talking about music with John and Harold[8] capering round him. However, it was a delightful party.

Friday 30 May 1930

Went to see Frank Dobson's 'Truth'. Very fine torso but rather boring head and legs. I gave a guinea towards the fund to purchase it for the nation, partly because I think it will be a good thing for the nation to have it, partly because people will see my name on the subscription list and say 'That young man is making good use of his money' and so buy more books and speak of them more tolerantly. Then to luncheon at Eddie Marsh's to see his collection of pictures. Bobbie Speaight, Lady Carlisle, Bryan and Diana. Good luncheon, good pictures. I don't think Eddie has any taste at all really; it is all part of his social

[1] Travel book about Waugh's Mediterranean journey of 1929; in the United States, the book was called *A Bachelor Abroad*.

[2] Maurice Bowra, Fellow of Wadham College, Oxford.

[3] William and Harold Acton.

[4] Robert Byron.

[5] *Red Wagon*.

[6] Bryan Guinness, later the 2nd Baron Moyne, to whom the Hon. Diana Mitford was then married and from whom she obtained a divorce in 1934.

[7] The Mitford children, all of whom were friends of Waugh, through his first wife, were: Tom, Nancy, Pamela, Diana, Unity, Jessica and Deborah.

[8] John Sutro and Harold Acton.

life. He likes Rex Whistler. After luncheon I went with Diana to see the mask she has had cast of herself by the German whom Harold Nicolson invented. It is very lovely and accurate. She has promised me a copy in white and gold plaster. Then we went with William to hear Robert[1] lecture on the Christians of Travancore. I can't think why he does these things. There was a scattered audience of about forty elderly people who none of them saw his jokes. The Greek minister was in the chair – why? – and made an exquisitely funny speech. My parents returned.

Saturday 31 May 1930

Went to two cinemas and read a few pages of a very interesting treatise on James Joyce's *Ulysses*. Corrected proofs of *Labels* – there are many misprints which were not in the galley proofs.

Sunday 1 June 1930

Luncheon at 108 Lancaster Gate. Desmond Parsons and Bridget – she looking very elegant and very lovely. Baby Jungman very late. She left early and sat at the other end of the table so I couldn't speak to her. Went to Audrey's and brought her to tea with my parents.

Monday 2 June 1930

Charming pencilled note from Wanda. Work and cinema.

Tuesday 3 June 1930

Wrote *Mail* article about OTCs. Cocktails at Wanda's. Dinner afterwards with Zena Naylor and David Herbert. We went on to the Blue Lantern – very squalid – but I enjoyed my evening.

Thursday 5 June 1930

Lunched with Diana[2] at Buckingham Street. Dined with Billy Clonmore and Harold at Quaglino's. We drank a lot. Eleanor Smith at the next table.

Friday 6 June 1930

I gave what should have been an amusing luncheon party at the Ritz but there was a horse-race that day and everybody chucked. In the end Eleanor Smith, Georgia and Sachie Sitwell, Bryan, Diana, Nancy, Frank, Cecil Beaton, William Acton and Liz Pelly[3] came. Luncheon was delicious. After luncheon

---

[1] Robert Byron.
[2] Diana Guinness.
[3] Elizabeth Ponsonby married Denis Pelly in 1929. She died in 1940, having obtained a divorce in 1933.

Diana and Audrey and I drove down to Poole Place.[1] Pilgrim made smells all the way down. How I hate dogs.

Audrey felt ill all the week and we left on Monday. We had a heavenly day on Saturday, bathing in the morning and visiting Bramber Museum in the afternoon. Tea in the gardens. Then we went to Bramber Castle and threw balls at coconuts and shot at bottles.

Whit Sunday 8 June 1930

Celia Keppel and Lord Bury[2] came over and stayed the night. He was a delightful P. G. Wodehouse character. Celia skinny. Spoiled little boy called Richard. Next day we bathed and sat in a haystack.

Tuesday 10 June 1930

We came up to London by train and lunched at Buckingham Street. After luncheon Bryan took me over Grosvenor Place – more unhomely than any marble palace would be. Deep gloom. Went back to change, dined Buckingham Street, went to Ruth Draper[3] – too humane and philanthropic. A brilliant artist if she was satirical but always sentimental and sympathetic at heart. A brilliant sketch of an American wife. Supper Savoy Grill. Full of people we knew.

Wednesday 11 June 1930

Wrote my *Mail* and *Graphic* articles. The *Mail* one all against Baby Jungman who chucked my luncheon on Friday with peculiar insolence.

Thursday 12 June 1930

Lunched at a women's club. Tea Olivia and Gwen.[4] Cocktails Sachie Sitwell. Dined Richard and Elizabeth. Small party afterwards. Paul Robeson passed out. Went back and slept with Varda,[5] but both of us too drunk to enjoy ourselves.

Friday 13 June 1930

Felt very ill indeed. Lunched with Billy Clonmore at Isola Bella. Harold and Peter Ruffer. Peter looking desperately thin and vicious. Cocktails at Lancaster Gate after one hour's sleep. Nancy Cunard[6] and her negress and an astonishing,

---

[1] Home of Diana and Bryan Guinness.
[2] Son of the 8th Earl of Albemarle.
[3] American monologuist (1884–1956).
[4] Olivia Plunket Greene and her mother.
[5] The separated wife of Gerald Reitlinger, art historian.
[6] Rebel daughter (1896–1965) of Sir Bache and Lady Cunard.

fat Mrs Henderson.[1] Michael Rosse. Later the party of Olivia Wyndham[2] and Ruth Baldwin on a Thames steamer. It was not enough of an orgy. Masses of little lesbian tarts and joyboys. Only one fight when a Miss Firminger got a black eye. Poor old Hat[3] looking like a tragedy queen. After the party to Vyvyan Holland's[4] where everyone fell asleep. Enid Raphael.[5]

Saturday 14 June 1930

Felt very ill. Got some sleep then went to dine with Richard and Elizabeth and arranged to take their flat during my parents' absence abroad.

Sunday 15 June 1930

Hamish[6] had a cocktail party in Oxford so I hired Miss Reid's Rolls-Royce and took Zena and Harold down to it. A delightful day. There was one row. Randolph Churchill threw a cocktail in Wanda's face. I came up after it had happened and made things no better by saying, 'Dear Wanda, how hot you look.' She left the party in a rage. Randolph was sent away and reprimanded by masses of young men in Bullingdon ties. We dined at the George with Frank and Elizabeth.[7] Elizabeth Pelly and John Betjeman joined us in the car. Arrived back at about 2.

Monday 16 June 1930

Feeling rather ill and vexed with prospect of work. I forgot to say that at this party John B. said, 'Yes, I noticed a cocktail in Wanda's face.'

Tuesday was Diana's birthday and I gave her an umbrella from Brigg which she broke next day.

Wednesday 18 June 1930

I lunched with Harold and William at Lancaster Gate and sat next to Nancy Beaton who said she kept a diary. I had tea with Nancy Mitford at the Ritz. She

---

[1] Wyn Henderson managed Nancy Cunard's private publishing and printing firm, The Hours Press, in Paris.

[2] Member of the Leconfield family (great-grand-daughter of the 1st baron). See Appendix of Names, p. 794.

[3] Brian Howard. The nickname was attached to Howard after a 1929 Bright Young People's hoax when Diana and Bryan Guinness staged an art exhibition of avant-garde paintings that purported to be the work of a German emigré genius, 'Bruno Hat', but were in fact pastiches by Howard. Waugh wrote the catalogue; Tom Mitford impersonated 'Hat'. The hoax was highly successful; Lytton Strachey bought a painting.

[4] Oscar Wilde's son.

[5] A girl celebrated for remarking, 'I don't know why people talk about their private parts. *Mine* aren't private.'

[6] The Hon. Hamish St Clair-Erskine.

[7] The Hon. Frank Pakenham and Elizabeth Harman.

was worried because Hamish had told her on Sunday evening that he didn't think he would ever feel up to sleeping with a woman. I explained to her a lot about sexual shyness in men.

Thursday 19 June 1930

Diana had a huge cocktail party I greatly enjoyed. Before it I lunched in the City with Anthony Russell and David Greene. Cecil Beaton told me that Frankau has written an attack on us both coupling our names with Godfrey Winn and Beverley Nichols. That comes of writing in the *Mail*. After cocktails, to dinner at Quaglino's with Audrey. She says she is not going to have a baby so all that is bogus. Then I joined a party at the Eiffel Tower given by Ruth Baldwin for Carl van Vechten.[1] He was so drunk he could not speak, only bark and bite. He bit Zena fit to kill. Then I went to a party at Audrey's. Nigel Playfair offered me a part in a play which I shall do. I waited for hours to sleep with Audrey but she was too tired.

Friday 20 June 1930

Attack, or rather counter-attack, on me by Charles Graves.[2] He too couples my name with just the same three. Clearly a conspiracy. My parents left England.

Sezincote, Saturday 21 June 1930

I lunched with Olivia at the Ritz and she came to see me off to Sezincote, where I spent a delightful weekend. Travelled down with John Betjeman and Frank Pakenham. Sezincote is quite lovely. Regency Indian style like Brighton Pavilion only everything in Cotswold stone instead of plaster. Fountains all playing and ferocious swans. A family pew which was like a box at a theatre with padded red balustrade above the heads of the congregation.

Colonel Dugdale said, 'The twenty-fourth of May is my day for haymaking.' 'Isn't that very early?' 'Yes, in fact the extraordinary thing is that I have never begun that day. Twenty-ninth this year. Thirtieth last year. Always well after twenty-fourth. Still I always keep twenty-fourth as my haymakin' day.'

Slept very badly all the weekend. There is a monument at Sezincote with huge plaques commemorating the Peninsular War, but it is also the chimney of the furnace which heats the orangery. The most lovely view in England.

London, Monday 23 June 1930

I left Sezincote by an early train and went to Birmingham. Visited art

---

[1] American author from Cedar Rapids, Iowa; music critic for the *New York Times*, then a highly successful novelist, influential in the so-called 'Negro Renaissance' of the 1920s. Wrote *Nigger Heaven*, *Peter Whiffle*, and *The Tattooed Countess*.

[2] Newspaper columnist.

gallery. Welsh custodian asked whether Augustus John was Welsh too. A new, very early Rossetti head of a Persian boy about which they couldn't tell me anything at all. Quite unlike anything else of Rossetti's. Lunch with Henry[1] and then on to his factory where I saw brass and iron casting. I was chiefly impressed by the manual dexterity of the workers. Nothing in the least like mass labour or mechanization – pure arts and crafts. The brass casting peculiarly beautiful: green molten metal from a red cauldron. Back to London and moved into Richard's[2] flat.

Tuesday 24 June 1930

Luncheon at the Savoy Grill. Afterwards to a matinée by an American woman called Angna Enters. Silent miming to a piano. Awful; went before the end. Dined at the Savoy in Ralph Straus's party at the Odde Volumes.[3] Sat next to a Lady Cromartie and a Mrs Mannin.[4] Also present a Lady Clonmel, Jimmy Stern,[5] and a soldier. Good dinner. Intolerable frippery and facetiousness. Enid Raphael next door with Vyvyan Holland. They tried to make me make a speech but I refused.[6] Slept very well.

Wednesday 25 June 1930

Luncheon Carl van Vechten. Rebecca West. Sovrani's. He collects autographs. I wrote, 'To Carl v. V. the playboy of the western world, who shares with the present Lord Rosslyn[7] the distinction of being the one man of letters who is also a man of the world, in sincere admiration from E.W.' Wrote an article on diaries for *Mail*.[8]

[1] Henry Yorke.

[2] Richard Plunket Greene's.

[3] A dining club whose programme-menu that night was headed: 'Ye 452nd Meeting of Ye Sette of Odde Volumes holden at Ye Savoy Hotel on Tuesday, Ye 24th Day of June, 1930; His Oddeship Capt. Ivor Stewart-Liberty, M.C. (Sciologist), in Ye Chair.'

[4] Ethel Mannin, writer and feminist.

[5] James Stern, short-story writer and translator.

[6] Possibly at the stage described in the programme as, 'Two guests will then be encouraged to say how much they have enjoyed themselves.'

[7] The 5th Earl of Rosslyn (1869–1939) married three wives and wrote two books: *Twice Captured*, about the Boer War, and *My Gamble with Life*. The song, *The Man who Broke the Bank at Monte Carlo*, was written about him.

[8] 'From time to time I purchase a thick notebook and record a few pages of my daily round, but I have a deep-rooted feeling that it is a mischievous and degrading habit to write anything that will not bring in an immediate pecuniary reward, so that the journal invariably languishes and dies in a week or two. . . . It is not necessary to be in touch with famous people in order to write a valuable diary. I still think that the funniest book in the world is Grossmith's *Diary of a Nobody*. If only people would really keep journals like that. Nobody wants to read other people's reflections on life and religion and politics, but the routine of their day, properly recorded, is always interesting, and will become more so as conditions change with the years.' 'One Way to Immortality', *Daily Mail*, 28 June 1930, p. 8.

Cocktail party Cecil Beaton. Audrey dined with me at St James's Square. Patrick Balfour and Mrs Condise [?] both had parties but we went to neither.

Thursday 26 June 1930

I lunched with Frank at Sovrani's. Audrey came to dinner.

Friday 27 June 1930

Diana had a supper party. Olivia and Inez dined with me beforehand. Inez said she was going to Patricia Moore's party. Soon it became clear that she did not even know where it was. She rang up several people all of whom refused to speak to her. There was nothing for it but to take her to Diana's, where she was insulted by Harold. I enjoyed the party, became very drunk and fought Randolph in the servants' hall. Olivia very drunk. All the usual people were there.

Coombe Bissett, Saturday 28 June 1930

Inez lunched with me. I said, 'How bad-tempered Harold was last night' to make things easier. Inez said, 'He was sweet to me. But then I know him so well he wouldn't think of being anything else.' Inez has taken to kissing me lately. I went down to Coombe Bissett by an afternoon train and spent a peaceful weekend at the Lambs.[1]

London, Monday 30 June 1930

Came up to London by a luncheon train and wrote an article. Intolerably hot day. Dined at the Duchess of Marlborough's. Sat next to Edith Sitwell. The dining-room was full of ghastly frescoes by G. F. Watts. Edith said she thought they were by Lady Lavery. She talked mostly about Ethel Mannin's book[2] and what she said and was going to say about what Mrs Mannin had said she had said. That evening Melba said, 'I read your books Miss Sitwell.' 'If it comes to that, Dame Melba, I have heard you sing.' There were two ambassadors and about forty hard-faced middle-aged peers and peeresses. The Duchess very battered with fine diamonds. The Duke wearing the Garter: also a vast silk turban over a bandaged eye from which his little hook nose protruded. When I left, the Duchess said, 'Ah, you are like Marlborough. He has such a mundane mind. He will go to any party for which he is sent a printed invitation.' I went on to a party given by Miss Watts in Charles Street. Harman[3] was there rather insistent and personal. Also poor Bobbie Roberts.

[1] Lady Pansy Pakenham married Henry Lamb in August 1928.
[2] *Confessions and Impressions.*
[3] Elizabeth Harman.

Tuesday 1 July 1930

I worked. Lunched at Ritz. Met Noel Coward.

Wednesday 2 July 1930

I went to luncheon with Patrick Balfour, Michael Rosse, Desmond Parsons, John Sutro. I forget who else. We went to the film with David Herbert in it. Frightfully bad. To tea at Alexander Square with Olivia. I said would she please find a Jesuit to instruct me. Maurice was to have dined with me that night and I had arranged a party for him but he spent the weekend injuring his hands on a rope. The dinner was good and I bought masses of fruit and *foie gras*, etc., which were not touched. It was quite a cosy little party really.

Thursday 3 July 1930

Basil Ava's wedding. I had Miss Reid for the day. I lunched with Nancy Mitford at Quaglino's. Then to the church. Very hot. Frank best man in hired morning suit. At the party afterwards Jim Laurence insisted on introducing me to Charles Graves. I went and bathed at the RAC with Patrick and Michael and John Betjeman. Then to a cocktail party at John Armstrong's. Lord Bury very sweet. Then back to change and to dinner at the Spearmans. Nancy Mitford and Clough Williams Ellis[1] and Doreen Jessel. Mary Pakenham was commissioned by Diana Spearman to do two frescoes in their drawing-room for £20 each. When she had done the first Diana said, 'I don't think we ever decided what we would pay you, did we?' Mary: 'No.' Diana, 'Well, you write on this piece of paper what you think we should give you and I'll write what I think we should give you. What have you written?' '£20.' 'Oh, well. I've written £15. Let's split the difference, shall we, and call it £17 10s.' Poor Mary has not yet been able to get even that out of them. They say, 'If you can find my cheque book you shall have it.' Clough Williams Ellis very jolly and chatty. He kept producing little books from an attaché case and showing me underlined texts. 'The Artist alone is the legislator' – that sort of thing. But he has a healthy enthusiasm for islands.

A very good example of the difference between Guinness and Mitford minds. Maureen was observed to be hopelessly drunk at the Redesdales' dance. Lord Redesdale, on having this explained to him: 'Drunk. Don't be absurd. Girls simply don't get drunk. And even if they did no one would mention it.'

Colonel Guinness in similar circumstances: 'Does she often get drunk?'

'Almost continually.'

'How very interesting. What does she drink?'

Friday 4 July 1930

Railway Club dinner. We met at Charing Cross Hotel. The waiter serving

[1] The architect and critic of urban sprawl.

cocktails was the witness in David's divorce.[1] Very comfortable Pullman car on slow train to Folkestone. I sat with Bryan. The manager of the hotel at Folkestone had not fully understood the nature of the gathering and had provided an enormous ballroom. Harold started lovemaking and Brocklehurst started breaking china. Incidentally he also broke my ebony cane. Bryan, Henry[2] and I left for Brighton in Bryan's cars. We went about fifty miles out of the way. Henry was sick twice. We slept at the Metropole.

Saturday 5 July 1930

Bryan and I went on to Poole Place. Nancy and Diana arrived later. Also Michael, Patrick and Lamb. Later Pansy. Later still Rupert Bowles. Diana and I quarrelled at luncheon. We bathed. Diana and I quarrelled at dinner and after dinner.

Next day I decided to leave. Quarrelled with Diana again and left. Arrived at dinner-time. Dined alone very expensively at Quaglino's. Invited Harold to join me. He went instead to the Ritz.

Monday 7 July 1930

I lunched at the Ritz with Noel Coward. He has a simple, friendly nature. No brains. A theatrical manner. We talked about Catholicism. He said, 'Go round the world.'[3] He said, what a shame he knew a Dominican prior who wanted all the time to be a play actor with the result that he was found quite dotty, in his hostess's underclothes. Quiet dinner Tom Balston's flat.

Tuesday 8 July 1930

Went to Father D'Arcy[4] at 11. Blue chin and fine, slippery mind. The clergyhouse at Mount Street[5] superbly ill-furnished. Anglicans can never achieve this ruthless absence of 'good taste'. We talked about verbal inspiration and Noah's Ark. I was to have lunched with George and to do so had refused invitations from Baby Jungman and Cecil Beaton. I sat in the 500 Club for an hour. Robert[6] was there, with his sister just returned from Holland. Finally I went away and took Audrey to Hyde Park Grill. Cocktail party at Grace Ansell.

---

[1] David Plunket Greene's divorce from Babe McGustie.

[2] Viscount Weymouth; later the 6th Marquess of Bath.

[3] 'He told me he was taking instruction and of his probable conversion. I advised him to take a leisurely trip round the world and think carefully before taking so decisive a step.' Noel Coward in a letter to the editor, 20 March 1973.

[4] See Appendix of Names, p. 794.

[5] The Jesuit clergyhouse off Grosvenor Square.

[6] Robert Byron.

All the inevitable people. John Betjeman brought Gerald Heard[1] to dinner who is said to be the cleverest man in the world. He was well informed about theology and spiritualism. Clearly an active and retentive mind. Personally unattractive.

Wednesday 9 July 1930

Lunched at Sovrani's with Frank after a morning with D'Arcy. Excellent cold duck with *foie gras*. I enjoyed this luncheon. Excellent cocktail party at the Beatons. Diana was there. I just said goodbye to her. Went to a theatre with Audrey. We went to see Nigel Playfair in his dressing-room. Such a bad play. Then to Quaglino's, then to St James's Square

Thursday 10 July 1930

Wrote *Graphic* article in morning. George sent a box of cigars as apology for cutting luncheon. Lunched with Lady Birkenhead. Baby's mother, Lady Lavery, Sachie Sitwell, Willie Walton, Chips Channon,[2] if that is how it is spelt, Eleanor,[3] Cecil Beaton. Just saw Lord Birkenhead going out in grey tall hat and grey frockcoat. Very sunburned, but an old, ill man. Mrs Richard Guinness said Baby was in tears after our tiff. Joined the Savile Club. Packed my clothes and removed them all to North End Road. Dined at Radnor Place with Henry and Dig. John Armstrong. The unmarried Ruthven twin and a Miss Labouchère. We went to *The Importance of Being Earnest* at Hammersmith. Supper at Rules.

Friday 11 July 1930

Went to Father D'Arcy and talked about infallibility and indulgences. Lunched at Ritz with Richard and Liza[4] and spent the day with them.

Saturday 12 July 1930

Father D'Arcy in the morning. Wrote letters all the afternoon. Dined with Gwen and Olivia at Alexander Square.

Monday 14 July 1930

Lunched with Beatrice Guinness. Sophie Tucker, Lady Birkenhead, Lady Ponsonby, David Cecil,[5] Frank, Eleanor, etc. I sat at a side table with Baby who

---

[1] Writer who went to California in 1937 and, with Aldous Huxley and Christopher Isherwood, helped to arouse in the west a new interest in eastern religion.

[2] MP and diarist.

[3] Lady Eleanor Smith.

[4] Richard and Elizabeth Plunket Greene.

[5] Lord David Cecil, Fellow of Wadham College, Oxford.

was sweet. Then a fat woman called Olga Lynn[1] was put down with us who said would I go to a 'book tea' at the Duchess of Rutland next day. I said no. There was a Levantine called Georges Katawi – if that is how it is spelt. He is Egyptian chargé d'affaires and a converted Catholic.

Tuesday 15 July 1930

Lunched with Lord Bury. A large party of very young men – friends, I suppose, of Celia's brother – and elderly relatives. The only people I knew were the Swiss minister and his wife. I never discovered the identity of either of my women. I had tea with Victor Cazalet[2] on the terrace of the House of Commons. On the way I met Oliver Baldwin grown fatter and Elmley grown a little thinner, I thought. The party at tea was Lady Oxford, Lady Clifford, Lady Russell, John Buchan and the Prime Minister. They talked of spiritualism. I thought MacDonald a nasty and inadequate man.

I went on with Lady Oxford to Olga Lynn's party because I hoped to see Baby but she had gone. I went on to cocktails at Diana's but she had left there too. Dined at the Savile with Harold and got drunk.

Wednesday 16 July 1930

Lunched at the Savile with Alec. Randolph Churchill. Peter Rodd. Went back and slept. Went to cocktails with Wanda who kissed literally everyone in the room except me. Came back to North End Road to work. Saw Audrey in the morning.

Thursday 17 July 1930

Lunched Savile with Frank and Father D'Arcy. Came back and went to sleep. Dined with Alec. Mrs Humphreys, Mr and Mrs Clifford Bax, Prince and Princess Galitzine and their daughter. Bad champagne at dinner. Went on with the Galitzines to the Sutros' party. I thought we had timed our arrival so as to miss all the music but there was about half an hour of it during which I talked to Douglas Woodruff.[3] After the music I drank a great deal of champagne and sat with Bryan in the garden. Diana was friendly and reproachful-looking. I wrote her a note when I got home trying to explain that it was my fault that I did not like her, not hers. I don't suppose that she will understand. Saw Baby in the distance, v. thick with Tom Mitford.

Friday 18 July 1930

Lunched at St James's Club with the Egyptian diplomat I met at Beatrice

---

[1] Singer; and prominent social figure.

[2] MP for Chippenham, 1924. Amateur squash champion, 1930. Liaison officer to General Sikorski, commander-in-chief of Polish army, in the Second World War and killed in a mysterious aircrash with him, 1943.

[3] Roman Catholic author and journalist. See Appendix of Names, p. 794.

Guinness's. Father D'Arcy and David Cecil. I was amused at the exchanges of diplomatic courtesies all over the club. Went to see Audrey and with her to A. P. Herbert's cocktail party where I talked all the time to Richard Hughes.[1] I never saw a man with fewer marks of success. Took two actresses, one hideous, one rather pretty, to their theatre. Dined at Quaglino's with Audrey – expensive, bad dinner. Cinema. Supper at the Savoy – Pansy and Frank. Frank fell asleep.

Saturday 19 July 1930

Slept well for the first time for a week. Dined with Gwen and Olivia and talked about religion.

Sunday 20 July 1930

Dined with Richard[2] at the Savile and drank a great deal.

Monday 21 July 1930

I went with Audrey to buy the puppy from Olivia. Then to a tea party at the Egyptian Legation. I was talking brightly about aeroplane accidents to Lady Dufferin when a footman called her away to the telephone. She came back greatly agitated to say that she had just heard that her husband was involved in an aircrash[3] coming back from Le Touquet. She asked me to go back with her, and I spent an hour with her, trying to get exact information from Croydon, the Chatham police, the Air Ministry, etc. Veronica Blackwood had gone off at once by car, so that Lady D. was quite alone. Eventually I got Lady Lowther to come round and see her. It has all haunted me since. Lady D. so lovely and both dignified and entirely discomposed at the same time, like a child in pain. No tears. I went later to dinner at Lady Cunard's. A very large party. Some of the young women did not see fit to turn up so that I found myself with an empty chair on one side and Gavin Henderson on the other. Opposite but too far to speak to Oswald Mosley, Princess Bibesco, Imogen Grenfell, Lord Ivor Churchill. A badly arranged table. Lady Lavery between the Sitwell brothers. The dinner was very good. After dinner we sat and drank and Lady Cunard made efforts to get us upstairs. The party seemed to be half for George Moore[4] and half for Nancy Cunard. Harold Nicolson[5] very disappointed with Keith

[1] Author of *High Wind in Jamaica*.

[2] Richard Plunket Greene.

[3] The Marquess of Dufferin and Ava, Viscountess Ednam, Sir Edward Ward, Mrs Henrik Leoffer, and Col. G. L. P. Henderson, the owner and pilot of a small aircraft bound for Croydon, were killed when the aircraft fell to pieces in mid-air near Meopham, south of Gravesend.

[4] Irish writer and critic (1852–1933); author of *Esther Waters* and *The Brook Kerith*. Devoted admirer of Lady Cunard; Nancy toyed with the idea that he was her father.

[5] The writer; six months earlier he had left the Foreign Office and joined the *Evening Standard*.

Winter but inflamed by Peter Howard.[1] Lady C. very restless throughout the evening, obviously dissatisfied with me as a lion. Lady Juliet Duff very dramatic in bereavement all in black and tearful.

Tuesday 22 July 1930

Went to Savile where everyone was talking of the air disaster. Then to luncheon at the Ritz with David Cecil. We talked about love, I think.

Wednesday 23 July 1930

Lunched at the Ritz with Billy Clonmore and Olivia Greene. Dinner in a Soho restaurant with Mrs Lucas, Audrey and Stephen Gwynn.[2] Very hot and stuffy. Bad wine. Found Gwynn a great bore. Then to a party given by Viola Garvin. Rose Macaulay. Intolerably hot and crowded. Then on to a party given by Donegall and Jim Laurence. Numerous rich old whores. I sat downstairs most of the time with Zena Naylor and Elizabeth Ponsonby.

Friday 25 July 1930

I went down to stay at Jim Laurence's house for the weekend. He drove me down. Before going I met Harold[3] in Fortnum & Mason's. He broke into a violent and crazy tirade against Harold Nicolson. Mad. Jim Laurence has two brothers, a sister and a father. The father a complete *Punch* profiteer with a voice that sounded sneering because he was trying to make it refined. A fine old house, very large and well furnished. Poor food. Good and copious drink. Everything run by a governess named Miss Somerset. While I was there there were two cricket matches. An odious little creature called Tommy Crossman, who used to be at Hertford, captained one side. When they were not playing cricket they played tennis, rackets, snooker, ping-pong and the gramophone. I sat and hid in my bedroom all the time, emerging for meals. On Sunday I could bear it no more and fled back to London, dined with Audrey at the Ritz and spent the evening with her.

Coombe Bissett, Monday 28 July 1930

Came with my mama to Coombe Bissett which I have taken from the Lambs for three weeks or so. Before coming I had to lunch with Dennis Bradley. He thinks he has placed the play[4] and there are difficulties over agents' fees.

I stayed at Coombe Bissett until Thursday 31 July sleeping very badly but

---

[1] In 1931, captain of the English rugby XV. Later, prominent supporter of Moral Rearmament.
[2] Irish writer, 1864–1950.
[3] Harold Acton.
[4] An adaptation of *Vile Bodies*.

getting through a certain amount of work. I think my mother enjoyed her rest from North End Road.

Forthampton Court, Gloucester, Friday 1 August–Tuesday 5 August 1930

Weekend at Forthampton with the Yorkes. Travelled down with Maurice[1] who said the food would be bad and no champagne. Both these predictions wrong. On the other hand, he said that the beds were comfortable and that there were enough bathrooms. This was wrong too. The party consisted of Maud, Vincent,[2] Henry and Dig Yorke, Dig's sister Mary and her husband Monty Lowry-Corry. This pair copulated incessantly. Hugh Wyndham, Mrs Y.'s brother, a typical ineffectual younger son. He had lost his money in South Africa and been rescued by the family. Now he spends his time drawing pear trees. His wife very shy and unattractive. Lilah Labouchère who started the day ugly and got pretty towards evening. It was a very agreeable weekend. No one did anything all the time except Henry who played a little billiards. Crosswords, Peggity, and halma. Copious conversation. Henry and Dig left for Knockmaroon protesting their detestation of Bryan and Diana. Maurice and I came to Coombe Bissett where we found Audrey waiting for us. Pleasant three days. *Daily Mail* do not wish to renew my contract. Theatrical producers do not wish to buy Bradley's play. I am spoiling for a quarrel with Bott [?], so with one thing and another I shall soon be poor.

Coombe Bissett, Saturday 9 August 1930

Audrey left. Chris Hollis and Douglas Woodruff arrived. We drank a lot during the weekend and they left behind several fleas. They are very settled in their minds on all debatable topics. Woodruff slightly more satirical than Hollis, who was shocked by my jokes about the *Universe* or individual Catholics. On Saturday evening, rather drunk, we drove to Tidworth Tattoo and saw the last twenty minutes of it. It is typical of military arrangements that we were able to walk into the grandstand without paying for tickets. Next day we went to see the phallic giant at Cerne Abbas. Two little girls with long bare legs sat on his testicles.

Monday 11 August 1930

Chris and Woodruff left. Richard and Elizabeth Greene arrived. Richard very boorish. One day we walked to a yew wood and a maze.

---

[1] Maurice Bowra.

[2] Henry Yorke's mother and father, respectively; his mother was a daughter of the 2nd Lord Leconfield, and a descendant of the 1st Earl Hardwicke who became Lord High Chancellor in 1737.

Friday 15 August 1930

Olivia arrived with her dog. A theatrical man wants me to start adapting plays. It seems to me a simple way of making quite a lot of money.

Saturday 16 August 1930

Frank came to call with an untidy, attractive girl called Lady Cranborne.

Sunday 17 August 1930

Elizabeth and I went over to tea at Cranborne. An exquisitely beautiful house full of plain, amiable guests with hooked noses. There was a religious service going on before the house.

Monday 18 August 1930

Richard and Elizabeth left. Olivia and I drove into Salisbury and bought some very good port from a slightly hostile wine merchant. That evening we got a little drunk and talked about religion. During the day I had a great number of telegrams from Auriol [?] Lee, Peters, and Gilbert Miller which ended in the project for adapting plays coming to nothing.

Tuesday 19 August 1930

Diana Cavendish and Betty Cranborne came to pick us up for a picnic in the rain but it stopped raining. Three Cecil boys and two Ormsby-Gore children – one a girl, very pretty.

Wednesday 20 August 1930

Lady Cranborne came to luncheon. I think she was a little disconcerted to find Olivia and me living there alone apparently in sin. Also disconcerted by Olivia's urban clothes and make-up. This last has had a sad affect on Pansy's cook who has in emulation bought a great quantity of cosmetics and goes off to Salisbury every afternoon looking like Lady Lavery. Audrey wants more money. I said no.

Thursday 21 August 1930

It rained all day. We did nothing. I wrote to Father D'Arcy.

Hampstead, Friday 22 August 1930

I returned to North End Road for the night. My father, on the eve of his birthday, has been severely bitten by his dog. My mother has just returned from visiting her relatives. Audrey seems to bear very little malice for my refusal to give her money. Kit Wood[1] has committed suicide. The Duchess of

---

[1] Christopher Wood (1901–1930), painter.

York has had a daughter. Birkenhead is still alive. I went to a cinema in the evening much to my father's sorrow.

Renishaw, Saturday 23 August 1930

Went to Renishaw.[1] Travelled down with Robert[2] who made me go third class. He says he only travels first class abroad because he thinks it is expected of Englishmen. We arrived at Chesterfield Station and found Sachie and Georgia[3] there to meet us. Also Willie Walton,[4] Harold Monro, a young man, very mad and conceited, called Gaspard Ponsonby[5] (son of Fritz). At Renishaw we found Francis Birrell, Arthur Waley,[6] a nasty man called Roderick and the entire family. Renishaw very large and rather forbidding. Arterial main roads, coal mines, squalid industrial village, then a park, partly laid out as a golf course, and the house; north front, discoloured Derbyshire stone, castellated. Very dark hall. Many other rooms of great beauty, fine tapestry and Italian furniture. Ginger[7] in white tie and tail coat very gentle. Ginger and Lady Ida[8] never allowed to appear together at meals. The house extremely noisy owing to shunting all round it. The lake black with coal dust. A finely laid out terrace garden with a prospect of undulating hills, water and the pit-heads, slag heaps and factory chimneys. Georgia exquisitely dressed among all these shabby men. G.P. in love with her. She got very much stouter during the ten days I was there chiefly because of bathing and the very good food (chef from Ritz) about which all the family complained. Most of the party left after the weekend. Robert shut himself in his bedroom most of the day. Later Ankaret and William Jackson arrived. I summoned Alastair[9] who had returned to England. The household was very full of plots. Almost everything was a secret and most of the conversations deliberately engineered in prosecution of some private joke. Ginger, for instance, was told that Ankaret's two subjects were Arctic exploration and ecclesiastical instruments; also that Alastair played the violin. Sachie liked talking about sex. Osbert very shy. Edith wholly ignorant. We talked of slums. She said the poor streets of Scarborough are terrible but that she did not think that the fishermen took drugs very much. She also said that port was made with methylated spirit; she knew this for a fact because her charwoman told her. The servants very curious. They live on

---

[1] Sitwell family seat.

[2] Robert Byron.

[3] Sacheverell Sitwell and his wife.

[4] William Walton, the composer.

[5] Son of Sir Frederick Ponsonby, courtier brother of Sir Arthur Ponsonby. Later, the 2nd Baron Sysonby.

[6] The sinologist.

[7] Sir George Sitwell, b.1860; the 4th baronet.

[8] Sir George's wife, daughter of the 1st Earl of Londesborough.

[9] Alastair Graham.

terms of feudal familiarity. E.g., a message brought by footman to assembled family that her ladyship wanted to see Miss Edith upstairs. 'I can't go. I've been with her all day. Osbert, you go.' 'Sachie, you go.' 'Georgia, you go', etc. Footman: 'Well, come on. One of you's got to go.' Osbert breakfast was large slices of pineapple and melon. No one else was allowed these. Osbert kept cigars and smoked them secretly. I bought my own. The recreations of the household were bathing, visiting houses, and Osbert's Walk. We went to Hardwicke – a vilely ugly house but full of good needlework. Osbert's Walk consisted of driving in the car quarter of a mile to Eckington Woods, walking through them, about half an hour (with bracken), the car meeting him on the other side and taking him home. He did this every day. There was a golf club where we had morning drinks. This too was a secret. Georgia is the centre of all the plots. Inez's father, Colonel Chandos Poole, came over to luncheon.

Ankaret could not bear it when Osbert read aloud, and kept joining in. 'That reminds me of something that happened to me. . . .' She also said, 'I can't see any point in being a Catholic unless one belongs to an old Catholic family. Now when I stay at Arundel I feel very Catholic. . . .' It was unsafe to mention any living author because they were all so vindictive about them.

After about ten days Alastair and I went on to Pakenham. Frank, John Betjeman and Elizabeth Harman were staying there. I spent about ten days there. John B. became a bore rather with Irish peers and revivalist hymns and his enthusiasm for every sort of architecture. I saw the only man who has been ostracized from West Meath society. He took a housemaid to Dublin in a first-class carriage. It would have been all right if they had travelled third. However they decided to give his son a chance so he played in the Cavan tennis tournament. 'Rotter' arrived and thought it was cricket. The organizer was Lord Farnham who lives by staying at Lunn's Swiss resorts all the winter. There was an agent of Lunn's there to see how well he organized things. We went to luncheon at Dunsany. Lord Dunsany[1] thinks his very nice eighteenth-century Gothic house is genuine medieval. He was rude to the servants and grossly boastful. He makes odious little faces of plaster. His house is full of the most awful kind of *art nouveau.*

The diary here breaks off for two months. During that time, on 29 September 1930, Waugh was received by Father Martin D'Arcy SJ into the Roman Catholic church. The diary resumes with Waugh's journey to Abyssinia for the coronation of Ras Tafari, the Emperor Haile Selassie. 'Six weeks before I had barely heard Ras Tafari's name', Waugh explained in

[1] The 18th baron, 1878–1957; author of nearly fifty books and eighteen plays; an uncle of Frank Pakenham.

Remote People. 'I was in Ireland, staying in a house where chinoiserie and Victorian Gothic contend for mastery over a Georgian structure. We were in the library discussing over an atlas a journey I proposed to make to China and Japan. We began talking of other journeys, and so of Abyssinia. One of our party was on leave from Cairo; he knew something of Abyssinian politics and the coming coronation. . . . A fortnight later I was back in London and had booked my passage to Djibouti.' The member of the party on leave from Cairo was Alastair Graham, who had been transferred to Egypt from Greece when Sir Percy Loraine, the ambassador in Athens, became high commissioner to Egypt and the Sudan. Graham, with another high-spirited attaché, Mark Ogilvie-Grant, occupied Sir Percy's outer office in Cairo and organized his official social life; and their duties one day required them to arrange a luncheon for two visiting crown princes from Abyssinia. The princes arrived wearing silk capes and bowler hats. They retained their hats during lunch. Still more disconcerting, it soon became plain – to the dismay of the attendant interpreters – that they did not speak any of the expected languages. The meal, with the help of Graham and Ogilvie-Grant, turned into a comic occasion; and it was this – his only – experience of Abyssinian politics that caused Graham to urge Waugh, whose tastes he knew, to attend as a spectator the coronation of the Lion of Judah. The advice was fruitful; the next part of Waugh's diary is a record, often in note form, of the African journey that produced both the travel book *Remote People* (1931) and the novel *Black Mischief* (1932).

London–Addis Ababa, Friday 10 October–Sunday 26 October 1930

In the train a French cinema photographer who took off his shoes but wore kid gloves all night. One gloved hand overhung his *couchette* and swayed with the motion of the train. The brass floor was nearly red hot. Marshal Pétain was in the restaurant. He and I alone observed the *jour maigre* and were rewarded with *oeufs au plat*.

Café de Verdun at Marseilles. Admirable luncheon.

Azay le Rideau. Shabby and not very clean. Uncarpeted passages. Double outside cabin to myself. Passengers: French colonials with inconceivably ill-disciplined children; officers of Foreign Legion, badly dressed, unshaven, pot-bellied, like dishevelled commercial travellers. Men sleep in hold, eat and live on deck. Very untidy like convicts. A bearded *sous-officier*. Mostly German; one American. Two jump out of port hole one hour out of Port Said and get away. Another jumps overboard in full view before luncheon near Suez; recaptured by Egyptian police but not brought to the ship.

Polish and Dutch deputations on board; busy with attaché cases presumably composing complimentary addresses. French and Egyptian come on board at Suez. Ras with son, two servants, and secretary-interpreter at Port Said; walks hand in hand with secretary, latter in European dress. English (half-Malay?) mother and daughter. Cannes to Madras. I thought at first the daughter would enliven the voyage. Both mindless. Daughter, Denise Harison, very much pigmented – crimson toenails, black rims to eyes – but not to attract males: simply child-imitation of smart people she saw at Cannes. Both so silly that although they spent all their time in nursery card games they could not even rationalize the rules. It was clear that all the games they taught us had become confused in their minds. Barton; brother British minister.[1] Retired banker [?] bore; slightly mercenary but well intentioned. Bloody American journalist who insulted servants. Italian proprietor of third-best hotel in Madras. Redhead Mason American off to sell agricultural machinery in Indo-China; no knowledge of any language – even restaurant French.

Port Said. All my acquaintances had gone.[2] Quarrel about cigar at Eastern Exchange. Port Office official noticeably less polite than eighteen months ago.

On board ship, those who habitually overeat, drink and smoke and take no exercise reap benefit; those who lead 'healthy' lives become ill at once.

I become slightly hypocritical as soon as I am away from my own background, adopting an unfamiliar manner of speech and code of judgements.

I oversleep Mass on both Sundays. Priests and nuns second class. No fish for dinner on Friday.

Dutch minister plays particular kind of bridge with a *misère* called Lulu.

Two days of fête: *Courses de chevaux*; only French played; *pari mutuel*; short odds. Ship decorated; a cinema film of more than normal ill-success. All stood up when Marshal entered; he very affable, distributing autographs; a signed photograph fetched 900 francs at auction. Second-class passengers come to ball and concert. Legionnaires' band; mouth-organs, drum and banjo; drum labelled 'Mon Jazz'. Girl sang, described by Barton as a 'Luscious Lucy'. Uncertainty about trains Djibouti–Addis; continual conflicting rumours due to Belgian consul's bad English. Hot wind. Those used to tropics succumb. Day before Djibouti rough sea. *Azay* very steady. Fight among stewards. Chinese put in cells; two soldiers there already. Always sweating. Presented bad review books to the library.

Djibouti arrived dawn. One couple still dancing, grey faces. Still uncertainty trains; purser assures everyone accommodation. There will be two trains, one early morning, one evening. Special for delegations. There will be one special train evening. Three P & O ships making connection, no possibility train. Barton and I go ashore and see British consul, young shipping agent Lowe; find in fact two trains, both specials for delegations, both evening. Says

---

[1] Sir Sidney Barton, KBE, CMG, Envoy Extraordinary and Minister Plenipotentiary at Addis Ababa.

[2] From Waugh's 1929 visit, with his first wife.

improbable obtain seats either. Heavy warm rain; no mackintoshes; topees suffered. Hôtel des Arcades, very amiable French manageress. Gave us room with balcony, change, wash. I leave behind sponge, razor, etc. Rain stops. We go for drive in waterlogged streets. Beggars, deformities, lepers. European quarter shabby stucco, broad streets; plaster peeling off; large quantities fall as we watch. Cannot understand sudden consternation crowd; discover this is an earthquake unnoticed shaking cab. Native quarter, mud huts; exchanged money, cheated exchange. Somalis partly shaven heads, partly dyed ginger curls. Returned hotel, Lowe said he had arranged accommodation train. Chasseur hotel assured us no customs examination baggage. Then recalled me Custom House, then said custom officer engaged party Government House honour d'Esperez, consequently no examination luggage. Dined terrace stars small boys fanned us hoping tips.

Left in train containing Egyptian, Polish, Japanese, Dutch delegations; empty first-class carriage. American photographers next door. Night journey. Arrived Dirre-Dowa early morning. Enormous retinue drawn up, irregular troops lining way to Governor's House where breakfast and champagne given to delegates. Barton and I breakfast in hotel. Zaphiro, Oriental Secretary, came to see us. First sight Abyssinian costumes. Throughout day guards of honour at all stations, varying size. Lunch Afdem; four meat courses. Dinner Hawash. Galla dancers please Egyptians; four hours' wait; lights won't work. Nowhere to go. More meat. Had been warned cold night but merely pleasantly cool; blankets lent from Hôtel des Arcades. Country between Dirre-Dowa and Hawash monstrous plain scrubbed trees. Rich soil. Train mounts steeply all night, woke up highland scenery native villages. Stopped dawn breakfast Modjo, later Akaki enable delegations change uniform.

Addis 10.30. Royal guard khaki bare feet presented arms, band black boys played all anthems at great length, official receptions. Barton's nieces appeared, deeply shocked that I had engaged no accommodation. First introduction hysteria Legation. Drove Hôtel de France, met Irene Ravensdale, got out to engage room, car drove away. Followed to collect luggage and leave cards. Met Troutbeck, asked appointment, interview, told impossible. Next days a nightmare attempting obtain information. People involved: Hall, halfcaste German in charge *bureau d'étrangers*; Collier, discreet head bank to be taken over Abyssinians January if they can pay; Taylor, Oriental Secretary; amiable second-rate wife. Awful Barton niece, pretty hysterical Barton daughter. British Mission arrived 28th. Garden party Saturday. Evening party Friday. —— arrived with Mission, dined with me Thursday, asked me to beat him. Sinclair, pathetic major Marine band, dined Wednesday. Lunched Colonel Sandford, unsuccessful farmer, general middle-man for *Daily Mail*; lunched Mathew, Anglican parson. Legation gave minimum information. Forgot invite me Durbar.

Addis broad streets unfinished houses. Casino unfinished. Chained people disappeared streets as distinguished visitors arrived. Italians Friday. Charles and Philimore, ADC Kittermaster, dined with me Saturday. Irene has odious American friend Mrs Harrison.

Coronation Sunday interminable service, 6.30–12.30. Ritual made ludicrous by cinema operators.

Addis Ababa, Monday 3 November 1930

Got up 7, went to Catholic church, island sanity in raving town. Returned, sacked my servants. Went to old palace, find Sandford who is distributing news of HRH. He said all asleep, no knowing what time would lay wreath Menelik's[1] tomb. Went to Hall and said I wanted to get into *gebbur*.[2] Said come back later. Went to hotel, got bill £20 odd. Went to mausoleum, hideous building, half-Byzantine. Went to Hall who I found with Balatingeta – just appointed Minister for the Press, after coronation! Sandford, complaining bad information, gave as example that if he now asked numbers troops reviewed following Friday, Balatingeta would not be able to tell him. Balatingeta had not so much as heard that there was a review of troops. Sandford giving both hell because Sir Percival Phillips's[3] wires had been held up. I said all right, will report spectacle disgusting barbarity. Cashed £25 cheques at bank, visited picture-dealer who had promised collect pictures for me. He had done nothing about it. Returned hotel, drank with airmen. Met Polish attaché whose driver had brought him to wrong address. Lunched. Wrote description barbarous *gebbur*. Went out to see what I could barbarous *gebbur*. 3.30 no signs barbarity. Changed, went to garden party American Legation. Went off with Professor Whittemore[4] to see church Haile Selassie, circular, thatched, painting inside ambulatory, outside oilcloth, exterior Turkish designs painted, fluted pillars. Sun set so rapidly unable see much. Went to shop and bought pictures of castration in battle; returned hotel, taxi-driver charged 18 thalers. Wrangle. Lost.

Irene returned greatest consternation; Mrs Harrison not invited British Legation reception. Long chat with drinks: 'What is my duty? After all Evelyn, you may think it's nothing but I *am* Daddy's daughter.[5] I *am* Baroness

---

[1] Emperor's.

[2] Feast.

[3] Ubiquitous foreign correspondent (born Brownsville, Pennsylavania, 1877: died 1937), and presumably the model for 'Sir Jocelyn Hitchcock' in *Scoop*. Covered Spanish–American War, 1898; revolution in China, 1927, etc.; *Daily Express*, 1901–22; special correspondent *Daily Mail*, 1922–34.

[4] Professor Thomas Whittemore, celebrated American ecclesiologist; he restored some of the mosaics in S. Sophia.

[5] Baroness Ravensdale's father was Lord Curzon, the statesman; his title of Baron Ravensdale devolved by special remainder on his daughter.

Ravensdale.' Later caught by Mrs Harrison: 'It's not myself I'm thinking of, Mr Waugh, it's Irene's dignity. She must *not* accept the so-called Lady Barton's invitation.' Parks American secretary dined with us. Proceeded reception Italian Legation. Europeans present enjoying fireworks, HRH in bar. Great upset Europeans distribution honours. Barton Star Ethiopia first class. Everyone else something better.

Tuesday 4 November 1930

Slept until 9, went to grandstand to see procession. Shown seats reserved for Press, consisted balcony immediately behind diplomatic tent no view of road. Sinclair sent me across with his bandmaster to the balcony of his hotel where I got an excellent view. Procession late, boring. Returned luncheon hotel. Went out to look at churches with Whittemore. Bloodthirsty frescoes martyrdoms. Wrote report procession; dozed; saw journalists. Charles Drage came in to have his hair cut. Cable arrived from *Express*: 'Coronation cable hopelessly late beaten every paper London.' Dined Charles Drage, went to bed early, others went out to Haile Selassie nightclub.

Wednesday 5 November 1930

Race meeting. Went with Irene and Mrs Harrison. Lunched with Troutbecks. Totalizator that gave 1–3 odds on all races. Prince Udine gave vast plated cup, Emperor astonishing object said to be for champagne. Great talk that the French Legation had not sold a single sweepstake ticket. No club spirit, etc. Went to party French Legation, very squalid and boring, after frenzied argument with American cinema photographer in which we all lost our temper in defence of royalty.

Thursday 6 November 1930

Slept late. Panic that Phillips had been allowed to use Legation wireless. Dispelled by note from Troutbeck. Read *Times* at bank. Invited dine by mayor of town but refused. English Legation reception. Talked Abyssinian politics most evening. Charles Drage pursuing Irene. Maffy [?] gets low order – Ethiopian. Noble [?] gets Selassie. Minister attempts affability. Somali dancers. Returned to find party going on in *tukal*[1] behind my bedroom.

Friday 7 November 1930

Slept well, went to see review of troops in plain near station, everything very late. Irene and Mrs Harrison entranced some troops we had seen everywhere. Slept afternoon. Great flea scandal started. English papers have published that Gebbi full of fleas and that Duke's cook gave notice before hunting expedition.

[1] Hut.

Had arranged meet Phillips and dinner at Casino Haile Selassie. Went there at
10. My taxi-driver laughed when I asked for the *carte de tarif* so I paid him
nothing at all. Sat down at table and ordered café cognac. Man like Nigel
Millett came and asked for 5 thalers entrance. At intervals European tarts
appeared in shawls and strode across stage. 10.30 I went away. Paid no more.
Walked home. Charles again took Irene out to dinner.

Saturday 8 November 1930

Went with Irene to see the new museum. The best-organized thing they
have done so far. Good guides. Irene riding-breeches, I in flannel suit. Came
back and at 12 received invitations luncheon palace. Changed into morning
coat and proceeded palace. Luncheon party rag, tag and bobtail of Addis.
American cinema men in green suits. French journalists in dinner-jackets.
Contractors, schoolmasters, missionaries. I sat between a photographer and a
British Flying Officer. Irene was put next to the Emperor and was translated
with excitement. Coming back she said, 'That has shown all those Bartons. I
have come out on top. I am Baroness Ravensdale in my own right.' Also:
'There was an idiotic woman on the other side who talked in platitudes. I knew
the Emperor wanted to talk to me. I was terrified, Evelyn, quite cold inside, but
I knew I had to find new subjects for him – new angles that would be of interest.
I saw everyone's eyes on me looking to see whether I was making a success of it.
Something outside me, greater than myself, came to my aid. Each time I was
able to find something original and appropriate to say.' I think I must be a prig,
people do shock me so. Another woman who shocked me was a Syrian Jewess
who at the end of luncheon strode forward and recited a long ode in Arabic – a
language unintelligible to His Imperial Majesty. This was apparently quite
unrehearsed and uninvited. The photographer next to me thought it was
*I*talian.

A man came to the hotel selling an enamelled *pot de chambre* and some
bootlaces.

Sunday 9 November 1930

Mass at the French church at 8 o'clock. D'Esperez the only other European
there. Black barefooted priests and black acolytes. 9 o'clock: set out with Irene
and Mrs Harrison to Jenjen [?] by car. The road as far as Addis Alem rather
boring. Derelict stable of Menelik. Three soldiers at Jenjen tried to get tips.
Picnic luncheons Irene Fortnum & Mason hamper. Set out to try and find
black and white monkeys, and walked in forest and blazing heat carrying
camera. Saw no monkeys. Lights of car broke. Borrowed bulb from other car at
Haile's nightclub. Most delegations left Addis.

Monday 10 November 1930

Set out at 6 with Whittemore for Debra Lebanos.[1] Empty bottles for holy water. Wonderful morning. Straight up Entoto then across plain broken many watercourses. Passed caravan donkeys carrying skins. Lunched about 11. Whittemore nibbled cheese. I ate meat and drank beer. Later, quite unbroken plain grazing land. Repeatedly lost way. Very able native boy sat on running board. Whittemore bowing to cowherds. About 2, suddenly came on deep ravine, river at bottom. Descended precipitous path volcanic boulders surrounded naked boys covered sores also baboons. Whittemore still bowing. Eventually semi-circle of ledge, some mud huts, one two stone houses and a church or two. Greeted fine bearded monk yellow sunshade unable read. Chauffeur went in search Abuna.[2] Sat in shade near church. Monk wrote on his hand fine script. W. pointed to letter like cross and crossed himself. Monk mystified. Led to Abuna, brown cloak, white turban, black umbrella, fly-whisk, led to square stone house. Waited. Crowd assembled. Half-hour let in. Pitch dark. Small windows high up hung sacking. Only light door. Twelve priests assembled; two stools covered rugs. Abuna read aloud letter of commendation. Grunts approval. Courteous chat via chauffeur. Books produced wrapped pretty shawls from whitewood cupboard. First two ghastly German prints stuck hinged boards. Later, illuminated MSS. All modern. Then taken to see sacred springs up hillside. Coffins – old packing cases or hollowed trunks – scattered under overhanging cliff. Holy water conveyed douche rusty pipes. Separate best room Menelik. Little hut Empress. Offered us hut full of goats, hornets. Said preferred tent; accordingly pitched; floor hay, covered rugs. Abuna supervised preparations. Should he kill goat, sheep or calf? No. Honey. Sat in tent. Native bread, beer, honey brought in, held for our inspection: all disgusting. Abuna sat down. Feared going share dinner. At last left. Ate from hamper. Little lamp hung on tent pole. Abuna came say goodnight, dusted Keating's[3] off rugs. Monk with rifle slept outside. Ghastly cold night. Little sleep. W. snored. Chauffeur took some honey and beer.

Tuesday 11 November 1930

Awoke dawn, ate corned beef, beer. Guard took honey and beer. Bible-reading in church, several at once. Seven thalers uncovered frescoes: vivid modern: rider saints on one wall, passion the other, childhood another. Pictures Ras Kassa, Tafari, etc., presumably done from photographs. Holy of Holies contained fumed oak tabor, old clothes, dust, umbrellas, suitcase, teapot, slop pail, hopeless confusion. Small shrine, prettier tabor containing cross that fell

---

[1] Debra Lebanos Monastery, and the centre of Abyssinian spiritual life; famous for its antique and sacred library.

[2] The Patriarch.

[3] Flea powder.

from heaven. Walked to look for baboons. Saw two. Rested. Guard came and examined everything, particularly clothes. 1 o'clock Mass. W. kissed everything, knew nothing. White gold vestments. Given carpet stand on 2.30 left. W. distributed half piastres. Walked up hill. Car ride began 3. Dark 6. Arrived Addis 11. Repeatedly lost way. W. lost head. Bivouacs all over plain. Ascent and descent Entoto perilous. Driver imperturbable. W.: '*J'ai décidé. Nous arrêtons ici.*' Driver: '*Ça n'est pas d'importance.*' Foxes, rabbits. Car called Rugby.

Wednesday 12 November 1930

Slept till 11. Chatted Irene. Slept. Dined Wright's bank. Got in rage with Cook's tout named Bertelli over Church.

Thursday 13 November 1930

Parks, secretary American Legation, dined with me. Talked of religion; very charming and quite different from the impressions I had formed of him.

Friday 14 November 1930

Lunched American minister. Excellent food, corn on the cob and *foie gras*. Slept after luncheon. Paid a few farewell visits. Packed.

Saturday 15 November 1930

Train left Addis 10. Large crowd on platform. Carriage with Chapman-Andrews, Major Cheesman, Plowman. Agreeable journey. Lunched with Irene on tinned food. She had read Mrs H.'s letter over her shoulder, describing her as 'crazy and selfish'. Very cold sleepless night.

Dirre-Dowa, Sunday 16 November 1930

Arrived Dirre-Dowa at dawn. Breakfast at Bollolakos'.[1] Saw off Irene and said goodbyes to everyone. Bath and shave. Went to Mass. Nosy French children. Incomprehensible sermon by priest with huge white beard. Came back and slept. Lunched with Plowman's governess and odious children. Slept. Tea with Plowman's governess and odious children. Went for stroll in town. Quite unremarkable. Plowman's horses had not turned up. I am going on without them tomorrow to Harar. Deformed beggars like spiders. Plowman shocked idea my not bringing dinner-jacket to Harar. Dinner. Mr Hall, half-caste Abyssinian, married to English old maid who fell in love with him when he was a prisoner of war. She wore large brooch presented to her father when Lord Mayor of London on the opening of Epping Forest. Hall no nationality. Also a Cypriot bank clerk. Hall admired Harry Lauder records because he could understand them.

[1] Hotel.

Haramaya, Monday 17 November 1930

Left Dirre-Dowa at 7 for Harar. Arrived Haramaya at 3. Very tiring. First river bed, then mountain with scrub. Other side of mountain rudely cultivated. Villages with lanes bordered flowering red and yellow cactus. Fine herds oxen. Stopped at native pub. It had been closed by order of the Emperor to prevent competition Haramaya. I took great dislike to my boys and sacked one at Haramaya. This whitewashed rest house side of lake thick every sort waterfowl. Delightful youth – Greek – manager, for uncle. Gave us good luncheon. French bank clerk also on way to Harar on leave lunched with me and advised Dar-es-Salaam–West Africa rail journey. I passed on road Plowman's smart ponies but want to make humble entry into Harar. Road full of caravan traffic, camels and mules. Slept afternoon. Room without glass windows – hospital cot. Dined with manager. When he wished to leave he said, 'You can't permit me.' He had been brought up in Alexandria. He is having an *affaire* with an Abyssinian lady of high rank who sent three soldiers to fetch him. He gave them three cigarettes while they waited.

Harar, Tuesday 18 November 1930

Journey to Harar very simple. Three hours grass downs. Much traffic on road, camels, mules and foot. Arrived at Harar at 12. Outlying villas, a church, Lej Yasu's[1] empty palace. Town approached from Haramaya seems in a hollow, but from Burton's side[2] on a hill. Rough stone walls. Market outside gates; gate decorated with flimsy triumphal arch entered through narrow tracks and high walls. Many ruinous houses, goats, poultry, etc. Broader street. Golden Lion Hotel. Armenian, fat, black skull-cap, seized my bridle. I came in and found the French bank clerk. Ate fair luncheon which gave me pain. Clean room ground floor built round garden courtyard. Hard pillow; rested. Went for walk in town with boy. Saw leper colony. Very cordial priest doctor. Little huts (because it takes several lepers to make a complete man). Catholic church. Crazy Capucin bishop greeted me with blessing. Sat on his divan and asked about Rimbaud. 'Very serious. Led a retired life. His wife left the town after his death probably for Tigre.' Returned hotel. Armenian took me and bank clerk to see a Greek grocer and went to Abyssinian musical party palace. Important guests because we brought an Aladdin lamp. Large empty room. Altar to Emperor, enlarged photograph over table, embroidered plush cloth. Green garden chairs. We sat here and drank whisky and soda. About fifty drunk Abyssinians sat on floor; already had *gebbur* and drunk bottled beer. Fat Abyssinian woman sang breathlessly patriotic songs about Haile Selassie, also complimentary references to notables. Accompanied three one-stringed

---

[1] Lej Yasu was the grandson (deposed in 1916) of Menelik II.
[2] The side described by the explorer Richard Burton (1821–90).

violins. Host very charming. We then said we must go. This signal for appearance of champagne and sponge fingers. Three other Abyssinians invited to join us in this. Complimentary speeches translated French-Amharic. Dined hotel. After dinner, Armenian and another Armenian haberdasher and French clerk went to a Harar wedding. Two parties. One bride's house, other bridegroom's. Bridegroom by far the richer. Raised dais on two sides room. Dancers – two men, covered mouths; one girl, covered head – shuffled up and down, sometimes tripped over. Girls of singular beauty crowded together singing. Drums. Clapping. Bridegroom's party, some streets away, similar but grander. Incense burned. Sacks of coffee on shelf, coloured basketwork hanging round walls. Armenian took revolver, also club. Boy and policeman. Party fled at sight of policeman because forbidden. Streets completely dead, completely empty. Doors shut sunset. Hyenas came in through watercourse.

Wednesday 19 November 1930

Armenian and his haberdasher friend took me for walk. Saw Arab drawing map, mouth green with *khat*. Went into palace and saw lion in minute hutch; frightful smell. Went into prison. Cells round a courtyard. Five or six in each cell. Chains, diseased. Went into three or four tedj[1] houses. Brothels. Red cross over doors. Ugly women. Saw exquisitely beautiful girls making basketwork tables and trays. Went into houses, looked at larders and kitchens, pinching girls and tasting food. Into all the Armenian shops. Lunched at the hotel. Gave me a pain. Went on by mule to the Plowmans. A large, attractive house, three storeys. Large drawing-room, thick pillars, good garden, glass in windows, Bronco in lavatory, all the Book Society selections for the last year. I was given a fine, three-roomed tent on the lawn. Three children a baboon called Grenadé. Three dogs. Numerous ponies and servants. I read Burton's *First Steps in Africa* and slept well.

Thursday 20 November 1930

Read Douglas Jardine's *Mad Mullah* all morning. Went with Plowman to attend Abyssinian party in palace. All sat down long table and drank *tedj* and champagne. Returned sundown. Whisky. Talked about painting.

Friday 21 November 1930

Went into town to see my Armenian who had promised me a *gebbur*, but since it was Friday that was clearly impossible. However it was the feast of St Michael and we went to church and saw procession round outer ambulatory. First, four acolytes (deacons, I suppose) walking backwards, one carrying cross, another a taper, another print of St Michael, another censer. Three

[1] Local drink made from honey.

others facing the one with censer. Ten dancing deacons with praying sticks and rattles swaying and singing. Two big drums, one at each end after vested priests. Deacons carrying cross, etc. Vast crowds. Crowds of slaves sitting on steps all round and Galla in rags squatting on the grass outside. One woman with no face. Her whole scalp had slipped sideways. Ugly.

Haramaya, Saturday 22 November 1930

Left Harar after luncheon riding consulate pony sent to meet Charles Barton. Rubbed my knees quite raw. Arrived Haramaya about 5.30. Nothing to do. Rather cold and disconsolate. 6.30 the Greek (Naxiŏte) proprietor arrived. He said now we will make the cocktail. Took large glass, added whisky, *crème de menthe* and an Italian tonic wine with quinine in it and soda. I felt a little better. We dined together and drank a lot. Slept badly. Blue birds.

Dirre-Dowa, Sunday 23 November 1930

Started at 7 am. This time I rode mule and arrived after uneventful but boring journey at 1.30. Found my train was on Tuesday morning not Sunday evening and therefore probably missed boat at Djibouti. Rearranged my luggage, rested, had warm bath, etc. Halls turned up for dinner. H. very boastful and pro-English. Mrs H. crazy and quite amusing. H: 'It is a great thing for my wife to meet an English gentleman.' Hall trying tell me he was an artist not a businessman. Went to his home after dinner. Picture King George on easel. Awful pastels by Hall. Hall admired [?] General Gordon, Sir George Newnes. Said he was on to valuable platinum concession. Said German farmer Addis humbug. Said his brother's wife jealous of his wife's jewellery. Lent me *John O'London's Weekly*.

Monday 24 November 1930

Cashed cheque at bank. In the evening Charles Barton arrived and the ugliest Miss Barton.

Djibouti, Tuesday 25 November 1930

Miss Barton and I left by train 7 o'clock. Rudely turned out of only comfortable carriage to make room for the tipsy servants of an Abyssinian princess. Throughout journey they threw bottles on to the line. Dirre-Dowa–Djibouti unparalleled desolation. Lunched buffet. In sight of Djibouti saw *General Voyson* still in harbour. She sailed just as we arrived. Went to hotel and saw Lowe the consul – stupid youth.

Wednesday 26 November 1930

Lowe said no boat leaving for Aden before Saturday. Italian boat due to leave that day. Spent day waiting for ship which eventually did not come.

Princess bought gong in store, green veil, also kimono. Evening went into native brothel with Movietone man and saw a little dance. One of most boring days of my life.

Djibouti–Aden, Thursday 27 November 1930

Ship arrived about 8. Was awake at dawn feeling ill. Vast bill at hotel, 325 francs largely the ugly Miss Barton's drinks. Ship named *Somalia*. Italian Transatlantic line. Never goes near Atlantic. Clean cabins. Bathroom. Four or five first-class cabins. Cargo sacks and skins. *Somalia* did not start until 4. Slept a little. Bored. Three other passengers: a French business agent, and a newly married Italian official and very pretty wife. Dined with captain. They talked Italian mostly.

Aden, Friday 28 November 1930

Arrived Aden about 7. Rocks and bungalows. Went to Hôtel de l'Europe, washed, and had breakfast. Left card Residency and visited airman who showed me interesting photographs of Arabia and map explaining politics. Saw Champion, political officer, who gave me permission to visit Mukalla. Received invitation dinner Residency. Met Welsh shipper (Pedder and Co.) and drank a lot of wine with him. Slept a little, dressed, and went to club. Nice terrace. Kind soldier invited me to drink – drank a great deal. Dined Residency. Symes most agreeable, wants Aden advertised. Played Wagner gramophone half-light. ADC Jackson, Mr Besse[1] shipowner, Champion and wife, a Miss Messiter. Drank too much. Came back and found Welsh shipper again. Drank more and he told me about Canon Braidie of Buenos Aires. It is nice to be on English ground again. Good laundry.

Saturday 29 November 1930

Visited Besse and arranged ship to Mukalla. He asked me to dinner. Lunched Residency. Symes wants advertisement and asked me to give up Mukalla and study his policy in the Protectorate. Consented. He lent me maps and texts of all his dispatches and several books. Vachell and Eccles dined with me at the club. Dance; election ballot boxes; bad dinner; champagne. Everyone drinks a great deal.

Sunday 30 November 1930

Went to Mass. Church full of Goanese. Wrote article on Abyssinian politics. Read books and paper of Symes. Dined Besse on roof. Two of his clerks present. Good dinner. Clever man. Lent me Gide's *Voyage au Congo*. Sent car for me. Proud of being rich. Disapproved alcohol.

---

[1] Millionaire merchant; founder of St Antony's College, Oxford, after the Second World War. See Appendix of Names, p. 794.

Monday 1 December 1930

Did not leave hotel all day. Read books and papers and made notes. Great lethargy.

Tuesday 2 December 1930

Wired *Times* asking if they were interested Lahej conference. Visited Champion who was very helpful and polite. Put me in touch with an interpreter. Afternoon visited Crater with interpreter. Took me to his club where they reclined and ate *khat*, then to public house where poorer Arabs were similarly employed. 'These poor people have their simple pleasures too,' said interpreter. Greatly struck variety of race and costume. Jews, bedouin, etc. Through lethargy fell into hands of my taxi-driver who drove me to Sheik Othman [?] boring. Then to a fair where I broke the bank at simple card game. Two to one odds on five to once chance. Saw dancers. Returned, bought two gold pounds [?] and dressed for Residency ball. Residency dance about 150 people; no male predominance; all ranks represented. Played bridge with a Protestant chaplain, Mr Ball, Blunt and Vachell. Ball asked me to stay.

Wednesday 3 December 1930

Lunch at Residency. Arranged to go by *Grandidier* on 10th after all. Talked politics with Resident. Evening met drunk, sex-crazed airman and got drunk with him. He kept saying how often he had had venereal disease and what a good athlete he was notwithstanding. There was a model dhow in his bungalow. His bathroom had '3d per call' on it. He assured me this came from 'the Troc'.[1] I think he had great respect for purity. A man turned out the lights because we were keeping him awake.

Thursday 4 December 1930

Woke feeling like death. Saw Champion and Lake, political officer. Arranged passage with *messageries*. Lunched at mess with Tapp, a gunner. Ball picked me up and took me to his house, large and ramshackle. Went to see a parade of Boy Scouts. One smart troop of Jews. Others Persian, Somali, Indian, Arab. Arranging examinations Scout law. Cooking meat on fires. Dined with Vachell, a sailor called Sinker, and a new airman called Harrison. Talked about courage. Went to cinema roof of Sailors' Institute. Everyone went to sleep and quite unable follow story. Saw Pathé Gazette of King leaving for Bognor Regis twenty months ago. Appalling English film *The Woman Who Did*. Went to club and drank beer. Met odious drink tradesman. Slept well.

Friday 5 December 1930

Padre Ball talked rot about India. He is a very kind, stupid man believing

[1] The Trocadero restaurant in London.

deeply in world brotherhood. Dined mess Willcox disgusting dinner. Went on to sapper dance but didn't stay long.

Saturday 6 December 1930

Went to Khormaksear and flew with Vachell 7 am. First drill, then we turned off and went up towards Dhamar but in barren hill country we found too many low clouds and had to go back. Excellent breakfast mess. Lunched with Maine, one of Besse's clerks at his hotel, Milner-Barry, a young man in Shell, and two other clerks. After luncheon we went for what Mr B. called a little walk in the hills. Luckily I had rubber-soled shoes, otherwise climb absolutely impossible. We drove to tanks,[1] then Besse gave a lithe skip and swarmed straight up a perpendicular cliff. Later loose stones. 'It is better to press with the feet than pull with the hands.' Very tired and scared for first half-hour, later got accustomed to it. We were bare to waist and very much scratched and bruised. Crossed crater, climbed another cliff, walked along edge, and then down over red-hot rocks. Then long walk on loose cinders to sea, where servants were awaiting us with towels and tea. Bathed in a warm, shark-infested bay. Drove back at great speed. Besse had change of clothes. Wore rimless pince-nez driving. Returned to Pedder, had warm bath. He came in full of having fallen in love with a Papist lady doctor. Dined Besse and his mistress and clerks. Excellent dinner and wine. Bed early, slept well. Gave Ball an Abyssinian picture of St Paul preaching at Athens.

Sunday 7 December 1930

Went to Mass at Crater. Turned out to be a concert odious Arab girls' mission school. After three-quarters of an hour we had reached epistle so went out. Met Ball, saw his church. Pretty Gothic building. Ball laments total absence congregation. Breakfast at the bank. Met Lake 10 o'clock with lorry and drove to Lahej camp.[2] Just as we arrived large square tent erected for Durbar collapsed. Lunched in camp with nice Irish soldier. Common colonel arrived later. Dozed in chair.

Rode camel into Lahej. Found resthouse, fairly clean but shabby. Two German engineers lived there two years doing odd jobs for sultan. One German fluent but very unintelligible English. Walked round town. Shower under little tap in petrol tin. Bad dinner, nothing to drink. Lights failed sometimes.

Monday 8 December 1930

Went for walk with shouting mechanic.[3] Interview with Sultan. Drank

---

[1] Reservoirs.

[2] Where the British Resident was holding a Durbar to coincide with a gathering of the Sultan of Lahej's tributary chiefs.

[3] One of the Sultan's two resident German engineers.

excellent coffee. H.H. wore turban, black overcoat, white linen trousers, patent leather shoes. Conversation no interest owing to shouting mechanic's bad interpretation. Went to see Sultan Achmed Fadl, H.H.'s brother. Haus Habi Sultan there. Mad. Achmed Fadl showed me ms. of his history of Lahej. He took me for drive in car. Plumes on hood. Armed guard. Everyone kissed Achmed Fadl's knees. He wore grey overcoat, grey veil, white shorts, khaki stockings, black and white shoes. He gave me honey and flowers. Pretty garden. Trees and water. Slept. Lake and Richards visited me. Went to camp for drinks. After bad dinner, shouting mechanic showed me photographs. He and friend left Dresden age nineteen, worked their way doing odd jobs Greece, Spain, Abyssinia, etc., on way to India. Make dams, palace WCs, mend stranded taxis and tractors, etc. Two years Lahej.

Tuesday 9 December 1930

Before breakfast drove to see shouting mechanic's dam, mended pump and plough. Back. Developed rash. Very irritable. Thought it was sandflies. Shaved. Changed white suit. Went to palace. Chiefs all assembled looking like carpet sellers. Some barefooted, all rather awkward. Fine dagger hilts protruding from bellies. Sultan of Ad Dali [?], beautiful child ten, eyes painted with indigo (the best part of his territory still in Zaydi hands). 11, Resident arrived. Chiefs announced one by one and greeted. Sat round. Resident made excellent speech. Translated. Lahej made speech. Sat about till luncheon. Meal of many courses. Asparagus and onion sauce, lemon squash to drink. Only Lahej and Prime Minister present. More chat after luncheon. 2.30 Resident drove away. I went with Reilly. Had tea with him. Went up and drank with Resident and talked Arabian politics. Parson came to dinner bringing Bryce Bennet [?] who asked for article again for Scout magazine. Went to call on odious people called Bethel.

Aden–Mombasa, Wednesday 10 December 1930

Ship came in 6. Went aboard 9. Made porter do transit free. Odious people at table. Excellent cabin but shared Frenchman.

A fairly agreeable voyage to Mombasa; calm seas with flying fish; warm but not too hot. A lovely American Kiki Preston who never rises before dinner. A plump English girl, student of biology, on her way to marry a man twenty years older. Mind fully occupied with contraceptions. Her mother. A redheaded girl. A good-looking clerk in Shell called Smith. In second class a Turk and an Englishman called Wilwood.

English Club, Zanzibar, Monday 22 December 1930

Last week we reached Mombasa at sunset. I went ashore with a Shell Oil agent named Smith and dined at the club. Good dinner. Saw nothing of

Mombasa except green – the first for months – and a good harbour.

On Tuesday at sunset we reached Zanzibar. Passport inspectors suspicious of bona fides. Ekrem Bey the Turk at Hotel Africa. Awful hotel. Declined letter introduction to a Captain O'Morghal who turned out to be one of the suspicious passport officers. He got me rooms at club. During the last six days I have been too hot to take much pleasure in the town. I have seen more than I wanted of Mohammed Ekrem Bey. Sultan's acting secretary has been amiable. There is a good library and I have spent most of the time reading. No one knows much about local politics or history. Everyone very placid. Yesterday went to Mass. Lunched Resident but women were present so could not talk of anything interesting. Tea at Arab country home. Old furniture, flowers, tea and biscuits and ginger. Ekrem will talk about women all the time. I think he is collecting money for the Kalif. He expects to return to Constantinople. Zanzibar convenient in closeness of all buildings. Surprisingly clean. Large Arab houses supposed by tourists to be of great antiquity actually seventeenth-eighteenth centuries. Amiable Papist archaeologist named Doctor Spanier. Vast numbers Indians. Bought suits and shirt and pyjamas. Wired for money but have received no reply so far. Setting out this evening for Pemba, returning Christmas Day.

Left 10 o'clock evening little steamship called *Halifa*. Trader called Grazebrook dined with me first and gave me champagne. Two other Europeans in ship. Arrived dawn Mkoani green hillside, well-designed bungalows by architect Harris. Chief man on island called James. He drove me to Weti but very sleepy. Stopped several times on way to talk to people. Slept afternoon (lunched with fat people called Murray with three gross daughters). Then went to call delightful doctor and wife called Semple. Dined there on lawn under electric light and they returned to ship with us, Mrs S. and French chum in smart pyjamas.

Friday 26 December 1930

Next day sailed to port for Chake. Bathed delightful couple called Poncian. Dined three tipsy bachelors, who fought over the distribution of Christmas presents to children. Next day stopped early morning Mkoani and sailed for Zanzibar. Met by invitation to dinner with nice lawyer. Also money from England. No mail. Excellent dinner. Caviare, turkey, etc., champagne. Before dinner went to Benediction, rather long. Ekrem Bey came after me again. He is bored. Pemba: good roads, rich clove forests, coconuts. Agreeable people, e.g. harbour clerk got me chair to sit on while waiting for a lorry to take me to Chake. Indian dishonesty in mortgages.

Zanzibar–Dar-es-Salaam, Monday 29 December 1930

Left Zanzibar in a large Italian ship *Mazzini* travelling second class as she is quite empty. The last days at Zanzibar chiefly occupied with the mail which arrived in bits during Saturday and Sunday. Mostly letters of congratulation or vilification about my having become a Papist. Religious controversy seems the occupation of the lowest minds nowadays. This ship is full of small black beetles. An English woman (who with her husband are doing the round trip, the first sight of the sea since they landed eleven years ago. He is a maker of bricks) told me that she was savagely stung by one but I don't believe that. We stopped at Dar-es-Salaam where I bought a *Pears Encyclopaedia* and two novels by Edgar Wallace. There is a war memorial – pugnacious black man with inscription, 'If you fight for your country, even if you die, your sons will remember your name.' Altar in Catholic church given by Kaiser. His arms obliterated. Hot in ship. Brickmaker has pain. Cinema, *Tarzan*, in the evening.

Tuesday 30 December 1930

Left Dar-es-Salaam.

Mombasa–Nairobi, Wednesday 31 December 1930

Arrived at Mombasa early morning. Immigration clerk made me pay £50 before I was allowed to land. This wasted a great deal of time, but I was able to cause him some inconvenience later in the day by making him do two more journeys to Kilindini and back. I called on the Apostolic Legate, Archbishop Hinsley, a very agreeable man with an admirably informed chaplain. Together they gave me a great deal of assistance in arranging my journey across the Congo. Lunched at the club with Smith and spent afternoon reading paper. 4.30 train left for Nairobi. Second class. Clean and quite comfortable *couchettes*; two fellow-travellers in carriage – a Belgian and a Scotsman. Dined with young lady on her way to be married. She said she had been a clerk at Scotland Yard for four years and that that had coarsened her mind a lot, but she had worked in a bank at Dar-es-Salaam and that had refined it again.

Nairobi, Thursday 1 January 1931

Train hour and a half late at Nairobi owing to three derailments. Very cool morning. Changed into flannels. Great luxury not to sweat. Drove straight to Muthaiga,[1] lot of toughs round the bar. No bedroom for me, but made member. Returned and took room at Torr's Hotel. Large and modern with many similarities to a good European hotel. Slept in the afternoon and went later to a pantomime given by amateurs: *Babes in the Wood*, full of local jokes and local patriotism. People behind said 'Dem good bay jove' and clapped their hands. Nairobi architecture surprisingly good, but rendered insignificant by great breadth of streets. Taxis very expensive. Muthaiga 10s, Government House 6s.

[1] Muthaiga Club.

Friday 2 January 1931

Out to Muthaiga where met Raymond de Trafford,[1] the Prestons, Gerard de Crespigny and others. Lunched with them. Everyone drank about ten pink gins before lunch. Went to races. Bookies didn't want ready money. Barman didn't want ready money. Backed one winner but down on the day. Raymond had party in evening. Hideous Diana Guest. Continual flow champagne.

Saturday 3 January 1931

Interviewed Indian leaders in the morning. Stupid men. Mr Varma particularly disagreeable. Lunch Muthaiga, Raymond. Races. Tea in Governor's box and watched races from there. Back to Muthaiga, drank champagne with Boy Long. Met Lady Delamere[2] who asked me to stay. Brawl in bar at Torr's. Dinner party Major Grogan; hideous Miss Guest; lovely Miss Buxton.

Naivasha, Sunday 4 January 1931

Mass 8.30. Goanese choir. Lunched at Muthaiga, Raymond, etc. Went with young architect called Hooktip (I think) to look at houses he was building. Saw aeroplanes. Went picnic from Government House into the game reserve to a place called Lone Tree, made a camp fire and most of us fell asleep. Saw herds of zebra, wildebeeste, etc. Little jumping creatures like kangaroos, hyenas, etc. eyes lit up as they awoke like windows of house. Wildebeestes' seem to stand out from their heads like green globes.

Next day Jan 5th went with Raymond to stay with Prestons. Arrived very late for luncheon. Gerard de Crespigny staying there, one-storeyed very luxurious house on edge of Lake Naivasha; delicious food. Went to bed early. Canapés [?] with cocktails like Ritz. Duck shot on lake. Fish caught in lake.

Tuesday 6 January 1931

Bathed in the morning, slept after lunch, went for drive looking for game with Gerry Preston and saw many waterbuck. Got very drunk in the evening.

Njoro, Wednesday 7 January 1931

Bathed before breakfast. Left Kiki after luncheon. She and Gerry de Crespigny setting out on safari. Drove to Raymond's house; incomplete; good furniture, books, etc. Dined at club. Early bed.

Stayed with Raymond Wednesday, Thursday, Friday, Saturday. Dined Friday night with neighbours named Grant and agreed to go on safari with them next week up a volcano. Lady Denman, who is here on birth control, and

[1] Ex-Coldstream Guards officer; son of Sir Humphrey de Trafford, the 3rd bart.
[2] Wife of 3rd Baron Delamere; later she became Mayor of Nairobi.

a nasty couple, Mr and Mrs Oliver Baring. Got very drunk most nights and talked about church. Saturday had meant to go and stay with Longs but telegram miscarried so came back and got tight. Boy called Dunston excellent servant. Met Lancing boy with brick-red face and pale pink suit. Bought large hat.

Sunday 11 January 1931

Long's brother Charles – very oppressed man – came to fetch me in car. Telegram had taken twenty-three hours to travel eleven miles. Arrived Elmenteita before luncheon. Three houses on top of hill, magnificent view over lake of flamingos forest and hills. Judy Denman[1] – red-faced cream-drinking girl in unbecoming trousers. Emaciated guardsman Charles Harford in love with her. Two bores, one knew Alec, who had come to buy cattle. Genessie Long well dressed. Went to lake and saw hippo. Harford shot duck which disappeared. Rose before breakfast next day. Most of party left. I now discovered that Delameres expected me at Nairobi not Elmenteita so I gave up visit. Drove over farm. Ayrshire cattle with monkeys playing among them. Bush fires. Raymond had arranged to meet me on Tuesday afternoon to take me to dinner Grants but did not come so I took a taxi from Nakura. Grants said safari off. Slept Raymond.

Wednesday 14 January 1931

Grants took me out for a picnic. Denmans and Barings too. Went to call on Sylvia Wilson in house with lovely garden and drank sherry. V. uncomfortable drive. Lady D. fished in lovely stream where I was stung by nettles. Caught nothing. Returned to find Raymond arrived. He got very drunk and brought a sluttish girl back to the house. He woke me up later in night to tell me had just rogered her and her mama too.

Kisumu, Friday 16 January 1931

Left Njoro having arranged meet Denmans and Grant at Kisumu. Went by train to K. Met ginger-bearded man in carriage – Irvine – who asked me to stay. Drove miles to his brother-in-law's house, clipped hedge cypresses. Then to his house. Arrived dark. Furious mother-in-law. 'Belinda's hindquarters totally paralysed.'[2] Swarm of bees in drawer. Ants on floor. Grey and scarlet parrot imitating Belinda's groans. Next day road surveyor drove us about talking culverts; bridge being constructed by small boy in gumboots. Left by afternoon train. Arrived Kisumu dark. Hotel proprietor let me share room with Imperial Airways young man.

[1] Daughter of the 3rd baron Denman, a former governor-general of Australia; her mother was a daughter of the 1st Viscount Cowdray.

[2] Belinda was a wolfhound bitch.

Jinja, Uganda, Sunday 18 January 1931

Drove round Kisumu. Negligible bungaloid mess. Waited until 3.30 for Denmans due at 12. Lunched at hotel and drove to stay with people named Swinton Home [?]. Small English country house with dressing-room, frilled dressing-table, white muslin behind washstand with pink bows. Family portraits, old silver, etc. Next day drove to Jinja. No room at hotel but slept in rest house. Met Raymond's lorry which had lost him. Took his blanket. Saw source of Nile and heard hippo. Good big-game talk in bar. 'Woman scalped by rhino, etc..' 'Buffalo don't put their head down till they're on you. After that aim at spine. Difficult shot.'

Kampala, Wednesday 21 January 1931

Father Janssen bearded Dutch priest in gaiters came to call. I drove with him to cathedral – not beautiful – and saw his own church he built himself and can't pay for, imitation carved wood in cement, etc. Heard his troubles with the Goanese. Went to hospital to visit venereal Catholics. He dined with me and put his leg out of joint. Other visitors – the editor of the *Uganda Herald* wanting an interview and a Motorways agent wanting me to pay £60 to go to Albertville.

Thursday 22 January 1931

Drove with Father Janssen to a convent of negresses. They train wives to be European in one house. Visited school where the boys can just speak English and are given a syllabus with such things as 'Explain the relations of Genoa and Venice in the 18th century.' Taught by teaching brothers and black masters. The negro nuns taught each other about Japan and Arabia.

Back at 4. Editor the *Uganda Herald* took me to Mutesa's tomb and the palace. Kabaka has many wives and his queen is a whore. Father J. had told me with relish of the excommunication of CMS[1] priests for fucking. He converts all criminals before they are hanged. Dined with Boby. Don from Makerere College, clever and common – also Papist.

Friday 23 January 1931

Attempts to organize journey across Congo. Difficult.

Lake Victoria, Sunday 25 January 1931

Mass at Father Janssen's. Dog in church. Packed. Boby drove me to pier still hoping for free copy. Embarked 12. Father J. came to see me off. Passengers one German, one transport official. Innumerable smart officers white and gold

[1] Church Missionary Society.

braid; blue at dinner. Entebbe about 3. Plague of small flies. Bad night noisiest ship conceivable. Tipsy Indian.

Monday 26 January 1931

Rusinga cargo boat with six cabins aft, saloon, bar. Deck passengers forward. Passage money does not include food. Read *Muster of Vultures*; people's faces burned away with juice of tropical cactus.

Tuesday 27 January 1931

Went to Bukota; large number of passengers including Grogan. Made to share cabin. Bukota German-built and slightly more character than other lake towns. Houses with white-pillared verandahs. Rocks. Catholic mission. Read more detective stories, including one about drug which made people tell truth and gorilla and secret passage. Cold.

Wednesday 28 January 1931

Arrived Mwanza. Large village with avenues of acacias and mango; mostly Indians; some Arabs. Hotel kept by Greek. CMS parson deeply interested native education. Tough egg from Manchester. Tactless to him about the sack. He told unsuitable story about a baboon; CMS went to write letters. Hotel Africa: maiden ferns; bar; dining-room built out with gauze sides; bedrooms across dirty yard. Cats made love in bedroom at night. Mwanza site of attack during war when schoolmaster couldn't hoist flag of surrender because of enraged bees. Bombarded by armoured lake steamer. Loot of town by English. Hot. Bored.

Mwanza–Tabora, Thursday 29 January 1931

Bored. Train left Mwanza in the evening 6.30. Travelled with CMS parson.

Tabora, Friday 30 January 1931

Arrived Tabora 12.30. Large station with neighbouring railway works. Walked five minutes to large hotel. Terrace. Large high hall – a few heads of game, advertisements, and 'Japanese' paintings. Board floor. Two large rooms, sliding doors, cement floor. Dining-room is one. Relics of band in the other. Pocketless billiard table. Photographs Lloyd George and Venizilos. Two very old men in bar. Pregnant woman, child. Young man with face in hands. Gaslight fittings and electric light. Bedrooms each with balcony and bathroom, but bath chipped. Tap dripping opaque water. Derelict car in yard and chaise longue on balcony. Goose.

Lunched hotel. Bath. Changed. Called on bishop, tea with him. Drove to ruined house where Stanley and Livingstone lived. Saw football match.

Pretty church, thatched roof and pointed windows; whitewashed walls, rough pillars.

English KAR[1] lines and public school. Football match.

Arab mango trees everywhere.

German acacia avenues converging on Boma.

Indian shops. Bicycles and soup.

Moravian chapel.

Square mud huts Swahili-style.

Austrian suffering from grievance about price of sisal.

Bishop came at 9.30. Drove to seminary and Tabora School.

Saturday 31 January 1931

Seminary. Dutch Father Superior, fine beard. Good woodwork by brother. Two-storeyed concrete building on site of first mission. Eight years' training to be priests. Three ordained. Laboratory with anatomical models, telegraph apparatus, etc.

Tabora school. Huge two-storeyed concrete building. Arcaded outbuildings for native teachers, old buildings, farm, etc. Bad soil. One class typing. Boys wore uniforms of khaki caps, vests and shorts. Band drilled by KAR sergeant-major.

Saturday morning school court. Honour boards with one boy a year's name. Dais. Carved shield-back chairs. We sat on dais with prefects, school on floor. Prefect of week shouts out 'Shari' (case). Three urchins called out accused of smoking. No defence. Laid on floor, held down, and given two strokes each with cane by sergeant who salutes after beating. Loud cries in most cases. A larger boy accused of refusing to plough a field. Said he didn't hear order. Witnesses called. Prefects discuss case and sentence him four strokes. An announcement made that epidemic of mumps in town over. Then we go out.

Went to Indian cinema with commercial traveller. Old Charlie in transition stage Keystone – *Goldrush*. Polishes his nails before meals. Food stolen. Eats grass with salt and pepper and delicacy, rinses fingers. In the end handsome lover turns up and Charlie goes off. Followed Indian film; fairy story; very ornamental. Beautiful girl greeted with shouts (no women in building) and is led from her bed to a precipice and thrown over. 'That is her dream.'[2] Supposedly beautiful youth gazes at her. 'He wants to take her into the bushes.' Later elephant with drunken attendant. 'That is an elephant.' Elephant escapes, wicked robber attempts entrap heroine. Her father dies saying he has never kept promise to irrigate desert, etc.

---

[1] King's African Rifles.
[2] A comment by Waugh's Indian companion.

Tabora–Kigoma (Lake Tanganyika), Sunday 1 February 1931

Mass at White fathers, excellent Gregorian singing. Spent most of day dicing for shillings with commercial traveller. Drove with bishop. Train left Tabora 9.30 for Kigoma.

Monday 2 February 1931

Travelled second class to Kigoma. Train full of Belgians and French, smells coffee at dawn. Kigoma predominantly Belgian; many Greeks. Natives savage. Unable buy tickets till 4. *Duc de Brabant* scheduled leave at 6. Captain invisible till 5. Fat untidy man with wife, and awful cabin. At 5, told impossible embark without medical certificate. Hurried in great heat up to doctor's house, found him eventually tinkering with motor boat. He gave certificate without looking at me. Rather in hurry to boat. She did not leave before 12. No cabins. No seats. Only little chairs. Purser Belgian, Greek, one bloody American who turned out to be a missionary. Lavatory locked in port. Warm, moonlit evening, found deckchair and just dozing when about 3 became deadly cold, suddenly all chairs blown over, clap of thunder. Downpour of rain. All dashed to little saloon soaking wet. Brought in luggage piled on deck. Continuous lightning; terrific wind and rain; two saloon windows would not shut; water came through roof in great quantities. Very rough till dawn; most people seasick. Dawn of unusual splendour; rain stopped and some drop in wind and sea. Deck passengers with goats and pig examined wrecked belongings. Engine room deep water. Breakfast. Very slow progress towing barge of cattle. Arrived Albertville about 10. Could not leave before 11 examination passports and medical certificates. Then to immigration office fill in duplicate forms. Age, mother's maiden name, etc. Day now very hot. Albertville: a line of houses on lake front with steep hill behind. Street untidy rather than dirty. Paper, etc.; grass growing in it. Scrubby palm trees. Many cafés and several hotels. Instead of Indians, amiable Greeks. White shopkeeper. Girls in railway office.

Bath, shave, change, decent Belgian hotel. Palace. Luncheon. Went to station to get ticket having found that aeroplane service discontinued. No one at station could tell me of connection Bukama–Port Francqui. Polite as though met interesting problem. Finally took 1st ticket, to Bukama. Slept afternoon, rose for dinner, and slept again. Very hot night at first and then heavy storm.

Wednesday 4 February 1931

Woke 5.30. Cool, heavy rain. Train left punctually 7. Further examination passports and cards of identity. Empty carriage. Very unsteady line. Shower bath in lavatory but does not work. Line runs through valley. Swamp and forest, high wooded hills on either side. River broken by swamp islands downstream. Grey sky. Mist in hills. Later plain, dense bush and occasional belts of forest. Many butterflies but no game. Luncheon at wayside restaurant.

Arrived Kabalo about 6. River broad and brown. Green bush on further shore. Cement, steep, quayside with two railway lines; two or three cargo boats, like suburban houses cut in two. Dirty little hotel with odious patrons. Dinner 8. *Prince Leopold* arrives. Large paddle-steamer. Native passengers on lower deck.

Thursday 5 February 1931

Woke river; green banks and palm trees either side; grey sky. Stopped at small trading station. Some change of passengers. Catholic cathedral in distance. Great shouting. Women long hair in series of tight braided strings; coloured handkerchief on heads. Passengers came on board carrying live fowls in circular, wicker crates; sugar cane, etc., bananas. Push one another off plank. Washing at edge. Heavy rain throughout the day. Cool. Stopped at two or three small stations. Some game – antelope – visible. Ship moved alongside when rain came on.

Friday 6 February 1931

Woke to find ship travelling through miles of swamp land without feature of interest. Occasional canoe drawing into side to avoid our wash. Kadia at 7 o'clock.

Saturday 7 February 1931

Papyrus swamps. Later riverside villages and clumps of fine trees. 'Some of them is palm trees and some of them is just trees.' Row with captain over bicycle. He employs his time wounding the passing game with small rifle. Hot day. We arrive about 3 at Bukama, a fever swamp with two or three houses, mostly derelict – a bank and Greek bar. A bridge over the river with some native huts opposite. Swarms of mosquitoes. No one knows time train due; no possibility of aeroplane. Went out to station, long way, about 8. No lights. Groups of natives with lanterns and little fires, some drumming. Train got in 9.30 and left 9.50. No mosquito nets. Carriages a model of bad building, windows jammed, etc. Extremely uncomfortable night.

Elizabethville, Monday 9 February 1931

Uncomfortable and boring day. Arrived Elizabethville 3. Hotel Globe. Expensive but well managed. Water in bedrooms, etc. Went to see Cook's. Aeroplane fare £100. No certainty of service. Motor junction discontinued during rains. Quickest route Europe via Cape. Accordingly booked ticket third class which should get me to England on 7 March.

These stimulating re-encounters with luxury! How often in London, when satiety breeds scepticism, one has begun to wonder whether luxury is not a put-up job, whether one does not vulgarly confuse expense with excellence. Then, with one's palate refined by weeks of (comparative) privation, of nameless and dateless wines, cigars from Borneo or the Philippines, one meets again the good things of life and knows certainly that taste, at least in these physical matters, is a genuine and integral thing. Reconciliation.

Visited excellent cinema.

Tuesday 10 February 1931

Worked quite well. Drank good wine and smoked good cigars.

Wednesday 11 February 1931

Hope to leave Elizabethville. Worked well and drank well. Left Elizabethville 10 o'clock in clean, new carriage. Found the American Seventh Day Adventist in the carriage.

Friday 13 February 1931

Very hot, crowded and dull train journey.

Saturday 14 February 1931

Arrived Bulawayo 6.30 and left at 5. Changed money and bought some books and toys. A dull town with flower shops.

Sunday 15 February 1931

More train. Half-caste boy in charge of bedding defrauded of 9s.

Monday 16 February 1931

Desolate country all day. Hot and dusty.

Cape Town, Tuesday 17 February 1931

Cape Town. Arrived 6.30. Bath, shave and breakfast at an hotel. Changed ticket at Cook's, bought a deck-chair and walked round Cape Town. Large Victorian buildings. Trams and buses. One or two early fourteenth-century buildings. Ill-conditioned half-castes everywhere. Embarked about noon travelling third class. Excellent, large, clean cabin for four with two occupants besides self. Good food though odd meals – meat tea at 5.30. Played bridge in the evening. Stewards jaunty. Too many children.

Cape Town–London, Wednesday 18 February 1931

Slight sea and many people sick.

Thursday 19 February 1931

Mr Harris was driven to the railway station in London by a friend's chauffeur in a Rolls-Royce. He gave the porter 5s. He said the man was flabbergasted. 'Of course,' he added, 'seeing me come out of a Rolls-Royce he expected at least a quid.'

Two young men discussing Edgar Wallace found him deep and difficult to follow. There were so many converging plots.

The African journal ends at this point, and there is no diary for the next twenty months. When it resumes, Waugh is again on the eve of a long journey. The entry of 4 December 1932 supplies a glimpse of the life he led in England during the intervals of foreign travel. He still lacked a fixed base; and wrote his books in the houses of his friends. *Decline and Fall*, his first novel, had been partly written in the Graham's house at Barford. By the early 1930s, following his divorce, his old friendships had fallen into disrepair and he spent his time in socially grander circles. Much of *Black Mischief* was written during 1932 at Madresfield, Lord Beauchamp's moated house near Malvern; Waugh had known Beauchamp's sons, Lord Elmley and Hugh Lygon, at Oxford, and the book is dedicated to two of the Beauchamp daughters, Lady Mary and Lady Dorothy Lygon. Lady Diana Cooper was acting in *The Miracle* during a provincial tour, and Waugh visited her frequently at weekends, when the pair of them would drive about visiting country houses. His most impassioned attachment, however, was to Teresa (Baby) Jungman, the daughter of Mrs Richard Guinness. He would have liked to marry her, but by becoming a Catholic after divorcing his first wife he had, he thought, permanently debarred himself from marrying again, for the Catholic church does not accept divorce. Teresa Jungman herself was a Catholic.

The journey to Brazil, on which he embarked in the winter of 1932 with 'a heart of lead', contains a hint of penance. As the diary shows, Waugh in the South American jungle inflicted discomfort and tedium upon himself in a way that was not normally part of his character; the diary also shows Waugh's capacity for physical endurance. To the subsequent travel book he gave a bleak title, *92 Days*, and its reviewers complained that travel seemed to bore him. The most important literary consequence of the journey was that his encounter with a religious maniac in the wilds of British Guiana led him to write a short story about a man trapped by a similar maniac. He later explained how this story grew into *A Handful of Dust*, often considered his best novel: 'I wanted to discover how the prisoner got there and eventually the thing grew into a study of other sorts of savages at home and the civilized man's helpless plight among them.'[1]

En route to Georgetown, Sunday 4 December 1932

Bright sunlight, slight breeze, and the ship rolling heavily enough to keep

[1] *Life* magazine, xx (1946), p. 58.

the children sullen and most of the women in their cabins. Two clergymen, one black, both Protestant, but the weather prevented them holding a service. The black clergyman, a prebendary and I think professor at some West Indian university. English cathedral voice and diction and bland clerical humour. I sit at the captain's table next to a Trinidad negress with purple lips. Opposite her a stout black mother. The girl has been in her cabin since dinner last night. Other passengers; two or three very old men doing the round trip; English general's wife and daughter. Ship comfortable, though far from luxurious; very noisy, creaking like a pair of new boots; hard little bunk but three-berth cabin to myself.

The last week before leaving was not really busy, but I was able to give that excuse for not seeing many people. Left Edinburgh, after strained hour in Diana's[1] dressing-room, for Madresfield – a journey as uncomfortable as anything I anticipate in Guiana – changed at Crewe at 4 am with an hour to wait. 7.15 at Birmingham where I was able to hear Mass and breakfast; 10 o'clock at Worcester. Arrived at Madresfield to find everyone still in bed. Three girls and Hubert[2] in the house. Bloggs[3] and Thom Lea[4] to luncheon, later Lord Dudley, very jaunty. Saw Mr Harrison and Captain Hance[5] and left early next morning with Hubert in his car. Lunched at Buck's. Found several telephone messages from Hazel,[6] and Hazel herself sitting in the vestibule of the Savile. She drove me to North End Road, where I collected clean clothes, and to a passport photographer's for photograph for Venezuelan visa. Henry Yorke invited me to stay. Dined with Teresa[7] at the Savoy Grill. Next day walked with Teresa in park and lunched with her and Ivan Davson at the Ritz. She sat quiet while he and I spread a map on the table and talked of Guiana. Dined with Henry and Dig – Teresa having gone to Northampton for a dance; later we went to Quaglino's.

Next day Dig came shopping with me. Lunched at Ritz with Beatrice Guinness. Tea with Peter Fleming[8] to talk of equipment for forests. Dined Savoy with Teresa and Simon and Golly Elwes.[9] Thursday last day. Shopped with Dig, lunched with my parents and packed. Am taking only suitcase and grip. A few tropical suits, camera, books, a pair of field boots and settler shirt

---

[1] Lady Diana Cooper's.

[2] Hubert Duggan. See Appendix of Names, p. 794.

[3] 'Bloggs' Baldwin, 2nd son of Stanley Baldwin, the statesman.

[4] Later the 3rd baronet; a contemporary of Waugh's at Lancing.

[5] Owner of local riding school, where Waugh took lessons.

[6] Hazel Lavery, second wife of Sir John Lavery, the portrait painter.

[7] Teresa Jungman.

[8] The writer (1907–71); brother of Ian Fleming. He had just returned from Brazil as a special correspondent of *The Times* attached to an expedition searching for the explorer Colonel P. H. Fawcett.

[9] Simon Elwes, portrait and flower painter, married Gloria, sister of Peter Rodd.

and shorts. Cocktails with Lady Colefax but arrived as almost everyone was going. Then dinner Teresa at Quaglino's; *caviare aux blinis*, cold partridge, marrow on toast. Friday. Mass at Spanish Place with Teresa and breakfast in Slip-In opposite where she gave me a gold St Christopher medal on a chain.

Down to the docks in Beatrice's car. Deadly lonely, cold, and slightly sick at parting. Heavy rain. Ship at first sight unattractive; like an Irish packet-boat with the second-class decks removed to leave a clear deck for the accommodation of two prize bulls, a race horse, a couple of fox hounds and some hens. Crew all coloured. Heating apparatus not working. Teresa drove off to lunch with Lady Astor in London. We sailed at about 2.30. Down the river in heavy rain and twilight. Heart of lead.

Yesterday more cheerful reading books on Guiana which leave me in alternating panics that the journey to the interior will prove impossibly wild or impossibly tame.

The ship still rolls heavily and makes every movement onerous. Conversations universally dull and respectable.

Monday 5 December 1932

Little sleep last night. Ship rolling heavily, and foghorn early morning.
Steward's attempt to regularize my life.
'What time would you like to be called?'
'I'll ring.'
'What time will you ring?'
'At different times. It depends how I have slept.'
'Will you want tea, coffee, cocoa, or fruit?'
'Sometimes one, sometimes another. I will tell you when I ring.'
'What time will you want your bath?'
'Sometimes evening, sometimes morning.'
Despair lightened by present of cigar.

Tuesday 6 December 1932

A calm night but heavy swell again today. Bitten by bed-bug. Last evening took up with melancholy young man – engineer, probably Portuguese–Indian origin – who offered help in journey up-country and knew a little about it. He is on his way to prospect for gold; his parents have timber concern near Bartica. Sensitive about local patriotism. Also took up with redhaired widow now recovered from seasickness; the mother of the little girl who has been so noisy. She speaks in a scornful way of Georgetown.

Sunday 11 December 1932

Two days ago the weather improved. We were promised fair weather after the Azores, but our worst night was the one immediately after that. It is now warm and calm and should be highly enjoyable, but I am incapacitated by a severe cold. I find it impossible to say anything in the dining-room, won't play deck games, and think that on the whole I must be giving the impression of a pretty dull young man – as indeed I feel. I read detective stories – fascinated by Van Dine's vocabulary, six misformed words in four pages in *Canary Murders*. Wrote first page of novel. Reading Maritain's *Introduction to Philosophy*.

I had not thought before – probably the delirious symptoms of hemlock poisoning described by Plato are largely due to Socrates' advanced age.

I feel less tied to London than when I started and have thrown off all the hesitations about the jungle which I felt driving down with Teresa. A certain inclination to take up being a highbrow again.

It is only as it gets calm that one can appreciate how very slowly this old ship moves. Magnificent skies, particularly at sunset, nearly every evening.

Antigua, Thursday 15 December 1932

My cold lasted until today and made the last few days of really beautiful weather perfectly wretched.

As we got near the end of the voyage – after Antigua the life of the ship disintegrates – there was an appearance of collecting-boxes. First the son of the black parson came round to collect for the Wesleyan Mission. Later the white parson attempted to raise £4 to buy Christmas presents for his parishioners. As these presents were already on board (incidentally, shipped free by the line) he presumably wished to reimburse himself for his own generosity. Mrs Johnson, the mother negress at our table, gave £1, but the rest of the ship were laudably unresponsive.

We were in sight of Antigua from 10 o'clock this morning and anchored at about 2.30. A lovely day, brilliant sun and cool breeze. Hilly coastline, vivid green – trees, sugar cane, palms, scrub, etc. The cathedral very prominent with shining cupolas. Collinses, white parson, and Carson (interesting young man from Fiji) left ship here. I went ashore with Willems[1] and three others and bathed in St John's Bay[2] – hard silver sand, deep water, bathing raft with springboards, café where we drank swizzles afterwards. Ice arrived by bus which was to take us into town. Black woman conductress. Pretty drive into town through sugar plantations; people riding ponies. Wide streets of small detached houses – little negro cabins at outskirts, but more substantial in centre with steps leading to them. Practically all of wood with balconies on wood and iron colonnades. Trees and flowers everywhere. Inquisitive and rather impertinent ragged black populace. Globe Hotel kept by English woman. Cathedral interior of pitch-pine, very fine. Sense of massiveness; galleries

---

[1] Almost certainly the 'melancholy young man' mentioned on 6 December.

[2] MS reads 'St James' Bay'. There is no St James' Bay in Antigua; Fort James guards St John's Bay.

supported by substantial pillars; candelabra; round-topped windows; a few memorials and in yard outside fine marble tombs of planters (pre-emancipation). People mostly carrying fish (pink and blue) or fruit. Conductress of bus pointed at sights: Government House where tennis party in progress, 'taverns' with great disgust. Crowds of little girls round the chapel with 'Jesus died for you' outside.

Barbados, Saturday 17 December 1932

Dropped anchor about 7 and went ashore to Aquatic Club to bathe and drink rum swizzles. Returned to ship for breakfast and later went ashore to Bridgetown. Hot and crowded little town. Intermittent rain. Very little to see in town. Statue of Nelson in Trafalgar Square. Gothic government offices. Cathedral with timber interior and numerous memorial tablets, many to victims of yellow fever – some to young wives who died almost as soon as they landed to join their husbands. Later met Willems and drove with him through sugar plantations to St John's Church. 1830 Gothic of best pre-Ruskin kind. Pink coral rock with pitch-pine roof and cedar pillars; tomb of Paleologus. From there to Codrington College; fine building at end of palm avenue (and lake) destroyed by fire 1926 and now being rebuilt on old plan but with shoddy workmanship, e.g. stalls in chapel badly fitted. About twenty students of theology. Fine views on this side of island. Drove to Willems's old school and met dreary headmaster (late principal Wycliffe Hall) then to luncheon at Crane Hotel and back into town stopping on way at Christ Church – castellated – where is vault in which coffins were disturbed. Called on Jesuit priest of great age named Besant and listened to lecture on theory of golf. Then to amateur dramatic club's performance of a play by Wodehouse called *Baa Baa Black Sheep*. Purely white audience and very slow acting. After play, dinner at Windsor Hotel. Heavy rain. Barman said no demand for West Indian drinks. Martini cocktails preferred. He made swizzles in shaker. Back to ship in pouring rain.

Sunday 18 December 1932

We were to have sailed that night but owing to rain cargo had to be taken off by day and it was not until 11.30 that we left, thus spoiling chance of seeing Grenada by daylight. Usual boys diving for pennies including one poor white of great beauty. After a time they produced a diving girl, but she was only a decoy for the others and did not do any diving. Arrived Grenada midnight and left before I was awake.

Postcript to Barbados. On leaving the ship the black parson said, 'This has been a great fellowship.'

Tuesday 20 December 1932

Arrived at Trinidad. On landing, a young man greeted me whom I did not recognize. His name was Bartlett and he reminded me that Ruth Baldwin had brought him to Richard Greene's and we had played poker dice. I remembered not liking him, but I liked him better in Trinidad. Willems and I went for a drive to St Joseph to see the church which Sir Algernon Aspinall[1] commends as containing some very fine old stained glass. It was quite modern and nothing in St Joseph at all interesting. Smooth black road there lined with little frame cottages among 'luxurious vegetation'; occupied hobbledehoy negroes and puny Indians; not at all agreeable. We went to Queen's Park Hotel (called QPH by Bartlett) and drank several swizzles. It is large wooden building with fine verandah and numerous servants. Alec insulted it at length in *Coloured Countries*. Bartlett said manager (named Marshall) wished to see me, I supposed to throw me out. He was very like Alec to look at. He gave me six or seven swizzles and invited me to stay the night as his guest, lending me silk pyjamas and a brilliant dressing-grown. Joined by pleasant-mannered Trinidadian, ADC named John de Voisier. We drove to a country club, drank more swizzles and finally dined. Trinidadian society turned up to dance. I left early. Except for the bed, which was new, the hotel had all the defects Alec complained of, notably noise and slow service.

Next morning continuous rain. Willems joined me. We played billiards, scoring eighty in just under an hour. Then de Voisier joined us in car with woman and we were taken to drink rum punch and eat oysters in what proved to be a police station but looked like an hotel. Police officer playing billiards. One adulterer. Bartlett disclosed fact that he was Teresa's first cousin. Lunched at QPH. Foul full cocktail bar: 'New Age'. Took car for drive over the Saddle: 'fine bamboos'; 'tropical vegetation'. Visited Benedictine monastery. Shown over by Belgian foreman of works building concrete guest house. Painting in refectory by Chinese lay brother who had no vocation. Bees. Orphan cobblers. Fine view, like all Benedictine houses. Brother at work on wash basin had helped build Buckfast. Bad false teeth like all ecclesiastics. General impression of Trinidad that I don't want to see it again.

Friday 23 December 1932

First sight of Guiana, misty palm-fringe through pouring rain and a few factory chimneys. We turned in the estuary and came down with the current to our mooring. Dreary wind-swept wharfs; some corrugated iron roofs of warehouses. 'Tropical vegetation'. One pretty vista of creek; opaque water with 't.v.' edge very green, seen through rigging of schooners. Smell of brown sugar and clouds of bees round customs sheds. Easy landing so far as immigration officers and customs concerned; passport, illiterate black seaman in ye olde straw hat. Got into taxi and drove through heavy rain to Sea View

[1] Secretary of the West India Committee; author of *Pocket Guide to the West Indies*.

Hotel where Davson's agent had booked me a room. Large boarding house. Female servants. Pretty, colourless, quite incompetent white girl in charge. Ate pineapple, fish and eggs. Went for walk in town, hot and tiring. Broad streets with detached wood buildings. Some quite considerable villas. Sordid emporiums. Scotto–Flemish town hall in matchboarding and cast iron. Various letters and messages of welcome. One from a Mr Maggs born in Midsomer Norton. Wrote name in book at GH. Visited club – huge, dilapidated barn, with billiard tables and bar; dilapidated museum of faded photographs and badly stuffed fauna. Met very agreeable priest who pointed way to bishop's house. Left letters of introduction. Called on Maggs. West country voice, fat, slow and rather deaf. Charming. Lives in room in Tower Hotel with an organ brought out from Midsomer Norton. 'Mr Maggs usually comes in about 4' means, wakes up.

Was interviewed by two black reporters. Wrote home. General impression of Georgetown that I don't mind how soon I leave it. Too diffuse.

Saturday 24 December 1932

Left Sea View Hotel and moved to Tower. Black chambermaid said, 'We shall miss you for your beauty.' Lunched at Government House. Denham cheerful, unaffected man of rather nautical air. Had the good luck to mention futility of compulsory Kiswahili in East African schools and found it was pet subject of his. As a result some cordiality and invitations to Christmas dinner. He looks like Winston Churchill. Had some further talk with Maggs whom I like particularly and with the manager, an Irish–Portuguese named Hernandez. Dined alone and sat up till 11.30 when Willems came to fetch me to midnight Mass at the cathedral. Very tired and service intolerably long. Gounod music. Not over until 2.

Christmas Day 1932

Sat about all day alone or in casual conversation. Found Maggs in state of great despondency and loneliness so gave him a copy of *Remote People* as a Christmas present. It seems to me rather a foolish action now. Dinner at Government House. No tail coat, so compromised with mess jacket and white tie and no doubt looked very odd but didn't mind. Rather a pathetic evening of the Denhams' charming attempts to be homely among childless officials; many jokes – imitation rolls which squeaked, a spoon which was hinged in the middle. There was a large male predominance. I sat between a black attorney-general and a white archdeacon. Toasts to the King and 'absent friends'. After dinner was trapped in conversation by a curate, and by a saturnine official with a decoration who spoke about Somalis. Some human moments with a tall, ginger-headed ADC and a pretty secretary.

Sunday 1 January 1933

On Monday of last week I went to tea with the Willemses and met Dr Roth, an opinionated and rather disagreeable old man who said he was willing, if I paid his expenses, to take me to the only place where unsophisticated Indians are still to be found – in the head waters of the Essequibo. He estimated that this would take three months and £300. At first I was not attracted by the proposition, but later grew more enthusiastic and saw the possibility of a good book in it. Next day the Governor had invited me to go with him to Mazaruni and throughout the trip, until the last evening, I became more determined to go with Dr Roth.

The trip was agreeable and comfortable. We motored to Parika where after ten minutes or so in heavy rain the *Tarpon* came into sight. Large steam launch with cabins on upper deck, two bathrooms, etc. Lunched early and arrived at Bartica at 3. Mr Wood, forestry man at Mazaruni, came on board. We landed at 4 and walked round the town while H.E. talked to various groups of 'pork knockers',[1] etc. Ramshackle little town: one principal street full of rum shops and 'Surprise Boarding House'. Visited small garden full of orchids. Small hospital with very ill doctor. Left for Mazaruni settlement; former convict station now headquarters forestry. Mrs Wood and Mr Davies came on board for drinks, went back to change and returned to dinner and bridge. Settlement pretty collection of buildings – one stone – on hillside; small clearing in forest.

Next day went for a walk in forest through track of tree-trunks laid in swamp. Saw countless ants, some flowers, fine butterflies and tortoise; slept after luncheon. Went to Kyk-over-al, earliest Dutch fort, on island up river. Nothing to see except one repaired arch and countless ants. Dined ashore with Woods and Davies. Davies told me Roth irresponsible traveller; no sense of time or money; nearly kills himself whenever he goes up country through neglecting rudimentary precautions. He and H.E. and Woods all strongly advised against going with him.

Next morning we visited Fort Island – diamond-shaped fort, Dutch tombs – and returned to Georgetown 12.30. After luncheon I visited Roth at museum who seemed less keen on expedition. Anyway I did not like him enough to spend three to four months in his company. I then went to see Haynes, the commissioner for Rupununi district. Very dotty – tells fantastic stories about submarine horse, communicative parrots, etc. He has a boat going up to Kurupukari (which I took to be Yupukarri for some days) with room for me.

Friday. Lunched with Jesuits; good food; rum swizzles; cigars, etc.

Friday–Saturday. Given up to making arrangements and getting stores. First arrangement. I should leave for Bartica Tuesday morning, embark for

---

[1] Diamond workers.

Kurupukari Wednesday. Then discovered no steamer to Bartica till Wednesday. Then Haynes decides include policeman and a clerk in boat. Agent says open boat in heavy rain already overloaded, impossible for me to travel in it. Haynes then offers to lend me horse to ride trail from Berbice to Kurupukari with him, leaving early Tuesday morning. Meanwhile half stores I had ordered must be countermanded as no room for them. Also many things not ready and Monday a holiday. Eventually decide to leave by Berice train[1] Tuesday. Meanwhile I buy bush-clothes, hammock, net, gun, flour, sugar, stores, etc.

Saturday was New Year's Eve and Georgetown full of parties. I went to cinema and returned to find Tower Hotel scene of Scottish orgy with pipers and quite elderly men sitting on the floor. I had received an invitation to another ball at the club so went there and drank whisky with various people and had supper. Fancy dress. Returned about 1 am with a doctor and drank with him. Scottish party still in full swing. Secretary asked me to join 'hectic' party with two fine tarts, but they all seemed too dumb and drunk so went to bed. Slept little owing to noise and when I went out to Mass at 7 there were four youths in fancy dress still singing. The servants did not get any sleep all night on that day. Felt ill all day. Lunched at Government House and said goodbye to Denhams. Went for dinner with Willems to road house Bel Air where we saw one of the tarts from last night with Portuguese chap; both heavy hangover and she less pretty by daylight. Later in the evening felt really ill; assumed I had malignant malaria; was sick; took a large dose of chlorodyn and slept eleven hours.

Monday 2 January 1933

Holiday. Awoke feeling a little better. Perhaps not malignant malaria. Went to races with Willems. Heavy rain and poor racing. Two or three entries each race. 'Gentlemen's hack race' all professional black jockeys. After dinner went out with two police officers in attempt to find low life; but not successful. Some masqueraders in Camp Street; one dressed as lion had large following. Dance at the King George Hotel. A few whore shops in Tiger Bay but everything very flat, presumably because money spent so late in holidays. Whittingham told story of tart who worked at Bartica, came back with a wad of notes in her garter and cartridge case of diamonds, married, and turned so respectable that she hit a man with hatchet who solicited her. But later both she and her husband murdered.

Georgetown–New Amsterdam, Tuesday 3 January 1933

Went to Mass at 7. Busy morning packing and making final purchases and arrangements with Garnetts who proved infinitely unbusinesslike. Ordered

---

[1] For New Amsterdam down the coast.

few more stores from Bookers. Freight $6\frac{1}{2}$ cents per lb. Willems took charge of luggage for me and arranged send it to England if I do not return Georgetown. Left hotel in some displeasure as service broke down after holidays.

Left Georgetown at 2.30 by slow little train for New Amsterdam. Pretty country of sugar estates fallen into decay and planted with rice or coconut palms. As we got into Berbice, people grew blacker. Haynes says in Berbice they call their fathers 'Sir'; in Georgetown they slap their faces. He talks all the time but I find it hard to understand. He has been mining engineer, surveyor, soldier, dredger-master. Is now temporary officer but hopes become permanent. Seems to have suffered from sexual timidity. Told story of lost opportunity with Venezuelan beauty: 'figue like butterfly'. Also stories of courage with Brazilian bandits. Expect he is a coward. Later at sunset became suddenly quite cold and plague of mosquitoes.

Arrived New Amsterdam about 7. Crossed with nuns in ferry. Walked to Lynch's Hotel. Asked whisky but little gent with long moustache refused it. So went to bar. Uncomfortable dinner; beset by mosquitoes, cold, and sweating. Reminded of Congo. After dinner went back to bar and tried to get car but no one would open. (Haynes talked to himself during night.) Heard Jordanist[1] preacher. Black beard, white robe and turban. Message that blacks must be dominant race but must first purge themselves of immoral habits. Great Pyramid and Lost Tribes of Israel jargon. Quotations from Jeremiah led by tiny boy with Bible, who became inattentive. Tepid interest in crowd. 'When a man come with pale skin and blue eye you are frightened.' He carried metal wand. Jordanites have started colony on land in Demerara. Jordan died quite recently. Very suitable for Betjeman.

Wednesday 4 January 1933

Boat left for Takama 7.30. Rainbow. Very pretty old Lutheran church.

Kurupukari, Wednesday 11 January 1933

Arrived at Kurupukari at 12 o'clock noon. I have marked stages of journey in map. For first three days it was savannah country – sparse grass on sandy soil, slight undulation. Every ten or fifteen miles rest houses, some with wired enclosures for cattle. Every half mile or so, dead cattle; some with carrion crows, some skeletons with heap of grass between ribs. Hart had lost 100 head in last drive, they told us at Takama. 'Eaten by tigers,' said Haynes. 'Surely not.' 'Yes, when they are dying tigers eat them.' This typical of Haynes's stories. 'The man was court-martialled and shot.' 'Shot for not saluting?' 'Yes, he went to France immediately afterwards and was killed.' Dead cows near rest houses intolerable stink.

[1] Sect deriving its name from a Mr Jordan of Jamaica.

Journey from New Amsterdam–Takama uneventful. Long sunny day. Rancher and Indian wife and children. Talk of horses, praised for bucking and bolting. Awful food on boat. 'This is last of civilization': Haynes. Black rancher Yearwood and wife sleeping in rest house at Takama. No hammock for Haynes. Man in charge was at 'party'. Went down dark river in boat. Arrived at party. Thatch house, open sides; solid Indians and talkative niggers sitting round. Two guitars. Girl with bowl of liquor and cup walking round and giving drinks. Hostess greeted us with 'Goodnight'. Danced foxtrot. First night in hammock fairly comfortable. Read *Titus Andronicus*.

Rode to Yearwood's ranch. Table and chairs a rare comfort.

After that no furniture. Houses often in bad repair. Blacks using floorboards and walls for fires. Pony v. slothful. Chief discomforts: lack of light and chairs after riding; proximity of blacks particularly when wet; smelled. But always creek to wash. Strong sweet tea. Rum; limes.

Luggage on pack-oxen; one and a half to three hours' wait at each place. Forest trail large trees left, but many trees and undergrowth cleared. Few flowers. Great noise of birds but no sight of them. Butterflies. Occasional animal like hare. One 'bear'. Armadillo holes. Drank creek water and bathed. Fresh horses at Canister. Efficient Constable Price looks after me. Arrived hoping to find the boat with stores waiting for us but no news of it.

Kurupukari Station;[1] wood house; convicts underneath some outhouses. Single large room equipped for court with dais, witness-stand and dock. Two tables in verandah laden with official forms. Sergeant's room, Haynes's and two others, low wood partitions; bed; girls from magazine covers on walls. 'I have this girl because I know her. People say is not beautiful but she has a beautiful soul. This one I have because it is such a voluptuous type.' All rooms liable to occupation by travelling ranchers. Haynes has no private residence of any kind. Berbice chair.

Throughout the week's ride Haynes did not once stop talking, except at night when he kept me awake with asthma and retching. Mostly boasts about his own honesty, courage and efficiency and generosity. Horsemanship. Physical prowess in knocking out Brazilians, niggers, etc. Repetition of complimentary remarks made by people. Description of how he 'hugs up', 'loves up' girls. Does not fuck. Speech full of 'de', 'plenty', etc. The black man has 'a very inferior complex'. 'I do all this for my King – for my two Kings. The one above too.' Sometimes he lapses into reviews of the world's history. 'Look at Napoleon. He was a little corporal. But he wanted to marry a princess so he divorced his wife. The Bolsheviks will soon start that too.' 'Boer war prolonged by British desire for a good scrap so they let all prisoners go.' Lectures on morality and speculation about transmigration of souls, etc. Great respect for

---

[1] The headquarters of the district commissioner.

British character; honour of Dagoes. Voice sometimes inaudible drone, sometimes wildly dramatic.

Pretty Indian girl named Rosa. Haynes flirtatious in old-womanly way. Said I could sleep with her but hedged when I tried to bring him to point.

Thursday 12 January 1933

No sign of Garnetts's boat.[1] No tobacco. Went to Indian family settled on other side of river. Haynes diagnosed worms in child. Pinched and patted; not enthusiastically received. Haynes gossips and explains everything to subordinates.

Another boat expected down river but no sign of it yet. Haynes too tired to proceed Annai. Bored and impatient. View magnificent. Haynes says, 'Whom God has joined, etc. Yes, but who is God? Love, therefore, etc.'

Friday 13 January 1933

No sign of boat. Decide to leave tomorrow without stores. Went out with gun in search of game but found nothing. Bored.

Stories low, no potatoes, sugar, rum, tobacco, tinned stuff. Haynes offered provide biscuits and dry meat, and then appeared with a tin of milk and Ovaltine saying he had more. Found out later they were his last. At 6, however, boats were sighted coming up river which proved to be Garnetts.

Saturday 14 January 1933

Had to delay another day as Haynes prepared mail for Bon Success, but worth waiting to have stores. Very dull day, reading T. Aquinas. Stores in hand are: one bag sugar; one bag flour; one bag potatoes and onions; lamp; oil; cooking pots; three rum (gave three Haynes); five tins tobacco; ten cakes common soap; two tins herrings; nine bully beef; one jam; one biscuit; two tea; two cocoa; twelve Milkmaid milk; six Nestlés milk; one Bovril; two pineapple; five fruit; four salmon; three sausage; four meat and veg; four butter; two tongues; six tomato soup.

Sunday 15 January 1933

Set out[2] after breakfast having sent Price and Yetto on at 10 am. Just as starting, boatman Duggin arrived with large tin of tinned foods saying pack-horse had refused to start and had had to be lightened. Started in displeasure and one mile along trail found pack-horse tethered to tree, packs beside him. Price and Yetto chatting. They said pack-horse still refused to go. Took off another large pile of stores. Set out and rode ahead. After ten miles found pack

[1] Bringing up stores.
[2] Waugh's destination was Boa Vista, in Brazil; he was accompanied by a police constable, Price, and one of Haynes's servants, Yetto.

not following and turned back. Price and Yetto and horse at eight-mile point. Horse had lain down four times. Left packs; rode back, telling Yetto to follow with horse. Dark before reached Kurupukari.

Kurupukari–Bon Success, Monday 16 January 1933

Made fresh start with a donkey called Maria and youth named Sinclair. Took a few of stores but had to leave great deal behind. Arrived at eight-mile point and found rancher named Major Weller and two entomologists named Myers and Fitzgerald. Myers dysentery. They had killed a bush turkey; gave them rum; lunched with them. Myers employed by Empire Marketing Board. Made camp rest house fourteen miles.

Tuesday 17 January 1933

Twenty-one-mile day. Boys late at breakfast, Sinclair malingering. Caught in heavy rain and soaked before reaching dissolute house. Made fire using floor, and dried clothes. Driver warned us of ferocious bullock but did not see him. Found one killed by tiger. Boys arrived 5.45. Good water. Washed at lemon tree so had hot rum and lemon. Talked Yetto in evening. He had once shaken Prince of Wales's hand. Also been robbed by Grenadian named Adams on his way to Cuba; had to return. Went to diamond fields. Made $800. Had six girls in motor car driving all night; drank whisky and gin; gave them gold ornaments.

Wednesday 18 January 1933

Dull ride; horse very tired. Ass followed. Yetto came on with me carrying hammock, etc. Reached Indian settlement in small savannah named Surama. Slept empty Indian house. Mud walls.

Thursday 19 January 1933

Dull ride. Arrived at Annai 12.45. Good house, glass windows; fine views of savannah. 'Air so healthy you shiver all de time.' Hired new horses; pack and blind in one eye riding horse. Counted stores. Dealer [?] arrived with wife, daughter of Melville. Also Syrian shit named Thomas who told me war had broken out England Germany.

Friday 20 January 1933

One-eyed horse played up on being bridled and threw himself over backwards. Five miles out stopped; repeated performance twice more, finally reared and fell over. Lost trail once but found it. Intolerably hot ride. Arrived at Christie's ranch [1] 4 o'clock. Christie told me he was warned of strangers in

---

[1] The inspiration for Mr Todd's ranch in *A Handful of Dust*.

dream. He had dreamt of a harmonium before my coming; gave me tea; told of iniquities of popes and Freemasons – VOL on arse[1] – and of 110 seen in sky in 1924 prefacing end of world. Questioned him about theology. 'Believe in Trinity. I couldn't live without them. But they are no mystery. It is all quite simple. It is in OT where – married his mother.' Told me Adam only lived to be 960. Spoke of Fifth Kingdom, etc. After had washed, got tight on rum. Christie family collected. Daughter married to East Indian, three sons. One of his sons had got a child by an Indian who had no cultivation and wouldn't sing in church. He had been to see the 'elect'; found them few but hard to count as no bodies.

Saturday 21 January 1933

Left 6.45 and reached Wong's ranch[2] 11. Delightful Portuguese manager D'Aguiar and Indian wife who cooked me eggs, coffee, mince beef, oranges. Little mud cottage thatched verandah with breast-high walls for hammock. Kabura flies. River. Pathetic decorations of cigarette cards, snapshots, and magazine covers. Great heat afternoon. Lost time on way here and saved by A. of Padua. Brazilian neighbours came to call with numerous children; all came in and shook hands with me. Two Indians – one like Mr Hyde – leant over the parapet and stared at me for some hours.

Sunday 22 January 1933

Started early on warty but strong chestnut mare and arrived at Hart's ranch at 11; several large buildings; the living house with ceilings and floors. Library of ill-assorted ant-eaten books – *Young Visiters*, *Sinister Street*, Mill on Liberty, *What a young man ought to know*, *Practical Joinery*, etc. Shower bath. Hart away. Mrs Hart (Amy Melville), a brother, six boys and a dotty bastard nephew, son of John Melville by his three-quarter sister (went off with a Mr King). Luncheon several plates of meats, farine.

Governess in shorts. Lent me journals with Carey Elwes's diaries in it.

Interesting meeting with Christie: 'Who would have thought the love of God to be circular?' 'Why should I wear an image of someone I speak to daily? Besides it is not the least like her.'

Boys arrived v. late, Price looking very thin. They had had no proper meals all the journey because they quarrelled so much as to who should cook.

Bon Success, Monday 23 January 1933

Left Hart's ranch with Mr Hart and two children by Ford truck, and reached Bon Success 10. Teddy Melville, government officer with pretty

---

[1] Christie maintained that you could always tell Freemasons because they had VOL branded on their buttockes. He conjectured that VOL meant 'Volunteer'.

[2] The property of a Georgetown Chinese, Mr Wong.

Brazilian wife, gave me beer. Breakfasted there. Mud house, concrete floor. Left at 1 and, crossing deep creek with ropes and pulleys, arrived Ignatius Mission at 2. Thatched two-storey dwelling house; two bedrooms and storerooms, gallery; downstairs stores and dining-room. Tame toucans, ponies, mocking bird, toad (eats cigarette cards), etc. Father Mather infinitely hospitable and kind; talked of Stonyhurst.[1] Church tin sides, thatched roof, mud floor. Open school, rest house and Indian dwellings scattered in neighbourhood. Keary[2] on rounds. Went to bed (not hammock), glad to have few days' rest.

Tuesday 24 January 1933

Mass at 7. Entire day reading in easy chair in gallery and gossipping with Father Mather. Reading C. Graham[3] on Jesuits in Paraguay.

Wednesday 25 January 1933

Mass at 7. Spent day reading. Took few photographs.

I stayed at Father Mather's until February 1st, my departure being delayed until the return of David Max y Hung, the head *vaquero* whom Father Mather was lending me as guide to Boa Vista. He is half Chinese, half Arawak-Indian; speaks excellent English and Portuguese; very quiet and efficient. He came on the Monday and arranged to have horses and another guide by Wednesday. Meanwhile Father Mather was continually busy doing me acts of kindness – finding me a piece of snake-wood and shaping it roughly for a walking-stick; also making a case for my camera which began as a loose leather bag and ended as a very elaborate construction of galvanized iron, calfskin, deerskin and an old duster.

On Sunday we paddled down to Figueredo's store and lunched with him, and from politeness ate too much. Visited the store where there was nothing one could buy so I got some Brazilian *crème de menthe* for the mission cellar. Figueredo gave us beer and *crème de caçao*. Gore, an English rancher, married to Indian, who spent most of his life in New Mexico, came to dinner and talked of Wild West in the cinema days. He took mail for us to the coast so I wrote exceedingly silly article on Rupununi. Camera case finished five minutes before leaving on Wednesday. Father Mather also gave me stone axe-head and two cigarette holders to take to J. B. Priestley.

Bon Success–Boa Vista, Wednesday 1 February 1933

Left Father Mather at 1.30, riding sturdy grey with hammock behind saddle. David's brother-in-law led on young bright bay wearing rucksack full

---

[1] The Roman Catholic school in England.
[2] Father Mather's colleague at the St Ignatius Mission.
[3] R. B. Cunningham-Graham (1852–1936), the Scottish adventurer and writer.

of books and tins and carrying umbrella and snake-wood. David came behind, on brown horse already galled in the withers, holding my grip in front of him. We rode through intermittent rain until 1.30. Forded Takutu and another stream. Country same as Rupununi; sand; grass; sandpaper trees. No cattle or horses anywhere. Reached first stage in darkness. Open thatched barn also in darkness. A man and numerous male children in hammocks. I sat down on a box and waited while David and Francisco watered horses. Presently a small cup of excellent coffee was brought by little boy. Later a lamp − small wick in open dish of beef fat giving as much light as candle but less easily extinguished. Smell of wet thatch appalling. Meal set on table, of farine and stewed *tasso* (dried beef). Ate very little and slept badly.

Thursday 2 February 1933

David said journey of over twenty-four miles. Saddled and packed at dawn and left after thimbleful of coffee at 6.45. Reached cottage at 8 and made tea and I ate piece of dried bread. Rode steadily through great heat and desolate country for about eighteen miles. Then we reached stagnant pool in sandy watercourse and meagre shade of palm. David said, should we stop here to rest horses and breakfast? 'Would it not be better to wait until we reach destination?' 'Francisco says long way.' 'How far?' 'We are nearly half way.' So I ate some dried bread and tinned sausage; drank nothing; sat among ants for an hour and then started again. Great heat and suffering from thirst. David's horse badly galled, and necessity of frequent repacking and saddling. Brazilian saddles supported by rags and straw. Eventually reached house about 5.30. Drank three or four mugs of water. Washed and changed. Amiable bearded young Brazilian of negro features and son. Wife invisible. Another dinner of farine and *tasso*; too tired to eat. David made me cup of cocoa. Lay in hammock too tired to undress. Fell asleep and dreamed I was paralysed. Woke at dawn dead tired.

Friday 3 February 1933

Ate piece of chocolate and drank cup of tea. Rode fifteen miles − my horse now galled − to larger farm. Manager away. Wife entertained us. Solid walls to room; some brickwork; roof of shingle; barn with carpentry bench. Fresh pork for luncheon and banana; besides, *tasso* soup and farine; rice. After luncheon, ladies of house sat in a row and stared at me. Another hour's ride through belts of bush brought us to farm where we were to spend night. Another large and solid house with wood shingles and mud walls. Much coming and going of *vaqueros*. Two little boys on one saddle. Mechanic with handsome saddle-bags. Attached to house, sugar-mill of primitive kind made hard cakes of brown candy-like substance, also treacle and refined sugar. Black bottle aroused anticipation but proved to be treacle. Washed and lay down in outbuilding.

Dinner at 6; uneatable; farine and *tasso* harder than yet encountered; then farine and treacle. Four relays of diners at table with lantern; deaf and dumb Indian; one-eyed negro, and elegant man with hiccups. Mostly travellers like ourselves. A dozen to sleep in little shed. I got David to hang my hammock in dining shed. But little sleep, *vaqueros* retching and coughing all round. Sugar-mill began work at 2.30 am. Moreover bad attack of diarrhoea.

Boa Vista, Saturday 4 February 1933

Rose feeling ill and very tired. Three hours' ride through alternating bush and savannah to Rio Branco, little farm opposite Boa Vista. Broad shallow water with islands between. Waited an hour till owner of farm came in little boat. Then crossed over in his boat (gratis) with two *vaqueros* who had spent the night at same house as us and come on with drive of bullocks.

Boa Vista first sight: red and thatch roofs among trees on (now) high bank. Sandy beach with girls washing clothes and bathing. Steep climb to Benedictine priory. Father Mather had given me Latin letter of commendation. Priory (built as hospital) seemed very solid and smart; tiled roof; wood floors and ceilings with lower floor on one side where ground sloped away; little fence between concrete pillars and garden of symmetrical beds in brick borders. Carved wood front door, etc. Glass windows; concrete steps and big verandah. Waited ten minutes or so on steps. German poked head out of window and talked Portuguese to David. He also guest. Presently priest in white habit appeared from the side of road; led us into very neat and stiff reception room with artificial flowers on table and wicker furniture; Swiss, speaks a little French. He said no boat for Manaos for indefinite period, possibly weeks. Sent David out to enquire. Meanwhile had shower bath and changed and lay in coma on bed. Presently priest returned to say breakfast was ready. Food cooked by nuns and brought from convent. Cold but delicious – soup, stewed meat, rice, beans, pancakes, and lemonade of peculiar, medicinal flavour. He sat opposite me as I ate; difficult conversation. Lay down for two hours after luncheon.

David returned with news that there was a boat on 10th belonging to Boundary Commission, and public one on 20th. Decide to remain. David unpacked and servants prepared room. Sat about still comatose and bad headache. Dinner at 6. Excellent and varied food. Conversation difficult particularly as German's English quite unintelligible. He is local planter. Walked up and down terrace after dinner until I insisted on sitting. Bed 8 o'clock. Took large dose of chlorodyne and slept heavily with vivid dreams.

Sunday 5 February 1933

Mass at 7. Congregation mostly girls in bridal veils and all kinds of ribbons and medals. A few men standing at back. Church seemed sumptuous after

Takutu. As usual where there is convent school, much sugary hymn-singing during Mass. Avenue leading to church cracked mud and sand. Small stores and private houses dirty and shabby. Great conversation difficulties as German planter talks little English and less French, priest no English little more French. Even their German not wholly intelligible to each other; explanations involved in Portuguese. The German makes no difference of accent in any language. The Swiss has most of the longer words but none of those in general use. We sometimes speak of the news – Atlantic disasters, etc. Is it true everyone starving in Georgetown? Sometimes general subjects. Would King George be king if he were not Freemason? Suspect priest of thinking out phrases. Benediction very hot, 7. Later to café and drank beer with German and a lonely storekeeper.

Monday 6 February 1933

Vet named Silva speaks some English. No one seems very helpful about journey to Manaos. German bought two frightful rifles, one loaded. He wears blue suit, sandals and boater, and carries silver crook cane. Conversations intolerable.

Friday 10 February 1933

Four days of degrading boredom. Nothing to read except some lives of the Saints in French and Bossuet's sermons. The German's conversation unbearable. The priest confined to his room with fever. Yesterday found young man who speaks English. Turns out the bastard son of Dr Roth married to Brazilian; works as blacksmith, chiefly tinkering up old firearms. He came out with me to drink some beer yesterday evening. Not the café I frequent because 'I gave the owner a licking just now and promised him another.' Roth held it unlikely I should get passage in Boundary Commissioner's boat and proved to be right. After coffee this morning the German announced that the Commissioner was here and could be found in the telegraph office. I went there and found him amiable but immovable. His boat was already full. Meanwhile I hear the possibility of another on the 15th and have found a French book of travel with such chapter headings as Le jardin du paradis, A l'ombre de mes dieux, To be or not to be, Sous le signe de Mystère, La mort qui romp, La Vierge des solitudes.

Sunday 12 February 1933

Wrote bad article yesterday but thought of plot for short story.[1] General opinion that boat will not leave before 20th.

---

[1] *The Man Who Liked Dickens*, which later became the chapter in *A Handful of Dust* called 'Du Côté de Chez Todd'.

Tuesday 14 February 1933

Finished short story. The boat is announced to arrive tomorrow but no certainty of its departure or arrival at Manaos. I have decided to go back to Guiana and try to return to Georgetown via Kaieteur and Bartica. John Roth had a son born to him and offered to conduct me to Kaieteur but by a route which seemed bound to end in exasperation.

Wednesday 15 February 1933

Morning and afternoon I visited Martinez[1] but the guide and horses were not there. Nor has the boat come from Rio Negro yet.

Thursday 16 February 1933

There seems little hope of leaving today. Martinez takes little trouble. Suddenly Steingler, the German, began to work for me and took me to see a 'collecteur', whatever that is, who sold me a grey cob for £5; I also bought a decayed saddle and bridle from Steingler for another fiver. Then visited Martinez and said all we needed was horse for guide. Priest willing to lend him saddle. After luncheon, Martinez said guide had found horse already, other side of river at Sao Pedro farm. Everything seemed fixed. Went down to river in afternoon to cross with luggage and horse. Said goodbye at priory. Sat in canoe with luggage and two small boys until it was dark. Guide couldn't find my grey horse. Returned late to priory. New prior had just arrived, cross after journey; just off to fête in his honour in school. Paulo got me some food and I went out with Steingler and drank beer, arranging for guide to call me at 4.30 next day to start for Dadanawa.

Friday 17 February 1933

Guide did not come; awoke at 5.30 and went to river. Infinite difficulty crossing horse, but at last by aid St Christopher accomplished. Put luggage in Sao Pedro, children went off in canoe. Guide went to find his horse. Returned about 9 to say no horse. Conversation impossible. No canoe. At 11.30 canoe arrived from Boa Vista, crossed and arrived late for luncheon. New prior forming low opinion of me and Dom Alcuin trying to explain me. Went to Martinez. He at last roused and ordered motor boat which eventually arrived and crossed with me. *Vaqueros* sent to scour countryside for horse and found him at 5. Later, boy appeared who offered another horse for pack animal for £1. All seemed well. Arrived late for dinner. Prior convinced I am mad and undesirable. Went with Steingler to clinch [?] pack-horse and drink beer with owner – bearded species of town clerk I think. Very amiable and asked me to coffee next morning.

[1] Local trader.

Saturday 18 February 1933

Up 5.30. Arranged motor boat with vile Roth. Went to coffee with town clerk who presented me with handsomely bound French volume. Hope he was unaware of his son's villainy over horse. Crossed with son and found horse; miserable animal. Son made off quickly. Moment we started pack-horse went lame, off fore badly swollen. Only possible get him along with great cruelty but what else to do? Started from Sao Pedro about 9. Rode infinitely slowly until 4, when we put up night at house where I now am writing. My horse lay down once on way. Stopped for half hour's rest in bush. Tried to eat bread and cheese but no water. Reached Indian house about 2.30 and had water and coffee. This house fair size and decrepit. Woman in charge with several daughters who fetched me chair and coffee and were kind. I think guide has found a second pack-horse but can't tell. If so, possible proceed tomorrow.

Sunday 19 February 1933

Have now got as far as small outpost *vaqueros* hut. One amiable bearded *vaquero*. I don't the least know how far we came today – no watch – but he says six hours from Takutu so we can't have done more than fifteen miles or so. Very tiring and horse extremely weak. He started well for first hour but like all these horses soon lost interest. We suffered a good deal from lack of water. The farm we hoped to reach is four hours away. Yesterday evening was pleasant enough; numerous females who giggled at me and one-eyed *vaquero* to whom I gave tip in hope would get better horse. But they gave me horse anyway, though bad one. Up at 5.45 but could not leave before 9.30 as horse had to be caught. Too tired to write. Chap bare waist with hairy chest, very fine arms. But saw fresh meat which induced me to stay.

Monday 20 February 1933

Up before dawn and off by 6. Rode about four hours across grass country; horse going badly; v. hot. Reached a ranch but found it empty and went across to another three-quarters of a mile away named Nova Cintra where a *vaquero* with face like El Greco's Ignatius was making an elaborate pair of leggings. Put up hammocks and rested. Asked if he could lend us fresh horse and he said no. No coffee and lunch of farine and dried beef. I opened tin of sausage and gave him some and I think this sausage softened him, for after lunch he went off with my boy and returned with a strong little piebald grey. We rode on another two miles to banks of Takutu having got lost in crossing creek. Crossed into British territory by survey mark, over smooth dry rocks. Rode up creek for a mile and stopped for night at Indian house. I got out map and tried to find where we were. Mountains on either side and I decided we had come a long way north and were between Kanuku and Kusad mountains. Indian confirmed name of creek as Sowariwau. We were thus four or five hours from St Ignatius, and much farther from Dadanawa, so I decided to go there on the next day. Opened what I hoped would be tin of tongue and found horrible sausage. No bread and very tired so ate nothing and went to sleep.

Tuesday 21 February 1933

Up before dawn, explained change of plan to guide with difficulty. Drank a cup of milk and reflected with pleasure that I should have a meal at Ignatius soon. Set off on Nova Cintra horse going well and soon left guide behind. Confident that I couldn't miss way between mountains and river; soon lost trail but kept on. Stopped at two Indian houses; one giggling women. Other man rode off at my approach. A little after noon horse dead beat and riding over baked marsh and feeling deadly tired, came across wide creek which I assumed must be Moru-moru [?]. Rode down it expecting find mission houses. Saw roof which turned out to be Indian hut. Old Wapishiana spoke a little English, said he was taking bullock to Bon Success that day. It was far away the other side of mountains, i.e. Kanuku mountains are another six hours away. I had gone round Kusad. Sowariwau was half a day's journey further on. Meanwhile my horse was worthless and I had lost guide, luggage, and had not even my hammock. I asked for food and he had some, bringing me three eggs and half a fowl which I ate with great relief. Rested in his hammock and about 3 o'clock set out, he riding bullock and his son bareback on game little grey mare. I effected a change with son and jogged along effortlessly for two hours or so when we came to a ruined house with my guide on the roof. The Indian now put the pack on the ox and rode my white horse. An hour after dark we reached Indian houses. No food and no room for us so slung hammock in open and spent cold night with little sleep.

Wednesday 22 February 1933

Rode Indian's mare and went on with him, leaving pack to follow. Very faint with hunger. Reached Gore's ranch 11.30 and sent a message to Father Mather announcing my coming. Mare unable to proceed. Lunched at Gores. Mrs Gore Indian; eggs and dry mince and water and cassava bread. No chairs. Pack arrived. Took Nova Cintra horse, which was rested by being ridden bareback, and arrived at St Ignatius about 2, very tired and painfully sunburnt. Father Keary back.

Monday 27 February 1933

Have spent agreeable time resting, reading *Dombey and Son*, eating and sleeping a lot. Father Keary went off on Saturday. Hope to leave on Wednesday for Kurupukari with Teddy Melville.

Saturday 4 March 1933

Had arranged to leave here today, but horses could not be found so am starting tomorrow. I have changed my route and instead of going to Kurupukari am trying to cross Pakaraima mountains to Kaieteur. Since this decision I have been busy trying to trace the track on various maps and have made tracings but no one here knows the route and I am dependent on getting guides and carriers at Tipuru.

Father Mather has done innumerable things for me, mending saddles, making a pack-saddle, measuring out farine, flour, etc., making bags, cutting walking-sticks, packing films, mending watch-glass, etc. We went to Figueredo but heard dismal *nao hà* in answer to most enquiries. Learned a little barter: 4 caps[1] equals 1 egg; 1 tin gunpowder equals 1 chicken; 1 tin farine equals $1.50, etc. Expect several difficulties on way but shall pass Father Keary. Father Mather took photographs of me today and is developing them. Have been found Macushi guide named Eusebio who says 'Yes, Father' to everything and has no personal property – no clothes, no cup, no knife. Says he can cook. Am starting with pack-bullock. Medicines in Figueredo's store: 'Radways Rapid Relief', 'Canadian Healing Oil', 'Lydia Pynkham's Vegetable Product', with American engraved labels. Borrowed aneroid and *Chuzzlewit*.

St Ignatius Mission–Hart's Ranch, Sunday 5 March 1933

Woke at 5.30. David and Eusebio already had horses and bullock saddled. Arranged packs and had coffee; started 7.15 grey sky. Weather throughout day remained pleasantly dull with slight rain until 3 pm. Travelled at walking pace with bullock until we struck the Bon Success motor road, not cattle trail, known as Mission Road as leads direct for carts to Yupukari. Followed motor tyres and went on ahead of bullock, crossing Manari and Nappi; continued on motor tracks crossing two creeks until 2.10 when sighted village with corral and outstation in distance. Enquired and found I was well off the Pirara track. Learned later should have turned off at Nappi. Tracks made by Hart's car transporting Commission stores. Sat on doorstep while Indian watered horse; drank some brandy and took snaps; no food. Indian produced marriage licences to amuse me. Village called Marakanata. Started again 2.50. Broad trail, straight. Horse very tired. Self tired and thirsty; sighted Pirara 4.45 and arrived at 5.30. Hart gave me tea and cheese. Lent me towel, pyjamas and hammock. Supper 7. 8 Hart suggests Rosary. Whole family and old Indian woman walked up and down in moonlight reciting Sorrowful Mysteries aloud. 8.30 Eusebio and bullock arrived having taken things easily. Decided stay one day here, rest horse and self. Hart says old woman at St Ignatius Piai woman. Pretends to fly. She had been through earlier in day and announced my coming.

[1] Gun caps.

Monday 6 March 1933

Slept heavily and woke stiff. Sent Eusebio off to Manuel Luiz. Coffee 7. School began at 8. Heard my name being invoked by negress governess to reprove children. Many tears and multiplication tables. Teddy Melville arrived in the evening, very conveniently for my journey next day. Rosary again, indoors this time. Brandy with Hart who told me of German who 1913 put three new launches on Rio Branco and raised price of cattle and was shot by his beneficiaries, the excuse being that he was taking turtle eggs out of season.

Tuesday 7 March 1933

Left at 8 with Teddy Melville and reached D'Aguiar's soon after 12, having stopped ten minutes at Manuel Luiz. Uneventful agreeable ride, horses going well. Manuel Luiz has painted front of his house 'Santa Fé, Manuel Luiz da Silva's Ranch, British Guiana,' with two pictures of horse and bullock, making it very like booth at a circus. Inside repainted with marbled objects [?] and some pictures. He lame old negro talking only Portuguese. He asked us to luncheon but I refused, remembering D'Aguiar's mistress was a cook, and we were rewarded with fresh pork stewed in milk. Found Eusebio eating. He reports bullock slow so I sent him on ahead on Karasabai road with the other Indians walking from Bon Success. D'Aguiar not here. Many *kabouras*[1] on river suggests disagreeable time ahead. Height by aneroid 300.

Wednesday 8 March 1933

Left D'Aguiar 7.40 with mounted guide. Rode till 8 towards two small grass rills at right angles to Ireng. Bore right towards Mount Egerton reaching fort at 8.20 leaving small swamp on left. Mount Egerton wooded summit on left (facing as I came) slope. Bore half-left with large swamp on left. 8.30 entered narrow swamp, pass between Mount Egerton and small hills. Level 275. 8.35 emerged into open swamp and rode towards hills reaching foot 8.45. Bore right. Path led between hills left and swamp and large, long lake left. Name Morero; surrounded by hills; conical bush-covered hill at end. Reached end at 9.05 (lake at 9) and turned left into swamp valley between grass hills. Later hill of right bush and savannah opened on left; distant grass hills all round. Ireng probably on left. 9.23 creek across trail, practically no water; level 275. Slow travelling from 9.05, rocks and numerous dry gullies. 9.43 bush. 9.47 Ireng on left very close trail and bush hill. 9.55 emerged into large open savannah enclosed by bare hills. 10.10 cross Yowari creek. Hut on further bank with Indian family reported bullock slept there last night and proceeded early in morning. 10.30 Ireng again. 10.42 bore half-right between two hills, left large

[1] 'Odious insects so small that they easily penetrate any ordinary mosquito curtain.' Evelyn Waugh, *Ninety-Two Days*.

hills in front. Level 300. Bore right and dismounted, led horses up rocky hill. Summit 10.55, level 400. Rising on right and continuing on left. Bore right again and proceeded down further slope and alongside of spur. Ireng visible from summit between bush hills on left. Savannah extended in front and right. 11.15 entered bush. 11.25 crossed Yurora, emerged into savannah. Bore half-left to Karasabai, arrived 12 o'clock noon. Eusebio and bullocks just unsaddling.

Learned Father Keary left this morning. Chief and large gathering shook hands and stared. No supplies so ordered sardines, bread, marmalade and tea. Wanted to wash so was led back to Yurora by little boys. Returned, lunchèd in chief's hut. Hammock on loom, rested. Ten houses, one with upper storey; two skeletons under construction; one ruin; three outlying houses quarter mile distant; very small wood-fenced corral; church.

Thursday 9 March 1933

Hills to north of Karasabai all bush; others bare except single bush hill south. Left 6.30 am with Indian boy as guide and rode NNE up valley. Top of valley swamp; one wet patch at 7 and another few minutes later; otherwise dry. Entered small valley 7.15 and crossed creek Wajei [?]. 7.25 dry creek. Proceeded up right-hand side of valley, bush on both sides. 7.28 bush. Crossed two creeks (or same). Travelling good savannah trot. 7.55 small open swamp (dry) bush. 8.20 open country; valley; short steep climb, going right (due north [?]). Found Indian family. Man wearing red cap; he and boys carrying bows and arrows; women hid behind rocks. Small hill with two huts on left; still bearing N. 8.30 rough bush between hills. Stiff climb (dismounted) 8.35 to 8.50. Descended valley and turned left (NW). 9 valley between large, forest hills. Two grass hills in centre one with village three huts. Mutukeyiping. Crossed creek 9.07 running R–L. Valley narrows down to bush. Small clear place 9.55. Bush again 10–11. Very slow; exceedingly rough trail. 11 emerged and bore right over undulating grass hills. Arrived Tipuru 11.30. Some difficulty find position Karasabai on map. Boy says half day's walk (eight miles?) from Ireng, half hour from Kara-Kara. Father Carey Elwes's map of position of Karasabai must be very wrong.

Found Father Keary here. Bathed in delightful rocky creek, Tipuru, and had luncheon; chicken very badly cooked and yams. Father Keary held instruction at 3, all the children chanting airs [?] in Macushi. Later he and I and his boy Marco went round looking for guide, hunters, and droghers[1] for me. Great difficulties as no one had gun or knew the way or answered consistently, so Father Keary very kindly changed his plans and decided to start with me tomorrow. This will make everything very much easier though

[1] Boats.

perhaps less exciting. Took some photographs. The men mostly wear quills or pins in their lower lips and have villainous Chinese faces. Killed cow so fresh meat tonight. Tipuru houses walled on account of *kaboura*, therefore hot and dark. Level 925. Villagers keep skulls of Arekunas, original inhabitants, among the rocks.

Friday 10 March 1933

Left 8.52, crossed Tipuru 9. Bush till 9.17. 9.50 crossed Kara-Kara. Up Kara-Kara five minutes. Into bush 10.16. Steep descent to Awarabirin. Up creek on left of trail. Bore right into open 9.30. Followed small creek crossing it twice. 10.57 village of five houses named Shimai. Rested until 11.15. Soon entered bush going up creek crossing three times. Very steep descent on rocks into wooded valley. Leading to Ireng. Followed this until 1.30. Bush at first, last half-hour in open. Made camp by half-finished house and empty palm hut near creek. Maripakanu. Passed Patamona family in bush. Man with bracelet on biceps and shoulder straps. Family footsore. Ate fresh meat, rice, dates. Brandy tea. Pleasant bathing place infested *kabouras* who made afternoon rest difficult but better muffled in handkerchiefs. Naked porters' sweat spoilt shirt.

Saturday 11 March 1933

Impossible trace course of journey on map until I have Tipuru village correctly placed. Left camp at 7 and walked through alternate bush and savannah patches for hour and half at fair pace. From 8.35–9.20 steep ascents with flat stretch between. Ireng visible in front on right. Bore right descending through bush. 11 open country and 11.30 creek and home inhabited by negress, mistress of King, Boundary Commission transport foreman. Several Indian passers-by. She gave us fresh milk and four addled eggs. Lunch and slung hammock and rested until 2. Crossed Echilibar 2.45 almost at its mouth and proceeded along Ireng bank until 3.22 when we turned off left through rising valley. At summit, Ireng visible in front having curved. We had now made a circle round Towailing and Towailing mountains which are marked on map as some miles separate but according to our guide are peaks of same spur. At 4.30 we came on three houses where inhabitants welcomed us and sold us a black cock for a Woolworth necklace and put house with leaky roof at our disposal. *Kabouras* very bad. Father Keary baptized a child and married the parents. Very tired. Name Karaparuta.

Sunday 12 March 1933

Very bad night as moon kept *kabouras* awake – also great number of fleas, some mosquitoes, and old bites itching intolerably. Early morning rain and boys came in to shelter but water came through roof. Father Keary said Mass in large circular house – dank and smoky and full of *kabouras*. Left at 8.20 and in half an hour were at Ireng bank again. Went through small valley to avoid curve in river, rejoining it 9–9.15. At 9.30 climbed steep hill of spur. Small creek at top. Hung hammocks and rested 10.30–12.35. Mounted further hillside and proceeded along spur. 1.20 descended and crossed Yowangparu at 1.40. Another climb at 2.05 and descent into broad valley at 2.20. Made camp at large creek at 3. Creek presumably Kowa. *Kabouras* frightful. Bathed in fine smooth rocks and sat muffled in handkerchiefs until sundown. Had been too tired to eat anything except a banana and cup of Bovril at luncheon. They now killed cock and in spite of great discomfort of *kabouras* ate large meal. Moon scarcely penetrated forest and flies disappeared at 6.30. Bell-bird. Hunter went out and came back with one bird size of partridge.

Monday 13 March 1933

Woke feeling infinitely better from long, uninterrupted sleep. Started 6.45 crossing creek and proceeding up it through bush. 7.20 open country. Climbed hill 7.40. 8.10 descended bush and creek. Two dry creeks. 9.30 creek. 10 dry creek. 10.35 fair-sized rocky creek Orinoco [?] proceeded up it 10.50 and crossed it after luncheon rest 12.45. All this through bush. Emerged open valley 1.20 with bush both sides and 1.45 began ascent of middle of three great spurs. Reaching second summit at 2.25. Crossed flat tableland crossed by single creek and at 4.45 reached three houses. Village of Kato on Klementi map. Welcomed with *casiri*, cassava bread, peppers, and green vegetable like spinach. Very tired and footsore. Slept in open shelter, very cold and damp. Badly bitten by fleas and found feet full of jiggers.

Tuesday 14 March 1933

Mass after bad night. Foolishly had six or seven jiggers removed and was lame in both feet in consequence. Started 7.45 proceeding across two small creeks to Chiung which we crossed at 9.05 by two houses. An hour later we reached creek Sipari and went up it, crossing it five times sometimes in bush. Walking very painful; frequent stops and swigs of brandy. After fifth crossing climbed hill, circling left then right and arriving dead beat 11.45 at Kurukubaru. Sat on church steps until hammock swung in small hut divided by bark partitions into four rooms. Fell asleep immediately. Later washed and dressed feet and lay in hammock all day without leaving hut. Had clothes washed.

Wednesday 15 March 1933

Awoke after long sleep, very stiff and sore but feeling better. Dispatched note to Mr Winter at Anandabaru warning him of approach. Looked at Kurukubaru. Thirteen houses and dissolute, large church, people impoverished and site bleak. Height 2875. Hills all round. Short of meat but hunters came with venison. My bearers had only been engaged to go to Kurukubaru and wished to return so I paid them off and engaged another, one of Father Keary's loads having become lighter. Paying off complicated as of course no one had any change and they wanted part-payment in gunpowder caps and shot. Result of rest, feet much better.

Thursday 16 March 1933

Started off 9.15 delayed by redistribution of loads. Cold morning and some rain. Feet fairly well at first but after an hour went dead lame with inflamed little toe. Cut piece out of boot and hobbled to Santa Monica arriving 12.20 in great pain. The village is now reduced to one shabby house surrounded by litter and rendered more desolate by the ruins of a modern shed left by the Boundary Commission last year. Rough ugly scrub round. No water but some stagnant puddles. We hung our hammocks in the trees surrounded by various kinds of biting fly.[1] The old women brought out some greens and pepper and a bowl of warm half-fermented *casiri*. Absolute impossibility of finding position on map as contradictory information that we have come directly away from Roraima and are within half an hour of Tumong.

Our route lay entirely through bush and mostly downhill. 9.35 bush and slight ascent. 10 big descent, followed down creek Owsawa [?] (runs into Tumong) on right, crossed it and followed it on our left. At 11 we came to a fine waterfall and left creek. 11.20 ascent, down to small creek, up again, open patch, bush again, open patch, bush again, open and the red asbestos ruin of Santa Monica in sight. Height 2100.

Friday 17 March 1933

Whenever Father Keary gives up the idea of saying Mass with special intention for our journey we have a better day. He threatened to do so this morning but I dissuaded him and we made a reasonably early start. Through bush all day. There was a plump grey stallion belonging to the Indians which I was able to hire. No saddle or bridle so sat him bareback and Marco led him. I was able to ride for about half the distance, continually mounting and dismounting. Apart from the normal discomfort of an hour's bareback there were the additional pains of a trail cut head-high for foot passengers only, and the feet, particularly the bad one, knocking against trees. However, all this brought into play an entirely new set of pains, so that by looking forward to the relief of walking when riding and vice versa the journey was tolerable. We travelled up the Tumong in defiance of the map, crossing it three times and leaving it on our right. Stopped for lunch at rocky ford; arrived about 3.30 at Anandabaru house, wood house built by Haynes when he was prospecting for

---

[1] 'Flie' in MS.

diamonds. A messenger from Winter met us on the road. By delaying a night on his way from Kurukubaru he had arrived just too late to delay a boat leaving for Kaieteur that morning. Anandabaru surrounded by bracken where a government botanist started a forest fire. The ground round it is so thick with fleas that simply by walking across it our trousers were covered with them. Winter had sent us the key of the bedrooms, so we slung our hammocks and bathed. There was a lime tree so we finished the brandy with lime juice, ate the last sandwiches and last corned beef and last rice, and retired to bed fairly content. At 9 o'clock torrents of rain came on and the roof proved valueless. Found one dry corner where it was possible to hang the hammock in a U and sit up or crouch all night in great discomfort, Father Keary snoring next door above the noise of the storm.

Saturday 18 March 1933

Still raining in morning, and rained all day, with brief intermission in forest when dripping from trees maintained downpour. Breakfast off bananas. In view of muddy condition of trail and swollen streams decided not to try and bring horse, and set off by myself with one guide only, leaving Father Keary to come on with the droghers. Up and down trail through bush 7.30–11.30 over *tacubas*.[1] Less painful going than previous days. Arrived at Mr Winter's prospecting camp – a stone house, hut and house under construction. Winter extremely hospitable – but no hope of boat within week or ten days. Bacon, eggs, bread and butter for luncheon. Father Keary turned up three-quarters of an hour after me. Dined stewed smoked hog. Winter full of good conversation. Slept in partially built house. Children watched me unpack. Gave them rubbish.

Sunday 19 March 1933

I had coffee with Winter while Father Keary waited boys to assemble. Mass in unfinished house. Father Keary went off at 9. Glad to see last of him. Spent restful day in hammock. Found positions on map. Tumong inaccurately drawn and Marapay [?] totally wrong. We are just under north-west corner of Kowatipu.

Tuesday 28 March 1933

Winter began to make arrangements to send me down with a few men to collect sugar and flour, to make a raft at Kaieteur. However yesterday a black man arrived with mail, etc., and it is arranged that I leave tomorrow with full reloading squad. The last ten days have passed uneventfully with gradually decreasing rations. The hunters have brought in very little. An excellent bird

[1] Creeks.

like a pheasant to eat. Also a water-rodent tasting like pork called *labba*. Some venison and pretty dull bush turkey; also wild hog.

Have been to diamond-working once or twice. The bed of a creek is being put through a sieve. Twenty or thirty Indians, men and women, with a few children playing round and lending a hand occasionally. They dig up gravel and take it in barrels up a path to the sieve which consists of three cylinders of wire-mesh. The fine sand goes below and passes through mercury to collect gold dust, large stones shoot out at end, gravel containing beryls, gold-nuggets and diamonds go into sieves where women work lever that washes the clay out by forcing water up and down through it. Water comes through canalized stream from dam made of clay and logs tied to trees with bush wire. Pipes all hollow wood. Pump worked by girl supplies more water. Two girls rotate cylinders. All waste resifting next day. Winter takes out trays and searches. Average yield seven carats a day in twenty-five or so stones, many discoloured either in skin or throughout. Black sand washed by hand that has collected on sacking stoppers.

'Aint you be got' = used you not to have. 'This side' = over here.

Indians all have pets; parrots, fowls, trumpet birds, *waracabra* whose legs get broken, wild hog, *accouris*, etc. My hat, blanket and handkerchiefs create new demand at store. Wrist-watch attracts attention. Indian craze for any new thing.

Winter conversation – genial abuse officials and stories of corruption and incompetence, stories of diamond that is sold and resold to each newcomer, surface cracks having given dull white tinge. Buyers give agent back bad stones and stop out of wages.

Thomas, who builds home with help of little boy and wears white vest and sometimes drawers and always hat and sandals, left wife because of twins. Attempt to carry him away by girl and family frustrated.

Agnes, educated Georgetown, came back and couldn't stand mother or lover, so lover married mother and gave her hell so slept with Portuguese catechist.

Necessity of coaxing Indians to work.

Made cocktails out of over-proof spirit bought for liniments.

Nail came off toe Sunday and consequent complete recovery.

Objections Governor's road; build on sand surface over root basis; upkeep bound to be expensive. Nigger reports lorry service has not worked for fortnight. Impossible cultivate borders of ridge road.

Jig = washing sieve. Battel = washing pan. Trommel = whole machine.

'Story' is used in wide sense. 'Story finish' = that is the end of the matter. 'Bad story', etc.

Wednesday 29 March 1933

Some cassava bread came in unexpectedly, but no meat except one macaw.

We live on eggs, and I am taking eggs and a little bread and one tin salmon as rations. The black man, Sobers, gloomy about prospects at Amatuk where Portuguese named Diabolo controls means of transit. But contradictory in his reports. Also says impossible make Kaieteur–Kangaruma in one day. Naked girl came across clearing but ran at sight of camera. Sobers disposed to take gloomiest views of the facilities of reaching Georgetown before next Friday. Paid Winter $15 for mess wages and $2 for my rations. Halved *Martin Chuzzlewit* with him. Was to have taken down diamonds, but they have to be boiled in aqua negra first and soaked in hydrochloric acid. Tip to servants, red cotton handkerchiefs. Have £110 and $110 in wallet and $30 for expenses to Georgetown. Rain off and on all day.

Thursday 30 March 1933

Left Mikraparu at 7.30 and arrived Chinapeng mouth at 2.30. Line led direct east until 11.15; then down deep hillside, sliding from tree to tree, turning north. Crossed broad stream running left to right. Boy said Chinapeng but obviously not. Rested an hour and ate three hard eggs and some bread. Left at 12.45, crossed another creek running left to right, probably Wang. Between creeks passed empty Indian huts. Trail became very hard where Boundary Commission had crossed. Reached Chinapeng at 1.50. Climbed hill and descended into remains of plantation. Forest trees cleared away and fruit trees growing among high weeds, also bamboos. Large abandoned store: counters, cupboards, a weighing machine, floor of sawn planks full of jiggers and fleas, thatch roof full of spiders, bats, etc. Continuous falls in Chinapeng from where we met it to here. Water deep and fast and cold. Indians turned up 4.10, those who left today before those who left yesterday. Bathed, drank rum. Rations supplemented by yesterday's kill = $1\frac{1}{2}$ macaws. Tired but no blisters or real trouble. I walked with the two blacks, Sobers and Gerry. Winter has given me generous rations considering his condition. I think he was really sorry to see me go. Probable day arrival Georgetown Friday (tomorrow) week.

Friday 31 March 1933

Starting delayed by Indian apathy until 7.30. There is a family, wife, husband and small boy who insist on bringing dog. Other two diamond-boys quite satisfactory. We crammed ourselves into flat-bottomed boat and made slow progress, the two blacks pulling very hard with improvised oars, the two good boys paddling a bit, the bad family eating. I said I would take paddle for hour and regretted it in ten minutes. Blacks use 'meet' for 'arrive'. We ate in the boat and slowly went downstream, very smooth rapid water giving detailed reflection except where strewn with pink, white and yellow petals.

Reached Kaieteur landing at 5.10. Left the men to get the luggage up and hurried across to see the fall, arriving there 5.30. One comes on fall quite suddenly. The light was poor but the whole gorge and basin absolutely free from mist. Saturated green cliffs, white river with cataracts visible for miles. Water just overflowing as if from over-filled bath. Brown at lip, then white, then all mist, descending very slowly, smoking, much like muslin drapery. At bottom, foam and rising spray and waves breaking like sea over boulders. Row scarcely audible from rest house a few hundred yards away. Rest house, large and in fair repair, carved with names. Sobers urged me to add mine, but Gerry scoffed saying, 'Half of dey is dead already.'

Saturday 1 April 1933

Revisited fall at 6. Hung with white clouds. Went down to lip with Sobers. He has passed nine times and always visits fall. Bad family did not leave hammocks until after 7. Decided to leave them behind. Hurried down to Tukeit landing. Very stiff descent but good rock footholds. Made descent in one hour and five minutes. Bathed at bottom. Confirmed in decision to abandon bad family by finding boat far too small to accommodate them. Even as it was, we were very low in the water.

Left 9.15 and paddled slowly down gorge. Cliffs not continuous but series of precipitous hills, densely wooded. Beached Waratuk cataract at 11.45. Beached boat, dragged it over rapids, cooked breakfast on sandbank the other side. Left 12.45. Very slow progress to Amatuk – same scenery. Here trouble was anticipated from Portuguese named Diabolo who had acquired the only boat on lower stretch of river, but while we were setting out to walk down and shout across to him, Sobers saw black pork-knocker friends fishing. Diabolo had not arrived and they had appropriated boat. They brought us down to Diabolo's house, and secured boat next day for dollar tip. Then on to McTurk's house on island and abandoned store. Polite old caretaker. Fell out with Gerry. Furniture and some books. Perched on water at high tide. Very bad night worried by flies inside net and bats outside.

Sunday 2 April 1933

Left at 7 and arrived 10.45 at Kangaruma. McTurk's store. Polite manager Wilson. Bought butter, beer, tobacco, marmalade, sugar, etc. Found several *Overseas Daily Mail*s up to February 28th. No world-shattering events. Several deaths.

Monday 3 April 1933

Left Kangaruma 9.15 in Ford van. Soon reached Potaro landing where Minehaha van and launch were waiting. Long delay; quarrel between two men over spanner. Attempts to take wheel off car. At length started down Potaro; took in cargo at Garraway Stream where beginnings of bridge and large camp visible. Engine often stopped. Reached Tumatumari at 1.30. Ramshackle village. Decent rest house. Catechist lent me books. Shopped evening to buy gold and real rum. Fresh bread; rum; limes.

Tuesday 4 April 1933

After some threatening and bribery I managed to induce launch to start at 10.45, two hours forty-five minutes after scheduled time. Comfortable, tedious journey sitting under little shelter amidships with three negresses who ate and one who had thermos and sand shoes and gold earrings and a bag of peppermints. Aged captain. Arrived Rockstone 8.30 at night, and left 11.30. Clerk in difficulties counting tickets, engineer in difficulty starting engine. Travelled herded together with the luggage (about twelve of us) in one truck. Slung behind motor tractor. Arrived Wismar 4 am. Slung hammock on board the ship and slept two hours despite horde of mosquitoes. Rockstone completely derelict. Wismar busy little black, East Indian, Chinese community.

Wednesday 5 April 1933

Paid various bills promised last evening. Ship left 8.30 am. Impossible telegraph Georgetown.

Waugh was back in England in May 1933. In September, he met for the first time Laura Herbert, who became his second wife; he went on a Hellenic cruise with Alfred Duggan, and through him visited the Herbert family at their villa, Altachiara, at Portofino near Genoa.

In October and November 1933, the Westminster Diocesan Court began the hearings into Waugh's first marriage that eventually led, in June 1935, to its annulment.

The next section of the diary describes an expedition to Spitzbergen in 1934. It was intended by its 'leader', Sandy Glen (later Sir Alexander Glen, chairman of the Scottish Tourist Board), to be a reconnaissance for the Oxford University Arctic Expedition of 1935–6, but an unexpected thaw cut the journey short.

London, Thursday 5 July 1934

I woke up in time to go to tea with Gerald Berners.[1] When he asked me he said, 'It is a *tea* party you know', with a little giggle. 'Don't you think that it is an amusing idea?' I said, '*Very* amusing.' It was intensely hot. I sat for a time

[1] The 9th Baron Berners, musical peer; as a composer, admired by Stravinsky. Built a piano in the back of his Rolls-Royce.

with Bridget and then told her that her lipstick was all over her face. It made her look as though she were smiling. Sitwells, Dianas Cooper and Guinness, Paulie Sudley,[1] Oggie,[2] Lady Alexander, etc. After tea I did not know where to go so I walked across Belgrave Square to see if anyone was at home at Halkyn House.[3] Hugh[4] was in the library drinking gin. I asked why he was in London and he said he was going to Spitzbergen on Saturday with Sandy Glen who had come over to Madresfield[5] for the day at Sibell's[6] Chepstow Races party. Coote[7] was there and later Maimie[8] and Poppet Jackson.[9] I said I would go to Spitzbergen too. Then I went back to dress. While I was in my bath Sandy Glen rang up and came to see me. We had some champagne while I dressed. He said it was all right my going to Spitzbergen with him. I gave him £25 for fares and he gave me a list of things I should need.

Dined with Lettice Ashley Cooper. Hamish[10] was there. He said he had been drunk and did not feel well. Then he opened the peerage and asked Lettice about her aunts. Poppet and husband there too. I was thinking all the time about Spitzbergen. We went to David Tennant's[11] party in the country. The drive took an hour. Someone had removed the signposts David had put up to show the way. It was a very bad party. I met Colin Davidson who said it was a bad party so we left together. I got to bed soon after 3.

Friday 6 July 1934

Met Hugh at Halkers[12] and drank gin. Bought skis and ice axes and balaclava helmets at Lillywhite's. Sandy was very pleased because he had got a crate of chocolate and some morphia. Lunch at Simon Harcourt-Smith's. Came away with Lady Jowitt. Then in great heat tried on windproof clothes at a shop in Holborn. There were hikers in the shop buying a tent. When I arrived the salesman said, 'The Spitzbergen Expedition.' I got a sleeping bag and a mackintosh cover. I dined with my parents and collected more luggage. Returned to Savile at about 10. Rang up the 43[13] and asked for Winnie. They said she had not yet arrived so I went to her flat. She put up a good show of being sorry for my departure.

[1] Viscount Sudley.
[2] Olga Lynn.
[3] The Beauchamp town house.
[4] The Hon. Hugh Lygon.
[5] The Beauchamp house near Great Malvern.
[6] Lady Sibell Lygon's.
[7] Lady Dorothy Lygon.
[8] Lady Mary Lygon.
[9] Augustus John's daughter, then married to Professor Derek Jackson.
[10] The Hon. Hamish St Clair Erskine.
[11] Son of the 2nd Baron Glenconner; married to the actress Hermione Baddeley.
[12] Nickname for Halkyn House.
[13] 'Half a speak-easy and half a brothel.' Alec Waugh, *The Fatal Gift* (London 1974), p. 16.

Saturday 7 July 1934

To Farm Street to confess Winnie. A few more purchases including a birthday cake for Teresa.[1] Waited at the Savile for parcels to arrive, drinking with Tom Burns.[2] A billiard cue came for another member and it was put with my luggage. At 12 to Halkers. Tom came too. We drank gin and waited for news from Lillywhite's. Susan Carnegie came too. Winnie sent me a telegram of good wishes. Nothing from Madresfield. We got to King's Cross five minutes before the train was due to start. A man was there from Lillywhite's with the rest of our goods. Sandy taking particular care of the chocolate.

The train left at 1.5. At first we were in high spirits, drank a jug of black velvet in the dining car, and several liqueurs. Then the heat began to get us down. We drank gin all through the afternoon and the steward got tired of going to and fro. By 6 o'clock we were silent and exhausted. We sat in shirt sleeves and a clergyman's wife stared at us. The train was over an hour late at Newcastle.

Sandy had permission from the Home Office to export morphia. He had to show it at the customs. They had been warned to expect him.

We were travelling second class. The cabins were good but there was no bar and too few servants. We did not get dinner until after 9 o'clock. Then the table was covered with little metal dishes of sardines, tomatoes, cheese and so on. We thought at first that these were *hors d'oeuvres*. Then we discovered a dish of tepid stew and realized that this was the whole dinner.

A Norwegian sat at our table. He said, 'Do you like Norwegian herring?'

'Yes.'

'They're very cheap.'

Later we offered him a plate of them. He said, 'There is too much talk about fish. It is *very* cheap.'

Upstairs in the smoking-room Sandy got into talk with a man from the Outer Hebrides and Hugh with a doctor on his way to join the *Rodney*. I was tired. Went to bed early with a dose of Dial.[3]

Sunday 8 July 1934

The Norwegian who had complained of the cheap fish was drunk before breakfast. He sat in the smoking-room singing folk songs and calling 'Cuckoo. Cuckoo.' At first it was funny. He tried to walk along the top of the seats and broke an electric bulb with his head. It exploded with a great noise. After that he was aggrieved because the steward spoke roughly to him. He kept saying that he had paid as much for his ticket as anyone else, that we were given beer

---

[1] Teresa Jungman.

[2] Of Burns, Oates, & Washbourne (later Burns, Oates), Catholic publishers.

[3] Sleeping pill.

and cigarettes because we were English. 'It is not correct. It is not correct,' he kept saying. He took up with another drunk and they danced together. The second drunk had a sweetheart waiting for him, he said, and showed us a bottle of 'parfoom' he had bought for her. Then he tried to pick a quarrel on the grounds that we were 'college men.' After luncheon both drunks were sleepy. At Bergen, at 6 o'clock, they looked torpid, but they kept up their joke about 'cuckoo'. There was a man in a kilt, and a couple in green leather shorts.

There was half an hour of fjord before we reached port. At first Bergen seemed ugly, red gables dotted among green hills and square Thames-side warehouses. Sandy's *laissez-passer* was effective and we got our baggage straight to the Tromso ship without customs; an inferior ship to the *Venus* in every way, with surly officers and a badly equipped, four-berth cabin. We did a lot of carrying ourselves. When everything was fixed we went ashore. The waterfront is built with charming eighteenth-century timber houses with semi-classical gables. We looked for a gay restaurant but found nothing except a large empty hotel, with an orchestra, called the Rosencrantz. Good dinner and bad Chianti. Afterwards looked for a café without success. Hugh went to sleep on shore. In our ship they turned out the lights at 12 but it was only twilight. At 10.30 it had been broad day.

Monday 9 July 1934

I woke up at various times in the night. It was noisy and very stuffy in the cabin. At 9 I dressed without shaving and went round to breakfast with Hugh at his hotel – prawns and cheese and eggs. Sandy went to the shipping office and got permission for us to use the first-class quarters on the *Prinsesse Ragnhild*. It is Teresa's birthday. She ought now to be receiving a series of parcels from me with no name attached. It is more fun for her that way.

A slight drizzle of rain; the people in the town glum and drab, except for a few epicene hikers; a few ruddy and flaxen children. Everyone speaks some English – not only waiters and people behind the counters in tourist shops, but stevedores. They look and smell English – and in point of fact a great number of them *are* English, for two big cruising ships are in harbour. Only here the tourists and natives are indistinguishable. Brilliant green grass. An old church with seventeenth-century carving, a 'cocktail' bar forbidden to sell spirits, shops full of standardized ready-made clothing and hideous ornaments.

We sailed in the evening. High tea at 8. We sat at the end of a long table, laden with salted and smoked meats and fish. The ship has no licence to sell spirits.

10, 11 and 12 July 1934

Steamed slowly north, threading between islands and up fjords and stopping three and four times a day at little, wood-built villages. I cut my head open getting ashore at our first port and bled extravagantly. Drove in great cold from Molde to Gjemnes and crossed by ferry to Kristisund where we picked up the ship again. At Trondheim we had baths and breakfast in an hotel with a palm court. It rained all that morning and the cathedral with St Olav's tomb was locked. The scenery becomes more Arthurian as we get further north. At this moment – on the way to Bodö – the sun is shining (it rained all yesterday) and the mountains on the starboard bow like a Doré engraving.

The ship is very full. The third class noisy with children. A Lutheran pastor from Providence, Rhode Island, shares our cabin. He sleeps in his cloth and lies all day in his bunk reading mystical works in English. There are Americans, English, and even French on board, but most of the passengers are Norwegian. They are attractive in childhood and old age. We read Edgar Wallace, look at maps and play cards – Hugh and I picquet, and cut-throat bridge for the three of us. Our chief interest is in the growth of our beards. Hughie's is golden and even. Mine appears to be black and patchy, with the making of fine Dundreary whiskers, but too little on the chin. Sandy shaves. What with my bloody bandage and our chins we look very disreputable and the English passengers have ceased making friendly advances. The pastor thinks we are college boys on vacation. The towns where we stopped were mostly dry. At some it was possible to buy bottles of spirit. Nowhere were there any bars or cafés.

On Friday 13th we reached Tromoso and left the *Prinsesse Ragnhild*. By the end of the voyage we had become very unpopular with the other passengers, particularly with the women who did not scruple to make unfavourable judgements on us in our hearing.

At Tromso a series of old men became important in the leader's life. At the moment of our landing he disappeared, murmuring that he must look for a splendid old man. Throughout the twenty-four hours of our stay there he prosecuted the quest with varying success, returning drunk in the evening with incoherent stories of a particularly fine old man who was the best ice skipper in the Arctic, had got through £60,000 in drink and had rescued a Rothschild from death. It was intensely hot at Tromso so that we sat in our shirt sleeves when we played cards. One of the leader's old men was named Reathe – a deaf Norwegian who had served in the American army and was now British vice-consul. He was immensely helpful to us, doing our shopping and cashing our cheques, but he would not drink or even come to the drink shop. We went to a cinema with him in the evening. We had a few purchases to make – potatoes, oranges, rum, socks, etc.

In the early afternoon of the 14th – attended to the quay by various old men of the leader's – we sailed in the *Lyngen*. The leader had warned us that this was to be the most disagreeable part of the expedition, but like most of his predictions – notably that Tromso was a cosmopolitan resort full of bars and hotels – this proved wholly inaccurate. I was able to hear Mass on Saturday morning. The *Lyngen* is a small ship subsidized by the government. She does five trips a year – fortnightly during the summer months. In winter Spitzbergen is cut off from all communications with Norway. There are only three or four passengers on board so we each have double cabins to ourselves. A warm afternoon through the islands to Hammerfest which we reached soon after midnight. Golden sunlight streaming into the cabin all night and sleep almost impossible.

Next day it was overcast and colder. The ship rolled a certain amount and all the passengers including Hugh and the leader were seasick. I spent most of the day in my cabin reading Saki. At night I took a treble dose of Dial and slept for thirteen hours. Tuesday 17th was cold but calmer towards evening and Hugh and the leader appeared to play picquet, Hugh constantly winning. At about 7 we came into sight of south cape of Spitzbergen and from then onwards had land on the starboard bow. Black mountains with glaciers flowing down to the sea between them – occasionally a magnificent burst of light on a narrow silver strip between iron grey sky and iron grey sea, the glaciers brilliantly white, the clouds cutting off the peaks of the mountains. The sea perfectly calm from supper-time onwards. Writing now at about 11 in the expectation of disembarking at Advemt Bay at about 2.

18 July 1934

We arrived at Advemt Bay in early morning. A very desolate prospect. Low clouds and a circle of hills, colourless and dark, except at the water's edges where there was grass; the higher slopes below the clouds were marked like zebra with white streaks of snow. Small copper-green icebergs floating near the banks. We unloaded the stores and Hugh and the leader elected to row them down to our whaler which was unable to start for seven or eight hours. I went to my cabin and slept. We left before 11 and arrived a little before 5, spending most of the day in the forecastle periodically drinking weak tea and eating cheese. We disembarked at a spot known alternately as Scottish Camp and Bruce City, which consists of four huts at the foot of a glacier – derelict but in good condition. The largest hut had been used last year as base camp by the Oxford Expedition and we found a number of stores left behind them – also a sketch book, lying in the open with a watercolour drawing of no merit, uninjured by twelve months' exposure – six of them under snow. The camp was built in 1907 by a bogus mining company. There is a length of trolley rail and we were able to push our stores up. We returned to the whaler and drank some rum. The leader gave the bottle to the men – it caused very little pleasure to them and great concern to Hughie and me. Terns are nesting all round the huts and they make a hostile demonstration whenever we appear, swooping down within a few inches of our heads with shrill abuse.

No diary exists between July 1934 (the 'Spitzbergen Expedition' returned to the United Kingdom at the end of August) and July 1936. The opening entry, when the diary resumes, refers to a telegram from Archbishop Godfrey telling Waugh that Rome had agreed to the annulment of his first marriage. With this news, Waugh's prospects changed. In 1933 he had met Laura Herbert in Italy, and by 1935 he was in love with her. She was born in 1916, the daughter of Mary and Aubrey Herbert MP of Pixton Park, Somerset. Mary Herbert was a daughter of the 4th Viscount de Vesci, a member of a family that had been prominent members of the Protestant Ascendancy in Ireland since the seventeenth century, but after her husband's death in 1923 she had been converted to Roman Catholicism. Aubrey Herbert was a half-brother of the Earl of Carnarvon who discovered the tomb of Tutankhamun, and also of Evelyn Gardner's mother. Laura Herbert was thus brought up as a Roman Catholic, and, as it happened, was a first cousin of Waugh's first wife.

In 1934 Waugh published *A Handful of Dust* and began a biography of Edmund Campion, the Jesuit martyr. In 1935 he paid his second visit to Abyssinia, this time to cover the opening stages of the Italian–Abyssinian war for the *Daily Mail*, one of the few newspapers in Britain sympathetic to the Fascist cause. On his way back to England from that assignment, which he had not taken wholly seriously, Waugh in January 1936 interviewed and was impressed by Mussolini. The purpose of his return visit to Abyssinia in the summer of 1936, which the next section of the diary describes, was to round off his book *Waugh in Abyssinia*.

London, Tuesday 7 July 1936

Holyhead midnight; sleeper and sandwich. Euston 5.30 daylight. Drove through empty streets to St James's where I found telegram 'Decision favourable. Godfrey.' Bath, shaved; lay down but did not sleep. At 8 rang up Bruton Street and was told that Laura had gone out to church. Dressed and went to Farm Street. Laura and Mary there. Knelt behind them and told Laura news in porch. Walked back to Bruton Street to breakfast. Took Laura to her Academy,[1] then bought her handkerchiefs. Message to call on Diana;[2] found her with face expressionless in mud mask. Took Laura to lunch at Paganis; she with paint on face. Went to see her act in mime, drove back with

[1] Royal Academy of Dramatic Art.
[2] Lady Diana Cooper.

Mary. Dined Burns at Simpson's and went to film *Fury*. Saw Laura for hour (red dress) after she had been to ball.

Wednesday 8 July 1936

Slept heavily; had drink with Jessel. Lunched with Count del Balzo at Claridge's and colleague. He was hopeful but uncertain about permission for Abyssinia. Cocktail party Simon Elwes – full of family and Russian ballet. Dined at Boulestin: Jennifer Fry[1] and Mrs Belloc Lowndes and other gossips. Chef described Laura's soufflé of spinach as a fantasy.

Thursday 9 July 1936

Downpour of rain. Went to be photographed. Chris lunched with me at St James's, called for Laura at 3.30 and spent afternoon with her. Dined Hubert[2] and Maimie[3] at the Maison Basque and had supper L. at Café Royal.

Friday 10 July 1936

Wrote review of Aldous Huxley's *Eyeless in Gaza*. Lunched with Hugh[4] and Maimie. Called for Laura and gave her high tea. Dined Bruton Street Mary, Gabriel,[5] C. Mendl, Belloc and went to L.'s play. She looked lovely – as though on the way to the guillotine and spoke well. About third best of the girls. Remarkably good girl named Lott. Supper at Café Royal.

Saturday 11 July 1936

Spent day entirely with Laura. Crossword in Bruton Street; luncheon. Went to Kew Gardens and were caught in storm. Dined before gas fire in Nancy Rodd's bedroom. Both felt sick. Dined at Jardin des Gourmets. Film Curzon.

Sunday 12 July 1936

Spent day entirely with Laura. Mass at Farm Street at 12. Luncheon St James's. Afternoon Bruton Street until evening when we went to the park to hear orators. Dined Bruton Street. News cinema.

Monday 13 July 1936

Gave Laura early lunch and lunched with D'Arcy. Cocktails Christopher Sykes. Dined Patrick[6] – Yorkes, Bowra, Coote. 10.30 Bruton Street.

[1] Daughter of Alathea and Geoffrey Fry, and niece of Waugh's first wife.
[2] Hubert Duggan, Alfred Duggan's brother.
[3] Lady Mary Lygon.
[4] The Hon. Hugh Lygon.
[5] Gabriel Herbert, one of Laura's elder sisters; she married Alexander (Alick) Dru in 1943.
[6] The Hon. Patrick Balfour.

Tuesday 14 July 1936

Early Mass at Farm Street, breakfast with L. Bruton Street. Drinks Hubert and Maimie. Luncheon Claridge's Violet Clifton for Sheikh of Bahrein. Drove with Diana[1] into Hertfordshire looking for house. Came to Highgate.[2]

Wednesday 15 July 1936

Highgate. Slept beautifully and again afternoon. Odd jobs, crossword, small walks.

Thursday 16 July 1936

Great difficulty getting man for dinner tonight, asked Simon Harcourt-Smith who said he and his wife would come to supper. Hubert at last accepted. Went to tea at Bruton Street for interview with Mary who arrived late and agitated with Auberon[3] and headache. She says we must wait until October before being engaged and Christmas before being married. Sidney Herbert[4] pounced on Laura two nights ago. We found him with Betty Cranborne at Buck's. My dinner very boring indeed but fun for Carolyn.[5] Irene Ravensdale talked of God, Jews, King and Simpson and was tight. We went on to the Savoy Grill where Hubert rejoined us. Poppy and Georgia, having a night off from their husbands, took us to the Nest. Black man dressed as woman. David Herbert and party. Clark-Kerrs there. Went on to Manhattan. Hubert tipsy. B. Fisher avaricious [?]. Back to St James's sober but tired 6 am.

Friday 17 July 1936

Up at 8 for breakfast with Laura. Then to Highgate. Crossword with my father. Slept in afternoon. Saturday, Sunday: Highgate.

Monday 20 July 1936

Came into London; luncheon with Laura. Day and dinner Laura. *Seagull.*

Tuesday 21 July 1936

Lunched Laura beastly face Simpson. Saw her act *Macbeth.* Sherry Grants.[6] Cocktail party Maimie. Dinner Ritz Grill. Fury all day culminating waiters.

[1] Lady Diana Cooper.
[2] Waugh's parents moved to Highgate from Hampstead in the summer of 1933.
[3] Auberon Herbert, b.1922; Laura's brother.
[4] Presumably Sir Sidney Herbert, a Conservative MP.
[5] Mrs Cobb, proprietress of the Easton Court Hotel.
[6] Laura Herbert's sister Bridget married Capt. Allister Grant in 1935.

Wednesday 22 July 1936

Lunch Lady Gainsborough; sat next enchanting Maureen Noel.[1] Afternoon L. Dined Katharine; supper Dru and Gabriel. Permission Abyssinia. L. perm.

Thursday 23 July 1936

Luncheon Buck's Bridget and L. Herbert madly jaggering[2] Howards cocktail party. Saw Laura off to Clonboy.[3] Cocktails Mrs Clifton. Dinner Travellers Club: Billy, Chris,[4] D'Arcy; jolly evening; drunk at the end (lie).

Pixton Park, Friday 24 July 1936

Train 9. Breakfast with Chris. Met L. Reading. Tedious journey. Pixton luncheon: Mary, Auberon. Lovely afternoon and evening. Grants arrived late.

Saturday 25 July 1936

Last night poor little Laura terribly scared by bat in bed. Storm. Lovely day, raining continually. Capt. Goad arrived. Phil-Italian. Grants. Picked vegetable named pompion.

Sunday 26 July 1936

Early Mass at Minehead. Fine day particularly afternoon and evening spent pottering with Laura. Played picquet after dinner and stayed up after others had gone to bed. Grants and Auberon left.

Monday 27 July 1936

Mary left early. Breakfast with Laura. 9.35 train to Westbury where Chris met me. Luggage lost. Lunched Mells:[5] Chris, Father David Mathew. Returned London in time for dinner with Burns and cinema.

[1] Lady Maureen Noel (b.1917), daughter of the 4th earl of Gainsborough.

[2] Private-language word used by Lygon family and Waugh meaning 'eager to please'. Also used as a noun: e.g. Boswell was Dr Johnson's 'jagger'.

[3] Surrey home – at Englefield Green – of Laura's grandmother, Lady de Vesci.

[4] Lord Clonmore; Christopher Hollis.

[5] The Manor House at Mells, some fifteen miles south of Bath, had been held by the Horner family since the dissolution of the monasteries. Katharine Horner married Raymond Asquith, the elder son of the statesman; after Raymond was killed in the First World War, she became a Roman Catholic. They had three children: Lady Helen (b.1908); Julian (b.1916), known as 'Trim', who became the 2nd Earl of Oxford and Asquith after Asquith's death in 1928; and Lady Perdita (b.1910), known as 'Per', who married in 1931 the Hon. William (Billy) Jolliffe, later the 4th Baron Hylton. Katharine Horner was a friend of Hilaire Belloc; and Monsignor Ronald Knox, whose biography Waugh published in 1959, spent the last ten years of his life at the Manor House. Waugh's old Oxford friend Christopher Hollis lived in Mells village; so did Conrad Russell, a great friend of Lady Diana Cooper. On his frequent visits to Mells, Waugh sometimes stayed in digs with Mrs Long.

Tuesday 28 July 1936

Busy day seeing Peters, Curry [?], collecting clothes at Highgate, tickets, money, etc. Grants and Helen Asquith dined with me Boulestin. Later to Savoy where found Perry and Kitty.[1] Had arranged to meet Hubert at Halkyn House but Lady Beauchamp had just dropped dead so my arrival, tipsy and with Brownlows, was not opportune. Went alone to the Nest where I found Peter Rodd and Mary Sewell. Drank with Olivia Greene, she very drunk. Put her to bed. Back to St James's very late and drunk.

London–Rome, Wednesday 29 July 1936

Awake early and still drunk; morning passed in trance. Got Rome Express at 2. Pleasant journey in empty sleeper. Sent perhaps indiscreet telegram to Laura.

Rome, Thursday 30 July 1936

Read Fleming's new book[2] for review. Arrived Rome at 8.10. Came to Russie. Stampa rang up, asking me to call tomorrow. Walked in breathless streets.

Friday 31 July 1936

Went to see Straneo [?] at the Press Ministry – polite but not cordial. Saw the minister – cordial and polite in intention, but unattractive chap. They passed me on to the Ministry of Colonies where the man I have to see, Ceralli, was out. Wrote the review of Fleming's book. Ate spaghetti in hotel. Went out at 4 and after delay saw Ceralli who gave me visa for Ethiopia, arranged for me to travel to Mogadishu and so to Harar, but raised suspicion that the Italians expect me to pay for this trip myself. In the evening walked to *biblioteca* feeling strong desire to drink Acqua di Trevi but found it shut so ate bad dinner at Colonna.

Saturday 1 August 1936

Lonely and a little peevish. Again visited Straneo who hedged about expenses. Went to the Vatican exhibition of the Press and was obliged by officious attendants to go through entire pavilion containing exhibits of Catholic periodicals of entire world, decorated with diagrams showing activities of journalists; pathetic historical section; new art; steps of variegated marbles; vast plaster tablets of papal pronouncements, oddly incorporated in building [?] rococo fountain with ship spouting water from rigging. Decided to

[1] The 6th Baron and Lady Brownlow. Lord Brownlow was a personal Lord-in-Waiting to Edward VIII from July 1936 to the abdication in December 1936.
[2] *News From Tartary*, by Peter Fleming.

go to Assisi on Monday evening. Studied *Osservatore* with aid of dictionary. Dined on Pincio.

Sunday 2 August 1936

Mass at San Silvestro. Spent day swotting Italian. Great difficulty with definite article. Kept awake by mosquitoes. Obliged dope at 3.

Assisi, Monday 3 August 1936

Went to Ministro Stampa. Kept waiting long time then told nothing decided about my fare. Minister in Berlin. Chucked for luncheon by Livia Sergio. Had refused Villari but caught him at his club and lunched there. Returned to pack and caught afternoon train Foligno–Assisi. Hot and crowded journey. Last stage by motor rail. Came to find delightful old hotel with big stone balcony opening on cloistered square. Church of St Francis opposite. Moonlight. Charming *maître d'hôtel*. Good wine. Almost sleepless night mosquitoes.

Tuesday 4 August 1936

No promised telegram from Stampa. Very hot. Spent morning sightseeing. Lovely town. Bells and Giottos. Heavy luncheon, then slept. Missing Laura.

Wednesday 5 August 1936

Hotter, missing Laura more. An evening of indescribable beauty. Visited San Damiano.

Assisi–Naples, Thursday 6 August 1936

Left Assisi 7.30 am and stood up in streamlined motor train Foligno–Rome. Enormous speed. Went straight Stampa where Straneo [?] had no news about me from his minister or from London. He tried to persuade me to stay on another week. Only one place left in ship – *Leonardo da Vinci* – and that in cabin for four. I became angry and he gave in and agreed to pay my fare on his own responsibility. I hope he doesn't get into trouble. Returned to Russie. Manager said, 'Do you wish to take a bath?' I must have looked hot. Lunched on Pincio, wrote letters, returned Stampa to collect letters of introduction, and ticket. Caught 7.35 pm to Naples. Lovely journey – cool and empty carriage and bottle of Frascati. Ghastly night in Grand Hotel bitten by mosquitoes.

Friday 7 August 1936

Feeling low after bad night. Ship due to leave at 5. Long formalities with passport, etc., before embarking. Minute, ancient, densely crowded ship. My cabin appalling, but everyone extremely agreeable. All Italians except one Belgian.

En route Naples–Djibouti, Monday 10 August 1936

Even now, when it is agreeable on deck, our cabin is uninhabitable. God knows what it will be like in the Red Sea. We spent most of Saturday at Messina taking on cargo. We are now heavily loaded and slow. The ship was clearly not built for the tropics. No ventilation in our cabin except one port hole. But the food is simple and the chaps at my table have realized I am not good at general conversation. One officer parades the decks in riding boots and spurs. Another in my cabin sleeps in a hairnet. At intervals they fire at and miss clay pigeons. Mass yesterday on deck attended by the second-class passengers, but few first. Four or five children seem to fill the ship. A cinema in the evenings. I peg away at my Italian, but so far have succeeded only in losing every word of French.

Tuesday 11 August 1936

Arrived at Port Said midday and sailed 5 o'clock. The Italians forbidden to land; only Belgian and I allowed privilege visiting Simon Arzt[1] and walking for an hour on seafront.

Wednesday 12 August 1936

Cool in the canal, but soon got hotter in Red Sea. Cabin intolerable. Still struggling with Italian lessons.

Thursday 13 August 1936

Sent radio to Santini, governor Mogadishu, to ask whether transport available for Harar. Limp and sticky as a pack of old playing cards.

Friday 14 August 1936

Decided cut losses on trip and go straight to Addis Ababa. Slept night on deck. Stopped Port Sudan. Very orderly. Officious young harbour officer ordering passengers not to sit on rails of ship. At Port Said English police sergeant, seeing my passport: 'Hullo, British? Can you speak any English, I wonder.' At Port Sudan, asking to land, 'Well you've come in an Italian ship you know.' Kind of concert in evening with ices and amateur singing.

Massawa, Saturday 15 August 1936

Massawa. Arrived about sunset. Dusty, crowded, noisy – lorries and wireless all night (Assumption). Ice-cream cart with palm canopy.

Sunday 16 August 1936

Day of blistering heat. No wind. Stayed at Massawa until 8 o'clock. Passengers who disembark replaced by new. Ship fuller than ever. Four in

[1] Emporium.

cabin but totally uninhabitable anyway. Sleeping for few hours on top deck. Reading *Pickwick Papers*. No reply from Santini. French-speaking geologist making himself agreeable. No cold bath water. On lower decks, in fact everywhere out of wind, hot to touch.

Monday 17 August 1936

Day of intolerable heat and boredom. Stopped Assab.

Djibouti, Tuesday 18 August 1936

Arrived early morning at Djibouti. Long delay in landing. Hotels Arcades and Continental full. At last got room at Europe a few minutes before arrival of Italian officer who slept in dormitory on the landing. Saw highly agreeable Wop consul. Went to Continental where found Lee and Moriatis.[1] Latter lately expelled ex Addis: full of stories starvation at Addis, withdrawal of all outpost garrisons, bets Addis will be in Ethiopian hands before Mashal [?] if only for few hours, says execution of Abuna[2] Petros [?] grave mistake. Truth appears to be Wops in jam. Last month train derailed and looted at Hadina [?]; passengers marooned in store thirty-six hours; telegraph cut and bridges above and below so that relief train unable get through; four days before reached Addis, several dead; Greek woman and two children under train throughout looting only black eye. Sharp reprisals Eritrea troops sent clear up district.

Wops have no control over Dessye road. Doubtful if they haven't evacuated Dessye and Debra Birhan. Fighting few weeks ago in woods round British Legation. Heavy lorries lately ambushed. Heavily and well-armed *shiftas*[3] throughout entire country. Gravest feature no crops planted so that famine imminent. Addis meanwhile entirely supplied by train.

Wops arriving very much passengers – luggage thoroughly searched,[4] obliged remove rank badges and medals. Refuse accept payment in lire. Thaler has been fixed at 5 lire and is consequently hardly procurable as all transactions bootleg. Silver dollar smuggling more profitable than ever. Difficulty and two per cent loss in changing 500-lire notes for lower denominations. There are these six currencies – French francs, Indochina francs, paper thalers, silver thalers, lire of less than 500, lire of more than 500. Dined with Lee who told me details of the looting. Says 50,000 troops in Addis. My impression that if Addis had held out another six weeks Wops would have had to fall back on Adowa–Makale [?] line. Aeroplanes unable take off Addis and good neighbouring aerodrome in *shifta* hands.

[1] Former proprietor of Le Select, a place of entertainment in Addis Ababa.
[2] Patriarch.
[3] Marauders.
[4] By the French Somalia authorities at Djibouti.

Wops sitting about all over Djibouti like slightly bewildered cruise-boat trippers.

Dirre–Dowa, Wednesday 19 August 1936

Foul journey. Train two and a half hours late at Dirre–Dowa but met Trapman [?] and French consul on platform. Also Wops sent by Resident. They had got me room in hotel which everyone said was impossible. Frog-Frasso [?] – asked me to dinner. Very agreeable. Trappers offered me lift to Harar so going break journey. Eight hundred French troops in Dirre–Dowa. Main airbase; huge 'prefecture'. Train from frontier and all trains we passed guarded by machine guns. Shabby unshaven white soldiers all along line.

Thursday 20 August 1936

Unsuccessful attempt purchase dollars Mohammed Ali. Great ease and speed getting pass for Harar. Drove over greatly improved road, arrived consulate about 6. Chapman-Andrews recuperating after bad go of fever. Long talk about situation. Local Wops are clearly being extremely amenable but the British peevish – in their language, 'browned off'. During war Wahib [?] Pasha's defence line never used because army already broken before they fell back on them and no one to man them. Nasshu [?] fled with the first. Gas used four or five times on southern front and caves [?]; some blind brought back to hospital. Harar was entirely empty of troops at time of bombardment, but important supply centre and some arms found hidden there later by looters. When town first taken by Italians handed over to savage bands [?] who killed all Christians they found, including three priests within short distance British consulate. Bandi since sent back. Usual complaints of interference with telegraph and posts. Weaver birds opposite my window.

Friday 21 August 1936

Went to call on Monsignor Jasseran [?] who was expelled but brought back again amid tears of populace. Throughout looting he remained at his house refusing rescue. He spoke with undisguised sorrow at the changes. After luncheon went for conducted stroll in town. Conductor lip-sealed Greek. People seemed thriving. Tried to see jug but shown lions instead. Wops giving me lorry to return in.

Saturday 22 August 1936

Returned lorrywise Dirre–Dowa. Dinner Lesca, old Frog. Later joined Wop officers, cinema man, Czechoslovak and German Jew. Jolly evening. Dinner to celebrate arrival of a Camembert cheese. Lesca left asking me to stay with him in the Gironde and showed me picture postcards of his house. I gave him *Campion*. The Czech sold me 50 thalers for 7 francs each. Lorry-driver asked about wages in Kenya. He gets 6 lire a day.

Sunday 23 August 1936

Bad journey. No first-class seats. Contrary to fears, bedroom at Awush [?]. Typical Frog employee of line keeping his seat in first-class coach. Frightful food at both buffets.

Addis Ababa, Monday 24 August 1936

Worse journey as carriage filled up with soldiers. Pouring rain. Pathetic waterlogged camps along line. At one, heard Italian soldiers talking to each other in English – American volunteers. Fighting yesterday near one station before Mojjo. Met at station by Wop and car took me to Heft's,[1] now Pensione Germanica Bar-dancing. He has taken in with him an English-speaking Wop. Smart bar and whole main building converted to lounge and dance floor – propeller with electric bulbs. My old bedroom is dining-room. Received me with utmost geniality. Servants seem scared. Foul and minute dinner. Many forms to fill in. Notices everywhere in Italian giving controlled prices. Heft has to pay natives in thalers; in town, all shops have Italian names and many of them photographs of Duce. Heft says he fought like a lion. Also that he was due for expulsion.

Tuesday 25 August 1936

Called at Legation with mail. Wops have given me car. Driver fed up with Addis. He gets 10 lire. Breakfast consists of bread and potted meat, tea no milk. Went to station to see departure of Black Shirts for Rome. Ras Sayman [?] seeing them off beaming. Those who were turned out before now proud of it. Everyone afraid of expulsion. Everyone says Italian officers don't spend money. Heft dresses up in boiled shirt 'because there are so many communists about.' Lunched Bosdari two Wops. English Besse [?] agent Davidson, octagonal spectacles. B. anxious get me out of Addis as soon as possible. Had talk with Moussili [?], still struggling small trader. Prices of foodstuffs about four times normal, eggs ten times, milk and vegetables very scarce and expensive. Natives must be paid in thalers. Wops never established exchange to give confidence, though they might easily have done so and collared large store silver in bank vaults.

One café named Vulpa di Roma. Davidson dined with me and we went round the town. Georgitis now chauffeurs' dive. Jacobson big hotel fairly chic.

[1] The Heft's establishment was formerly the Deutsches Haus; it was the headquarters of most of the Press during the early stages of the war, and features, as the Pension Dressler, in *Scoop* (1938).

Everywhere else dead at 11.30. Heft large Wop party. Contradictory accounts what garrisons maintained interior.

Wednesday 26 August 1936

Fascist meeting in honour of German consul. Speeches in praise of Hitler and the unforgettable friendliness of Germany during the outrageous pro-barbarian sanctionist campaign. Rows of uniformed schoolchildren sang *Giovinezza*.[1] Talk with Nistrom [?]. Said possibility victory December held back by Emperor bombed daily, troops melted and turned *shifta*. Gas only caused eighteen deaths, but great moral effect. Army retreated under continuous fire from own people. Went to stinking mud-logged camp of the marines in farm beyond Gebbi. Later drove call on Ras but found him occupied with a battle. Emperor got away with about £10,000. His wife has a few hundred a year, so have children. Most of Rases got away with very small fortunes. Fighting all night. Heavy firing guns towards dawn, aeroplanes up all evening.

Thursday 27 August 1936

Firing at breakfast-time. I thought last night that I had never been in a city so full of unhappy people. Went to call on Graziani[2] at the little Gebbi. Place very shabby. He sitting among relics of Tafari's furniture.[3] Very fresh and businesslike. No Fascist speeches about Roman civilization and the wickedness of sanctions. He asked where I had been, where I wanted to go, how much time I had. Offered me a tour in the south, and the chance of joining a column operating towards the lakes. Six months ago it is the kind of thing I should have jumped at. But now I simply shirked it. Luncheon with Bosdari [?]. Guest of honour the German chargé d'affaires, Strohm, who is very popular because just become consul-general. He began saying that there was only one book, etc., *Black Mischief*; spent much of afternoon with him, von Waldheim, Cramp; also gave me pillaged Order of Trinity. Dined Roberts, chargé d'affaires, military attaché Taylor, and Lee. Wops gave me guard with machine gun to go to dinner. Pensione Germanica full of apprehension attack and rising in town.

Dirre–Dowa, Friday 28 August 1936

Grim journey to Dirre–Dowa. Train left 7 arrived Dirre–Dowa at 11. Cold and crowded. No regrets in leaving Addis Ababa.

[1] The Fascist youth song.
[2] Marshal Graziani, the Italian commander-in-chief.
[3] Haile Selassie's furniture.

Gura, Saturday 29 August 1936

Grim journey. Was told plane to leave Dirre–Dowa at 7.15, take me Asmara by luncheon-time. Went to aerodrome and waited two hours. Finally set out in three-motor Caproni. Sat in gun-turret most of time. Impossible see country. Arrived blazing heat at Assab where hospitably entertained at clean, fairly cool RAF mess to vile luncheon and told flying conditions Asmara impossible. I induced pilot to push on to Massawa where we arrived at 4. Heat frightful. Very reluctant sleep there. No telephone, no cars to get to town. At last we found a good-natured captain who was going to station Gura near Asmara. Set out in crowded little car. Magnificent road; gradually grew cooler; moonlight. Stopped for dinner at wayside café of which several on road. Democratic. Officers and lorry-drivers, cheap and bad food, but fine view over hills, wine. Engineer fellow-traveller insisted on paying. Two punctures, one of which needed mending. Arrived Gura at 11, very tired. Was hospitably received and housed in sectional bungalow in considerable comfort. Slept heavy.

Asmara, Sunday 30 August 1936

Was able to see surroundings in morning. Very large aerodrome now largely empty and used for the postal service. Clean bungalows, very clear running water, metal furniture. Fine sycamores and granite boulders and euphorbia gave impression ornamental tropical garden in park. Fine, cool weather. Waited on colonel with my friend the captain of previous evening. Waited was the word. But he lent us his car. Some talk of Mass but never materialized. Highly agreeable dinner on fine road with civil aviators.

Arrived 11.30 Asmara. Franchi, head of Press Bureau, fat and jagger, received me and took me to bungalow in grounds of hotel. Poor chap, he had had many telegrams about me and thought I was a woman and had waited all yesterday in a fever of excitement. Lunched with him at hotel. Bad luncheon. He appears to be arranging everything for me very obligingly. Thank God I have borrowed some books in Addis Ababa. Walked round profoundly depressing town. Built for 2,000 whites, occupied now by 60,000. Dense crowds, all men. My bungalow absolutely disgusting – no light or water. Bed full of fleas.

Monday 31 August 1936

Have effected a few reforms and feel like Elizabeth Fry. New lamp, carbolic in the bathroom, new bedding. Otherwise a day of doing nothing. When taxed with filth of town Italians say, 'We are in Africa.' Bad omen if they regard tropics as excuse for inferior hygiene. Reminded that they are race who have inhabited and created the slums of the world.

Tuesday 1 September 1936

Up at 5 am, off at 5.30 am with Franchi and another officer driving at headlong speed to Aksum. My cold very bad. Mists. Road really magnificent being done in sections by various commercial concerns. Tarmac, concrete parapets, cuttings, graded, cambered, cuttings faced with stone, little beds of patterned pebbles. At 6 am workmen going to work. Sun hats, overalls. Paid £40 a day and most of their keep. Middle-aged. Many bearded. Big steel bridge over Mareb. Passed cemetery of seventy workmen murdered in bed last February by band led by monk at Mai Alada [?].

Aduwa. Many signs of antiquity. Houses stone, built often of two storeys, solid timbers. Houses in clusters, inside good stone walls with gate towers. Sycamore trees, including the one where the 1896 Askaris[1] were mutilated. Red flags everywhere and yellow for officers' brothels. No signs of bombardment. Huge camp outside. People clearly on friendliest terms with Wops. Children singing *Giovinezza*. Drove on to Aksum. Stopped at filthy camp where elementary Boy Scout precautions of hygiene neglected. Soldiers unshaven, loafers crumbling crusts of bread.

Aksum like Aduwa built in series of encircled clusters of huts. Many fine trees. Lake with steps cut in rock – pool of Queen of Sheba. Numerous stiles; some standing, others in bits; very ugly and looking as new as the clock tower in Addis. Lunched with very hospitable officers' mess and afterwards went to see church. Very shabby but finely planned. Traces of good masonry. Not shaped in usual octagon. Afterwards climbed hill to see underground tombs of king about 500 AD, height of Axonite civilization. Finely jointed stones. Again natives obviously well inclined to invaders, but marked shortage of men. Perhaps they're with Imru in the west. Drove back to Asmara at enormous speed, arriving 8 o'clock for uneatable dinner. Heavy sleep, comparatively free of fleas.

Wednesday 2 September 1936

Intensely boring day. Bad cold. Poor luncheon in intolerably crowded restaurant. Itching and sneezing and reading American novels borrowed from Wright in Addis Ababa.

Makale, Thursday 3 September 1936

Drove to Makale via Adigrat, starting 9.30 am arriving 6.30 pm. Road, where finished, magnificent: little gardens at corners with flowering cactus, trees; devices in pebbles; milestones carved with wolves, eagles and foxes. Often crossed two other routes, the rough soldiers' route looking like dry

[1] Menelik II defeated the Italians in 1896; the Askaris were indigenous troops recruited by the Italian army.

watercourses and the caravan paths. In one place, miles of laden mules. Stream of traffic. Wild West wooden towns springing up. Makale through rain and dusk seemed full of castles. Theodore Palace, and an isolated fort a mile away castle of Gugsa's father, perhaps Theodore. Slept in house of engineer – tin replica of my house in Asmara. Dined well at officers' mess. One tubby captain de Franchi commander Gugsa's guard spoke American.

Friday 4 September 1936

Drove to Maichew. Officer at Maichew described battlefield in greatest detail. Apparently fought chiefly by white troops at close quarters. Aeroplanes turned retreat into rout in pass between Maichew and Ashangi but not decisive at Maichew. Government posts both Maichew and Makale very like old Abyssinian chief's house, with crowds of gossips, litigants, petitioners, etc., squatting about outside. At both messes chief talk was of women. Emperor seems to have forfeited chance of victory at Maichew by delaying three days until Italians in position. Waited at table by spy who worked in Italian army and brought news of attack. Returned to Makale for the night.

Asmara, Saturday 5 September 1936

Went promenade of town with de Franchi. Well-built stone houses. Theodore's Palace made in the 70s by Wop architect; bad repair but imposing neo-Gothic. Balconies. Fine carved throne. Rush-strewn courtroom. Abyssinian officials madly jaggering. Was shown chief tart of town. Not bad. Uneventful drive back to Asmara, arrived dinner-time. Doubt of vacancy in aeroplane Monday but certainty free ticket.

Sunday 6 September 1936

Attempted to go to Mass but impossible enter church. Hung about gloomily until evening when Franchi had arranged a little party in my honour, complete with dumb naval officers and imitation champagne. After dinner we visited the brothel where seven girls work from 9.30 in the morning until 11.30 at night, with two hours off for luncheon. They give each man five to ten minutes for 25 lire. After three months they take a holiday. When we arrived there were about eighty men waiting in a large hall and two smaller writing-rooms, in the corridors and halfway upstairs. No furniture except the benches on which they sat and a large table piled with military caps.

Monday 7 September 1936

Up at 5.30 am for aeroplane. Gave batman 100 lire and he was a feather-knocking-down case. Arriving at aerodrome, had furious row about a 500-lire note and won it. Waited until 10 when we got some coffee and sausage. At 11, told flight off for the day because Kassala under water. Sudan authorities will not allow flight direct to Khartoum. Day of ineffable boredom.

Cairo, Tuesday 8 September 1936

Up at 4.30 am. Aeroplane, fine three-motor Caproni, did start soon after 6. Stopped at Kassala, Khartoum, Wadi Halfa and reached Cairo by sunset. Very delightful flight, unhurried and full of interest in both stages. Slept at hotel decided by Littoria but dined well at St James's restaurant.

Tripoli, Wednesday 9 September 1936

Flew to Tripoli where great uncertainty about planes for the next day. But by visiting Press Bureau was able to fix it. Fine town, good hotel.

En route London, Thursday 10 September 1936

Flew to Ostia arriving 4 o'clock, having lunched at Syracuse. Half-hour Naples. Very interesting and agreeable flight. Had intended to bathe, change, fuck, and eat a luxurious dinner. Instead spent the evening driving to pay my debt to the English College in smuggled lire. Caught 9.20 train after single Dial[1] at station buffet. Shared sleeper with priest.

Friday 11 September 1936

All day in train. Delicious luncheon. Slept at Lotti.

London, Saturday 12 September 1936

Flew to London, arriving Highgate in time for luncheon. Huge mail but no worries. Dined Buck's Burns; oysters, grouse. Met Belloc after dinner. Heard of Hughie's death.[2] Wired Mells.

Sunday 13 September 1936

Mass at Highgate. Wrote large number of letters. Went with my mother to film after dinner.

Mells, Monday 14 September 1936

Spent morning shopping, mostly for Laura from whom sweet letter. Caught 3.30 to Frome. Met by Helen. Called on Chris. Dined at Manor. Everyone enchanting. Living at Mrs Long's.

Tuesday 15 September 1936

Corrected proofs. Walked in thunderstorm. Drank at Talbot. Hollises and Chris's brother Roger came to dinner. Agreeable and dull evening.

[1] Sleeping pill.
[2] The Hon. Hugh Lygon died suddenly while travelling in Germany.

London, Wednesday 16 September 1936

Came down to find letter from Laura saying that I might see her and that Mary[1] is proposing further postponement of wedding. Rang up Chris to pick me up on way to station, changed and caught train unshaven and without breakfast. Got to London about 12 and fetched Laura at Academy. Spent day with her, lunching at Scott's, dining at Lansdowne. She was ill and loving. Spent day at Bruton Street. Decided nothing except to be civil.

Mells, Thursday 17 September 1936

Having slept very little at St James's, caught 9 o'clock train and breakfasted with Chris. Talked to Katharine, answered letters. Odious new experience – fan telephone call from youth who said he wanted to hear my voice. No work. Walked with Chris, called on Conrad, dined alone, bed early.

Friday 18 September 1936

Little work. Dined at Manor, Per, Billy, Trim, Helen, Sir James Barrie.

Saturday 19 September 1936

Michael Trappes-Lomax staying with Chris. Went with them to Bath to see Prior Park, dined there with Katharine. Thinking of joining Gabriel in Spanish trip.

Sunday 20 September 1936

Church with Katharine and little Jolliffe at Downside. Lunched with Conrad. Chris dined with me. Worked myself into rage with Mary at night and had to take dope.

Monday 21 September 1936

Rage justified by letter from Laura saying would I decide if I wanted to share London house with Mary. Mind boggled. In the afternoon went to see houses at Nunney and Whatley which Katharine spoke of. Whatley Rectory is quite agreeable, but like a thousand other houses in England. No decent drawing-room. The housekeeper Mrs Haynes showed us over. I asked of a tap whether it was hot or cold water. 'I must ask the canon.' 'Why not try?' 'Oh, no water ever comes out.' The house at Nunney is enchanting. Very small, next to the castle and farm buildings. Exquisite eighteenth-century façade. I went to the door and asked if it was for sale. A pretty girl came and said, 'How did you know? We only decided at luncheon today. We haven't yet given our notice.' She, her mother and apparently some other relatives sublease it from Mr Young the farmer on condition he keeps a room there. Inside and out it is very dilapidated but of the highest beauty. Panelled rooms, very fine oak and walnut staircase, Norman cellars. For a considerable sum it could be made one of the

---

[1] Laura's mother.

loveliest small houses in England. Walking back I met Trim who had motored out to meet me. We went back to the house and met the farmer. A shock, as he's young and a gentleman. I had imagined putting him up a bungalow, but clearly that won't wash. The castle excellent and whole village very attractive. Dined at Manor. Too little to eat. Cook must be lent to the Benensons. Chris talked too much and Lady Horner felt it.

Tuesday 22 September 1936

Did some work and the crossword. Maidie Hollis[1] taken ill, miscarriage feared, taken to Bristol.

Thursday 24 September 1936

Mary Herbert came to tea and later to see Nunney and the rectory at Whatley. Seems quite reconciled to Laura's marriage; only serious difficulty now Aunt Vera.[2]

London, Friday 25 September 1936

Drove to London with Mary. Lunched with Gabriel who is off to Spain to relieve insurgents. Spent afternoon with Laura. Went to meeting at Westminster of Archbishop's Spanish Association. Committee was appointed of Lord Fitz Alan, Lord Howard of Penrith, etc. Gabriel read report of her talk with Duchess of Laguna. I moved for her to be sent out to advise best means distribution. Dined Bruton Street, Francis Howard, Gabriel, Mary. Cinema and supper with Laura. Slept St James's.

Mells, Saturday 26 September 1936

Caught 9 o'clock train for Frome and found to our horror no breakfast car. Laura bore no ill-will. Delightful day, though wet. Went to look at Whatley rectory and Nunney Farm. Laura seemed to like farm. Lunched and dined Manor. Longmans bothering about their manuscript.[3]

Sunday 27 September 1936

Mass at Chantry. Morning with Laura at my lodgings. Called with her on Conrad. Acton and Chris to luncheon. Afternoon at Manor and evening.

Monday 28 September 1936

Saw Laura off by early train. Did some work. Wrote to Major Shore about Nunney Farm.

[1] Mrs Christopher Hollis.

[2] Lady Victoria Herbert; she was the aunt not only of Laura Herbert but also of Evelyn Gardner, Waugh's first wife. When she heard that Waugh wanted to marry Laura, six years after he had divorced another niece, she remarked, 'I thought we had heard the last of that young man.'

[3] *Waugh in Abyssinia.*

Tuesday 29 September 1936

Went to Bristol to see Maidie. Unsatisfactory reply from Shore.

Wednesday 30 September 1936

Went to see another house at Nunney belonging to people called Wilbraham. Poky but pretty. Longman still fussing about his manuscript.

Thursday 1 October 1936

Did some work. Saw wholly unsuitable house with Katharine.

Friday 2 October 1936

Finished *Waugh in Abyssinia* in morning and spent wholly delightful day. Lunched in Bristol with Christopher, the Woodruffs and Michael Trappes-Lomax. Went sightseeing with Michael. Church of Mary Redcliffe hideously clean. Drove to Bath. Got mildly tight on champagne, dined at Empire and home in the best of tempers.

Saturday and Sunday. Prize bore Sir Almroth Wright[1] staying at Manor. Spent most of the time there. Took evening train to London and dined with Laura. Read life of Marie Bashkirtsev for review.

London, Monday 5 October 1936

Wrote review. Lunched with Laura, Simpson's. Dined with Patrick who is suffering from unrequited love. Drank with Hubert at Buck's and talked about politics. Saw Maimie in afternoon, fat and sweet and inconsequent. Told me details of Hughie's death. Grand news that Linton Shore may let me have Nunney.

Tuesday 6 October 1936

Lunched at Phyllis's with Hubert and Maimie and a redheaded woman. Spent afternoon with Maimie. Cocktail party at Mrs Cobb's. Took Laura out to dinner with my parents. Seemed to go quite smoothly. Corrected final proofs of *W. in A.*

Wednesday 7 October 1936

Luncheon Laura Buck's, ordered pressed duck. Afternoon with Diana[2] who was at first in tearing form imitating the King and Mrs Simpson, then, when Laura came to fetch me, suddenly became foully rude. Very shocked and

---

[1] Pathologist, 1861–1947; originator of anti-typhoid inoculation. After a conversation with him, Shaw wrote *A Doctor's Dilemma*.

[2] Lady Diana Cooper. She had recently stayed with the King at Fort Belvedere.

exhausted. Julian[1] and Helen[2] and Laura dined with me at Buck's and went to extremely funny film. Laura melancholy. Sleeping badly every night.

Thursday 8 October 1936

Luncheon with Mary and Laura in foul restaurant near her Academy. Julian, Per and Billy came later. No food. Agitation. Later talked to Mary about Nunney. They want me to take on forty acres. Went to drink sherry with Grants who were frightfully dull. Laura very tired and gloomy. Foul dinner at Bruton Street. Heavily drugged sleep.

Friday 9 October 1936

Completely restored by good night's sleep. Lunched with Laura at Fleming's after happy morning in bed reading P. G. Wodehouse. We caught trains within five minutes of one another at Paddington, she to Pixton, I to the Woodruffs.

Saturday 10 October–Sunday 11 October 1936

Fair weekend. Too many Actons and Rospigliosis. Agreeable conversations with Douglas. Church where the priest denounced infidelity of Newbury. Anti-Jewish hooliganism in East End.

Mells and London, Monday 12 October–Friday 16 October 1936

Returned to Mells feeling boorish and despondent. At Mells constantly disturbed by telegrams and trunk calls from London about business. On Thursday 15th made a very good start with the first page of a novel describing Diana's early morning.[3] Went to Bristol one afternoon. Saw Young at Nunney who was very good-natured and eager to convenience everybody. Saw Linton Shore who is a footler but not the bully I had expected. He will not sell, but will let on a long lease. On Friday 16th was summoned to London in the morning to confer with Mary about furniture. Lunched Bruton Street. Felt ill. Had Turkish bath, felt better, dined Bruton Street went early to bed with dope.

Saturday 17 October 1936

Went to Longman Green to find they had composed a blurb giving exactly the impression of *W. in A.* which I had tried to suppress. Lunched at Simpson's and went to enchanting Soane Museum. Dined first on oysters at Buck's, then on a delicious hare at Boulestin's. Several telegrams and telephone messages re Gabriel and Mary.

---

[1] The 2nd Earl of Oxford and Asquith.
[2] Lady Helen Asquith.
[3] Waugh's fifth novel, *Scoop*, opens with a visit by John Courtenay Boot to Mrs Stitch at her Hawksmoor house near St James's Palace.

Cambridge, Sunday 18 October 1936

Early Mass at Farm Street. To Cambridge. Laura saw me off, coming as far as Hatfield. Met at station by polite undergraduate. Found sherry party including Father D'Arcy at Father Gilbey's. Lunched, not badly, at Union. Went round several colleges sightseeing. Gilbey admirable guide. Day of great beauty, sun after rain, leaves just turning, etc. Old man in bowler hat watering aspidistras in conservatory. Huge and rather horrible tea party of Catholic undergraduates. Too early dinner in Trinity. Not bad. Then I talked to full house at Fisher Society. Mostly anecdotes strung together. Not much of a paper but it kept them amused. They are used to worse. A few questions afterwards.

London–Mells, Monday 19 October 1936

An hour's further sightseeing then to London to make row at Longman Green. Was quite unnecessarily truculent. Went to Charlotte Street and lunched with Laura and Lady E. Paget. Then by a very bad train to Frome.

Tuesday–Friday. Working at novel. Took Katharine and Lady Horner over Nunney. Next day they went to London for the winter. Lunched at Christopher's with Conrad and Lord Churston. Friday Laura and Bridget came to luncheon at 2.30 with spaniel. Went over Nunney again. Laura slept at Christopher's.

Saturday 24 October 1936

Leaf-catching with Laura. She took afternoon train to Reading. Troubled with bad fingers. Saw doctor.

Sunday 25 October 1936

Mass at Chantry. Worked on novel.

Monday 26th–Tuesday 27th dined with Christopher. Mrs H. came back from hospital. Wrote offering Shore (*a*) £3,000 down (*b*) Wilbraham's house in exchange (*c*) £50 a year for seven years, then £150. During seven years I to spend not less than £700 in restoration.

Wednesday 28 October 1936

My 33rd birthday. Lunched at Midsomer Norton with my aunts. Hands slightly better.

Thursday 29 October 1936

Finished second chapter of novel and sent it off to be typed.

Ostend, Friday 30 October 1936

Morning train London, delightful journey with Conrad. Met by Laura. Cashed £30, ate bread and cheese at Buck's, caught 2 o'clock train with Woodruffs and Actons[1] for Ostend. Smooth passage, Ostend empty, most hotels shut, windswept promenade. Two tables working at casino. Very pleasant. Good dinner at restaurant named Renommé. Won £5 at roulette.

Saturday 31 October 1936

Drove to Bruges where was horrified by Flemish Gothic. 'Doctor Livingstone I presume' to Michelangelo. Good spherical pulpit. Chauffeur showed us poison gas factory with great pride. On to Ghent in pouring rain for luncheon and visit to gloomy castle which delighted Douglas and Daphne.[2] John had stayed behind to play system of minimum stakes on the even chance. Played a little before dinner and lost yesterday's £5 and £15 more. Good dinner. Went back to casino and bet further £10. Then played my own method seriously and won back about £20.

Ostend–London, All Saints' Day 1936

Played again after Mass and won another £5. So gambling proved cheap. Delicious luncheon. Proceeded to ship in happy vinous haze. Pleasant journey home but late. Arrived 9. Supper at Berkeley. Later to Bruton Street to meet Laura returned from Ampleforth after messenger boy had missed her at station.

Monday 2 November 1936

Lunched with Lady Horner where great abuse of the King as everywhere in London. Afternoon and evening with Laura. Called on Phyllis and Hubert[3] and drank champagne late after French fancy dress boring film.

Tuesday 3 November 1936

Opening of Parliament. Abuse of King on all sides. Wrote review for *Morning Post* and lunched with Phyllis and Hubert, and heavy drinking. Laura bought me birthday present of knife. Cocktails P. Balfour and Penelope, he leaving Europe in very low spirits. Dined Fleury's.

[1] Douglas Woodruff, editor of *The Tablet*, married in 1933 the Hon. Marie (Mia) Acton, sister of the 3rd Baron Acton, and granddaughter of the historian.
[2] Daughter of Lord Rayleigh, FRS, Professor of Physics at the Imperial College of Science; she married Lord Acton (John) in 1931, and became a Roman Catholic and a close friend of Mgr. Ronald Knox.
[3] Phyllis de Janzé and Hubert Duggan.

Wednesday 4 November 1936

Good luncheon Boulestin with Laura. Bought stamps for book binding. Woman regarded it as great sacrilege use stamps for so low a purpose. Clonmore and Dig Yorke dined with me at Buck's. Laura now living at Mulberry Walk with boring Grants. Painful evening with Belloc who wants free work for his paper and had persecution mania at Buck's.

Thursday 5 November 1936

Went to see editor *Nash's Magazine* and accepted money for jam job, 30 guineas a month for less than 2,000 words on anything I like. Gave Laura oysters and lunched Peters at St James's. Afternoon train home feeling lonely on return. No letter from Shore. No typescript from McLodden.

Friday 6 November 1936

Slept till 11 so felt grand. Wrote review of book about Albuquerque. In evening wrote free stuff for Belloc: hope I get to heaven that way. Decided to go to Oxford Sunday.

Saturday 7 November 1936

Appeal for cash from Gracie.[1] Sent her £5. Hope I get to heaven that way.

Oxford, Sunday 8 November 1936

Went to Oxford with Chris who had to lecture to the Newman. Lunched with Knox to whom our visit was very distressing. Found Douglas, Mia, Hugh Fraser[2], a dumb soldier and an undergraduate. Foully cold. Tea with Julian in Balliol. Went to Campion Hall and saw D'Arcy's latest *bric-à-brac*. A fine Murillo, probably genuine, fine vestments, a lot of trash including watercolours by undergraduates and reproductions cut from books, bits of china. A statue of 'a queen' which D'Arcy chooses to regard as a Madonna. A bogus Lely of Nell Gwynn. Dined at Campion. Painful scene between Father Walker and D'Arcy with regard to a cigar. Went to Newman meeting. Chris spoke very badly about Roosevelt's election as though it were Battle of Lepanto. Heckled but desisted seeing he was ill. Madrid reported fallen.

Oxford–Mells, Monday 9 November 1936

Madrid not fallen. Went to bookbinder's and walked about Oxford. Lunched at Campion and returned to Mells.

[1] Gracie Ansell.
[2] The Hon. Hugh Fraser, later a Conservative MP.

Tuesday 10 November 1936

Wrote quite a lot of novel. Went to look at outside of Warminster Manor. Beastly surroundings. Rain and cold. Slept badly.

Wednesday 11 November 1936

Low spirited. Went to see good Georgian house at Timsbury with appalling decorations. Agents have sent me notices of two houses that sound excellent, one near Exeter; one at Stogursey near Bridgwater.

Thursday 12 November 1936

Worked a little. Low spirited. Sleeping badly.

Pixton Park, Friday 13 November 1936

Joined Laura in train at Westbury and went to Pixton. Grants there.

Saturday 14 November 1936

Went in car to see charming house at Stogursey. Bright and well conditioned. Delightful country. Mary came down also, bringing ex-governess of Bridget's. Servants frightful.

Sunday 15 November 1936

Long drive to Mass. Walk with Laura. Caught fresh cold. Felt ill. Slept in afternoon and went to bed early. Wrote offering to buy Nunney but withdrawing offer to take on lease.

Mells, Monday 16 November 1936

Bad cold. Mary and Laura dropped me at Mells. Went to bed early with hot whisky.

Tuesday 17 November 1936

Spent day indoors, feeling foul. Wrote article for *Morning Post* and some novel. Wednesday–Thursday. Stayed indoors and wrote.

London, Friday 20 November 1936

Went to London. Lunch with Laura at Boulestin. Went to Korda's studio and was told plot of vulgar film about cabaret girls which he wants me to write.[1] John Sutro motored me back to London. Dined with Laura and Mary at Mulberry Walk. Gabriel, returned from Spain, was to have come but too ill. Francis[2] was to have come but too vague. Discussion with Mary about Spain made her violently abusive. Left early and had drink with Hubert.

---

[1] Sir Alexander Korda, the film director, wanted to make a film called 'Lovelies from America.' The idea perished
[2] The Hon. Francis Howard, later the 2nd Baron Howard of Penrith.

Saturday 21 November 1936

Bitterly cold. Some shopping, lunched with Laura at Simpson's. She cried. Cinema alone. Went to see Gabriel, fervid [?] and fanatical. Drank bottle of Château Yquem with Laura after brief visit to Mia and John in Cambridge Square. Dined Berkeley Buttery, returned Mulberry Walk where Laura again cried.

Sunday 22 November 1936

Went to church at Highgate with Laura and later to luncheon with my parents. Returned to tea with Katharine. Dined new restaurant which used to be Blue Train.

Mells, Monday 23 November 1936

Lunch and afternoon with Laura. Evening train Mells. Cold, tired and very low spirited.

Tuesday 24 November–Thursday 26 November 1936

At Mells attempting to work but doing nothing much. Went with Conrad to see the Hermitage, St Catherine. Dark, poky, Gothic. Stogursey withdrawn from market. Mary wrote to say it was an illusion of Laura's that engagement was to be postponed further. Sleeping badly and too late all week.

London, Friday 27 November 1936

Went to London for Katharine's charity ball. Laura picked me up with bad cold. Very dull dinner indeed, two men short. Sat next to dumb Cécile Howard. Laura went home after dinner. I to dance where I found chums and got a little drunk. Later with Mrs Connolly to crowded nigger joints. Left her there impolitely.

Tetton House, near Taunton, Saturday 28 November 1936

Laura worked in morning, I shopped and had pick-me-up with Belloc. 1.30 train to Taunton to stay Tetton, Elizabeth Herbert.[1] Agreeable house full of fine pictures and furniture.

Sunday 29 November 1936

Early Mass. Laura ill, went to bed after breakfast. Spent day in her room except for brief excursion to see house where owner had just had a fit and would not let us in.

---

[1] Laura Herbert's aunt; daughter of J. E. Willard, a former US ambassador to Spain.

Monday 30 November 1936

Stayed on at Tetton to succour Laura. She seemed better. Malnutrition.

Mells, Tuesday 1 December 1936

Went to see the Hermitage, St Catherine, but Laura ill so after luncheon took her back to Taunton where her mother picked her up. Bloody journey back arriving Mells at 9.

Wednesday 2 December 1936

Worked.

Thursday 3 December 1936

Times leader about Mrs Simpson.

Friday 4 December–Tuesday 8 December 1936

The Simpson crisis has been a great delight to everyone. At Maidie's nursing home they report a pronounced turn for the better in all adult patients. There can seldom have been an event that has caused so much general delight and so little pain. Reading the papers and even listening to announcements that there was no news on the wireless took up most of the week. I did a review of Aldous Huxley's dull essays and struggled through the film scenario to a dull and premature end. Tomorrow, Wednesday, I go to London. Mells has become oppressive. Laura, having been in a state of collapse on Tuesday, and having promised to lie quiet at Pixton all the week, went to London on Wednesday, and Thursday reports she was 'too rushed' to write, and on Friday sat up till 2 am in a restaurant. Conrad lunched with me on Sunday, very happy with the crisis. Perry[1] is out with Simpson in Cannes. If it had not been for Simpson this would have been a very bitter week.

London, Wednesday 9 December 1936

Came to London. Lunched Diana. Cocktails Hubert. Got drunk. Dined with Laura at Yorkes.

Thursday 10 December 1936

Went with Laura and sense of guilt to Stroud and saw two pretty houses. Back by Cheltenham Flyer.

Newton Ferrers, Callington, Cornwall, Friday 11 December 1936

Went with Laura to Newton Ferrers by morning train. Sat and did nothing. Youth came.

[1] Lord Brownlow; then Lord-in-Waiting to the King.

Saturday 12 December 1936

Walk. Nellie Eliot to luncheon. Did nothing. Bertie[1] gave us Yquem. Saw lovely Regency house not for sale.

Sunday 13 December 1936

Laura made me miss train. Returned. Did nothing. Laura left with youth.

London, Monday 14 December 1936

Returned London. Visited parents.

Tuesday 15 December 1936

Laura shamming toothache. Went to party of Mary Dunn. Laura looked belle of party.

Wednesday 16 December 1936

Lunched Hubert. Dined Bertie and Diana[2] and went to Beits' party. Got tipsy, stayed to end, enjoyed myself v. much. Miss J. Fry also had party.

Thursday 17 December 1936

Lunched with Chapman-Andrews who says Government alarmed re Wops in Hadhramaut establishing spy consul at Djibouti. Dined Simpson's with Laura and called to say goodbye to Gabriel who is returning Spain.

Mells, Friday 18 December 1936

Ritz luncheon Hubert and Laura. Afternoon train buffet car to Mells, Laura slept Chris, I Long.

Saturday 19 December 1936

Chris took us houses Batcombe, South Wraxall [?] and Eagle House. All possible. Eagle House superb but suburban. Went by train to Swindon. Faringdon, dined well and went cinema with R.H.P.[3]

Sunday 20 December 1936

Mass with old women at Buckland. Afternoon saw two no-good houses. Betjemans, Fulford, Sparrow[4] dined. Laura v. flirtatious with R.H.P. Was bloody to her, she very nice to me owing to her feeling of guilt. Gerald joke re elephants.

---

[1] Sir Robert Abdy, owner of Newton Ferrers; art collector.
[2] Lady Diana Abdy.
[3] Robert Heber–Percy.
[4] Roger Fulford; John Sparrow, then at the Chancery bar, later Warden of All Souls College, Oxford.

Pixton Park, Dulverton, Monday 21 December 1936

Mary picked us up in motor. Saw two no-good houses then Piers Court, Stinchcombe. Absolutely first-rate, delighted. Late luncheon pub. Pixton at 6. No one else here – except Auberon.

Tuesday 22 December 1936

Wrote letters, did crossword, walked with Laura and bought stock.[1] Grants came. Hiccoughs at night.

Wednesday 23 December 1936

Family fun. No sleep.

Thursday Christmas Eve 1936

Father D'Arcy came, very dotty. Laura and I made crib. Exeter shopping in morning. Felt very low. Midnight Mass in main room. Wine and biscuits.

Christmas Day 1936

Church again. Felt very ill. Family fun. Afternoon to Tetton to Christmas tea party of Howards. Nearly sick on way home. Champagne slightly helped.

Boxing Day 1936

Hunted and galloped into two gateposts.

Sunday 27 December 1936

More church. D'Arcy still here and dottier. Saw Diana's eye-apple Bydown not so good as Piers Court. Captain Grant went.

Monday 28 December 1936

Started work again. D'Arcy went.

Tuesday, Wednesday, Thursday, Friday (Footman Willie sick on way to church), Saturday. Work. Hunted with stag hounds in blizzard. Heard that Korda likes film treatment. New Year's Eve Elizabeth and girls came, also Grants again. Did some beating for pheasants. Made mulled claret. Alick Dru came with poodle and was amusing.

Sunday 3 January 1937

A. Cecil and Captain Fletcher came. Drank Yquem after church with Alick and Laura and dregs for Mrs G.

[1] A hunting stock.

Monday 4 January 1937

Drove with Dru and Laura to Stinchcombe, lunched Wotton-under-Edge. They left me at Stroud pub. Went alone to appalling cinema, dined alone and drank champagne. Architect came 9. Dull competent man.

Tuesday 5 January 1937

Spent day at Stinchcombe with architect examining rafters, etc. Saw superb summerhouse *again*. Endless train journey to Pixton. Mrs Hancock dining, gentlemen having quarrelled. Played bridge not well.

Wednesday 6 January 1937

Hunted in gales feeling ill. Mary H. very decent re Stinchcombe.

Thursday 7 January 1937

Algernon Cecil proposed steal my bedroom at Mells. Furious.

Friday 8 January 1937

Went to Mells in A.C.'s motor. Bedroom difficulty solved. Did nothing.

Saturday 9 January 1937

Lesbians Hudson and Hall arrived. Visited Conrad and Hollis and was tipsy and laughed at H. and H. at luncheon. Walked with Helen and had tea with Hollis.

Sunday 10 January 1937

Church with Cecil. Hollis dined, fainted.

Monday 11 January 1937

London circus with D'Arcy. Bought engagement ring. Supper Savoy Grill.

Tuesday 12 January 1937

Driberg upset Laura re engagement, bought seed pearls and pierced her ears.

Wednesday 13 January 1937

Engagement in paper *Times*. Lunch Ritz Hubert. Laura left. Dined H. and P.[1]

Thursday 14 January 1937

Saw Korda who accepted film. Luncheon Rodds. Went to sales with Dig. On diet, dined Burns.

[1] Hubert Duggan and Phyllis de Janzé.

Friday Saturday 15th 16th. Dined with Olivia[1] one evening. Very depressing, stark crazy and roaring drunk. Went to see my parents. Yorkes lunched with me at St James's Sunday.

Monday moved to Alick Dru's flat. He with terrible hangover. Went to Turkish bath and took Mia[2] out to dinner.

Tuesday 19 January 1937

Shopped with Alick. Saw insurance man. Bought clothes.

Wednesday 20 January 1937

Laura came to London to see a Miss Price actress.

Thursday 21 January 1937

Laura went to Clonboy.[3] I dined Alick and Miss A. Throgmorton.

Friday 22 January 1937

Went to luncheon at Clonboy. Dined with Hollis, Woodruffs, etc. Odious brother of Chris. Very expensive and sad evening. Offer Stinches accepted, £3,550 plus cottage.

Saturday 23 January 1937

Vile arrangements of Mia greatly inconvenienced me. Went with Laura to stay Betjemans.

Sunday 24 January 1937

At Betjemans. Laura sang. Given ink by Butlers.

Pixton Park, Monday 25 January 1937

Very early start met Mary Bristol and Katharine went Stinkers. Margaret, Laura and I saw builder Malpas and kind lawyer Milward and came to Pixton by train.

Tuesday 26 January 1937

Terrible suffering Pixton.

Wednesday 27 January 1937

Laura went London day to see actress Price. Hideous sufferings.

[1] Olivia Plunket Greene.
[2] The Hon. Mrs Douglas Woodruff.
[3] Surrey home of Laura's grandmother.

Thursday 28 January 1937

Bad cold. Snowing.

Easton Court Hotel, Chagford, 4 February 1937

I went to Chagford[1] where I remained off and on until Tuesday before Easter. Korda sent a very brutish American named Kerrell to work with me on the film. He contributed nothing, but I was able to rough out and later dictate in London a third long treatment. Since then I have heard nothing from Korda and have been at work on the novel which has good material but shaky structure. Laura went twice to Paris to buy her trousseau. I went to see her in London once or twice. Haunted Willis's rooms and bought a chimney-piece and mirror, both Adam, and two very fine carved pedestals which I am having converted at enormous expense into bookcase ends.

I became a director of Chapman & Hall: there were some speeches by Inman[2] and later the presentation with great pomp of an utterly worthless box of knives and forks. Wedding invitations went out and have been almost universally refused. Presents have come in, mostly of poor quality, except from the Asquiths who have given us superb candelabra, sconces, and table. Long colloquies with lawyers resulting in Piers Court being conveyed to me. Came to London before Palm Sunday. Dined with Elizabeth on Monday and Lady Tweedmouth on Tuesday. Went to Ampleforth by train Wednesday. Auberon, away from Pixton, slightly more agreeable. Pleasant unrestful Holy Week, visiting Castle Howard and entertaining dumb little boys and monks. Returned London on Monday and stayed at Highgate. On Thursday took my mother to see Piers Court to see how Malpas's work was progressing and found nothing done at all. Came on to Chagford very tired. Norman[3] again causing anxiety.

Week at Chagford, correcting proofs, writing articles for *Nash's* and attending to prodigious correspondence with lawyers, architect, insurance company, etc. Ran amok at village shop and bought a great deal of old furniture, fenders, etc.

[1] The Easton Court Hotel, Chagford, on the edge of Dartmoor. Became a literary retreat in August 1931 after Alec Waugh, with Marda Vanne and Gwen Frangçon Davies, visited the hotel while touring the west country and a maid, unable to resist a uniform, fell for their chauffeur in his cap. The chauffeur persuaded the group to make the hotel their base for the rest of the tour. Subsequently, the hotel was used by Patrick Balfour, Pamela Hansford Johnson and Beverley Nichols, among others. Evelyn Waugh wrote *Brideshead Revisited* there in 1944. The proprietress was an American, Mrs Carolyn Cobb.

[2] Philip Inman (b. 1892) had been brought in to Chapman & Hall as a 'company doctor' to arrest the firm's decline. He was created a baron in 1946 and served briefly as Lord Privy Seal in 1947.

[3] Helped Mrs Cobb run the hotel.

Pixton Park, Thursday 8 April 1937

Went to Pixton with Carolyn and Norman for luncheon. Cocktail party that afternoon for Laura's neighbours – not much pleasure to me.

Friday 9 April 1937

Laura's party all chucked for ball but substitutes arrived. Ball beastly at newly rebuilt, badly redecorated house of Lord Fortescue.

Saturday 10 April 1937

Suggested going to London but Laura obdurate. Hunting impossible but *very* pleasant ride with Laura on Mrs Fitzherbert. Beastly Lord Rankeillour [1] self-invited bore.

Sunday 11 April 1937

Mass in laundry, thank God. Alick full of fun. Mrs Hancock, who is nice, came to luncheon. Beat Laura at chess. Tried to be matey with F. Howard.

London, Monday 12 April 1937

Very pleasant journey London Laura. Horrible luncheon in Viennese restaurant. Opened new presents, some delightful. Slept Highgate.

Tuesday 13 April 1937

Arranged books and clothes Highgate. Lunched Cornwall Terrace, Father D'Arcy and Father More O'Farrell. Both sensationally ignorant of simplest professional duties.[2] Slept Highgate.

Wednesday 14 April 1937

Left Highgate for good and lunched at delightful Bridget, delicious luncheon. Dined Cornwall Terrace. Went first-night film and supper later Diana[3] and Kommer,[4] slightly tipsy.

Thursday 15 April 1937

Lunched Cornwall Terrace after arduous morning shopping. My mother, Father M. O'Farrell, sweet Bridget. Arranged presents at Gloucester Gate without unpleasantness. Dined with Hubert at St James's, rather tipsy. In morning chose lovely carpet with Diana[5] and in evening another from Gerald B.[6] Turkish bath.

[1] As James Hope, Conservative MP for Sheffield Central, 1908–29; baron, 1932.
[2] There had been a wedding rehearsal that day.
[3] Lady Diana Cooper.
[4] Rudolf Kommer; associate of Max Reinhardt, producer of *The Miracle*.
[5] Lady Diana Abdy.
[6] Lord Berners.

Friday 16 April 1937

Cleansing morning chez Woodhouse. Lunched Buck's and enjoyed it. Came on to 2.30 to 8.30 cocktail party, mostly highly enjoyable. Rather tipsy. Dined Yorkes.

Saturday 17 April 1937

Early Mass: D'Arcy, with Laura and Herberts and Woodruffs. Breakfast St James's, Douglas and F. Howard; Henry came later. Changed and pick-me-up at Parkin's and to church where got married to Laura. Reception Gloucester Gate. Bachelor gathering in bedroom: Henry, Francis, Douglas, Sutro, Perry, Billy, Hubert. Drove Clonboy, saw Lady de Vesci.[1] Farewell Lady de Vesci, threw rice, caught aeroplane Croydon, Auberon and Mary last moment arrived see us off. Elizabeth and her foul son in aeroplane. Picked up dress of Laura's in Paris, dined Tour d'Argent, pressed duck, wild strawberries, Musigny '14. Caught Rome Express in exact time.

Portofino, Sunday 18 April 1937

I slept well, Laura not. Customs, passport, etc, very jaggering. Lunched from paper bag, drove in horse cab from S. Margherita to Portofino. Lovely day, lovely house, lovely wife, great happiness.

Monday 19 April 1937

Delicious days at Portofino somewhat marred by torpor and diarrhoea. Bathed from motor boat Wednesday, Thursday, Friday. Improvement in health.

Friday 23 April 1937

Eve of St George. Bonfire seen from Patchie's [?] window.

Saturday 24 April 1937

St George. Day of Laura's accident 1931. Both very happy. Missed Mass owing to Laura's sloth. Cooking improved, have broken austere traditions of house by importing brandy, strega and chianti. Went S. Margherita afternoon, shopped. Laura gave me St George's medal. Had cards printed to leave on Arciprete.[2] Health improving.

Sunday, Monday, Tuesday, Wednesday. Went to Rome. Uncomfortable journey. Russie very full and very enjaggering. Secured small suite. Dined Ranieri, searched all hotels for better rooms but found them full.

Thursday. San Silvestro. Called on Lord and Lady Howard. Called on by

---

[1] Laura Herbert's grandmother.
[2] In English, archpriest; an honorific title.

Howards very welcoming and went very cold drive with them after tea. Monsignor Richard Smith dined and told us his sister was afraid of pigeon. Very fine 1911 claret.

Friday. Laura very bad temper indeed. Also I. Confessed, saw sights. Lunched Mrs Strang, facetious don and treacherous Dago and pansy professor. Long motor drive with Howards round Lake Albano, tea Frascati. Dined Johnny Walker III in pretty little house. French brandy. Rather tight. Dial.

Saturday. Audience at Vatican on dais of public audience arranged by Lady H.'s very decent sister. Pope very ill spoke French not about us. Lunched on Piazza San Pietro. Train to Assisi. Bad room.

Sunday. MOSQUITOES. Secured royal suite. Mosquitoes. Drunk at luncheon.

Monday 3 May 1937

Laura tears. S. Chiari and Damiano. Mosquitoes.

Tuesday 4 May 1937

Communion. Will Hayes[1] priest and server. Train to Florence. Hopelessly tired but grand suite Excelsior.

Wednesday 5 May 1937

Walked round. Goad lunched with us and was very upset by our visit. Filthy luncheon. Filthy dinner.

Thursday 6 May 1937

Ascension Day. Sightseeing. Good *cannelloni* at Paolis. 4.50–7.50: Fancy dress football match, Laura delighted. Laura very drunk at dinner in cellar bought cat (clockwork). Band jaggered.

Friday 7 May 1937

Returned Portofino, very hot journey. Food better.

Monday 10 May–Sunday 16 May 1937

Cooking variable, health improving. Bathing daily. Working fairly hard and fairly well.[2] Friday. Tea party of promiscuous Jews from Casteletto and arciprete (much travelled). Sunday (Whit) jaggering and avaricious first communicants.

[1] Perhaps he looked like Will Hay, English comedian.
[2] On *Scoop*.

Monday 17 May 1937

Wrote novel very badly all week. Friday 28th news came of Bridget's baby Polly. Visited tenants. Sunday 30th. Castello Americans wanted to see house and us and succeeded. Train to England. No sleep. Wet.

London, Monday 31 May 1937

Morning in Paris. Took midday aeroplane, arrived London soon after 3. Went to Fleming's Hotel. Bath. Dinner Captain Grant at Cornwall Terrace.

Tuesday 1 June 1937

Went to Denham with Peters, wild goose chase. Gabriel to lunch. Moved to Mulberry Walk. Cocktails Hubert, dined Simpson's feeling low. Burns later. Dutch girl and crazy painter.

Wednesday 2 June 1937

Derby Day. Dr Haire. Lunched Cornwall Terrace. P. Sudley, Gabriel, Mary. Went to Highgate in low spirits. Dined Mulberry Walk, very rich.

Thursday 3 June 1937

Shopped. Mrs W.[1] lunch, very good. D. Yorke[2] dinner. Y.[3] later. F. Howard sherry.

Friday 4 June 1937

Maurice lunch. Bridget afternoon. Shopping and telephoning. Laura's ears re-pierced.

Piers Court, Friday 12 November 1937

I have been surprised again and again lately by blanks and blurs in my memory, being reminded by Laura of quite recent events which delighted me and which I have now completely forgotten. I have therefore decided to try once more to keep a daily journal.

I went to bed resolving to wake early and prepare my speech for the afternoon. I woke with Poulteney shouting to his cows in the field below my windows, but did not get up or prepare my speech; instead lay dozing till I was called. We got off by 9.30 and reached Englefield Green a little before 1. Lunched there, Gerry Liddell saying that Lady de Vesci had taken a dislike to toast, believing the holes to be made by worms. To London by train, meaning to spend a quiet hour at the St James's thinking over what I had to say; found,

[1] His mother.
[2] Dig Yorke.
[3] Henry Yorke.

instead, that through a muddle between Ellwood[1] and the telegraph office the book of Calder–Marshall's was not there, so I had my hair cut and went straight to the book exhibition to get a copy there from Chapman & Hall's stall. Was shown a room where I could sit quiet and where in fact I was ceaselessly interrupted by various officials of the exhibition and photographers. Finally by Douglas Woodruff. Having an empty mind I drank two huge whiskies to stimulate it: paralysed it instead. Was led at last into a huge hall full of young women − 700 or more of them. Began to speak − 'ideological writing' − and heard my voice like someone else's droning and stumbling; felt, 'if only I could sit back and think of other things'; and realized that I must keep this thing in motion. At last, in an awful blank, I looked at my watch; I found it was 5 o'clock so shut up sharp. The audience missed any point, but they had come to stare, not listen. It was a shoddy speech anyhow. Went to Chapman & Hall's stall and signed a dozen or so copies of books – mostly for the trade. The new 5s edition is excellent. My mother and Lady Upcott[2] were there; talked to them, lost Douglas, had a sandwich at St James's, back by train. Talked before and after dinner to Lady de Vesci, she showing great spirit and style. To bed early with headache.

Englefield Green, Saturday 13 November 1937

Mary was coming to luncheon en route for Hatfield. Laura and I tried to stay and meet her but G.L. drove us out. Drove to Oxford via Abingdon, lunched at the Randolph – new management and vivid enamels – and afterwards called on D'Arcy at Campion Hall where we saw many new acquisitions. Home soon after dark. Two sets of callers, both with double-barrelled names.

Piers Court, Sunday 14 November 1937

Mass among cigarette stubs at the Dursley YMCA. As the men were away I had the run of my own tools and spent a happy day in the garden, where the new trees are in.

Monday 15 November 1937

Cater said the man from Prince of Wales garage reported very badly of the electric light plant; would I go and see him. I went. He said the big end was going of the motor and that the dynamo must be cleansed; I said come and do it. Returned to tell carpenter I was disappointed shelves were not finished. Ellwood asked would I come and see the Esse cooker. Was shown a glowing, red-hot plate. Mrs Ellwood: 'Ellwood, stand so that Mr Waugh can see the crack in your shadow.' There did seem to be some flaw so wrote to complain.

---

[1] Manservant.
[2] Wife of the Comptroller General of the Exchequer and a resident, like Mrs Waugh, of Highgate.

Worked in garden and ordered the clearing of all laurels round the gates.

Tuesday 16 November 1937

Read review books – Nicolson's *Helen's Tower* and a novel about sex obsession in the lower middle classes. After luncheon to Bristol to broadcast. Victor Bridges was waiting there, both deprecating and self-assertive; an inclination to anecdotes about the Savage Club which come out painfully in his broadcast. When we came to rehearse at 5 o'clock we found our joint talk was about ten minutes short, most of the deficiency being mine. We tried to devise some questions and answers, then went out with Stucley for a drink. Stucley did not want Bridges to come; I rather think he had prepared dinner for Laura and me at his flat; we had asked Bridges to dine with us, so Stucley sat rather sulky while we dined at a restaurant. Then back to run through talk with new additions. Still too short. Further additions. We mooned about for half an hour. Then read our stilted conversation. It was just as short but no one seemed to mind. An easy £13. We then went up to a studio and watched the rehearsal of an unseen cast by an animated producer at a switchboard.

Wednesday 17 November 1937

The man from the Prince of Wales came again and cleared the dynamo. It made no difference at all to the charging. He says it must be the driving belt. I tell him to get another. Carter and Prewitt are doing prodigies of destruction in the shrubberies. To call on a neighbour at a house called Isle of Rhé. Then to tea with the Miss Leighs to meet their pet tenants – a Mr and Mrs Renshaw. The Miss Leighs acute and decided and amusing.

Thursday 18 November 1937

The carpenter says he has now mended the light plant by playing with the switchboard. He has finished the shelves which look superb. I wrote my page for *Night and Day* and half my article for *Harper's Bazaar*. Greene[1] rang up to say that *Night and Day* is on its last legs; would I put them into touch with Evan Tredegar,[2] whom I barely know, to help them raise capital. They must indeed be in a bad way. I moved two castor-oil plants and a holly and some berberis to the corner of the field-gate under the laburnum trees. The clearing of the slopes above the gates is having the best possible effect.

Friday 19 November 1937

Had a very singular accident while working in the garden this afternoon. I jumped to cut a holly branch over my head and got a stunning blow in the eye

[1] Graham Greene.
[2] The 2nd Viscount Tredegar.

and nose – as far as I can remember from my own left fist. Inexplicable. A monk would have put it down to an assault from the devil. Anyway it hurt atrociously and has made a nasty cut. Wrote an article for *Harper's Bazaar* on the new Palladian craze and its perils. Delicious wine given by Alex – Château Lafaurie–Peyraguey 1924.

Saturday 20 November 1937

Bill for £150 from electricians. Douglas and Mia came to luncheon; arrived late and left early. Douglas wandered about the house picking up and perusing books. We took Mia round the garden in great cold, lost Douglas and found him sitting on the floor behind the piano. Mary came for the night and arrived half an hour before her time.

Sunday 21 November 1937

All felt ill. Mass in Dursley YMCA. Garden planning. Mary left soon after luncheon and I fell asleep, exhausted by hospitality. Dug a little, read Sunday papers, chess.

Monday 22 November 1937

Work continuing in clearing drive and entrance of laurel and bramble. Started work again on novel. Another lady with double-barrelled name called.

Tuesday 23 November 1937

Pegging out circular lawn in front of house. More work on novel which is taking some shape.

Wednesday 24 November 1937

Cut down big Portuguese laurel on line of front door. Gates being rehung in field. Planted hollies by laburnums at field-gate. The Misses Leigh and the parish priest from Nympsfield came to tea. I fetched them and drove them back. Sticky party. Men working on electric light proclaim it is mended.

Thursday 25 November 1937

Wrote reviews for *Night and Day*. It seems likely that this paper is coming to an end as they lately rang up to ask if I would give them an introduction to Lord Tredegar with a view to borrowing money. Gabriel telephoned to say she had come to England to see a dentist at Bath. Could she stop here on the way. She said she would arrive at Stroud at 9. Baskerville would come from Pixton to meet her there, bring her here and sleep here too, take her to Bath. We got nursery ready for him and bought additional blankets. At 6.30 Mary rang up to say Baskerville was held up in fog. Accordingly we got Steel's Garage to meet her. She arrived at about 10, ate some dinner, and went to bed early.

Friday 26 November 1937

Gabriel left at 8.30 in station taxi, having seen us for one hour and travelled from 6.30 pm to 10 am rather than catch the morning train to Bath. Laura and I then went to London. Board meeting at Chapman & Hall's where the month's figures showed a perceptible improvement. All directors accordingly highly sceptical. Returned in the evening. Cold foggy drive home.

Saturday 27 November 1937

Miss Reynolds returned an article I had written her about architecture on the grounds that her paper stood for 'contemporary' design. I could have told her all about Corbusier fifteen years ago when she would not have known the name. Now that at last we are recovering from that swine-fever, the fashionable magazines take it up. New fence set back from gates immensely improves entrance. Carpenter has now taken three days on gate-post. Milwards came to dinner – every dish intolerably bad.

Sunday 28 November 1937

Mass at Nympsfield. Afterwards by appointment I took Laura into the convent. Mother Superior, talking of very generous benefactor: 'She gave us £1,200, poor soul.' We drank coffee in a group of nuns. I was reproved by Mother Superior for suggesting that time of Dursley Mass was inconvenient. 'You could have arranged things differently.' Luncheon with Bazleys at Hatherop. Spacious home in Tudor style – as far as one could see hurrying through mostly nineteenth-century work. Pleasant furniture. Sir T. and his sister and undergraduate step-brother. Too little to drink at luncheon. Highbrow talk about continental economists. After luncheon Laura felt ill so we drove back and she went to bed. We had meant to have tea at the Awdrys. Miss Awdry had come 'tacking in', as she expressed it, with an elocution teacher whom we had seen her greet in an extravagant way on Stroud platform.

A quiet week at Piers Court. Weeping willow planted. Visits from local county council horticultural expert who knew nothing, representative of electric light company. Worked a little at novel and learned that *Night and Day* is coming to an end, at any rate as far as I am concerned. Father D'Arcy came to us for Saturday night. Snow. I think he enjoyed talking about Aldous Huxley, etc. He had great difficulty with his car and left his luggage behind.

London, Monday 6 December 1937

We had to go to London. Missed train at Stroud and spent an hour and a half in bitter cold in Gloucester. Lunched on train. I went to Chapman & Hall where the sheets of my limited edition were not ready; to Peters where there was no good news for me; to my club where I found a notice to say the subscription had been raised; to Cornwall Terrace where Gabriel was unable to decide whether or no to leave immediately for Spain, and Mary was in anxiety about Auberon's education at Ampleforth where he is allowed to cut classes, games, and OTC and will only go to Mass on days of obligation and then only if he can serve for the headmaster; to dinner with Laura to my parents whence I emerged full of guilt.

Tuesday 7 December 1937

Wrote my last review for *Night and Day*. Drank with Hubert. Lunched at Admiralty House – Diana, Duff,[1] Venetia[2] and Sir Cuthbert Headlam. Red journalist expected but did not come. Diana spoke, as I thought, of a 'morning with the electric'; she said it was a play everybody was excited about and she made me feel a bumpkin and wanted to. Got back a bit towards the end. Conrad[3] came in with baby-face of guilt and self-consciousness. Luncheon very nasty. House superb. We also went into board-room. Laura saw doctor. Mary hard to convince that everything is satisfactory. Took evening train and arrived home, both exhausted and rather ill. Dial night.

Wednesday 8 December 1937

Had to present prizes at Dursley Secondary School. Struck by deep gloom just before, but speech went all right in the end. Peter Stucley came to drink, and carol-singers.

Thursday 9 December 1937

Laura had to go to Bath to dentist. Very bad day. I lunched with Christopher Hollis who told me Daphne Acton has been rolling in nettles. Two neighbours, doctor and wife, to tea. Cocktail party, half in our honour, at Awdrys. Neither of us feeling very sociable. Many more people with double-barrelled names.

Friday 10 December 1937

Woke after wonderful night's sleep in very good humour and as a result have done no work at all, but concentrated on making things agreeable for Laura.

Monday 10 January 1938

Several visitors during the last month. Father D'Arcy who had difficulty with his motor car and finally drove off without his luggage. Alick Dru who arrived with a very serious hangover after Peter Acton's wedding, Julian Oxford and Christopher Hollis. Helen Asquith. Carolyn Cobb. On the day

[1] Duff Cooper became First Lord of the Admiralty in Chamberlain's national cabinet of May 1937.
[2] Montagu.
[3] Conrad Russell.

before Christmas Eve, Laura and I went to Pixton for a week and from there to Mells, two expeditions to London for Chapman & Hall board meetings and visits to Dr Oxley. At Chapman & Hall's we are threatened by action from the Gas, Light, and Coke Company for publishing a book on the thesis that cancer is caused by coal gas.

Work in the house: stripping, not with perfect success, of the library chimneypiece; building of cupboards in the night nursery. I have engaged Evans, one of Mr Jotchman's carpenters, at £3 5s 0d a week. In the garden we have planted a weeping ash, a tulip tree, a copper beech, and a scarlet oak which I propose to move again. We have begun levelling the land outside the drawing-room window, and I propose to level the slope, bringing the lawn opposite the front door. Negotiations with the West Gloucestershire Power Company go on slowly; I have agreed to pay £120 if they will connect me by the end of March. Mrs Awdry threatens to build a cottage in the further of the two arable fields which originally went with Piers Court.

Work on *Scoop* going slowly, with infinite interruptions and distractions. *Night and Day* ends as a weekly; my own connection with it ending in some bitterness on my side. A dozen each of the new edition of my works have been printed on large paper and I have given away six. Duchess of Rutland died. Contradictory reports of fighting round Teruel have sunk to unimportance in the news.

Waugh's acquisition of Piers Court in 1937 marked the beginning of an attempt to lead a settled country life; but he soon interrupted it when in the following year he travelled first to Hungary and then, with his wife, to Mexico – subsidized by the Cowdray family, which had large interests at stake there – in order to observe the dictatorship of General Cardenas. The book he wrote about his visit, *Robbery Under Law: The Mexican Object-lesson* (1939), was the only one of his five pre-war travel books that he did not include in the anthology of his travel writings, *When the Going Was Good*, published in 1946. He was content to leave his Mexican book 'in oblivion', he wrote, 'for it dealt little with travel and much with political questions'. Its theme he described as 'notes on anarchy'. Mexico, he concluded, was a 'waste land, part of a dead or, at any rate, a dying planet'. The 'object-lesson' was as follows: 'Even at the time of writing when tempers are gloomier, the air is one of nervous vexation that progress should be checked by malicious intervention; progress is still regarded as normal, decay as abnormal. The history of Mexico runs clean against these assumptions. We see in it the story of a people whom no great disaster has overwhelmed. Things have gone wrong with them, as they have gone right with us, as though by a natural process. There is no distress of theirs to which we might not be equally subject.'

The diary resumes in June 1939, two months before the outbreak of the Second World War.

Piers Court, Wednesday 28 June 1939

Meeting at Nympsfield to inspect orphanage and start debating class at school. Dined with Lady Featherstone Godley. Bad dinner, bad wine, middle-aged military men boasting about their ancestry. Diana[1] rang up in the middle to say she must stay the night Thursday.

Thursday 29 June 1939

Diana and Conrad arrived two and a half hours late without baggage, with rambling story of having been to bed in barn. At dinner Diana tried to talk about crisis but was deflected rather abruptly.

Friday 30 June 1939

Review in *Daily Mail*, very well intentioned, saying that my book[2] is full of repulsive stories about the immorality of priests and nuns. Took Diana and Conrad to see Stancombe grotto.

Saturday 1 July 1939

Set off in new car to lecture on Mexico to Birmingham Catholic graduate association at Sion House. Car failed to start after luncheon in Tewkesbury, arrived rather late and found Archbishop Williams there, talked to him about birth control. Lectured to pleasant audience in tropical conservatory. Hostess Mrs H. Watts as funny as could be. Good early Victorian furniture, fine grounds. Crasus [?] Watts came in time for dinner. Delightful evening talking about Pugin (Watts's great-grandfather).

Sunday 2 July 1939

Left after Mass, breakfast and viewing some Blenheim guns. Drove to Malvern to meet Coote, Maimie, Vsevolode,[3] and Pat Hance at Hornyold. Lunched with Coote at Upton-on-Severn, commodious, nondescript, very cheap house. Coote typically has concentrated on vegetable garden.

Monday 3 July 1939

Continuous rain. Dug new path in woodland.

[1] Lady Diana Cooper.
[2] *Robbery under Law.*
[3] Prince Vsevolode Joannovitch of Russia, who in 1939 married Lady Mary Lygon ('Maimie').

Tuesday 4 July 1939

Continuous rain. Began correcting errors of measurement in long net of tennis court.

Wednesday 5 July 1939

Continuous rain. Continued work on tennis court. Letter from Diana saying why she was not allowed to talk about crisis. Wrote long explanation, also further protest to *Mail*. Letter from Carter clearly indicating that he proposes to bring action for recovery of wages at his convenience.

Thursday 6 July 1939

More rain and tennis court.

Friday 7 July 1939

Cinema. Milward telephoned to say he could not explain on telephone what he proposes to do tomorrow night during the ARP 'blackout'. Told him I should be out that evening, so he sent someone in my absence to explain that no one knew what was to happen in the blackout.

Saturday 8 July 1939

Lady Featherstone Godley called in the morning to ask where first aid post was and complain of Lady Tubbs's change of venue from boilerhouse to stable. Count d'Oyley rang up to ask us to weekend at Berkeley. Refused, controlling temptation to explain that I do not go visiting the immediate neighbours. Letter from *Mail* clearly taking too casual a line re libel. Telephoned Milward to ask about 'blackout' arrangements. 'I can't tell you on the telephone. I will send a special messenger.' Lady Plymouth and Lady Phyllis Benton[1] to luncheon in pouring rain. Milward messenger came with note marked 'secret' in red chalk saying, 'General report at 0215 hours to Mrs Collins at Old Parsonage Garage who will give you final instructions.' Soon after 11, Red Cross party arrived and were settled among blackbeetles in the back kitchen. Rain stopped. A misty moonlit night. Went out at two and found Mrs Baldwin and two farmers' boys at Old Parsonage. Waited half an hour. Presently two special constables arrived, then some air raid wardens, then Mrs Collins who attached labels to us specifying injuries. Then more officials gathered and presently someone let off a firework. Then the wardens copied particulars of our injuries in notebooks. We walked to Piers Court where the Red Cross squad, who had had nothing to do till then, put our arms in slings. Then I produced some beer and port and we were having a drinking party when Mrs Day-Fayle appeared to inspect us.

[1] 'Lady Phylis Bentham' in MS.

Sunday 9 July 1939

Very sleepy. Father Murtagh has spent £40 on some plaster stations of the cross. Leightons and a Catholic fellow called Nichol and wife to luncheon. Slept in afternoon and went to garden party Stancombe.

Monday 10 July to Thursday 13 July 1939

Engaged among flowers in making paths and semi-circular terrace round chestnut and lime on NE corner of house.

Friday 14 July 1939

House closes down for three weeks. Drove with Laura to Pixton, arriving lunch-time where we found Gabriel, Titania Herbert, Lady Lucas and daughter. Eddie and Bridget[1] arrived about 9 during beginning of dinner.

Thursday 27 July 1939

After two weeks of Pixton life I leave for a few days' rest. There have been various guests – Sir Robert and Lady Hodgson, Sir Cecil Periera, various Amorys and Horners popping in and out, children all over the house, incessant rain, unpunctual uneatable meals, incessant telephoning and changing of plans. I have rewritten the first chapter of the novel[2] about six times and at last got it into tolerable shape. The *Daily Mail* have refused to publish any apology for their libel. We lunched at Dunster[3] one day and saw lemons and olives ripening in the open, a room of Spanish–Netherlands leatherwork, some fine furniture and Charles II carving, a host who told us in some detail of his successes at roulette. IRA bombs, surrender to Japanese, comic dependence on Russian negotiations fill newspapers.

To London by dinner train and to Highgate for tonight.

Friday 28 July 1939

Went to see Jewish lawyer about bringing pressure on *Daily Mail*, lunched alone at St James's, and to board meeting.[4] Inman has expelled St Johnstone from board, having secured election to Athenaeum. 'We remain good friends.' He expressed himself satisfied with the negligible books we have published lately. My father told me he, Inman, has been promised a peerage. After the board meeting I went to a bookshop in Cecil Court and purchased three dilapidated copies of Halfpenny's[5] and a fine copy (needs rebacking) of

---

[1] Grant; Waugh's sister-in-law and her husband.
[2] *Work Suspended*, published in 1942.
[3] Dunster Castle, Somerset; held by the Luttrell family since 1376.
[4] Chapman & Hall's.
[5] William Halfpenny, eighteenth-century architectural designer.

Chambers' *Civil Architecture*, the whole for a few pounds. Slept at Highgate.

Carlton Towers, Goole, Yorks, Saturday 29 July 1939

Walked with my father in Kenwood and attempted to undo the rather unamiable impression of my former two evenings. Went to King's Cross, where in a crowded train Miles[1] had happily engaged a carriage which we had to ourselves with two other members of the party, Loftus and Lewis. Tedious journey to Selby, arriving Carlton about 5. First sight of the house is staggering, concrete-faced, ivy-grown, 1870-early-Tudor bristling with gargoyles, heraldic animals carrying fully emblazoned banners, coroneted ciphers; an orgy of heraldry. Two prominent towers, water and clock, the latter in the style of a Flemish belfry, which from the younger Pugin's original drawings were to have been mere turrets compared with a vast Norman tower which was to complete his wing, leading to church and 'Hall of the Barons'. The inside gives every evidence of semi-amateur planning; space where none is needed, cramped arches and windows where one cries out for space, harsh light everywhere from bad stained glass. The main corridor is completely lightless, except for little, stained windows in the ceiling which give into a box-room attic above. All state bedrooms face north over stable yard while servants' quarters command the south terrace. Large numbers of indifferent paintings ascribed to Italian masters. The great drawing-room wainscotted in sham ebony with, above, sham Spanish leather, atrocious paintings in the panel of Shakespearian characters, more escutcheons with countless quarterings. Closer inspection, however, reveals many charms: the relics of two earlier houses below the 1870 shell, some 1830 Gothic, some first-class pre-Adam Georgian and bits of pre-Tudor rooms. A fine music library with some fairly interesting books. The whole Howard family are together. I never discovered exactly how many, seven or eight of them, each with a Christian name beginning with M. A nice chap called Gavin Maxwell[2] and Maureen Noel were the rest of the party. Lord Howard has little importance in the house and twitches painfully. We played 'the game' after dinner. Maxwell, to be civil to me, chose clues from my books which no one recognized. I stayed until Tuesday. On Sunday night we used the Emperor of Abyssinia's gilt plate which Lord Howard bought for £40, and which I last saw used at Addis Ababa for the journalists' banquet. I think they were only once used after that, at the Red Cross dinner, then packed for transit and flight. They looked very shoddy beside the fine English silver. Daily Mass but no tiresome piety.

---

[1] The Hon. Miles Howard, son of Lord Howard of Glossop, the owner of Carlton Towers, Goole.

[2] Author (1914–69) of *Harpoon at a Venture*, 1952, an account of an attempt to establish a shark fishery on a Scottish Island, and *Ring of Bright Water*, 1960, the story of two pet otters.

Pixton Park, Tuesday 1 August 1939

Travelled straight through to Pixton where I found Gabriel, Auberon, Coney and Ralph Jervis[1] and everyone in a ferment about the fête.

Wednesday 2 August 1939

Lord Howard of Penrith died. Mary put off poor John Awdry who is, I suppose, the sole living being to whom a visit to Pixton is a treat, to make room for the ex-minister of Albania who speaks no English and is losing his sight.

Thursday 3 August 1939

Mary's fête more or less successful. I bought a number of useless objects at extravagant prices at an auction. Household machinery more than usually inefficient.

Piers Court, Friday 4 August 1939

Returned home to find the rain had stopped all work in the garden, weeds had grown prodigious, Prewitt's only effort had been to kill all the grass on the circle with an application of soot, the whole place looked as neglected as it did when we first arrived two years ago. Also that Cook had bought for me at Sir Charles Prevost's sale a large lot of calf-bound sermons which I don't want and an enormous pair of portraits, George III and wife, which are disconcerting. They were presented by the King to the first baronet who was governor of numerous dependencies, including Canada, and were presumably shipped from Government House to Government House suffering considerably in the transit. The new telephone service is causing great interest to all.

Saturday 5 August 1939

Induced Cook to take back sermons. The George portraits cost £8. They will cost a good bit more before they are done with. I worked in the garden trying to rectify Prewitt's errors of judgement in the semi-circular terraces at the N. of the tennis court.

Sunday 6 August 1939

Church and spade.

Monday 7 August 1939

Spade, and Berkeley show. Bank holiday.

[1] Mr and Mrs ('Coney') Ralph Jarvis; in *Unconditional Surrender* 'Everard Spruce' has a secretary named 'Coney'. Ralph Jarvis (1907–73) was a merchant banker.

Tuesday 8 August 1939

Maria Teresa[1] returned. Took soap and water to the George III portraits and found them rather fine under their grime. Coney and Ralph to luncheon. Oldridges to sherry. The sham bookbacks arrived and I stuck them in place. They look very well.

Wednesday 9 August 1939

The *Daily Mail* is publishing an apology in my words and paying my legal expenses – a very satisfactory conclusion. Dug.

Thursday 10 August 1939

Wrote review for *Spectator*. Dug. Gradually cleaning the alley of thistle and dandelions.

Thursday 17 August 1939

A peaceful week of sunshine. Writing in the morning – novel going very slowly – and cleaning the avenue in the afternoon. On Saturday 12th I opened a flower show. In the library I sit opposite the portrait of George III and have decided to keep it there permanently. A Bath antiquary offered £12 for the pair. Prewitt came back to work from his holiday on 14th and has cleaned the kitchen garden. On 15th I went over to Sapperton to see Miss Bruce's system of making vegetable manure. Her garden is certainly remarkably fertile and the compost sweet and rich, though her explanations of the process have a great deal of metaphysical nonsense in them.

Friday 18 August 1939

My father and mother came to stay.

Saturday 19 August 1939

Drove my father to Bath to see the Assembly Rooms while Laura was at her dentist. Lunched at the Pump Room and drove to Corsham where Alec[2] was playing cricket against the Sappers in charge of the dump. Six thousand civilians were at work storing explosives in fifteen miles of subterranean trench under the ground. Alec made a good score and took some wickets. Laura and I drove to the mason's yard round Bath and saw some Gothic tracery which might make a balustrade in the garden. We took Alec back to Stinchcombe after the match.

Sunday 20 August 1939

Finished the weed-heap and covered it with soil. A neighbour called Selsby

---

[1] The Waugh's first child, born March 1938.
[2] His brother.

was brought in to sherry with a lovely girl who was granddaughter of Holman Hunt and consequently my cousin.[1] War seems more probable. Alec increasingly, abnormally inarticulate and engrossed in his profession.

Monday 21 August 1939

Took Alec to station and went on to sale where I bought a portfolio stand, 10s and some books. Laura bought a cruet stand and some plates for which we have no possible use. In the afternoon to Owlpen to show it to my father and to Ogleworth.

Tuesday 22 August 1939

Russia and Germany have agreed to neutrality pact so there seems no reason why war should be delayed.

Wednesday 23 August 1939

As in September of last year, it is difficult to concentrate on work at the moment. I spent a restless day, but am maintaining our record as being the only English family to eschew the radio throughout the crisis. I have purchased for £10 16s the thirty-foot run of Gothic balustrade from Box and have inserted Miss Bruce's distillation into the weed-heap.

Thursday 24 August 1939

Working in the afternoon in the garden, clearing the alley, I thought: what is the good of this? In a few months I shall be growing swedes and potatoes here and on the tennis court; or perhaps I shall be away and then another two or three years of weeds will feed here until the place looks as it did when we came here two years ago.

Friday 25 August 1939

The news shows no prospects of peace. The Pope's appeal was in terms so general and trite that it passes unnoticed here, where no one doubts that peace is preferable to war. Perhaps it may have more meaning in Italy where they have not heard the same sentiments every day of their lives. I have written to Basil Dufferin to ask if he can put me in touch with MI.[2] I presume they are in a feverish state in London. Worked well at novel.

Saturday 26 August 1939

Worked well at novel. I have introduced the character who came here to beg,

[1] Diana Holman Hunt. William Holman Hunt (1827–1910), the Pre-Raphaelite, married in succession Fanny Waugh and Edith Waugh, both of whom were daughters of Evelyn Waugh's great-uncle, a pharmacist of Regent Street, London.
[2] MOI: Ministry of Information.

saying he was on the *New Statesman* and an authority on ballistics, as the driver who killed the father.[1] I suspect he will assume a prominent place in the story. Confession.

Sunday 27 August 1939

Went to luncheon with Christopher[2] at Mells. Maidie seems solely concerned about the way war will affect her housekeeping. Communion. My inclinations are all to join the army as a private. Laura is better placed than most wives, and if I could let the house for the duration very well placed financially. I have to consider thirty years of novel-writing ahead of me. Nothing would be more likely than work in a government office to finish me as a writer; nothing more likely to stimulate me than a complete change of habit. There is a symbolic difference between fighting as a soldier and serving as a civilian, even if the civilian is more valuable.

Monday 28 August 1939

To Bath where Laura visited the dentist, I a house agent. Lunched with my aunts and took away some books from my great-grandfather's library. Evans back at work here hanging the picture of George III in the library. I think of putting 'scribble, scribble' on a ribbon across the top. Miss Metcalfe the schoolmistress came to tell me I was a billet. My heart sank. But it is not for children but for five adults who are coming to arrange for the children's arrival and go in a week's time.

Friday 1 September 1939

The week has gone very slowly. Household admirably calm. My offer of services rejected by MI. Have written, to please Laura rather than with any hope of result, to Sir Robert Vansittart[3] and Gerry Liddell. I have put the house into the hands of several agents. The stone Gothic balustrade arrived from Box. Evans at work adapting the panels in the library to the George III portrait. Evacuated children due here today; also the Nympsfield school treat. As we expected, rain. Yesterday Highnam[4] garden was open to public. We

---

[1] Possibly Henry T. F. Rhodes, sometime lecturer in criminology at the University of Lyons. He reviewed occasionally for the *New Statesman*, on the strength of three books he had written: *The Criminal in Society*, *Alphonse Bertillon*, and *The Criminals We Deserve*. He was said to be a handwriting expert, but also showed expertise in firearms and ballistics. C. H. Rolph of the *New Statesman* comments: 'One thing that inclines me to believe he might have seemed to Evelyn Waugh to have "come to beg" is that he seemed to do a lot of personal lobbying; he always wanted introductions here and there, or influence exerted on his behalf by people who scarcely knew him.'

[2] Christopher Hollis.

[3] Chief diplomatic adviser to the Foreign Secretary, 1938–41.

[4] Highnam Court, near Gloucester.

went and I was delighted with it and found many ideas for Victorian planting here.

Immediately after writing this I went to the vicarage and fetched the chairs which were being lent for the orphanage tea. Mr Page had just heard the 10 o'clock wireless news. Germany had begun bombing Poland. Borrowed chairs in two loads. On returning with the second, Ellwood told me the bus company had had the bus for the afternoon commandeered. Meanwhile Stokes, the Wotton confectioner, had left with tea. We decided to take it to Nympsfield. Loaded huge drum of ice cream, toys, cakes, etc., on car and took them to nuns. After luncheon I planted fritillary bulbs round the Spanish chestnut, then at 6 went to receive the evacuated children at the village hut. Most of the notables of the village were there; no children, and complaints that Mrs Barnett had changed all the reception arrangements. Meanwhile we listened to wireless in a Mrs Lister's motor car. It said the evacuation was working like clockwork. Still no children. Then some empty buses. Finally a police officer in a two-seater who said the children had come 400 short and there were none for Stinchcombe. Rain came on so we dispersed, dropping Page at vicarage.

Today Evans finished the new arrangements of panels in the library. The west wall is now symmetrical and, with the George III portrait, looks absolutely splendid.

Saturday 2 September *1939*

There is apparently no shortage of men for Forces. Except for an hour and a half delay on the telephones to London everything is normal. We began preparations for the evacuation helpers by removing all valuable objects from the rooms I am giving them. At 11 we learned that no evacuees were coming here today. An oppressive day. Wrote an advertisement of the house for *The Times*, and an offer of my services via Bruce Lockhart. Telephoned to Peters. He has moved to Information.[1] I am hopeful of getting a post from him. In the evening a certain number of mothers and children arrived. We went to the Dursley cinema where Baldwin was laughed at loudly on the newsreel. The 'blackout' was on. We were stopped twice and warned about our lights.

Sunday 3 September *1939*

Mass and communion. After breakfast the Prime Minister broadcast that war had begun. He did it very well. Various regulations followed concerning all places of amusement closed, air raid warnings, etc. Mr Page has a destitute woman, pregnant, with four children in his stable loft. We took them a bed and some clothes. The woman was sitting at a table in tears, Page ineffectually trying to put wire round the railings to keep the children, which the mother

---

[1] A. D. Peters, Waugh's literary agent, had just joined the Ministry of Information.

won't control, from falling through them. Little groups of children are hanging round the village looking very bored and lost.

Monday 4 September 1939

Some of the evacuees are under the impression that they are taking refuge from the IRA. Others are extremely discontented at not drawing more pay from the Government and are going home in a huff. Most are settling down. It is now clear that we are going to be immune. A civil note from Vansittart saying he was passing me on to Lord Perth[1] so I wrote long letters to Perth and Peters pressing my qualifications as liaison with foreign war correspondents. Began building operations on the erection of the Gothic balustrade. The evenings are very oppressive as we have to sit behind shutters, as, by all accounts, the police are interpreting the regulations with a minimum of good sense, bullying the cottagers for pinpoints of light that would be invisible from the lowest air-craft. On Sunday evening Eyre rang up that he could get Ellwood into his searchlight corps at Bristol. Accordingly Laura and I drove him there in the morning. There were queues of recruits waiting to join, others drilling, most of them young professional men. Eyre took us to the top of the queue and signed Ellwood on right away. We took him back to pack. Police rang up that the Mullers[2] must register at Staple Hill police station. Ellwood had a chicken for tea and a bottle of port and Mrs Harper as his guest. Then at 6.30 we drove him in and said goodbye to him. Mullers also in car to register. Greatest difficulty finding right police station in darkening streets and drive home with single obscured light exceedingly difficult. Laura drove with great calmness. Home at 10.

Tuesday 5 September 1939

War news more or less meaningless. Peter Stucley came over to consult about his National Service. There seems no demand for cannon fodder at the moment. I got a letter from the Ministry of Information saying I was on their list and must not apply for other National Service until I hear from them. A telegram and a telephone call in answer to my advertisement in *The Times* to let this house. Three women came in the afternoon; all smiles at the attractions of the house until I mentioned £15 as the weekly rent when they became glum. A happy time building the wall.

Wednesday 6 September 1939

Two more enquiries about the house, one from the keeper of an idiot school. Just before luncheon Mrs Phillimore came to see us. She took no interest in it at

---

[1] Then Chief Adviser on Foreign Publicity at the Ministry of Information.
[2] Servants.

all and tried to engage me in conversation about religion and spoke of the coming 'mutation', by which I suppose her to be American. I believe she had come all the way from Torquay to talk of this mutation and had no intention of taking the house. A further enquiry from a Northwood schoolmistress. The wall rising.

Thursday 7 September 1939

The newspapers suddenly empty of all reading matter. A letter from Lord Perth telling me to await orders. Further foolishness about lights. I spent some time whitening the buffers of the car and blackening the lights. A secretary came to see the house for her employer.

Friday 8 September 1939

It seems a very long time since the war began. No one seems anxious to take this house or to employ me on National Service. The discontent among the evacuees has increased. Seven families left the village amid general satisfaction. Those who remain spend their leisure scattering waste paper round my gates. Diana Awdry stopped in to say that a German submarine was lying berthed on the sand at Lyme Regis and was offended by our incredulity. Working in garden.

Wednesday 13 September 1939

A tedious time. No one wishes to take the house or to employ me. Peters answers no letters or telegrams. Perth has been removed from head of Information. The papers complain with increasing bitterness about the Press services. I did some wholly unsuccessful bricklaying, Prewitt some admirable work putting up the Gothic balustrade. Letters from London suggest that no one is finding work of the kind they want. Maria Teresa is being sent off today but Deakin pretends she is ill in order to make Laura drive her to Bristol.

Sunday 17 September 1939

Deakin proved right. Maria Teresa had a temperature and we were obliged to send her all the way by car, Evans driving. The last days have been very tedious. The war seems likely to develop into an attack on Great Britain by an alliance of Russia, Germany, Japan, and perhaps Italy, with France bought out and USA as sympathetic onlooker. Had I no garden to dig in I should be in despair with lack of occupation.

Today our immediate prospects seem lightened by the visit from a Dominican nun who thinks of bringing a school here, seemed to think the place big enough and the rent £600 p.a. small enough. It would be a great comfort to have the house provided for. Alec is back in the army.

Monday 18 September 1939

This morning, depressed at the war news and the confusion of English services, I came down to breakfast and found the registration book for my car, for which I had applied, arrived by return of post. I reflected that there was really a great deal which went through smoothly in England, that we made a great fuss when anything went wrong and disregarded the vast machinery that was working successfully all the time, etc., etc. I then looked at the book and found that it referred to a totally different car. I further found that the number-plates of my car and its licence were different. Consequently most of the morning passed on the telephone between Steel's Garage and the Gloucester Licence Office.

Tuesday 19 September 1939

Laura delivered the Mullers to Mrs Eyre. They left full of gin and with protestations of regret. An Ember Day and no dispensations.

Wednesday 20 September 1939

A letter from Ian Hay[1] at the War Office encouraging me to hope for a liaison post. Sibell Lygon[2] and her husband (in RAF uniform) arrived unexpectedly and stayed to luncheon. She in a great state of nerves, full of laments about blackout and rationing, which I unimaginatively took literally. Later Laura pointed out that she was apprehensive for Michael's safety. Michael encouraging about German flying. After luncheon we went for a farewell visit to Mells, taking six pullets for Maidie Hollis. Lady Horner attempted to take them from her. She told of the simple woman in Mells who had refused to take evacuated children, had defied first Katharine and Mr Higgins, later herself and Canon Hannay.[3] Hannay had threatened her with hell and she had remained obdurate. During the recital, sympathy remained strongly with the obdurate woman but Lady Horner recovered it by saying, 'So this afternoon at the Women's Institute tea I prevented her from getting a slice of Mrs Gould's cake.' We went to take Maidie her pullets. Chris[4] has taken on teaching at Downside and attributed the murder of the Rumanian premier to Russia's ambitions in Bessarabia. Hollis came to dinner. Chris remarked that for ten years in Napoleonic wars we stayed at war with France without firing a shot; when pressed dropped to six years; when pressed admitted there might have

---

[1] Pseudonym of John Hay Beith (1876–1952), who wrote one of the most successful First World War novels, *The First Hundred Thousand*, and had been made director of War Office public relations in 1938 with the rank of major-general.

[2] Lady Sibell Lygon had recently married Michael Rowley, a pilot officer.

[3] Who wrote novels under the name of George A. Birmingham.

[4] Christopher Hollis.

been some naval fighting; when pressed admitted Finisterre and Trafalgar as incidents during his period of unbroken peace.

Thursday 21 September 1939

Trim got a summons to London from the CO of the Grenadiers. Lady Horner is supervising the hanging of her pictures from London. We have visited Conrad Russell (at the farm) and saw the comic papers he had bought for his boy evacuees – *Dandy, Knockout, Radio Fun, Magic*. Douglas Woodruff came to luncheon bringing Peter Lunn, a boy with a nasty soft voice and an ill-assured manner. Mells looking supremely peaceful and spacious. Drove home to find the Gloucester CC had returned me the wrong registration book and a series of petrol ration books. Barbara Crohan came in to tell us about her evacuees.

Sunday 24 September 1939

Having delayed until after Ember Week, the Bishop of Clifton has dispensed us from fasting.

Monday 25 September 1939

The Dominican nuns confirm the taking of this house from October 1st. Preparations all day in garden and house. The papers are all smugly jubilant at Russian conquests in Poland as though this were not a more terrible fate for the allies we are pledged to defend than conquest by Germany. The Italian argument, that we have forfeited our narrow position by not declaring war on Russia, seems unanswerable.

Tuesday 26 September 1939

Two nuns arrived: Sister Theresa, whom we saw before, and another, the cook, timid and infirm. They have immediately begun asking us for additional advantages: that we should have them in on Friday instead of Sunday when they begin paying the rent; that we should keep two free till then; that they should take stores off us at wholesale not retail prices and so on. A telephone message that the Bishop is making difficulties revealed that they would not scruple to back out of the bargain at the last moment. Altogether they have been tiresome.

Wednesday 27 September 1939

Sister Theresa left for London leaving us the timid cook, to be joined shortly by a Quaker games-mistress. We gave the nuns breakfast in bed which they seemed to regard as a supreme luxury. They are bringing thirty children, two parents, six nuns, a mistress and a priest and seem to think they will be comfortable. Days of extraordinary beauty. Laura working heroically.

Thursday 28 September 1939

The games-mistress failed to arrive. The convent furniture came at 8 pm when Laura and I were setting out to dinner with the Eyres. They sent no one to help carry it in and the nun in charge had no money for tips.

Friday 29 September 1939

Laura and I left. The house in turmoil. The nun and the games-mistress impudently commandeering Prewitt's services. A telephone call from Pixton to say that an epidemic of dysentery was raging and that Laura and I should stop at Mells. This we did very readily and spent a most happy weekend there, discussing the ethics of voluntary service with Katharine and the development of Soviet foreign policy with Christopher. There were times when he talked on with no one listening. Per and Billy[1] in and out.

Pixton Park, Sunday 1 October 1939

Set off early and arrived at Pixton before luncheon. We found a household of fifty-four, including twenty-six evacuated children, six spinster 'helpers', and, most unexpectedly, a neighbouring doctor and his wife; he had been struck by mortal disease and brought up here to die. He was dying with unconscionable prolixity in the dining-room. We ate (and helpers) in the hall making a fine target for the children's spittle from the top landing. Eddie[2] in low spirits, without employment, spending the day poaching the syndicate's pheasants. The dysentery epidemic had never existed except in Mary's[3] imagination and is not mentioned. Mild flu and heavy colds are raging, however.

Monday 2 October 1939

Eddie got a telegram calling him to London to see General Beith[4] for 'immediate service abroad'. This was in fact in the liaison post which I had been promised. Ex-cavalrymen are being employed for it. We drank a magnum of Perrier Jouet 1921 before dinner. Gabriel is at work in the local garage having turned down two offers of excellent public employment.

Tuesday 3 October 1939

A letter from Beith saying it had not been possible to include me in the liaison corps. Reviewing a poorly edited, collected edition of Lewis Carroll.

Wednesday 4 October 1939

Eddie and Bridget returned. He in uniform, transformed by his job into a

[1] Lady Perdita and the Hon. William Jolliffe.
[2] Eddie Grant, a brother-in-law; married to Laura's sister, Bridget.
[3] Mary Herbert, Waugh's mother-in-law.
[4] See p. 442, note 1.

self-respecting fellow. Everyone with acute colds. Eddie says that Beith talks impatiently of Belisha's [1] zeal for publicity. I went for a very long walk and got lost.

Thursday 5 October 1939

I went for a long walk to clear hangover. Everyone low-spirited with colds. The 'helpers' are beginning to face the prospect of two or three years' continuous drudgery with some apprehension.

Friday 6 October 1939

No news from Beith or the nuns or Prewitt. Eddie and Bridget went to London.

Saturday 7 October 1939

A superb day. Cut timber in the morning and rode in the afternoon. Severe row with Gabriel re her Francophobia in the evening.

Sunday 8 October 1939

Mass in the iron [?] room. Bitter cold and rain. Laura bad cold, sent to bed.

Monday 9 October 1939

Letter from Carolyn, who has returned to England to share our war, describing her crossing.

Tuesday 10 October 1939

A Red Cross flag day. It seems supremely ridiculous that while an essentially charitable enterprise – giving refuge to threatened children – should be financed by taxes and enforced by the police, the provision of medical service for the army should be thought a suitable field for private charity. Mary and I rode through pouring rain to sell flags at a number of outlying farms; we raised about 8s. Mary said that the farmers would feel aggrieved if neglected.

Gabriel went to London. Mary caught her at Taunton and delivered two of the evacuated children to her who are going home. She is now eagerly canvassing for more children – to the 'helpers' alarm.

Wednesday 11 October 1939

Carolyn and Norman came to luncheon with me at the Carnarvon. Afterwards Mary and I worked in the woods. Lucia arrived with a gasmask for the weekend and proved ineffectual with the axe. Mary said, 'May I just show you something', took the axe out of Lucia's hand and hit her with all her might

---

[1] L. Hore-Belisha, Secretary for War.

on the shin. On the way back to the house the van was besieged by evacuated children whom Mary was unable to shake off. No news from Navy or Army.

London, Monday 16 October 1939

By first post a letter from the Naval Intelligence Division asking me to call when I was next in London. I decided to go up immediately and was dropped in Taunton at midday by Mary. The train was not unduly crowded and it carried a restaurant car. The journey took about one and a half hours longer than its normal time. After an ineffectual attempt to get into touch with Sir Aubrey Smith, who Mary thought might help, I drove out to Highgate. No difficulty about taxis. I dined and slept at Highgate. My father is taking the Sixth Form at Highgate Grammar School in a course of Victorian poetry – unpaid but apparently welcome work to him.

Tuesday 17 October 1939

Went to Admiralty where everything was shipshape. Saw Fleming[1] who told me there was no immediate chance of employment, but that my name was 'on his list'. From there to the War Office where everything was confusion. The main hall was like a railway station in holiday time. Men and women in and out of uniform milling about. A few officers like porters being besieged with questions on all sides. An officer told me that the only way to get upstairs was to go outside and telephone for permission. I did so and got my hair cut at the same time. A distraught youth named Captain Verreker received me. I sat in his room for half an hour and listened to the work of the department. There were two other officials in the room. Every single call and telephone conversation was about something that was lost or about telephone calls cut off. Incidentally my letter had been lost. Finally there was a dramatic moment. 'The Northern Command on the telephone' in a state of great indignation. 'Simpson has been going about wearing an armlet on mufti.'

I learned there was no job for me and left for the St James's where I had half a dozen oysters, half grouse, a whole partridge, and a peach, half bottle of white wine and half Pontet Canet 1924. From then my day began to improve. Cocktail party at Michael Rosse's. The blackout is really formidable – all the gossip is of traffic casualties – the night watchman of the St James's knocked down the club steps, Cyril Connolly's mistress lamed for life and Cyril obliged to return to his wife.

Supper at Quaglino's. Frank Pakenham in uniform with Gwen Farrell. Frank full of ambitions to serve in any capacity, civil or military, greatly dismayed by the obscenity of conversations among private soldiers and full of resentment that he was obliged to attend C. of E. church parades.

---

[1] Ian Fleming, author of the 'James Bond' novels.

Pixton Park, Wednesday 18 October 1939

Went to Welsh Guards, where two delightful officers of enormous age interviewed and accepted me. They thought there might be something for me in six months. So, more comforted, I returned to Pixton where a fresh wave of lice has effected an entry.

Thursday 19 October 1939

Sustained by inward satisfaction having arranged things with Welsh Guards. Work out of the question as the evacuated children are now admitted to the garden at the back of the house under my windows. Impetigo, thrush, and various ailments are rampant.

Saturday 21 October 1939

By the second post a letter from the Welsh Guards unaccountably telling me that their list had been revised and that they had no room for me. My first feeling was that there must be someone at the War Office occupied in blocking my chances; my second that Colonel Leatham had become notorious for his generosity in giving commissions and had been rebuked. Whatever the reason, I was thrown into despair. I now had no irons in the fire. That night I tried a new sleeping draught made by the local doctor. He admitted later that it was what he used to give mothers in travail.

I slept well but woke feeling on the verge of melancholy mania.

Sunday 22 October 1939

A bitter day. I wrote various letters, still niggling for a job.

Easton Court Hotel, Chagford, Monday 23 October 1939

Woke more depressed than ever. The doctor came to see Laura and said that it now seemed likely that the baby would be born next month. Accordingly I decided to leave for Chagford in the hope of getting my novel finished, or nearly finished, by the time I could take Laura from Pixton. I went by train. Norman met me in Exeter. The hotel is empty except for a nervous couple who are so affable and who bring the conversation round so often to Jews and refugees that I think they must be Jews.

Tuesday 24 October 1939

Wrote all the morning. The second chapter taking shape and, more important, ideas springing. A long and lonely walk in the afternoon. A little more work.

Wednesday 25 October 1939

Wrote all the morning and some of the afternoon. Eight-mile walk. A preposterous letter in *The Times* by H. G. Wells proposing the declaration of the new Rights of Man which is half nonsense, half mischief, and a handful of trivial, practical precepts such as 'No castor oil' and a hikers' charter to destroy the countryside.

Thursday 26 October 1939

Working well. Over 4,000 words done since I arrived. A letter from Humbert Wolfe[1] very kindly volunteering to push my fortunes with the War Office. Also one from the maligned nuns at Stinkers,[2] announcing that the contract is being signed. A letter from Brendan Bracken[3] saying that Winston Churchill had strongly supported my claim to a commission in the Marines.

Friday 27 October 1939

Working well. People beginning to speculate about German invasion.

Saturday 28 October 1939

My 36th birthday which Laura and I had arranged to spend together in Exeter. Left by an early bus and spent one and a half hours walking Exeter streets. Cold and brilliant; full of troops. The Clarence Hotel full of staff officers. A happy day with Laura. She did a little shopping, we lunched heavily and quite well, and sat in a cinema until it was time for her train. Then I drove the car back to Chagford where an unattractive brother-in-law of Norman's had arrived for the weekend. Bad night.

Sunday 29 October 1939

Drove to Mass and communion at Gidleigh and spent day without working. Two agreeable Devon women came to luncheon. Rain and bitter cold.

All Saints, 1939

Continuous rain for the last three days and, in consequence, the novel progressing well and myself not sleeping. I awoke this morning saying to myself, 'So you got to sleep after all.' I take the MS of my novel up to my bedroom for fear it should be burned in the night. It has in fact got to interest me so much that for the first time since the war began I have ceased to fret about not being on active service. Perhaps that means that I shall shortly get a commission.

They are saying, 'The generals learned their lesson in the last war. There are

[1] Civil servant, poet and essayist (1885–1940).

[2] i.e. Piers Court, Stinchcombe.

[3] Politician and publisher (1901–58); MP, 1929; ally of Churchill; he moved into Downing Street when Churchill became Prime Minister in May, 1940, and became Minister of Information in 1941.

going to be no wholesale slaughters.' I ask, how is victory possible except by wholesale slaughters?

Saturday 4 November 1939

A note from Bracken speaking well of his own efforts on my behalf with the Marines. I drove into Exeter to meet Laura, ordering luncheon first by telephone, oysters and partridges. She was not quite so well as she had been the Saturday before. I told her what I had learned of Trim's hiking [?] life and that cheered her. Sir Ronald Graham[1] says Ciano is wholly disillusioned with Hitler. We lunched well, spent the early afternoon in a cinema which we were obliged to leave at the moment the film showed signs of becoming interesting, and then separated at the railway station.

Sunday 5 November 1939

A humiliating drive to church. I got jammed with another car in a steep lane and persistently went forward when I wished to go back until we were interlocked and holding up a stream of traffic. Helpers then lifted the other car out of the way. I got stuck again on another hill and throughout Mass and a supremely prosaic sermon on the holy souls thought of little except my experiences. Driving away I got into the wrong gear and progressed in a series of sharp jerks as though on a bucking horse. Rudolph Messel came to luncheon. The war has depressed him so much that he has bought a farm and a hunting stable. What with pacifism, political disillusionment and sex obsession, he is in a confused condition of mind. It is as exasperating to him as to me that no one wants us to fight. Pouring rain. A little boy with whooping cough has appeared in the hotel.

The *City of Flint*[2] fills the news with its changes of fortune. A trawler sunk from an overdraught of sprats. Papers unreadable. Novel hanging fire.

Monday 6 November 1939

Started work on the novel once more with tolerable success.

Friday 17 November 1939

Two visits to Laura at Pixton, taking advantage of Mary and Gabriel's absence in London. We had our meals at neighbouring hotels – badly at the Carnarvon, better at the Lamb, best in a boarding house called The Green which smells of the slums and has genuine Chippendale chairs. I am to stay there while Laura's baby is born. I have been promoted to the condition of having a number at the War Office in the Emergency Reserve and I am

[1] A former British ambassador to Italy.
[2] Merchant ship seized by different countries.

applying for the Yeomanry again. I have also, through the kind offices of Winston Churchill, Bracken, and a former adjutant-general, got as far with the Marines as to be sent a form to fill up; this privilege was hitherto refused. Perhaps I shall be able to join the war yet.

I have written a further 6,000 words of the novel, with the usual consequence that the better I work, the worse I sleep. After a weekend full of rumours that Holland is on the verge of invasion, the war has settled down to reconnaissance flights. I have opened negotiations with Chapman & Hall's, Osbert Sitwell and David Cecil with the idea of starting a monthly magazine under the title of *Duration*.

November 11th this year was not observed by a two-minute silence. I remember nearly all the armistice days: the first when the school ran wild for some hours and was issued with a special ration of galantines, which we all particularly disliked, for tea; the second when the two-minute silence was a new idea and taken reverently with the bandmaster sounding the Last Post in the Upper Quad; one at Oxford when Hugh Lygon and I drank champagne in the New Reform Club; one at Aston Clinton when the headmaster refused to recognize it and some of the boys whose fathers had been killed asked me to keep it in school; one in Abyssinia where Steer kicked an Armenian outside the Legation chapel.

Dulverton, Saturday 18 November 1939

At 9 Bridget rang up to say Laura's baby had started. I drove over to Pixton. When I arrived soon after luncheon Laura had had morphia and was cheerful and in practically no pain. She grew worse and later in the evening the local doctor summoned help from Tiverton to induce the baby. A son[1] was born shortly before midnight.

Sunday 19 November 1939

Laura happier than she is likely to be again.

Wednesday 22 November 1939

The last few days have been delightful for Laura. She is drowsy and contented. I am living at a boarding house in the village where the women believe I was tipsy on Friday night. The Marines have sent me a long questionnaire asking among other things if I am a chronic bedwetter. It seems probable that I am going to get a commission there.

London, Friday 24 November 1939

I went to London for my interview with the Marines, leaving Laura in good health and spirits and the Dulverton pension in the hands of the shooting

---

[1] Auberon Alexander.

syndicate. I went first to the St James's and had my hair cut, then to Highgate where I dined and slept, finding my parents markedly unsympathetic to my project of joining the war.

Saturday 25 November 1939

Went straight to the medical board which was in a flat in St James's. In a tiny outer room there were three or four youths waiting and two bloods, already in the Navy, who were undergoing an intensive examination for the Air Arm. Doctors in shabby white coats strode in and out smoking cigarettes. I went first to have my eyes tested and did deplorably. When asked to read at a distance with one eye I could not distinguish lines, let alone letters. I managed to cheat a little by peering over the top. Then I went into the next room where the doctor said, 'Let's see your birthday suit. Ah, middle-aged spread. Do you wear dentures?' He tapped me with a hammer in various organs. Then I was free to dress. I was given a sealed envelope to take to the Admiralty. In the taxi I unsealed it and found a chit to say that I had been examined and found unfit for service. It seemed scarcely worthwhile going to the interview. I went and found the same youths waiting in another waiting-room. They went in nervously, one by one, and came out jointly. Finally myself. A colonel [?] in khaki greeted me in the most affable way, apologized for keeping me waiting and gradually it dawned on me that I was being accepted. He said, 'The doctors do not think much of your eyesight. Can you read that?', pointing to a large advertisement across the street. I could. 'Anyway most of your work will be in the dark.' Then he gave me the choice between Marine Infantry, a force being raised for raiding parties, and Artillery, an anti-aircraft unit for work in the Shetlands. I chose the former and left in good humour.

Peters lunched with me at my club and spoke grimly of the Ministry of Information. After luncheon I called on Phyllis and Hubert, found her obsessed by war news and both a little gloomier than when I last saw them. Returned to write letters and found a message that the editor of the American magazine *Life* was at the Savoy and wanted to see me. I nearly did not go, but finally went and found a lugubrious kind of baboon who commissioned two articles at the startling price of $1,000 apiece, a sum which, if it materializes, will go a long way to settling my immediate debts. Elated by this I drank a lot of champagne with various people sitting about in the club and took a magnum to dinner at Patrick Balfour's. He told me that my idea for a magazine had already been anticipated by the rump of the left wing under Connolly. I went on to the Slip-In and drank three bottles of champagne and a bottle of rum with Kathleen Meyrick. I was sick at about 5.

Pixton Park, Sunday 26 November 1939

The subsequent hangover removed all illusions of heroism. I went to confession at Farm Street and leaving met Theodora Benson[1] and had a cocktail. Then to the Ritz where I found the Churchill family, Richard Greene and others. Met Henry[2] and took him to luncheon. His life in the Fire Brigade sounds unendurable. A ghastly journey back, dark, cold, and feeling ill. I arrived to find Laura very much worse than I had left her, lachrymose and complaining of pleurisy.

Monday 27 November 1939

The boy's christening. Of the godparents only Katharine came, Christopher,[3] Frank[4] and Maimie being cut off. A wet cold day. Laura in abysmal spirits. I decided to move up to Pixton. A very bad night.

Tuesday 28 November 1939

Laura considerably better. Bridget and Mary away. A letter from the Admiralty calling me up on the 7th at Chatham. This is a blow as it gives me no time to do the work which would set my affairs in order. My pay is 6s 10d a day out of which I get 2s 5d pocket money when the deductions are made. Laura and the children are worth 7s 6d. I wrote fourteen letters and spent the time with Laura having my meals in her room. The last days at Pixton were spent uninterruptedly in Laura's room where I had all my meals, did crosswords and read aloud and watched her get slightly but appreciably better. The news has been mainly occupied with Finland. The *Daily Express* tried to be smart and came out with huge headlines 'Finland Surrenders' on the second day of the Russian campaign. That and the *Daily Mirror*'s 'Siegfried line broken in 12 places' in October are still the best examples of uncensored journalism.

Early Wednesday 6th to London, tried on uniforms at Hawkes and made myself obnoxious to the accountants' department. I went to Angela Kinross's[5] Wednesday salon and found a lot of foreigners, dined with Burns[6] at Garrick and had a bottle of champagne with Hubert. All this in rather low spirits at leaving Laura, and after a liverish week of inactivity at Pixton; also pink-eye. Next day to Chatham in civil clothes. In the train I recognized a man who had been at the medical examination on the same day as I, tall, bald solicitor from Plymouth named Bennett.[7] He was very much the type I had expected as his

---

[1] 1906–68; author of novels, short stories and travel books; a daughter of the 1st Baron Charnwood, author of a standard life of Abraham Lincoln.

[2] Henry Yorke.

[3] Christopher Hollis.

[4] The Hon. Frank Pakenham.

[5] Angela Culme-Seymour married Patrick Balfour in 1938; he became the 3rd Baron Kinross in 1939.

[6] Tom Burns.

[7] In fact, Messer-Bennetts.

leisure was devoted to sailing. When we came to meet our other companions we were puzzled: there are twelve of us chosen out of 2,000 applicants and it would have been hard to find a more nondescript lot. A mild accountant called St John, half highbrow, with a weak bladder; an ashen young man with a huge cavalry moustache from N. Wales, called Griffiths, who surprises the mess servants by drinking quantities of hot water at all hours and calling for French mustard; he had been a schoolmaster. A choleric-looking wine merchant of great girth named Hedley. These are the best. The others are pathetic youths for officers. It is very surprising for a force which is expected to be so tough.

The regular Marines are delightful people rather smugly obsessed by their obscurity. 'How on earth did you hear of us?' Our reception was totally unlike the book which Bridget lent me to cheer me up. All the senior officers greeted us like embarrassed hosts with a flow of apology for the discomforts of our life. Something too of oriental courtesy, 'Will the noble second lieutenant come into our humble mess and meet our ill-favoured brigade major', but, like oriental courtesy, based on great self-confidence. The barracks and mess are, in fact, extremely agreeable. I have a large bedroom with a large fire and one-third of a derelict batman. The architecture of the square is charming and the mess full of trophies, though the best pictures and silver have been locked up for the war. The food is delicious. There are almost continuous entertainments. The day we joined we did no work but walked in the fog through Chatham and Rochester and sat about in the mess being given drinks by senior officers. Next day we had a series of speeches from the Commandant and other officials. 'Gentlemen, when we enter the mess all differences of rank are left behind; all we expect is the deference due to age.' As I am older than most of the captains that seemed to me a happy note. We are under the particular care of a Major Blandford, who is very humane, and a decent Sergeant Fuller, who is full of *esprit de corps* and its praises. We spent endless time drawing various bits of equipment, going through poison-gas chambers, etc. On Saturday morning we did a little squad drill and saw our barracks. In the afternoon I went to London and spent the night at Highgate. On Sunday I went to Mass at Farm Street and lunched with Hubert and Phyllis at Quaglino's. After even so short a time it seemed odd to hear anyone talking of the war in its general aspects. Quaglino's was full of acquaintances, mostly in uniform. Back into the fog and the blackout in time for supper and a cinema in the garrison theatre.

5 The Wartime Diary 1939-45

Introduction

Keeping a diary on active service during the Second World War was a serious military offence; Waugh's diary for the years 1939–45 is extensive. His career, though, was by no means straightforward and is not always easy to follow from the diary; a brief summary may therefore be useful to readers.

Waugh joined the Royal Marines as a second lieutenant. After preliminary training at the divisional headquarters at Chatham, he went for further training to Kingsdown, near Deal, in Kent, and then to Bisley, near Aldershot. In July 1940, by now a captain in command of a company, he was posted to Haverfordwest, Pembrokeshire, where he and his men embarked in an ancient cross-channel steamer ready to forestall any German invasion of Eire. When this threat fizzled out, the unit moved to the defence of Cornwall. In August 1940 the unit travelled to Birkenhead, embarked in a troopship, the *Ettrick*, and sailed to Scapa Flow. Waugh became battalion intelligence officer. After assault training round Scapa Flow, he sailed to West Africa in the *Ettrick* as part of a British expedition, undertaken with General de Gaulle, the leader of the Free French, to seize the port of Dakar in French West Africa. The expedition was a fiasco. After returning to Scotland via Gibraltar, Waugh at his own initiative secured a transfer to Combined Operations, under Colonel Robert Laycock.

In February 1941 Waugh sailed with No. 8 Commando from the Isle of Arran to the Middle East. On 19–20 April he took part in a night raid on the German-held coastline of Libya, at Bardia. At the end of May and beginning of June, as Laycock's intelligence officer, he fought in the rearguard action that preceded the evacuation and loss of Crete. On 5 July, when the Commandos in the Middle East were disbanded, he was transferred back to the Marines and returned to England in a liner that took the long route round the Cape; during the voyage, according to his own account, he wrote *Put Out More Flags*.

Waugh in his diary described the following year, 1942, as 'a good year'. Having taken a company commanders' course in Edinburgh during January and February, he again secured his release from the Marines and returned to 'soldiering among friends' with the Commandos, first in Scotland and then, after a five-week photographic interpretation course, at Sherborne in Dorset, where he served as an intelligence officer at brigade headquarters.

He spent 1943, as he had spent 1942, entirely in the United Kingdom. Unlike 1942, though, it was not a good year. Laycock left for North Africa and the invasion of Sicily without him, and in Laycock's absence he was expelled, in July, from the Special Service Brigade; the diary incorporates the exchange of letters that preceded his forced resignation. In December 1943 he went on a parachute jumping course.

During the first half of 1944 he was on leave writing 'an ambitious novel', *Brideshead Revisited*. In July he left London with Major Randolph Churchill to join a British Military Mission to Tito's Partisans in enemy-occupied Jugoslavia. On 16 July the aircraft in which he and Churchill were passengers crashed in Jugoslavia; they were flown back to hospital in Italy, undertook a recuperative jaunt to Corsica, and returned to Jugoslavia in September. Waugh stayed in Croatia with the Mission until early December. He was then posted to Dubrovnik, on the Dalmatian coast, as liaison officer between British troops and the Jugoslav authorities. He was expelled from Dubrovnik by Partisan pressure.

In February 1945 he returned to Italy. On 2 March he had a private audience with the Pope about the Partisans' treatment of the Catholic Church in Jugoslavia. Later in March he returned to London. In May his application to return to Jugoslavia in a diplomatic capacity, as British consul in Dubrovnik, was turned down; he then started to write *Helena*. In mid-September 1945 he returned with his family to his home at Piers Court. On 18 September he was demobilized.

Of the gaps in the wartime diary, the longest occurs between November 1940 and the spring of 1942. This period is covered, however, by 'Memorandum on LAYFORCE', in which Waugh wrote a full account of his experiences in the Commandos, including his part in the Battle of Crete.

Chatham, Monday 11 December 1939

Our first day of work, none of it except PT at all formidable. As usual, a great deal of time wasted in standing about doing nothing.

Tuesday 12 December 1939

Breakfast 7.30; parade 8.15; infantry drill, a tour of the quartermaster's territory learning among other things how to distinguish cat from rabbit by the number of its ribs; 10.45 military law; 11.45 PT with degrading games that are designed to keep us gay and which in fact deny the natural dignity of man. Luncheon. Parade 2.30 and ID[1] till 4, after which all the squad fall asleep in armchairs except for the ambitious clerks who tried to ingratiate themselves with the sergeant by depriving him of his leisure with an extra drill 5–6. Dinner last night was very formal, with the removal of the tablecloth in a great tug from either end of the table, but no port passed round. A new officer has joined us from Oxford, and Griffiths threatens to leave for the RNVR. Bitterly cold with the threat of snow. The Finns fight while the League of Nations has, I suppose, its last meeting on the subject.

Tuesday 19 December 1939

A cold week in which the various mischiefs effected by PT have abated or changed their ground. We now have three evening parades a week. The length of our course has been shortened to January 12th which will leave us absurdly under-educated for Deal. I went to London on leave on Saturday. Took Mary and Francis Howard to dinner at Buck's, had some drinks with Judith at Wrights, slept at Cornwall Terrace, lunched with Tom Burns and dined with him and Anne Bowes-Lyon. Back by a late train feeling that I had spent a great deal of money without much pleasure. Poor Alfred[2] has been enjoying some Christmas leave. He telegraphed to Lady Curzon in the country to meet him for dinner at the Dorchester. She came up to London, dressed herself up, got tickets for a play and waited from 8 to 12 when she went to bed. At 3.30 she was telephoned for to come at once to the Slip-In bringing £3. I found at the St James's that a tick called Pakenham felt it necessary to explain why he was not in uniform. Outside news, the *Graf Spee*'s failure to become glorious.

[1] Presumably 'infantry drill'.
[2] Alfred Duggan, a son of Lady Curzon by her first marriage.

Pixton Park, Saturday 23–Sunday 31 December 1939

Eight days Christmas leave at Pixton culminating in a severe cold. Laura able to get about a little. We had our meals separately, either upstairs or in Bridget's sitting-room. The children, our own and the evacuees, were omnipresent. A nice, quiet young monk from Ampleforth as chaplain. The usual Pixton Christmas celebrations inadequately prepared at too short notice. I got to Bridgwater for luncheon with Christopher and Trim one day. The news of Chatham is that our course there is definitely curtailed and we go to Deal on the 13th or 14th of next month to train with the whole of the officers of the Infantry Brigade. I think we have finished with Sergeant Fuller and infantry training. Mary Pakenham engaged and married but I was unable to leave Laura for the wedding. Finns still resisting and raising unrealizable hopes.

Sunday 31 December 1939–Sunday 7 January 1940

A gloomy journey to London. Francis Howard travelled with me and had forgotten to get any luncheon, so, as there was no restaurant car, I was obliged to give him half mine. London was full of dirty snow and fog. I telephoned Henry and found him and Dig at home, had tea with them and enjoyed talking to them enormously. Then to dinner with Miles, Trim and a hanger-on of Miles's named Loftus. We dined at Buck's, drank a lot, and then I had to go to my train and sit, with the wine freezing in me, in a dark carriage full of smoke and sappers; no taxis at the station, a cold walk to bed. Slept badly.

Our new programme was small arms, which has meant continuous instruction in the range on the mechanism of rifle, Bren gun and anti-tank rifle, too little exercise, no fresh air, no interest – each in turn performing some mechanical trick with varying degrees of clumsiness. A charming colour-sergeant instructor who regarded the whole thing with undisguised contempt. Our future colonel spent a day or two here and gave us a sketch of our spring and summer, ending with our extinction in August. St John has been struck ill with gallstones.[1] I had to find him a doctor in the middle of the night. After half an hour spent at Guard Rooms, telephoning, walking to Melville Barracks, the doctor was discovered sleeping in a room immediately overhead. A good little pantomime in the garrison theatre.

In training at Kingsdown, Kent, Thursday 18 January 1940

Writing in the Deal–Walmer Union Club. The last days at Chatham were delightful. We did a course of firing various kinds of small arms, at which I was excessively bad, on a wonderfully dreary range at Gravesend. With the

---

[1] John St John, author of *To the War with Waugh* (London 1973), says that his illness, though never diagnosed, was certainly not gallstones; nor has he ever suffered from a weak bladder (see entry of 28 November 1939).

revolver, at ranges so close that I could see the target, I did better. I went to London for a weekend staying with Tom Burns. I had cocktails with Teresa [1] and was touched by our reconciliation and her new brightness – she sits up four nights a week in an ARP post and dances with Canadians at low nightclubs on other days, sleeps all day, and has lost her dog – and arranged a meeting after Mass next day which was a bitter disappointment to me, she at her busiest and most irritating. I saw members of Cazalet's battery – 'the monstrous regiment of gentlemen', G. Berners – in battledress and medals. Dined off snails with Burns and Stanley Morison. Burns lives in a land of wild make-believe at the Ministry of Information, where the only problem of the war is to decide precisely what sort of government shall be set up in Germany, immediately, bloodlessly. Belisha's dismissal talked of constantly, jubilantly by the old and well-born, indignantly by the young and plebeian. I lunched with Maimie and her prince. We had a guests' night at Chatham on the last evening of the course. Patrick came down for it and, I think, found the evening very surprising, particularly 'the strings' who came downstairs with the port and the elaborate ceremonies with the snuff horn.

On January 12th, Friday, I left Chatham and began the happiest forty-eight hours of my life. Met Laura at Fleming's Hotel where we stayed, dined early with Phyllis and Hubert (who wrangled) and Gerald Berners, went to an exquisite spy film, slept and woke in comfort, a little shopping, luncheon with Liz and Raimund,[2] tea with Mary Pakenham, now surprisingly married, dinner at Boulestin, the Little Review, supper at Fleming's. Another soft night and morning in bed with the papers, Mass at Farm Street, luncheon at the St James's to Phyllis, Hubert, Liz, Raimund. Everything went perfectly. It was a delightful preparation to the camp at Kingsdown.

We arrived there after dark on Sunday and found a derelict Victorian villa surrounded by little asbestos huts which were used in the summer as a holiday camp. One bath for sixty men, one washbasin, the WCs all frozen up and those inside the house without seats. Carpetless, noisy, cold. A ping-pong table makes one room uninhabitable, a radio the other. We are five in a bedroom without a coatpeg between us. The other detachments of officers from Deal, Portsmouth and Plymouth are so like ourselves in composition that it is like a 'hall of mirrors'. The first morning's work consisted of a series of lectures, mostly by the Brigade Commander, St Clair Morford,[3] who looks like something escaped from Sing-Sing and talks like a boy in the Fourth Form at school – teeth like a stoat, ears like a faun, eyes alight like a child playing pirates, 'We then have to biff them, gentlemen.' He scares half and fascinates half. We

[1] Teresa Jungman.

[2] Lady Elizabeth Paget, a niece of Lady Diana Cooper, married in 1939 Raimund von Hofmannsthal, a son of Hugo von Hofmannsthal, the Austrian poet.

[3] The model for 'Brigadier Ritchie-Hook' in *Men at Arms*.

had an early afternoon off and Hedley and I visited the club, a cosy little house for retired doctors, mostly, paid a guinea and became members. It was increasingly welcome as a refuge. We also bought oil-stoves and decided to move into huts.

On Tuesday we spent the morning on the downs, mostly in heavy snow, doing very simple tactical problems which I managed to fail. After luncheon we had another lecture and then marched through a blizzard to see some field latrines. I moved into my hut and enjoyed the privacy, but found it a cold night even with a fur rug and oil-stove. The Marines are suffering unendurably. Poor Marine Rose has become quite cheerful at the prospect of so much distress. This morning in deep snow and a keen wind to fresh, easy tactical exercises.

The prospect is extraordinary with white foreground and dingy sea background full of a hundred or more neutral ships awaiting the contraband control. One, an Italian, was wrecked last night.

Thursday 15 February 1940

The practical course is due to end Friday 16th when we go to Bisley, confident that we cannot be going to more unsuitable quarters than those we are leaving. Since 28th January I have lived out with Laura at the Swan Hotel and have lost touch more and more with the camp. In doing this, I followed the example of the senior officers. Kingsdown House has had a most discouraging effect on everyone. There has been a steadily increasing listlessness and noisiness accentuated, but not caused, by the long spell of snow and frost. Nothing could have been more unfortunate for the Brigade. We all left our divisions full of *esprit de corps*. I noticed that everyone has become much dimmer in character. In the mess only the radio and the ping-pong table assert themselves. The house is so oppressive that all the younger officers (and most of the older, too) are getting into money difficulties as they can only leave it by buying admission to clubs and hotels. Everything has been mismanaged – the mess bills incorrectly added up, our pay unexpectedly docked of the promised marriage allowance, the mess catering has been bad and the improvements suggested by the mess committee neglected after a day or two. The worst irritation is that nothing was done for us; every slight improvement was the result of agitation from below. Major Teak, when set in motion, has been fairly efficient, but initially did nothing. This makes an ironical point, which no one missed, on 'man-management'. The truth, of course, is that no one felt responsible for us; when the Brigade is formed that will be entirely different. Meantime, a lot of genuine enthusiasm has been lost.

We have had too little work. Leisure was expensive and tedious. An hour's drill every morning would have been excellent for physique and morale. Instead, there have been lectures and tewts,[1] the latter usually quite

[1] Tactical Exercise Without Troops.

interesting, long stand-easies throughout the morning, frequent free after-noons, no work ever before 9 or after 4. Result: everyone shabby and cross.

Laura and I went for a disastrous trip to Stinchcombe. We had arranged to stay with Barbara Crohan (now Bray) at Owlpen. Our train at Stroud was two hours late (11 o'clock and there were no taxis. The Imperial Hotel had been converted into an office. Rain was falling and freezing on the ground. At last we got a taxi which took us as far as the beginning of the hill up to Uley and then did not move. Half an hour spent in pushing it round on the ice. Then a walk at snail's pace to Owlpen where we arrived at 2 am. Next morning no taxis would go out. We walked and obtained lifts and at last reached Piers Court at 12 noon and spent an hour there. The house clean enough, the garden desolate, Prewitt shamefaced and in rags. We then drove to Stroud where we found it impossible to get luncheon for some time. At last we were directed to a café. No direct train to London. A long, long, bitterly cold wait at Swindon. We reached London at about 11 pm, slept at Fleming's in the first comfort we had met. The weekend cost about £12. At the end of it I got a note saying the nuns did not want to stay on. The only agreeable part of the weekend was a chance meeting with Douglas and Mia at Mass at Farm Street. We went on with them to luncheon and ate snails.

We have had a few small parties here and seen a few of the local neighbours, Lord Birdwood, Lady Sargent, a Miss Eliot, Hubert's sister Marcella Rice. We dined there, and Edward Rice and an acrimonious little Scotsman did their best to convince me that I was engaged in an unjust war with the certainty of defeat. I thought they showed more sense than manners and not much sense. There is no war news except the continued astounding success of Finland. Today, for the first time, the papers openly admit that recruiting is going on in England for a Finnish legion.

Bisley, Monday 26 February 1940

The change to Bisley was greatly for the better. We left on 16th by a train which arrived at the advertised time – the first of this kind I have seen since the outbreak of war. We were met by Colonel Lushington and a very decent adjutant called Houghton, driven to camp which is a collection of unrelated pavilions scattered about neat grounds; outside the camp are horrible little patches of gorse and pine and villas. Lushington greeted us with the news that we might all ship a second pip and go away until Monday, so I was able to surprise Laura at Highgate and spend the night there. We then moved into London to Fleming's and had a gay time with Phyllis, Hubert, Teresa, Patrick, Douglas and Mia, Liz and Raimund, etc. I came back early on Monday in time for breakfast.

The messing is atrocious, but in every other way life is tolerable. We are organized under battalion commanders and live apart. Our battalion has its own bar. We have done some rather farcical mutual training during which I gave a twenty-minute lecture on reconnaissance patrols. Digby-Bell told me that I am likely to get made a captain in April. Bailey was nearly expelled as a result of bad reports from Chatham and Deal but 'spoke up for himself' so well that he is staying on.

I decided to remain in camp this weekend as a measure of economy. On Thursday the Brigadier appeared in our tent where we were stripping the Bren and told Messer-Bennetts that we were to spend the day with him on Saturday. He picked us up at 12.30 and, driving all over the road, took us to a depraved villa of stockbroker's Tudor. I asked if he had built it himself. 'Built it? It's four or five hundred years old.' That was a bad start. He turns slate-grey instead of red when he is angry. Inside the villa there was evidence that the nucleus of the house had been an old cottage. Mrs Morford was pretty and bright. She seems to me to lead a peculiar life with the Brigadier. She told us with great relish how, the night before, she had had to get up several times to look after a sick child. Each time the Brigadier laid a booby trap against her return by putting his boots on the top of the door. He shouts, 'Woman, get the cigarettes!' and she trots off cheerfully. Most of the Brigadier's family reminiscences dealt with floggings he administered or with grave accidents resulting from various dangerous forms of holiday-making. After luncheon, we went for a walk in fine weather and fine country round Sutton Place. He said that he missed his hockey in wartime. Golf was not the same thing; nor rackets (at which his wife excelled). 'One has to play team games as long as one possibly can. Last war I was centre-half for my company. It was worth £100 a minute. You get hold of your men that way. I had hold of my men. If a man was brought up before me for a crime, I used to say, "Will you have a court-martial or take it from me?" They always took it from me. I bent 'em over and gave 'em ten, as tight as I could. My company had the best record for crime in the regiment.'

We went back to tea and a new daughter arrived from London, very large and attractive. The Brigadier turned grey several times with this daughter, who was by a previous madam and a Catholic. She has a job in London but, said the Brigadier, was infected by the younger generation's craving for change and pleasure. She told me that she had been a liftgirl in the Times Book Club and lost her job because, at Christmastime, she hung mistletoe in the lift. The Brigadier though it most unsuitable that she should tell me that. After tea the Brigadier produced a book of verses and drawings compiled by himself and his wife in imitation of the *Just So Stories* and the *Book of Beasts*. I had to read all these verses with the B. breathing stertorously down my neck. Many of them dealt with waking people in the morning with cold sponges. 'That really happened to my wife's brother Ivor,' he said. A number of majors came to dinner, all with their madams, all foreign, a coincidence on which the Brigadier did not fail to comment rather frequently. 'Extraordinary thing these Marine officers' wives – one Russian, one Swede, one a Hun. I pulled Mrs Mac's leg about Sweden the other day. Said they were all skunks. She was quite annoyed.' We had plenty to eat and drink. Candle-shades and table-mats painted by Mrs Morford, some with Japanese flowers, others with lanterns.

After dinner the Brig. and I talked of Africa. He told me of a Gyppy he could trust, the only one in the country, Hassamir [?] Bey, an adviser of Farouk's. This unhappy man had once had to spend a day travelling with the Brig. in a train from Luxor, single track, narrow gauge, desert on both sides and intense heat. The Brig. thought he would go mad. Luckily he had a golf ball with him so he and the Gyppy played ball all the way 'throwing it as hard as he could, so that it jolly well hurt'. The Gyppy kept it up all day. Not many could have done that. 'I never saw him again but it made a great impression on me. He was a white man.'

He drove us back all the way, picking up a number of Canadians, Guardsmen and assorted stragglers on the way, and then returned to start his office work at home.

Thursday in Easter Week, 28 March 1940

I have been to London every weekend since the day of my visit to the Brigadier, staying with Laura at Fleming's, dining and lunching at the Ritz and spending a very great deal of money. We are now about £500 overdrawn. I owe £200 in income tax and see no possibility of getting my finances square except by prodigious national inflation. I dined one Thursday at a Guards' mess at Pirbright, got a little drunk and came back to get very drunk indeed. Another Thursday at Minden where Alick Dru[1] and Peter Acton[2] were taking an intelligence course. We had long leave at Easter which we spent at Cornwall Terrace, Laura with German measles. Everyone was away, and Buck's and St James's both shut.

We have come to the end of our course here and are engaged with the NCOs in pitching tents for the troops who arrive on Tuesday. A decisive date in the course was a long Friday of route march and practical exercise which was disastrous from first to last, and at every stage of the disaster I occupied a conspicuous place. Until then I had been confident of getting second-in-command of a company and had been told as much by Digby-Bell. On the eve of our Easter leave the company lists came out, I with a platoon in B Company. The work would be more interesting but it means sharing a tent, subsisting on lieutenant's pay; also the knowledge of having disappointed expectations. At the moment, in the absence of the company second-in-command, with the company commander doing a brigade job, I am nominally in command, which means nothing except that I attend company commanders' conferences,

[1] Waugh's brother-in-law.
[2] Brother of the 3rd baron and the Hon. Mrs Woodruff.

where, today, I carried a point about training. The brigade plan is to start the militiamen on thirty days' unrelieved small-arms training which is certain to be depressing and may well be demoralizing. Bailey has been sacked from the brigade and transferred to Mobile Base Defence.

In order to inculcate a fighting spirit, no air raid precautions are allowed in camp.

The Finnish surrender had an acutely depressing effect on me. The war seems to be going badly in general, and in particular offering no possible front for our specialized types of warfare.

London, Saturday 30 March 1940

On Thursday, after writing my diary, I drank from 6 until midnight and awoke feeling liverish and eager for leave. Encouraged by Bell I applied to the Colonel who gave it to me immediately, before I had explained the various reasons why I thought myself entitled to it. There was a company commanders' meeting in the morning when the adjutant sketched the future organization of the battalion. 'We have to find thirty Marines for a pioneer platoon. Two of them arrived some weeks ago. I found them in the camp and asked what they were. They said pioneers. Since then they have not been seen again but no doubt they will reappear when we go under canvas.' Also: 'I am afraid that all except one of the CQMSs have been found medically unfit for service. The fourth was unable to undergo the examination as he is away sick.'

We have a capable CSM in B Company named Macy [?]. He and I were able to make all preliminary arrangements in a few minutes. Two of our Marines are already under close arrest for being drunk on parade in the early afternoon. The call to the Fleet for a stiffening of long-service men has been the opportunity for every captain of Marines to weed out his criminals. These old men, combined with the militia who applied for the Marines under the supposition that it would involve no fighting on land, made up the brigade.

I left camp at 4.30 on Friday and came to London to a new (to us) hotel recommended by Elizabeth Herbert, 12 Curzon Street. I had telegraphed for Laura. Intent on economy, I came by tube and went to St James's for a drink. I ordered it and then found Osbert Darell [?] tipsy with two friends. He asked me to join him. Intent on economy I did, as he wished to pay for my drink. After half an hour's acute boredom I was going when he called for more drinks. I had to pay. He and his friends were drinking brandy – bill 7s. 6d. As I was going the waiter said, 'Excuse me, your whisky has not been paid for.' I despaired of economy and took Laura to dinner at La Coquille. Osbert Darell was there too with an animated party.

Russell's private hotel is delightful. We have a large sitting-room – our room is on the top floor for 12s a night, up old stairs. From the window I see nothing more modern than Sunderland House. All round, shabby stucco; opposite, the entrance to Shepherd's Market, with whores tripping in and out; a flower stall. It is very unlike London. The furniture is late Victorian. On returning at night I found candles put out and a gas jet burning in a little brass jet for lighting them. Francis Howard is here too.

This morning a day of sunlight. A large breakfast, a bus ride to Fulham Road to look at an enamel watch which had taken Laura's fancy, bought a globe of shells for my mother's birthday. Luncheon at the Guards' Club with Miles Howard. Afterwards to Walt Disney's *Pinocchio*. Queues round Regent Street so we took expensive seats. Lovely landscapes, night scenes of great beauty.

In the interval between these diary entries, Waugh was promoted to captain, the troops arrived, and the battalion was formed at full strength.

Bisley, Friday 10 May 1940

Invasion of the Low Countries received with satisfaction in camp. 'The balloon is going up at last.' All weekend leave cancelled. D Company[1] went on night operations – a darker night than usual and an unfamiliar area. I tried out some new section commanders, explaining at length that the experiment had no direct connection with promotion. The operations were dilatory and confused. Back to camp at midnight and then to Street's Cottage.[2]

Saturday 11 May 1940

I arrived at camp for breakfast to find the parade was at 8.30 because everyone had been up half the night standing to for a parachute scare. The day was full of orders and counter-orders and standing by for orders about leave and 'emergency' duties. The maximum irritation having been caused, it was decided that there should be an emergency company permanently confined to camp; also an emergency platoon, for the extermination of parachutists. Final orders were not issued until after 7. There was too little time to have a bath and change for dinner with the Brigadier. A sad little party – the guests we were invited to meet were held up in London. The CO, the Brigadier and I too tired to talk. The Brig. suddenly dictatorial. 'You are getting too personal. Let us change the subject.' He spoke for the first time of our possibly losing the war and of Spain as a possible sphere of brigade operations.

Sunday 12 May 1940

To church at Pirbright. Then left Laura until luncheon while I tried to sort

[1] Waugh now commanded D Company.
[2] Where he was living.

out the various new orders and reconcile them with my company programme. After luncheon too weary for anything except sleep. Afterwards we took a taxi to Guildford and dined there.

Monday 13 May 1940

One of the best men in the company, Reynolds, under close arrest for camp-breaking. When charged, broke into some incoherent grievance about his section being taken away from him. He was to have been a corporal today. Instead I appointed Welsh. Confined to camp all day; slipped away late, after plans for a tewt had been changed, to say goodbye to Laura. Battalion very anxious about fate of Cowan's girl.[1]

Tuesday 14 May 1940

Confined to camp but got away in the morning to say goodbye again. Emergency orders make training almost impossible. Sodomy in C Company.

Wednesday 15 May 1940

The CO's tewt in the morning. In the afternoon drove to look at training areas for twenty-four-hour field exercise. Made administrative arrangements for exercise. Thought I had made myself clear but found all I had said was interpreted in an entirely contrary sense. The men only think of leave and promotion and are liable to persecution mania. Cowan's girl escaped alive from Holland, came to camp.

Thursday 16 May 1940

War going actively in France. Everyone whose sense of melodrama was disappointed last September now galvanized. New orders hourly, e.g. gas capes and Very cartridge. D Company went out for twenty-four hours' exercise. The men definitely enjoy the picnic part but are too keenly competitive to profit by the practical exercises. They simply wish to win the battle. We fought two advance guard actions from Bisley Common to Maristwood [?] Farm where we went into bivouac among large elms and pasture – a delight after scrub and birch. One Marine taken ill, a second shamming. Slept little.

Friday 17 May 1940

Awake from 3.30 am onwards. Marched off at 6.30. In camp soon after 8. Everyone sleepy. Hot day. Battalion given up to courts-martial. Row to be composed between Cowan and Newman over a servant. The French line broken and turned by tanks. No one in the least disconcerted.

[1] Pamela May, the ballerina, was in enemy-occupied Holland.

Saturday 18 May 1940

Emergency company and therefore unable to leave camp. An easy morning scrubbing tent boards, etc. Instruction to NCOs and platoon commanders. Superb weather.

Sunday 19 May 1940

Mass at 9.15 at Pirbright; afterwards sat in the sun at the Guards' mess, drinking beer, watching croquet, and talking about the extreme gravity of the situation. To camp for a football match which we won. Met the Brigadier at 5th Battalion mess. He said that the French failure is due to aircraft bombing driving gunners from their guns. The French were in the mood to surrender until Churchill went to hearten them. He said, 'Can't stop these tanks. The men have to get out sometimes to pee don't they? Shoot 'em then.' Apparently this simple precept impressed the French enormously and they decided to postpone surrender. Luncheon in the mess was a most peculiar spectacle. Some time ago Messrs. Bourne & Hollingsworth offered to adopt the Royal Marines and knit comforts for the troops. In thanking them the Brigadier expressed the hope that some of them would come and visit him some day. This was eagerly accepted, with the result that about thirty shopgirls suddenly descended on us for the day. It was inexpressibly painful. By good fortune they greatly overstayed their invitation so the senior officers do not wish to repeat the experiment. At 5 I went to look at training areas with Hedley and his sergeant, Cowan and his girl, Farmer and Sergeant Farrer. Later to dinner at Pirbright.

Monday 20 May 1940

A day out in training. Section training, platoons moving round the perimeter of a farm. A woman cutting cabbage stalks lost her dinner and the week's groceries and thought we had stolen them. We gave her some steak and onions but she remained dissatisfied. Returned to camp to find bad news of the war.

Tuesday 21 May 1940

Battalion field day; brilliant weather. Some slight personal friction between officers, and particularly between myself and the second-in-command, but a fairly successful day. Returned to camp to learn that Arras, Amiens and possibly Abbeville had fallen, the French having left the Meuse undefended and the bridges undemolished. Tanks and airplanes going ahead everywhere.

Wednesday 22 May 1940

Heavy rain all night and morning. Laura returned to Street's Cottage. I lectured to the company upon the international situation and depressed myself so much that I could barely continue speaking.

In the evening a lecture from Fitzgerald who has just come off the *Curaçoa* which was badly bombed in Norway. He described embarking a company and a half of the Leicesters who had the wrong baggage. When that was adjusted they sailed, examined their stores at sea and found the anti-tank magazines empty. This battalion when fully assembled numbered 600 and returned 150 strong. Fitzgerald then described lying in the fjords round Andenes being bombed hourly day by day. RAF constantly flew without their distinguishing signs and neglected to give answering signals; were constantly fired on and sometimes brought down. Andenes had no anti-aircraft defences, but the Royal Marine garrison lost only one man killed and one wounded. In *Curaçoa* a Vickers on a searchlight-mounting proved the most valuable weapon. She avoided being hit for some days by manoeuvre; keeping engine running, put full steam ahead or astern and wheel right over on approach of bomber. Bombs screamed. RAF several times came round ship stunting and showing off, and left her to shadowing Dorniers.

Saturday 25 May 1940

This morning, just as the battalion had decided that its training was so deficient that we must break up into cadres, the Brigadier, having boasted that we would have held Boulogne, reported us as trained and ready for service. Cadre training will continue. The major put in charge has eluded all responsibility and left me in charge of the NCOs' cadre. Defence measures made last few days' training null. I got Gavin Maxwell over to lecture on sniping. At midday Saturday, Laura and I set off for an idyllic weekend at Alton in the Swan Hotel. A charming town not only devoid of military but full of personable young civilians of military age. An hotel full of foliage plants and massive, elaborate furniture. We went to church, read P. G. Wodehouse (who has been lost along with the Channel ports), watched old men in panama hats play bowls, and forgot the war. Burns made strenuous efforts to get in touch. The second battalion has not yet arrived.

Monday 27 May 1940

The day set apart for preparing the corporals' cadre was entirely occupied with an exercise for the benefit of the signallers. As their apparatus could not be made to work they benefited little. The Ministry of Information required my attendance in London.

Tuesday 28 May 1940

Cadre started. I went to London. Arriving there I found the news of Belgian surrender on the streets together with women selling flags for 'Animal Day'. Had haircut and bought pants. Went to Ministry of Information where Graham Greene propounded a scheme for official writers to the Forces and

himself wanted to become a Marine; also Burns. I said the official writer racket
might be convenient if we found ourselves permanently in a defensive role in
the Far East, or if I were incapacitated and set to training. Returned to find the
camp in great despondency. The Commanding Officer went to Aldershot and
was told to prepare the troops for the blackest news of the BEF and to keep up
their morale.

Glorious 1 June 1940

The end of a bitter week, doubly embittered by a typhoid inoculation of
unusual virulence which has laid the camp in the lowest spirits. Some of the
troops fell into hysteria and fainted as soon as pricked. The cadre training was
carried out with the minimum of zeal, in particular a night exercise filled us all
with shame. We have had numerous grim exhortations about the gravity of the
situation. Duff[1] has dealt cleverly with the news and is putting out the
surrender of the Channel ports as a great feat of heroism. Arctic training is
recommended for the coming week. The move to Havant is cancelled. Eddie
and Alec[2] have both got home safely.

I returned from a happy day at Alton to find that one of the men in my
company had shot himself. He left a note for the CSM apologizing for causing
trouble and saying he is too sensitive to be a corporal – a promotion I had
encouraged him to expect. He was at pains to see that his bullet injured no one
else. Two stretcher bearers confronted with blood for the first time resigned
their posts. The consequences of this man's death took up most of the week.
There was an inquest and later a funeral with military honours. The sergeants
entertained his relatives. The funeral went off very smoothly. The men in the
suicide's tent had no objection to remaining there. He had kept the
ammunition by him since his training at Chatham.

Monday 10 June 1940

While the news from France gets blacker, our training gets staler. There was
an exhilarating Friday when we were ordered to stand by for an immediate
move; then a lull. Embarkation leave two weekends running – I remaining on
duty this weekend except for a happy night at Alton. A long and thirsty field
day, night and another day on Bagshot Caesar's Camp area near the criminal
lunatics at Broadmoor; all weary from it, and in despair at the incapacity of
Signals. Last night, on return from Alton, a late night signal to prepare to move
instantly to South Wales. Teak sent on ahead to provide billets. In hope for
Tenby and fear Haverfordwest. One air alarm during the past fortnight.

[1] Duff Cooper, Minister of Information.
[2] Eddie Grant, brother-in-law, and Alec Waugh, Evelyn's elder brother.

Pembroke, Thursday 4 July 1940

We went to Haverfordwest. Our departure was planned with customary unnecessary haste. The battalion shaken out of camp at 4 am and then left standing about until noon. The mess gave up trying for a week and fed us intermittently on bully beef and biscuits while the corporal of servants took to drink and theft. A long journey and late arrival. Marched in the dark to unlit, filthy billets; all settled in with utmost gloom. Daylight revealed a town of great beauty, full of people eager to be hospitable. Billets were cleaned and redecorated. D Company secured the drill hall and were the best housed of the battalion. Training came to an end and we settled down to a delightful ten days. The local squire turned out to be John Philipps who was brought over to Stinkers for luncheon last summer. He has one of the most beautiful houses[1] I ever saw and was very hospitable. His other guests were conscientious objectors and a friend of his sister's, who was impolite to me; but the splendour of the house – early eighteenth-century interior in a medieval shell – made up for this. The Brigadier had made an order against wives following us, which the Colonel immediately countermanded, so I telegraphed to Laura who arrived on Monday night and stayed in reasonable comfort at the Castle Hotel. We had a long forenoon routine so I was free from 2 until 8 next morning, which was a wholly agreeable interlude. At the end of the week we got orders to move again, marched to Neyland Ferry on Sunday morning and embarked in a small, dirty ship, the *Lady of Mann*, where we lived in gross squalor at six hours' notice to sail. Another ship, *St Briac*, has been moved alongside us and has relieved the crowding slightly. Laura came to Pembroke but I found it impossible to see much of her, and as the town and hotel were uninhabitable I sent her back to Pixton. We had a night ashore, greatly incommoded in all arrangements by the Flemish drifters which are our only connection with the shore, but a fairly good time was had by all.

Double Bois, Cornwall, Wednesday 17 July 1940

Company commanders busy producing 'appreciations' of the Irish coast, belated scheme in hand for field firing of mortars and anti-tank rifles, final stores still being embarked on Saturday and ordered to prepare for immediate disembarkation in Plymouth area. The Commanding Officer made an ill-considered attempt to combine field firing practice with unloading, which resulted in our marching thirteen miles to a waterless village, firing for three-quarters of an hour, marching back, and being rebuked sharply at the end of it. The disembarkation was planned, as all our moves have been, to cause the maximum inconvenience. Heavy drinking among the most senior NCOs. A fairly comfortable night journey and arrived at Double Bois near Liskeard.

[1] Picton Castle, Haverfordwest.

Summoned Laura to join me but have seen very little of her. Our task is the defence of Liskeard. None of us can quite make out why anyone should want to attack it. Even the CO says he cannot rid himself of a sense of unreality. On Saturday night he returned from a conference in high spirits having been given a mobile role repelling landers at his own discretion with a section of artillery, numerous lorries, the mobile company, etc., under his command. During the succeeding twenty-four hours all these except the mobile company were stripped from him. In addition he has had to send B Company to cover a battalion front on the Lynher and we are defending Liskeard again with road-blocks. It rained more or less continually and all washing and sanitary accommodation is shocking. On Sunday I went to luncheon at Port Eliot and spent Saturday and Sunday night in the dry at Webb's Hotel. Meanwhile we are being issued with tropical clothing.

Whitesand Bay, Tuesday 6 August 1940

After ten days in Double Bois, during which great quantities of public money and infinite Marine energy were spent on the defences of Liskeard, we suddenly got orders to move to the coast and at the same time send twenty per cent at a time on forty-eight hours' leave. This leave to be for forty-eight hours at home; no train guide; men going to all parts of the country. We, B and D Companies, moved to Whitesand Bay Hotel which would have been reasonably comfortable for one company. Sharp words with Colonel on subject of Aga cookers. We moved in and began elaborate defence of the coast, D Company holding over four miles.

I went on leave on the 30th. It was too short. A night at Pixton where we went by car. My daughter limp and affectionate, my son hideous and robust. Train to London to Russell's, dinner with my parents. Next day I saw Brendan Bracken and the late Adjutant-General. A new force of independent volunteer companies is being formed under Sir Roger Keyes to which I hope to get transferred. Diana Cooper came to luncheon with us. Dined in a slapdash way at a beastly restaurant with Phyllis and Hubert. The Woodruffs came in to drink champagne with us after the cinema. They were full of tales of the interesting jobs all my friends were getting – Tom[1] in Madrid, Chris[2] in Washington. I felt sad to be going back to the confusion of the Marines. Then my leave was over.

I came back to find that the military had suddenly woken to the fact that there was a coincidence of high tide and moon and that everything was in a state of tension. Company commanders' leave stopped, platoons bivouacking at their posts. A general had been round and re-sited a number of my sections.

[1] Tom Burns.
[2] Christopher Hollis.

Yesterday three move orders: one to Plymouth; one to battalion headquarters at Bake House [?]; one up the coast. No suitable camp sites anywhere. Farrer has been returned to me. Hedley has returned from leave in deep melancholy. Cowan scowling. The Marines in imperturbable good spirits cheerfully working long hours at defences which they must now know will never be manned. I await news of release from London.

Downderry, Friday 16 August 1940

Company under orders to relieve A Company at Downderry. Move began at 8 and was over by 11. Our many moves lately have accustomed us to this sort of thing and we do it without bother if left to ourselves. A Company had orders to stay in their quarters until 2, so we had a long wait literally on their doorstep. Eventually we moved in. Good billets, the best since Haverfordwest. We explained to the troops that the routine was to be one of keeping watch and patrols all night and rest during the day. Posts occupied at 10. Meanwhile a warning order came to be prepared to move on Sunday. I went out with Cowan's platoon by lorry to an empty picturesque house on the extreme west of our front. There was a full moon and the view across the shore magnificent. Presently two enormous flashes, followed at what seemed a very great interval by two explosions. We thought they were heavy bombs on Tor Point. I was detailed for a court-martial the following morning so, as there was to be no sleep for me in the morning, I turned in. Two mines had been laid on the golf course at Crafthole.

Saturday 17 August 1940

Left the company early for Bake House. The court-martial assembled late and adjourned early so that it was 4 before I got away. Marine Morley was being tried for sleeping at his post when sentry, a crime of which he had admitted guilt. But for this admission we – I as prisoner's friend – had a good case. I called medical evidence that he was suffering from sinusitis and that his behaviour, as described by the sergeant, was consistent with a severe headache; also evidence that when he slept, he slept like the dead and would not have woken at the orderly officer's approach. I had carefully schooled him in an explanation of his statement that he 'dozed' and was quite shocked when the judges found him guilty, the sentence to be promulgated later.

Meanwhile the order had gone out 'concentrate at Bake House forthwith'. It was 7 before the last platoon arrived and they then had stowage and loading to do until nearly midnight. We bivouacked in the farm.

The Warwicks who took over from us at Downderry had had eight moves since Dunkirk.

Birkenhead, Sunday 18 August 1940

Reveille at 2. We fell in by moonlight in our helmets, the men carrying their weapons, ammunition, full changing-stations order and two kit-bags – an enormous load. The lorries ran continuously backwards and forwards to St Germans. When we reached the station for the second train, the first had not started. We left one and a half hours late, at 7.30, with the promise of breakfast at Exeter. The troops spread themselves about and stored their gear and went to sleep. There was no breakfast at Exeter, but Bristol at noon provided a cup of contemptible tea and a few biscuits. From then on each station promised us dinner at our next stop. We arrived at Birkenhead at 7 pm having had nothing to eat except what the men could afford to buy for themselves at Crewe in a scurry and scramble. All this time we were carrying emergency rations of bread, margarine and corned beef which Teak, in command of the train, refused to break. At Birkenhead we found the *Ettrick*, a magnificent brand-new[1] troopship – a Belisha luxury. But the men were not allowed aboard until the nominal-roll had been checked, the equipment strapped down and all their luggage and weapons brought aboard. It was 10 before they got food, then they were kept loading until midnight while one platoon had to turn to at 2 am.

Monday 19 August 1940

A day of great comfort and conflicting rumours. The role on which the brigade staff had been working so secretly for so long was apparently off and another on. Then another. A miscellaneous force was assembled – the Argyll and Sutherland Highlanders, admirable-looking men, a great surfeit of doctors, some sappers, RASC, a naval detachment. The ship was overloaded[2] by 400 per cent of its capacity and after a morning spent in rectifying the mistakes of the loading in the dark, the ship's captain refused to sail. The Brigadier turned up with his staff and was quartered in the mental ward of the sick bay. Late at night an order was made for the Argyll and Sutherland Highlanders to disembark. Heavy drinking in the evening. Gin at $2\frac{1}{2}$d.

Tuesday 20 August 1940

The *Ettrick* sailed at 8 leaving [?] Hedley,[3] breakfastless, with a working party and steamed slowly round to the docks, berthing at 3. A lost LMC was found appropriated by the Argyll and Sutherland Highlanders. Careful watch was kept on all the weapons and stores and repeated attempts at scrounging were defeated. At Orderly Room I had to charge Sergeant Glover with obtaining a railway warrant in excess of his proper number with the

---

[1] Not brand-new; a newly converted P & O ship – hence (see 29 August) the Goanese stewards.

[2] By mistake two battalions had been embarked in the same ship.

[3] Leaving Hedley ashore on the pier, perhaps.

unexpected result of incurring an ill-supported denunciation of myself and my laxity. It seems clear that if there is an expedition, which becomes increasingly doubtful, I shall be left to take up my transfer to the Commando while an ungenerous attempt is being made to suggest that I am leaving under a cloud. Ely and Newman left under their clouds as soon as we berthed. Shore leave was given at 7 that evening. Hedley and I dined at the Adelphi and drank a quantity of good wine. The restaurant was full of sailors. The Argylls moved out taking a lot of our equipment and leaving all stores in desperate disorder. The Argylls' doctor, with whom I shared a cabin, said that the Brigadier had made himself extremely offensive to them by objecting to their eating good food on manoeuvres and lecturing them on their obligations towards their troops. Later I learned that their colonel had resigned his command and his commission rather than serve with him.

Wednesday 21 August 1940

Due to sail that day but held up by reloading, everything having been stowed incorrectly. Discoveries at last minute, e.g. that the ship's boats are run on Dieselite not on petrol. A company of the 3rd Battalion is joining us, while one from the 5th takes their place on their ship. Numberless odd detachments come on board with peculiar officers – a mysterious Dragoon in green trousers who is said to be a cypher officer, captains of Field Force [?], sappers, signallers, mobile units, countless doctors. All ammunition in hopeless confusion. Revolver ammunition of five rounds per weapon. D Company ten packs short; frantic search for them. The messdecks dark and crowded. I have a long talk with the Colonel about my future plans and part, or do not part, friends. Major Teak growing a moustache. Re-allotment of messes and cabins. Civilians in uniform everywhere but no more efficient than soldiers. A remarkable lack of curiosity about the purpose of all this expedition. It is now spoken of as an opposed landing.

Thursday 22 August 1940

The Polish ship in which the 5th Battalion is travelling lost its propeller. It was decided to wait for it. Searching all day for missing equipment. Corporal Bailey had stored the battalion mess drink in various officers' cabins. It is being drunk copiously. My CSM in exceedingly poor shape adds to my difficulties.

Friday 23 August 1940

Announced positively that we sail at 11 o'clock. At 11.30 announced that it is blowing too hard to get out of harbour. Leave chits therefore given. General atmosphere of jollity and drinking. Letter-censorship is sometimes on and sometimes off. The authorities realize they cannot disguise the simple fact that the Marines are in Liverpool. More than that no one can tell them. The

Brigadier says the mosquito nets have been loaded at the bottom. The rumour is that we are the reserve battalion of the reserve brigade. Rumour at 2 that we are sailing that night. Leave stopped. At 4 leave piped. I went ashore, found a Catholic church, went to confession, bought some shorts, went to a news cinema, dined at a restaurant called Crocodile – an impudent barmaid, poor and expensive dinner. Joined by Michael M.B. We went to the theatre and saw some very funny clowns in the review *Roll Out The Barrel*. Then to supper at the Adelphi. The French restaurant full of Marines.

Saturday 24 August 1940

Early in the morning a Marine from the 2nd Battalion headquarters reported to me saying he was Ross's servant and was joining D Company. This was the first I had heard that the company was being taken over. Later the Colonel explained that 2nd Brigade Headquarters was being broken up and sent back to Plymouth. Ross, as major, drafted to us. I was offered choice: (*a*) leaving ship at Scapa, which is our first destination, and returning to division for transfer to Commando; (*b*) becoming brigade intelligence officer; (*c*) battalion intelligence officer; (*d*) second-in-command of D Company. After some consideration chose (*c*), since I do not want to leave battalion when it is going into action and (*d*) would mean Farrer returned to subaltern which is deserved but bitter. Some difficulty about my rank, but it is decided I can remain captain in excess of what we are authorized to carry, pending casualties. The expedition seems to have become more modest in size and time. I doubt if it is now intended for tropics. We sailed at 10. Formed convoy when we got out to sea. Five destroyers. Depth charges dropped at 6 but without evidence of result. Cold, grey, calm weather.

Sunday 25 August 1940

Cold, grey, slight sea. Church parades in relays. Adjutant pinning up orders: 'a chain of prayer'. Last time we tried that we evacuated BEF. No work as intelligence officer today. Ross takes over company.

Scapa Flow, Monday 26 August 1940

Arrived in Scapa Flow at 0630 and began duties as intelligence officer which consisted in a dangerous climb along Swanbister Pier at low water with the Colonel and Adjutant. Thence in cartload of young pigs to Kirkwall where I arranged transport for an exercise on Wednesday. As things turned out, two-thirds of it was not needed. The Navy provided transport and the Gordons lent me a car to Stromness where I was in search of maps from the Army. Met the General, announced the presence of Royal Marines to him. 'Glad you fellows got in all right. The place is full of mines.' Lunched with the ADC and returned to *Ettrick* in General's launch. A general to command our expedition came on board. Anti-aircraft fire in the night. First waking thought that I must go and look after my company. Then the reflection that I had no company, so to sleep again. Various curious apparitions on board including a party of Frenchmen in Royal Marine uniform. Also two young Marine officers – 'Browne with an e' the Commanding Officer called one. They have done three weeks on the square at Chatham, seven days' signalling, twenty-four hours' small arms and seven days' military law and had been sent to command platoons in action. They are being sent back.

Tuesday 27 August 1940

In afternoon went ashore with the Commanding Officer and Adjutant and reconnoitred grounds for exercise. Brigade troops were sent ashore for night bivouac and route march. Half returned by midnight, the rest by breakfast. They had not liked the look of their rations. We did night tow exercise.

Wednesday 28 August 1940

Battalion exercise. I, now a complete non-combatant, was chief umpire. The exercise was primarily a long climb up Alla [?] through damp heather among charnel heaps. When we reached the summit it began to rain hard. The Commanding Officer wished to tighten up march discipline so he formed up the battalion and marched back; delay with the tows, choppy sea held us back. Boats came in at 7. Brigade exercise had been fixed for the night but Milner, an experienced naval officer, advised so strongly against it that it was cancelled. In afternoon I was initiated by Baxter into the brigade intelligence box of secrets and our future destiny.

Thursday 29 August 1940

Hacker's [?] dislike of 'that nigger' the Goanese steward more marked. Spent forenoon reading intelligence reports and afternoon in talking to one of the French liaison officers, Lamonte. Should be Lamond. He and another, Melville, have little information and come to us to ask more than to give. They cannot understand Marine indifference to the wider aspects of the expedition;[1] neither can I. If there is failure or grave loss it will be due to lack of liaison between us and the diplomats, etc., who are preparing the way.

Friday 30 August 1940

Reveille 1245 for brigade exercise. Calm night. Tows formed, we went to destination Scapa Bay and waited for one and a quarter hours. The troops had been given rum and fell asleep. At 4.15 we landed – a long, cold wade waist-deep inshore. Then, among mosquitoes, we climbed a hill across numerous

[1] The attempt by a British expedition, co-operating with de Gaulle, to seize Dakar, an important French port on the west coast of Africa.

fences. I, the chaplain, and a French officer under instruction trotted along behind battalion headquarters. I had seen no orders and knew little of our objective. By 6 the whole thing seemed over and we marched back, waited for boats, came aboard in drifters by 8.15. Bath, large breakfast, and morning with intelligence reports. These are scrappy and suffer from Baxter's copying out facts and figures without knowing their meaning. Old Gillette in green trousers, Baxter and I have the office largely to ourselves. Cameroons today reported as de-Gaulled.

Scapa Flow–Freetown, Saturday 31 August 1940

We sailed at about 11 in rain and mist with a strong headwind, sea choppy to rough. Soldiers when writing to their wives and sweethearts put SWALK, which means 'Sealed with a loving kiss', or ITALY, which means 'I trust and love you'.

Sunday 1 September 1940

Rough weather, continuous C. of E. services. At about 5 the cruiser *Fiji* next to us in convoy put up a signal which was variously interpreted to mean 'I am dropping depth charges at 800 feet' and 'I have been torpedoed and am proceeding to UK.' The latter proved correct. She made port under her own power, taking with her highly important people in the combined operations. The Brigadier registered pleasure for the first time for some weeks.

Monday 2 September 1940

Wind has dropped a little. There are said to be numerous submarines about. Working on battalion War Diary, my intelligence summary having been rendered superfluous by divisional summary. I am still in bad odour through not having read orders for brigade exercise.

Saturday 7 September 1940

Swell and mist until yesterday. Now calm weather, warm. The Liverpool convoy joined us safely. Leisurely work in music room, making up-to-date map. On Thursday, information received that enemy troops are battalions where we had companies reported. Plan accordingly modified. Company commanders mystified about their plans; present suggestion appears to be that in event of 'Plan Nasty' we settle down to a tropical campaign against acclimatized and vastly more numerous forces. Various recreations planned for troops. I lectured on Abyssinia. Debate on 'Any man who marries under thirty is a fool.' Lost by overwhelming majority. Discussion developed into personal testimony to wives and mothers. French examination for officers. Poker and heavy drinking. I visit the Chief Engineer and read a detective story. Permission to grow beards rescinded. Azores passed September 6th. Company commanders losing heart with training. Digby-Bell has sawn the barrel off a rifle. Concert in afternoon on deck. Crooning, tap dancing, a sergeant telling dirty stories, a knockabout fight, sentimental songs. The chaplain persuasively getting audience into place: 'Will people sit down please so that people at the back can see. We shall never get started if you don't do as you're told.' A very curious performance by the sergeants who formed a ceremonial party with names of beans – 'Silly Bean', 'Black Bean', 'Awful Bean', etc. A 'Chief Bean' in the centre to whom they make obeisance. The Silly Bean sang two slightly dirty songs of some antiquity, 'That's what we used to call it when I went to school.' Forfeits paid by the Awful Bean. Hedley says this traditional game is allied to 'Priest of the Parish'.

Saturday night at sea observed with hard drinking and tombola.

Sunday 8 September 1940

Day of undisturbed tranquillity. I suggested Lamond should lecture the officers on French politics: idea treated as shocking. Matins in two houses, identical. Drunk before luncheon. Sleep. PT under Teeling. Adjutant bottles junior officers for rowdiness of seniors.

Freetown, Tuesday 17 September 1940

We arrived at Freetown on 14th and found it cooler than was expected. There was no shore leave, but yesterday we landed as a battalion and marched about seven miles to a bathing beach, bathed, and back by same route. I enjoy being in Africa again and among niggers. Troops felt the heat on the return march and several fell out. We sweated a lot, but since Dr Watson lectured us we are now encouraged to drink.

The doctors have invented a yellow fever scare and are hard at work making mosquito veils. There was news on Friday that six French ships had left the Mediterranean. Our escort went to look for them, taking the General with them, but returned last night apparently unsuccessful. We still work away at plans Conqueror, William and Rufus, while there are rumours that the campaign has been abandoned. They are overfilling this ship, sending back the sappers we put in the *Kenya* to make room for another company from another battalion. The doctors all tried to resign because they were not told enough of our plans. I lunched on Sunday with two of the French officers who quoted Pascal.

Sunday 22 September 1940

We left Freetown at dawn yesterday. Numerous changes on board and strange faces. A second march to Lumley. Intelligence work consisted of: (1) carefully cataloguing all recent documents two days before they ceased to be secret and are scattered broadcast; (2) gridding maps. Commanding Officer, enamoured of coloured map, wanted to have it copied. He got some further misinformation from a naval officer and disbelieved in anything the naval officer forgot. Working till 11 pm yesterday in heat. Caricaturist major at our table.

Freetown, Friday 27 September 1940

We returned to Freetown at dawn this morning. The battle of Dakar took place in the following way. Our force, 'M', had the intention of installing General de Gaulle and the Free French in Dakar. We consisted of the Royal Marines Brigade, an independent company, and various attached troops, REs, sailors, etc. There was a large naval force including *Barham, Resolution, Ark Royal, Devonshire, Cumberland* and destroyers and French sloops. The Free French were in two transports, *Westmorland* with headquarters and *Penland*. We in four: *Kenya, Sobieski, Ettrick, Karanja.* There was also the brave little *Belgravia* laden with delicatessen from the British to the French people.

At dawn on 23rd we arrived in sight of Madeleine Bay. It was a calm and misty morning. Contrary to our intelligence reports the mist did not lift. It was very hot and humid. A board was put up on which signal news was posted and my section kept an intelligence log. By about 10.30 we saw from the exchanges between the admiral commanding the garrison and General de Gaulle that he was not having a cordial welcome. We commanded French ships and submarines to keep in port. General de Gaulle called on the French not to fire on him. They said, 'Go twenty miles away.' At 11 we could hear fairly heavy firing. Some servants claimed to have heard firing at dawn. As it turned out they were quite right but no one believed them.

The plan depended on one of three situations: 'Happy', when de Gaulle was received without opposition; 'Sticky', when the *Richelieu* or one or the other isolated units showed fight; 'Nasty' if negotiations were refused and resolute opposition shown. For 'Sticky' there was to be limited bombardment by our ships of specific targets followed by a French landing. For 'Nasty' the French retired out of range and we bombarded the town heavily and took it by assault. By lunch-time situation 'Sticky' was announced, with the recommendation to try plan 'Charles' – a Free French landing at Rufisque, where it was thought the soldiers might be sympathetic. De Gaulle was convinced that only the Navy was against him. That evening a warning was given that plan 'Conqueror', combined landings at Rufisque and Hamm, might be tried next day in its first (Rufisque) phase. By dinner-time it was pretty clear that the Free French landing at Rufisque had not succeeded and a signal announced *Westmorland* stopped two miles out by shore batteries. We turned in, expecting to land somewhere next day.

Tuesday 24th was again foggy with a slight swell. Flag Officer announced operations delayed by bad visibility. General Irwin commanded the making of

Bangalore torpedoes, an explosive rod for destroying wire. We remained without news all day, speculating as to whether the resistance was genuine or bluff. Early that morning we had issued an ultimatum calling on Dakar to surrender and got the answer, 'I defend Dakar to the end.' Later that night an order: 'No landing operations tonight. Bombardment may be continued tomorrow.' By next morning everyone had made up his mind that the operation was off and sure enough we were met by the fleet at about 10.30 and told to withdraw southwards. The whole armada was rendezvoused at sea and manoeuvring when there was an air attack. A bomb fell about a hundred yards in front of us. That afternoon we got the order to return to Freetown and hold ourselves in readiness for operations at short notice.

A very gay journey back. Very drunken evenings in the officers' mess. The troops less lighthearted about their reverse. This afternoon we got the news that the *Resolution* was being towed back and the *Cumberland* had beached at Bathurst. The talk is that the earlier operation 'Accordion' is on – an infamous plan for which I can affect no interest.

Saturday 28 September 1940

Landed with St John and spent day ashore. A town with no comforts for Marines on leave. Troops got drunk a little but behaved tolerably well. I enjoyed the market a little, but it is a place with nothing to show[1] except happy inhabitants.

Sunday 29 September 1940

Ashore again to get a range for the Commanding Officer. In the evening General Irwin gave a lecture on the Dakar fiasco. Facts I did not know before: (1) HMG wanted to call operation off but were persuaded by commanders. (2) On Monday morning, envoys landed in Dakar harbour, found the place deserted, were met by two officers who refused to allow them to enter, were fired on and wounded when leaving. (3) On Monday afternoon some French Marines succeeded in landing at Rufisque but met with opposition and withdrew. (4) All Monday afternoon no communication between *Westmorland* and *Barham*. (5) *Richelieu* now making eighteen knots to Casablanca. (6) Crew of captured submarine said sailors and special force brought in cruisers defending [?] Dakar. Submarines themselves had arrived [?] two days. (7) French employed listening apparatus on buoys.

General causes of defeat seem (*a*) initial misconception (*b*) faulty intelligence

[1] 'Later when he came to read *The Heart of the Matter* Guy reflected, fascinated, that at this very time "Scobie" was close at hand, demolishing partitions in native houses, still conscientiously interfering with neutral shipping.' Evelyn Waugh, *Men at Arms* (London 1952). Waugh omitted this sentence from the 'final version' of *Sword of Honour* published by Chapman & Hall in 1965.

(*c*) superiority of French gunnery (*d*) air inadequacy (*e*) signal inadequacy. Irwin did not comment on delays (*a*) at Liverpool (*b*) Scapa (*c*) Azores (*d*) Freetown. These clearly very important.

Freetown–Gibraltar, Sunday 6 October 1940

Left Freetown for Gibraltar with 5th Battalion, *Barham* and destroyers, with 'Accordion' probable. No work at Freetown. In idleness, brooding on general situation, as fighting troops never do. War will go on until it is clear to thinking observers that neither side can hope for victory in any terms approximating to the hopes with which they started. Fighting troops are not thinking observers. The first country to decide on a compromise will find that they have lost everything, while the other, surprisingly, will have gained everything. Therefore the most valuable thing is to stop the fighting and working part of the nation from thinking. Therefore the obstructions which the supply services, staffs, etc., put in the way of the fighting troops are a very valuable distraction and keep battalion commanding officers and company commanders in a continual state of parochial worry. Armies where things go smoothly at first and worse as conditions deteriorate are more likely to crack than our own chaotics.

Catholic major 'Hooky' Walker, with us for week, left behind Freetown.

No mail. Troops begin to suspect absurd plot to keep home news from them. Three cases of homosexuality in two days.

Pidgin English description of air raids. 'Steam chicken top side drop plenty no good shit.'

5 am nigger singing in canoe. Marine: 'Fuck off you black bastard.' 'Oh officer, sah, you have not taken your Eno's.'

Gibraltar, Tuesday 15 October 1940

Reached Gibraltar 6 am. The last ten days very tedious. We had read all the books in the library, drunk nearly all the wine, smoked all the cigars, and eaten most of the food. The buggery trials were the only thing of interest. I defended Marine Florence. He got eight months. His companion in pleasure got eleven. I did quite well for him.

On Sunday night we acted my unimaginative charades. The Colonel, in troubled innocence, speaks of stagnation. Interest in Plan Accordion seems to have lapsed.

Gibraltar–Gourock, Friday 18 October 1940

Sailed from Gibraltar, not at the first attempt. On Thursday night we put out under convoy of *Australia* and two destroyers, the Brigadier waving from the end of the jetty, a large party of passengers returning to England for promotion, transfer, etc. In two hours we were ordered back and kept all the day at four hours' notice to sail. Rumours rife that we are going on Accordion, but the passengers remain, joined by the Brigadier; mail arrived, including, for me, a letter from Bob Laycock saying he had a post for me in his Commando, but dated August 22nd. At last we sailed, late on Friday night.

Gibraltar has a garrison of 10,000 men and a local defence corps. The women have been evacuated, all but six or seven; there was no beer in the town. When the last Englishwoman has left, a corps of harlots will come from Tangier to amuse the troops. At the moment they have little recreation. I spent two pleasant afternoons ashore. The garrison library, soon, presumably, to be demolished, was delicious – a large collection of nondescript leather-bound books in a series of clubrooms with leather and mahogany furniture and a sub-tropical garden through the windows. One modern room full of novels, smelling of scent. I bought a silver velocipede, ridden by a bearded man in a tall hat, with a trailer for carrying toothpicks: £2 10s. To my great delight I found Father Gilbey the Dominican chaplain in *Renown*. Or rather he found me and took me off to his cabin where I read *Tablet* and *Times* up to the end of September. I arranged to lecture the wardroom discussion club – which seems immensely more cultured than anything that could exist in I Royal Marines – but our false start stopped that. The battalion did some ceremonial exercises in torrential rain in the Alameda gardens and got uncommonly drunk: Baxter, brigade intelligence officer, paralytic before tea in the Rock Hotel. We are now said to be returning merely to refit and then sail immediately. Hope to leave the battalion at Greenock either for Laycock or the 3rd Brigade or some job Walker may find for me. All letters from home were about air raids. Bobbie Longden[1] blown up at Wellington. Henry Yorke no doubt fighting fires day and night. The armed forces cut a small figure. We were like wives reading letters from the trenches.

Pixton Park, Tuesday 5 November 1940

On October 27th we reached Scotland and berthed at Gourock. The last day the convoy sailed close to the Irish coast. The *Empress of Britain* was sunk ten miles astern of us but we got through without incident. A rather flat party the last night on board. Up to Sunday morning we had no information as to our movements – whether we changed ship, remained on board, went into camp, or even returned to our divisions. Then we got orders to be ready to disembark, proceed to a camp at Kilmarnock, and go on leave. We fell in at 1.30 to disembark and reached Kilmarnock, a few miles south, at 7.30, the movement being hindered by all the usual military mistakes. We arrived in the dark with no rations, no camp. Billets. The people of Kilmarnock provided the supper for the troops. Officers in large modern hotel near the station.

[1] Robert Longden (1903–1940); Eton and Trinity College, Oxford; Master of Wellington College, 1937.

Next day, my birthday, difficulties over special train held up general leave, but I got off on representing that I might at any moment be called up for Commando. The army PO has given us no letters later than September 15th. The journey to Taunton took just twenty-four hours. Long waits outside all junctions, no attempt to run connections.

I arrived very happy to forget the war for a week. Got into civilian clothes, caught a sharp cold, but had a highly enjoyable week. Laura and I visited Stinkers and found the house full to capacity; the chaplain sleeping in the wine cellar, the garden breast-high with weeds, all the young hedges looking very unwell, many young plants completely lost. I got twenty gallons of petrol out of the Bristol control. Talk is all of air raids. Evacuation is very much better at Pixton as family life has now been separated from children and helpers. Laura lets the numerous rows pass over her. We drove to Chagford for luncheon. Bad accident on railway; over thirty killed at Norton Fitzwarren. Sunday papers full of Hitler's attempt to conciliate Catholics. Greek war beginning as Norway and Finland began. Good news seems so improbable that people seem rather to resent it. There are no signs of any shortage of supplies but great disorganization of communications. Three of our officers went on leave not knowing where to find their wives. Countless troops in the same position. Leave expires tomorrow.

Kilmarnock–London, Thursday 7 November 1940

I arrived, having neither dined nor breakfasted, at about 10 o'clock. The hotel where the officers were billeted was deserted. I left my gear at a shop and looked for Akam. Found him, no letters, no orders. Telephoned brigade. Parke-Smith told me he had seen Laycock in London and that there was a vacancy for me in the Commando; he would take this as authority to go. Akam was driving through Carlisle in a hired car. We set off together at seventy miles an hour. Twenty miles out of Carlisle there was a peculiar noise in the bonnet and the car stopped. We took a taxi to Carlisle where I dined in an hotel full of alluring girls and got a sleeper to London.

London, Friday 8 November 1940

At about 10 there was an air raid warning. I began the hunt for Laycock. They had told me he was at the War Office. No one could tell me anything of him except an old colonel who after long research informed me that he was a captain in the Blues. I tried the Admiralty who sent me to a secret office in Richmond Terrace where I found Major Walker and a civil brigadier. They told me that Laycock was in Scotland a mile or two from I RM's next destination. We tried to telephone him but without success. I lunched at Buck's, which has lost the annexe and the use of one room, and went to the RM office where an offensive fellow called Dawson told me that I had gone about my transfer in a most improper manner, that I had no business to have left IRM and so forth. I went back to the civil brigadier and tried again to telephone Laycock. 'Indefinite delay.' That was work enough for the day. I went to the Dorchester Hotel which was reported to be full of friends and, leaving my taxi, met Duff[1] who took me up to his suite. Phyllis and Hubert joined us. She lives in a peculiar way, in her house by day, in her room at the hotel in early morning and late evening, in Odham's vestibule at night. I asked about a room and was offered a bunk in the Turkish bath, Tancred Borenius's vestibule or Hutchy's[2] bed 'if Barbara Rothschild is not using it.' Then Lord Lothian and such people began to arrive to see Duff on duty, so we went below and dined foully. Saw more friends and went to bed in Hutchy's room.

Highgate, Saturday 9 November 1940

No news from Laycock. I went to see Maimie who has left her large house for a cottage behind Brompton Oratory where she lives serenely in acres of rubble. The little drawing-room full of luxurious litter – flowers, lapdogs, mechanical toys. She was giving a cocktail party at noon because 'people are so dutch about jaggering one in the evenings nowadays'. We lunched off oysters and two years (both ancient) of champagne of the kind Vsevolode and I like. Then with enormous cigars, Maimie with a small one, to a matinée with Pam Chichester who has been bombed and wounded. It was not at all what the neutrals imagine London life to be. Then to Highgate which has been heavily bombed. My father fears nothing but my mother is rather more disturbed. There was considerable firing during the night but no bombs near us.

Sunday 10 November 1940

As usual Haynes[3] made his Sunday call and after ten weeks of Marines he seemed highly intelligent. The evening before I had got on to Laycock and found that he was ready for me any time. To Mass at Highgate. Alec came for the day. He is engaged in 'petroleum warfare'. We went to the cinema. He had brought a bottle of champagne for me. Much firing at night but no bombs.

Monday 11 November 1940

Finally, I hope, picked up my transfer. Lunched with Betjeman who told me of Roger's suicide. Air raid warnings all the day.

Dined with Diana, Jean Norton, Hutchy, Windsors' Jew lawyer Monckton and a man from Duff's Ministry. The talk was mostly of bombs. H. Nicolson, after the Ministry of Information was hit: 'It is valuable at such moments to collect one's impressions – valuable I mean for *me* but for no one else. My own

---

[1] Duff Cooper, the Minister of Information.
[2] St John Hutchinson, K.C., father of Lady Rothschild.
[3] E. S. P. Haynes.

impression is predominantly that of "flash" rather than "bang".' Slept in Phyllis's bed and took an early train to the north.

Glasgow, Tuesday 12 November 1940

Travelling all day. A bombastic and indiscreet captain in my carriage told me a great deal, which has since proved fallacious, about Commandos. At Glasgow, where I arrived about 10, great difficulty in finding a bedroom. Finally I shared with a lieutenant-commander who wore his underclothes under his pyjamas and drank whisky in bed. I bathed and had supper in the French restaurant which has greatly deteriorated since the days Diana and I went there with *The Miracle*.[1]

Wednesday 13 November – December 1940

Went to Mass early, in black darkness and fog, and took the morning train to Largs. A smug, substantial, modern pleasure resort – or rather pleasure as the Scots conceive it – with a superb view across the water to Cumbrae and Arran. I went to the Marine Hotel where they had told me, incorrectly, that 8 Commando had its headquarters. The first person I met was Mary Campbell, who told me to my extreme surprise that Robin[2] was in the party. Various friends and acquaintances appeared – Phil Dunne, Toby Milbanke, Randolph, Harry Stavordale.[3] Robin took care of me, found me a room in the hotel, lent me his servant and led me to HQ where Bob Laycock failed to recognize me. There is no place for me in the troop so I was made liaison officer with Harry – a life of untroubled ease.

From 13th until December 1st I remained at Largs. Nothing could be less like the Marines than the Special Service Battalion. 8 Commando (ten troops of fifty, three officers to each troop, intelligence and three liaison officers, liaison section of six, a small orderly room staff, an administration officer (QM) and second-in-command) has just been added to 3 Commando and called 4 SS Battalion. Bob commands the battalion with an elderly Somerset Light Infantry major, Walter Curtis, as second-in-command. Dermot Daly[4], Scots Guards, commands Commando with Bones Sudeley[5] as second-in-command. The troops are mainly Household Cavalry and Foot Guards, with some specialists (sappers and gunners and Marines) and some odds and sods. Poor Godfrey Nicholson, a most unsoldierly figure, is a troop leader, with the only unattractive man, Graham Bartlett, as his subaltern. He asked me to join him, I

[1] In the early 1930s, when Lady Diana Cooper was touring Britain in *The Miracle*, Waugh used to visit her.

[2] Robin Campbell, son of the British ambassador to Portugal.

[3] Philip Dunne: man about town, of the poet John Donne's family, later an M.P.; Ralph (Toby) Milbanke, son of Lt.-Col. Sir John Milbanke, V.C., 10th bart.; Randolph Churchill, the Prime Minister's son; Lord Stavordale, son and heir of the 6th Earl of Ilchester.

[4] Grandson of the 4th Baron Clanmorris.

[5] The 6th Baron Sudeley.

refused, and he said, 'I quite understand.' Until the coming of Mary Campbell, the smart set – Peter Milton,[1] Philip, Harry, Dermot, Toby – got along very nicely with the more serious soldiers. On her first coming she drew Godfrey out to such an extent that he called them 'scum', a verdict which she promptly repeated with unhappy results. She had never found herself with dandies before and it went to her head so that the dandies greatly despised her, and, when their wives arrived, issued strict orders that they were to eschew her manners, which were matey, noisy, and mischievous. Pamela Churchill[2] was there too; Katherine Nicholson, Peggy Dunne and Nell Stavordale came later so that there was plenty of feminine company. The smart set drink a very great deal, play cards for high figures, dine nightly in Glasgow, and telephone to their trainers endlessly. I went to Glasgow once only; with Harry, Philip, Peggy and Patrick Ness [?], a pleasant troop leader from the Bays. We saw two halves of two reviews and had supper and a row with the police coming back. I have reverted to lieutenant again and am obliged to be very cautious about money. The hotel is expensive and avaricious. Randolph had a bill of £54 for a fortnight. Mine was a fifth of that, but even so too high. There are two manageresses, both like Mrs Ellwood but without her good looks.

The standard of efficiency and devotion to duty, particularly among the officers, is very much lower than in the Marines. There is no administration or discipline. The men are given 6s a day and told to find their own accommodation. If they behave badly they are simply sent back to their regiments. Officers have no scruples about seeing to their own comfort or getting all the leave they can. It would not work with HO Marines or with officers of the Teak, Farrer type, but with the particular men Bob has chosen it is, with very few exceptions, a workable system. In training the troops have worked alone, concentrating on field craft. They have no conception of battalion tactics or inter-communication. We have no contact at all with 3 Commando, who live at the other and more squalid quarter of the town and are reputed to be a rough lot who drink with their men. They regard us as 'cissy' and beat us soundly in a boxing match. They have done one operation – a raid in the Channel Islands – which proved a fiasco.

During this fortnight we were at forty-eight hours' notice for co-operation with 101 RM Brigade on 'Accordion'. On December 1st we were released from this and given two days' leave, after which we are to train for another operation. There is a stir, of the kind which has grown familiar, suggesting immediate action.

On Saturday night, November 30th, Mary telephoned to say that Laura had begun her labour. The child, a girl, was born at midday on Sunday and died

[1] Viscount Milton, son and heir of the 7th Earl Fitzwilliam.
[2] Mrs Randolph Churchill.

twenty-four hours later. It was an easy birth, very sudden at the end, and Laura is in good health. I travelled on Sunday night and Monday morning, arriving at Tiverton junction at 10.30. The baby died shortly after my arrival. I saw her when she was dead – a blue, slatey colour. Poor little girl, she was not wanted. Mary had had her christened Mary the day before. The funeral was this morning in Brushford churchyard. I spent the night at Pixton so as to be in time for Mass. The rest of the time I have spent by Laura's side, talking, doing crosswords, etc. Mrs Amory is very kind and very disconcerting in her abruptness and lack of femininity. The house is Tudor, full of peat smoke and uneven floorboards, but comfortable and with a good cook. Tomorrow at 9.30 I take the train for the first part of my return journey.

I am rapidly recovering from a cut mouth caused by hurrying into the blackout after dinner, for night operations.

Orthodox diary entries cease here until the beginning of 1942. The following 'Memorandum on LAYFORCE' records Waugh's service with the Commandos in 1940–1, including his experience of the Battle of Crete. Despite the title and numbered paragraphs, the Memorandum was evidently not intended for any official purpose.

Memorandum on LAYFORCE; July 1940–July 1941

1. Commandos were first raised in secret. Certain independent companies had been formed and used in Norway and a few of these remained in existence after the failure of that campaign. Commandos were originally intended to supply raiding parties, primarily against the occupied coast of France; they were largely sponsored by Sir Roger Keyes, whose criticism in the House of Commons was silenced by his appointment to the post of Director of Combined Operations. Commandos were originally intended to work directly under Sir Roger Keyes's office, independently of existing military and naval organizations; they were to be commanded by youthful officers, to consist in all ranks of volunteers for hazardous service, and to have an abnormally high proportion of officers and NCOs to men. Administrative staff was to be reduced to a minimum: this was effected by paying a special allowance and leaving men to find their own accommodation in England, an indulgence which made service particularly attractive. From the first these units developed individual peculiarities; they attracted divergent types and in all stages of their development it was found difficult to get suitable officers for colonel's appointments.

2. I heard of Commandos first from Brendan Bracken, whom I went to see at 10 Downing Street during forty-eight hours' embarkation leave from Cornwall, where the RM Brigade was engaged on coast defence while preparing for operation 'Accordion'. During the same leave I also heard of them from General Bourne, assistant DCO. Brendan said: 'You ought to be with Bob Laycock's tough boys'; General Bourne said, 'No one can see any point in these irregular units.' With Colonel Lushington's permission I wrote to Bob Laycock and was in correspondence with him when RM Brigade sailed for Dakar (Operation 'Menace'). Before sailing I once saw a Commando, No. 3, which was part of the defence of Plymouth. They were unimpressive to look at, but the umpires, on an exercise which we did with them, spoke enthusiastically of their endurance and enterprise. In fact on that occasion, after marching twenty miles, they made boobies of the directing staff by taking all the defended posts by subterfuge. There was an independent company in the Dakar expedition who sailed with the Free French in *Westmorland*. General Irwin caused great offence to the Marines by saying, 'If there is any Zeebrugge work to be done, the independent company will do it.' In fact neither Marines nor independent company saw action.

3. 1 RM landed at Gourock on October 27 and went into billets in the Glasgow area. Fourteen days' leave was given and during this period my transfer was arranged. I returned only to collect gear and reported for duty in London where the War Office was unable to tell me anything of Lt.-Col. Laycock's whereabouts. Eventually after an interview with Brigadier Haydon and some incivility at RMO I was posted to 8 Commando then at Largs, the date of seconding being Nov. 12.

4. When I joined 8 Commando they were in billets at Largs, temporarily attached to Operation 'Accordion'. Their establishment was ten troops of fifty men each, commanded by a captain and two subaltern section leaders. Lt.-Col. Laycock commanded, a major of SLI[1] was second-in-command. Harry Stavordale was just handing over as adjutant to an SLI captain. The troops were mainly regimental in composition. (1) Household Cavalry. (2) Grenadiers. (3) Coldstream. (4) Scots Greys. (5) Irish and Welsh Guards. (6) Composite (called 'Buffaloes' by Toby Milbanke who then led them). (7) SLI. (8) Composite (commanded by Godfrey Nicholson). (9) Line cavalry. (10) Specialists: RE, RA, RM. There were three liaison officers on establishment. At the time of my arrival 8 Commando was in process of being brigaded. Brig. Haydon had command of 1 SS Brigade of which 8 Commando formed B Company, 4 Battalion. 3 Commando was A Company. Bob Laycock was Battalion Commanding Officer. The brigading was for the purpose of operation 'Workshop' (Pantellaria).

5. The Commando before my arrival had been in training at Burnham-on-

[1] Somerset Light Infantry.

Crouch and later at Inverary. When formed they had been exceptionally zealous; discipline was already deteriorating when I joined. After RM Brigade the indolence and ignorance of the officers seemed remarkable, but I have since realized they were slightly above normal army standards. Great freedom was allowed in costume; no one even pretended to work outside working hours. Troop leaders never sent in returns required by the orderly room at the proper time or in the proper form. Officers took leave when their troops were not allowed it. The special lodging allowance did little to cover the very high standard of expenditure in No. 8. Two night operations in which I acted as umpire showed great incapacity in the simplest tactical ideas. One troop leader was unable to read a compass. The troops, however, had a smart appearance on inspection parades, arms drill was good, the officers were clearly greatly liked and respected. The men had no guard duties. After parade they were free from all restraint and were often disorderly. There was already a slight undercurrent of impatience that they had not yet been put into action (No. 3 Commando had done one ineffectual excursion to the Channel Islands). Roger Courtenay was attached to 8 Commando. He was organizing a *folbot* (canoe) section which, at the time of writing, is still in existence in the Middle East, doing reconnaissance from submarines. Courtenay himself got an MC for recon- naissance at Rhodes. Nell Stavordale, Pamela Churchill, Mary Campbell, Peggy Dunne and G. Nicholson's wife were in the hotel at Largs when I joined.

Setting out drunk for one of the night operations I fell down and cut my lip but no one thought the worse of me for this accident.

Peter Milton spent most of his time in Glasgow both before and after succeeding Toby in command of a troop.

The RSM, an Irish Guardsman, was usually drunk. Later he was reduced to the ranks.

At a boxing competition 8 Commando showed very bad training and lack of fighting spirit.

On the whole, however, I saw few symptoms of their later decay. They had a gaiety and independence which I thought would prove valuable in action. The whole thing was a delightful holiday from the Royal Marines. I was made a liaison officer as there was no room for me in a troop. I hoped to become a troop leader, but the system of regimental troops greatly reduced the chances of this. When G. Nicholson had to be sacked, his troop was superseded in entirety by one from 3 Commando. When the Buffaloes became vacant I was already at brigade HQ and Dermot Daly's brother-in-law, Billy McGowan, was given the job; this would have happened even if I had been still in the Commando.

6. At the beginning of December we were transferred from operation 'Accordion' to 'Workshop'. After two days' leave we embarked in HMS *Glenroy* and sailed to Arran for what was intended to be a brief period of intensive training.

Glenroy was one of three fast merchant ships purchased by the Admiralty and adapted for combined operations. The holds had been made into troopdecks, cabins built on the decks, to accommodate one infantry battalion. The decision to use them for nearly double this number, with the consequent disorder and discomfort, had a bad effect on discipline. The ships were equipped with thirteen ALCs and one SLC swung on the davits and two MLCs on derricks. A MTB was added later.[1] The Captain was a retired naval officer, Paget;[2] a man of irritable disposition and poor judgement. He quickly earned the nickname of 'Booby' and amply justified it by his subsequent conduct in the Middle East.

The First Lieutenant was an elderly, conscientious officer. The only other naval officer was the Pay Lt.-Commander who had dug himself into a position of authority and trust beyond his position or abilities; he was cordially detested by all. The remainder of the ship's company were RNR, some of whom had served in her in peacetime, and RNVR. The latter included Roger Keyes Jnr, another generally unpopular figure. The RNVR lieutenants and sub-lieutenants were a pathetic collection of youths straight from insurance offices, who had nothing in common with 8 Commando. Besides being dreary fellows to talk to, they were hopeless seamen. From the first the two services got on badly together; had either been efficient the other would have respected it; had both been inefficient in the same way they would have liked one another (as, indeed, the Navy liked No. 3 Commando); but No. 8 Commando was boisterous, xenophobic, extravagant, imaginative, witty, with a proportion of noblemen which the Navy found disconcerting; while the Navy was jejune, dull, poor, self-conscious, sensitive of fancied insults, with the underdog's aptitude to harbour grievances. Six weeks after the event they were still resentful about some magazines which got trodden on. Moreover we were not equal partners in the same mess; the military were guests in a naval mess with no influence on its management and very definite ideas on the subject. They aired their grievances loudly, referred to the Captain as 'the old bugger on the roof' (Eddie Fitz-Clarence). There was a meeting of reconciliation between representative officers which embittered relations still more, chiefly by Philip Dunne comparing the Navy to the guard on a train and the Army to a first-class passenger. Wardroom and anteroom were so overcrowded that it was impossible for either service to keep to itself.

7. The plan of training was for each Commando to go ashore alternately for two weeks while the other did boat training on Holy Island and Arran. The boat training consisted of packing into ALCs which the military seemed to consider an esoteric art requiring great practice, and letting the naval officers make a nonsense of the navigation. Again and again they ran boats aground and

---

[1] Types of Landing Craft, and a Motor Torpedo Boat.
[2] Captain Sir James Paget, Bart., RN.

let them get left by the tide. Some likeness to the coast of Pantellaria had been traced in Arran and an attack exercise planned which, at the expense of tactical verisimilitude, gave each party a march and climb of about the size required for 'Workshop'. At the beginning of January we did a rehearsal which high officers from the Admiralty and War Office came to see. It was a failure owing to 3 Commando having bunks to sleep in while we sat up in the anteroom, drunk but awake. No. 3 Commando could not be woken, were late and without equipment in the boats and entirely disorganized on the shore. We spent Christmas on board *Karanja* which was no improvement for the officers, an immeasurable improvement for the numerous sergeants who got second-class cabins, stewards, and a wet canteen and consequently were paralytically drunk all the time, and a hardship to the men who found their quarters intensely cold, objected to having their food prepared by Goanese, and anyway were out to have a grievance. In January it became known that the likelihood of the operation coming off was less. Finally it was cancelled. Sir Roger Keyes made a speech promising to 'put us across the enemy' at the first opportunity and urging us to 'keep our spearhead bright'. It made little impression. Meanwhile the ban on having wives to Arran was removed and for a week we had a series of parties. Then we were given two weeks' leave. There was a rumour that after leave we should be going abroad, but we were all sceptical of that kind of rumour by now. In fact (I did not know it at the time) 'Workshop' had been cancelled. The three 'Glen' ships were wanted in the Middle East for 'Cordite' (Rhodes)[1] and there was a struggle going on at the War Office whether or no we should go out with them.

8. After leave we again embarked in *Glenroy*. 4 Battalion 1 SS Brigade ceased to exist. We again became No. 8 Commando, a part of 'Z' force under Bob's command, with No. 11 (Scottish Commando) commanded by a Major Pedder and another commando under a Major Colvin. 'Z' force was split between *Glenroy* and *Glengyle* with a few individuals in *Glenearn*. As soon as stores were embarked we sailed for Egypt, Feb 1st (?). The conditions of overcrowding were worse than ever. No. 11 Commando were very young and quiet, overdisciplined, unlike ourselves in every way but quite companionable. They trained indefatigably all the voyage. We did very little except PT and one or two written exercises for the officers. Bob took me for Force HQ as adjutant, to be promoted brigade major if we became a brigade. There was very high gambling, poker, roulette, chemin-de-fer, every night. Randolph lost £850 in two evenings. We stopped at Cape Town where the people treated all ranks with the most notable hospitality. Harry ill-treated the ostriches in the zoo. Randolph lunched with Smuts. Dermot got very drunk.

On March 8th we reached Suez and proceeded up the Canal, which was

---

[1] The invasion of Rhodes; the operation did not take place.

reported to be mined, to Kabrit in the Bitter Lakes. The Germans at this time were dropping sacks of salt in the Canal; their fall was reported and the area closed until they were found which, since they dissolved, they never were.

At Kabrit General Evetts came on board and spoke to the officers. He said we were to serve with his division (6th) and promised us a 'bellyful of fighting'. This speech greatly dismayed F—— who from then on made no disguise of his wish to get an office job in Cairo. Next day we landed and went into camp at Geneifa.

9. The unit's name was now changed again. 'Z' force became 'Layforce'; No. 8 Commando became 'B Battalion'; the use of the word 'Commando' was prohibited. Bob became a colonel, Dermot and the other battalion commanders, lieutenant-colonels. A brigade major was supplied by CHQ and I went down to intelligence officer. We had something not unlike a brigade organization. Training for 'Cordite' followed the usual course. A line was marked out in the desert and routes to objectives. We were just beginning serious rehearsals in this area when in the first week in April the German reoccupation of Cyrenaica put Egypt in a fluster. The Guards Brigade were taken out of 6 Division and sent west and 6 Division was practically dissolved. 'Layforce' was ordered to move in a hurry to Alexandria area with the 'Glen' ships. *Glenroy* was taken to Port Said and sent to evacuate Lemnos. In the meantime a D Battalion was formed at Geneifa consisting of the remnants of two Middle East Commandos, one of which had seen action in Abyssinia and the other, discreditably, in Castello Rosso. This Commando included a troop of denationalized Spanish socialists of very low quality. The battalion commander was a sapper, Colonel Young, who was unimpressive in appearance but proved to be a good officer. In Alexandria area the brigade was divided between Sidi Bish and Amiriya. Here the morale of B Battalion began to deteriorate very rapidly; the six months' special service, a renewal of the original period for which we had volunteered, was nearly up; this renewal had been made at the time of 'Workshop' under the promise of immediate action. Men had not volunteered to leave their regiments in order to do general defence duties in the Middle East and they now began to ask for the promises made them to be implemented. Negotiations were now begun with General Headquarters Middle East chiefly through Arthur Smith, which continued for three months, during which a series of non-committal and mutually contradictory statements were made. In B Battalion the older officers were homesick and the younger impatient to get into action. All spent every available hour in Alexandria leaving their troops in an uncomfortable camp. In C Battalion the discontent was personal, against Col. Pedder, whose peculiarities came very near megalomania. 'D' were working hard reorganizing and retraining. 'A' were a shoddy lot without any particular characteristics.

10. Various staffs – Desforce, C-in-C Med, GHQME, LTC Kabrit, etc. –

mainly animated by a Lieut. Colonel Maurice Hope, now devised a series of minor operations against the enemy's lines of communication on the coast of Cyrenaica; these had names taken from theatrical farces, 'Rookery', 'Nook', 'Walls', etc.; they consisted of ambushing enemy motor transport, putting oil into water, destroying aircraft on the ground, etc. As a result of various misfortunes none of these was ever carried out and B Battalion was mainly, and later exclusively, charged with them. 'Layforce' was made part of the general reserve of MEF in the middle of May. Wishing to do the best for his old friends, Bob had B Battalion exempted from this and kept on special service. They moved their headquarters to Marsa Matruh, maintained advance parties at Tobruk, and exhausted every means of getting into action. They repeatedly set out for operations in the Aldwych farce sequence and were always turned back. At the same time they pressed for a classification of their position as volunteers. The feelings of the battalion were well summed up by an inscription found on the troopdecks of *Glengyle*: 'Never in the history of human endeavour have so few been buggered about by so many.' It was also suggested that the name should be changed to 'Belayforce'.

All the operations of the Aldwych farce group should have been practicable if put through with dash. Co-operation with the Navy proved cumbrous; weather was not propitious; the Eureka boats detailed for the work were too fragile. There was always a perfectly good reason why each individual excursion was cancelled; the conclusion was that we had the enemy at a great disadvantage in the matter of lines of communication; we had a special force designed to harass him, and this force was never used, except in the Bardia raid, where the intelligence supplied was so faulty as to make the operation futile.

11. The Bardia raid was first conceived as an operation for two battalions; then modified for one, A Battalion. It took place from *Glengyle* on the night of 19/20 April. It was a dark night; the sea was moderate, getting rougher towards morning. Our information was that 2,000 enemy troops held the town and that there were large concentrations of transport there; also one or more coast defence guns. All this proved to be entirely false. The town was deserted, the only vehicles were abandoned trucks, the guns had been destroyed some weeks before when we evacuated the town. The only enemy seen were a motor-cycle patrol. No other use was made of the road, which had been reported as frequented, during our three hours' occupation. In the circumstances the raid fell flat, the only incidents being caused by our own incapacity. Strategically, however, the raid fulfilled a purpose by drawing off forces from the front. *Glengyle* lay four miles out and would not approach closer even when it was clear that there was no opposition; their reluctance caused the loss of sixty men, the precise circumstances of whose capture are not yet known. The ship arrived at rendezvous at 2205 hours and the landings were timed for 2320. The boats were overcrowded and many men were seasick. One boat failed to get

into the water, and the boat which was to have followed it to B Beach preferred to go to A Beach. B Beach thus never had a landing party. A Beach, where four detachments and battalion headquarters landed, proved to be a good landing place but the wadi was steeper and rougher than was expected. After a check at an unexpected ditch all detachments moved up to the top. The covering party fired a few shots at their officer, killed him, and disconcerted the parties climbing the wadi. No detachments got into the town itself but were content to burn some motor tyres in the camp. One party returned down the wrong wadi and were left ashore. A motor-cycle patrol passed through two parties who failed to stop it; one man injured himself slightly with his own grenade (he reported it as enemy action until the fragments removed from his rump disproved the tale). One boat from A Beach had got grounded and had to be destroyed. The MLC in which I re-embarked could not raise its ramp for half an hour and drifted about the bay in the light of the burning MLC, full of disorderly troops and a seasick brigade major. Eventually the cable which had fouled the winch was cut and we reached *Glengyle* at 0415. The party at C Beach further SE destroyed a small trestle bridge but failed to reach the water supply. One boat from this beach failed to rendezvous, but got into Tobruk safely. The D Beach party was perfectly successful but found their guns already spiked.

After this operation there was a good deal of talk among the more responsible A Battalion officers that Colonel Hound[1] had behaved badly. I thought no one had behaved well enough for them to be able to afford a post-mortem and did not pass their criticism on to Bob. Perhaps if I had we might have been saved some shame in Crete.

I wrote a short memorandum trying to show that night favoured the defender and that only the smallest parties should be used in minor night operations.

12. In May, C Battalion was removed from Layforce and sent to Cyprus. With A and D detailed for general reserve, B Battalion now became the sole special service unit. Various officers volunteered for individual reconnaissance and demolitions and for parachute work. A substantial majority of C Battalion officers tendered resignations before leaving for Cyprus, but were refused. At the end of May, during Bob's absence in Crete, Dermot went out of his mind, rushed to Cairo, saw Smith and Wavell and on his return told his men that (*a*)

[1] 'Hound' has been substituted, by the editor of the diaries, for the real name of this officer, whose crack-up during the Battle of Crete is described by Waugh later in the 'Memorandum on LAYFORCE'. In Waugh's novel, *Officers and Gentlemen*, the collapse of the military machine in Crete and the behaviour of its officers ends the illusion of the hero Guy Crouchback that the war is being fought by men of principle, officers and gentlemen. The disintegration of 'Major Fido Hound' closely parallels the conduct of the officer whose real name has here been suppressed. Protective dashes – used elsewhere in the diaries – might in this instance have confused the reader.

those with units in Middle East might return to them; (*b*) those without were to go to infantry base depots with the exception of a small force which he proposed to make into a long-range desert patrol; (*c*) that 'special service' was off. All B Battalion's efforts in future consisted in drawing up and cancelling lists of the various categories and intriguing to be sent home. They were so occupied with this that they announced themselves incapable of mounting one of the farce operations. Dermot also in this period split up troops between Marsa Matruh and Tobruk so that troop leaders' leadership practically ceased. During this period I met a Grenadier subaltern in corduroy trousers and silk shirt in the Union Bar; he had been given sick leave by the Church of England chaplain in order to go into hospital but felt better in Alexandria and so was engaged in courting a Greek lady. At Marsa the Commando gave up all pretence of military work and spent the day bathing and fishing. A Scots Guards sergeant came on parade with a fishing rod. Robin Campbell remained in his tent all day and emerged at nightfall. The officers' mess had no regular meals and lived on sardines and biscuits. Randolph worked ardently with the Air Force to try and organize a combined operation. The gunboat *Aphis* was attached to the Commando; they made two or three trips in her attempting to land but failing.

13. I think that it was on May 14 that I went by aeroplane to Cairo from Alexandria to try and get some 'time-pencils'[1] from Peter Fleming, persuaded him to return with me, dined with Julian Oxford and Anne Palairet, and flew next day to Alexandria where we got a truck and Sir Walter Cowan, and drove, a very painful drive, to Marsa Matruh. Peter stayed two nights there. He found a poor audience for his booby traps. 8 Commando were just preparing an attack by Foot Guards from *Aphis* on Gazala aerodrome. Randolph discovered, what Maurice Hope did not know, that there are two aerodromes at Gazala and that the one we proposed to attack was the less frequented. For a week he tried to arrange a separate attack from the air by himself and Philip but could not get it sanctioned by the Air Force. He was greatly exhilarated in these days by the belief that the parachute attack on Crete[2] had been defeated. After a rehearsal for the Gazala landing Bob went to Cairo and I remained at Marsa, very content to be with old friends again.

On 20th (?) Dermot's party sailed and returned on evening 21st without having landed, after severe attacks from bombers all day; they sailed again at

[1] Type of fuse.

[2] As soon as Italy attacked Greece in October 1940, the British occupied Crete, which Churchill thought 'invaluable' to the defence of the Mediterranean, particularly Egypt. Six months later the Germans struck south, overrunning Jugoslavia and Greece. On 20 May 1941 they attacked Crete with parachute forces: a new sort of war. Two days later they controlled the airfield at Maleme, and ten days later the Battle of Crete was over. Laycock's Commandos were sent in to reinforce the garrison, commanded by General Freyberg, on 26 May; Waugh accompanied Laycock as his intelligence officer.

midnight in good spirits to try another attack. At 3 in the morning Bob woke me and said we must leave immediately for Alexandria. He had arrived at camp from Alexandria half an hour ago to find the telephone in the orderly room ringing and Freddy Graham[1] on the line telling us to come at once as A and B Battalions were under orders to move. We motored until the morning and arrived at Sidi Bish at about 10 am. We found that A Battalion was to leave by train at 2 pm, embark in destroyers, and land at Suda Bay in Crete. When this was in order and A Battalion actually in the train a signal came cancelling the move and leaving them at four hours' notice. GHQ then telephoned to say that a party of 200 men were to embark that afternoon in *Abdiel*. Two boobies arrived from Cairo; we went to *Abdiel* and made arrangements. She is a very fast forty-knot, mine-laying cruiser. We saw them off. The last order that evening was putting the remainder of the force at six hours' notice. I was on telephone duty that night. At 5 am C-in-C Med's office asked whether we could embark by 7 am. As we had no transport I said no. The sailors seemed surprised but believed us. From now until 8.30 am our telephone was constantly ringing with messages from GHQME, Movement Control Alex, C-in-C Med, alternately cancelling and ordering the move. Meanwhile troops packed up. We were told to take stores, etc., for a long stay. We therefore packed office stores, including many files, whose loss was later an incon-venience. We got to the port at 10.30 and, joined by a party left behind by *Abdiel* the night before, embarked in four destroyers; brigade HQ was in *Isis*, whose captain, Lieutenant-Commander Swinley, showed us every possible kindness and hospitality. The sea was rough. We saw no enemy aircraft either on this or any subsequent crossing. Our orders were to land at one of three points on the western section of the south coast, and march inland to join Creforce at Suda. It was found impossible to land; had we done so our column would have met the retreating rabble on the roads that night and would have had the greatest difficulty in getting through; it is doubtful if we should have been able to take any part in the battle.

After lying off for an hour we returned to Alexandria arriving after dark next night. Here naval staff officers came on board and gave us new orders. These stated that the situation in Crete was 'well in hand' but that 'the Maleme aerodrome garrison was hard-pressed', suggesting wrongly that the aerodrome was in our hands and was being attacked from outside; in fact it was in enemy hands, and was being contained in a half-hearted manner by the New Zealand Brigade. At the moment these orders were given us, the enemy had spent a day pouring new troops into Maleme and were prepared to move outward at dawn. We were instructed to base ourselves at Suda for a sea-borne counter-attack. We transferred to *Abdiel* and one destroyer, brigade HQ in the former, where

---

[1] Major (later Major-General) F. C. C. Graham was Laycock's brigade major.

we were shown no hospitality; the ship's officers were tired out. I was able to get a large cabin to myself and spent the day in great comfort and contentment.

At about 11 o'clock that night we sailed into Suda Bay. We had three hours to land ourselves and stores. Lighters should have come alongside immediately but did not do so for three-quarters of an hour. When they did, they were full of wounded. The first indication which we received of conditions in Crete was the arrival in the captain's cabin, where HQ were waiting, of a stocky, bald, terrified naval commander named Roberts or Robertson. He was wearing shorts and a greatcoat and could not speak intelligibly on account of weariness and panic. 'My God, it's hell,' he said. 'We're pulling out. Look at me, no gear. O My God, it's hell. Bombs all the time. Left all my gear behind, etc., etc.' We took this to be an exceptionally cowardly fellow, but in a few hours realized that he was typical of British forces in the island.

No light could be shown on deck and there was confusion between the wounded and runaways and our troops waiting in the dusk to disembark. The ships could not prolong their stay because they had to get as far clear as they could before light. It was soon plain that we had barely time to get the men ashore and would have to leave most of our stores. A large quantity of valuable signalling stores – 9 and 18 wireless transmitting sets – was wantonly thrown overboard. We landed in tank landing craft which we heard were to be scuttled behind us. The quay on which we landed seemed to have been badly bombarded; it was full of craters and littered with loose stones, burned-out vehicles, abandoned stores, etc. There were groups of wounded sitting about and swearing moodily.

Liaison officers met us from General Weston[1] and Lt.-Col. Hound. They said the Germans were in Canea. Weston had sent a truck so Bob and I set off to find him, leaving Freddy Graham to look after the troops and get them to the defensive positions Bob chose off the map in a shed with a torch. In the dark Suda seemed to be burned out but this was, I think, a trick of the starlight. We drove forward into the country somewhere between Suda and Canea to a farm building which was Weston's HQ. He was asleep on the floor. A Marine told us that the New Zealand Brigade had packed up at Maleme and were in retreat. There was also an Australian Brigade in retreat, also various British and Greek units. The Marines and ourselves were to form a rearguard covering their withdrawal to Sphakia on the south coast. This was barely thirty miles but the road led through the mountains and was longer than it looked on the map. We then went to Hound's headquarters, gave him his orders for the line he was to hold next day; his liaison officer spoke in a quavering undertone which I learned to recognize as the voice of the force. Hound himself did not seem particularly nervous that night; I think he was encouraged by our coming and

[1] Royal Marine general commanding the rearguard.

thought he would now be able to leave things to Bob. He spoke of unremitting bombing but had suffered no serious casualties.

We next went to Freyberg's[1] headquarters; he was in a camouflaged tent off the Suda–Heraklion road, east of the junction with the Sphakia road. He was composed but obtuse.

Bob said he was worried about his left flank which was in the air.

'My dear boy, don't worry about that. The Boche never work off the roads.'

Bob asked if it was a defence to be held to the last man and last round.

'No, a rearguard. Withdraw when you are hard pressed.'

It was now light. We kept our truck and drove to the further side of the first rise of the south road where we found Graham and brigade HQ and D Battalion. All the road which we travelled was densely packed with motor transport and marching men. When we were going forward we had to plough slowly through them; coming back they climbed onto the truck presuming we were heading for Sphakia.

We picked up one man in colonel's uniform who spoke in the most affected voice I ever heard, saying, 'By Jove don't cher know old man.' He said he had been in charge of a transit camp at Canea. It was too dark to see his face but he seemed quite young. I wondered at the time and have continued to wonder since if he were a German. I had decided to make investigations when the truck got stuck temporarily and he disappeared into the dark and the mob saying, 'Thanks no end.' It occurs to me now he may have been a private soldier masquerading as an officer to get transport.

Our headquarters were off the road on the side of a hill, facing south, covered in rock and gorse. Freddy made an attempt to arrange tactical groups of the sort he had heard about at the Staff College. The signallers were useless since their apparatus was all sunk in Suda Bay. Sergeant Lane had shown intelligence in getting hold of a few tinned stores. We each got a packet of biscuits and some bully beef. Most of us were already tired and thirsty but not hungry. Besides our usual headquarters we had attached a Presbyterian minister and a caddish fellow, sacked by Pedder, called Murdoch.

At 8 o'clock the German aeroplanes appeared and remained in the sky more or less continually all day. There were seldom less than half a dozen or more than a dozen overhead at a time. They were bombing the country to the west of us and in Suda Bay, but did not trouble us that morning. As soon as they appeared the rabble on the roads went to ground. When there was half an hour's pause they resumed their retreat.

Bob produced some written orders for a timed rearguard action lasting two days. A Battalion was to fall back through D and take up an intermediate position, etc. Bob sent me forward in the truck to give Hound his orders. I had

[1] General Freyberg, Commander-in-Chief Crete.

rather vague memories of his position from the night before and drove about for some time in no-man's land. There were plenty of aeroplanes about. When they came directly overhead we pulled into the shade and sheltered in the ditch.

At one point in our journey General Weston popped out of the hedge; he seemed to have lost his staff and his head.

'Who the hell are you and where are you going?'

I told him.

'Where's Laycock?'

I showed him on my map.

'Don't you know better than to show a map? It's the best way of telling the enemy where headquarters are.'

It did not seem worth pointing out that we were not headquarters, just two lost officers meeting at the side of the road. He said he wanted a lift back to Laycock. I said I was going forward to find Hound. 'I used to command here once,' he said wistfully.

At length I came across a Layforce anti-tank rifleman concealed in the hedge about a mile east of Suda on the coast road. He said that headquarters were vaguely on his left. I put the truck under the best cover available, left my servant and the driver, and went forward on foot. There were vineyards and olive groves south of the road running up to the edge of the hills where the country became scrub and rock.

Quarter of a mile off the road was a domed church and some scattered farm buildings. The olive groves were full of trenches and weapon pits. I walked about for half an hour trying to find Hound. Some of the trenches had stray colonials or Royal Army Medical Corps details in them; some had Layforce. A Battalion kept no lookouts although they were not being directly bombed. They just crouched as low as possible and hid their heads. The bombing was all going on in the hills, three-quarters of a mile or more to the south; here the enemy were systematically working over the scrub with dive-bombing and machine-gunning. I knew there were no British there, except a few stragglers taking a short cut for home, and thought that a way was being cleared for an infantry advance. I reported this later but we had no troops to spare and nothing could be done. Late that evening the Germans worked through and cut off a company of D Battalion holding the road between Suda and the junction. I do not know if this company surrendered or fought it out.

After asking two officers who made excuses for not leaving their holes I found one who cheerfully consented to take me to Hound. He took me to the furthest of the farm buildings and went back to his company. I went into a tin-roofed shed and found two NCOs sitting at a table.

I said, 'I was told Colonel Hound was here.'

'He is,' they said.

I looked round, saw no one. Then they pointed under the table where I saw their commanding officer sitting hunched up like a disconsolate ape. I saluted and gave him his orders. He did not seem able to take them in at all.

He said, 'Where's Colonel Bob? I must see him.'

I said I was on my way back there now.

'Wait till the blitz is over. I'll come too.'

After a time the aeroplanes went home for refreshment and Hound emerged. He still looked a soldierly figure when he was on his feet. 'We had a burst of machine gun right through the roof,' he said half apologetically. I think this was a lie as the aeroplanes were concentrated on the hillside all that forenoon.

I took him to Bob. He showed no inclination to go back to his battalion but could still talk quite reasonably when there was no aeroplane overhead. Soon they came back and he lay rigid with his face in the gorse for about four hours. If anyone stretched a leg, he groaned as though he had broken all his limbs and was being jolted. 'For Christ's sake keep still.'

A squadron of dive-bombers now started work to the east of us; they came round and round regularly and monotonously like the horses at Captain Hance's.[1] Just below us there was a very prominent circular cornfield in a hollow and they used this as their pivot so that they were always directly overhead flying quite low, then they climbed as they swung right, dived and let go their bombs about a mile away. I do not know what their target was; Freyberg's headquarters had been somewhere in that area. At first it was impressive, but after half an hour deadly monotonous. It was like everything German – overdone.

It was intolerably hot on the hillside; blankets served the double purpose of camouflage and protection from the sun. It was then I learned that the most valuable piece of equipment one can have in action is a pillow. From then on I always carried mine under my arm and did not relinquish it until it went into the captain's wastepaper basket in Alexandria harbour; it was then threadbare and soaked in oil.

At sunset Hound went back towards his battalion who were to withdraw that night to a position about seven miles inland. D Battalion moved out to a position in their rear. Hound's second-in-command, with the newly arrived A Battalion detachment, were to hold the most forward position. There was also the company which got cut off, of D Battalion, which should have fallen back through A Battalion's forward position. I think that was the plan but I have no copy of the orders and, anyway, it did not work out that way the next day. Bob and Freddy went out in the truck to look for Weston. We did not once, in the five days' action, receive an order from any higher formation without going to ask for it. The rest of HQ settled down to sleep. An hour or two later – I think

[1] The riding school at Malvern, near the Lygons, where Waugh learned to ride in the early 1930s.

about 9 o'clock – Bob moved HQ to the road. The Germans had worked along the hills to our flank and were very close, he said. We took up firing positions along the road facing east, posted sentries and went to sleep.

Within an hour, Bob having gone off again in the truck, we were woken up. Hound had arrived with a confused account of having been ambushed on a motor cycle. His battalion was fiercely engaged he said (this was balls), and without explaining why he was not with them he gave us the order to withdraw. It all seemed fishy but Murdoch was in command of brigade HQ troops so off we set, I presumed to fall back about a mile.

We marched on and on all through the night, through two villages. I protested but Hound kept saying, 'We must get as far as we can before light.' The roads were full of troops retreating without any discipline. All the officers seemed to have made off in the motor transport. After the second village the road ran along the side of a valley with steep bare slopes on either side. When I suggested a halt Hound said, 'We must find cover.' Nothing but daylight would stop him. The moment that came he popped into a drain under the road and sat there.

I got an hour's sleep. When I woke up the road was full of a strange procession carrying white sheets as banners; they were a ragged, bearded troop of about 2,000. I thought at first it was some demonstration by the local inhabitants. Then I realized that they were Italians, taken prisoner in Greece, and now liberated. They advanced towards freedom with the least possible enthusiasm.

Some troops of A Battalion now arrived with a few wounded. One man had marched all the way with a bullet through his guts. When he lay down he stayed down and the doctor finished him with morphia. I asked Captain Mackintosh-Flood what the situation was. He said, 'I don't know and I don't care.' So I went off to look for myself, leaving my servant and the intelligence section behind.

It was always exhilarating as soon as one was alone; despondent troops were a dead weight on one's spirits and usefulness. I set off along the road we had come. Presently I met a subaltern (not one of ours but, I think, English) accompanied by, one could not say in command of, half a platoon. He was in a great hurry.

He said, 'You can't go any further on this road. The enemy landed parachutists in the night. They're firing on it with machine guns.'

I asked where they were firing from.

'I don't know.'

'Were any of your men hit?'

'I didn't stop to look,' he said, laughing at me for asking so silly a question.

So I left the road and cut across the hills to the village we had passed in the night. It was a pretty, simple place with a well in the square. I wanted to fill my bottle but the rope had been cut and the bucket stolen. I asked a peasant, in gesture, for water; he went away grumbling a refusal but I followed him into his cottage and after a bit he gave me a cupful from a stone jar.

In the square a peasant girl came and pulled at my sleeve; she was in tears. I followed her to the church, where in the yard was a British soldier on a stretcher. Flies were all over his mouth and he was dead. There was another girl by him also in tears. I think they had been looking after him. There was also a bearded peasant who shrugged and made signs that might have been meant to describe the ascent of a balloon, but which told me what I could already see. Again with signs, I told them to bury him.

Then I went on through the next village at the furthest house of which a motor cyclist had told me I should find some sort of headquarters. The enemy were being held about half a mile up the road from there. In an arbour of sweet jasmine I found Bob and Freddy and two brigadiers; they had had an adventure, being attacked at close quarters by tommy-gunners. Bob had jumped into a tank and Ken Wiley, second-in-command of A Battalion, redeemed the Commandos' honour by leading a vigorous and successful counter-attack. A few New Zealanders, mostly Maoris, had rallied and were joining us in the rearguard. A plan was decided on which I cannot now remember and, anyway, was never put into effect.

Presently Bob, Freddy and I got into the truck and drove back to where I had left Hound. A number of his battalion had got together there but he was still in his drain. Bob as politely as possible relieved him of command saying, 'You're done up. Ken will take over from you.' Then we went to set up brigade headquarters in the next village back. This was called, I think, Babali Inn.[1] There was certainly an inn there with some tipsy stragglers and pools of wine spilled about but some jars still full. We had had no food that day, and two mugs of the wine, brown and sweet, made us all more cheerful. We broke into a house and called it brigade HQ after Bob had rejected a very nice barn I found him. D Battalion took up a line on the edge of the village in a deep ditch near a well. Presently A Battalion appeared at a good pace. They should have been covering D while they took up position but Hound had gone forward and told them to withdraw. Bob now relieved him of command in terms which could not be misunderstood. (The Presbyterian minister had also taken his part, telling Christie Laurence, 'It's *sauve qui peut*, now.') If the enemy had cared to push on they could have caught D Battalion before they were in position, but they were tired by now and, anyway, seldom advanced far without air preparation. From now on the air support slackened a great deal. There were frequent reconnaissance planes and some desultory attacks but no longer the skyful of the preceding week.

[1] Babali Hani.

After Hound's unexpected retreat Babali Inn became the front line so brigade HQ withdrew a mile or so to a place of great beauty. It was a little roadside shrine with a spring running down to a brook. There had been a kind of terrace there once and the spring was built round with stone, and fell into stone basins. Presumably the place had some medical properties once. There was a grove of five trees round the spring and although there were gross evidences of previous occupation it was still an enchanting spot. Sergeant Lane had prudently filled a large bottle with wine. We kept it cool in the spring. Bob had a box of cigars and a book of crossword puzzles. We had a few hours' rest here. Fatigue and hunger were beginning to affect us.

At about 5 in the afternoon Bob and I went up to visit George Young. He was still in his ditch at Babali Inn in uncomfortable circumstances, being shot at from three sides by sub-machine gunners in the trees. The enemy also had a four-inch mortar ranged on him and on the road which was accurate and damaging. Bob and I had some bullets near us in getting to the trench and bombs very close on the return journey. We found Young's headquarters, and all of his battalion whom we saw, in the steadiest condition. He was now commanding what was left of A Battalion. He held his position until told to withdraw when it became dark.

As night fell stragglers emerged from the ditches, like ghosts from their graves, and began silently crawling along towards the coast. None that I saw in this area were under any kind of control, but the majority still had their rifles. They had all thrown away their packs, had beards and the lassitude of hunger and extreme exhaustion; a pitiful spectacle.

Orders, now, were to fall right back to Imvros over the other side of the mountains and the troops marched for over twelve hours. Brigade HQ went on in a truck through a burned-out village where a party of sappers were waiting to blow the bridge after the last vehicles; this was our one tank we still had with us. For some reason this bridge was never blown; about two miles further on, however, the road had been cratered, without orders, at a narrow place and a party were at work trying to fill it in. There was a great confusion here of vehicles blocked by the crater and Bob and I were able to get some sent back to lift troops. We also arranged a distribution of rations which had turned up from somewhere. At this point Bob put his hand on a great rock and said, 'This is a bloody big tank.' There was a Greek general and his staff at the crater and I got his bus for our troops. Those that we met on the way were practically insensible when they arrived. We gave out rations, loaded wounded and one hysteric (not ours) on our truck, and drove down to Imvros. It was day before we arrived; one reconnaissance plane shot at us but otherwise we were unmolested.

At Imvros there was some attempt at organization. There was a first-aid post at a church and areas in the surrounding vineyards were allotted as assembly areas. There was a great quantity of motor trucks in the village and I went forward to try to get some sent back to lift our men down the mountain.

An officer leaped across the road shouting at me, 'Get back there.'

I asked him who was in charge of movement control.

He said, 'I am. You can't come any further.'

I began asking him about the trucks. Then he said he had nothing to do with movement control.

I said, 'You mustn't let your nerves affect your manners.'

He grew combative and said, 'What exactly do you mean by that?'

I told him exactly. 'You may be very frightened but you must try to be polite.'

'I am not frightened,' he said like a sulky little boy and told me where the officer in charge of traffic was. I began to tell this officer what I wanted but an aeroplane came over and he leaped into a ditch. I followed him, still explaining, but while there was an aeroplane buzzing anywhere in the sky he could not take anything in. He thought I was trying to get transport to go down to the sea and muttered monotonously, 'No motor transport beyond this point.' He passed me on to General Weston who had set up headquarters in a cottage. Weston said he had sent trucks.

We lay up all that forenoon under the walls of the vineyard. I think there was a good deal of machine-gunning from the air but we slept. Bob went to Weston who told us to wait until dark, then fall back to the end of Imvros gorge and hold that while the stragglers went through. We had left the tank at the top of the road where the crater was, its engine running, its water emptied out. This seemed to have frightened the enemy off all day. Murdoch detached himself from us at this stage, preferring to make his own way to Alexandria.

After Imvros the road ended in a series of exposed hairpin bends. A track to the left diverged and ran through the gorge to the coast; between the mouth of the gorge and the foot of the road was a village and another small gorge; then an open rump of hillside and a further gorge, full of caves, which led down to Sphakia, the port of embarkation. All these points were quite close together, but at this stage all distances seemed enormously increased by our exhaustion; half a mile's climb was a laborious undertaking.

Soon after midday we got bored with lying up in the vineyards and as there were few aircraft about Bob decided to move brigade HQ by daylight. The gorge was magnificent, narrowing and deepening until it looked like a seventeenth-century baroque landscape; halfway down it opened into a circle with a well of cold sweet water. At the end it opened a little and was full of caves.

All the caves were full of ragged, starving, neurotic Australians who had run away earlier. Whenever an aeroplane was heard, often when it was not, they shouted, 'Aircraft, take cover!' and shot at anyone who moved about. One could hear the wail being passed from cave to cave down the gorge. Some of them had Cretan women living with them in the caves; at night these men sallied forth to raid ration dumps. Some were starving but some had large stores of food they stole in this way.

We found a green patch, with some large rocks and olive trees near the path up to the village, and established brigade HQ here. That at least would be the military expression, but in fact we simply rested; of HQ, Murdoch and the staff captain had disappeared and were not seen again until we reached Alexandria; the signallers were depleted by stragglers and were useless in any case; the intelligence section had not been used except once or twice as runners; there was no situation map, file of messages, or log.

The Presbyterian minister had made his own way home; as far as I know he never attempted any ministration of any kind; when he got back to Alexandria he put in a huge bill for kit lost in enemy action, asking £1 for a Bible, half a guinea each for hymn books, two suits of khaki service dress, 'shirts (superfine)'. He then took leave to Palestine and never returned. We found when we came to work out mess accounts that he did not sign for a tenth of his drinks. He was a corpulent young man whose name I had forgotten. I think his friends address him as 'Andrew'.

In the evening Bob and I went to look for a naval embarkation officer who was said to be in the village. This village was a steep, picturesque little place with two churches and some wells. The wells were getting dry and the place stank. It was always full of stragglers filling water bottles. We found no embarkation officer but learned that Freyberg was in a cave on the west slope of the hill below the hairpin bends in the road. To get there we had to cross another small ravine, whose sides were terraced for olive trees. This was thronged with Greeks and Australians who hoped to get taken off. They said that only wounded were to be taken off that night.

We found Freyberg just as it was getting dark. He was sitting outside his cave surrounded by miscellaneous staff officers, saying goodbye to New Zealanders who were leaving that evening. Some had photographs of him which he signed. He gave us half a cupful of sherry and a spoonful of beans for which we were very grateful. He seemed to have lost all interest in the battle, spoke of his earlier successes against the parachute landings in the east with satisfaction. Bob asked him about order of embarkation and he said, 'You were the last to come so you will be the last to go.'

There was a one-eyed booby with DAQMG[1] on his arms. He said to me, 'When the enemy shows his head, hit him; drive him back.' He was himself getting out by air next day. I interrupted his exhortation to ask for food. He pressed a great parcel of Greek notes into my hand and said, 'Buy it, buy a caique.' I then said our men had had nothing that day and that we had no stores

---

[1] Deputy Assistant Quarter-Master General.

of our own, so he told us to draw some from Sphakia quay. He wrote out a chit authorizing this, at the same time adding the odd enjoinder to picket the ration dump. I tried to explain that our position to the east made that impossible. He said, 'I don't know anything about the east.' I think this ass was called Brunskill.

Bob and I then began our return journey; the crossing of the ravine proved impossible in the dark and after an hour or two's scrambling and a bad fall for Bob, we spent the rest of the night at a little shrine on the hilltop, from where we could hear the embarkation at Sphakia. The sailors made a prodigious noise; at the end they were shouting, 'Any more for the boats?' for they could have taken off some hundreds more than they did, had the embarkation been better organized. At dawn we returned to our HQ and Freddy was sent off to find Weston and ask for orders.

There was a continuous trickle of stragglers down the gorge all day and the recurrent wails of 'Aircraft! Take cover fuck you!' from the men in the caves.

In the afternoon we moved HQ to a deep cave opposite us. Here we found a dozen of the Spanish socialists who had fled in a body at the first shot. We had thought hardly of them but they greeted our arrival with the gift of a pilaf of rice and goat's meat, a roast pig and two boiled fowls; all our criticism was disarmed; meanwhile our own party went foraging and found some potatoes, dry bread and two fowls, so that day all ate heartily. Freddy brought back orders that next day we were to leave the gorge and cover the Sphakia gorge.

We slept in the cave and spent the forenoon there. Air activity was now very slight. In the afternoon, the 31st of May, Bob and I went to get further orders and find a place for headquarters. Freyberg had gone but Weston had set up in his cave. The wireless was no longer working. Its last order had been that that night was the last night for evacuation. Weston ordered that those who were left behind, of whom there would be about 8,000, were to drift eastwards and look for boats. Before leaving, Freyberg dictated an order of priority for disembarkation which said Layforce was to be last, but all fighting troops had precedence over others. We interpreted this to mean troops who had retained their arms and organization, but I believe he may have meant soldiers as opposed to civilian refugees. Anyway no attempt was made to enforce the priority.

We found a cave full of blankets, rations and weapons which had been left by Australians and sat there till dusk. Meanwhile fantastic optimistic rumours were being spread saying that Syria had declared for Free France, America had taken over the Atlantic and our Atlantic fleet was in the Mediterranean, 300 Blenheims had bombed Berlin for three hours leaving it in ruins, six leading Nazis had landed by parachute in Scotland, etc. These were believed by many. A well-intentioned naval officer appeared to have invented them.

At dusk Layforce took up position in Sphakia region. There was some firing inland where the Marines held a line; it was said the Germans were close on our left flank. Weston now decided that the morale of the troops, the lack of rations and munitions, and the impossibility of further naval help made further resistance hopeless, and he dictated a capitulation[1] to be handed in at dawn the next day. He first charged Bob with the task but later realized that it was foolish to sacrifice a first-class man for this and chose instead Hound,[2] who had lately attached himself to brigade HQ, where he was a nuisance owing to his having thrown away his water bottle in his flight. Bob and I had resigned ourselves to being captured but now got slightly more hopeful of escape. Weston said that we were to cover the withdrawal and that a message would be sent to us by the embarkation officer on Sphakia beach when we could retire.

At about 10 o'clock that evening there was no sign of the enemy and the approaches to the beaches were thronged with non-fighting troops. Bob and I and Freddy, with servants, therefore set off to find the beach officer, Colonel Healy, and ask authority to withdraw. We pushed our way through the crowds who were too spiritless even to resist what they took to be an unauthorized intrusion and arrived on the beach to find that there was no one in charge, Colonel Healy having left earlier by aeroplane. Bob then took the responsibility of ordering Layforce to fight their way through the rabble and embark. My servant Tanner took this order back. The beach was a little harbour approached by narrow lanes through the village of Sphakia. I rescued a party of Greek boatmen whom the Australians wished to shoot as spies. As there was nothing further he could do, Bob ordered brigade HQ to embark, which we did in a small motor boat. We reached the destroyer *Nizam* at about midnight and sailed as soon as we came aboard. There were no 'fighting troops' among the officers in her and few among the men. We were given tea, of which we drank a great quantity. Bob, Freddy and I were given the captain's quarters. We did not see any of the ship's officers and arrived at Alexandria at 5 in the afternoon, June 1st, after an uneventful voyage during which we were too exhausted to do more than shave. I think I was the only man in the ship to bring his pack away with him. The only piece of equipment which I had jettisoned was my steel helmet, which, contrary to what I was told in training, gave me no illusion of protection.

Tanner was on another destroyer with about 120 officers and men of A Battalion who had got to the beach by a side lane. Colonel Young and the rest of his men were unable to force a passage through the rabble. We had put 800 men

[1] Could Crete have been held? The conclusion of the most thorough study of the battle is that Wavell, in command of the Middle East, 'could have rendered Crete impregnable' during the six months that Britain occupied the island before the German attack; and that, despite Wavell's failure, 'Crete might still have been held' by Freyberg. See I. McD. G. Stewart, *The Struggle for Crete* (London 1966), pp. 478–83.

[2] Colonel 'Hound' then disappeared. The capitulation was effected by Colonel Young.

of Layforce into the island. Most of our wounded had been taken off the evening before. Two men from brigade HQ and five from D Battalion made their escape by MLC.

14. Two MLCs escaped from Crete on 1st June. Pattison, of the intelligence section, gave me an account of his adventures. On the morning of 1st June the remaining troops looted the rations and destroyed their arms. They spread sheets from the cottages on the ground but the aeroplanes bombed them that morning. German troops occupied Sphakia. Pattison took refuge in an MLC with an assorted party of Australians and marines; they set out at dusk with petrol for about fifty miles, some tins of water and a few tins of food. They landed at the island south of Crete and left behind two or three men who despaired of the attempt; the islanders gave them a sheep. An Australian private soldier took charge of the party, all of whom started the voyage in extreme exhaustion. When petrol was exhausted, they hoisted a sail made of blankets. They had no map or compass and steered by the sun and their memory of their map. They were nine days at sea and at the last gasp. One man had died and one shot himself. They held a religious service and sang 'God Save the King'. An hour later they sighted land, drifted onto a sandy beach near Sidi Barrani and found a Royal Army Service Corps lorry full of food a hundred yards from them. One of them was killed that evening by a bomb on his 21st birthday. Pattison, who was a solicitor, was put in for an OCTU[1] as a result of this exploit.

15. C Battalion, though nominally a part of Layforce, were now outside our control. At the beginning of the occupation of Syria they were taken from Cyprus to Port Said and given the task of landing north of Litani river to prevent the bridge from being demolished by the French. They sailed in *Glengyle* but on the night appointed Captain Petrie considered it too rough to land. The operation was repeated two or three nights later, by which time the bridge had been destroyed. They were ordered to form a bridgehead to allow Australians to come through them. Half the force were landed at the wrong side of the river. One half, however, under Pedder took the port, battery and barracks successfully. The Australians were afraid to come forward and our battalion was left thirty-six hours without support under heavy fire. They had about twenty-five per cent casualties including Pedder, who was killed. They were then returned to Cyprus for garrison duty.

16. I was instrumental in sending a peculiarly futile little party to Cyprus. Soon after our return from Crete, Freddy Graham was moved to another brigade. Bob was in Cairo and I was in charge at headquarters. I was sent for by C-in-C Med's office. The C-in-C wished to send a party to Cyprus to sabotage enemy aircraft which were expected to land troops at Nicosia; the plan was that

---

[1] Officer Cadet Training Unit.

they would lie up in the neighbourhood of the aerodrome, destroy aircraft at night and escape as best they could. I sent a party of a dozen volunteers from A Battalion which was called 'Pencil Party' because it was hoped, vainly, that they could be provided with 'pencil' time fuses. When they got to Cyprus they found C Battalion returned there, themselves unwanted, and the ground round Nicosia totally devoid of cover. They were, however, retained.

17. B Battalion meanwhile was half at Marsa Matruh under Dermot, half at Tobruk under 'Bones' Sudeley. The latter were to put oil in some enemy wells down the coast. At the end of June, when Bob was in Cairo, Bones arrived un-expectedly at Alexandria by destroyer. He was in a poor state of nerves and got hopelessly drunk that night. He had a confused story of the men being disheartened by postponements, the sea and tide being unfavourable, the operation being cancelled and Maurice Hope being unreasonably critical. Even in his version it was clear to me that Hope's criticisms would be universal if the matter became known. The simple facts were that Bones had spent his entire time in an air raid shelter, had been drunk on reconnaissance, had been told to wait ten days until the moon was right for his landing, had asked instead for the operation to be cancelled, and had himself left first, leaving his troops to follow at their leisure. Beresford Pierce at Desforce had already made a failure of his Salum push on 15th and was ready to be disagreeable to everyone. Navy and Army at Tobruk were contemptuous. Hope sent a signal offering to raise another SS force for Bones's operation. Dermot rushed to Arthur Smith, got the file copies of signals destroyed, promised to send another force at once to Tobruk under his own command. An advance party under Philip Dunne left Alexandria for Tobruk on 6th July. Dermot's force were following next day but their move was cancelled just as they were entraining by a signal from GHQME. This was due to a suggestion from England that Layforce should return home as a body. There the matter rested at the time I transferred to HMS *Nile* for draft to UK thus severing my connection with the Army. My transfer took place on July 7th. On 9th I left for Kabrit camp and 12th embarked at Taufiq in *Duchess of Richmond*.

18. Bob flew home to England. Brigade headquarters ceased to exist. At the time that the order to stand fast arrived, the condition of Layforce was:

A Battalion: about 150 all ranks under Captain Nichols. Some of these volunteered for special service in Far East; some were already being returned to units in the Middle East; some had put in for return to UK on compassionate grounds.

B Battalion: a few casualties from bombing at Tobruk. The Coldstream had already rejoined their regiment. Most line-regiment personnel had been sent to IBCs.[1] A number of odd officers had joined the Cheshire Yeomanry; others

---

[1] Infantry Battalion Centres.

were pursuing individual careers. A great number had put up slender compassionate grounds for their return and were being generously treated. Morale of all ranks very low but they responded readily enough when Bones compromised their honour. Philip particularly debonair still. Dermot half crazy. I spent an alarming evening playing billiards with him, Harry, and Peter Milton, when he insulted Harry continually, and chased a black waiter in the dark during an air raid. Randolph had been doing liaison with Harriman but came tumbling back at the chance of returning to Tobruk.

C Battalion: 350 men under Major Keyes at Cyprus. They were to be allowed to disband when relieved.

D Battalion: a few men under the second-in-command, who had been wounded in Crete, including one or two Spaniards. Staff Captain F—— was appointed to the Joint Planning Board. No doubt he will rise steadily on the G. side[1] where his incapacity and ignorance and timidity can do most harm.

Of the Glen ships, *Glenearn* had a bomb down her funnel at Crete and was useless. *Glenroy* had an inglorious career. Setting out for the evacuation of Greece, she ran on a rock in the entrance to Alexandria harbour. Later she was sent to take reinforcements to Crete, was bombed and shaken, but could have fulfilled her task; instead she turned back. She had been slowed down a lot and needs many repairs. *Glengyle* is still in service.

19. Some individuals connected with Layforce:

Pedder. We shall never know who killed him. Many of his men had sworn to do so and he was shot in the back by a sniper. He had, however, just led a successful assault and it seems an unlikely occasion for murder. All his officers feared him, and most hated him. He had carefully weeded out anyone of character or maturity and had a bunch of youths who put up with his idiosyncrasies, but abused him behind his back. His intelligence officer, killed at Litani, used not to dare to come and talk to me in public. He worked everyone very hard, and saw to their welfare. He was half mad but seems to have done well in his final action.

Admiral Sir Walter Cowan.[2] A very old, minute hero who came out as a kind of mascot to Pedder's Commando and was left behind with gross discourtesy

---

[1] Intelligence side.

[2] Admiral Sir Walter Cowan, Bart., KCB, DSO, had commanded a river gunboat on the Nile during the Sudan campaigns of the 1890s; thereafter he had been on Kitchener's staff in South Africa, when Kitchener was C-in-C. He had taken over the Devonport Destroyer Flotilla from Roger Keyes (later, Admiral Sir Roger Keyes) as long ago as 1902. In 1941 he was seventy-four. Earlier he had been attached at his own request to the Indian Cavalry (Mechanized) Regiment with the 8th Army in the Western Desert and had been captured, taken to Italy, and then repatriated as being 'of no further use' to the British war effort. Incensed by this slight, he got himself posted to the Commandos as a naval liaison officer; he was entitled to wear an admiral's insignia, but instead dressed as a naval commander, in khaki battledress, with a green Commando beret.

when they went to Cyprus. B Battalion then adopted him. Most of his experience had been with the Army and he showed great intolerance of sailors, particularly of signalmen, who he could not bear anywhere near him. He neither smoked nor drank wine, and ate all his food on the same plate – porridge, fruit, meat, eggs in a single mess. He was exquisitely polite, almost spinster-like in conversation; church-going with a belief in British-Israel. He sat behind me in the boat at Bardia bearing the weight of fifteen men. I could feel him fluttering like a bird in the hand. Later he said, 'Young Waugh is uncommon heavy.' He read nothing but Surtees. He was popularly believed to spend his leisure in sniping at Italian prisoners with a catapult. He certainly loathed them almost as violently as he loathed signallers. I was once talking to him when a group marched past us with distinguishing patches in the seats of the trousers. He had been asking solicitously, like an aunt, after my health. He suddenly broke off and said with extravagant venom, 'That's the place to mark the sods.' He went with the *Aphis* party on their abortive raids and greatly enjoyed the bombing. 'They ought to have got us,' he said very regretfully.

Peter Beatty[1] was attached to us in an undefined capacity. When everyone else was intriguing to get sent home Peter wished to stay. In his lucid moments he had a very shrewd appreciation of the collapse of 8 Commando. In his less lucid moments he said and did innumerable funny things. I heard him tell the hall porter at the Cecil Hotel to find out which was the best military hospital and book him a room as he thought he should lie up for a day or two. On another occasion, at Amiriya camp, Harry had to go and interview the Commandant. Peter came loping after him, followed him into the office dugout and without a word to the Brigadier or any explanation from Harry took a newspaper off the desk and sat in a corner reading it. Both Harry and the Brigadier pretended to ignore his presence. Harry finished his interview, saluted and left. Peter finished the newspaper and wandered off, still carrying it.

He has three habitual gestures; one is to press his upper teeth with his thumbs as though they were false and loose; one is to rub his hands together as though they were freezing; the other to finger an imaginary beard. He gave Bob a long lecture on his, Bob's, unpopularity which was taken to heart. Freddy Graham fascinated him. He used to come to the office window just to see him and would go away giggling and chafing his hands.

F—— looked like a Hollywood hanger-on and in fact had been one. He had a swagger and great felicity in choosing nicknames. He has been married three times and kept by rich women continually. He studied psychoanalysis and had a set of opinions formed from American magazines.

---

[1] Younger son of Admiral of the Fleet Sir David Beatty, who commanded the Battle Cruiser Fleet at the Battle of Jutland. See Appendix of Names, p. 794.

When I met him at Largs he was a fire-eater, talking of shooting Germans like rats. As 'Workshop' became likely he became restless, saying with perfect frankness, 'You know, old boy, I don't like this idea of a spot being "forever England".' When he saw Evetts, whom he called 'Death and Destruction', and heard his speech about a 'bellyful of fighting', he immediately applied for special leave for Cairo and asked Arthur Smith to get him a staff job. He wished to make himself propaganda chief in charge of the morale of MEF. He returned very jubilant, saying that the generals 'fell for him like a ton of bricks'; they did not give him a job but at least he got himself sent on a security course. 'I passed out with every distinction,' he said. 'Extraordinary thing was they said they didn't think I was suitable. Then they offered me a post as security officer in the Western Desert. Of course I turned that down.'

He then settled in Cairo sharing a flat with Ian Collins's uncle whom I had known in Addis Ababa. Both thought the other rich, and lived happily together until accounts fell due. He seldom drank but did so in Cairo once with Momo Marriott and made a scene with a taxi-driver and got his name taken by a PM. When he heard that Layforce was being disbanded he appeared at Alexandria with a letter in his pocket from BTE saying that he had never left Layforce, had been merely seconded for a course and was now returned to us. Dermot then ordered him to Tobruk. He then produced an alternative letter from the other pocket saying that he was now in security. Bob, later, refused to forward his application to return to UK but I have no doubt that he will get there.

Sergeant L—— came to us as a corporal from 3 Commando at Arran, and was put in charge of the liaison section. He was a small, tubby, cheerful fellow who before the war was a 'commercial artist' employed by Lever the soapmakers. He was exceptionally neat and industrious. When he was given any task such as making a plan of the sleeping space on deck it was always done in half the time and with twice the finish that one expected. His willingness to please would have been slightly ingratiating had it not been combined with such sunniness. In his spare time he filled sketch-books with painstaking and atrociously vulgar drawings of anything he saw. When he went ashore he made the best possible use of every minute.

On my recommendation he was promoted sergeant and, when I was made adjutant of the force, at his request I took him with me as orderly room sergeant. Eventually under Freddy he became staff sergeant; a great deal of confidential paper passed through his hands. He always received orders with, 'I most certainly will sir.' We thought him a little comic and wholly estimable.

In Crete he was still cheerful and resourceful. He was left behind a prisoner. When we came to go through his possessions to see what should be disposed of in what way, we found two large volumes of diary, which he had kept daily, in great detail, since he joined us. It was written in horrible style, usually ending each day with 'So goodnight, everybody' and was illustrated with drawings and photographs. It consisted of three elements: a prosaic travel narrative with descriptions of all the trees and birds and ships he saw; a running criticism of the officers of the unit; and a selection from every confidential document which had passed through his hands. His resentment against officers was enormous and extraordinarily unreasoned; it did not seem to have any political basis; his attitude was one of intense personal envy of each officer individually. There was plenty that might be said against most of the officers he came into contact with; he complained about their going ashore at Port Said in service dress instead of battle dress, and at their breakfasting later than the other ranks. Every instance of ignorance – when George Jellicoe did not know the capacity of a service water bottle – was carefully recorded. He had even taken the trouble to get the wine bills from the mess servants. Freddy Graham commanded his entire respect, and he seemed to have some liking for me. His particular butt was Randolph. He also had a fiery resentment of Dermot's occasional attempts to restore discipline. The theft of confidential documents was, of course, a grave crime but I was the more shocked at his meanness of spirit and spite. We were in some doubt as to what to do with the volumes. Finally we cut out all the confidential matter and took the rest back to England where he can obtain it at the end of the war. We censored nothing except on grounds of military security.

Return from Middle East. On July 5th I left the Army and returned to the Royal Marines on the strength of HMS *Nile*, being allowed to live in an hotel until the draft for UK was ready. On July 9th late at night we left Alexandria for Suez but were taken out of the train at Geneifa and put into the naval camp at Kabrit for three days. This was a beastly camp. Of the ships going home *Georgic* was said to be the most comfortable. Tony Connolly and I put our names down for her but later learned that *Duchess of Richmond* was sailing a day ahead so transferred. *Georgic* was bombed and sunk in the harbour at Suez the day we sailed. *Duchess of Richmond* was almost empty after Durban where we put down a large party of Maltese civilian refugees (who were treated by the South Africans as 'non-European') and South African troops on leave from Mombasa. We had 1,400 Italian prisoners who were very docile. One crime – four men conspired to steal a bottle of soda water in the Red Sea, and wept on conviction. The escort used to say, 'I'll *acqua pane* you.' One night a rating got drunk and beat up some prisoners in the cells. We put him under arrest. The doctor in charge of the Italians interceded for him, saying it would be distressing if any ill-feeling arose between the two races. We travelled 20,000 miles to get home, stopping at Cape Town, Trinidad, and following the American coast, with air escort, to Iceland and so to Liverpool arriving September 3rd.

I took a weekend's leave at Pixton and reported on the Monday to Plymouth Barracks – band playing in the square, drill sergeants in blue, vintage port.

Found Major Sinclair of Addis Ababa brigade major who sent me on fourteen days' leave. On returning to Plymouth I was detailed to the MNBDO2[1] at Alton and from there to the 12th Battalion Land Defence Force.

12 RM Land Defence Force commanded by a Lieutenant-Colonel ——, the only regular Marine officer. It was with this battalion that I first realized the quality of the new troops and officers they have trained during the last year. With the exception of the commander of the machine-gun company, there was no officer who would have been worth making a corporal. One had been a sergeant but had deteriorated by promotion. The chief topic of conversation in mess was complaints about rates of pay. They are living in very considerable comfort at Hayling Island. Training ended sharp at 4 daily and at noon on Saturdays. It consisted mainly of three-rank drill. The senior NCOs were mainly youths fired from Exton. Colonel —— was insane. When I joined I was kept standing to attention throughout the interview, rated for coming, marched out by the Adjutant like a defaulter and given a week's leave. I returned to find him wildly welcoming. I became adjutant and later Director of Instruction, in which office I shook up the company commanders. As soon as I saw the battalion I applied to Morford for a move which finally came through on my birthday. I took another day's leave and travelled up November 1st to Hawick, where the brigade was in camp, in the last sleeper I was to have, for they were shortly afterwards taken off.

Officer Commanding Troops, Duchess of Richmond: a dipsomaniac named ——. He drank so heavily that the skin came off his eyelids. He used to address the Italian prisoners in execrable French saying, '*Attendez-vous*' to mean 'Pay attention'. He would ask large numbers of guests to his cabin and then say, 'When you've had a drink, go away.' He was removed from his command at Cape Town.

Lieutenant-Colonel W—— who drank very hard. When tipsy he talked endlessly and facetiously. His chief humour was the employment of dated solecisms. 'Cast asparagus' for 'aspersions' and 'viva voce' for 'vice versa', etc. He had a black dog to whom he talked in the same manner. In his office he fell into maniacal rages and turned a very nasty colour. He, too, was removed from his command.

Bones Sudeley died in the Red Sea. He was alone in his ship. The news of his death appeared in the papers the day I landed.

Bob[2] was reported missing December 15th. He had landed with a detachment south of Benghazi on November 23rd to cut communications behind Rommel's line. There were various stories of what happened. Some say they met opposition on the beach and the submarines made off, leaving half the

---

[1] Mobile Naval Base Defence Organization.
[2] Colonel Robert Laycock.

party; others say that the ship that was coming to take them off was torpedoed. Writing on December 20th, it looks unlikely that he has survived; but in White's everyone says he is too 'fly' to be caught.

5th Battalion Royal Marines. Colonel Reading, an able, ambitious, smug, conceited, active, quick-witted little man with no single interest outside his profession. The battalion has now been in existence for nearly two years and is still training intensively. Nothing connected with tactics bores him. He is like Pedder, but without passion or eccentricity. He has no friends. One morning, embarking at Gourock for a week's exercises, I met the 1st Battalion and felt homesick for them, although they had lost two-thirds of their original officers.

November 1941

Writing an article. On my first leave home I was asked by American *Life* to write an article on the Commandos. I said I must get leave first and the editor arranged it with Brendan Bracken. I wrote about the Bardia raids and got £200 for it. Then, without my knowledge, Peters sold it to the *Evening Standard*. It was announced; the other papers complained; the War Office then issued my article as a news bulletin. The Marine Office became agitated, Brendan backed out of his responsibility, and I got reprimanded.

December 1941

Leave in London. No sleeping cars. Train grossly crowded. London crowded and dead. Claridge's slowly decaying. Wine outrageous in price and quality, sent round daily from the Savoy. Newspapers always late and usually deficient. Everyone justifiably depressed by the news from the East.

Company Commander's School, Scottish Command: Colinton,
Monday 5 January – Saturday 7 February 1942

I went to the course with as much relish as though I were going on leave. Colinton is an old suburb of Edinburgh, twenty minutes' car drive out. Officers were billeted about the village in varying degrees of comfort. The mess was spacious. The school was at Bonaly Tower, my great-great-grandfather's house.[1] I discovered this by recognizing the Cockburn coat of arms on the staircase.

After a few days Laura joined me and we lived mostly in Edinburgh at the Caledonian Hotel. I took a daily taxi out in the morning. For ten days we lived with a local Catholic lady named Mrs Bury in fair comfort. Food and wine were scarce in Edinburgh. One smart, crowded restaurant called Apéritif. The old

---

[1] 'In the Second World War, I was sent on a company commanders' course held in a pretty, sham castle in the outskirts of Edinburgh where I noticed the Cockburn arms in a stained-glass window. This, I learned, was Bonaly Tower, which Lord Cockburn built in emulation of Abbotsford.' *A Little Learning*, p. 11.

Café Royal with its fish bar and three tables admirable, but liable to sell out of oysters in the first hour of opening. The Caledonian Hotel execrable in every respect downstairs, but still with a flavour of better times in the bedrooms.

Michael Messer-Bennetts (now a major) was on the course, but broke his collarbone early and disappeared to hospital. The teaching staff were admirable. The Commandant, Buchanan-Smith, a former professor of agriculture, fancies himself as a personality with some reason. He quoted Descartes in his lectures and dramatized war, danger, death in a way that was needed. My syndicate instructor, Major Caulfield, a good type of regular. The course was normal: lectures, tewts, sand-table demonstrations, etc. The chief oddity was the psychoanalysts. The Army has become alarmed at the poor type of officers coming from the OCTUs, a large proportion of whom, after passing out, are sent away from their regiments as unsuitable. So, like Romans consulting Sibylline books, they decided in despair to call in psychologists. As these unhappy men had never met an officer in their lives and had no conception of what they were expected to look for, they were set loose on us with the idea that we are presumably more or less satisfactory types. I think they found us very puzzling. I was interviewed by a neurotic creature dressed as a major, who tried to impute unhappiness and frustration to me at all stages of adolescence. He had presumably been cautioned to keep off sex, as no word was said of it. He also neglected to mention religion and I gave him a little lecture about that at the end. He was chiefly surprised to learn that I chose my friends with care and drank wine because I liked it ('Most drunkards find it repulsive'). We had a series of intelligence tests, printed forms with simple questions to be answered, such as are, I believe, issued to elementary schoolchildren. On another occasion he had a magic lantern and displayed a series of blotches which we were supposed to find like objects. Most of us made a mockery of this.

Most of the instruction was based on defence of Britain and was not particularly applicable to Marines. The other students were drawn from Scottish regiments and seemed to me superior to the English. A sadist gave us a gas demonstration.

I returned to Stobs for a month of acute depression. Every day D Company gave evidence of low morale. The men mean-spirited, lazy, untruthful. My senior subaltern, Hand, a Lancashire solicitor, fat, garrulous. I found him one day carrying his equipment up to the company lines. 'Why don't you make your servant do that?' 'Well you know how it is. If you get on the wrong side of them they take it out of you in other ways.' I asked him how he felt when war broke out. 'It came as a complete surprise. I was quite happy because I thought we were so weak we should have to climb down again.' He had waited until called up and then got a commission by direct entry. Sydney Massie had committed suicide while I was in Edinburgh in the belief that he was losing his reason. The other subaltern, Gale, was garrulous and slightly touched.

Reading left to become a brigadier in charge of naval air bases, taking Collier with him. Tailyour was sent to the Third. Cutler came to take command over the head of a very decent man, Phibbs. He is a pompous booby, more human than Reading, with no interest in the war or in warfare. Penfold, the FRMO from Alex., turned up too.

Friday 13 March 1942

I was told by my NCOs that Tim Porter was taking over D Company. I asked the Commanding Officer if this was true and he said it was. I asked to see the Brigadier and saw him next day. I stated my case that I was qualified to command a company and asked to be transferred somewhere to do this. The Brigadier, to the Commanding Officer's embarrassment, was most sympathetic but said I was only suitable to command one in battle. I said I was still less qualified to be a second-in-command. Cutler made himself ridiculous by saying I could not salute and raising a frivolous point about a street-fighting exercise with B Company which he had misconceived. I wrote to the Brigadier pressing the point and dined with him on the following Tuesday. We had a long intimate conversation in which he promised me a company with the minimum of delay. He spoke of his own disappointment, the futility of the division, which was formed to gratify ambitions, the lack of ships for a serious invasion and the lack of any plan for victory, quoting a description of the elder Pitt as an inspirer of men but a futile strategist as being Winston's capacity.

Since then I served Woolley as second-in-command and respect his conscientious management of his company though finding him second-rate and boring. I have little to do, live with Laura at the Tower Hotel and take a cab in and out of camp for working hours only.

Sunday 29 March 1942

The Brigadier addressed all officers, few of whom knew him personally, and bade us a poignant farewell. He is leaving in disgrace having quarrelled with everyone. With him the last relic of the spirit of the original brigade seems to be gone. I had a letter from Bob, now in command of Special Service Brigade, and asked if there is any post for me with him. Meanwhile I am going on leave for Easter – Brains Trust at BBC, Mells, Pixton, Diana.

Leave: Wednesday 1 April–Saturday 11 April 1942

I arrived in London in a sleeping car which Laura and I found easy to get. People seem to have given up applying for them in despair. I dined that night with Diana. I arrived rather tipsy from drinking champagne at White's,[1] where

[1] Waugh was elected a member of White's on 18 March 1941; his proposer was Captain D. R. Doby and his seconder Lord Milton.

wine is now rationed – no port in the bar and only one glass in the coffee room. We dined at the Carlton Grill and she was so anxious to talk about Singapore and I about the Middle East that we both talked continuously and neither listened to the other. Wine plentiful.

Next day I was due to speak at the BBC as guest of the Brains Trust. I had refused to lunch with them first and lunched instead with Frank Pakenham. Arrived at BBC simultaneously with them. The other guests were Sir William Beveridge, don-civil servant, and an inconsiderable clergyman, the Dean of St Paul's.[1] The professionals were Campbell, vulgar, insincere, conceited, and Joad, goatlike, libidinous, garrulous.[2] I was delighted to observe the derision in which he was held by all the BBC staff. Even the electricians and photographers grimaced behind his back and the compère constantly refused to let him speak. We had some trial questions to test our voices. We sat in a windowless cabin round a small table with the microphone in the centre. The questions were too general to allow proper discussion within our limits. 'Does knowledge lead to happiness?'; 'How should you answer the child's question "Who is God?"?' Joad bounced in his chair with eagerness to speak. I missed the chance to crush him over the question of compulsory church parades. One question we had was on the subject of equal pay for soldiers and civilians. Beveridge and Campbell strongly supported it, so I suggested that if they felt like that about it they had better make a start by accepting one-third for their afternoon's work. Then there was a question about 'radio glamour', and the frightful conceit of Joad and Campbell, who assumed they were the embodiment of glamour, made me increasingly impatient so that at the end, when the machine was switched off, I raised the question again and asked whether we were all agreed to give our £20 to a war fund. The savants were aghast. Beveridge said, 'It would be a gesture.' 'No, simply a test of sincerity.'

Campbell: 'Well of course I'm ready to do what the others will but I think it would be impossible from the point of view of BBC administration.'

BBC official: 'No, not at all. Perfectly easy.'

Joad whined: 'I never gave an opinion on that question.'

'Does that mean you refuse to come in?'

'No, I will agree if the others do.'

So I left them saying, 'I am sorry you have had such an unprofitable afternoon.' But I knew they meant to go back on their word and they did. It may be added that I was obliged to waste the forenoon in going from Admiralty to War Office to RM Office to get permission to broadcast.

[1] The Very Revd. W. R. Matthews.

[2] Commander Campbell, ex-Merchant Navy, and Professor C. E. M. Joad. Both men were regular members of the Brains Trust, a panel of more or less well-known people who answered questions submitted by listeners.

An afternoon train to Frome and to Mells at 9, where I found Laura and Helen, Perdita, Katharine.

Good Friday. Mass of the Presanctified at Downside. Fasted. I had been to confession in Farm Street where a woman with blazing eyes marched up and down the aisle until ejected, saying 'Filth and poison! Filth and poison!'

Saturday Mass in Frome. Katharine brought Ronnie Knox from Downside for the weekend. The Mells visit passed happily with good food and talk, churchgoing, visits to and from Conrad and Hollises. The north court is under plough.

On Monday afternoon we went to Pixton, finding Gabriel absenting herself from farm duties. Dined off bacon. Next day Bridget left and Auberon[1] arrived with Bishop Mathew and a Scottish friend. Auberon has managed to plough both his groups and his future was widely and wildly discussed. I found Teresa, contrary to accounts, a civil, intelligent and self-possessed little girl, inarticulate and pasty-faced. I am sending her to my mother for a long visit which may, I hope, undo some of the mischief of Pixton neglect. My son was sanguine and self-confident.

On Thursday Laura and I returned to London, I to St James's, she with Teresa to Highgate. I dined that night with Frank Pakenham and Maimie Lygon, getting tipsy first at White's. Dined at Wilton's, where Marks of Buck's has taken charge, and ate £2 pot of caviare and drank black velvet. The bill was a little over £7 for the three of us, without cigars or liqueurs, or indeed anything much to eat. Then we went to Vsevolode's air raid wardens' post and drank port and sat some time in his house. On returning to St James's I was so tipsy that I supported Auberon's candidature for the club. Next day I met Laura and ate oysters with her, saw part of a film, went to tea with the Yorkes; then separated. I dined at White's and caught the evening train for Hawick, again getting a sleeper without difficulty. The happiest leave of the war.

Edinburgh, Saturday 11 April 1942

Preparing with admirable calm to move to Glasgow. The Commanding Officer told me that the Royal Marine Commando had applied for me by name and was likely to go to the Far East soon. Bob Laycock had also applied for me. Poor Cutler was greatly puzzled at this sudden demand for me. I went down to see the new brigadier, Nick Williams, who was most friendly, shooting a socialist line, deploring the Government and the Royal Marine Office. He will assist me to Laycock.

Ardrossan, Tuesday 26 May 1942

Took just a month to get to Special Service Brigade headquarters and my

[1] Auberon Herbert.

position is still irregular as I can't be appointed CSO3I until I am in the Army, and my transfer seems to be indefinitely delayed. The camp at Pollock is a housing estate cut out of a park with concrete roads and no houses. A few smoke-blackened trees remain. We had huts, without water this time, and I was obliged to sleep with the company subalterns. Glasgow was all round us, but a long and crowded train journey took us to the centre of the town. The only island of comparative decency was the Western Club, who made us temporary members. Here I spent most of my available leisure drinking vintage port.

Towards the end of my days with 5 RM I fell into a fever of claustrophobia and irrational hatred of poor Cutler. Now I have escaped I cannot remember him. My last activity with them was a combined operations landing. 5 RM were enemy. We moved out in trucks to the Troon area on Thursday afternoon and dug defensive positions against a dawn landing. At tea that evening the landing was postponed for twenty-five hours. Men slept out, I in the golf house, which alleviated our sufferings throughout the exercise. Next day we 'improved' our defensive positions, slept out, and at dawn some landing crafts appeared and from them a brigade of sullen and soaking soldiers who proceeded inland without bothering about our defences at all.

We were declared dead at 9 o'clock and went to breakfast, where Bob found me and promised to help rescue me. We then moved to another place five or six miles away and bivouacked in some woods. Next day we went into the battle again, but by now another exercise called 'Daffodil' had started between tanks and Home Guard on the same ground, so we were called off. Marched back to the beach, bivouacked again, and returned at midday to Pollock, having slept out four nights for half an hour's exercise.

On return I learned that the Adjutant-General had ordered my loan to Special Service Brigade pending transfer to Army. On Monday 11th I got a truck and came to Ardrossan where I found Bob and Philip and Peter Laycock, Peggy, —— living in surprisingly open sin with ——, a BM and his bride, an old booby full-colonel who rapidly descended to lieutenant-colonel, established in a black-market hotel called Glenfort. My work at Seafield Towers is negligible and the routine a pleasant holiday from Cutler and his Marines.

End of May Miss Virginia Cowles came, as 'special assistant' of the American ambassador, to visit the brigade. I had to arrange her programme and laid on a number of amusements for her. She played the part of admiring female with great astuteness. She has seen more action than most of our Commandos but she treated them with 'Oh you great strong man how brave you must be. We would be scared stiff,' which went down well. Bob we think failed to sleep with her.

My daughter Margaret was born about 11th or 12th June. I arrived on

Saturday morning at Pixton and found Laura very well and the asparagus in season. I had meant to take my ten days' leave, but was recalled for a course of photographic interpretation which I had put in for and been told was full.

The course is at Matlock, five weeks beginning 16th. We live in Intelligence Training Centre where other courses are in progress, in a huge hydro called Smedleys. The atmosphere is very different from the company commanders' course at Edinburgh. The student officers are Jews and Canadians, mostly of a very half-baked kind and the instructors like well-meaning schoolmasters. No suggestion of a military establishment. No orders are given. 'I say, would you mind sort of getting round.' The opening address was given by the vice-commandant, Casson,[1] a Hellenic cruising don. He spoke in a way to induce the greatest priggishness in any of his hearers who took him seriously, saying how it was the duty of intelligence officers to educate their commanders, etc. He gave some instances of disasters arising from the neglect of intelligence and quoted Bob's attack on Rommel as an example. 'Then there was that raid when Roger Keyes's son was killed. All very gallant and quite useless. *We* knew perfectly well Rommel was away in Rome, but did anyone trouble to consult us? No. So young Keyes's life was thrown away.' This to an audience of very junior officers and NCOs. At question-time I asked him about this raid and was impolitely answered. He then made a wholly irrelevant attack on Commando security. So I reported the matter to Bob who called for a special report and is going to have an inquiry, which may be fun.

My own course consists of peering into stereoscopes for some hours a day and instruction from a glib Jew and a shy schoolmaster – both quite inoffensive.

Messing is very poor and the place too crowded. The directing staff live apart from students. It is altogether less good than Colinton.

Tom Driberg has been elected Independent Member for Maldon by a large majority. The newspapers have behaved very curiously over this by-election, giving no news of what any of the candidates are saying. In recording the result they simply describe him as a journalist and a churchwarden, which gives a very imperfect picture of that sinister character.

Graham Eyres-Monsell is an instructor here. I have also taken up with a jagger named David Elias and a busted-flush oil and secret service man called Goodwill who was in charge of all intelligence in the Balkans and did so badly that they have put him on to teach others. He is very likeable. The students are quite without interest. Matlock Bath has a series of 'Lovers' Walks', cairns and petrified bowler hats. The custodian of the petrified bowlers told me, with surprise that I should not know, that they found a ready market among 'estates' where he said they adorned garden walls.

[1] Stanley Casson, 1889–1944; reader in classical archaeology at Oxford.

At dinner I talked to an officer about Army forms and said it would be easier to remember them by their names than their numbers. 'At least,' I said, 'I find it easier.'

'Ah, there you introduce the personal equation.'

'?'

'With better educated officers the difficulty wouldn't arise.'

'Educated?'

'Yes. I mean with experience as clerks.'

Laura joined me in the third week and I went to live out, illicitly, at the new Bath Hotel. We led a pleasant, quiet life. We visited Chatsworth with Anne Hunloke,[1] dined at the widow Rangers [?], and got tight there. The course ended 23 July. My interest slackened towards the end. Casson was had up to London and reprimanded for his remarks about the Rommel raid and ordered to withdraw the statement, which he did astutely so that no one in his audience – except those I had warned to expect it – could have noticed.

There was an unhappy man named White, typical of Intelligence Corps, with whom I shared a room at Matlock. He had just returned from a long spell as censor at Gibraltar where he was sent, he believed, because he was a Protestant and the Intelligence Corps was run by Roman Catholics. He unwrapped his chocolate so that the mice might eat it without disturbing me. He had arranged to go on leave to Nottingham to sleep with a barmaid and, after eagerly looking forward to it, gave it up because, after surmounting a few tiny difficulties about being duty officer, he found he had forgotten to put his name in the book. 'It's the last straw,' he said, and stayed at home.

After the course I came on a week's leave which has been prolonged to over a fortnight by my taking up a little work at CCO's[2] office. I met Head in Marks's fish-bar and he called me in to find a special training area. This meant a visit to ISTU at Oxford. I also visited CIU at Medmenham. I found an office where father and son worked together, the son as group captain and the father as squadron leader. CCO's office full of funny faces including Bennett and Zuckerman[3] of the Spearman circle.

A funny interview with Casa Maury. 'Why do you particularly prefer this operation, sir?' 'It is quite captivating. The ISD report gives the most enchanting details of just who sleeps with whom.' Then in front of some serious staff officers he fell into gossip about the Abdys.

Laura and I gave an expensive dinner party to ill-assorted friends. We spent a great deal of money. Laura has become perceptibly more luxurious since the austerity regime.

Randolph returned in a straight waistcoat full of exuberant confidence in

---

[1] Lady Anne Hunloke, sister of the 10th Duke of Devonshire, owner of Chatsworth.

[2] Chief of Combined Operations.

[3] Basil Bennett; and Solly Zuckerman (later Chief Scientific Adviser to the government).

American production. It is a bitter thing for Pamela[1] to have him speaking of three months' leave of absence to devote himself to politics. She hates him so much she can't be in a room with him. Lord Digby was in conference with her yesterday, I suppose urging her to bear her burden bravely. David's[2] prodigies of courage become more legendary every day. Randolph had a run with him to Benghazi. A man has bicycled to Ardrossan to teach us how to eat grass.

I went to Bognor for a night and fell out as usual with Duff.[3] Since then he has been spreading it about that I am pro-Nazi. I told him I could see little difference between Hitler's new order and Virgil's idea of the Roman Empire. White's closed on August 1st. I miss it sadly.

Ardrossan, Thursday 27 August 1942

I finally returned to Ardrossan by air with Phil and Bob on 24th. During the last week in London there was nothing at all to do. On the day after Laura left I had a hard day's drinking, starting with a cocktail party in Vsevolode's, then luncheon at St James's with Phil. We drank port and brandy until 6, then we went to cocktails with Maimie, then with Randolph, and finally dinner at the Ritz with Angie and Bob,[4] Pamela, Randolph and his sister Sarah.[5] From that evening I began to trace a decline in my position in Bob's esteem. The next ten days I wandered aimlessly in the triangle Ritz, St James's, Claridge's, spending most of the time with Randolph or Phil. Finally I moved into Montpelier Walk and stayed with Maimie.

I first heard of the Dieppe raid on the morning after it was mounted, arriving at the St James's for breakfast to be greeted by the porter with, 'We thought you would be in Dieppe, sir.' Fragments of news came out during that day and the day after, 21st August. Saw the film at Combined Operations Club and heard a fairly full account of the operation from Ian Collins. Shimi Lovat[6] did brilliantly, the only wholly successful part of the raid. B Commando ran into E-boats on the way to the beach and were dispersed. Peter Young landed with twenty headquarter details and carried on the battle ashore, sniping the battery for two or three hours. The Canadians were stuck on their beaches, the tanks were a failure, and the Royal Marine Commando was put in to reinforce failure. Titch Houghton, Picton-Philips and Billy and Bobby Park-Smith

[1] The Hon. Pamela Digby married Randolph Churchill in 1939; the marriage was dissolved in 1946.

[2] David Stirling's. He was operating behind enemy lines in North Africa with the Long Range Desert Group.

[3] Duff Cooper.

[4] Laycock.

[5] Sarah Churchill.

[6] Lord Lovat, son of the Lovat who raised the Lovat Scouts in the Boer War; in 1943, as deputy commander, Special Service Brigade, he was later instrumental in the removal of Waugh from Combined Operations.

among the dead. The public, to judge by the papers, are a little puzzled to know whether the raid confirms the practicability of the Second Front or the reverse.

I returned to Ardrossan to find headquarters indignant that they had not been employed in the raid. Bill Barkworth has returned from the Middle East and is unemployed. Basil Bennett is taking over camp commandant; the Q side has proliferated with Hunt as DAAG and DAQMG with numerous subordinates. I occasionally hear him ordering about three times as much equipment as is needed. I suppose that that is being done all over the country to the great detriment of production. We now have a mess at the Kilmany Hotel for Brian, Basil, Bill, Bob, Phil[1] and myself, and play poker dice for low stakes. Maimie had a fair and circus on Hampstead Heath in aid of Yugoslavia. She has no means of using the money she raises so lavishly. The circus, when I went with Coote and my godson Jonathan Guinness,[2] a personable child, was a success in so far as Maimie sold the tickets twice over and indignant crowds were turned away.

This headquarters had now had all its functions usurped by CO Headquarters, and exists, as I see it, simply to wait until Bob is made a force commander. That is certain to happen before the end of the war. Meanwhile I can wait more patiently than most.

Yesterday Bob and Phil returned to London.

Trouble at Kilmany Hotel. First Katie the crazy Irish maidservant gave notice. Then Miss Sneddon the manageress said that she wished us to move out of our private room into the main dining-room. Pressed for a reason she said the other guests objected; further pressed, she said Mrs Fawcett objected. Mrs Fawcett, by reason of being the wife of the manager of the local chemical works, is the first lady in Ardrossan; she thinks that in seclusion we eat more heavily than she. Brian interviewed Mr Leahy, the ex-manager, and it was agreed that we stayed in our room. Father Basil propounded a theory that English soldiers surrender in battle because they fear hell. He found no support for this theory.

Friday 28 August 1942

It is believed that Katie inflamed Mrs Fawcett by saying 'It's Government House now,' referring to our occupation. A chaplain is trying to take my servant, Hall. I have spent the day in complete idleness, having no share in or knowledge of the current operations.

Monday 14 September 1942

Ten days at Ardrossan playing dice and drinking a great deal.

[1] Brian Franks, Basil Bennett, William (Bill) Stirling, Robert Laycock, Philip Dunne.
[2] Son of the Hon. Diana and the Hon. Bryan Guinness.

Brigade headquarters is split, one half going under command Guards Brigade with Glendinning.

Monday 28 September 1942

Most of the brigade staff have gone away to be experimented on by Dr Zuckerman with a new stimulant. (This was good cover for a projected operation: EW, 22 Oct.) I have spent the day in the Brigade Major's chair but have had little more to do than in the Intelligence Room. I mainly open the letters and send them on to DAQMG. One or two I address to myself, post them in the OUT tray; they disappear for about three hours into the 'Central Registry' and return to the IN tray. I write a letter and put it in the OUT tray; many hours later it comes back typed; I sign it and put it into OUT: it then disappears forever and much, much later the office addressed gets it in an IN tray, whence it goes to a Central Registry and so on.

On 14th we went to London by the night train. I met Laura and we spent the night at the Hyde Park Hotel in the suite where the 'Mayfair men' attacked M. Bellinger [?]. Next day Bob, Brian and I flew to the Isle of Wight and spent the day with the Marines, slept at Portsmouth, saw *Victory*, next day drove to see 12 Commando and Bob and I went to Diana's[1] at Bognor for the night. Conrad was there. 18th we visited 3 Commando and drove back to London. I slept at Brian's flat. 19th spent all day at White's and took night train to Glasgow. Embarked on yacht *Sister Anne* and had a very rough trip to the Depot with Air Vice Marshal Robb and General Haydon. All were sick except Bob. A fine series of exercises and demonstrations by the passing-out squad of police recruits. Bullets whistling everywhere. They had killed a man two days earlier. It was less remarkable than a street-fighting demonstration we saw some days earlier in Glasgow, when 6 Commando fought in a populated area and put a smoke bomb through a bakery window. It was a great change from the enormous precautions of Bisley in 1940. The local laird, Cameron of Lochiel, turned up draped in tartan and wanted to take the general salute on the grounds that he represented the King in those parts. There was a squat, silent, Communist journalist with a pasty mongol face and boils. He kept asking when we were going to open the Second Front. Another rough voyage but no one sick this time.

Friday 24th. We went to visit 1 Commando at Dundee. Bob and I stopped the night at Keir[2] – a great palace with massive Italian terraces, too much shiny white paint, some splendid pictures mostly Spanish, and a chapel by Boris Anrep. The greater part of the house was a hospital. Bill's wife is extremely pretty and self-conscious and amorous to Bill. When Bob and I arrived we were

---

[1] Lady Diana Cooper's.
[2] Keir, Dunblane, Perthshire: William (Bill) Stirling's house.

shown into her where she sat over a dead fire in a semi-circular sitting-room. She leapt like a deer, said, 'Oh. I don't know where Bill is. He's always disappearing when strangers arrive,' and fled from the room. Later she played poker dice, wholly absorbed in Bill, and won consistently. Mrs Stirling full of charm and humour. They have heard no news of David; we had heard, but from the doubtful source of Randolph, that he was missing after the Benghazi raid. We held our peace. Francis Howard is missing from a small boat raid in which the commanding officer was killed.

Basil Bennett[1] brought large quantities of liquor for us. I think we are the only mess in Europe which constantly drinks claret, port and brandy at dinner.

Honesty of brother officers. I went to Matlock leaving a fine library of brand-new books chosen for me by Cyril Connolly, few of which I had had time to read. When I can back over half had been stolen.

Assault Intelligence Unit now being formed, vaguely under our command, takes the only interesting tasks which the 1 section of the brigade might have done. Bill Barkworth has gone to it but remains with us in a highly nervous state.

Americans will take instruction only from Commando officers. They are very unsoldierly and have peculiar names.

Sherborne, 12 October 1942

At the end of September Bob went to London for Richard Sykes's wedding. Two-thirds of headquarters went to a course to try out a secret stimulant which was treated with fantastic secrecy. On the Wednesday, about October 1st, Bob sent a message that he was not returning. Later, on the scrambler, he gave orders for a move. All the hysteria of a 'flap' broke out. I remember my first experience of it at Bisley and how stimulating it was. Now, after so many, I suffer nothing but boredom. For five hours Roger Wakefield and Colonel Atkinson ran about the office like two hens.

Presently it was disclosed that our move was to Sherborne so I went there ahead of the main party on 5th October. Passing through London I found Randolph preparing a speech on Army reform for a secret session and gave him notes recommending virtually the abolition of conscription. Sherborne is fine. We use the castle for headquarters. After two or three oppressive and expensive days at the Digby I moved to lodgings and Laura joined me. Jacob Astor is here with a detachment of his Phantoms. Various odd bodies get attached to us. I made up my mind that this is an army deception exercise to take their minds off the big operation. This is confirmed by Bob briefing us for the most futile and fantastic operation imaginable yesterday, 11 October.

[1] Later a close friend of Waugh. See Appendix of Names, p. 794.

October 1942

The operation was cancelled. Whether it was ever seriously projected I do not know but believe not. Brigade headquarters in the Rectory, Closworth, the house of the Rev. Neate and his bearded wife. An enchanting couple. He was convinced the Germans would land in his garden and wanted more ammunition. His wife wanted petrol. 'They think the world of that' – showing features of the church. 'They' was 'a professor of London.' 'Can any of you fellows mend an old pump? Mrs Neate's old pump wants mending.' (Her heart.) We all caught fleas in his outhouse. After sitting up all night Bob and I went to luncheon with Nell and Harry[1] at Emshot and drank a great deal of wine. I saw myself in a mirror afterwards, like a red lacquer Chinese dragon, and saw how I shall look when I die.

Sharp and triumphant row with Shimi on a matter of maps.

Laura returned to Pixton 17th. Basil Bennett came to live at Mrs Maxwell's.

I am reading what I take to be one of the vulgarest books written – a life of Landor of all subjects. I wrote a review of Graham Greene for the *Spectator* and meditate starting a novel. I have reached my last Havana cigars – fifty left in reserve. And my last case of claret. I am still being paid as lieutenant – cannot get captain's pay or staff pay. I suppose it will come one day.

Brigade headquarters as usual in trouble with hotels. Bob, Nell, Daphne Weymouth, Phil, etc., arrested in Plume of Feathers for drinking after hours. They moved from Digby to Plume of Feathers who promptly reported the latter hotel for illicit meat ration. They are pawns in some civic chess game – no doubt connected with the Rotarians.

Bob gave a conference to the troop leaders on the exercise, warning them that their training was elementary and their discipline weak, and threatening to disband them. Where he excels and commands all my admiration is that he is able to say this without a sting, so that he rouses no resentment. If I did it I should be sarcastic and so, with people like that, do no good at all but only harm.

Saturday 24 October 1942

Brian, Basil and I, also Tom Churchill and Johnny Atkinson went to umpire a field day at Sherborne School. The exercise, needless to say, was in withdrawal; the boys correspondingly pusillanimous and protection-minded. I spoke to some, asking what regiments they hoped to join; they all wanted to be government chemists or public health officers. The exercise dragged on without incident until nightfall, when all the umpires quietly slipped away to their dinners. Basil and I drank a bottle of Dows 1920 before dinner and another after it. Then we remembered we had been asked to 'sandwiches and

[1] Lord and Lady Stavordale.

beer' with Colonel Randolph the Commanding Officer. We found him sitting behind mountains of food none of which, having cigars in our mouths, we attempted to eat. I was full enough of wine to believe the evening a success but the general opinion is the reverse.

Sunday 25 October 1942

Brian and I went to spend the day with Nell and Harry at Emshot. Phil and Daphne already there. A beautiful day of overeating and overdrinking. In the afternoon we went to Melbury. That evening I was very drunk indeed and enjoyed myself enormously. When I left the house at about 2 I fell down some steps. Later I woke Basil up and plagued him for about an hour. In the evening I had orders to come to London. Sergeant O'Brien of 12 Commando just returned to England from Norway after a successful little raid.

London, Monday 26 October 1942

Called at 6.30. Still very confused with drink and smelling of 'orange gin'. Drove as far as Camberley in a stupor where we had a collision which destroyed the car. Got a lift to Combined Operations HQ where I arrived four hours late where they said O'Brien was still in Stockholm. Went to see Maimie and, in a daze, walked round exhibition. Oysters at Wilton's, then to Combined Operations HQ where O'Brien had been caught. Interview in a daze. Still in a daze to White's, Blondie's,[1] White's and Blondie's where I slept. Dined with Bill Stirling and intelligence experts. Sat up late with Blondie.

Sherborne, Tuesday 27 October 1942

Returned to Sherborne in good humour.

Wednesday 28 October 1942

My 39th birthday. A good year. I have begotten a fine daughter, published a successful book,[2] drunk 300 bottles of wine and smoked 300 or more Havana cigars. I have got back to soldiering among friends. This time last year I was on my way to Hawick to join 5 RM. I get steadily worse as a soldier with the passage of time, but more patient and humble – as far as soldiering is concerned. I have about £900 in hand and no grave debts except to the Government; health excellent except when impaired by wine; a wife I love, agreeable work in surroundings of great beauty. Well that is as much as one can hope for.

Saturday 20 March 1943

A calm cold day, misty at early morning and evening but full of brilliant sun at midday. Almond, daffodil, all the flowers of April in bloom and the

[1] 'Blondie', like 'Mamie', was a nickname for Lady Mary Lygon.
[2] *Put Out More Flags*

hedgerows coming into leaf. In my heart winter, born of idleness, loneliness, and a heavy cold in the head. It has been a drab week with Bob, Brian, Phil and Angie away and the office work going on in corners. Myself without any task except to open the letters and in a kind of condition of Coventry. The week before – at Weymouth with Laura and, at the weekend, on exercise – was full of incident, and last week seemed the drearier in contrast.

Domestic difficulties at Westbridge House, aggravated by Basil's and my failure to eat sheep's hearts on Wednesday evening. On Thursday Mrs Maxwell at her drawing-room window calling that she would no longer feed us; we must dine out. Basil for some time has been showing unreasonable despair saying, 'I must chuck it. We can't go on here. I have become a marionette. You make me do the most extraordinary things. I have never twiddled clocks anywhere else. I am going mad. Why should I pay that ridiculous woman for telephone calls? I am going to leave the Army. You want to go to the snake-house. I shall live at Weymouth. It's all over with us here.' And so on at length. We discussed the situation and made out a list of minimum demands on which to base a concordat. We consented to occasional fish dinners and vegetable broth, demanded the unrestricted use of the bathroom, and bread-and-cheese luncheons in the billet. Basil took on him to negotiate the treaty, funked it, and left everything undecided. On the night Mrs Maxwell said we could not dine, we induced Louie to give us fish cakes, and a dish of eggs and minced meat which was better than could be got in London. It is the belief of our servants that Louie is trying to drive us out in revenge for the locking up of our gin to which she has recently become addicted. But there is an artistic decency about the woman which, once she is at the range, prevents her from cooking badly.

Meanwhile we drove to Purse Caundle to see Aunt Vera's house[1] which is spacious and full of splendid furniture. We intend to move there.

Basil went to London for the weekend leaving me alone. After dinner I drank Crofts 1927, which is sweet and heady after the Dows 1912, and finished *The Man who was Thursday* which I had not read since Lancing days. It is painful to realize that Chesterton introduced 'the Century of the Common Man'. It was easy in 1908 to believe in the basic wisdom and wholesomeness of the common man and to think all wrongheadedness confined to prigs and cranks. It is harder now after the stampede of silliness and vice in half Christendom.

Sunday 21 March 1943

A night disturbed by a sort of nightmare that is becoming more frequent

---

[1] Lady Victoria Herbert's house: The Manor House, Purse Caundle. Lady Victoria was the mutual aunt (b. 1874) of both Waugh's wives who thought she had 'seen the last of that young man' in 1929.

with me and I am inclined to believe is peculiar to myself. Dreams of unendurable boredom – of reading page after page of dullness, of being told endless, pointless jokes, of sitting through cinema films devoid of interest.

After Mass to the Castle,[1] where I found nothing for me to do. Luncheon alone with Roger at the Plume of Feathers. At 9 o'clock the Prime Minister spoke on the wireless in order to assure people that he was not oblivious of the problems of peace. He was quieter in tone than usual and Mrs Maxwell thought him depressing.

Monday 22 March 1943

A day of ineffable boredom ending pleasantly in a carouse. Basil and I got drunk and went over to call on Bob and Phil just back from London. On the way home we ran into a pile of stones and incapacitated the car.

Tuesday 23 March 1943

Headache. Basil and I drinking gin and tonic by 10.30. Two sharp blows to professional pride in finding Churchill[2] sent to Shetlands to brief Fynn for the operations and John Selwyn appointed assistant brigade major with hints that he will take over in near future when Brian is to go away. Later in the morning Bob explained to me that I am so unpopular as to be unemployable. My future very uncertain. The first seed of the trouble was my telling Churchill weeks ago that I did not think there was any function for intelligence officers in the brigade. This, of course, is the worst blasphemy to staff officers of his type whose entire life is built up round the system and emphasizing the importance of their appointments. It is their object to make work for themselves, if possible so much that it justifies the appointment of a subordinate and their own promotion. It is not the military system to see where there is work that needs doing and to send someone to do it, but to start with the men and try and find something for them to do. Consequently there is a shortage of manpower in one quarter, and idleness, or worse still unnecessary work, in another. There was not time to say this yesterday. I hope to today.

Bob, Phil, Brian off to Torquay. Basil and I went to Purse Caundle again where we found nothing but welcome and kindness. Stopped to eat eggs with Angie and then home.

Wednesday 24 March 1943

A summons to Combined Operations HQ, to write a 'personality handout' for USA about Hilary Saunders[3] the recorder. A most singular request.

---

[1] Sherborne Castle, the unit's HQ.

[2] Tom Churchill, a brother officer.

[3] Hilary St George Saunders, 1898–1951; secretariat, League of Nations, 1930–37; during the war, wrote official publications; librarian, House of Commons, 1946–50.

London, Thursday 25 March 1943

To London by the 8.45 train. Went to Nancy's bookshop[1] where I was told that it is now a daily occurrence for enormous majors in the Foot Guards to come in and ask for the works of sixteenth-century Spanish mystics. At White's I met Ran Antrim and Ed Stanley and with them went to luncheon with John Sutro at the Bagatelle. After luncheon to Combined Operations HQ where I was first interviewed by Col. Neville who assured me that it was at the CCO's request, not the recorder's, that I was to write the 'personality handout'. This document apparently is sent out with the American Book of the Month. Recorder's very flat pamphlet *Combined Operations* is to be Book of the Month. He was greatly embarrassed, or professed to be, by the business. I had my hair cut at Trumper's and returned to White's to drink a bottle of champagne with Brian; then to Montpelier Row to dine and sleep with Maimie and Vsevolode.

Sherborne Friday 26 March 1943

In the morning to Combined Operations HQ again to get some information about 62 Commando's future operations. I saw the new chief intelligence officer and told him I thought intelligence officers in the Special Service Brigade quite redundant. Oysters with Perry Brownlow, luncheon at White's with Vsevolode, 2.50 train back in which I stood as far as Andover. Dined at Westbridge. After dinner summoned to Milborne Port to drive tart to dance.

Saturday 27 March 1943

Wrote praise of Saunders. Laura came to take Basil's place at Westbridge House, looking fifteen years old and very grubby. She spent the weekend with me and left early on Monday morning.

Monday 29 March 1943

I was busy all day reducing the verbosity of the proposed reorganization of the Special Service Brigade (which puts us nearer an infantry division, in form, with advancement for Shimi, and makes brigade HQ static and political, or so it seems). On Monday we dined with Angie and on Tuesday we drank port at home. The news from Tunis seems good. A sharp rebuff from the solicitors of the tenants of Purse Caundle.

In our cups Basil and I found a drawerful of letters and photographs belonging to the Maxwell children and, reading Margaret's schoolgirl diary, were struck with shame and put it away. This morning, sober, we regretted the generosity of the evening before.

Roger has added to the curious legends of his career by claiming to have been

---

[1] The Hon. Nancy (née Mitford) Rodd worked in Heywood Hill's bookshop in Curzon Street, Mayfair.

trained as a spy and once to have got as far as embarking in a canoe to land as an agent, but was recalled at the last moment on the grounds that he would always look an Englishman. This morning gazing from his window at a leafless flowering almond, he said, 'I have planted three double cherries like at at home.' 'But that's an almond tree, Roger.' A long scrutiny. 'Yes I see now the leaves are much coarser.'

Wednesday 31 March 1943

We went to see Lady Victoria. She said, among other things, 'I wish dear Mr Barker (of Winkworths) were still alive. He was so very kind – looked like a fox. There is a man there *called* Mr Fox but I think you had better see Mr Bush as he knows all about it.' She had a palsied lady's maid as her woman of business: 'She is *so* clever. Such a head for affairs.'

London, Thursday 1 April – Tuesday 6 April 1943

In London working on 'Operation Coughdrop', which, as fresh intelligence came in, seemed less practicable. I applied for the appointment of force commander, feeling it dishonourable to brief people for a task one was not sharing, but I was ridiculed as too old for parachuting. The matter is not yet decided.

I stayed a night at the Hyde Park Hotel and then moved to Maimie and Vsevolode. I visited my mother on her birthday and found her alert and more cheerful now that her cook has come back and relieved her of continuous duty by my father's side. He is infirm and very deaf; his face seems fallen away at the side as though he had had a stroke. I am told that is not the case. I conversed with him by writing my replies on a sheet of paper and this seemed to cause him amusement.

Hubert is lying ill at Phyllis's house with what the lower classes call palpitations. Maimie says he will die in two years, but when I saw him he was talking vigorously about Renaissance history.

Meals at White's, Buck's, the Savoy, Ivy, Combined Operations HQ Club, and at Maimie's. Plenty to eat and still some wine at a price. Maimie had a dinner party for a merchant prince from whom they seek some commercial advantage, his nymphomaniac wife, and the mistress of the King of Greece.

I returned to find Basil had left for Scotland. Luckily Laura was free to come so she arrived today.

Sherborne, Wednesday 7 April 1943

Laura arrived looking very plain and dirty but in good spirits.

Thursday 8 April 1943

It was learned that Bob proposes establishing an advanced HQ in Scotland, leaving Shimi to see to Sherborne. I see little room for myself in this arrangement and decided to go to London as Bob's representative at Combined Operations HQ. Mrs Maxwell has a cage full of chickens to whom she addresses herself at length in nauseating terms. Slept very badly.

Friday 9 April 1943

A day of complete idleness with good news in the papers and general uncertainty here of our future use. Bob returned late at night.

London, Friday 16 April 1943

Three unusually active days in London combined with an austerity regime self-imposed in the hope of getting into air-bearable condition. I came to London on the 12th, leaving Sherborne with all gear and the expectation of not returning. Bob left on leave in a hurry, leaving 'Coughdrop' and numerous minor matters in my hands. There is a difficulty about the size of Bob's proposed advanced HQ. I wanted, heaven knows why, to go to the Virgil Society opening meeting, failed, and failed for a long time to find Douglas[1] but eventually dined with him at White's and returned to the penitential ant-heap[2] where he lives, and where he put me up for three nights before moving to Maimie's. My notes on what I have done during these days show that most of my work has been unnecessary, but it has prevented me sleeping, since Sherborne accustomed me to undisturbed repose during the day. The sort of thing that happens is that someone telephones and says can he come and see me right away. I say yes. Nothing more happens. Or a young woman brings in a technical pamphlet.

'I was told to show you this.'

'Are you sure it's meant for me?'

'Oh yes sir.'

'Right, put it down and I'll look at it.'

'Oh I can't do that.' Takes it away again. I believe I am more efficient than most here; that is because it is new to me. Lushington is consistently helpful. I have dined with Douglas and Mia and with Eddie Sackville-West.

I said to Hall at Park West, 'This is the kind of place the planners will make us live in after the war.' 'Oh, sir, won't there be gardens between the blocks?' 'No, Hall. No gardens.'

Everyone I meet is despondent of the future and unduly hopeful about the immediate battles, except Douglas who is also hopeful of the future and a few knowledgeable soldiers who are despondent of the battles. 'Monty' has been making himself intolerable in the papers.

---

[1] Douglas Woodruff.
[2] Park West residential flats in the Edgware Road, near Marble Arch.

Thursday 22 April 1943

I find the work at Combined Operations HQ increasingly fatiguing. Last night on returning to Maimie and finding Prince Bernhard of the Netherlands, Chips Channon, and others all chattering to the dogs in so small a room I felt near collapse; and later, dining with more people talking French in a smaller room at Mrs Chichester's, I had to leave and go home alone and early to bed.

General Haydon shows himself ill-intentioned. Everyone here sees everything through frosted glass and hears through stuffing, so that they never quite get the point of what is said or done and write minutes to each other always just off the point. Haydon through overwork is the worst at this, and then falls into a temper.

The operation I am engaged on looks less probable daily as more and more forbidding intelligence comes in. An immensely secretive humbug from MI9 came and went off with the draft plan and left it in a taxi-cab. Meanwhile heroic Mickey Rooney is at work training his detachment.

Bob had a birthday party, all his family; apart from that I have had a Lenten time lunching most days on sandwiches at the office.

Good Friday, 1943

Having it at some stage fixed in my mind that Easter was the 24th, I have been led into a series of painful mistakes – one of which resulted in Rooney's party travelling to Ringway on the wrong date and starting their co-operation with the Air Force on the unhappiest basis. I managed to get to Communion on Thursday morning and to the last half of Tenebrae on Friday.

Everyone is leaving the office for Easter.

Saturday 15 May 1943

After days of rain, brilliant summer. London shabbier and shoddier in the sunlight than in shadow. The crowds uglier and more aimless, horrible groups of soldiers in shabby battledress with their necks open, their caps off or at extravagant angles, hands in pockets, cigarettes in the sides of their mouths, lounging about with girls in trousers and high heels and filmstar coiffures. I never saw so many really ugly girls making themselves conspicuous. Restaurants crowded; one is jostled by polyglot strangers, starved, poisoned, and cheated by the management; theatres at an early hour of the afternoon when it is unnatural and inconvenient to go; even so they are all crowded.

Laura has made two visits to London – one when Maimie and Vsevolode left the house for us, one at the Hyde Park Hotel. She is in good looks and great good health.

Planning and training for Rooney's operation still goes on as if it were to be mounted – though most of us are decided against it, I have the fear that we may suddenly find it approved by the Chief of Staff.

Bob has been occupied with his reorganization which seems to involve enormous calculations – I don't know why. He was due to sail to North Africa the day after tomorrow taking everyone except me, who was to follow on. Now the move has been suddenly postponed.

The victory in North Africa took us by surprise. Our own soldiers just back from there said it would be a long campaign. English and American newspapers studiously avoid all mention of the other's share in the battle.

I dined with Henriques to celebrate the publication of his unreadable book.[1] Good food, bad company. I have come to prefer it that way, rather than bad food and good company. J. B. Priestley, pathetically vain, jealous even of Noel Coward, trying, unsuccessfully in my presence, to lead the conversation to higher matters. He sees himself as a man of great responsibility as the epitome of the Common Man. A vulgar fellow called Frere,[2] a friend of Alec's, and a pert wife I used to know under the name of Pat Wallace.

Henriques has now gone, like so many others, to North Africa, so that all my efforts to be agreeable to him produce no tangible advantage at this HQ.

A curious dinner party with the Sea Lords, Diana, Emerald,[3] Crinks Johnstone, given by Lord Queensberry. Emerald saying to Sir Dudley Pound, 'Evelyn here is with Dicky[4] planning the Second Front.'

The Poles are generally blamed for minding about the murder of 8,000-odd officers by the Russians.

Last night I returned to Maimie to find a dinner party. A Serbian diplomat told with great drollness the story of a Mr Brown, a Moravian minister of religion, who has been attached to the Serbian Legation since 1916.

Shimi has alienated the affections of the entire brigade by a series of astoundingly caddish actions.

Basil has raised a great stir by launching the Commando Benevolent Fund without consulting the public relations department here. Also by going about the Stock Exchange in his cups and telling a totally false tale of a legless officer who was given 28s a week pension. The Lord Mayor of London took a prominent part in the business.

I see myself faced with extreme penury if I am obliged to live much longer in London.

The last entry proved erroneous. I got my passbook and found myself to be buoyantly solvent. Accordingly I invited Laura to London and moved with her to the Hyde Park Hotel on May 22. We gave a small, expensive, and not very

---

[1] Robert Henriques. His 'unreadable book' was *Captain Smith & Company*.

[2] A. S. Frere, publisher.

[3] Lady Cunard.

[4] Lord Louis Mountbatten, chief of Combined Operations.

luxurious dinner party at the Savoy – Maimie and Vsevolode, Liz and Raimund just back from America, Ran Antrim, Nancy Rodd.

I lunched with CCO,[1] arrived rather tipsy, found the house a nest of Communists and behaved rather badly.

I found my work more and more exhausting so demanded leave which was grudgingly given after I had made Shimi send a man to my relief. Bob went to Scotland on 28th so that I had no friends in London of the brigade. I have taken Verschoyle's[2] flat in St James's Place for two months.

On 29th I went to Campion Hall where D'Arcy was having his annual dinner. Ned Lutyens[3] very gaga, making his old puns and obscenities but without gusto or relevance; David Cecil. Frank, who was coming, went to speak to Labour men in the north instead. My visit coincided with Ronnie Knox, who gave a brilliant conference next day at the Old Palace, every word of which seemed directed at myself. I called on Rachel, lunched with Maurice at Wadham, went for a walk with Ronnie,[4] dined at Campion with John Rothenstein.

Hall[5] had come with me and I had a scholastic detailed as his guide to show him the colleges. He asked for instruction about the Faith.

Monday 31 May 1943

Came to Pixton by a grossly crowded train and spend the time resting, so far as the habits of the household allow.

My leave was on the whole very disappointing. The best part of it was the exhilarating twenty-four hours between leaving Combined Operations HQ and setting out for Oxford. I spent the last weekend at Mells and returned to London to the flat in St James's Place I had taken from Verschoyle. I found that I had inherited a feud with the management which resulted in my getting no breakfast the first day and in wasting many hours with lawyers before the thing was settled. The flat is quiet but feminine in character and too small for two.

Wednesday 9 June 1943

Peters told me that Alexander Korda has made a proposal which should solve all peacetime difficulties of income, if conditions allow of anyone's

---

[1] Lord Louis Mountbatten.

[2] Derek Verschoyle. Literary figure, formerly on the *Spectator*, who had been a boy at Arnold House school when Waugh was a master.

[3] Sir Edwin Luytens (1869–1944), architect. He designed St Jude's church, Hampstead Garden Suburb, which Waugh attended as a boy.

[4] Rachel Cecil, Lord David Cecil's wife; Maurice Bowra; Ronald Knox.

[5] Waugh's soldier-servant.

difficulties being solved – a contract of ten weeks' work a year at £200 a week. That should leave me leisure in the rest of the year to write exactly as I please on what I please. My first thought, however, was that inflation may make £200 a week negligible.

I read a report in the *New Statesman* of an interview with returned Serbian guerillas – anti-Mihailović propaganda. It read like an official interview and my first thought was, 'How has this been allowed to appear?' That, on second thoughts, showed how used one has become to governmental tyranny.

On July 24 my father died and brigade HQ left London for 'Operation Husky'. It was an unfortunate coincidence as I was distracted from one by the other. I was angry with Bob for leaving me behind so easily. My father died with disconcerting suddenness. I spent most of the next few days at Highgate. The funeral was on 27th at Hampstead. I spent some weary hours going through my father's papers and destroying letters. He kept up a large correspondence with very dull people. My mother's mind seems clouded by the business. Laura and I had Bron brought up to interest her.

Shimi has made a successful and dastardly attack on John Selwyn; also an attempt on me to post me to the Depot, which still hangs in the balance. Probable sailing date August 7th to 10th. My chief pleasure in the last few days has been having some bookplates engraved by an aged but brilliant engraver called Osmond.

Inserted in the diary at this point is a series of letters bearing on Waugh's forced resignation from the Special Service Brigade.

CONFIDENTIAL

8 May 1943

To: The Deputy Commander
      Special Service Brigade
        SPECIAL SERVICE BRIGADE LIAISON OFFICER AT COHQ
It is my intention that Capt Waugh shall join 'HUSKY' Force in North Africa as soon as it can be arranged. I am therefore appointing Capt Bray to take his place. This officer will require far closer acquaintance than he has at present with the Special Service Brigade and I therefore suggest that he shall spend some time at Rear Headquarters, acquainting himself with all branches there and then make a brief tour of the Units in order to know the personnel. He should also spend a short time with Capt Waugh at COHQ in order to learn the procedure there. Capt Waugh will remain as Liaison Officer at COHQ until his embarkation orders arrive.

The appointment of Liaison officer at COHQ is to be maintained as I require an officer to act as my representative at the HQ during my absence.

(Sgd) R. E. LAYCOCK
Brigadier
Commanding Special Service Brigade

MOST SECRET

24 June 1943

To: The Deputy Commander
    Rear Headquarters, S.S.Bde
Copy to: Capt H. Bray
    Advance Headquarters, S.S.Bde
Subject: CAPT E. WAUGH, ROYAL HORSE GUARDS
    & FUS. HALL

Please include the above-mentioned officer and other rank in the first reinforcements to the Theatre of Operation 'HUSKY'.

(Sgd) R. E. LAYCOCK
Brigadier
Commanding Special Service Brigade

PERSONAL

5 July 1943

To: Lt.-Col. The Lord Lovat, DSO, MC
    Rear Headquarters
    Special Service Brigade
Dear Shimi,

With further reference to your letter of the 29th June, I now learn that it will probably be six weeks before there is a passage available for me.

This is clearly too long a period to keep two liaison officers at this Headquarters. I suggest, and George Mills agrees, that it would be best if he were to be attached to your Headquarters at Midhurst for the next four weeks. This would both be convenient for him personally, would be valuable experience for him in learning the work of Brigade Headquarters to which he has not yet done an attachment and also, I should think, a convenience to you, who must be short of 'G' officers at the moment.

If he returns here for the last ten days or fortnight of my stay, that should prove ample time for him to be in touch with all that is on hand.

Yours sincerely,
(Sgd) E. WAUGH

9 July 1943

To: Captain E. Waugh
    Combined Operations HQ
Copy to: Camp Commandant (who will please arrange billet for
      Captain Mills)
Subject: LIAISON OFFICERS – COHQ
    Reference your letter addressed to Lt. Col. The Lord Lovat, will you please instruct Captain G. Mills to report to this HQ on Monday, 12th July.
    He will remain here until Captain A. D. C. Smith returns from a course, when he will return to COHQ.
    You will then report to the Commando Depot.

(Sgd) J. G. SOOBY
Captain
ADAA & QMG
Special Service Brigade

12 July 1943

To: Lt.-Col. The Lord Lovat, DSO, MC
Dear Shimi,
    I have to-day received a letter from your Headquarters SS/305/A.2./Mills of 9th July, signed by Acting DAA and QMG from which it is clear that my position as Liaison Officer at COHQ is not fully understood.
    Could you please explain to this officer:—
    (1) That I am appointed Liaison Officer here by the Brigade Commander and have his explicit orders to remain at this post until my embarkation.
    (2) That these orders were confirmed in writing to you in his Confidential letter of the 8th May in which he states 'Captain Waugh will remain Liaison Officer at COHQ until his Embarkation Orders arrive'.
    (3) That the question of my going to the Depot was raised by yourself solely with a view to my own welfare, the suggestion being that if it could be fitted in, it would be beneficial after so long at an office desk, to spend a short time in the open air in order to get physically fit for the Theatre of Operations.
    (4) That I have good personal reasons for wishing to remain in London as long as possible.
    In these circumstances, a week is the most I can reasonably take away from duty at the Depot and I suggest that I notify Colonel Vaughan and Captain Mills as soon as a definite date for embarkation is known.

Yours sincerely,
(Sgd) E. WAUGH

To: Captain E. Waugh
    Combined Operations HQ

13 July 1943

Dear Evelyn,

Reference your personal letter dated 12th July, my SS/305/A.2/Mills of 9th July, 1943, signed by A/Q holds good. If you require further instructions on the matter, please notify me.

Your letter, ref. para. 1. I recently (10th June) requested permission from the Brigade Commander in the presence of the GOCO for Captain Mills to act as Liaison Officer with Rear Headquarters. This was accepted.

Reference para. 2. The confidential letter written by Brigadier Laycock on 8th May is automatically cancelled by para. 1.

Reference para. 3. A harmonious liaison has never been established between your department and Rear Headquarters; I saw fit to apply for Captain Mills, for this reason, see para. 1. Two Liaison Officers are not considered necessary. Further, it is considered essential you become physically fit before proceeding overseas.

Reference para. 4. I understand that your private affairs were progressing satisfactorily, and you told me you did not require much more time to complete them.

Finally, I wish to add the following remarks:

I have shown your letter to the GOCO, who confirms:

a. Two Liaison Officers are unnecessary at COHQ, and directs:

b. You will report to the Depot on 1st August.

c. You will not proceed overseas unless passed physically fit by Achnacarry.

I hope I have made myself clear.

   Yours
    (Sgd) SHIMI

16 July 1943

CONFIDENTIAL

To: GOCO

Reference attached D/O letter from Deputy Commander, Special Service Brigade to L.O. S.S.Bde., para. 6(c). If doubt exists about the fitness of an officer for foreign service, it is usual to refer him to the Medical Authorities.

2. I do not understand why an exception is being made in my case.

3 May I please come and see you about this?

    (Sgd) E. WAUGH.

PERSONAL

17 July 1943

To: Lt.-Col. The Lord Lovat, DSO, MC
      Rear Headquarters,
      Special Service Brigade

My Lord,

I have the honour to inform you that I have this morning had an interview with the GOCO in which he advised me to leave the Special Service Brigade for the Brigade's good.

I therefore have the honour to request that I may be posted to the Royal Horse Guards.

    I am
        My Lord,
            Your Lordship's obedient servant,

                      Evelyn Waugh
                      Captain GSO3
               Special Service Brigade

19 July 1943

PERSONAL

To: Brigadier R. E. Laycock

My dear Bob,

I am sure you are too busy to worry about my personal problems but I should like you to be in possession of the facts relevant to my leaving the Brigade so that when you have leisure to look at them, you will know that it is not I who have let you down.

The attached papers show the course of events up to my interview with the GOCO on the 17th July.

I wished to see him for two reasons:

a. I did not believe the Deputy Commander's statement that on the 10th June you had authorised him to supersede me in this office before my embarkation.

b. I was reluctant to go to the Depot because

1) Since my father's death my mother, aged 74, is entirely alone in London. A request has been made for my brother's return from the Middle East (a Captain aged 45 – the Waughs have no aptitude for pushing themselves in the army) on compassionate grounds and until that is arranged I have heavy responsibilities and I know that my duty is to spend as much of my time as I can with her.

2) I have lately spent £5.5s. on a Harley Street doctor who, I am advised, is the best Consulting Physician in England and in any case is a better opinion than Lt.-Col. Vaughan and he has passed me fit for Foreign Service.

I regard my posting to the Depot as unprecedented in the history of the Brigade and only explicable on grounds of personal malice. If I could be spared for special training for my duties with you, this should clearly have taken place here and at Norfolk House in the intelligence of the present and future campaign.

By the time I saw GOCO the question of the date of my going to the Depot was not of importance since the latest information about the time of sailing suggested that if I went on the 1st August, I should not be at the Depot longer than 10 days.

When I saw the GOCO he was already in a highly excited condition. He stated 'Your Brigadier has made a great mistake in asking for you at all and I shall see that you don't go until I am satisfied that you are fit'. I asked him what he meant by 'fit' and he said that he required me to do the Depot course and also an Intelligence course.

This would have postponed my sailing by at least three months and have rendered me useless for your immediate requirement.

He then became more agitated and gave vent to a volume of general abuse from which I was able to extract only the following concrete charges:

1. That his PA had complained of my rudeness.

2. That two days previously I had failed to give a telephone message to the Deputy Commander.

3. That GOC Southern Command had complained that in November last I had failed to stand to attention when he came into your Headquarters during Exercise 'Blackmore'.

With regard to these charges:

1. I immediately went to apologise to Miss Lawrie who was dumbfounded by what I told her, said that she had never complained nor, as I well know, had cause for complaint and that she would immediately clear the General's mind of this misconception.

2. On the day in question the Deputy Commander was absent from his Headquarters on an Exercise and was inaccessible. The GOCO was informed of this at the time. The matter on which I had to telephone him was completely trivial.

3. I do not believe that General Lloyd made any such complaint and in the interests of truth, not with any hope of changing the GOCO's opinion, I have written to him to confirm these facts.

The GOCO ended by saying that I had done nothing but discredit to the Brigade since I had joined it and that for the Brigade's good he advised me to leave as soon as possible.

I have therefore tendered my resignation to the Deputy Commander.

Yours sincerely,
Evelyn Waugh

Extract from a Letter from GOC Southern Command to Captain Waugh, dated 20 July 1943.

Your letter has surprised me a lot, and there must be some mistake. I have never made any report on this incident to General Haydon either directly or indirectly.

I remember the occasion, but I did not notice you were drinking claret, nor did I notice who stood up or who did not. One naturally expects the usual courtesy from officers, but I do not expect officers at Headquarters to stand up during training on all occasions: they often have headphones on and obviously cannot do so.

A few days after the incident I was asked by some officer – I cannot remember who – what I thought of your drinking claret at 4 am: the query was made in jocular fashion, and I thought nothing more of it.

You are at liberty to shew this to General Haydon if you wish.

A fine pompous letter to Lord Louis Mountbatten should follow here but Diana Cooper lost it. E.W.

Tuesday 10 August 1943

The foregoing letters give the sequence of events which led to my leaving the Special Service Brigade. On Wednesday last, August 4th, I saw Lord Louis Mountbatten on terms so cordial as to be almost affectionate. Result, none. The reasons: (1) That Shimi had adroitly shifted the blame to the poor, mad General and any enquiry that was made was bound to discredit him more than Shimi.[1] (2) Lord Louis was going away for six weeks so that any enquiry would have to be conducted by the General. (3) The war in Sicily, and probably in Italy, will be over before I could arrive. (4) The indignation I felt a month ago has subsided and I have got bored with the whole thing. My military future is vague. I should quite like to join Bill Stirling[2] but learn that his position is very insecure. I went with Hubert to Windsor and found the barracks full of

[1] Lord Lovat (in a letter to the editor, 28 October 1975) comments: 'Nobody wished to have him. Laycock left him behind in London during an operation in Italy, a prolonged affair, with the promise that he would be sent for in due course. I do not think he had any intention of having Waugh back on his staff where he was the cause of constant trouble. In the interval Waugh spent a week to ten days at the bar at White's and I suggested to General Charles Haydon (the "poor mad general" – as Waugh calls him – in Combined Operations Headquarters) that Waugh and his soldier-servant would be better posted to the Depot and do some soldiering while there was a war on our hands; this was done, and Waugh resigned.'

[2] Colonel Stirling (a cousin of Lord Lovat) was attempting to raise a new unit: the 2nd Special Air Service Regiment.

fine paintings and middle-aged, embittered subalterns. I suppose I shall go there.

Laura left on Thursday and I find the flat in Curzon Street desolate. On Friday I went to Bognor for the weekend. The Duchess of Westminster was the only guest; Weal the only servant. Diana with grimy hands fretting about coupons and pig-swill. Fine wine, *Vice Versa* read aloud, gin rummy. Only one row with Duff, but continuous friction with Diana. I returned to the desolate flat, lunched and dined at White's.

Written at Windsor, Sunday 29 August 1943

I spent a lonely and bibulous week in London and returned for a night to Bognor where Desmond MacCarthy and Katharine Asquith, Maud Russell were staying. Desmond had just read *Work Suspended* and was full of praise for it. That evening a great number of bombers passed over the house continuously from 9 till after 10; the noise so loud and close that we might have been sitting in one of them. There was no exultation in any of us. At 4 in the morning we had them again. They had been to Milan. At breakfast Diana was in a state of high excitement because of a report that the Italians were sending British prisoners to Germany. I pointed out that this was precisely what we had expected the French to do with German pilots in 1940 and that Pétain's failure to do so was then denounced as the basest betrayal. Logic in the early morning was more than Diana could bear and the irritation she had been suffering for some time made an outburst of ill-temper and I left sad and cross with no inclination to be reconciled.

I telephoned for Laura to come for the weekend and we had two wholly happy days at Curzon Street. On Monday I went down to Windsor where I have now spent nearly two weeks. There are only the old and the young here. Most of the old have lost interest in the war and are thinking of peacetime careers. The two squadron leaders, Henry Broughton and Jacky Ward, are dull fellows. Miles Manton rarely appears. There is a gloomy fellow whom I have a kinship with, Jones, expelled from the Middle East for gambling. There is an amiable ginger-headed fellow called Mick Dillon who is under a cloud, I think for bad temper. Everyone else seems to be named Shannon, Shore or Sandford.

I dined with the Grenadiers at the Hind's Head and got very drunk. It was the first evening of the return of my room mate, a young man called Korah who has taken a Pelman course in personality and intellect without any noticeable effect except that he lacks shyness.

I have dined with Angie and called on Nan Daly.[1]

Yesterday was typical of my present life. At 9 I strolled round to the signal office and found them starting on a wireless scheme, so I climbed into the

[1] Wife of Dermot Daly and daughter of the 1st Baron McGowan. She was found murdered, in March 1976, at her home at Witney, Oxfordshire.

control car with two schoolboys who were part of cadet party visiting us. We drove about fifteen miles talking signal jargon and halted. I went into the inn and sat with a very old man who believed that the Duke of Windsor was commanding the allied forces in the field. Presently we drove back, talking signal jargon. One of the armoured cars drove off the road for no apparent reason and broke its axle. Late luncheon in the mess with Lagrange 1928. Fell asleep after luncheon and was woken by Gwyn Morgan Jones suggesting we go driving, so we took a taxi to his house and had some tea, harnessed the pony to the governess cart and drove over to Hawthorne Hill where Angie was expected but had not arrived. We drank some of her whisky, reharnessed the pony and drove to Gwyn's house, drank more whisky and returned in a taxi to barracks. Dined, Lagrange 1928, and then took a bottle of port to the billiard room, since the Colonel has forbidden port-drinking, and sat up till 12 talking about religion and socialism and whether or not the Berrys are Jews. It will be difficult for our descendants reading of the titanic war effort of 1943 to realize that this is how active and fully trained officers, yearning to get to the front, are obliged to spend their time and money.

Fusilier Hall has become Trooper Hall and spends his day hanging round my room to pop in whenever I am in to ask, 'Any news, sir?', meaning, are we going out to North Africa.

I had a day in London. Met Basil at the Ritz who was unable to hide his exuberance. He has got his move order to join Bob. In order to do so he has (*a*) taken Angie's flat from her at £500 a year and let her a room facing the park at his hotel[1] for £2 a week (*b*) engaged Sooby to work for him after the war (*c*) promised Mills employment (*d*) given a case of whisky to Ronnie Todd. I think England is the only country where people resort to bribery to get *into* the war.

I lunched with Maimie and dined with Basil and returned to Windsor.

The appointment of Louis Mountbatten as Commander-in-Chief South-East Asia (Japan) came as a surprise to all at Combined Operations HQ. It is generally thought that this will be the end of that HQ and most of them will move to Ceylon. Bob is now intimate with 8th Army and is getting reinforcements. It looks to me as thought justice may be done and that the final reshuffle, after all the intrigue, may be that he will command a Mediterranean Commando Force under AF while Shimi will be packed off to the Far East under Marine command. Nothing could be funnier than that.

I have bought a number of architectural books at Mrs Brown's in Eton, among them a splendid Palladio for £5 10s. I have engaged Osmond to engrave a letter-paper heading for Maimie.

I am going to an interview on Wednesday for AMGOT.[2] I have got so bored

[1] Hyde Park Hotel.
[2] Allied Military Government of Occupied Territory.

with everything military that I can no longer remember the simplest details. I
dislike the Army. I want to get to work again. I do not want any more
experiences in life. I have quite enough bottled and carefully laid in the cellar,
some still ripening, most ready for drinking, a little beginning to lose its body. I
wrote to Frank[1] very early in the war to say that its chief use would be to cure
artists of the illusion that they were men of action. It has worked its cure with
me. I have succeeded, too, in dissociating myself very largely with the rest of
the world. I am not impatient of its manifest follies and don't want to influence
opinions or events, or expose humbug or anything of that kind. I don't want to
be of service to anyone or anything. I simply want to do my work as an artist.

Thursday 2 September 1943

I spent a wholly delightful weekend with Angie, Pempie and Bobby Casa
Maury[2] being cosseted. Two film people who are apparently part-owners of
Put Out More Flags came on Sunday.

On Tuesday 31st I went to the castle and was shown over the library by the
librarian Mr Morshead who gave me permission to return when I wished.
Korah came back from his course. His first act on being called in the morning is
to cram his mouth with chocolate creams.

Yesterday's day in London was a great failure. I went to Anderson &
Sheppard to try on clothes which were not ready, then to Peters to sign a
contract that was not yet ratified, then to Bush House to be interviewed for
Amgot. I was first taken to see a civilian named Gudgeon who said, 'Why are
you anxious to join Amgot?' I said I did not yet know I was anxious to do so,
but wanted details of the terms of enlistment. He said he couldn't do that in his
office and sent me to a Jewish major who asked if I had ever worked with a
secret department. I named about six and he said I must see Col. Sutton who
was not available until Friday. And so away to St James's Club where I had
asked Basil to luncheon. He had not received my invitation. So I went up to the
dining-room with Willy Teeling and found the steward in a sulk because no
one would keep tables; luncheon very bad and port full of crust. Then Basil
came and drank brandy with me and I took the afternoon train to Windsor.
Dined with the Colonel, two doctors and Korah and Brian Rootes – ineffably
gloomy.

Basil says Shimi is being sent to the Far East.

Written on 23 September 1943

After a few days at Windsor I decided to ask for indefinite leave pending

[1] Pakenham.

[2] Angela (née Dudley Ward) Laycock; Penelope (née Dudley Ward) Pelissier; and the
Marquis de Casa Maury (Spain), who in 1937 married their mother, Freda Dudley Ward, as her
second husband.

posting and got it. Laura came to London, then I went to Pixton, then I returned to London alone and homeless, staying sometimes at the St James's Club, once at Maimie's, now in a squalid bedsitting-room in Ebury Street. I have been very drunk on several occasions, once on Cyril Connolly's 40th birthday, about which I remember nothing except that I enjoyed it, once lunching with Maurice Bowra on the day White's reopened. I went to the christening of Angie's baby. Lord Louis Mountbatten was the other godfather. We had rather an incongruous luncheon afterwards.

A further interview with PWE[1] and another arranged for today.

My day normally is to go to St James's Club for letters, then to Nancy's bookshop for gossip, the air heavy with Trumper's 'Eucris', Osbert Sitwell, Sergeant Preston,[2] Cyril in and out, shabby little new books and sumptuous old ones, the proprietor's nasty little Victorian nick-nacks. Luncheon at White's, usually with Ran and/or Freddy.[3] (Ran is becoming formidably eccentric; he sits in the main hall making loud comments to himself about the members, 'This used to be a gentleman's club. How did that man get in?' 'That man's got no neck.' 'What's a gunsmith doing here?' 'Those men look crooks to me.') After luncheon, bookshops in search of lithographic books. Then dinner, usually with friends, often tight.

Bill Stirling appeared for two days and left again, promising me an appointment but making no definite offer.

Yesterday I went to High Wycombe with Chris Hollis to see a collection of furniture belonging to a Mr Snell. He had some fine pieces but praised them so extravagantly that there were no words left for his guests. 'This is very important – unique – I have been asked time and again to name my own figure for this,' etc. What he most prided himself on and what he most conspicuously lacked was 'atmosphere'. The structure of every room was bogus. Nothing was in the right proportion. The chimney-pieces and panelling were pickled and waxed, the walls tinted plaster; rugs and polished boards and the grille of a Quaker meeting house and a Sheraton sideboard. Nothing could have been more remote from a real room of the period as one finds them in a thousand country houses with a thousand anachronisms.

Bill Stirling arrived at White's before luncheon and I was able to get ten minutes alone with him. He promised to take me back when he went, but his own position is clearly precarious – so precarious that he is thinking of going straight to the Prime Minister over the Army's head. I lunched with Osbert Sitwell in a private room at the Écu de France – Nancy Mitford, Alice von Hofmannsthal, Sergeant Preston, Waley the Chinese translator, and his mistress. Plenty of good red wine and fair luncheon. Osbert said, 'The

[1] Political Warfare Executive.
[2] Art historian serving in US Army; appears in *Sword of Honour* as 'the Loot'.
[3] The 8th Earl of Antrim, and the 2nd Earl of Birkenhead.

daughter of the Emperor of Abyssinia applied for the post of a matron at Eton. When asked her qualifications she said she was a widow of nineteen with six children.' Of Mrs Strong, who has just died in Rome: 'She had a signed photograph of the Parthenon.'

In the afternoon I went for a further interview with Political Warfare. This time a tableful of examiners, mostly civilians. As usually happens I found myself asking the questions instead of them and made a bad impression. Walking back I met Chris Hollis in the street and took him and Betjeman to St James's for drinks. He stayed on to dinner – excellent – and we drank till the bar shut at midnight. I cannot remember what we talked of, except, at one stage, the obligation of charity to love mankind in general – an obligation we both find it impossible to meet. During the day I bought a pretty little illuminated book of poems – 7s 6d.

Friday 24 September 1943

My usual round – St James's, Nancy's bookshop, where Debo[1] appeared for an electric five minutes, and White's, where I found Phil[2] in the barber's chair returned an hour before from Italy. Lunched with Ran, met Bob, met Bill Stirling who appears confident but non-committal, dined with Audrey[3] and Phil and left them early. Phil has all the vitality of the battlefield, full of genuine soldiers' talk. They have all done well and are proud of themselves. I wrote a letter to the *New Statesman* in reply to a very silly one on Catholic education from Marie Stopes.

Saturday 25 September 1943

I offered myself the day before to help Bill Stirling in getting out his project for an expanded SAS. Accordingly I spent most of the day with him. He is vastly different from Bob – a romantic, more imaginative, more moral, less alert, less concrete. My chief value to Bill is to give him someone he can trust to discuss the project with. I lunched with John Betjeman and we went together to see the books that have been accumulating at the Hyde Park Hotel. They did not seem impressive in quality. Mia and Douglas, Susan and Bill, dined with me at the Ritz. Bill and I went to White's and kept the barman and underporter up till 2 playing slosh[4] with them and drinking hard. I gave the underporter a lecture on mezzotinting and then to bed. In the morning I called on Hubert[5] and found him frightfully ill.

---

[1] The Hon. Deborah Mitford in 1941 married Lord Andrew Cavendish (later the Duke of Devonshire).
[2] Philip Dunne.
[3] Audrey Rubin.
[4] Game played with balls on a billiard table.
[5] Hubert Duggan.

Sunday 26 September 1943

More work with Bill, Mass at Farm Street; a little light-headed with the drink of the night before and of the morning. Luncheon with Susan at Claridge's. American soldiers at the next table drinking champagne. Miriam Rothschild, bandaged and married. Virginia Cowles. Dined at White's with Bob Boothby, fresh from an all-party Communist rally.

Monday 27 September 1943

I went to visit my mother who was quiet and dull.

Tuesday 28 September 1943

Too much drinking at midday and at night. White's all the time.

Wednesday 29 September 1943

Low health. Visited Hubert who was in despair. Bought third edition *Rustic Ornaments for houses of taste*. Dined Frank Pakenham and Mr and Mrs Toynbee. Catholic talk. Visited Frank earlier in the day at Beveridge's[1] office. He lives in Bruton Street in an office decorated like a hat shop with silk draperies and rickety Empire furniture. Bill has fixed luncheon with the Prime Minister to discuss future of SAS. I hope to get appointed G2, though, war-weary, I dread the prospect of organization and training and a hundred new acquaintances. But after my treatment by Haydon I must 'make good' as a soldier. Nothing can upset him more than to find me promoted as a result of his intemperance.

Sunday 3 October 1943

Rather pleasant days spent largely with Hollis and Woodruff. Purchased Owen Jones's *Victorian Psalter* for £1 and Wicks's *Spires and Towers* with the supplementary volume for 37s 6d. Sent an SOS for Laura who is coming to Claridge's today. Nancy now speaks of Peter[2] as though he were 'the late Colonel', quoting proverbial wisdom and worse with 'Peter always used to say . . .'. A very unsuccessful dinner party last night with Phil and Audrey, Maimie and Vsevolode. The Russian's intolerable. A funny, boisterous letter by me in *New Statesman and Nation*. I call often on Hubert who is pathetically ill. Freddy says John Betjeman is on the make. Bill has disappeared to Scotland with nothing settled. Row with Maimie over Allies Club.

Monday 4 October 1943

A day of great happiness. The expectation of Laura's visit. Taking rooms at

---

[1] Sir William Beveridge was working out plans for post-war social security.
[2] The Hon. Peter Rodd, the Hon. Nancy Mitford's husband.

Claridge's, moving there, getting my hair cut, ordering *The Times*, theatre tickets, table at Marks's and so on. She arrived in great good looks and high spirits. We went out to Highgate to help order a gravestone for my father. Returned to dine at Claridge's and an early bed-time. This was the end of it. Next day Laura was not well and the preparations made for her fell flat. We called on Hubert but saw Lady Curzon instead. The play was excellent. We dined with Frank Pakenham and Father D'Arcy. Next day, Wednesday, all left, and I returned to my futile hanging about White's and port-drinking with Pat Smith.

Tuesday 12 October 1943

I spent the weekend at Pixton where the trees were splendid but Laura ill and my children uninterested. I returned to find Bill Stirling fled and Hubert very much worse. This morning, for the first time, he began to talk of religion and of returning to the Church, but he has no strength for reasoned argument and needs the presence of someone holy. I suggested a nun but nothing seems to come of it much, though Lady Curzon seems sympathetic. It seems in Hubert's mind that it would be a betrayal of Phyllis to profess repentance of his life with her.

I am having a controversy with Marie Stopes in the *New Statesman* and wrote a very funny letter about it last night.

Wednesday 13 October 1943

I went to see Father Dempsey who is the Catholic chaplain for West London District, to consult him about Hubert. He was a big fat peasant[1] who said, 'I know a priest who is a fine gentleman. Would it not be better to get him? I should put my foot in it.' He telephoned some Irish nuns: 'It's a great work of charity you will be doing Mother . . .' to have a sister available in case she was needed. He gave me a medal. 'Just hide it somewhere in the room. I have known most wonderful cases of Grace brought about in just that way.' When I got to Chapel Street Lady Curzon told me that it was not expected Hubert would live through the day. As Dempsey had gone out I went to Farm Street and brought back Father Devas. Marcella[2] did not want him to come in. She and Ellen were sitting by him supporting him in a chair saying, 'You are getting well. You have nothing on your conscience. 'I brought Father Devas in and he gave Hubert absolution. Hubert said, 'Thank you father', which was taken as his assent.

The middle of my day was different. Randolph is just back and he and I sat drinking until late afternoon. I hear of nothing but defections from Bill.

[1] Father Dempsey came from Dublin; during the war, he was a regular attender at Sadler's Wells Ballet seasons at the New Theatre.

[2] Marcella Rice, Hubert Duggan's sister.

Christopher Sykes is now talking of ratting. I went back to Chapel Street. Numerous doctors – one particularly unattractive one from Canada – Marcella more than ever hostile. Father Devas very quiet and simple and humble, trying to make sense of all the confusion, knowing just what he wanted – to anoint Hubert – and patiently explaining, 'Look all I shall do is just to put oil on his forehead and say a prayer. Look the oil is in this little box. It is nothing to be frightened of.' And so by knowing what he wanted and sticking to that, when I was all for arguing it out from first principles, he got what he wanted and Hubert crossed himself and later called me up and said, 'When I became a Catholic it was not from fear', so he knows what happened and accepted it. So we spent the day watching for a spark of gratitude for the love of God and saw the spark. Then I dined with Peter Fitzwilliam and his wife Phil and his mistress and a man with a beard and Peter's influence was enough to get us a square meal at a fashionable restaurant and he gave me a box of cigars. They went on to gamble and I to bed.

Thursday 14 October 1943

Lunched with Charles Scott; dull company, splendid wine. Dined with Cyril, Raymond Mortimer, Patrick,[1] Dick Wyndham. Quennell and various ladies came in later. The food and wine were copious and delicious. The talk good – mostly of patent medicines and drugs. The highbrows cannot understand why science has not produced elixirs that will give them innocent and unclouded happiness. They spoke of the neglect of 'the pleasure principle'. Host and hostess went to bed, the party seemed to wake up. I walked home in fresh air and moonlight.

Friday 15 October 1943

Bill Stirling returned. I ate oysters and lobsters with Randolph. It is entertaining to read now of the cession of the Azores under our fourteenth-century treaty with Portugal when since 1940 we have had a force standing by to assault our old allies. No news of Hubert. I have done all in my power in that matter.

Pixton Park, Monday 25 October 1943

Writing at Pixton where I came on Friday 22nd and intend to stay and start writing. Events of the last week were: Bill left, but at the last moment I was able to drag him to adjutant-general's office and fix my posting. He also left me with a list of other officers and men to collect. Having done that, I thought myself free to come here. Bob has been made Chief of Combined Operations. I wrote to congratulate him comparing him, not quite sincerely, to the righteous

---

[1] Lord Kinross.

flourishing like a green bay tree. There is no shade for me under those wide branches. We lunched together on Thursday but there was a curtain of reproach between us. A curious dinner party on Thursday evening – Andrew and Debo Cavendish, Peggy Munster, Phil and Audrey, Daphne Weymouth, and (again, after all) Robert Cecil. Not a success. Andrew and I went and drank a bottle of champagne at Pratts and forgot it. I saw Randolph regularly, who is developing an antiquated sort of competitive national patriotism which will not help with the electorate nor with the elect. Russian victories are somehow not as welcome as they were a year ago.

Saturday 30 October 1943

I went to Newton Ferrers[1] for my 40th birthday. I got few presents and no letters. Returned to Pixton.

Oxford, Tuesday 2 November 1943

Left Pixton for Oxford where Father D'Arcy met me. I was the only guest at Campion and came in for more attention than on their more social evenings. The talk after dinner was not as good as usual, for there are now a number of secular priests up reading the humanities and these introduced the air of the presbytery. They spoke of impostors who preyed on the devout and each in turn told his story. 'Why Father that is very like what happened to Father Freeman in Bradford . . .' and indeed it was all too like. Later Frank came in with more of the outer air.

London, Wednesday 3 November 1943

Hubert's requiem. A Low Mass at Farm Street unintelligible to most of the congregation. The trumpets of the Life Guards sounded splendid. All understood that and in the hush that followed a voice sounded imperiously, 'In the forty years I have held the King's commission I never saw an officer fail to stand to attention when that was sounded.' I turned and saw poor Basil Dufferin being reprimanded by an unknown veteran. Instead of saying, as he should have done, 'Sir, I am here to pray for the soul of a friend. Do not defile this holy place with your parade ground insolence', he said, 'Sorry. I didn't know the tune.'

Thursday 4 November 1943

Robin,[2] one-legged but otherwise unchanged at first sight, lunched with me at White's. That evening we had a dinner for him at the Savoy of all who were available of No. 8 Commando, organized very well by Randolph.

[1] Home of Sir Robert Abdy.
[2] Robin Campbell.

Friday 5 November 1943

Luncheon with Phil and Audrey. Dinner with Angie. I saw Baby[1] and her baby and bought it a grotesque piece of Dutch silver.

All this time there was difficulty with the draft I was to take to North Africa. The joining order had been held up in the adjutant-general's branch of the War Office. I managed to straighten this out and get the party sent on leave.

Saturday 13 November 1943

On 8 November Laura came to London to see me off and at once became slightly ill. After a night of discomfort in Ebury Street I moved her to the Hyde Park Hotel. On 9 November came a cable from Allied Force HQ cancelling our journey and ordering us to await Bill's return.

This morning, 13 November, came a further order sending us back to our units. I have spent two or three days – at least, one or two hours a day for two or three days – trying to get us properly posted, but we have no one in this country responsible for us and SAS is in process of absorption by Airborne Corps with, I think, the elimination of Bill. Randolph has flown away and I have no status from which to negotiate. Bill's signal required preparations to be made for return of SAS, but no one acts.

There is a great deal of talk at the moment about the rocket guns which the Germans are said to have set up in France, with a range to carry vast explosive charges to London. This fear is seriously entertained in the highest quarters. I have accordingly given orders for the books I have been keeping at the Hyde Park Hotel to be sent to Piers Court. At the same time I have advocated my son coming to London. It would seem from this that I prefer my books to my son. I can argue that firemen rescue children and destroy books, but the truth is that a child is easily replaced while a book destroyed is utterly lost; also a child is eternal; but most that I have a sense of absolute possession over my library and not over my nursery.

Written on Thursday 30 December 1943

None of us except one subaltern in the Coldstream Guards went back to his regiment; the rest of us stayed in London on various pretexts, and with Phil's help I was able to arrange a parachute course at the secret house near Ringway kept by SO(E).[2] Six weeks ago on a Saturday we had a preliminary medical exam, from which I feared the worst. Instead we all passed and went exultantly to White's. We collected several cases of wine and spirits from Justerini and Brooks. Nothing could have spoiled the elation of our journey except what in fact happened. We all developed heavy colds, I influenza.

[1] The former Baby Jungman; Mrs Teresa Cuthbertson.
[2] Special Operations (Executive).

The secret villa was comfortable and the commandant charming – a songwriter in private life, it was said. Christopher Sykes was drunk all the time; for that reason and because it helps his impediment of speech he spoke always, very loudly, with either an American or a French accent. As most of the instructors and students were either American or French they were puzzled. Altogether we puzzled them rather. Through my 'flu I missed the first two days' 'synthetic' training – jumping through fuselages, swinging on ropes, etc. Did one morning's light training. Next day, Thursday, we waited all day at Ringway for the wind to drop and on Friday we did two jumps. The first was the keenest pleasure I remember. The aeroplane noisy, dark, dirty, crowded; the harness and parachute irksome. From this one stepped into perfect silence and solitude and apparent immobility in bright sunshine above the treetops. We were dropping at 700 feet only, so that the pleasure was brief. All too soon the ground seemed to be getting suddenly nearer and then, before one had time to do all one had been told, one landed with a great blow. The first time I kicked myself; the second somehow sat on my left leg and limped off the field thinking I had strained a muscle. Later in the day my leg got stiffer; the doctor saw it that evening and ordered it to be put in a splint.

From now for a week I was in the hands of a listless young RAF doctor who never called till after dinner. On the Monday I insisted on being X-rayed and it was found I had cracked the fibula. I went for two days to an RAF sick station, run with great squalor by a dishevelled corporal, escaped back to the secret villa where Phil, Christopher, etc., had returned for their final three jumps. Then, in plaster, to London where, after wandering and indecision, I landed up at the Hyde Park Hotel where Laura joined me. I spent a happy two weeks there (£71 exclusive of wine) entertaining continuously. I thought my friends would have been less attentive if I had been in Millbank hospital.

From there I went for Christmas to Maimie where I was exceedingly unhappy. I find my dislike of Vsevolode so overwhelming that I cannot sit in the room with him. I don't like their friends or their dogs and Maimie is lost to me. I moved out again and came yesterday to the Hyde Park Hotel, having had my bank account and learned that I have more than £1,000 lying at hand.

War news is consistently good. Everyone talks of peace next year. Some of peace in a matter of weeks.

An absurd incident; Ann O'Neill[1] left messages for me asking me to take part in her 'brains trust' on Wednesday. I knew that she and Esmond Rothermere always gave a dinner party on those evenings so I accepted simply so that I might have the chance to refuse dinner, explaining what I felt about a host who denied his guests wine. She took my acceptance and then said that she would be out of London next week so my malice has undone me.

[1] Ann Charteris married Lord O'Neill in 1932; he was killed fighting in Italy, 1944. She then married Lord Rothermere. She married Ian Fleming in 1952.

Chagford, Devon. Written on 31 January 1944

The 'brains trust' referred to above was more painful than I expected. Bill Astor shone in a horrible sort of way. Two seedy socialists, the editors of *New Statesman* and *Evening Standard*, were outstandingly bad. Hugh Sherwood cocky. I was sulky and cross, the audience very unintelligent. Next week, however, an authentic brains trust under the same auspices was a greater failure. Augustus John tipsy and inaudible, Connolly, Quennell, Eleanor Smith, Sergeant Preston in the chair and fifteen bored doughboys as audience, most of whom had missed their way to an all-in wrestling match.

After hanging on in London alone (Laura down with mumps) leading a more and more limited life in the vicious spiral of boredom and lassitude, I decided to escape, put in an appeal to write a novel,[1] was headed back by Col. Ferguson with an order to train the Home Guard at Windsor, persevered, and finally suceeded in getting three months, qualified by the promise of doing part-time (a very small part) for Ministry of Information. On Saturday I left the Hyde Park Hotel and my uniforms and went to Pixton. Today, Monday, I

---

[1] In a letter dated 24 January 1944, to the Officer Commanding, Household Cavalry Training Regiment at Windsor (copies to the Secretary of State for War and Brendan Bracken):

'I have the honour to request that, for the understated reasons I may be granted leave of absence from duty without pay for three months:

1. I have reached the age of 40 and the rank of Lieutenant in the Royal Horse Guards. My service since 1939 has been with: a) The Royal Marines, b) Number 8 Commando, c) Lay Force, d) Special Service Brigade Headquarters, e) Combined Operations Headquarters, f) SAS (Parachute) Regiment.

I have thus not acquired the technical training to render me of use to my regiment in their present mechanized role.

2. I have no longer the physical agility necessary for an operational officer in the kind of operations for which I have trained.

3. I have not the administrative experience necessary for the type of appointment normally given to a regular officer of my age.

4. I have not the knowledge of foreign languages necessary for an appointment in the Intelligence or para-military Departments.

5. In civil life I am a novelist and I have now formed the plan of a new novel which will take approximately three months to write.

6. This novel will have no direct dealing with the war and it is not pretended that it will have any immediate propaganda value. On the other hand it is hoped that it may cause innocent amusement and relaxation to a number of readers and it is understood that entertainment is now regarded as a legitimate contribution to the war effort.

7. It is a peculiarity of the literary profession that, once an idea becomes fully formed in the author's mind, it cannot be left unexploited without deterioration. If, in fact, the book is not written now it will never be written.

8. On the completion of the writing I shall be able to return to duty with my mind unencumbered either by other preoccupations or by the financial uncertainty caused by the necessity of supporting a large family on the pay of a lieutenant. I shall be able to offer myself in the hope that some opportunity will then have arisen in which I can serve my regiment.'

came to Chagford with the intention of starting on an ambitious novel[1] tomorrow morning. I still have a cold and am low in spirits but I feel full of literary power which only this evening gives place to qualms of impotence.

Tuesday 1 February 1944

Up at 8.30, two and a half hours earlier than in London, and at work before 10. I found my mind stiff and my diction stilted but by dinner-time I had finished 1,300 words all of which were written twice and many three times before I got the time sequence and the transitions satisfactory, but I think it is now all right. I have bought a very expensive concoction of halibut oil which I hoped would restore my vitality but on reading the label I find it to be a cure for chilblains. The hotel is full of elderly women who do not distract me from my work. Carolyn has given me the room they call 'the middle lounge' for a private sitting-room but the fire smokes so badly that I must choose between freezing and going blind.

Wednesday 2 February 1944

Score at close of play 3,000 words odd. Went to tea with two girl friends of Carolyn's, one with a past full of pansies and sudden death.

Tuesday 8 February 1944

Working steadily; much rewriting; 1,500–2,000 words a day. Today an arduous revision, rescription and reordering. A disquieting note from the Ministry of Information suggesting that my leave is far from certain. Norman has gone today to fetch me some of my claret from Stinchcombe. I find the cider a poor substitute.

Sunday 13 February 1944

My wine arrived on Thursday. There seems to have been theft in the cellar; only three bottles of Yquem where I left eleven. The Pontet Canet '34 is not good but I drink it with pleasure after so long with cider.

I have fallen into a slough of rewriting. Every day I seem to go over what I did the day before and make it shorter. I am getting spinsterish about style.

The battle at Nettuno looks unpromising. It is hard to be fighting against Rome. We bombed Castel Gandolfo. The Russians now propose a partition of East Prussia. It is a fact that the Germans now represent Europe against the world. Thank God Japan is not on our side too.

Monday 14 February 1944

Yesterday, after a day of tinkering and reading the papers, I sat down after dinner and wrote 3,000 words in three hours. Today I have treated myself as a

[1] *Brideshead Revisited.*

kind of invalid as a result, but I shall have the third chapter done before I go to bed. Reading Haydon's autobiography with great pleasure – the miniaturist Cross who 'retired from society' when Mrs Haydon refused his hand. The ostrich plumes in the soldier's helmet to make the hero more 'ponderous'.

Friday 18 February – Wednesday 23 February 1944

Laura came to stay with me. 23rd Ash Wednesday.

Saturday 26 February 1944

This morning I finished my third chapter, 33,000 words in all, and took it in high good humour to the post office. I was just about to start on the fourth after luncheon when I was called to the telephone. Col. Ferguson speaking from Windsor: the War Office had turned down my application for leave. I was to be found employment. I had been found employment as ADC to a general whose name Col. Ferguson had forgotten; he was a very good little chap. I was to lunch with him on Monday at 12.45 at the Apéritif. So that ends my hopes of another two months' serious work. Back to military frivolities.

London, Thursday 2 March 1944

I came to London on Sunday where I found everyone scared of air raids and, in contrast to my own health, very grey and old. On Monday I spent all day drinking at White's except for an hour at the Ritz with Audrey and Phil, tea with Maimie, and luncheon with General Thomas, who accepted me as ADC in spite of my warnings against it. I thought him a simple soldier but heard later that he is a man of insatiable ambition and unscrupulous in his means of self-advancement. On Tuesday I went to his headquarters for a week's trial – today returned unaccepted. This is a great relief. The primary lack of sympathy seemed to come from my being slightly drunk in his mess on the first evening. I told him I could not change the habits of a lifetime for a whim of his. The HQ was architecturally deplorable and the staff glum and drab. I now find that the War Office has refused my application for leave so I must return to Windsor. My sole interest now is in my novel.

Thursday 9 March 1944

No sooner was I quit of one general than a second was produced for me like a rabbit from a hat – Miles Graham, on the surface a more human fellow than Tomkins.[1] I went to Pixton for the weekend and got up on Monday morning with the old, glum feeling I used to know at Stobs camp and have not really known since. I saw the general at 3.45 and he held out hopes that he might not

---

[1] *Sic.*

want me for six weeks and would be able to let me off to write until then. That seems too good to be true. Meanwhile I have renewed my application to Brendan for full leave but have heard nothing of it. Dined last night with the McEwens and Dick Stokes at Ritz. Phil and White's unchanged.

Chagford, Saturday 11 March 1944

I telephoned General Graham, accepted his offer of becoming PA to him, and was given six weeks' leave. It is better than I could possibly hope. I telephoned to Chagford and Pixton and came here yesterday, picking up Laura on the way. For three days I have been in a state of intense nervous excitement which must be calm before I start work. I spent the last days in London in and about White's. No raids.

Monday 13 March 1944

A wholly delightful weekend at Chagford with Laura, getting into a calm state to begin work today. Yesterday I walked by myself and planned the work of the next five weeks. This morning a letter arrived from General Graham cancelling his whole arrangement with me.

Wednesday 15 March 1944

Had I not been stunned on Monday morning I would have persuaded Laura to stay on with me here. I have done little work and been in a continual fret. I have had to change rooms too because Lord Grantley arrived with a film actress and wanted my sitting-room which, since I was taking it free, I could make no claim to. Now his tart has taken him away and I am back in the same rooms but not with the same heart I had three weeks ago. One day, believing it to be the first of a long period of work, is worth a week of odd days of which I expect the summons to move.

Thursday 16 March 1944

I have at last got into stride again and wrote 2,700 words today, 700 of which will need to be rewritten tomorrow. Weary, but I don't sleep and have taken drugs every night this week. No news from Windsor except a note from Hall that he is back there. London under fire again. In Italy we advance through a desolation we make as we go.

Tuesday 21 March 1944

Today I sent off another 13,000 odd words to be typed, and have my teeth well into a new chapter. English writers, at forty, either set about prophesying or acquiring a style. Thank God I think I am beginning to acquire a style.

No news from the War Office. It is just that, having so often suffered so sharply from their dilatoriness, I should at length profit by it.

Wednesday 22 March 1944

It is always my temptation in writing to make everything happen in one day, in one hour on one page and so lose its drama and suspense. So all today I have been rewriting and stretching until I am cramped.

Friday 24 March 1944

Sent off another 8,000 words.

Monday 27 March 1944

Sent off another 7,800 words.

Wednesday 29 March 1944

Another 8,500 words. End of Book 11 (27,000 words, 62,000 in all). Laura came for the last visit before the birth of her baby.

Saturday 1 April 1944

A telegram from Windsor ordering me to report to a Col. Tufton or Tusnon in London on Tuesday morning. It is not quite as disastrous as it might be for I have come to a suitable halting stage in the book and a week or two away from it may do no harm. I wrote a funny review of a new book by Prof. Laski for *The Tablet*.

Sunday 2 April 1944

Palm Sunday. Completed the corrections of the first batch of typescript.

Monday 3 April 1944

Came to London to the Hyde Park Hotel and spent two weeks idle in London waiting for an appointment to conduct journalists round the Second Front. Most of my day at White's. Saw a number of friends, drank a great deal of good wine which is getting scarcer daily but still procurable by those who take the trouble.

Pixton, Sunday 16 April 1944

Wrote to Public Relations that they could find me at Pixton.

Grace, Lady Wemyss is here. Auberon surprised her in her bath and is thus one of the very few men who can claim to have seen his great-great-grandmother[1] in the raw. I have completed the revision, with many changes, of the first two books of the novel.

---

[1] Grace Blackburn married the 8th Earl of Wemyss (1818–1914) in 1900. His daughter, Lady Evelyn Charteris, married the 4th Viscount de Vesci; and their daughter, Mary Vesey, who married Aubrey Herbert, was Auberon Waugh's grandmother.

Written at Chagford on Thursday 4 May 1944

On Friday last, in London, I had a letter from 'public relations' saying they had no employment for me, which inflamed my persecution mania to the extent that I wrote to Bob, who was on leave, asking for his help in getting me six clear weeks to finish my work. Phil, now doubled up with arthritis (Reddie[1] at White's said, 'You *will* laugh when you see Captain Dunne'), and other friends all said I should be safe now that I had overcome my pride. I lunched with Freddy Birkenhead and got drunk with him, Dermot and others, slept an hour, returned to White's to find Maurice Bowra dining with Bob Boothby; they and I and Maurice Bridgeman drank heavy and late; Maurice Bridgeman walked with me to the Hyde Park Hotel telling me at length the circumstances of Lord Bridgeman's last illness. Next day, or the day after that, I felt the effects of this day's drinking. On the Saturday I ate oysters with Raimund von Hofmannsthal and returned with him to lunch with Liz, lovely but seldom in the room; Isaiah Berlin came later and I saw them off to Oxford longing to go too and, until the train started, half considering it. That night I was just feeling drowsy after my sleeping draught when I was called on the telephone. Cyril Connolly asking me to join him and Robin and Mary Campbell and Alice Obolensky in the country, naming a train. I gratefully accepted. Another dose of bromide and chloral, again growing drowsy, again the telephone, again Cyril. He had told me the wrong train; I must be at Victoria next afternoon at 4.26. Less grateful acceptance. Sleep at last. Ill next day. Mass at Farm Street and the reading of a long pastoral about sex education. Lunch at White's. A very hot afternoon, the streets crowded with a parade of adolescent prostitutes, no taxis. To Victoria by tube. At Victoria I learn that the train Cyril found for me did not exist. Back to the Hyde Park. An hour's sleep. Dinner at White's. A day of great gloom.

Next morning a call from Bob. His office is less imposing than in Lord Louis's day. Phil and Harry[1] eating gulls' eggs at his door. A wholly unsatisfactory interview. Bob unable or unwilling to help. He feels, I think, a little of the resentment all generals feel at the apathy to the Second Front. The papers would have us believe the country is on its toes, straining at the leash, etc. My observation is that people say either, 'There won't be a Second Front', or, 'It will be a disastrous failure because the Americans will run away.' Admittedly I consort most with the middle-aged and embittered. That night —— and John Sutro dined with me. I gave them a fine dinner – gulls' eggs, consommé, partridge, haddock on toast, Perrier Jouet '28, nearly a bottle a head, liqueur brandy, Partaga cigars – an unusual feast for these times. I found their company delightful. ——'s descriptions of service life as seen by a bugger were a revelation. He combines his pleasures with keen patriotism. That day I

[1] The Senior Hall Porter.
[2] Philip Dunne and Lord Stavordale.

made arrangements to go back to Chagford and wait there until again summoned.

On Tuesday 2 May Liz lunched with me at Wilton's, ate nothing, looked ill and nervous, and when later Raimund joined us seemed overcome with aversion. He, too, discomposed and morose. Perhaps a climax of some kind in their lives. Osbert Sitwell at St James's Club openly demanding peace, as could not have been done a year ago.

That evening, May 2, was the dinner given by Douglas Jerrold for the new Archbishop of Westminster[1] to meet the flower of Catholic literature. We assembled in the hot afternoon (save that a wind was blowing grit in our eyes) at 6.30 (4.30 Greenwich) at the Dorchester. I saw no one I knew save Speaight[2] and Graham Greene. A tipsy Scotsman of vulgar appearance reminded me he had once greatly surprised me by calling at Ardrossan and leaving a card in which he described himself as Spanish consul in Glasgow and knight of St Columba. Colm Brogan joined us and the consul made jokes about whisky I could not share. I felt very ill at ease in these Rotarian surroundings. Chris and Douglas, whom I relied on, had gone to Claridge's. Presently we went to dinner, which was eaten at such a rate that the table was clear by 7.45 when I should normally be thinking of my second cocktail. Compton Mackenzie, disguised as Cunninghame-Graham, made an emotional speech. 'Here we are together, all different, all divided on every issue except one – our love and homage to His Grace. I humbly beg His Grace to give us a lead in our work.' His Grace had clearly never read anything except a text-book in his life, but was not nonplussed. With complete self-assurance he praised the conduct of the House of Commons on the Education Bill and of Amgot in Sicily, said that censorship was designed to help the author not to hinder him, said what an august lot we were – and by God we weren't – and sat down. He is a man of mean appearance, sly, pleased with his job, absolutely philistine, absolutely charmless. After dinner he was moved round the table talking to each in turn. He said nothing at all interesting to us. During dinner I had Graham Greene on my deaf ear and on my right Halliday Sutherland,[3] who boasted of his triumphs with publishers. He said the only trouble with grammar he had was with his prepositions. 'Any prepositions in particular?' 'Yes. "Lest".' I implored him to read Fowler. After dinner the guests stood about and since they were of a type who habitually finds itself one of the principal speakers at a public meal and had that night been kept silent, they now began quoting to one another juicy bits of previous successful speeches. I left, with Graham Greene, before His Grace, and hoped the Archbishop thought I was called to military

[1] Cardinal Griffin.

[2] Robert Speaight, actor and biographer of Hilaire Belloc (1957) and Eric Gill (1966).

[3] Scottish doctor-administrator (1882–1960) and prolific author, mainly of travel books; bestseller *The Arches of the Years*, 1932.

duty. Next day, yesterday, I came here and to my delight found Deirdre Balfour, and to my sorrow found that Carolyn had sent all my clothes to Pixton. Today I painfully picked up the threads of a very difficult chapter of love-making on a liner.

Friday 5 May 1944

Lay in bed this morning sadly realizing that I must rewrite all I did yesterday. Urgent message to go and see Carolyn. Found her and Norman in consultation over his will. The situation as first explained to me was that Norman wished to leave everything (which I presume is the half-share in the hotel the money for which, and all the goodwill and hard work, was supplied by Carolyn) to his own family, one of whom, Mrs Price, is destitute. Carolyn professes to be alarmed lest Mrs Price's promiscuous generosity should dissipate the fortune immediately, and proposes that she should hold all or half in trust. I say that I see no advantage in this as Mrs Price's character is unlikely to change and that there is no point in having two instead of one dispersal. Norman then goes to his air-spotting (from which I gather he is shortly off on more dangerous duty – hence the interest in his will) and Carolyn begins to talk of her own family and her duty in seeing her money returned to them; in fact it is clear at last that she is not at all fretting about Mrs Price's imprudence as it affects Mrs Price, but in the Cobb children's share in the minute legacy. She also spoke of the sentimental value of some pearl studs and of a gold watch of her brother's which she gave to Norman. An odd little incident to start the day – rather a grim one.

Later a telegram from Windsor ordered me to report to a room in Hobart House on the afternoon of the 11th.

Saturday 6 May 1944

A letter from Windsor making it clear that the telegram is not their doing. I have hopes that it may be Bob at work to get my release. Norman left for Second Front at 8.30 and returned at 10. Work on the book slow.

Sunday 7 May 1944

Work at a standstill. Why? Mass at Gidleigh. Reading *Pride and Prejudice* which is not the stuff to work on.

Tuesday 9 May 1944

Today I finished and despatched Book III Chap. 1 (12,000 words) – the most difficult part of the book so far, and in spite of some passages of beauty I am not sure of my success. I feel very much the futility of describing sexual emotions without describing the sexual act; I should like to give as much detail as I have of the meals, to the two coitions – with his wife and Julia. It would be no more or less obscene than to leave them to the reader's imagination, which in this case cannot be as acute as mine. There is a gap in which the reader will insert his own sexual habits instead of those of my characters.

Yesterday there was a telegram from Bob confirming that he had talked to Bill about me. There was also some deplorable amateur theatricals in the village. An absurd Brazilian named Lady Peel[1] came to reveal what had hitherto been kept from the villagers, that their money was to go to the Free French. She made a singularly infelicitous speech in which she reminded the audience of the village hall how much they had enjoyed buying their clothes in Paris. I had put her out, intentionally, before dinner by asking how far the Communists are in charge of the de Gaulle movement. She answered me, equivocally, from the platform by telling the story of a woman of respectable antecedents who now pushed a pram full of dynamite about and peddled *L'Humanité*.

London, Wednesday 10 May 1944

To London.

Thursday 11 May 1944

Interview in the afternoon. I found the room at Hobart House full of the scourings of the Army, pathetic old men longing for a job, obvious young blackguards. We were seen in turn by a weary but quite civil lieutenant-colonel and a major. The colonel said, 'We've two jobs for you. I don't know which will appeal to you the more. You can be a welfare officer in a transit camp in India.' I said that was not one I should choose. 'Or you can be assistant registrar at a hospital.' I said if I had to have one or the other I would have the latter. Then he said, 'By the way are you educated? Were you at a university?'

'Yes, Oxford.'

'Well, they are very much in need of an educated officer at the War Office, G3. Chemical Warfare.'

'My education was classical and historical.'

'Oh, that doesn't matter. All they want is *education*.'

As soon as I left them I hustled round to Bob at Combined Operations HQ and said, 'Get me out of this quick.' So he telephoned Hobart House and said Bill Stirling wanted me. Then I took Angie to have a drink and after a bath dined with Robin and Toby Milbanke at White's and drank champagne at £5 a bottle.

Chagford, Friday 12 May 1944

Saw Bill Stirling who confirmed my appointment and six weeks' leave. Returned to Chagford.

[1] Wife of Sir Arthur Peel, British envoy in Rio de Janeiro.

Saturday, 13 May 1944

Telephone message that Laura has had a daughter and is well. A dull day's work. Norman Webb's last evening before going to sea as an aircraft spotter.

Sunday 14 May 1944

In Norman's absence walked to Mass at Gidleigh – delicious fresh morning and beautiful path by river. A dull day's work rewriting yesterday's. Book III Chapter II.

Sunday 21 May 1944

I have written about 15,000 words in the last week and am in alternate despondency and exultation about the book. Anyway it is very near the end now. I think perhaps it is the first of my novels rather than the last. Today I walked to Mass and back. Tomorrow I go to Pixton to see Laura and my new daughter. A nervous wreck named Beverley Nichols has arrived. Not a man of strong understanding. A mercenary, hypochondriacal, flibbertigibbet who doesn't take in one of six words addressed to him – but civil to the old ladies.

Tuesday 30 May 1944

I went to Pixton yesterday week and found Laura in excellent health and her baby also. My children were much in evidence and boring. On Whit Sunday the baby was christened Harriet Mary, the godparents being Bill Stirling, Countess Coudenhove, Basil Bennett, Nancy Rodd and, by an inexplicable whim of Laura's, Miss Haig, the young woman who was sent to take charge of refugee children and is now my mother-in-law's secretary. There was no wine at Pixton and at the end no beer or cider, but copious food. I did little work except decide that long passages must be rewritten in Book II, Today I returned, being assured by Bill Stirling that I might rest assured of as long as I needed to finish the book. I wrote in the afternoon during a refreshing storm of rain but in the evening came a telegram ordering me to Windsor to report before proceeding to my new unit. It is a great waste of time, energy, and money.

London, Wednesday 31 May 1944

Travelled to London and thence to Windsor in order to be told the address of 2SAS Regiment to which I had written daily for weeks, which the Life Guard adjutant said was too secret for the post. I saw Basil for one minute in which he told me that Bill had been sacked and succeeded by Brian.[1] It was hot and I was tired. I went to White's, dined with Bill; the wine went to my head. I joined Hugh Sherwood. He had a drunken row with Kenneth Campbell, each

[1] Stirling was forced to relinquish his command after disagreement with his seniors. He was succeeded by Colonel Brian Franks. See Sykes *Evelyn Waugh* (London, 1975), p. 201.

saying to the other 'You're no gentleman, sir.' Then Hugh and I went to Pratt's where I was given some poisonous port, had great difficulty in walking home, fell down in my bedroom and was sick.

Thursday 1 June 1944

Woke half drunk and had a long, busy morning – getting my hair cut, trying to verify quotations in the London Library, which is still in disorder from its bomb, visiting Nancy. At luncheon I again got drunk. Went to the Beefsteak, which I have just joined, with Christopher and Freddy.[1] Basil Dufferin stole my cab and made me miss my train to Chagford. Back to White's – more port. Ed Stanley arrived. Went to Waterloo in an alcoholic stupor, got the train to Exeter and slept most of the way. Arrived in poor shape at the Rougemont where I was well received and slept ill. I should add that I saw Brian who gave me leave to finish my book.[2]

Chagford, Friday 2 June 1944

Returned to Chagford still in poor shape. Slept in the afternoon. Took a treble sleeping draught and went to bed early.

Saturday 3 June 1944

Started work again, retarded two weeks by my visits to Pixton and London, and finished the rearrangement of Book II, took it to the post, and started once more on the chapter I was doing when I got the summons to London. Maltby, the Oxford binder I have dealt with since I was an undergraduate, more than twenty years ago, writes that he is too busy with 'local government work' to attend to my orders.

Monday 5 June 1944

Yesterday walked to Mass. An Air Force honeymoon couple over my head made work impossible all day. Today I had the couple moved. I have now tidied up all the interpolations and am in the straight, in the last chapter. Hope to finish it by Corpus Christi.

Tuesday 6 June 1944

This morning at breakfast the waiter told me the Second Front had opened. I sat down early to work and wrote a fine passage of Lord Marchmain's death agonies. Carolyn came to tell me the popular front was open. I sent for the priest to give Lord Marchmain the last sacraments. I worked through till 4 o'clock and finished the last chapter – the last dialogue poor – took it to the post,

[1] Christopher Sykes and Lord Birkenhead.
[2] 'Colonel Franks felt the undesirability of Evelyn as a regimental officer even more strongly than his predecessor had done.' Sykes, p. 201.

walked home by the upper road. There only remains now the epilogue which is easy meat. My only fear is lest the invasion upsets my typist at St Leonard's, or the posts to him with my manuscript.

Ardchullery Lodge, Strathyre, Perthshire, Saturday 24 June 1944

On Corpus Christi Day 1944, having been to communion at Gidleigh, I finished the last version of *Brideshead Revisited* and sent it to be typed. Next day Laura came from Pixton and spent a week with me, during which I corrected the typescript which McLachlan made with tremendous speed. On the Friday, June 16th, I came to London. On the day before, though no news had appeared in the papers, the bombardment by 'pilotless planes' had begun. I remained in London until Wednesday June 21st. There were nearly continuous 'alerts' and occasional explosions. The chief inconvenience was at night when one found oneself unwillingly listening for the sounds of the planes which are indistinguishable to an ear like mine from the noise of a motor car. This made sleep very difficult and I was obliged to shut the hotel windows and drug myself. At about 1.30 on the night of Monday June 19th–20th I heard one flying near and low and for the first and I hope the last time in my life was frightened. Thinking this disagreeable experience over I think it was due to weakening my nerves with drink (I was drinking heavily all those days in London) and have therefore resolved today never to be drunk again.

On Wednesday night I travelled to Scotland with Basil to join 2SAS Regiment, now commanded by Brian. I started in poor shape and am now recovering my composure in surroundings of great beauty – Bill Stirling's shooting lodge, on the edge of a loch surrounded by deer forests and grouse moors, depopulated and demilitarized. HQ consists of us, Christopher, a licentious youth who says 'my old dad is a martyr to his prick', and frequent guests. Phil has left, leaving his servant who says, 'I have decided I am not a fighting man.' The most curious feature of the HQ is a pair of Italians who are personal slaves of the regiment having been captured in North Africa and introduced here with forged AB64s in battledress having never been entered as prisoners of war. They are the cooks (one had a restaurant in Milan).

Pixton, Sunday 2 July 1944

The work at Ardchullery was restful but not wholly agreeable, for the house was frequently invaded by young philistines and Brian was so shy of having me under his command as to be almost hostile. He had no work for me in his regiment and wanted me out of the way. I was in some doubt as to my future when on June 28th a series of messages arrived that Randolph was in London and searching for me. I returned to London arriving on the morning of St Peter and Paul and after going to Mass at Brompton Oratory I went to see him at the Dorchester. He asked me to go with him to Croatia in the belief that I should be able to heal the Great Schism between the Catholic and Orthodox churches – something with which he has just become acquainted and finds a hindrance to his war policy. I accepted eagerly but, until yesterday, thought it unlikely to come off. I have had so many setbacks in the last three years. Now, however, I have had a telegram to say that everything is fixed. We leave on Tuesday by air. I am here saying goodbye to my family and go to London tomorrow, Monday.

Randolph Churchill had been asked to lead a military mission to Croatia by Brigadier Fitzroy Maclean, who was in command of British aid to Tito and his Partisans.

Jugoslavia in 1944 had been occupied by the Axis for three years. After the German–Italian invasion of 1941, there had at first been only one resistance movement: the Četniks – Serbian royalists – led by a former Serbian staff colonel, Draža Mihailović. Britain sent him a military mission and what help they could. After the German invasion of Russia, a second – and, as it soon turned out, rival – guerrilla organization emerged: the Partisans led by Josip Broz (Tito), the secretary-general of the small and long-proscribed Jugoslav Communist Party. For many months the outside world knew little about Tito, until in 1943 two British officers parachuted in to his headquarters: first F. W. (Bill) Deakin, an Oxford don, and later Fitzroy Maclean, a former diplomat. Their reports on Tito's anti-German zeal, and the ruthlessness of his guerrillas, were enthusiastic. Mihailović, by contrast, appeared to be less interested in fighting the Germans than in waiting his chance to restore the fortunes of Serbia. The British accordingly abandoned Mihailović and put their full support behind Tito; more cautiously, the Americans followed suit. Maclean attached a series of military missions to local Partisan commanders; and a special unit of the RAF, called Balkan Air Force, was set up on the Italian mainland at Bari – where Maclean also established his rear headquarters – to provide the Partisans with supplies and air support. With each of these missions, there was usually one American.

In Croatia, the situation was particularly complex. Jugoslavia, formed in 1918 from the ruins of the Austro-Hungarian empire and its neighbouring states, was divided in religion between the Eastern and Western churches; the Orthodox Christians were concentrated in Serbia, the Roman Catholics in Croatia. The Germans in 1941 dismembered the whole country, setting up in Croatia an independent Fascist state under Ante Pavelić, a terrorist who had been closely connected with the assassination of the Serbian King Alexander of Jugoslavia in 1934. The Pavelić forces – the bloodthirsty Ustashe – were equally hostile both to the Četniks of Mihailović and to Tito's Partisans. The Germans were strong on the ground in Croatia, and indeed still held large tracts of it at the end of the war.

Churchill's and Waugh's first destination on leaving London was Bari. From there they were bound for Vis, an island off the Dalmatian coast that had been seized by the Royal Navy in 1943 and was firmly held by a combined garrison of British and Partisans. Tito himself was also temporarily on the island; he had been evacuated there in a hurry after a successful German airborne attack on his base at Dvrar, in Bosnia. Negotiations were about to begin between Tito and the supreme allied commander in the Mediterranean, General Maitland (Jumbo) Wilson; it was becoming plain that Jugoslavia would be inherited, when the war ended, not by the Royalists and the young King Peter (Alexander's son) whom the British had at first supported, but by Tito and his Partisans.

Tuesday 4 July 1944

Left Hyde Park Hotel, writing this now only nine days later[1] it sounds odd, amid flying bomb alerts. Took luggage to Randolph's hotel. Lunched Beefsteak and told Harold Nicolson I was off and saw how much he would have liked to come too. Drove with Randolph to Hendon, flew to Swindon, long delay in comfortable rest house, left in York aeroplane, padded seats and cups of tea, at midnight.

Wednesday 5 July 1944

Arrived at Gibraltar for breakfast, lunched in the air on currants and sandwiches and chocolate; arrived at Algiers early afternoon. Wholly American city. Hotel for officers over rank of full colonel only. To Embassy, charming Arabesque villa, partly old. Duff, Diana, Bloggs Baldwin, a peevish [?] attaché from my regiment, Virginia, Mrs Hemingway, Victor Rothschild, all staying in house.[2] Good dinner at house. Randy to Jumbo.[3] I was asked too but preferred to stay at home.

Thursday 6 July 1944

Lunched with Bloggs in town at bistro black market where mystery man listened to our conversation. Dinner party at embassy. Deadly air vice-marshal. Bedroom parties in dressing gowns.

[1] Waugh wrote up his journey to Italy after he had arrived, working backwards from 13 July to 4 July. To avoid confusing the reader, these entries are here printed in chronological order.

[2] Duff and Lady Diana Cooper (Duff Cooper was Britain's representative, in effect ambassador, to General de Gaulle's Committee of National Liberation); Bloggs Baldwin, younger son of Stanley Baldwin, the former Prime Minister; Virginia Cowles, war correspondent; Mrs Hemingway – Martha Gellhorn, war correspondent; 3rd Baron Rothschild, former Fellow of Trinity College, Cambridge.

[3] Randolph Churchill's visit to General Wilson.

Friday 7 July 1944

Diana and Bloggs went out for day. I lunched with Hermione Ranfurly[1] at her house. That evening, expedition to ruins by sea an hour's drive away. Large Anglo–American–French party, songs by moonlight in ruins. Home at 2.30.

Bari, Saturday 8 July 1944

Left Algiers embassy at 7, flew to Catania, hole aeroplane, got no lunch, but on to Naples, by good luck, which was misfortune for others, got seats on Bari plane, arrived 7. Randolph arranged to dine out leaving me dine alone, no bedroom, amorous New Zealand with arm above her head and nurse at same table. Drunk strega and sleeping draught and slept well.

Sunday 9 July 1944

Woke on Randolph's bathroom floor, found church, returned to find message to join Randolph at Philip Broad's[2] flat. Appuleian Aqueduct Company's Fascist luxury. We were to leave that morning for Vis but weather inclement. Picnic lunch with Broad, Foreign Office debauchee, secretary, Bill Deakin (Hindu legs, ascetic face). I think genuine Tito enthusiast. Cocktail party that evening. Air vice-marshals, etc.

Vis, Monday 10 July 1944

A delay at Broad's office, then flight to Vis. Many Jugs in plane and a Hungarian dancer. A great banquet for Tito at HQ (a modern villa with all conveniences except water), a bagpipe band, much gin and wine and kümmel. Tito and staff an hour and a half late for luncheon. He in brand new cap and uniform of Russian marshal[3] with Jug badge. Hammers, sickles and Communist slogans everywhere. Tito startled all by going back on his agreement to meet Jumbo Wilson at Caserta. Randolph very drunk; bathing. All a little affected by wine in the evening. Maclean[4] dour, unprincipled, ambitious, probably very wicked; shaved head and devil's ears. I read his reports in one of which he quoted Lawrence of Arabia saying it was a victory to make a province suffer for freedom. Too early to give any opinions but I have as yet seen nothing that justifies Randolph's assertion to the Pope that 'the whole trend' was against Communism. Subsequent conversations have increased my

---

[1] Personal secretary to General Wilson and wife of the 6th Earl of Ranfurly.

[2] Head of a small Foreign Office outpost in Bari dealing with Jugoslav affairs.

[3] Tito's uniform was that of a Jugoslav, not Russian, marshal; it had been specially designed for the occasion.

[4] Brigadier Fitzroy Maclean took over the British military mission to Tito from Deakin in September 1943.

scepticism.[1] Orphans singing and rolling tins. Partisan girls. Omladinas.[2] Maclean jealous of extraneous elements in 'his' territory. Air Commodore Carter jolly drinking man. Mild Ranfurly. Gordon Alston. Two dreary SOE men. Tom Churchill[3] anxious to be civil and show the antiquities of the island. Tito like Lesbian. Randolph preposterous and lovable [?]. HQ in beautiful bay – oleanders and vines, red earth, aromatic shrubs; no road to villa; walk through mined vineyards. Jack Churchill[4] piped 'Will you no come back again?' to fleeing Marines.

Tuesday 11 July 1944

Vis. Brig. Maclean saturnine and Nazi. A day of whispered conferences, pairs pottering about the terrace. The water so nasty that nothing except the wine was drinkable. Slept badly for Randolph talked till 3 and the flies woke at 4. Thunderstorm.

Wednesday 12 July 1944

Vis. Changes of plan ended in Brigadier and Randolph not lunching with Tito and Brigadier going alone to Caserta to explain to Jumbo Wilson his protégé's rude behaviour. I went to the airfield with Air Commodore Carter to see off Jug delegates for London. They turned up one man short and as Baltimore could only hold five and make two trips I popped in too. A speedy flight and long delay at airfield at Bari. Too late for luncheon; visited HQ and saw sights: S. Nicola's tomb, and dined with P. Jordan[5] and Brooke-Hunt both of whom are coming with us. Jordan at pains to explain his newly found detestation of Communists.

Bari, Italy, Thursday 13 July 1944

Randolph returned; inoculations; visit to 399 HQ and stores; numerous odd gadgets.

Our trip put off until Sunday. Dined with Jordan who wants Pope to lead anti-Communist Europe in crusade.

---

[1] In a letter to the editor (January 1976), Fitzroy Maclean comments: 'From this entry it looks rather as though the diarist, in spite of what he says to the contrary, had joined my Mission with his mind made up on a number of subjects.'

[2] Anglicized plural of Serbo-Croat 'omladina': young people.

[3] Brigadier commanding 2nd Royal Marine Commando Brigade.

[4] Colonel Jack Churchill, DSO and bar, MC. Had been captured leading a raid from Vis on the neighbouring island of Brac; last seen playing his pipes in the forefront of an attack. Elder brother of Tom Churchill.

[5] Philip Jordan, war correspondent.

Friday 14 July 1944

Last cigar. As a result I am consumed with hunger and find myself popping furtively into the snack bar and eating sausage rolls at all hours. We drove to a town beginning with P for luncheon at a black-market restaurant in what appeared to be a private house. Tough *tagliatelle*, delicious little fish, nauseating *zabaglione* made I think with stolen American ice-cream powder. Sightseeing afterwards – a fine old church San Vito; tiny seminarist acted as guide; perhaps future pope. Slept. Charlie Brocklebank turned up. We dined at an officers' club with Bill Deakin. Randolph has gone to Caserta. Winston has signalled very angrily about the Tito fiasco. The Russians seem to be behind it. When Tito went for an hour's cruise in a destroyer they tried to go too and, being refused, pressed Ronnie Tod to say whether he had been meeting King Peter at sea.

Saturday 15 July 1944

Bari, visits to HQ signalling office, etc. Dinner at club. Randolph returned.

Croatia, Sunday 16 July 1944

Bari. Communion 7.30; packing.

Started in low spirits as the result of indigestion. We got into the aeroplane – a large Dakota transport – at nightfall. Randolph, Philip Jordan, I, Air Commodore Carter, some Jugoslav partisans (one girl), two or three Russians added at the last moment which necessitated our offloading much of our stores. Randolph consequently in a rage. We sat about in and on the luggage. The Russians had a large basket of peaches and grapes and oranges which they passed round. As soon as we flew out to sea the lights were put out and we flew in darkness, noisy, uncomfortable, dozing sometimes. After some hours I was conscious by my ears that we were descending and circling the airfield, then we suddenly shot upwards and the next thing I knew was that I was walking in a cornfield by the light of the burning aeroplane talking to a strange British officer about the progress of the war in a detached fashion and that he was saying 'You'd better sit down for a bit skipper.' I had no recollection of the crash nor, at the time, any knowledge of where I was or why, but a confused idea that we had made a forced landing during some retreat. The next thing I knew was sitting on a stretcher in a hut. Randolph in tears because his servant had been killed. A good deal of confused talk about who had escaped and who had burned. I was in no great pain though burned on hands, head and legs. Randolph lame in both legs, Philip Jordan with cracked ribs, one Jugoslav with bad burns and an arm broken in two places. I kept saying, 'Don't let them put margarine on my burns, it is the worst thing.' Randolph shouting for morphia.

Monday 17 July 1944

At dawn we were moved in an ambulance to a village called Topusko[1] and put on beds. A savage Jugoslav woman tried to give me a tetanus injection. The village barber tried to give me brandy. Another young woman in trousers tried to give me roast lamb. All the morning people came and peered at me. An armed guard stood outside. Philip Jordan and I were in cabins of what must have been an inn, single-storeyed with a verandah built round a farmyard; privy of awful filth. After a few hours Philip Jordan and I tried our legs and went to visit Randolph in a neighbouring house, lying side by side with a badly hurt Communist commissar of asiatic appearance. He was protesting furiously at our having been moved from the airfield. He had signalled for a fighter-conducted day plane. A Hungarian Jew from Cricklewood appeared who told me he had been a 'Fine Art Dealer' in Bond Street and solicited help in escaping from the country. The place was misty, a curiously suburban agricultural landscape. A bombed-out bathing establishment. All this time no pain[2] but fatigue and no sleep. Later in the day we went by ambulance back to the airfield; visibility not good enough for landing. Dying air commodore snoring and groaning. An American in charge at the airfield. Randolph upbraided him for moving us. 'It is golden rule, etc.' At last we bedded down in some straw outside and woke next day very stiff, particularly in the neck, no appetite or energy, no pain.

Bari, Tuesday 18 July 1944

A Scottish doctor turned up on a motor cycle and bandaged me up. Long medical conferences dominated by Randolph as to whether they should try to operate on Air Commodore Carter who was now becoming paralysed, or take him to Foggia. Randolph drinking brandy hard. One German plane over. Randolph shouting orders to all. At length Spitfires and a Dakota transport and returned to Bari before dark. Taken to 98 General Hospital.

Remained in hospital until August 2, reasonably happy; no appetite. Food suitable for troops undergoing heavy training in the highlands of Scotland. Dinner at 6 pm in great heat. Ate almost nothing except breakfast while I was there, but suffered nothing until in the last day or two a boil began to grow on the nape of my neck. Randolph in hospital like 'the man who came to dinner', drinking, attacking the night nurse, wanting everyone's medicine and all treatment, dictating letters, plastering the hospital with American propaganda photographs with Serbo-Croat captions. Soon he left for Algiers and I found

---

[1] A small spa that served as political and military headquarters for the Partisans' 'liberated' area of Croatia.

[2] MS reads 'to pain'; but the context suggests that 'no pain' was intended.

things more restful. Force 399 absolutely useless in giving us any help; Air Force excellent; Foreign Office (Philip Broad) excellent.

Rome, Wednesday 2 August 1944

Flew to Rome suffering from boil on neck. Mondi Howard[1] arranged for me to stay with John Rayner[2] whom I hardly knew in charming flat, 5 Via Gregoriana.

I spent two days in Rome seeing Mondi, Philip Jordan, Virginia,[3] with neck getting worse. Took it to Castellani[4] who said it was a carbuncle and needed surgical treatment.

Therefore went to bug-infested 48 General Hospital where M and B treatment reduced me to a condition of despair. Suffering was intense and continuous. At the end of four days I complained and tried to change my doctor. Instead they changed the treatment to injections of penicillin every three hours. This worked and by 15 August I was able to leave. Coote[5] came to visit me in Bari and spent her leave in Rome with me.

Rome, Tuesday 22 August 1944

A week of easy living, getting stronger and eating better. Rome short of water, light and transport. The few restaurants madly expensive. Ranieri open for luncheon only. Most of the hotels taken for various messes. My day, on the average, has been to wake at 7 to the bell of S. Andrea del Frate, tea with John Rayner in pyjamas, read the enemy broadcast news, dress slowly and go out, either by foot or in a borrowed car to see one of the churches; lunch either at Ranieri or alone at the Eden, now an officers' leave hotel. Back to sleep and in the evening read a little before the light failed. Usually dinner at Via Gregoriana, electric light every four days, on other days a single candle or a storm lantern. Often official guests of John.

The loss of my luggage in the fire has left me destitute of many things now irreplaceable. At the moment I feel most the loss of shoes and go about in 'creepers'. When we get in the field again I shall miss my Dunlopillo bed.

The news from France continues to be consistently good; the Americans apparently working efficiently and courageously. Appalling Russian behaviour to Warsaw rebels. Tito saw Churchill.[6]

[1] The Hon. Edmund Howard; during 1944–5 attached to Psychological Warfare Branch of Allied Forces HQ in the intelligence section.

[2] Head of one of the sections of Psychological Warfare Branch of Allied Forces HQ.

[3] Virginia Cowles.

[4] Sir Aldo Castellani, Mussolini's consultant doctor during the war. Before the war, he had been head of the Ross Institute in London.

[5] Lady Dorothy Lygon, in Italy with the WAAF.

[6] Tito and Churchill first met on 12 August 1944 in General Wilson's villa overlooking the Bay of Naples.

On August 20th, Sunday, Randolph arrived still rather lame. He is much calmer, talks of going to Corsica before returning to duty. Rome full of chance encounters – Jimmy Reynolds, Hermione Ranfurly, Ian Campbell-Gray. No sign of Chris whom I expected to find. A box of fifty cigars from Bloggs.

Saturday 26 August 1944

A busy, hot week. Rome full of bigwigs for a series of conferences and the Grand Hotel like the Kremlin with guards everywhere. Luncheon party with Alice di Robilant, cosmopolitan, polyglot, querulous about minor discomforts of war. On Tuesday Diana arrived with Bloggs. Her visit was a failure. The heat overcame her, she deserted Bloggs at first, he replied by going sick on her. Randolph left her to go north with his father, Virginia had already left, I was turned on to write a report on the food conditions of Rome which kept me busy and, except for a luncheon party of Randolph's (which he attempted to give in Jumbo Wilson's private dining-room) and two hours' sightseeing from 7.30 to 9.30 am, saw little of her. The report, with which Mondi Howard helped enormously, took me into the poor quarters to scenes of pitiful distress which gave me the less relish for my own meals.

I lunched with Princess Bandini[1] – a modern house of great splendour. We lunched amid tapestry and Empire furniture[2] and white-gloved footmen and ate American ration sausages. Both her sons have died since the war and the family is extinct. All Romans of the upper classes live in fear of Communism. There is some evidence that the fears are well founded. Yesterday, having sent some days previously to Bari for my letters, I got the disquieting reply that I was expected there on the 25th and therefore letters would be held. Besides the annoyance of missing my post, I suffered alarm that Randolph had failed to arrange my attachment to him during the remainder of his sick leave. This was indeed the case but I put things right today. Meanwhile we should have left for Corsica but he has not appeared.

Lunched yesterday with William Rospigliosi who, as the result of having done time in a 'concentration' camp, is for the first time in his life perfectly *bien-vu* by everyone. He was dressed as an American war correspondent and showed no nostalgia for Helen and England.

Monday 28 August 1944

The hospitable intentions of Alice di Robilant have caused me great annoyance. On Friday I accepted an invitation to dine at her farm, leaving the question of transport open until I knew if Randolph were coming. At 8 I rang

[1] Possibly Edmund Howard's cousin Maria Sofia, Countess Gravina, who before her marriage was of the princely family of Bandini (more properly Giustiniana-Bandini).

[2] There was damask but no tapestry on the dining-room walls of Countess Gravina's house and the furniture was not Empire but Italian *settecento* and *ottocento*.

up from a cocktail party at Mrs Murchey's to find neither host or hostess in. Then the heat of the evening and an invitation to dine from Eric Linklater made me give up the idea. Later I heard that a carload of young ladies had called for me and searched and I felt badly about it. Then I was asked to dinner Saturday night when there was no transport. Then again last night. I determined on no account to fail them this time. As telephone calls are rationed to four a day I was left to fix my journey with a diplomat. He was out all day but expected back. I sat at home by candle light until 9.15 when Andy di Robilant telephoned to say all his guests had arrived – not got my messages. He would send a car. I waited and finally, very hungry, reached them at 9.45 to find an Italian-speaking dinner. I returned very weary at 2 but slept better. My neck is painful and I am full of fear that I may get a return of my carbuncle.

Yesterday afternoon Randolph telephoned from Naples that he would come today, Monday or Tuesday. Had I known of this extra four or five days I could have been a better companion to Diana and written a better report. Dined Saturday with Hugh Montgomery,[1] neurotically anti-Italian and anti-clerical from his confinement in the Vatican. Saturday communion at S. Andrea delle Frate. Yesterday Mass at S. Maria del Popolo.

Isle Russe, Corsica, Friday 1 September 1944

On Tuesday 29th August, after luncheon at the Vatican with D'Arcy Osborne, Randolph and I drove in a jeep to Naples through a devastated countryside. At Cassino there were notices everywhere forbidding traffic to stop. Here we stopped while Randolph made water before a group of women. When asked why he chose this place he said, 'Because I am a member of parliament.' We spent that night and the next (owing to a failure to book airplane tickets) at Harold Macmillan's villa, a house of peculiarly vicious design. The Minister was away the first night and out the second. Roger Makins and a Treasury official were our only company.

Yesterday Randolph awoke fighting drunk. We arrived at the airfield two hours too early and then discovered that the machine stopped at Rome anyway so that we need not have come to Naples at all. Our only link with Corsica was that Randolph had lived there in sin eight years ago and a letter of introduction from someone on Wilson's staff to an American general with a Hungarian name. At Bastia we found ourselves two or three hundred miles from the general's headquarters at Ajaccio. An English military captain at the airport had unfortunately known Randolph as a sergeant at the beginning of the war and had great relish in refusing to help. After half an hour we found transport to the town, called at American headquarters and succeeded in getting a revolting luncheon and the loan of a car. We drove to Isle Russe and found all

[1] First Secretary at the British Legation to the Vatican under Sir D'Arcy Osborne, the minister. After the war he left the diplomatic service and entered the priesthood.

accommodation requisitioned by the USA.[1] Randolph persisted in believing the island to be rich in lobsters and luxury hotels. We drove on to Calvi where we found the same situation. No rooms, no restaurants. At last we found an RAF officer messing with sergeants in the Bishop's Palace. He gave us gin and the use of his telephone. Randolph rang up the US general at Ajaccio and found he was in France but that his staff had been 'alerted'. A most eccentric colonel with a Polish name came to pick us up, drove us to his camp where we drank whisky in his bedroom. He had a chest full of good things which he pressed on us. 'Just say what you want. How are you off for underclothes? Have some chewing gum. Take a pocketful of cigars.' He seized the telephone and ordered rooms for us at Isle Russe, 'the best in the house', 'the best dinner – go out kill a turkey'. Then we drove back on a dangerous corniche road, preceded by two police on motor cycles. No doubt previous bitter experience had led the colonel to send these men ahead, but they did not make the drive much safer since the cars they passed all swung back into the centre of the road behind them just in time to collide with the colonel's jeep and we had many hair-raising escapes.

At Isle Russe we were installed in a suite of rooms each with a sitting-room in the hotel taken by Americans as a rest camp. The food is the kind one sees pictures of in American magazines. We were joined by a desperately smug American Red Cross girl and the fat major who had been detailed to look after us. His name is Martin. We talked about Anglo–American relations *ad nauseam*. The colonel's eccentricity became less marked. Neither he nor any of his country-people were able to take in any expression of opinion they had not previously read in a digest, and assumed they had misheard anything that was unfamiliar.

Topusko, Croatia, Saturday 16 September 1944

Our journey to Croatia was very different from our last. We set off in brilliant sunshine after a luncheon party at Elliot's.[2] Bloggs saw us off. G. Selwyg, an American captain, met us. There was a youth meeting near the airfield[3] and the raised track, formerly a railway, like a Dutch dyke, was lined with girls in peasant costume who Randolph at first thought were there to greet us. We drove fifteen miles or so in a jeep over bad dirt tracks to our camp, passing Topusko on the way which seemed quite different from my memories of it. Camp was in a chestnut forest on a hillside with a beautiful valley below us. Randolph and I had a newly built wood cabin. John Brooke-Hunt, a doctor, and Selwyg, had bivouacks. We ate under a shelter which was also the kitchen,

---

[1] In the MS, the word 'enemy' is crossed out and 'USA' written above it.
[2] Air Vice-Marshal William Elliot, commander-in-chief Balkan Air Force.
[3] i.e. the airfield serving Topusko.

a delicious meal of eggs. It was cool and I slept very well. The Jugoslav HQ Croatia were out of sight in the same woods. The General very German; no clenched fists or Communist signs. We spent three nights in the woods. Then Randolph and I, returning from a luncheon in Topusko with the politicians – the Communist and Croat peasant leaders who live in slightly flirtatious amity; an aged monsignore[1] from Zagreb who though feeble defended his Archbishop; a sculptor pupil of Mestrović – found that a sudden move had been ordered and that we had to move into a farmhouse on the outskirts of the town. Four rooms, a little verandah, a farmyard, two tents in an orchard for the men, a loft for the Jugoslav guards and servants. The work of the farm seems to be mainly in the hands of a little girl of five or six. Our work – breakfast, I at 8, the others 9. 10.30, go and visit HQ and ask if there is any news; possibly write a signal for enciphering. Large luncheon. Randolph sleeps. I read. We have a large library given by the British Council – dinner at 8. Storm lanterns too feeble to read or write. Wireless news hourly. Randolph drunk and rhetorical. At 10.30 I go to bed and sleep very well.

Topusko is a town laid out for leisure and suitable to our habits. The woods are full of ornamental walks, there is one pretty little garden kept fairly tidy, with the arch of ruined abbey in it and a little shelter, another garden with a weeping willow and overgrown paths near the bath. Many buildings are ruined and the shops are all gutted and put to other uses. No inhabitants except soldiers and Jews awaiting evacuation who give the Communist salute and write illiterate appeals to Randolph. Permission has been granted to take them to Bari. Plane trees down the street, pretty cobbles in centre, plinth without statue (king?). Baths brand new, clean and still working. We go and take them most days, no charge. The evidence of elaborate therapeutic machinery in surrounding buildings. A few callers – local Communists whom Randolph rags in a salutory way. He is absorbed in electoral possibilities and undeterred by language limitations. Shouts them down.

Note on Jugoslav soldiers: simple blue eyes, fair hair, cheerful and respectful, always singing and joking. After the sulkiness of British troops it is extraordinary to see the zeal they put into fatigues.

Note on Jugoslav policy: they have no interest in fighting the Germans but are engrossed in their civil war. All their vengeful motives are concentrated on the Ustashe[2] who are reputed bloodthirsty. They make slightly ingenuous attempts to deceive us into thinking their motive in various tiny campaigns is to break German retreat routes. They want Germans out so that they can settle down to civil war. Communist leaders are all out for United Front. 'The people will vote for Communists not for Communism.' The two local bosses,

---

[1] Monsignor Svetozar Rittig; mentioned below.
[2] Croatians allied to the Germans.

Gregorić[1] and Hebrang,[2] have spent the years before war in prison. Gregorić has a kind of holiness; not so Hebrang.

Typical Partisan action. Day before yesterday, 5,000 Partisans attacked 500 Ustashe at Cazin (near Bihac) saying their aim was to hold it in order to attack German road communications. Successful liquidation of Ustashe. Yesterday same party made a half-hearted attack on neighbouring Ustashe village but fled before reinforcements. Today they evacuate Cazin.

Sunday 17 September 1944

Mass at 9 at Topusko church; half a dozen bourgeois, including two politicians of the Croat peasant party and a Dr Snoj of the Slovenian clerical party, and two soldiers. The remainder forty or so old devout peasant women. Randolph then drove me to investigate religious practices elsewhere – Glina, a church like Topusko but with a would-be baroque altar where Mass was over but a christening taking place, and a village where Mass was about to begin with a country audience assembling. Four priests within six miles; no hindrance to worship except rival state organizations for youth and the military. John Brooke-Hunt left by a Russian aeroplane. Gregorić and Mondić [?] visited us and Randolph roared at them about Communism.

Monday 18 September 1944

Three planes came in. We met them on the dark airfield in bitter cold; slight mist at times; line of burning oil tubs; groaning wounded. Thirty Jews who have occupied much of Randolph's attention. Randolph blind drunk from Communist dinner party.

Tuesday 19 September 1944

Decided to go trip to Slovenia with clerical Dr Snoj. Saw church carvings [?] by Croat sculptor.

Sunday 24 September 1944

No air sorties until next month and therefore no mail. I was headed off from Slovenia on the excuse of the crossing of enemy territory being difficult but I think to stop my travelling with Snoj. The staff have shown anxiety about our activities, primarily, I think, Randolph's drunken political conversations and

[1] Pavle Gregorić; doctor and Communist leader from Zagreb.

[2] Andrija Hebrang; one-eyed Croat Communist leader of working-class origin; friend and later a rival of Tito. Believed to have worked for the Russian secret service. While engaged in underground work in Zagreb, was arrested by the Ustashe and later exchanged for Ustashe and Germans captured by the Partisans. Became Secretary-General of the Croat Communist Party, and the most important political figure in Topusko. After the war, he sided with the Russians in their 1948 dispute with Tito, and was their candidate to succeed him. Arrested and later reported to have 'committed suicide' in prison.

our acquaintance with Košutić and young Radić[1] who have come from Zagreb to negotiate, as they think, a coalition with the Communists. They seem in ignorance of the Communist domination.

Time passes slowly. This fortnight seems very long. I wait for the end of the war and tire of the war news. But I sleep as never before. I have no cigars or wine and therefore neither smoke nor drink, perhaps I owe my sleep to that. George Selwyg fled Randolph's conversation and visits the air base. Interpreter phrases. 'The commissar means' for 'says'. 'Never mind' for 'not at all', i.e. *prego*. Our food is dull; meat cooked in fat and sardines. No fruit or fresh vegetables but we eat pills supposed to compensate for the deficiencies.

Every morning lying in bed, rejoicing in the mass of vine outside my window and the light coming through the leaves, I have thought of Midsomer Norton. For a fortnight I have compared it to the border round a text, to my grandmother's illumination, to the tones of chromolithograph. I have just realized that it is quite simply the light through the vine that used to hang round the smoking-room verandah and all these other associations are removed [?] from the direct one of straight memory.

Sunday 1 October 1944

The week has gone slightly quicker but still very very slowly. For the last few days it has rained ceaselessly. On Monday last we were asked in the morning to a banquet that evening, given to celebrate an exchange of decorations between the general staff and the Russian mission. We met at 9 pm and found elaborately decorated tables and covers for at least a hundred. I sat next to the monoglot commissar and a dreary English-speaking Communist journalist. Dinner, very good, took three hours; then there were speeches and then a theatrical entertainment of gruesome character. We got back at 4 am. The entertainment consisted of rousing choruses in Russian, Jugoslav, and a language said to be English; a propaganda playlet from the Russian about a boy getting a medal from the state school; a dialogue between Hitler and Reaction, played by a kind of witch; and a play about a cowardly soldier who becomes brave through shooting a German. My Communist neighbour said, 'You see in spite of war we have the arts.'

Next day, a splendid autumn day of brilliant sunshine, we drove to see a battle at Sunja, Randolph abusing the driver and the guide all the way there and back. We stopped a mile short of Sunja and picnicked, with peasant

---

[1] Son of the murdered founder of the Peasant Party. The Croat Peasant Party was the largest political party in pre-war Jugoslavia. Some of its members collaborated with the Pavelić regime. Maček, its leader, remained passive. August Košutić, who had come to Topusko to propose a political coalition between the Peasant Party and the Partisans, was his deputy. As Waugh anticipated, the Communist leaders of the Partisans had no wish to dilute their authority and they rejected the proposals.

women like illustrations from fairy tales pottering about their farmyards on bare feet and a desultory inconclusive little battle raging below us. We returned to find the telegraphist paralytically drunk wandering round without trousers and finally collapsing. No aeroplanes and after that Tuesday no sun. George Selwyg ran away from us and was brought back. Randolph's servant, who has had to suffer much, yesterday asked to be returned to his regiment and all today has been drunk.

We had Monsignore Rittig to luncheon today. His story is less gallant than I thought. He originally took refuge from the Ustashe among the Italians, and only went to the Partisans when Italy fell. But he is treated with great honour by the Partisans, says Mass with great reverence and is a valuable link between them and decency. Also at luncheon, asked at the last moment, August Košutić, Peasant Party leader of Maček's party who came from Zagreb to discuss an alliance with the Communists. As he left our luncheon he was carried off by the secret police. Randolph, half drunk, rushed off to see Hebrang, the Communist boss, and has been typing endless signals ever since. I go for walks in the mud and think of starting to write a mystery story to pass the time. With the new month there is a hope of mail.

Sunday 8 October 1944

The past week has gone like a fortnight – a great improvement. It rained until Wednesday, stopped for three days and began again. No aeroplanes landed, though some dropped supplies for Partisans. The Russian advance has lowered our prestige. There are numerous small signs of deterioration of our relations with Jugs. Randolph's servant took to drink and has been sent to the airbase to await removal. G. Selwyg is under orders to go. Jugs report our rocket attack on Sunja (first opportunity weather allowed) futile. We have had two canvas chairs made by local carpenter. Unstable but more comfortable than those we have. I should like to start writing a novel but have not the opportunity unless I can persuade Randolph to go to Belgrade when it falls. The maple trees in the single street have turned pale yellow and twilight lasts an hour.

Monday 9 October 1944

Randolph summoned to HQ and rebuked for various minor faults of men under him. Part of policy of pin-pricks. Last night aircraft flew low and went back without landing.

Friday 13 October 1944

Randolph and I at dinner – I wondering how long I could bear his company, even he I think faintly conscious of strain – a telephone call from the airfield: Major Clissold and Major Birkenhead had arrived. Freddy could not be more unexpected if his coming had never been suggested. We had both despaired of him. Randolph's elation was extravagant; he leaped about chuckling and slapping himself, making it plain to me that he had found the restraints of my company irksome. Major Clissold (a gentle ex-schoolmaster from Zagreb, political adviser to Maclean) had very much the second place. Alone, he would have been a welcome and honoured guest; now he was in the way. Not much in Randolph's way, who got uproariously drunk at once. Freddy looked, and was, very ill, having had a fortnight of dysentery in Bari.

Saturday 14 October 1944

I took charge of the gentle Clissold. Freddy had brought cigars and two letters from Laura, shoes, hairbrushes, enough to warm my heart; there was a month's mail still missing. At and after luncheon Randolph and Freddy became paralytically drunk, made an exhibition of it in the lane and went to bed. I made excuses for Randolph who was due to dine that evening with the general commanding 'Croatia'.

Sunday 15 October 1944

Mass, walk, happy with my cigars. Freddy remained in bed all day.

Monday 16 October 1944

Clissold and I drove to a hospital in Petrova Gora forest to visit US airmen. They are coming through our hands in large numbers now. Byrd arrived with the rest of the mail.

Tuesday 17 October 1944

I had meant to spend a happy day with my letters alone in the mission as the rest were to visit HQ in woods but they came back, the expedition cancelled. But I wrote six or seven letters hoping Clissold would take them out. In the evening we went to the showing of the films we had brought in in Glina; failed after four dull newsreels. Supper with Squadron Leader Ruffle [?]. Hosts and guests had all dined before so that nothing was eaten of fine preparations. No aeroplanes.

Wednesday 18 October 1944

Another disappointment. I had looked forward to being left alone all day while the rest visited a lake in the south. That expedition too has been cancelled. But Freddy takes a lot of Randolph's company off me. Have conceived idea of keeping my aunt's home at Midsomer Norton as a working studio.

Monday 23 October 1944

Every evening last week Major Clissold has hoped for an aeroplane and has been disappointed, sometimes on the airfield itself. On Friday we took fifty-six Jews out in intense cold and sent them back to their straw after two hours' wait. There are also fifteen American aircrew, three of them injured in their jump, waiting to get away. Randolph sends petulant signals 'personal for Air Vice-Marshal' believing they will cause consternation at Bari.

On Friday Belgrade fell and there was a great discharge of rifles. On Saturday the celebrations were more formal. A religious service by seven orthodox popes[1] lately arrived from Dalmatia, a temporary altar in the frescoed tea house, tattered vestments, incense, a few chants and then a purely political and patriotic sermon. The General there, all the Communist bosses and editors, Clissold and I by chance. Then the whole party, priests included, adjourned to the Catholic church. HQ troops formed up outside. Monsignore Rittig preached, introducing, Clissold told me, an element of religion, then a *te deum* in the church. None of the congregation seemed familiar with the usages of the place. The priests are said to be got together for a discussion. It seems to me conceivable that Broz[2] aims at a national secularized church.

Randolph got drunk in the early afternoon and had an endless argument with Mates,[3] going round in ponderous circles, contradicting himself, heavily humorous, patronizing, appalling. Mates was even worse, showing a fiery and insane patriotism side by side with his Communism. He spoke of Istria in exactly the terms Hitler youths employed about the Sudeten Germans; he showed the same mystical interest in 'blood' both as a racial bond and as a sacrifice; he showed a more-than-German small-state sense of dignity (and vulgar esteem for physical toughness). And he is a likeable youth, typical of what is best in the Partisans. Later there were torchlight processions, more oratory, a Russian aeroplane, expected, which never came.

Yesterday we awoke to an air-raid – six or seven slow machines dropping small bombs and machine-gunning the village without opposition. Randolph became greatly overexcited. This, he said, was just how the Dvrar parachute attack[4] had begun, and the raid of itself seemed so pointless that I gave some credence to this. However they flew away and Clissold and I went to look for damage and found little. There was a direct hit on the tea-house and the anti-

[1] i.e. priests. *Pop* is Serbo-Croat for priest.

[2] Tito.

[3] Leo Mates: young Communist from Zagreb attached as English-speaking liaison officer to the British mission. Later, Jugoslav ambassador to the USA and vice-minister of Foreign Affairs.

[4] In late May 1944 Tito's headquarters at Dvrar in Bosnia were heavily attacked by a German parachute and glider force, preceded by air bombardment. Escaping encirclement, Tito, some of his staff, and a handful of British officers built an airstrip which allowed them to be evacuated by air, first to Bari and then to Vis.

Fascist fresco was untouched. In church at 11 o'clock there was an aeroplane buzzing round and several bursts of machine-gun fire. The congregation were a little apprehensive at first but the priest was admirably self-possessed and from the moment the canon of the Mass started no one looked from the altar. I half thought there might be a Ustashe attack and that we should come out to find the place in their hands or suddenly find the church invaded by bloodthirsty Croats. Freddy, whom I found alone and morose at the mission, believed a parachute attack was due at any moment. I packed my rucksack and haversack but we did not have to move. Heavy rain fell all the afternoon and evening; the light failed; Randolph and Freddy lay in bed; I strained my eyes re-reading *Quest for Corvo*. This morning I was awake early and dressed, not wanting to be caught in bed by air-raiders again, but there is heavy mist everywhere so I am writing this instead in the sitting-room that reeks of *rakija*.

Randolph got up at 8 through restless fear of air attack, so that his conversation and telephoning and typing and clucking over the signals like an old hen began two hours earlier and I lost the part of the day I value. Clissold and I called on the HQ and got information about a Partisan attack on an oil refinery near Zagreb. Then to Glina in the jeep, taking cigarettes and old magazines to the American aircrews. The three injured men, particularly the former funny man who is hurt internally, were in low spirits and despair of getting taken out. It rained heavily all day and the airfield was pronounced unusable until it had had three days' clear weather.

At luncheon Randolph and Freddy became jocular. They do not make new jests or even repeat their own. Of conversation as I love it – a fantasy growing in the telling, apt repartee, argument based on accepted postulates, spontaneous reminiscences and quotation – they know nothing. All their noise and laughter is in the retelling of memorable sayings of their respective fathers or other public figures; even with this vast repertoire they repeat themselves every day or two – sometimes within an hour. They also recite with great zest the more hackneyed passages of Macaulay, the poems of John Betjeman, Belloc, and other classics. I remarked how boring it was to be obliged to tell Randolph everything twice – once when he was drunk, once when he was sober. Two hours later, in a fuddled state, with a glass of *rakija* in his hand, he came to my room to expostulate with me for unkindness. Later he cooked kidneys for Zora[1] making loud appreciative kisses and whistles when the dish appeared – these, his American slang, his coughing and farting make him a poor companion in wet weather. At least I have not to endure his snoring as Freddy must. Finished *Quest for Corvo*.

Tuesday 24 October 1944

Went with Clissold to visit Monsignore Rittig in the house of the parish

[1] The cook.

priest. A spacious little house with the usual decorations and furniture of a presbytery – a reception-room with hideous dining-room furniture, historical chromolithographs, pious postcards stuck about, an encyclopaedia. The house had the unusual character of a museum also, for the parish priest had assembled and lovingly arranged a number of cut and inscribed stones – Roman and medieval – found in the town. I asked Rittig a number of questions about the position of the church. Did the priests in liberated territory recognize the authority of their bishops? Yes, etc. Bishops had done nothing to hinder their work. How many priests were there? He did not know. Were there in fact any chaplains? Yes, not many. How many? Did not know. And so on. I asked about the plans for education; would the teaching orders be allowed back? The Franciscans had behaved badly, inciting the Ustashe. None of this was quite satisfactory and I began to think the Monsignor put politics, or, as he would call it, patriotism, above his religion. Then I asked about the religious practices of the Partisan soldiers. He began to praise their sobriety, purity, courage. I said, Is it better to be a courageous heathen or a cowardly Christian? At that he quite changed, chucked the patriotic line, quoted the 9th beatitude, remarked that it was St Raphael's day and we must all be like St Raphael, and humanely said it was the priest's duty to stay with his people however hard it was, and that we had the assurance that evil would not prevail over good. I left him with the assurance that he was a sincere priest. The parish priest then showed us his stones.

Rain stopped and there is some hope of the field being serviceable in forty-eight hours. Clissold rather presumptuously invited Captain Byrd to luncheon. A boring young man with few social graces. Jews called to complain of their priorities and about supplies. They said that a Jew had been killed by the bombing and his body robbed and stripped at once by the Partisans. This does not accord with what we know of them. Troubled by piles.

Wednesday 25 October 1944

Drove to Glina with Clissold, picked up Squadron Leader Ruffle and visited waterlogged airfields. Then to IV Corps HQ to see the commander who was said to be in a rage about the miscarriage of his supplies but whom we found in a condition of humorous resignation remarkable for his extreme youth. It was plain from the figures he gave us that supplies are sent haphazard as they become available without reference to the laboriously prepared tables of priority. No rain and the ground drying. Spent the afternoon and evening indoors. Randolph and Freddy went to supervise the reception of parachute stores at Gajevi [?] but returned at once having found the thing in good order. Clissold predicts that this country will be closed to travellers after the war. Yanks fighting naval battle in Pacific. Elsewhere war seems to have begun hibernating.

Thursday 26 October 1944

Drizzle began at midday, developing into heavy rain in the afternoon. It rained all night. The hope of air landings is therefore further postponed. Meanwhile thirty-three airmen have arrived at the field. Spoleto has fallen – perhaps it will soon be possible to leave by sea. Corporal Jasper again drunk.

Friday 27 October 1944

A day of continuous rain. We did not leave the house. Further 'tiffs' with Randolph resulting in his making a further appeal to me for kinder treatment. It left me unmoved for in these matters he is simply a flabby bully who rejoices in blustering and shouting down anyone weaker than himself and starts squealing as soon as he meets anyone as strong. In words he can understand, he can dish it out, but he can't take it. However, as we are obliged to live together I must exercise self-control and give him the privileges of a commanding officer even though he shirks the responsibilities. I have felt less inclination to hide my scorn since his loss of self-control during the air-raid on Sunday. The facts are that he is a bore – with no intellectual invention or agility. He has a childlike retentive memory and repetition takes the place of thought. He has set himself very low aims and has not the self-control to pursue them steadfastly. He has no independence of character and his engaging affection comes from this. He is not a good companion for a long period, but the conclusion is always the same – that no one else would have chosen me, nor would anyone else have accepted him. We are both at the end of our tether as far as war work is concerned and must make what we can of it.

Yesterday the Moslem 'Brigade' marched through Topusko, a battalion strong, mostly without boots or baggage, ragged, with a few songleaders trying to stir them to sing about youth. They were very young and thin. Had they worn long mustachios and outlandish clothes like their fathers and borne weapons with a Byzantine cut they could have marched through this cosy landscape without disturbing. But there was too near a kinship to ourselves – their weapons and tattered uniforms were ours or Italian; they had come too from our sort of action at Cazin – an attack in overwhelming superiority, the loot our kind of loot – an X-ray apparatus and operating table – their failure ours, they could not stand the counter-attack. They were treacherous, too, had followed their leader in three changes of allegiance and had then murdered him for money. This is Europe, I thought.

Saturday 28 October 1944

My 41st birthday and the glummest I have had for eleven years. There was a drizzle of rain all day and I left the house only once – a journey to the baths which were said, untruly as we found, to be open again. It has been a good year

– a daughter born, a book written, a narrow escape from death. I pray God that next year I am at my own home, at my own work, and at peace.

Sunday 29 October 1944

Mud underfoot, grey skies overhead, intermittent rain, drizzle, mist. To Mass at 9, to the baths at 11, where the water was not as deep or as hot as I should have liked, where there was a strong smell of marsh gas or worse and where anti-Fascist women rattled the windows and cried '*Avion!*'. After that all day indoors straining my eyes over bad modern print in the failing light and the flickering electric lamp.

Monday 30 October 1944

A signal to say there will be no 'pick-up' operation for ten days.

Tuesday 31 October 1944

We remarked when we got the foregoing signal that the rain would now stop; it did; a sunny day and clear moonlit night. Clissold and Freddy proposed travelling overland to Split, were told it was feasible, and an hour later that it was impossible. Randolph cooked dinner consisting of one enormous, raw potato each with a hard egg in the centre – uneatable. Muddled reply to signal about journalists; muddled discussion about law of libel.

All Saints' Day

Fine. Large number of peasant women in gala dress. Mass at 10.30. Mail expected in the evening but did not come.

Thursday 2 November 1944

Rain began at 4 am and continued most of the day, postponing hopes of air landing. Byrd rode over to luncheon to tell us that IV Corps are complaining again about Sergeant Pavelić, this time apparently because he asked the mayor of a village to meet a pig[1] at tea, and have asked for his deportation; they also complain of lack of supplies. There is no gratitude to us among the Jugoslavs nor need there be, for we have no generosity to them. We pursue a policy of niggardly and near-sighted self-advantage and then whine when we fail to secure universal love and esteem.

Randolph fretting and fuming over his signals; rushing out to ask the telegraphist if there is anything in, saying, 'Perhaps I shall hear on the next contact.' 'Hear what?' 'That Corporal Crooke' (who was expected to parachute last night) 'is safe.' 'But have you any doubts?' 'No, of course not. But *why don't they tell me?*' He is planning to go to Belgrade, which will give me a welcome holiday also.

[1] The MS is clear; the meaning is not.

Friday 3 November 1944

A number of contradictory signals have given us the fear that our mail may have been dropped wide some nights ago, robbed, and lost. It would be insupportable to me. In the evening Mates came on Randolph's summons. Randolph was already drunk and got drunker – a shameful conversation with Randolph haranguing Mates and demanding silence from everyone, Mates retaining his wits and his dignity. Randolph went supperless to bed. Mates was quite explicit about Communist aims here, contrasting the movement here with that in Greece where they had attempted to seize power first and then beat the Germans; here they fought the Germans first and were now prepared to seize power. 'The time has come when we can begin to ask those who have fought with us what their aims are after the war.' Randolph was too drunk and too eager to speak himself to appreciate what was said. Freddy, more sober, very repetitive, sat up complaining about having to share a room and recounting over and over again a row of the previous night.

Saturday 4 November 1944

Randolph, with ostrich-cunning, stayed in bed hoping to give the impression that he had been ill, not drunk, the night before. It was not, however, so peaceful a day as I hoped. Byrd rode over and stayed five hours with inane gaucherie, neither at ease, nor ill enough at ease to go. I was intolerably rude to him, felt ashamed and then realized that he simply did not notice. Then came a signal that forty-eight aeroplanes were dropping at Kladusha and Randolph was so excited that he leaped out of bed. Then Mates called. Then there was a further signal giving a different time for the air operation and no cancellation of the earlier message. So Randolph, who had decided to go out to the drop, was still further excited and spent hours on the telephone and fussing like a hen over the telegraphists. I went to bed at my usual time but could not sleep till they at last left. Freddy woke me to get my key of the box but I find this morning that he did not lock it.

Sunday 5 November 1944

The drop at Kladusha was successful; a more important event for me was a small drop at Glina which brought our mail, intact, not lost as we thought, a pile of air-letter cards from Laura, books from Nancy, a box of inferior cigars from George Selwyg. Unhappily it also brought a vast assortment of PWB material and Randolph made the living-room uninhabitable apportioning it. Weather remained very fine and there is every hope of Clissold leaving shortly with our outward mail. Mass at 9. Randolph returned from Kladusha 11.30; mail at 1; goose at 8. The appearance of this bird galvanized my companions a little. I should have preferred our normal dinner. Rain.

Monday 6 November 1944

Drove to Kladusha with Randolph who wished to lick up all he could of the vicarious esteem of the mass drop. Kladusha is a Moslem village – in a mile or two we drove from central Europe into the Balkans – an impoverished collection of half-ruined houses round a large green, rows of chestnut trees, leaves pale yellow, a conical hill with a ruined castle on it, standing over the town and the sun setting behind it. Men with red fezzes and straggling beards, military age, dour and suspicious manner. A ruined mosque and chapel. Two stores with sodden army stores lately dropped. Drove back with the sun setting behind us down the Glina valley, all the hills rusty with autumn leaf. Another letter.

Tuesday 7 November 1944

Celebrations of Russian revolution. Many soldiers with new, gilt, Russian-made medals. Stari[1] fighting drunk in the evening. Dry but overcast day. Promise of Dakotas landing tomorrow. Ironical comments on possibility of rain.

Wednesday 8 November 1944

Woke at 4 am. Heavy rain. Stari in tears. 'Mr Captain I ain't agoing to do it no more. I'se fixed up those other guys' – indicating other-ranks' quarters – 'they say you go and see Mr Captain, he make it all right.' Later he told Randolph that if he were sent back to his unit under arrest, he would be shot. Rain most of the day and no flying. Bakarić[2], the new Communist boss of Croatia, came to luncheon. A solicitor's clerk with a suitably diffident manner – completely non-committal. Randolph and Freddy got drunk. I left the party when Randolph began explaining the British Foreign Office. Two hours later Freddy was talking gibberish to himself in the earth closet. Randolph broke into maudlin reproaches of my failure of friendship and cruelty to him. 'It can't go on. It can't go on.' 'All right then I'll go back to Bari.' 'I'm still fond of you. In spite of all your beastliness to me. I am wounded and grieved....' I did not feel the smallest stir of compunction. Randolph and Freddy went to bed before dinner and did not appear again. Peaceful evening with Clissold.

Thursday 9 November 1944

Mates called with two loutish youths in uniform. 'This' – pointing to the more loutish and pockmarked one – 'is the commander of the HQ battalion. This' – a cleaner cad – 'the commissar. We are come about the incident of Sergeant Stari.' They then proceeded with great solemnity to say that they had

[1] A peasant attached to the mission as handyman. *Stari* is Serbo-Croat for 'old man'.

[2] Dr Vladimir Bakarić; Croat Communist leader in Zagreb, a close colleague of Tito's, and, for three decades after the war, the leading politician in Croatia.

investigated the matter and found that an incident had taken place, which affected not only the discipline of the army but their relations with their allies. Before sending the matter up for court-martial, which would result in Stari being shot, they would like to know Major Churchill's wishes in the matter. Randolph said he thought Stari was scared and that he was prepared to overlook the matter. The Partisans clearly wished to point a contrast between our drunken army and their sober and disciplined men. They said that they would consider a more lenient punishment in view of Randolph's great clemency, and would send Stari to prison. Stari when he heard the news was overjoyed and grateful. After dinner it began to snow.

Friday 10 November 1944

Snow and thaw.

Saturday 11 November 1944

Clissold and I went for a long walk, starting on crisp, frozen ground and returning, when the sun was up, through deep mud. In the afternoon a bath. Thinking the money well spent if it would keep Randolph quiet, Freddy and I have bet him £10 each that he will not read the Bible right through in a fortnight. He has set to work but not as quietly as we hoped. He sits bouncing about on his chair, chortling and saying, 'I say, did you know this came in the Bible "bring down my grey hairs with sorrow to the grave"?' Or simply, 'God, isn't God a shit.'

The first of a large party of escaped prisoners of war[1] arrived here.

Sunday 12 November 1944

A request from HQ. Could we please tell them the dates of British national festivals? What could we say? St George, King's birthday? Empire day? We had to tell them we had no festivals except those of the church.

Monday 13 November 1944

More escaped prisoners arrived. Clear weather but the ground still soft.

Tuesday 14 November 1944

Woke once in the night to rain, later to heavy snowfall. I think it my plain duty to move to Glina and act as camp commandant to the prisoners daily increasing in numbers but in the sixth year of war wait to be ordered there.

---

[1] Topusko was a final link in the Allies' hazardous escape route across the Balkans. Some escaping Allied prisoners of war, who had been told that at Topusko they would reach a British military mission commanded by the Prime Minister's son, were bewildered at what they found: Randolph Churchill in bed, a cigar in one hand and a glass of *rakija* in the other, reading Lord Birkenhead's very large family Bible.

Wednesday and Thursday 15–16 November 1944

Did not leave the house until Thursday evening when we went to an entertainment given for the ex-prisoners in Glina. A revolting American patriotic film, some folk dancing, choruses, and patriotic songs. 'That is a love song made by a partisan soldier to his Bren gun.' A project for overland journey to the coast.

Friday 17 November 1944

Report of large German mechanized force moving up through Bihać; possibility of *pokret*.[1]

Saturday 18 November 1944

Freddy, having doubled his bet, is now anxious to win it, so that instead of purchasing a few hours' silence for my £10 I now have to endure an endless campaign of interruption and banter, both reader and heckler drunk. Light failed for lack of petrol.

Sunday 19 November 1944

I returned from Mass to find the mission in great excitement as an order had come to move all the prisoners of war and pilots to Udbina where the airfield was serviceable. Randolph got fuddled and attempted to direct things. After many hours of confusion he eventually drove off in the jeep with Freddy, Clissold, and a Jugoslav colonel, followed by three trucks carrying about sixty passengers each and doomed to break down. That was an hour before sunset with seventy miles to make of rough country, some of it precariously held. I was delighted to see my letters home go at last. I get more pleasure from seeing my own letters leave than in receiving those from home. I now settle down to a peaceful twenty hours. Clissold's patience broke at the last and he refused to embroil himself as interpreter in Randolph's drunken negotiations. He and Freddy both promise to secure my recall and I think Clissold's final loss of temper a surety for his good offices at Bari.

Monday 20 November 1944

An enemy aeroplane at 6 and again at 8. Partisans fired everything they had, including our sentry who loosed off a tommy gun under my window at a target a mile high; they have been in an excitable state all the morning disturbing my one day's rest with continual fusillades. My rest did not last long. Randolph returned at 4 bringing a confused account of failure at Udbina and four American officers. My proofs came of B.R.[2]

---

[1] Partisan expression meaning 'a military movement'.
[2] *Brideshead Revisited*.

Tuesday 21 November 1944

Americans in and about the house all day. I corrected proofs in the cold of my bedroom.

Wednesday 22 November 1944

The Americans still with us. Randolph got drunk at midday and abandoned his Bible reading. The Americans got drunk at cocktails with the Russians and one was sick on the floor during dinner.

Thursday 23 November 1944

Americans made as though to go but returned in full strength at nightfall.

Friday 24 November 1944

Americans at last left. Busy with proof corrections in Randolph's rare absences from the room.

Saturday 25 November 1944

Proof corrections. Randolph soaking all the afternoon and attempting to compose verse. He sat with a glass of *rakija* stinking beside him, grunting, counting the syllables on his fingers and in the end produced the line: 'Nostalgia for the limbo of the oblivion of your love.' Later he became abusive, and later comatose.

Sunday 26 November 1944

Freddy and Clissold arrived Bari 20th. I am delighted that my letters are on their way home. Finished final proof correcting at 6 in the evening while Randolph was at a cinema show at Glina which failed to happen.

Monday 27 November 1944

Heavy fall of snow; a truck of airmen and escaped prisoners left for the Lika. Randolph drunk.

Tuesday 28 November 1944

Heavy snow, thaw; authorization for my departure; road closed; Partisan jubilee.

Wednesday 29 November 1944

Snow and thaw; the party who left on Monday stuck at Slunj. At night a dinner of Zavnoh[1] to celebrate the anniversary of its foundation. 6.30–12 midnight we sat in a little lamplit room, with Christmas decorations and

[1] Regional Anti-Fascist Council for the Liberation of Croatia.

colossal charcoal drawings of Tito on the walls. Excellent dinner with no attempt at speed in the service; pretty girls waiting. One woman guest (hostess), the monoglot President of the anti-Fascist Women who sat on my right; on my left, an Istrian doctor of fine Italian beauty who was learning Serbo-Croat with difficulty; he and I talked in halting Italian; opposite, Mgr. Rittig who muttered to me in barely audible and barely intelligible French; most people made speeches, many of them spoke twice. A gruesome evening and another like it tonight with the Americans, who are celebrating Thanksgiving a week late.

Thursday 30 November 1944

American dinner postponed as Col. Huntingdon returned from Slovenia worn out. Signal arrived posting me to Ragusa – wholly acceptable but staff now report road cut south of Korenica by Germans.

Friday 1 December 1944

Staff now report road cut between Slunj and Korenica and between Korenica and the coast. The Americans gave their dinner – many tepid courses in a frigid hall. Speeches.

Saturday 2 December 1944

Found American colonels breakfasting on the remains of the chocolate cake from last night's dinner. Thaw almost complete but snow again threatening. Anxious about getting my proofs home – otherwise resigned to long delay.

Bari, Monday 11 December 1944

On the evening of Saturday 2nd news came from the HQ that the road to Split was again open. Accordingly I started at 10 o'clock on Sunday, after Mass, in the jeep with a driver and a Partisan major. The Americans were on the move also, not very sure where they wanted to go but quite sure they wanted to be up and doing. I met them at Slunj where the snow was not kind to what must in other conditions be an impressive series of cascades. After Slunj the road led up to Plitvice lakes through forest country, deep snow and scores of mines. We got stuck once or twice and were glad of the Americans' help in pulling us out. After Plitvice we went into the Lika, a very desolate country, a broad flat valley under snow, bare hills all round us, ruined villages, no civilian inhabitants except a few barely human creatures who crept out of houses to stare at us. We reached Korenica at 3.30 pm, a large village with several substantial buildings, all in ruins except for two or three houses at one end. Here in two tiny rooms was a joint mission, officers and men, American, English, crypto-Croats, an elderly woman and a young girl all living together and sleeping on the floor. There were no British officers there. The Americans found me some hay and space for my sleeping bag in a communal dormitory across the road. Hard frost that night. The women up before dawn making a little fire and cooking a sort of porridge.

I got off at 9 on Monday morning and drove on through the Lika, through Udbina, all ruins, to the foot of the pass over the Dinaric Alps. Here we were warned that Cazin had been evacuated by the Germans and that a large German column was advancing down the road towards us. We drove on and up through an ice-hung forest of intense beauty until at 11.30 we reached the summit and the stone marking the frontier of Dalmatia. The change was abrupt. Snow and ice suddenly ended, the stone became tawny, green plants in the crevices, trees below us with their autumn leaves still on them – red vines, yellow oaks, green olives and far ahead a patch of blue and gold and the sun on the Adriatic. We went down and reached Obrovac at 12.15, a pretty little coloured town with clean streets, red roofs, colour-washed stucco. At last I began to feel confident in arriving safely. The bridge was down but a landing craft was acting as ferry. We delayed, fussing over a defective wheel, and drove on to Benkovac where we waited an hour and changed our major, who was bound for Zara, for two others who said they were bound for Šibenik but were in fact joy-riding. Neither knew the way and a rather tedious hour followed when we drove through the coast plain down roads which proved to be blocked. At last we came to the sea at Biograd and along the coast to Šibenik at dusk. Lights came on in the town as we waited for the ferry. At Šibenik we again changed passengers and drove down an execrable road – an incomplete new one – to Trogir, and then very fast to Split, arriving at 8.30. Here I presumed our difficulties were over but at the town major's office no one knew where the mission was, misdirected us until we came to a requisitioned hotel where we found a RNR lieutenant who said, 'You go to the end of the Prom. Keep straight on till you meet the first Jug sentries, turn right, it's a cul-de-sac, you can't miss it.' These instructions, by daylight, proved to be entirely misleading. That night we drove about for half an hour, returning twice to the sailor. Then we telephoned and the British Liaison Officer (Scott) sent a jeep to guide us. He was a hospitable fellow in a decent villa some way out of the town. He gave me dinner and a bed.

It was here I first heard what have been continual since – complaints about the deliberate rudeness of the local Partisans. They are ill at ease in Dalmatia, where the cultured townsmen dislike them heartily. The Partisans react by a regime of suspicion, arrests by the secret police, and discourtesy to the BLOs. A British cruiser is moored in the harbour, the *Delhi*, and greatly resented.

Next morning, December 6th, I wanted to go into the town and revive my memories of the Diocletian Palace but instead was obliged to hang about waiting to see Wintour, whose place at Dubrovnik I am taking over. He, also, was full of resentment at his treatment, but assured me he was leaving me the best house – a villa I once went to with the Infanta Beatrice. At 1 pm I embarked in the *Hai Lee* [?], an adapted trooper flying the Norwegian flag, which was employed in returning to the starving coast the children and old people who had been sent as refugees to Italy. There was a gale warning out but we had a smooth passage rendered more agreeable by the hospitality of the doctor who let me use his cabin.

Wednesday 6 December 1944

At 7 am we docked in Brindisi. It was not until 3 pm that a car came for me. We reached Bari in the dark and very much in the dark for the lights had failed and I found the Imperiale lit by a few candles and no reservation for me. I went on to BAF,[1] also candle-lit and saw John Clarke[2] who told me that as soon as Wintour left the Partisans confiscated the villa at Dubrovnik. I was feeling a little depressed when George Jellicoe turned up a little tight, carrying a candle. Then the lights came on, he and I went back to the Imperiale and later dined together at the Club.

Thursday 7 December 1944

A very busy day visiting officers, barbers, priests, shops. British at war with Partisans in Athens.

Friday 8 December 1944

Also busy. Lunched with Constant Lambert; dined, an excellent dinner, with Jonathan Blow.

Saturday 9 December 1944

Busy and rather weary. Sent a signal to Fitzroy Maclean seeking authority to make an enquiry and a report on the religious situation. It seems highly probable to me that the Maclean mission will soon disband. Partisan refusal to accept Unrra or AML[3] help, if distributed by our observers, causes one crisis, the fighting in Athens another. The Russian advance towards Zagreb puts us in the shade. Clarke and I dined together and ordered a banquet for Coote Lygon next day.

Sunday 10 December 1944

Communion at a little church in the slums. Lunch with John Clarke and various mission officers. Lay down very weary but Coote arrived, rather inopportunely, at 3.30. I had a rather sticky time with her until 6, failed to get a bath, took two Benzedrine tablets, found I lost all appetite through fatigue and could eat little of the very fine feast we had arranged. For myself I found it a

[1] Balkan Air Force.
[2] Regular soldier and one of Waugh's superior officers at the Allied HQ in Bari.
[3] Allied Military Liaison.

dull evening and wondered whether Coote found it worth her long hitch-hike.

I had meant to go to Dubrovnik tomorrow but am delayed and in no great hurry to go. There is a rumour of Bob, Phil and Harry Stavordale arriving here soon.

Wednesday 13 December 1944

I remain in Bari seeing people in connection with my mission at Dubrovnik and collecting stores. I keep meeting old friends – yesterday Father Basil, just retiring from Commandos, this morning Taffy Rodd,[1] just back from Athens. He reports our force there is beleaguered in a small quarter of the city, with a precarious hold on the airfield and no communication with the coast. Yesterday the Communists cut the water supply from Marathon. *Union Jack* hints that the Greek crisis is splitting the Labour Party at home. Everyone here is worried about Greece. This is no time to embark on a full-scale operation, nor could such an operation be permanently successful. The best we could do would be what the Germans did in Jugoslavia – hold the towns and roads and leave the Communists waiting in the hills to revenge themselves on our friends when we retire. The fault has come through the papers and politicians in England refusing to recognize that the Partisans everywhere are a homogeneous revolutionary army – instead we have called them 'patriots' and 'resistance groups' or 'armies of liberation' and put the word Communist, when used at all, in inverted commas as a German propaganda lie. In England apparently the thing is seen as an attempt by us to force an unwelcome royalist government on a democratic nation. Only an overwhelming display of strength could do any good now and we have not the men for it even if the country would support it.

What else have I talked about? Mostly abuse of the Jugoslav Partisans from all sides, prophecies of Italy going Communist as soon as the Germans move out, a certain amount of architecture talk. The sight and sound of so many people exhausts me after the months at Topusko.

Thursday 14 December 1944

Freddy Birkenhead, Bill Deakin, John Clarke and I in a mood of black despair – the war going the wrong way, the situation in Greece insoluble, the casualties in Italy approaching last war level, the Americans becoming unfriendly, Italians watching for the chance to come out against us, no personal future for any of us. Dined alone at the Imperiale and fell into conversation with three policemen who told me there were 2,000 armed deserters loose in Italy from British forces alone.

By December 1944, when Waugh left Bari for Dubrovnik, the German army was rapidly withdrawing from Jugoslavia, Greece, and Albania. To help the

[1] Younger brother of the Hon. Peter Rodd.

Partisans cut off the German retreat, the British in late 1944 had assembled 'Floydforce' – a unit of brigade strength comprising the 43 (Royal Marine) Commando, a detachment of the RAF Regiment, a regiment of the Royal Artillery, and an RASC transport company – and transferred it to the mainland, with its rear headquarters at Dubrovnik. Waugh, still part of Brigadier Maclean's military mission, was posted to Dubrovnik as the mission's representative, his task being to urge on the Partisans against the Germans. Maclean himself was meanwhile in Belgrade, the Jugoslav capital, which had fallen to the Russians and the Partisans in October; Maclean had reopened the British Embassy and was seeking to regulate dealings between Britain and Tito, now established in the White Palace. With Tito incontestably, by this stage, the *de facto* heir to Jugoslavia, the Partisans in Dubrovnik, as elsewhere, began to treat their British allies in an increasingly peremptory manner.[1]

Dubrovnik, Friday 22 December 1944

For the last three nights at Bari I moved out to John Clarke's villa in San Spirito where the aeroplanes gave me no peace. I went into Bari by day, making final arrangements for Dubrovnik and seeing Bill Deakin, his wife embarrassingly named 'Pussy', and Michael Trappes-Lomax, who turned up unchanged and a little futile as permanent president of courts-martial.

On Monday December 18th I sailed, taking with me a sergeant-major from 12 Commando, still illicitly wearing their badges, and a Scots Guards corporal, John Clarke's servant, a temporary attachment until Gourdie gets his permit to come. We were warned to sail at 10 am but it was 6 pm when we did so. Our ship a TLC[2] with a small cargo of evil-smelling sacks and some shabby-looking RASC[3] men. I had been warned to expect no hospitality from the Navy but found the juvenile RNVR[4] sub-lieutenants (the senior addressing the other as 'No. 1') most welcoming. Their accommodation was tiny – a bunk in a passage, a minute square cabin with another bunk. The cabin was also the wheelhouse and wardroom. All they could do, they did for us. Corporal Pearson, Clarke's servant, showed signs of dissociating himself from our party and travelling as a private passenger. When, at 10 o'clock, I found my way in the darkness to the hole where I was going to sleep, I found two men sprawling among my luggage and no bed laid out for me, so I returned to a chair in the wheelhouse where the steersman carried on a continuous, liturgical conversation into the speaking-tube and I slept little. Our hosts (there were two other officers travelling) were again enormously kind, but there was nothing I could say to them or they to me

[1] See Donald Hamilton-Hill, *S.O.E. Assignment* (London 1973), pp. 171–9.
[2] Tank Landing Craft.
[3] Royal Army Service Corps.
[4] Royal Naval Volunteer Reserve.

which was intelligible, and the noise of the engines made all small talk a great effort.

We sailed into Dubrovnik at 10 next day, following a narrow channel along the coast which had been swept of mines, and berthed in the harbour where I was greeted by a youthful captain in the Rifle Brigade, named Earle, and driven to the mission house. This was a very small hotel on a narrow alley, one dining-room and a few bedrooms, no bath or heating. The major discomfort arose from the lack of an officers' mess. I had been assured in Bari by Randolph and the mission at VIII Corps that orders had been given to provide a suitable house at once, but the next twenty-four hours were spent in convincing me that no such order had been received here.

On the day of my arrival I lunched with Major Hamilton-Hill, the DAQMG, a dapper, rather common fellow, at a frigid villa in Lapad; a bad army-ration lunch in the company of the RC chaplain and a silent paymaster; bad wine. That evening we dined at home; excellent fried fish and chicken, very well-cooked vegetables, good wine – everything delightful except Corporal Pearson, who showed signs of being not only an independent individual but an independent mission; his offences culminated in his saying casually to Earle, 'I shall be coming up to Nikšić with you when you go.' 'Really, Corporal,' I said, 'what is your reason for doing that?' 'I am looking for some things for Colonel Clarke. That is the real reason for my coming.' So next morning, after a tour of the churches at first light, all of them full, I had Pearson up to my room and talked to him briefly and severely, saying that since he was now under my command he must understand me or he could find himself looking very foolish; that he was here for my convenience, for as long as I wished to keep him; that he was the junior member of the mission and must behave as such; that he must never leave the house without permission from the sergeant-major, must dress properly and so forth. Since then he has been cowed and docile and quite useful.

My next step was to have the beds cleared out of the main bedroom and some furniture put there so that I now have my own sitting-room where I work and eat. My own, indeed, only since this morning, for on the afternoon of 20th we met a peculiar-looking officer, a toothless Armenian named Major Karmel[1] of the 60th. I began my relationship with my customary loathing but in the two days he stayed with us formed a warm liking for him. He is quick-witted, funny, fond of wine and cigars, and with the adaptability of his race quickly dropped his original line-regiment heartiness and became human and civilized. He was of service to me in numerous ways, notably in taking me to a cave where I bought a large quantity of excellent wine for 10 lire (6d) a litre. Earle left yesterday and Karmel stayed on.

[1] A barrister before the war; Recorder of the Crown Court, 1972.

Last night Hamilton-Hill and the Brigadier dined with us. The Brigadier, an Irishman with a singular name which is pronounced Twigg, gives an impression of extreme artificiality for he has the eyes and forehead of an orang-outang, a moustache like Osbert Lancaster's, and a voice which blends Aldershot and Irish in a way which made me repeatedly think he was being facetious only to find my smile frozen on my lips by the gleam of his little ape eyes. Dressed in the beret and hackle of his regiment he looks wholly absurd, but he has a row of good medals and all acounts of him make him a first-class soldier. Like everyone I have met for some time, he spoke of the coming war with Russia as something inevitable and imminent. I thought it a dull evening. I thought, moreover, I antagonized my guest by correcting his history in the first few minutes. Karmel, however, professed to think the occasion a success.

The city of Dubrovnik is entirely unravaged by war but has a depressing air; the shops empty, the market full of little groups bartering household ornaments against potatoes and home-made soap, the people pale and scared. They are hungry and sulky. The Partisans look revolting – figures which seemed plausible enough in the Lika seem preposterous in the street here, and the fine architecture does not easily bear its burden of red stars and Partisan inscriptions '*Živio Tito*'[1] '*Živio Stalin*'. All accounts agree that the English landing[2] was greeted with joy; there has been bitter disappointment now it has been discovered that they are merely a small military force with a limited function and no intentions [?] to 'take over' the place and feed it. The Partisans have succeeded in reducing the British staff to nervous impotence and completely rule the roost. The British soldiers preserve a higher spirit, and recently forcibly disarmed a Partisan officer who was kicking a wounded German. The function of the mission here seems primarily to be an intermediary between Floydforce and the Partisan authorities; the work I have done so far has been billeting, welfare, listening to complaints from both sides (and in that matter I find little to choose between them).

Today: breakfast at 8 – fried egg, bacon and sausages. 9.30 went with Karmel to the brigade HQ for the meeting between the Brigadier and the town commander. A cordial meeting: the Brigadier in his hot-potato voice explaining his force orders; the town commander, insolent eyes, a large fair moustache, a fair, rosy complexion, smiling appreciation; a hulking moron interpreter, ex-sea-captain from Vancouver. The interview ended with sweet tea laced liberally with whisky. Then to Ensign 'Tony', the interpreter, to get a telephone put into his office, to complain that a ship had sailed without due notice to the Port Liaison Officer, to arrange a time for billeting in the afternoon; offered him twenty-five tons of diesel for the power station, giving

[1] Long live Tito.
[2] Of Floydforce.

the impression it was my doing; back to the mission to see Karmel off; then a visit from a tearful middle-aged English lady, married to a Jugoslav, who wants to be evacuated; gave her no comfort except a packet of cigarettes, a cake of soap, a copy of *Time*; she kept saying, 'I am so afraid there will be an upheaval'. Found my telephone was out of order. Luncheon fried fresh sardines, raisin tart, white wine.

2.30 at Tony's office who arrived late and overexcited after drinking champagne with a boy and girl youth leader from Moscow just arrived by motor car from the Montenegrin Youth Congress. We went with the Force Billeting Officer, Nairn, to look at stores. Then I went in search of a dismantled German lorry which lay in our workshop area which the Partisans wished to dismantle further and found it so dismantled as almost to have disappeared. Then I discussed the Christmas party which the British troops wish to give for the local children; the Partisans wish to give it themselves for their own Communist youth organization. I said, 'The men are far from home and are thinking of their own little children. They are giving up their own rations to entertain the children of Dubrovnik.' I tried to make clear that rows of uniformed infants chanting '*Zivjela Britanija*' was not their idea of Christmas. I then went to the district Partisan store to bargain over the wine for the soldiers' Christmas. Hamilton-Hill, who has a niggling mind, wished to beat them down. He offered 50 gallons of petrol and 50 kilos of flour for 800 litres of wine and 25 litres of spirit. The commissar began by saying there would be no payment but if we liked to give anything it would be acceptable. I suggested our price and he said that was enough for the wine only. I said then the deal was off. Then he said he would bestow the *rakija* on us so I left feeling the worse for the bargaining. Then I learned that after the Brigadier this morning promised 25 tons of diesel, we could only supply 17. I went to Hamilton-Hill and explained how unfortunate this was and that the Brigadier should be informed. He agreed and telephoned half an hour later to say he would make it up to 20 tons, hoping thereby to avoid informing the Brigadier. I have accordingly made a signal to Karmel leaving it to his discretion to raise the matter at Nikšić.[1] Returned to find an inarticulate message about a Canadian who wants to leave the country and another about a naval officer who wants to go for a drive. Dined alone and sat with a greatcoat on my knees until 10 and then to bed.

Saturday 23 December 1944

Awoke at 3 and fretted myself into a dislike for Major Hamilton-Hill. Visited liaison office and had stormy interview with Tony. The Partisan terms for the Christmas party are that the Communists shall be hosts and shall say

---

[1] Advance HQ of Floydforce, ninety miles from Dubrovnik.

that the provisions come from England, that one Englishman may come too. Our men had looked forward to an afternoon's fun and are disappointed; they had given up their own NAAFI rations for it. So the party will not take place unless a signal I have sent to VIII Corps headquarters produces results.

Further disagreements about patrolling the town; I said we might give up the patrol but not the right to do so. Meanwhile the news from the outer world is depressing – Germans advancing in Belgium, street fighting in Athens, another large call-up for the Army. It will not be a happy Christmas. It was snowing when I awoke this morning and there has been snow in the air all day. I asked the squadron leader who commands the RAF Regiment here to luncheon. He was dull and said nothing of much interest except that his men were increasingly pro-German. It was deadly cold in the afternoon and I sat wrapped in overcoats until 4.30 when an oil stove reached me which I had been trying for days to get from Hamilton-Hill and now obtained quite easily in his absence. He returned at 5 and I went to explain the situation of the picket to him. Then returned to a slightly warmer evening, interrupted by Hamilton-Hill on the telephone – could he send his orderly officer and sergeant round the town? – and various dull signals.

Sunday 24 December 1944

Called by Hamilton-Hill. He now wishes not only to fall short by 5 tons of diesel of the 25 promised for the electric plant but to get back 2,500 gallons, about 10 tons, of what has already been handed over, as he has given more than can be spared. He also wishes to go back on his liquor deal – not to take the *rakija* or to give money for it, on some point of conscience connected with its sale to officers – a point of conscience which will be quite unintelligible to Partisans, as indeed it is to me. Very beautiful Mass at the Franciscan church. Earle arrived at lunch-time, sent in alarm at my signal about the patrol. After luncheon a tour of empty villas with billeting officer, then an interview with town commander who took the loss of diesel in good part. At this interview Hamilton-Hill showed curious obliquity, raising the amount required back to 3,000 gallons and evading the undertaking to return it. At 6, first Mass of Christmas at the cathedral, attended by bourgeois – much dressing and undressing of the bishop and operatic music. Guns and rifles firing all over the town, bells ringing. Dinner with Earle.

Christmas Day 1944

Mass at Franciscan church at 8 and communion; a bright, cold day. The Czech woman who claimed that Wintour owed her $39 proved to be an impostor. I reported to Tony, 'She needs either medical or police attention.' 'I think it will be police.' Cocktails with a group of proletarian officers at HQ. Luncheon alone. After luncheon Rolf Elwes's son called on me. Sleep. Dinner alone. A letter from Nancy[1] and a dubious-looking cheque from Randolph for his Bible bet. Nothing from home. Dinner alone and bed.

Tuesday 26 December 1944

A day of brilliant sun. I walked to Lapad in the morning to investigate the claims of a family named Mustapić to be British subjects. I took the HQ interpreter with me. We walked full circuit of the peninsula before we found the house, a rather shabby little villa. I then sent the interpreter home and was admitted. At first I thought I had come to a house of ill fame; the shadowy hall seemed full of personable young women, some of them in dressing gowns. I was shown into a stiff little parlour with a Christmas tree in the corner, and the crowd of women resolved itself into four – the ladies Mustapić – who entertained me with engaging grace until their father arrived. On reflection I am still not sure that perhaps my first impression may not have been right. An atmosphere of extreme sexuality pervaded the meeting. It was a peculiarity of this family that the only members who were unquestionably Jugoslav spoke fair English, while those who were unquestionably British spoke not at all. It took time to sift their affairs. Mustapić père had been born an Austrian, had emigrated to New Zealand and prospered modestly there as a dairy farmer. He claimed to have been naturalized in 1903. He married a Jugoslav in New Zealand named Bulog who had three brothers – Tom, Joe and Steve – somewhere in the antipodes. The girls were undoubtedly born in New Zealand. They had two birth certificates and one passport (issued by the consul in Sarajevo in 1937) between them. The girl with the best papers, birth certificate and passport, had lately married an Orthodox upholsterer, who was now engaged singing[2] to 29 Division of the Partisans. Her older sister was also married, to an installateur of chauffage. They pouted prettily when told they were no longer British, and asked to be divorced. The two younger girls were certainly British but spoke no English. In spite of this, one of them, the father confided, hoped to marry an English soldier. These two girls were afraid of being impressed into the Partisan army. The family had Palmerstonian ideas of the value of British citizenship and thought once they had their 'papers' they would be exempt from all annoyance and fraud. I have written a full account of their affairs for attention in Bari. They gave me *rakija* and sweet biscuits and sent me off with many smiles. I wonder if it was a brothel.

Jeremy Elwes dined with me – a pleasant-mannered youth with a large appetite and the looks of a mulatto. He aspires to lead Catholic Action underground and to make violent propaganda for an increased birth-rate.

[1] The Hon. Nancy (née Mitford) Rodd.
[2] The MS reading seems plain; the occupation unlikely.

Wednesday 27 December 1944

Brigadier Taowig[1] returned. He wore a monocle which I do not remember having seen before and looked more than ever simian. I had a hot bath. A youth from Nikšić came for the night.

Thursday 28 December 1944

Brigadier Davy[2] arrived from Bari. I had an appointment with town commander and intelligence officer which the latter failed to keep. Major Wintour and a journalist, Harrison,[3] arrived. Wintour had indigestion, Harrison had pro-Partisan sympathies. A dull little military cocktail party for the two brigadiers.

Friday 29 December 1944

Conversation with Wintour's interpreter who told me that all schools in Dubrovnik had been closed by the Partisans while the teachers took a two months' course in the new educational aims under Communist instructors. Complaint by Partisans that in a café the previous evening four British NCOs were seen in conversation with a German in Partisan uniform, who, with their approval, said the Partisans were bandits and spat on his red star. The Partisan police attempted to question the German who escaped with British assistance. I suspect *agents provocateurs*.

Saturday 30 December 1944

Wintour left at dawn, leaving me with an appointment to go sightseeing with a guide. He proved to be deaf and nearly witless, half-starved, dazed. He insisted on getting police permission before coming with me; the police sent us to the town commander where the guide explained that he had been a friend of the Dukes of Windsor and Westminster and Lord Dudley; that he had had unpleasant experiences lately. Only the other day the Italian town major had engaged him to show a German general over the town, which he had done with great skill. 'As you know they are all pro-German in this town', so all the applause during their tour had been 'Heil Hitler' not 'Heil Mussolini'; the German general had been delighted but the Italian commander had put him, the guide, in prison for a week. This did not endear him to the simple Major Bogdan[4] who said we might go together that morning but that in future I must

---

[1] *Sic*. Here and elsewhere in the MS, Waugh seems to have misspelled the Brigdier's name deliberately.

[2] Brigadier George Davy; in command of Land Forces Adriatic; formerly brigadier of the celebrated 7th Armoured Division of the Eighth Army during the Western Desert campaign.

[3] Hubert Harrison, head of Yugoslav Section of BBC during the war; later, Reuters' correspondent in Jugoslavia.

[4] Major Bogdan, the Partisan town commander.

apply for a guide who had a closer grasp of the party line. Then we started on a tour, tottering through the wind-swept streets; at moments the poor old man remembered bits of his recitation, at others his mind was a blank; he was clearly very much set back by the town commander's refusal to give him a general licence. We could not get into the reliquarium at the cathedral; in fact we saw little that was not familiar to me. One would have thought that with so much to trouble him the old man might have been unencumbered by a mother; but no, he had one of ninety, starving and praying for 'Major Winterbottom' who had given her some food. So I had a small parcel made up for him and sent him back with a pathetic flush of excitement.

Other tasks today: can I give the president of Montenegro a pair of tyres; can I arrange the funeral of a German prisoner, dead in hospital; can I find a store for the LRDG; can I dine with Brigadier O'Brien Twoigg.

I forgot to mention yesterday a long call from Brigadier (about to become General) Davy; his strategic plan was to delay the German retreat by shooting at their rearguard. This delayed them, he said, because they stopped to collect their wounded. Having hustled the Germans out of Podgorica, he is now going to hustle them out of Mostar. He said, 'I do not believe the Partisans have any intention of taking a serious part in the war once their country is cleared. They want to get on with politics.'

Written on Tuesday 2 January 1945

Harrison remains with me, held up by the storm, and is a great bore. Yesterday to communion, today to Mass at the Franciscan church. The weather very cold and windy. Little to trouble me. No mail in from Bari. Dominicans state fourteen priests shot here by Partisans.

Typical of my day. A man calling himself Preticic, claiming to be, alternatively, President of Montenegro and of Southern Herzegovina, has lately been importunately demanding motor-tyres. I telephone Tony to establish his identity. After inquiry Tony says he can find out nothing about him. 'But has he car? Then he *must* be a big shot.'

Friday 5 January 1945

Last night Harrison at last left. I was able to avoid a quarrel with him only by submitting to being bored all day long by his vanity and acrimonious wrong-headedness. It is a relief to see the last of him. The only service he did was to introduce me to an elderly sculptor named Paravicini – a bad sculptor to judge by the only visible work of his, two bas-reliefs on the bank – who as local Director of Fine Art is able to show me things that are otherwise locked: the museum, a pleasantly nondescript collection Paravicini purposes to reduce to standard provincial model; and the archives, kept by a racial bore so busy explaining the fact that all his documents are in Italian that he has no eyes for the beauty of the building he works in.

Last night I dined at the hospital – a mess of home-made squalor and bad company. Brigadier O'Brien Twoigg has returned from his scamper to Split with nothing accomplished; VIII Corps refused to see anyone connected with his force. Brigadier (General) Davy has settled down in Split to have his bust carved by a local sculptor. Unless these soldiers are up to something, they are being particularly futile. What I rather think is that they believe themselves, wrongly, to be up to something – a forgotten fragment of the general strategic plan which would have come into operation if the North Italian campaign had revealed a soft underbelly.

9 o'clock pm. I have dined alone and happily on fresh fried sardines; the wind is howling outside. A futile day. First with Paravicini to see the cathedral treasury; the civil guardian arrived with his key and three pupils, but the ecclesiastical guardian failed us. Priests blessing the houses today. After luncheon a wrangle with v Sector Partisan HQ about diesel for the power station. I said the welcome in the town had not inspired us to illuminate it, but we are threatened with the failure of the water supply also, and Brigadier Twoigg refuses to discuss the matter. The arrival of three Anglo-American ML[1] officers is threatened for tomorrow; perhaps their arrival may be opportune; meanwhile their schooner is being unloaded and, it appears, their stores seized by the Partisan army, I think unwittingly.

Saturday 6 January 1945

Communion at the Franciscan church. I had never before realized how specially Epiphany is the feast of artists – twelve days late, after St Joseph and the angels and the shepherds and even the ox and the ass, the exotic caravan arrives with its black pages and ostrich plumes, brought there by book learning and speculation; they have had a long journey across the desert, the splendid gifts are travel-worn and not nearly as splendid as they looked when they were being packed up at Babylon; they have made the most disastrous mistakes – they even asked the way of Herod and provoked the Massacre of the Innocents – but they get to Bethlehem in the end and their gifts are accepted, prophetic gifts that find a way into the language of the Church in a number of places. It is a very complete allegory.

A day of raging storms and official indecision.

I wrote first a signal then a letter protesting against the impertinence of a Q signal about soap; destroyed both; six months ago I should have sent them. A meeting at 12.30 between Bogdan and Brigadier O'Brien-Twoig and various mutes. There was a great deal of soldierly good fellowship – 'The fellows on top

---

[1] Military Liaison.

decide all this over our heads. We simple soldiers manage to muck along' – drinks, and impatience to get to luncheon, which we failed to do until after 2. I regard the meeting as a further milestone on the road of deterioration of Anglo-Partisan relations. A number of complaints were made against British troops – shouts of 'Fuck Tito' in a café and so forth, including rather improbable tales of jeep-loads of English soldiers beating up Jugoslav officers – followed by demands (1) that all British troops shall be liable to inspection of papers by a 'specially chosen' Partisan force (2) that they should only use the town three days a week. Brig. O. Twoig, with military pacifism, assented to both. The process is now nearly complete – first we are asked to withdraw our patrol and thus to resign the right of supervising our own discipline on the grounds that it is no longer needed and that the Partisans are withdrawing theirs; then incidents are reported (perhaps fabricated); then we resign the right to use the town at all, except by Partisan grace, three days a week, which can clearly be reduced at will after suitably arranged incidents; the OZNA[1] meanwhile take over control. No question was raised by our appeasing soldiers and I left Brig. O. Twoig beaming self-satisfaction and plainly believing that relations had been substantially improved.

It is interesting to note workings of military mind. At 1 pm today Brig. O. Twoig asked Bogdan if he could provide house for canteen. At 3 pm DAQMG telephoned to ask if house can be opened tomorrow afternoon.

He continued telephoning off and on all evening and in the end got no house.

Sunday 7 January 1945

Orthodox Christmas; spasmodic firing, a thunderstorm; my telephone snapping and croaking and filling the room with blue fire at every clap of lightning. A ship in with soap, a dull letter from Laura and a bright letter from Nancy Rodd, the first yet about *Brideshead Revisited*. Asked to tea by 11 Corps at 3 in the afternoon. One never knows what to expect in this country. I expected a crowd, a stage, a concert. Instead a small room, tables on three sides, perhaps forty present of whom thirty-five guests, English, American civilian. First there was green chartreuse and ham sandwiches, then tea and cakes, then cherry brandy and cigarettes, then two speeches about Montenegrin liberty and the expectation that the thing was over. Not at all. Next there appeared cold mutton and red wine and general conversation of a sort until 6.30.

Monday 8 January 1945

Brig. O. Twig sent David Karmel to Bogdan to try and wriggle out of the surrender of Saturday; no result. A bitterly disappointing letter from Laura.

[1] Secret police.

Tuesday 9 January 1945

In obedience to a letter from Bari I went in quest of a Dutch lady, to a house well-called 'Solitudina' on the end of Lapad peninsula with a boat-house and landing-stage but no road to it, only a path between palm trees – a fine old house with old furniture, both dilapidated and ravaged by military occupation. I found two middle-aged ladies, one German, one Dutch, and a little girl living alone. The Dutch, whom I had come to see about renewing her passport, could claim extradition but will not leave the German. They are well-off for food, comparatively, but lonely and apprehensive. The German said she would sooner be in an English concentration camp than in what the Partisans termed freedom. 'For two years we said "if only the English would come!" Now they have come and we are not allowed to speak to them.' I could do nothing except promise help with their mail and some sweets for the little girl. In the afternoon I took a parcel of food to a starving old priest. Two little parcels of books from Nancy including an authentic breath of Bloomsbury air – Cyril's *Unquiet Grave*. A letter from Nancy proclaiming *Brideshead Revisited* as a classic.

The motto of privilege: 'Liberty. Leisure. Privacy.'

Tuesday 9 January – Wednesday 10 January 1945

Two days of storm culminating last night in hours of sleeplessness with thunder like an air-raid and hail like the fall of broken glass; it seemed to be pelting down inside the room. I read Connolly's *Unquiet Grave*, half commonplace book of French maxims, half a lament for his life. Poor Lys; he sees her as the embodiment of the blackout and air raids and rationing and compulsory service and Jean as the golden past of beaches and peaches and lemurs. It is badly written in places, with painful psychological jargon which he attempts to fit into service of teleological problems. I also read a dull American 'thriller', sadistic, full of eyes that 'snap' and 'flick', absurdly stamped 'Welfare'. It is sad that pornography has ceased to appeal to pleasure in the last decade and raises the penis by cruelty only. I have written a number of sharp notes to Bari and done something to subvert Karmel.

Thursday 11 January 1945

I lived all day in the smell of the oil stove and the noise of the storm.

Friday 12 January 1945

I commissioned my portrait bust from Paravicini, who needs food more than money, for £50 and some rations while he is at work. I doubt his ever getting the stone or finishing it; if he does it will be the next best thing to having myself stuffed. I told him I had the taste of Prince Paul. Some ML officers arrived; the colonel lunched with me; an affable Kenya man. They have 40 tons of food to distribute among 20,000 people, and little prospect of an agreement to send more. A frightened Bohemian woman came, fresh from prison, asking for freedom. I gave her a cake of soap.

Saturday 13 January 1945

A South African citizen who has been here before and been given food came with her son; I sent them off rudely and was sorry for it before they had been gone ten minutes. Later in the day a scared Jugoslav came; I sent her off politely; later still a Partisan colonel, full of professional goodwill. I have slept badly lately so that afternoon went for a long walk on Lapad and slept better as the result.

Sunday 14 January 1945

I have omitted to say that yesterday I got the treasury of the cathedral opened – a difficult business requiring three keys, one held by the bishop, one by the canons, one by the mayor. It was dark in the treasury and the treasures were very dirty but were a fine collection of medieval and renaissance metalwork. I said to Paravicini, '*J'ai le gout de Prince Paul. Faites-moi comme un oeuvre de Roubillac.*' '*Mais mon capitain, vous manquez le perruque.*'[1] Mass at the Franciscans. Karmel to luncheon. Another soporific walk, a tepid bath in a house that smelled.

Monday 15 January 1945

Mr Paravicini came, stronger for two days' full diet. His conversation in guttural French painful to follow. He set up a rough wooden stand with toggles on wire at the top like leaves of a palm, began scooping handfuls of grey mud out of a rucksack, and in an hour had made a head. I was fascinated to watch him and full of wonder at the result.

Tuesday 16 January 1945

Gourdie came; Pearson goes. I sought out the woman whom I insulted on Saturday and promised her regular rations; advised her to get the hell out of here with her son. I am annotating Cyril's lament. Second sitting for Paravicini; the head becomes like my head. Dinner with O. Twigg.

Wednesday 17 January 1945

Looking back on the last two days I find that everything I have done, which is not much, has been benevolent – giving jobs to the needy, food to the hungry, arranging to get a Canadian moved towards Canada, helping a Dominican

---

[1] Prince Paul was regent of Jugoslavia on behalf of King Peter, 1934–41. Roubillac, French sculptor, 1695–1762. Waugh wrote 'un oeuvre' instead of 'une oeuvre', and 'capitain' instead of 'capitaine'; if he wrote 'perruque' (an alternative reading is 'personnage') he got the tense of that wrong also.

priest swap wine for flour. There are few in the Army can say this and also say they have been solitary and comfortable. The Paravicini bust takes the shape of an Anglican divine of the Matthew Arnold epoch.

Thursday 18 January 1945

Communion at Franciscan church. Signal that Floydforce returning to Italy forthwith. Poor Mr Paravicini's bust grew much less like me. I have now on my hands a Jewish interpreter who knows no English and for whom I have no work. He sits downstairs all day long and I hope enjoys his food.

Friday 19 January 1945

Interview with Bogdan. My poor Mr Sen got a cold reception and the threat that his permission to work for me would not be renewed. I asked him to talk to the cook and tell her I always wanted three courses for dinner. He told her I should always have three guests for dinner. He was a man of substance in Zagreb and all his family save one daughter is dispersed and probably murdered. David Karmel returned and lunched with me. At the end of this afternoon's séance Mr Paravicini began to work by electric light. Suddenly the bust which had become a lump of dead clay began to look like me. It is a different process of growth from a picture, which is like the pantomime scene of lifting gauze curtains, the fairies becoming lighter and more precise at each layer being raised; it is the transformation scene when the thing changes in a twinkling to its extreme opposite.

Floydforce expect to be clear of Ragusa in a week, leaving me with a mass of stores and a wireless set. I told poor Mr Sen to tell the kitchen that toast, as soon as made, must be stood on its edge or it would become flabby. Tonight my bread appeared precariously balanced.

Saturday 20 January 1945

I had the great pleasure of arranging with the brigadier for the gift of 1,000 rations to the hungry Dominicans. I also adopted a Maltese widow, castigated a Canadian for concealing his marriage, made the acquaintance of a Belgian bookbinder to whom I entrusted *Unquiet Grave*, found Roddy Douglas, Zena Naylor's half-brother, in charge of DID, a great convenience, and watched my bust change scarcely perceptibly. A good day.

By choosing preposterous objects as possessions I keep them at arm's length.

Poor Mr Sen is literally an agoraphobe; he led me to the hills by back alleys, from the habit of fear.

Sunday 21 January 1945

Farewell 'tea' (chartreuse, mutton, etc., as on Orthodox Christmas) at

Commandant Grada[1] which O. Twigg left too early. In the evening at the theatre a performance of the Korčula 'Mauresque' dance for the Youth Movement followed by some children boxing; Communist salutes from the stage; raffish young Communist audience. Fourteen Masses said for Twigg. Karmel: 'Why don't they pray for me?' The news of the ML pact being signed is welcome.

Monday 22 January 1945

Illiterate Montenegrin Armenian called and was given clothes. I called on prior of Dominicans, with clothes. I am now on very loving terms since the rations were delivered, and gave in Karmel's name for prayers.

Tuesday 23 January 1945

Brig. O. Twig left.

Wednesday 24 January 1945

A Berlin stockbroker, a Norwegian widow called for help. The latter married a Jugoslav, speaking no common language except a little English; he died slowly of tuberculosis leaving her penniless in a foreign country during a revolution, her own country occupied by the enemy; she cheerfully set about teaching English. A Partisan came to say he had a pain, could I give him jam to cure it. The nuns got a fine load of mixed foodstuff and twittered like sparrows. I went to the Dominican convent to meet the Bishop of Kotor, a timid shabby old fellow who is giving me a great deal of useful information and for whom I am preparing a questionnaire. The clergy are undecided how to observe St Blaise's day, February 3rd; whether to boycott the town in memory of the fourteen murdered priests or assert its Catholicity. A walk with Karmel on the sea front in cold wind and drizzle; a bad night's sleep in spite of this.

Thursday 25 January 1945

Communion at Franciscan church. The burning of coffee is one of the myths of the decade. It was reported to me that the town has it that British troops did their cooking on burned coffee because the Partisans gave them no wood.

Two cases of English bilking Jugoslavs – one for a clarinet, the other a novel. I told Paravicini that I would go on feeding him after the sittings for my portrait were finished; the effect was galvanic; the shuttles flew back and forth on his Penelope's loom and my head suddenly took form. An exhausting interview with Miljanić, president of Montenegro, who is obsessed with the problem of introducing a Scottish female doctor into his country. A visit from a Communist French widow of forbidding appearance who wants to go home to

[1] Town commander.

France. An unwelcome present from M. Albert Bonniz [?] of a black book in stained and gold-printed vellum with ribbon ties. Such a thing as I have no use or liking for. I did not know how to reward him so gave him a pair of old shoes which apparently he liked. I walked to Lapad and back in rainy weather and gave a lot of unwanted medical supplies to the Jugoslav navy.

Friday 26 January 1945

The female Partisan came dressed as a woman with a ribbon in her hair and a woman's dress. I gave her soup, chocolates, cigarettes, and an embarkation card to Bari. She was still hideous. An exquisite Italian bride, a bearded Croat poet who became tipsy on a glass of *rakija*, a naval surgeon, also came. The bust grows in finish but is not at all like me. Wintour threatens to come. I wrote that I could not put him up, that his journey was quite unnecessary. All I could do to put him off.

Saturday 27 January 1945

A delicious smell of cut branches in the Franciscan cloister in preparation for St Blaise's day. The tea mixed with coffee in our store. Squalls. Karmel queasy.

Sunday 28 January 1945

Ships in Floydforce embarking; poor post; an encouraging demand from Foreign Office for report on Church affairs. A morning séance with Paravicini, the bust very unlike me. A long afternoon with the Bishop of Kotor and the Prior. The continual unsatisfied thirst of all small neutrals for British policy. '*Mais monsieur que voudra faire la Grande Bretagne en Bulgarie?*' Have we a plan for the Adriatic? Have we a plan for the Danube basin? Why must we give Croatia a Karadjordjević[1] king? '*Mais monsigneur les Anglais sont un peuple humain et commercial. Nous n'avons aucun plan.*' And then knowing shakes of the head. Ah, the captain does not trust us. I drank the best part of a bottle of very strong white wine and left a little tipsy. I dined with Karmel and grew tipsier. Not drunk but forgetful today of what I said last night.

Monday 29 January 1945

A series of absurd problems. Mustapić arrested. Gjoratović beaten. A totally new character – a distracted Chilean engineer whose daughter aged seventeen had stowed away on a British ship and sailed for Bari. Twenty-six Italian deserters disappeared with Floydforce. I wrote hasty notes on the Church in Croatia.

[1] Serbian royal dynasty which became the royal family of Jugoslavia.

Tuesday 30 January – Wednesday 31 January 1945

Food situation becoming very much worse. I sent a series of signals of increasing gravity; finally asking for permission to distribute DID stores.

Thursday 1 February 1945

Another visit from the insane Czech woman who claims to have lost $39.

The circumstances of Waugh's expulsion from Jugoslavia, with which the next part of the diary deals, are not easy to follow from the text.

Tito had never wanted Floydforce on the mainland; after its withdrawal, the Partisans became increasingly hostile to any British presence whatever. The dispute with Waugh formed part of a general deterioration in Anglo–Jugoslav relations; but it is reasonable to conjecture that the Dubrovnik authorities particularly wished to shift him because of his contacts with Croatian Catholics. Waugh declined to move, and appealed to his superiors in Bari for support. His superiors, however, who were fully occupied with a rapidly moving situation throughout the Balkans, including a civil war in Greece and Tito's territorial claims to Venezia Giulia and Trieste, were disinclined to add even a minor dispute with the Partisans to a growing list. Besides, some of those in Bari did not share what they took to be Waugh's conviction that all Croatian Catholics deserved Allied support; at least some of these Catholics had collaborated with the pro-Fascist regime of Pavelić. Waugh's superiors in any case resented his habit of sending comparatively trivial signals to headquarters prefixed by four 'Q's, which meant that a senior officer must decode them; a colonel who had got to bed at 4 am was unlikely to be amused when he was woken up an hour later to decode a Waugh signal about, for instance, supplies of soap. When, therefore, the Partisans applied pressure for Waugh's removal, his superiors did not resist.

Monday 12 February 1945

The last evening in the Pension Lovrijenac, all the stores packed and some of my personal belongings; tomorrow at 7 or soon after (Shrove Tuesday) we start for 11 Corps[1] HQ at Gačko. Today has been this: awake from 4; at 6.30 I got up and wrote a letter for Brigadier Maclean suggesting I should devote myself to the affairs of the Croatian Church and take them to England, giving a very modest account of the ill-behaviour of the Partisans in the last few days. Received a sheaf of signals at 9 all saying my journey to Gačko was not

[1] A Partisan corps.

necessary. No orders from Macmis.[1] Gave orders for the disposal of mission stores and got the loan of two trucks from RASC. Said goodbye to Mrs Dezoubovic. Saw RASC officer about debt of half a million krona to garage proprietor, Roddy Douglas called to say the girl he had rescued from OZNA now wanted repatriation to Dubrovnik, he lunched with me, set company of partisans to work carrying stores, received visit from Mrs Arena – 'I wept all last night that you are going. Since my husband died no one has looked after me. So I have brought you my husband's cigarette holder' – amber and damascene.

Went to say goodbye to the good and dignified ladies of La Solitudina, called in at signal office and found signal[2] saying 'Return to Bari at once.' Ships had now sailed; everything was finished [?]; I wanted to destroy Antoravic.[3] I went to Tony and asked him to telephone Antoravic saying I had been recalled; might I wait for ship in Dubrovnik. As I hoped he said no. This satisfactory from all points of view (1) Antoravic has gone too far (2) I can continue trip (3) Macmis through delay have put themselves wrong with me. I then went (6.30) to Dominican Priory. Prior gave me heady white wine and told me that a letter has been sent to GSH recommending the execution of all connected with St Blaise fête on grounds that it was religious. He half believed this himself. He also attempted a lie about priests being called up in Split. I caught him up and he had the grace to be confused. Within an hour I heard it asserted and denied that children were now sent compulsorily to Mass. I returned to the mission 7.30 to find (*a*) Mustapić with three presents from his daughters (*b*) the Norwegian Moslem who had dropped in for literary talk. I gave her books, soap, food and sent her away smiling but bewildered (*c*) a Jew engaged to a cousin of Peter Lunn's who had a 'delicate' letter to send. I have forgotten to mention the visit from a girl who claimed to be Australian with the only evidence of divorce papers.

To go back. The origin of my move. February 7th David Karmel and I returned from a country walk to find a written signal from 11 Corps ordering me to go Trebinje and stay there. I replied that I was VIII Corps mission, and signalled Bari. On 10th they renewed the attack. I refused to go, saying if I left Dubrovnik it would be for Italy. No answer from Bari. Ships leaving (or thought to be) 1600 11th. At lunch-time signal ordering me to obey 11 Corps orders. I at once wrote to Commandant Grada capitulating and demanding work parties. Meanwhile I had highly secret letter to Mgr. Tardini[4] – at

---

[1] Short for 'Maclean mission'; i.e. the headquarters of Brigadier Maclean's military mission to which Waugh was attached.

[2] From his superior officers in Bari.

[3] Partisan who replaced Major Bogdan as town commander of Dubrovnik.

[4] During the war, Under-Secretary of State for Foreign Affairs at the Vatican together with Mgr. Montini, later Pope Paul VI. Later, Cardinal and Secretary of State.

Vatican – from bishop here. I gave it to an ML officer called Cavan to give to 37 M Mission,[1] to give to Archie Lyall to send to Mondi Howard to give to Mgr. Tardini.

To go back further: 3 February (Saturday) was St Blaise's day. Partisans ordered it to be observed with customary ritual and next day, having got all they wanted from bishop, called up his seminarists. The structure of the feast was charming (*a*) early rising (*b*) greeting friends courteously outside the gates (*c*) quiet prayer (*d*) grand prayer (*e*) religious procession (*f*) high jinks. This year the Church did its part, and the civic dignitaries did theirs in tall hats, and two bands did theirs, but the peasants did not come in in large numbers and in spite of setting and genuine ceremony it fell flat.

David Karmel gave a tea party where the Partisans ate like hogs.

The mediocre town commander Bogdan gave place to a pubescent cretin named Antoravic.

The Paravicini bust, removed from my little room where he had worked in half-light with his nose touching it, was removed to his bright villa where it looks awful. He began again and the thing was better; went well. My being called away stopped him tinkering. I made him take the clothes seriously.

Sunday 25 February 1945

Rome. Hotel Continentale (a recent hotel near the railway station now taken over by the Army. Well-run, absurdly cheap: 350 lire for a week with all meals. Wine 150 lire a bottle. By contrast horse cabs yesterday in search of the Vatican legation cost 1,200 lire).

To go back. On 13th I drove to Gačko, a brilliant morning, snow for the last few miles and destroyed villages. Gačko about half destroyed, HQ of 11 Corps. Few civilians. I spent three nights there in David Karmel's house, scarcely moving out of doors, reading Trollope. David went for the day to Sarajevo, just 'liberated', saw a hundred corpses all executed, forty per cent civilians, the women busy stripping them of loot. On Friday 16th returned to Dubrovnik in the expectation of a boat on the next day, but this was postponed first by the arrival of more craft, later by weather until 20th. Major S—— was being expelled also, for fornication. Most of the girls who slept with English officers, and in one case the little sister of such a girl, have been rounded up by OZNA. We saw bourgeois girls breaking stones on the road near Trebinje. I stayed in the Komodor Hotel, now the ML mess. Very squalid officers with no will to help. No food ships have yet appeared. I walked about Lapad but kept away from the town where I had made my adieux. This did not prevent Antoravic giving his staff, in the presence of Wintour's interpreter, the account of a

[1] Another name for the Maclean military mission.

purely imaginary interview in which he upbraided me for not reporting to him daily and in which I was speechless with shame.

At last we sailed on the afternoon of 20th in great discomfort in an LCI and arrived next day at Bari. I found the mission HQ friendly and idle. John Clarke approved my propositions of coming to Rome to see the Pope and then of writing my church report and returning to England. Meanwhile a proposition has been made that mission officers may become consuls. It would be highly gratifying to return to the place I was expelled from, with great authority; it will give me the chance to help some of the unhappily stranded people of the place. So I have put in for this.

I enjoyed my three nights in Bari. I found three boxes of cigars waiting for me and a delightful pile of letters. I dined with Archie Lyall twice and Jonathan Blow, lunched with Bill Deakin (sympathetic to my consular ambition) and Peter Lunn. Saw the Unrra representatives, no good.

Yesterday I left Bari aerodrome at 7.15. The whole journey to Rome took six hours from door to door, about two hours less than if I had gone by car. The immediate arrival was discouraging; a surly town major who grudgingly gave me a room, no car, I walked carrying bag and greatcoat in the wrong direction. Then to my great good fortune Dan Ranfurly appeared, drove me to my hotel. I lunched with a Palestinian Jew and spent the afternoon in the spring sunshine driving round and failing to find Mondi Howard, Hamish Erskine, Hugh Montgomery. I went to the remote suburbs to the private house of D'Arcy Osborne instead of to his office and scribbled a note. Then returned and found Adrian Daintrey, dined with him drinking quantities of red wine and talking aesthetics. Rome still densely crowded with oafish Americans, the shops emptier than in August, the prices absurd. All restaurants shut to the military, all hotels run as messes, the occupying army developing a barrack life quite divorced from the life of the town, the buildings splendid in the spring sunshine. Topics – brigandage, the 12,000 (new figure) armed deserters mostly American, the thefts of cars, acts of violence, the incompetence of the government, the certainty of Communism when our armies move out, the uselessness and selfishness of the Italian upper class. I lunched with Dan Ranfurly today; at his small AC mess English and Americans occupy different sides of the dining-room. His job seems to give him access to everyone in Rome and he promises to help me with my Croat appeal.

Monday 26 February 1945

Early Mass. Moses in Peter-in-chains. At 10 to Dan Ranfurly who took me to D'Arcy Osborne. He had already made an appointment for me with Tardini, lent me his car. Utley,[1] secretary, most helpful. An hour with Tardini,

---

[1] James Utley, for many years a resident attaché to the British Legation to the Holy See, with great knowledge of Vatican personalities and politics.

gesticulating Neapolitan, French and English. He took the matter seriously and bade me return. Luncheon Ambassadors with John de Salis,[1] a likeable original; then met woman in the street who told us Mia Woodruff had arrived. Went to see her, looking very young and pretty and thin. Then to the US Legation to Holy See, long talk with Titman[2] and arranged interview with Myron Taylor for tomorrow. Dinner with Mondi Howard, to his mess afterwards to meet the foreign Minister also same man, leader of Christian Democrats. All at Howard's mess cosseting Christian Democrats and hopeful that Communists will not prevail in Italy.

Tuesday 27 February 1945

Vatican legation at 10 where Utley took me to Propaganda to interview Cardinal Fumasoni-Biondi, a gentle old man in a room full of Chinese junk, thence to Tardini for another interview. Luncheon with Sir D'Arcy Osborne alone, good luncheon, I was reminded of Lord Beauchamp even to his having a taste for Mr Rankin's pictures. At 4 to Myron Taylor, elderly, handsome, obtuse. I grow a little weary of my own story of Croat church affairs, then to a cocktail party at Mrs Murchey's to meet John Rayner where I drank rather too much gin, back to Continentale to give dinner to Mia Woodruff and Utley who enjoyed it and Dan Ranfurly who did not.

Wednesday 28 February 1945

Walking past the Grand Hotel with the intention of visiting S. Maria della Vittoria I found a stretcher being carried out heavily laden with Randolph and went with him to a hospital where he was to have his knee operated on for the injury sustained in the airplane accident. Then to Utley's office to get him to arrange interviews with Montini[3] and Pope. Lunch with Mr Leigh-Smith very ugly and unpopular First Secretary with vehement Slav wife. Wop highbrow named Moravia.[4] I got more weary of my Jugoslav tale. To J. de Salis to meet Mgr. Moscatello, Jug accredited to Vatican, who was forty minutes late and very despairing, then to Bernard Wall, to meet former editor of *Osservatore* now editor of *Popolo*, Christian Democrat party, asked him to write an article in *Osservatore* about Croat church affairs, returned to my room very weary and glad to have no engagements.

Thursday 1 March 1945

To the Vatican to present the Prior of Ragusa's card to Mgr. Cordovani,

[1] Colonel with Allied Forces HQ as liaison officer.
[2] Harold Titman, assistant to Myron Taylor, President Roosevelt's personal representative at the Vatican.
[3] Monsignor, later Cardinal, Giovanni Battista Montini; later Pope Paul VI.
[4] Alberto Moravia, the novelist.

Maestro di Palazzo, a civil Dominican. In the two hours' wait I went to the Vatican museums but found the crowds of soldiers and guides unendurable, most particularly in the Sistine Chapel where I was startled to find that most of the paintings were invisible to the naked eye, colourless and full of those painful spaces where the paint seemed to have sunk into the wall and disappeared; the Last Judgement infinitely inferior to its photographs. I lunched with Bernard Wall and sat exhausted in my room until it was time to go to cocktails with Mgr. Hemmick.[1] Mia, William Rospigliosi, Dan Ranfurly, Jim Utley, an American woman and a Russian couple. Hemmick told us that the Dorias[2] will buy nothing on the black market and walk to the opera rather than use government petrol for anything not wholly official. This edifying example seems ludicrous to most Romans. Dined at Valadier's, now a Naafi, with Mia and William. I got my invitation to a private audience in the afternoon.

Friday 2 March 1945

Private audience at 9.30. Just time to step into St Peter's and pray for guidance. Then into Cortile Damaso, up the lift to the second floor, through a series of dazzling anterooms full of men who looked like the general staff of King Bomba, then without waiting at all into the presence. A white figure at a table in a general background of splendour but I was unable to look about. Genuflected three times and sat by his side. I was warned that his English was parrot-talk so loudly asked to speak French. Embarked at once on Jugoslav church affairs, gave him a brief resumé, mentioned Rittig. He took it all in, said *'Ca n'est pas la liberté'*, then gave his English parrot-talk of how many children had I and that he saw the naval review at Portsmouth. Gave me rosaries for my children and a 'special' blessing. But I left him convinced that he had understood what I came for. That was all I asked. I saw Tardini who gave me two letters to smuggle to Jugoslavia. He and the Pope said polite things about my work for the 'church and civilization': *'continuez'*. I lunched at the Grande with Bridget Vesey,[3] a fellow Wren, John de Salis, Jim Utley, then called on the Duchess of Sermoneta[4] at the Orsini palace – she wanted a few inches of

---

[1] Sociable American, a canon of St Peter's.

[2] Prince Filippo and Princess Gesina Doria-Pamphilj; he was one of the leading anti-Fascists among the Roman nobility and became first mayor of Rome after the Allied liberation in June 1944. She was a Scotswoman. Both went into hiding during the war, running considerable risks in the Allied cause.

[3] Second cousin of Laura Waugh; married Lt.-Gen. Sir Terence Airey, acting supreme commander in Italy, 1946, and later Military Governor of Trieste.

[4] Marguerite Caetani, American-born wife of Roffredo Caetani, Duke of Sermoneta; publisher of two celebrated literary reviews: *Commerce*, between the wars in Paris, and *Botteghe Oscure* (in which Dylan Thomas's *Under Milk Wood* was first published) after the Second World War in Rome.

sticking plaster for a vaccination. John de Salis dined with me and on this last evening I found that I might all the time have been drinking fine claret which was on sale in the bar. John and I drank three bottles.

Naples, Saturday 3 March 1945

Aeroplane to Naples where we were told there was no flying that day to Bari. Telephoned Bloggs Baldwin and stayed the night with him in a flat up some hundreds of steps, shared by two dull airmen and a Grenadier actor.

Bari, Sunday 4 March 1945

Bloggs looked after me very kindly. I took an afternoon aeroplane and, after a cold, rough flight in which I was despondent and nervous, arrived at Bari. Everything smooth here. Room in hotel, good mail, report from Bishop of Šibenik. Bad news from Jugoslavia. Forty-five priests murdered at Mostar. Gross discrimination shown by Partisans in food distribution; British collaboration assumed for attack on Trieste and Istria.[1]

Monday 5 March 1945

Fruitless morning calling on people who were out.

Friday 9 March 1945

After five days at the Imperiale, during which I developed a sharp cold in the head, I drove out to the villa at San Spirito carrying my luggage in the back of a 15 cwt truck. I asked the driver whether he was sure it was safe and lazily accepted his assurance that nothing could happen to it with the side curtains closed. When we reached San Spirito my bag was missing; it was itself a loved object, being the one I originally bought to take to Abyssinia in 1930, since when it has gone everywhere with me in all sorts of conditions, much patched and repaired. Inside it were all my more useful clothes, my diaries for the past six months, and the leather wallet containing all my private papers and all my notes for my report on the church in Croatia. I was in despair. The military police were offensive and listless; no one, however sympathetic, offered any hope of restitution. Luggage thefts are continual at Bari they said, you haven't a hope in hell old man. My memory was good enough to note a few general conclusions but the report would lose all its authority without my papers. I was in despair. Dined alone and went to bed with the resolve to return immediately to England with the report unwritten.

Saturday 10 March 1945

A morning clouded by the discomfort of having lost most essential toilet

[1] In fact the British strongly opposed these attempts by Tito to assert Jugoslav territorial claims.

articles. After luncheon a telephone message informed me that the military police had recovered my bag intact.

Sunday 11 March 1945

I propose to start writing my report.[1]

Monday 12 March 1945

Remained at San Spirito working off and on.

Tuesday 13 Marvh 1945

On hearing that Maclean was coming out of Jugoslavia and going straight to London I decided to leave tomorrow. Report half-finished.
Charlie Brocklehurst dined with me at San Spirito.

Wednesday 14 March 1945

Up at 5, arrived airport 6.30, plane put off till 8.30, arrived Naples at about 10. No plane on that day. Telephoned Bloggs. Lunched, dined and slept the night with him.

Naples–London, Thursday 15 March 1945

Up at 4.30, but at 5, aeroplane at 7.30. Flew straight and smooth over the cloud which opened at 12.20 to reveal Versailles below us. Lunched at Lympne at 2. London at 6. Hyde Park Hotel. Dinner White's Peter Beatty. Telephoned Laura who will join me tomorrow; also Basil who has lent me his suite.

---

[1] To write a report on the condition of the churches in Jugoslavia was Waugh's own idea. It was entitled 'Church and State in Liberated Croatia' and submitted to Fitzroy Maclean and the Foreign Office at the end of March 1945. The conclusion of the report stated that the Tito régime 'threatens to destroy the Catholic Faith in a region where there are now some 5,000,000 Catholics', but added that Tito, if subjected to Allied pressure, 'might be induced to modify his policy far enough to give the Church a chance of life'. The report itself, together with Foreign Office comments, is now in the Public Records Office, and a summary of it may be found in Christopher Sykes's *Evelyn Waugh*, pp. 273–6.

6 The 1945-56 Diary

Hyde Park Hotel, London, Holy Saturday 31 March 1945

Over a fortnight in England, mostly at the Hyde Park Hotel. Expense enormous so that it seemed a great economy the day before yesterday to buy a gold watch for £50. We average £15–20 a day in living, eating and smoking. Comfort very fair and, it seems, better than a year ago. Good claret £2 10s. Luncheon at Marks's oyster bar on Thursday for Maimie, Nancy Rodd, Basil and myself, only stout and port to drink £7 14s. But I have plenty of money that has accumulated during my absence. Rocket bombs fall two or three times a day within hearing distance; one took out the windows of our sitting-room on Sunday morning, falling at Marble Arch. The war news is consistently good. Everyone expects the end in a few weeks but without elation; all conditions expect worse from the peace than they have had in the war. I have had interviews at the Foreign Office with Chapman-Andrews, an old friend from Abyssinia, who is now in charge of consular personnel; he is very hopeful of my getting an appointment if I wish it. Also with Douglas Howard,[1] a timid but civil bureaucrat who could not give an answer to my request to circulate my Croatian report among Catholic MPs, bishops and editors. 'Please don't think I am being obstructive.' How often I have heard that; how often I shall hear it again. I saw the Archbishop of Westminster, shrewd, vain, common, not humourless. I went there after drinking a bottle of champagne with Basil, rather tipsy and mixing my words but I don't think he noticed it; anyway he is to take his Easter luncheon with us.

I went to Pixton for two nights to find my boy more personable and manly. I drew pictures, played games, climbed the roof and was exhausted. Then to Midsomer Norton where my mother is living in considerable care and great kindness with my aunts. She has been given notice to leave her flat in six months' time and thinks it the end of the world – helpless and hopeless, unable to give a clear answer to the simplest question. I found her company wholly disagreeable and left with shame that I had not treated her more gently.

[1] Head of Southern Department in the Foreign Office, dealing with Albania, Yugoslavia, Greece, Bulgaria, Romania and Turkey.

Henry[1] has written an obscene book named *Loving* about domestic servants. I went to Warwick Street church yesterday and was made to carry the canopy. I was alarmed at the sketches for the redecoration of the place and have written to ask for an interview.

Easter Day 1 April 1945

Mass at Warwick Street, saddening attempts to get breakfast afterwards, everything either shut or attended by queues. The Archbishop at luncheon, genial and sharp, unable to keep august names out of his conversation: 'I said to Lord Beaverbrook I said . . .'; 'Alexander said to me "*cui bono?*"'; but he ate heartily and left in a good temper I think.

Monday 2 April 1945

A matinée at Victoria Palace. Henry Yorke and Dig to dinner. He talked nonsense about symbolism in his book and sense about the lower classes and Russia, which he thinks will collapse from internal corruption in ten years.

Tuesday 3 April 1945

Luncheon at Maimie's. Signed large cheques to Inland Revenue. Went to see Father More O'Ferrall about the disastrous suggestions for redecorating Warwick Street. Dined with Basil in our suite, he having given up his to Marshal Smuts. No bombs for some time now. No exhilaration anywhere at the end of the war.

Low Sunday 8 April 1945

A quiet week. On Wednesday we had Laura's mother to entertain and on Thursday mine. Mary only needed dinner; my mother needed legal advice. Both visits passed off successfully. No further rockets or bombs. The war news continual successes in the destruction of central Europe. No answer from Windsor, the consular department of the FO, or the department who have hold of my Croatian church report. I bought some Victorian books of engravings and a gold watch. Most days I go to White's for an hour, otherwise live in our rooms at the Hyde Park Hotel.

Tuesday 10 April 1945

Laura went back to Pixton for a few days. I lunched at the Beefsteak and returned mildly fuddled, slept, went to White's where I found a message from Kitty Brownlow, went down the street to see her and stayed till midnight. Ursula Manners came in; it was odd to find a third generation talking of 'Max', how she had telephoned to him to get news of her brother's wound, etc.

[1] Henry Yorke, who wrote under the name of 'Henry Green'.

Wednesday 11 April 1945

Luncheon at Beefsteak again. Clive Bell very ingratiating; walked with him most of the way home; slept; dined at Turf with Basil; went to see Bob and Angie later; drunk.

Thursday 12 April 1945

Hangover. Sent flowers to Angie, chucked appointment to show London to insignificant Yank named Edmund Wilson, critic; spent afternoon at White's with Connolly; dined there, drank bottle of champagne and felt better, went to Connolly's where I met E. Wilson mentioned above. It was the next day I chucked him. Augustus John, Elizabeth Bowen, Bohemian girls.

Friday 13 April 1945

Hangover. Laura returned. V. and A. Powell[1] and Dru came unexpectedly to dinner. All the days of Laura's absence have been befogged with drink and insomnia, mostly the result of being poisoned early by Kitty. In the course of the week I visited AG17 and found them civil, promising to regularize my position. I also learned from Maclean that I shall have permission to inform MPs, editors, etc., about Croatian church. Roosevelt died and was succeeded by a wholly comic man, delight of Lord Sherwood. Armies monotonously victorious. Gloomy apprehensions of V Day. I hope to escape it.

Saturday 14 April 1945

Still shaken by Kitty's poison. Angie to luncheon. Oppressive heat wave.

On Tuesday 17th Laura returned to Pixton. I bought a little Mulready at Hugh Walpole's collection.

Wednesday 18 April 1945

Basil Dufferin's memorial service. White's turned up in good numbers. 'Do I look too much like Christmas?' Afterwards to luncheon at Belgrave Place with Korda. Some dull knights. K. intelligent and agreeable. Good luncheon, hock and Havana cigars. Afternoon 4.45 to Oxford with Frank[2], advised him to stand for Parliament as eccentric foreign nobleman who had beaten the record for demobilization. Stayed at Campion Hall two nights. Very hot. T. S. Gregory[3] staying there. Conversation mostly despondent at the collapse of Europe, the advance of Russia, heathenism. T. S. Gregory talking big about our policing Europe. I pointed out we had not the men to police England, that garrison towns were not centres of good order. Recommended catacombs. Father D'Arcy believed he had supernatural guarantees of the future Christianity of Europe.

[1] Lady Violet Powell and Anthony Powell.
[2] The Hon. Frank Pakenham. He had been invalided out of the Army.
[3] Roman Catholic journalist and author.

Thursday 19 April 1945

A pleasant day in Oxford. Chestnut and lilac in flower. Bought books. Lunched with Frank and John Betjeman, called on Rachel Cecil (mumps) sat in Maurice's garden[1] and heard harsh reports on *Brideshead*: 'Cecil Beaton's favourite book. Connolly does a funny imitation of Marchmain's death bed. I didn't know you had been in love with Auberon.' Dinner at Campion.

Reported after complicated train journey at Windsor and got twenty-eight days leave from acting commander. Arrived White's 1.30. Perry motored me down to Belton. They have one corner of the house open, the small library, the only sitting-room. A stock jobber called Waddington; champagne and delicious young asparagus. Next day Kitty, a novelist named Valentine Williams and industrialist Prince Poniatowski. Great commercial chat. Sunday Ursula Manners came to dinner with news of Debo's party.

Pixton Park, Monday 23 April 1945

Early train to London. Weather now cold. Bought repeater watch £125 – have not told Laura yet. Afternoon train to Dulverton, empty carriages.

Tuesday 24 April 1945

Mary and Gabriel left. Grant children away. I made conversation with my children and worked out Laura's descent from six or seven dukes.

Chagford, Tuesday 1 May 1945

Arrived at Chagford last night. A disagreeable journey as a lunatic female porter took my luggage from the train at Taunton and I was obliged to wait three hours in Exeter amid squalls of sleet and snow. I bought some books of engravings.

At the weekend Laura took to her bed with a high temperature. Magdalen Eldon arrived and took to her bed with aches. Dru alternated between bed and armchair suffering from distended liver. Eddie[2] looked as though he should have been in bed and poor Mr Belloc as though the grave were the only place for him. He has grown a splendid white beard and in his cloak, which with his hat he wore indoors and always, he seemed an archimandrite. He lost and stole and whatever went into his pockets, toast, cigarettes, books never appeared, like the reverse of a conjuror's hat. He talked incessantly, proclaiming with great clarity the grievances of forty years ago: that the English worshipped the Germans and respected only wealth in one another; that the rich enslaved the poor by lying to them; that the dons at Oxford were paid by the rich to lie. Perhaps in forty years' time I shall make myself tedious denouncing

[1] Maurice Bowra's garden at Wadham College.
[2] Eddie Grant.

Communism in this way. 'The Bank of England would not let Napoleon found an empire.' 'The French are a Catholic people.' At times he was coaxed by the women to sing and then, with face alight with a simple joy and many lapses of memory, he quavered out old French marching songs and snatches from the music halls of his youth. He is conscious of being decrepit and forgetful, but not of being a bore.

I have the news that my application to go back to Jugoslavia has been refused and I am well content. Honour is satisfied. I am glad to have done all I could to go back and glad not to be going. The end of the war is hourly expected. Mussolini obscenely murdered, continual rumours that Hitler's mind has finally gone. Communism gains in France. Russia insults USA. I will now get to work on St Helena.[1]

Sunday 6 May 1945

I have done enough reading to start tomorrow on *Helena*. All day there was expectation of VE Day and finally at 9 it was announced for tomorrow. Carolyn resentful that she does not feel elated. It is pleasant to end the war in plain clothes, writing. I remember at the start of it all writing to Frank Pakenham that its value for us would be to show us finally that we were not men of action. I took longer than him to learn it. I regard the greatest danger I went through that of becoming one of Churchill's young men, of getting a medal and standing for Parliament; if things had gone, as then seemed right, in the first two years, that is what I should be now. I thank God to find myself still a writer and at work on something as 'uncontemporary' as I am.

London, Monday 28 May 1945

The day of publication of *Brideshead*. A charming letter from Desmond MacCarthy this morning promising to review it in the *Sunday Times*.

I got deeply depressed at Chagford and after a week's work came to London by way of Pixton. A pleasant week in London during which I was offered and accepted a diplomatic post in Athens and a castle in Wicklow. I wrote a letter to *The Times* denouncing Tito's claims on Trieste which has evoked an answer I think from Fitzroy Maclean. I have switched the argument solely to the persecution of the Church and look forward to tomorrow's issue with eagerness. I bought a repeater watch and broke it at once: £120. I had some new photographs taken by Howard Coster. All my friends and enemies are standing for Parliament. I do not envy them at all. Wednesday–Friday last week at Mells. Trim home, wine flowing, Katharine happy, Trim still European. Christopher Hollis radiating happiness at his certain seat for Devizes. A house for sale near Mells – Southfields Whatley, home of the lately

---

[1] Mother of the Emperor Constantine and, according to legend, the discoverer of the Cross on which Christ was crucified. Waugh's novel, *Helena*, was published in 1950.

homicidal Elderton.[1] A very charming house in a friendly district – Jolliffes, Hollises, Asquiths, Weymouths. I am quite ready to chuck Peter Fitzwilliam's castle and move there.[2]

Pixton Park, Sunday 1 July 1945

Back at Pixton after nearly a month in London leading the life of an old man pottering between the Hyde Park Hotel, White's and the Beefsteak. I had a splendid set of rooms which were delicious in the hot weather, and most of the afternoons were spent dozing on the sofa. Every day I went to Nancy Mitford's bookshop and usually found Osbert Sitwell or Gerald Berners there. I made no attempt to work. *Brideshead* has been a success; sold out in the first week and still in continual demand. Most of the reviews have been adulatory except where they were embittered by class resentment. The Americans have made it their Book of the Month, which is worth £10,000 down and a probable further £10,000 from ordinary sales and cinema rights. In order to avoid paying four-fifths of this to the State I am arranging, if possible, to fix my gross income for the next five years at £5,000 a year.

Cyril Connolly has moved into Regent's Park in a decent house of which he has taken every decent room; the rest go to a Mrs Lootit. I scared him by saying the Crown authorities would expel them all for living in sin and have made up for it by the gift of a jardinière. I also bought Laura a 100-guinea cashmere coat. As I was spending nearly £100 a week on my own living expenses I felt generous. The General Election is being a great bore to all.

I had a curious journey here on Saturday. I had a military warrant which said: 'This must be exchanged for a ticket.' I took it to the booking office, ordered a ticket, and gave the warrant in exchange. The man with great rudeness told me to give back the ticket and use the warrant itself, so, being out of patience, I walked off with the ticket, settled in a corner seat and was eating my sandwiches when the loudspeaker began saying, 'Will Captain Waugh, passenger to Dulverton, please report to the RTO immediately.' I did not move but everyone in the carriage looked at the name on my bag and at me with

---

[1] 'Major Elderton and Major Shaw were two eccentric retired majors who lived near Whatley. They conducted a game of persecution against the parson, a Mr Evans, giving the choirboys two and sixpence to sing out of tune and letting down his car tyres while he was preaching. Elderton also used to terrify the villagers by asking them questions and falling into an ungovernable rage if they did not give the right answers. It was from this that they derived the habit of saying 'Up to a point' when they could not agree – a device which Evelyn pilfered for the employees of Lord Copper in *Scoop*. All this I heard from the anecdotes of Lady Horner. I doubt Evelyn himself ever met Elderton. Myself I found him a mild eccentric but by no means as extreme as Lady Horner portrayed. I fancy that she exaggerated to make a good story, but even in her anecdotes there was no suggestion that Elderton was "homicidal".' Christopher Hollis, in a letter to the editor, November 1975.

[2] The 8th Earl Fitzwilliam owned a house in Ireland that Waugh thought of buying.

curiosity. The voice kept on calling me every five minutes for half an hour till we started, while I began to fear a search of the train by military police. When we steamed out I thought I was safe, but at Taunton four hours later the voice caught up with me. When I reached Dulverton the ticket collector had been warned to take the other half of my ticket. I expect I shall hear more of it.

The purpose of this visit was to see a farm Laura thought suitable for us. I went yesterday afternoon – Clem Barton near Tiverton, a ramshackle house entirely devoid of any tolerable feature, a fine view, rich land. I said no. Auberon here with a distressed Pole, the Grants and Gabriel; all have now left.

Ickleford, Hitchin, Saturday 28 July 1945

A period of sloth at Hyde Park Hotel ended today with my coming here with Randolph. The house is only part furnished with whatever Pam[1] chose not to take. The plan is to stay until White's reopens but I am not confident that we shall live harmoniously so long.

Election day, the day before yesterday, was a prodigious surprise. I went to White's at about 11. Results were already coming in on the tape, and in an hour and a half it was plainly an overwhelming defeat.[2] Practically all my friends are out. Chris[3] and Hugh Fraser the hope of the Catholics. 10,000 votes against Winston in his own constituency for an obvious lunatic. At 12.30 Harry Stavordale and I went to the Rothermeres' party – a large, despondent crowd joined later by a handful of the defeated candidates. Watered vodka and exiguous champagne, rude servants, a facetious loudspeaker. Back to White's. Dinner with Pam Berry, Virginia, who is to marry one of the newly elected Labour agitators on Monday[4] (Winston had said to her a few days before, 'You are a bird of ill-omen. Your arrival in any European capital presages disaster') and Christopher Glenconner. Then, a mark of despair, up to a party of Emerald's[5] where I explained Christian marriage laws to Kick Hartington[6] and my style of writing to Desmond MacCarthy.

Yesterday Randolph arrived in my room at 7.30 am, dazed by adversity but full of hope of being adopted at Bromley. Winston is trying to get used to being a private citizen, fretting about coupons for curtains and petrol, homeless, without his despatch boxes and aeroplanes. Max Beaverbrook giving ill advice to the last, urging on him the joys of opposition. Nothing could be more unfortunate for his reputation than for him to start a clause-by-clause heckling

[1] The marriage of Pamela and Randolph Churchill was dissolved in 1946.
[2] For the Conservative Party.
[3] Christopher Hollis, who had been elected MP (Conservative) for Devizes.
[4] Virginia Cowles married Aidan Crawley, Labour MP for the Buckingham division of Bucks.
[5] Lady Cunard's.
[6] The Marchioness of Hartington; eldest daughter of the former ambassador to London, Joseph P. Kennedy, and Rose Kennedy.

opposition. There are many people puzzled about their futures, even Dan Ranfurly who was on the point of becoming a lord-in-waiting. The Conservative benches will not only be empty but without talent – Chips Channon, William Teeling, Juby Lancaster, etc. A great chance for Bob Boothby. Douglas Woodruff dined with me and we discussed how to groom Chris for personal importance.

Sunday 29 July 1945

To Mass in Hitchin in a church which smelled. To luncheon with the Melchetts. Lord Melchett kept his room. We ate well but unattended, Lady Melchett carrying out the plates. Five or six strangers to luncheon including a Hungarian who abused Jews inappropriately. Later Randolph left for the last family party at Chequers and I spent a quiet evening alone.

Monday 30 July 1945

A quiet morning cooking my breakfast, reading a barely readable detective story, eating alone cold bacon and cucumber. Interrupted only by telephone calls to and from Randolph. Then to London by an empty train and to dinner with Douglas, Mia and Chris at Park West. Chris spoke of Wessex as the redoubt of Englishry, of the Church of England as the guardian of national life, and it became plain to me that he was not destined for national prominence. But it was a friendly evening with plenty of wine and Mia near collapse from exhaustion. I lay that night on a camp bed and slept little, for that frightful block of cells is so constructed that the walls hum all night like a ship.

Tuesday 31 July 1945

Dressed and shaved at dawn and spent a long morning waiting for Randolph to call for me. Then we drove to Hertfordshire to lunch with Audrey James, variously called Coates, Marshal Field, Pleydell-Bouverie, a strained, nervous cross-patch of a woman in a beautiful Queen Anne house named Julians with the first garden which I have seen in good order for five years. Everything was very expensive, full of Sisleys and Beatons, splendid wine, all the materials of luxury but no ease. She had the impudence to show us a number of books bound by Sutcliffe[1] with his imprint and claim to have bound them herself, but she gave us a bottle of Haut Brion '24 to take off with us. We returned to find our cook, a frail gnome of immense age who cooked us a fair dinner. Afterwards we drank Armagnac and I attempted to explain to Randolph that he had reached a grave climacteric in his life and must now grow up or perish. He will perish. I slept naturally and heavily.

[1] Sutcliffe and Sangorski, of Poland Street.

Wednesday 1 August 1945

Miss Buck came for the day. I wrote some letters and went for a walk through the depraved quarters of Hitchin. Randolph arranging his few books and calling for continuous applause.

Thursday 2 August 1945

Randolph's retching drove me from the room.

Sunday 5 August 1945

Momo Marriott[1] drove down to luncheon. Emerald's pursuit of me becomes more furious daily.

Monday 6 August 1945

Dinner with the Melchetts. News published by 6 o'clock wireless that an 'atomic' bomb had been dropped on Japan. Randolph overexcited, got drunk, drivelled about redressing of balance of power. I asked, if we knew early this year that we had this power, why did we betray Poland to Russia? Randolph painfully offensive to chauffeur.

Tuesday 7 August 1945

Newspapers, as often miles wide of public conscience, jubilant about bomb, forecasting vast benefits to world by its discovery. *Queen Mary* crossing Atlantic on handful of new fuel, etc.

Wednesday 8 August 1945

Randolph to London. Russia declared war with Japan.

Thursday 9 August 1945

Papers, catching up with public opinion, now express consternation at new bomb. Everyone seems impelled to make a public statement about his own opinion of the atom bomb. Even I, left alone, began to write a note for *The Tablet* on the subject, but recovered my good sense and destroyed it.

Hyde Park Hotel, Friday 10 August 1945

To London in order to avoid arrival of Randolph, son and nurses. Dined at St James's with Bob Boothby who says there is serious questioning in Tory party of Winston's position as leader of opposition. We drove to look at small crowds of drunks celebrating premature announcement of Japanese surrender.

---

[1] Lady Marriott, daughter of the American banker Otto Kahn, married to Major-General Sir John Marriott.

Saturday 11 August 1945

Laura came to Hyde Park Hotel. We went to a poor review and to dinner at Claridge's with the Marriotts.

Sunday 12 August 1945

Nancy Rodd and Hugh Fraser lunched with us. Dined at Allies Club.

Monday 13 August 1945

Father D'Arcy dined with us. He has just become Jesuit Provincial. I asked lightly, 'Does this mean you will be next General?' He answered gravely that he hoped not.

Tuesday 14 August 1945

Most of the day spent in collecting wine. Chris, Hugh, Magdalen,[1] Kick Hartington to cocktails. Bob and Angie[2] to dinner. Drunk.

Ickleford, Hitchin, Wednesday 15 August 1945

Peace declared. Public holiday. Remained more or less drunk all day. Collected the boy Auberon[3] at the Eldons and drove him to Ickleford. He behaved very politely.

Thursday 16 August 1945

Another public holiday. Hangover. Winston[4] a boisterous boy with head too big for his body. Randolph made a bonfire and Auberon fell into it. American came to luncheon and signed R. up for highly profitable daily column. Some village sports and damp bonfire and floodlit green.

Written on Friday 31 August, Hyde Park Hotel

The boy Auberon stayed a week at Ickleford and won golden opinions on all sides, even mine, so that I was encouraged to have him for a few days in London and show him some sights.

On the day we returned, Wednesday, I took him to the Zoo, which was crowded with the lower classes and practically devoid of animals except rabbits and guinea pigs. On Friday I devoted the day to him, hiring a car to fetch him from Highgate and to return him there. I wore myself out for his amusement, taking him up the dome of St Paul's, buying him three-cornered postage stamps and austerity toys, showing him London from the top of the hotel,

---

[1] Christopher Hollis; the Hon. Hugh Fraser; the Countess of Eldon, daughter of the 14th Baron Lovat.

[2] Robert and Angela Laycock.

[3] Waugh's son.

[4] Randolph Churchill's son, later an MP.

taking him to tea with Maimie, who gave him a sovereign and a box of variegated matches. Finally when I took him back to Highgate my mother said, 'Have you had a lovely day?' 'A bit dull.' So I felt absolved from paying further attention to him and sent him back to Pixton in Gabriel's charge on Monday. I have resumed the normal life of Hyde Park Hotel, White's, Nancy's shop, the Beefsteak. At the latter I have a new *bête noire* in the person of the Lord Chancellor.[1] I dined with my Communist cousin Claud[2] who warned me against Trotskyist literature, so that I read and greatly enjoyed Orwell's *Animal Farm*.

I also reread with immense respect E. M. Forster's *Passage to India*. The only details I had remembered beyond the main themes were the eggs at the picnic and the cries of 'Esmees-Esmoore' at the trial. Odd.

Emerald's attempts to get me to dinner have relaxed. Connolly is back from Switzerland, having, it is said, done much unspecified mischief among French intellectuals. Nancy has written a novel[3] full of exquisite detail of Mitford family life, but planless and flat and hasty in patches. There is talk by Randolph of my becoming a columnist in the *Daily Telegraph*.

An enjoyable and drunken evening at the House of Commons with Christopher and Hugh and Kick Kennedy. Evenings at White's; one with George Selwyg[4] who has appeared here. In an hour of vinous geniality I have promised to take him to Oxford on Monday.

A few Tate pictures on view at the National Gallery. I met Father D'Arcy at the private view.

Unreasonable resentment against USA about the end of Lease-lend. Workmanship so bad. A pair of trousers 'invisibly mended' comes back to me cobbled; two pictures framed with joints that do not close. The arming block[5] at Zaehnsdorf again rejected as inferior cutting.

Saturday 8 September 1945

Last days in London. The valet at Queen Anne's Mansions is packing my books and uniforms for transit to Stinchcombe. Laura is packing, I hope half as thoroughly, at Pixton. The Army seem to have lost all records of my RM service and my 'release' is delayed, but this does not upset me. On Monday I go to the inn at Berkeley Road and on Wednesday sleep at Piers Court. Nancy has gone to Paris leaving a grave gap in my morning's routine. Alec has gone to New York leaving my mother lonely. I go to her tomorrow. I went to a lovely presentation (Cecil) of *Lady Windermere's Fan*. Father D'Arcy, Toby Jessel,

---

[1] The 1st Earl Jowitt (1885–1957).

[2] Claud Cockburn.

[3] Waugh suggested its title, *The Pursuit of Love*, and helped to revise it before publication.

[4] An American who had served with Waugh in Jugoslavia.

[5] Metal bearing engraved design for decorating the covers of a book.

Baby Jungman have dined with me. One evening, Tuesday last, I was very drunk and taken home from White's by Randolph. I thought this a grim indication. I went to Oxford for the day last Monday with George Selwyg. It began badly, everything shut, St Giles's Fair filling the streets, the George, where I had taken the trouble to order luncheon, closed, the Randolph full. In despair I went to Hertford where the old servants received me warmly, gave us luncheon in Hall and the porter offered to return my Shakespeare which I lost twenty years ago and have often thought of. We went to Merton, shut. I asked what Fellows were in residence. 'Mr Deane-Jones'; I knew [?] him and reintroduced myself. 'I wonder what became of that not so nice friend of Clonmore's, Byron?' 'He was drowned on the way to Greece.' This jolted the don and he became more affable, showed us the library and chapel. I then gave Selwyg a bottle of champagne at St James's and felt I had done much for Anglo-American friendship.

Sunday 9 September 1945

I went out to Highgate to say goodbye to my mother, went to Mass there, where a ranting Irish Passionist threatened hell-fire to anyone who left before the last gospel; left before the last gospel and lunched with my mother. Alec has just sailed to America and she is a little lonely but so slow in all she does that her days go fast. My eyes were sore from too much sleeping draught. I walked across the Heath to Muriel Silk's and collected my Guadeloupe madonna, very clear and bright – 7 guineas – and took it to the Hyde Park Hotel. Then to dinner on guard at St James's Palace with Michael Rosse, two giggling subalterns, and Mark Ogilvie-Grant. Very drunk.

Stinchcombe, Monday 10 September 1945

To Prince of Wales's Berkeley Road. Passengers at Paddington herded about like animals but, thanks to a porter, a seat in the train. Arrived on a grey, fly-infested, heavy evening with a hangover and the excitement of homecoming contending. It began to rain as I walked up to Piers Court to fetch Laura. At first sight the garden was rank, the paths lost, the trees stunted or overgrown irregularly; inside everything damp but superficially tidy. Slept ill.

Piers Court, Tuesday 11 September 1945

Nuns half out, ourselves half in. Laura saying how perfect everything looked, I detecting losses and damage everywhere. Romeo's sword broken again and an explanation by the nuns which made no sense.

Wednesday 12 September 1945

Nuns left at 10.30. The last seven of them in one car with their luggage and two birds in a cage. A day of feverish activity moving furniture, unpacking books and silver (all apparently cream jugs), stocktaking in the cellar – four dozen Dows 1922, six dozen assorted claret; caught cold. Mrs Muller arrived for fortnight. No water supply.

Thursday, Friday and Saturday. Very heavy work, very heavy cold. The auctioneers who are checking the inventory distracted to find everything moved. Lady Bowlby called with circular letter wanting signatures to complain about lack of water supply. At midday a summons from Windsor to be demobilized on Tuesday. A great nuisance. By Saturday night the library was in order and the tanks full enough for a hot bath. It was curious to find sumptuous commonplaces of prewar life – writing paper, old magazines. My hunting boots furry with damp turned up in the beer cellar, also Rossetti's *Spirit of the Rainbow*. Mrs Muller attempts to feed us a vegetarian diet.

Sunday 16 September 1945

Cold slightly better. To Mass in Dursley. We expected some welcome from our neighbours but have had none. Sorting papers, writing letters. Continuous soft rain. No difficulty about regaining Culverhay for Laura's cows. Tomorrow to London.

London, Monday 17 September 1945

I took my cold with me to London; a day of humid heat. The train crowded, a few first-class carriages at the head, off the platform, locked up; got a guard and eventually a seat. To Trumper's to have my hair cut, to the Hyde Park for a bath and a change of linen, to White's where Randolph consulted me on a point of 'honour'. Some days ago he dined with Beaverbrook who said, 'Don't tell your father, but the whole secret of the Conservative failure at the polls was his personal unpopularity.' A day or two later Randolph lunched with Esmond[1] and Anne Rothermere and Duff, and repeated the story. He also saw Alastair Forbes, a smart-allick employee of Esmond's, and says he does not remember whether he told him or not. Knowing Randolph I think he did, and many others as well. On Sunday the *Dispatch* had an article by Forbes saying, 'The latest party line from Leatherhead is that Winston's unpopularity, etc.' That afternoon Beaverbrook rang up Randolph and asked if he had told Forbes. Randolph said no. Beaverbrook: 'That's fine. I'm taking action against Rothermere. I can prove malice. I am going to call anyone who has been to Cherkley[2] since the election to give evidence for me.' I told Randolph, first, that I did not believe that Beaverbrook had any intention of bringing an action, was testing his power, had traced the story to Randolph anyway and was teasing him; secondly, that it was his plain duty to inform Beaverbrook at once that, if

---

[1] Esmond Rothermere, chairman of Associated Newspapers.
[2] Beaverbrook's country house.

called, he would tell the truth. Randolph sought Camrose[1] who told him the same thing. Feeling ill I went to bed early.

Piers Court, Tuesday 18 September 1945

Hired car to Windsor, got my release papers, perfunctory medical examination, back to Albany Street Barracks where the Dispersal Centre is earning golden opinions by doing a very little, quite unnecessary, business with great expedition. I was given a quantity of printed directions about unemployment benefit and medical aid and such nonsense. Got away at noon and decided not to bother about the clothing issue at any rate for that day. Phil and Audrey's wedding party[2] at Hyde Park, designed for a dozen, grew to about twenty. Most of us went to luncheon with Randolph – turtle soup, prawns, lobsters, asparagus, melon, ices; champagne flowed at both parties but I felt too ill to enjoy it. Old gang, Harry Stavordale, Ed Stanley, Sykeses, Rose Warwick, Bob and Angie, Anthony, etc. The evening train back to Stroud, not overcrowded, weary, very happy to have a home to come to.

Wednesday 19 September 1945

Rain again. Cold still oppressive. Laura's 'companion' Sanders came from Dulverton on trial (of us).

Tuesday 25 September 1945

Gradual restoration of order in the house. Mrs Harper and Mrs Muller working heroically cleaning up. No calls of any kind by neighbours. Yesterday Laura went to London for a fête organized by my mother-in-law. She, Bridget, Mary, Maria Teresa, the two Grant girls, Mrs Anderson and her son all transported to London and distributed between the Ritz and the Great Western Hotel, Paddington – a trip to Hampton Court, a film of Henry v, a dinner party at the Ritz, a visit to the Zoo, then the girls go to the convent at St Leonard's and Laura and Bridget return here. It sounds a nightmare.

Yesterday I read my Lancing diaries through with unmixed shame.

Tuesday 2 October 1945

News from the outside world becomes more horrible daily – chaos and tyranny and famine and sheer wickedness throughout two-thirds of Europe and all Asia, but my life seems more placid and happy than ever. I have begun a novel of school life in 1919 – as untopical a theme as could be found. Laura

[1] Principal proprietor of the *Daily Telegraph*.
[2] Philip Dunne; he married, as his second wife, Audrey Rubin.
[3] Rosa Lewis, the model for 'Lottie Crump', the proprietress of Shepeard's Hotel, in *Vile Bodies*.

came back from London with Bridget. Maria Teresa had had her last luncheon, before going to school, at the Cavendish and was kissed by Rosa.[3] With Bridget, Mrs Muller left; since then we have had the house to ourselves. Laura grapples vaguely but pertinaciously with her household tasks; most of her day is spent boiling potatoes for her chickens, who now lay three eggs a day, and making little milk cheeses we do not eat. On Saturday night we dined at the inn at Berkeley Road. Last weekend was exactly six years since our last Sunday here in 1939. I found myself by chance engaged on the task I was doing then, digging a path behind the yew at the north-east corner of the house to lead to what was to have been my formal garden.

We have practically no meat – two meals a week – and live on eggs and macaroni, cheese (made by Laura), bread and wine; very occasionally we get a rather nasty fish. But we have some wine left. When that is gone our plight will be grave.

Sunday 7 October 1945

We are now without hot water as the result of the boiler springing a leak. Laura spends all day in the kitchen and hen yard, I in library and garden. On Wednesday last Lady Bowlby assembled a meeting to protest about the water supply. All the village was there. Diana Oldridge talked sense. A Scottish dentist kept saying 'a file has been opened at the Ministry of Health' as though this were access to boundless prosperity.

On Thursday Father Murtagh came to tea, holy and abstemious. 'I am preparing a paper on the love of God. That's a good subject, now, isn't it?' And he began to give us his reflections in a curiously naïve and didactic way. Suddenly: 'Do you like the Mass being in Latin? Now the Mass is a great act of love, isn't it?' He should have been a monk I think. He kept saying he was not lonely as though to convince himself. He is very obtuse in personal contact.

News from the world still horrible.

Sunday 28 October 1945

My 42nd birthday. The last three weeks have been happy and uneventful: Laura cooking better, wine lasting out, weather splendid. I have written more of the school story, a review of Connolly's *Palinurus* which on rereading I find feeble, a paper to read aloud at Cambridge, Oxford and London which I think will need rewriting. I went to London last week for two nights and drank a vast amount of champagne, first with Basil,[1] then with Randolph and Peter Fitzwilliam, I went to a board meeting at Chapman & Hall. Eleanor Smith died suddenly and Frank is trying to use the occasion for Freddy's[2] conversion.

[1] Basil Bennett.
[2] Lord Birkenhead was Eleanor Smith's brother.

They cremated her before anyone knew it was illegal. I am preparing a version of my travel books for a single volume. I have fixed on Mr Dix for Bron next term.

Wednesday 21 November 1945

Pleasant days at Stinchcombe. After long correspondence and threats of legal action I have at last had a boiler installed. Ellwood has returned, and silver, boots and furniture shine. I went to London on Thursday last to address the Catholic graduates of London University. A day devoted entirely to duty; luncheon with my mother, dinner in a horrible restaurant with Catholic graduates, mostly female. Douglas and Mia were there and made the evening tolerable. My paper was gloomy in tone but lively in expression; and the discussion afterwards, though it seemed flat to me, was said to be unusually vigorous. Dr Letitia Fairfield made an angry speech. Afterwards to Park West to drink port with Douglas, Mia, John Acton.

On Friday Laura came for the night on her way to St Leonard's to visit Teresa. I got a little tipsy at the Beefsteak at luncheon and very tipsy at White's at dinner, having won some money on the races.

Next day, Saturday, to Cambridge carrying lobsters and a guinea-fowl for Father Gilbey. Felt ill. Dined *tête-à-tête* with him. Felt ill next day having slept badly. Father Gilbey's fear of his cook drove us out to all meals that day, so I never ate my lobsters or fowl. An hour's sightseeing was the sole recreation in a day devoted to irksome duty: visiting sick Poles in hospital, talking to humourless, grubby undergraduates. The audience at the Fisher seemed largely non-Catholic. I was asked many questions, mostly irrelevant or unintelligible; again I was assured with apparent sincerity that the paper had been an unusual success. Afterwards I was pursued by two neurotic, agnostic poets and kept up until midnight.

To London next day and happily found that an MP who had asked me to luncheon was ill so I was able to go to the Beefsteak and hear the pundits praising de Gaulle's sagacity in the French crisis. Returned with joy to my own home. Found letter and telegram from the Duchess of Atholl requiring me to speak on Jugoslavia at an anti-Soviet meeting. Refused collaboration with so dubious an ally. Well pleased to be back in my own bed (the Haynes' four-poster at last erected). Sent off the fragment of four books that are to make *While the Going was Good*. My review of *Palinurus* seems to have caused a mild sensation in a small circle. Cyril: first: 'I will not read it. It will spoil my friendship with Evelyn'; Secondly: 'I do not mind for myself. It makes Ann Rothermere look ridiculous.'[1]

---

[1] The review asserted that *The Unquiet Grave* was the kind of work that appealed to the circle round Ann Rothermere.

Saturday 1 December 1945

Eddie and Bridget Grant came for last weekend. I gave them champagne and claret and port and sherry and gin and I think they enjoyed them. On Sunday I left them to go to Oxford to speak at the Newman. Oxford were better hosts than Cambridge. Father Corbishley met me at the station. Campion Hall still has the atmosphere promoted by D'Arcy. I promised to write a note on Campion Hall hospitality for their golden jubilee book, and today wrote it. Two young men and a girl took me to dine at the Mitre and were more self-possessed than the Fisher boys. The meeting was full of girls. I was touched to see Frank Pakenham and his wife. The discussion was quite amusing. The chaplain did little to contribute. He seems to give dances and nothing else. After the paper I escaped to Campion Hall and drank whisky in the Stuart Parlour as of old. Next day to luncheon in London, as it seemed the quickest route home. Busy pruning and training the beech avenue. Reading *Ulysses* and a preposterous commentary. I still get echoes of my Connolly review. Raymond Mortimer advised Cyril to read it by saying it was so flattering.[1]

Friday 21 December 1945

A mild winter; sunshine half the day. Laura and I dine without fire or central heating in complete comfort. I have done no writing except for a letter in *The Times* joining in the baiting of Picasso and a note of reminiscence for the Campion Hall jubilee book. The last few days have been taken up with preparations for Christmas – expensive trash in the shops. I sent off a dozen early Victorian albums and American *Bridesheads* as presents. Today Laura has gone to Taunton to meet Bron and Teresa and bring them home. A week ago No. 8 Commando gave a dinner to Bob at Buck's. It had been largely talked about as an orgy but it was an evening of quiet reflection. Dinner – caviare (brought from Moscow by Randolph), chicken soup, grilled soles, roast turkey, cold beef, plum pudding and mince-pies all in very large quantities – vodka, champagne, port, brandy, Havana cigars. It would not have been remarkable even four years ago but was very remarkable this year. Nancy came for the weekend and remained seated before the fire for two days. A large and expensive parcel of old books from Lowe of Birmingham has proved a disappointment – battered and dirty. A theatrical performance at Uley – semi-professional village art; that is to say, a producer-leading actor is sent about the country to stimulate local talent. A nativity play with an apology on the programme, 'Whatever our beliefs we can appreciate the simple faith of the Chester Cycle . . .'

---

[1] Raymond Mortimer denies the story, pointing out that his relations with Connolly remained cordial until the end of Connolly's life, which would scarcely have been the case had the report been true.

In London I saw a fine replica by Frith of his *Railway Station* on sale in Mount Street for £1,250 and nearly bought it.

The Manor House has been sold to a Welsh couple who first excited our interest by having a string of polo ponies and three young children. They prove on enquiry to be respectively experts on folk dancing and housing, so all interest evaporates.

Wednesday 26 December 1945

Maria Teresa and Bron have arrived; he ingratiating, she covered with little medals and badges, neurotically voluble with the vocabulary of the lower-middle class – 'serviette', 'spare room'. Only on points of theology does she become rational. On Christmas Eve we went to midnight Mass at Nympsfield. I was moved to remit the sums owing by the nuns for the losses and break-ages of their six years' tenancy of this house. We managed to collect a number of trashy and costly toys for the stockings. We had a goose for luncheon and a tasteless plum pudding made for us by Mrs Harper, a bottle of champagne. By keeping the children in bed for long periods we managed to have a tolerable day. My only present, a very welcome one, a box of cigars from Auberon. I have seats for both Bath and Bristol pantomimes. The children leave for Pixton on the 10th. Meanwhile I have my meals in the library.

Though I make-believe to be detached from the world I find a day without post or newspapers strangely flat, and look forward to tomorrow's awakening with Ellwood laying the papers by my pillow.

Home for a cold New Year's Day. My children weary me. I can only see them as defective adults; feckless, destructive, frivolous, sensual, humourless. I began the New Year without previous resolutions by resuming work on *Helena*.

Wednesday 9 January 1946

Laura left today to cope with some nursery crisis at Pixton. I have had a postponement of my call-up from MGM and am steadily at work on *Helena*.

Saturday 12 January 1946

Yesterday I had to mention the fall of Palmyra. Longinus was executed there. I brought this in as decoration and made Helena have heard of him. Today I rewrote a paragraph of the first chapter making the tutor mention him. Then, because Mr Hodges, my nurse's father, was a fabulous figure to me, I gave Helena two fables: first of the nursery, the exemplary soldier; secondly of the schoolroom, the stupendous pundit. Then I introduced to the Longinus paragraph the fact that Helena felt his death as a bereavement, the final end of her education. Then I introduced into the passage about Tetricus's betrayal the sense that Helena thought the grave of her nurse's father dishonoured. So the book prospers.

Saturday 26 January 1946

Last night I had eight hours' natural and deep sleep and today feel restored after a visit to London on 23rd and 24th in which I drank great quantities of champagne and made myself conspicuous in a fashionable party of unloved acquaintances. Laura is still away and has postponed her return for a week. I miss her grievously. The first book of *Helena* was finished last week and sent to be typed. I am reading hard for the second and third. I lunched with Diana last Wednesday, fully reconciled after seven years' estrangement.

This morning the *Itinerary of Bordeaux* arrived from the London Library, and all day off and on I have been fretting about the date of its composition and Helena's journey, and finding it mentioned pompously and slyly in Gibbon. Then, quite suddenly, while I was reading something else, the solution came to me – absolutely simple. He didn't mention the Cross because he never saw it; it was not on view. I have been to Rome many times and not seen the Cross there. It was only exposed on Good Friday and he was not in Jerusalem more than a few days. And Eusebius did not mention it because he hated it.

Monday 28 January 1946

I drove to Bristol in Prothero's car, met Laura looking bowed with work and illness, collected Bron, a midget in new school outfit, and took him to Mells, where Katharine and Helen received him with the utmost kindness and he behaved well. Next day I took him to his school which was in a rudimentary state of preparation – ladders and paint-pots everywhere. Dix had little presence. Mrs Dix seemed trustworthy. I put him in the hands of a clean-looking matron and returned to Mells. Katharine was gayer than I have seen her for years, the house full of very old servants. I brought wine. Next day I returned here by hired car, stopping in Bath to examine some wholly repulsive religious busts. The poor old man who owned them seemed so crestfallen that I bought some mouldy Ionic columns to cheer him up.

Saturday 2 February 1946

American mails are in with the letters they write to authors. The magazine *Life* blithely proposed to publish a series of photographic illustrations of my books based on the originals from whom the characters were drawn. I answered threatening them with imprisonment. Father Murtagh came to tea and I lent him Bernanos's *Diary of a Country Priest* from curiosity to see how he will take it. I was able to go to confession and communion at Mells. There is a hope that Laura may return today, a fear she may bring Margaret.[1]

[1] The Waugh's second daughter, then aged three.

Saturday 9 February 1946

Laura returned a week ago today bringing Margaret, an egotistical little girl who has improved slightly during the week she has been here. Yesterday a nurserymaid arrived with Harriet.[1] Robert Henriques came to call bringing the *Jewish Encyclopedia*; he was full of his adroitness in managing to obtain privileges from the State. I have hopes of his conversion to Christianity.

London, Thursday 21 February 1946

To London 9.20, a very cold stormy morning. There was a restaurant car on the train, the first I have seen since the war. At Paddington a long queue for taxis so to Hyde Park Hotel by crowded tube carrying my bag. On the steps of the hotel met Dig Yorke and arranged to call that evening. To White's full of friends. A letter from Deats, whose name is spelt Deitz,[2] and Deitz himself who asked me to call that evening. Horrid luncheon with Christopher Sykes, Simon Elwes, etc., then to Golders Green to see Professor Marmostein [?], a Jewish authority on the fourth century, venerable, guttural, vague. He tried to convince me that a legend of a sword falling from heaven at a peasant's feet and being used for his decapitation was identical with the story of the Empress digging a bit of wood out of the ground and taking it to Rome. Returned to London to find shops all shutting at 5. Caught Vsevolode in his office and persuaded him to let me have wine in fair quantity. (One case sherry, two cases 'pool' Burgundy.) To Deitz at Ritz, pink champagne, the gift of a handful of cigars. To the Yorkes – no hospitality of any kind. Their parsimony has become morbid. They described dining with Cyril. 'Of course we can never ask him back. We have no wine.' 'Couldn't you get some from the cellars at Forthampton or Tewkesbury?' 'Oh no, that would *never* be allowed.' 'Then why not do what Cyril does and buy it?' '*Buy* it!!!' To White's where Frank dined with me. He was in a daze of hero worship of Mr Ernest Bevin's defence of the Poles.

The King never sees him. He has only seen him once since he has been in office and is not asked even to the Uno parties. Joined by Randolph and drank till 1 o'clock. Back to the Hyde Park Hotel where I found a note from Basil soliciting peace. Next morning I went to see Maimie. Then to White's where I found Basil abject. He said that for a fortnight he has felt hunted. His surrender has been absolute – gin and wood port on the way and two bottles of gin as a present to Laura in his hands. Hurried luncheon at Beefsteak where Ed Stanley's candidature is ill looked on. To Chapman & Hall's board meeting where the project of Moray MacLaren's book was welcomed and I was able to put in a

[1] The Waughs' youngest daughter, then aged one and a half.

[2] Howard Dietz (not Deitz), publicity director of MGM and husband of Tanis Guinness, who in 1937 jilted the 6th Earl of Carnarvon (a cousin of both Waugh's wives) on their wedding eve and instead married Dietz.

little library to which Duff intends to present his books. Diana has taken the Borghese apartments on the *piano nobile* for her suite. Miss Penelope Thomas, Diana's secretary, a compact little creature, met me affably. Auberon was there. He has apparently established himself in the house. A cocktail party assembled. The first three hands I shook were Mme Pol Roger, M. de Polignac, Philippe de Rothschild, so that I was immersed in wine. They tried to speak of my books, I of their vintages. Mme Pol Roger promised and gave me half a dozen of her '28. Quennell arrived that day and did badly (1) by sending a telegram announcing his arrival and adding, 'Afraid Evelyn will not like it'. Hostesses, least of all ambassadresses, do not like it thought that guests dictate their company. (2) At dinner saying in piping tones, 'I wonder if anyone ever reads Browning nowadays?' upon which Duff swelled, purpled, and recited for twenty minutes *Sordello*. (3) Late in the evening we discussed next day's dinner party. I asked for Nancy. Peter: 'I've more or less asked a girl to dine with me but I don't know where I shall take her.' Pause. Diana: 'Do I know her? Name! Who is she?' 'Well she's the joint property of myself and Ali Forbes.'

At dinner, primed with champagne and general good feeling, on Diana's advice, I pursued Auberon downstairs (on his way to Brussels) and told him I liked him. He believed it. Next day met Maurice Bowra, sat in the sun in Tuileries gardens, drank champagne cocktails, drove up the river with Diana to lunch at a terrace restaurant, then with Nancy to the salon of a Mme Bouquet who has her Thursdays. I was a fish out of water. They were all very flattering, mostly buggers. A large dinner party that night. I sat next to an adventuress. Next day John Julius[1] came, the Amerys (father and surviving son),[2] and an entirely bloody Professor Huxley[3] who put Quennell in the shade. Shopping with Nancy, sightseeing with Diana.

Great difficulties changing money. Ali Forbes had boasted: 'I never get less than 820 francs to the pound.' Auberon: 'I get 1,000.' Pinned down, he gave a Pole's name and the wrong address. John Julius and I set out to find him. A polite fellow talking English, in a shady hotel. He led us through darkness to a bedroom where a Pole in battledress lay groaning in hangover.

He (first Pole): 'It is my brother who arranges the money. He is at the dentist. He will be back at 3.30.'

'It is now 4.'

'Then he will come at once.' We sat for twenty minutes. We were pressed to accept coffee, did so. None came. He told me Auberon owned the Cavendish Hotel. He talked of Duff's imminent removal until I was obliged to introduce

[1] Son of Lady Diana and Duff Cooper.

[2] Leopold Amery (1873–1955); MP, 1911–45; Colonial Secretary, 1924; it was said of him that he might have been Prime Minister if he had been half a head taller and his speeches half an hour shorter. His 'surviving son' was Julian Amery, MP.

[3] Professor Julian Huxley, Director-General of Unesco 1946–8.

John Julius. He left. He said his brother would telephone. At 6.30 he did so, fixing a meeting at the Crémaillère, not the Opera.

When he came I said, 'You are very like your brother.'

'I am he. I have had to make contact with a Jew. How much do you hope to get?'

'Auberon said 1,000 francs.'

'1,000? He has ideas like Lord Byron. I have 720.'

'Very well.'

'You are disappointed?'

'No, I know Auberon.' The exchange was effected.

'Where shall we dine?'

'I have to dine at the Embassy.'

'Oh, then you *are* disappointed.'

Maurice dined that evening and Nancy again. I was a little drunk every evening; quite drunk on Saturday night when Diana, John Julius and I drove to their home at Chantilly. Woke at dawn to find a waterfall in the middle distance, an exquisite day and a lovely park. Mass at the village church, then a drive to Senlis, Ermenonville, and the Mer de Sable. A luncheon party, Diana in trousers after wrangle; also Randolph, Mme de Montgomery [?]. Amery *very* funny with animal stories. It was very agreeable to see Huxley, who is head of all education and science for Uno, a crypto-Communist who regards himself as a world force, treated on all sides as a zoo-keeper, by myself from malice, by everyone else in genuine goodwill. 'Don't you find it difficult to get bamboo shoots for your panda, Professor?' On Sunday night Quennell had palpitations of the heart brought on by sexual excess.

Monday: a slight cloud owing to Diana's declaration that no food would be provided in the Embassy. As all restaurants are shut on Mondays it caused grave inconvenience. In the end Bowra and I went up the river to the place where Diana and I lunched the first day. Late in the afternoon, laden with hats and cheese and wine, I took the aeroplane to London, slept at the Hyde Park Hotel, and returned with a glad heart to home.

Piers Court, Saturday 13 April 1946

The children's holidays have begun. Teresa taller and more personable. It is a great surprise to see how nice they are to one another. Bron has been robbed of 10s by a boy called Lavery. My mother came for two nights' visit. We put ourselves out for her and I think she was happy. My article in *Life* looks well and has attracted attention.

Friday 26 April 1946

I fasted and gave up wine during Holy Week and attended a number of religious services. I made the disconcerting discovery that Bron's tale of

Lavery's theft was pure invention. I have become involved in a tedious game with the children of correspondence in a crack in a cedar tree between them and Bad Basil Bennett, captain of the robbers.[1] That and a fantasy about 'Dr Bedlam's School for Mad and Bad Children' occupy most of their conversation. They have a pet lamb. I spend many hours a day weeding the lawns.

Yesterday to London for the day. Luncheon at the Beefsteak. I have had a letter from Evan Tredegar asking me to join a committee consisting of himself, Marie Stopes, an unknown B.Litt., and 'we hope Harold Nicolson', to proclaim Alfred Douglas the greatest sonneteer since Shakespeare. I replied that considering Milton and Wordsworth I could not agree with the judgement and that anyway I thought Marie Stopes a preposterous person to propose it. At the Beefsteak I met Harold. He said he had replied to Evan saying that considering Milton and Wordsworth he could not agree with the judgement and that anyway he thought Marie Stopes a preposterous person to propose it. Am I developing a Beefsteak mind? Going out I found Douglas Woodruff crouched at the end of the table like a dying orang-outang. I chid him about *The Tablet* but his face crumpled with woe. I struck no spark and said he seemed low-spirited. Yes, he said, his chinaware had been stolen from store and fictitiously sold. Many things had lately gone wrong with him, he said. To Chapman & Hall board meeting where the year's figures showed nearly £20,000 paid in excess profits tax. I raised the point whether we could not have found a way to spare this. Opposition from Chamberlain, timid support from Bale and Neale. It appears Matthews cannot shake off the habit of profit-making at everyone's expense, even when the profits are confiscated. To White's, drank with Stirlings and Perry Brownlow. Home by the evening train.

Tuesday 7 May 1946

Teresa left yesterday for school. Bron goes the day after tomorrow. I found their company increasingly irksome as the holidays dragged on. On Sunday they dined with us and were obstreperous. Yesterday I went to London to have my hair cut. The news of the French constitutional plebiscite is the first good news out of Europe for a year. Margaret has had her adenoids removed. I have dug a broad passage leading to the centre of the balustrade in the garden.

Saturday 11 May 1946

Douglas Woodruff came for the weekend. Leighton came to do homage with gifts of books. I tried to persuade Douglas that a magazine had influence simply so far as it was readable. He is making *The Tablet*, confessedly, a 'clearing house' for supplying foreign papers with titbits taken from the British wireless monitoring reports.

[1] Waugh told the children that Bennett, his Commando brother-officer and a family friend, would do very bad things to them unless they sent him messages via the cedar tree.

Wednesday 15 May 1946

At work on Saccone & Speed's advertisement with my mind distracted by phrases from my speech at the Oxford Union next week.

Thursday 16 May 1946

To my surprise and annoyance the Golden Cockerel Press do not wish to publish my 'Dowager Empress'. I must fall back on Burns.

Oxford, Thursday 23 May 1946

Having felt ill since Sunday I set out for Oxford in a hired car, stopping for a draught of opium at Mrs Cope's on the way. I bought Maurice two bottles of Roederer '28. We drank one at 6 before I went to the Union. There was wine of a sort at a dinner; two dons and the speakers; young Noel in a white blazer; a negro with a beard. All very civil. The debate crowded – a record attendance they said. It was nearly 10 before I was called on to speak. They laughed and applauded my speech as they had done at the other speakers. I accepted under the promise of John Betjeman being my opponent. Instead a dull liberal named oddly Aubrey Herbert. Walked home. A glass or two of port. Slept badly though drugged.

Friday 24 May 1946

At Oxford. Ill most of the day. I visited chemists constantly for sedatives. I went round to bookshops and bought a few nineteenth-century illustrated books. Luncheon with Maurice, a fine hock and a Camembert cheese. Went to see a clerical schoolmaster who had a hideous bookcase to sell in a fine Betjeman interior. The Deakins and Cecils came to dinner. Highly enjoyable evening. Bill Deakin full of guilt about Tito.

Piers Court, Saturday 25 May 1946

Returned home by hired car. An invitation to go to Salamanca next month. Accepted.

Saturday, 8 June 1946

Victory Day. At home, having refused an invitation from the *Empire News* to report a masquerade which Mr Attlee is organizing in London. He is driving round in a carriage with Churchill, behind the Royal Family, at the head of a procession of Brazilians, Mexicans, Egyptians, Naafi waitresses and assorted negroes claiming that they won the war. It has rained most of the day. I hope it rained hard in London and soaked Attlee. None of the 'Communist' countries sent representatives. I have finished as much of my treatiese on Saccone & Speed as I can do without further material. Fourteen dozen bottles of champagne to date. Prewitt is back working well for me building up the haha wall. All the grass looks ghastly and my motor mower is still under repair. Food is so dull that I have lost all appetite. After some days of doubt I have secured an air passage to Madrid on 15th. It is said Liz will be there too. Some books I have sent to be bound in Bristol came back very ill done. I am wrestling with Father D'Arcy on love. Lucid and graceful; a subject of which I am grossly ignorant but so much of it consists of criticism of modern philosophers of whom I have never heard. I feel stale and bored and look forward greatly to the change of going abroad. My nephew Robin Grant is here; a pusillanimous child who seems to give great pleasure to Margaret. Auberon came for a night – first fruit of the declaration of love Diana forced from me. He was very dull and barmy. Laura drove to Taunton and returned with a cow in great spirits.

Monday 10 June 1946

Bill Deakin and his wife came for the night. Maclean had that morning published an apologia in *The Times*, dishonest in two ways: (*a*) in claiming to have originated the mission and discovered Tito when in fact Bill had done all the early and dangerous work; (*b*) in saying no pretence was ever made that the movement was not Communist, when in fact at the crucial time Randolph was empowered by him to act as public relations officer and sent to Rome and London, seeing the Pope and Winston, to assure them that the 'whole trend' was towards liberal democracy.[1] Meanwhile the trial of Mihailović is being

[1] Fitzroy Maclean comments in a letter to the editor, January 1976: 'The origination of British liaison with the Jugoslav Partisans is a matter of history. No one (least of all myself) has ever suggested that I was the first British officer to make contact with Tito or the Partisans. Contact with Tito was first made by Captain Hudson as early as September 1941. In May 1943 Captain Hunter and Major Jones were dropped as Liaison Officers to the Partisans in Croatia and Slovenia. Soon after Captain (now Sir William) Deakin and Captain Stewart were dropped to Tito's Headquarters in Montenegro. In July 1943 Mr Churchill appointed me his Personal Representative with Tito and Brigadier Commanding a British Military Mission to the Partisans (Macmis), controlling all British officers attached to Partisan formations. In September 1943, with several other officers, I was dropped into Jugoslavia as its commander. Full details can be obtained from the relevant official documents, from Sir William Deakin's *The Embattled Mountain*, from my own *Eastern Approaches* and *Disputed Barricade* and from Richard Clogg's *British Policy towards Wartime Resistance in Yugoslavia and Greece*.

Deakin and Stewart reached Tito's Headquarters at the height of the enemy's Fifth Offensive. Stewart was killed and Deakin wounded shortly after their arrival. For the Partisans this was the worst moment of the war. Bill Deakin's cheerful and courageous conduct during the Offensive won him the lasting respect and affection of all who were with him, including Tito himself. This and the first hand information which he and the other officers already in Jugoslavia were able to give me were of the greatest value to me when I took command of the Mission in September. This I emphasized most strongly in my official reports at the time and have made abundantly clear in everything I have since written on the subject.

What emerges no less clearly from the official documents since published, from *The Embattled Mountain* and from several of the contributions to Richard Clogg's book is the extent to which,

staged as a fraudulent 'exposure' of British intrigue. The General has plainly been offered his life if he will pretend he was put up to fight the Partisans by English Fascists.

The last days have been wet and I have been idle and restless, looking forward greatly to my trip to Spain.

Footnote 1 continued

from Hudson's time onwards, such information as became available about the Partisans was deliberately suppressed in London and Cairo. Indeed it was only the direct intervention of the Prime Minister that finally broke what amounted to a conspiracy of silence. Mr Churchill's purpose in sending me to Jugoslavia was, as he himself put it, to find out who was killing the most Germans and how they could be helped to kill more. Thanks to the information I received from Bill Deakin and others on arrival and from my own observation at first hand, I was able during the year and a half I spent in Jugoslavia to reach a number of very definite conclusions on this subject. These I duly transmitted by signal and whenever possible by written despatch to the Prime Minister and Supreme Allied Commander, making as sure as I humanly could that they reached their destination. My conclusions were, briefly, that the Partisans were militarily most effective, that they were managing to contain a score of enemy divisions which could otherwise have been deployed against the Allies on other fronts, that they deserved all the help we could give them and that in my view we should stop supporting the Cetniks of General Mihajlović, many of whom were actively collaborating with the enemy, and transfer our support to Tito. It was on the strength of these reports and of the verbal report which Bill Deakin and I made to the Prime Minister in Cairo towards the end of 1943 that the decision was taken to drop General Mihajlović and give Tito all possible support.

On the political side my reports (now made public) were equally definite. They made it absolutely clear that Tito was a self-proclaimed Communist, that the Partisan Movement was Communist-controlled and that Tito's ultimate aim was to seize power and establish a Communist system of government in Jugoslavia, an aim in which he seemed to me very likely to succeed. Knowing this and knowing what I did about Communism after spending the years 1937 to 1939 in the Soviet Union, I could naturally never have suggested to anyone that "the whole trend was towards liberal democracy". Nor did I authorise Randolph Churchill to say anything of the kind to the Pope or to his father. On the political as on the military side the reports from my Headquarters went out in my name and on my responsibility and, as anyone sufficiently interested can now see for himself, were perfectly clear on this point. Beyond saying that in my view the Partisans were almost certain to come to power in Jugoslavia after the war, the only speculation I allowed myself in regard to the future was to say that, from my observation of him and from my knowledge of the Russians, Tito might in the long run prove impatient of Soviet control. "Much," I wrote to Mr Churchill in a despatch in November 1943, "will depend on Tito and whether he sees himself in his former role of Comintern agent or as the potential ruler of an independent Jugoslav state."

Moving on to June 1946, my reason for recalling in a *Times* article the rationale of the War Cabinet's decision to drop Mihajlović and support Tito was that it seemed important to establish the truth on this subject, by this time in serious danger of becoming blurred. In 1946 Tito was extremely unpopular in Great Britain and America; the decision to support him (which had been taken on my recommendation) was under violent attack from all sides; and no one else showed any wish whatever to defend it. In June 1946, against my friends' advice, I finally decided to join the fray, thereby, as they had rightly foreseen, only incurring further odium. Even after all these years, the suggestion that I was trying to steal the credit for such an intensely unpopular decision has a somewhat ironical ring.'

Friday 14 June 1946

To London. Bought some charming nineteenth-century books from Jew in Cecil Court; dined and slept at Park West.

London–Madrid, Saturday 15 June 1946

Left Park West with Douglas at 8.[1] He was still in doubt about the nature of the congress we were attending and our own position there. At Croydon we met Mary Campbell travelling with unknown, handsome young man; Professor Brierley of All Souls on his way to Francisco de Vitoria celebrations;[2] Lady Cope, who put under my charge her daughter travelling to Pax Romana Congress. At Madrid Professor Brierley was met by suave lawyers, later known to us as Antonion de Luna [?] and Castanon, and conducted in car to Palace Hotel; Miss Cope was met by friends; Douglas and I by gauche Pax Romana students who took us by bus to low-class Hotel Nacional. It then became plain that Francisco de Vitoria Association was a luxury tour for international jurists in which Douglas and I were not included. All celebrations had been postponed five days. Organizers were busy getting their people out of Madrid. Saturday evening so everyone away. Douglas telephoned to countless friends all of whom were away. We dined at a small restaurant and had our first acquaintance with Spanish prices, which are enhanced by government taxation and an adverse exchange (41 pesetas to £1) to a preposterous level. After dinner (we had had no luncheon) we called on Brierley at the Palace and met a Swiss professor and Professor Russ Hoffman [?], a morbid Yank, and a sham who was bluffing his way to government support with the excuse for doing research work at Simancas. We learned that these learned people were off next day on a tour of Castile and decided to join them.

Valladolid, Sunday 16 June 1946

Turned up at Palace Hotel with our luggage at 10 o'clock to mild surprise of Luna. Dutch couple did likewise. I think Luna, having represented to Spanish Government that he could collect distinguished cosmopolitan party, was prepared to welcome interlopers. Only other genuine professor was large, comic Swede from Upsala. After various breakdowns we drove to Valladolid arriving there at 5, very tired and hungry. Lunched and were swept off to official reception at the university from which Douglas and I escaped to visit the English College, where the rector has spent the war years without students collecting and arranging interesting archives. Thence to a *vin d'honneur* at the town hall. Here and elsewhere the *alcades*[3] all seemed young shits, not worthy

---

[1] It was this journey with Douglas Woodruff to Spain that inspired *Scott King's Modern Europe* (1947).

[2] Spanish theologian (*c.* 1485–1546), often regarded as the 'Father of International Law'.

[3] Mayors.

burgesses. After dinner the *alcades* took us to the theatre at midnight and put us into boxes where flamencos sang. I was too tired to stay to the end.

Burgos, Monday 17 June 1946

Professors Brierley and Hoffman failing in health. A vigorous sightseeing tour in the morning including very splendid museum of ecclesiastical sculpture. At 2 o'clock a mayoral banquet. Immediately after banquet drove to Simancas to see Royal Archives where there was a Boston woman who had worked there for forty years discovering two facts. She complained later, on many occasions, that one of us had stolen her fountain-pen. Wine and macaroons with the mayor. Back to Valladolid, off to Burgos, arriving about 10. After dinner drank with Prof. Dering and wife. He was a professor of law at Lvov, had spent the war in Switzerland, now had a chair in Madrid. Spanish policy seems to be to appoint all literates to professorships and pay them too little to support life. They are then offered supplementary work by the Foreign Office. Dering's job was to form 'Universitas', an international league of 'professors' and 'intellectuals'. When not discussing this drab project, he was a jolly man. At the banquet I sat next to a monoglot, deaf octogenarian.

Vitoria, Tuesday 18 June 1946

Vin d'honneur at town hall with fifteenth band at 10 in morning. Drove to see two monasteries. Las Huelgas would have repaid much closer study. Douglas at constant cross-purposes in conversation and seldom aware of it. In order to establish my bona fides I gave a copy of *Brideshead* to C——, weary old queen, and of Spanish edition of *Handful of Dust* to subservient professor. Another mayoral banquet. Nasty food. Hoffman and Brierley both sickening. After banquet a tour of cathedral with cross canon [?] who lost all his audience. 7.30 Drove off to Vitoria. Dined at hotel. Joined by professor of Santiago and wife. Very heavy pidgin-French conversation. After dinner to the theatre where we saw the last act and a half of *Lady Windermere's Fan* in Spanish, played as grand melodrama.

Wednesday 19 June 1946

Woke feeling ill. Felt worse. We left wreaths at hideous Vitoria memorial. Children did folk dancing in main square. Felt worse. Left before banquet and retired to bed for the day. Mayor of town and two aldermen dispensed a medicine for me which worked a cure.

Salamanca, Thursday 20 June 1946

Long drive to Salamanca, stopping in Burgos for Corpus Christi celebrations but too late for main procession. Arrived Salamanca late at night but before Pax Romana students, who got in at 4 am next day. Saw procession of Blessed Sacrament with fireworks flung at it.

21st. Salamanca full of priests and students. We stayed there five nights. After a few experiments we gave up the sessions of the various congresses, which were ineffably tedious and pointless, more particularly those of 'Universitas'. Did sightseeing. Went on day's expedition to Ciudad Rodrigo, particularly beautiful town, and saw farm bull-games, selecting heifers for maternity by playing them.

Luna returned from Madrid having done nothing about getting Douglas and me a passage back.

On 26th we went to Avila and were deposited in Madrid at Palace Hotel in the evening, after which Luna sequestered himself. We spent the next six days in Madrid in increasing heat and uncertainty about means of getting home. Victor Mallet[1] away. I saw a lot of Peggy. Embassy staff wet. Fan consul lent me money and took me to bullfight. I bought a little expensive trash. It seemed we should have to go by train, an odious journey, but Douglas persuaded the Foreign Minister to put two officials off the aeroplane for us. The Embassy was outraged. On the last evening Randolph turned up with a showy tart. We dined with him and sat too long.

London, Tuesday 2 July 1946

Home in comfort by air to find London almost as hot as Madrid. A telegram awaiting me to say Laura was delivered of a son.[2] A cocktail party at Lady Beaumont's in honour of David Mathew; dinner at Mia's. A hot night.

Wednesday 3 July 1946

A hot day. Ordered clothes. Lunched Beefsteak, dined Brian Franks.

Tuesday 4 July 1946

Maimie lunched with me. We drank three bottles of champagne in the afternoon. I was drunk and, after wandering about White's, went early to bed.

Friday 5 July 1946

Lunched with Peter Beatty. Dined with Ran. He very drunk.

Pixton Park, Saturday 6 July 1946

Had arranged to go to Pixton. Funked train and took taxi. Rather tedious journey. Found Laura well and the house cool and smelling of lilies and roses. I had meant to write against Connolly who has perpetrated a fatuous article in *Horizon* on the marks of a civilized state, but I left *Horizon* and many books at White's.

[1] British ambassador in Madrid.
[2] The Waughs' fifth child and second son, James.

Returned to London Wednesday 10th. Lunched next day with Peter's caviare. Extreme heat.

Saturday 13th. To Mereworth to stay with Peter Beatty. A house of enchanting beauty, gardens in disorder, Peter almost stone-blind. Phil Dunne and the Murrough O'Briens [?]. Drove up with Phil on Monday morning. Heatwave over.

Tuesday a drunken day; lunched at Beefsteak. Ben Nicolson full of discovery of a new Raphael. Went with him and Harold to see it. Drinking in White's most of afternoon. Then to Beefsteak again where I got drunk with Kenneth Wagg and insulted R. A. Butler. Then to St James's for another bottle of champagne where I insulted Beverly Baxter. Was sick on retiring to bed.

Wednesday. Confession. Maimie and Susan Carnegie to luncheon at Hyde Park Hotel. Very crowded cocktail party at Simon Elwes', full of royalty and all too squashed to curtsey. Dined quietly at White's and read Osbert Sitwell's second volume of autobiography.

Thursday 18 July 1946

Communion and called on Vsevolode to discuss his wine book. Received two dozen Roederer 1928 from him.

Piers Court, Thursday 8 August 1946

Returned to Stinchcombe very thankfully in Prothero's car. The last three weeks in London passed like three months in lassitude. After 1st August White's was shut and I saw few friends. I had people to drink champagne with me at the Hyde Park Hotel most evenings, chiefly the same gang, David Stirling, Ran Antrim, Christopher Sykes, Bridget Parsons, etc.

At the end of July Diana came to London, lunched with me in great melancholy before she left for the weekend, arranged to dine together on Tuesday. By Tuesday all was changed – Louise de Vilmorin,[1] Countess Palfi, was coming to London. A series of letters and telephone calls – she was coming by air, she was coming by sea, she was coming in the morning, she was coming at night. Finally I went to dinner at the Dorchester at 8 to find Diana, June Capel, Raimund. Champagne flowing. Before they had had their soup Diana and Raimund were off to Northolt to meet the poetess – I protesting vainly that even a poetess cannot get lost on arrival at an airport – and I was left alone with Miss Capel for two hours. She struggled bravely to make conversation, but could think of nothing but Vilmorin. We sat like a far too long protracted first act waiting for the appearance of the Great Actress. At last she came, lame, wizened, flashing eyes – Toulouse Lautrec, Laurencin, the Spirit of France, egocentric maniac, Diana and June dancing attendance. In spite of her record of long married life in USA she affects not to speak English. If the talk became

[1] French light novelist (d. 1969).

general for a moment she recalled it to herself with squeals of pain or perplexity and ran into the bedroom for private conversations. The hell of a woman. I can understand Diana's passion for they are doubles and it is the Narcissus in her – another Iris[1] – and June is naturally loving and giving, but next day I found tough old eggs like Venetia and Daphne[2] fallen victim. Daphne, with running eyes, 'She had a mother called Melanie.'

David had a dinner party for Liza Maugham whom he loves. He asked me to bring a girl friend. I asked June who, on second thoughts, accepted. She came in a splendid black and cream dress. We dined in great din at Bagatelle. Peter Stirling drunk. Later we went to Orchid Room, separated and I sat with June until 3 talking of religion. I dined with Liz and Raimund and found her becoming a scold. I stayed with the Jessels in the suburbs. Helen unfeminine but pleasant, Teddy the model smug businessman, censorious of others' drinking. Not a lavish host; nice children.

Tea with Frank at the House of Lords. An old lord whose name I didn't hear sat with us. Frank said I was a writer. 'My young brother wrote a book the other day which sold a million copies.' It was Lord Maugham.[3] Later Frank behaved badly, chucking dinner with me at White's and sending Henriques. Baby Jungman is on her way home with her children, repudiated. We had anxiety for two days about Trim's safety in the Jerusalem explosion.[4] He is alive and engaged to be married. The only work I did in the last month was an article exposing Connolly which has had great popular success.

Returned home to find Bron and Teresa, the rest still at Pixton. Laura making plans to move house to Taunton and at the same time buying two fields here.

Tuesday 13 August 1946

Laura and I went to see the house, Culmhead [?], to which she wants to move. It is a large, early Victorian house standing in woods and moorland. It will need acres of carpets, tons of mahogany, hosts of servants, but after a parish meeting at which it was plain that they all want to make Stinchcombe a suburb of Dursley, I want to move too. The present owner is a speculator who is making a profit selling it off in bits. The price about £8,500 for 160 acres; not expensive.

This house was shortly afterwards withdrawn from the market.

Saturday 24 August 1946

In answer to a telegram appealing to me to help quieten Randolph I went to

[1] Iris Tree, bohemian daughter of the actor Sir Herbert Tree.

[2] Venetia Montagu and Daphne Bath.

[3] The 1st Viscount Maugham, then 79; brother of Somerset Maugham; Lord Chancellor 1938–9.

[4] 'Trim', Lord Oxford, was Asst. District Commissioner in Palestine 1942–8.

stay with Pamela Berry in a luxurious ranch-house near Reading. Randolph had quarrelled with her in the meantime and was not there. Instead Seymour and Freda Casa Maury. Peter Fleming came to dinner in a dazed condition. He has built himself an atrocious villa on a large estate he has in the district. Although he farms two thousand acres he never has a pat of butter or an egg and lives on rations from the co-operative store. John Betjeman came to luncheon and read his erotic poetry aloud. Painfully crowded journeys there and back.

A tedious three days among my children. Then on 29th to London for Chapman & Hall's board meeting and to fetch my mother here. A typical day. Left at 8 in heavy storm and arrived in rain and wind at 11.30 at White's. To chemist to have sleeping draught made up and Heywood Hill's where at 12 both assistants were out to luncheon. To Trumper's where my man was on holiday and a crowd waiting, to White's where Geer[1] could not take me till 1 o'clock. Talked to Perry and Randolph. Nowhere to lunch. Everything still shut. Randolph undertook to 'arrange something'. When I emerged from the barber's chair he led me through the rain to Quaglino's where we had an absolutely awful luncheon and a bottle of undrinkable hock for which they charged £4 8s. No taxi. I had to hire a car to take me to Essex Street and accordingly was quarter of an hour late. An entirely new figure, fat with a shiny plebeian face and crescent-shaped glasses, was in the chair. The usual dull business of Bale explaining the character of technical books. Then on the agenda: 'Appointment to the board of Mr McDougall.' I asked who this was and learned that a new man was being put in over Walker's head to manage the 'general' side and was to have a place on the board. I protested. They looked smug and said it had all been decided by Methuen. Bale and Neale looked guilty. I put it on record that I disapproved. Then set out to find drawing materials. Then to meet my mother whom Prothero had picked up and was waiting for me in St James's. A tiring drive home.

Friday 30 August 1946

To Gloucester with Laura who bought a cow for more than £100. I went to a junk shop and bought a lion of wood, finely carved for £25, also a bookcase £35, a painting of the baptism of a Jewess £15, a charming Chinese painting £10, a Regency easel £7; all good things and at reasonable prices. Then I lost my reason. Among a pile of old paintings was a very pretty watercolour and gouache of Durham Cathedral. I asked the price. '£150', said the aged shopkeeper. I bought it.

Saturday 31 August 1946

I wrote to resign from the board of Chapman & Hall.

[1] The club barber.

Friday 13 September 1946

To my intense annoyance Ball, the carpenter on whom I depend so much, has gone off his head again and been locked up. I have written an article on Mrs Trollope's *Father Eustace*.

Monday 23 September 1946

Laura taking children to school. I to London for three nights to settle final business with Saccone & Speed and to drink large quantities of champagne.

Friday 4 October 1946

To London again for one night for Debo's ball. Dermot and I got very drunk and I suppose cut inglorious figures, but I enjoyed it.

Monday 7 October 1946

Gabriel and Alick came for night. For the last ten days the weather has been delicious and my grass sown above the haha is willow-green everywhere. I wrote a short story about a murder and turned my thoughts to a jaunt in USA.

Monday 28 October 1946

My 43rd birthday. I start the year with the resolution to be urbane and industrious and to keep, for one year at least, a full diary. Had I been writing a novel and wished to fix my hero's position in life a summary of my morning's post would have done it conveniently. (1) A reply from the Dublin house agent to my enquiry about Gormanston Castle – 1806 Gothic, fifteen bedrooms, chapel, seductive 'unfinished ballroom', 124-acre park. (2) BBC Third Programme offering me a three-weeks' tour of European capitals as bait for introducing their Christmas programme. (3) *La France Libre* containing an unauthorized translation of an extract from my forthcoming travel book. (4) A nun thanking me for giving her copies of *Brideshead* and *Campion* for a library in France. (5) The Beefsteak Club reminding me to find seconders for Maurice Bowra and Ran Antrim. (6) An Owen Jones illuminated book from a Birmingham bookseller. (7) The *New Yorker*.

The day was cold and sunny; the leaves just turning. Laura did all she could to make it peaceful. We drank a bottle of champagne before dinner, ate haddock for breakfast, pilaf for luncheon made with a packet of rice Peters gave us, roast chicken for dinner. I wrote letters, read Henry James, put lawn sand on the grass, walked.

Oxford, Tuesday 29 October 1946

I began a week's tour overshadowed by a sharp cold. I drove to Oxford to find Campion Hall en fête, the Cardinal and the Vice-Chancellor, dignitaries with little in common, closeted in an inner room and clearly at an end of their conversation, with dons and women drinking sherry outside. The Cardinal, graceless and affable, does not improve on acquaintance. Dinner comprised many un-needed courses – *vol au vent* of tinned salmon, etc. I sat next to the Vice-Chancellor and later in the library with Douglas, Ronnie Knox, and the Master, who is bitter with D'Arcy's zeal for collecting and has acquired a handsome tapestry for the chapel.

Wednesday 30 October 1946

A day that would have been delightful but for my cold. High Mass at St Aloysius with a brilliant sermon from Ronnie and generous indulgences for a congregation full of heretics. Douglas, with his habitual attraction for bores, inflicted first Father Walker and then Professor Zulueta on me. Elizabeth Pakenham lunched with me. I dined at Wadham high table with Maurice Bowra and Bill Deakin. The senior common-room full of a new hybrid – pupil-teachers.

Wantage, Thursday 31 October 1946

In the late afternoon to stay with the Betjemans in a lightless, stuffy, cold, poky rectory among beech woods overlooking Wantage. Harness everywhere. A fine collection of nineteenth-century illustrated books. Delicious food cooked by Penelope. I brought sherry, burgundy, port. A daughter of grossly proletarian appearance and manner.

Eton, Friday 1 November 1946

Cold severe. Glad to be relieved of obligation to hear Mass. By motor to Eton in the evening. I dined and stayed with a schoolmaster named Hedley and his pretty wife and at dinner heard myself doing my familiar turn about my patriarchal attitude to my children. They found it droll and original. I lectured the boys and failed to recognize my godson Jonathan Guinness. They asked quite bright questions afterwards.

London, Saturday 2 November 1946

To London, to Hyde Park Hotel in a suite, newly reopened on the first floor, of ingenious hideosity.

A dull weekend spent in White's and the Beefsteak where there was no one I much wanted to see. On Sunday I dined with Dick Stokes[1] and ineptly twitted him on his reputed engagement to Miss Ward. At the Beefsteak the ever-present, Landseer, hangdog Lord Chancellor, who affected to consult us in a man-to-man way about reform of the divorce laws. 'I'm frankly at my wits' end. What would you fellows do? When I was first called to the bar there were 800 cases a year. Now there are 7,000 a term.' —— appeared in his usual daze of guilt at having stayed too long in Paris and not being home, with the usual sheaf

[1] Richard Stokes, Labour MP and Roman Catholic.

of acid telegrams from ——. A pile of letters brought further tidings of prosperity and the promise of February in Hollywood.

Monday 4 November 1946

White's a little more enjoyable after the weekend. At 12 a Mr Heppenstall came from the BBC to discuss terms for sending me on a tour of European capitals. I pitched my terms high, as I did not really want to go – £300 payable in foreign currency. He drank two champagne cocktails and seemed disposed to talk about his own literary ambitions. My mother lunched with me and I behaved well to her. I read most of Henry Yorke's new book *Back*, which is marred by a dismally unsuccessful pastiche inserted in the middle. I called on him and Dig in the evening. Frank Pakenham and Pansy Lamb came to dine.

Tuesday 5 November 1946

I stayed in London for no other reason than that Laura was entertaining her mother at Piers Court. I spent most of the day with Maimie Pavlovsky[1] ending rather fuddled with wine. In the morning I went to Harley Street to consult a pile specialist who advises an operation.

Piers Court, Wednesday 6 November 1946

Returned very wearily to Stinchcombe.

Thursday 7 November 1946

A day spent in answering letters, correcting proofs, unpacking books and eating practically nothing. The BBC, as I expected, have refused my terms. Christine Longford sends encouraging reports of Gormanston.

Friday 8 November 1946

The interest of the postbag, the huge irritation and boredom of the daily newspapers.

Saturday 9 November 1946

Throughout the day constantly recurring thoughts of Ireland. Not so much of what I should find there as what I should shake off here. The luxury of being a foreigner, of completely retiring from further experience and settling in an upstairs library to garner the forty-three-year harvest. The certainty that England as a great power is done for, that the loss of possessions, the claim of the English proletariat to be a privileged race, sloth and envy, must produce increasing poverty; that this time the cutting down will start at the top until only a proletariate and a bureaucracy survive. As a bachelor I could

---

[1] Lady Mary Lygon, through her marriage in 1939 to HH Prince Vsevolode Joannovitch of Russia, was formally titled Her Serene Highness Princess Romanovsky Pavlovsky.

contemplate all this in a detached manner, but it is no country in which to bring up children. But how long will Liberty, Diversity, Privacy survive anywhere?

Sunday 10 November 1946

Reading these thoughts above, so generalized and so tritely expressed, I ask what I really mean, personally, by them. Why do I contemplate so grave a step as abjuring the realm and changing the whole prospects of my children? What is there to worry me here in Stinchcombe? I have a beautiful house furnished exactly to my taste; servants enough, wine in the cellar. The villagers are friendly and respectful; neighbours leave me alone. I send my children to the schools I please. Apart from taxation and rationing, government interference is negligible. None of the threatened developments of building and road-making have yet taken place. Why am I not at ease? Why is it I smell all the time wherever I turn the reek of the Displaced Persons' Camp?

Monday 11 November–Tuesday 12 November 1946

Working an hour or two a day on a long short story *Scott-King's Modern Europe* which has gathered momentum and is now bowling effortlessly along to its end. My mind aflame with Ireland. Laura thinks in terms of Auberon's succession. I of a possible fifteen years' ease and industry.

Thursday 14 November 1946

This morning a long cable from Peters[1] in America offering these terms: a month's trip to Hollywood for Laura and myself, all expenses paid, for me to discuss the film treatment of *Brideshead*. If we cannot agree, they forfeit their money. If we agree, they pay $140,000 less what they have already spent. These terms are acceptable and funny because I was under contract to this very firm to let them have the rights of any novel I wrote for $20,000 and they paid me £3,000 free of tax to be released from this contract.

Friday 15 November 1946

Patrick Kinross came to stay, large and plump and dishevelled from Ireland. I gave him plenty to drink and smoke and Laura found oysters and a chicken for his dinner. He showed some slight guilt at his ease in accommodating himself to the bureaucratic regime, but spoke without any irony of so-and-so having had 'a good war' by which he meant a series of safe and comfortable para-military appointments. Laura finds him painfully common and was delighted when he drawled, *à propos* of his coming interview with a Foreign Office Selection Board, 'I suppose I must pretend not to be a gentleman.' He had visited Gormanston at my request but had arrived in the dark and seen it by candlelight so that his impressions were chiefly of vastness and emptiness.

[1] A. D. Peters, Waugh's agent. The offer was from MGM.

Sunday 17 November 1946

Bron's birthday. Laura and I drove to take him out to luncheon at Mells. Katharine and Helen were welcoming, but liable to distractions. It is difficult to know how welcome one is there nowadays. The boy was well grown and well mannered. I think on the whole it was a dull expedition for him, sitting silent by the fire while we discussed the horrors of Trim's position in Palestine.

Patrick left on Saturday afternoon. What an enormous, uncovenanted blessing to have kept Henry James for middle age and to turn, as the door shuts behind the departing guest, to a first reading of *Portrait of a Lady*.

Tuesday 19 November 1946

This morning I received a questionnaire from an American schoolgirl and wrote as follows to her headmistress:

Dear Madam, I regret that I am obliged to report a misdemeanour on the part of one of your pupils, Mary Lester, who has addressed the enclosed letter to me.

I am sure that you will agree that to write in this tone to an unknown foreigner, asking him details of his personal appearance and of his relations with his wife, is an offence against modesty. Moreover by signing her name as 'Camelot Interviewer' she does a grave disservice to your institution by suggesting that she has some approved status in making this application. I know that the encouragement of this kind of activity is entirely contrary to the great Ursuline tradition.

I know, too, that the greatest triumphs of your Order have been among savages. If, as seems possible, Mary Lester is a Red Indian, is it not sad that she should have found contact with the lowest instead of the highest manifestations of white civilization? I trust you will mete out condign punishment to this unhappy child but not take the grave step of expelling her to her Reserve.

Thursday 21 November 1946

I tried my customary evasive tactics designed for invitations to lecture, and told Bristol Grammar School that I would lecture to them in my own home. The headmaster, an old queer called Garrett, called my bluff and they came in a charabanc about twenty strong. I had intended showing them my collection of books, urbanely. Considering afterwards what I had said, it seemed to me that I simply gave vent to peevish and otiose complaints about modern times. To escape testiness – that is why I am going to Ireland.

Saturday 23 November 1946

The French called the occupying German army 'the grey lice'. That is precisely how I regard the occupying army of English socialist government.

Sunday 24 November 1946

A stormy day. Frank and Elizabeth Pakenham came to luncheon – very late. Frank was more at his ease and off his guard than I have seen him in London lately. They have no eyes for the house or anything in it. Frank on hearing we were going to Dublin: 'Who can I give you introductions to? You must call on De Valera.'

Wednesday 27 November 1946

This morning I received the offer of £50 for fifty words from America. It is the price I had for writing the life of Rossetti twenty years ago.

Saturday 30 November 1946

All in order for our visit to Dublin – passports, tickets, bank credit. This morning comes the disquieting information that there is an aerodrome within a few miles of the castle. Muriel Silk came to luncheon bringing the *Baptism of a Jewess* which she has cleaned very nicely.

Monday 2 November 1946

A hurricane blowing and bitter cold. Midwinter is no season to prospect for a house. We travelled in smoky, dirty, ill-lit carriages to Liverpool and boarded the boat where there was a tang of civility in the air and ample provisions in the dining-room. The usual St George's Channel personnel – colonels' wives covered with regimental badges, priests, drunken commercial travellers. This time a number of Jews, presumably tax-evaders.

Dublin, Tuesday 3 December 1946

On deck early to see the ship berth, breakfast by lamplight, a dawn drive to Shelbourne Hotel, baths and second breakfast. Then with an hour or two spare before the house agent came to fetch us, into the square in the soft Dublin luminance. There was a letter from Billy Wicklow commending a solicitor to us, Terence de Vere White[1]; a letter from a rival house agent who approached us on T. de V. White's suggestion; a letter of welcome from a friend of Patrick Kinross, Moragh Bernard; a call from Christine Longford. At 11 we started for Gormanston by car with a man from the house agents and an architect named Hendy. All the way – twenty miles of flat, swampy country – they told us funny stories about Dublin 'characters'. At last the castle, which was reached by a back-drive through stables and outhouses. It was a fine, solid, grim, square, half-finished block with tower and turrets. Mrs O'Connor, Lord Gormanston's widow, opened the door, young, small, attractive, common. She had lit peat fires for our benefit in the main rooms, but normally inhabited a small dressing-room upstairs. The ground-floor rooms were large and had

[1] Terence de Vere White (b. 1912), a novelist as well as a solicitor. He later became literary editor of the *Irish Times*.

traces of fine Regency decoration. Pictures by Lady Butler everywhere. There were countless bedrooms, many uninhabitable, squalid plumbing, vast attics. On the whole I liked the house; the grounds were dreary with no features except some fine box alleys. The chapel unlicensed and Mrs O'Connor evasive about the chances of getting it put to use again. She gave us a substantial luncheon. My hirelings drank brandy and seemed disposed to tell funny stories till dusk, but I routed them out and we paraded the wet fields. Then drove back at nightfall. The house agent came into the hotel with us and began to tell funny stories till I turned him out. That night, very weary, we dined at the hotel, drank a bottle of champagne, went for one act of an unintelligible peasant comedy at the Abbey Theatre, and then to bed.

Wednesday 4 December 1946

Visits to the bank, to solicitors, to a shop where I bought Laura an astrakhan coat which from then absorbed all her interest. The shopwoman warned her that it was illegal to export it. Designs to deceive the customs and to dispose of her exciting fur coat agitated her until we were in the train at Liverpool. We lunched heavily with Edward and Christine Longford[1] at a restaurant called Unicorn where I was forced to drink more port than I wanted. In a sort of stupor I interviewed Hendy and White. He produced a report valuing Gormanston at £13,000 and £5,000 necessary repairs. I gave White written instructions to bid at the auction. Then Laura and I went to dine at Jammet's where we found Billy Wicklow and a BBC pansy at the next table, joined them, drank great quantities of champagne and went to bed quite drunk.

Thursday 5 December 1946

A new character entered our lives named Mr Roper who wrote to us from a house agent's but proved to be a crypto-solicitor. He wished us to buy a castle in Waterford called Strancally. We lunched at Jammet's with Moragh Bernard, a most obliging fellow, White, and the Killanins,[2] then went to see the owners of Strancally, a wistful, defeated old couple. The house looked lovely from their photographs, taken I suspect in Victorian times, but it is alarmingly remote. The belief in England that there is an abundance of skilled labour in Ireland is an illusion. Laura and I walked the beautiful streets till dark, then to the packet where she passed the customs without question, and so home. On boarding the ship I bought a local evening paper and read that Butlin had acquired a stretch of property at Gormanston and was setting up a holiday camp there. This announcement made us change all our intentions. It came just in time for us, disastrously for poor Mrs O'Connor.

[1] The Earl and Countess of Longford (the Hon. Frank Pakenham's brother and sister-in-law).
[2] The 3rd Baron and his wife.

London, Friday 6 December 1946

In London by luncheon-time. Dined at White's with Bob Boothby after visiting house agent's to put Piers Court on the market. Laura went to retreat.

Belton House, Grantham, Saturday 7 December 1946

To Belton to stay with Perry Brownlow. The house[1] is in reduced scale but still very considerable luxury. Lady Beatty told us of her son who shows every sign of sanctity. Perry has filled his house and littered his exquisite furniture with revolting electrical devices – wireless, intercommunication sets, and apparatus for recording the voice.

Sunday 8 December 1946

Walked to Mass. Sachie and Georgia Sitwell arrived. An afternoon and evening of uninterrupted gossip.

London, Monday 9 December 1946

Returned to London. A day at White's.

Tuesday 10 December 1946

Laura returned from retreat. I went to confession, lunched at the Holland Park to see T. S. Eliot's new play *Family Reunion*. It approached parody at moments but the audience was devout. The programme said it was the story of Agamemnon. Except for a Greek sense of doom and a Greek technique in the use of choruses there was no connection apparent to me. The main fault was that it aroused too much intellectual curiosity about the details of the plot. I think a story must be well known before it can be treated in that way.

Piers Court, Wednesday 11 December 1946

Returned home gladly, travel-worn. I am sluggish now about moving and I have postponed a second visit to Ireland until I return from Hollywood. I saw Ian Collins who wishes to publish my cheap editions and proposes a system of payment which will escape taxation. I think Winston is like Agamemnon in his hubris and in destroying the altars of Troy.

Thursday 12 December 1946

A day of letter-writing, mostly to Dublin. In consequence a bad night.

Saturday 14 December 1946

John Betjeman gave a 'talk' about me on the wireless. We borrowed Deakin's apparatus and listened. Too much of it was quotation. He read a long passage from *Vile Bodies* and succeeded in breathing life in those dry old bones.

[1] Built in 1685–9; designed, according to some authorities, by Sir Christopher Wren.

Monday 16 December 1946

I seem to be in the way of a good deal of critical attention. This morning *Horizon* arrived with a long article by Rose Macaulay advising me to return to my kennel and not venture into the world of living human beings.

Thursday 19 December 1946

I went to London by the early train. I have now reached an age when any disturbance of routine is disagreeable, and I sat misanthropic, smoking cigars, while the train lost more and more time until it halted for three-quarters of an hour in a snowstorm just outside the Paddington station. I had time to try on a suit which has taken six months to make and then went to luncheon at the Beefsteak where I talked to Harold Nicolson and Clive Bell and drank enough wine to fuddle me slightly. In that condition I went to Duckworth and signed sixteen copies of *When the Going was Good* for Christmas presents. Also to the travel agency who are sending me to Hollywood. At 5 o'clock there was the Beefsteak committee meeting. My candidates Maurice Bowra, Ran Antrim and Randolph Churchill all got in – the latter after long discussion in which Hugh Sherwood made a spirited defence and overbore two men who had come with the firm purpose of blackballing him. During the meeting I drank a lot of whisky and went rather drunk to a cocktail party given by John Murray[1] where I got very drunk. Rose Macaulay attempted a serious conversation in which I did not shine. I spent most of the time with Hermione Ranfurly jeering at people who were introduced to me and ended by bearing off a diminutive man called Gibbings to White's for champagne cocktails. From then my memory is vague but I went to bed early I think at the Hyde Park Hotel.

Piers Court, Friday 20 December 1946

Peter Oldfield of Knight, Frank & Rutley drove me home. The roads were covered in ice and we took nearly five hours on the journey. I showed him the house and rejected the suggestion that I should advertise it at my own expense in *Country Life*. He thinks I shall be lucky if I get £15,000 for it. Laura arrived for dinner with three chickens, a nursery maid and a turkey.

Monday 23 December 1946

The presence of my children affects me with deep weariness and depression. I do not see them until luncheon, as I have my breakfast alone in the library, and they are in fact well trained to avoid my part of the house; but I am aware of them from the moment I wake. Luncheon is very painful. Teresa has a mincing habit of speech and a pert, humourless style of wit; Bron is clumsy and dishevelled, sly, without intellectual, aesthetic or spiritual interest; Margaret is pretty and below the age of reason. In the nursery whooping cough rages I

---

[1] The publisher.

believe. At tea I meet the three elder children again and they usurp the drawing-room until it is time to dress for dinner. I used to take some pleasure in inventing legends for them about Basil Bennett, Dr Bedlam and the Sebag-Montefiores. But now they think it ingenious to squeal: 'It isn't true.' I taught them the game of draughts for which they show no aptitude.

The frost has broken and everything is now dripping and slushy and gusty. The prospect of Christmas appalls me and I look forward to the operating theatre as a happy release.

Christmas Day 1946

Drove to midnight Mass at Nympsfield very slowly on frozen roads with Teresa, Bron and Vera[1] in the back of the car. The little church was painfully crowded. We sat behind a dozen insubordinate little boys who coughed and stole and wrangled. The chairs were packed so close that it was impossible to kneel straight. Drove home very slowly and did not get to bed until 2.30 am. Laura has imprudently sent Saunders and Kitty for holidays so that she and Deakin are grossly overworked. I made a fair show of geniality throughout the day though the spectacle of a litter of shoddy toys and half-eaten sweets sickened me. Everything is so badly made nowadays that none of the children's presents seemed to work. Luncheon was cold and poorly cooked. A ghastly day. I spent what leisure I had in comparing the *Diary of a Nobody* with its serialized version in *Punch*.

Laura gave me a pot of caviare which I ate a week ago. My mother gave me a copy of the *Diary of a Nobody*. But for these I have had no presents though I have given many. I should like to think that from 29th October[2] onwards friends in all parts of the country were thinking 'What can we give him for Christmas?' and hunting shops and embroidering and continuing to find me unique and delectable presents. But it is not so.

En route to New York, Saturday 25 January 1947

Embarked in the *America* full of cocaine, opium and brandy, feeble and low-spirited. One of the reasons for my putting myself under the surgeon's knife was to wish to be absolutely well and free from ointments for Laura's American treat. All the reasons for the operation appeared ineffective immediately afterwards. The pain was excruciating and the humiliations constant. The hospital was reasonably comfortable and the nurses charming – the grace of God apparent everywhere. But I had ample time to reflect that I had undergone an operation, which others only endure after years of growing agony, when I had in fact suffered nothing worse than occasional discomfort. I

[1] Nurserymaid, later promoted to nanny.
[2] The day after Waugh's birthday.

took no advice, either from a physician or fellow sufferers, just went to the surgeon and ordered the operation as I would have ordered new shirts. In fact I had behaved wholly irrationally and was paying for it. My last visit to the surgeon on the day before sailing was more painful than anything which had gone before. I was in hospital three weeks. Laura came up to see me, looking worn out with the company of the children. Later she fell into a neurotic state over a feud between Deakin and the rest of the servants. She needed a holiday and has already profited by it enormously. Christopher Sykes, Elizabeth Pakenham and Douglas Woodruff came to see me – Maimie often, Alec once. I went home for two days, travelling in an ambulance, lay quiet, then to London where I felt ill all the time and in pain most of the time. No treat for Laura there. At last we got on board.

A warm seaworthy ship full of Americans, mostly Jews. Laura and I secured a retired table far from the band and were beginning to tame our steward when we were summoned to the captain's table to sit with an admiral and ambassador, a colonel, Lady Jersey and a woman with a face like a pie. The only English on board – Patsy Ward, Isobel Mills, a Crawley – are travelling second class, a sign of the times. There was also a curious proletarian colony of GI brides – trousers, babies, cockney accents – travelling first class, another sign of the times. A smooth crossing. We landed at New York on 31st January in warm sunshine.

New York, Friday 31 January 1947

A feeble young man sent to meet us by MGM failed to find us until we had got through the customs and the battle was over. I avoided the journalists by the simple expedient of ignoring a message sent by a page boy – 'Mr Waugh to report at once to the Press on the sundeck.' I was feeling ill that day. We drove to the Waldorf Astoria, an enormous hotel where we had a minute suite so ill-planned that half the area was taken by corridors. We never went to any of the restaurants. Ate in our rooms. The food was tasteless and all French wine except champagne ruined by bad cellarage.

On the first evening we went to the theatre (arranged by MGM) and sat through two acts of a three-act comedy shot through and through with socialist propaganda. I went to the drugstore and asked for Dial. I learned later that New York State has lately become alarmed at the suicides and has enforced a strict ban on the sale of barbiturates. The chemist said I must have a doctor's prescription.

'I am a foreigner here. I have no American prescription.'

'We have a doctor on the 17th floor.'

'I have to go out. I can't go and see him.'

'I'll fix it for you.'

He telephoned the doctor, 'Dere's a guy here says he can't sleep. OK to give him Dial, doc?' Was given a box of twenty tablets 'to the prescription of Dr Hart'. '$3 medical attention.' That was the best piece of service I have yet met in USA.

Saturday 1 February 1947

I had a stenographer in my room and dictated a preface for Christie Lawrence's book of adventure.[1] She produced a typescript so full of mistakes that it was apparent she cannot have ever expected it to make sense. In the evening we dined with the Brandts. An absolutely delicious dinner in a pretty little house. Mrs Brandt is a woman of no intellectual interests. Brandt three-quarters civilized with a taste for Trollope. Mrs Brandt is a secretary raised to its highest power. She did not disguise that her services to us were personally distasteful but she performed every service brilliantly. She introduced Laura to a good dress shop where Laura spent $2,000 in a very few minutes. (Matson[2] had $3,500 in hand for us.)

Sunday 2 February 1947

Mass at St Patrick's – densely crowded. Lunched with Mrs Kermit Roosevelt in a pretty little house in Sutton Place. A party of good-mannered people. Later Pempy Ward came to dine with us – her looks enormously improved, fat from good living and the great success she is having in *Lady Windermere's Fan*. She had also become rather more acid – full of malice about Cecil Beaton, Eric Dudley.[3] In fact altogether improved.

Monday 3 February 1947

Bought champagne, brandy and sherry for use in the West. A strange modification of American liberty that the wine merchant could not send it to Hollywood for us. He had to pack it in disguised cases for us to take in our compartment. I then went to see Mr Mays the editor of *Good Housekeeping* which is the most prosperous paper in the continent. He was an emaciated Jew lately promoted within the Hearst organization from editing a weekly paper devoted to commercial chemistry. I explained that we got electric shocks at the Waldorf when we touched metal.

'It is the carpets.'

I said we had carpets in England too.

'Not so thick.' He then tried to demonstrate the galvanic properties of his carpet, shuffled across the room and tried to make a card adhere to the wall, failed. He showed me a very commonplace illustration that he is using for a story of mine in his next issue. I called it *Tactical Exercise*; he has changed the name to *The Wish*.

'Why?'

[1] Lawrence had served with Waugh in Crete.

[2] New York literary agent.

[3] The 3rd Earl of Dudley.

'People would think it dealt with the war.'

I marvelled at a people who had not the patience to read a sentence or two of a story in a magazine.

He said: 'This illustration is by the very best artist in the country.'

'What did you pay for it?'

'$2,500.'

'But you could have got a real picture for that.'

Laughing that off he said, 'What's more, this illustration is about the story. Often they have nothing to do with it.'

'Why?'

'Artists as important as —— are so busy they don't get around to reading what they illustrate. Maybe they have a secretary makes them a synopsis. Then maybe they get mixed. We can't control artists as important as ——.'[1]

Then he said, 'Would it be a convenience to you if I gave you $4,000 for expenses? I know you have tax troubles same as us.'

'Yes, but what for?'

'In advance for a story.'

'But I may not write another story suitable for you.'

'Well it won't break us if you don't. We're easy people to do business with. Maybe in two-five years you'll write us something.'

I said I would take half in the form of a new motor car to be delivered in Ireland.

'That'll be all right. I'll fix it with one of our advertisers.' He did not want to use *Scott-King's Modern Europe*. 'It's a little satirical for our people. But I'd like to show it to Miss Cousins and see what she says.'

'We love your Royal Family. The greatest moment of my visit to London was to see Queen Mary in a theatre . . . London is so clean and hopeful.'

Then Laura and I went to luncheon with Harry Bull, editor of *Town and Country*. H. Bull knew all about everyone – Kitty Miller's sister's will, Sergeant Preston's English reputation. He clearly bore a grudge against *Good Housekeeping* for buying me. He is not allowed to increase his circulation and prices. The reasons he gave seemed strange – that Hearst wanted the paper to be exclusive. He is always having his discoveries bought up by *Good Housekeeping*. I did not tell him the details of my interview with Mr Mays. I asked what the *New Yorker* paid for their excellent covers – $250. He gave us to think that Mrs Brandt lived and entertained entirely on MGM expenses. Then he took me to a bookshop and bought me half a dozen new novels on his Hearst expenses. A girl in the bookshop: 'You must read this. It is about incest.' 'Brother and sister or mother and son?' Girl regretfully: 'No, only father and son.'

The same young man who had met us saw us to the train. Mrs B. thought it

[1] Dashes in MS.

odd I insisted on this, knowing I had travelled far in youth.

The *20th Century* is the pride of the US railways – rightly. A red carpet is laid down the platform. The compartments are full of gadgets but it is all thin aluminium and one hears coarse native laughter through the walls. The dinner absolutely excellent.

New York–Los Angeles, Tuesday 4 February 1947

We reached Chicago at 10 and saw only snowbound marshalling yards. Our coach was hitched onto another inferior train, *The Chief*, and left at 2. The *maître d'hotel* is small, shrivelled, swarthy; perhaps Italian or Greek. I said to him, 'I am a foreigner.' He answered surprisingly, 'We are all foreigners in this country.'

A swarthy, flashy man with a bright wife, whose names later appeared to be Cullman, introduced himself to us on the train. These and Mrs Marshall, who used to live at the Castello at Portofino, made themselves our companions on the journey. After Chicago we left the snow and next day were running through mountain country.

Los Angeles, Thursday 6 February 1947

Arrived at Pasadena at 9 am and were met by a car from MGM. We drove for a long time down autobahns and boulevards full of vacant lots and filling stations and nondescript buildings and palm trees with a warm hazy light. It was more like Egypt – the suburbs of Cairo or Alexandria – than anything in Europe. We arrived at the Bel Air Hotel – very Egyptian with a hint of Addis Ababa in the smell of the blue gums. The flabby manager had let my suite to a man suffering from rheumatic fever – a prevalent local affliction – and we have a pretty but inadequate bedroom and bath. We unpacked, sent great quantities of clothes to the laundry, bathed and lunched. A well-planned little restaurant, good cooking. We drank a good local red wine, Masson's Pinot Noir. We were the only people in the room drinking. Two tables of women with absurd hats. Rested. At 6 sharp we were called on by the two producers Gordon and McGuinness, who were preceded with fine bunches of flowers – with their shy wives. We sat in our bedroom and drank. Conversation difficult. Bed early, after dining without appetite in the restaurant, and slept badly; woke in pain.

Friday 7 February 1947

Exhausted and in pain. A cold, misty day. Gordon called for me at 11 am. We went to Culver City to MGM building and sat in his office. The publicity men came to interview me and proved amenable to my suggestion that nothing should go out until we had decided to make the film. I keep it in Gordon's mind that I have agreed to nothing. Gordon, whom I call 'Leon', and I talked about *Brideshead*, then went to luncheon in a huge canteen where there was a high table for producers and stars but the same trashy food for all but no wine. We then went to what was called a 'conference' which consisted of McGuinness coming for ten minutes and talking balls. Then the 'writer' was called in who proved to be Keith Winter whom I last knew at Villefranche. He wore local costume – a kind of loose woollen blazer, matelot's vest, buckled shoes. He has been in Hollywood for years and sees *Brideshead* purely as a love story. None of them see the theological implication, though McGuinness says that 'a religious approach puts an American audience on your side'. There was something a little luxurious in talking in great detail about every implication of a book which the others are paid to know thoroughly. Laura meanwhile was lunching at Romanov's with Mrs Gordon and going to a dress show. Returned weary and hungry with no appointment until Monday. At the studio they deplored that here too the profit motive had ceased to operate. Taxation is so high that stars cannot be induced to act except from motives of vanity. This means that they must appear constantly in a heroic light.

Thursday 13 February 1947

Laura and I are still living in an attic bedroom in spite of all the efforts of MGM to get us properly housed. The restaurant is excellent and since we have given this as our address for all letters it would be inconvenient to move. I wage a war of nerves against the flabby young man who acts as manager, but without success. We spent a quiet weekend, visited the cinema and some shops, had our photographs taken at the studios. Laura has done some extensive and extravagant shopping and looks smart and young and happy. Keith Winter shows great sloth in getting to work. He came to luncheon with us in native costume and was refused admittance to the restaurant until I provided him with a shirt.

On Tuesday I was trapped by nuns to luncheon at a fine convent school in the hills; found myself exposed to autograph collectors, amateur photographers, and finally to a 'brains trust' before the entire school. That evening I went to dine at Loyola University. I was asked for 5 so ordered my car for 9 and plainly outstayed my welcome by an hour; but the Jesuits were more human than anyone I have yet met in California. Gordon gave a dinner party for us and asked medical men and women to meet us, presumably as representing the intellectual élite of MGM. People keep very early hours here. The city is quarter-built, empty building lots everywhere and vast distances. Since the war they have succeeded in spoiling even the climate by inducing an artificial and noxious fog. The women's shops are full of good clothes. It is impossible for a man to find anything wearable – no collars or shirts. I could not even get hair lotion. A few nondescript invitations reach us but there is laudably little effort at lionization. The women lunch together in large loud parties with elaborate hats. Laura gets asked out to luncheon alone. The men lunch in wineless canteens. Jovial banter prevails between the hotel servants and the guests, but our insular aloofness is respected. We have trained the waiters in the dining-room not to give us iced water and our chauffeur not to ask us questions. There is here the exact opposite of the English custom by which the upper classes are expected to ask personal questions of the lower.

On Thursday afternoon Gordon proudly showed us his last film – *The Green Years*; it was awful. Mercifully the cinema was provided with push buttons to stop the film, so when Gordon had gone I stopped it. We went a long drive to dine with a friend of Bill Stirling – a surly, handsome Irishman, whether actor, writer, or businessman we never discovered, married to a lady who proved to be Helen Wills the tennis champion. We met the actor who plays Dr Watson.

Friday 14 February 1947

We were told we had won our battle of nerves with the hotel and were to move into a suite. We went to tea with Anna May Wong in a remote, odd house full of Chinese, Koreans, an Alsatian dog, the old dancer Dolin and his ferocious mother and dim partner. Then we went to dine with an agreeable American couple called Allen. She proved to be a well-known novelist called Helen Howe. Her father (like my father) was there, and a disgruntled Jewish producer. A civilized evening. The host collected American Gilbert-and-Sullivana.

Saturday 15 February 1947

The manager informed me that the invalid in my suite was worse. Our beds had not been made at 2. I became disgruntled and went to pay my respects to the Archbishop. A very old boy. He had asked two ladies and three clerics to meet me. We had a glass of wine and awkward polite conversation. We spent the morning in ordering food parcels for Europe.

Simon and Golly Elwes have arrived in a house directly opposite the hotel but we have not yet seen them.

Piers Court, Easter Monday 7 April 1947

I returned to Stinchcombe without exultation. Before the war I used to come home after an absence eager to see what plants had grown and what progress the workmen had made in the house. Now the expectation is that something has decayed further. There are great patches of damp on the ceilings, fallen walls outside, but the general impression was one of bright colour, leather bindings, gilt frames, polished mahogany, oil paintings full of incident – wholly attractive after the grey of Downside and the shapeless, dun, functional plastic, linoleum and steel nullity of the *Queen Elizabeth*. America seems very remote and the diary I had meant to keep in detail, to be a store of literary material, is a blank.

Our lives in Hollywood changed greatly with the arrival of the Elweses.

Their hostess, Andrea Cowdin, appointed herself our hostess for all practical purposes. We lunched or dined there every day, went with her to parties and met all the most agreeable people at her house. MGM slipped more and more from the scene. Gordon, I think, lost heart as soon as I explained to him what *Brideshead* was about, until in the end when the censor made some difficulties he accepted them as an easy excuse for abandoning the whole project. I was equally relieved. Winter remained in a kind of trance throughout. MGM were consistently munificent and we left as we had come, in effortless luxury.

Our chief friends in Hollywood besides Andrea were Iris Tree and her boy Moffat, Mrs Hugo Rumbold, Merle Oberon, the Reggie Allens (Helen Howe), and Sir Charles Mendl.[1] After a month we moved to the Beverly Hills hotel to a large suite of rooms where we spent a further fortnight. We saw a highly secret first performance of Charlie Chaplin's brilliant new film *Monsieur Verdoux* and went to a supper party at his house later which comprised mostly central European Jews. We also went over Walt Disney's studios. I was thus able to pay my homage to the two artists of the place. We antagonized most of the English colony who were guiltily sensitive of criticism. Randolph came for a rather disgusting two days – excellent on the platform but brutishly drunk in private. I found a deep mine of literary gold in the cemetery of Forest Lawn and the work of the morticians and intend to get to work immediately on a novelette[2] staged there.

Laura grew smarter and younger and more popular daily and was serenely happy. I was well content and, as soon as the danger of the film was disposed of, almost serene also. Our passage home was in doubt until the last minute. At five minutes before the time of sailing Laura and I were asleep in the Waldorf Hotel with engagements made for the evening and for next day. Then the telephone summoned us to the docks and the gangway went up as we struggled on board the *Elizabeth*. The ship rolled heavily in an apparently calm sea and no one slept much. There was good company on board and fair comfort.

I had five days in London overshadowed at first by the loss of an essential piece of Laura's luggage and throughout by the irksome consequences of my operation, not yet fully relieved. On Wednesday of Holy Week I drove with Simon to Downside and went into retreat, consulting a monk, Tusky Russell, about the welfare of my soul. Then, yesterday, home, joined late in the afternoon by Laura, Bron and Teresa from Pixton.

Saturday 19 April 1947

In the past ten days I have painfully written a humdrum essay on Hollywood for the *Daily Telegraph* – £200 – and begun an essay for *Life* about death. I

---

[1] Press attaché at the British Embassy in Paris, 1926–40. Married celebrated American interior decorator, Elsie de Wolfe.

[2] *The Loved One* (1948).

have also made arrangements for my children's futures, removing Bron's name from Ampleforth and putting him down for Downside, and taking Teresa from St Leonard's and transferring her in the autumn to Ascot. The gentle effects of Easter have worn thin and my temper has been short, my prayers tepid.

Lords Pakenham and Inman have joined the cabinet. Sharper famine is foreseen the next winter. I have no human contacts here. Laura is busy and happy with agriculture and has lost all her Californian chic. My children afford me no pleasure. At Tusky Russell's instance I am reading Thérèse of Lisieux's autobiography, with none of the repulsion I anticipated and none of the revelation. Mystics spend half their lives in doubt and despondency, half in exultation. How can one claim that one half is valid evidence and not the other? But to aim at anything less than sanctity is not to aim at all. Oh for persecution.

Tuesday 22 April 1947

To London to have my hair cut and arrange my passage to Ireland. Successful in these aims, but the rest of the fifty hours passed in a vinous mist. White's is a curious spectacle now, lit during the day by two candles. It seemed entirely populated by drunks. Ed Stanley has reported Lionel Tennyson[1] for being drunk on the steps and taking the porter to conduct him home. Randolph is home dead broke, selling all his possessions. After, as I was later informed, playing billiards with an umbrella, I went to his house where were Robin Campbell, Momo Marriott and some others.

On Wednesday I felt ill, slept in the afternoon, and went to the Saintsbury Club with Vsevolode where there was too little wine and too much oratory. Then to John Sutro's birthday party.

On Thursday I felt ill and decided to return home. Luncheon of caviare and champagne with Peter Fitzwilliam who tells me I have chosen the worst possible week to visit Dublin as there is an agricultural show in progress. A magnum of champagne in the afternoon with Randolph who tried to sell me £100 gold cigar case. Instead I bought £20 edition of Pope.

Monday 28 April 1947

Today I go to London, tomorrow to Dublin, in low spirits to look for a house. I am uncertain whether duty or interest makes this move desirable. Yesterday two people came to see this house; one couple liked it but thought it expensive, the other was rich but wanted a suitable soil for rhododendrons. I am thinking of giving up smoking: (*a*) mortification, not only the pleasure of smoking but the swagger of it; cigar in hand I become more boastful and ribald; (*b*) the saving of money which I could give away without affecting the position of Laura or my family; (*c*) health, particularly in the way that smoking

[1] 3rd Baron Tennyson; grandson of the Poet Laureate; England cricket captain v. Australia, 1921.

makes for sloth. I put off doing things until I've finished my cigar. I have often determined to give up getting drunk but never for long with success.

Dublin, Tuesday 29 April 1947

I flew to Dublin and arrived to find it cold and crowded. Peter Fitzwilliam had secured me a room at the Dolphin, an inn frequented by jockeys, which reeked of whisky and wine. I dined with Terence de Vere White at the Kildare Street Club. We returned to the Dolphin, where a drunken Irish authoress engaged us in talk.

Wednesday 30 April 1947

By taxi to Mullinger where I saw two houses, Levington, charming but scarcely larger than Piers Court, and Mears Court, large but charmless. Owing to Punchestown races I was able to go round in the owners' absence. I dined with Bryan Moyne and his wife at Knockmaroon. He is very barmy, consumed with parsimony but rather gay in attire and attending a hair specialist to prevent baldness. He collected twigs in the garden, took charge of a goat.

Thursday 1 May 1947

Trains have practically ceased to run in Ireland. I travelled by taxi to Tipperary seeing a seedy Victorian house called Viewmont and a vast castle at Kilkenny, on the way. Lunched at Kilkenny and arrived in early afternoon at Kiltinan. An avenue of fine oak, medieval, Tudor and Georgian castle of great beauty on the edge of a cliff with river and springs below; the owners a Mrs Grub and Mrs de Sales de la Terrière, mother and daughter living in dire poverty and squalor; twenty-seven dogs in the house. Mrs de Sales de la Terrière had lost all interest in life, she and her mother told me. The whole place was romantic and inconvenient.

Slept that night at the inn at Cahir where I met two English refugees whom I did not feel kinship for.

Friday 2 May 1947

Drove to an ugly Italianate villa on the shore of Loch Derg, and then to Dublin where the cold was intense. I had nothing to read and my attempts to get in touch with Billy Wicklow failed. Dined alone and sadly and went early to bed.

Saturday 3 May 1947

Drove to Lerm's [?] old house, horribly redecorated, at Templeogue. Drank with Billy and T. de V. White, lunched with T. de V. White. Peter Fitzwilliam was expected all day and at length arrived after the races and bore me off to Coollattin where we found various invalids and a no good brother-in-law.

Sunday 4 May 1947

Drove five miles to Mass and spent the day indoors. Various masters of hounds arrived for a puppy show.

Monday 5 May 1947

Went to luncheon with Lady Rathdonnell at Lisnavagh, a large prosaic early Victorian house which took my fancy.

Tuesday 6 May 1947

Saw a perfectly beastly house near Shelton.

Wednesday 7 May 1947

Left Coollattin. Lunched with Perry, More O'Ferralls, Lady Beatty at Jammet's; caught the aeroplane to London.

London, Thursday 8 May 1947

Douglas Woodruff's 50th birthday dinner. I expected a grim evening but it was quite agreeable.

Friday 9 May 1947

Maimie and Coote lunched with me, Basil insulted me, I insulted Malcolm Sargent.[1]

Saturday 10 May 1947

To Downside.

Mells, Sunday 11 May 1947

Lunched with Chris and Maidie, who is overshadowed by Conrad Russell's death; tea at the Manor. Talked to the boys about Hollywood in the evening.

Piers Court, Monday 12 May 1947

Laura fetched me for luncheon at Ammerdown. We went to Bristol to pick up Bron who has been having his squint excised. They now say he has diphtheria.

Thursday 15 May 1947

Laura's brother Auberon came for the night at his own invitation. He wished to discuss his career in journalism. We made him tell us something of his courtship of Elizabeth Cavendish. I bought my son Auberon a white mouse. Ascension Day never passes without my thinking of the day now thirty years ago at Lancing which was the most miserable of my life.[2]

---

[1] The conductor.

[2] A whole holiday for the school, when all the other boys dispersed, leaving Waugh alone. See *A Little Learning*, p. 110.

Friday 16 May 1947

Christopher Sykes came after a series of contradictory messages caused, we learned, by his son's escape from Roper's school.

Saturday 17 May 1947

Coote Lygon and Camilla Sykes to luncheon. A hot sunny day. A painful hour in the open in deck chairs. Two ascents of Stinchcombe Hill. Camilla intent on sending her delinquent son to Eton. Christopher feebly inclining to Downside.

Sunday 18 May 1947

Mrs Brandt and John Foster,[1] bursting with success, came to luncheon. We went to tea with Max Beerbohm who is in a little house near Stroud. A delicious little old dandy, very quick in mind still. He at once said, on learning of Mark Sykes's escapade, 'Perhaps it is like the case of Mr Bultitude and I am now entertaining Mark.' A touch of Ronnie Knox and of Conrad and of Harold Acton. 'The tongue has, correct me if I am wrong, seven follicles in adult life.' Much of what he said would have been commonplace but for his exquisite delivery.

My little boy is home. Very good. Hatty is the horror of the nursery.

Chinese servant's description of Good Friday: 'Belong long time Sassoon men chop Englishman's joss. Englishman still plenty sorry.'

Tuesday 20 May 1947

Finished Forest Lawn essay.[2] Not much good.

Wednesday 21 May 1947

Began *The Loved One*. Very slow.

Thursday 22 May 1947

Communion. Not well today.

Friday 23 May 1947

The Loved One goes very slow, snakes and ladders progress. Some time ago an American from Cambridge wrote to ask me for an interview. I said if he would come here I would see him. Today he came. A very very humourless Boston Irishman. All the topics he raised bored me so much I would only say, 'No, No.'

'Do you consider that in a democratic age the radio and cinema will develop into great arts?'

'No. No.'

[1] Lawyer; later Sir John Foster, QC.
[2] For *The Tablet*.

'Do you think the renaissance villain represents the individual at war with society?'

'No. No.'

'Do publishers have an influence on modern writing comparable to the patron of the eighteenth century?'

'No. No.'

Then I ordered him eggs for tea as he had a long journey back and he spilt one on his trousers. I gave him sherry and a copy of *Campion* and sent him back on his long journey to Cambridge.

Monday 2 June 1947

I have decided to try a new method of work. When I began writing I worked straight on into the void, curious to see what would happen to my characters, with no preconceived plan for them, and few technical corrections. Now I waste hours going back and over my work. I intend trying in *The Loved One* to push straight ahead with a rough draft, have it typed and then work over it once, with the conclusion firmly in my mind when I come to give definite form to the beginning.

Eve of Corpus Christi. I decided my new method of work left me with an itch to get things into shape. Accordingly I shall begin rewriting at once what I hastily jotted down.

Low-spirited, so took a long walk through sunny lanes, woods – Wick, Nibley, Stancombe, and over the golf course. Everything like Birket Foster. Sweated heavily. Returned to a bath and change, a glass of burgundy, fruit juice and soda and a story by Henry James. And a cigar – which was contrary to my resolution and very sweet.

Wednesday 11 June 1947

Laura and I went to London en route for Ireland. I met Seymour Berry in White's who asked me to do a grand tour for the *Telegraph*. We lunched with the Rathdonnells at the Cavalry Club. He is a scatter-brained, slangy, rather seedy-looking young man whose hopeless ambition seems to be to build a new house as large as what he is selling for the price of the old and improve his farm and also I suppose pay off a mortgage.

In the evening we took the aeroplane to Dublin. All arrangements I had made worked well. A car was at Collinstown airport, a table reserved at Jammet's, a bedroom and dressing-room of the greatest comfort waiting us at the end of our long drive to Shilton. We spent two nights at Shilton. The first day was wasted on a visit to a house near Bagenalstown which was entirely unsuitable. Next day we went to Lisnavagh[1] where the agent gave us luncheon and tried to induce us not to purchase the place. Laura liked it and so did I. We

---

[1] House owned by Lord Rathdonnell in Co. Carlow.

drove next to Dublin and gave dinner to the de Vere Whites, slept in a great smell at the Dolphin and took an early aeroplane to London, lunched at Buck's with Randolph and drove with him to Mereworth. A large party for the times – Anthony and Dot Head, Mrs Tree, Bill and Susie Stirling, Randolph, Brendan Bracken, Joan Aly Khan. Poker in the evenings. I lost £21. Randolph and Brendan barely on speaking terms. Randolph amusing about a party at Anne Rothermere's where the girls had been put up to auction. Liz[1] fetched £40. We drove back with Peter on 16th and took the evening train home, very tired.

Monday 23 June 1947

On my instructions Laura purchased a wireless set. Sir Max Beerbohm had made me think that the Third Programme might interest us, particularly when we are in Ireland. I have listened attentively to all programmes and nothing will confirm me more in my resolution to emigrate.

Sunday 29 June 1947

Bron's first communion was postponed because of ill-health. Laura and I had meant to go to Ammerdown. Instead I asked Cyril Connolly and his concubine to stay. They came on Saturday afternoon and proved pleasant guests, showing more than polite interest in the house. I think it was in his mind to buy it. His joint tenure of the house in Regent's Park is proving irksome. He maintains his habitual bewildered resentment when bohemians behave like bohemians which he satirized so well in *Rock Pool*. He was offered £3,500 a year to take Agate's post[2] on the *Daily Express*. Christie Lawrence wrote and telephoned in distress because his publishers have mis-spelt his name on the cover of his first book. Cyril recanted his socialist opinions, saying that his father's death had liberated him from guilt in this matter. Miss Evans came to luncheon and there was some friction of rival French snobberies. Cyril is now obsessed by porcelain and silver gilt and nauseated by books.

The late hours we kept and the brandy we drank left me exhausted yesterday (30th). Today (1st) I resume work on *The Loved One*.

Weekend of 6 July 1947

Simon and Golly Elwes came to stay. We did nothing to entertain them and they bored us.

In subsequent week I finished the first draft of *The Loved One* and began the rewriting, much delayed by the slowness of the typist.

Weekend of 20 July 1947

Ronnie Knox came to stay and talk about the article I propose writing about

[1] Lady Elizabeth von Hofmannsthal.
[2] Book critic.

him for *Horizon*. Frank and Elizabeth Pakenham came to luncheon. I read in the papers that Frank has since cancelled all engagements on account of fainting fits. Elizabeth again pregnant. Ronnie remembered her only as the unmarried girl who had spoken at the Union[2] in favour of birth control.

Monday 21 July 1947

Laura went to London to collect French governess.

London, Wednesday 23 July 1947

I went to London for Daphne Bath's ball. I stayed with Randolph. Dined with Anne Rothermere. I greatly enjoyed the ball, stayed late and drank heavily.

Thursday 24 July 1947

Cocktails in the morning with Pam Berry. Luncheon at Kick Hartington's. Then by train to Mells where Laura and I stayed the night for Bron's first communion.

Friday 25 July 1947

Bron's communion. We took him to Mells for luncheon, discussed Trim's wedding with the bride [?]. Returned to Piers Court very much exhausted. Weather oppressive. I found a letter from Lord Rathdonnell asking £20,000 for his property.

Tuesday 29 July 1947

'It is not Christmas upsets the children but what they eat.' In this way, too, I explain the three or four days suffering which follow my rare visits to London. The symptoms are constant; insomnia, a disordered stomach, weakness at the knees, a trembling hand which becomes evident when I attempt to use the pen. They are at their worst on the day after my return home. I tell myself I have drunk too much, smoked too much and kept late hours. But I grow sceptical of this glib excuse. On this last occasion for instance, 23rd July, I had an easy train journey as far as bodily comfort was concerned. I drank perhaps three cocktails before luncheon, lunched lightly, took things easy in the afternoon, drank perhaps three cocktails before dinner. From then onwards I drank fairly steadily – champagne, with a little brandy at the end of dinner – until 4 o'clock; but I doubt whether in those eight hours I consumed more than a bottle and a half. Next day I began drinking at 11 and drank two glasses of brandy and ginger ale, later two glasses of gin, and at luncheon practically nothing – half a glass of white Bordeaux and two tiny glasses of port. This is not enough to make a healthy middle-aged man ill for four days. No, it is the excitement –

[2] The Oxford Union. Elizabeth Pakenham was in fact married at the time of the debate.

which began in the train when I remembered that I had not told Ellwood to pack a stiff evening shirt for me. Would he have had the sense to do so? I search my bag and find he has not. Then half an hour's agitation. Should I telephone from Paddington to have a shirt put on the next train? It will entail great trouble for Laura and for myself who will have to come back to Paddington at the crowded hour to collect it. What are the chances of buying a shirt ready-made? The train is late, I begin to calculate what will have to be done at Stinchcombe – Laura fetched from the fields, she may be out, the shirt wrapped and labelled. There will not be time. Who at White's can lend me one? So I am in a fever by the time I reach London. There are no cabs. I take an underground train which involves me in long walks with my bag down crowded hot tunnels. I arrive at Piccadilly and find a cab at the exit. I drive to White's, leave my bag, drive to Turnbull & Asser. A young shop assistant tells me it is impossible to get a shirt. An older one is more hopeful. The young and the old search the basement and return, the younger in triumph. I ask them to try other shops. They telephone; presently I hear the older man say: 'Yes, a plain linen front, two studs', and I know I am saved. Then I go to White's. An urgent message from Ellwood to telephone at once. He has remembered his mistake and is putting the shirt on a train. Then I find Harold Stavordale; more and more friends come in, most of them up in London expressly for Daphne's ball. I am entirely sober but flushed and exalted when I reach the Beefsteak. My behaviour there is exemplary, but I am flushed and excited again at Duckworth's, where I go to sign copies of the limited edition of *When the Going was Good*. I puff cigar smoke about and my hand trembles on the pen. I am sure the young directors think I have lunched too well. I puff out and buy a book at Seligman's. Back to White's. Randolph is there. My memory is now becoming vague as to whom I meet or what I say. Randolph animates me, repeats what I say with relish, makes me feel jolly. I go back with him to his house where I am staying and have tea. I go to see Maimie who has not been asked to the ball. Then I dress. The day is getting hotter, it seems. I am amusing and dignified at dinner. After dinner the men shout at one another over the brandy. I do not shout but am I becoming supercilious? to my host? to an American journalist named Forbes? Guilt is beginning as my memory grows feeble. I suppose I was at least five hours at the ball. How did I spend the time? My memories all pieced together would not fill an hour. There is this intellectual problem that still frets me six days later. What did I look like? I have a plain memory of countless faces, particularly of my contemporaries, looking red and damp, with their ties askew and their shirts disordered. I never thought about how I looked from the moment I left my bedroom before dinner. It is probable that I looked like those repulsive memories. I sat with people – Debo, Venetia, who else? – for long periods. Were they bored by me? I kissed people – Liz and Liza, Angie and Clarissa, Daphne and Kitty;[1] who else? Did they like it? I became captious of people I did not know. Were my strictures well received? But the overriding intellectual puzzle – how did I spend five hours in that house? Then a brief night and an awakening feeling fairly well. A good breakfast. White's in the peculiar 11 o'clock stale gloom it always has after a party. I am with Cosmo Crawley, Dermot Daly, and the drunks. A morning call on Pam Berry. Luncheon with Kick Hartington. I talk a great deal – do the young people like it? An afternoon train to Bath which I catch with two minutes to spare. I sleep on the way down. I am bad-tempered on the drive to Mells. At Mells I believe I am quite agreeable. Up early next day for Bron's first communion. Shall I go to confession? A day with Bron, a long drive home, and then collapse and the mind working all the time pulling out facts like sea-urchin spikes from a foot.

Wednesday 30 July 1947

To London again, staying at St James's Club. I dined with Ann Rothermere, a large party where to my delight I found Diana Cooper. Afterwards a private showing of the exquisitely funny old Marx Brothers film *Night at the Opera*.

Friday 1 August 1947

Spent the day reading up Ronnie's contributions to *The Tablet*. Dined with Douglas and Mia. The Scandinavian project is in train.

Saturday 2 August 1947

By hired car to Pam Berry. Maurice Bowra and Oliver Stanley.[2] Sumptuous food and drink, tender cosseting, delicate flattery from Pam. Stanley modest and funny. Bowra greatly lacking in frankness and it came to me that all his appreciation for foreign poetry is an imposture. I questioned him sharply on his knowledge of Lorca and found his answers unsatisfactory. Pam talks chiefly of the sexual act.

Sunday 3 August 1947

Sybil Colefax and Eddie Marsh. Angie came for the night.

Monday 4 August 1947

To Farnborough to make my peace with the Betjemans. Successful in this. A drive with John looking at 1860 churches. Penelope seems resolved to enter the Church in the autumn.

[1] Elizabeth von Hofmannsthal; Liza Maugham; Angela Laycock; Clarissa Churchill; Daphne Bath; Kitty Brownlow.

[2] The Rt. Hon. Oliver Stanley, son of the 17th Earl of Derby; he had been Secretary for War in 1940, and Colonial Secretary in 1945.

Piers Court, Tuesday 5 August 1947

Returned weary to Stinchcombe.

Wednesday 6 August 1947

Laura and all children returned.

Saturday 9 August–Monday 11 August 1947

Laura and I went to stay with Bob and Angie in their new house – an old vicarage in deplorably suburban surroundings near Ascot. No servants except their old cook. Bob making mayonnaise and splicing ropes.

Wednesday 13 August 1947

Victor Mallet came to luncheon to see the house with a view to buying it. He was useful in promising letters of introduction to Swedes.

Thursday 14 August 1947

I discovered by chance that I had miscounted the days and was due to leave for Stockholm on Sunday, not Monday as I had supposed. This caused reorganization of plans.

London, Friday 15 August 1947

I was obliged to come to London a day earlier than I had intended, in order to see the editor of the *Daily Telegraph* – an interview which took four minutes. I arrived at Paddington at 10.45 and went straight to St James's Club to leave my luggage, then to Trumper's to have my hair cut, then to Burlington Arcade having resolved in the train to buy the silver-gilt cabbage leaf dessert service which excited me some weeks back and to give a few pieces to Trim for his wedding present, but to my disappointment I found it sold. Then to Mass at Farm Street. It was a very hot day. I took a cold bath and dozed after my return from Fleet Street. Douglas Woodruff came to dinner with me. As always he knew everyone in the room – more than this, remembered them – while I caused offence by failing to recognize D'Arcy Osborne. We drank a bottle of champagne each and Randolph joined us. The two journalists, like swordfish in a tank, interviewed one another and went on interviewing one another elsewhere after I had gone to bed.

Saturday 16 August 1947

I anticipated a day of bitter boredom but fortunately Douglas was in London and unoccupied. I bought a gold hunter for Trim. At noon Soldati the Italian film producer came to see me. A nervous man like Groucho Marx. I had supposed from his wishing to make a film of Newman's life that he was a zealous son of the Church, but found him a typical commercial cinema man only superior in quickness of mind and humour to his American counterparts. His favourite English writer was Samuel Butler (*Erewhon*). His ambition, which he ill concealed, was to make a fortune in Hollywood. Douglas lunched with me and afterwards we went to see the Wellington treasure in South Kensington. Some rude Portuguese plate and Prussian crockery, an obscene Jan Steen, a fine Lawrence. Later I dined at Park West, and Douglas insisted on listening to Winston Churchill's thick tones enunciating clichés.

Stockholm, Sunday 17 August 1947

A very hot day in London and Stockholm where I arrived at 11 at night, found a note directing me to the Carlton Hotel, a small, modern, noisy place in a main shopping street. But the restaurant was still open and I had half a bottle of champagne and a beautifully cooked sole.

Monday 18 August 1947

I spent the day looking at Stockholm, a city of startling beauty, water on all sides, bridges, trees, some lovely buildings. My change of address necessitated rewriting to all to whom I had sent letters of introduction. An admirable luncheon at Opera Keller. In the evening to an expensive restaurant called Bellmansro where I was too tired to eat. The *Telegraph* agent came to see me. A cheerful, civil good-looking fellow who is sick of Stockholm and wants to go to Berlin. First impressions of Stockholm Paradise, second Limbo. Girls very pretty and not disfigured by paint and hairdressing. All look sexually and socially satisfied.

Tuesday 19 August 1947

More sightseeing. Splendid German woodcarving of St George and princess. The town hall the last building of importance in Europe designed to be picturesque. Not my taste but everything carefully designed with aesthetic intent. I lunched with Viklund, the *Telegraph* correspondent and the literary editor of his paper – an ugly man enormously well informed about modern English writers. After luncheon a dull young woman, fat, came to interview me. Later when the interview appeared it was headed 'Huxley's Ape makes hobby of graveyards'. That evening Mrs Holmquist, to whom I was introduced by both Victor Mallet and Randolph, dined with me at Opera Keller. Very pretty, shy, gluttonous. I should think passionate. She said Randolph had greatly alarmed her by his bad temper. She has a beautiful little flat at the top of a building in Strandvägen and from her I began to get some impression of the straightened circumstances of the upper class. After dinner we walked through the old town and had beer in a cellar where a man was singing Bellman to the lute.

Wednesday 20 August 1947

More sightseeing. Luncheon with Assarsson, head of the Foreign Office, an old pansy with a pretty modern bungalow full of works of art. With us Grafström head of political department FO. Assarsson had no car, but he had caviare and a Hepplewhite table.

Thursday 21 August 1947

Three invitations to dinner of which I accepted the first, Karl Asplund, a poet antiquaire. Mrs Holmquist came to luncheon with me bringing a son and daughter and picking up a pert tart. We went first to the House of the Nobility, one of the finest exteriors in the city but modern renovations inside (pretty chimneys). A great hall full of coats of arms. Mrs H.: 'But this is funny. I find here the names of so many friends I did not know were nobles.' Arplund's dinner was in an old inn some way out of town. Delicious food and drink. Pen Club company all most knowledgeable about English books. They apologized for Prince Wilhelm's absence (his uncle Eugen the painter is just dead).

Friday 22 August 1947

A day's outing with my publisher, a dull fellow. Swedes are bloody dull.
He said: '*I Chose Freedom* has sold 35,000 copies. A great sale.'
'That is good.'
'It is very bad.'
'Why? Do you not think it truthful?'
'I know it is quite truthful but it will be a terrible thing if it caused feeling here against Russia.'
The Swedes have a very disadvantageous trade agreement with Russia. They resent it being disadvantageous, not on other grounds. Communism to them is simply Russian aggression. They cannot conceive its mystique. Eighteen per cent of town council are Communist.

We saw Gripsholm Castle, a pretty building with masses of portraits. A drive through rich farmland and lakes. Insolently bad service in the hotel at Gripsholm.

In the evening Arplund had invited me to join a little party for the French Legation to see the pavilion Haga (Gustav III) which is being renovated very carefully by a French enthusiast. I found it included a dinner party. Again delicious food and wine, but a great lack of imagination and curiosity in the conversation. A French woman with carmine lips tried to be the life and soul of the party. I was weary and glad when the restaurant closed. Drink regulations here are not oppressive.

Saturday 23 August 1947

To Upsala by train to visit Engströmer, the Chancellor who lives in a tiny Park West flat. The Professor of English joined us and we went to visit the

Faculty House, full of English and American books. The Chancellor told me without reserve that most of the girl students live in concubinage. The town is delicious and many of the buildings good. Cathedral awful. Queen Christina's silver bell is still rung daily for her 'luck'. I am astonished by the lack of curiosity displayed by all types of Swede in all subjects.

Sunday 24 August 1947

In the evening my publisher asked me to dine to meet two young poets. One was my age and very drunk. They call themselves the '40 group', admire Kafka, Sartre.

Oslo, Monday 25 August 1947

Left Stockholm by the morning aeroplane and arrived at Oslo at 1 o'clock. Everything very shabby, the town airless and dusty in unusual heat, the inhabitants straggling about the streets in their shirt-sleeves eating ice-cream. The Grand Hotel in the builders' hands; constant hammering. But they have the agreeable Scandinavian habit of serving constant meals. Dinner lasts from 12 till 6; at 6 supper begins, lasts till 12. A midget female socialist came to introduce herself as my agent and took me to see my publisher, who hasn't published anything yet. A press conference was arranged for 6.30 that evening. Half a dozen journalists came, of whom two or three knew no English. A girl was quite drunk. The press attaché from the British Embassy did all the talking. Dined with agent and publisher.

I stayed in Oslo until Friday 29th. The weather was oppressive, the food poor, the noise of trams under my window intolerable, the city hideous. Their town hall when complete will be the ugliest building in Europe. The only unique thing is Vigeland's extraordinary phallic shrine, where I spent some time. I dined with the publisher to meet Mrs Undset[1]. She never spoke except to ask if I had read 'Julie Noitch' (Julian of Norwich,[2] it transpired), drank a lot, and looked like a malevolent boarding-house proprietress.

I left with pleasure on 29th and arrived at Copenhagen in the late afternoon. I found I was a highly popular writer among the Danes. The *Telegraph* correspondent, two publishers, a dozen journalists and cameramen met me at the airport. That night I dined with the publishers at a public gardens named Tivoli – a unique institution one hundred years old where there is a circus, a concert, traditional Italian pantomime, sideshows, switchbacks and places of refreshment from workmen's beer cafés to luxury restaurants, the whole thing well frequented and orderly. The Angleterre Hotel was pleasant and old-fashioned. I stayed at Copenhagen till 2nd September when I left with regret. I saw the sights in company either of my young publishers or a literary jagger

[1] Sigrid Undset, the writer.
[2] St Julian of Norwich, mystical writer of the early fifteenth century.

called Kragh-Jacobson, visited Elsinore, Baroness Blixen,[1] a Catholic rally at Forum.

During my tour I decided to abandon the idea of settling in Ireland. Reasons: (1) Noble. The Church in England needs me. (2) Ignoble. It would be bad for my reputation as a writer. (3) Indifferent. There is no reason to suppose life in Ireland will be more tolerable than here. My children must be English. I should become an anachronism. The Socialists are piling up repressive measures now. It would seem I was flying from them. If I am to be a national figure I must stay at home. The Americans would lose interest in an emigrant and the Irish would not be interested.

I came to London to the Hyde Park Hotel and spent two nights. The *Daily Telegraph* has no idea what they want me to write. I shall write a comic series of dialogues for them. In London I bought a mechanical Gothic organ and drove down with it.

I found Laura just released from a school treat. Teresa in a hideous dress. The French governess speaking English. The children pleased to see me. I called on Andrea Cowdin in London, gave her some Heywood Hill antique nonsenses and received a ham, a box of cigars, and countless good things. I took the painting of cattle out of my library and sewed [?] up the frame as part of the plan to make the house habitable now I am to inhabit it.

Piers Court, Thursday 2 October 1947

I returned home to find the house clean and silent and waterless. Eddie Grant died on Saturday 27th after a week's illness. Laura went to comfort her family. I therefore had a gloomy evening celebration with Bron, Teresa and the French governess and took Teresa to Ascot next day by car. She had a hangover. I delivered her to the charge of Monica Hollis, and the French governess to some crypto-nuns in Sloane Street. I remained ten days at the Hyde Park Hotel with the time heavy on my hands, seeing my old little circle of White's and Connolly and Maimie, Pam, Bridget Parsons, Sykeses, Liz, etc. Some tedious meals at the Beefsteak. I became reconciled with B. Bennett who celebrated the event by taking a shower-bath in his clothes. The Woodruffs seem beside themselves – Mia with vain-glory, Douglas with delusions about the Ark of Noah.

Thursday 2 October – Wednesday 8 October 1947

Alone and low-spirited. I dug the garden and became so painfully stiff that I was obliged to stop. On the 7th Trim Oxford and his bride came for the night and on 8th I went with them to Mells, slept in a room so cold and damp that my stiffness turned to torture and was later dubbed fibrositis. Since then I have lived as an invalid.

[1] Karen Blixen, author of *Out of Africa*.

9th. Henriques came to luncheon. 10th Laura returned.
A week of invalid life, large fire in library and never setting foot outside.

Tuesday 21 October 1947

To London apprehensive of a relapse – unnecessarily. White's full of distressed peers in starchless collars contemplating the abolition of the upper house with resignation. Cyril obsessed with French eighteenth-century *objets d'art*. 'I want to make a mausoleum where I can lie surrounded by the finest works of the period where students will come to peer through a window at me and them.' An evening – surely fruitless – at 58 Sloane Street: a Catholic brains trust with an audience devoid of curiosity. Slept at Highgate. Luncheon with McDougall at Boulestin's. An extremely bad luncheon with no attempt at *grande cuisine*.

Tuesday 28 October 1947

My 44th birthday. I am a very much older man than this time last year, physically infirm and lethargic. Mentally I have reached a stage of non-attachment which if combined with a high state of prayer – as it is not – would be edifying. I have kept none of the resolutions made this day a year ago. I have vast reasons for gratitude but am seldom conscious of them. I have written two good stories – *Scott-King's Modern Europe* and *The Loved One* – in the course of the year and have decided to remain in England. I have added a number of beautiful books to my collection and a few valueless pictures. I have given large sums to church funds and been drunk less often. I have been more comfortable than most Englishmen.

Friday 31 October 1947

Jack (to me now) McDougall and his wife came to stay. She a quiet American lady. They had a dull weekend but enough to eat and plenty to drink.

Friday 7 November 1947

Laura went to Nutcombe to help kill a pig, I to Dursley to be enrolled as a trustee of Stinchcombe Hill. During the weekend I finished the article on Ronnie Knox.

Sunday 16 November 1947

Carol Brandt came to luncheon bringing John Foster. She brought rice and fat, having already sent children's shoes. We gave her lists of things wanted from USA and a book, proofs bound, to take to Loyola College, Baltimore, who have offered me a degree.

Wednesday 19 November 1947

By car to Oxford to address the 'writers' club'; called first on Maurice and had tea, brandy and gossip from him. Then to my host, a humourless, gentlemanlike fellow called Kennedy. We dined in the senior common-room at the House – a good consommé, roast chicken, sweet mousse, shockingly bad wine. David Cecil arrived with the port. My address was well received and David made the subsequent discussion agreeable and intelligent.

Thursday 20 November 1947

A rather gloomy morning. Snow and bitter cold succeeded by humid warmth. I had intended a morning in the second-hand bookshops but found them all closed for Princess Elizabeth's wedding. Also great difficulty in finding a glass of beer. I had to walk as far as the station to find an inn open. I lunched with Christie Lawrence whose circumstances are not easy, with a wife and child, no house but lodgings, a rack-rent government allowance which makes it not worthwhile winning a university prize. His health and sanity are enfeebled by Gestapo torture. His book[1] was well received, sold out, not reprinted. It brought him £180. His purpose is to go to Uganda in the colonial service. I have offered to finance him if he decides to stay in England. Home by car.

Sunday 23 November–Monday 24 November 1947

A sale at an old house in Tetbury. Laura and I spent two frigid, happy days there and at the cost of about £100 acquired some worn curtains and carpet, a fine urn and hall seats, and a variety of battered toys and odds and ends.

Friday 28 November 1947

Some days of anxiety about the safety of the MS.[2] of *The Loved One* – Cyril ill, his secretary incompetent, his colleague Watson mischievous, but in the end all right. Ronnie Knox sent me a paper on translating the Bible which has necessitated retrieving the MS. of that too and rewriting. Hungry days. Living mostly on bread, cheese from America and thank God wine.

Monday 1 December 1947

Stuart Boyle[3] came for the night. Short, highly nervous, older than I expected, stocky. Touching respect for his poet wife Vera. Very much conscious of Jews; perhaps a Jew with assumed name. Born in South Africa. Not used to wine or food. Potential convert to Catholicism. Clearly a hard-working, penurious draughtsman of great technical skill and little imagination or taste. Just what I want.

[1] *Regular Adventure.*
[2] *The Loved One* was to be published in the magazine *Horizon* edited by Cyril Connolly.
[3] Illustrator of *The Loved One.*

Tuesday 2 December 1947

A morning discussing the illustrations and decorations of *Loved One*, which resolved itself into Boyle taking dictation. I supplied every detail and if the book is a failure it will be my fault alone.

Sunday 7 December 1947

Sunday is not the happy day it should be. There is no rest for me because I do not work. I get up earlier instead of later and for a man of middle age and set habits this is disturbing. There is a drive to church. An ugly suburban church, bare and comfortless. No letters, which are for me now, as for my deaf father, the link with the world. No papers until noon and then papers that fill me with gloom and disgust. A weekly joint seldom edible. For quite other reasons, and in quite another form, the Victorian Sunday has returned as a day of wrath.

Tuesday 9 December 1947

Correspondence with Boyle about the details of *The Loved One* gives me an interest.

Sunday 14 December 1947

Another Sunday. This time with Bridget visiting us – enveloped in wool in spite of the mild weather. A prolonged drinking-bout of her and Laura.

Boxing Day 1947

Mild weather. On December 19th Laura and I drove to Ascot to fetch Teresa and took her to luncheon with the Laycocks. She was at once committed to a den of obstreperous children while Bob and Angie gave us very good sherry and white burgundy and an excellent game paté which Bob had concocted. He was walking lame, his face thin and aged; Angie blooming. A large luncheon where Teresa cut a wretched figure, mincing her words and rolling her eyes like a nun. We drank a great deal and reached home in the dark to find Bron returned. The family had already been increased by Margaret's arrival in quarantine for whooping cough. So here we have been all together. I find the children particularly charmless. I am attempting to give Bron some extra lessons. He is lazy but not very stupid.

Press cuttings pour in, mostly laudatory. I am annoyed to find myself continually described by people whom I have never set eyes on as bad-tempered. I was disappointed to find my story reviewed by a young man called Russell in the *Sunday Times* after Desmond had expressed unqualified pleasure in it. The standard of modern reviewing is lamentably low.

I have been suffering from the effects of too many narcotics and am stopping them.

We began Christmas with midnight Mass at Woodchester Priory. We had a fine turkey and the children had good presents. Laura bore the brunt of it all.

Written on Sunday 4 January 1948

On Sunday 28th my disgust with my family grew past bearing. On Tuesday 30th I went to London by the early train for refreshment, drove to White's and found it in the hands of the painters. However I got drunk there, at the Ritz with Maimie, and at the Beefsteak Club, where Maurice Bowra was making his first appearance. I think I talked loudly and loosely. Then I continued drinking all the afternoon and arrived at Maimie's for dinner to find a cold welcome from Vsevolode which later became active hostility when I broke a decanter. Went to bed early and drunk at St James's Club and slept little.

Next day I telephoned Diana, went to confession and then to the Dorchester to help her in the hunt for a Highlander's full dress bonnet for a carnival ball that night. I spent the afternoon with Christopher Sykes, collecting a painting – *Une question embarrassante* – and taking it to be framed, calling on the Jungman sisters who live in frightful squalor next door to the Sykeses, and giving my godchild a Teddy bear which cost £7 10s. I dined with the Woodruffs – a tremendous spread of food and wine. Helen Rospigliosi[1] and Sir Noel[2] and Lady Charles. Helen and Lady Charles frightfully drunk – far drunker than I had been the day before. Roger Hesketh arrived at 8, saw the table and said: 'Oh I didn't know there was dinner'; a place was hastily set for him. He ate hugely and at 9 said he must leave because he was dining out.

Thursday 1 January 1948

Bought a watch for Laura in Holborn, called on Diana, went to Mass at Farm Street, took Diana to luncheon at Wilton's and caught the afternoon train home, having arranged various pleasures for myself next week in London.

I found a pile of letters, mostly agreeable. Derek Jackson has bought my car for £700, a tax-free sum that is very warming. Planning vicarious benefactions for Christie Lawrence and direct benefactions for Mrs Percy Waugh. No sign of life from Stuart Boyle. *Scott-King* sold 14,000 up to Christmas. Connolly is getting nervous about *The Loved One*.

My temper is the softer for my jaunt to London.

Written on Saturday 17 January 1948

O the flat boredom of writing compared with the exhilaration of telling events!

On Wednesday 7th I went to London staying at St James's Club, dined at Victor Rothschild's table at the Savoy. Twenty-six. The girls pretty and well dressed, the men shabby and celebrated. The host, whom I only knew as a

---

[1] Douglas Woodruff's sister-in-law.
[2] Sir Noel Charles, KCMG, MC: the 3rd bart. and diplomatist.

bumptious, exuberant fellow, paralysed with shyness and shame. I sat beside Diana, opposite him, Pam Berry on my right. As good a dinner as the times allow, plenty of wine, a conjuror who would have been absurd in a village hall.

Thursday 8 January 1948

To Brighton with Diana and Duff to lunch with Hugh Sherwood and Daisy Fellowes in a sunny love-nest. Caviare, cold pheasant, Camembert cheese, fine claret, port, brandy, a brief drive to visit the church at Rottingdean (to verify Forest Lawn replica[1] and find it entirely false) and M. Baring's[2] villa. Back to London. Trains empty. Nancy Rodd dined with me at the Ritz Hotel.

Friday 9 January 1948

To Chapman & Hall's to see Jack McDougall, who had a bottle of sherry and the Boyle drawings for me. Apart from a few easily corrigible defects, they are quite admirable. To the Beefsteak to induct Betjeman, but he had taken ill or frighted and would not come. Instead I found Lord Reading inducting Frank. A jolly luncheon. Rested on my bed. During all these days never quite drunk or quite sober. I bought two enchanting paintings by a man aptly named Joy. £150.

Dined with Cyril. The Sykeses, Mrs Cameron. I see Cyril's boom fading, *Horizon* losing subscribers, income-tax officials pressing him, inertia, luxury and an insane longing to collect rare things. He was in 'good form', giving spirited imitations of Logan Pearsall Smith, and I am sure when we all left collapsed into melancholy. As always a supremely good dinner.

Saturday 10 January 1948

Took Diana to see my Joys and bought another delicious painting by a Czech. 1840 *The Connoisseurs*, £130. Went to tea with my mother and was irreproachably genial. To Graham Greene's film *Brighton Rock* and dined with Woodruffs.

Sunday 11 January 1948

Mass at 12 at Farm Street where I met the shambling, unshaven and as it happened quite penniless figure of Graham Greene. Took him to the Ritz for a cocktail and gave him 6d for his hat. He had suddenly been moved by love of Africa and emptied his pockets into the box for African missions. Diana

---

[1] The Church of the Recessional at the Forest Lawn, Los Angeles, cemetery was built in its exterior lines as a replica of St Margaret's, Rottingdean; originally, the sponsors of Forest Lawn offered to buy the church and re-erect it, stone by stone, on the Pacific coast. Kipling wrote 'The Recessional' while living at The Elms, Rottingdean.

[2] Maurice Baring, the Catholic writer; he signed the register at Waugh's wedding to Laura Herbert, and lived for a time in Steyning Road, Rottingdean.

lunched with me. Both tired. Not a success. Slept. That evening I gave a curiously ill-assorted party at the Ritz – the Pakenhams, Daphne Bath, Elizabeth Cameron and Christopher Sykes.

Monday 12 January 1948

Lunched with Bennett luxuriously. He has given Chris Lawrence £300 and had a sharp note in reply. Why? That evening Angie gave a party. Small, pretty, a pianist, a waiter, champagne, turkey but not what was needed. I kissed everyone.

Tuesday 13 January 1948

Returned home to find that the children had greatly enjoyed my absence and that their manners had deteriorated correspondingly. Played billiards with Laura in the evenings.

Sunday 25 January 1948

I drove to Oxford leaving Laura crippled with fibrositis, and was charmed with the warmth of my reception at Campion Hall. Frank Pakenham was leaving as I arrived and delayed to apologize for the delays of his office over the importation of Maltays [?]. He is going to see the Australian High Commissioner about them. Father Corbishley had arranged a sherry party for me – Maurice Bowra, David Cecil, Mrs Graham Greene, several dons. I became pleasantly exhilarated and went to the Old Palace from which the Newman officials took me to a bad dinner at the Carlton Club. Afterwards I spoke about Hollywood. Four hundred turned up, nearly ten times the normal audience. They seemed amused by what I said. Afterwards I had a drink with the Jesuits and was presented with a crocodile cigar case, the property of a Jesuit lately dead.

Laura fell into a melancholy during the subsequent week.

Tuesday 3 February 1948

I took Margaret to London. Dined at Beefsteak slept Hyde Park Hotel. Next day 4th was photographed, had my hair cut, gave McDougall luncheon, saw the Indian exhibition, saw Peters, dined with Phil and Audrey, drank late with Basil.

Thursday 5 February 1948

Returned home after sending Margaret and my mother to the theatre and giving them luncheon.

During the subsequent days a cook and kitchen maid who later transpired to be mother and daughter and later still mother daughter and granddaughter, of

French origin and high pretensions in their art, failed to come.

Laura's melancholy abated.

Lent began. I have 'given up' wine and tobacco. Laura wine. As a result we drank heavily on Sunday 15th. A youngish man named Hiram Winterbotham came to call. Mrs Strutt had spoken of him as a collector and friend of Sybil Colefax. He spoke of himself as a friend of almost everyone. A talkative handsome fellow with a knowledge of Georgian domestic architecture which took me back ten years. He has assumed the name Winterbotham for reasons of self-advancement.[1] He was born Hague. On Monday 16th we drove to luncheon with him at Woodchester in a house Laura and I once looked at but thought too small and suburban. His furniture was not remarkable, his pictures modern. He has made structural changes all of which are deplorable. But the hall looks nice.

My Lenten resolution to start work on *Helena* has not come to much. I wrote instead a silly article, some letters to papers, numberless letters.

On 23rd February the McDougalls came for the night.

On 29th Winterbotham came to dinner with three friends.

Monday 1 March 1948

A hangover from Sunday's remission of Lenten abstinence. Laura left for a visit to her family. When the hangover is over I shall work on *Helena*.

Wednesday 3 March 1948

Patrick Kinross came for the night and left next day to see a dentist. He languidly expresses the desire to be married. I suggest Coote. He has thoughts of Diana Campbell Grey.

Friday 5 March 1948

Laura returned. A disappointing day.

Tuesday 9 March 1948

Priest (?) came to tea and stayed to dinner. Drank heavily.

Wednesday 10 March 1948

I went to London to see Andrea who is there ill and to get my hair cut.

[1] Hiram Winterbotham comments: 'I was particularly devoted to my uncle, Arthur Winterbotham, and when he expressed in his will the hope that I would change my name from Hague to Winterbotham, I did so to give him posthumous pleasure. There was no question of inheritance, as he pre-deceased his wife, or other self-advancement that I know of.' Letter to the editor, November 1975.

Bought glass at Goode's, they have only oddments and failed to buy a book at Maggs. Returned in the evening to entertain Patrick and Coote.

Thursday 11 March 1948

Patrick and Coote left. I went to Bristol BBC to record my essay on Forest Lawn. Very civil young man.

Wednesday 24 March 1948

Set out with Laura to drive to Downside. Four miles from home the back axle of our car broke. We summoned Prothero and after a delay set out with him. In sight of Downside *his* back axle broke. Another taxi took us to our destination, I to monastery, Laura to stay with Agnes Holmes. Tenebrae. Simon Elwes arrives later with two protégés – young Wavender and old Emmott.

Maundy Thursday 1948

A long day of churchgoing. I visited my aunts at Norton. Simon swaggering about like an impresario.

Good Friday 1948

Churchgoing. I called on my old nurse Lucy Hodges, now old and a grandmother and rich and not much elated by my visit.

Holy Saturday 1948

The fast over I smoked and drank. Laura gave a cocktail party. The boys at the school acted an indecent farce.

Easter Sunday 1948

We returned after Mass. —— brought a lot of middle-aged pansies to cocktails.

Easter Monday 1948

A morning catching up with letters. The printers in Bristol at work on *The Loved One* have been burned down.

Tuesday 4 May 1948

At last the holidays have come to an end. In my most miserable schooldays I did not welcome the end of term more gladly. Teresa left a week ago and I supposed I should be happier for her absence but its only effect was to transform Margaret, who had been attracting my affection, into an entirely obnoxious little girl. Today Bron returns to All Hallows, Margaret to

Nutcombe, Harriet to Pixton, where she is welcome as an adjunct to the nurserymaid Vera. Reason resumes its sway.

I have not, as a matter of fact, spent an inordinate length of time at home. For the weekend of Low Sunday I went to the Baths[1] where there was no sleep, Daphne keeping up drink and jazz until 3 am and at 6 am her children bicycling round the house with loud cries. Mary Campbell, Robin and John de Forrest in the house – Robin fat, vain, opinionated, offhand and generally spoilt. From Sturford Mead[2] to Mells for a night, the time chiefly spent with Ronald. Then to London for my usual Hyde Park Hotel, White's round. Back to London the following week. An absurd party was given for Diana which I have described in so many letters that I cannot bear to do so again.

While at Daphne's we visited the Greenes. Olivia[3] 1/3 drunk 1/3 insane 1/3 genius. I have been involved since in a long correspondence with her in which she claims to be guided by God to give Gwen's money to the Communists.

I have bought a preposterous painting and a fine silver candelabrum.

Monday 16 August 1948

I have not been well since July 9th, troubled off and on with nettle rash which the Wotton doctor has been unable to cure and only alleviates by the use of very depressing drugs. A brief heat wave, otherwise a cold wet summer. The children all home. Teresa's voice odious, Bron lazy, Margaret stupid but charming, Harriet mad. During the last week my mother has been here adding hugely to my depression by her incessant praise of everything. If she complained all the time as most old people do she would be no more tedious and would relieve the necessity of trying usually fruitlessly to be civil. Any effort, physical or social, seems to make my itch worse. I do nothing. Success has brought idleness as its dead fruit.

Thursday 19 August 1948

My aunt Lilian's funeral at Shirehampton. I am told that I met her in early childhood but have no memory of it. The time of the funeral was changed fairly frequently by telegraph. Eventually it was 3.30 pm. Laura and I drove there, she in astrakhan, I in tall hat and tail coat. Shirehampton is now a district of the City of Bristol housing 16,000 factory hands. The church was burned down some fifteen years back and entirely rebuilt in a spurious, light, and ugly fashion. The only feature of interest was a number of pieces of calligraphy done by a Miss Base. The Raban vault is in good order with ample room for the surviving members of the family. A curious feature: my aunt Henrietta died in

---

[1] The Marquess and Marchioness of Bath.

[2] Home of the Baths.

[3] Olivia Plunket Greene, who was living in seclusion, with her mother, Gwen Plunket Greene, in a house on the Baths' estate.

1880 aged eight and it is so recorded in the vestry. In the vault is no child's coffin but a full-sized one bearing the name Henrietta Raban aged nineteen, 1889. I suppose there will never be an explanation of that. My aunts Mildred and Emma were the only mourners. Uncle George was prevailed upon to assist in the service because, as Aunt Mildred explained, he has 'such a sweet voice'. The service was brief and seemly. Afterwards the vicar, a gentlemanlike old man named Dixon, invited us to tea. The house where my great-great-aunts lived has great charm, though the gardens are ill kept, the gates removed during the war by government agents and the property diminished and built over. Mrs Dixon complained of a ghost in the upper regions and Mr Dixon boasted of a secret passage in the cellarage.

London, Monday 23 August 1948

To London by the midday train, had my hair cut dined at White's and took Maurice Bridgeman[1] to a coloured film about the ballet at the expense of the *Daily Express*. Slept at Hyde Park Hotel.

Tuesday 24 August 1948

Unimposing consulting rooms near Paddington. Imposing doctor. Egyptian (?) said he was French and a great collector. Talked like Poirot. He told me nettle-rash was not in any way connected with diet. 'Eat and drink as you like.' He must find what poison was in my blood. Injected some stuff. From him to dentist. To White's; lunched with Patrick Kinross and Christopher Sykes. Patrick gave me his novel to read. During the next few days I read it and carefully annotated it. Everything about Angela excellent, the rest dreary.

Another cinema. Doctor in afternoon. He said 'Drink less' and tried to sell me 5-guinea book about his collection of works of art.

Wednesday 25 August 1948

Dentist. Doctor. White's. Patrick's novel. Dinner at the Woodruffs with two abbots.

Thursday 26 August 1948

Doctor, dentist. Enormous and excellent luncheon with Tony Bushell and two cinema colleagues at 16 Duke Street to discuss a film for Lady Olivier. No business discussed but many grouse eaten and many bottles of wine drunk. In the evening I took Douglas to what purported to be a film supper. We arrived at a private theatre in Soho and found K. Clark, Miss Lejeune, Miss Winn, a very pretty editor's wife (who, I learned, had been a Wren selected for her beauty and sent to the *Express* during the war to be publicized. She married the assistant editor before her leave was up). There was a table of *hors d'oeuvres* and

[1] See Appendix of Names, p. 794.

cocktails which promised well and a horrible old photographer with a flashlight. We saw a film in colour about Danny Kaye and came out for supper. There lay the remains of the *hors d'oeuvres* and half a bottle of gin. That was the supper. The editor of the *Express* had come hoping for champagne and quails. K. Clark and Miss Lejeune left to dine. We saw an admirable Italian film *Paisa* and left very hungry. Mia produced a four-course dinner in four minutes.

Friday 27 August 1948

Doctor, dentist (who having worked for hours to produce a false tooth confessed to failure), White's, Patrick's novel, film.

Saturday 28 August 1948

Tom Burns gave me enthralling task of cutting the redundancies and solecisms out of Tom Merton's *Seven Storey Mountain*.[1] This took a week and resulted in what should be a fine thin volume. I gave dinner to Mia, the Pakenhams and Burns. Bill £26. But lavish.

Sunday 29 August 1948

Mass Farm Street. Father D'Arcy dined with me. Full of love but ill and scatterbrained.

Monday 30 August 1948

Doctor. He had now learned who I was and was much more enthusiastic. 'You must come and see me as a friend. I will give you wine. I will bring you a little blonde from Paris, yes?' Lunched at Ritz with Frank and Elizabeth. He proposed I should go with them to Ireland, to stay with Maureen Dufferin. I said I would if she asked me and he arranged the passage. From then on for three days there were a series of telephone calls from him and his secretary. It transpired that Maureen had a luncheon for the Governor-General on Saturday which Frank was shirking, sending me in his place without her knowledge. He seems to have told a great many lies which resulted in my being expected and not going. I took Christopher to the cinema and found him insane.

Tuesday 31 August 1948

A luncheon party by Mia for T. Burns's in-laws. I took Christopher to cinema and found him more insane. Before that he took me to see a crippled man of letters named Hayward whom I met years ago at Tours.

Wednesday 1 September 1948

White's shut. I sent Christopher tiger lilies to acknowledge my faults of the

---

[1] Fr Thomas Merton, American Cistercian monk, whose book, amended by Waugh, was published in Britain with the title *Elected Silence*.

evening before.[1] A meeting at Dropmore Press to discuss Ronnie's book.[2] Shanks showed an unattractive parsimony. He wishes to print 750 copies. Too many. His typographical expert had never heard of Owen Jones. Film. Dined with B. Bennett.

Piers Court, Thursday 2 September 1948

Returned very gladly to Stinchcombe, full of love for Laura and family.

Friday 3 September 1948

Coping with correspondence.

Saturday 4 September 1948

Coping with correspondence. Donaldsons[3] dined and the women got drunk.

Sunday 5 September 1948

Communion. Badminton court.

London, Tuesday 28 September 1948

To London by early train in order to be in time for luncheon. Graham Greene suggested the meeting and refused to come to my club. The idea was Catherine Walston's who was curious to meet me. Graham's flat is next to hers at 5 St James's Street. The paralysed John Hayward was there, tenderly and candidly petted by Mrs W. Luncheon plainly had been brought from her flat for there was no salt. She sat on the floor and buttered my bread for me and made simple offers of friendship. Twice a year she and her husband give a great feast primarily for Hayward. I was asked to the next, in January. Finally, I was asked to go with her to the country. I couldn't that afternoon as I had to dine with the editor of the *Daily Express*. Very well they would pick me up after dinner. I couldn't do that as I was lunching with Father Caraman next day. Very well she would send a car for me at 2.30. That evening a good dinner at the Savoy – Kenneth Barnes, Kenneth Clark, Leigh Ashton, Miss Lejeune, Miss Winn occasionally and some *Express* people. A friendly discussion of the film tribunal's choice and a victory for foreign films being eligible for first prize.

I woke next day 29th September with a pleasant sense of having an interesting time ahead. Prayers at Maiden Lane and then to the press show of Graham

---

[1] 'Hardly had I introduced Evelyn and John than a rather uncannily well-placed remark by John excited Evelyn to an explosive outpouring of religious polemics, wholly unsuited to the occasion and grossly insulting to the memory of my father.' Sykes, *Evelyn Waugh*, p. 315.

[2] *Sermons by Monsignor Knox, selected and edited by Evelyn Waugh*, published by the Dropmore Press in a limited *de luxe* edition, 1949.

[3] Lady (Frances) Donaldson in 1967 published *Evelyn Waugh, Portrait of a Country Neighbour*.

Greene and Carol Reed's film *Fallen Idol* which was clever and funny and original. Father Caraman to luncheon. We talked about the *Month*.[1] Then Mrs Walston's car came but driven by a lout who did not know the way so that we were hours reaching Thriplow. Her house has been confiscated by the socialists so she lives in a farm buildng, one storey, modern, wood. A living-room with modern books and gramophones and wireless and modern pictures, a little dining-room, magnificent Caroline silver, a kitchenette, a bedroom, two bathrooms, two dressing-rooms. No servants except a nurse named 'Twinkle' who dined with us very neatly dressed as a nurse and talked about masturbation, incest, etc. Three children out of five were at home. Mrs Walston barefooted and mostly squatting on the floor. Fine big eyes and mouth, unaffected to the verge of insanity, unvain, no ostentation – simple friendliness and generosity and childish curiosity. Two bottles of champagne before dinner in silver goblets. Usually they have a supper of shredded wheat and boiled eggs. Tonight for me there was bisque of lobster, partridges, cheese, fine claret, port, brandy. Not drunk but tongue pleasantly loose. We talked all the time of religion. She and Graham had been reading a treatise on prayer together that afternoon. Then she left the room at about 1 and presently telephoned she was in bed. We joined her. Her bedside littered with books of devotion.

Thursday 30 September 1948

Woke after four hours' sleep and presently walked their flat, well-kept fields among Arab horses. I left at 10 by car and came to London in time to order luncheon for Laura and McDougalls and Patrick Kinross at Bon Viveur. Glad Patrick was there to enliven it. Very weary in the afternoon. In the evening Ronnie 6oth birthday party. I tried to get out of making a speech but failed and made a bad one but everyone had a good time chiefly Ronnie.

Friday 1 October 1948

Lunched with Laura at Wilton's, sent her to *Fallen Idol*, joined Magdalen[2] and Asquiths, sat in White's just reopened with new carpet and looking-glasses and nearly missed train home.

Piers Court, Saturday 2 October 1948

Busy coping with correspondence. Donaldsons came to dinner and got tight.

Sunday 3 October 1948

Communion. Ellwood gave notice. I will let him go without attempting to hold him. His going will make a great change in our way of life. I shan't replace

[1] Roman Catholic periodical.
[2] The Countess of Eldon.

him but settle myself into a simpler way of life for the century of the common man.

Tuesday 5 October 1948

Ellwood withdrew his notice so my simple life is postponed. The American Catholic from *Life* Emmet Hughes came to stay and discuss my trip to USA.[1] Very dull civil fellow. We seemed in agreement about the article.

Saturday 9 October 1948

I received a cable from New York confirming the invitation from *Life* to go there at the end of this month. Dined with Donaldsons and Harfords [?].

Thursday 28 October 1948

My 45th birthday. An unproductive and unhealthy year. The start pray God of a better.

Given the relative assiduity with which Waugh had been keeping a diary during the preceding years, the gap between the last entry and the resumption of the diary nearly four years later, in September 1952, is surprising. No explanation except a change of habit presents itself.

Sunday 28 September 1952

Drove to visit Belloc, prearranged with letters and telephones, with Jebbs. Kingsland, Shipley. Farm house, brick at corner of lane; dilapidated windmill near it. Some milk churns suggestive of dairy farming. Greeted by two Jebb boys, one handsome in sailor's sweater, other small, natty, cherubic, paralysed hand. Very welcoming. Decanter of sherry. Fair-sized hall, book-lined and prints of sentimental interest; photographs. Clean and comfortable. Younger boy went to fetch 'Granda' [?]. Sounds of shuffling. Enter old man, shaggy white beard, black clothes garnished with food and tobacco. Thinner than I last saw him, with benevolent gleam. Like an old peasant or fisherman in French film. We went to greet him at door. Smell like fox. He kissed Laura's hand, bowed to me saying, 'I am pleased to make your acquaintance, sir.' Shuffled to chair by fire. During whole visit he was occupied with unsuccessful attempts to light an empty pipe.

'Old age is an extraordinary thing. It makes a man into a shuffling beast, but his mind remains clear as a youth's.'

He noticed my stick near the door and told the boys to put it away. Also a leaf

---

[1] To lecture at Catholic universities.

that had blown in, which he had expelled. He looked hard at Laura and said: 'You are very like your mother, are you not.'

'She is taller.'

'English women are enormous. So are the men – giants.'

'I am short.'

'Are you sir I am no judge.' He could not follow anything said to him, but enjoyed pronouncing the great truths which presumably he ponders. Great zeal over wine – a rarity. 'Wine. What next? A man should drink a bottle a meal, etc.' 'It is a good thing to write poetry. That is the thing to be remembered.' 'Very few poets nowadays.' 'I write poetry constantly, great poetry. Not much at a time.' 'These things are not come by easily.' He lapsed into French, telling a story for whose indelicacy he apologized. He spotted that I didn't understand it. 'Would you rather have two languages, sir, or one.' Conversation trailed off. Complained that Nancy Astor did not ask his wife to dinner. Told Lord Astor dying; couldn't take that in. Still talking of arrogance of the rich. Nothing about religion. 'Sunday? What next?' 'How long have all men dressed alike?' (We were a singularly heterogeneous lot.) 'Is it since the French Revolution?' Attempts to remark on extreme fashions of the Directoire not understood. 'What do they say about Napoleon now? Do they say he was a rascal?' but like jesting Pilate would not stay for an answer. Physical – pleasure in wine, annoyance with pipe. Authentic pleasures few. Showed terrible etching of Beauvais Cathedral with great pride; 'the largest ever made.'

Drove on to Frank and Elizabeth. Floater in coming at all. Mistakenly had thought it more convenient; plainly wrong. Children everywhere. Frank had 'hardened' about his book[1] and said he was sick of it and wasn't going to bother any more, quoting with derision Tony Powell's dilatory and delicate habits of authorship. We both got cross. I overstated the badness of the writing. I said I wasn't shocked at a politician writing like that, but at a don's. It might be work of a second-year undergraduate at BNC. I had in the preceding days taken a physical revulsion of the MS. and couldn't bring myself to touch it. When challenged to find clichés, failed. Left on bad terms and with the feeling that all Frank's protestations of friendship are blarney, and his sense of Catholicism, 'uplift'.

Bombay–Goa,[2] Thursday 18 December 1952

Rose 5.15. Bus came to Taj Hotel and drove in darkness to aerodrome. Sleeping figures on Bombay pavements. In aeroplane some rich Indians on way to Poona villas. English 'geographer' from Bangalore. Arrived Belgaum 9

[1] His autobiography, *Born to Believe*.

[2] Waugh went to Goa, a relic of the Portuguese Empire, for the celebrations of the 400th anniversary of the death of the missionary St Francis Xavier (1506–52), 'Apostle of the Indies', whose body is enshrined there in the church of Bom Jesus.

am. No aerodrome. Merely a level strip of earth bordered by old trees and the atmosphere of a picnic assembled round waiting car and bus. An Indian told me I need not take the train to Goa. A 'luxury' bus was going straight there. We drove in the bus to a little hotel. I asked him the way to lavatory. 'You must use my house.' He led me to minute bungalow in hotel grounds, through an unmade bedroom to a thunderbox. He was the manager of the hotel. At bus station in Belgaum a youth distributed leaflets in English denouncing tyranny of Portuguese rule in Goa. No one paid any attention. Two hours' drive to frontier. Goan youth vomited. Wireless at frontier post and little restaurants. Long puzzle over my passport. New, better bus beyond frontier. Portuguese post very easygoing on control. Booth selling beer and whisky. Drove two hours downhill through jungle. Then a glimpse of Old Goa, a good waterside road to Panjim. Goan youth went out of his way to show me my hotel. Mandovi. Manager out. I was not expected until next day. 5 o'clock hot but not insupportable. Went shopping. Ordered a suit 94 rupees – $6\frac{1}{2}$ guineas. Vainly sought cigars. Currency all Indian. Have not seen Portuguese notes. Hotel small steel and concrete skyscraper with marble enrichments still under construction. Noise inside and outside (where the quay is being built with mechanical drill) appalling. Very weary. Wrote notes to Governor and Patriarch. Early bed with sleeping draught. Sailing ships outside window – dhows from Muscat collecting betel and rice and bringing petrol.

Friday 19 December 1952

At 9 took taxi to Goa. Entered Bom Jesus, full of pilgrims. Tuscan tomb very cramped. Convent adjoining full of pilgrims cooking in the cloisters. Space between B.J. and cathedral full of booths selling refreshments and objects of piety. Great crowds, 25,000 daily, children and women in Indian clothes, men European clothes some with sodality capes. Queues for 'kissing', i.e. veneration of St Francis. On steps of cathedral greeted by priest – Father Ribeno. 'Mr Way?' The Patriarch had driven round Old Goa seeking me. With Ribeno and Mr Merese, half owner, editor, and writer, with his brother, of the single-sheet evening paper. Ribeno showed me Franciscan convent full of pilgrims, remarkably clean, and old Patriarchal Palace adjoining. Some fine rooms and gallery of good painting. Franciscan church occupied by Exposition of Religious Art. Natives still reverence statues, kissing and leaving coins even when in museum. (St Catherine in Bom Jesus has lately had her feet set on a cloud instead of on a Mohammedan.) Veneration of body in cathedral sanctuary, panels removed from silver reliquary, body (now spoken of simply as 'the relics') protruding and one brown stump of toe emerging from white wrapping. Body fully vested, one grey forearm and hand, and grey clay-like skull visible. I postponed my own veneration until I could make it more privately.

Mr Merese drove with me and solicited call at his office – charming wooden verandah. Brother. Woman purchasing festival stamped envelope. Beer, sandwiches. Elderly tieless toothless man Dr Fred Da Sa joined us. He said he spoke all languages perfectly and had saved Gandhi's life by performing illicit operation when in prison. He said, 'All English gentlemen like shooting. You will shoot with me on Sunday. I have a beautiful place with a tennis court.' 'I always miss when I shoot.' 'Then you like pigling?' I took him to mean pig-sticking but he meant sucking pig. He insisted on me and the editors lunching with him on Sunday.

Returned hotel to find Indian Vice-Consul with invitation from Indian Consul-General. I agreed to have tea with him that afternoon. Also humble official, also Da Sa, from Government House to ask if I wanted anything. I said I wanted a car and gave him a copy of *Holy Places*. Heavy siesta. Invitation to lunch next day with Patriarch. Tried on a suit and ordered shirt and pants. 84 rupees. Tea with Indian Consul and wife (broken arm) very elegant and cultured and lonely in Goa. Returned hotel to find Merese again, presenting me with copies of his evening paper containing description of my morning's visit to Goa. All I could read were my own comments. 'Beautiful. Magnificent. Really fine.' Gave him *Campion*.

Da Sa dropped in to present me with a life of Churchill written by himself in Portuguese and to show me W. Churchill's autograph. Then a tremendously boring journalist who wanted to improve his education by asking me my opinion of H. G. Wells as a thinker. I told him C. Sykes and R. Knox were greatest English thinkers. He stayed with me until 9. After dinner Goanese manager of hotel (drunk?) told me he wished to write a book about the theory of politics with special application to Goa. He was well content with the political condition of Goa. Slept well and naturally.

Saturday 20 December 1952

Government car came 6.30. Drove through exquisite cool morning to Goa. Already as crowded as day before though booths not open. Communion in cathedral. Recognized and accosted by bearded Jesuit who led me to head of the queue for 'kissing'. Kissed. Drove back to shave and breakfast. While shaving Da Sa popped in to say, 'All the people in Goa are asking if you have slept well.' Noise absolutely infernal. 11 o'clock to Government House. Brief interview in French with Governor-General. Met many officials including Hindu archivist Pissurlencar. Fine old house.

I should mention all my callers slip into my room without notice. Perhaps they knock but in the hubbub I have no warning of their approach and the door will not fasten.

Lunched at Patriarch's Palace. Patriarch fine-looking spruce alert old man. Archbishop coadjutor there and Bishop of Madura. Three household priests.

Five courses. Five wines including Portuguese champagne. I gave him *Holy Places*. Not impressed. Bishop of Madura rather tight. After lunch straight into chapel and straight downstairs. Uninterrupted siesta. Indian consul sent guide book. White visitors are as rare here as in Ireng country.[1]

Learned that Indian Consul is Christian so left card. Vincent Coelho.

Sunday 21 December 1952

Mass at 8.30 in Panjim Church. Men in choir or porch. Body of church all women and children. At 10 o'clock Merese brothers arrived in car with Jesuit Father Irenere Lobo. Ferry across river. Populous shore of well-kept bungalows. Goans houseproud. These largely residences of absentee servants in Africa or Bombay. Mr Fred Da Sa modest house. Wife and five children. He joined party and we drove to Calangute, stopping on way at prosperous house of Pinto family for beer. They were cousins of Merese and, it transpired, of Lobo too. Visited a fine old Franciscan church and convent now secular priests' house. Wine and compliments. Luncheon prepared with pigling from Da Sa's in rather horrible bathing-beach . . .[2] among half-naked policemen. Father Lobo entirely delightful. He has established a retreat house, one of several, at Baga where strict weekend spiritual exercises include Friday penitential via dolorosa with leader carrying heavy teak cross. Lobo full of smiling goodwill. 'Here we have no courtships. It is all Christian.' The parents arrange the marriage, inquiring about piety, dowry and syphilis. The castes do not intermarry. The husband is usually abroad for most of his life and mother becomes head of household. No divorce. Even under Masonic rule pre-Salazar when divorce was legal very little used.

Siesta and left Lobo returning with Merese 5.50 to find message that car will call for me at 6 to take me to Governor's Palace. Bath, change, drove long distance to seaward to governor's fine villa in park. Picturesque ancient soldiers. Smart ADCs. The rest less smart. The ladies sat in two rows in the centre of the drawing-room with Governor-General's wife at apex. Shook hands with each in turn then led by His Excellency to verandah, given whisky and surrounded by journalists. One rough fellow seizing food, 'The Governor's house is *our* house.' Left at 7. Accosted in hotel by a Mr da Costa, engineer of ancient family. Ostensibly to consult me about his children's education. Sly conceited fellow. Took me out for some 'good coffee' into what proved to be a government-sponsored exhibition. Portuguese products – dentists' chairs, etc. – round a bright square with wireless coming from Albuquerque's statue. Other statue in city is remarkable bronze of Goan (died 1815 in Paris) hypnotizing a woman (check).

[1] The River Ireng, on the border between Brazil and British Guiana; visited by Waugh in 1930.

[2] Illegible.

We sat in café frequented by Portuguese officers and officials. Youth with insolent-pansy manner named Hall. I took a great dislike to him and told da Costa he was probably a deserter from the army. He has married the wife of the Indian C-in-C Capiana. Drank brandy. Boy Hall sat with us ostentatiously *distrait*.

Monday 22 December 1952

By arrangement with Archbishop coadjutor to Old Goa at 9. Tall, bearded, genial, from Azores. He had no interest in antiquities and was indeed visiting many of them for the first time. I gave him, as he gave me, an exhausting day, visiting churches and convents, some ruinous, some under restoration. Wherever we went people darted like carnivorous fish on shoals to kiss his ring. There were groups of dozens, some hundreds from all over India led by their priests. One group of monkey-like figures newly baptized in the jungle. Their priest said: 'Until now they thought there were no Christians except the Fathers. They are greatly surprised.' Well so was I. Fishermen descendants of St Francis's original converts. Ancient pockets from Malabar and Travancore turned out and mixing with every kind of Indian. Collecting water from well where St Francis Xavier is believed to have bathed, touching and kissing every stone and stick. Taking off shoes to venerate weeping crucifix in S. Monica. German 1689 stigmatic. Convent of S. Monica vast and fascinating. Belloc 'Europe and the Faith' my foot. Foiled in attempt to cross river to fine-looking church, part remains Hindu temple. That evening Hall drinking in hotel with Coelho. He invited me to join him after dinner. I did so and found him most engaging. He is bored with Goa, but in his present matrimonial position can't go elsewhere. Da Costa had repeated all my strictures of the previous evening. He took it in good part when I assured him I had indeed made them. We visited an elaborate, empty exhibition of modern art and trades organized by exhausted and disappointed Portuguese from Lisbon.

Canons of Goa only ones in East(?), not much share in celebrations. Old men devoted to Opus Dei. Black cassocks edged red, red stockings.

Tuesday 23 December 1952

Abortive return to Goa in morning. After luncheon Dr Pissurlencar, Hindu archivist, drove me to temples in New Conquests. Mangesh, eighteenth century. Fine tank and courts. Pilgrims' hostel. Wives of children of Brahmins. Inside rather like Turkish baths, marble floor and plump men with towels round their middles. Silver gates, two pairs. God in river shrine barely visible. Nautch girls gliding about inside, not out.

Magesha. Older.

Palace of Rajah of Suridem, pensionary. Well-kept spacious house adjoining Temple of Peace.

ShantaDurga. Sacred trees. And sweet-smelling shrub in pedestal, also in gardens.

All temples similar plan. Always ornamental cart for procession.

Siroda [?]. Formerly village of half-caste whores. They have now all moved to Bombay according to Pissurlencar.

Back via Ponda. Military centre black and white troops, early bed and dope at 4.

Christmas Eve 1952

Slept late and spent morning writing these notes. Fast.

A very dark priest appeared at 6 with a resonant unintelligible voice to show me an apologetic work he has composed directed to the Hindus. I rashly said I could not read Portuguese so he expounded it to me.

Poor children given a small loaf of bread and biscuit and four sweets at church. 5.30.

A Dr Rego has announced his intention of calling. I have ordered another suit as the insidious red dust covers everything. Dr Rego called to apologize for not asking me to his house.

Statue of Abade Faria hypnotist erected 1945. By Goan sculptor in Bombay.

Midnight Mass in cathedral densely crowded. I hot and weary was given a fine armchair in the chancel among nuns, priors and St F.X. himself, but communion later too difficult. I had brought four servants from the hotel and lost one. Gave the surviving three beer in a booth.

Christmas Day 1952

Very hot and airless. Call from journalist and government official. Otherwise lonely and torpid. Town very quiet. A few paper lanterns and firecrackers, paper flowers, sweets. Pleasant to escape holly and mistletoe.

Goan servants, silent, smiling quickly, nervous brown fingers playing chess with the salt and pepper.

No map of India except wall-map.

Bookshop: detective stories and popular rationalist education. No English religious books.

Friday 26 December 1952

Woke up feeling fine and whisked Renato Da Sa, abject jagger, off for drive. English cemetery disappointing. Goan cemetery remarkable for graves of the freethinkers – two of them: a judge, died twelve years ago, marked by boulder; a disciple by classical stone. Nearby a heretical Syrian with cross. Drove to Santanna. No invention in Portuguese seventeenth-century façades. But a fine church finely placed in what was once a populous place, now uninhabited. Da Sa asked whether I thought the BBC would present a translation of his life of

Winston. He could not understand that they would be more likely to take something about Goa. Winston seemed to him more topical and popular subject. Dined with Coelho. Evening dress obligatory. Dr Rego and elegant cosmopolitan wife and another couple I have met before. Pro-Indians?

Saturday 27 December 1952

To Margao with Pissurlencar. Tedious wait at river crossing. No great interest in drive. He talked a great deal about Brahmins. Drove back with Chief Justice who seemed to command no awe among people. That night I tried to go to Hall's bar, but found the square given over to a ball in aid of lepers.

Sunday 28 December 1952

Mass and communion in room over Central Café. 8.30 *Herald* editor Prazeres da Costa (deformed hand) and small son drove me across river Bicholim.

Sanguem, Valpoi, Ponda. Great change from Old to New Conquests. We called on the only nobleman – a gunner major in tumbledown house next door to temple (hideous). Building new house, delayed by demand for skilled labour in iron mines. Da Costa provided a picnic, red wine, sardines, bully beef, which we ate in a deserted barracks. He said Hindus 100 per cent pro-Indian, Christians 50–50, African Goans pro-Portuguese. Bombay doubtful. Editor of *Times of India* Goan. In 1947 twenty to thirty agitators were arrested and liberated in Portugal. Must ask whether Goa used for African agitators. I chose this jaunt in preference to climbing 4,000 steps for a good view with Merese.

Monday 29 December 1952

Hotel full of Indians and showing strain. Went to Old Goa to see exhibition of ecclesiastical art. Still shut.

Goanese now insist on being called Goans. When I first became aware of their existence twenty-two years ago they insisted that they were predominantly Portuguese. Now all insist that they are pure Indian. They have no idea of the horrors of Hitler's or Stalin's regime and recount as a great cruelty the mild Portuguese rule of law.

The bookshop here, Hindu-kept, has three-quarters books in English, no Catholic writers. All popular sex psychology and old rationalists.

Spitting and knife-waving professor from Bombay came to luncheon with me. Later drove to island Divar with Merese and ate sweets with his mother-in-law.

Priest, about the queue system introduced this year: 'The people are becoming a little more civilized through queueing for rations.'

Mysore, Monday 5 January 1953

I awoke wondering whether to have my moustache removed and after breakfast was accosted by ancient barber whom I accepted as an omen. He practically shaved my head and manipulated my spine and squeezed my skull. Was less happily treated by tedious student guide. Drove wth him to Somnathpur, deserted thirteenth-century temple, returned by Chamundi Hill, where fine huge seventeenth-century bull. After luncheon drove to Seringapatam. The mausoleum of Hyder Ali and Tipu Sultan and Tipu's summer palace are exactly like Brighton Pavilion. Many youths begging, saying they are students. I scolded one and then thought of Igantius in Paris – too late to make amends. Am taking taxi to Belur tomorrow. Manager of Tourist Bureau (and editor local paper) insists on my taking his son with me.

Taxi controversy as follows: first I take hotel station-waggon to Government Tourist Bureau (Mr Swamy) to enquire about facilities Belur and Halebid. Then I engage same driver to take me there. After luncheon Swamy appears and says how much am I paying. I say I don't know but presume hotel rates. Swamy says station-waggon more expensive than taxi. He goes away and returns with son and taxi to say that hotel waggon costs 12 annas a mile. His taxi 8. His son will accompany me free. I must take taxi. I agree and tell waggon-driver this. He says he has beautiful new car he can let me have for 8 annas. We drive to his garage and go to Seringapatam in beautiful new car which is very uncomfortable. My heart sinks at prospect of long day in it but I stick to bargain. After dinner Swamy arrives in great stealth and agitation to say it has come to knowledge of police that hotel driver has no licence for beautiful new car. I shall be in danger from police if I go in it he warns. I send him away.

Tuesday 6 January 1953

I start for Mass at 6 in b.n.c. Swamy's taxi follows. A hundred yards down road police stop car and arrest driver. I walk to Mass followed by Swamy's car offering services. At end of Mass my driver arrives in waggon. He will take me in waggon for 8 annas. At breakfast Swamy's son arrives. I send him away. My driver has to go to court, so deputy takes me. I thus have every advantage: a comfortable car for the price of an uncomfortable one and the company of a driver with no pretensions to English.

Twelve-hour day 7.30–7.30. First to Sravanabelagola, two hills like immense smooth grey boulders lying on the green, dun and chocolate plate. Both have temples on summits. Great tank in village and pilgrim hostels. The larger hill has the colossal statue of Gomateshwara fifty-foot-high single stone. Up smooth face of hill, six hundred cut steps with two arches. Shoes off. Ascent in wicker chair on shoulders of bearers. Very uncomfortable. The colossus was under repair and surrounded with scaffolding which I climbed painfully in stockinged feet.

Then via Hassan, where fair in progress, to Belur, arriving at noontime rest and everything locked and people said they did not open to Moslems and Christians. It then transpired that my car was Moslem-owned. Hence the Hindu hostility. Walked round temple. Mass of carving as fine as ivory chess men. Gods, dancing girls, and usual friezes of Amazons, elephants. Thence to neighbouring Halebid. Almost identical. Hoysaleshwara, thirteenth-century. Some pilgrims there and place open. The inner shrines, two, in the centre of all this froth of carving contain each a single stone cylindrical object on an altar, like biscuit box on . . .[1] or one of knobs on quays. Phallic? Then back to Mysore through Hassan now densely crowded.

Memory of road dust, huge trees with ash grey trunks, monkeys, flamingoes(?) a few brilliant birds, ox cart, women with baskets.

Bangalore, Wednesday 7 January 1953

Wasted morning waiting for permission to see Maharajah's palace. Afternoon train back to Bangalore.

Madura, Thursday 8 January 1953

Early start, circuitous flight to Madura arriving 12.30, cloud and some rain. No hotel. Stayed in 'Retiring Room' at station. 'Gentlemen's Waiting Room' had 'Gentle' painted out and 'Upper Class' substituted. Took tricycle rickshaw to call on bishop who was away in Madras but Jesuits friendly and one Visuvasam offered services as guide. That evening I walked round huge temple by electric light. Tenth-century sculpture greatly inferior to Mysore thirteenth-century, but size impressive and vivacity of beggars, students, fortune tellers, shop keepers, etc.

Friday 9 January 1953

Father Visuvasam came in car and took me over temple in detail. Obscene sculptures very small and unobtrusive. Many of statues had grubby aprons – innovation. Elaborate code of *post hoc* symbolic explanations. Law courts, former palace, very dull. Tanks. Vegetarian luncheon at bishop's house. Then to tea with aged Christian historian-statesman now in obscurity. Horrible Swiss photographer. Then we visited slums, cinema. Teetotal meals in station expensive and very poor. Old bearded priest came to visit me late at night. Christian 'matron' wanted Goa water for stomach, gave her handkerchief.

Trivandrum, Saturday 10 January 1953

Strolled about city. Left for Trivandrum 1420 arrived there in an hour.

[1] Illegible.

Modern red-roofed town with well-kept gardens. Very hot. No drink. Unsuccessful attempts to talk to secretary European club.

Bangalore, Sunday 11 January 1953

After Mass went to visit Mgr. Ivanios who was finishing his Mass. Immensely aged since I met him in 1930. Reported insane proclaiming fourth member of Trinity but he seemed lucid. Dreary visit to College. Returned Bangalore by air.

Monday 12 January 1953

Dull half-day in Bombay, bought trinkets for children. Aeroplane – Australian – 'hostess' seemed hoyden after Indian girls. Three hours' delay at Karachi.

Rome, Tuesday 13 January 1953

Little sleep. Arrived Rome 3. Sight not seeing tour. Returned to learn that flight was off because of fog. Poor Alfred's[1] wedding. Slept Plaza Hotel, dined Russells.

Wednesday 14 January 1953

Early arrival aerodrome. Told further twenty-four hours delay. Took train. Oh the pleasure of sleeper and wagon restaurant after air.

London, Thursday 15 January 1953

Arrived London by Golden Arrow. If I had stayed in Rome I should have been able to fly and return home that evening. My regrets at missing my children were allayed by a telephone call. Mrs Harper assured me that they were all at Stinchcombe still in quarantine for mumps. Dined Pratt's and talked to Randolph at White's.

Piers Court, Friday 16 January 1953

A warm day in London. Saw Peters. The editor of *Good Housekeeping* tried to dun me for an advance. My Goan article unpublished. My story unsold in America. Went to an exhibition of pitiable modern 'sculpture' illustrating the theme of an unknown political prisoner. Home by train. Met by Laura and Margaret.[2] Cheerful dinner.

Saturday 17 January 1953

Margaret left. Mary[3] arrived. A busy morning opening and answering letters.

[1] Alfred Duggan.
[2] Waugh's daughter.
[3] Waugh's mother-in-law.

Sunday 18 January 1953

Bitter cold. Mary left, after luncheon with James.[1] I had half remembered a cut[2] in a set of Canova's Works which might be adapted to decorate *Love Among the Ruins*. With dazzling eyes and a magnifying glass and razor blade I attempted adaption.

Monday 19 January 1953

More letters to write. Persuaded Downside to take Bron back. Bitter cold. Tried to be genial. Correspondence mostly demands for speeches.

Tuesday 20 January 1953

Bron and Teresa left. We set out to motor to Bath and Downside but motor broke and Laura proceeded in small taxi. I read. Jack McDougall's sister-in-law suicide.

Wednesday 2 January 1953

Paid out £1,300 in cheques which only include a fraction of tax due. Eric Linklater sent me his new book. Reading old weeklies to catch up with news.

Thursday 22 January 1953

Bitter cold. Letters. Linklater's book. Clare[3] made ambassador Rome.

Tuesday 27 January 1953

Warmer but dark all day. I eat less and less and drink little but get no thinner. I try to work and have completed some collages from Moses's engravings after Canova which, if they can be reproduced, will be amusing and ornamental and should determine the form of *Love Among the Ruins*. By the time I have written my letters the papers come and when I have read them it is nearly noon so I do little work before luncheon and then don't get out after luncheon and then have tired eyes by 8 o'clock and don't want to sit up reading and not sleepy so take drugs at 11. A flaw somewhere. I suggested to Mother St Paul that Harriet should remain here this term if they would remit her fees. The nuns leaped at it, remarking that many little girls at the school are terrified of her.

Thursday 5 February 1953

Succeeded in preventing Salmen [?] and his wife of Little Brown, Boston, from coming here at the price of visiting them in London, I to give him

[1] Waugh's son.
[2] Engraving.
[3] Clare Boothe Luce, wife of Henry Luce, the head of *Time Inc*.

luncheon at White's, Laura to entertain her at the Hyde Park Hotel. I had pictures to fetch – Augustus Egg's *Afternoon in the Rain* and the *Pleasures of Travel* trio[1] reframed – so we went by car driven by Prothero. An early start in bitter cold. St James's Club where I had an appointment with Mr Thrusal of Cambridge who is a model of punctilio but can't make shoes. Well, I prefer punctilio. Saw Willy Teeling who told me Eden looks worn out, had a very poor reception at a private Tory meeting and might resign that afternoon on Formosa. Discussed indecent artefacts with Leigh Ashton. Then to two shops and White's where Salmen already sat like a guinea pig. Drank a lot. Luncheon saved by Cyril Connolly who joined us. We – Laura and I – then drove to Highgate to see my mother who was alert but very weak indeed – alarmingly so. Drove to Winkfield to dine with Angie. Emma, a very pretty girl, licks the pug's tongue. Fine wine; a drive of awful cold. Home at 1 o'clock.

Friday 6 February 1953

Weary and shaken by the day before.

Saturday 7 February 1953

The proofs arrived of the collages' enlarged plates for *Love Among the Ruins*. I anticipate happy hours at work on them.

London, Friday 13 February 1953

A cold happy week. Trim and Anne Oxford came to luncheon; otherwise saw no one. Went to London early train and straight to White's where started drinking with Ed Stanley, Ran Antrim, etc. Lunched with Jack McDougall at Brooks's, continued drinking all afternoon with a break to discuss Queen Anne Press with Harling[2] but too tight to make much sense. Went to cocktail party given by *Life* magazine to show off their new office. I had decided to go as a means of making friends with them. I don't think I can have achieved my object. Went to dinner with Diana in an oyster restaurant. No memories of the evening.

Saturday 14 February 1953

Woke early, thirsty. Went out to Highgate to call on my mother. Stayed an hour. Back to confession at Farm Street and White's. Late afternoon train to Robertsbridge to stay with Lady Curzon, Alfred and his bride. Bodiam a small house in the castle park sumptuously furnished with the remains of Montacute,

[1] *The Pleasures of Travel 1751* and *The Pleasures of Travel 1851* by Thomas Musgrave Joy illustrated the benefits of the replacement of the stage coach by the train; Waugh commissioned a third painting, *The Pleasures of Travel 1951*, by Richard Eurich, RA, which depicted alarmed passengers inside an aircraft about to crash.
[2] Robert Harling; typographer, magazine editor, and author of *The Paper Palace*.

Hackwood, Carlton House Terrace. Good food, excellent wine. I have the impression of a genial evening. Some people came in later. I don't know who.

Sunday 15 February 1953

Sobering down. Rather ill. Mass. Lady Milner and an old pansy came to luncheon. Cold; snow. Drove to Harold Nicolson's for tea. Back to entertain starving young publisher Hardinge and wife.

Piers Court, Monday 16 February 1953

Early train. White's until time to come home. Weary.

Shrove Tuesday 1953

Randolph and June[1] came to luncheon. Very good luncheon.

Ash Wednesday 1953

Ashes. Proofs. Resolved to give up opiates for Lent.

Writing at Stinchcombe, Monday 16 March 1953

Have abandoned resolution to give up narcotics and am giving up wine instead (since yesterday).

Lent began well. I wrote first pages of novel,[2] very good too. White's in an air raid. Then the fog closed in and my chimney smoked and I wrote a review of Tito's book and corrected proofs and fiddled with the collages for *Love Among the Ruins* which are becoming more and more my own work.

Downed tools on March 4th and drove to Mells. Fog and cold. Laura took me to Downside where on water and uneatable fish I was called to address some scattered yawning boys in a science lecture room on the subject of Tito, which has already become tedious to me. Then to a parlour where the stove failed to give heat, to drink whisky which I hate and chat to boys who smoked cigarettes and drank sherry. My taxi was three-quarters of an hour late and the monks eager to be rid of me. At last I reached Mells hungry, cold, and too full of whisky and sat up till nearly 2 with Trim, getting warm and drinking more whisky. Much extra business going on – a solicitor and agent about the place.

Next day felt ill. Bron came over. Tedium in spite of great sweetness of Asquiths. Took him to revolting unfunny film in Frome and then off.

One night at home and then by early train with Laura to London. A very cosy White's day – all friends there. Took Laura to *Woman of No Importance*, charmingly staged and acted.

The next morning, train to Glasgow – clean, hot. Good heavy luncheon.

[1] Second wife of Randolph Churchill.
[2] *Officers and Gentlemen.*

Arrived torpid at 6.30 met by a friar and three well-intentioned natives. Hasty bath and cast my underclothes. To dinner, without appetite, in a clearly very expensive and smart restaurant where my hosts were ill at ease. Heat oppressive and noise made me deaf. Later taken to a hotter and noisier drinking den named 'Press Club'. Drunk woman kept saying, 'Oh are you *really* Evelyn Waugh? I am so frightened of you.' The reception committee had planned a drinking bout but I slipped back early.

Next day March 8th I had a quiet morning, walking to Mass, then writing the opening paragraphs of my oration. A dozen fried oysters. The meeting was at 3. A great hall densely crowded with an overflow in a basement – well over 3,000 who had paid to come. As Archbishop (Campbell) was speaking, the loudspeaking apparatus broke. I was in despair but it started again before he had finished. The whole thing was well planned. My speech was not bad and the audience was sympathetic. Colm Brogan spoke too. Then we went to the CTS shop to drink. I was given £20 which more than covered my fares and hotel. (I had just got £185 prize too, free of tax.) An old man assured me that Eden was the Grand Master of the Grand Orient and had been responsible for the murder of the Archduke at Sarajevo. A solicitor then took charge of me. I was hungry by now and ate a good dinner (having refused to make a second lecture to the university students) and sleeping train to London.

Monday 9 March 1953

Arrived early in London, breakfast and shave. Then to Chapman & Hall's office for a two-hour consultation with the printer about the layout of *Love Among the Ruins*. He gave me a charming old type catalogue. Then with Jack to White's, Brooks's, White's again, drinking cheerfully. Met Laura at the train, drank a little more in the tea car and returned tired out and a little tight.

Most of this week has been spent recovering while Laura sickened with 'flu. In London I wrote to Muggeridge to ask if he would print an article declaring Tito to be a woman. He telegraphed back he would. I wrote it; not very well. He hedged and said it must appear after Tito leaves, so I am cancelling it.

On Thursday a very decent reporter came to interview me for the *Sunday Chronicle* on the subject of Tito. He told me that the security police are appalled at the task before them and insist on a bullet-proof car, a secret residence, a secret list of engagements. The Duke of Norfolk has been prodded into presenting a remonstrance. Sick as I am of the affair, the politicians must be sicker. He comes by sea and already has cost us three aircraft who showed off to him at Gibraltar.

Yesterday I finished the decorations for *Ruins* and am now clearing decks for action to get my novel finished before I start for Argentine in September.

Wednesday 1 April 1953

Spy Wednesday.[1] Children arriving home. I went to Downside. My life lately has been so solitary that the Holy Week retreat is no longer the refreshment it used to be. A rather cantankerous Jesuit gave the conferences. The weather was severe. An American–Jewish convert named Milton Waldman attached himself to me.

On Saturday 4th I dined at Mells with Chris Hollis; returned Easter Day. The Gregorian Society elected me a member. I was greatly pleased.[2]

London, Wednesday 8 April 1953

I had to get my hair cut so went to London taking Bron and Teresa for the day. Lunched at Wilton's.

Piers Court, Thursday 9 April 1953

To Midsomer Norton where —— has been most dilatory. Agnes and I interviewed him and received a promise of immediate action. The house had failed to sell at £3,000. I instructed him to accept any offer over £2,000. Paid a final visit to the house without emotion. Collected a few objects and papers. Margaret greatly enjoyed herself among the oddments.

London, Thursday 16 April 1953

To London with Laura for the first night of Graham's[3] play, *The Living Room*. Champagne first at Claridge's. Odd party – Korda, Eddie Sackville-West, Matthew Smith, Barbara Rothschild. Went to play in high spirits which the performance failed to dispel. More champagne between acts. With result that I was rather inattentive to the final scene which presumably contained the point of the whole sad story. On reflection I felt the tone was false. The piety of the old Catholic ladies wasn't piety. The tragic love of the heroine wasn't tragic; her suicide clumsy. But as I didn't listen to the last ten minutes it is not fair to judge.

Eddie, Chris Hollis, Raymond Mortimer and someone dined with us afterwards.

Chantilly, Friday 17 April 1953

To Paris. I did not know it, but the Golden Arrow has been changed to a late afternoon train. At Calais there was one crowded first-class coach attached to the sleeping-car train. Could not get luncheon until 3. By that time faint with hunger. Drank a bottle of burgundy and a glass of brandy and felt better. Was

[1] Wednesday before Good Friday.

[2] Waugh's grandfather, Dr Alexander Waugh, the doctor of Downside Abbey and School, had been the first Protestant elected to the Gregorian Society (of Downside old boys).

[3] Graham Greene's.

met at Paris by Diana, Juliet Duff and her boy. Drove to Chantilly. Exhaustion and wine confused me. Found Duff and Rupert Hart-Davis.[1] No dinner. A tiny sandwich and a lot of drink. Then a circus (with Communist Chinese performers). I was overcome by exhaustion and wine and left half-way through. Finally dinner at midnight.

Saturday 18 April 1953

Heatwave. Weary, Pattens,[2] Flemings, IsaIah Berlin[3] to luncheon.
was going to London on Tuesday. Duff had alarming outburst of rage and hate.

Sunday 19 April 1953

Heatwave. Weary, Pattens,[2] Flemings, Isaiah Berlin[3] to luncheon.

Monday 20 April 1953

Chantilly. Wretched.

Paris, Tuesday 21 April 1953

Paris. Luncheon Frank and Kitty Giles.[4] Nice Americans – Joyce – and horrible Italian Jews. Called on Momo at Ritz at 7. Dined alone Quai d'Orsay. Horrible night in horrible room at 69 Rue de Lille.

Wednesday 22 April 1953

Telephone from 9 am. Fled to Ritz. Train to Versailles. Luncheon with Nancy[5] who is there to complete work on Pompadour. Drove round park in expensive fiacre, rough grass, newly planted trees, public works on the water pipes – awfully ugly. Back to Travellers to drink with Mary Ormsby-Gore's husband. Then dinner at Gileses. Tony Rumbold.

Thursday 23 April 1953

Day of complete rest between Travellers and Ritz. Dined Momo.

Chantilly, Friday 24 April 1953

Norwiches[6] returned. Much against my will I had agreed to return to Chantilly to help them with Douglas Fairbanks who was guest of honour for St George's dinner. He and awfully boring wife arrived Saturday. Also Gileses.

---

[1] Publisher; his mother was Duff Cooper's sister.
[2] Bill Patten, an attaché at the US Embassy, and his wife, Susan Mary.
[3] The Oxford political philosopher.
[4] *The Times* correspondent in Paris and his wife.
[5] Mitford.
[6] Duff Cooper was created 1st Viscount Norwich at the end of the war.

Sunday 26 April 1953

Large luncheon party – mostly Americans. Norwiches had left Fairbankses to find own hotel rooms after St George's dinner.

London, Monday 27 April 1953

Returned by night ferry. My dreariest trip abroad since Christopher and I went to Paris together.

Piers Court, Tuesday 28 April 1953

Signed *edition de luxe* of *Love Among Ruins* at Chapman & Hall. Printing defective. Luncheon at Marlborough Club with Jack and May, his daughter just half-blinded, an awful optician peer Charnwood, Teresa and Mme Bisch – Edith de Born – bright gushing Belgian. Home and very pleased to be there.

Much letter-answering. Disquieting news that Treasury are still pursuing 1945 MGM payments and have won case in court.

Sir Winston new KG exemplified liberal chivalry by stating that it is better to be bribed than to be killed.

Margaret had a friend to stay – a dull little girl called Julia Whyte. I exhausted myself in efforts to be agreeable.

Monday 4 May 1953

They left. Fine spell. Flowers coming out. All the printing of the *edition de luxe* has had to be condemned. So much for the amiable printer who gave me album of types.

Wednesday 20 May 1953

Margaret's letters from school piteous. I began to make enquiries about another convent for her and on 23rd visited Lechlade – children happy, education poor, fees barely lower than Les Oiseaux [?]. To tea after with Jungmans. Their destitution has been greatly exaggerated.

Saturday 30 May 1953

Daughters returned for Coronation holiday. Downside was sterner. Teresa brought charming friend Annabel Hennessy. They remained until Corpus Christi June 4th. Grave talks with Margaret persuaded Laura and me to withdraw her from Westgate and to send both her and Hattie to Ascot next term.

On Sunday 31st Miss St John Mildmay told Laura that 'the village' resented our lack of decorations. I devised a triumphal arch with our curved lion on top which Robinson erected next day. That day, Monday, we gave a cocktail party for the Dursley Dramatic Society and some of the village. The Silver Band played and got very drunk. The children, both ours, Donaldsons, and Annabel, behaved admirably.

Coronation day. Mass. Then great upheaval providing fancy dresses and decorating the mare and cart. Cold and windy but no rain. Sports. After dinner elder children drove with Donaldsons looking at bonfires.

Wednesday 3 June 1953

Susan Mary Patten arrived. Gala dinner.[1]

Thursday 4 June 1953

Children dispersed. Day devoted to Susan Mary. Gloucester Cathedral, Stanway where Letty and Benson were just returned from Coronation full of funny stories about coronets. Saw house. Early dinner at Stratford and Redgrave's performance of *Antony and Cleopatra* not all it is cracked up to be.

My book getting foully offensive reviews from Beaverbrook press.

Friday 5 June 1953

Susan Mary left. Settled down to recuperation and work but disturbed by (*a*) summons from Frank for dinner in praise of Father Corbishley (*b*) Graham Greene proposing himself for visit. When I accepted Frank's invitation I supposed dinner to be in Oxford. It proved to be in London which enabled me to study Victorian paintings and meet Reynolds, curator of Sheepshanks bequest. White's full of Americans.

Graham came June 12th. He is full of theatrical projects but, it seemed, in an unhappy state. He told the Italian ambassador, as excuse for not visiting conference at Florence, that he was 'no longer a practising Catholic'. He asked for a biscuit before Mass as though to provide (like his hero in *Heart of the Matter*) a reason for not taking communion, but went off to early train fasting on Monday. He told me the plot of his new play is a priest who 'sacrifices' his faith in order to restore a boy to life. But very sweet and modest. Always judging people by kindness.

Francis Howard dined Saturday. Donaldsons Sunday. Much champagne drunk.

I have accepted an invitation for Laura and Margaret and myself to Belton out of compassion for bereaved, lonely, ageing Perry to whom I am indebted for so much gay hospitality in the years before I married.

Some kind reviews of *Love among the Ruins*. Mostly positively abusive.

[1] 'Laura was wearing a ball dress and a tiara, Evelyn a white tie and decorations. . . . Evelyn announced that I would give a speech describing the Coronation. . . . Of course I had been nowhere near the Abbey.' Susan Mary Alsop, *To Marietta from Paris, 1945–1960* (London, 1976), p. 225.

No work done except one review. Everyone eagerly on the watch for failing powers.

Friday 1 January 1954

8 o'clock Mass in Dursley. We arrived at the end of the epistle. Sunless morning, white frost. There is no rejoicing on feast days in England. No best clothes. Simply cold early rising, annoyance at children being late. A day all indoors. Writing letters, reading papers and weekly reviews, dozing, drinking gin to induce good temper. Read Max Beerbohm aloud.

Saturday 2 January 1954

News of Duff's sudden death in Vigo Bay. My last words with Diana, when she telephoned to say goodbye, were sharp.

Clocks barely moving. Has half an hour past? no five minutes.[1]

Curious illusion (comparable to Maurice Bowra's recent vision in Ashmolean of Hughes's *Home from the Sea*) in connection with the Burges-Poynton wash-handstand given me by John Betjeman. When I examined it at Patrick Kinross's house in Warwick Avenue I saw and handled an ornamental serpentine bronze pipe which led from the dragon's head in the tank to the bowl below. It arrived here lacking this member. I protested to Pickford's and wrote to Patrick to confirm its previous existence. He replied: 'Missing member in post. Blame me not Pickford's.' I accordingly apologized to Pickford's only to receive, delayed by Christmas presents, a kind of zinc funnel. I wrote to John asking him to confirm that there should be the pipe I saw. He has replied that it never existed. Either I have suffered a complete delusion or I saw the pipe as originally designed by Burges. The latter seems more probable if the dragon's head tap is meant to be practicable.

Sunday 3 January 1954

Church again. My prayer is now only, 'Here I am again. Show me what to do; help me do it.' My dispute with Roper[2] in the *New Statesman* becomes tediously pedantic.

London, Monday 4 January 1954

Intense cold at Kemble station, where I took the train to London with Bron and Teresa for their Christmas treat. Bron is staying the night with me at the Hyde Park Hotel; Teresa, Laura and Margaret at Auberon's house. I gave them luncheon at the Ritz, joined by Jack McDougall, had my hair cut, saw Mr Stopp the Cambridge critic who is going to write my 'life'.[3] He is earnest,

[1] These three sentences exactly reproduce the MS.
[2] Hugh Trevor-Roper, Regius Professor of Modern History at Oxford.
[3] Frederick J. Stopp, *Evelyn Waugh: Portrait of an Artist*, London, 1958.

Germanic, bald. Back to Hyde Park Hotel to find Laura and small children already assembled. Tedious and complicated arrangements for dressing and dispersing to various entertainments. At White's Auberon's green cheese moon face. He had joined Cooper's corpse in the aeroplane and apparently forgotten that he had lent his house to my family. I took three children to Freda's party, round dances well organized by professionals, left them for dinner at Pratt's and returned later. Drank a terrible champagne named Bourgeois Père et Fils. Slightly tight. Returned to Carol and Pempy Reed's and then saw Bron home.

Tuesday 5 January 1954

Feeling ill, whether solely because of Freda's wine unable to say. White's morning full of fun. The obituaries treat Cooper as a mixture of Fox, Metternich, Rochester, and the Iron Duke. Ed Stanley told me that Diana was desperately seeing everyone she could. Sent her note by his hand. He told me later that she said she hadn't the patience to open it as I had showered her with letters of condolence beginning 'My dear Diana' and signed 'Yours sincerely, Evelyn Waugh'. However she did open this and was enchanted because I wrote 'Darling Baby – Bo',[1] and immediately telephoned asking me to come and see her next day (funeral day). Lunched at St James's with Alfred Duggan and Tony Powell. I tried desperately to arrange an adolescents' dinner for Freda's second party. Pakenhams seemed safe. One acceptance: Frank himself, whose motive as later transpired was to enlist my support for his candidature as Belloc's biographer.[2] I think he would be worse than anyone. Dinner at Hyde Park. Freda's dance not so well organized as the children's party. She and daughter doing no introductions. It seemed Teresa would have no partners until I captured an angelic woman called Lady Ronaldshay and her sister who had numerous sons and nephews. I left her in their charge and visited White's, returned to collect them.

Wednesday 6 January 1954

Mass at Brompton Oratory. Visited Diana in the morning. Found her in John Julius's[3] dressing-room. Susan Mary ('I am wearing this red hat because Diana has a thing about mourning. I have a black one downstairs.') and Kitty Giles. Juliet Duff popping in and out and taking swigs of vodka. She had written off her own bat to ask Winston and Bobbity[4] to read the lessons at memorial service; Diana appalled first telephoned Lady Churchill to disclaim all responsibility. Next to Lord Salisbury and without giving him a chance to

---

[1] 'Bo' was a Waugh nickname originating with the Lygon family in the early 1930s.
[2] Lord Longford denies (February 1976) that he wanted to write Belloc's biography.
[3] Lady Diana's son; the 2nd Viscount Norwich.
[4] The 4th Marquess of Salisbury.

speak poured out endless apologies. 'Of course I should never have thought of asking you . . . the last person . . . etc.' Only when she had to stop for breath did she learn that he thought the suggestion highly appropriate and longed to comply. I had an hour alone with Diana. She was very wild and witty, full of funny stories – Paul- Louis's[1] wreath mistaken for the President of France's, etc.

Plans. Rome, Madrid, Tangier, Athens. 'Must keep nomadic.' A feeling of 'Home they brought her warrior dead.' Contemptuous annoyance at letters of condolence and offers of help. Eager to drive John Julius out of Foreign Office. Intention to live on capital in England. When I left, Juliet, who had popped in for vodka, sent after me. A hoarse whisper: 'Pray for my poor Duffy.'

In order to pick up Ronnie[2] at Swindon we travelled by slow train. Intense cold. Ronnie very amiable and news of Katharine good.

Piers Court, Thursday 7 January 1954

Intense cold. Sat like hibernating badger all day. Donaldsons to dine.

Friday 8 January 1954

Intense cold. Mass. Ordered central heating and donned woollen underclothes.

Saturday 9 January 1954

Intense cold but house warm. Ronnie and Laura and older children left yesterday.

Sunday 10 January 1954

Frost breaking. Comatose.

Monday 11 January 1954

Wet and chilly but no frost. Hollises to luncheon. Chris seeking information about Holy Land and Holy Places. Wrote final letter in Roper controversy.

In the second half of January 1954 Waugh left England on the voyage to Ceylon that produced the hallucinations described in *The Ordeal of Gilbert Pinfold*. On balance, it seems more likely that he kept a diary of the voyage – which was his usual, though not invariable, custom – and later destroyed it, than that he did not keep one at all. The existing MS has no entry between January 1954 and June 1955.

---

[1] Paul-Louis Weiler, Alsatian millionaire.
[2] Ronald Knox.

Monday 20 June 1955

Thomas Pakenham[1] came for the night at his invitation, brought by Dick Girouard's son, Mark.[2] He is a handsome lad marred by spots, awkward in manner, painfully self-assertive. Girouard outshone him, recognizing Burges's wash-handstand as soon as he saw it, and exhibiting remarkable knowledge of English nineteenth-century art. Both boys refused champagne saying they were surfeited with it. I sent them off to bed early as Thomas bored me.

Tuesday 21 June 1955

A telephone message at breakfast: could Miss Spain and Lord Noel-Buxton of the *Daily Express* come to call. They were told not to. I loosed the boys into the library and got rid of them before luncheon. That evening at 7.45 a hullabaloo at the front door. Miss Spain and Lord Noel-Buxton were there trying to force an entry. I sent them away and remained tremulous with rage all the evening.

Wednesday 22 June 1955

And all next day.

London, Thursday 23 June 1955

I went to London by the breakfast train – the first time for many weeks. Straight to Trumper's to get my hair cut – Thomas Pakenham's tousled mop had made me conscious of my own – then to Chapman & Hall's to send out copies of *Officers and Gentlemen*. Owing to the railway strike this has been left too late. I should have sent inscribed copies to Mortimer, Nicolson, Betjeman, etc., weeks earlier. Jack McDougall took me to luncheon at Brooks's where I was shown two columns in the *Express* describing her[3] escapade of Tuesday. It lays her open to ridicule. I sent a message to Muggeridge asking whether he would like a reply in *Punch* and he said: yes. Tried on clothes in Albemarle Street, then, weary, took refuge in White's where I sat until 7 drinking and talking to a succession of friends – mostly to Randolph who, fiery with whisky, poured out the story hitherto unknown to me of——'s adultery with——, how the butler photographed them in the act, how —— attempted suicide and was evacuated by —— with a stomach pump. All this during the time that —— was supposedly pregnant by him. I had an invitation to meet Cardinal Gracias at the Indian Embassy but preferred Randolph's wild denunciations. Dinner with Ann Fleming. Nigel Birch[4] the only other guest. He was one of the cronies I had just left at White's. We had said all we had to say to one another. Great exhaustion came on me early but I slept extremely ill.

[1] Frank Pakenham's eldest son.
[2] Later Slade Professor of Fine Art at Oxford.
[3] Nancy Spain's.
[4] Conservative MP.

Piers Court, Friday 24 June 1955

I spent the morning drinking in White's. Lunched at Brooks's again with Jack McDougall. Jack Donaldson was there. Back to White's with him, more drinking. To the train. More drinking in the train. Rather drunk and very weary. Home, to find many letters, among them a request from Tom Driberg to come next day with a photographer.

Saturday 25 June 1955

Driberg and photographers came and spent most of the day here. I said to Laura: 'Very soon, perhaps the next time I write a book, I shall be humiliated by the lack of interest shown and shall look back on these as years of plenty.'

Sunday 26 June 1955

Late Mass. Delayed hangover from London. I wrote the essay on Lord Noel-Buxton for *Punch*. Reading Quennell's *Hogarth's Progress*, a perfunctory work obsessed by prostitution. Q. imputes debauchery to Hogarth with the slightest evidence. His huge, efficient output alone proclaims him a temperate man. I am saying so in a review for *Time and Tide*.

Monday 27 June–Wednesday 29 June 1955

Delicious weather. Laura in the hayfields. An invitation for the weekend from the Heads, to dinner from Lord Kemsley.[1] The latter is very rum as I have never met him. A poignant hope that this might mean the Kemsley Literary Prize was dispelled by Ann. 'He just takes names for his dinner parties out of a hat.' *Punch* rejected my article. Rereading it I could see why. A telegram from Gilmour[2] asking for it for the *Spectator*. A request by an American television company to send a team here. Fee only $100 but Peters says it is a good advertisement for the book. Quarter of an hour's question and answer did not seem exorbitant. Accepted.

Thursday 30 June 1955

The television people came at 10 and stayed until 6.30. An excruciating day. They did not want a dialogue but a monologue. The whole thing is to be cut to five minutes in New York and shown at breakfast-time. They filmed everything including the poultry. The impresario kept producing notes from his pocket: 'Mr Waugh, it is said here that you are irascible and reactionary. Will you please say something offensive?' So I said: 'The man who has brought this apparatus to my house asks me to be offensive. I am sorry to disappoint him.' 'Oh, Mr Waugh, please, that will never do. I have a reputation. You must

[1] Newspaper proprietor (including the *Sunday Times*).
[2] Ian Gilmour proprietor of the *Spectator*.

alter that.' I said later, not into the machine: 'You expect rather a lot for $100.'
'Oh, I don't think there is any question of payment.'

Friday 1 July 1955

I rewrote my article on Noel-Buxton, greatly improving it.

Saturday 2 July 1955

Laura went off to All Hallows, Mells, Downside. I wrote my review of Quennell and at luncheon ate a dish of our first peas, late this year, but delicious. As good as I have ever eaten. In the afternoon I took Prothero and drove to Winkfield to Dot and Antony Head.[1] They are leaving that house soon and settling in Wiltshire. With the Laycocks gone too I suppose I shall never revisit that maze of drab expensive villas. Dot was loving and jolly and mad. Angie appeared neat and fresh and on the spot. Antony is becoming genuinely high-minded, unambitious, full of care for his soldiers and his own hobbies. At dinner the conversation was almost entirely about religion – Philip[2] and Sally Hardwicke and a mute local couple. We sat up late in Angie's bedroom. She undressed seductively behind a muslin screen. I drank very little and at 2.30 had to tiptoe down to look for dessert spoon in order to take paraldehyde. But that and sodium amytal gave me less than four hours' sleep. The bed was too small and the blinds too flimsy.

Piers Court, Sunday 3 July 1955

I went to Mass at Eton with Sally Hardwicke. There were about twenty boys there. None had a missal, few followed the service at all. The sermon was the reading of an encyclical. It seemed a very poor religious training for the boys. After Mass I went to the house Philip has just inherited on the golf course. A costly decorator's hall. 'Can't sell it,' Philip complains in bewildered tones. 'Cost my grandmother sixty thousand. Can't get an offer.' Twelve acres of roses, a horizon of military training areas, the interior all wrought iron, sham rococo, old velvet. 'I thought some Indian rajah was bound to jump at it.' Back to luncheon at the Heads. They are dining with Princess Margaret for Andrew's[3] river party on Thursday. Angie dines with the Astors. They kindly suggested I should take Lettice Ashley-Cooper, who is now stone deaf. I shan't go at all.

Home in time for dinner through a storm of rain. Dined Tresham. Fine old champagne.

Monday 4 July 1955

Letters of thanks for my book and some reviews, none of them exactly what I

---

[1] Secretary of State for War, 1951–6.
[2] The 9th Earl of Hardwicke.
[3] The Duke of Devonshire's.

should have wished. Cyril[1] remarks on my 'benign lethargy' and condemns me to the role of Maurice Baring.

I told Dot that the most exciting thing that ever happened at Stinchcombe was an invitation to dine with the Morgan-Jones. An invitation came for Saturday. Eagerly accepted.

Tuesday 5 July 1955

Proofs from *Spectator*. I have further polished the article which causes me more pleasure than anything I have written for a long time. An indignant and rather insolent protest from the Director of the Wolverhampton School of Art asking what I mean by saying his students damaged Ceccarini's Rafael. Splendid weather. Laura in the hayfield. I went for a long walk and returning sweating by the lane was accosted by a village woman who said wasn't it a shame the buses did not come that way.

Wednesday 6 July 1955

Warm brilliant haymaking days. I idle. Ann Fleming, to my horror, has telegraphed 'Presume Ivor Claire based Laycock dedication ironical'. I replied that if she breathes a suspicion of this cruel fact it will be the end of our friendship.[2] I am planning to stay at the hotel near her in August to write the account of my late lunacy.[3]

Thursday 7 July 1955

A sultry day heavy with elderflower. I went to the cinema and saw again the film of Graham's *End of the Affair* – most of it, that is to say. I could not face the detective a second time. Then I came home and reread the book. Hardly a sentence from it occurs in the film. It has the obvious faults of elevating the social status of the characters and losing the inimitable Clapham drabness of the original. It also misses the entire point of the story – the events which follow Sarah's death and are the real end of the affair. The heroine alone was moving. After the film a visit to the church.

Friday 8 July 1955

A letter from Jeanne Stonor telling me that David Mathew[4] is very ill. We

[1] Cyril Connolly, reviewing *Officers and Gentlemen*.

[2] 'Evelyn did not know what fear meant, and he worshipped the sort of physical courage epitomized by Bob Laycock. When the war trilogy appeared, I pretended to identify the caddish Ivor Claire with Bob, and his response was violent indeed but not wholly simulated.' Ann Fleming, contribution to *Evelyn Waugh and His World*, ed. David Pryce-Jones, London 1973. *Officers and Gentlemen* was dedicated 'To Major-General Sir Robert Laycock, KCMG, CB, DSO. That every man in arms should wish to be'.

[3] The hallucinations he experienced on his 1954 voyage.

[4] Bishop David Mathew.

had talked of him at Winkfield, Dot and Angie denouncing him as a snob. He had made a joke which they took amiss about his precedence in Malta. And we had just been joking at length about Angie's precedence in England. They comprehend one idiom only, and are shocked at heart by his sexlessness.

It is always now said that puny men are pugnacious because of their weakness. It is more plausible that God makes pugnacious men small because of the greater harm they could do if powerful.

Saturday 9 July 1955

Lawns being mown, once a lovely drone and delicious scent, nowadays the roar of an engine and stink of exhaust gas.

The *Spectator* came. My article gives me keen pleasure still.

Confession in the afternoon. Dinner at the Morgan-Jones, Krug and roulette, two couples and an odd man. Morgan-Jones in velvet, the odd man in white linen. A snobbish lady from Malmesbury on my right, Lorraine jolly but inaudible on my deaf side. Smoked salmon, lamb cutlets, a cheese soufflé that lay flat, strawberries.

Sunday 10 July 1955

Communion. Mario and Tina too. Also Vera's family in force.

Monday 11 July 1955

Bad reviews of *O. and G.* in England, good ones from New York. A number of fan letters about Lord Noel-Buxton including General Templar and a private soldier in Canterbury. Splendid weather still, gates being painted and everything looking neat as Forest Lawn. Ann telephoned yesterday to say that Gilmour was uneasy about Amis's[1] review of *O. and G.* He need not have been. It did not disturb me at all and came unfortunately for him in the same issue as the Noel-Buxton article which shows there is life in the old dog – more than in the young. I am quite complacent about the book's quality. My only anxiety is about American sales. It would be very convenient to have another success there.

Tuesday 12 July 1955

High summer continues. I shall not go to London until it breaks. This is a pleasant house in the heat. For the first time since I planted it the honeysuckle outside my bedroom window scents the room at night. I don't sleep naturally. I have tried everything – exercise, cold baths, fasting, feasting, solitude, society. Always I have to take paraldehyde and sodium amytal. My life is really too empty for a diarist. The morning post, the newspaper, the crossword, gin.

[1] Kingsley Amis's.

Wednesday 13 July 1955

A sultry day of unrelieved boredom.

Thursday 14 July 1955

A letter from Edith Sitwell saying that she is under instruction from Father Caraman and hopes to be received into the Church next month. Laura and I went to vicarage which is being sold up. The village in force buying souvenirs. Nothing of any interest. Stinchcombe is now without a parson and the house Isaac Williams[1] built is up for sale.

Saturday 16 July 1955

Great heat continues. Tony Powell came to luncheon. We were unable to find anyone to meet him. It was an unrewarding long hot drive for Tony. I opened a case which I thought contained champagne and found only Anjou Rosé. In the evening Laura and I drove to Gloucester to see *Murder in the Cathedral*. The clothes and properties were very shabby by daylight but as the cathedral darkened they brightened. We were in the front row. The amateur actors were all better than the professional who played Becket. One very pretty girl among the women of Canterbury, two fine fat charade actors among the knights. The candlelight procession at the end was very showy. The Donaldsons came back to supper with us. We talked of Lord Noel-Buxton who, in this week's *Spectator*, rounds on the lady he escorted here and publicly calls her a liar. Has she no brother with a horsewhip?

Sunday 17 July 1965

Communion. Heat. Repose.

Monday 18 July 1955

The joys and sorrows of a simple life. Joys: I found that a pseudo-Sheraton table from Highgate fits perfectly over the radiator of the dining-room window and only needed the knocking away of four wooden bosses. A drop in temperature. The arrival of the long-awaited mechanic from Atco to put new blades in the lawn mower. The fine close mowing of two of the front lawns. A telephone call from Diana proposing herself for Friday night. A new Agatha Christie story which began well. Sorrows: The failure of the lawn mower after an hour's use. The staleness of Monday's bread. The deterioration of Mrs Christie's novel a third of the way through into twaddle.

Tuesday 19 July 1955

Cool and bright. The postman tried to charge me nearly £8 duty on my

---

[1] Tractarian poet and theologian, 1802–65.

weekly box of cigars which normally costs £1 18s. A letter from Edith saying she is to be received into the Church in London makes me uneasy that she intends making an occasion of it. I wrote, officiously, to Caraman urging the example of St Helena. Laura went out to luncheon. Nothing to read or do.

London, Thursday 21 July 1955

I went to London by the breakfast train from Kemble and drove straight from Paddington to Garrard's carrying the Vuillaume movement for regulation. Walking back along Vigo Street I turned into Albany on impulse and called on Graham Greene. I found him alone and *désoeuvré* having completed a novel and a play, now waiting to take his daughter to Canada in search of cattle and a husband. He told me he has the beginning of cirrhosis of the liver and is on a strict regime. Also that he has broken with Korda who guillotined the Monte Carlo film just as it was ready for shooting.[1] Also that Edith Sitwell has just learned of Osbert's connection with —— and is profoundly shocked, fearing an immediate police raid. Also that Mrs T. S. Eliot's insanity sprang from her seduction and desertion by Bertrand Russell. He is coming to stay for the night next Thursday. I tried on clothes in Albemarle Street, then to White's for a three-hour session. Randolph sober and on a regime. Not so Seymour Camrose who was hopelessly drunk before luncheon. Cosmo Crawley told me of a series of horrifying motor accidents, poor little Tessa Head badly cut about, Miss Hennessy paralysed and totally defaced, old Fred Cripps on his feet concussed, the Duchess of Buccleuch recovering – a catalogue of injuries. After luncheon I spent an hour in the park with Ann. Ann told me that —— and his wife were dining before a party for James Thurber. He said: 'You have always asked me to tell you, so I will do so. Your breath is terrible this evening.' She left the table soon after and he followed to find her telephoning, giggling '. . . so my breath was all right this afternoon.' He then knew he was being cuckolded. At the party she disappeared, he followed and found her in bed with ——, who apparently is enraptured and wishes to marry her. It is thought she must have some oriental tricks in bed.

There was a garden party at Buckingham Palace and all the streets impassable. I took a cab outside the Dorchester Hotel and fifteen minutes later was still in Park Lane so I despaired of my train, walked to the St James's and waited for the next. Dined on the train and had a long heavily drugged night.

Piers Court, Friday 22 July 1955

The start of holidays from Ascot and Downside. Also Diana's visit. A most

[1] 'I suppose I was having a bit of liver trouble and dramatized it to Evelyn. Just as he dramatized my visit to Canada which was in search of a small ranch and not of a husband. I had a temporary quarrel with Korda, who refused to allow Alec Guinness to play a part in a film *Loser Takes All* – part based on himself.' Graham Greene in a letter to the editor, November 1975.

successful day. The girls arrived pretty and loving, Bron tall and polite. Diana arrived in the early afternoon from Stanway and we went to the Press at Wotton-under-Edge to arrange for the reproduction of Lavery's portrait. Diana read me a letter from June Churchill describing a gruesome evening at Chartwell, Randolph drunk at dinner calling Soames[1] a shit, enraging Winston by diatribes against Jerk Eden.[2] Winston so shaken with fury that June and Clemmie[3] feared another seizure. Randolph storming up saying he would leave at once and never see his father again. June, already in bed, forced to dress and start packing. Then at 1 am Sir Winston padding down the passage in pyjamas, saying: 'I am going to die soon. I cannot go to bed without composing a quarrel and kissing them both.' Randolph next day sober and obsequious at luncheon at Cherkley with Lord Beaverbrook.

A gay dinner with speeches and charades afterwards, first the children then Diana joined Laura and me acting and dressing up and singing with gusto. I have not seen her so jolly since she left the Embassy, still less since Cooper's death.

Saturday 23 July 1955

Diana left for Juliet. She told me Nancy has cooked her goose with the *gratin* by referring to Marie Antoinette's 'traitor's death'.[4] Very funny and odd. The *Spectator* has amusing letters about Lord Noel-Buxton. He comes out of the affair very ignominiously. In the evening Laura and I went to Tresham to meet the Gileses who confirm the report of Nancy's ostracism. After dinner we read aloud Kipling's *End of the Passage*.

Monday 25 July 1955

Bron left early to travel by bus to London to stay with a school friend and go to the Downside dance. At 2 o'clock Laura and I took the children to the cinema in Dursley. We were greeted by the manager saying that the Stroud police wished to speak to us. They said that a youth had been arrested incapably drunk carrying Bron's suitcase. From their description it was plain that the prisoner was Bron. We drove to Stroud and found him white and dirty eating a bun. He had a third of a bottle of gin, of the brand I drink, in his possession. We took him home and sent him to his room. Later he said that he missed his bus in Gloucester, spent all his money at the White Hart buying a bottle of gin, drank most of it at Gloucester station, conceived the idea of travelling to London without a ticket and with 2d in his pocket. When arrested

[1] Christopher Soames, the politician, was Randolph Churchill's brother-in-law.

[2] 'Jerk' was a soubriquet attached to Sir Anthony Eden, the Prime Minister, by Randolph Churchill and the anti-Eden faction of White's Club.

[3] Lady Churchill.

[4] Nancy Mitford had written an article justifying the execution of Marie Antoinette.

he gave a false name and address and was identified by correspondence in the suitcase. Inquiries at the White Hart in Gloucester elicited the reply that no bottle of gin had been sold that day. We told Teresa and Margaret, leaving the rest of the household, I hope, in ignorance. An evening of ineffable gloom.

Tuesday 26 July 1955

We took Bron into the Juvenile Court. He was fined 10s without any enquiry. He behaved sensibly, pleading guilty and apologizing. A day of gloom. In the evening old Hale turned up and stayed to dinner. His presence was a welcome relief. He boasted that he had 'graduated in the university of life' and flirted with Meg.

Thursday 28 July 1955

To Bath to meet James[1] and Graham Greene. We reached Stinchcombe to find the Jesuit who is taking duty during Father Collins's holiday, waiting for luncheon. He seemed disposed to spend the afternoon with us and addressed Laura twice as 'mummy'. On the first occasion I thought my hearing was playing a trick on me. The second was unmistakable. Graham was genial and full of repose, deep in a condemned book by an Italian theologian who holds that mankind was created to redeem the Devil.

St Margaret's Bay, Friday 29 July 1955

The *Spectator* has a dull letter from Lord Noel-Buxton closing the incident ingloriously. I had much to carry so took Prothero to London, arriving with Graham at White's at midday. He set off to Albany carrying his suitcase. I bustled about in the heat trying on a suit, taking *Into the Cold World* to be relined and reframed, Vivian's *Spanish Scenery* to be rebound. Diana picked me up at 3.30 and we drove at an easy pace to St Margaret's Bay where we found Ann, Raymond O'Neill,[2] Freddie Ashton the choreographer and a painter named Ironside. Her London servants were not there and the boy O'Neill made little effort to fill their places. White Cliffs is gruesomely small and ill furnished but the party, excepting O'Neill, was gay.

Saturday 30 July 1955

No one gets up in the morning. When they do they immediately sprawl on sun mattresses on the strip of rank grass which only a low brick parapet separates from the shingle beach covered with similarly supine proletarians. As there was no cook we were obliged to lunch at a dreary hotel at Sandwich, but I had a keen appetite and ate two helpings of boiled beef. There was a helicopter advertising Hennessy's brandy on the lawn. I paid for luncheon. Afterwards

[1] The Waughs' second son, then aged nine.
[2] The 4th baron O'Neill, Ann Fleming's son by her first marriage; he was 21.

Diana and I drove through the streets of Sandwich looking at antique shops empty of anything desirable. Daphne Straight came to supper of cold lobster and brawn.

Sunday 31 July 1955

Diana up at 7.45 in night dress to drive me to Mass. Her day and ours was complicated by a series of telephone calls from a lunatic American journalist who eventually arrived at the wrong station, borrowed £2 from the garage keeper, and took the next train to London. We dined at Noel Coward's sham Tudor farmhouse at Aldington. He had his little entourage and an American actor. We had to turn Raymond's sullenness into a joke, pretending that he was depressed by the fact that all our talk turned to death. We worked this joke hard for the rest of the visit and it helped to ease things. Diana pointedly (and in the circumstances of Bron's disgrace ironically) praised the charming manners of my children.

Monday 1 August 1955

All sprawling in the sun. Luncheon at an hotel. I did not pay that time. More sprawling. Lady Clark choked off a visit. Uneatable dinner but plenty of champagne. I read Aldous Huxley's latest story.[1] I find his scientific imagery very flat and ugly.

Folkestone, Tuesday 2 August 1955

Diana brought me early to the Grand Hotel Folkestone – Edwardian brick, very much like the Hyde Park Hotel, polite old servants, very dull kitchen and clientele. They showed me into a large suite with a piano in the parlour and I thought their charges modest for such space. Later they told me the parlour was not for me. The upper part of Folkestone where this hotel stands is very prosperous and genteel, finely kept gardens along the cliff edge and all traffic running behind the hotels. The eastern part must be pleasant outside the holiday season. Densely crowded now. I walked there for a short time, dined early, did the crossword alone, two words missing, and went early to bed.

Wednesday 3 August 1955

Woken early by workmen hammering all round me. Changed my room for one on the first floor. Walked into town under grey skies, found the Catholic church, wrote letters. It scarcely seems worth while starting to write until after Edith's reception. The sun came out after luncheon and I fell asleep in my room. Everyone is very civil and obliging in this hotel. If only the cook and the patrons were better it would be admirable.

[1] *The Genius and the Goddess.*

Thursday 4 August 1955

A brilliant day. I took the train at 9 in a clean carriage holding a man who read the letters of Cicero and looked like a lawyer and a ginger-whiskered giant who looked like a farmer and read the *Financial Times*. A cinder blew in on this man and burned a hole in his tweed coat. From Charing Cross I walked to White's buying a carnation on the way and drank a mug of stout and gin and ginger beer. Then at 11.45 to Farm Street where I met Father D'Arcy and went with him to the church to the Ignatius chapel to await Edith and Father Caraman. A bald shy man introduced himself as the actor Alec Guinness. Presently Edith appeared swathed in black like a sixteenth-century infanta. I was aware of other people kneeling behind but there were no newspaper men or photographers as I had half feared to find. Edith recanted her errors in fine ringing tones and received conditional baptism, then was led into the confessional while six of us collected in the sacristy – Guinness and I and Father D'Arcy, an old lame deaf woman with dyed red hair whose name I never learned, a little swarthy man who looked like a Jew but claimed to be Portuguese, and a blond youth who looked American but claimed to be English. We drove two streets in a large hired limousine to Edith's club, the Sesame. I had heard gruesome stories of this place but Edith had ordered a banquet – cold consommé, lobster Newburg, steak, strawberry flan and great quantities of wine. The old woman suddenly said: 'Did I hear the word "whisky"?' I said: 'Do you want one?' 'More than anything in the world.' 'I'll get you some.' But the Portuguese nudged me and said: 'It would be disastrous.' After luncheon I walked to White's through empty streets and smoked a cigar until it was time for my train back to Folkestone – again clean and fast and empty. But I was weary when I got back, bathed, dressed, drank Pimm's and felt a little refreshed, sent £2 to the chef with a note saying all dishes for me must be cooked specially, never kept warm. Ann arrived at 7.45 and we spent a restful evening. She is worried because Fiona[1] is not in love and talks about the universe.

The engagement is announced of the youngest Clifford sister to a low-born man with no legs and two wives. A girl with any sense of humour could not choose to name herself Atalanta Fairey.

Friday 5 August 1955

I am bored with Folkestone, spending too much, getting too little for my money, doing no work, not even feeling very well. Laura writes that she cannot join me. With her I might explore the amusements. Alone I read and smoke and do nothing. The man at the next table to me has introduced himself as

---

[1] The Hon. Fiona O'Neill, Ann Fleming's daughter by her first marriage.

Lord Mersey,[1] Matthew Ponsonby's father-in-law. He tells me funny stories. I ate a simple Spanish omelette for luncheon and suffered indigestion all the afternoon.

Saturday 6 August 1955

A wasted day. I dawdled and read and in the evening went to dine with Patrick and Bettine Broughshane.[2] I had settled to go by train. In the afternoon I listlessly decided to take a car which cost me £3 instead of a few shillings. They live in Sandwich in a tiny, pretty, flimsy, pokey Queen Anne house like those in Westminster inhabited by Heads and Berrys. The other guests were a desperately dull colonel of the Foot Guards and Elizabeth Wynne who was bright but kept from contact. Crème Vichyssoise (good), steak (bad), fraises du bois, champagne. Later Mark Ogilvie-Grant came in from a jaunt by bus to a dance hall in Ramsgate. He arrived with iridescent homosexual high spirits but soon sank into the gloom of the little party.

Sunday 7 August 1955

To late Mass where an old priest ranted against the dangers of seaside holiday-making to an elderly and juvenile congregation – 'filthy practices of courtship permitted only to the married'. No withers wrung in that church, I think.

Monday 8 August 1955

I gave my notice to the hotel to leave on Wednesday. The persecution by Lord Mersey has made my mealtimes unendurable. I shall slink home with much money squandered and no work done. I went in the evening by train to Ann's. At the station, Martin Mill, an idiot of about eighteen was playing in the yard with a paper dart. Ann said he had been there when she arrived home that morning. I dined with her and Fiona. She gave me some particulars about abortion in wartime for my next volume.[3] I returned by train, the first-class carriages full of drowsy louts. Ann had been spending the weekend among sodomites in Wiltshire. The Edens came to luncheon. Jerk confessed that as a boy at school he sat upon and killed a pet mouse in order to escape punishment.

Tuesday 9 August 1955

I went by train to luncheon with Ann. There was no one in the booking office at Folkestone to sell me a ticket and no one at Martin Mill to ask for it, so I travelled free in an entirely empty train. Uneatable luncheon. Afterwards we

---

[1] The 2nd Viscount Mersey (1872–1956). Chief Liberal Whip in the House of Lords, 1944–9.
[2] The 2nd Baron and Lady Broughshane.
[3] *Unconditional Surrender*, published 1961.

drove with Fiona and Caspar[1] to the funfair at Folkestone. He is a very obstreperous child, grossly pampered.

Piers Court, Wednesday 10 August 1955

Left Folkestone, glad to escape the stories of Lord Mersey and Caspar. Lunched at White's where all was lightness and kindness, home by train. To my annoyance Bron is still here. I was promised his absence. The children greeted my return with illuminated addresses and Septimus[2] in fancy dress presenting the key of the front door in a silver casket.

Thursday 11 August 1955

I begin a modest regime of drinking nothing between breakfast and 6 o'clock except a cup of black coffee.

Saturday 13 August 1955

Wrote a review of the new edition of the *Cruise of the Nona* with Ed Stanley's excellent introduction. Read a novel by an American who says he has formed his style on mine. Can't see it. The Vuillaume movement came back from regulation at Garrard's. I patiently fitted it into its case and set it going. It stopped.

Sunday 14 August 1955

Walked to Mass and communion praying for kindness towards Bron.

Monday 15 August 1955

Early Mass. Bron and Hatty left to Nutcombe and Bickham respectively. Teresa returned from Somerset. In spite of my earnest prayers I was delighted to see Bron go. The household became happy once more and we began to plan an outing to Birmingham Art Gallery and Stratford Theatre. Displeasure takes the shape of boredom with me nowadays.

Tuesday 16 August 1955

White's procured us a box for Stratford. The play turns out to be *Titus Andronicus*, most unsuitably. Laura says that the Oliviers will not act in it. But the girls are gleeful about the jaunt. I wrote to propose our calling at Stanway on the road. In the evening the Donaldsons came for cocktails. I find I watch the clock for my 6 o'clock gin and that I am growing perceptibly thinner. The Donaldsons seemed to be on bad terms with one another and they cheerfully stayed on to dinner. At luncheon we had entertained Father Prince [?] who arrived at 12.15. He called me 'Daddy'.

[1] Caspar Fleming, son of Ann and Ian Fleming.
[2] The Waughs' third son and youngest child, born July 1950.

Wednesday 17 August 1955

The morning papers reveal that the Oliviers are acting at Stratford. A letter from Jack McDougall saying that *Officers and Gentlemen* is selling briskly. Eight hundred last week. Reviews clearly have little influence on sales. I think the little stir about Spain–Buxton may have helped. Even *Men at Arms* has raised a drooping head and sells a hundred a week.

Birmingham, Thursday 18 August 1955

The original day's visit to Birmingham to see the Pre-Raphaelites became extended. With Laura, Teresa, Margaret and £30 we drove off in the afternoon. A letter to propose our stopping at Stanway brought no answer so I presumed Letty Benson to be away. I also wrote to Lady Olivier telling her we shall be in the audience on Friday. We stopped in Evesham while the children had tea. As we approached Birmingham the evening became hotter and heavier. Birmingham was humid and overpowering. We arrived at Queen's Hotel where I found that our rooms for the night would cost £9. The children had 'bubble' baths, the salts for which we had purchased in Cheltenham. Laura and I drank Pimm's No. 1 Cup in the cocktail bar where there was a cool breeze and an intoxicated dwarf. A ham sandwich and then on foot to the theatre where we sweated through a tedious farce. Back to dinner. The servants very civil in the hotel, the rooms poky, airless and shabby. But the girls in high spirits.

Piers Court, Friday 19 August 1955

After a distressed night to the museum before opening time. We went to the curator's office where a pretty and obliging girl, who proved to be the daughter of Professor Bodkin, greeted us and led us to the cellarage where, in the manner of modern museums, the gems were hidden. Their version of the *Lost Child* proved to be a small sketch for our painting. Holman Hunt's *Shadow of Death* was there. I had never seen it except in reproduction. A superb painting grossly defamed by Ironside. The light and shadow on the legs is the finest achievement of the period. In the gallery upstairs were many beautiful Hugheses, a painful replica of *Work*, Hunt's *Finding in the Temple*. But the *Last of England* was away on loan. There was also a special exhibition of Italian masters, including Katharine's Bellinis. The experts are all excited by a Titian *Ecce Homo* which left me unmoved. We lunched at the hotel, suffering for our faith, and drove to Stratford stopping to see the Beauchamp Chapel and Leycesten Hospital in Warwick. Still very hot. I drank a bottle of Bollinger on the terrace of the theatre where we dined early. I had been cast down to find we were to see *Titus Andronicus*. I was enthralled by it. So much so that I itch to write an appreciation. There is only one real dramatic scene – Aaron with his blackamoor baby defying the Gothic princes – brilliantly performed by a Mr Quayle. Sir Laurence soldiered manfully through his part. Lady Olivier played hers with delicious nonchalance, full of wit in the dumb show, demure as an early Victorian bride when attending the murder of her ravishers. The ceremonial done with gravity and solidity. When it was over I took the children behind and briefly presented them to Lady Olivier. She was friendly but weary. The small boy who played Lucius came in and she kissed him provocatively. A swift cold drive home and to bed very tired.

Saturday 20 August 1955

I slept seven hours without chemical aid. Spent all day indoors. Meg very dreary. She drank too much at luncheon at Birmingham.

Sunday 21 August 1955

Communion, praying again for charity towards Bron. By telephone the glad news that he is prolonging his stay at Nutcombe.

Sunday 28 August 1955

A week of great heat, hunger and thirst, growing thinner daily and more active in mind. Wrote an essay on the Stratford *Titus* which I hope will give pleasure to Lady Olivier but now fear may give pain. It appears she is morbidly sensitive to criticism. I have read a dull American life of Alfred Austin – a close parallel to Stephen Spender – and made a gaffe amadyonene for anadyomene in the *Spectator*.

There is a letter in this week's *Tablet* calling attention to a house near Winchcombe which is for sale with a pre-Reformation Catholic chapel. After luncheon Laura and Teresa and I drove to see it: Portlip Hall, a square capacious Jacobean house beautifully secluded on the slope of a valley, a long lime avenue, large stables, a very fine walled garden, the rooms numerous, low, oak-panelled. A view of open hillside above wooded slopes. I could be very private there. The chapel is detached and locked. We were told the keys were at the presbytery in Winchcombe. The housekeeper gave us keys but not ones capable of letting us in. She told us that the chapel belongs to the diocese and is endowed for two Masses a year. None of our furniture or pictures would look well in that house. It should sell very cheap. I am greatly agitated by the prospect.

Monday 29 August 1955

Laura took children to London, leaving Teresa in her London lodging, fitting Septimus and Harriet with bridal fripperies.

Tuesday 30 August 1955

A youth wearing Lancing colours presented himself at 11 am asking whether I would like to hear news of the old school. Sent him away. Sweating and trembling I put back the Vuillaume movement. It ticks for quarter of an hour, then stops. I have found the reason: the library chimney-piece is not level. Two strips of cedar wood at the back of the clock-case have caused the trouble.

Laura said last night that she would be pleased if any or all of her children became priests or nuns. A few years ago the thought revolted her. She attributes her change to lack of zest for life rather than to zest for Heaven.

Saturday 3 September 1955

Bron and Margaret returned on Wednesday. They behave very well, but the spectacle of so many children sitting in the drawing-room makes me long for space. A man came from Knight, Frank & Rutley who held out little hope of our getting more than £10,000 for this property. He made enquiries and later told me that Portlip would go for about £9,000– that is, the two lots we should need. The choice seems to be: remain here in increasing discomfort in a property fast depreciating in value for another ten years, then sell for a few thousand and move to Brighton; or embark on huge disturbance and expense now in a larger house.

Mario is causing annoyance by losing his reason. He is obsessed like a character from Renaissance drama with suspicion of his wife's infidelity, pretends to go out and conceals himself under the bed to spy on her. Under the strain her cooking has become unendurable.

Tuesday 6 September 1955

A letter from Daphne from Debo's house in London and the notice of an exhibition of Victorian paintings in Peckham decided me to go to London.

Wednesday 7 September 1955

Breakfast train from Kemble. Laura came too, to shop with Teresa. White's shut so I went to St James's where I learned that Daphne left for Tangier yesterday. A blow. When I had had my hair cut in Trumper's and consulted the man at Garrard's about my clock I had a lonely day ahead. A light luncheon of ham mousse and melon. A taxi to Peckham where the pictures proved to be all second-rate costume pieces. Two pansies were going round. One proved to be —— the critic so I took him back to St James's for a drink. Then sat doing nothing until it was time for the dinner train. Laura very exhausted. I ordered champagne and the steward spilled most of it in his refrigerator. More champagne. An expensive dinner.

Sunday 11 September 1955

Mario's insanity has kept Laura busy. Yesterday she sent him and Tina and a brother to London as preparation for his entry to a loony bin.

Monday 12 September 1955

After much coming and going of magistrates and alienists Mario was removed to the lunatic asylum. It is hoped that the cooking may improve.

Wednesday 14 September 1955

Bron was returned to Downside. I drove with him and Laura to visit my Raban uncle and aunts in their new home – a village shop, the two main rooms having shop windows on the village street, a little garden at the back, the rooms full of Victoriana and relics of India. My uncle very absurd, my aunt Emma endearing. Then to Mells for a drink. Katharine says she will be dead in five years. Laura professes to see signs of failing affection between her and Ronnie. We then dropped Bron at Downside. Clusters of unprepossessing boys were lurking round the drive and gates. Laura gave him £4, his allowance for a quarter in advance, most imprudently. He immediately joined the corner-boys, perhaps to drink and smoke. A cheerful dinner in his absence.

Thursday 15 September 1955

Laura's lunatic gardener threatens to liberate himself. Much of her time is occupied in this affair. We drove over to luncheon with Sibell Rowley to meet Maimie who has been deserted by Vsevolode, very poor and pretty. I drank port for the first time for months with great enjoyment. Teresa proposes to bring Annabel Hennessy for the weekend.

Friday 16 September 1955

Notification that a colonel is interested in buying Piers Court. I feel dismayed rather than stimulated at the prospect of starting a new life. Sibell told us yesterday that Portlip has a black record of disasters to previous owners.

Monday 19 September 1955

Various other possible purchasers of Piers Court announced. The most promising Sir Anthony Lindsay-Hogg who is insane and I think rich. Mario has released himself from the asylum but says he is unfit for work. He thinks he has lost a brother. Two American fans forced an entry.

Tuesday 20 September 1955

Veronica's wedding day. We all travelled to London by train, I bearing a clock for her. Since it has been cleaned it seems too handsome a present. Laura took Harriet and Septimus to the Hyde Park Hotel to dress as page and bridesmaid with Teresa's help. I took Margaret and James to luncheon at the Ritz. Yesterday's American fans were there. St Paul's, Knightsbridge, well filled with young people, flowers, choirboys and girls and a bishop. Veronica and Septimus looked very nice. The Bishop cut 'the avoidance of fornication' and substituted a genteel periphrasis. The reception at the Hyde Park Hotel. I did not think there were so many people in London I did not know. Alec also was at sea. I sat in an anteroom. Carolyn Cobb sat with me and embarrassed me by saying that Lady Upcott told her that my letters to my mother were the most beautiful ever written.

Home by dinner train. James dispatched to stay with Speaight.

Brighton, Wednesday 21 September 1955

Lindsay-Hogg frantic to see house. Portlip not sold by auction. We drove Harriet and Meg to Ascot, then on to Brighton in the rain, greatly refreshed by smoked salmon at Guildford.

Thursday 22 September 1955

Royal Crescent Hotel its old dowdy friendly self. We sat in our hideous suite while the rain fell. Then ventured out to the theatre but left after the first act and went to a cinema. Supper upstairs.

Friday 23 September 1955

Rain in the morning but fine later. A stroll on the pier. Then round the Lanes where I purchased a Gothic clock for £27.

Saturday 24 September 1955

A curious lack of appetite for food and drink. A letter this morning to say that Portlip has been sold. I have spent many hours planning its decoration and Victorianization. In the afternoon Laura and I drove to Petworth, which is open to the public. Perhaps it is merely a symptom of my general lack of appetite, I found the place dull and ugly, most of the pictures badly hung – the Fuselis invisible – and many in poor condition, the façade and surrounding landscape deplorable, the interior decorations lavish but not splendid. I see from the guide that it lacks a dome. The blank grass expanse to the west is deadly. In the evening to the theatre for the third evening in succession. This· time on the pier, an adaption of *Sally Bowles*, enjoyable.

Sunday 25 September 1955

To Mass, rude [?] and scolding priest. The pier. An ill-cooked grouse.

Wednesday 28 September 1955

Laura and I returned to Stinchcombe stopping on the way to look at a house near Calne which proved to be appalling. The Brighton visit was healthful and restful. Jack McDougall and May came on Monday. Apart from them we saw no one. We went to two more plays and visited Arundel Castle – only the library remarkable, but that a gem. One curious incident. My cheque book disappeared from the writing table one day. Laura, I, and the chambermaid searched the room diligently and came to the conclusion it must have fallen into the wastepaper basket and been carried away. That night it reappeared in its place on the writing table. Inexplicable. We stopped at Burghclere to see the splendid paintings.[1]

After dinner the Italians, who had been told to pack and had not done so, arrived from London where they had lived in vagabondage. Mario declares he is cured. Laura's soft heart will not allow her to expel them. So there they are.

Sir Anthony Lindsay-Hogg came to luncheon bringing Dudley Delavigne.[2] They are both very agreeable and I thought we had sold them the house but no, no good. The Italians have disappeared for the day promising to return.

Saturday 1 October 1955

I wrote my letters and began a little description of my first meeting with Max Beerbohm. After luncheon with Laura and Vera to confession but Father Collins did not turn up so we went to the cinema and later found him on duty. Laura drove the Italians away with their luggage to Tetbury. I fear it is not the last of them.

Sunday 2 October 1955

Communion. The clocks should have been changed. We remembered to get up late but lunched early by mistake.

I must ask experts: is prayer one of the activities which are unimpaired in senility? Or do people pray best at their full strength and are apparently prayerful dotards just blank? The point arises in the treatment of Mr Crouchback in the final volume or volumes of work in progress.

Tuesday 4 October 1955

The mystery of the clock deepens. The local clock-maker called and pronounced it free of 'knocking'. He told me he sold on an average one £25 diamond engagement ring a week to the workers of Dursley.

---

[1] By Stanley Spencer, in the Sandham Memorial Chapel near Whitchurch, Hampshire.
[2] An estate agent.

Wednesday 5 October 1955

I wrote a little memoir of my first meeting with Max Beerbohm.

Thursday 6 October 1955

To London for the day to meet Nancy. White's first. Ed Stanley and the usual habitués. Then to the Ritz to meet Ann. We gossiped about the Edens. A man whose name I did not know came up to us and said: 'I am sorry you didn't put anything about Lady L—— into your novel.' 'I barely knew her.' 'She was my mistress for three years.' Even Ann was surprised. She told me that *Encounter* are eager for a reply to Nancy's articles on the aristocracy.[1] News had already reached Nancy of my intention and she was resentful and apprehensive. Ann also said that P—— had been invalided out of the army for insanity. That Mrs Johnny Churchill telephoned Clarissa at Downing Street from the police station where Johnny[2] was incarcerating and he could be heard on the line barking like a dog in his cell. That Pam Berry thinks she is the reincarnation of Lord Northcliffe and cannot understand why Jerk does not report regularly for instructions.

Luncheon at Hill Street – just Momo, John, and Nancy, very cosy. Home by the 4.55 after looking round Mrs Franks's shop.

Sunday 9 October 1955

Cyril has an article in the *Sunday Times* that reeks of insanity.

Written on 20th October. I wrote a long refutation of Nancy's mischievous article in *Encounter* dealing very little with her glossary of plebeian expressions, which has caused all the stir, and much with her misrepresentations of the English class system. Mr H. Hamilton (who impudently refers to me as 'Evelyn' in his correspondence) wants to issue a booklet on the subject.

In spite of having no servants we entertained extravagantly during the weekend. Mrs Harper and the village rallied loyally. Teresa and Alice Jolliffe and the Pakenhams stayed in the house, Donaldsons and numerous Cheltenham young ladies came to cocktails, the Sykeses and Leslie Hartley[3] to luncheon. A ham and a whole smoked salmon helped, but Mrs Harper cooked excellently. Frank made a splendid entrance to Sunday breakfast his face, neck and shirt covered with blood, brandishing the Vulgate, crying, 'Who will explain to me second Corinthians five sixteen?' (or some text). Of every name mentioned Frank asked: 'What chance of their coming in?' (to the Church). He

---

[1] The article classified English speech-patterns into 'U' (upper class) and 'Non-U' (non-upper class).

[2] John Spencer-Churchill, painter; nephew of Winston Churchill and brother of Clarissa Eden, the Prime Minister's wife.

[3] L. P. Hartley, the novelist.

was much concerned for the welfare of Trevor-Roper's soul. A particularly silly article on the Oxford martyrs was in that day's *Spectator*. Elizabeth described Edith Sitwell's confirmation at Farm Street – a large invited congregation, the cream of Catholic London, whom Archbishop Roberts took for one of his mission schools in Bombay, saying: 'Now I want you all to learn a very useful prayer and say it every day if you don't do so already. Repeat after me – O God – pour down – we beseech thee – thy grace . . .' He made them go through it in chorus three times. Afterwards there was a cocktail party at the Connaught Hotel paid for by the Jesuits. After Edith left, Father Caraman announced: 'Before we separate I just want to say that any of you who would like to ask Dame Edith to a meal, is free to do so.'

The fine weather is over, first frost, now heavy rain. Laura's cowman broke his leg with his motor bicycle and she has to milk twice daily. Bron, I learned from Christopher, has been boasting at Downside about his drunkenness and imprisonment.

Friday 28 October 1955

My 52nd birthday. Condition unchanged since last year. One letter – from my Aunt Emma. Nothing from Teresa or Bron. Margaret, James and Harriet left presents behind them at the end of the holidays – a collection of coloured inks from Meg which must have taken all her pocket money, a cake from Hatty, a crucifix from James. I have been doing neat little literary jobs quite industriously during the last fortnight – reviews, etc. and am reading up R. H. Benson with interest for an American preface.

As the day wore on poor Laura, who was trying her best in extreme exhaustion, aches and cough, had to give up and take to her bed. So I spent a lonely evening.

Saturday 29 October 1955

Laura still far from well, we set off for Ascot. The car was far from well and it was after 2 when we arrived at the Berystede Hotel. Margaret and Hatty voracious. They ate huge luncheons, teas and dinners and for relaxation drove round the cemetery at Brookwood. Laura early to bed.

Sunday 30 October 1955

We drove the children to London to Mass at Farm Street and luncheon and Teresa at the St James's Club. They gorged. Margaret is top of her form, robust and popular at school, full of new common tastes. My Pre-Raphaelite preference is for the wistful and difficult. We had meant to stop at Stonor but Jeanne and Sherman were ill so we drove straight home to a cold house and no dinner prepared. Boiled eggs and narcotics.

A very gloomy birthday.

Monday 31 October 1955

Slept until 10.30. Laura better. Read Benson and Corvo for the American preface.

Thursday 3 November 1955

The post was five hours late because the post van was attacked by robbers at 5 am at Cambridge and all registered mail stolen.

Monday 14 November 1955

After rather a busy week writing literary snippets, I went to London for the luncheon given by Burns & Oates[1] for Ronnie and his Bible. Two hundred male guests at the Hyde Park Hotel. Several heathen, including Eccles and Kenneth Clark[2] next to whom I sat. The wines were copious and good, the speeches delightful except the Cardinal's. He read a dreadful sort of testimonial. After luncheon I went to the Portuguese Art Exhibition at the Academy but was overcome by heat and boredom. Then to various stationers' shops trying to buy writing-paper. Instead of the bulging albums of samples one used to be shown, there were three or four square blocks, nothing I wanted. Then at 5 to 5 to Coles to order wallpaper only to find it was just closing so I quickly ordered the cheapest. Very weary to the Hyde Park Hotel, bathed, dressed and to White's where I found the usual habitués. Thence to the Ritz where Ann was dining with me. Caviare, crème Germiny, Tournedos Rossini, pears, white and red Burgundy. Foolishly I drank some spurious chartreuse. The bill was £10. A good dinner in an almost empty room. Ann told me of ——'s matrimonial fiascos. His wife has had vast 'fibroids' removed from her womb in order to enable her to conceive – by whom? —— asks everyone he meets. Ann had the Edens to luncheon next day and invited me. I was spared the need to decide as I was engaged to meet Clare Luce at Momo's. A night of suffocation in steam-heated hotel bedroom.

Tuesday 15 November 1955

A morning in White's. Not feeling particularly well. At luncheon Clare, Patrick Kinross, Randolph and an empty chair where Joan Aly Khan should have sat. Her absence and Randolph's presence spoiled my meeting with Clare. It became a press conference with her giving full and satisfactory answers to a hostile cross-examination. She has become slow in the uptake and verbose as an American rotarian, but is pretty as ever. Diana called for me and we went to the Tate to see the Stanley Spencer exhibition where I should have liked to linger but she rushed, missing the point and thinking him quaint and whimsical,

---

[1] The Roman Catholic publishers.
[2] Sir David Eccles, the Conservative politician; Sir Kenneth Clark, the art-historian.

where I see him realistic and proletarian, with the remnants of nineteenth-century non-conformity such as Betjeman has popularized. Winter came on suddenly and by the time I reached Kemble station the cold was bitter.

Wednesday 16 November 1955

Bitter cold again. Begging letters. Garrard's report the library clock keeping perfect time, very mysteriously. Mrs Attwood has sprained an ankle. A doctor's wife from Wotton has become part-time cook to us.

Thursday 17 November 1955

Resolved: to regard humankind with benevolence and detachment, like an elderly host whose young and indulged wife has asked a lot of people to the house whose names he does not know.

Today's sad story. Waking shortly after 7 (one sodium amytal: no paraldehyde) I thought: 'There is a pleasure in store for me today. Laura and I are going to a Jules Verne-Disney Film.' It was *20 Leagues*[1] *Under the Sea* and absolutely *awful*.

Saturday 19 November 1955

An offer from *Life* of $5,000 for an article on St Francis of Assisi. It is sad that the Americans are only interested in hackneyed topics. What can one say of St Francis that has not been said better and often? But half the sum can be paid as travelling expenses and it is too good to refuse.

Monday 28 November 1955

All last week ruined by the common cold. On Saturday Teresa returned to us having taken her Somerville entrance and presumably failed. Graham Greene's new novel for review – a masterly but base work.

Written on 6 December 1955

Ill, sad, in and out of bed until 1st December when I went to Oxford by way of London. I had my hair cut, ordered a new suit, ate a substantial luncheon at White's and felt better. To Oxford by 4.45. Father Corbishley did not send to meet me at the station, nor did he make me welcome at Campion. Next year I shall break the habit of going up for what each year becomes a less cordial celebration. The Master of Balliol, a large, personable Scotchman, with a vulgar interest in education, Nevill Coghill, David Cecil were the guests. In hall I was deaf, but heard better in library and common-room. We were all bustled off to bed at 11 as usual.

Next morning Corbishley seemed willing to redeem his lack of welcome and spent two hours with me visiting the Ashmolean, which has been transformed

[1] *Sic.*

into a series of elegant reception rooms, all pictures of interest kept out of sight, and the *Light of the World* at Keble. I lunched with Maurice at Wadham. He had forgotten it was Friday. We talked chiefly of Cyril's relations with his concubine. Patrick Kinross has a file of all the cables and most of the letters sent to Conk from the Greek islands. Cyril is keeping an elaborate record which he hopes to make his *magnum opus*. To London by train, refreshed myself with smoked salmon sandwiches at White's. Then to the play about the Jesuits in Paraguay – very theatrical. Dick Stokes was there with an undistinguished woman. They took me to supper at Boulestin.

On Saturday I went by train to Frome – appalling luncheon on board – and was met by Laura and Bron. We went to see a mansion for sale, but no use for our purpose, then to Mells. Katharine in bed. The Powells to cocktails. A happy evening with Ronald. Next day, feeling very well, Mass, morning call on Hollises, James to luncheon, home by motor car to find Teresa entertaining Alice Jolliffe and a disgusting young woman named Gregory. Yesterday I remained in my room until they had left the house, then wrote letters, hung pictures, unpacked wine. The repainting of the back quarters is transforming them.

Written on Sunday 11th. The past week largely occupied by Teresa's hopes and fears over Oxford. For the first two days she was constantly called to the telephone by friends saying they had been telegraphed for to be vivaed. On Wednesday she got a letter summoning her for a weekend. This was construed to mean that she was in the running for a scholarship. On Saturday we took her to Somerville which proves to be a handsome building at the top of St Giles next door to St Aloysius. I was convinced that it was merely from civility to Maurice that she was asked to an interview, but it appears that she is really certain of acceptance. A scholarship is worth only £30 a year and of small significance. We took Polly Grant to luncheon at the Randolph. She has failed and pretends to sour grapes. She speaks as though reading aloud.

On the way home from Oxford we stopped at Swinbrook to look at the church. Bobo's[1] grave is inscribed: 'Say not the struggle nought availeth.'

I have tried to make some Christmas cards by sticking drawing-paper on the backs of mid-Victorian prints.

Monday 12 December 1955

A letter from Peters's office saying that *Life* objects to advancing me travelling expenses for the article on St Francis. A letter from Bron saying he has been invited to stay a week in London with a Mr Mathew. This proved to be false. A sad, sleety morning.

[1] The Hon. Unity Mitford.

Tuesday 13 December 1955

The news came that Teresa has been elected scholar of Somerville. My mind goes back thirty-four years to the December when I got a scholarship and my father wrote, as I have been writing today, letters of thanks to all my schoolmasters. In less than a year he had lost all happiness in me.

Wednesday 14 December 1955

To London with Laura and Teresa. I gave them and Jack McDougall and Sweet Alice luncheon at the Ritz – Lobster Newburg and Tournedos Rossini. Excellent. Later I went to cocktails with Debo. She said she and Diana Mosley were alone. I found all the Astors, all the Trees, all the Cavendishes, Mrs Hammersley and others in a tiny stifling room. Diana and I crouched over an open window as over a fire. Debo has written a delicious, dotty contribution to the 'U' controversy about hens and hons. Smoked salmon with Ian and Ann and an early bed, having arranged for Teresa to go to the Roman Holiday party.

Thursday 15 December 1955

The Hyde Park luncheon. We sat down sharp at 1 and left the table at 5. A magnificent banquet. Then to dinner at the Ritz for the Roman party. I imprudently drank two bottles of Vichy water before starting, felt ill, sat between Liz and Caroline Freud and had to leave the table to be sick. Ate and drank nothing. Ann dressed Teresa prettily for the ball. Many of the women looked nice, all the men quite awful. I left about 2, again having eaten and drunk nothing.

Friday 16 December 1955

Luncheon at the Birkenheads. Dinner at White's with Graham Greene and Cyril Connolly. Cyril obsessed by his cuckolding and very bad company.

Piers Court, Saturday 17 December 1955

Had Bron to see me and gave him a lecture and £5. Returned home to find the little girls. I had a sore throat.

Sunday 18 December 1955

Went to bed after Mass.

Monday 19 December 1955

Spent most of the day in bed.

Tuesday 20 December 1955

Morning in bed. Laura's strength fading. News from *Life* magazine that the St Francis 'commission' is no commission at all. Christmas cards in abundance.

Wednesday 21 December 1955

Laura's strength failed. Teresa to London to try on clothes. She stayed in the train at Kemble where Prothero was meeting her and had to come out from Stroud by bus and walk in bitter cold from Dursley. But she set to and cooked supper and then made Christmas cards. A laudable girl.

Written January 3rd 1956. Christmas was less painful than usual. All the family were home and all in good health. I escaped midnight Mass on the excuse of seeing that Septimus was not kidnapped and walked by myself to church at 8.30. The children spent the morning opening presents. The turkey was a good bird. I had no present from outside the house except a pot of Strasbourg pie from Jack McDougall. An uneventful week. No news from *Life* magazine. I have agreed to contribute £500 to Angela Antrim and Rose Baring in order that Teresa may share their ball with them on July 5th. I have read light novels and done no work and seldom left the house. One day we went to the pantomime in Bristol. Harriet and I by train, to the Art Gallery where Hogarth's triptych is on view for the first time, to luncheon at a decent restaurant called Hort's but no oysters.

Thursday 5 January 1956

A man from Garrard's came and installed the clock at last.

Epiphany 6 January 1956

Early Mass. Bron went to communion. We burned a chair.

Sunday 8 January 1956

I went to Mells stopping at Bath to meet Diana[1] who was coming from London but she was not on the train and I drove on arriving just before dinner. She came at quarter to 9 having got into the 5.5 instead of the 5. She left next afternoon; I stayed until Monday morning. Katharine very infirm. Ronnie showing her little attention, letting her wander out into the wind to call her dog, and totter about the room finding matches and cigarettes. He merely complained that she dropped her stick often. I think he resented the fact that Diana and I were there to see Katharine, not him. The central heating failed and the house was very cold. I called on the Hollises on Sunday morning, read bits of the newspaper aloud. The door had not shut on Diana when Ronnie produced the scrabble board and in the face of my obvious reluctance made me play. I won heavily but he cooked the score.

I drove home on Monday to find a letter from *Life* which seems to make it plain that the St Francis commission is off. My personal appeal to Henry Luce was read and answered by the man of whose conduct I was complaining.

[1] Lady Diana Cooper.

Tuesday 10 January 1956

Auberon has failed to get the seat at Taunton. I was told at Mells by Diana that Pandora Jones,[1] who brought her husband into the Church, is separated from him and being divorced. The Clifford girls are nothing to me but this lapse of the last of them depresses me. Every week it seems I hear of a desertion. I used to see the Church as peculiar people bound by human and divine loyalties. At times it seems a nondescript crowd with comings and goings haphazard. Clarissa's apostasy was the sharpest wound of course.

Wednesday 11 January 1956

Bron's last night of the holidays. Meg insisted on making a celebration of it, carrying it through with champagne, speeches, and one-woman charades with touching vigour.

Friday 20 January 1956

The last child has gone back to school, leaving only Teresa unemployed. Wet, windy, dark, not very cold weather. Low spirits; idleness.

On Tuesday 23rd at luncheon Laura revealed that Derrick, the former cowman, was incapacitated from factory work for a week but fit for milking. I decided to take her to Brighton. In one minute she looked ten years younger, telephoned the Royal Crescent Hotel, arranged for Rose Donaldson to keep Teresa company, and next morning we were off, driving at thirty miles an hour to run in the new engine. The weather darkened but our spirits rose as we approached the coast to find fog and rain. The hotel manageress deftly rearranged the rooms to give us our usual suite. That evening we went to the theatre to see Shaw's *Misalliance*.

Next day shopping and eating and drinking and the cinema. Our usual Brighton regime. Next day another theatre at Worthing – a play about Burgess and Maclean. Laura has had her hair cut and her clothes repaired and is generally rejuvenated. Septuagesima Sunday at Mary Fitzherbert's church. Today 30th, I have induced her to go to London to see Margot Howard de Walden to get advice about Teresa's début. We have got our Gothic clock from the dilatory antiquary.

Tuesday 31st Laura and I separated after breakfast, she to drive home, I to take the train to London where I had to dine and speak at the Staff College at Greenwich, an engagement I made months ago for the insufficient reason that the secretary wrote such a pleasant letter of invitation. For weeks I had been dreading it. We left Brighton in warm sunshine. Before I reached London

[1] Pandora Clifford married Timothy Jones, eldest son of Sir Roderick and Lady Jones (Enid Bagnold, the writer).

snow was falling. I went to White's which was full and jolly. A mot of Andrew Devonshire's: Randolph boasted he was going to Washington 'to keep Jerk in order'. 'Ah', said Andrew, 'the last camel to break the straw's back.' I invited myself to luncheon at the Savile with Peters and my American publisher – a dull dog. There was an aged, snowy-haired, grey-faced, shabby man opposite me who did not look like anyone I had ever seen before. Peters said: 'Have you quarrelled with Peter Rodd?' It was he. The evening papers reported sudden intense cold everywhere and traffic stopped all over the country. I was anxious for Laura, telephoned and found she had got home with difficulty. Then I was anxious for myself and decided to stay in London as long as the frost lasted. It broke on Sunday 5th and I returned home on Monday. My London visit followed the usual manic-depressive curve – manic until midnight on Friday, then an abrupt fall. The Greenwich evening was quite enjoyable. Half an hour's heavy enforced drinking in the anteroom, then dignified dinner in the Painted Hall. Then we adjourned to an anteroom where I spoke for half an hour. I don't know what I said, nor I am sure did my audience – a small club of senior officers – but it seemed to be a success. Then an hour of heavy enforced drinking. Next morning I still was on the up-grade, White's in the morning, I gave Ann luncheon at the Ritz, went round some galleries with her in euphoric mood, dined with Daphne and her new husband[1] in Debo's house. We had tickets for the theatre *Waiting for Godot* – but did not get there until the last interval. I could make no sense of the last act. Daphne and her husband came back to supper with me at the Hyde Park.

On Thursday Ed Stanley and Maimie lunched with me. Harry Stavordale dined with me at Pratt's and we went to a party at Patrick Kinross's for Daphne which lasted until 3. Not many memories of who was there or what I said.

On Friday I went to look at houses for Teresa's ball and lunched with Jack McDougall at Brooks's. I went to tea with Maimie and Coote. She was in very poor shape. I took her to cocktails with Daphne and later I found myself entertaining a lot of strangers to dinner. Maimie stayed on and began to say that she could not face the divorce court, that it was 'against her principles', that she was 'nervous'. She was far from sane.

On Saturday morning all my high spirit was exhausted. White's was empty. I had no appetite for food or drink and this condition persisted. I wandered from club to club, saw Maimie and Coote often. Coote has accepted the post of governess to a Greek family in Constantinople.

I returned to find that Teresa has made all her plans through Stopp to go to Germany. She left this morning – Wednesday. Alec Waugh has sent me his bestseller.[2] It is highly enjoyable.

Yesterday a man with a wooden leg and a very pretty wife came to see the

[1] Daphne Vivian married first the Marquess of Bath and, second, Xan Fielding.
[2] *Island in the Sun.*

house with a view to purchase. I think it is altogether beyond their means, but he has to live in the district as he is employed at Scott's bird sanctuary. He talked vaguely of letting the land and dividing the house. They did not seem a very businesslike young couple.

There is keen excitement about the election of the Professor of Poetry – Auden and Nicolson, both homosexual socialists, and an unknown scholar named Knight. I wish I had taken my degree so that I might vote for Knight. John Sparrow and Maurice Bowra have put up Nicolson, Enid Starkie and David Cecil, Auden.

Dublin, Thursday 9 February 1956

I left for Ireland in low spirits. The aeroplane from Bristol was nearly empty and we arrived at dusk to find intense cold. A slow sad drive through the suburbs. At the Shelborne a letter from Billy[1] saying he expected me at the Kildare Street Club at 7.30. For two hours I sat in my bedroom reading the manuscript of a first novel which seemed wholly cribbed from me. I went to the dinner expecting I don't know what. I found Father D'Arcy and Billy and a little man who looked like Attlee whom they had picked up. He never spoke. Then came a father and son, surgeon-professor and pugilist-barrister; Terence de Vere White the solicitor I once employed when I was looking for a castle; and a neat, baldish youth who never spoke. That was the whole party. It was not, it transpired, the anniversary of Billy's reception, nor very near the date. I can only think Father D'Arcy was in Dublin on other business and proposed the dinner. We sat in the public dining-room and had an excellent dinner with many good wines. I sat between Father D'Arcy and White. White had read the reviews of every book published in English and many of the books themselves. Poor Father D'Arcy's memory is so defective that he begins anecdotes and forgets their point, loses every name. We sat until midnight. For the last hour the talk was on that deadliest of topics – Nancy's 'U' controversy. I walked back to the hotel in a bitter, snowfall wind. Billy had arranged a drive on the Saturday. Otherwise there seemed no pleasures in store. It was not the weather to walk the streets as I should like to have done. I decided to leave at once.

Friday 10 February 1956

A bad night, an early start, Bristol at 12.20 with Laura there to meet me. We lunched at Hort's, drove to Bath to have the car attended to, then home. I found a letter from Bron of the kind I used to send my father at his age, asking to leave school.

Saturday 11 February 1956

Snow. A morning writing letters – exhortation to Bron, instruction to Father

[1] The Earl of Wicklow.

Aelred[1] on how he should rewrite the story of Maria Pasqua [?], thanks to Alec for his bestseller.

Monday 13 February 1956

In the hope of understanding Bron better I read the diaries I kept at his age. I was appalled at the vulgarity and priggishness.

Ash Wednesday 1956

I resolved to make a visit to the Blessed Sacrament daily during Lent and to eschew gin and paraldehyde.

Friday 17 February 1956

I have been successful so far in the first resolve. With great difficulty I have kept the second. Last night I was obliged to resort to paraldehyde.

Saturday 25 February 1956

A week of intense cold. I have two large new oil radiators in the library but by the time I have answered my morning letters I am too frozen to write any more and slink back to the drawing-room. I have kept my Lenten resolution to eschew gin and visit the church daily. Sometimes I walk back. Last night we went to Bristol to see Moira Shearer in *King Lear*. She is no good at all, nor were most of the actors, nor the scene painters. *King Lear* should be filmed.

Tuesday 28 February 1956

The frost has at last broken. My fingers and brain begin to thaw and I can get to work. Bridget and her two daughters came to tea on their way to London. They spoke of nothing but debutante balls and were exceedingly depressing.

Wednesday 29 February 1956

Laura was taken by Diana Oldridge to Uley to consult a witch about the health of a cow. This witch not only diagnoses but treats all forms of disease, human and animal, by means of an object called 'the Box' – an apparatus like a wireless set, electrified, and fitted with dials. She puts hairs or blood in one cavity while in another she inserts various medicaments observing the reaction of a needle. Apparently there are many hundreds of these boxes in operation, mostly in the south and west of England. Laura seems quite confident in their efficacy. Well, Wesley cured himself of pleurisy by rubbing garlic on the soles of his feet.

[1] The Revd. Aelred Watkin, Headmaster of Downside School, 1962–75. Edited the *Great Chartulary of Glastonbury*, 3 vols., 1946–58.

Melbourne Hall, Derby, Saturday 3 March 1956

I set off alone for Melbourne feeling that middle age was no time in which to visit new houses and make new friends. Warm day. Train from Gloucester to Derby – empty carriage. Peter Lothian[1] met me at the station in a small, shabby car and we drove to Melbourne – a fine, Queen Anne stone house on the side of a lake, with a Victorian glass-roofed billiard-room, hall built into what should be the forecourt. A Norman church, a good group of old houses and a dower-house, all on the side of the lake. I was taken straight to luncheon at the dower-house, which is inhabited by an uncle. The dowager lives in the big house, which is open to the public all the summer and not greatly used by Peter and Toni. Jock and Bridget McEwen were at luncheon and two young neighbours. I sat next to an idiot aunt. Good luncheon and good wine. Afterwards we drove to Staunton Harold and walked back part of the way. Staunton Harold has lately been saved from destruction partly by the Pilgrim Trust who took over the church and partly by Cheshire VC who took the house. The church was the first Protestant church to be built – very fine with a roof painted as though by Blake. Lord Ferrers died during the sale of the house. His heir is married to Toni Lothian's sister but lives in Norfolk. The house very dilapidated. Little groups of volunteer labourers are at work on repairs. A few rooms are already occupied by Cheshire's destitute old people. After tea the Haddingtons arrived and a youngish couple named Hay[2] – courtiers. Young neighbours came to dinner, called — —. I asked him whether he was any relation to ——. 'Son.' 'I know your uncle well.' 'We are not speaking to him because of his cruel treatment of Prod.'[3] He then began to speak of Prod whom he sees a great deal and as I talked I suddenly saw in the rather dingy youth a hint of Prod's own expression and I wondered whether he was not Prod's son. Peter Lothian played the piano a little but no one listened. Early and sober to bed. The Blessed Sacrament is kept in an improvised chapel among the bedrooms.

Sunday 4 March 1956

Mass (and communion. It was agreeable to be called by the butler with 'You are going to communion, sir?') at the village church; modern and full of armorial devices of Kerrs. A lazy morning indoors. The Protestant Bishop of Derby and his wife ('call me Cuckoo') came to luncheon. He was the Mr Rawlinson who came to Lancing in 1918 as a fiery young don from the House; a modernist, one of the authors of *Foundations* whom Ronnie attacked in *Some*

---

[1] The 12th Marquess of Lothian.
[2] Lady Margaret and Alan Hay; Lady Margaret Hay was Lady-in-Waiting to the Queen.
[3] The Hon. Peter Rodd.

Loose Stones[1] – whose agnosticism first unsettled my childish faith. He had no memory of me. I remembered coming top of his Divinity set and his giving me back a paper in which I proposed something very near agnosticism with the words, 'No mean theologian, Waugh.' After luncheon we went to Kedleston to visit Lord Curzon's tomb (of which I found my memories curiously distorted and enriched). The church was shut, and looking for a housekeeper we ran into Lord Scarsdale who welcomed us, ten strong, with remarkable geniality and took us round the state-rooms – all in splendid condition. A quiet evening. Everyone flattering to me, a new audience, purring a little.

Piers Court, Monday 5 March 1956

The Hays drove me to London. We stopped for a drink at Aston Clinton and – new audience – I told them about my schoolmastering days. Ann Fleming lunched with me at the Ritz. I tried on clothes, had hair cut, visited the wine merchant. Ran shows curious anxiety to get everything for the ball ordered now. The talk at White's all of motor accidents. Diana Abdy very seriously hurt. Young Gage in it again. Home, tired, by the dinner train.

Tuesday 6 March 1956

Piles of letters and bills.

I forgot; yesterday at White's everyone with long faces because of the international disgrace into which the country is put in Cyprus, Jordan, and everywhere. Randolph in great glee: 'Jerk's very shaky.'

Sunday 11 March 1956

Ann proposed herself for the weekend and then fell sick. Meanwhile we had taken tickets for the theatre in Bristol and saw a clever, blasphemous, indecent play about Don Juan translated from the German. On Sunday the Henriqueses came to luncheon and Coote to tea. She was here to say goodbye before going to the Levant as governess to a Greek family who live half the year in Athens and half in Constantinople. We have today arrested Archbishop Makarios in Cyprus and there are anti-British riots everywhere. Poor Coote will be massacred in Athens as an Englishwoman and in Constantinople as a Greek. She has been engaged because her charge, aged four, is too much advanced and needs retarding. Diana Abdy is lying unconscious in Bristol after a motor accident ten days ago. Her son Valentine is in Truro probably lame for life.

Thursday 15 March–Friday 16 March 1956

Irene Ravensdale was giving a cocktail party for debutantes. I thought I

---

[1] R. A. Knox, *Some Loose Stones, Being a consideration of certain tendencies in modern theology illustrated by reference to the book called 'Foundations'* (London 1913). Knox was then Fellow and Chaplain of Trinity College, Oxford.

could be helpful to Teresa so offered to take her. Since Laura had fittings at
dressmakers I was obliged to take the early train which was crowded –
Thursday being a day when the Duke of Beaufort does not hunt. Uncomfortable journey. Arrived tired with nothing to do in London and, because of my
Lent, nothing to drink. I sat in White's where horrible Randolph imposed
himself on me, boasting of his friendship with Father D'Arcy. He said: 'Annie
says you have not forgiven me for talking too much at luncheon with Clare
Luce.' I said: 'That is the least of the things I have against you.' I did not know
how black his record was until I went to Ann's whom I had asked to luncheon
but who asked me to lunch at her house. A horrible party – Loelia
Westminster, Sir Solomon Zuckerman, a madman and a common musical
couple. They all yelled in Ann's minute dining-room till my head span. She
said that Randolph the previous evening had given Father D'Arcy an account,
which must in its nature be spurious, of my correspondence with Clarissa at the
time of her wedding,[1] adding a totally untrue story that he with a group of
adherents had discomfited me at White's by challenging me on the subject.
After luncheon Ann and I went to an art gallery. Who should be there but
Clarissa with Bridget Parsons. I greeted them but passed politely on, Ann
trying to call me back and later behaving just as Randolph claimed to have
behaved – discomfiting me by challenging my conduct. As disgusted as Mr
Pooter I returned to rest at the Hyde Park Hotel but had no sooner sat down with
my cigar than Laura came in to use my room for rest. I had a bath. I was not
dressed when Teresa arrived to use my room between debutante tea and
cocktail party. I fled to White's, drank a lot of Bollinger '45 and felt better. At
Irene's house there was a crowd so dense I did not attempt to enter the
drawing-room but sat with the butler in the hall. Irene came and sat with me.
Making little sense and drinking champagne, I remember Lady Curzon telling
me that she had to warn clergymen not to give her the chalice at communion
because one nip of wine drove her to dipsomania. Fled very exhausted. Patrick
Kinross came to dine with Laura and me. He is on his way to America for his
first visit.

Next day I had nothing to do except try on trousers. Sat in White's. Home
by the 4.55.

Saturday 17 March 1956

A paragraph in the *Daily Express* which I hope may prove libellous. Bertie
Abdy came to luncheon by train from Bristol. Diana is still unconscious after
more than fourteen days. The surgeons thought she could not live so long.
Bertie professes hope of her complete recovery. His accounts of Valentine (in
hospital at Truro) are more vague. The boy has been delirious, upsetting Bertie
by praying and singing hymns. 'I don't know where he learned such things.' As

[1] To Sir Anthony Eden.

to what limbs are broken he seemed to have little idea. But here he was as happy as a cricket looking at books and pictures and talking without a stop – an inconsequent flow of inaccurate historical information – 'they had no salt in the Middle Ages' – combined with a distinctly bawdy turn. A naïve interest in English art of which he knows not even the leading names. Pugin's *Contrasts* an unknown book to him. He talked for five hours and left me limp.

Easter 1956

I went to Downside on the Wednesday of Holy Week and stayed until after the High Mass of Easter. There were no friends staying at the monastery this year so that the triduum was without distraction. It was indeed rather boring since the new liturgy introduced for the first time this year leaves many hours unemployed. Father Illtyd Trethowan, a bright, youngish philosopher, gave a series of conferences which were outstanding compared with any I have heard at Downside. I found myself in violent disagreement with almost all he said and resentful of the new liturgy. On Thursday, instead of the morning Mass, mandatum, tenebrae and night vigil at the altar of repose, there was an afternoon Mass with the mandatum interpolated after the gospel and the altar of repose emptied at midnight. On Friday, instead of the Mass of the Presanctified, stations of the cross and tenebrae, an afternoon adoration of the cross and general communion. On Saturday nothing (except the conferences) all day until the Easter vigil at 10.30 in the same form we had suffered the last two years. I lunched at Mells on Saturday. Trim and Anne home, he very white, she very black. In spite of all I found the triduum valuable.

Easter week, the family home in full force. Bron behaving admirably. I had good accounts of him from all at Downside. Margaret in great beauty except for her huge feet. I am taking her to Chantilly in Low Week to avoid Teresa's first house-party. Poor Harriet very uncouth and shabby. James quaint. I am hoping to get him educated free by the Jesuits. Much correspondence with Rubinstein[1] about my suit against the *Daily Express*. We went to luncheon with David and Tamara Talbot Rice and I bought a charming little Augustus Egg for £30. On Saturday a dubious young man called Graham came to luncheon ostensibly to photograph Teresa; also Chris.

Low Sunday 8 April 1956

Moira Shearer and Ludovic Kennedy to luncheon. Margaret yawned at Mass like the shadow of the Valois so I made her walk back to church in the afternoon to pray.

Tuesday 10 April–Wednesday 18 April 1956

I took Meg to Paris in some doubt whether it would be a success. It was. She

[1] Of Rubinstein, Nash, solicitors.

was sunny, intelligent, tireless, affectionate, polite. We drove to London airport and took the 'Epicure' luncheon aeroplane. Diana met us in Paris and took us to tea with the Gileses, we looked at the Madeleine and drove out to Chantilly. Margaret and I the only visitors. Next day we went over the Musée Condé, the Louvre, tea with Nancy, cocktails with Pam Churchill. Next day Nancy came out to luncheon, we went back with her to Notre Dame and Sainte Chapelle, tea with Momo who was lying sick in the Ritz. The weather now turned nasty but not so as to damp Meg. Next day to Compiègne with Diana, next day to luncheon with Gaston[1] and to the Musée Grevin. Sunday was cold. Maud Russell came to stay and Tanis[2] and her latest husband to luncheon. Diana forgot to order any food. The high spot was a visit to Senlis in the late afternoon. We dined with jolly racing people.

On Monday Diana went off to Monte Carlo for Prince Rainier's wedding. Meg and I moved to an hotel, where we found John Sutro and Graham Greene. We lunched at Malmaison, went over the palace, went up the Eiffel Tower, to Nancy for an odd whisky party of lesbians and to dinner in Pam's gilded cage with little Winston and various fast and fashionable Frogs and Geoffrey Lloyd the political failure. We went to Cousteau's lovely under-water film.

Next day to Versailles, which Pam arranged for us to see privately. In the evening a delightful dinner party at Susan Mary's – the Gileses, Odette Pol Roger, Lady Jellicoe. Next day Napoleon's tomb and back to London. The English rival luncheon service was even better than the Frog, and more open-handed with the wine and more comfortable machine. Saw Meg on the train home.

Piers Court, Thursday 19 April 1956

An interview with the headmaster of Downside – curiously sanctimonious – who will take James for £100 a year as a candidate for the priesthood. Home that evening.

On Saturday 21st Father Aelred Watkin came to stay. A very agreeable guest.

Tuesday 24 April 1956

Talbot Rices to luncheon.

Thursday 26 April 1956

Bron back to school. He has behaved well.

London, Friday 27 April 1956

I had to go to London for the night for a conference with lawyers over my

---

[1] Gaston Palewskí, French ambassador in Rome, a friend of Nancy Mitford.
[2] Tanis (née Guinness) Phillips; previously Mrs Howard Dietz.

libel action against the *Express*. They appear quite confident of victory. Teresa's social season began. Maimie dined with me. We each drank a bottle of Krug.

Piers Court, Saturday 28 April 1956

Home weary. Prospective purchasers came to see house.

Sunday 29 April 1956

Further prospective purchasers for house. My children show nothing but glee at the prospect of moving.

Monday 7 May 1956

Children have all returned to school. The weather is delicious, the house is silent, there is no reason for me not to work. I will try one day soon.
I did a little work.

Laura's cowman came back to duty. To celebrate her deliverance from the milking parlour we went on a little tour. Had we allowed ourselves two days more it would have been more restful.

Harrogate, Friday 18 May 1956

We drove off at 10 o'clock and reached Rugby at 12.45. The inn was full of Rotarians and Orientals and we had sandwiches in the bar in low spirits. At 4 we reached Doncaster where the Whitsun traffic had made a complete block. We backed out and made a long detour wasting a full hour. We reached Harrogate at 7. A fine old-fashioned hotel, the Majestic. We were both weary. Baths, champagne, salmon, crossword, bed.

Saturday 19 May 1956

An easy journey through splendid country to the McEwens at Marchmont arriving there at 4. I had not seen the border towns since the snows of 1941–2. In spring they were enchanting. Marchmont is a fine Adam house, before Adam invented the style named after him, cleverly enlarged by Lorimer when Jock's father bought it. The furniture was most unworthy of it. Nothing of value or character. No pictures worth glancing at. Bedrooms by Maples. It would be a wonderful house for a collector. Party comprised the Schwartzenburgs, Austrian ambassador – he a pipsqueak, she very elegant, the Lothians, Kistie Hesketh, very quick and clever. Food adequate, wine not copious. Paper games and parlour games.

Sunday morning late Mass in the house, twenty-five minutes. It did not seem like a great feast. In the morning I finished the gin. There was no more in the house. In the afternoon we drove to and failed to enter the Haddingtons' house. On the way back we stopped at East Gordon, the farm from which my great-great grandfather emerged 200 years ago. A good solid house on a hill, one of the largest farms of the district. In Gordon churchyard we found several Waugh tombs.

Whit Monday at breakfast R. A. Butler[1] arrived, squinny-eyed, awkward, given to horrible outbursts of 'Yo ho ho'. He was afraid of assassination by Cypriots but said he was used to that from his Indian childhood but thought it had no part in our democracy. In the afternoon to Abbotsford where I revived memories of 1941. The pretty daughter of the house is now a lonely divorcée, her sister's heart is broken. The two live there quite alone except for the daily flood of tourists which is their sole support.

Cambridge, Tuesday 22 May 1956

Mass and communion in the house and immediate departure. A long day's uneventful drive to Cambridge where I had proposed ourselves to the Walstons. We found a family gathering, Catherine's horrible American mother, a horrible socialist brother, a son and his tutor, late naval Protestant chaplain; Harry[2] provided good wine which I spilt. Their house was a great contrast to Marchmont; Bohemian, profuse, full of objects of beauty and interest.

Piers Court, Wednesday 23 May 1956

Left early and drove to London where Laura went to take duty at Neville Terrace, I spent the day at White's and took the evening train home.

Thursday 24 May 1956

Letters. The house is scoured and polished by Mrs Harper and her circle.

Tuesday 29 May 1956

Delicious weather. Everything looking beautiful. Laura in London. I act as Teresa's social secretary. Various nibbles from prospective purchasers of this house.

Corpus Christi 1956

Twelve years ago I walked to Mass along the banks of the stream to the Maynes' having the day before finished writing *Brideshead*. Today, an equally beautiful day, with nothing to celebrate, I walked through the motor bicycles to Dursley. At midday a youngish couple came to see the house.

Sunday 3 June 1956

Laura, Teresa and I drove over to see a house near Stroud – quite hopeless and inhabited by a poor mad German chemist.

[1] Then Leader of the House of Commons.
[2] H. D. Walston, Labour MP and agriculturalist.

Monday 4 June 1956

Laura and Teresa busy with lists for dance and dinner parties. In the evening Father D'Arcy came for one night only. The Donaldsons to dinner. Not a very exhilarating evening.

Tuesday 5 June 1956

Took Father D'Arcy to the station. A middle-aged New Zealand couple – Catholic fans named Barr – came to luncheon. Another woman came to see the house. We heard of a cheap house in Montgomeryshire.

Wednesday 13 June 1956

Today I accepted the offer of a Mrs Gadsden to buy this house for £9,500.

London, Thursday 14 June 1956

To London early. A very full and happy day in White's. Drinking with Ran and Angela at 6.30 and no details fixed about bed. In the evening a dinner party at Hyde Park Hotel for Bridget's dance. Pretty civil girls, awful young men. I went as far as the house in Chester Square, which was for sale, up a narrow crowded staircase and away to White's. Met Andrew Devonshire who took me off to Liz and Raimund where we drank champagne and talked theology.

Friday 15 June 1956

Chucked Mogs Gage and stayed in London. Happy White's. Took Laura to theatre. Slept during performance.

Saturday 16 June 1956

Laura ill. Day wet. To Ascot. Luncheon at Beefsteak. Laura went to bed. I played ping-pong with little girls and walked with them in the rain. No room in the inn, so to London to sleep.

Piers Court, Sunday 17 June 1956

Communion Brompton Oratory. Little girls came to London by train. Met them at Waterloo. Luncheon at St James's Club. They ate great quantities of crab, gulls' eggs, asparagus, strawberries, etc. National Gallery. Margaret showed great taste, intelligence and memory. Long drive home.

Pixton Park, Tuesday 19 June 1956

Set out on house-hunting tour. Saw decayed, odd house named Bridon [?], near Nutcombe. Slept Pixton.

Wednesday 20 June 1956

Laura's birthday. A day driving round Devon and Cornwall looking at houses. Saw one that was just tolerable. All the rest useless.

Thursday 21 June 1956

Another day's ineffectual house-hunting. Lunched 1½ hours late with Bertie Abdy. No that was yesterday. Today we lunched at Bideford. Saw two or three useless houses. In the evening Auberon arrived and was bland and genial and rather likeable.

Piers Court, Friday 22 June 1956

Home. A letter from Mrs Gadsden confirming the sale of this house which I had begun to suspect.

Saturday 23 June 1956

Teresa entertaining Alice Jolliffe and some awful youths for a local dance. She wore hideous dress. All late for dinner.

London, Tuesday 26 June 1956

I went to London in the early train wearing my grey bowler hat and feeling jaunty. I fell in with a happy drinking set in White's and drank. Later I gave a dinner party at the Hyde Park Hotel. I was enchanted by Alexander Weymouth. Otherwise I have little memory of anyone there. I went for a few minutes to the Hyltons' ball in St James's Square and then to Dot Head's at Chelsea Hospital. The whole royal family were there and all the knights of the garter. The young did not enjoy it but the old did.

Wednesday 27 June 1956

Went with Ran to see the police in Kensington – a strange matinée idol superintendent. Andrew Devonshire gave me a cigar case. Angela lunched with me at the Ritz.

Thursday 28 June 1956

Sobering up. I went to a cocktail party at Simon Elwes. Then to dinner at Ann Fleming's. Ian passed a stone some days earlier. Without appetite or hearing at dinner. Nicky Gage wore no tie. Thomas Pakenham wore Arab fancy dress. We went to Tanis's party which was like a nightclub – all old noisy people in cramped surroundings and to Lady Nicholls's which was airy and youthful. Back to Tanis. Walking at 2 or 3 from Cadogan Square to Knightsbridge London was full of men in white ties strolling about.

Friday 29 June 1956

Early Mass. Then to Max Beerbohm's funeral in St Paul's. Ill attended. Lunched at Ritz with Teresa and Osbert Lancaster – raw steak. Teresa Jungman lunching with David Margesson.[1] Returned by train very exhausted.

---

[1] 1st Viscount Margesson; Secretary of State for War, 1940–42.

Saturday 30 June 1956

A long drive to Radnorshire to see Pencraig House – 1860 domestic Gothic, very attractive. Wretched agent had no idea how much land, which cottages, etc., were for sale.

Sunday 1 July 1956

Laura gallantly went to take out Bron and James.

Monday 2 July 1956

Laura very busy with holocaust of capons for ball. I wrote my letters.

Tuesday 3 July 1956

Laura to London. Architect condemns Bridon [?] House utterly.

Now as I move about the house and garden nothing irks me as it used to do. It is Mrs Gadsden's house not mine so I don't care if the stone crumbles and the tap drips and the weeds smother the beds. I am soon going. There is a meditation to be made on death on these lines.

London, Thursday 5 July 1956

After two dreary days alone at home I went to London by train for Teresa's ball. It was dark with some drizzle after a stormy night, but I had sent £2 to the Poor Clares at Looe asking them to arrange good weather from 7 pm onwards and at 7 it cleared and remained fine throughout the night; a remarkable performance by these excellent women to whom I have sent another £3. Most days since have been wet. Rain would have ruined everything as there were far too many people for the tents and house and the square gardens were crowded. Angela[1] had arranged the tents brilliantly and her painted arch was funny and clever and pretty. We were photographed in the tent in the afternoon. Angela's party dined in the square. Laura and I gave a dinner party at the Hyde Park Hotel. I sat between Maimie and Nell Stavordale. Ed Stanley was very jolly. The young people – except Raymond Bonham-Carter – looked seedy. One dreadful youth was in a dinner jacket as were also many others at the ball – including Phil Dunne and John Marriott[2] who should know better and have not the excuse that they wished to 'jive'. I spent most of the evening in the house, fairly cheerful at first but with deepening boredom. By 3.30 it was plain that the party was a great success and that no untoward incidents threatened, so I slunk away. The rest danced on until after 5.

Piers Court, Friday 6 July 1956

Laura and I drove home, very weary.

[1] The Countess of Antrim; sister of Christopher Sykes.
[2] Major-General Sir John Marriott, DSO, MC.

Saturday 7 July 1956

A small house party assembled for a ball at Sudeley Castle.

Sunday 8 July 1956

House party would not go. Instead it grew in numbers.

Pixton Park, Monday 9 July 1956

Laura, Teresa and I drove to see the house at Combe Florey that is for sale – cosy, sequestered, with great possibilities – and slept at Pixton.

Piers Court, Tuesday 10 July 1956

Home, stopping again at Combe Florey and another house (hopeless), lunching at Wells. Teresa shows marked deterioration.

London, Wednesday 11 July 1956

Feeling better. To London by motor. A very enjoyable White's. Lunched with Dick Stokes. Dinner party that evening for the Norfolks' ball. For the first time Teresa had collected some presentable young men. The Hyde Park Hotel was full of dinner parties for the ball. The ball at St James's Palace was a splendid parade of the ancien régime. I enjoyed it very much.

Piers Court, Thursday 12 July 1956

Good White's. Good Ritz where Pam Berry came to luncheon with me and soothed [?] me with flattery. Drove home with Laura leaving Teresa to her own devices. I have decided that the duties of chaperonage are too painful for Laura.

A quiet weekend eating and sleeping badly, corresponding with house agents.

Monday 16 July 1956

Mrs Gadsden came to luncheon bringing her solicitor son who seems to have married a negress. Mrs G. was most accommodating, expressing willingness to take over cows and peasants if required. All she will not accept is the statue of Rafael.

Wednesday 18 July 1956

Laura and I drove with Mrs Donaldson to see a house named Buckshaw (not much good) lunched at Yeovil (no good at all) saw Ston Easton again (most seductive).

Friday 20 July 1956

Margaret and Harriet returned from school.

Thursday 26 July 1956

This is the last quiet day before Teresa is on us with debutantes and dances.

Friday 27 July 1956

Christina McDonnell arrived from Ireland before luncheon. Teresa was not home to entertain her since she had neglected to take her driving lessons in London and was therefore taking two on her last morning. She arrived at tea-time in a motor car driven by a civil young man who drove away at once leaving beind a deleterious half-wit who had neither money, luggage, nor an invitation for the night. He decided to impose himself on the Mitchels twenty-five miles away, whose house he had passed on the way here, to which Teresa expected Laura to drive him between her milking and going out to dinner. When we left at 8 the young Donaldsons had arrived but not the three young men from London. Laura and I went to dinner at Tresham and on returning learned that Teresa's dinner party had sat down at 9.15.

Saturday 28 July 1956

One of the young men, having reached the house at 7 am required to be driven away by Laura at 8.30. I never saw him. He was Simon Elwes's elder boy. At luncheon-time two civil young men named Turton and Bowes-Lyon appeared. We sent them all away in the rain to a fête at Altrincham's, whose brother Christina is courting. After dinner the young men were serious about politics and sent early to bed.

Sunday 29 July 1956

Both young men went to the Protestant church at 8. We sent them to luncheon in Gloucester and to see sights. A champagne party developed on their return. After supper the young men departed. Bron returned from visit.

Mells, Monday 30 July 1956

Christina stayed on. Diana came to luncheon in exuberant spirits having driven from Ramsbury in dark glasses claiming mescalin vision. She was the life and soul of luncheon with an appreciative audience, climbed to the top of Stinchcombe Hill and had forty winks. Then she and I drove off to Mells. Her spirits sank as she approached. 'Don't want to get there.' We found Katharine stronger. All Oxfords and Asquiths and Ronnie present but not a very cheerful evening, Diana taking against Oxfords, Ronnie doing crosswords and asking the meaning of recondite words in dictionary, Trim making us late for dinner which as a result had to be gobbled.

Piers Court, Tuesday 31 July 1956

Large picnic of children and Christina and all Mells and Diana at Ston Easton. Children in high spirits. The house seemed rather more formidable and forbidding.

Wednesday 1 August 1956

General exodus. Christina to Griggs, Margaret to Nutcombe, Teresa to Bickham. We dropped Christina and Teresa, and with Bron, Margaret and Hatty drove to Combe Florey, very cosy and welcoming. To my surprise the children seemed to prefer it to Ston Easton.

Thursday 2 August 1956

Weary. Laura went to London to fetch James. Another house, an episcopal palace near Exeter, has presented itself.

Friday 3 August 1956

Rain and storm.

Wednesday 8 August 1956

An early start for Bishop's Court. A letter from Meg passionately pleading with me to buy her Combe Florey. The car broke down, as only ours ever does, but we arrived at 11.45 to find a solid spacious house in a fine park. The interior is 1868 with some art nouveau additions. Could it be Burges? An untruthful fellow showed us over. The weather was oppressive. We lunched with the nearest neighbours Griffith-Williams at a very elegant Regency house, had hock which gave me a stomach ache, picked up Meg in Exeter and went back to Bishop's Court. She was immediately wildly enthusiastic about it and demands that I buy it. A long, tiring drive home enlivened by a call on Agnes Holmes. I looked up the Garratt family and find that the owner responsible for the 1868 restoration married a de Salis and named his son Challoner, which points to papistry.[1] In the evening Eden made a plaintive whine on the wireless about Suez.

Whitchurch, near Aylesbury, Saturday 11 August 1956

I took Margaret to stay with Pam Berry at Oving. She was in low spirits perhaps because I had struck her the evening before for breaking my 'acme' chair the second time. Laura drove us and we arrived for luncheon. Oving is not an imposing house from outside. Pam has created an elaborate interior of plaster work and made it luxurious and ornamental. No other visitors. Nicholas

---

[1] Richard Challoner (1691–1781); Vicar Apostolic of London 1758; author of *Garden of the Soul*, 1740, a favourite devotional book of English Catholics.

Berry has become an attractive boy, Adrian a gangling creature, who has disgraced himself in France by giving all his money to the Poujadiste Party and is now filling in time before going up to the university driving a lorry for £9 a week. We played childish poker. The white Bordeaux at luncheon griped me.

Sunday 12 August 1956

Pam civilly drove Meg and me to Mass in Aylesbury. The family party pottered about the bathing pool. Weather was bad. In the late afternoon we drove to look at neighbouring house. Meg won money off Adrian at cards (did he perhaps lose his francs in that way?) and he insisted in playing on in the hope, unrealized, of winning it back.

Piers Court, Monday 13 August 1956

Pam very civilly sent us all the way to Reading. The train which Laura looked out for us proved to be 'Saturdays only' so we had two hours to wait. Meanwhile Meg's school friend, Fanny, an uninteresting child, had arrived at Stinchcombe.

Saturday 18 August 1956

A week of depraved idleness. Continuous storms. Laura and I went to London on Thursday and had our hair cut and ate caviare, grouse and peaches at the Ritz, to cheer ourselves up. I await news of Bishop's Court survey. A Canadian Jew came to interview me for the wireless.

Tuesday 11 September 1956

Today after weeks of uncertainty, during which Bishop's Court was bought for the full price asked, and Mr Banks proved less sympathetic as a trustee than I had hoped, I heard that the Batchelors will accept £7,500 for Combe Florey with the land in hand less an outlying plantation. I had begun to have real fears that we should find ourselves back at the start of house-hunting again with the winter coming on and no shelter. As it is there are annoyances – the Batchelors won't move until the end of November.

Laura and Bron and Hatty are at Portofino, James and Septimus at Bickham. I had a happy two days alone with Margaret. Then Teresa returned bringing Annabel Hennessy. The two girls sit all day in the drawing-room, Teresa working a little, Annabel extremely idle. Meg sulks. I have resumed work on *Pinfold*. The Donaldsons have been to see me twice. No car. Dark, wet, cold weather to match the news in the papers. The film company who should have paid £5,000 this month have failed. But at least I am sure of a roof at Christmas.

Friday 28 September 1956

There has been one fine day and many foul, three days of industry, many of idleness. Annabel left, Laura and Margaret and Harriet and James returned. Margaret and Harriet went away. James went away. Laura and I went to Combe Florey where Col. Batchelor hid from us. I found the plans I had made for a new drive impracticable. The sale and purchase of houses takes up much time. But *The Ordeal of Gilbert Pinfold* progresses. A bill for a further £250 for Teresa's ball was a crippling blow.

Saturday 29 September 1956

Laura and I had an engagement to visit Mrs Gadsden in her Cotswold cottage. We went first to David Rice, who gave us a brace of partridges. Mrs Gadsden had made great preparations with half a dozen different titbits to eat. I mistook – again – her major-domo for her architect. Two people, nameless, from near Chard. Other guests came as we left. We dined with Francis Howard at Hatherop. Various cousins there. Vintage port before dinner.

Monday 1 October 1956

Unsatisfactory letters from all business associates. Worked hard. No cigars.

Wednesday 10 October 1956

I have worked hard and easily, seldom writing less than a thousand words a day. The book is too personal for me to be able to judge it. I have also had much correspondence with lawyers, etc. This house is sold, Combe Florey is bought, but every day seems to bring more need for negotiation. And there is all the business of moving furniture to order. Laura has been rather ill. Teresa went to Oxford today with Alice Jolliffe who has been a lot in the house. A nice-mannered girl.

A week ago having run out of gin I went to the Prince of Wales for a bottle, tendered £2, and was given a handful of silver in exchange. Later I thought too much. Yesterday, again out of gin, I went back and said: 'Did you find your money lacking in the till when I bought a bottle?' 'No.' I again gave £2. '34s 6d' said the barmaid giving me 15s 6d change. 'I hope you don't mind all silver' just as she had said before. I gave her back 10s and she seemed not much surprised.

Thursday 11 October 1956

To London for the day to have my hair cut, give salt cellars to Plante to be gilded and lunched with Lady Curzon in Alfred's honour. It was all slightly better than I expected. Cyril was at luncheon and came back to White's. Since

P. Watson left him £1,000 he spends his time talking to his stockbroker. He said that after Dunkirk he feared a Fascist rising led by Harold Acton.

Sunday 14 October 1956

Mary came to luncheon. The Donaldsons to dinner bringing Robin Campbell who was surly, opinionated, and under-dog.

Tuesday 16 October 1956

I have worked hard every day lately. Not today. Rebecca West has libelled me, according to the *Daily Express*.

Sunday 28 October 1956

My 53rd birthday. A charming present of marble eggs from Bron, otherwise no recognition. The house is half empty of furniture. On Wednesday we shall sleep here for the last time. My 'novel' has progressed well but is not finished. Laura has moped a little at seeing her house dismantled. I am exhilarated. We have had some rather gruesome farewell visits. The removal of library shelves reveals deplorable condition of walls behind them. Mrs Gadsden made a last-minute attempt to knock £500 off the price of the house. Odd.

7 'Irregular notes' 1960-65

Introduction

With Waugh's move to Combe Florey House, near Taunton, the diary breaks off for four years. *The Ordeal of Gilbert Pinford* was published during the summer of 1957. Waugh spent 1958 researching his biography of Ronald Knox, visiting Southern Rhodesia early in the year to discuss Knox with Lady Acton and to consult her collection of Knox's letters and papers. Waugh made a further visit to Africa in 1959, as a tourist, writing newspaper articles to pay his way. During 1959 and 1960 he was also occupied with the third and final volume of his wartime trilogy, *Unconditional Surrender*.

December 1960.[1]

Fading memory and a senile itch to write to *The Times* on all topics have determined me to keep irregular notes of what passes through my mind.

The Cooper Memorial Prize. Princess Alexandra brought off a good left and right thanking 'Sir Horace Bowra' for his speech of welcome and remarking that Duff would always remain illustrious for his slim volume *Operation Handbrake*.[2]

What was Mrs Morris doing in 1872 when Rossetti went mad? There is no mention of her seeing him, attempting to, getting or seeking news of him.

I must have given my hat many hundreds of times to the old porter at the Ritz (London). The other day when I came to leave after luncheon he was not on duty, so I went behind his counter and collected my belongings. In my hat he had put a label with the one word 'Florid'.

Archbishop Roberts had an audience with the Pope a week after Dr Fisher. Pope asked: 'Who was that other English Archbishop who was here last week?'

Betjeman's biography.[3] John demonstrates how much more difficult it is to write blank verse than jingles and raises the question: *why* did he not go into his father's workshop? It would be far more honourable and useful to make expensive ashtrays than to appear on television and just as lucrative.

---

[1] In the final section, a notebook rather than a diary, Waugh's own style of dating has been reproduced.

[2] According to Anthony Powell, it was not Princess Alexandra but the recipient of the prize, Canon Andrew Young, the poet, who made the error. See *London Magazine*, August–September 1973, p. 72.

[3] *Summoned by Bells*, written in verse.

Christmas. All that remains of Bethlehem is the breakdown of communications; no room in the inn. We adopted the heathen festivals. We must not whine now that the heathen are taking them back again.

Cyril Holman Hunt left a family of Eurasians in Bridport.

28 December 1960   Laura and I drove to luncheon with the Sykeses at Donhead St Mary – our first visit. A solid unimposing house on the village street. Inside Camilla's brilliant taste much compromised by poverty. Mark was there looking quite presentable. He had a Japanese girl posing as an Australian, long black hair, tight black trousers, but surprisingly well mannered. Other guests were Bell and American wife. Christopher and I talked of our luncheon with Claudel which was dim in my memory. He had taken me there on the day of our jaunt to Paris after we had drunk heavily *en voyage*. The old man was deaf and dumb. All his family – wife, sons, and daughters-in-law – sat round the table. He greeted me by putting into my hands a newly printed *edition de luxe* of some verses of his. A present? I began to thank him. He took it away and put it on a table. I had the impression it was to be my prize if I behaved well. Lively conversation mostly in English. Every now and then the old man's lips were seen to move and there would be a cry 'Papa is speaking!' and a hush broken only by unintelligible animal noises. Some of these were addressed to me and I thought he said: 'How would you put into English "*potage de midi*"?' I replied: 'Soup at luncheon.' It transpired that he was the author of a work named *Partage de Midi*. His tortoise eyes glistened with hostility. After luncheon there was a good deal of fuss among the womenfolk as to whether or no papa was to have cognac. He got it, brightened a little, called for an album and made me sit by him as his arthritic fingers turned the pages. It was like one of Maimie's albums; anything that caught his fancy had been pasted in. Some were humorous, some not. There was a group of the Goebbels [?] family. 'That's funny,' I said, feeling on safe ground. 'I think it *very* sad,' he mumbled. The flat in Passy was dark and ugly with objects brought from Japan. When we left he came to the drawing-room door and laid his hand on the *edition de luxe*, gave me another look of reptilian hate, and left it on its table. Next day he told a daughter-in-law that both Christopher and I were 'très gentlemen'.

At luncheon with the Sykeses I felt euphoric and facetiously told a story in my absurd French, but returning home to my coughing children and the litter of chocolate boxes all the cafard of Christmas returned in force.

31 December 1960 – 1 January 1961   The *Daily Mail* sent me an advance copy of Graham Greene's *A Burnt-Out Case* asking for a review for which, I suppose, they would have paid £100. I have had to refuse. There is nothing I could write about it without shame one way or the other. Coming so soon after his Christmas story it emphasizes a theme which it would be affected not to regard as personal – the vexation of a Catholic artist exposed against his wishes to acclamations as a 'Catholic' artist who at the same time cuts himself off from divine grace by sexual sin. The hero of *A Burnt-Out Case* is a bored, loveless voluptuary who hides his despair in the most remote place he can find – a leper settlement in the Congo – recovers a spark of humanity but not his 'faith' and dies in an absurdly melodramatic way. The efficient doctor is an atheist. The faithful missionaries have given up all attempt to impose the moral law and are interested only in building and finance. A grotesque Catholic layman seeks to impose mystical ideas on his adolescent wife. There is an excellent sermon by the Father Superior and a splendid creation of the heat and remoteness of the leproserie. The journalist intruder is a sham – 'Quote – Wordsworth'. It is the first time Graham has come out as specifically faithless – pray God it is a mood, but it strikes deeper and colder. What is more – no, less – Graham's skill is fading. He describes the hero's predicament three times, once, painfully, in a 'fairy story' which is supposed to take up a whole night but is in fact told in ten minutes. The incident of Deo Gratia's attempted escape and rescue is poorly handled. Graham can't carry corn [?]. His early books are full of self pity at poverty and obscurity; now self pity at his success. I am not guiltless as one of those who put him in the odious position of 'Catholic artist'. He complained of the heat of his sexual passions, now at their coldness. A book I can't review.

4 January 1961   I wrote to Graham saying that taken in conjunction with his Christmas story, his new novel makes it plain that he is exasperated by his reputation as a 'Catholic' writer. I told him in all sincerity how deeply sorry I am for my share in this annoyance. Twelve years ago a lot of Catholics were suspicious of his good faith and I officiously went round England and America reassuring them. I pray that the desperate conclusions of 'Marie' and 'Querry' are purely fictitious. It has been a bad year for the old steeplechasers – Elizabeth Bowen, John Betjeman, Lesley Hartley down and out of the race; Nancy Mitford and Tony Powell just clinging in the saddle. *A Burnt-Out Case* will be a heavy fall.

6 January 1961   Writing to *New Statesman* to defend his country against the charge of being unprogressive, the Persian ambassador quotes as evidence of modernity that domestic servants are unprocurable.

Letters not written to *Observer* January 22nd. (1) to ask Mrs Gilliatt[1] how one decapitates a head (2) to point out to Mr Pavey, who says that capital punishment was forbidden by rabbinical law 2,000 years ago, that at that time they had no authority to inflict it and that when the Zionists murdered Lord Moyne (and others) they justified their acts by calling them 'executions' by a sovereign state.

30 January 1961　An absolutely barren day. I just sat reading American detective stories. In the evening an offer of 50 guineas for my aunt Elspeth's copy of *The World to Come*, a deplorable set of verses in the metre of *Hiawatha*, aping the theme of the *Dream of Gerontius*, written when I was twelve. I accepted.

Much fuss about *10 Rillington Place*. No one has pointed out that Evans, a lapsed Catholic, was hell-bent. As a result of his conviction he returned to the Church and died shriven. This exactly illustrates the point I made in a letter to the *Spectator*.

4 February 1961　To Mells arriving at 6. Christopher Hollis was there. He announced that he had just seen on the television a report of Edward Longford's[2] death. Quarter of an hour later the telephone rang. Frank. Would I write a panegyric for *The Observer*. I had not seen Edward for twenty-five years and knew nothing of his activities in Dublin. I told him to tell *The Observer* to write to me about it in as chilling a manner as I could assume. Then Magdalen telephoned Katharine to propose herself to tea next day. Hearing I was there she wailed: 'He hates me.' Endless 'no he doesn't' 'yes he does'. Finally she said she would not come.

5 February 1961　Magdalen came. She looked gravely ill, fleshless and transparent under a fuzz of blue hair. She was on her way to Oxford to conduct a conversation at the Old Palace about Ronald for the American television – a project I declined to take part in weeks ago. 'Tell me what I'm to say.' 'If I knew what to say I should be in your place.'

To dinner with Tony and Violet Powell. Any scruples we felt about approaching a house of mourning instantly dispelled by ribaldry. Frank had spent the previous evening telephoning to everyone he knew seeking publicity for Edward. Pansy, when told he fell dead at the luncheon table, remarked, 'Just like Charles Dickens.' When asked to the funeral: 'He never came to any

---

[1] Penelope Gilliatt, *The Observer* film critic.
[2] The 6th Earl of Longford: elder brother of the Hon. Frank Pakenham, Lady Violet Powell, and Lady Pansy Lamb.

of *our* funerals.' Great uncertainty about Edward's will, Chrstine's future residence, the fate of Pakenham. Frank had roped in two hired mourners – Tristram Powell and young Mount, both from Oxford.[1] I was reminded of Pansy's story of her mother's announcement in the nursery: 'Children, your father has been killed in action and in future your brother, Silchester, will be addressed as "Edward".'

6 February 1961 A letter from David Astor asking for a panegyric of Edward. *The Observer* had already printed an ample obituary.

7 February 1961 Wrote a brief description of Edward as a young man. I said it was done at the request of the new head of the family. I hope they retain that sentence.

12 February 1961 A great pleasure resulting from being rid of servants – one can throw away all the presents they have ever given one.

24 March 1961 Reading the report of the *Lady Chatterley* trial I found quoted the ludicrous scene between Mellors and Lady C.'s father. I must have read it years ago. It had entirely gone from my mind, but I recognized in it the germ of the hallucination I suffered and described in *Mr Pinfold*. This father of Lawrence's was the father I had heard urging his daughter to my cabin.

4 May 1961 It is a common feature of all but the most recent fiction that a character is falsely suspected of a misdemeanour and is able to recognize his true friends from the false by their irrational belief in his innocence. How many of my friends should I believe innocent of what crimes? If I heard, e.g., that Andrew Devonshire was arrested for sodomy, Ann Fleming for poisoning her husband, Bob Laycock for burglary, should I not think: how surprising and amusing?

3 June 1961 RECESSIONAL[2]
The tumult and the shouting dies;
The D'Armses and the Waughs depart;
Still stands thy mound of dough and ice –
Fond product of the baker's art.
Thy wedding-cake is with us yet,
Lest we forget; lest we forget.

---

[1] Nephews.
[2] Written after the marriage of Teresa Waugh.

21 June 1961 Fiona O'Neil has decided to marry Mr Morgan. When struck, Fiona tells me, he emits a sound like a steam locomotive *through his ears*.

I was the guest in London of the BBC, Christopher Sykes acting as host. Unlike other great businesses they have no motor cars available. Christopher had to stand at street corners waving at taxis. They were unable to obtain theatre tickets for me. The Director-General, Graham's brother,[1] had me to dinner at Shepherd's Bush in a new 'Television Centre'. This was well-found. Graham in a state of euphoria such as I have never seen him in. He spends Christmas in Addis Ababa. We may expect a Communist rising there before Easter.

I am reminded of the time Graham and I went to Rheims with a mixed party of celebrities to visit the champagne houses. At the air office we were given a list of fellow-guests. Alan Pryce-Jones among them. Graham said: 'I am not coming. I won't go with that man Jones.' 'What do you mind about him?' 'I absolutely detest him.' 'Well, he isn't here. He always accepts all invitations and decides on the most attractive at the last moment. He's obviously chucked.' So Graham got into the bus. But Alan was at the aerodrome, having motored there. It was then too late for Graham to escape. He had a bottle of whisky with him and swigged for comfort. He swigged throughout the *vin d'honneur* and the banquet. At 11 o'clock the dinner party broke up. Graham wanted to find a brothel and would not believe they had all been closed. I went to bed early. We had an early start for Epernay in the morning. Alan Pryce-Jones was in the hall, fresh and elegant, looking eighteen years old. Graham lurched out of the lift with bloodshot eyes and pallid face and trembling hands. 'I sat up till 4 drinking whisky,' he said. 'Who with?' 'Alan Pryce-Jones.'

15 July 1961 Hemingway's suicide has made me reread *Fiesta*. It was a revelation to me when it first came out – the drunk conversations rather than the fishing and bullfighting. Rereading I was still impressed by the writing but the construction is imperfect. The opening gives a full description of Cohn in detail allowed to no other character. It was clearly intended to be the tragedy of Cohn but he fades away at the end.

18 July 1961 I have spent some days clearing up papers, preparing to start on my autobiography (with some misgivings about what Alec is going to say in

---

[1] Sir Hugh Greene.

his). I found a number of scraps of paper on which I had jotted down thoughts and anecdotes during the last fifteen years. I transcribe them here without dates and without order.

A profoundly immoral principle: 'It will all be the same in 100 years time.' All morality depends on causality to the nth degree. Every act of free will, good or bad, attenuates its consequences to the end of time.

After Ronald Knox's death Douglas Woodruff visited Mells and asked Katharine for a little souvenir to carry away. Of course; had he anything particular in mind? What he would most value, said Douglas, was the typewriter on which Ronald wrote his translation of the Vulgate. 'Alas,' said K., 'that broke down and was thrown away. He got this new one just before his death and hardly used it.' 'That'll do,' said Douglas, picking it up there and then and making off with it.

Tugboat Annie Rosse,[1] being conducted round the estate at Birr, was taken to a turf cabin where a crone sat in pig dung smoking a pipe and complaining of the roof. 'My dear, don't change a thing. It's simply *you*!'

Reading the papers, and especially the literary reviews, is like sitting in a railway carriage and hearing a fellow-passenger pointing out to a companion passing objects of interest and getting them all wrong. 'There's the white horse,' he says at Westbury, 'that Chesterton wrote about.' One's instinct is to put him right. Reason opposes: 'What the hell?'

Loup. The fish that is grilled, stuffed with fennel, flambé in brandy and remains quite tasteless.

The pagan soul has been compared to a bird flying through a lighted hall and out into the darkness. Better, to a bird fluttering about in the gloom, beating against the windows when all the time the doors are open to the air and sun.

Politicians are not people who seek power in order to implement policies they think necessary. They are people who seek policies in order to attain power.

We are all American at puberty; we die French.

Doppelgängers don't recognize one another.

---

[1] The Countess of Rosse, née Messel.

If one writes: 'sloe eyes' one is trite. If one writes: 'eyes like bullaces' one pleases and instructs. The meaning is identical.

It is impudent and exorbitant to demand truth from the lower classes.

'My dear young lady, you are going to get many, many offers of marriage.' 'How exciting! How do you know?' 'Murderesses always do.'

House-maids' nerves.

When Osbert's ancestor HURT assumed the ancient name of Sitwell he went the whole hog and called his son Sitwell Sitwell. Perhaps his hypersensitive descendant should resume the patronymic and call himself Sir Hurt Hurt.

The King was the sacrificial victim; later the object of betrayal and assassination. The People have assumed the crown. Their heads lie uneasy.

Where are you dying tonight?

Robert Byron was like Belloc in his banging about of ideas and a few facts. Belloc represents a tradition. He thinks himself the voice of Europe. There is no personal arrogance in his slapdash manners. Robert represented nothing except his own groping foibles. His march east would have taken him to Communism.

Politicians thrive by concealing the price-tags.

Nations have no adult life. They sicken and die the day they come of age.

Christians of this latest age are beholden to their infidel neighbours for reducing society to a condition in which many sins have lost their allure and many false opinions their plausibility. In the time of our grandparents avarice was rewarded with popular esteem and with power; luxury took many delicate forms; the world wore so fair a face that the warnings of the prophets sounded archaic and neurotic; hedonists were happy and atheists gave evidence of virtue; no one seemed deserving of Hell. It took heroic Faith to renounce the world and the flesh and fear the Devil. Now all we need for the renunciation is elementary common-sense. But that virtue has grown scarce lately.

10 August 1961   Wanted: two more English pronouncial possessive adjectives; one (like 'their') which can be used for both 'his' and 'her' and would render unnecessary such awkward phrases as 'everyone receives his or her reward'; also something corresponding to 'suus' and 'ejus'. 'Fox watched his son breaking *his* gold watch' instead of 'his (Fox's)' or 'his (the son's)'.

In speaking of contemporary art and architecture 'late' should be used instead of 'modern'.

2 September 1961   Reminiscence. When Ducker of the Turl died I told Catherine Walston that I must find a new bootmaker. She took me to Thrusal of Cambridge (with whom I have dealt ever since). On my first visit he was measuring me for my last when Catherine suddenly drew attention to Thrusal's own boot which was almost circular, like the boots ponies wore on their hooves when drawing lawn mowers. 'That's exactly the kind of shoe I have been looking for all my life.' 'I regret to say, madam, that I am obliged to wear it because of a deformity of the foot.'

Mushrooms are a flavour, not a food. This is also true of blackberries (Oct).

18 September 1961   On Saturday Janet Kidd gave a ball that was very lavish. The horses in their boxes were floodlit and a stallion bit an American pornographer. There was an oyster bar in the harness room. I knew barely six of the people there. Girls outnumbered men. Janet had a 'special' bottle of champagne for me – 1928 and completely *madérisé*. Today she announces it in *The Times* incorrectly calling herself 'The Hon. Mrs Edward Kidd'[1]. She lists as hosts and hostesses of dinner parties Hinchingbrooke, who brought a daughter and one pansy, Laura who brought Sibell Rowley, Bron and Teresa, Ronald Duncan who had had no dinner at all having just arrived by train to stay with Janet, and Barbara Colyton who wasn't there at all.

Reminiscences. Randolph reading the Bible for the first time: 'My God, what a shit God is!'

5 October 1961   Dinner at the Garrick to celebrate the publication of Harold Acton's second volume of Neapolitan history. Dinner, chosen by John Sutro, excellent; the book unreadable. I sat next to the old Bloomsbury sinologue Arthur Waley who told me that Miss Compton-Burnett's father was a doctor in Hove and that all her rural scenes are entirely imaginary. I reminded him we had met forty years ago at Renishaw (nearly) and that he had then shown

[1] The Hon. Janet Aitken, daughter of the 1st Baron Beaverbrook, married in 1943, as her third husband, Major Thomas Edward Kidd.

superior knowledge of winter sports to Gaspard Ponsonby. He said: 'Oh, dear. I am sorry.' It is seldom I have heard the voice of Bloomsbury.

21 November 1961   Violet Clifton. RIP. I stayed with her only once. She objected to a telegraph boy whistling as he came up the drive.

24 November 1961   An irrational satisfaction in the news that Teresa (Waugh) is pregnant. If similar tidings came from D'Arms I should merely reflect 'another American'.

14 March 1962   Were I tempted to believe in the transmigration of souls, I should find support in the observation that people like Quennell seem soulless. The population of the earth is multiplying. There are not enough souls to go round.

Clarissa writes to Ann Fleming: 'The Haileses[1] found Evelyn W. rather a bore.' I thought I had charmed and delighted them.

24 March 1962   White's. 7 pm. I sit alone in the hall. A member known to me by sight but not by name, older than I, of the same build, but better dressed, said: 'Why are you alone?' 'Because no one wants to speak to me.' 'I can tell you exactly why; because you sit there on your arse looking like a stuck pig.'

26 March 1962   There is a technical, pharmaceutical term for a medicine containing no curative properties. I came on it the other day and have forgotten. What was it? Very useful metaphorically.

Easter. 'Perfectionist' means one who believes in the perfectibility (in the eyes of God) of human nature. It is now used of one whose aim is to perform a task perfectly, i.e. the artist. Drunkenness, despair and suicide among artists comes from their concentration on the task rather than on their own souls.

Punctuality is the virtue of the bored.

In all discourses on prayer one is told not to expect an answer or a perceptible sense of nearness to God. Only very rarely are 'consolations' given

[1] With whom Waugh had stayed during a visit to the West Indies.

and they are not to be sought or highly valued. 'You cannot pray? Did you mean to do so? Did you try? Do you regret failing? Then you *have* prayed.' To the sceptic this must be the essence of deception.

There are girls who think of chastity as a private piece of property which they should protect from theft. They can exhibit its value. In a moment of extravagant generosity they can give it away. That is not chastity.

9 May 1962 I have found the following notes made some twelve years ago, when I hope to emulate *Trivia*. (1) Keeper of the King's Conscience. I meet the Lord Chancellor (Jowitt) frequently at the Beefsteak. He is a man of striking looks, as a Great Officer of State should be cast in Hollywood. Whenever we meet he asks kindly what I have in hand and what new books I can commend. There is a doggy droop in his eyebrows and all the sensibility of a painting by Landseer. He has risen to take precedence over all subjects save the Primate by accepting all preferment offered. Now he speaks of his position as being above all political faction. He does this in order to avoid disputes which he has not the wit to sustain. The lawyers in the club treat him with respect; members not of that calling regard him (wrongly) as a Communist agent.

Abjuring the realm. To make an *interior* act of renunciation and to become a stranger in the world; to watch one's fellow-countrymen, as one used to watch foreigners, curious of their habits, patient of their absurdities, indifferent to their animosities – that is the secret of happiness in this century of the common man.

The sixteenth-century revolution succeeded (where it did) largely because men without religious vocations (e.g. Luther) were in monasteries. The twentieth-century revolution is succeeding because men with religious vocations are outside monasteries.

The ball Mary is giving at Pixton for my daughter. Never do a kindness unless completely and in isolation. Never worry others with attempted kindness.

Yesterday I saw the film of *Tender is the Night*. I had never heard Fitzgerald's name until after his death, after the war, when a film producer remarked that I must have been greatly influenced by him.

(*a*) The American self-killers – Fitzgerald, Hemingway were apostate Catholics.

(*b*) *Litera scripta manet.* The impression of eye and ear is transient.

Re-reading the book, which I admire only moderately, I found myself saying: 'Oh, so that's what really happened. So she was really like that, was she?' The film, in all parts except Abe and the film actress, was well acted. It was false but ingenious to give the sister a dominant role. Fisticuffs introduced to make Diver the new type of American hero. The rural privacy of the Villa Diana, whose outrage is one grand theme in the book, was outraged by the producer at the start. The whole negro incident lost – also the police. Minutes, it seemed hours, of kissing between what might be any two players without relevance to the story. The whole point missed of Diver *not* being the man who cured Nicole. All changes for the flatter and feebler – and this is a very good film of a rather poor book. The enormously expensive apparatus of the film studio can produce nothing as valuable as can one half-tipsy Yank with a typewriter. But we novelists should remember that our 'characters' and our 'dramas' are mere shadows compared with those of the real world.

The artificiality of Kipling is far greater than that of his 'decadent' contemporaries. 'When 'Omer smote 'is bloomin' lyre' – what barrack-room balladist had heard of Homer or lyres?

The Church, in our last agony, anoints the organs of sense, sealing the ears against the assaults of sound. But nature, in God's Providence, does this long before. One has heard all the world has to say, and wants no more of it.

26 June 1962   Scratch Bowra and you find Muggeridge.

The grandson of Field-Marshal Lord Chetwode is going on a three-year course of instruction to Boston, USA, with the aspiration of graduating from being a 3rd Class to a 2nd Class Bandsman.

Letter addressed to editor *Sunday Telegraph* but suppressed by me at Prime Minister's request:

Sir, Please publish the following comments on your paragraph about myself in your issue of July 1st: (1) It is entirely false to say that I enjoy 'particularly cordial relations' with the Prime Minister. I have not met him for some four years and have never made any claim to his friendship. (2) I received an official invitation to meet U Thant which I was unable to accept because other business kept me at home in the country. (3) The attempt to identify the Prime Minister with a minor character in my life of Ronald Knox was made in a socialist paper at the time of the book's publication. I then replied suitably. Your contributor, [Pam Berry][1] 'Albany' has merely transcribed a

[1] Square brackets as in MS.

stale impertinence. Kindly refer him (or her) to the rebuke it incurred. Your obedient servant.

Mrs Belloc Lowndes used to be reported as having said: 'Always be polite to girls. You never know who they may become.' I have just found this, illustrated by du Maurier, in *Punch*, August '72. It would be an interesting investigation for someone with a lexicographer's mind to trace the first mention, and subsequent attributions, of jokes.

Punch, Nov. 1872. Of a child 'Go and see what she is doing and tell her she mustn't.'

1 September 1962 Vernacular version of the Salutation suggested by a correspondence in the *Catholic Herald*. 'Hiya Moll, you're the tops. You've got everything it takes, baby, and that goes for junior too. Look Moll, you put in a word for us slobs right now and when we konk out.'

5 October 1962 Driven from home by the local celebration of Polly Grant's marriage, I went to London and found that Ann was celebrating a still more preposterous event – the first night of Ian Fleming's film *Dr No*. At her home at 7 was a small, bizarre party – Andrew and Debo, Maugham and Clarissa, the Chancellor of the Exchequer and Mrs Whatever she's called, the American ambassador and Mrs Bruce, Diana and I. I greeted Clarissa and we talked briefly about the West Indies. Then I sat with Mrs Whatever she's called who had just returned from America in *a ship*. She spoke of it as though it were an unique experience like riding a horse from South to North America. When we reached the theatre there were ninety other honoured guests – two front rows of the circle. We entered in darkness and left unobserved by the paying audience; not at all like a gala performance of opera with tiers of boxes, promenade and tiaras sparkling under chandeliers. The film was totally fatuous and tedious, no mystery, not even erotic. When it was over Ann's party went to the Ambassadeurs – a very expensive restaurant and gambling hall. She had the lower room but the superior guests refused to crowd into it and went upstairs where there was a glum table of youngsters presided over by O'Neill and a jolly table of oldsters. Poor Cyril Connolly wandered up too and got cold chicken. He was still in tears next day. As I was leaving at 2 am I found myself next to Clarissa in the hall. She said: 'I'm very fond of you.' 'And I of you' and we kissed in a brotherly sisterly manner. The party must have cost £1,000. It was not, so far as I know, mentioned in a single newspaper. The critics had already had a press view and written their opinions and weren't asked. No photographers, thank God. But what conceivable purpose did the party accomplish?

One can write, think and pray exclusively of others; dreams are all egocentric.

Those who most reprobate and ridicule their fellows – e.g. Samuel Butler and Osbert Sitwell – were not fathers themselves.

Growing up and growing old are a continuous process of learning what one cannot do well.

25 December 1962   My daughter, Margaret, leaving Farm Street after Mass, of her engagement ring: 'It is just right for church. It glitters so.'

One of the rarest experiences: to find a man or woman in any position capable of the job. All calculations are based on the assumption of other people's efficiency.

One forgets words as one forgets names. One's vocabulary needs constant fertilizing or it will die.

10 January 1963   Septimus: 'Did Uncle Auberon once try to get into Parliament? I thought he was only a business man.'

5 May 1963   How to invent names for fictitious characters without fear of prosecution? This morning's *Times* has births to Clague, Fimbel, Futty and Prescott-Pickup.

5 June 1963   The most difficult dogma to reconcile with reason is that of baptismal regeneration. Accept that, and the whole sacramental system is acceptable. But most heretics accept it and then deny transubstantiation.

10 June 1963   We cherish our friends not for their ability to amuse us but for ours to amuse them – a diminishing number in my case.

The Profumo case; newspapers and politicians are hysteric; 'the greatest scandal of the century'. In my lifetime there have been two adulterous Prime Ministers, Lloyd George and ——, and almost certainly a third, Balfour. Every cabinet has had addicts of every sexual vice. Rufus Isaacs lied to the House of Commons in a personal statement on the Marconi case and ascended to high honours.

3 September 1963   Re-reading Robert Byron. It was fun thirty-five years ago to travel far and in great discomfort to meet people whose entire conception of life and manner of expression were alien. Now one has only to leave one's gates.

All fates are 'worse than death'.

28 October 1963   Bibliographical note. Chapman & Hall forgot the half title page of *Basil Seal Rides Again*. I had one printed for the fifty copies which I was giving to friends. When the books came for signing and addressing there were more than fifty. I did not observe this. Thus some of the copies I sent to friends lack half-title, some of the 'out of series' copies for review have it. The numbers of each were not recorded.

25 October 1963   A two-day visit to see what Ann[1] has been up to. Laura and I arrived after dark by the wrong road over a cart track. The full horror of her edifice did not appear until next day. That evening we were ushered by a butler who had arrived only a few minutes before us, through a little dining-room (the only means of access) into a lofty drawing-room with a good carpet, otherwise sparsely furnished. A log fire (the only one in the house), a mean chimney-piece, a good fire-back, the sole surviving feature of the demolished house. Ian Fleming, near death, in a woollen sweater drinking heavily the whisky forbidden him by his doctor. No curtains. Appalling echoes everywhere much magnified by Maurice Bowra's voice. He and I deaf. Ian too bored to listen, saying: 'It is kind to have Maurice here. One must be kind.' Ann too worried about his condition to attend to her guests. A narrow staircase (the only one) led to a few minute rooms and bathrooms; a plethora of beds. No chairs or tables or writing materials. Narrow little built-in cupboards. The walls so thin as to admit every sound. Liquefied caviare for dinner left over from a London party. Next morning Ian left for the golf links and many Charterises came to luncheon. We were able to inspect the property – a strip of swamp 100 yards

---

[1] Ann Fleming.

wide and $\frac{3}{4}$ mile long, which she is attempting to drain and level with imported soil. Of the house only one Caroline wing survives, the dining- and drawing-rooms; at right angles a low stone edifice, the bedrooms. On this Ann has spent twice the price of any of the most beautiful houses in the kingdom. I got Baby and her daughter Penelope (who needs a haircut and elocution lessons) to dinner. Penelope momentarily cheered Ian. He provided excellent champagne. Next day he again left for the golf links. Laura and I to Mass and back to Baby's cottage. Clarissa to luncheon. She has developed a look of Doris Castlerosse.

14 November 1963   Since John Sutro's visit here on August 16th we have been in almost daily correspondence about the 40th anniversary celebration of the OU Railway Club. This evening we dined on the Brighton Belle. John,[1] Harold Acton, Bob Boothby, Henry Bath, Roy Harrod, Christopher Sykes, Cyril Connolly, Ran Antrim and, as junior guests, Bron,[2] Giles,[3] Desmond Guinness and two young Harrods. Also Terence Greenidge who has had large parts of his brain removed by a surgeon and was very talkative. The sexagenarians were really not up to it all. We sat in comfort. Harold made a very long speech with his back to most of us. The general verdict: 'Anyway John is enjoying it.'

March 1964   Randolph Churchill went into hospital (Sister Agnes's, thus keeping me away who had arranged to go for two days' examination as the result of being taken ill at Mentone) to have a lung removed. It was announced that the trouble was not 'malignant'. Seeing Ed Stanley in White's, on my way to Rome, I remarked that it was a typical triumph of modern science to find the only part of Randolph that was not malignant and remove it. Ed repeated this to Randolph whom I met on my return from Rome, again in White's. He looked so pale and feeble and was so breathless that we there and then made up our estrangement of some twelve years.

Easter 1964   Compare the Mass to the hunting-field. The huntsman's (priest's) primary task is to find and kill foxes. He is paid for this if he shows good sport to the followers. Some keep up with hounds if they are well mounted and know the country, and are in at the death; others coffee-house [?] at coverts and trot about lanes.

   When I first came into the Church I was drawn, not by splendid ceremonies but by the spectacle of the priest as a craftsman. He had an important job to do which none but he was qualified for. He and his apprentice stumped up to the

---

[1] John Sutro.
[2] Auberon Waugh, Waugh's eldest son.
[3] Giles FitzHerbert, Waugh's son-in-law.

altar with their tools and set to work without a glance to those behind them, still less with any intention to make a personal impression on them.

'Participate' – the cant word – does not mean to make a row as the Germans suppose. One participates in a work of art when one studies it with reverence and understanding.

1 April 1964   Returning to London after the turmoil of Rome I found Barchester.

Easter 1965   A year in which the process of transforming the liturgy has followed a planned course. Protests avail nothing. A minority of cranks, for and against the innovations, mind enormously. I don't think the main congregation cares a hoot. More than the aesthetic changes which rob the Church of poetry, mystery and dignity, there are suggested changes in Faith and morals which alarm me. A kind of anti-clericalism is abroad which seeks to reduce the priest's unique sacramental position. The Mass is written of as a 'social meal' in which the 'people of God' perform the consecration. Pray God I will never apostatize but I can only now go to church as an act of duty and obedience – just as a sentry at Buck House is posted with no possibility of his being employed to defend the sovereign's life. Cardinal Heenan has been double-faced in the matter. I had dinner with him *à deux* in which he expressed complete sympathy with the conservatives and, as I understood him, promised resistance to the innovations which he is now pressing forward. How does he suppose the cause of participation is furthered by the prohibition of kneeling at the incarnatus in the creed? The Catholic Press has made no opposition. I shall not live to see things righted.

On Maundy Thursday appeared a notice in the paper under the heading 'Death of Former Unionist MP'. I did not recognize this as Phil Dunne until Christopher Sykes told me on Saturday. He was my age. I last saw him just before Christmas, elegant, gay, and I thought how little he had aged compared with myself. He was completely selfish without an element of conceit or self-assertion, debonair, never boring, never morose; a finely controlled temptation to malice; chivalrous, with a sense of private honour uncommon nowadays. Though I saw him seldom in late years, a deeply valued friend whom I shall miss bitterly.

The diary ends here. Evelyn Waugh died, after attending Mass with his family, on Easter Day 1966.

Appendix of Names

Abdy, Sir Robert, the 5th Baronet (b.1896): educ. Charterhouse and Sandhurst; wealthy and much-married art collector.

Acton, Harold, (b.1904): educ. Eton and Christ Church, Oxford; spent seven years in Peking, taking a special interest in Chinese classical theatre; served with RAF in World War II; author of poems, two volumes of Neapolitan history, several novels, two volumes of autobiography, and a memoir of Nancy Mitford (q.v.). Acton was the dominant undergraduate aesthete of his Oxford generation; deploring the Georgians, he proclaimed instead the merits of T. S. Eliot, Gertrude Stein, Ronald Firbank, and the Sitwells, and helped to start the fashion for Victoriana later popularized by John Betjeman (q.v.). Waugh said that Acton, at Oxford, 'led me far away from Francis Crease (q.v.) to the baroque and rococo and to the *Waste Land*.' Strong traces of Acton appear in 'Anthony Blanche', in *Brideshead Revisited*. He inherited a celebrated villa, La Pietra, outside Florence. A lifelong friend of Waugh's. Knighted 1974.

Antrim, Randal ('Ran'), 13th Earl of (b. 1911): educ. Eton and Christ Church, Oxford; married Angela Sykes, sister of Christopher Sykes (q.v.); Royal Navy, 1939–45; Chairman of National Trust, 1965.

Asquith, Mrs Raymond (Katharine Horner); daughter of Sir John Horner of the Manor House, Mells, Somerset; she married in 1907 Raymond Asquith (son of the statesman) who was killed in the Battle of the Somme. The mother of Lady Helen; Julian ('Trim'), the 2nd Earl of Oxford and Asquith; and Lady Perdita, who married in 1931 the Hon. William Jolliffe of Ammerdown (later the 4th Baron Hylton; he died 1966). She and her brother, Edward Horner, were close friends of Lady Diana Cooper (q.v.) before the First World War; also a friend of Hilaire Belloc (q.v.). Became a Roman Catholic after Raymond Asquith's death. At her invitation, Mgr. Ronald Knox (q.v.) in 1949 moved to the Manor House in Mells.

Baillie-Hamilton, Wanda; née Holden; married in 1929 Charles Baillie-Hamilton, MP for Bath, 1929–31. Marriage dissolved, 1939. She inspired, in *Put Out More Flags*, 'Sonia Digby-Vane-Trumpington', who (like Tallulah Bankhead) entertained young men in her bathroom while she bathed. According to Randolph Churchill, she threw a bun at the mayor in her husband's constituency, and 'after this Charlie decided to abandon his political career'. Randolph Churchill, *Twenty One Years* (London 1965), p. 95.

Balfour, Patrick (b.1904): educ. Winchester and Balliol College, Oxford; succeeded as 3rd Baron Kinross, 1939. Journalist and author: *Society Racket*, 1933; *Ataturk*, 1964. Covered Abyssinian war for the *Evening Standard* while Waugh worked for the *Daily Mail*, the assignment that produced *Scoop*. In World War Two, served with the RAF in the Middle East; from 1944–7, Press Counsellor at the British Embassy in Cairo. He has said he detects traces of himself in 'Lord Kilbannock' in *Sword of Honour*.

Beatty, the Hon. Peter (1910–45): younger son of Admiral of the Fleet Sir David Beatty (cr. Earl Beatty, 1919). A friend of Waugh's in the Commandos. An awkward, likeable figure with a capacity for saying unsayable things. In later life, he saw a psychiatrist, and on one occasion Waugh happened to be present when the psychiatrist called. Indicating Waugh, Beatty said in a helpful way: 'His trouble, doctor, is that he wants to be a Cavendish'.

Belloc, Hilaire (1870–1953): combative poet, versifier, journalist, Liberal MP, historian, social theorist, and Roman Catholic propagandist. Of Anglo–French descent; served in the French Army. President of the Oxford Union. Author of more than a hundred books, including *The Path to Rome*, *The Cruise of the Nona*, *The Bad Child's Book of Beasts*. Waugh was introduced to him by Duff Cooper. He was a close friend of Mrs Raymond Asquith.

Bennett, Basil (1894–1966): educ. Charterhouse and Magdalen College, Oxford; Rifle Brigade in

World War One, wounded; golf, racing, and riding between the wars; after Munich, joined Territorial Army searchlights (uncommissioned), discharged from Army as unfit; succeeded in getting back into Army as Camp Commandant to Commandos. Shared digs in 1942 with Waugh when stationed at Sherborne, Dorset, which began a lasting friendship. After the war, became Chairman of Hyde Park Hotel (started by his father) and appointed his ex-Commando brother officer, Colonel Brian Franks, managing director. Waugh and family often stayed at the hotel when in London.

Berners, Gerald, the 14th Baron, (1883–1950); a composer thought well of by Stravinsky; became friends with Waugh in thirties; had a piano built into the back of his Rolls-Royce. Also a painter and writer. Lived at Faringdon House, Berkshire.

Berry, Lady Pamela (b.1914): daughter of the 1st Earl of Birkenhead and brother of the 2nd (q.v.); after World War II, Waugh relied on her to keep him in touch with London gossip. She married in 1936 the Hon. Michael Berry, who became editor-in-chief of the *Daily Telegraph* and *Sunday Telegraph* and in 1968 was created 1st Baron Hartwell of Peterborough Court by the Labour Government. One of the last London hostesses to maintain a *salon*.

Besse, Antonin (1877–1951); merchant, and founder of St Antony's College, Oxford. Born Carcassonne; went to Aden as junior clerk in a French firm, 1899; started own business, exporting coffee, 1903; traded with hides and skins with Abyssinia; severe financial loss after First World War, but recovered and built up commercial empire encompassing Port Sudan, the three Somalias, Abyssinia, and Arabia; also Shell agent. Twice married, second time (1921) to Briton. Had intended to finance college in France, until he encountered Oxford Vice-Chancellor; St Antony's College started 1950. Knighted 1951, shortly before death.

Betjeman, John (b.1906): poet and architectural writer. Educ. Marlborough and Oxford. Schoolmaster, staff of *Architectural Review*, film critic of *Evening Standard*. In 1933 married Penelope, daughter of Field Marshal Sir Philip Chetwode, then Commander-in-Chief, India. In World War II, press attaché in Dublin (where he learned Erse); Admiralty, 1943. Literary editor of *Time and Tide*. Lifelong enthusiast for Victorian architecture. In later life, acquired national fame as television performer. Numerous books include architectural guides to Berkshire and Buckinghamshire (with John Piper), and a two-volume guide to English Parish Churches, and *London's Historic Railway Stations*. The third enlarged volume of his *Collected Poems* was published in 1970. He was knighted in 1969, and appointed Poet Laureate in 1972. A friend of

many members of Waugh's circle, including Randolph Churchill, Maurice Bowra, and Lord Birkenhead (q.v.). Waugh tried and failed to convert him from Anglicanism to Roman Catholicism.

Birkenhead, Frederick ('Freddy'), the 2nd Earl of (1907–1975): the son of the statesman F. E. Smith and Margaret, second daughter of the Rev. H. Furneaux, a Fellow of Corpus Christi College, Oxford; godson of Winston Churchill. Educ. Eton and Christ Church, Oxford; Parliamentary Private Secretary to Secretary of State for Foreign Affairs, 1938–9; Lord in Waiting to King George VI, 1938–40, and again from 1951–2; joined 53d (Oxfordshire Yeomanry) Anti-Tank Regiment, 1938; Captain, 1940; Major, 1941; British Military Mission to Jugoslavia with Waugh and Randolph Churchill (q.v.), 1944. A conscientious biographer: *Frederick Edwin, 1st Earl of Birkenhead*, two vols., 1933 and 1935 (revised 1959); *Strafford* (1938); *Lady Eleanor Smith–a Memoir* (1953); *The Prof. in Two Worlds*, a biography of Professor Lindemann (1961); *Halifax* (1965); *Walter Monckton* (1969). In 1935, married the Hon. Sheila Berry, sister of the Hon. Michael Berry who married (1936) Birkenhead's sister, Lady Pamela. In conversation with the editor of these diaries, in 1974, described Waugh as a 'viper'. In Jugoslavia, he said he was confronted with the alternative of sleeping in the same room with Randolph Churchill or outside with the rats; 'I chose Randolph by a narrow margin'. He was known to Randolph Churchill, his fag at Eton, as 'Freddy Breadsauce'.

Bowra, Maurice (1898–1971): classical scholar, audacious wit, and powerful influence for fifty years on successive generations of clever Oxford undergraduates. Son of an administrator of the Chinese customs. Educ. Cheltenham College and New College, Oxford; fellow of Wadham College, Oxford, 1922; Warden, 1938. Publications include: *The Oxford Book of Greek Verse*, 1930; *The Heritage of Symbolism*, 1943; *Heroic Poetry*, 1952; *Problems in Greek Poetry*, 1954; *Pindar*, 1964. In *A Little Learning*, Waugh wrote: 'He [Cyril Connolly] and Maurice Bowra were both acquaintances who became friends after I attracted some attention as a novelist'. Christopher Sykes describes Waugh's relations with Bowra as 'of the utmost ambivalence . . . sometimes admiring and sometimes contemptuous.' *Evelyn Waugh*, pp. 52 and 408. 'Mr Samgrass', the Oxford don in *Brideshead Revisited*, was modelled on Bowra. 'A Waugh to end Waugh', he said of *Sword of Honour*. Knighted, 1951.

Bridgeman, the Hon. Maurice, (b.1904): Chairman of British Petroleum Company 1960–9 and White's Club friend of Waugh's. Third son of

1st Viscount Bridgeman, landowner and politician; educ. Eton and Trinity College, Cambridge; Anglo-Persian Oil Company, 1926; senior government oil adviser and strategist in London and India during Second World War. Rare example of an aristocrat becoming a leading industrialist. Knighted 1964.

Brownlow, Peregrine ('Perry'), 6th Baron, (b.1899): educ. Eton; European War, 1918; Personal Lord-in-Waiting to King Edward VIII, 1936; Parliamentary Private Secretary to Lord Beaverbrook, 1940. Married in 1927 Katherine ('Kitty'), who died in 1952, daughter of Brig.-Gen. Sir David Kinloch. 'After Munich, Perry Brownlow gave Chamberlain a cigarette case on which was engraved a map of Europe with three sapphires marking Berchtesgarden, Godesberg and Munich.' Harold Nicolson, *Diaries and Letters, 1939–45* (London, 1967) p. 357. Owner of Belton House, near Grantham, Lincolnshire, where Waugh often stayed.

Bushell, Tony: actor celebrated for his good looks; as a young man, understudied Ivor Novello and appeared in film of *Disraeli* with George Arliss; in World War Two, commanded a squadron of the Guards Armoured Division; after the war, associate producer with Laurence Olivier of *Hamlet* and *Richard III*. Later became director of the Monte Carlo Golf Club.

Butts, Mary: *avant-garde* twenties hostess with a house in Belsize Park; writer of short stories.

Buxton-Noel, Noel, the 2nd Baron (b.1917): educ. Harrow and Balliol College, Oxford. The son of Ramsay MacDonald's Minister of Agriculture, he emerged briefly in the public arena during the 1950s as a result of (a) his row with Waugh, and (b) his attempts to walk across Britain's three principal rivers to prove a point about the sites of Roman fords: he walked all the way across the Humber, partly walked and partly swam across the Thames at Westminster, and narrowly escaped being swept away by the Severn Bore.

Byron, Robert (1905–41); educ. Eton and Oxford. At Eton, used to go to the cinema disguised as an old woman. In 1920s, travelled extensively in Near East with David Talbot Rice; in 1930 they published *The Birth of Western Painting*. Established a reputation as a Byzantinist with *The Byzantine Achievement*, 1929. Best-known book, *The Road to Oxiana*, a study of Islamic architecture. Violently anti-Catholic; his Oxford friendship with Waugh died in the 1930s largely for this reason. Commemorated by Christopher Sykes (with whom he travelled in Persia and Afghanistan in 1935) in *Four Studies in Loyalty*. Torpedoed in Second World War, the only one of Waugh's close Oxford friends to lose his life in the war through enemy action.

Carew, Dudley (b.1903): educ. Lancing; published first novel, encouraged by J. B. Priestley, in 1924; taken up by J. C. Squire (q.v.) and *London Mercury* group; *The Times*, 1926–63; author of six novels and two cricket books; three times married, in 1974 to a woman to whom he had been briefly engaged in 1926 and had not seen since. Carew came under the influence of Waugh at Lancing in 1920 and possessed from the start an unshakeable belief in Waugh's genius, saving every scrap of his writing. Waugh described him as 'a born hero-worshipper'. Introduced Waugh to Evelyn Gardner (q.v.), his first wife. Published in 1974 *A Fragment of Friendship*, which set out to correct the 'distortions and omissions' of *A Little Learning*.

Churchill, Clarissa (b.1920): daughter of Major John Spencer Churchill and Lady Gwendoline Spencer Churchill. After Second World War, worked on *Contact* magazine, published by George (later Sir George) Weidenfeld. Married Sir Anthony Eden (Earl of Avon), 1952.

Churchill, Randolph (1911–68): lifelong journalist; only son of Winston Churchill; educ. Eton and Christ Church, Oxford; at Eton, was fag to Freddy (Viscount) Furneaux (later the 2nd Earl of Birkenhead) and best friends with his second cousin Tom Mitford, the only brother of the six Mitford sisters; aged 15, in love with Diana Mitford, who married Bryan Guinness and later Sir Oswald Mosley; at Oxford drove a golf-ball out of Peckwater Quad using a mashie niblick; first met Evelyn Waugh in 1929, introduced by Basil Ava (q.v.). After Oxford, shared house in London with John Betjeman. Conservative MP for Preston, 1940–5. Married first the Hon. Pamela Digby, who later married Averell Harriman, the American politician and diplomatist, and, second, June Osborne. Extremely rude to servants and newspaper proprietors; disdainful towards intellectuals: asked why White's Club had admitted Cyril Connolly (q.v.) and Peter Quennell (q.v.), he replied: 'We like them to see how we live'. In later life retired to East Bergholt, Suffolk, where he landscape-gardened all day and telephoned all night. A leading critic of Anthony Eden's premiership; also pursued a vendetta against R. A. Butler. Incessant talker; generous host; impossible guest. Waugh used to present him with leather-bound copies of his books and dedicated *Put Out More Flags* to him.

Clonmore, Lord ('Billy') (b.1902); succeeded as 8th Earl of Wicklow, 1946; educ. Eton and Merton College, Oxford. Became Anglican clergyman, then converted to Roman Catholicism. Editor *Dublin Review*, 1937–40. Royal Fusiliers in Second World War. Publications include *Pope Pius and World Peace*, 1937, and *Fireside Fusiliers*, 1959.

Cockburn, Claud (b.1904); born in Peking, China, where his father was 'Chinese Secretary' at the British Legation; educ. at the universities of Oxford, Budapest, and Berlin. A cousin of Evelyn Waugh. In the thirties, served as correspondent of *The Times* in the United States, 1929–32; founded *The Week*, a mimeographed news-sheet; fought in Spain; and acted as Diplomatic Correspondent of the *Daily Worker*. In 1947, settled in Co. Cork, Ireland. Publications include *Beat the Devil*, a novel, and three volumes of autobiography.

Connolly, Cyril (1903–74): author and critic; educ. Eton (a contemporary of George Orwell, Anthony Powell, Henry Yorke ('Henry Green'), John Lehmann, and Harold Acton) and Balliol College, Oxford (Brackenbury Scholar). Sir Maurice Bowra (q.v.), when Vice-Chancellor of Oxford, remembered him as the cleverest boy of his generation. Began journalistic career under Desmond MacCarthy and Raymond Mortimer on the *New Statesman and Nation*. On eve of World War II, founded (with Peter Watson and Stephen Spender) the monthly magazine *Horizon*, which published *The Loved One. Horizon* appears in the *Sword of Honour* trilogy as *'Survival'*; it ceased publication in 1950, when Connolly became a regular reviewer for the *Sunday Times*. Publications include *Enemies of Promise* (1938), *The Unquiet Grave* (1944–5), *The Modern Movement* (1965). He was three times married and died heavily in debt. 'As he himself well knew, he never fully lived up to his gifts'. *The Times* obituary, November 1974.

Cooper, Lady Diana (b.1892); an 'exceptionally brilliant social figure' (said Waugh) who became one of Waugh's closest friends in the early 1930s and so remained. Third daughter of the 8th Duke of Rutland; married 1919 (Alfred) Duff Cooper (later Viscount Norwich), who resigned as First Lord of the Admiralty over Munich, and in World War II became Minister of Information and later British Minister in Algiers; after the war, British Ambassador in Paris. Lady Diana described her formal education as 'erratic'. In her teens, a member of the circle that included Raymond Asquith, Patrick Shaw-Stewart, Julian Grenfell, Ivo Charteris and Edward Horner, all of whom died in World War I. During World War I she worked as a nurse at Guy's Hospital; in the twenties she went on the stage, notably in Max Reinhardt's spectacular, *The Miracle*, to finance her husband's political career. The inspiration of 'Mrs Stitch', who appears in *Scoop* and *Sword of Honour*. When Waugh apologised for having made Mrs Stitch behave badly by tearing up an official letter of Guy Crouchback's, she told Waugh that she did not mind at all, since she would have behaved in exactly the same way as Mrs Stitch.

Close friend of Mrs Raymond Asquith (q.v.). Author of three volumes of autobiography.

Crease, Francis: unworldly amateur scribe of mysterious origins and effeminate manners who lived in rooms near Lancing during Waugh's schooldays, and gave Waugh private lessons in writing techniques. In 1928, he published a folio of thirty-four decorative designs to which Waugh wrote a preface. From Sussex, Crease moved to the village of Marston, near Oxford, and later to Bath, where he died during World War II.

D'Arcy, Very Rev. Martin, S.J. (b.1888): educ. Stonyhurst and Oxford. The Master of Campion Hall, Oxford, 1932–45; Provincial of English Province of Society of Jesus, 1945–50. Publications include: *The Mass and the Redemption, Catholicism, Christ as Priest and Redeemer*. He received Waugh into the Roman Catholic church in 1930 and officiated at his wedding in 1937.

Dawkins, R. M. (1871–1955): eccentric professor of Byzantine archaeology and modern Greek at Oxford. Once observed by Osbert Lancaster perched in the upper branches of a large chestnut tree in Exeter College garden. Ordered his suits by postcard from the general store of a small village in Northern Ireland. Lived in Denbighshire.

Deakin, F. W. (Bill) (b.1913): Before 1939, Fellow and Tutor in Modern History at Wadham College, Oxford, and literary assistant to Winston Churchill. On 28 May 1943, he parachuted into the highlands of Montenegro with Captain Stuart and a small party to make the first British contact with Tito and the Partisans. In September 1943, now a Colonel, Deakin handed over command of the British Military Mission to Tito to Brigadier Fitzroy Maclean (q.v.). In December 1943, in Cairo, when asked by Smuts what he did, replied, 'I think I am some sort of bandit.' Next day, on 10 December, in Churchill's bedroom at the house of the resident minister in Cairo, he was interrogated by Churchill for two hours about the evidence for Mihailović's links with the Axis; this evidence was decisive in causing the switch of British support from Mihailović to Tito. In 1944, seconded to the staff of Harold Macmillan, the Cabinet's representative in the Mediterranean theatre. Warden of St Antony's College, Oxford, 1950–68. Retired to France, 1971. Publications include: *The Brutal Friendship: Hitler, Mussolini and the Fall of Italian Fascism* (1962). Co-editor, with Alan Bullock, of the *Oxford History of Modern Europe.*

Douglas, Robert Langton (1864–1951): educ. New College, Oxford; son of a clergyman; local secretary of the Church of England Temperance Society; took holy orders; British chaplain in Siena; pioneer in the history and criticism of Siennese art;

wrote standard history of Siena, *Storia della Politica e Sociale della Repubblica di Siena* (1902), and *Fra Angelico* (1900). A principal discoverer of Sassetta. Collected early Italian paintings and then dealt in them; sold a number to J. Pierpont Morgan. In December 1914, enlisted as a private in the infantry. Director of the National Gallery of Ireland, 1916–23. After World War II, moved to New York with his third wife. Died in Fiesole, after being received into the Roman Catholic church. His many children included Marshal of the Royal Air Force Lord Douglas of Kirtleside and the illegitimate Zena Naylor.

Driberg, Tom (b.1905): educ. Lancing and Christ Church, Oxford; *Daily Express*, where he helped to create the modern newspaper gossip column as 'William Hickey', 1928–43; MP Maldon Div. of Essex, 1942–55; MP for Barking, 1959–74; Chairman of Labour Party, 1957–8. Publications include: *Beaverbrook*, 1956; *Guy Burgess*, 1956; *Hannen Swaffer*, 1974. Driberg and Waugh were sacristans together at Lancing; in 1930 Driberg, though an Anglican, was the only person whom Waugh invited to attend his reception into the Roman Catholic church; Driberg speculated that Waugh hoped he would report the event in the *Daily Express*. Baron, 1975.

Dufferin and Ava, (Basil), 4th Marquess of, (1909–45): educ. Eton and Balliol College, Oxford (Brackenbury Scholar); succeeded 1930; Parliamentary Private Secretary, during the 1930s, to the Under-Sec. of State for India, the President of the Board of Education, and the Secretary of State for War; Under-Sec. of State for the Colonies, 1937 to May, 1940. Killed while serving with the Royal Horse Guards near Fort Dufferin in Burma, a territory that had been annexed by his grandfather while Viceroy of India (1884–8). Elegized by John Betjeman (q.v.): 'Friend of my youth, you are dead.' Married Maureen Guinness, 1930; a daughter, Lady Caroline (b.1931), who married as her third husband the American poet Robert Lowell.

Duggan family: In 1902 Alfred Duggan, whose father owned fifteen large *estancas* in the Argentine, married Grace Hinds, from Alabama, daughter of the US Minister to Brazil. The Duggan family were devout Roman Catholics of Irish origin. Alfred and Grace Duggan had three children: Alfred Leo (q.v.), b. 1903; Hubert (q.v.), b. 1904; and Marcella, b. 1906. Alfred Duggan became hon attaché at the Argentine embassy in London in 1903, and died in 1915. In 1917, Mrs Duggan married Lord Curzon, the statesman, then Leader of the House of Lords; he died in 1925. When her son Hubert first stood for Parliament in East Ham (1930), Lady Curzon (the Marchioness Curzon of Kedleston) took a furnished house in the constituency, toured it

in a chauffeur-driven Rolls-Royce, and lived on hampers sent from Fortnum & Mason. When Marcella married Edward Rice at St Margaret's Westminster, Sir Thomas Beecham and the London Symphony Orchestra provided the music. The marriages of Hubert Duggan to Joan Dunn, and of Marcella Duggan to Edward Rice both ended in divorce. Lady Curzon was also step-mother of Lady Cynthia Curzon, Sir Oswald Mosley's first wife.

Duggan, Alfred (1903–64): born in Buenos Aires of mixed Irish, American, and English descent; step-son of Lord Curzon, the statesman; educ. Eton and Balliol College, Oxford. Crossed Atlantic under sail on natural history expedition to South Seas, 1924; London Irish Rifles, 1940; invalided out of army, 1941; schoolmaster, machine operator in aeroplane factory. In mid-forties, began to write historical novels: *Knight with Armour*, a novel of the First Crusade; *God and My Right*; *Leopards and Lillies*; *Thomas Becket of Canterbury*. At Oxford, he was the richest of Waugh's contemporaries: 'we were often drunk, Alfred almost always.' He continued to drink heavily in later life. When he turned to historical novel-writing, he was greatly helped and encouraged by Waugh.

Duggan, Hubert (1904–43): younger brother of Alfred Duggan (q.v.), and step-son of Lord Curzon, the statesman. Educ. Eton. Regular soldier in the Household Cavalry (Life Guards), 1924–8; MP (Conservative) Acton, Middlesex, 1931–43; Captain, Life Guards, 1940. His death inspired the description of Lord Marchmain's final hours in *Brideshead Revisited*. One of Waugh's closest friends.

Dunne, Philip (1904–65): educ. Eton and Royal Military College, Sandhurst; 11th Hussars, 1924; Royal Horse Guards, 1929–33; MP (Unionist) for Stalybridge & Hyde Division of Cheshire, 1935–7. Married Audrey Rubin, 1945. Liked shooting, racing and hunting.

Fagan, Joyce: modern-minded girl who in the twenties came to Bloomsbury from the provinces; at one time secretary to Clifford Bax; member of the 1917 Club, of which Ramsay MacDonald was the first President. In 1924, Evelyn Waugh introduced her, disguised as a man, to an Oxford party, which was interrupted by the University Proctor and his bulldogs; they did not penetrate her disguise, and fifty years later Alec Waugh (q.v.) wrote, in *The Fatal Gift* (1974): 'I have never seen, in a whole half century since, anything that looked so denegerate.' She married Donald Gill, of the US Embassy in London.

Fleming, Ann: (b. 1913): granddaughter of the 11th Earl of Wemyss; married first (1932), the 3rd Baron O'Neill, who was killed in action in 1944;

second (1945), the 2nd Viscount Rothermere (Esmond), nephew of Lord Northcliffe and head of the *Daily Mail* group; and third (1952), Ian Fleming, author of the James Bond novels, who died in 1964. With Lady Pamela Berry (q.v.), one of Waugh's principal sources after 1952 of London gossip. Waugh twice provoked her to physical violence (see *Evelyn Waugh and His World*, p. 327): once when she struck his ear-trumpet with her soup spoon, and once at the Grand Hotel, Folkestone, when he frightened her three year-old son by pulling faces, when she slapped his face, overturning a plate of éclairs.

Fulford, Roger (b. 1902): educ. Lancing and Worcester College, Oxford; President of the Union, 1927; Liberal candidate 1929, 1945, 1950. Publications include: *Royal Dukes*, 1933; ed. with Lytton Strachey *The Greville Memoirs*, 1937; *The Trial of Queen Caroline*, 1967.

Gardner, the Hon. Evelyn (b. 1903): Waugh's first wife, whom he married secretly on 27 June 1928 and divorced in 1930. Her mother was the eldest daughter of the fourth earl of Carnarvon; her father, a successful politician, was the 1st Baron Burghclere; her uncle was the 5th Earl of Carnarvon who discovered the treasures of Tutankhamun. At the time of her first meeting (1927) with Waugh, at a party in Portland Place given by the Ranee of Sarawak, she 'resembled a ravishing boy, a page', wrote Nancy Mitford, Harold Acton described her as 'a fauness with a little snub nose'. She shared rooms, before her marriage, with Lady Pansy Pakenham (q.v.); Nancy Mitford (q.v.) was her closest friend. After her divorce from Waugh, she married in 1930 John Heygate (q.v.), (later the 4th Bart.), from whom she obtained a divorce in 1936; in 1937 she married Ronald Nightingale.

Gielgud, Tasha (d. 1972): the step-daughter of the Grand-Duke Michael, the brother of Tsar Nicholas II, who had eloped with and afterwards married her mother, who was given the title of Countess Brassov. They both escaped from the Crimea in a British ship in 1919 and came to live in East Sheen. She married Val Gielgud, Head of Sound Drama at the BBC 1929–64, in 1921; they separated formally in 1928. Subsequently she married a man named Marjolier. Her parents are buried in West Hampstead Cemetery.

Graham, Alastair (b. 1904): educ. Wellington and Brasenose College, Oxford. Apptd. hon. attaché at Athens, 20 February 1928; transferred to Cairo, 2 September 1929. Resigned from diplomatic service in 1933 and thereafter lived a reclusive life on the Welsh coast, after 1958 at Newport, Cardiganshire. Attached to US Navy in World War II. Graham was Waugh's closest friend from 1924 until 1929, and

appears in *A Little Learning* under the name 'Hamish Lennox'. Waugh testified that Graham contributed to the character of 'Sebastian Flyte' in *Brideshead Revisited* (see Sykes, *Evelyn Waugh*, p. 252).

Graham, Jessie (d. 1934): Alastair Graham's American mother, and the model for 'Lady Circumference' in *Decline and Fall*. Waugh described her as 'high-tempered, possessive, jolly, and erratic.' Her father was Andrew Low of Savannah, Georgia, who emigrated to the United States from Scotland and made a fortune in cotton; he was gaoled during the Civil War as a northern spy; he died in Leamington Spa. Her mother was the daughter of W. H. Stiles, American chargé in Vienna during the revolution of 1848. Her brother Willie inherited £750,000, which he very soon spent; he was a friend of Rosa Lewis of the Cavendish Hotel and it was through him, Alastair's uncle, that Waugh was introduced to the Cavendish. Rosa Lewis figures in *Vile Bodies* as 'Lottie Crump'. The picture Waugh drew of Lady Circumference, in a felt hat, at the school sports in *Decline and Fall* is 'quite a good likeness', according to her son Alastair Graham (q.v.).

Grant, Mark Ogilvie-: Etonian; appointed honorary attaché at the Residency in Cairo in December 1929; distinguished career in World War II; prisoner of war, Italy. Later employed in Athens as an adviser to BP, the oil company. Close friend of Nancy Mitford (q.v.); appears in her novel *Pigeon Pie* (1940) as the 'Wonderful Old Songster of Kew Green'.

Greene, Graham (b. 1904): educ. Berkhamsted and Oxford; author of some twenty novels and five plays. Waugh described him as an 'honoured friend'; he wrote of his love for Waugh. A Roman Catholic convert. In later life, settled in France. Publications include: *Babbling April* (poems), 1925; *Stamboul Train*, 1932; *England Made Me*, 1935; *Brighton Rock*, 1938; *The Power and the Glory*, 1940; *The Third Man*, 1950; *The End of the Affair*, 1951; *The Quiet American*, 1955; *Loser Takes All*, 1955; *A Burnt Out Case*, 1961; *The Honorary Consul*, 1974.

Greene, Gwen Plunket (b. 1878): daughter of Sir Hubert Parry, the musician, and Lady Maud Herbert; niece by marriage of the theologian Baron von Hügel, whose letters she edited in 1928. Her elder sister, Dorothea, married Arthur Ponsonby, aristocrat and Labour politician, who became Lord Ponsonby of Shulbrede; their children, Elizabeth and Matthew (q.v.), were both friends of Waugh's. Gwen in 1899 married Harry Plunket Greene, an Irish singer, from whom she later separated. She was a Roman Catholic convert.

Greene, David Plunket (1904–41); second son of Gwen and Harry Plunket Greene. Nearly seven feet tall; 'more than anyone else, he was representative of the age of jazz that shook Oxford in the twenties', Daphne Fielding, *Mercury Presides* (London 1954), p. 107. Accomplished blues pianist. Committed suicide by drowning in Shearwater lake on the Longleat estate.

Greene, Olivia Plunket (1907–55): daughter of Gwen and Harry Plunket Greene; the first girl with whom Waugh fell seriously in love, during the winter of 1924–5. Harold Acton, in *Memoirs of an Aesthete*, refers to her 'minute pursed lips and great goo-goo eyes'. Some friends of Waugh believed that it was she who turned him against his family. Important influence on Waugh's conversion to Roman Catholicism; she had, according to Father D'Arcy, 'a peculiar and inimitable cast of faith of her own'. In later life, a recluse and near-alcoholic, combining her Catholicism with Communism, and living with her mother in a cottage on the Longleat estate. She died unmarried.

Greene, Richard Plunket (b. 1901): elder son of Gwen and Harry Plunket Greene; robust contemporary of Waugh's at Oxford, and occasional bodyguard to Harold Acton. Taught with Waugh at Aston Clinton; taught music at Lancing. Served with RNVR in World War II; thereafter retired, with his second wife, to Barnstaple. Married in 1925 Elizabeth Russell, great-granddaughter of a duke of Bedford; Waugh's first book was dedicated to her.

Greenidge, Terence: educ. Rugby and Hertford College, Oxford; eccentric contemporary of Waugh's at Hertford, and introduced him to the Hypocrites Club; bought a stuffed dog which he and Waugh set up in the Hertford quadrangle as a sexual temptation for the Dean, C. R. M. F. Cruttwell. With Waugh, made the film *The Scarlet Woman*. Author of '*Decadent Oxford?*' During World War II, worked at the Playhouse, in Oxford, and wrote sonnets, often containing railway train images, to actresses.

Harman, Elizabeth (Countess of Longford) (b. 1906); the daughter of a Unitarian opthalmic surgeon; in 1931, married the Hon. Frank Pakenham (q.v.), and converted him to socialism. Became Roman Catholic six years after her husband (in 1946); she felt the first strong pull of Catholicism while reading Evelyn Waugh's *Edmund Campion*. Biographer of Wellington and Queen Victoria. Eight children, of whom one – Catherine, Waugh's god-daughter – died in a car accident in 1969.

Harmsworth, Desmond, the 2nd Baron Harmsworth (b. 1903): educ. Eton and Christ Church, Oxford; married the daughter of an Ohio state senator, 1926; succeeded his father, Cecil Harms-worth, a younger brother of Lord Northcliffe, 1948; newspaperman, book publisher, painter.

Haynes, E. S. P. (d. 1948): lawyer and author; educ. Eton and Balliol College, Oxford. Friend of Alec Waugh, and solicitor in Evelyn Waugh's divorce. Author of some 30 books. Struck off the solicitors' rolls in 1948 for improperly kept accounts. Rarely finished lunch before 4 p.m. and at his end of the table maintained a store of bottles, jars, and tins containing garlic biscuits, sauces, etc. which may have inspired the description of the eating practices of the Boot family at Boot Magna Hall in *Scoop*. He died after his shirt-tails caught alight while he stood in front of his bedroom gas fire.

Head, Antony, 1st Viscount, 1960 (b. 1906): educ. Eton and Royal Military College, Sandhurst; married Lady Dorothea Ashley-Cooper, daughter of 9th Earl of Shaftesbury, 1935; MP (Conservative) Carshalton, 1945–60; Secretary of State for War, 1951–6; High Commissioner, Federation of Nigeria, 1960–3; High Commissioner, Federation of Malaysia, 1963–6.

Herbert family: the Hon. Aubrey Herbert, MP (1880–1923), 2nd son of the 4th Earl of Carnarvon, married the Hon. Mary Vesey, daughter of the 4th Viscount de Vesci and Lady Evelyn Charteris, daughter of the 10th Earl of Wemyss. They had four children: Gabriel (b. 1911) who married Alexander Dru; Bridget (b. 1914) who married Major Allister Edward Grant; Laura (b. 1916) who married Evelyn Waugh; and Auberon (b. 1922).

Heygate, Sir John, the fourth Bart., (1903–76): second son of A. C. G. Heygate, an assistant master at Eton; educ. Eton and Balliol College, Oxford. Assistant news editor BBC, 1926–9; forced to resign from BBC by the director general, Sir John Reith, after being named as co-respondent in Waugh's divorce; married the Hon. Mrs Waugh in 1930 (marriage dissolved, 1936); writer at UFA film studios in Germany; served Royal Artillery in Second World War – an article in *Horizon* in 1941 about the training of army officers prevented him, he thought, from getting a commission. He published a number of novels, including *Decent Fellows* (about Eton), *White Angel, A House for Joanna*, and *Love and Death*. In later years lived in Co. Londonderry and described himself as a 'retired author'. Close friend of Anthony Powell (q.v.). As his second wife, he married in 1936, Gwyneth Lloyd (two sons); this marriage was dissolved in 1947. In 1951 he married Dora Luz Harvey, who died in 1968.

'One realizes one was the rather feeble villain in *A Handful of Dust*', he wrote to the editor of these diaries in February, 1975. 'But much later on EW used to ask Tony Powell about me in a friendly manner. Nor must one forget his taking of sides against Arthur Calder Marshall when he had attacked my anonymous article in *Horizon*.'

Hollis, Christopher (b. 1902): son of the Bishop of Taunton; educ. Eton and Balliol College, Oxford; assistant master Stonyhurst College, 1925–35; married Margaret Madeline King, 1929; Royal Air Force in World War II; MP (Cons.) for Devizes, 1945–55; numerous publications, including books on Eton and George Orwell. Resident of Mells, Somerset. Chairman of Hollis & Carter, publishers.

Howard, Brian (1905–58): of American parentage; educ. Eton and Christ Church, Oxford; *First Poems*, published by Nancy Cunard at her Hours Press, Paris, in 1931; peripatetic life in Europe; early and articulate anti-Fascist; occasional reviewer for *New Statesman*; RAF aircraftman in World War II; committed suicide by an overdose of drugs; buried Nice cemetry. A notorious and extravagant aesthete-homosexual, described by Waugh, borrowing Lady Caroline Lamb's words, as 'mad, bad, and dangerous to know'. He largely inspired the character of 'Ambrose Silk' in *Put Out More Flags*, and there are traces of him in 'Anthony Blanche' in *Brideshead Revisited*.

Howard, the Hon. Edmund, (b. 1909); son of 1st Baron Howard of Penrith and Lady Isabella Giustiniani-Bandini. Educ. Downside School and New College, Oxford; served Second World War with KRRC; diplomatic service, mainly in Italy, 1947–69. Publication: *Genoa*, 1971.

Griffith-Jones, Mervyn (b. 1909): educ. Eton and Trinity Hall, Cambridge. Waugh's host at the Nuremberg war crimes trials in 1945, where he was one of the British prosecuting counsel. Achieved brief notoriety in the Lady Chatterley case when, as prosecuting counsel, he asked: 'Is it a book you would have lying around in your own house? Is it a book you would even wish your wife or your servants to read?' Common Serjeant in the City of London, 1964.

Jungman, Teresa ('Baby'): one of the two daughters of Mrs Richard Guinness (whose first husband had been Nico Jungman), hostess and talent-spotter (Noel Coward and Cecil Beaton). In the early thirties, Waugh wanted to marry Teresa Jungman. Aged 15, she dressed up as 'Mme Anna Vorolsky', a Russian refugee, borrowed a jewel casket and her mother's Rolls-Royce, and went about describing the Red Terror and pretending she had to sell her jewels to educate her 'poor little boy', deceiving, among others, Beverley Nichols and the Duke of Marlborough. As Mme Vorolsky, she attended a garden party leading two borzois and, on being introduced to a distinguished soldier and his wife, told him that she would never forget the night they spent together in Paris during the war. The general

coldly replied that he had spent one night only in Paris during the war. 'Zat,' said Baby, 'was zee night.' A Roman Catholic.

Kendall, Guy (1876–1960): educ. Eton and Magdalen College, Oxford; double first, in greats and theology; master at Charterhouse, 1902; headmaster of University College School, Hampstead, 1916–36. Became a friend of Arthur Waugh's after reviewing Alec Waugh's *The Loom of Youth* for *The Journal of Education* in 1917. At Charterhouse, taught J. F. Roxburgh (q.v.), Richard Hughes, and Robert Graves; at UCS, taught Stephen Spender. His regular Sunday visits to the Waugh home with his friend E. S. P. Haynes (q.v.) reminded Alec Waugh of the Sunday visitors in *The Diary of a Nobody*. In *A Headmaster Remembers* (London, 1933), Kendall recalls a UCS parent who used to put up her ear trumpet when she herself was speaking and lower it when others spoke, a device used by Evelyn Waugh in later life. Kendall's daughter, Ursula, attracted Waugh's attention during adolescence.

Knox, Monsignor Ronald Arbuthnott (1888–1957): son of a prominent evangelical bishop of Manchester; educ. Eton and Oxford. Ordained as Anglican clergyman, 1912; chaplain of Trinity College, Oxford; received into Roman Catholic church, 1917; entered Roman priesthood, 1919; Roman Catholic chaplain to the University of Oxford, 1926–39. He published a new translation of the Bible, based on the Vulgate text, New Testament, 1945; Old Testament, 2 vols., 1949. His writings include *Some Loose Stones*, 1913; *A Spiritual Aeneid*, 1918; *Essays in Satire*, 1928; *Let Dons Delight*, 1939; *Enthusiasm*, 1950; and detective stories featuring 'Miles Bredon'. Became a close friend of Waugh's after World War II; Waugh published his biography, *The Life of Ronald Knox*, in 1959.

Laking, Sir Francis (1904–30) the third and last Bart; his grandfather had been a royal physician. A cousin of Dudley Carew (q.v.), and brother of Joan Laking (q.v.). In the middle 1920s, became secretary and court-jester to Tallulah Bankhead, the actress, to whom in his will he left 'all my motor-cars', though in fact he died (from drinking yellow Chartreuse) in debt and motorless. 'His eternal complaint was, "Whath the good of having a baronethy if one doethent have any money?"'. Lee Israel, *Miss Tallulah Bankhead*, (New York, 1972), p. 94.

Laking, Joan (b. 1900); sister of Sir Francis Laking; moved to South Africa on the outbreak of World War II to ensure, she told her circle, a supply of gin; in South Africa, became a friend of Field Marshal Smuts, and died there.

Lanchester, Elsa (b. 1902): red-haired actress; during the 1920s, ran with Harold Scott a celebrated club in Charlotte Street, The Cave of Harmony, which combined dances and cabaret (one act plays, character songs, etc.) and which was visited regularly by Evelyn Waugh; the club figures in Aldous Huxley's *Antic Hay*. Married Charles Laughton, 1929. Her many films include *The Constant Nymph, The Private Lives of Henry VIII, Mary Poppins*. Became an American citizen, 1950; settled in Beverly Hills, Los Angeles.

Laycock, Robert (1907–68): Waugh's commanding officer and patron during the middle years of World War II. Called Robert after his grandfather, a Notts MP; his father was Brig.-Gen. Sir Joseph Laycock, a fine shot, a friend of the King, and the husband of the divorced wife of the 6th Marquess of Downshire. Laycock was a Household Brigade officer with a rare combination of upper class nonchalance and professional efficiency: after commanding 'Layforce' at the Battle of Crete, he led an attempt to kidnap Rommel at his headquarters and returned across the desert on foot. He became Chief of Combined Operations in succession to Lord Mountbatten, 1943–47, and ended the war as Major General Sir Robert Laycock, KCMG CB DSO. Governor and C-in-C Malta, 1954–9. *Officers and Gentlemen* is dedicated to him 'that every man in arms should wish to be'. 'Tommy Backhouse', in the Sword of Honour trilogy, shares many points of resemblance with Laycock.

Long, C. F. D. (1902–24): educ. Lancing and Gonville and Caius, Cambridge, where he read engineering. A speleological pioneer, particularly in Yorkshire, in 1921 he stayed underground at Stump Cross for 168 hours and found many new passages. In 1923, he pioneered White Scar Cave, at that time little more than a stream flowing from the base of a limestone cliff. Long killed himself before the cave was opened to the public in 1925.

Lovat, Simon ('Shimi'), the 15th Baron Lovat (b. 1911): educ. Ampleforth and Magdalen College, Oxford; son of the Lord Lovat who raised the Lovat Scouts in the Boer War. Brilliant career in Second World War, winning DSO and MC; as Waugh's commander after Robert Laycock (q.v.) left for North Africa in 1943, played key role in Waugh's enforced resignation from the Special Service Brigade. A cousin of the Stirling brothers, William and David (q.v.), and brother-in-law of Fitzroy Maclean (q.v.).

Lucas, Audrey: daughter of E. V. Lucas, the man of letters. Married Harold Scott, who had run the Cave of Harmony club with Elsa Lanchester (q.v.); close friend of Waugh's in the early thirties.

Lygon family; the 7th Earl Beauchamp in 1902 married Lady Lettice Grosvenor a grand-daughter of the 1st Duke of Westminster; they had seven children: (1) William (b. 1903) who was MP for Norfolk E. as a Liberal 1929–31 and as a Liberal National 1931–8, and succeeded as the 8th Earl Beauchamp in 1938; as Lord Elmley, he was President of the Hypocrites Club when Waugh was at Oxford, and took part in the film *The Scarlet Woman*; (2) Hugh, a close friend of Evelyn Waugh's who died suddenly during a motor tour of Germany in 1936, and who is sometimes said to have helped to inspire 'Lord Sebastian Flyte' in *Brideshead Revisited*; (3) Richard; (4) Lettice; (5) Sibell; and the two younger daughters, (6) Mary ('Maimie') and (7) Dorothy ('Coote'), who became Waugh's particular friends. Lady Mary Lygon in 1939 married H. H. Prince Vsevolode Joannovitch of Russia, who worked for Saccone & Speed, wine merchants. Lady Dorothy did not marry. The Lygon family have been commonly supposed to have inspired the Marchmain family in *Brideshead Revisited*, and Madresfield Court, the Lygon home at Great Malvern, has been identified with 'Brideshead'. Lady Dorothy Lygon has recalled a conversation with Evelyn Waugh in 1944 in which he talked about Brideshead: 'It's all about a family whose father lives abroad, as it might be Boom [a family name for the 7th Earl] – but it's not Boom – and a younger son: people will say he's like Hughie, but you'll see he's not really Hughie – and there's a house as it might be Mad, but it isn't really Mad.' (See *Evelyn Waugh and His World*, p. 53). The only direct physical resemblance between 'Brideshead' and Madresfield is the art-nouveau decoration of the chapel. Lord Beauchamp and 'Lord Marchmain' both lived abroad, Lord Beauchamp because of an accusation of homosexuality made against him by his brother-in-law, the Duke of Westminster.

Maclean, Fitzroy (b. 1911): educ. Eton and Cambridge; 3rd Secretary, Foreign Office, Paris (1934) and Moscow (1937). Resigned from Diplomatic Service in 1939 and enlisted as a private in Cameron Highlanders; joined 1st Special Air Service Regiment, 1942; fought in Western Desert; Brigadier Commanding British Military Mission to Jugoslav Partisans, 1943–5. Married 2nd daughter of 16th Baron Lovat, 1946: thus a brother-in-law of Lord ('Shimi') Lovat (q.v.). MP for Lancaster Division of Lancs., 1941–59; and thereafter for Bute and N. Ayrshire. Parliamentary Under-Secretary of State for War, 1954–7. Baronet, 1957. Publications include: *Eastern Approaches*, 1949; *Disputed Barricade*, 1957; *Back to Bokhara*, 1959.

Molson, Hugh (b. 1903): educ. Royal Naval Colleges, Osborne and Dartmouth; Lancing; and New College, Oxford; President of the Oxford

Union, 1925; first in law; Barrister, 1931; MP 1931–61, except for 1935–9; Minister of Works, 1957–9. Cr. Baron, 1961. Rebellious friend of Waugh's at Lancing who was later talked about as a possible leader of the Conservative Party.

Mitford family: the 1st Baron Redesdale was a diplomatist (one of the first two foreigners to be presented to the Mikado), later appointed (1874) by Disraeli to be secretary to the Commissioners of Public Works and Buildings; he knew Garibaldi, Brigham Young, and Richard Burton. His son, the second baron, succeeded him in 1916 and married, in 1904, Sydney Bowles, daughter of the MP for King's Lynn.

They had one son and six daughters: (1) The Hon. Thomas, (1909–45): educ. Eton; called to the bar, 1932; deputy Judge Advocate, 1938–9; killed in Burma in Second World War. (2) The Hon. Nancy (q.v.), (b. 1904). (3) The Hon. Pamela, (b. 1907): married 1936 Professor Derek Jackson, FRS, divorced 1951; settled in West Country. (4) The Hon. Diana, (b. 1910): married 1929 the Hon. Bryan Guinness; divorced 1934. Married 1936 Sir Oswald Mosley, 6th Bart., founder of the British Union of Fascists, 1932. Both imprisoned during Second World War; thereafter lived in France. (5) The Hon. Unity Valkyrie ('Bobo'), (1914–48): Member of the British Union of Fascists and a friend of Hitler. (6) The Hon. Jessica ('Decca'), (b. 1917): married 1937 Esmond Romilly, who was killed on active service 1941. Second marriage to Robert Treuhaft, lawyer. Settled San Francisco. Publications include *Hons and Rebels*, and *The American Way of Death*, an exposure of undertakers. (7) The Hon. Deborah ('Debo'), (b. 1920): married 1941 Lord Andrew Cavendish, later the 11th Duke of Devonshire.

Mitford, the Hon. Nancy (1904–1973): the eldest of the six celebrated daughters of the 2nd Lord Redesdale. Brought up at Asthall Manor in Oxfordshire; educ. Frances Holland Day School, 1910–14, and the Hatherop Castle finishing school. As a girl, two of her closest friends were Lady Pansy Pakenham and the Hon. Evelyn Gardner (q.v.), Evelyn Waugh's first wife; she was living in the Waugh's Islington flat when the break-up occurred. Became one of Waugh's regular correspondents. Married the Hon. Peter Rodd, 1933; marriage dissolved, 1958. Began writing novels before World War II (*Highland Fling, Christmas Pie, Pigeon Pie*), but had her first success at the end of the war with *The Pursuit of Love*, which sold over a million copies. Worked during war in Heywood Hill's bookshop (which figures in Waugh's diaries as 'Nancy's Bookshop') in Curzon Street. Moved to Paris after the war. Strong anti-American opinions. Publications include *The Blessing, Voltaire in Love, Love in a Cold Climate*, and a celebrated article in *Encounter* (1955) on English modes of speech, which she classified (following Professor Alan S. C. Ross of Birmingham University) as 'U' and 'Non-U' – upper class and non-upper-class.

Otter, Gwen: Chelsea hostess, whose heyday was in the 1890s; her house was lined with Beardsley prints, the walls painted to resemble a Moorish palace. Friend of Aleister Crowley, the satanist. Waugh described her in *A Little Learning* as 'an inexhaustibly hospitable, unmarried woman of middle age and slightly reduced means, with the appearance of a Red Indian'.

Oxford and Asquith, 2nd Earl of, Julian ('Trim'), (b. 1916): educ. Ampleforth and Balliol College, Oxford (first in Greats); succeeded his grandfather, the statesman, 1928; married Anne Palairet, daughter of the late Sir Michael Palairet, KCMG; Lieutenant, Royal Engineers, 1941; Asst. District Commissioner, Palestine, 1942–8; Adviser to Prime Minister of Libya, 1952; Administrative Secretary, Zanzibar, 1955; Governor of the Seychelles, 1962–7.

Pakenham, the Hon. Frank (b. 1905); succeeded as the 7th Earl of Longford, 1961; educ.: Eton and New College, Oxford; Conservative Party economic research department, 1930–2; Oxford don; converted to Roman Catholicism after promptings by Evelyn Waugh, 1939. Personal assistant to Sir William Beveridge, 1941–4; Lord in Waiting to the King, 1945–6; Minister of Civil Aviation, 1948–51; First Lord of the Admiralty, May–Oct., 1951; Secretary of State for Colonies, 1965–6. Founder of New Bridge organisation for helping ex-convicts. Chairman of Sidgwick and Jackson, publishers. Nicknamed 'Lord Porn' by newspapers following his anti-pornography campaigns of the 1970s. Married Elizabeth Harman (q.v.), 1931. Publications include *Born To Believe* 1953; *Humility*, 1969.

Pares, Richard (1902–58): son of Sir Bernard Pares, the Russian scholar; educ. Winchester and Balliol College, Oxford. A contemporary of Waugh's to whom Waugh was deeply attached. Fellow of All Souls, and professor of history at Edinburgh University; specialised in the history of the sugar trade in the eighteenth century. But for his early death, 'would probably have been elected Master of Balliol', *A Little Learning*, p. 192. Christopher Hollis (q.v.) first met Waugh in his rooms in Balliol. He married the daughter of Sir Maurice Powicke, the medieval historian, and had four daughters.

Ponsonby, Hon. Elizabeth (1900–40); only daughter of the 1st Baron Ponsonby of Shulbrede; a leader of the Bright Young People; one of the first girls to have her hair shingled; married in 1929 John Denis

Pelly, from whom she was divorced in 1933. Model for 'Agatha Runcible' in *Vile Bodies*.

Ponsonby, Matthew (b. 1904): 2nd Baron Ponsonby; married 1929 the Hon. Elizabeth Bigham, daughter of the 2nd Viscount Mersey. Brother of the Hon. Elizabeth Ponsonby (q.v.).

Powell, Anthony Dymoke (b. 1905): educ. Eton and Balliol College, Oxford. Worked for Duckworth, the publishers, 1927–35; film scriptwriter, 1935–6; served in World War II in the Welch Regiment, and the Intelligence Corps; Major. Publications include: *Afternoon Men*, 1931; *From a View to a Death*, 1933; and the 'Music of Time' series of novels, published between 1951 and 1975. Married Lady Violet Pakenham (sister of the Hon. Frank Pakenham, q.v.) in 1934.

Quennell, Peter (b. 1905): educ. Berkhamsted and Balliol College, Oxford; critic and author. Numerous publications include: *Poems*, 1926; *Byron*, 1934; *John Ruskin*, 1949; *Hogarth's Progress*, 1955; *Samuel Johnson, His Friends and Enemies*, 1972. A friend of Waugh's at Oxford, Quennell subsequently 'joined the ranks of his favourite bugbears' (Quennell, contribution to *Evelyn Waugh and His World*, p. 24).

Rice, David Talbot (1903–74): educ. Eton and Oxford. Joined staff of Oxford Field Museum expedition to Kish, Mesopotamia; field director of the British Academy excavations in Constantinople, 1927; with Robert Byron (q.v.), author of *The Birth of Western Painting*. Professor of the history of art at Edinburgh University, 1934. Served in Intelligence Corps in World War II. His many publications include: *Byzantine Art*, 1930, and (with his wife, Tamara Abelson) *The Icons of Cyprus*.

Rodd, the Hon. Peter (1904–68): husband of Nancy Mitford (q.v.), 1933–58; the principal model for 'Basil Seal' of *Black Mischief, Scoop, Put Out More Flags*, etc.; described by Christopher Sykes (in *Evelyn Waugh*, p. 41) as possessing 'intellectual abilities which can be compared with those of the greatest minds' and by Harold Acton (in *Nancy Mitford, A Memoir*, 1975) as 'a very superior con man'. Often called 'Prod'. Educ. Wellington and Balliol College, Oxford; worked with Spanish refugees during Spanish Civil War; Welsh Guards during Second World War. His father was ambassador to Italy 1908–19, and created Baron Rennell, of Rodd, in 1933. As a young man Peter Rodd possessed, Waugh wrote (*A Little Learning*, p. 204) 'the sulky, arrogant looks of the young Rimbaud'.

Roxburgh, J. F., (1888–1954): educ. Charterhouse; master at Lancing; created Stowe School virtually single-handed and became its first headmaster. Tall, handsome, with an actor's voice in which he used to read Shakespeare, Latin, and particularly French to the boys with great effect. At Stowe, he prided himself on knowing all the boys (over 500) by their Christian names; and exercised great charm with parents. During the 1931 political crisis, he turned off the wireless on which Stowe sixth form boys were listening to the Prime Minister on the grounds that no gentleman would wish to waste his time listening to a Socialist (Ramsay MacDonald). 'J.F. was markedly virile, but... homosexual.' *A Little Learning*, p. 160.

Smith, Lady Eleanor (1902–45); a daughter of the 1st Earl of Birkenhead (F. E. Smith); she developed passions for Gypsies, ballet, circuses, and Spain. As a child, fought a village boy she found blowing up a toad with a bicycle pump. With the Jungman sisters, in the early twenties, she started the fashion for treasure hunts that became a characteristic pastime of the Bright Young People (a phenomenon she detested). Wrote a gossip column which she described as 'publicising a loathsome clique of advertising nitwits'. A Roman Catholic convert. Her books included *Red Waggon, Flamenco*, and *Ballerina*.

St Clair-Erskine, the Hon. J. A. W. ('Hamish'), (1909–73): son of 5th Earl of Rosslyn; educ. Eton (Oppidan Scholar) and New College, Oxford. Engaged to the Hon. Nancy Mitford (q.v.) before she married the Hon. Peter Rodd (q.v.). Served courageously in Brigade of Guards in Second World War. 'Hamish, in his day, was a Bright Young Person and his life, for the last thirty years, exemplified the difficulty of taking on from there', A. P-J. (Alan Pryce-Jones) in *The Times*, 12 January 1973.

Squire, J. C. (1884–1958): educ. Blundell's; poet, critic, and literary journalist; a considerable literary force in the 1920s as chief reviewer for *The Observer*, editor of the *London Mercury*, and leader of the literary establishment known as the 'Squirearchy', opposed to and by the Sitwells, T. S. Eliot, and the 'moderns'; he said that *The Waste Land* was 'scarcely worthy of the Hogarth Press'. Gave the first BBC commentary on the Oxford and Cambridge Boat Race. Captained literary cricket team, The Invalids, described by A. G. Macdonnell in *England Their England*, which sometimes included Alec Waugh and Edmund Blunden. Knighted 1933.

Stanley, Edward ('Ed'), the 6th Baron Stanley of Alderley (1907–71); educ. Eton and Balliol College, Oxford; married (1) Lady Victoria Chetwynd-Talbot, 1932 (divorced, 1936); (2) Mrs Sylvia Fairbanks, 1944 (widow of Douglas Fairbanks, and formerly Lady Ashley, and originally Sylvia Hawkes; she married Clark Gable in 1949); (3)

Therese Husson, 1951 (marriage dissolved, 1957); (4) Lady Crane, 1961.

Stavordale, Edward Henry ('Harry'), Lord Stavordale, succeeded as 7th Earl of Ilchester, 1957 (1905–64): educ. Eton and Christ Church, Oxford. Married 1931 Helen ('Nell') Ward, a granddaughter of the 1st Earl of Dudley and a relation of Angela Dudley Ward, who married Robert Laycock (q.v.). Captain in Royal Horse Guards in Second World War.

Stokes, Adrian (1902–1972); philosopher of art. Educ. Rugby and Magdalen College, Oxford; publications include *The Thread of Ariadne*, 1925; *Stones of Rimini*, 1934; *Venice*, 1945; *Art and Science*, 1949; *Monet*, 1958; *Painting and the Inner World*, 1963; *Reflections on the Nude*, 1967.

Sutro, John (b. 1904): rich contemporary of Waugh's at Oxford and a lifelong friend. In his London home, in St John's Wood, Waugh first tasted plover's eggs (see *Brideshead Revisited*). Founded the Oxford Railway Club, which used to hire trains to drive about England, with chefs hired from London restaurants and fine wines on the menu. Through Sutro, whose family had financial interests in the film industry, Waugh became involved in writing filmscripts for Sir Alexander Korda (see Waugh's short story, *An Excursion in Reality*).

Sykes, Christopher (b.1907): educ. Downside and Christ Church, Oxford. Author and Waugh's authorised biographer; second son of Sir Mark Sykes, the 6th Bart., of the Sykes–Picot agreement that in 1916 partitioned the Middle East – Syria to France and the rest to Great Britain. Married (1936) Camilla, daughter of Sir Thomas Russell Pasha, for many years head of the police in Egypt. In Second World War, served in 7 Battalion The Green Howards; SAS Brigade (despatches, Croix de Guerre). BBC 1948–68. Has identified himself as 'Roger Stillingfleet', the writer in Waugh's *Work Suspended*. Publications include *Innocence and Design* (with Robert Byron), 1936, *Four Studies in Loyalty*, 1946, *Orde Wingate*, 1959, a biography of Lady Astor, 1972, and *Evelyn Waugh, A Biography*, 1975.

Stirling, David (b. 1915): son of Brigadier-General Archibald Stirling of Keir, and of the Hon. Mrs Margaret Stirling, a daughter of the 13th Baron Lovat; a cousin of Lord ('Shimi') Lovat (q.v.); educ. Ampleforth College, Yorkshire. In World War II with No. 3 Commando and went with this unit to the Middle East, where he subsequently served with the First Special Air Service Regiment, and performed legendary feats behind German lines with the Long Range Desert Group; DSO, 1942; prisoner of war, 1943–5. After the war, went to Africa and became President of the Capricorn Society, which attempted to preserve the Central African Federation (Northern Rhodesia, Southern Rhodesia, and Nyasaland). In 1974, set up a UK citizen's defence organization intended to assist in the maintenance of public order in the event of crippling industrial action by trade unions; this organization was dissolved in 1975. Tall, imperturbable, ingenious. Brother of William (Bill) Stirling, Waugh's senior officer in 1943.

Vivian, the Hon. Daphne (b. 1904); daughter of the 4th Baron Vivian; she married (1) Viscount Weymouth, 1927, later the 6th Marquess of Bath, and (2) Alexander ('Xan') Fielding. Author of *Mercury Presides* (an autobiography), *Emerald and Nancy*, a memoir of Lady Cunard and Nancy Cunard, and a life of Rosa Lewis of the Cavendish Hotel.

Waugh, Alec (b. 1898): educ. Sherborne; published *The Loom of Youth*, July 1917; prisoner of war in Germany, March 1918; married Barbara Jacobs, daughter of W. W. Jacobs, the short story writer, July 1919; settled at Ditchley, Sussex, 1920; worked part-time for Chapman & Hall, until 1924; in April, 1924, invented the cocktail party to fill the gap in London social life between 5.30 and 7 (see *Esquire*, July 1974); travelled widely, usually in search of material for his books; served in Middle East during World War II. Author of over forty books; his two most successful novels, *The Loom of Youth* (1917) and *Island in the Sun* (1956) were separated by an interval of forty years. Three times married; second (1932), to Joan Chirnside of Victoria, Australia (d. 1969), 2 sons, 1 daughter; third, to Virginia Sorensen of Utah, writer of children's books. In later life, settled in Tangier, usually revisiting England in early summer to attend the Lord's test match.

Woodruff, Douglas (b. 1897): educ. Downside and New College, Oxford; *The Times*, 1926–38; Editor of *The Tablet*, 1936–67. Married the Hon. Marie, daughter of the 2nd Lord Acton, 1933; Chairman, Burns and Oates, publishers, 1948–62; Director, Hollis & Carter, publishers, 1948–62. Publications include: *Plato's American Republic*, 1926; *The Story of the British Colonial Empire*, 1939; *The Tichborne Claimant*, 1957; *Church and State in History*, 1961.

Wyndham, Olivia (1897–1967): a great-granddaughter of the 1st Baron Leconfield; became caught up with the 'Blackbirds' in mid-1920s, fell in love with a black woman, and moved to New York, where she died. She was an aunt by marriage of Waugh's godson Jonathan Guinness, the son of Diana and Bryan Guinness (Lord Moyne).

Yorke, Henry Vincent (1905–74); descendant of the earls of Hardwicke; educ. Eton and Magdalen

College, Oxford; as an undergraduate, described by Waugh as 'lean, dark, and singular'; married in 1929 the Hon. Adelaide Mary ('Dig'), daughter of the 2nd Baron Biddulph. Became managing director of H. Pontifex and Co., Birmingham manufacturing firm. Auxiliary Fire Service in Second World War. Under the name 'Henry Green', the author of a series of highly-regarded novels, including *Loving, Caught, Back, Nothing* and *Doting*. Described by W. H. Auden as 'the best English novelist alive'. A recluse in later life.

Index